The Rise of Western Power

The Rise of Western Power

A Comparative History of Western Civilization

Jonathan Daly

B L O O M S B U R Y
LONDON • NEW DELHI • NEW YORK • SYDNEY

Bloomsbury Academic
An imprint of Bloomsbury Publishing Plc

50 Bedford Square
London
WC1B 3DP
UK

1385 Broadway
New York
NY 10018
USA

www.bloomsbury.com

Bloomsbury is a registered trade mark of Bloomsbury Publishing Plc

First published 2014

British Library Cataloguing-in-Publication Data
A catalogue record for this book is available from the British Library.

ISBN: HB: 978-1-4411-8901-1
PB: 978-1-4411-6131-4
ePDF: 978-1-4411-1851-6
ePub: 978-1-4411-4475-1

Library of Congress Cataloging-in-Publication Data
A catalog record for this book is available from the Library of Congress.

Typeset by Deanta Global Publishing Services, Chennai, India
Printed and bound in India

For My Sofia:
God put you in my life for a reason.

CONTENTS

PERMISSIONS

The author is grateful to the Florida Center for Instructional Technology for permission to use Maps 0.1, 11.2, and 14.1 and to The Probert Encyclopaedia (a division of nsdk.org.uk) for permission to reproduce Maps 4.2, 5.1, 5.2, 7.1, 10.1, 10.2, 10.4, 11.1, 12.1 12.2, 12.3, 13.1, 13.2, 13.3, 13.5, and 14.2. Maps 1.2, 1.3, 1.4, 2.2, 3.2, 4.1, 5.4, 5.5, 9.1, and 10.3, were reproduced from H. G. Wells, *The Outline of History: Being a Plain History of Life and Mankind* (New York: Macmillan, 1920; images digitalized and placed in the public domain <http://outline-of-history.mindvessel.net/copyright.html>). I am especially grateful to Peter Bull for creating Maps 1.1, 3.1, 3.3, 3.4, 5.3, 8.1, 9.2, and 13.4.

LIST OF ILLUSTRATIONS

PROLOGUE: WHY THE WEST?

A traveler to Baghdad around the year 1000 A.D. described a vast and flourishing city of broad streets and spacious gardens, abundant markets and marble-clad palaces, efficient sanitation and water-supply systems, innumerable mosques and thousands of watercraft, some from distant India and China docked along the Tigris River banks.[1] Córdoba, the capital of the Umayyad Caliphate in the Iberian peninsula, another of the world's biggest metropolises at a half-million people, boasted by far the richest library on the planet, vibrant commercial relations in every direction, and a reputed 1,000 mosques, including the grandest in the entire Islamic world, the Great Mosque with its 856 columns of polished stone. Scholars flocked to these and other Islamic centers of learning in search of wisdom and knowledge.[2] Four thousand miles to the east, the splendid capital of the dawning Song Dynasty, Kaifeng, soon bested Baghdad and Córdoba in population and wealth. The world's first economy to use paper currency, it produced iron at a rate achieved in Europe only 700 years later. Of this fabulously wealthy city, a resident a century or so later recalled 72 large and many more small restaurants where one could dine indoors or in pleasant gardens.[3]

In those same years, only two cities in all of Western Europe may have had around 40,000 inhabitants—Venice and Regensburg, Germany, then the capital of the Duchy of Bavaria.[4] London, not yet the capital of England, and Paris, the capital of France only since 987 and still largely in ruin from the Norman siege of 885–886, were smaller still. These and other Western European cities were often just aggregations of parishes or small towns and villages still interspersed with forests, marshlands, fields, and vineyards. Here one presumably found few if any restaurants with pleasant gardens.

By contrast, in 1793 Great Britain's first envoy to China, 1st Earl Macartney, an otherwise sympathetic observer, noted the absence even in the richly decorated "houses of the better sort" of numerous conveniences to which the English were widely accustomed, such as dressers, light fixtures, mirrors, interior doors, bed sheets, table cloths, napkins, knives, forks, spoons, glasses, comfortable mattresses, and swift carriages.[5] While it is quite likely that a Chinese traveler to Britain would have found much to deplore in its material culture, the contrast with Marco Polo's marveling at China's opulence 500 years prior is striking.[6] Britain in particular and Western Europe in general—at least in their own eyes—had caught up materially to China and other advanced societies.[7]

A century later still, the West, especially Europe and North America, was without peer technologically and economically—something no one would have predicted in the year 1000. The West also brought to life a host of cherished goods, including representative government, the free enterprise system, individual liberties, modern science, and the rule of law. When one takes into account the West's negative contributions to world history, such as the physical and cultural genocide of tens of millions of native peoples in the Americas, the systematic and dehumanizing Atlantic slave trade, an arrogant and often vicious worldwide imperialism, the Holocaust, and two frightfully destructive world wars, it is obvious that no other region, empire, culture, or civilization has ever left so powerful a mark upon the world.

How can one explain the unexpected rise of a small promontory at the end of the Eurasian land mass? My book aims to answer this question.

Some 15 years ago, Jared Diamond's *Guns, Germs, and Steel* showed that complex societies first emerged with writing, metallurgy, sophisticated technology, and specialized systems of government only in those regions well endowed by nature with domesticable plants and animals. The land from the Eastern Mediterranean to the Fertile Crescent boasted 32 of the world's 56 most productive wild grasses (compared to only six in East Asia), and four of the five major domesticated animals—sheep, goats, pigs, and cows—compared to only one in East Asia—a region far more richly endowed than other parts of the world.[8] That is why civilization first emerged in West and East Asia and then spread to India, North Africa, and Europe. Yet Diamond failed to explain why of all the leading candidates for rapid and powerful advancement, only Europe broke away startlingly from the rest.

Scholars have offered two basic explanations for the West's rise: one material, the other cultural.[9] Some scholars, including many world historians, emphasize economics, class conflict, control of natural resources, and imperialism. Europe rose, they argue, thanks to its close proximity to the Americas, subjugation of overseas colonies, rapaciousness, borrowing of technology and ideas from Asia, easy access to large coal and iron ore deposits, and violent militarism. The West did not triumph because of any cultural superiority. Its rise, moreover, was a mere temporary and quite late displacement of Asia. In the words of one historian, the West "used its American money [i.e silver from mines in South America] to buy itself a ticket on the Asian train."[10] China had remained richer, more populous, and generally more developed right down to the 1850s, when Europe finally achieved the number one position.[11] Although these factors help explain the West's rise, they do not account for its rapidity. It was as if the greatest juggernaut in history appeared out of nowhere.[12]

Others, often disparaged by their opponents as Eurocentrists,[13] have pointed to Europe's cultural dynamism, inventiveness, openness to the outside world, intellectual curiosity, respect for individual rights, defense of private property, and the relatively high status of women. Many scholars with this basic outlook emphasize the influence of distinctive Western institutions, typically viewed as concrete manifestations of culture.[14] Often important in such explanations is the political fragmentation of Europe following the collapse of the Roman Empire and the subsequent powerful influence of the Christian Church.[15] Among the interstices that opened between the church and various secular lords, all fighting for political and social dominance, there emerged, some argue, a uniquely vibrant and creative society in which individuals enjoyed great autonomy and associations banded together to advance their interests against powers and principalities. The West rose, in this perspective, because Europeans (and then also Americans and other Western settler peoples) unleashed human creativity more than any other civilization in history.[16] Yet most of these interpretations fail

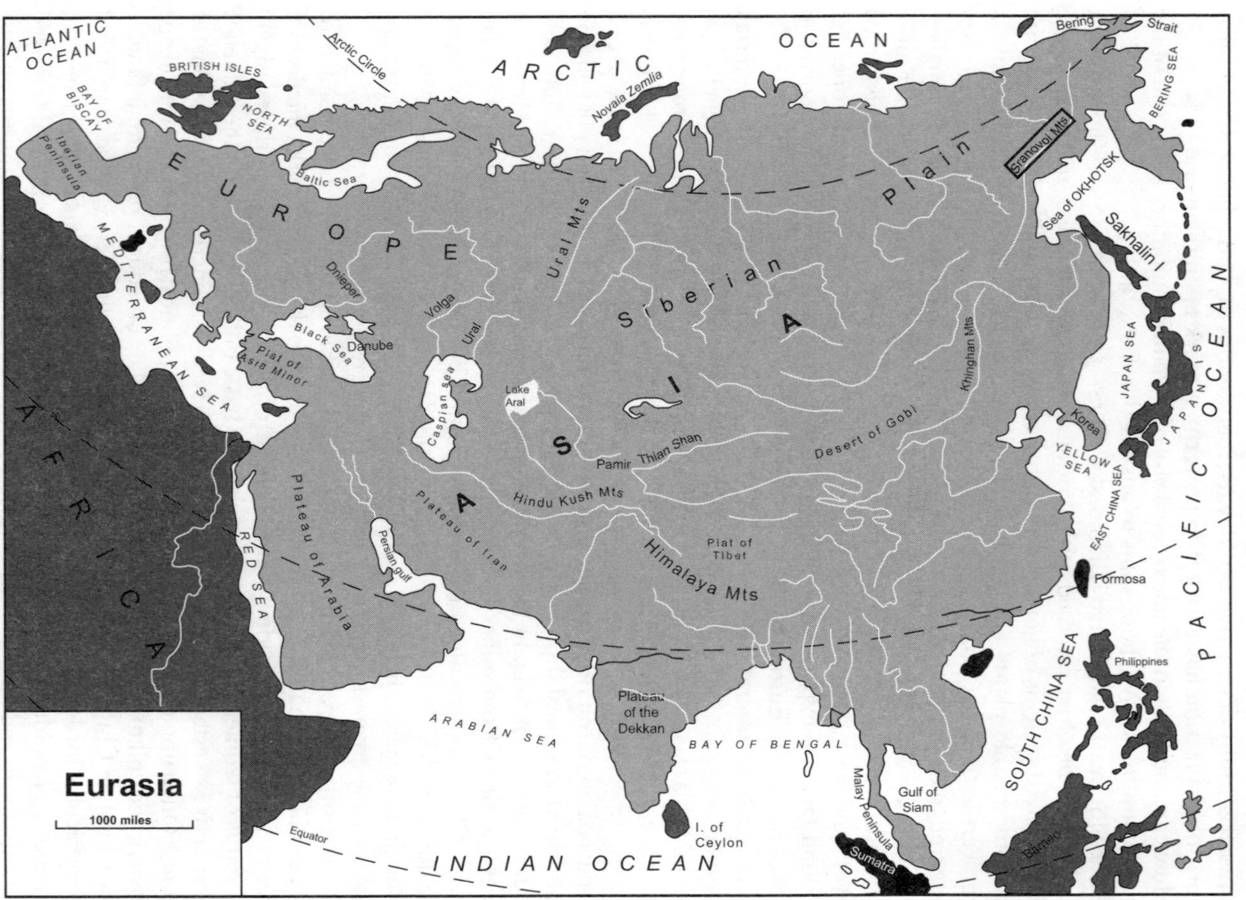

MAP 0.1 *Eurasia: Earth's biggest and most interconnected landmass.*

to credit adequately the contributions of other peoples to Europe's rise. From the perspective of such scholars, it was as if the West rose in a vacuum.

One strain of evolutionary biology helps to elucidate the nature of human creativity. Being alive and evolving over time means interacting with one's environment. All living things—from bacteria to humans—are phenomenally creative in their ability to adapt. At every moment, we must process almost infinite data relating to our surroundings and our own bodies and mental processes. We create from this manifold an awareness of our corner of the world.[17] On this basis, we act, react, invent, build, and collaborate. If each individual displays such extraordinary creativity on its own, imagine how much vastly more he or she can achieve in communities. All human collectives—from hunter-gatherer bands to sophisticated civilizations—connect organically among themselves and with their environments. This alone makes them all worthy of the profoundest respect and even awe.

According therefore to an ecological model of evolution, no living thing can thrive in isolation but only in intricate interplay with the widest range of living and nonliving things.[18] At various points in their development, however, the leaders of a host of cultures and civilizations found many reasons to impede further experimentation and innovation. One can point, for example, to decrees by the Ming Emperor Zhu Yuanzhang (r. 1368–1398) forbidding private voyages overseas and trade with foreign countries.[19] Such prohibitions presumably hampered innovation; they could not stifle it altogether. China under the Ming Dynasty flourished in nearly every sphere.[20] Yet Europe, despite its smaller population, was rising faster, developing more ecologically, more organically—was more open to other cultures and to its physical environment—than the other great civilizations. Therein lay the secret of its success.

Yet why did Europe develop so organically? The key explanations are geographical, historical, and cultural. For tens of thousands of years, following the emergence of *Homo sapiens*, humans across the planet connected with their ecology in similarly creative ways. With the rise of urban culture and civilization several thousand years ago, however, diverse peoples established a wide variety of social patterns and political organizations. Communications and exchanges among them impelled much if not most human advancement. Thus, the peoples living on the earth's biggest and most interconnected landmass, Eurasia, had an advantage over all others (see Map 0.1). Partly for this reason, the most complex civilizations first arose there—specifically in Asia. Europe's position at the extreme opposite end from the world's richest and longest continuously thriving culture—China—was highly favorable: sufficiently isolated to avoid conquest, the European peoples nevertheless were exposed to insights, wisdom, technology, inventions, concepts, cultural achievements, religious visions, and knowledge from across Afro-Eurasia. A key fact was the Europeans' willingness to embrace these riches.

Europe itself is divided into many separate regions by an intricate web of waterways. They provide excellent transportation routes, but none was so important as to foster the development of a centralized state. On the contrary, Europe's geography favored political fragmentation.[21] Aside from the unification of much of the continent in Roman times and three brief interludes of centralized rule by Charlemagne, Napoleon, and Hitler, Europe has been divided into dozens of highly independent polities. Intensive competition, exchange, interaction, and mutual emulation created hothouse conditions for innovation, the scale and vigor of which increased over time.

ıltural explanation for Europe's extraordinary openness to outside influences elusive, though is surely conditioned by its geography and history. Its peoples among themselves during the past thousand years more than the peoples of other regions—partly because so many of its founding cultures stemmed from the waves of nomadic warriors migrating across Eurasia. Goths, Huns, Vandals, Franks, and other aggressive, self-governing peoples formed the ruling elites for centuries throughout much of Europe. At the same time, European intellectuals embraced the rationalistic heritage of the Greeks, the Roman imperial model and conception of the individual person enshrined in both thought and law, and several key values handed down by Judaism and Christianity. These values placed spiritual and moral goods above material ones, advocated resistance to unjust authority, substituted linear to cyclical time, called people to the improvement and even the perfection of themselves and their institutions, insisted on the intrinsic goodness of material reality, and defined the universe as rational and the human mind is capable of understanding it.[22] The absence of centralized rule enabled Europeans to challenge authority and pursue innovation and change in every sphere of life.

The Europeans' willingness to learn from others and to try new things began in the Middle Ages and then gradually increased in scale, scope, and intensity. Throughout the past thousand years, Europe was shaken repeatedly and, in later centuries, continuously by major transformations. Some were dramatic and swift; in other cases, small innovations gave way cumulatively to broader transformations. Over the centuries, they fused into a continuous transmutation,[23] like a controlled chain reaction, an extraordinary concatenation that continues through to our day: a human society hardwired for constant innovation and change.

The Europeans got their inventiveness from human nature: all people in the aggregate are equally ingenious. Their competitive spirit, aggressiveness, and ambition, however, came from accidents of geography, history, and culture. These factors made them successful economically and militarily, often terrifying and cruel to their enemies and horribly destructive of traditional cultures and societies, but also the founders of many cherished goods of the modern age: individual rights, acceptance of religious diversity, equality before the law, and gender equality. For millennia, people had learned to build upon past achievements. The European peoples benefited from this vast human patrimony and continued to add to it. In the midst of this development, however, their natural human creativity and inventiveness reached a critical mass of accomplishment that other peoples could not easily imitate both for technological reasons and because of commitments to value systems emphasizing communitarianism, closeness to nature, and spirituality, among others.

Far be it from me, however, to suggest or imply that the West's unique emergence to preeminence in the modern age overshadowed the achievements of other human cultures. Not only did many of those achievements make possible the West's rise; they deserve admiration in their own right. As Marshall Hodgson argued decades ago, whether the Islamic world "'led to' anything evident in Modern times must be less important than the quality of its excellence as a vital human response and an irreplaceable human endeavor."[24] In other words, the great non-Western cultures have value both for their obvious influence on the emergence of the modern world and for their intrinsic worth as extraordinarily successful human ventures.

Definitions

Several key concepts—Europe, the West, Western civilization, and civilization—should be defined at the outset. "Europe" is not only a geographical entity but also a social construct. No natural boundary separates it from Asia, and many people disagree about what countries it encompasses; in particular, Russia's inclusion is often seen as problematic.[25] Until the 1700s, Europe was usually called "Christendom," a term that developed partly in opposition to the Islamic Middle East.[26] Geopolitics involving alliances with the Ottoman Empire and the secularizing thought of the Enlightenment gradually fostered a preference for "Europe." Public intellectuals now began to scrutinize the nature of their continent.

Montesquieu was the first, in 1748, to delineate Europe "as a geographical, cultural, political, and intellectual entity with its own history and its own distinctive features." In 1752, the Scottish philosopher David Hume emphasized the importance to European culture of a strong middle class. Four years later, Voltaire argued that several other features distinguished Western Europe from the Ottoman Empire, including climate, government, and religion, but especially the treatment of women. The European self-image that began to emerge thus highlighted temperate climate, political liberty, property rights, an aristocratic check on despotic government, a dynamic middle class, the relatively high status of women, scientific advancement, and later also economic prosperity.[27]

Scholars have also defined Europe with reference to the cultural streams that influenced its development, including ancient Egyptian and Babylonian foundations, the Persian doctrine of good and evil, the Arabic lyric sensibility, Judeo-Christian ideals of self-examination and universal justice, Greek philosophy and the ideal of harmony, Celtic mysticism, Roman law and citizenship and ideals of empire, and Germanic self-governance, among many others.[28]

One historian has pointed to specific movements that transformed Europe—such as the Reformation, the Enlightenment, Romanticism, nationalism, imperialism, communism, fascism, and totalitarianism—as a way to characterize what it means to be European.[29] It is also possible to define Europe as those countries that participated in key historical events, such as the Crusades, the Age of Discovery, the Scientific Revolution, and the early development of mechanical printing, railroads, and political representation. To a large extent, the peoples from Portugal to Scotland, from Sweden to Poland, and from Russia to Gibraltar would fall under this classification. So would former European colonies like the United States and other lands considered part of the "West."

The idea of the "West" as a geographical and cultural entity opposed to the "East" emerged in ancient Greece. European intellectuals later took up this idea, often with derogatory attitudes, as of a superior West and an inferior East.[30] In reaction, peoples of non-Western lands have rightly challenged such views.[31] Such rhetorical disputes are unfortunate. Even so, the term "West" has come, often without any discussion or prejudice, to mean Europe, along with the United States and other European settler societies, like Canada and Australia.[32] This is the sense implied here.

"Western civilization" has the same meaning in this book as "the West," though it also has a long and often checkered past. One scholar dismisses the very idea as a set of "intellectual constructs" devised for political and propaganda purposes.[33] Still, most historians consider it a valuable concept. The "Western Civ" course emerged in the United States since World War I.[34] With their European brethren slaughtering one another in the trenches, one could even say destroying their civilization (see Chapter 13), it seemed to many American academics that the essence of their culture had to be grounded in something better than modern European history. Scholars from several academic departments at Columbia University, therefore, anchored the development of the American ideals of liberty, the rule of law, political participation, and individual rights back through European history to ancient Greece and Rome or even ancient Egypt and Mesopotamia. Theirs was a vision of progress through time, which in an epoque of violent nationalism was meant "to keep civilization alive."[35]

Civilization can mean several things. First, high standards of behavior, politeness, manners, self-restraint, and the like, in the sense in which Norbert Elias understood the "civilizing process."[36] Second, complex societies made possible by the domestication of plants and animals beginning 10,000 years ago and displaying sophisticated economies, cities, written language, sharply differentiated sociopolitical hierarchies, labor specialization and exploitation, multifaceted systems of mythology or religion, and significant artistic and scientific achievements.[37] Third, coherent cultural spheres in which all the members share some specific attributes, such as values, outlooks, historical consciousness, linguistic and ethnic affinities, social norms, and sometimes political unity.[38] A civilization in this sense is "a culture writ large," such that "none of their constituent units can be fully understood without reference to the encompassing civilization."[39] Such is how I understand "Western civilization" in the present book. The English historian Arnold Toynbee enumerated 21 distinct civilizations, from the Egyptian and Sumeric to the Chinese, Islamic, and Western, as well as the Andean and Mexic.[40] Naturally, scholars have compiled a wide variety of such lists.

Civilizations and cultures interact in many ways, both positive and negative. For example, their intermingling has stimulated innovation. William H. McNeill considers this the main source of progress in history.[41] They have also collided. In the medieval and early modern period, Christian Europe and the nearby Muslim peoples defined each other as hostile camps—thus, the Dar al-Islam (territory of submission) and Dar al-Harb (territory of war), in Muslim terminology.[42] Only in the late eighteenth and the nineteenth centuries did some Muslims begin to view Europe as worthy of respect and emulation.[43] Early modern Europeans tended to be far more curious and well informed about the Islamic world, yet they were equally hostile to it.[44]

Recent studies have illuminated these interactions in modern times. The American political scientist Samuel P. Huntington has identified eight major "civilizations," of which the three most important to him are the West, China, and the Islamic world. What divides them and also unites each of them separately, he argues, is culture and, in particular, religion. Yet these cultures are so different, and the populations, resources, and territories encompassing them so great, that violent clashes between them are nearly inevitable.[45] The American political theorist Benjamin Barber has presented an equally grim analysis of the fate of civilizations. In his view, while many countries are fragmenting into petty religious and tribal enclaves perpetually at war with one another, much of the world is being transformed "into one homogenous global theme park, one McWorld tied together by communications, information, entertainment, and commerce."[46] One need not agree with either assessment to conclude that understanding the past development and present configuration of world cultures is an urgent necessity. This book aims to contribute to this understanding by providing a comparative history of Western civilization, the most dynamic modern culture.

* * *

My gratitude cannot be adequately expressed to the colleagues and friends who have read and commented on parts of this book in their areas of expertise—Michael Alexander, George Huppert, Nanno Marinatos, Deirdre McCloskey, Rachel Fulton, Esther Klein, Guity Nashat, Roman Yukilevich, Richard John, Scott Palmer, Willemien Otten, Rick Fried, Dan Smith, Robert Johnston, Mark Liechty, Scott Smith, an anonymous reviewer, and the staff of the Core Course in the History of European Civilization at the University of Chicago. I am especially indebted to those who critiqued the entire manuscript—James Sack, Philip Devenish, Steven Marks, and four anonymous reviewers. Others kindly shared their knowledge and expertise, including Steven Fanning, Sergei Maksudov, Leon Fink, Leonid Trofimov, Donald Holtgrieve, Kenneth Sawyer, James Cracraft, Richard Levy, David Morgan, Martin Tracey, and J. P. Brown. Thanks to all the suggestions and insights of my dear friends and colleagues, this book has turned out far better than it could otherwise have been, though for any mistakes they missed or in which I have stubbornly persisted I bear full responsibility. I would also like to acknowledge Zane Elward and Amy Zimmerman for their diligent research assistance.

My wife Sofia prompted me to investigate the rise of the West, helped me create a successful undergraduate colloquium as a laboratory for its exploration, and inspired me to write this book. She inspires me in every aspect of life—emotional, intellectual, and creative. I dedicate this book to her.

QUESTIONS FOR REFLECTION

What do world historians argue about the Rise of the West?

How do "Eurocentrists" explain it?

In what sense can we say Europe developed more ecologically than other cultures?

Why did the societies in Eurasia have an advantage over others?

How did political fragmentation influence Europe's development?

What factors influenced the development of European culture?

1

Innovation in world civilization

In the years from 32,000 to 12,000 B.C., Cro-Magnon artists north and south of the Pyrenees Mountains painted thousands of pictures of horses, bulls, deer, and other large mammals on cave walls. Some remain among humankind's most stupendously beautiful artistic creations.[1] When Pablo Picasso visited the newly discovered cave near Lascaux in 1940, he exclaimed: "We have invented nothing."[2] In the subsequent Neolithic Age, humans across the globe subsisted in hunter-gather bands scarcely differing from one another in their technology and cultural achievements.[3] Once civilizations emerged in the Near East, India, and China, however, Europe would have seemed a stagnant pond to any wanderer from the banks of the lower Nile or the Fertile Crescent.

What can explain the rise of one civilization or the decline of another? Why were migrants from Asia 40,000 years ago able to build seaworthy boats and to colonize New Guinea and Australia, while apparently no other people on earth for the next 30,000 years managed to reproduce such a technological feat?

It seems that innovation—conceiving and bringing to life brilliant ideas—can largely explain the rise of civilization and the successes of human cultures. People who devised ways to stretch available resources, to outsmart their enemies, to boost their confidence and camaraderie, to build up and deploy knowledge and information—in a word, to make themselves more powerful—flourished. Others who clung to routine and tradition and failed to open new pathways failed to keep up with the innovators.

Nature endowed some places more richly than others, but resources do not explain success. Consider the third-biggest economy, Japan, with its limited resources, or the earth's natural treasure chest, Russia, a land of more woe than fortune. No, more important than resources was the ability of peoples or societies to find it within themselves to achieve great things. Available resources, geography, climate, values and beliefs, habits and traditions, talented leadership, individual genius, and blind luck all played a part in the success or rise of a given people.

Yet success can follow only if several of these things line up and lead to innovation. Just as random mutations that enter a species' genome can enable it to thrive in a given environment, so random innovations that strengthen a people's cultural make-up can determine its success in its corner of the world. I write "random innovations" in the sense that humans are always trying new ways of doing things in the hope of making our lives easier, happier, healthier, and more abundant, but only the occasional innovation proves historically pivotal. Indeed, as with genetic mutations, the vast majority turns out useless or even harmful. The key difference, though, is that biological species do not arbitrarily reject genetic mutations with the capacity to increase their adaptability, whereas human societies throughout history have repeatedly spurned potentially valuable innovations. They have done so at their peril, however, for the most innovative societies have typically become the most successful.

Prehistory

Humankind's first innovations contributed to all later achievements.[4] Despite fragmentary evidence and ongoing debates, researchers agree on the following. Around 7 million years ago, our remotest ancestors began to speciate, or separate genetically, from other hominids in sub-Saharan Africa. Our closest ancestors could both swing from branches and walk upright by around 4 million years ago. They continued to evolve through several stages, some of which bear exotic names like *Australopithecus africanus*. Their descendant, *Homo habilis* ("handy-man"), began crafting simple stone tools in East Africa some 2.3 million years ago, thanks to the gradual evolution of their hands. No other hominid ever figured out how to do this. (Interestingly, this does not mean that hominids cannot be taught to flake stone, something Bonobos or "pygmy chimpanzees" have learned to do since 1990.)[5] Roughly a half-million years later, *H. erectus* began migrating to Asia and then to Europe.[6]

So far, we have noted three big innovations: walking upright, making tools, and probably relatively complex thought, all thanks to favorable genetic mutations. It is also possible, as some scholars now argue, that our ancestors began from the time of early tool-making to use hand gestures to convey messages, a skill that may have preceded and influenced the far later development of vocal language. To take one example of gestural communication that remains with us even today, human babies learn to point fairly early, whereas other primates never do.[7]

Later still—at least 790,000 years ago—one or more beings of the genus *homo*, probably including *erectus*, learned to harness and then to make fire.[8] The world's first great nonbiological advance, it also introduced the first powerful tool, enormously extending the abilities of those who wielded it. Fire in the long run could be used to clear forests, to ward off predators, to maintain warmth, to illumine the darkness, and to unlock nutrition from many foods, particularly tubers and meat, and to make them easier to chew and to preserve.[9] Yet it could also destroy habitats and kill populations if improperly used.

All human transformations, which substitute tools or ideas for instinctive behaviors and thus separate us from the reign of nature, are two-edged swords. An essential feature of being human is to decide how to act and what to value at each step, rather than to follow clear-cut instincts, as our nonhuman fellow creatures do. Our tools, including conceptual ones, enable us to overpower the animals and some humans to overpower others. They allow us to come to terms with our environment in myriad ways, both good and bad. The mastery of fire to some extent therefore prefigured not only the rise of great civilizations through innovation but also the endless human story of conquest and subjugation.[10]

The next breakthrough came roughly 200,000 years ago through biological evolution, when anatomically modern humans, or *H. sapiens*, began to evolve in East Africa.[11] They had more rounded skulls, less protruding brow ridges, greater intellectual ability, and smaller, far less muscular and powerful bodies than their ancestors or the contemporaneous Neanderthals, who evolved in parallel to *H. sapiens*.[12] Evidently, nature reoriented *H. sapiens*'s physiology from strength to intelligence. These developments took tens of thousands of years to bear fruit.

Our ancestors' greatest transformations either dramatically enhanced their power or enormously increased their ability to use information. The first two major advances so far mentioned—control of fire and evolution toward *H. sapiens*—are instances of each. Fire constituted an extraordinarily powerful new tool, while becoming modern humans allowed our ancestors to process vastly more information. The revolution that now occurred, between 100,000 and 50,000 years ago, the emergence of spoken language, thanks to the evolution of the necessary vocal apparatus, intensified this ability.[13] No transformation has been more momentous. Complex language enabled our ancestors to work better together, to share insights, to interpret the universe, and to store up and to pass on knowledge and culture—in fact to become human. (Like all human advances, it naturally has a "dark side," for example, unavoidable miscommunication.[14])

The new being was extraordinarily adaptive to diverse environments. Further genetic leaps, moreover, were unnecessary (though they are presumably continuing at the same slow—to us—pace as before).[15] Instead, our recent ancestors began to use culture to replace biology. While nonhuman animals follow their instincts in nearly all instances, humans began to develop cultural patterns, including customs, lore, traditions, values, and ideas to guide their behavior. They handed down this patrimony, so that each succeeding generation learned from the former one and, occasionally, was better equipped to adapt than their forebears.

Our direct ancestors began to display more sophisticated behavior roughly 100,000 years ago and what many scholars consider fully modern behavior 50,000 years later. During this period, *H. sapiens* began to migrate from Africa into Europe and Asia, leaving behind many deadly maladies and discovering much healthier environments teeming with wildlife.[16] Beginning around 50,000 years ago, they developed a practice of ritual burying, commemorating the life and passage into death of members of their community. At this time, they began to catch fish and craft stone tools displaying regular patterns. A bit later, tools made of bone and antler appeared. Gradually, tools serving a much wider set of functions were crafted, including projectile points and instruments for engraving, cutting, drilling, and piercing.[17] It would probably have been difficult to fashion such specialized devices without language, which made possible cooperation on a high level. The creatures with these capacities formed a new subspecies, ours: *H. sapiens sapiens*. Many paleoanthropologists call this transformation the "human revolution."[18]

By roughly 32,000 years ago, human society in some places had achieved an extraordinary degree of sophistication and cultural mastery. The most stunning signs of this development are the cave paintings mentioned above. In some 350 known caves, prehistoric artists painted or sketched tens of thousands of scenes from nature, mostly a wide variety of animals, some of fabulous beauty. Viewers today marvel at their "modern" appearance. Scholars dispute their meaning—mythological?

ritualistic? We will almost surely never know. Beyond dispute, however, they bear witness to a refined civilization, the first ever, which endured, apparently unchanging, for some 20,000 years.[19] Lost are the myriad other cultural artifacts that must have accompanied the cave art, like poetry, music, mythological stories, and religious beliefs. Can one conceive of communities so artistically sophisticated without them? Such prehistoric cave art has been found only in Europe, yet it seems likely that peoples throughout Eurasia and Africa had at least here and there achieved awesome feats of cultural refinement, some of which enabled the emergence of later known civilizations.[20]

This burst of creativity marked a qualitative leap forward, the emergence of a new being. Our earlier biological ancestors fashioned stone tools, made and wielded fire, and probably communicated with rather sophisticated hand gestures. In these ways, they differed significantly from all other living creatures. Yet the gap between them and *H. sapiens sapiens* was far greater. For well over 1 million years, the first members of the *Homo* species learned to fashion slightly more efficient tools and possibly to communicate in more effective ways. Then suddenly, in the space of 100,000 or perhaps only 50,000 years, anatomically modern humans—in reality the only true humans—invented complex verbal language, created stunningly sophisticated art, domesticated plants and animals, founded the great religions, and built up the early civilizations.[21] In all sobriety, it is hard to see much in common between these beings and their biological ancestors.[22]

Some scholars argue that the key distinguishing feature of the new being was not material prowess or even intellectual dexterity but rather spiritual perception. David Martel Johnson has suggested, for example, that the key shift in human evolution was the emergence some 100,000 years ago of "religious consciousness." This shift, he argues, made possible the so-called human revolution.[23] Certainly, the late Stone Age cave paintings seem to have conveyed more spiritual than materialistic meanings. Is it not likely that the experience of awe at the grandeur of reality struck them more powerfully than sharing the pleasures and successes of the hunt, admittedly a matter on which their lives depended?

Around the time of the first cave paintings, the longevity of *H. sapiens sapiens* increased sharply, followed by the extinction of his closest competitor in Europe, *H. neanderthalis*. Lacking both complex language (scholars debate whether they could talk at all) and sophisticated tools, the Neanderthals apparently could not for long survive in the same habitats as our ancestors. (Scientists are uncertain about the ancestral relations between these two species and exactly how much genetic material they had in common; it may have been up to 25 percent.)[24] Scholars have put forward many theories about their demise. The most convincing emphasizes that they were less adaptable than our ancestors, perhaps in part because they lived in far smaller social groupings.[25]

Over the next several thousand years, our ancestors constructed more and more refined tools and instruments. Bones etched with tick marks dating to 25,000 years ago may have served as a form of calendar. Sewing needles began to appear from the same era, and pants, shirts, and shoes sewn from animal skins and dating from a few thousand years later have been discovered near Moscow. Spear-throwers appeared next, and by 15,000 years ago spears, hooks, and nets grew more common. The most sophisticated weapons of prehistoric times, bows and arrows, were invented around

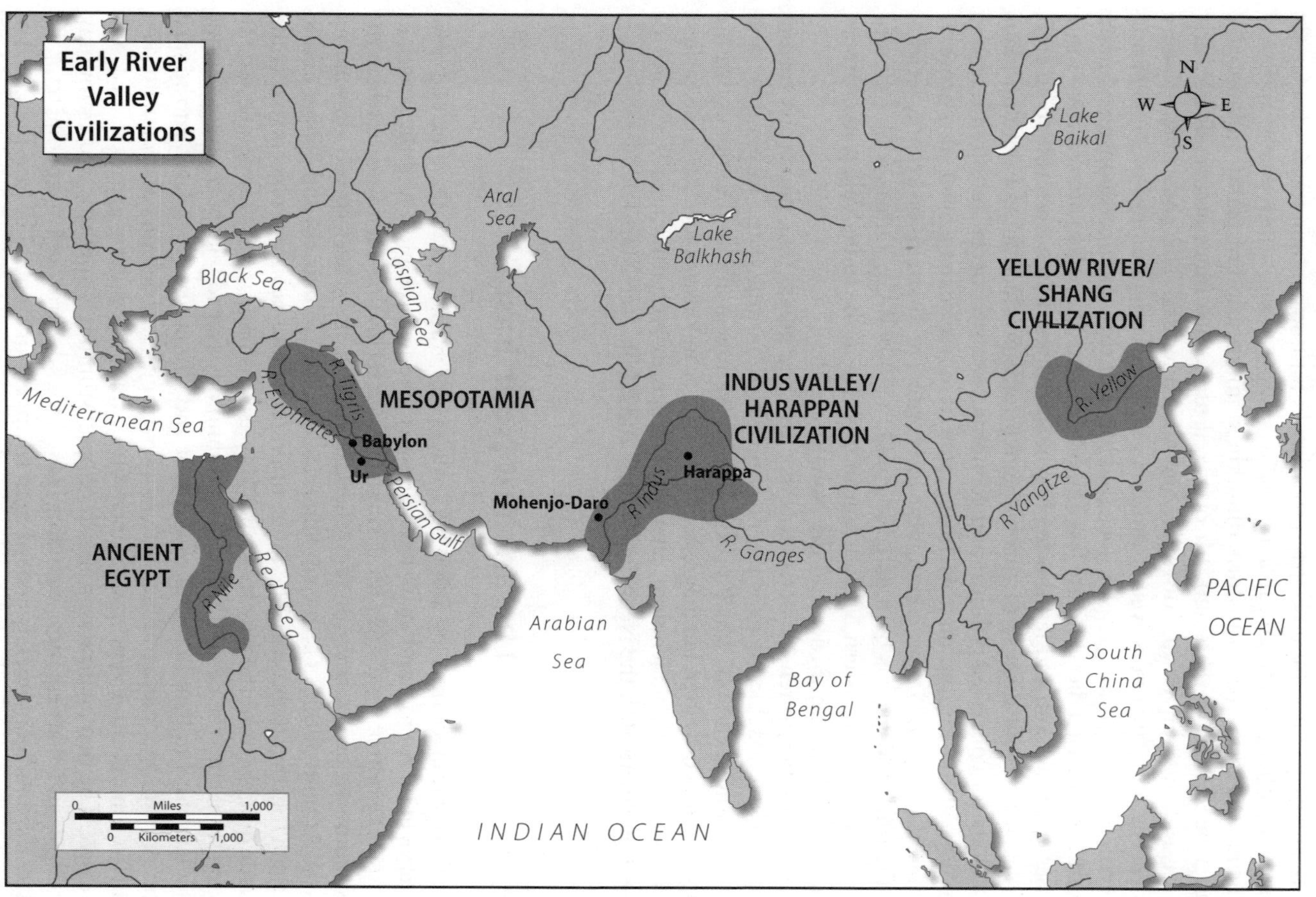

MAP 1.1 *Civilization first emerged in the ancient Near East, Egypt, India, and China.*

10,000 B.C. All such advances resulted directly from our acquisition of language. Periodic contacts during millennia among communities scattered throughout the globe's inhabited spaces must have resulted in fruitful exchanges of technology and lore. In any case, innovation occurred too slowly for one community to advance far beyond any other in material capacity.

The next great human transformation, the domestication of plants and animals, began around 10,000 years ago.[26] It occurred numerous times independently, first in Asia and then in Africa, Australia, and the Americas. The consequences were momentous. Our ancestors went from living in small communities of hunters and gatherers to larger, more complex societies. Most of their members consumed more uniform, grain-based diets and ate less animal protein. They also suffered from more diseases, grew weaker, and led shorter, less healthy lives. Elites were able to emerge, however, who could dispose of surplus agricultural production and develop plans and visions for concerted political and economic activity. Specialization in learning, technological innovation, manufacturing, and resource management also arose. It did not take long for larger communities to form. The first city on record, Jericho, near the Jordan River, has been dated to roughly 9,000 B.C.[27] Others soon followed not only around the eastern Mediterranean but also in the Indus Valley, in northern China, and at length in Africa and the New World.[28]

It was in cities, often clustered together in core areas, that numerous further innovations were achieved over the next several thousand years. Ideographic and early mnemonic symbols, which probably conveyed meaning but did not constitute a fully developed written language, began to appear in various localities, the earliest of which is seventh millennium Henan province in western China.[29] Cradles of civilization emerged in the Near East, India, and China (see Map 1.1).

The ancient Near East

In southern Mesopotamia, by 5,000 B.C., olives and grapes were cultivated and wine was fermented. A thousand years later, artisans invented the plow and the wheel, at first to make pottery and soon for cartage. A huge technological advance, which the pre-Columbian civilizations of the Americas lacked, the wheel spread throughout Eurasia. Around 3000 B.C., ancient Sumerians learned to melt tin and copper and to cast them together as bronze. The range of practical and beautiful objects that could be made quickly from the new substance was astonishing, at least for people used to hacking stone into the desired forms. The technology spread widely, reaching Europe by the late third millennium B.C. and Africa and China not much later. At the start of the Bronze Age, pictographic systems of writing—hieroglyphs and cuneiform—began to emerge in Egypt and Sumer. Over time, they grew more refined and expressive. The two civilizations also developed stunningly sophisticated astronomy, metrology, and mathematics, including geometry, algebra, and trigonometry.[30] By the late third millennium, law codes began to appear in Sumer. The best preserved of them, which was promulgated by the Babylonian ruler Hammurabi, dates back to around 1790 B.C. Most of its 282 laws concern crimes against person and property (including slaves and livestock); many also regulate the institution of marriage.

Since most of the Egyptian writings on papyrus perished from the effects of time, one cannot understand the ancient Egyptian society and culture fully. From an analysis of indirect evidence, however, Martin Bernal has argued that their contributions enabled ancient Greece—and by extension Western civilization—to flourish.[31] His assertions have sparked an intense and ongoing scholarly debate.[32] Whatever its eventual outcome, few scholars would deny that the sophisticated technologies and institutions of modern times could not have emerged without ancient Middle Eastern and North African social, economic, political, cultural, and scientific foundations.[33]

Yet in these great ancient civilizations, something was missing. Writing was the preserve of only highly educated people. Perhaps the centralized nature of political and economic power gradually impeded further development. These societies had hit a dead end, it seems, even before mysterious "Sea Peoples" from the north invaded and conquered them around 1200 B.C.[34]

Henceforth, smaller cultures would bear the mantle of innovation. Some contributions were relatively small, others great. The Celts, for example, created the first pan-European Iron Age culture by 300 B.C. and left behind a powerful storytelling tradition, which included the heroic tales of King Arthur and Tristan.[35] More important was the discovery of how to smelt iron, first in Anatolia or the north Caucasus and then throughout the eastern Mediterranean and Africa and beyond, by the twelfth-century B.C. Though weaker than bronze, iron could be sharpened, whereas bronze had to be recast. Also, iron ore was far more abundant than copper or tin.[36] Around the same time, the Phoenician people established a seagoing trading culture on the easternmost coast of the Mediterranean. For this purpose, they invented the galley ship with two rows of oarsmen (the bireme) and, far more important, a phonemic system of writing dating to roughly 1000 B.C. Unlike hieroglyphics, which consisted of many hundreds of ideographic characters, the Phoenician script is limited to 22 letters (see Chapter 6). People with less leisure time than elites could readily master it. Since each letter represented a distinct phonetic sound, other languages could easily adapt it. The Greek alphabet, which added vowel sounds, probably made possible the flourishing of ancient Greek culture.[37]

The next set of transformations occurred in what the German philosopher Karl Jaspers called the Axial Age. During this period, from 800 to 200 B.C., thinkers and prophets in China, India, the Middle East, and Europe developed most of the great religious, philosophical, and ethical systems of world history. These included Confucianism, Daoism, Hinduism, Buddhism, Jainism, Zoroastrianism, Judaism, and the philosophy of Plato and Aristotle. No other half-millennium has seen a more astonishing and creative profusion of ways of apprehending the world and the human place within it. "Since then," Jaspers adds, "there has been only one entirely new, spiritually and materially incisive event . . . the age of science and technology [of the modern West]."[38] Some Axial worldviews aimed at universal applicability; others related mostly to a small population or territory. Several laid the foundations for some of the world's great civilizations, including China, India, and Persia. From two of them, Israel and Greece, flowed great cultural streams shaping much of European civilization.

The ancient Hebrews were the first people on earth who experienced a concrete, personal, loving relationship with a being utterly beyond human understanding and completely transcending all contingent reality, whom they called Yahweh or God.[39] Most humans, it seems, have perceived mystery in the world, a reality beyond what we see and feel. They have represented such things as forces, spirits, beings, even persons. Yet none previously had experienced this reality as a single all-powerful deity, who created all things and personally and continually intervenes in the historical world in an effort to perfect creation. Scholars, recognizing the influence of Judaism on the rise of the West, have pointed to its various specific contributions to Western civilization, such as the first consciously developed written history of a people,[40] respect for manual labor, the subordination of nature to humanity, and a sense of linear as against cyclical and nonprogressing time.[41] Of course, without Judaism, the other two Abrahamic religions—Christianity and Islam—could presumably never have emerged. Yet without a personal sense of being chosen by a creator who wishes to perfect the world through the instrumentality of his creatures, it is hard to imagine either Christians or Muslims taking up the stupendous challenges of spreading their faith across the globe or striving rigorously to comprehend the secrets of nature and the life of the mind.

The classical world

The ancient Athenians supplied the tools. They, more than any other ancient people, pursued a rational and systematic investigation of the world. Theirs was a true revolution of the mind. No doubt the Greek achievements would have been impossible without Mesopotamian, African, and Egyptian cultural foundations and probably even specific contacts—Plato and many other cultivated fourth-century Greeks studied in Egypt and marveled at its culture.[42] Yet the Greeks and no other people integrated these precious influences to conjure a unique cultural synthesis.

It occurred in the bosom of a highly practical society. A mercantile, seafaring people emerging from a broader Greek civilization with many hundreds of city-states and colonies—mostly facing the sea—all around the Mediterranean and Black Sea basins, the Athenians established the world's first rule-governed, participatory democracy. In this context, the major Greek philosophers, especially Plato and Aristotle, subjected to rigorous, methodical analysis nearly every aspect of life and reality. First, they established rules of thought—logic and rhetoric—and then worked their way through fundamental questions of esthetics, ethics, law, medicine, politics, faith, social relations, psychology, metaphysics, nature, and many other areas of knowledge. Other cultures had posed questions about the world but none ever furnished such lucid answers to them.[43]

One can even argue that no other humans on earth ever again achieved such an intellectual transformation, except the Europeans with the Scientific Revolution (see Chapter 8), which itself would have been impossible without the foundations laid in Athens 2,000 years before. Any civilization that has truly assimilated ancient Greek thought has experienced a mental revolution. Yet this was rare. Islamic scholars drank rich drafts from the wells of Greek thought, and their brilliant achievements in philosophy and science owe much to that elixir. Yet most eventually recoiled in fear of the dangers that relying on pure rationality posed to their religious faith.

The Greek legacy did not end with Athens. Alexander the Great (356–323 B.C.) conquered a vast empire from North Africa to the Indus Valley. Influenced by Egyptian, Persian, and Indian culture, Hellenistic civilization arose. Its most important city, Alexandria in northern Egypt, founded in 331 B.C., became a great center of learning. It boasted the world's first research library, where Greek, Egyptian, and Jewish scholars made important breakthroughs, especially in textual analysis. Around 300 B.C., Euclid systematized the vast store of mathematical knowledge in his 13-volume *Elements* and established both Euclidean geometry and the axiomatic method upon which he based it. Later in the third century, Archimedes, who probably studied in Alexandria, calculated the value of pi and the volumes and areas of circles, parabolas, cylinders, spheres, and other solid and plane figures. Eratosthenes (ca. 276–195 B.C.), a chief librarian at Alexandria, calculated the Earth's circumference relatively accurately.[44]

Greek culture continued to shape the world of ideas and artistic creation for centuries throughout the Mediterranean world. As the Roman Empire expanded, its elites became thoroughly Hellenized. In the words of the poet Horace (65–8 B.C.), "Captive Greece took captive her fierce conqueror and introduced her arts into rude Latium."[45] He meant that serious Roman education followed the Greek curriculum, copied Greek institutions, and was often conducted in the Greek language.

The Romans may have learned philosophy, science, and mathematics from the Greeks, but their own immense contributions lay elsewhere. An eminently practical people, they established efficient administrative sway over the entire Mediterranean world and united these lands with a system of roads still in use more than a thousand years later. Many of their technological innovations in the fields of engineering and hydraulics facilitated later breakthroughs by Muslims and Europeans. They instituted a strong and stable monetary system (though inflation had become a big problem by the third-century A.D.) and developed a trading network reaching right across the Eurasian continuum. To administer a far-flung and ethnically diverse polity, the Romans created the world's first refined and complex legal system, one that eventually involved means of resolving disputes between peoples of an extraordinary variety of customs, religions, and ethnicities.[46]

Roman experts in the law (*iurisconsulti*) elaborated precise and clear legal definitions and distinctions using an abstract legal vocabulary. Law professors composed procedural manuals, commentaries on the law, and collections of jurisprudence. The Greek (Stoic) ideas of a universal human nature and a natural law common to all powerfully influenced the development of Roman law. The legal system generally accommodated local customary law even after citizenship was granted to all freemen under Roman rule in 212 A.D. Judges throughout the empire not only applied statute law but also enjoyed the power both to follow and to set legal precedents. Over the centuries, they created a vast and systematic but supple corpus of law that set out most of the main branches and sub-branches of our modern legal systems today, though until recently only Western law had incorporated it.[47]

The Romans—uniquely, according to one scholar—invented the concept of the human individual.[48] In ancient Greece and other earlier cultures, each person was above all a member of a family, a clan, a tribe, a city-state, or other community. Individual identity, except in the philosophical reasoning of thinkers like Socrates, was deemed relatively unimportant. Roman legal culture challenged this view. Laws defining the concept of the "legal person" and prescribing detailed rules governing private property provided a framework in which elite individuals could advance private interests and carve out private space. This shift in understanding found expression in the highly individualized personalities created in Roman literature and art.

Ancient China

At the other end of Eurasia, history's longest-enduring society had already emerged. The Qin Dynasty (221–206 B.C.) and its successor for some 400 years, the Han Dynasty, established China as a unified state.[49] Despite frequently devastating invasions, civil wars, and rebellions, it has endured for over 2,000 years.[50]

Practical philosophy, political institutions, scholarship, mathematics, technology, and science flourished. Emperor Wu (156–87 B.C.) imposed Confucianism, with its emphasis on a familial model of hierarchy, deference to authority, humility, and sense of social place, as the ruling political philosophy, following centuries of competition with other schools of thought. Detailed knowledge of the Confucian classics became the main criterion for entry into the highly prestigious civil service. The emperors established a common currency and standard weights and measures; administered censuses; built roads, canals, and defensive fortifications; and sent many embassies and expeditions toward Central Asia, laying the foundation of the famed Silk Road to the Mediterranean. Scholars compiled vast historical works tracing the Chinese rulers back to mythological times (the third millennium B.C.). Mathematicians laid out methods for solving complex problems (but did not posit axioms),[51] anticipated a few proofs not achieved in Western mathematics until several centuries later, and discovered the crucially valuable concept of place value.[52] Scholars made significant advances in meteorology and astronomy, for example, accounting for both solar and lunar eclipses. Artisans and craftsmen invented paper, the seismoscope, the crossbow, the blast furnace, the horse collar, the seed drill, and the stirrup—all by the early centuries of the Common Era.

During the Tang (618–907), the storied civil service exam was instituted, and the mandarin class emerged.[53] Both survived until the early twentieth century. Scholars compiled vast historical works, encyclopedias, books on geography, and refined maps and star charts. Artisans invented wood-block printing, the escapement mechanism for clocks, and natural-gas-powered stoves.[54] The greatest age for Chinese poetry, the Tang, also saw the emergence of painting as a highly developed art form. Scholarship, science, technology, and mathematics continued to flourish in the Song Dunasty (960–1297), as did material culture, industry, and the economy.[55] Two other great Chinese inventions came into use during this era: gunpowder and the magnetic compass. Iron production in the late eleventh century approximated that achieved in Europe seven centuries later—as did China's population of 125 million.[56] Social life became more "civilized" in general, with a greater emphasis on cultural refinements and courtly pursuits. Unofficial writings, such as notebooks, diaries, and descriptions of daily life, proliferated.

China temporarily declined following devastating invasions by northern nomadic peoples in 1127 and 1271–79, yet rose again to great heights of wealth, power, civilization, and prestige during the Ming Dynasty (1368–1644).[57] Literacy expanded enormously, fueled in part by a printing boom. Scholars compiled vast digests, commentaries, encyclopedias, and compendia of facts and knowledge, both abstract and practical. Chinese applications of algebra during the early Ming were probably the most advanced in the world. Painting, drama, prose, poetry, and calligraphy flourished. A large number of elites adorned their homes with exquisite lacquerware, porcelain, enamelware, embroidered silks, and decorative objects carved from jade and ivory, among other esthetic delights. Silver flooded into the country in pursuit of such goods, as well as of commodities like tea, making China by far the world's biggest economy. The population apparently surged to well over 150 million in 1600, when all of Europe had only around 100 million souls. After the collapse of the Ming, however, China slowly declined relative to the civilization rising at the other end of Eurasia.

Two factors help explain China's extraordinary inventiveness for over 1,000 years. Most important was its enormous population, which was bigger than any other in history. If all human beings in the aggregate possess similar ingenuity, then a society with more people will produce more innovation. Second, good communications, a shared culture, flourishing educational opportunities, and a huge and relatively unified market gave China's vast pool of talent myriad opportunities for sharing ideas and learning from one another.

Yet after the Northern Song era, Chinese artisans crafted no more world-changing technologies (though they made incremental improvements in many areas, especially agriculture).[58] Why? After all, the population kept growing bigger, and opportunities to learn and innovate remained superabundant. Perhaps most importantly, the greatest Chinese inventions, including printing, gunpowder, and the compass, transformed the world, but not China. One can thus hypothesize that something in Chinese culture prevented the compass, say, from leading to transoceanic voyages.

What features in Chinese culture may have exerted this influence? It seems that over time Chinese elites concentrated more and more of their talent on literary endeavors. The main focus of these efforts was the civil service examination—for over 1,000 years the world's most rigorous method for assessing human talent.[59] For most of the examination's history, any male who passed a practice test could take the examination, whatever his social background. No wonder democratically inclined European commentators in the eighteenth century lauded the system.[60] Students spent 6 years memorizing the Confucian classics—431,286 characters—and then studying commentaries and other philosophical, historical, and literary works. If a qualifying candidate passed the week-long county-level examination, by demonstrating skill at calligraphy, poetry, and literary writing concerning topics of public policy and ethics, then he could advance to the triennial provincial examination. The successful—a tiny fraction—were guaranteed employment within the imperial bureaucracy. The ambitious usually went on to the even more grueling empire-wide examination in the hope of becoming an "advanced scholar." One could achieve no higher or more remunerative honor in society. Some brilliant men studied mathematics, astronomy, and law, but they received only scant official encouragement. Some literati pursued research and reflection in other nonliterary fields, but without much institutional backing. The examination system was thus a unifying force in Chinese culture but at the cost of stifling much creative thinking.

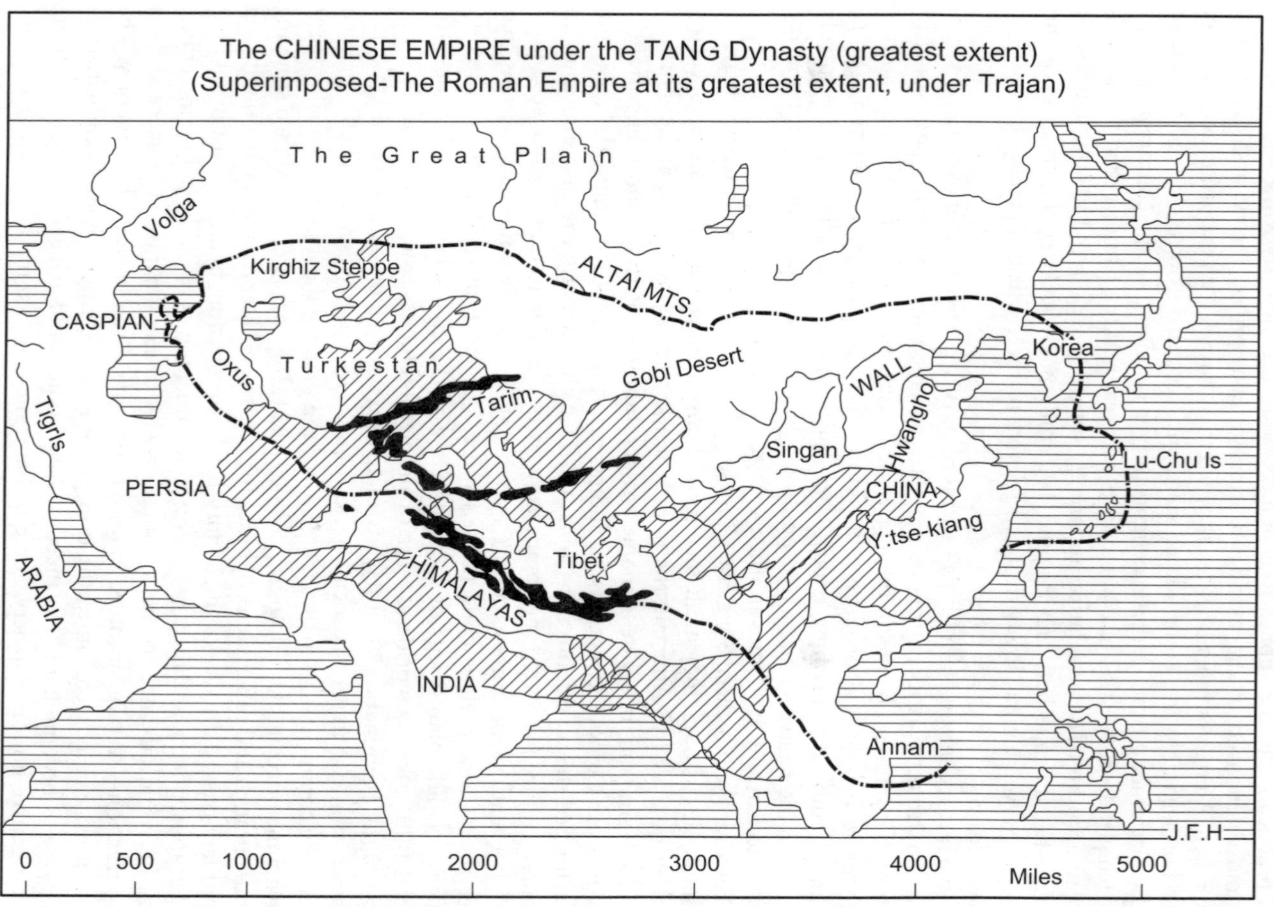

MAP 1.2 *Two vast, early Eurasian empires: China and Rome.*

So how did China compare to the Roman Empire? (see Map 1.2)[61] For one thing, Chinese civilization endured, whereas Rome collapsed by 500 A.D. The Roman economy was more highly monetized, but probably not by much. Rome, one might say, was an empire of property holders; China, an empire of officeholders. The population at the time of Augustus (63 B.C.–14 A.D.) was roughly similar to China's contemporaneous 55 million. In terms of engineering, the Chinese during antiquity probably never matched the Roman aqueducts. Rome had increased its wealth over several centuries by expanding its tributaries, as had ancient China, whose higher birthrate also raised aggregate wealth. The Song may even have experienced modest intensive economic growth, a feature that is central to modern economies but virtually unknown in previous centuries.[62]

Comparing the contributions to world history of China and Rome—and Greece—is a trickier business.[63] China's four greatest inventions alone—paper, printing, the magnetic compass, and gunpowder—probably surpassed those of any people until eighteenth-century Britain or nineteenth-century America. The Chinese administrative model was a marvel. It influenced many states in East Asia and, in the nineteenth century, inspired the British and other Western governments to institute civil service examinations. Scholars often point to the insatiable appetite for silver of China's vast domestic market as the main catalyst for world economic development beginning in the sixteenth century. Looking at other aspects of life, however, did China raise up any ideas, systems, or institutions that inspired global change? Aside from its important contributions to Buddhism and its undisputed cultural leadership in East Asia, China's influence in the wider modern world, despite its wealth and prestige, remained surprisingly modest.

Unlike the Greeks, the Chinese developed no influential philosophical systems or approaches that fueled anything so momentous as the Scientific Revolution (see Chapter 8). The frequent constitutional changes in the Greek city-states; the adversarial culture in law and politics, which involved being able to argue both sides of any case and led to intellectual skepticism; and the strenuous search for axiomatic mathematical and philosophical certainty played only a modest role in Chinese history. There the elites mostly shared a single ideal vision of a wise and benevolent ruler. Confucianism, China's greatest Chinese intellectual contribution, underpinned this vision by emphasizing harmony, stability, and community-mindedness rather than innovation and critical thinking. It was before the ruler that the most powerful arguments were made, not before the law courts, which were mostly avoided like the plague; and flattery more than rational proofs tended to achieve the best results.[64] Criminal and administrative laws (a holdover from Qin times and tolerated by Confucian thinkers) were both highly developed in China, but not civil law. In general, Confucianism favored conciliation, persuasion, custom, and example over rules or sanctions. Of course, the Chinese achieved marvels of social organization, cultural longevity, technological advancement, and artistic refinement all without elaborate civil law. Yet given the crucial role in modern times of civil law in the emergence of civil society, of sophisticated commercial systems, and of constitutional government, its absence in China was probably to be regretted.

Rome made one more huge contribution. By unifying a vast territory from North Africa to Armenia and from Scotland to the Persian Gulf under a single ruler, legal system, administrative apparatus, and official language, the Romans facilitated the rise and spread of Christianity. The English historian Edward Gibbon (1737–94) argued that Christianity caused the fall of Rome by weakening the people's martial spirit, sowing religious divisions, and diverting wealth to priests who preached chastity in an age of declining birthrates. In fact, the empire was already in decline when Emperor Constantine (r. 306–37) decreed an end to the persecution of Christianity in 313. If anything, the faith exerted centripetal pressure on the crumbling empire just as it proved Europe's strongest unifying force and its greatest inspiration for reform over the next several hundred years. In any event, the Roman church embraced Rome's administrative structure, civilizing mission, and imperial ideal.

Other great civilizations

Other peoples imparted valuable innovations to world civilization. The Indians founded one of the most ancient and sophisticated civilizations, dating back almost 7,000 years. Before the Birth of Christ, it had achieved breathtaking advances in medicine, engineering, agriculture, textile manufacturing, and industry. Over 2,000 years ago, Greek and Chinese scholars made pilgrimages, toward the headwaters of the Indus River, to the school in Taxila, perhaps the first institution of higher learning on the planet.[65] Emperor Ashoka (r. 269–232 B.C.) is famed for both great military conquests early in his reign and the promotion of peace, toleration, and social inclusion during the majority of his years on the throne.[66] Indian scholarship, science, and mathematics reached their peak during the culture's Golden Age, when the enlightened Gupta Dynasty ruled northern India from 280 to 550. Thereafter, a centuries-long series of invasions from Central Asia and Europe shattered the people's unity and muted its glory.[67] The subcontinent remained wealthy, thickly settled, and industrious, and there were some periods of glory. Akbar, the Mughal emperor of India from 1561 to 1605, a military strategist of genius, promoted religious toleration (but not for the faith of his youth, Islam), argued for the supremacy of reason, and abolished the discriminatory taxes on non-Muslims.[68] Indians continued to produce the world's most beautiful cotton prints, using secret methods developed millennia before. By the 1600s, the prints took Europe by storm. In 1680–84 alone, the Dutch and English East India Companies imported well over 1 million lengths of cotton cloth, including brightly colored calico and chintz.[69] Unlike China, however, India retained neither its independence nor its prestige. Within 200 years, it was a jewel in the crown of Britain.

Yet India's contribution to world history may almost have equaled China's. Someone once devised a computer metaphor to compare the two cultures. China, it was argued, produces hardware; India writes software. Aside from the fact that this description corresponds accurately to current commercial reality, it also makes a good historical point.[70] Whereas the Chinese made repeated and stupendous material breakthroughs, the Indians transformed the soul and the mind. Siddhartha Gautama, a wealthy prince born in far northern India (present-day Nepal), around 400 B.C., set off wandering at age 29 and achieved spiritual enlightenment 6 years later sitting under a banyan fig tree. The Buddha, or "enlightened one," devoted the rest of his life, nearly a half-century, to imparting spiritual knowledge, winning disciples, teaching proper discipline, and forming monastic communities.[71]

His teachings were open to all, irrespective of race or caste and, eventually, gender. The first universal religion,[72] Buddhism spread over the next several centuries to Afghanistan and throughout Southeast and East Asia.

Buddhism thrived in China, in particular. At the start of the sixth-century A.D., roughly 3,000 Buddhist monks from India and Central Asia were actively spreading the doctrine there. By the end of the Tang Dynasty in 907, despite some fierce official persecution, a syncretic Buddhism mingled with elements of traditional values and beliefs became an integral part of the Chinese identity and worldview and surely inspired much of the cultural ferment of the subsequent Song era.[73] Confucianism laid out practical principles of life, but for many Chinese only Buddhism could stir the soul.[74] Neither doctrine, one should point out, favors the transformation of the world; both advocate social harmony and even quietism.

India's second great contribution to human cultural evolution was in mathematics.[75] From ancient times, Indian scholars advanced human knowledge in nearly every branch of mathematics. Their arithmetic breakthroughs involved inventing place value (independently of China), fractions, negative and irrational numbers, and one of the mind's simplest yet most profound advances, the concept of the number "zero." Indian achievements in geometry included calculating square roots, cube roots, and Pythagorean triples; in algebra, expressing quadratic, cubic, and quartic equations; in trigonometry, defining the functions of sine, cosine, and inverse sine; and in calculus, discovering concepts of the derivative and infinitesimals. Aside, perhaps, from the Greeks, who learned from and influenced them, no people advanced mathematical knowledge as much, until the modern European age.[76]

A remnant of the Roman Empire survived in the eastern Mediterranean, centered on Constantinople, the city of Constantine.[77] The Byzantine Empire, which stretched from Asia Minor and North Africa to Italy until the mid-600s, maintained one of the world's highest levels of culture, with achievements in the arts, science, scholarship, and commerce. Yet its greatest contribution to world history, aside from preserving ancient Greek learning, was shielding Europe from attacks by crusaders of the last of the three great universal religions, Islam.

Originating on the Arabian Peninsula, Islam drew upon the traditions and beliefs of the world's two other Abrahamic religions, Judaism and Christianity.[78] The founder, Muhammad (c. 570–632), was a charismatic merchant and military leader with a prophetic gift. Revelations he received during the final two decades of his life were later compiled as the Quran. It proclaimed that there is only one God, that Muhammad was his final and the greatest prophet, and that to achieve salvation, one needs to perform several simple religious duties. The most important of these was regular prayer and physical purity. The Prophet led several battles to impose his religious vision against the established authorities, until, by the time of his death, the entire peninsula was under his rule. Internecine strife, involving assassination, rebellion, and civil war, broke out among his followers. Yet the first four successive Muslim leaders, or caliphs, swept by force of arms to Afghanistan in the east and to the Atlantic Ocean in the west (see Map 1.3). Islamic law required the faithful to engage in jihad, meaning in part armed struggle to expand Muslim territory. Thus, the Islamic armies kept pushing. The Frankish leader Charles Martel (c. 688–741) turned them back in central France, at the Battle of Tours (or Poitiers) in 732. Decades after this loss, the Muslim dominions still extended from the Pyrenees Mountains

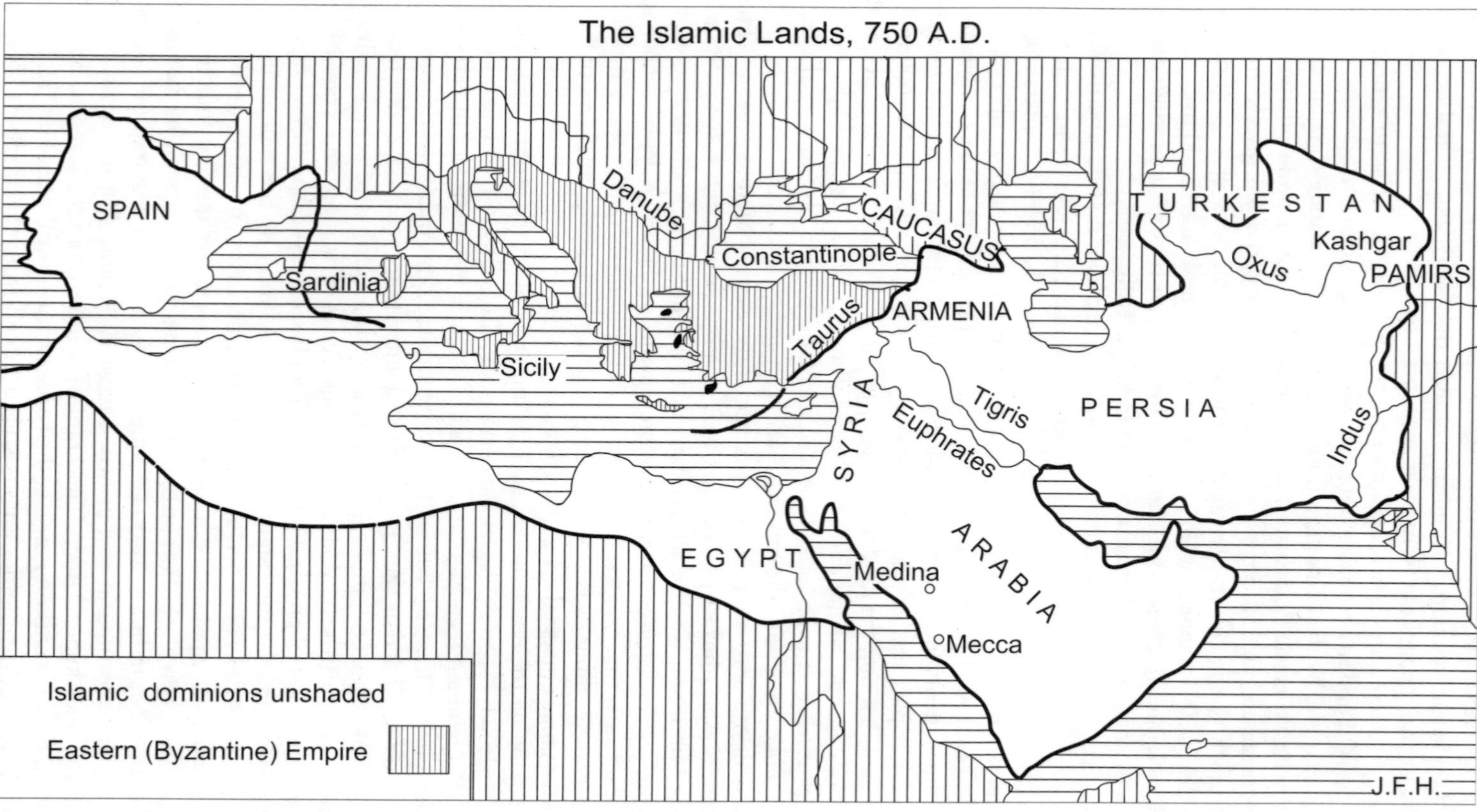

MAP 1.3 *The Muslim and Byzantine Empires overshadowed politically fragmented Europe in 750 A.D.*

to the Indus Valley. Still, Muslim rulers did not hasten to convert the conquered (the higher taxes imposed on non-Muslims were too lucrative), and indeed for centuries Christians constituted the majority of many nominally Muslim lands.[79] They, Jews, and other non-Muslims often enjoyed broad tolerance, if not active acceptance.[80]

The violence of Islam's early expansion contrasts with that of Buddhism and Christianity. These spread mostly by persuasion and conversion. Monasticism, an institution lacking in the Islamic world, also played a key role in the other two faiths, by slowly establishing spiritual outposts, further and further from the religions' birthplaces.[81]

The Muslim rulers, typically warriors and merchants with a cosmopolitan outlook, presided over one of the most splendid civilizations in the world. Their rule fostered tremendous social mobility and a practical tolerance of peoples of other faiths, who contributed much capital and talent. Islamic religious law, which regulated nearly all aspects of life, was highly egalitarian (though not in gender terms). Its detailed business and contract law greatly fostered the development of trade. Islamic societies, in fact, were largely meritocratic with very little inherited status. Individual personality and leadership mattered far more than institutionalized legitimacy.[82] Bonds of continuity were weak; social and political catastrophe, frequent. Elites depended on personal success and official favor. They could amass colossal fortunes but also quickly lose them. Slavery was deeply entrenched in Islamic society precisely because the elites lacked other obvious status markers.

Trading caravans had crossed the Arabian Peninsula since antiquity. The entire eastern Mediterranean, despite the fall of Rome, had remained a commercial crossroads going back to ancient Mesopotamia.[83] Building on this foundation, Muslim traders developed a commercial network extending far beyond the already enormous Islamic world.[84] They opened up trade routes and outposts through the Sahara Desert, down the eastern coast of Africa, across the Indian Ocean, and into the China Sea. In many instances, the further spread of Islam followed business relations. This network facilitated the diffusion of important crops from Asia to the Mediterranean world, including citrus fruits, rice, cotton, and sugarcane. Muslims imported silk and paper from China and learned to make them. They exported refined pottery, glassware, paper, sugar, soap, textiles, perfumes, cosmetics, medicines, and other goods of their invention or manufacture. In addition to luxury goods from Asia, the most profitable trade was in slaves captured or bought from the Mediterranean region, the Eastern Slavic lands, and Africa. Giant marketplaces sprang up in Baghdad, Cairo, and other major cities. In some cases, they sold contracts to buy future crops. Credit, bills of exchange, and commercial trading companies developed.[85] The adoption beginning in the late 900s of the Indian numbering system, which we call "Arabic numerals," facilitated keeping accounts and measuring goods and services. Yet Muslim rulers were not above despoiling entrepreneurs in times of need, even those who lent them money in the good times. Urban commercial interests, generally, enjoyed neither independence nor political influence. They, like everyone else, were at the mercy of the rulers.

Muslim craftsmen possessed impressive technological skill. Across the Islamic world, they harnessed the power of water mills to grind meal, saw logs, crush raw materials, and other industrial uses. Artisans invented or improved a wide range of practical items, including bars of soap, the fountain pen, metallic-glazed ceramics, stained glass, the refined oil lamp, various string and woodwind instruments, the alidade for a surveying land, timekeeping devices, and the astrolabe for calculating astronomical position.[86]

The Islamic world's greatest contributions were in mathematics and science. Greek philosophy profoundly influenced Islamic thought.[87] Muslim scholars also translated the great heritage of Chinese, Indian, and Persian learning.[88] In fact, Islam was the first civilization in history that synthesized learning and technology from all the great civilizations of the old world, either directly or indirectly. Mathematicians developed the use of symbols for unknown quantities, a technique that is still called by its Arabic name, *al-jabr*. Muslim scientists essentially invented chemistry using precise and careful observation, experimentation, and record keeping.[89] They developed dozens of chemical processes like distillation, crystallization, sublimation, and purification and discovered thousands of chemical substances and derivatives. These led to many practical applications, including perfumes, dies, and cosmetics, and to culinary, medicinal, hygienic, and household uses.

Muslim scientists made significant accomplishments in medicine, optics, and astronomy. Developing rigorous methods of observation and experimentation, they advanced medical knowledge in the full range of disciplines, including anatomy, the treatment of diseases, physiology, pathology, obstetrics, pharmacology, ophthalmology, and surgery. Refined surgical techniques were made possible in part by the invention of precision surgical instruments. The Persian polymath Ibn Sina (981–1037) consolidated all of this learning, along with Ancient Greek and Indian knowledge, into his *The Canon of Medicine* (1025), a work still taught in European medical schools in the seventeenth century. Breakthroughs in nearly every aspect of optics were brought forward by Ibn al-Haytham (965–1039), the "father of modern optics," in his multivolume *Book of Optics*. At the Maragheh observatory, built in 1259 in northwestern Persia, the Arab astronomer Ibn al-Shatir (1304–75) anticipated many of the discoveries of later European scientists, including heliocentrism and the theory of lunar motion (see Chapter 8).

The Achilles' heel of Islamic intellectual life was philosophy. In order to win over the still largely Christian peoples of the Middle East, Muslim theologians drew on systematic Aristotelian thought to make their own faith intelligible. From the eighth to the twelfth century, philosophers of the Islamic world undertook refined studies into major questions raised by the ancient Greeks regarding logic, ethics, theories of knowledge, and metaphysics. Ibn Sina, for example, concluded that faith and reason were fully compatible. A century and a half later, the Andalusian polymath Ibn Rushd (1126–98) argued further that rational investigation of the natural world could help man to understand God, as the creator of all things. Yet a powerful strain in Islamic thought ran counter to these views. Best articulated by the brilliant Persian scholar al-Ghazali (1058–1111), who advocated direct mystical experience of God (the Sufi tradition of Islam),[90] its main thrust was to cast doubt on the trustworthiness of reason as a means to approach the most important realm of understanding and experience, Islamic faith.[91] Mathematics and the natural sciences, insofar as they were kept entirely separate from religion, could be pursued. Implementing this stricture, however, required purging the Islamic world's only institutions of higher learning, the religiously based madrasahs, of Greek philosophy and natural science. For several centuries, it remained possible for powerful elites to fund brilliant scholars.

Without reliable institutional support, however, the Islamic world's achievements in philosophy and science gradually dwindled, though Muslims continued to make significant advances in a variety of scientific and scholarly endeavors, such as astronomy.[92] One can also mention the *Muqaddimah* of Ibn Khaldun (1332–1406), which the English historian Arnold Toynbee considered the most brilliant philosophy of history "that has ever yet been created by any mind."[93]

How can one characterize Islamic contributions to world history? The preservation and further development of Greek learning must rank very high. Extensive practical achievements in technology and science were equally important. The Muslim peoples were less industrially developed than the Chinese, yet during their Golden Age (mid-eighth to mid-thirteenth centuries) they were probably just about as inventive and, thanks to the Hellenistic inheritance, even more philosophically oriented. To return to the metaphor suggested above, the Islamic world's advances occurred in both software (the life of the mind and of the soul) and hardware (the material realm). The Chinese, by contrast, assimilated and synthesized the cumulative achievements of previous and contemporaneous civilizations far less extensively and successfully than did the Muslims—in large part because they considered their own civilization the pinnacle of human achievement. The Chinese therefore influenced the next great civilization to rise, the West, far less than did the Muslim world. It helped that the cultural and political superiority of the nearby Muslims deeply stirred the imagination and challenged the ingenuity of the Europeans.

None of this is meant to argue that the Chinese, Muslim, Indian, Byzantine, or other peoples created absolutely superior cultures or civilizations. Such judgments are impossible to make. Each achieved wonders of originality and inventiveness expressing its particular values and ways of life. Some flourished longer than others or were more powerful or richer. They all deserve deep admiration. Each contributed in its own way—albeit some more than others—to the fund of knowledge and technology of the modern world. More importantly for this study, of all the marvelous cultures throughout history, three contributed the most to making possible the European and ultimately Western synthesis of recent centuries: the Islamic world, China, and India, perhaps in that order.

Astonishing human ingenuity

Yet, to repeat, every people and culture on earth has achieved miracles of adaptation and innovation. Each deserves the profound and undying respect of every thinking person. Even the most isolated, tiniest, least developed, and apparently most impoverished peoples on earth have worked astonishing feats of creativity and inventiveness in learning to thrive in whatever circumstances nature has given them. Jared Diamond came away awed from his years among the tribal peoples of New Guinea. Their social organization, minute knowledge of the flora and fauna of their area, and extraordinary powers of observation led him to attribute to them a higher average intelligence than people in developed Western countries.[94] One does not need to share this opinion to believe that people the world over all possess impressive levels of creativity and intelligence.

If all people, as collectives, are equally creative, then how can one account for their differing contributions to world civilization? No region contributed more in this regard than sub-Saharan Africa, whence modern humans first emerged. Without Africa, there would have been no civilization, no West, no Industrial Revolution, and no computer to write this book on. Yet several geographical factors disadvantage the oldest continent. Desert makes up 40 percent of its area. Consistently high temperatures enable disease-causing microbes to flourish across much of the continent. Nearly everywhere the soils are poor. One might almost argue that Africa was historically more hospitable to animals, insects, and bacteria than to humans.[95]

At nearly 12 million square miles, Africa is three times bigger than Europe, yet 2,000 years ago it had only around half the population, or 16 million inhabitants, about half of them in North Africa and the Nile Valley. Since all humans are extraordinarily creative, and all their cultures adapt ingeniously to their environments, higher population densities lead to more inventiveness. That factor by itself was probably going to make Europe the site of more innovation than Africa during those 2,000 years, especially given that Europe was part of the Eurasian land mass, home to a total of 146 million people at the birth of the Common Era. Yet another major stimulus to technological and other forms of advancement is human interaction. The more opportunities we have to learn from others, to share ideas, to exchange handiwork, and to experience other cultures, the more breakthroughs we will make.[96] Inevitably, all the greatest early civilizations emerged along the vast, highly populous, and easily traversable Eurasian continuum. They arose because of these geographical factors and not because their founders and inhabitants displayed greater creativity or intelligence than people on other continents.

Thus, the peoples of Africa founded hundreds of fortresses and towns, forged intricate regional and transcontinental trade routes, developed myriad cultures expressed through 2,110 of today's nearly 7,000 living languages (though making up only 12 percent of the world population),[97] built up sprawling empires, and deployed sophisticated metallurgy and other technologies.[98] For most of its history, however, communications and transportation across the continent were weakly developed, given geographical constraints, in particular, its predominant north–south axis. The movement of animals and humans is far easier along an east–west axis, because it does not require crossing climatic zones.[99] As a result, except along the northern and eastern coasts, the fruits of human ingenuity did not circulate anything like so rapidly as across Eurasia.[100] Even so, African peoples domesticated the available wild plants—sorghum, African rice and yams, the oil palm, and coffee. Although the land teemed with wildlife, few animals proved domesticable. We know for sure only that Africans first domesticated the guinea fowl, a pheasant-like bird.[101] In comparison with the emergence of modern humans and the flourishing of ancient Egypt, these may not seem like huge contributions to world civilization—though many coffee lovers might disagree.

The South and Central American peoples made some important advances, entirely independently of the world's other great core areas, including pictographic writing from at least 500 B.C., sophisticated calendars, the concept of the numeric "zero" (before the East Indians), and formidable social efficiency. Great civilizations arose: the Mayan, Incan, and Aztec.[102] Indigenous peoples domesticated a wide variety of plants (and a few animals), probably their greatest legacy to world civilization: corn, potatoes, squash, beans, cocoa, tomatoes, peppers, rubber trees, and many others.[103] They also imparted to Europeans ideals of living in harmony with nature. In recent times, the Latin American peoples have strongly influenced worldwide popular culture with innovative musical styles popular the world over, like salsa, mambo, samba, bossa nova, tango, merengue, and rumba, culminating in the Latin Pop Explosion of the late 1990s.[104] The continent's north–south geographical orientation impeded development. Yet their contributions would surely have been greater had contact with pathogens carried by Europeans not ravaged their populations and cultures.[105]

"No people in history have been so 'naturally' expert in war as the nomads of the Eurasian steppe;"[106] so wrote an eminent authority on their history. Until the gunpowder age, few sedentary peoples—not even the Persians, the Romans, or the Chinese—could readily withstand them. In nomadic societies, every adult male was a warrior, instead of roughly every tenth man as in sedentary communities. The nomads' horses, essential for their work, gave them a decisive advantage in war. When hundreds or even thousands of half-ton mounted beasts bore down on an enemy in one vast formation, who could stop them?[107] Given their lifestyle, the nomads rarely conquered the adjacent sedentary states, yet they exerted constant military pressure on them for many centuries. From the Scythians in the sixth-century B.C. to the Huns and Visigoths in the fourth-century A.D., and from the Avars and Magyars a few centuries after that to the most awesome of these warrior-peoples, the Mongols, in the thirteenth century, the steppe nomads terrorized and extorted "protection money" along every margin of their territory.

The nomadic Mongol warriors forged history's largest contiguous land empire (see Map 1.4). It stretched from Eastern Europe and the Middle East to the Sea of Okhotsk and the South China Sea.[108] Everywhere they went they pillaged and destroyed but also united, most notably perhaps in reuniting the disparate Chinese lands for the first time in centuries. Within the vast Mongol Empire, trade and cultural exchange flourished for a century starting in the early 1200s.[109] They opened the commercial routes along which Marco Polo, Ibn Battuta, and countless others journeyed. The Mongols also spread technology, for example, gunpowder, the Chinese concoction perfected in Western Europe. Ironically, precisely that substance enabled sedentary societies finally to develop weaponry that rendered the steppe warriors all but harmless and decisively shifted the balance of military power between the sedentary and nomadic worlds (see Chapter 4).

Another people contributed richly to the rise of the West without ever founding an empire or ruling a large territory: the Jews.[110] They conceived the earliest monotheistic vision of the universe and set down the first narrative of the emergence and development of a single people.[111] Throughout their history, prophets vehemently denounced injustice and called the rich and powerful to account. A moral code and a set of laws, granted to the Hebrew people by God himself, they affirmed, stood above all men and rendered every person equal in the eyes of God. In the other religious traditions of the time, humans could become gods and the gods acted like humans with all their passions and vices.[112] Upon the foundations of Judaism, two civilizations centered on monotheistic religion emerged, Christianity and Islam.

To these civilizations, the Jews added a leaven of astonishing creativity in business, medicine, letters, science, the arts, and a variety of other leadership roles. When commerce began to flourish in Europe in the eleventh century, Jews were the chief

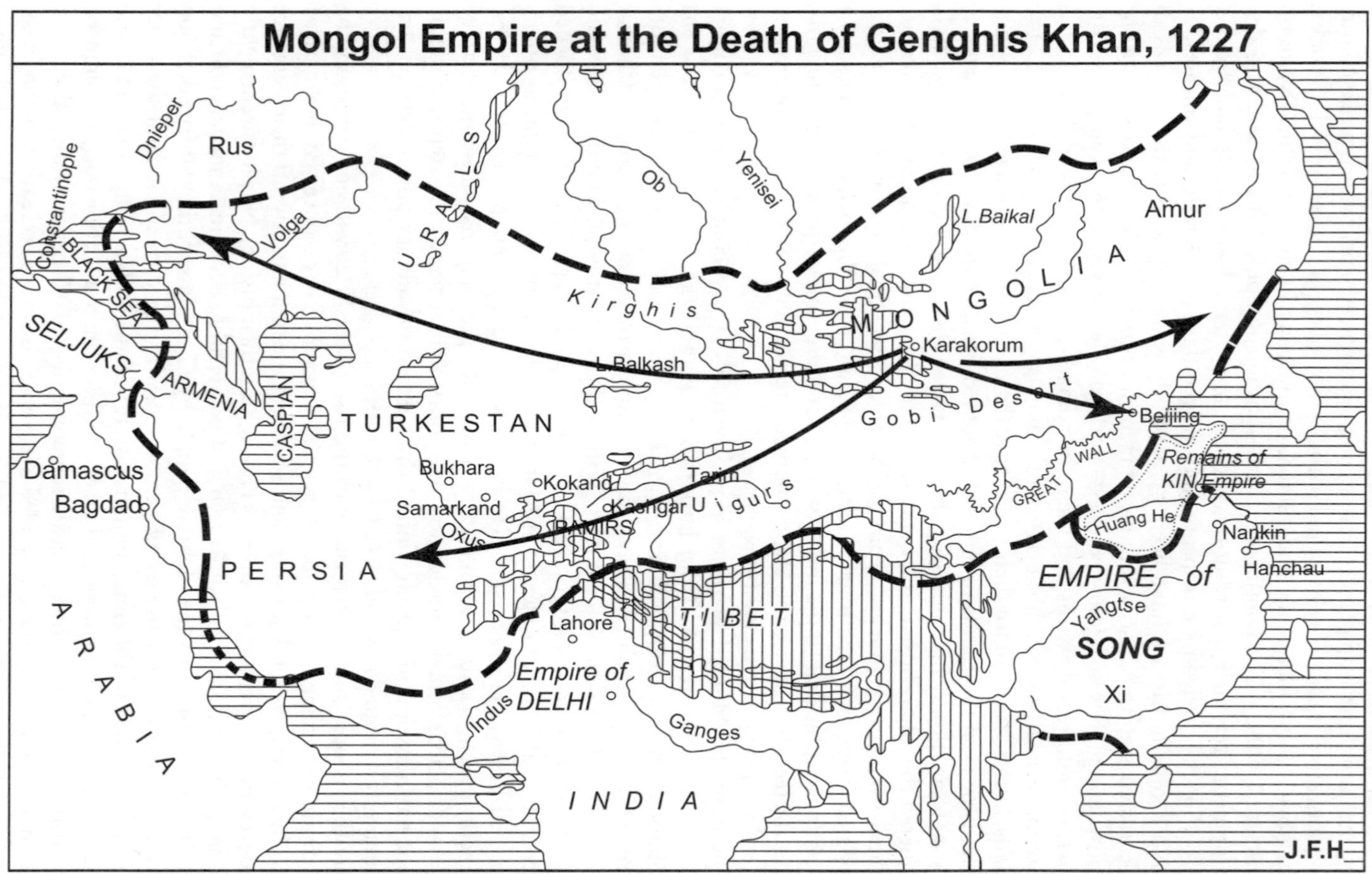

MAP 1.4 *The nomadic Mongol warriors forged history's largest contiguous land empire.*

moneylenders, a trade that Christian laws encouraged them to practice.[113] During the high Middle Ages, Jewish scholars translated key works of science and learning from Arabic into Latin. Dozens of thinkers and writers in the early modern period, from Michel de Montaigne to Baruch Spinoza, were at least part Jewish. Other major figures probably descended from converted Jews, like Christopher Columbus. Despite ferocious and almost continuous persecution, Jewish entrepreneurs amassed both the capital and business experience to play important roles in the emergence of capital markets, banks, overseas trading operations, and stock exchanges in Europe's leading commercial centers. The emancipation of the Jews in Europe, beginning with the French revolution, launched them on an extraordinary career of success in every field of endeavor. The story of the rise of the West is therefore inextricably intertwined with that of the West's Jews.

Across the globe, one can find dozens of sites bearing witness to the breadth, depth, and height of human vision. The religious temples in classically proportioned twelfth-century Angkor Wat, in today's Cambodia, spread over one square mile of grounds and boast 10,000 square feet of carved-stone bas-reliefs depicting scenes from Hindu epics.[114] Consider the hundreds of stone sculptures, many weighing over 50 tons, erected on Easter Island 2,400 miles off the coast of South America over 500 years ago.[115] Yet another marvel is the gigantic bronze Great Buddha completed in 751 in the city of Nara, Japan. It stands 52 feet high and weighs 500 tons—a wonder of the world for centuries.[116]

The enormous influence China exerted throughout East Asia is evident in the case of Japan, an island country roughly the size of Germany. The Chinese impact began through Korea, which lies 100 miles distant at the nearest points—five times closer than China. (By contrast, only 21 miles separate the British Isles from mainland Europe.) Thence Buddhism arrived in the sixth century.[117] For 200 years, Japan's rulers sent large embassies of scholars, merchants, officials, Buddhist monks, and artists directly to China.[118] They returned with the full range of Chinese ideas and practices—from Confucianism and the yin-yang duality to the tea ceremony and urban planning—which took deep root and radically transformed Japan. Dominated by a military aristocracy throughout much of its history, the Japanese grew economically prosperous from trade, efficient agriculture, and a work ethic promoted by Confucianism. Like Europe, the country was close enough to the great centers of civilization to learn from them but far enough to avoid easy conquest. In 1281, Japanese warriors—assisted by a powerful typhoon—halted an invasion force of nearly 200,000 attackers in some 4,500 ships launched by Kublai Khan, the emperor of China and great khan of the Mongols.[119] This felicitous event appeared to the victors as a sign of divine favor and Japanese exceptionalism.

For several more centuries, feudal lords (*daimyo*) ruled their regional domains, even after the Tokugawa overlordship (shogunate) was established in 1603, though now internecine wars ceased.[120] Xenophobic policies dating from this era largely excluded Europeans—and even European books until 1720—and thus isolated Japan. Despite official restrictions on trade, such as the outlawing of wheeled vehicles, commerce flourished and cities grew. By 1750, Edo—Tokyo—was perhaps the world's second-biggest urban center (after Beijing). As in China and Korea, however, technology and innovation lagged behind Europe.[121] Even so, knowledge of Western development seeped in, and many Japanese were positively impressed. When the United States

Navy sent a small fleet of steam ships armed with the latest exploding-shell cannon to Edo Bay in 1853, Japan's ruling elites felt they had to agree to open up their country to foreign trade.[122] Fifteen years later, the Tokugawa Shogunate collapsed, and two *daimyo* who vigorously adopted Western military technology restored full power to the newly enthroned Meiji Emperor, Matsuhito.

Within a few decades, the Japanese had assimilated nearly every idea, institution, and technology the West had to offer, from warships and banks to modern science and political parties. As one scholar has argued quite persuasively, this "was the most massive shift which has occurred in human history in the last 10,000 years."[123] By the later twentieth century, Japan had become the second-richest and most technologically innovative country on the planet. It seems that, beyond a well-ordered society with a decentralized system of government, the greatest Japanese advantage was their willingness to adapt the great achievements of other cultures—first from China starting in the 600s and then from the West 150 years ago.

Thousands of other peoples throughout the world, on every continent and in every inhabitable ecological niche, have for centuries astonished scholarly and amateur observers with extraordinary displays of ingenuity, daring, perseverance, and creativity. Canoes, toboggans, kayaks, snowshoes, boomerangs come to mind. Native peoples the world over disclosed to explorers the secrets of the flora, fauna, and ecologies surrounding them. Inuits, for example, taught the American naturalist Clarence Birdseye how to preserve fish with flash freezing. He went on to found a frozen food company that still bears his name. All of these largely anonymous innovators contributed in ways great and small to the development of our modern civilization. Only near-perfect geographical, cultural, and historical conditions made possible the explosion of innovation achieved in Europe.

After the millennium, the competing but culturally unified European peoples began, very gradually, to pull together and synthesize the abundant achievements of cultures around the Mediterranean, across Eurasia, and ultimately throughout the wider world. Humans had always learned from one another and shared their learning. But now the members of one civilization figured out how to build continuously upon these achievements and to create toolkits of power and pathways of knowledge reaching ever-greater heights of complexity and sophistication. In other words, they engendered or stumbled upon what we now call the modern age.

A latecomer

Europe was never one of the core areas of civilization. These were three: China, India, and, the oldest of all, the region between the Nile and the Oxus (Amu Daria) Rivers. Each had known continuous development at a high level for several millennia. No other region of the world could match them for innovation, riches, or power. Around the turn of the first millennium A.D., however, a new core area began to emerge north of the Mediterranean Sea.[124]

After the fall of Rome, Europe was impoverished and backward, compared to the core areas of civilization, but it was not entirely undeveloped. Nor did it lack all natural advantages. Even if a major civilization had never taken root, the European

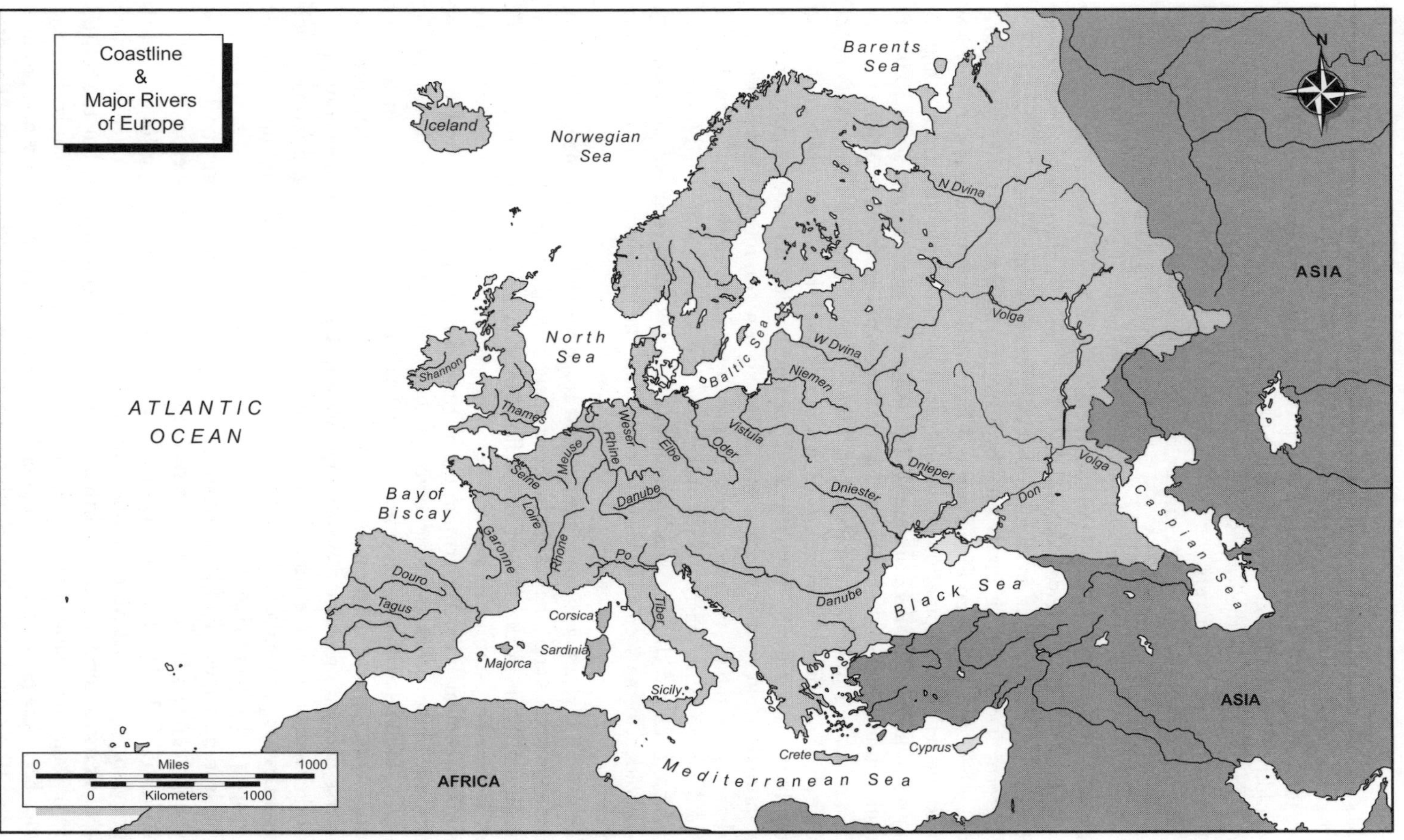

MAP 1.5 *Europe's long coastline and numerous rivers gave Europeans the greatest access to waterways for transportation and travel.*

continent had been continuously inhabited for thousands of years. Here one finds the world's oldest known cave paintings, hundreds of massive prehistoric stone rings dotting the British Isles, and remains of peoples who fashioned beaker-shaped pots and made copper and bronze tools across much of the continent by 2000 B.C.

In addition to the geographical advantages discussed in the Prologue, Europe's meandering coastline is the longest of any continent. This meant that, together with numerous and extensive rivers, the Europeans had the best access to waterways, until recently the cheapest and most efficient means of transportation (see Map 1.5).[125] Most of the land is relatively flat, too, which also facilitated movement of people and exchanges of goods. Rainfall is moderate but reliable; the climate, temperate, so the tropical diseases that plagued the equatorial regions were absent. Europe, among continents, also faces the fewest natural disasters.[126] Finally, the Americas were easier to access from Europe than from any other continent, except Africa.

The term "Dark Ages" is rarely used by historians nowadays to refer to the early Middle Ages, but the material and cultural level of the continent was certainly low after Rome fell. The population of the imperial city itself plunged from a high of perhaps 1 million in 200 A.D. to roughly 100,000 in the year 450 and some 20,000 at the millennium. Most of the continent's other large cities grew less populous too. The Roman roads and aqueducts deteriorated. Illiteracy became almost universal outside the church. Epidemics of disease struck frequently, and the climate grew colder and wetter. Eking out a living from the land became harder. As independent farming grew more difficult, former yeomen sought out security on manors and estates. The "barbarians" who had swarmed across Europe and shattered the weakening empire settled down and intermarried with indigenous elites. They established hundreds of rulerships. Even the church, which might have made claims to universal authority, was beholden to the secular lords who controlled the appointment of bishops and even clergy.[127]

For over 200 years in Europe, the greatest force for civilization, the preservation of ancient texts, and the cherishing of beliefs and nonmaterial values was monasticism. Born in the Near East, it flourished in Europe from the early 500s when St Benedict established a new type of monastic order at the Abbey of Monte Cassino in central Italy. Prescribing equal times for prayer, study, and work for monks, the Rule of St Benedict enjoyed enormous popularity and, somewhat ironically, facilitated the achievement of material success. Also important for later developments, female religious orders opened a path for women's advancement in diverse occupations, albeit mostly only within the confines of their convents.[128] Few other societies at the time or before (e.g. Tang China) offered women such possibilities for personal development. This social feature played an important role in Europe's subsequent rise.

The leading tribes of northwestern Europe in these times were the Franks, a Germanic people. A few of their kings succeeded in uniting these tribes, for example, Clovis I (466–511). The greatest was Charles the Great, or Charlemagne (r. 768–814), the grandson of Charles Martel. Sometimes called the "father of Europe," he united most of France, Germany, and northern Italy. It has been argued that the mortal threat of Islam necessitated the rise of a counter force in Europe.[129] In reality, had Charles been less great, the Carolingian Empire could never have risen. Certainly, Pope Leo III recognized the Frankish king's significance and crowned him "Emperor of the Romans" on Christmas day in 800. In return, Charlemagne promoted the Christianization (in some cases by force of arms) of his still largely pagan empire, patronized scholarship and the arts, and fostered what scholars have called the Carolingian Renaissance.[130]

Yet this one relatively successful attempt to unite the European continent collapsed almost as soon as Charles died. His lands were divided between his three grandsons, who fought among themselves, and then were further divided in subsequent years under less charismatic and forceful rulers. The Frankish kings paid their servitors in land, which soon became the inalienable property of aristocrats. They fought incessantly among themselves, further dividing the realm politically. Some great kings still emerged, for example, Alfred the Great of England (849–899). He not only united the various kings of the English under his rule and defended the realm against Danish Vikings, whose king he persuaded to adopt Christianity, but also vigorously promoted learning and scholarship and personally translated into Old English the Roman philosopher Boethius's *The Consolation of Philosophy*, among many other learned writings.[131] Still, Europe disintegrated politically and remained impoverished economically. Learning and culture were still treasured in isolated localities, yet in the year 900 no one would even remotely have predicted Europe's extraordinary ascendancy a thousand years later.

A millennium may seem a vast expanse of time, yet for nearly all of human history innovations diffused slowly. Truly dramatic transformations were few and separated by tens of thousands of years. The three most important were the mastery of fire, the emergence of language, and the domestication of crops and livestock. Other changes, like the development of writing, the emergence of metallurgy, the invention of the wheel, or the rise of religions generally started in one civilization and then spread continentally over the course of a few thousand or several hundred years. Most cultures managed to adapt and assimilate, or to reject, them before new ones emerged. No one culture could achieve absolute preeminence. None until Europe, drawing on the achievements of the rest of the world, effected transformations in many areas of life simultaneously and thus forever changed the rules of the game.[132]

QUESTIONS FOR REFLECTION

What key factor explains the rise of civilizations?

How did the domestication of plants and animals change human societies?

What did the ancient Greeks contribute to human development?

Why was Roman law a valuable achievement?

What impact did Chinese inventions have?

What constituted the Islamic cultural synthesis?

Chapter 2 Chronology

Early eighth century:	Peasants begin three-crop rotation system in Europe
742–743 A.D.:	Last of frequent and great epidemics strikes Europe
~700–955 A.D.:	Successive raids limit population growth of Western Europe
Mid-ninth century:	Earth begins cyclical warming period, enabling higher crop yields
Tenth century:	Horse collar usage spreads to Europe after originating in China
989 A.D.:	"Peace of God" instituted by church to limit wars and conflicts
~1050 A.D.:	Large-scale construction of castles begins throughout Europe
Late eleventh century:	Burgher class begins to form in urban centers of Europe
1135 A.D.:	Discoveries of silver begin in Europe, infusing capital into Europe
1140 A.D.:	St Denis Cathedral completed in Paris
Late eleventh century:	Musical notation and polyphony become widespread in Europe
Twelfth century:	Hanseatic League started, furthers trade between Northern European cities
Mid-twelfth century:	Giovanni de'Dondi's inventions begin "revolution in time"; Northern Italians begin to spread commercial systems across Europe
1300 A.D.:	Forest cover of Europe reduced to 20 percent from apex of 95 percent; 10 percent of Europeans live in towns; in commercial areas, about 25 percent
1308–21:	Dante Alighieri's *The Divine Comedy* written
Mid-thirteenth century:	Most bourgeois/burghers no longer submit to a feudal lord
Late thirteenth century:	Reading glasses invented in Northern Italy

2

Medieval transformations

In early 1258, the Mongol army of Hulagu Khan laid waste to magnificent Baghdad for seven days, killing at least 200,000 men, women, and children. The attackers destroyed vast quantities of books, demolished innumerable buildings, looted every precious or useful object, and carried off thousands of slaves. Abdullah Wassaf, a Persian historian and tax collector for the Mongols, described the plunderers as sweeping

> through the city like hungry falcons attacking a flight of doves, or like raging wolves attacking sheep, with loose rein and shameless faces, murdering and spreading fear. . . . The massacre was so great that the blood of the slain flowed in a river like the Nile . . . Beds and cushions made of gold and encrusted with jewels were cut to pieces with knives and torn to shreds; those hidden behind the veils of the great harem . . . became a plaything in the hands of a Tatar monster.[1]

The Islamic world, already in decline since the fall of the Caliphate of Córdoba in Andalusia over two centuries before, never recovered its former splendor. Similarly, the slow conquest of China by the Mongols throughout the thirteenth century ended the flourishing Song Dynasty.[2]

Europe's trajectory was heading in the opposite direction. An agriculture revolution, begun just before the millennium, spurred a boom in commerce and urbanization. Involving the rise of banking, some technological innovations, double-entry bookkeeping, and regional and international trading networks, this economic efflorescence powered a burst of construction projects, in particular, dozens of immense Gothic cathedrals, for centuries the world's tallest buildings.[3] European society in this era eradicated slavery, conferred on women relatively high status in world-historical terms, and produced a stupendous flowering of literature, art, and music. Here one finds the foundations of Europe's later rise to world preeminence.

Much recent scholarship into medieval history has focused on the strangeness of the Middle Ages. Many historians dwell on the violence against the Jews, the predation of lords and rulers, the bizarre superstitions infusing all of life, the grotesque habits and customs, the monstrous appetites, the harsh living conditions, the marginalization and persecution of gays, the corrupt but pervasive authority of the church, and other phenomena modern Western people would consider "exotic."[4] All such topics deserve attention and certainly characterize the medieval period, which in most respects could not be more different from modern life in developed countries. Yet the modern age did not emerge at some instant, like Athena bursting from the head of Zeus. An earlier historical tradition, first developed in the United States by Charles Haskins at Harvard in the 1920s and carried forward by his student Joseph Strayer at Princeton into the 1980s, understood and emphasized the indebtedness of modern institutions and values to medieval developments.[5] Our understanding of history has been deeply enriched by the newer scholarship, yet something important has been lost: a more holistic view of our past.

Agricultural revolution

People living a country where fewer than a half-million workers produce enough food to feed 317 million Americans along with tens of millions more abroad can be forgiven for straining to imagine a time when nearly every man, woman, and child tilled the land. Yet for thousands of years after the domestication of plants and animals that is how nearly all humans lived. They hovered at the edge of subsistence, their life expectancies short. Famines struck often, and infectious diseases carried away young and old, rich and poor. Diets consisted mostly of cereals with occasional meat, fish, or other sources of protein and fruits and vegetables seldom. In Carolingian times (ca. 800–900), Europe's peasants ate mostly coarse grains, like millet, husked wheat, barley, oats, and rye. Inhabitants of the southern climes had some fresh fruit, of course, and those close to rivers and the sea enjoyed fish.[6]

Three factors gradually altered this picture. Periodic calamitous epidemics ceased to strike the Eurasian continent after the pestilence of 742–743.[7] Second, the earth experienced a cyclical warming trend from the tenth century, which extended the growing season and opened more northerly latitudes to husbandry.[8] The third factor alone depended on human agency. New technologies in agriculture increased yields by 50 percent or more.

As so often with European technological innovations, crucial assistance came from elsewhere. The horse collar was imported into Europe from China in the 900s. Muscular horses, bred in Carolingian times, though frailer than oxen, could work longer and faster and therefore gradually replaced them. Of course, horses were first domesticated north of the Black Sea.[9] Horseshoes, apparently descended from the Roman era, protected the hooves from softening in the wet earth and improved traction.[10] More important still was the heavy wheeled plow, of northern European fabrication (though the Chinese had invented a heavy iron plow nearly a millennium before). The soil north of the Alps is generally rich in nutrients but dense. The light-duty plows used in the south scarcely made a dent there. Creating furrows required a sharp iron plowshare, followed by a curved iron moldboard to turn the soil over. A change in agricultural technique rounded out the other innovations. Starting as early as the 800s, northern European peasants figured out how to plant crops in two-thirds of their land, leaving only one-third (instead of one-half) to rest and regain nutrients. This gradually put roughly 17 percent more land under the plow.

Any big increase in food output, throughout history, has tended to spur population growth. For this reason, early economic expansion eventually struck against the constraints of the so-called Malthusian Law. As the Rev Thomas Malthus

(1766–1834) argued in *An Essay on the Principle of Population* (1798), human reproduction will always outpace food production unless new technologies permit higher crop yields. Yet even then, more mouths will appear and force the issue again. "Famine," he writes, "seems to be the last, the most dreadful resource of nature. The power of population is so superior to the power of the earth to produce subsistence for man, that premature death must in some shape or other visit the human race."[11] Historians now realize that his concern was somewhat exaggerated. Instead of repeated, devastating famines, most of human history has known very slow economic growth punctuated by occasional, moderately destructive famines.[12] Still, continuous economic growth had never occurred anywhere in history for long. Europe was no exception—it lost one-third of its entire population during the Black Death (1347–51). For most of the Middle Ages, however, Europe avoided catastrophe, partly thanks to available virgin territory. Peasant communities in 1000–1300 reduced Europe's forest cover from 95 to 20 percent, drained vast swampland, and began reclaiming some 2 million acres of land from the sea in the Low Countries. Overall, these pioneers doubled the continent's arable land.

What scholars often call the medieval "agricultural revolution"[13] launched a massive population increase, a commercial boom, a burst of urbanization, and a scintillating cultural flowering—all duly covered below. Yet comparatively, China's population increased just as dramatically, rising from 66 million in the year 1000 to 115 million just 200 years later. The explanation is similar. The Chinese increased their agricultural output and productivity massively, though for the most part by putting new land under the plow and by introducing new higher-yielding crops, rather than through new technological innovations (they had invented various iron plows, a horse harness, the seed drill, and other technologies centuries before).[14] Malthus was right, though: all such successes were fragile in premodern times.

The rise of feudal society

Meanwhile, Europe had been experiencing a sociopolitical transformation that set the stage for other radical changes. Beginning in the early 700s, catastrophic invasions overran the continent—Muslims from the south, Vikings from the north and west, and Magyars (or Hungarians) from the east.[15] Soon after the millennium, the raids ceased. The Norsemen and Hungarians gradually adopted a sedentary life and converted to Christianity. The Muslims were pushed out of southern France and, a bit later, from Sicily. Many of the Slavs and Baltic peoples of Eastern Europe also adopted Roman Christianity, resulting in a huge expansion of Christendom. In the long run, the new territory would give the continent massively more resources and, in the short term, the ability to withstand the Mongol attacks of the 1200s.

Two centuries of invasions and havoc had undermined public order.[16] To take but one example, in 980 the Count of Macon swore fealty to the Duke of Burgundy but was perfectly independent of him.[17] Neither lord paid more than formal obeisance to the King of France. Thirty years later, the petty lords in the region of Macon, essentially any strongman possessing a castle, had broken away and established complete sway over their domains. It is scarcely an exaggeration to say, at least on the Continent, that no lord's actual power extended much beyond 30 miles of his castle walls. (Kings, dukes, and other lords continued to enjoy widely acknowledged formal legal authority, in some parts of Europe, for example, England, more than others.) The main social distinction was now between those who could afford to equip themselves for battle and those who could not. Constant minor warfare and the brutal pillaging and exploitation of the defenseless became the norm. This was a rude and barbarous time in European history.

From this chaos and anarchy, however, emerged a truly remarkable social order, often called "feudalism."[18] Marxists and world historians sometimes mistakenly believe that merely owning tracts of land and forcing peasants to work on them define the system or that it was merely economic in nature. In reality, this practical arrangement (many historians nowadays reject the term "feudalism" as implying overly uniform legal relations)[19] fostered social stability and was characterized by dense ties of mutual dependence. In an environment where authority came to be based not solely on legitimacy or legal right but also—and often mostly—on raw power and where all weak and poor people fell under the fist of the castellans, no one was secure. Gradually, many castellans themselves pledged with all the lords in their region not to fight with each other. The ties were both horizontal and vertical, as lesser lords also pledged with greater and greater with lesser. A sort of complex multilateral peace treaty arose, whose variegated structure has been likened to a Gothic cathedral.

Of course, the powerful did not guarantee the security of the weak for nothing. Knights pledged fealty, meaning military and other services, to counts, while counts pledged the same to dukes. The dominant lord exercised "banal lordship," or the right to demand payment of taxes and tolls and the use of his oven or mill from all who lived within his sway. In return, and this point is both crucial and astonishing in a world-historical sense, the senior member of the relationship granted to the junior some benefice, usually called a fief, which typically consisted of a piece of land. In this way, through an intricate web of vassalic ties, European society halted the spiraling chaos and, by individuals banding together, created a modicum of order. The relations throughout the system, moreover, were secured for the most part by legal writ, or at least by duly witnessed oral agreement, establishing the foundations of a legal culture unique in global terms. These contractual bonds, which also encompassed ecclesiastical authorities, were often cemented by means of elaborate ceremonies with multiple witnesses and official seals pressed into wax.[20] A social revolution in its own right, feudal society marked the triumph of social over state power.

True, over the next few centuries, Europe's monarchies, reasserted themselves—thanks in part to the military revolution (see Chapter 4) and new techniques of bureaucratic management—and even tried beginning in the 1500s to assert absolutist power. These attempts ultimately failed because European society could not be overcome by any state, no matter how powerful or aggressive (see Chapter 10).[21]

In fact, many scholars consider medieval political fragmentation one of the most important factors in the subsequent development of Europe.[22] Almost perpetual warfare among small states spurred innovation in military technology and trained the European polities to project military power more and more forcefully (see Map 2.1). The power vacuum circa 1000 A.D. also opened the door to competition between church and state. For example, churchmen asserted their authority by forbidding slavery in Venice in 960. An institution and practice as ancient as human memory,

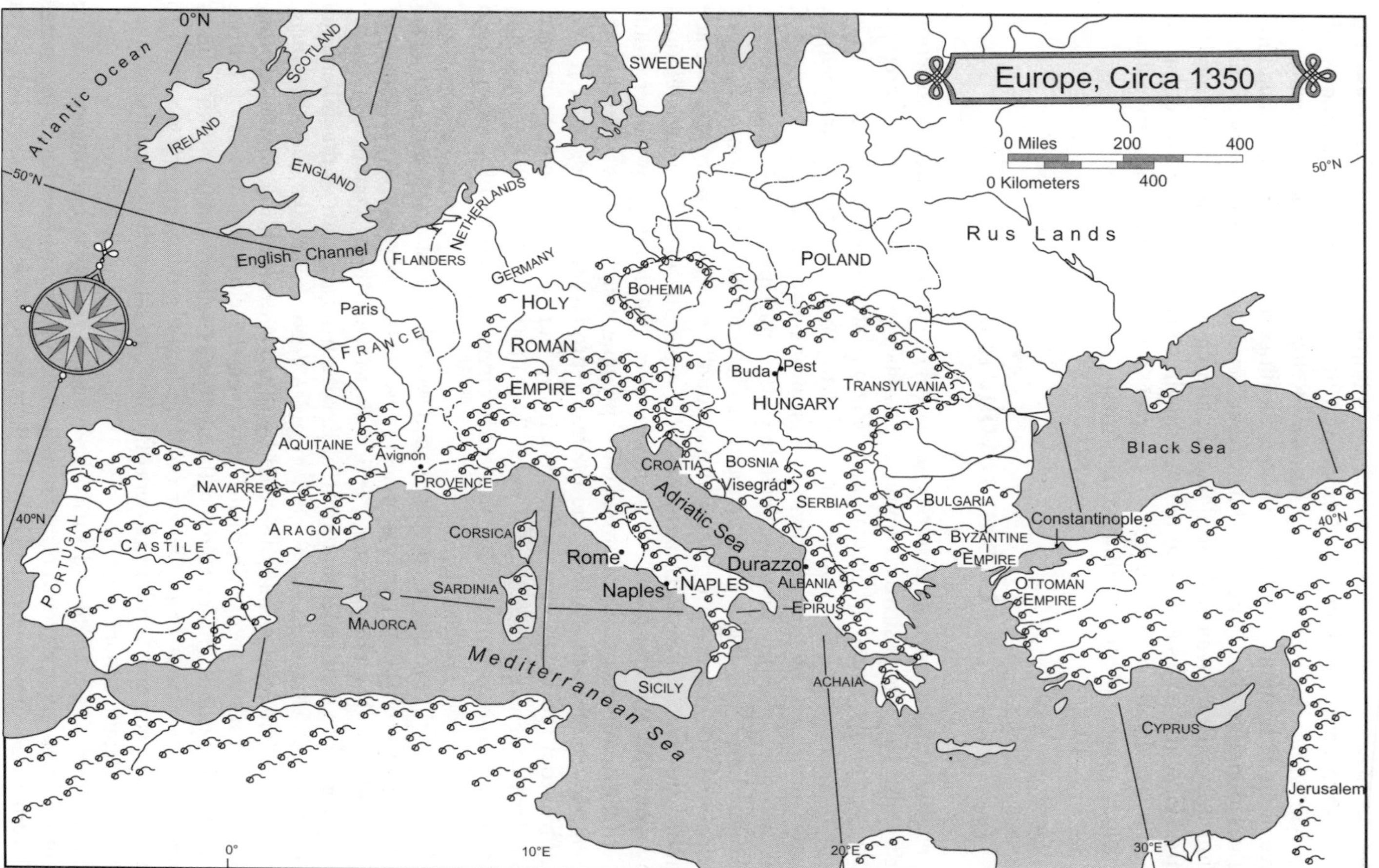

MAP 2.1 *Medieval political fragmentation: A key factor in European development.*

which remained deeply entrenched throughout the Islamic world (though never in the dehumanizing form it took centuries later in Europe's New World colonies), had all but disappeared from Northern Europe by 1200.[23] Why? Slaves could not easily find places within the web of feudal relations.[24] Religious authorities also imposed a "Peace of God" beginning in 989 in various localities to curb fighting among lords and their looting of villages by appealing to conscience and the fear of God. Violence continued, but the movement showed that the church was concerned about the "big picture." How the ecclesiastical authorities sought to impose a universal dominion from the late 1000s is the subject of Chapter 3. Also contributing to political fragmentation were relatively autonomous cities.

Urban revolution

The invasions of the previous centuries had wreaked havoc and sowed destruction, but they also had one positive economic effect. They put vast amounts of precious metals, previously stored in secular and religious strongholds, into circulation. This massive infusion of capital, combined with increased agricultural output, strongly stimulated economic activity.[25] Europeans had for centuries imported small quantities of costly luxuries, including silks and spices, from Asia through the Middle East. Now they had more money to spend. The production of Europe's principal exports, especially woolens, also gradually increased. International trade expanded slowly, too. Mediterranean seaports, especially in Italy, whose relations with Byzantium and the Islamic world were never sundered, grew busier. Trade fairs sprang up in strategic locations, like Champagne, roughly halfway between the shipping centers of northern Italy and the textile producers of Flanders.[26] For over a century from the 1180s, the six yearly fairs in four towns of Champagne were the greatest commercial venues in Europe. The 1100s also saw the emergence of contracts for business ventures, big and small, often with dozens of investors, each putting up relatively small sums.

A "commercial revolution" occurred in towns all across Europe.[27] Cities had first emerged over 10,000 years before. In most places, they had served mostly as administrative and military centers, and only secondarily as commercial hubs.[28] The type of urban civil order that arose in Europe from the turn of the millennium was entirely new. Until then, urban settlements in Europe were like those elsewhere. Dominated by the local nobility or ruled by officials of distant governments, they paid taxes to various lords. Gradually, however, the cities and towns of Europe threw off those bonds and established themselves as self-governing polities almost completely autonomous from the surrounding lordly powers, paying no taxes to king or anyone else and deciding matters of policy in a relatively democratic manner. How did this come about?

The process was gradual and varied from region to region but in general went like this.[29] In the later eleventh century, well-to-do urban dwellers began to emerge as a distinct class of people, often later called "bourgeois" or burghers, though as yet without any special legal status. The towns in which they lived still fell under banal lordship. Over time, an aristocracy of wealth grew up, centered on the bourgeoisie who lent money to lords and even kings. They bought up land in the surrounding area; some became lords of fiefs and were thus freed from taxes. By the middle of the 1200s, most burghers had liberated themselves from banal lordship. The next step was securing charters of liberty for their cities from kings or other great lords. The first known charter north of the Alps was secured by the Walloon city of Huy, which received free urban status in 1066 from the Prince-Bishopric of Liège. Granting these documents was in a prince's or a king's interest for two main reasons. First, it weakened the nobility by eliminating an important source of its income: preying on towns. Second, it increased the wealth of the most important royal creditors—the burghers. While sensible from the prince's point of view, granting liberties to subject populations was extremely unusual and, on the scale at which European rulers practiced it, utterly novel in world history. Rulers everywhere and always had preferred to keep their subjects fully subordinate.

What emerged was a unique polity. Proudly autonomous and clearly separated from the surrounding countryside, the European city was not part of a larger organism but was an organism in its own right.[30] The social atmosphere in the towns was open to ambition and talent. People of different social standings and wealth were united into new institutions, including guilds, universities, and the guild of guilds, the "commune."[31] The commune was a self-governing body, whether incorporated or not. The merchants, professionals, and craftsmen, who ran the show (as members of the craft fellowships, or guilds, however, and not as individuals), had never before enjoyed a socially prominent position in Europe or, it seems, in any other civilization or region. Unusually in human history, in fact, labor was given an intrinsic dignity and worth. A high percentage of journeymen could hope to rise to the position of master craftsmen. Such a rich artisan could be just as high and mighty as a merchant or, within the city walls, a nobleman. Talented people engaged in manual labor and commerce inevitably discovered innovative ways to ply their trades, to everyone's benefit. The commune was, in short, a voluntary association of artisans, merchants, and professionals, and, legally speaking, nothing and no one stood above it. Moreover, anyone who lived in the city for a year and a day had a legitimate claim to membership. In this way, one said, "city air makes you free."[32] No wonder city dwellers in Europe were bursting with pride, jealously guarded their political autonomy, and frequently celebrated and commemorated their status. They were after all members in some of the most exclusive and influential clubs in the world.[33]

Here, it seems, is an important area where Europe started to differ from the other great civilizations. Merchants played a vital role in China and the Middle East but enjoyed high status in neither.[34] China boasted many vibrant cities. Each one contained a dense network of guilds.[35] Chinese guilds were often wealthy, many maintaining temples, gardens, theaters, and schools. Yet neither city nor guild exercised political authority, enjoyed autonomy, or possessed charters of any kind. The urban dwellers themselves felt strong allegiance to their families and ancestral villages and therefore never identified fully with the cities in which they lived. The government officials who administered the towns and regulated the guilds strenuously impeded any efforts to form the kinds of associations that distinguished European urban life. The Chinese social structure was so rigid that merchants had little hope of achieving independence from close government supervision. The dominant Confucian philosophy, moreover, disparaged business, even if government officials often accepted bribes in exchange for leaving merchants to their affairs.[36] In other terms, Chinese cities did not shelter people from the oppressive weight of governmental power.

The Islamic tradition favored commerce, since Muhammad was himself a merchant. Individuals in the Islamic world also enjoyed a high level of social mobility, thanks to a meritocratic social structure. In Europe, professional advancement was open to talent, but rising in urban communities and the higher reaches of power generally required adhering to detailed rules of seniority or legitimacy. There thus emerged a unique balance between ambition, on the one hand, and strict procedures, on the other. This result, it seems, enabled European communities to harness to a very great degree their human capital. In the words of Marshall Hodgson, Europeans could "act far more effectively, as members of a group," than could other peoples of the world.[37] One might think of the Crusades, but in general networks of Europeans acting for religious, scholarly, commercial, or political reasons became more and more effective for mobilizing human ability. In the absence of strong central government, Europeans had for centuries—from before Carolingian times—founded guilds, charitable societies, monasteries, burial clubs, and other collective organizations and had gained recognition for them as corporations under established and still valid rules of Roman law.[38] European society, in other words, had learned to organize itself.

A literary example helps illustrate this point. In *Decameron*, by Giovanni Boccaccio (1313–75), seven women and three men—none related by birth or marriage—have fled plague-infested Florence and, lodged in a country villa, agree to amuse themselves by telling stories each in turn. One of their fellows, Pampinea, a woman, proposes the following:

> But when things lack order they cannot long endure, and since it was I who began the discussions which brought this fine company together, and since I desire the continuation of our happiness, I think we should choose a leader from among us, whom we shall honor and obey as our superior and whose only thought shall be to keep us happily entertained all. And in order that each one of us may feel the burden of this responsibility together with the pleasure of its authority, so that no one of us who has not experienced it can envy the others, let me say that both the burden and the honor should be granted to each one of us in turn for a day . . .[39]

Delighted by her proposal, the company with one accord elects Pampinea queen for the first day with authority to appoint her successor of the following day. The book has a distinctly modern feel. Of course, European society remained strictly hierarchical, and the more talented and ambitious inhabitants of Muslim countries enjoyed greater social mobility.[40] Yet the comparison hints strongly at a significant difference in social organization, in which Europeans displayed a greater capacity for taking initiative and organizing themselves than people in the other great civilizations.

Technological innovations

Europeans also began gradually to excel at innovation. Until then, the greatest inventors were Chinese. By the eleventh century, they had given the world paper, wood-block printing, porcelain, iron smelting, gunpowder, and the compass. Already, though, the Europeans seemed poised to catch up. In some cases, they improved or perfected existing technologies. Take gunpowder. Concocted as early as the 900s in China, the formula was used mostly in fireworks though also in incendiary bombs. Europeans improved the recipe and launched a military revolution beginning in the 1300s (see Chapter 4).

Even earlier, the use of wind- and water mills enabled Europeans to begin to liberate themselves significantly from reliance on muscle power. Finding alternative forms of energy has plagued humankind since the beginning of time. The mastery of fire and the domestication of animals were solutions to this problem. So, too, was the use of coal as a fuel in ancient China 10,000 years ago. Nine thousand years after that, around the end of the first millennium, the Chinese developed a mighty coal-fired iron industry, as noted in Chapter 1. This operation dwindled, however, after the Jurchen conquest in 1126. Yet neither the Chinese, nor the Indians, nor the Muslims, nor any other people systematically and extensively used labor-saving devices before the medieval and early modern Europeans. The main reason, it seems, was the availability of relatively inexpensive human labor, thanks to the institution of slavery and to low food-production costs, especially in China and India.[41]

Invented in the ancient Near East, water mills began spreading widely across Europe from the fall of Rome.[42] There were at least 5,624 in England in 1086 and surely vastly more on the Continent, along with thousands of windmills.[43] The reason for relying heavily on the devices in Europe was manifold. First, slavery had gradually been replaced by serfdom, under which dependent rural workers nevertheless enjoyed some legal rights.[44] Second, the depopulation of core areas of the Roman Empire had engendered a labor shortage. Third, Europe enjoys an abundance of continuously flowing rivers and streams. Fourth, the European aristocracy had the authority to dam up waterways and to force environing peasants to use their mills, giving them a material incentive to construct mills and develop mill technology. Fifth, the ideal of economic independence of monastic communities spurred them to rely heavily on waterpower.[45]

Even the early European water mills saved a huge amount of labor. Each mill produced roughly two horsepower or the equivalent work of up to 60 persons.[46] Before the millennium, they were employed chiefly to grind grain into flour. Then over the next few centuries, thanks to improvements in the design of cams and crankshafts, which convert rotary into back-and-forth motion, water mills (and to a lesser extent windmills) were put to use in dozens of processes, including mining, sawing, stone-cutting, tanning, metallurgy, and the production of many products, such as olive oil, cutlery, hemp, paper, and, most important, textiles.[47] The immense value of water mills can be easily understood in the case of fulling, or the cleansing and finishing of woolen cloth. One man operating a European fulling mill could produce as much finished woolen cloth in a day as three men using traditional methods could do in seven.[48] Similar savings were achieved in other areas of production, leading the economic historian Joel Mokyr to argue that "medieval Europe was perhaps the first society to build an economy on nonhuman power."[49]

Medieval Europeans developed many other technologies. Some were rather lowly but valuable, like fastening buttons.[50] Among the most significant were eyeglasses, mechanical clocks, and double-entry bookkeeping and other tools of commerce.

Corrective reading lenses mounted in a frame were apparently invented in the second half of the 1200s, probably in Italy. These simple glasses effected a minor revolution in productivity. At around age 40, most people's close vision begins to decline. Unfortunately, the peak performance of scholars and skilled artisans generally coincided with the onset of presbyopia. Corrective spectacles, thus, extended the working life of these valuable toilers sometimes by as much as 20 years. Further advances in grinding lenses led to the development of other important technologies, including glasses to correct for myopia, in the 1400s.[51] European glassmakers, for example, on the Venetian Island of Murano, became among the world's finest and most innovative. By the 1400s, they exported large quantities of glassware across Europe and the Middle East, including mosque lamps with Quranic inscriptions.[52]

Historian David Landes considers the mechanical clock the most revolutionary innovation of the period.[53] Invented in China in the early 700s and developed into sophisticated chronometric and astronomical instruments by the late 1000s, the technology was apparently adapted by Europeans in the following century or so and subsequently lost to China. By the mid-1300s, Giovanni de'Dondi had fashioned a timepiece that marked days, months, years, and the movement of the known planets. The mechanical clock had enormous significance for Europe. First, European craftsmen became masters of miniaturization—portable timepieces were available by the 1430s—and inventors of fine instruments, including gauges, micrometers, and eventually telescopes and microscopes. These advances would play an important role in the Scientific Revolution (see Chapter 8). They also led toward constructing other complex articulated devices, such as calculating machines in the 1600s and steam engines in the 1700s. Second, by the mid-fourteenth century several northern Italian cities had erected large mechanical clocks as symbols of the secular municipal authority; most other European towns soon followed suit. These technologically sophisticated marvels boosted the pride of urban dwellers and enabled them to schedule their lives as they saw fit. Finally, the ability to plan ahead and keep track of time helped Europeans develop a sense of productivity, efficiency, and time management.

Other great civilizations had known regular timekeeping. By far the most sophisticated was China.[54] No other culture developed such a profound historical sense or devoted so much effort to preserving the known historical record. Concretely, all Chinese cities and towns from at least the Tang era employed officials who used sundials and water-powered mechanical clocks to mark the "hours" (actually every 2 hours) day and night with drums, gongs, bells, or trumpets. The intervals were named, however, but not numbered. This official time served to reinforce the emperor's sovereignty, just like the calendar, which was worked out anew at the start of many reigns. No independently tended clocks existed, and certainly no individuals owned clocks in China. An autonomous culture of timekeeping controlled by individuals and authorities at every level of society simply never emerged in the Middle Kingdom. When Jesuit travelers in the late 1500s and early 1600s bestowed intricate clocks upon Chinese mandarins, they denigrated them as mere toys and curiosities, perhaps so as to defuse their potential threat to centralized authority.[55]

Using refined astronomical techniques to determine the months and days of the lunar calendar, to establish the times for the daily prayers, and to calculate the proper observance of Ramadan was the job of *muwaqqits* or timekeepers in mosques throughout the Islamic world.[56] Yet this practice never fostered a broader public sense of time, an hour-by-hour awareness of time's passage, or an individual's ability to plan out the day. Bernard Lewis cites the ambassador from the Holy Roman Empire to Istanbul writing in 1560 that "if they established public clocks, they think that the authority of their Muezzins and their ancient rites would suffer diminution."[57] No, for several centuries the "revolution in time" affected only Europe.[58]

Commercial revolution

Meanwhile, a commercial revolution was taking hold in the northern Italian city-states.[59] History is full of contingency, with accidents sometimes playing an important role. From the middle of the thirteenth century, Florence and other inland cities were riven by often-violent factional struggles dividing most political actors into Guelphs and Ghibellines. To protect their interests, businessmen needed to stay close to home. To carry on with international trade, therefore, the biggest Italian merchants developed a set of tools allowing them to operate at a distance.[60]

First, they trained agents to represent them in other localities or to accompany merchandize abroad. Most were close family members—people they could trust fully. Some also set up branch offices abroad. In order to keep track of their far-flung operations, merchants developed sophisticated accounting practices, in particular, double-entry bookkeeping, which first emerged in Tuscany in the thirteenth century. Its key feature was to separate debits from credits and capital from revenue. Merchants also worked out elaborate schemes for managing risk. The two principal forms were partnership contracts and maritime insurance. In the former, investors and traders would team up, one furnishing most of the capital, the other assuming the responsibility for conveying money and goods to foreign ports and back. Sometimes multiple investors shared the risk. These partnerships first developed among Islamic traders in the Mediterranean with whom the Italians carried on most of their commerce.[61] Maritime insurance contracts were bought and sold in ancient Greece and Rome,[62] and the word "risk" probably derives from the Arabic *rizq*. Even so, Genoese merchants perfected these operations, and they played a significant role in international trade by the 1300s. Italian merchants also developed long-term business partnerships owned by shareholders. Each Italian trading city boasted hundreds of them in the 1200s.

One major impediment to the smooth development of business in medieval times was the restricted money supply. For two centuries after 1135, however, discoveries of silver deposits in Northern and Central Europe infused capital into the market. Dozens of mints struck coins effecting a "monetary revolution," in the words of the French medievalist, Marc Bloch.[63] One means of further increasing financial liquidity was through credit extended by savings banks. Bankers evolved from money changers who were experts in rates of exchange among the enormous diversity of coins in circulation. Trusted Italian bankers received deposits of monetary assets and extended credit to their owners. Far more important, as a way to deploy existing specie more efficiently, were bills of exchange. Like most early financial instruments,

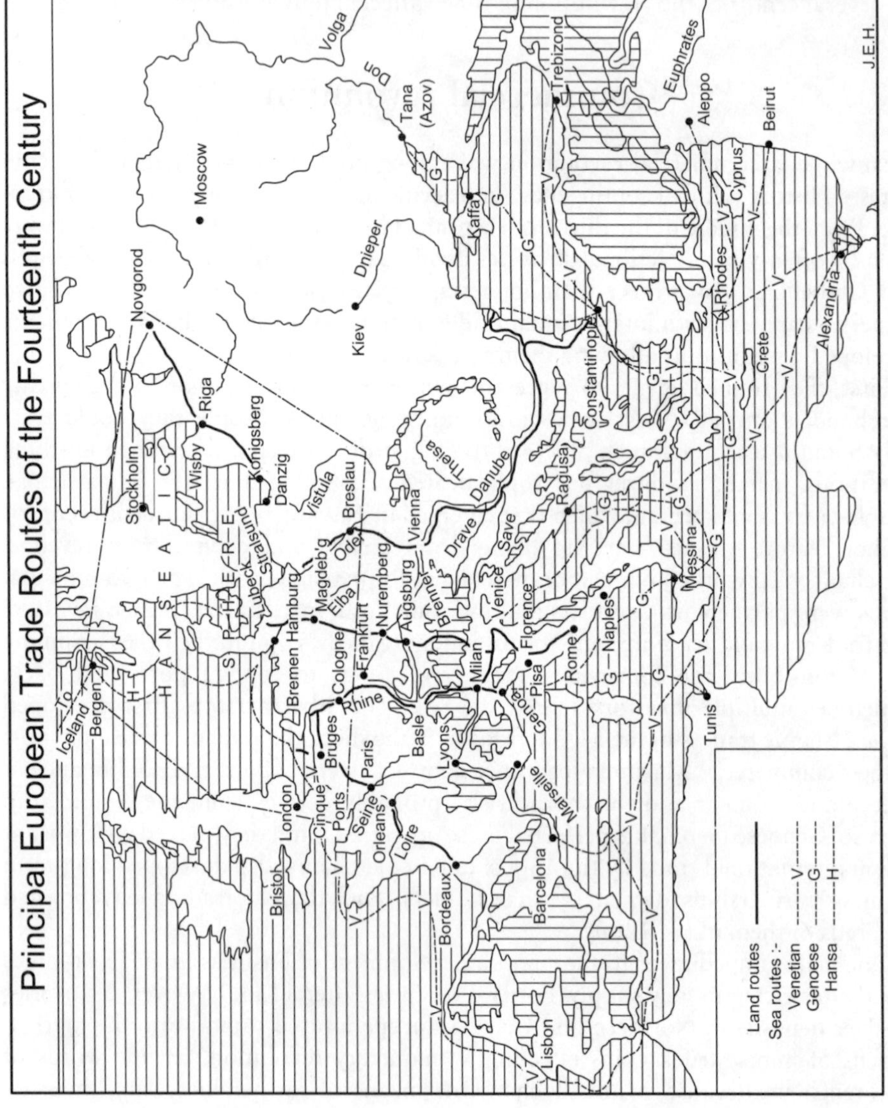

MAP 2.2 *The Hanseatic League dominated trade in Northern Europe while Italian merchants dominated the Mediterranean.*

they emerged in the ancient Middle East and were further developed by Muslim traders.[64] With bills of exchange, money changed hands in one locality in one currency and then again in a second place in another currency. Italians dominated this trade. There were by the fourteenth century roughly 140 Italian banks, several, including the houses of Bardi and Peruzzi, with hundreds of agents and numerous branches in the major cities of Europe.[65] Thus, until quite recently the headquarters of most banks in the United Kingdom were located on Lombard Street, named after Italian moneylenders from Lombardy.[66]

All of these innovations, along with improved sailing techniques (see Chapter 5), powered an expansion of long-distance trade with China and the Middle East. By the 1200s, Byzantine manufacturing began to decline in the face of expanded Italian production of cloth, soap, and glass.[67] Still, the Italian merchants were far from commercial domination. The volume of trade linking Europe to the Near and Far East paled in comparison with the commercial traffic of the Indian Ocean.[68] Moreover, most European exports were produced in the textile workshops of the Low Countries. Finally, a trading consortium of the north, the Hansa, controlled a big portion of European commerce. Linking dozens of cities on Europe's northern littoral, from Holland to Novgorod in Russia, it provided security for its members, won for them exemptions from taxes and fees in major trading centers including London, and helped promote Germanic colonization into northeastern Europe (the famous *Drang nach Osten*).[69]

By the 1200s, Europeans formed interconnected commercial networks and continent-wide economies, drawing together highly innovative and productive cities from Italian colonies in the eastern Mediterranean to the British Isles and from southern France to the Baltic region (see Map 2.2). Though far less rich or populous than China and boasting a smaller level of trade than East or South Asia, Europe nevertheless was emerging as an important and powerful civilization. It expressed this prowess through many cultural achievements.

Construction boom

Surely the most awesome achievements were Gothic cathedrals. Not merely the tallest buildings in the world for many centuries, they were also monuments to a human spirit seeking unity with the transcendent and an expression of the divine spirit infusing the material realm. The religious figure who led the quest for this new architectural form was Abbot Suger (1081–1151). Born into a poor family, his brilliant mind and rigorous study enabled him to become a counselor to both kings and popes. As the abbot of St Denis, near Paris, he oversaw the construction of the first monument of Gothic architecture, the abbey church of St Denis (narthex completed in 1140). Powerfully influenced by the Neoplatonic writing of Dionysius the Pseudo-Areopagite, Suger concluded that man and the realm he dwells in can be made whole only if transformed by the divine spirit. His purpose was to allow sanctified light to render the material world immaterial. His church therefore celebrated soaring height, radiant color, vast unity of space, and gloriously suffusing light.[70] As architects across Europe adapted the style in their own ways over the next three centuries, these elements remained pervasive.

Two technologies made them possible. First, the horse collar enabled teams of horses and oxen to haul loads up to 5,000 pounds—10 times more weight than earlier arrangements.[71] Second, new engineering techniques played a key role. The pointed or ogival arch, perhaps borrowed from Islamic architecture and used for creating vaulted ceilings in Gothic churches, suggested visually a movement toward heaven.[72] Four to six narrow ribs, running from the corners to a central point, strengthened each vault, enabling it to rise higher than previously possible. Thin exterior walls, held in place by buttresses and exposing vast windows, merely enclosed the interior space and were not load bearing. "Flying buttresses," which soared outwards from these walls, allowed engineers to increase overall height still further.[73] It seems that no previous—and few later—architectural styles or achievements could rival the Gothic in grandeur.

A few numbers will show just how ambitious these projects became. For four millennia, the world's tallest structure, the Great Pyramid of Giza, proudly rose to 481 feet (455 feet today due to erosion). Two English churches, the Lincoln Cathedral and Old St Paul's, London, both completed circa 1310, edged past that record, with ground-to-spire-tip heights of 525 and 460 feet, respectively.[74] No man-made structure reached as high as the Lincoln Cathedral until the erection of the Washington Monument in the late nineteenth century.[75] Several other European church towers built in this era rose well over 300 feet. A few pagodas in China and Japan may have equaled them in height. Yet these towers and spires cannot rival the magic of experiencing Gothic churches.

For one thing, the interiors, attaining in several cases 136 to 158 feet, for example, at Beauvais, Metz, and Notre Dame of Paris, created an open space bathing in light. Outside of Western Christendom, only the patriarchal basilica of Hagia Sophia in Constantinople constructed in the 500s A.D. could rival them. The interiors of the grandest buildings of the other great civilizations were either cramped, narrow, and divided into numerous stories like Japanese and Chinese pagodas or relatively low lying, albeit at times immense and beautifully adorned, like the most splendid mosques. Stupas in the countries with large Buddhist populations can be tall, but, conceived primarily as reliquaries, they are mostly closed on all sides. Gothic cathedrals, by contrast, welcomed worshipers into a soaring, unified space often tinted with myriad hues when light streamed in through thousands of square feet of brightly colored stained glass all telling the stories of the Christian faith. Esthetically, the experience must have been stunning.

The number of churches constructed in the period 1050–1350 astonishes—over eighty cathedrals and more than 500 large and 10,000 small churches in France alone, requiring in the words of one historian "more stones than the pyramids of Egypt, and more labor than the roads of Rome."[76] These edifices, though built mostly of stone, were often damaged by fire, storms, or lightning and had to be rebuilt, in many cases every half-century. This was truly an age of vast building efforts.

The construction of fortified castles, also begun around 1050, was if anything even more prolific, because of the breakdown of public order. For a similar reason, most cities put up high walls with towers and battlements. Some were truly vast, for example, at Carcasonne in southern France. Here the double walls, which stand yet, stretch nearly a mile in length and are punctuated by 45 towers.[77] By the 1250s, Europe's nobles began to set themselves apart from urban upstarts, the burghers, and other commoners by building still more castles outside the fortified urban walls and by establishing a cult around their lineage and family histories.

Great public buildings were erected especially in Italy but also in Flanders, as were bridges all across Europe. The immense Cloth Hall (completed in 1304), in the city of Ypres, testifies to the wealth and influence of the Flemish woolen industry. All the great northern cities of Italy, wealthy from expanding commerce, built grandiose town halls, like the Palazzo Vecchio in Florence (completed in 1322), as well as many imposing palaces of rich citizens.[78] Facilitating trade across long distances required replacing many old wooden bridges. Medieval engineers surpassed the Romans in design and building techniques, for example, by temporarily diverting water courses in order to lay foundations, building pointed abutments against the load-bearing piers, and using pointed arches in order to elevate the passages below.[79] Bridges in the countryside were usually fortified, given the violent nature of the age, while those in cities were often built up with residences and shops.

Literary flowering

Medieval Europe also witnessed a profusion of literary innovation and creation. Imaginative writing began to appear in the vernacular, paving the way toward the rise of both national consciousness and national literatures. For the first time in Europe, women began to play a significant role as writers.[80] Some literary genres exerted a powerful social influence. Many literary works recounted heroic tales and mystical experiences. Allegory was ubiquitous. Not only did people in the Middle Ages see the world and all its manifestations as pregnant with signs and meanings of other aspects of reality and the transcendent realm. They also conceived them as complex and interconnected. Finally, a few authors penned some of Western civilization's masterpieces, including arguably its greatest one, Dante's *Divine Comedy*.

One important source of inspiration for many writers and storytellers was Arab poetry encountered during battles to reconquer Spain and in the earlier Crusades.[81] Muslim and indigenous sources inspired troubadours, who recited or sang poetry, first in southern France around 1100 and then gradually across much of Europe. Men and women, generally well born, composed verse in vernacular languages. They dealt with topics both serious and merely entertaining, involving both philosophy and storytelling. Perhaps the most distinctive and socially important genre was the art of courtly love.

This tradition, which grew out of the poetry of troubadours, was incorporated into the works of some of the greatest masters of the age, including Chrétien de Troyes. Its main goals, following Neo-Platonic conceptions, were to ennoble carnal love and to elevate the mores, values, and behavior of courtiers and other well-born men. Andreas Capellanus codified its main principles in *De Arte Honeste Amandi* (1174).[82] Above all, love should impassion and consume a man. It should impel him to exalt and to revere a worthy, though often unattainable, noblewoman. He should crave to please her in every possible way and to displease her in none. He must remain devoted to her. The lover will inevitably suffer pain and tribulation as he pursues his love. Finally, the relationship will often, perhaps usually, remain platonic.

Women's social status

David Landes has argued that "the best clue to a nation's growth and development potential is the status and role of women."[83] It does seem likely that the more a people draws upon and validates the talents and capabilities of the female half of the population, the greater its potential for innovation and success (see Chapter 14).

The ideal of courtly love strengthened or at least confirmed the relatively solid position of elite women in medieval European society. They not infrequently ruled over castles, led soldiers to battle, or governed polities. Eleanor of Aquitaine (1122–1204), for example, ruled as Duchess of Aquitaine, took part in the Second Crusade, and served as regent while her son, Richard the Lionheart, the King of England, fought in the Third Crusade.[84] It was she who introduced the art of courtly love to the English court. Her granddaughter Blanche of Castile (1188–1252) helped the future Louis VIII of France organize an invasion of England in 1216 and then ruled as regent for 8 years after his death in 1226.[85] Many elite women, while their husbands were away at battle, especially during the Crusades, took charge of household and castle.

In China during these same years, most elite women and even many from lesser families underwent the debilitating process of foot binding. Husbands and families, moreover, regularly sold women like commodities. With well-to-do men typically dividing their affections and attention among various wives and concubines, few elite women wielded the range of authority their European counterparts often possessed.[86]

In both law and custom, European women of the Middle Ages enjoyed high status and extensive legal rights by world historical standards. According to canon law, marriage without the consent of both parties was impermissible. Therefore, women could not legally be compelled to marry against their will, even if in practice family pressure often did overpower individual wishes, especially among the well to do. A medieval woman could sometimes remarry freely after her husband's death. She could inherit property, run a business, or work for wages.[87] It bears emphasizing that, unlike in other major civilizations, in particular, the Islamic world and China, men could not practice polygamy. Nor could they legitimately keep concubines. Thus, women in Europe enjoyed relatively high status in the realm of marriage law and the rules of cohabitation. Again, unlike in the other great civilizations, one found ordinary European women in the workforce and in the marketplace on a much more regular and substantial basis, not hidden away in harems (or in separate thread-markets, as in the Islamic world). Of course, it would be wrong to imagine that women in Europe enjoyed a social status even remotely equal to that of men; in no culture of the time was that the case.

There were many accomplished women of letters in medieval Europe.[88] Several were interpreters of the faith, such as the German prioress, natural philosopher (scientist), and author of mystical writings, Hildegard of Bingen (1098–1179), one of the greatest composers of her age. Another was Mechthild of Magdeburg (1210–ca. 1285), a German mystic whose seven-volume description of her visions may have influenced Dante's *Divine Comedy*. There were also St Gertrude the Great (1256–1302), a German writer of devotional literature; Marguerite Porete (d. 1310), who wrote a highly popular work on Christian spirituality in Old French; and the English mystic Julian of Norwich (1342–ca. 1416), whose writings the former Archbishop of Canterbury, Rowan Williams, calls "what may well be the most important work of Christian reflection in the English language."[89] The abundance of acknowledged and revered female mystics confirms that women in medieval Europe occupied a relatively high social position, when one considers that people's religious experience was, aside from physical survival itself, the most important aspect of life.

The highly prized writing of some medieval women was purely secular in nature. The German nun Hrotsvitha (ca. 935 to 975) wrote sophisticated and learned plays modeled on the comedies of the Roman satirist Terence, but more chaste.[90] The Florentine ambassador, reformer, and papal envoy St Catherine of Siena (1347–80) wrote dozens of letters now considered masterpieces of Tuscan vernacular prose. Margery Kempe (c. 1373–after 1438) dictated the first autobiography (not just by a woman) in the English language.[91]

Women enjoyed less worldly success or renown in the other great civilizations of the time. Taoism offered women something like equality, even access to mastership and the freedom to travel, but this was a minority tradition in Chinese society.[92] Numerous women during the Tang Dynasty (618–907), China's high point of gender equality, excelled at the country's most prestigious cultural pursuit, poetry,[93] as did a few in the Song and Yuan periods.[94] Yet, whereas in Europe women scholars, scientists, philosophers, and writers slowly grew more numerous over the centuries, one must wait for the seventeenth century to encounter another "high tide of women" poets again in China.[95]

Women's status in the Muslim world also declined. Many women engaged in the intellectual professions, including law, medicine, and teaching, during the life of the Prophet. There were also many female merchants, including Muhammad's first wife Khadija (555–623).[96] One finds evidence during the medieval period of female professionals—midwives, doctors, wet nurses, teachers (typically of the "female arts"), secretaries, peddlers, and prostitutes—as well as some women engaged in commercial activities, though "the morals of contemporary society made it impossible for them to be present at gatherings of a commercial nature attended by males." In other words, they were mostly segregated by sex, which was not at all the case in Europe. Women could also work in the crafts, for example, as dyers, weavers, and spinners, though again for the most part not when men were present.[97] By law, Muslim women enjoyed relatively secure property rights (even, to some extent, reproductive rights), though traditionalist practices often curtailed their exercise.[98] Muslim women, because they had the same talents and creativity of women everywhere, despite the restrictions imposed on them by society and culture, played influential and active roles in their societies in medieval times, yet not as much as women in Europe. Widows in medieval Europe in particular often played a very active role in economic life.[99] European women's legal status—for example, in terms of property rights—declined in early modern Europe owing in part to the spread of Roman law, which defined women as mentally weak.[100] Even so, as noted above, European women's participation in public and intellectual life gradually expanded (see Chapter 14).

Muslim women writers were rare, though one can name the mystic poetess Rabi'a al-'Adawiyya (d. 801).[101] Women sometimes played significant roles in Islamic religious life, in particular, in the transmission of prophetic sayings and occasionally as experts in other religious fields of knowledge.[102] Several women wielded power as rulers, including Sitt al-Mulk (970–1023) who served briefly as regent of the Fatimids and Shajar al-Durr (d. 1257), Sultana of Egypt for seven years. Yet, as in China, the number of women active in public life or in the world of letters declined markedly over time, leading one scholar to assert that "women's exclusion from the political realm was, in the Middle Ages, almost complete."[103] The reasons for this change in the Muslim world are not fully clear (in China a proximate cause was the expanding popularity of female foot binding), though they are probably related to the decline of Islamic philosophy from the 1200s, following three centuries of brilliant speculative thought, second until then only to that of the ancient Greeks.

The *Divine Comedy* and medieval culture

The greatest literary work of the Middle Ages was Dante Alighieri's *Divine Comedy*. A massively long and complex poem written in the early 1300s in terza rima and divided overall into three books, each composed of 33 cantos, it tells the story of the author's imaginary journey through Hell, Purgatory, and Paradise. Guided by the Roman poet Virgil, Dante descends a deep abyss marked by nine concentric segments, the final three further subdivided into 17 bands. As he enters the gates of Hell, he writes:

> Here sighs, with lamentations and loud moans,
> Resounded through the air pierced by no star,
> That e'en I wept at entering. Various tongues,
> Horrible languages, outcries of woe,
> Accents of anger, voices deep and hoarse,
> With hands together smote that swell'd the sounds,
> Made up a tumult, that forever whirls
> Round through that air with solid darkness stain'd,
> Like to the sand that in the whirlwind flies.[104]

At each level, he encounters famous dead people condemned according to the nature of their past sins. At the very bottom, caught bodily in frozen ice, thrashes Satan. Thence, the poet and his guide descend further and, passing the Earth's center, ascend to its surface. There they begin to scale Mount Purgatory across its seven terraces, where they encounter dozens more dead, each purging away their sins in specific ways intended to counteract lifetimes of evildoing. At the summit, Virgil stays behind, while Dante is led forward into Heaven by his one true love, Beatrice, whom he had adored from afar. This realm is divided into nine concentric spheres, similar in structure to the traditional medieval geocentric cosmology. Every heavenly body, from the Moon to Saturn, is attached to a crystalline sphere, each orbiting the Earth. To an eighth sphere are attached all the stars, beyond which lies the abode of angels. Again, the poet proceeds through each sphere, conversing with famous deceased earthlings. At the ninth sphere, Beatrice, who personifies theology, remains behind, as St Bernard, the famed Abbot of Clairvaux and mystic, leads Dante toward an immediate experience of God.

The *Divine Comedy* is important for three reasons. First, it exemplifies the creative genius of the age with its soaring beauty, imaginative power, and synthetic conceptualization. Not only a work of astonishing loveliness, Dante's masterpiece represents a unified conception of reality that finds places of relative honor for "noble pagans" like Aristotle and even for Islamic philosophers like Ibn Rushd. Europe's military elites may have been trying for two centuries to conquer the Islamic Middle East by force of arms, but its own philosophical elites were being won over by Muslim thinkers in the universities (see Chapter 3).

Second, the work's complexity and capaciousness astonish. Scholars have likened it to a Gothic cathedral. One might argue that the medieval European mind itself, at its most developed, also bore this character, as a study of the thought of St Thomas Aquinas would attest. Indeed, most serious medieval writing was infused with multilayered meanings, including allegorical, moral, historical, and anagogical (or spiritual). Such philosophical and literary works were complex, yes, but also rigorous, highly lucid, and at their best intended to encompass and assimilate multifarious counterarguments and intellectual challenges. This approach enabled the medieval mind to come to terms with extremely threatening ideas. Among the most important was the tension between faith and reason. It seems that precisely this problem caused Islamic philosophers to abandon their unfettered quest for truth, starting with al-Ghazali (1058–1111), for fear of compromising their commitment to faith.[105] In traditional China, a similar role was played by the emphasis on historical continuity and reverence for traditional values and canonical texts, which often made it difficult for Chinese intellectuals to develop and propound radically new ideas.[106]

Third, by conceiving as intelligible to human reason every corner and realm of the universe save one, the Divine, Dante was formulating a powerful idea of the Christian West. True, neo-Confucian philosophers a century or two before pursued an "investigation of all things." Yet despite a steady and almost exponential growth in the knowledge of natural phenomena from the early centuries of the Common Era until the end of the Ming Dynasty—efforts often conducted by teams of naturalists and funded by the Chinese government—Chinese thinkers never developed a concept of "laws of nature." The culture's devotion to the study of concrete historical development may have even prevented the emergence of systematic sciences of nature.[107] By contrast, precisely this idea in Europe helped pave the way toward the Scientific Revolution. After all, if God endowed mankind with the capacity to comprehend the material world, then studying his handiwork had two benefits. It both opened nature's secrets and revealed clues about the nature of the Creator himself.[108] The medieval tendency to interpret the world allegorically helped as well. Perceiving deeper meanings in things, while keeping sight of the things themselves, probably made it easier for natural philosophers of the Middle Ages to begin to make the astonishing leaps of imagination necessary to posit scientifically unseen forces. Jean Buridan (ca. 1295–1358), for example, a French priest, anticipated Isaac Newton's theory of inertia.[109]

Music and art

The European economy expanded after the millennium, especially in the years 1250–1340. Then the population level crashed. During the following half-millennium, the continent repeatedly suffered devastating wars and material hardships, before modern economic growth began in the 1800s. Yet high culture, which bloomed in the medieval period, flourished without surcease into the twenty-first century, reaching astonishing peaks of creativity and undergoing often radical transformations for a millennium—from the often stylized but spirit-infused Gothic to the nonrepresentational art of recent times. No other civilization expressed itself in such radically different artistic styles in a similar span of time. Of course, no other civilization went through so many transformative changes and yet remained a single civilization.

Europe's musical development demonstrated Western man's increasing ability to function effectively in concert. Polyphony, two or more distinct voices sounding together, dates from the late eleventh century in Europe. This development gave rise to rudimentary musical notation, also a European invention.[110] Previously, most music was improvised; henceforth, it would mostly be composed. It also grew ever more complex. By the early 1200s, Pérotin (1183?–1238?), choirmaster at the church of Notre Dame in Paris, was composing sacred music for three and four distinct voices whose melodic lines were woven together like a rich tapestry. Often two secular songs in the vernacular were superimposed upon a sacred Latin text and melodic line, typically from Gregorian chant. Again, this stemmed from the medieval tendency to grasp disparate elements of reality into one whole. By the next century, European composers were producing more secular than sacred music. Musical notation grew more precise, paving the way toward more and more complicated compositions. Guillaume de Machaut's (ca. 1300–77) four-part *Mass of Our Lady* is a notable example. Over the next few centuries, European composers added still more voices and then, gradually, new forms emerged, including the sonata, concerto, and symphony, calling for complex instrumentation. The culmination of this trajectory probably occurred in 1844 when Hector Berlioz and an assistant, along with five choir directors, conducted a "mega-concert" in Paris with over 1,000 performers.[111] The entire musical tradition seemed to be moving toward a crescendo.

Bernard Lewis finds it significant that the Islamic cultures rejected Western polyphonic music categorically. In such compositions, he writes, "Different performers play together, from different scores, producing a result that is greater than the sum of its parts."[112] Lewis believes this collaborative action was related to democratic politics and team sports, both of which involved the cooperation of individuals according to specific rules and competition within distinct structures. Polyphony also requires synchronization—as do so many other modern endeavors, such as scientific research. These features were central to Western development but did not easily take root in other cultures.

The plastic arts also underwent transformations but in the direction of showcasing the individual—as both artist and subject. During the Gothic era, sculptures carved by anonymous artisans, along with stained glass adorning churches, dominated. The art of the fresco, kept alive from Roman times, remained important in Italy. In the late 1100s, painting on wood panels also reemerged. In these media, mostly anonymous artists told stories from the Bible and the lives of Christian saints. They sought neither realism, nor true proportion, nor perspective. Human forms were typecast to represent either religious figures or human qualities, not individuals. Modern European painting began to emerge in Italy only in the early 1300s with Giotto di Bondone (1267?–1337), an artist recognized in his own lifetime for his charisma and creative originality.

Cenni di Pepo Cimabue (ca. 1240–1302), Giotto's teacher, still worked in the Byzantine tradition, creating brightly colored ensembles of religious figures, adorned with golden haloes, and all occupying the same plane. Giotto broke radically from this style.[113] The golden haloes remain, but his individualized figures recede in depth within a three-dimensional framework. Giotto's characters are not only more realistic, but also reveal distinctive personality traits, emotions, and purposes. A few lack any claim to religious or other fame, like his *Girl Spinning Wool*. Not only did Giotto represent nature in new, sympathetic ways, he also captured human interaction with it, as in his *St. Francis Preaching to the Birds*. From Giotto onward European painters, passing through many styles, media, and periods, gradually achieved stupendous realism, technical virtuosity, and almost microscopic detail, along with profoundly original ways of representing both external reality and internal experiences.

Beginning close to the millennium and continuing for three centuries, first in literature, then in music, and finally in painting, geniuses began to break free and embark in new directions. What is perhaps most striking, from a world historical perspective, however, is that European artists continued to transform their media (e.g. Jan van Eyck invented oil-based paint in the early 1400s),[114] to push the boundaries of the acceptable, and to experiment with genres, materials, and techniques until by the twentieth century they had seemingly exhausted all the imaginable potentialities of their crafts—before inventing still more.[115]

***

This process may serve as a metaphor for the development of all of Western civilization. From the millennium, an agricultural revolution yielded vastly greater food production, which fostered urbanization and the growth of trade and industry. Technological innovation helped each sector of the economy and society to continue to grow. Greater prosperity freed up artistic talent. Breakthroughs, both minor and major, occurred simultaneously and continuously in many areas of human development. Yet no single sphere predominated; no social or political elements overwhelmed any other. Indeed, powerful new social institutions, in particular, feudal contracts and incorporated cities, helped create and sustain a balance of forces. A political and ideological struggle between ecclesiastical and secular powers, brewing since the start of the millennium, might have upset the balance and aborted the equilibrium, as will be recounted in the next chapter.

QUESTIONS FOR REFLECTION

In what sense did the feudal system mark the triumph of social over state power?

How were medieval European cities different from those in other cultures?

How did Confucianism influence social and economic developments in China?

Contrast the role of clocks in European and other major cultures.

What philosophic ideas lay behind the design of Gothic cathedrals?

In what ways was the status of women higher in Europe than in other major cultures?

Within the Christian worldview, why was studying creation important?

What does the emergence of polyphonic music say about European culture?

Chapter 3 Chronology

337:	Emperor Constantine converts to Christianity
392:	Pagan religions banned by Emperor Theodosius I
~500–1000:	European "dark ages" of instability and almost universal illiteracy
530:	Emperor Justinian orders compilation of Roman legal codes
782:	Focus of Palace School in Aachen redirected to Seven Liberal Arts
787:	Imperial decree by Charlemagne dictates that all abbeys must have a school
800:	Pope Leo III crowns Charlemagne emperor
909:	Ownership of Abbey of Cluny conferred to Sts Peter and Paul, that is the Papacy
975:	Bishop of Le Puy declares first "Peace of God"
1054:	Great Schism
~1070:	Texts of Roman law rediscovered in southern Italy
1075:	Pope Gregory VII declares that only Pope may select bishops
1075–76:	Pope Gregory VII's decrees lead to open hostility with Holy Roman Emperor
1080:	University of Bologna founded, specifically to study Justinian texts
1098:	Cistercian order established
Twelfth century:	Rediscovery and reintroduction of Greek philosophy begin
1109:	Approximately 2,000 monasteries now subordinate to Rome via Cluny
1122:	Concordat of Worms ends Investiture Conflict
1140:	Gratian completes "Concordance of Discordant Canons"
1179:	Third Lateran Council selects Pope without Imperial confirmation

Early thirteenth century:	Professionally staffed law courts exist throughout Europe; Dominican and Franciscan orders established and quickly expand
1231:	Papal Inquisition established by Pope Gregory IX to suppress heresy
1241:	At least eight more universities now exist, dozens more follow
Mid-1260s:	Aristotle's *Politics* rediscovered
1265–74:	St Thomas Aquinas writes *Summa Theologica*
1300:	Approximately 100,000 monks and nuns active in Europe
1305:	Avignon papacy established

3

Papal Revolution

In January 1077, Henry IV, the Holy Roman Emperor, secretly crossed the Alps into Italy. On the 28th at Canossa, in the garb of a penitent—shoeless, without food, and in a hair shirt—he entered the fortress of Countess Matilda of Tuscany, a staunch ally of Pope Gregory VII. For three days he pleaded with Gregory to lift the excommunication that separated him from the saving embrace of the church. The previous year Henry had publicly denounced the pope as a "false monk" and called for his resignation. Gregory responded in kind, forbidding the king's subjects to acknowledge his rule. At issue was the emperor's right to appoint bishops in his realm, a right the church was fighting to wrest from his control. For the moment, with most of the German princes shunning Henry and flocking to the pope, the church appeared supreme. The pontiff therefore absolved the emperor, lying prostate before him, and invited him to take Holy Communion.[1]

Historically, the idea of a spiritual leader without a military force dictating terms to a powerful ruler and humiliating him publicly seems absurd. Either the secular lord ruled incontestably over a country's spiritual or moral authorities, as in Byzantium and China, or the two powers were merged into one, as in the Islamic world. Europe's political fragmentation allowed its religious leaders to challenge the state and assert their superiority even in the temporal sphere. The secular rulers fought back, of course, and both sides developed legal and philosophical arguments, founded institutions like assemblies of the realm and religious orders to enhance their power, granted support and immunities to universities and monasteries, and enlisted allies among secular and ecclesiastical lords. These developments imposed limits on Europe's monarchs, fostered a division of loyalties, moved the civilization toward a separation of church and state, and in the long run encouraged the rise of constitutional forms of government.

The early church

Christianity was the first universal monotheistic religion. Scholars trace its lineage to ancient Near Eastern traditions and myths. For over 2,000 years, prophets and mystics in the lands between the Tigris River and the eastern Mediterranean Sea had struggled to comprehend their place in the world, the deeper purposes of life, and the creative forces of the universe. In so doing, they nearly always built upon—or reacted to—insights and religious experiences of their forebears, even those of traditions and peoples alien or hostile to their own. Thus, the Israelites adopted the story of the Flood, which first appeared in the Sumerian *Epic of Gilgamesh*, but vehemently rejected the idea of the arbitrary deities of ancient Egypt and Mesopotamia in favor of a loving God who never changes and is always faithful and just toward the creatures he has made.[2]

Judaism's signal contribution to world history was, therefore, the utterly original idea and experience of a personal relationship with the creator of all things.[3] God was not a flesh-and-blood ruler, but a being beyond all understanding who nevertheless loves and cares for all his creatures, especially a few chosen tribes in the region of Jerusalem. As recounted in the book of *Genesis*, a man named Abram was born in the Sumerian city of Ur in southern Mesopotamia and later settled in Canaan on the Mediterranean coastal plain. After many years of religious experiences, he prepared to sacrifice his son Isaac to prove his devotion to the Lord. This willingness to sacrifice his most precious blessing sealed his covenant with God, won him the name of Abraham ("Father of Nations"), and laid the foundation of Judaism. On that foundation, some 2,000 years later, arose the second Abrahamic, monotheistic religion, Christianity.

From the start, this new faith concealed powerful tensions. In his efforts to win disciples, Jesus, as understood by the earliest witnesses,[4] appealed to both reason and the heart. His teaching was radically accepting. "Come to me, all you that labor and are heavy laden," he urged, "and I will give you rest" (Mt. 11:28). His most important assertions, usually presented in parables, furthermore, were neither the commandments of Judaism and Confucianism nor the mind-challenging texts of Taoism and koans of Zen Buddhism, though Jesus' stories, too, often challenged the intellect. For the most part, understanding what Jesus asked of his disciples was simple enough; fulfilling his demands was another matter. The Kingdom of God he likened to a "pearl of great price" that a rich merchant sold all he had in order to purchase (Mt. 13:46). This precept is very straightforward, but hard. Indeed, elsewhere Jesus warned that "it is easier for a camel to go through the eye of a needle than for a rich man to enter the kingdom of God" (Mt. 19:24). As if this were not demanding enough, Jesus called on his disciples to "be perfect, as your heavenly Father is perfect" (Mt. 5:48). This radical perfectionism contrasted starkly with the apparent universal, welcoming appeal of Jesus' message.

Another stumbling block for many potential followers, especially among his fellow Jews, who had been awaiting the coming of a king, was Jesus' ethic of nonviolence and his refusal to assume political authority. "He also whoever slaps you on the right cheek," proclaimed the Nazarene, "turn the other to him as well" (Mt. 5:39). This doctrine often lacked appeal among Jews chafing under the oppressive hand of Roman rule. Jesus even recommended to "render unto Caesar the things that are Caesar's, and unto God the things that are God's" (Lk. 20:25). Far from advocating quietism, however, here Jesus was building into the new doctrine a strict division of loyalties, secular and religious, which would evolve into profound clashes of authority in medieval Europe. Jesus, or more likely the evangelist Matthew, increased the potential for conflict by promising to found his church upon one of his disciples, Peter, and to entrust him with "the keys of the kingdom of heaven" so that "whatsoever thou shalt bind upon earth, it shall be bound also in heaven: and whatsoever thou shalt loose on earth, it shall be loosed also in heaven" (Mt. 16:19). The papacy would base claims to political supremacy and universal authority on precisely this text. Of course, a powerful institutional church was necessary to make such claims, and no such institution existed for many centuries. During Christianity's first 300 years, in fact, the complete absence of any higher political or ecclesiastical authority meant that no single interpretation of Jesus' teachings could be imposed on anyone.[5]

Heeding Jesus' call to "make disciples of all nations" (Mt. 28:19), his disciples and their followers sought to spread the new faith by appeals to the heart and to the intellect. They preached salvation from sin and emancipation from death and, most importantly, faith in a loving God. As the author of the First Epistle of John wrote in a letter to fellow believers, "God is love, and the person who abides in love abides in God, and God abides in him" (1 Jn 4:16). Fervent Christians traveled all around the eastern Mediterranean region and then to Rome and beyond, winning converts, establishing Christian communities, and occasionally rekindling the faith by means of letters or "epistles." They wrote them in the lingua franca of the Mediterranean world, Hellenistic Greek. The faith thus spread far more readily than if the New Testament had been written in Hebrew or even Latin.

St Paul (ca. 5–67 A.D.) in particular traveled thousands of miles (see Map 3.1) and wrote several letters incorporated into the New Testament. Paul conversed widely and may have disputed with Epicurean and Stoic philosophers in Athens. According to a scholar who recently interpreted Paul's letters in the light of Greek and Roman literature, "More than anyone else Paul created the Western individual human being, unconditionally precious to God and therefore entitled to the consideration of other human beings." No person therefore had the right to treat others as objects.[6]

Indeed, Christians showed great compassion for the sick and the weak. Women in particular, who enjoyed relatively high status within Christian communities, were active proselytizers of the new religion.[7] It spread quickly also, thanks to favorable conditions established by the Roman Empire, including political stability, civil peace and the rule of law enforced across an immense territory, a network of excellent roads, and the widespread use of the Greek language. Despite persecution by both Jews and Romans, Christians made up perhaps 8–10 percent of the entire Roman population of 55–60 million when Emperors Constantine I and Licinius jointly granted them full rights in 313.[8]

The doctrine continued to gain adherents mostly through persuasion and debate. Several early Church Fathers placed their trust in both reason and faith. Far from rejecting Greek philosophy, Clement of Alexandria (d. circa 215) argued that God himself had been its source. Tertullian of Carthage (d. circa 230) claimed further, "*Reason*, in fact, is a thing of God, inasmuch as there is nothing which God the maker of all has not provided, disposed, ordained *by reason*—nothing which He has not willed should be handled and understood *by reason*."[9] Finally and more boldly still, Origen of Alexandria (d. 254) believed that since the Lord is "pure intelligence, or something transcending intelligence and existence, we can never say that God is apprehended by any other means than through the intelligence which is formed in his image."[10] The essence of these arguments was to affirm the rationality of God, the orderliness of his creation, and the ability of man to comprehend much of both through reason.[11] This trend might have continued, but worldly success got in the way.

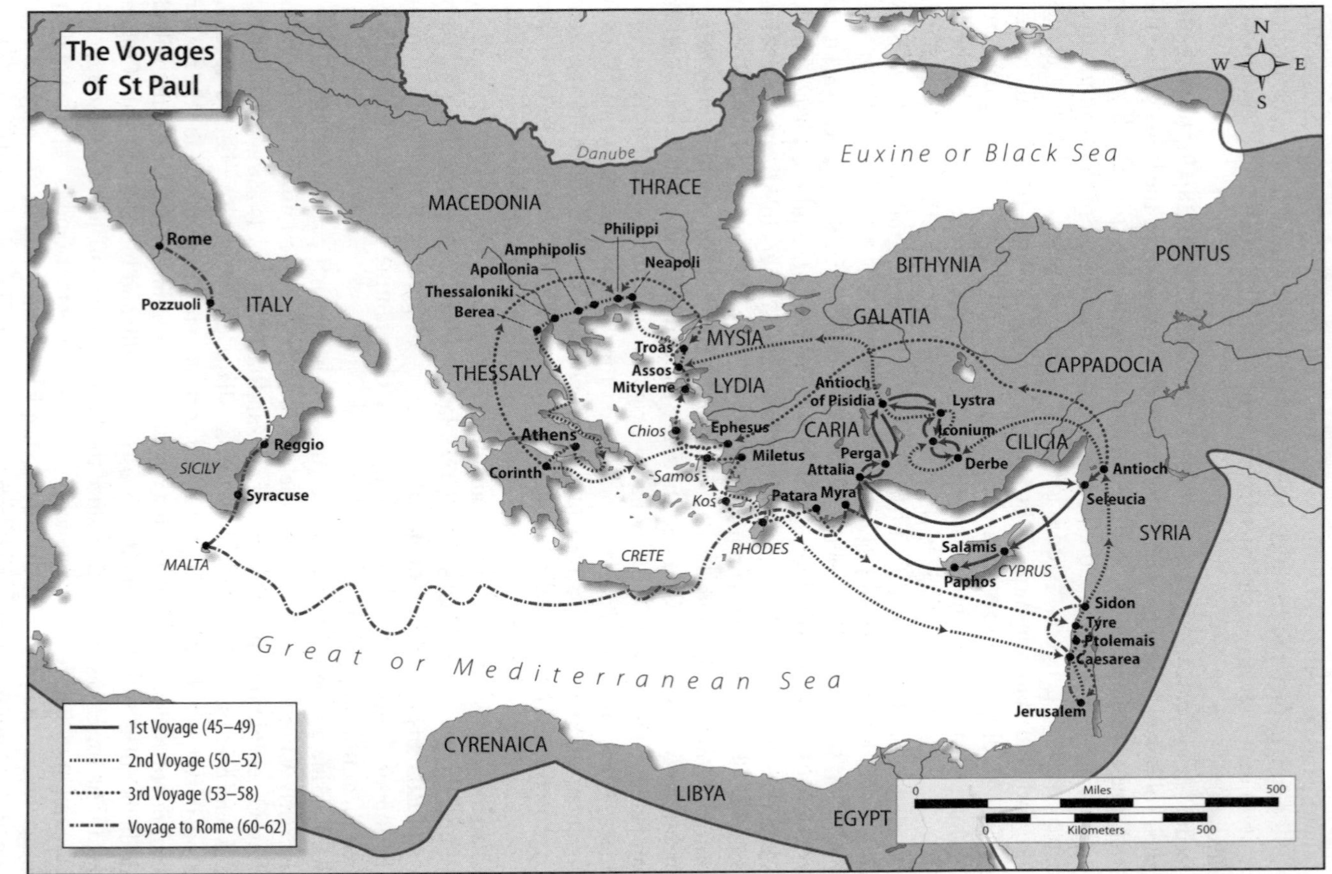

MAP 3.1 *St Paul traveled thousands of miles throughout the Roman Empire spreading Christianity.*

Christianity's status rose when Constantine converted in 337 and Theodosius I banned pagan religion in 392. Why did Constantine adopt the new faith? With barbarian tribes attacking, the economy stagnating, taxes and labor obligations increasing, the population and its life expectancy sinking, and epidemics escalating, the Roman Empire, now ruled from the eastern capital, Constantinople, was crumbling. Constantine apparently hoped the faith, which stirred the souls of millions, would provide a unifying principle for his empire.[12] Indeed, it probably enabled the Eastern Empire to survive for over 1,000 years as Byzantium. Most importantly, the Byzantine emperor could enforce doctrinal and institutional conformity, whereas in the West no single political authority ever existed, apart from Charlemagne and Louis the Pious (r. 814–40). It was precisely the absence of political centralization that made possible the titanic struggle between church and state resulting in what historians call the Papal Revolution.

The Western church

The collapse of the empire based in Rome in the 400s brought down the entire civilization. Over the next few centuries, the population crashed, economic activity nearly ground to a halt, and literacy plummeted. The rulers of Byzantium could draw on a large pool of men educated in secular schools (they were open to women as well). In the West, by contrast, clerics staffed the administrative institutions of both church and state. Senior church leaders—the bishops—possessed enormous moral authority, thanks to their literacy and the memory of Rome. Constantinople, though richer and more powerful, could not boast a more glorious heritage or a mightier claim to primacy over the entire church than the papacy's descent from Peter, the first bishop of Rome. Thus, Pope Gelasius I (r. 492–96) asserted that primacy in a dispute with the Patriarch of Constantinople. He also claimed to possess an authority higher than the emperor himself. In defining these relationships, Gelasius formulated succinctly and forcefully what came to be called the theory of the two swords.[13] As he wrote to the Eastern Roman (Byzantine) emperor Anastasius in 494: "There are two powers, august Emperor, by which this world is chiefly ruled, namely, the sacred authority of the priests and the royal power. Of these that of the priests is the more weighty, since they have to render an account for even the kings of men in the divine judgment."[14]

Although Gelasius argued that these two powers complemented each other, defining their interrelations was a thorny matter. In principle, each related to its own sphere: one temporal, one spiritual. Yet living one's life and finding a path to salvation overlapped, for any deed could either advance or impede one's way to heaven. Since eternal life was more prized than life temporal, the pope had a potentially stronger claim. Indeed, church theorists later asserted that the pope had received both swords from Christ and had merely entrusted the temporal sword to secular authorities.[15] The latter surely felt that the state must either dominate the church or be dominated by it. In Byzantium, the emperor indeed reigned supreme. In the West, no single power existed.

Allegiance to secular authority was further weakened by Christian flight from the world. In *The City of God*, St Augustine (354–430), a bishop of North Africa, argued that believers inhabit two realms, a city of man and a city of God.[16] Augustine predicted the latter's eventual triumph, but it was now a lonely citadel in a hostile world. For many Christians, only monastic life offered citizenship in the divine city.

Following the example of Jesus, who often withdrew to pray, some early Christians in Egypt in the third century began to seek spiritual refreshment on the margins of society and in the wilderness. Monastic communities formed around the more spiritual hermits in Egypt and the Near East. St Basil (329–379) imposed common hours for meals, work, and prayer.[17] This model spread to the West and inspired St Benedict (ca. 480–547) to formulate the church's most long-lived monastic rule. He aimed to help ordinary people to seek the Kingdom of God through spiritual and personal discipline. In an age that disparaged labor as the fate of slaves, Benedict proclaimed that "to work is to pray" (*laborare est* orare).[18] As a result, many communities following his Rule grew rich and gave out alms to the poor. The monks were supposed to read 4 hours on ordinary days and even more on Sundays and holidays. This type of monk, as one scholar noted, "was the first intellectual to get dirt under his fingernails."[19] They were probably also the first elites in history who did not scorn manual labor in general.[20] Benedictine monks were to own nothing individually but did not have to live in poverty. They would pray, eat, read the Bible, and work together as a community or even a household, always under the spiritual guidance of superiors, to whom they owed absolute obedience. Social distinctions were to play no role in the selection of superiors, so that in theory a former slave could dictate to an aristocrat. Public prayers were said seven times daily, though a prayerful attitude was expected at all times.[21] The monks were expected to devote much effort to learning and teaching.

The struggle for the faith included preaching, argument, the self-sacrifice of believers, appeal to popular sources of belief, and at times even violence. Everywhere the deeds of Christian martyrs were commemorated and celebrated. Monks like St Martin of Tours (316–97) physically destroyed pagan shrines, altars, and temples. Others incorporated elements of such shrines and practices into the new institutions. Such approaches probably seemed unavoidable, since unbelievers and pagans outnumbered Christians in Europe for centuries.[22] Christianity also faced a huge problem with heresy.

Intellectual splintering was natural because of the faith's complex theology.[23] Of the great world religions, none has more sophisticated philosophic underpinnings. Jesus, whose teachings were uncomplicated, did not work out this set of doctrines. They emerged for two reasons. First, things claimed about him, for example that he is the Son of God, required careful explanation in order to be taken as reasonable. Second, Christianity arose within the Hellenistic intellectual world. When St Paul disputed with Athenian philosophers, he was doing what came natural to an educated Hellenized Jew.[24] Thus, a religious teaching that began with Jesus' simple teachings gained persuasive power from the need to win converts within a sophisticated cultural sphere and intellectual power from brilliant theologians steeped in Greco-Roman high culture. At the center of disputes about the faith was the nature of Christ himself. The Arians asserted that God created him, whereas the Church Fathers agreed at the Council of Nicea in 325 that the Father and Son were of the same essence.[25] The importance of such disputes was not that they led to the affirmation of dogma but that they placed highly rationalized thinking at the heart of Christian religious life.

The early Christian leaders rarely resorted to violence against heretics or non-Christians.[26] Gradually, fervent and painstaking mission work increased the ranks of orthodox believers. As the faith gained prestige, it also advanced in great bursts. Rulers like Clovis (ca. 466–511), king of the Franks, adopted Christianity, as did entire tribes, through mass conversions.[27]

Yet a deep division between church and state had also begun to emerge. The Christian message proclaimed that worldly power and wealth meant nothing; heavenly riches and God's favor—everything. Christ's entreaty to care for the poor became a central focus of the church, along with praying for Christian souls. In Roman times, the elites had shown generous civic-mindedness. As Christianity became the established faith of Western Europe, in the later fourth century, they gave lavishly to the church. In fact, everyone with the means gave. In exchange, priests and monks interceded with God. "Even the smallest gift to the poor or to the church," in the mind of contemporaries, "brought about a miraculous joining of heaven and earth. In such gifts, time and eternity were joined."[28] The "poor" included the clergy, and the gifts often involved building churches. As secular institutions declined, therefore, religious authority increased. Those who gave demanded that the recipients—the mediators between them and heaven—be spiritually worthy. This meant that priests and monks should not marry and should not indulge in sexual relations. As lay people pressed for clerical chastity, the clergy gained moral superiority in their eyes. Real wealth, secular influence, and moral authority all combined to make the church the equal of—if not superior to—secular rulers and lords.

The power of the Church of Rome increased further, thanks to the leadership of Gregory the Great (r. 590–604), the first monk to accede to the papacy.[29] He expanded the papal estates, maintained cordial but distant relations with Constantinople, supported extensive missionary work throughout Europe, and in general redirected his attentions away from the East and toward the north, where the Frankish sphere of influence gradually expanded, reaching a high point when Pope Leo III crowned Charlemagne emperor on Christmas day in 800 A.D., long before the Byzantine Empire's glory had faded.[30]

One might mark the start of Europe's rise at this point. The territorial unity of the Carolingian Empire shattered soon after the death of Charles in 814, but the cultural foundations he laid endured (see Map 3.2). The "Carolingian Renaissance" involved the establishment of a school in every abbey in the empire by a decree of 787, the adoption by these schools of a classical curriculum, the attraction of some of the age's greatest scholars to the court in Aachen, and the assertion of ecclesiastical power and righteousness.[31] The clergy were to be set apart from the laity through their administration of the sacraments, ritual purity, and celibacy (though priests were not yet prohibited from having wives).[32]

Yet in this period, bishops also came under secular control. Generally appointed and invested with the symbols of their authority by lay rulers, bishops exercised political influence, ruled over land and even churches as fiefs, rendered services for these fiefs to secular lords, and occasionally wielded arms. Carolingian bishops in fact became a pillar of the secular order, helping to administer justice, acting as diplomats and emissaries, and checking the ambitions of powerful noble families, besides their religious duties. Many bishops rarely resided in their dioceses. As public order broke down following the death of Charlemagne's immediate successors, there

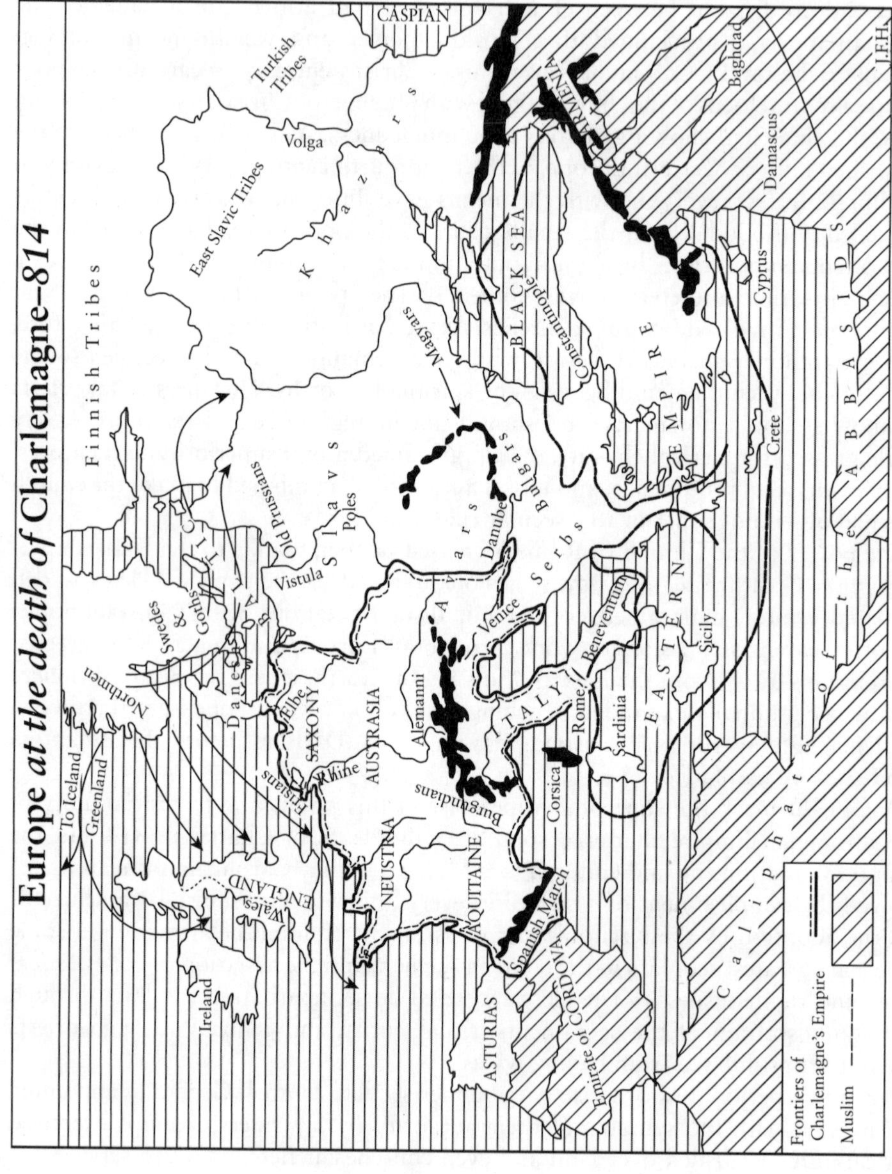

MAP 3.2 *The empire forged by Charlemagne was the closet Europe came to being united during the Middle Ages.*

arose territorial lordships encompassing the offices of both secular and ecclesiastical lords. Although many bishops and priests remained committed to the faith, the church as a whole lapsed into relative weakness.

The religious institutions that best preserved the spirit of the Gospel on the eve of the millennium were monasteries. Some enjoyed legal protection and thus political autonomy. Charlemagne's son, Louis the Pious (r. 814–40), extended his protection to all the monasteries of the empire. As central authority declined, other secular lords also endowed monastic houses. Most of these lords retained a proprietary interest in the institutions, at the very least expecting to play a role in the selection of abbots. Some lords granted them exemption from taxes and other obligations to ensure their complete devotion to spiritual things.

The Benedictine Abbey of Cluny in Burgundy was a paragon of this development.[33] In 909, William I, Duke of Aquitaine, endowed the abbey with land, conferring its ownership upon the Apostles Peter and Paul, the patron saints of the papacy. The abbots of Cluny were thus to answer directly to the popes in Rome. In subsequent centuries, Benedictine houses had hired labor to replace the monks in field and workshop. The reformers of Cluny rejected manual labor almost entirely in favor of continuous prayer. Lay magnates who thirsted for salvation bestowed vast wealth upon the abbey in exchange for inclusion on its prayer lists. Thus, the institution grew rich, which further enhanced its political and institutional autonomy.

The Abbey of Cluny played a key role in paving the way toward reform in the church. First, it sparked a powerful renewal of religious life across Europe. Second, by subordinating itself and its growing number of dependent monasteries to central authority, Cluny upheld the ideal of papal supremacy. Third, the Cluniacs strenuously defended the superiority of spiritual over secular power. Finally, when reformers gained control of the papacy in the late eleventh century, they found willing and effective allies in the abbots of Cluny.

Reform builds

Christianity experienced powerful movements for renewal throughout its history, far more frequently and consequentially than any other major religion.[34] Why? First, it was heir to the Hebrew prophetic tradition. From the time of Abraham, several dozen seers imparted to the Jewish people divine revelations of God's wrath, promises of glory and protection, impending destruction, calls to righteousness, and assurances of the coming of a messiah. Christians enthusiastically embraced these stories of intimate connection to God and saw their complete fulfillment in the person of Jesus, whom they proclaimed the Messiah. Yet, secondly, Jesus himself presented a vision of apocalyptic redemption beyond anything foreseen in the Old Testament. Instead of earthly success and political security, which most Jews hoped for, Jesus promised a Kingdom of God to all who believed in him, including and most especially the meek. This Kingdom would bring love, peace, and justice for eternity at the time of Christ's second coming. In the meantime, Jesus imposed on his followers demands all but impossible to fulfill: to love one's enemies, to attach little importance to material things, and to become a servant to others. Inevitably, the ecclesiastical institutions that arose to promote these deeds fell woefully short.

It was not surprising, therefore, that movements for a return to Christ's precepts time and again wracked the institutional Church.[35] Medieval European people of all social origins thirsted after religion in many different forms, both organized and popular. Sometimes secular or religious leaders led the charge, for example, Constantine or Gregory the Great. In many other cases, beginning largely in the 700s, intellectuals, laypeople, and clergy advanced reformist claims, guided by ideals of spiritual purity, indwelling faith, personal transformation by the Holy Spirit, or emulation of apostolic example. Thus inspired, they repudiated the wealth and power of the institutional church, condemned the impure behavior of the clergy, and demanded the purification of both. Still others, idealizing established institutions and practices, clashed with the reformers. Many struggles to return Christendom to the true ways of Christ and his Apostles emerged from the monasteries, prompting one historian to dub these struggles an "effort to monasticize the entire Church."[36] The Eastern Church experienced powerful and even violent movements for reform, such as the Iconoclast controversies in the 700s and 800s.[37] Yet the calls for spiritual transformation were far more frequent, popular, and insistent in the Western Church.

The breakdown of order before the millennium sparked a wave of popular religion, heresy, and calls for church reform. By any measure, renewal was sorely needed. All pretense of clerical celibacy had vanished. Bishop Ratherius of Verona (890–974) once remarked that enforcing this canon would leave his diocese entirely without priests.[38] Church offices and buildings faced a real danger of becoming hereditary property. The amount of ecclesiastical holdings at stake was immense, thanks to centuries of bequests. The clergy everywhere were allied to and even dominated by the secular powers. Bishops rented out parishes for money or payments in kind. The Marquis Boniface of Tuscany (d. 1053) once held 13 parish churches from the Bishop of Reggio. He shared the revenues of 14 other churches with local knights.[39] Reformers called this the crime of simony, or trafficking in the Holy Spirit for money. Equally deplorable, many "princes of the church" basked in their power and glory. Archbishop Manasses of Rheims (1069–80), for example, supposedly quipped that "the archbishopric would be a fine thing, if only one did not have to sing Mass for it."[40] Each episcopal see, in the eyes of many prelates, was thus a mere "honor," a fief requiring homage, fealty, or military service. At the turn of the millennium, control over the 77 bishoprics in France was divided up among the king and various dukes, counts, and viscounts, sometimes "in ways that can look very close to 'owning' them," according to one scholar.[41] Secular lords "invested" bishops with their symbols of authority, in exchange for feudal homage.

Organized opposition to these practices built throughout society and the church. It was manifest in the "Peace of God" movement aimed at curtailing attacks on churches and villages by marauding castellans.[42] In 975 in Le Puy in south-central France, the bishop called together townspeople, peasants, and secular lords in a field. Flanked by his nephew's armed men but acting without papal sanction, Bishop Guy threatened the lords with excommunication should they refuse to maintain the peace. Over the next two decades, similar meetings occurred in other French towns. Most participants were enthusiastic commoners, including women, who believed they were making an eternal covenant with God. Again, ordinary Europeans were displaying an unusual ability to coordinate their activities for positive action. These local initiatives spread widely—throughout France and into Catalonia—and grew in sophistication and rhetorical power.[43] Processions, liturgies, and the presentation of the relics of saints became the standard practice, and miracles common occurrences.

Now the councils came more under papal and secular control.[44] Knights and castellans pledged a Truce of God, beginning in 1027 in southeastern France, which limited the days on which they could fight. This trend also spread. In 1049, Pope Leo IX at Reims presided over a council that proclaimed the peace as universal. Aspirations of ordinary people and reforming clerics merged in demands for more righteous spiritual leaders. At such councils, calls rang out for a reformed priesthood. Men of the cloth should be celibate, should not hunt or carry weapons, should have no women in their houses, and should not traffic in the Holy Spirit. Reformers appealed to the laity to protest corrupt priests by avoiding their churches. Rousing mass support for the movement increased its influence but also brought to life popular activism that sometimes veered off toward unsanctioned forms of piety. In any event, ordinary people in Western Europe were, as in founding and administering urban communes, drawn into organized, grassroots activity that over time enhanced their social power.

Only the universalist institutions, customs, celebrations, and ideas of Christianity gave coherence to Europe as a whole.[45] True, most secular elites shared the code of chivalry and nearly everyone was imbricated in the network of feudal relations. Yet what united most Europeans' hearts and minds was the Christian faith. There was the mass with its beautiful and uniform liturgy, standard rites of passage throughout life, numerous holy days and religious festivals, the veneration or remembrance of hundreds of saints and other holy men and women, common given names, the diffusion of monastic orders, the taking part in pilgrimages that most people at least aspired to, a sense of common enemies (Muslims) and "others" (Jews), and in general shared religious and spiritual traditions. In all these ways, Europeans experienced a unity of civilization, which never took political form.

Even the Holy Roman Emperors, who exercised nominal rule over the vast territory that lay roughly within the present-day boundaries of Germany, Switzerland, northern Italy, the Czech Republic, Austria, and the Low Countries, owed their political authority symbolically to the church, since the pope crowned each emperor, from the first one, Otto the Great, in 962, until the 1200s. The emperors, who claimed the title temporal vicar of Christ, were the principal agents of reform in the church and confirmed the election of the popes until this practice was abolished during the Investiture Conflict at the turn of the eleventh century.[46]

Revolutions in the church

From its earliest days, the church aimed at transforming the world. The first Christians expected Christ's imminent return in glory. When he failed to appear, an institutional church emerged. Christ would come again someday, as the Nicene Creed teaches, but concern with when should preoccupy believers less than seeking to lead a godly life in this world. Yet great expectations of spiritual apocalypse remained vital throughout the medieval period. The approach of the millennium heightened these expectations because the New Testament book of Revelation speaks of how Christian martyrs "came to life and reigned with Christ a thousand years" (Rev. 20:4). Many people believed and hoped the year 1000 would mark the Second Coming.[47] Renewal and reform were thus perceived as a means of preparation, just as Jesus had foretold that the Kingdom of God would be won by those who prepared for its coming (Mt. 25:1-13). The Peace movement and a massive campaign across Europe to build new churches and monasteries and to repair existing ones were two aspects of grassroots preparations.[48]

The only body capable of large-scale, coordinated, continental renovation was the papacy. Situated in the Eternal City, the site of the earthly remains and tombs of Sts Peter and Paul, boasting establishment by Christ himself, the church stood at the apex of order and authority in the West. Elites and ordinary people came to Rome from all over Europe seeking the church's guidance and judgment. The papal reformers of the eleventh century seized the initiative to extend the Holy See's authority over the whole church and all of society.[49] They deployed four main instruments to this end: appeal to tradition, the monastic orders, ideas, and the law.

A tradition of separationism was deeply rooted in the Bible. Jews kept separate from Gentiles. Levites and other temple officials kept themselves aloof from ordinary people. One key thrust of the reform movement was to purify and consecrate the priesthood. The clergy should not marry women and father children, who required material support from church funds, but should "marry" the church and devote themselves to their flocks. Nor should priests have contact with impure things like money, sex, blood, and weapons. Graphically, the reforming Cardinal Peter Damian (ca. 1007–72) warned against the befoulment of the holy sacraments by hands that had touched the genitalia of a trollop. Other reformers explained that priests engaging in sex relations with parishioners or monks with novitiates committed spiritual incest. All such perversion must be repudiated. By purifying themselves, lay and monastic clergy not only elevated the church and more fully carried out their divine calling but also demonstrated their greater fitness to exercise authority.[50]

Separation of the clergy found further affirmation in the Judeo-Christian tradition of dualism. The Bible sharply distinguishes between spirit and flesh, soul and body, faith and works. Our dual nature disallows the Christian from inhabiting solely the spiritual realm.[51] Imitating Christ, who fuses the mortal and divine natures, is our only means to combine and thus overcome these dualities. Since the clergy and, in particular, monks were best able to achieve this divine emulation, they alone could lead the church's efforts to infuse purity into society.

Papal grants of immunity and protection to monasteries augmented the church's influence in society and the political realm. Thanks to papal support and the spiritual fervor of the age, the network of monasteries associated with Cluny rose from about 60 in 1049 to some 2,000 in 1109 (see Map 3.3).[52] Each of these monastic houses (technically priories and not abbeys) answered directly to the abbot of Cluny who himself was subordinated to the pope. Gregory VII (r. 1073–85), who supported them staunchly, urged monks to work directly in society in order to transform it spiritually.

The institutional reform began with the pontificate of Leo IX (r. 1049–54).[53] A product of the reforming monastic movement, he recruited a dozen like-minded

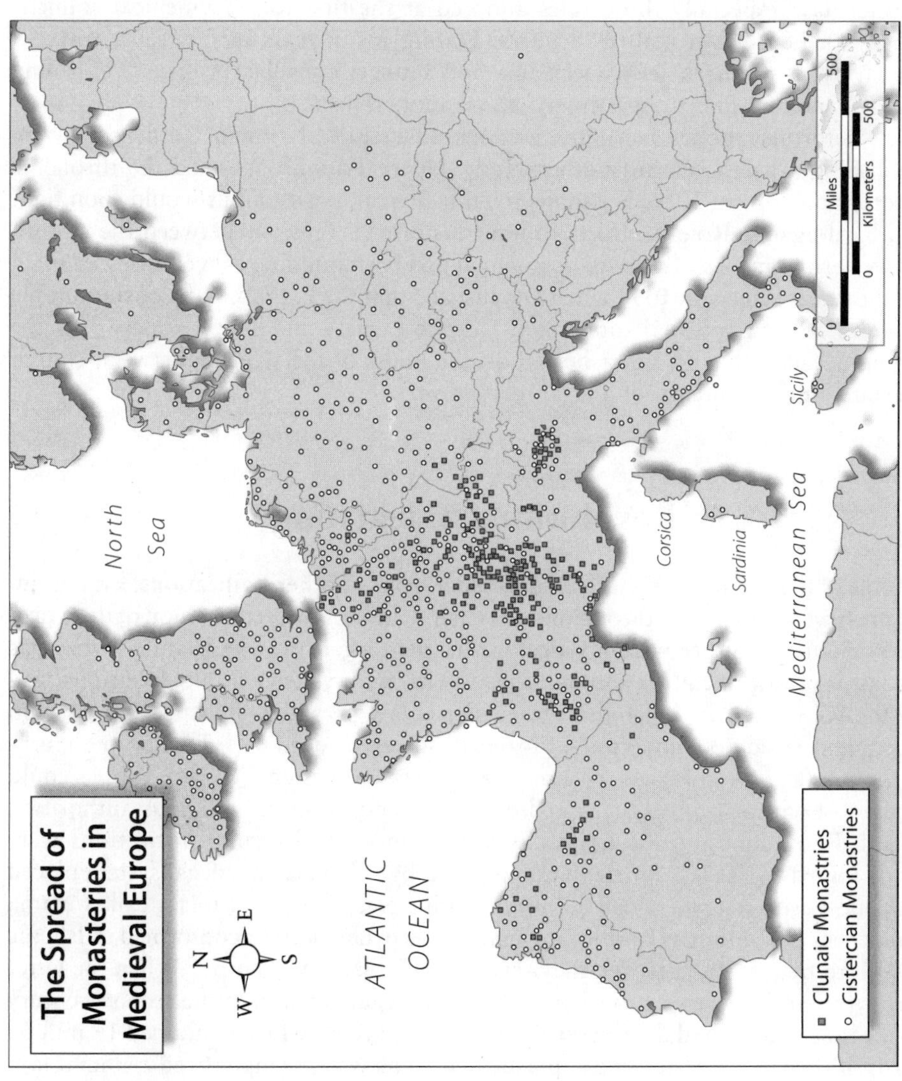

MAP 3.3 *With the support of the papacy, monasteries quickly spread throughout Europe.*

reformers, mostly bishops and abbots from around the Holy Roman Empire, and appointed them to senior positions in Rome.[54] All these men had fought against simony, clerical marriage, and the tradition of imperial influence in ecclesiastical affairs. For the next half-century, they worked to purify and to emancipate the church. A charismatic leader, Leo IX preached powerfully against simony and other abuses of things spiritual. Under the influence of Peter Damian, Leo advocated a return to canon law, especially those rules adopted at the first four ecumenical councils (325–451). Leo was a man in a hurry. During his 5 years in office, he traveled extensively in northern Italy, Germany, and France; convened a dozen reforming councils; and sent many papal envoys to promote reform.

The reforming popes faced tremendous adversities. Norman conquerors were establishing a harsh rule in southern Italy. Henry IV, who assumed the throne as emperor at age 16 in 1056, began his reign in a weak position but would soon fight back hard against Rome's efforts to limit his power. Tensions between the eastern and western branches of Christianity, which had been building for centuries, erupted into the Great Schism in 1054 when Leo insisted that the Patriarch of Constantinople recognize Rome's spiritual supremacy. Despite earnest diplomatic efforts over the coming decades, this rift never healed. In the midst of the struggle between church and state, Europe underwent a legal revolution.

Revolutions in learning

The role of the law in the West distinguished it from all other civilizations. Byzantium had preserved Roman law throughout the early Middle Ages, yet its vision of the world and its political culture were mystical rather than legalistic. The Islamic world was strongly legalistic in culture and outlook, and its legal system was highly rationalized like the West's, yet the religiously based *sharia* law pervaded all aspects of Muslim society and faced no competitors. European society, indeed each European country by the 1200s, was governed by not one but several systems of law. People could appeal to each for protection or redress against political and religious authorities. In both Byzantium and the Islamic world, religious and secular institutions were tightly joined by the law rather than separated by it. The Islamic legal system placed everyone—even rulers—under the law. In principle, religious scholars called ulama could check the authority of rulers by making sure their actions conformed to Islamic law. More frequently, however, they served their rulers obediently.[55] When the latter were tyrannical, there was nowhere to turn for legal defense. In the second-century B.C., China's rulers had developed a complex legal code, which contained 17 million words 400 years later. Yet this sophisticated legal system emphasized criminal law, while commercial law developed only weakly, in marked contrast to the Roman Empire.[56]

The rediscovery of key texts of Roman law in southern Italy around 1070 sparked a legal revolution that made the Papal Revolution possible.[57] This discovery was not accidental. At mid-century, jurists of both the papacy and the empire began scouring libraries and archives for remnants of the ancient law in the hope of gaining an advantage in the struggle for primacy between church and state.

Most important were law codes originally compiled on the orders of Emperor Justinian around 530. These texts, for example the Digest, which contained thousands of pages of Roman case law and legal opinions resolving particular disputes, touched on diverse topics but were very loosely organized. In order to build upon this foundation and even to make sense of the vast Justinian corpus, a system of analysis and synthesis was required. An approach called "scholasticism" filled the bill.

Conditions for its development began to emerge during the Carolingian Renaissance.[58] First, in 782 Alcuin of York redirected the focus of the Palace School in Aachen from military training to academics, specifically the seven liberal arts.[59] A few years later, Charlemagne decreed the establishment of similar schools in every monastery and cathedral. Other important schools opened in northern Italy, such as the school of rhetoric in Pavia, which dated to 825. A few scholars active in these centers of learning translated texts from the Greek, for example the Irishman John Scotus Eriugena (ca. 815–77), a successor to Alcuin. This intellectual flowering declined with the Carolingian Empire.

A second intellectual revival began at the start of the millennium with the reopening of Carolingian cathedral schools. A few became celebrated centers of learning, especially at York in England and at Reims, Orleans, Paris, and Chartres in France. Brilliant scholars like Fulbert, bishop of Chartres from 1006 till 1028, attracted students from all over Western Europe. They wrestled with texts of Plato, Aristotle, and the Christian Neo-Platonists. For example, Fulbert's cathedral school was famous for Neo-Platonic learning.[60] Drawing on a translation of Plato's *Timaeus*, scholars distinguished between divine, natural, and positive law. Justice is divine, they argued; since man makes law, which is a part of justice, then by enacting laws man is able to understand the will of God.

The scholastic method developed as a means to resolve contradictions between texts, ideas, and arguments. The approach was called "dialectical," or dialogic, because it sought to reconcile divergent or contradictory positions—ancient Greek and Christian, divine and human, Muslim and pagan, practical and theoretical, and ultimately faith and reason.[61] Scholars used the method of *quaestiones disputatae*, whereby each text, idea, or concept was objectively asserted, sympathetically defended, and rigorously critiqued, before a doctrinally but also logically defensible resolution was reached. It was an extraordinary venture, derived from a profound belief in the power of the intellect to comprehend every aspect of reality. This method permitted scholars to harmonize Greek philosophy, which tended to emphasize the universal, and Roman law, which emphasized consistency and the particular, and then to bring both into accord with Christian theology.

Scholars and legal practitioners applied this method first and foremost to the Justinian texts. In fact, Europe's first degree-granting institution of higher education, the University of Bologna in Italy, was founded in 1080 specifically in order to study and teach them. Jurists, by means of dialectical probing, worked to systematize the vast body of Roman legal rules into a single integrated whole. First, they found general principles under which these rules could be subsumed. Second, they classified general cases as species of a common genus. Here they drew upon the system of classification developed most effectively by Aristotle.

Peter Abelard (1079–1142), a foremost logician who taught in Paris, contributed powerfully to this development.[62] Following several Eastern Church Fathers, from

Clement of Alexandria to John of Damascus (ca. 676–749), he argued that all knowledge is good because it comes from God. Abelard recognized inherent flaws in the philosophical approaches of Plato and Aristotle and overcame them in a manner that permitted a harmonization of both. For Plato, universal concepts, like the True and even the Table, truly existed as eternal "forms" or "ideas." All particular existing things could best be understood, according to Plato, through deductive reasoning, as instances of these forms. By contrast, Aristotle employed inductive reasoning in order to work his way from existing things toward external qualities by which to classify the things. Abelard rejected both approaches in favor of "nominalism," the view that categories and qualities are merely names (*nomina*) conceived by the mind in order to classify things. It might seem like a petty distinction, but literalistic and fetishistic medieval thinkers might have devoted all their mental power to analyzing the concepts themselves had they not accepted them as tools for organizing the vast store of knowledge available to them.

Among the oppositions to reconcile in regard to the law were general principles and exceptions, justice and mercy, divine (revealed) law and positive (man-made) law, customs and statutes, and religious and secular ordinances. Within each element of these binary sets, there were still more contradictions and even paradoxes to bring into consonance, for example, between God as terrible Judge and as merciful Redeemer. In synthesizing all these oppositions, therefore, scholastic legal scholars also had to harmonize the underlying worldviews and philosophical doctrines. Their efforts culminated in powerful new systems of law and philosophical syntheses.

The birth of universities in Europe made them possible.[63] In Bologna, the students incorporated as a guild and then hired experts in the law to teach them.[64] The Bologna native Irnerius (ca. 1055–1130), for example, was a star professor to whom students flocked from around the continent. By the mid-twelfth century, roughly 10,000 students were studying the law in Bologna under the imperial protection of Frederick I Barbarossa who declared: "the world will be ruled and illuminated by learning."[65] A few decades later, a guild of faculty emerged from well-known schools in Paris. Whether controlled by the students or the faculty, these institutions enjoyed immunity from prosecution by local secular authorities and oftentimes even ecclesiastical authorities. By 1241, at least 12 more universities had been founded in England (Oxford and Cambridge), Spain (Salamanca and Palencia), Italy (Salerno, Arezzo, Modena, Vicenza, Padua, Naples, and Vercelli), and France (Toulouse). Dozens more appeared over the next two centuries (see Map 3.4).[66] The institutions conferred the right to teach only upon those who fulfilled the criteria approved by the masters. Some, like Paris, had four faculties: liberal arts, theology, philosophy, and law. Others offered only graduate study in the latter three. In each case, students had to complete a study of the seven liberal arts, whether in a cathedral school or in a university, in order to matriculate in the higher programs of study.

The European university was a pioneering institution. The professors worked together, established curricula in concert, and were largely free to disagree with one another. Higher schools in antiquity had been dominated by a single teacher. Islamic madrasahs were similar.[67] Each of the hundreds of madrasahs was established through an act of piety as a private religious foundation (*waqf*).[68] Teaching and

MAP 3.4 *Systematic higher education in the Middle Ages was a pan-European phenomenon.*

learning were therefore of utmost importance in Islamic society. If the university was a guild that brought together several masters, however, the madrasah was like a workshop headed by a single master who directed a few or several journeymen and apprentices. Here one studied theology, history, and above all, Islamic law, but not natural philosophy, logic, mathematics, or Greek texts.[69] In the Islamic world, these subjects—aside from astronomy, which one could study in the mosques—were taught only under the auspices of a private master, who depended on the largess—and often the whims and political fortunes—of powerful benefactors. Knowledge was often transmitted orally and informally, to a large extent by rote memorization of religious works and standard textbooks, in personal interaction with a master whose legitimacy stemmed from an unbroken chain of learning from master to master down the generations.[70]

The same was true of China, which boasted an older and even more elaborate system of education. From the National University founded well over 2,000 years ago and specialized colleges emerging over the centuries to a network of schools following established curricula in every town of the empire beginning in the Song era, no culture in history had so highly prized or more generously supported education.[71] Much of the learning involved memorizing classic texts and practicing calligraphy, but students also received rigorous training in textual interpretation and analytical writing. For the most part, however, the entire system of learning focused on preparing candidates for the civil service examination, for most of Chinese history the single most important avenue toward worldly success.

What made Europe's universities unique were their diverse, influential, and relatively autonomous faculties. They maintained uniform academic standards and allowed for a continuous exchange of ideas and scholars across the continent, thanks in part to the lingua franca spoken in every country, Latin.[72]

Paradoxically, Europe's political fragmentation made possible the emergence of an institution that transformed learning. Why this was the case requires another comparison.[73] Muslims enjoyed full rights anywhere in the Islamic world. In Christendom, by contrast, no political or religious authority had the power to enforce such uniformity, and therefore people lacked rights outside their hometown. When students and faculty, who hailed from many lands, joined together in guilds, they gained power in numbers and could threaten to decamp for more welcoming localities. The loss of so many consumers could devastate a city. Such threats often won privileges for the fledgling academies from secular and ecclesiastical authorities. Each madrasah was a rooted institution, by contrast, generally one of many in a given city. Threats to relocate thus meant little. Second, the absence of a unified political authority in Europe allowed the flourishing of diverse legal bases. The corporation, a social organization grounded in Roman law, and the trust, a customary English association, were both recognized as legal entities with full juridical rights just like persons. Islamic law, by contrast, acknowledged only physical, natural persons; it denied such status to the *waqf*.[74] The unified legal and power structures of the Islamic world made it possible to ban "institutional persons," which might have provided greater shelter to autonomous educational (and charitable and commercial) institutions and entities. Ultimately, an incorporated or chartered university wielded vastly more clout than any madrasah, with its lone patron, no matter how eminent.

Revolutions in the law

People living in hyper-litigious modern societies where plaintiffs contest even apparently reasonable policies or practices may believe there are too many lawyers, but few would be happier, more prosperous, or more secure without the rule of law. Under this legal regime, law transcends politics and binds the ruler, even the law he or she makes. The modern Western legal order with its procedural guarantees, checks and balances, constitutional restraints, and respect for individual and group rights emerged from a protracted struggle between tenacious secular and ecclesiastical authorities in medieval Europe.[75] Emperors, princes, kings, incorporated cities, and nobles fought for influence and control among themselves and against popes, bishops, and abbots seeking to assert their moral superiority. All the contestants drew upon the available logical methods, conceptual tools, and intellectual systems, including Greek philosophy, Roman law, Germanic legal codes, Christian theology, and even custom, tradition, and legend. Out of these confrontations emerged a set of multifaceted legal frameworks.

The cornerstone of the papal framework was canon law, the rules by which the church was governed. It consisted of Divine Law (revelation), pronouncements of church councils, papal letters (decretals), and episcopal statutes. By the millennium, the vast number of canons was not even gathered together in a single place. Few legal experts had the capacity to organize them. Within several decades, however, a powerful body of canon law was preserved, categorized, interpreted, and applied by hundreds of jurists.[76] Now the church could regulate minutely the life and activities of the clergy; impose and administer rules governing sacramental, moral, and religious behavior, commitments, practices, and offenses of the laity; and, finally, clarify its relations with secular rulers and authorities, with which the church shared many overlapping jurisdictions.

First, Popes Leo IX and Nicholas II (r. 1059–61) reemphasized the canons calling for morally pure clerical behavior. In 1059, Hildebrand, the future Pope Gregory VII, asked Cardinal Damian to comb the papal archives and gather all the texts relating to the rights and powers of the Holy See.[77] It seems his work led to an anonymous collection of canons, the *Seventy-four Titles*, which stressed papal supremacy. Over the following decades, scholars produced much systematic analysis and several more canonical compilations. Two key themes were the pope's authority and rules for spiritual purity.

By far the most important compendium was the *Concordance of Discordant Canons*, completed by the Bolognese canon lawyer and monk Gratian around 1140.[78] He analyzed thousands of canons from a thousand years of Church history, reconciling and systematizing them by creating a legal framework based on theological and philosophical doctrine and Roman law. The result was both a holistic legal treatise and a textbook. The treatise presented a comprehensive hierarchy of the law from the noblest and most supreme, divine law, to the humblest and most subordinate, customary law. On this spectrum, canon law was of course superior to princely law, though natural law (what is inherently just according to human reason and conscience) stood above both. A revolutionary aspect of Gratian's understanding of natural law was his insistence that "princes are bound by and shall live according to their laws."[79] They could change old laws if they followed legal procedure but could not disregard them. Within Gratian's framework, all existing and conceivable law either had its place or was rejected, if it contradicted divine, natural, or ecclesiastical law. Obviously, Gratian's treatise augmented the authority of the church, as interpreter and enforcer of divine and canon law.

As a 1000-page textbook, the Concordance was taught in law schools alongside Roman law, which remained valuable for its vast fund of cases and legal concepts. Canon law, as the actual functioning legal system of Europe's most sophisticated polity, influenced the study and evolution of secular law—royal, urban, feudal, manorial, and commercial. The second half of the twelfth century witnessed the publication of books on legal procedure, both Roman and canon; treatises on criminal law; and law codes and monographs on specific branches of local secular law in the various polities of Western Europe.[80] By the early 1200s, Europe had authoritative, hierarchically organized law courts, both ecclesiastical and secular, staffed by a highly regarded class of university-trained lawyers.

A unique system of law developed in parallel with Roman and canon law but with only minimal influence from either: English common law.[81] The most flexible of the three and the most protective of the individual, it began to emerge when Henry I (r. 1100–35) appointed traveling royal judges who earned a reputation for fairness. Over the next several decades, and especially during the reign of Henry II (r. 1154–89), the issuance of royal writs established speedy, evidentiary- and common-knowledge-based procedures for trying property and other civil cases. Henry reinstituted the Anglo-Saxon custom of jury trials, where 12 jurors conducted the investigation and decided claims of wrongful dispossession of land. The crown thus protected individual property rights. The number of writs multiplied over time but never exceeded 80 (*habeas corpus*, still a part of American jurisprudence, was one). They defined the limits of royal judicial authority: no writ, no jurisdiction. How different from the (Roman) civil law tradition, which spells out in great detail what is lawful and unlawful. Judges in all English royal courts based their opinions on both local custom and legal precedents established by earlier court decisions. By contrast, the civil law judges on the Continent simply applied existing laws.[82] Of course, judges everywhere in Europe limited the power of rulers.

A variety of courts continued to exist across Europe, including ecclesiastical, manorial, urban, and private. The expansion of royal control over justice in both England and on the Continent generally reined in, but did not abolish, these courts, which therefore continued to limit the authority of rulers. For one thing, people could contest the laws of one jurisdiction by simply fleeing to another. In general, the modern concept of the separation of powers grew out of this competition of separate legal jurisdictions in medieval Europe.[83]

The same was true of corporations and, even more so, of English trusts.[84] Perpetual endowments, perhaps inspired by the Islamic *waqf*, trusts possessed the rights of a juridical person whose charter neither church nor state could revoke.[85] Since the members of both corporations and trusts owed allegiance to the larger body, rather than to each other, these institutions fostered the development of a public space separate from individuals, social estates, and rulers.

All that held Europe's thousands of competing jurisdictions and institutions together, it seems, was the Christian faith. Indeed, the most marked characteristic of all the prevailing European law was its manifestly religious character. The famous *Sachsenspiegel* (1220), which codified both civil and criminal law and remained in force or at least influential across the German-speaking lands for centuries, declared that "God is himself law; and therefore law is dear to him."[86] How, therefore, could the church not have triumphed in its struggle for supremacy of authority, at least until the most powerful secular rulers could consolidate their power?

The investiture conflict

Tradition did not favor the papacy. The Holy Roman Emperor, following Byzantine and Carolingian practice, was considered the head of the church, even the temporal vicar of Christ.[87] By custom, bishops were beholden to secular lords who physically bestowed on them their ring and staff, giving each bishopric the appearance of a fief.[88]

Ideas often trump custom, however, and most learned men favored the church. The millennial era witnessed a powerful religious revival, a yearning for spiritual purity, and a widespread abhorrence of the pollution of holy things. Church reformers vehemently denounced fornication by priests and their dependence on lords who obtained their power from "pride, rapine, treachery, and murder." Dramatically, the reformers symbolically likened the church to the soul and lay power to the body.[89]

Gregory VII, elected pope in 1073, launched a campaign against clerical impurity.[90] He sent dozens of letters urging bishops to punish—and parishioners to boycott—priests and bishops involved in sexual activity or simony. In early 1075, Gregory opened a campaign affirming papal supremacy. In February, he decreed an end to lay selection and investiture of bishops, something no king could possibly agree to, as it meant a huge loss of power and authority. A month later came the *Dictatus papae*.[91] The Pope alone was universal, thundered Gregory, and he alone could appoint, move, and depose churchmen; could grant priests the right to judge superiors; could nullify sworn oaths; could be called universal and use imperial insignia; could be judged by no one; and—here Gregory cited no canonical precedent whatsoever—could depose kings and emperors. Thus began the Papal Revolution. Emperor Henry IV had apparently been willing to support and even to promote the campaign for church reform. Gregory's assertion of papal supremacy, by contrast, meant war.

They joined battle in late 1075 and early 1076. Henry rejected the papal candidate for the bishopric of Milan and proposed his own. Gregory replied that the papacy stood above all earthly rulers who, in accordance with their Christian faith, were bound to respect the pope's decrees and to kiss his feet, according to the ancient custom. The emperor in turn, as noted above, denounced the pope as a usurper and a "false monk" and reaffirmed his own position as grounded in a theory of the divine right of rulers. Gregory then excommunicated his rival and declared him deposed. Henry had miscalculated. The German princes and bishops flocked to the pope, abandoning the emperor who felt compelled to travel to Canossa in a hair shirt. Gregory absolved the emperor and lifted the excommunication. He misjudged the situation, however, since now many German princes returned to Henry, while others elected a new emperor. A civil war ensued, which many blamed on Gregory. Soon Henry named as "anti-pope" Clement III, who outlived Gregory. Henry invaded Rome the following year, and the Normans sacked the city in 1085, the year of Gregory's death. Civil war continued in the Empire as German aristocrats built castles and multiplied their feudal lordships, thus undermining the authority and power of the emperor. Civil strife broke out on similar grounds in France and England.

Subsequent popes continued Gregory's fight along somewhat different lines.[92] Whereas his main goal had been the election of bishops by church officials, his successors emphasized rooting out only lay investiture. By the Concordat of London (1107), for example, Henry I of England renounced his right to invest bishops and abbots with their symbols of authority (ring and staff) so long as they would observe the custom of swearing fealty and homage to him like any secular vassal. Moreover, the English kings persisted in controlling the appointment of bishops. Henry II in particular rewarded his supporters with bishoprics and abbeys. He went too far, however, when he tried to subject the clergy to his unified judiciary. He had to back down on this point in 1170, though only after his supporters had murdered the Archbishop of Canterbury, Thomas Becket, creating a wave of antiroyal sentiment. Still, in its contest with the papacy the English monarchy came out stronger. So did King Philip I of France, who renounced both investiture and homage but retained the right to grant ecclesiastical fiefs to bishops and to receive fealty from them.

The situation in the Holy Roman Empire was far more complex and intractable, mostly because the emperor's political position frequently shifted.[93] In 1111, Henry V, enjoying staunch support in the German lands, imposed a very favorable settlement on Pope Paschal II (r. 1099–1118) through force of arms. In 1119, however, under pressure from the German princes and bishops, Henry met with the new pope, Calixtus II, ready to give up his right to investiture "of all churches." At the Concordat of Worms (1122), the emperor abandoned nearly all his authority over the church in Italy. In the German lands, the clergy were to select bishops and abbots, the emperor to invest them with the *regalia* or symbols of secular power, and finally the church invested them with the ring and staff of spiritual authority. This was little more than a symbolic victory for the church.

It took another half-century for the papacy to win full independence from the Holy Roman Emperor. The Third Lateran Council (1179) empowered the College of Cardinals to elect the pope without imperial confirmation.[94] Two decades later, the power and prestige of the papacy reached its apogee under Pope Innocent III (r. 1198–1216).[95] According to one scholar, his "curia never slept," with decretals flowing from Rome in torrents. His activity culminated in the Fourth Lateran Council in 1215, which brought together representatives of eighty ecclesiastical provinces and nearly two dozen prelates from Constantinople and the Middle East.[96] Among the 70 canons adopted were strict rules for punishing heretics, leading to the establishment in 1231 of the Inquisition.[97]

Spiritual revolutions in the church

The Papal Revolution demonstrated the supremacy of moral authority and ideas over tradition and temporal might. This was the first instance of a tendency of the West in which physically weaker actors claiming moral superiority have contested the right to dominance of mightier forces. Within Christianity, the justification for such claims stems from statements by Jesus, for example, that it is the violent (the fervent) who take the Kingdom of God "by force" (Mt. 11:12) and that the meek (the weak) will "inherit the earth" (Mt. 5:5). These assertions—absurd by worldly standards—may account both for the Christian West's interminable impulses to reform—an impossible standard can never be fully realized in an imperfect world—and for the repeated asymmetrical battles engaged on moral grounds in the Western world, from Luther's shattering of the church's unity to the Bolsheviks' aim to bring down the entire liberal capitalist world. In each case, moral and mental fervor gave the underdogs extraordinary influence.

The evangelical and spiritual awakening, which began just before the millennium especially in the region between the Rhine and Loire Rivers, set people's hearts and souls on fire. Presumably, the economic expansion discussed in Chapter 2 helped fuel the era's cultural and social optimism, though it would be crass to imagine them merely a by-product of material improvements.[98]

Throughout the Middle Ages, Christians were taught to see life as a pilgrimage, a journey toward union with God.[99] This is the sense in which Dante began his *Divine Comedy* with the words: "Midway through the journey of our life." Devotional travel to holy places, sporadic from the first centuries after Christ, became common after the millennium. The main destinations were Jerusalem, Rome, and the alleged tomb of St James the Apostle in Compostela in northwest Spain. As the practice expanded, many new sites drew pilgrims—millions in all. The main attractions were allegedly miracle-working physical remains, mostly bones, of holy men and women. Some journeys were local. Others covered thousands of miles. The church integrated the practice into institutional devotion, imposing obligations to undertake pilgrimages as penance. Pilgrims usually traveled in groups and under the protection of the religious authorities. Monasteries across Europe established way stations to welcome pilgrims and even built chapels and churches to house holy relics and to accommodate devout visitors.[100] The practice expanded cultural horizons, increased personal freedom, improved lines of communication, and brought large numbers of European Christians to the Holy Land.

The expansion of pilgrimage to Jerusalem led to the establishment in 1080 of the Knights Hospitaller to care for sick and destitute pilgrims.[101] Fifteen years later, Pope Urban II called for a crusade to take back the Holy Land from the Muslim conquerors. A key justification was to protect and to keep open the pilgrim routes. Christian fighters departed full of enthusiasm and in 1099 captured Jerusalem. In that year the Hospitallers were reconstituted into a military and religious order charged with the care and defense of the Holy Land, and the Knights Templar were instituted to organize further pilgrimages and crusades. They established a Europe-wide network and arranged letters of credit for well-to-do pilgrims. Over the next two centuries, Europeans conducted a dozen more crusades (see Chapter 5).

These journeys across Europe and especially to Muslim-dominated lands, probably the world's biggest migration till then of people from one developed society to another, exerted powerful effects on Christian Europe. This was not surprising, given William McNeill's persuasive argument that in premodern times the "main drive wheel of historical change was contacts among strangers."[102] Most significant for Europe, it seems, were new attitudes, in particular, a chastened awareness of the greatness of the Islamic and Byzantine civilizations. It seems likely that feelings of inferiority spurred the Europeans to strive to achieve more, to fight more aggressively, and to try and adopt every new technology, institution, idea, or practice they encountered abroad. Finally, they gained not only control over some Mediterranean trade routes and a sense of commonality, but also a perception of intra-European cultural differences (protonationalist sentiment).[103]

For nearly three centuries after the millennium, spiritual fervor spurred monastic growth all over Europe. In 1098, the birth of the Cistercian Order gave the most self-denying believers a home.[104] Unlike the Cluniacs, the Cistercian brothers themselves put plow to field. Ironically, rejecting worldly ways and the riches of Cluny, they also gained immense wealth and, under the inspired and inspiring leadership of Bernard of Clairvaux (1090–1153), won papal privileges of immunity and great political influence. At the time of Bernard's death, there were some 350 Cistercian monasteries scattered across Europe (see Map 3.3 above). A half-century later, in the early 1200s, two new monastic orders burst onto the scene.[105] The Dominicans and Franciscans were mendicants: men and women dedicated to serving others, to denying self, and to living in poverty, chastity, and obedience. Most importantly, they committed themselves to working in the growing cities, caring for the poor and sick and serving as pastors, teachers, preachers, and missionaries. Overall, in the thirteenth century there were probably well over 100,000 monks and nuns in Europe, since one estimate reckons some 25,000 in England alone.[106]

It was an age of associability, of frequent contacts, of social density. Male Franciscans traveled constantly. The monastic houses communicated regularly with one another. Individual priests and religious were routinely transferred as considered necessary by church authorities. Scholars often trained and taught at different universities. Learned professionals, chiefly doctors, lawyers, and accountants, multiplied. As the commercial economy accelerated, men skilled in math and logic enjoyed high demand and infused rationality into the broader culture. Most of these educated elites could easily communicate in Latin, Europe's lingua franca. Latin was in fact enjoying a revival as a spoken language and a golden age in poetry, hymnody, religious writing, and philosophy.[107]

Educated Europeans began to see their world differently. The individual, hitherto submerged in the collective, now began to seek self-expression. Artists wrote biographies and prefaces and identified themselves in their works. Writers set themselves at the center of many stories.[108] Key reasons for this behavior were to attract patronage and recognition but apparently also simply the joy of setting oneself apart. Similarly, philosophers felt and promoted the dignity and nobility of human nature, the underlying value of nature, the meaningfulness and rationality of the natural order, and the belief that this order is intelligible to the human mind.[109]

Religious belief and doctrine also bent in these winds of change. Christ began to appear not in glory but as a human suffering in the world. His mother, Mary, was increasingly represented as mediator between her son and the world.[110] In the late twelfth century, purgatory began to be conceived as an actual physical place where ordinary Christians—those who were "neither very good nor very bad"—could purify themselves in anticipation of entry into heaven.[111] Not only was the inherent worth of millions of people thus being affirmed; the church clearly also wished to gather most of Christendom to its bosom. In the 1200s, ordinary people responded in part by claiming to experience countless miracles.[112] Everyone, not only the tonsured and ordained, was called to change the world through action.

These intellectual and cultural changes have been called the "Twelfth-Century Renaissance."[113] It laid the foundation for a burst of philosophical speculation in the next century.

Important for these developments was the recovery of ancient Greek philosophy. In the early Middle Ages, the learned knew some writings of the Church Fathers, of Latin thinkers such as Cicero and Seneca, and of Neo-Platonists like Boethius. Indeed, Étienne Gilson wrote, "Plato himself does not appear at all, but Platonism is everywhere."[114] The late eleventh century saw increased interest in translating texts, fueled in part by exposure to the Greek and Islamic worlds during the First Crusade. Sicily and Toledo, now recovered from Muslim domination, became great centers of translation of Greek science and mathematics, including Euclid and Ptolemy, and of Aristotle, at first from the Arabic rather than the original Greek.[115] A few European scholars traveled to Constantinople, like James of Venice who translated Aristotle's *Posterior Analytics* and other writings from the Greek in the second quarter of the 1100s. By the end of the century, nearly all his works dealing with logic, grammar, metaphysics, science, and cosmology had been translated—a vast and mighty corpus; a hundred years later, they were well known.[116]

Other scholars, like Adelard of Bath (ca. 1080–1152), traveled and lived among Muslims and translated and popularized works of science, philosophy, and mathematics by Muslim scholars.[117] Some of these works not only built upon Greek philosophy and science but also advanced and interpreted them in a monotheistic theological framework. European scholastics especially esteemed Ibn Rushd or Averroes, one of the few eminent Muslim proponents of the harmony of faith and reason.[118] The Latin philosophers called him "the Commentator," for his extensive and brilliant commentaries on Aristotle and other Greek philosophers.[119] One scholar has even argued—though he has not convinced all his colleagues—that the scholastic method developed under the direct influence of Islamic precedents.[120]

Aristotle and Ibn Rushd took the universities by storm. Some of their ideas were unacceptable to Christians, for example, Aristotle's rejection of divine providence and his belief in the eternity of the universe or Ibn Rushd's repudiation of the Trinity. Thus, in the early 1200s the religious authorities of Paris, Europe's greatest center for philosophical speculation, prohibited lecturing on Aristotle. Yet some university masters continued to teach him in private. By the 1250s, the ban had been lifted and Aristotle had become a key element of the curriculum.[121] Ibn Rushd was far more revered in Europe than in the Islamic world, which had turned away from philosophy.[122] Thinkers like Thomas Aquinas (ca. 1225–74), a Dominican, and Roger Bacon (d. 1294), a Franciscan, embraced both "pagans" and "infidels," constructing vast syntheses based on the belief that nature and Divine Law are in harmony and, in the case of Bacon, that mathematics are necessary for understanding theology. Some scholars believe the recovery of challenging texts can explain this stupendous flowering of philosophy and logic. Marie-Dominique Chenu points instead to an astonishing "hunger of spirit" inherent in the age.[123] Whatever its cause, the result was an almost unbounded faith in man's ability to understand the universe.

Surely the greatest intellectual achievement of the Middle Ages, and one of the most astounding of all time, was Aquinas's *Summa Theologica*.[124] Encyclopedic treatises called *summae* were all the rage beginning in the twelfth century, the result of that "hunger of spirit." St Thomas wrote two. His key work, *Summa Theologica*, gathered together systematically all the main questions of theology, doctrine, ethics, political theory, canon law, and Christian philosophy and resolved them in the light of writings of dozens of Greek, Roman, Christian, Jewish, and Muslim philosophers and theologians. In all, he addressed 612 topics, divided into 3,120 subtopics. His method was to state the topic, present possible objections (10,000 all told) to his conclusion, cite a supporting authority, develop his argument, and answer the objections.[125] The result was a complex synthesis of reason and faith, philosophy and theology, demonstrating a deep faith in human reason to pierce the secrets of the universe.

Such optimism troubled the religious authorities. In 1277, the Bishop of Paris condemned 219 "propositions" then being discussed at the University of Paris, beginning with two: "That there is no more excellent state than to study philosophy" and "That the only wise men in the world are the philosophers."[126] Many of the propositions limited the power of God, for example, "That God cannot be the cause of a newly-made thing." Even some teachings of Aquinas, who was later declared a Doctor of the Church, fell temporarily under the condemnation.[127]

The speculation of the great medieval thinkers was, indeed, a two-edged sword. It has been argued that the condemnation inspired subsequent philosophers like Duns Scotus (ca. 1266–1308) and William of Ockham (ca. 1288–1348), two Franciscans, to adopt a more skeptical approach toward Aristotle's scientific theories, several of which were incorrect.[128] Moreover, Ockham argued that human reason cannot demonstrate the immortality of the soul, or God's existence, or any religious propositions, paving the way toward a radical separation between faith and science.[129] Religious authorities and theologians in the Islamic world, particularly al-Ghazali, also condemned both Aristotle and what they considered excessive confidence in human reason. The results, however, differed markedly. Speculation, questioning, skepticism, and endlessly pushing the bounds of knowledge continued in Christendom but fell off in Muslim lands.[130] Stubborn political fragmentation in Europe was probably the main reason for this divergence.

Political revolutions in Christendom

Some historians argue that Gregory VII and other reformers created a "papal monarchy."[131] It was, they say, an independent government spanning Christian Europe with the continent's most sophisticated bureaucracy and legal system, a large diplomatic corps on temporary and permanent mission in every European country and even many non-European lands, representatives in every town and village of Christendom, exclusive jurisdiction over thousands of educational and religious institutions and tens of thousands of pilgrims, and the primary initiative in a half-dozen large overseas military ventures. Without permanent military or naval forces, the papacy nevertheless commanded enormous power, played great kings against one another, and enjoyed more political authority and influence than any other polity in Europe for at least two centuries. The recovery of Sicily and northern Spain from the Muslims increased the papacy's strength relative to the Holy Roman Empire, which had no navy and therefore was unable to enforce its will in these regions.

Although the church jealously guarded its authority and even insisted on its superiority, in some regard church and state reinforced each other's power and prestige. Most areas of crime and punishment, for example, were in the purview of the state. Everything related to the soul fell to the church. Yet intersections of the two spheres occurred in various places, including the Inquisition. The millennium witnessed an explosion of heresy. Among the most menacing were the Cathars.[132] Usually, prelates imposed only spiritual punishments, such as excommunication. The influential abbot, St Bernard of Clairvaux, for example, urged winning heretics back to the faith through persuasion.[133] By the early 1200s, however, canon lawyers and theologians began to justify capital punishment for convicted heretics.

In response to a canon adopted at the Fourth Lateran Council, prescribing that heretics be excommunicated and punished by secular authorities, Emperor Frederick II launched a systematic campaign against them. Partly in order to prevent him and other lay lords from becoming the chief enforcers of religious orthodoxy, Pope Gregory IX (r. 1227–41) set up the Papal Inquisition in 1231.[134] He appointed permanent itinerant judges, mostly Dominicans and Franciscans, who operated under the supervision of bishops. They were active in France, Italy, Aragon, and Germany, though not in England. A papal bull of 1252 empowered them to use torture, though in principle only as a last resort, in order to ascertain guilt or innocence. A few were fanatics, like Robert le Bougre. He had put a few hundred people to death before he was relieved of his duties and imprisoned in 1239. In principle, inquisitors could apply no harsher punishment than expulsion "from the bosom of the church," though with the understanding that the secular authorities would then burn the person at the stake. Thus, when it came to the most extreme threat to the very foundations of Christendom, church and state were as one. In countless other ways, they remained rivals.

As a result of the Papal Revolution, kings were no longer the heads of their churches, and the pope was their lord with regard to things spiritual. The weakening of the empire brought on by the papal challenge doomed any near-term prospect of a Europe-wide secular empire or even of German or Italian unity.[135] Throughout the German lands, localized rights of lordship over peasants grew, increasing serfdom. Even before the Investiture Conflict, the emperors had few sources of income beyond their own estates. Now local taxes and levies increased, while royal and imperial revenues declined further. Not only did the church declare and assert its autonomy, so also did universities and urban communities. These institutions, taken together with transcontinental commercial enterprises and semi-independent religious organizations, like the Templars, created multiple zones of public and private autonomy. The expansion of the legal profession, of rules of due process, and of conceptions of legal rights all mediated among these various interests and further strengthened the bonds of society. Thus restrained and challenged in every direction, the European state required some radical measures just to maintain itself.

Above all, Europe's rulers imitated the papacy.[136] No other political entity—not even the relatively centralized Anglo-Norman monarchy in England[137]—could furnish such powerful models of central leadership or of bureaucratic government. The papacy's arsenal of coercive and persuasive instruments also included a vocabulary of authority, influence, and power; philosophical treatises interpreting and justifying rulership; and a reinvigorated Latin language. Europe's rulers in turn deployed them forcefully in order to centralize their realms, to undermine the ties of feudalism, to challenge the decisions of feudal courts, to legislate, and to impose new taxes.

Like the papacy, secular rulers appealed to legal and philosophical arguments. Most European monarchs had for centuries advanced legal and moral claims to territories much greater than their administrative and military capacities allowed them to enforce. As the sinews of secular government strengthened, many sovereigns gained full dominion in fact and not only in right.[138] Marrying into powerful families could achieve the same end, a potentiality unavailable to the papacy. Further, princes and kings commissioned scholars to advance justifications for their rule, including the theory of "divine right," a doctrine that remained vital for centuries, in part because a king's subjects found it hard to perceive him as a mere layman.[139] Finally, the recovery in the mid-1260s of Aristotle's *Politics*, which grounded rulership in keen observations about existing forms of government and the nature of man, also opened the door to further secular justifications of monarchy.[140]

An entirely new—and uniquely Western—mechanism for solidifying kingship were the assemblies of estates, parliaments, diets, and other like bodies that emerged all over Europe in the thirteenth and fourteenth centuries in the context of military revolution (see Chapter 4).[141] Some were regional or provincial; others, territory-wide. These institutions, in conjunction with influential bodies like universities and religious organizations, gave rise to the *Ständestaat* or "polity of estates."[142] The three main estates, or status groups, were the church, the nobility, and the commons, of which the main power were the towns. The monarch called representatives of the estates periodically in order to raise taxes and seek advice on grave policy decisions.

These assemblies of estates differed in several ways from feudal assemblies of barons and other secular lords who had for centuries met to offer counsel to the king.[143] First, they included representatives of the clergy and the towns. Second, they gathered and deliberated both in three separate chambers and as a unified body according to fixed rules and procedures. Third, they expressed the interests of an entire territory, not merely of individual members of a given territory. Fourth, whereas the feudal lords viewed the ruler as their overlord, the estates confronted him as partners in governance. As such, the assemblies, which flourished in the later Middle Ages, both instituted a mechanism for raising revenue and imposed limits on the royal capacity to levy taxes. They also established a forum for promoting interests and rights of the status groups and thereby institutionalized a constitutional division of powers.

With the power of the major European states increased, papal supremacy could not long stand. The turning point came during the reign of the French king, Philip IV the Fair (r. 1285–1313).[144] Boniface VIII decreed in *Unam Sanctam* (1303) that the spiritual authorities had the right to judge secular rulers but could themselves "be judged solely by God not by man."[145] A few years later, however, a French-born pope, Clement V (r. 1305–14), took up residence in Avignon in southern France and expressly granted the kingdom of France and its subjects an exemption from his predecessor's decree. Most French kings exercised strong influence during the 67-year-long Avignon Papacy.[146]

This turn of events was less surprising than the period of papal supremacy. After all, the expansion of agriculture, commerce, and urbanization had for three centuries vastly increased the population and wealth of Western Europe. The resulting increase in fiscal resources everywhere fueled an enormous growth in the number of government officials, mostly trained lawyers. In the thirteenth century, most were still clerics, but gradually their ranks swelled with laymen, especially in Italy.[147] The transition from charismatic monarchy to secular, bureaucratic kingdom—and even toward the nation-state—had begun.[148] In the long run, this new polity would not only overshadow the papacy, but also take the world by storm.

* * *

The confrontation of church and state in the first 200 years of the new millennium destroyed imperial pretensions to unite all Europe under one secular ruler. It also established church and state as separate and distinct, albeit complementary, entities. Such a balanced political division never occurred in the other great civilizations, probably because in no other civilization did the power and authority of religious institutions so nearly approximate those of the temporal sphere. None of the great Eastern civilizations was dominated by a single religion. Each either developed two or more or melded these into a syncretic unity. The Muslim world confessed a single faith, yet lacked a doctrine or tradition of resistance to secular authority.

Under the protection or at least the shadow of the two main European powers arose a third force—urban society—based on wealth, technological innovation, and commercial sophistication, not moral authority or martial prowess. Yet endless competition among Europe's hundreds of polities drove kingdom, duchy, canton, and even town to push the limits of military technology and tactics in order to stave off conquest, as will be recounted in the following chapter.

QUESTIONS FOR REFLECTION

Describe the mighty tensions within Christianity.

Why did Christianity develop such a complex theology?

Why did Christianity experience powerful movements for reform?

How did the role of the law differ in Western Europe and the Islamic world?

In what ways was the European university a revolutionary institution?

How did legal fragmentation foster the development of freedom in Europe?

Why were medieval Christian philosophers so open to non-Christian thought?

What role did assemblies of estates play in medieval European political life?

Chapter 4 Chronology

~3500 B.C.:	Weapons first designed specifically for war
~1400 B.C.:	Iron begins to replace bronze in weaponry
~600 B.C.:	Cavalry becomes integral in military tactics, replacing chariots
Fourth-century B.C.:	Philip and Alexander of Macedon begin combined-arms doctrines
732 A.D.:	Charles Martel defeats Muslim invasion force at Tours
~800–1000:	Vikings expand to Slavic lands, Western Europe, and North America
814:	Charlemagne dies and his empire splinters
900:	Cavalry now dominant military force in European armies
Twelfth century:	Normans begin expansion, taking over England and southern Italy
1100:	Armor increasingly complex and protective
1200:	Trebuchets prevalent, replacing catapults as siege weapons
Thirteenth century:	Mercenary bands increasingly common and successful
Early fourteenth century:	Pike-based armies begin to challenge armored knights
1302:	Battle of Golden Spurs; First Estates-General called in France
1320s–30s:	Wars, floods, and famines diminish wealth of Italy
1337:	Black Death begins to ravage Europe
1346:	Battle of Crécy: infantry defeats mounted knights
1370:	Major breakthroughs in sailing move commerce to sea-based trade routes
Late fourteenth century:	Economic boom in Europe
1420s:	Artillery increasingly effective
1439:	Charles VII of France establishes Europe's first standing army

Mid-fifteenth century:	Field artillery allows large states to expand further
1453:	Fall of Constantinople
Late fifteenth century:	Infantry revolutionized by new tactics and weapons
Early sixteenth century:	New fortifications let small states remain autonomous
1618–48:	Thirty Years' War
Early seventeenth century:	Gustavus Adolphus moves from *tercio* to linear tactics
Mid-seventeenth century:	Central, absolutist authorities begin to rise in Europe

4

Military revolutions

"The English archers then advanced one step forward, and shot their arrows with such a force and quickness," that it seemed as if it they were blanketing the earth with "snow."[1] Thus, Jean Froissart, the French chronicler, described the commencement of the battle at Crécy on 26 August 1346.[2] That conflict marked a turning point in military history, when highly disciplined foot soldiers armed with longbows and pikes defeated the finest aristocratic mounted knights, for hundreds of years the masters of every European battlefield. Though numbering only around 20,000, the English army not only routed French forces three times as great, but also slaughtered a vast number of them, while themselves suffering only minor losses. Again Froissart: "in the English army there were some Cornish and Welsh men on foot, who had armed themselves with large knives; . . . and falling upon earls, barons, knights, and squires, slew many."[3] Previously aristocratic warriors had spared one another's captives. The common-born infantrymen felt no such compunction.

Of all the regions of the world during the medieval era, Europe witnessed the most ferocious combat. Just as the lack of central political authority invited a political contest between church and state, it also led to almost continuous warfare among the hundreds of European rulers, fueling a series of interlocking military advances.

As commoners (typically in the service of kings or at least led by noblemen) learned to challenge armored knights, the larger monarchies developed expensive siege and field artillery, enabling them by the mid-1400s to reestablish their preeminence. The early 1500s, however, saw the emergence of sophisticated fortifications by which smaller states could preserve their autonomy. During the following century and a half, the major European states built up huge, yet highly disciplined and even scientifically articulated, armies. Relatively small countries, like the Dutch Republic, if they were rich, could hold their own in this belligerent environment, for money was truly the sinews of war. For two centuries, these states warred among themselves while gradually projecting their power abroad. Eventually no power on earth could stop them.

Ancient and early medieval warfare

As with so many other achievements of civilization, the Mediterranean region and China were the first crucibles of the military arts. The earliest known defensive bastion was erected 9,000 years ago at Catal Huyuk (Anatolia).[4] Although spears, bows, and slings had been wielded many tens of thousands of years earlier, the first dedicated offensive weapon, the mace, appeared in the Middle East around 3500 B.C. Smiths began to forge tips, blades, and smashing surfaces for weapons from copper and, several hundred years later, from bronze, a more durable metal. The Bronze Age began a bit later in the Indus Valley and in China. A huge proportion of the artifacts extant from this time are, in fact, weapons.

The most sophisticated new innovations were the chariot and the sword, which appeared in Mesopotamia around 2500 and 2000 B.C., respectively. Over the next several centuries, the level of craftsmanship increased. The war chariot evolved into light, two-wheeled vehicles with spoked wheels and a friction-reducing hub-and-axle design. Nomads of the Central Asian steppes, with their expert horsemanship and cultivation of powerful steeds, made the best use of them. They overran the entire Eurasian civilized world between 1800 and 1500 B.C., slowing development in India and creating sharply differentiated social structures in China. The Assyrians, the dominant power in the Middle East for centuries, deployed light chariots with archers and heavy ones bearing spearmen. Egyptian charioteers held sway throughout the Nile Delta region.

Iron gradually replaced bronze in the eastern Mediterranean region from at least 1400 B.C. Since iron was abundantly available, its advent increased aggregate wealth and democratized warfare. The great monarchies fell or faced fierce challenges from mostly unknown peoples migrating from the northeast. Some consolidated and strengthened themselves, thanks in part to the new, inexpensive material. The Assyrian Empire, after a century's decline from 1230 B.C., became the most powerful military and administrative force the world had ever seen. Up to 100,000 highly trained soldiers equipped with iron weaponry, armor, and chariots took part in some campaigns. By the time of Tiglath-Pileser III (r. 745–727 B.C.), Assyria, a state whose entire purpose was to make war, still dominated the region.[5]

A cavalry revolution began in the 600s B.C. among nomadic peoples of the Central Asian steppes. Equine herding communities constituted formidable military forces. Whereas sedentary populations could sustain at most one soldier per ten agricultural workers, every nomadic horseman was a warrior. For nearly 2,000 years, they made repeated incursions on the margins of China, the Middle East, and India. In time they mingled with settled peoples and founded such empires as the Median centered on present-day Iran and, later, the Jurchen stretching north of China, continuously threatening established states. Even the Great Wall of China did not ensure protection. Tribute payments forestalled many attacks, but not all.

The combined-arms force of Philip II of Macedon (r. 359–336 B.C.) was the most sophisticated and adaptable in the ancient world.[6] His army blended mercenaries and citizen-soldiers, aristocratic cavalry and lower-class but marvelously well-trained infantry, professional support staff, and siege weapons like catapults. The infantry divided further into three types. There were heavily armored *pezhetairoi* who wielded 13-foot pikes, agile *hypaspists* with their 10-foot pikes, and lightly armored archers and javelin throwers, the *peltasts*, all highly disciplined and arrayed in strict formation. Most importantly, Philip and his son Alexander the Great (r. 336–323 B.C.) raised tactics, training, organization, and military science to a high level of refinement. Each phalanx, composed of over 8,000 men, was a self-contained fighting unit of combined arms, similar to the modern division, which emerged some

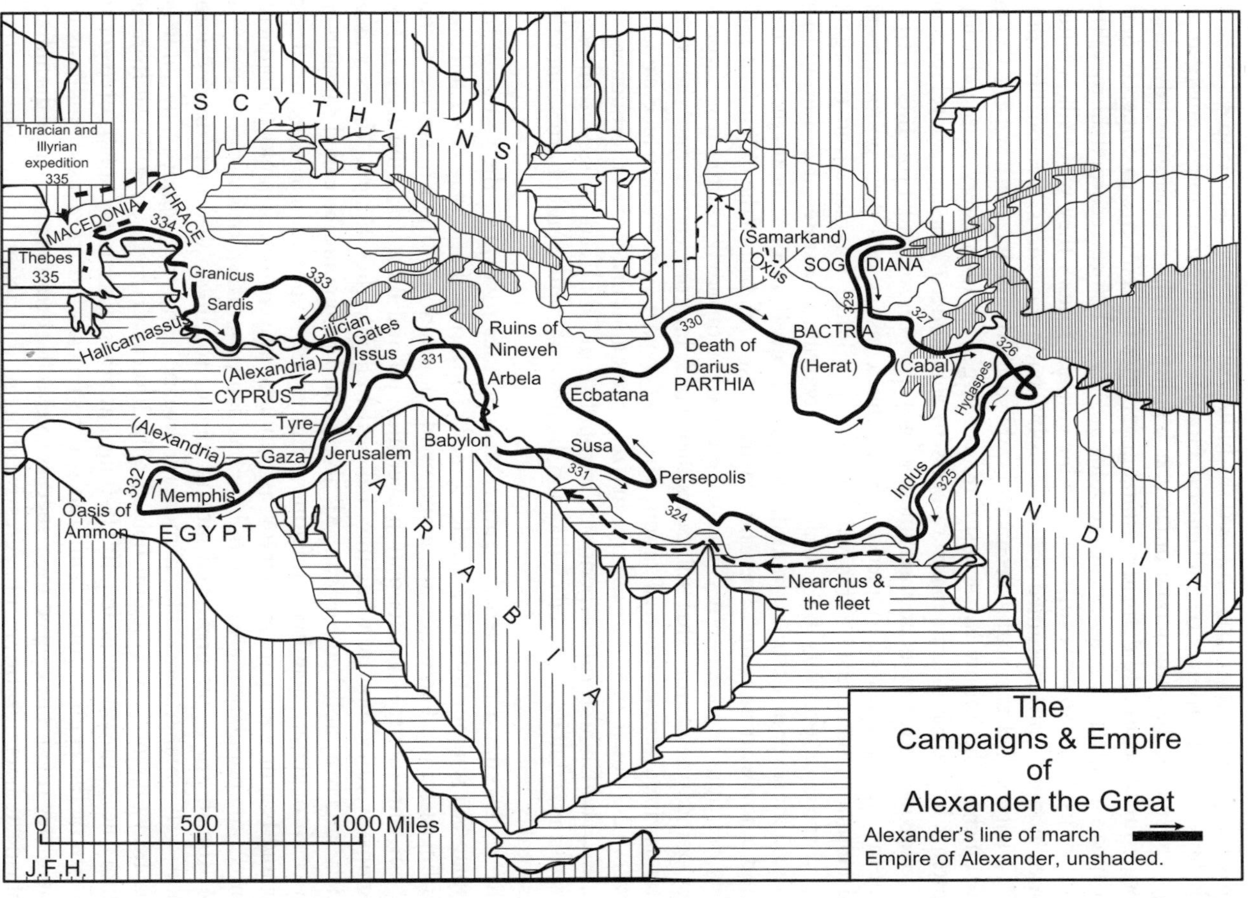

MAP 4.1 *Using superior tactics, Alexander the Great conquered Asia Minor, Egypt, Persia, and northwest India in less than a decade.*

2,000 years later. Probably no fighting force before the gunpowder revolution could have withstood its onslaught—especially on flat terrain—so long as Philip and Alexander lived. With these forces, and his strategic brilliance, Alexander devastated the numerically superior Persian army on its own territory and then pressed through Central Asia and into the Indian subcontinent (see Map 4.1).

Following the decline of Hellenistic Greece, two great empires emerged at opposite ends of the Eurasian landmass. Each polity laid the foundation of dynamic, prosperous societies and defined regional geopolitics for centuries to come.

China's civilization was far more ancient.[7] Even before recorded history, the Chinese displayed some readily identifiable cultural traits—they wove silk, crafted refined pottery, and consumed millet, possibly with chopsticks. By roughly 1600 B.C. a tribe called the Shang began to establish its dominance in northern China over much of the Yellow River basin, thanks largely to its mastery of the chariot. Written Chinese, similar in many respects to the modern language, developed in the following centuries as an instrument of governance. Around 1100 B.C., a tribe from the west, the Zhou, toppled the Shang but consolidated their political gains and cultural achievements. This was an era of political fragmentation that gave way in the eighth-century B.C. to a chaos of warring city-states, a condition that persisted for several centuries. Indeed, the epoch from 403 to 221 bears the name of Period of the Warring States. The Zhou Dynasty itself fell before the Qin in 221 B.C. These warriors from western China were armed with newly crafted iron swords. They unified the country that still bears their name into one empire and, thanks to a standardized script, one civilization. The next dynasty, the Han, which came to power in 206, built an empire as large in size—if not administered so thoroughly—as Rome's. The Chinese rulers, periodically toppled and replaced by restive elites or invaders, maintained a unified civilization, by force of culture and of arms, until the present day.

Rome, by contrast, united the entire Mediterranean world to the shores of the Caspian Sea without forging a single unified civilization. Latin was never adopted as a lingua franca. Culturally, the empire-wide imposition of the Roman law—and later of Christianity—was its only powerful bond and most enduring legacy. The Romans prevailed not by what they believed but how they fought. Theirs was a society largely established for war.[8] All able-bodied men could be called to military service throughout their lives. Lifelong training was expected. They prepared for war and fought with patriotic fervor, as only free citizens can. Thanks to frequent combat, the population always numbered a high proportion of seasoned veterans. The Roman army was organized into legions of roughly 5,000 men divided into successively smaller units, like a modern division. The vast majority of soldiers were heavy infantry: each legion fielded only 300 cavalrymen. Overall, the Roman military never greatly exceeded 400,000 men at arms, a relatively small force given the size of the empire—over 2 million square miles—and the tens of millions of people they ruled. They owed their success to excellent training, superior discipline, sophisticated organization, and aggressive strategy and tactics. Continuous warfare, and consequent rapacious taxation, however, took their toll on the empire. By the third-century A.D., it was in decline.

Rome faced powerful threats in the east and north. From the time of Julius Caesar (100–144 B.C.), fierce Germanic tribes continuously attacked Roman positions across the entire northern frontier.[9] Huns and other nomadic warriors of the Central and East Asian steppes challenged the empire from the east. Many of these mostly Germanic "barbarians" were gradually Romanized, so that by the time of Emperor Theodosius (r. 379–95) the majority of imperial soldiers and officers descended from barbarian tribes. They, therefore, did not conquer Rome but merely inherited it. After 400 years, the greatest empire until modern times collapsed, giving way to political fragmentation on a massive scale. Unity was never recovered.

The Eastern Roman Empire, or Byzantium, declined more slowly. It could still field 60,000 troops in 1071 (down from 150,000 in 550 A.D.), something no Western ruler could manage until two or three centuries later.[10]

Medieval warfare

The systematic recovery of the art of war in Europe began in Carolingian times. Charles Martel, a brilliant military commander who turned back a Muslim invasion in 732, created Europe's first heavy cavalry. His grandson, Charlemagne, a ruler of enormous charisma and energy, consolidated vast lands across Western and Central Europe through continuous military campaigns.[11] The Franks he ruled were fierce warriors but anarchic and unreliable, constantly disputing booty, living from plunder, and warring among themselves. He imposed discipline and order. Grants of landed estates to his military commanders ensured their loyalty and laid the economic foundation of a self-sustaining standing army. Charlemagne established logistical support and supply and siege trains enabling his forces to campaign hundreds of miles from home and to conduct sieges for months on end. By founding well-stocked frontier posts connected by roads to each other and back to established forts, he both protected his realm and set up beachheads from which to extend his territory farther. In a series of decrees issued from 802 to 813, Charlemagne established rules governing military recruitment, training, and service; the organization of units; and the equipping of soldiers. For example, each infantryman had to carry a lance and a bow, a spare string, and 12 arrows.[12]

The disintegration of Charlemagne's empire after his death in 814 returned the continent to warring chaos. His military reforms—even the use of the bow—were largely abandoned. What remained were the heavily armored, mounted knights subsisting from their estates and plundering their neighbors.

Often descended from bellicose Germanic warriors, these knights displayed a furiousness in battle unusual on the world scene. William McNeill has advanced a simple explanation. Europeans raised far more livestock than other peoples, including large animals like pigs and cattle. Each fall, they slaughtered vast numbers of the beasts. Shedding blood, in other words, was like second nature.[13] In the great rice-producing lands of Asia, by contrast, livestock was less abundant, and in warm climates killing it before winter was unnecessary. Another reason for the particularly bloody quality of European warfare, at least after the millennium, was the absence of slavery. In societies that kept slaves—nearly all others besides Europe—taking prisoners to enslave them was a central feature of war. The Europeans, by contrast, fought over territory, not over prisoners, and therefore aimed to destroy or to completely subdue the enemy.[14]

Among the fiercest warriors to take the field as Charlemagne's empire disintegrated were the Vikings.[15] These Germanic people were dynamic, ruthless, ingenious, and consummate explorers. Moving easily throughout the periphery and the interior of Europe by means of long, swift boats, Viking raiders began to appear on the English and French coasts in the late 700s. The absence of powerful naval forces in the Mediterranean or near the Atlantic gave the Norsemen close to free rein. When a hundred or more ships each carrying over thirty warriors appeared unexpectedly on one's shore, few settlements could withstand them. They plundered towns and monasteries, seized vast numbers of victims for ransom and to sell into slavery to Muslim traders, extracted tribute, and even captured major cities, for example, Bonn and Cologne in 881.

Yet the Vikings also founded communities, commercial outposts, and cities. Swedes beginning in the 850s conquered much of the East Slav lands, established trading colonies along the great rivers, and laid the foundations of the future Russian state. Others traveled west to Iceland, Greenland, and even, around the year 1000, Newfoundland to establish colonies. Others still founded settlements in Ireland, Scotland, Wales, England, northern Germany, and northwestern France. In 911, Charles the Simple of France created the Duchy of Normandy in order to win the fealty of the Viking leader Rollo. His successors launched vigorous military expeditions. First they expanded their domains in France. Then, Duke William of Normandy invaded and conquered England by sea in 1066, achieving a feat that eluded both Napoleon and Hitler many centuries later. Less dramatic but historically just as significant was the Norman conquest of the southern third of Italy during 150 years after the millennium, in the process expelling Muslim rulers from an important region of Europe.

The Vikings did not so much decline as gradually assimilate to the peoples they conquered, mostly adopting Christianity, imparting their fierceness and energy to these lands.

Stirrups and solidly constructed saddles with raised pommel and cantle, introduced in the years 200 B.C. to 300 A.D., enabled mounted knights to become the dominant military force throughout Eurasia, including Europe by 800 or 900 A.D. (but not China whose rulers feared independent knights).[16] Military necessity did not alone cause the rise of heavy cavalry in Europe.[17] As political authority devolved to the local level in many regions of Europe, especially the former Carolingian Empire, a new class of local magnates arose with castles as their power base.[18] In the face of continued raids from abroad and the breakdown of public order, kings and princes made land grants to vassals in exchange for oaths of fealty and military service. The vassals in turn subinfeudated their lands to lesser vassals. Most knights also banded together laterally, giving pledges of loyalty to one another (see Chapter 2). Aside from in England and other lands where public order remained strong, this arrangement, called "feudalism," helped maintain a modicum of order in Europe for three or four centuries.

Heavily armored knights dominated partly because cities were few and politically inconsequential. Foot soldiers and bowmen played a role in battles throughout this time but only as an auxiliary to knights: to soften the enemy and to protect the cavalry.[19] Mounted knights alone possessed the discipline to charge in concert. The cavalry charge with lances gripped horizontally, followed by an infantry attack, was the most effective military tactic of the age.[20] Even where infantry played a significant role, as it did during the Norman Conquest, cavalry charges decided the outcome.

Chivalry, or the culture of knighthood, characterized the age. Most of the great literature of the early Middle Ages glorified courage, even fearlessness in the face of death. Indeed, seeking to avoid battle was deemed cowardly. Tournaments, jousting, and training for combat were the principal occupations of noblemen. Only knights enjoyed the leisure for these activities, ate a meat-rich diet that made them strong, and could afford to outfit themselves for battle.[21] Indeed, a knight's full armor, weaponry, mounts, and equipment cost as much as 20 oxen or the income from 300 to 450 acres of good arable land.[22] Kings and other lords were doubtless happy that this heavy expense did not fall on them, the more so as they lacked the resources to shoulder it.[23] When a king planned a war, he summoned his knights to a council. If they agreed to fight, they called up their vassals and infantry levies organized into militias from their estates and rode to battle.

Knights were not typically the heedless warriors depicted in the *Song of Roland* (late 1000s). They fought few pitched battles and rarely fell in combat. One can name several major battles, in which hundreds or even thousands of noblemen faced one another, resulting in the death of fewer than ten knights. For example, only one died of battle wounds during the year-long Flanders War (1127). Of course, medieval knights were heavily protected. Body armor grew more abundant and sophisticated starting in the 1100s. Chain mail, and from the late 1200s plate armor, often covered the entire body.[24] Moreover, the code of chivalry required putting up for ransom fellow knights captured in battle.[25] Even heroic literature gradually shifted away from glorifying death in battle. In fact, one interpretation suggests that a purpose of the *Song of Roland* was to denounce the hero's failure to blow his horn before the cause was lost.[26] The rise of the courtly love tradition also justified avoiding battle, seeking peace, and devoting oneself to wooing ladies as much as to training for war.

Nor did the noble warriors always loyally serve their liege lords.[27] Over time, vassals came to view their fiefs as private property and not as a pledge of fidelity to the lords whose ancestors had originally granted them. Thus, many simply did not heed the call to battle. Knights generally lacked discipline and often could not coordinate their efforts. Many pillaged, marauded, and raided, contributing to the breakdown of public order discussed in Chapter 2. The feudal elites responded in two main ways to this scourge: church-enforced cease-fires and the building of castles.

France was the richest kingdom of Europe and therefore had the greatest number of armored knights.[28] It was probably also the land most devastated by lawlessness. It is not surprising, therefore, that the Peace and Truce of God, mentioned in Chapter 2, originated in France. The Second Lateran Council, which officially instituted the Peace of God in 1139, also quite specifically banned the use of crossbows against Christians.[29] Such efforts bore some fruit because many knights felt a reluctance to shed Christian blood or to fight battles unsanctioned by the church. History records numerous devotional exercises preceding battles, especially during the Crusades.[30]

Yet in practice, European society remained bellicose and riven with conflict. Despite strong prohibitions against priests shedding blood, enforced more assiduously during and after the Papal Revolution, some priests continued to fight and even lead battles. A few master-warriors, who happened to be clergy, even took on trainees and wrote learned treatises on war.[31] Others preached sermons summoning the faithful to "holy war." Many English clergy who held benefices from the king were obligated to heed his call to arms, a practice that ended only after 1418. Yet even into the 1400s, it was still the custom in at least one church for knights, at the reading of the Gospel, to raise their naked swords in a sign of readiness to defend the faith.[32]

The most effective defense against lawless knights was the stone castle.[33] They proliferated after the millennium in the face of political anarchy, ceaseless raiding, and strife caused by the Investiture Conflict. A castellan ruled the lands surrounding his castle, typically a private stronghold erected in defense of private interests. In the basic design, a single tower stood amid high protective walls.[34] Sometimes the walls—especially in wealthy Italy, a land fragmented into some 200 independent polities—"encastellated" (encircled) towns and cities.[35]

Where castles stood, the only viable military tactic was to lay siege. Around 1,100 numerous military forces in the Mediterranean region possessed rudimentary siege engines, including catapults and traction trebuchets, a device invented in ancient China that used the weight of a few or several dozen men to lever projectiles weighing roughly 150 pounds up to 75 yards.[36] Beginning in the early to mid-1100s, counterweight trebuchets that functioned like giant slingshots also began to proliferate in the Mediterranean region. Perhaps first developed in Byzantium, the biggest of these devices could hurl a stone of 200 pounds some 400 yards. The counterweight trebuchet, by far the most powerful weapon in history until the gunpowder revolution, was the cumulative achievement of four civilizations—the Chinese, the Islamic, the Byzantine, and the Western. It could play a decisive role, for example, by demolishing fortress walls in the siege of Acre (1189–91) during the Third Crusade. The Mongols, who learned siegecraft from the Chinese and the Persians in the early 1200s, quickly became the world's most successful besiegers.[37]

From the mid-1100s, especially in Iberia and the crusader states, a new castle design emerged with concentric walls punctuated by towers but no central defensive structure. Over time, the inner walls rose higher and higher. Thanks to these improvements and also to the difficulty of maintaining a siege, the advantage in Europe generally rested with the defenders. So long as they had stored up provisions, as most habitually did, then the attackers often starved more quickly than the besieged.[38] Indeed, the vast majority of the many thousands of fortifications constructed throughout medieval Europe actually faced no attackers at all.[39] Thanks to their fortifications, smaller and poorer polities were often able to resist incursions by more powerful ones. There thus emerged a unique balance of power among European states and polities. Other regions of Eurasia, by contrast, tended to endure domination by single great powers.[40]

European arms race

The Eurasia-wide commercial upturn apparently fostered by the postmillennial warming trend gradually transformed Europe's fractured political landscape into a scene of unremitting war and a hothouse of military innovation. Thus began the world's first arms race—one that has never ended. It broke out in the 1300s in Italy, thanks to its vast commercial wealth and welter of competing city-states. For roughly a century, the Italians defended themselves well,[41] until consolidated monarchies emerged in France and Spain in the early 1400s. They turned the Italian peninsula into a battleground and precipitated its political and economic decline.

By the late 1200s, as noted in Chapter 2, Italian merchants and bankers dominated Europe's commercial economy. They bought and sold wholesale and brought new technology, financial instruments, and methods of trade to the outlying areas of the continent. Merchant-bankers in inland towns of north and central Italy funded clerical, royal, and princely administrations and long-distance trade, mining, shipping, and other big commercial operations. They linked manufacturing and financial centers in northwestern Europe with agricultural regions of the Mediterranean basin and import–export businesses around the known world. The biggest companies gained concessions and monopolies from secular and ecclesiastical lords in exchange for big loans. By the early 1300s, the Bardi, Peruzzi, and Acciaiuoli houses of Florence controlled such vast agglomerations of trading, manufacturing, and banking over so great a territory that scholars have referred to them as "super companies."[42] Although most German cities from the lower Rhine to the Baltic region had banded together in the Hansa, a loose trading confederation, they remained in every way outclassed by their southern competitors.

Italian success in business financed almost constant warfare among the peninsula's city-states. Following a tradition dating to late Roman times, the city communes of Italy imposed military service on all adult males. Nobles and wealthy burghers were obligated to provide horses and train for cavalry service, while all others had to serve in the infantry. Paid outsiders supplemented these forces.[43]

Mercenaries had fought ubiquitously in Europe from the time of Justinian (r. 527–65). Many took part in the Norman Conquest of 1066. The commercial revolution after the millennium greatly expanded their number. In the 1200s, mercenary hosts sprang up to fight for the highest bidder. Some were extraordinarily effective, like the Catalan Company, which won most of its battles from 1282 to 1311 in Italy, the Balkans, and Anatolia.[44] Such companies were particularly numerous in Italy by the 1300s. Indeed, in the middle of the century most military forces in Italy fought solely for wages. Yet as their employers discovered, lacking the funds to pay them invited pillaging and marauding. Like the sorcerer's apprentice, the Italian city magistrates had conjured a power they could not control. Although rulers all over Europe faced a similar problem when hiring mercenaries, it was most acute in Italy until city administrators devised a clever means to reassert their authority.[45] First, towns began to impose more taxes on themselves in order never to fall behind on their payments. Second, they would contract with small private military units or, better yet, with their captains so that, with any luck, they would never face a united front of disgruntled soldiers. The Venetians played this game most successfully and thus avoided major upheavals in their lands. Florence and Genoa, by contrast, did not.

Over the next few centuries, to survive, a polity needed to raise taxes and to master the art of war. Those that did thrived; the rest often went under. It was possible to increase taxation dramatically, since taxes were so low to begin with, without inhibiting economic development. Indeed, nearly all the tax money went to pay soldiers who spent most of their money locally, which stimulated economic activity.[46] Some mercenaries used their fighting expertise to win independence for their people, for example the Swiss mountaineers, about which more below.

The fourteenth century marked an important transitional period in the history of business and of war and of the business of war in Europe. A series of wars, famines, and floods in the 1320s and 1330s brought down the Italian "super companies." Worse, the Black Death struck Eurasia in the mid-fourteenth century. Originating north of China, it wreaked havoc first in East and South Asia in the early 1330s, carrying away some 25 million people.[47] In 1347, it raged from Constantinople to the farthest corners of Europe over the next 5 years, killing up to one-third or even one-half of the population in many regions, for a death toll of some 30 million. Recurrent epidemic outbreaks for over a century impeded population recovery.[48] The social and even geopolitical effects were devastating. One scholar argues persuasively that the Black Death helped precipitate the fall of the Mongol Empire and the Chinese Yuan Dynasty and in general weakened all the great powers of Asia, opening up a path for Europe's rise.[49] In Europe, the great fairs languished or shut down, and a labor shortage forced wages up and accelerated the disintegration of feudalism.[50]

Commercial activity was reoriented toward the sea. Beginning in the 1370s, a series of breakthroughs in sailing vessels, navigational methods, and systems of armament for ships sparked a frontier boom in the Baltic lands and launched Europe on a career of world discovery and exploration (see Chapter 5).

The economy surged again in the late 1300s. The woolen-cloth trade increased, greatly benefiting producers and merchants in Bruges, Ghent, and Ypres. The technology for hard-rock mining spread throughout central Europe. Silver, copper, tin, coal, and iron poured onto the market, commencing a cycle of commodity-price booms and busts.[51] Many governments, worried about food shortages sparking revolts, set up grain reserves. Grain prices fell drastically, as did the price of meat and fish. A middle class began slowly to emerge, especially in southeast England, the Low Countries, and northern Italy—the major centers of economic growth.[52]

Entrepreneurs strived for greater efficiency.[53] First, they sought to cut costs by finding new suppliers, establishing operations close to the source of raw materials, and producing goods themselves. Second, they set up new accounting practices. For instance by 1368, the Del Bene company kept three separate sets of books, recording the cost of raw wool, the cost of the labor to produce cloth, and the wages of their dyers. The greatest innovator in record keeping was Francesco di Marco Datini (ca. 1335–1410), an arms trader and purveyor of luxury goods. He calculated the ratio of overhead costs, established debits/credits ledgers throughout his company by 1393, and made sure all the ledgers were balanced annually and the resulting general financial statements given to him. Datini also worked fanatically to diversify his risks. A century later, the Franciscan mathematician Luca Pacioli (1446/7–1517) published the world's first treatise on accounting.[54]

Institutions fostered economic development as well. In the 1400s, trade fairs emerged again. The world's first stock exchanges appeared in the Flemish cities of Bruges and Antwerp by 1450.[55] By that time much of Europe's agriculture and manufacturing were market oriented and cost-effective. Shipping rates in the Mediterranean fell by 25 percent in the 1500s.[56] Businessmen found ways to circumvent the religious prohibition on lending money at interest (usury). Thus, the cost of borrowing fell to around 5 percent or even lower in the century after 1450. Capital grew abundant and accumulated into great fortunes. Many of the super-rich, such as Jacob Fugger (1459–

25), a brilliant entrepreneur, funded the war making of Europe's rulers.[57] Others made money from war directly, such as by constructing fortifications, rebuilding destroyed structures, shipbuilding, mining, and iron production.[58]

Infantry revolution

Economic expansion doubtless fired Europe's arms race, but the ingenuity, discipline, and democratic action of ordinary people triggered its first dramatic stage. In this story, poorly armed foot soldiers from hilly, mountainous, or agriculturally impoverished lands challenged and defeated richly accoutered noble warriors. In other terms, Western Europe's periphery rose up against its core and transformed the nature of war.

The shift began slowly, with the rise of communal (urban) armies of the Low Countries and northern Italy in the 1100s. These forces relied primarily on infantry. Early on, such troops demonstrated their power in 1176 at Legnano. There some 3,500 foot soldiers of the Lombard League, arrayed in a rectangular formation and armed with pikes, stood their ground against some 2,000 knights of the empire.[59] The Italians won the battle, though only thanks to cavalry reinforcements that enveloped the enemy, and knights reigned supreme for more than a century.[60]

Still, the wealth and thirst for freedom of merchant societies grew.[61] Take Flanders, one of the wealthiest regions in Europe; it fell under French rule in the late twelfth century. As the woolen trade flourished, commercial relations with England intensified, challenging French hegemony. The main Flemish cities fielded infantry-based militias whose troops were organized by guilds and very well equipped and trained. Following an uprising and massacre against the French in May 1302, Philip the Fair sent his knights to crush the rebels. At Courtrai (Kortrijk in Dutch), in July, Flemish infantry armed with long pikes awaited the heavy cavalry's advance.[62] They had chosen their battlefield carefully. The ground was marshy, and the defenders had dug ditches across the terrain. The Flemings stood in ranks—eight deep—pikes bristling forward. When an initial French attack by infantry and crossbow failed to move the enemy, the cavalry charged recklessly across the bog, expecting the opposing infantry to break ranks. They did not. Knights fell at full tilt against the steel tips of pikes held secure by man and earth. Over 1,000 knights died that day. The triumphant Flemings seized gold spurs from their enemies' boots, giving the fight the sobriquet "Battle of the Golden Spurs."

Yet this battle did not mark the triumph of the infantry. The heavy French cavalry had fallen to defeat largely because of the uneven, marshy terrain. Plus, they gave up head-on attacks.[63] Two years later, the French won the Battle of Mons-en-Pévèle and took back their spurs. Then in 1328, they crushed the Flemish infantry at the Battle of Cassel, slaughtering over 3,000.[64] Even so, an infantry revolution was underway. One of its key features was to make war far bloodier. Unlike the chivalrous knights, foot soldiers found it dangerous to take prisoners or hostages when to do so required laying themselves open to a devastating cavalry charge. Probably just as important were class antagonisms.[65] Surely the lowborn infantry relished sticking it, quite literally, to their social betters on horseback.

Swiss foot soldiers enabled another peripheral region of Europe to emerge as a powerful military force.[66] High in Alpine valleys, several urban and rural communes had enjoyed some autonomy from the surrounding principalities for centuries until three rural communes formed a confederation in 1291. Over the next century, these and other Swiss cantons fought with great fierceness against armies of the Holy Roman Empire.[67] Like the Flemings, the Swiss mountaineers formed tight, mutually supporting bodies of infantry armed with 12-foot pikes. In disciplined square ranks, they would advance steadily and fearlessly against the enemy. Thus arrayed and so long as none lost his nerve, they could stand against any cavalry charge. Crossbows in their midst reinforced their defense. When necessary, in case of attack from all sides, they could quickly turn their pikes in all directions, in "hedgehog" formation. When their ranks broke, they furiously wielded halberds (battle-axes) for hand-to-hand fighting. In four important battles of the fourteenth century, beginning with Morgarten (1315) and Laupen (1339), Swiss forces routed Austrian and Burgundian heavy cavalry.[68] In 1394, the Habsburgs recognized Swiss independence within the Holy Roman Empire. Swiss fighters went on to become the most successful and celebrated mercenaries in Europe.

The crowning moment of the Infantry Revolution was achieved by another peripheral land, England. Its ascendancy began with Edward I (r. 1272–1307) who defeated rebellious barons and later conquered Wales and Scotland. From the Welsh he adopted the longbow, an individual weapon more powerful and decisive in battle than any other until then, the crossbow included. Invented by the Chinese centuries before Christ, the crossbow was widely deployed in Europe from the millennium. Its advantages were high velocity and simplicity of use. The English longbow combined even greater striking power with a higher rapidity of fire. A skilled archer could loose several arrows before a horseman had completed his charge, piercing his armor.[69] In the early decades of the 1300s, thousands of Englishmen gained this expertise.

Sheer numbers of archers, coupled with brilliant tactics, gave the English army a devastating victory at Crécy in northern France in 1346. Edward III (r. 1327–77) led some 14,000 archers, light infantry, dismounted men-at-arms, and cavalry against roughly 20,000 French knights, undisciplined infantry, Genoese mercenary crossbowmen, and light cavalry (see Map 4.3).[70] This asymmetrical victory—the English losses were around 200 compared to perhaps several thousand on the French side—marked a turning point in the history of warfare.[71] Henceforth, all who had eyes to see grasped that highly disciplined infantry, armed with pikes or longbows and backed up by minimal cavalry cover, could defeat the finest heavy cavalry in Europe. It was also clear that training, tactics, discipline, and cooperation by all the main military branches mattered more than valor and armor. The art of war trumped any single element of warfare taken alone. Experimentation, analysis, rationalization, and further innovation almost inevitably followed.

The mounted knight did not immediately disappear from the battlefield. For one thing, long-dominant France hesitated to transform its military radically. Thus, English forces continued to devastate the French until late in the Hundred Years' War (1337–1453), even when outnumbered significantly, as at Agincourt (1415).[72] Also, noblemen abhorred giving up their horses, which conferred enormous prestige.[73] Certainly, aristocrats remained key players on the battlefield, preserving their codes

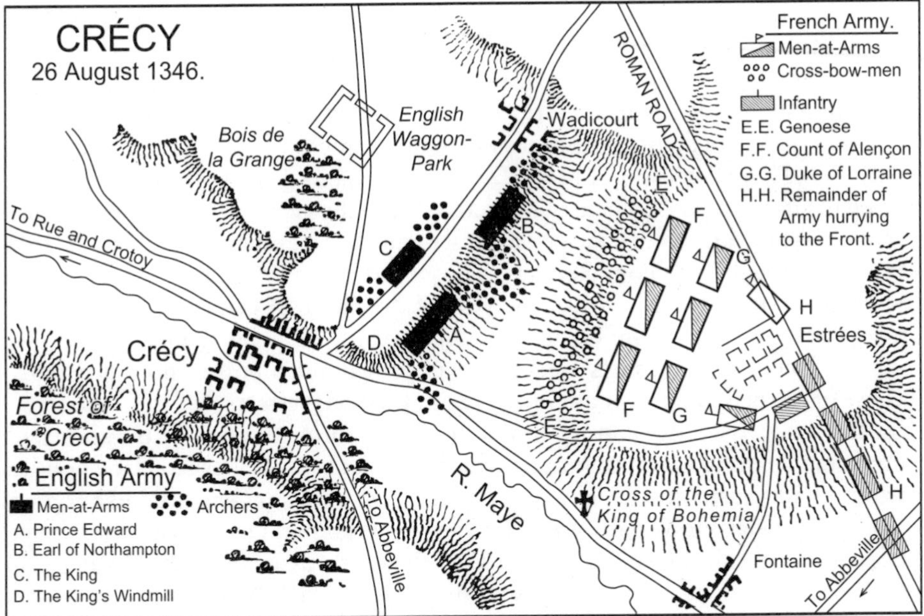

MAP 4.2 *At the Battle of Crecy, English soldiers armed in part with longbows defeated a larger French force.*

of behavior in war right down to the eve of the French Revolution,[74] and generally dominating the European officer corps until World War I and even World War II.[75] But military organization and tactics had changed radically and permanently with huge consequences. Shifting to infantry meant that governments had to raise taxes and fund the new forces themselves. This was harder to achieve for a decentralized realm like France than a more centrally governed one like England.

War and the origins of representative government

The move toward infantry empowered the commons in Switzerland, England, and Holland by giving rise to representative institutions. Only the commons—merchants, yeomen, and peasants—could supply the funds and soldiers needed to form an infantry. Wherever the commons were well organized, literate, articulate, moneyed, cohesive, and conscious of their important role in society, they could also express and enforce demands for a voice in government—taxation only in exchange for representation.

As early as the millennium, the need to raise troops for war had prompted European princes to convoke the continent's first secular assemblies. Armies were spoken of as being "assembled."[76] The early Capetian (French) kings summoned assemblies of vassals only for war. In Norman England, assembled armies largely represented the realm. One of the main vassalic duties, moreover, was to give one's lord military counsel (*consilium*). In time, this obligation evolved into a right. The first conciliar summons of representatives in both England and France in the early 1200s followed patterns already established for military summons.

The increasing incidence of warfare in the thirteenth century entailed higher taxes and more requests for military counsel. This led to the emergence of political assemblies of estates across Europe, as noted in Chapter 2. Desperate for money, the French king Philip Augustus (1180–1223) sent out hand-picked officials (*baillis* and seneschals) to raise taxes. Their richest targets, the thriving towns, many with their own militias, often received charters of royal immunity in exchange for financial help. A political struggle with Pope Boniface VIII moved Philip IV the Fair to convene the first French Estates-General 1302, the year of the Battle of Courtrai.[77] A few years later, constantly short of funds, he despoiled wealthy Knights Templar, Jews, and Lombard bankers. The Estates-General never gained much power in France, partly because of the persistent strength of the realm's regional estates.[78]

England was the success story in this regard.[79] Through much of the thirteenth century, the English kings met with secular and ecclesiastical elites to decide political matters, to administer justice, and to raise taxes. On occasion, knights and burgesses (municipal officials) took part. When Edward I was preparing to wage battle against the Scots in 1295, he convoked the first English general assembly, called by posterity the Model Parliament. Each county sent two knights, each borough two burgesses, and each city two citizens, making the assembly fairly representative of the country as a whole. In exchange for war funding, they demanded and received the right to bring grievances to the king. For decades, the composition and duties of the assembly remained fluid. The Commons won the right to attend all meetings in 1327, and to meet separately from the Lords in 1341. In the following decades, the Commons gained control of the power to tax. It seems likely that the rise of the Commons stemmed from their tactical importance in the king's army. Certainly, the financial demands of the Hundred Years' War augmented the significance of Parliament. This interminable conflict also increased the power of provincial governments in France, weakening the king. The next revolution in military affairs, this one initially perfected by France, returned its army—and king—briefly to preeminence in Europe.

Gunpowder revolution

For centuries, Chinese Daoists had been working their way systematically through available organic and inorganic substances in search of an elixir of eternal life.[80] One of them invented an explosive powder using saltpeter in the mid-800s. Gradually, Chinese artisans learned to make fireworks and explosive devices, though these and other sophisticated weapons did not prevent China's conquest by Jurchen and Mongol nomadic warriors over the next few centuries. Travelers from the Mongol court apparently carried the recipe across Eurasia early in the 1200s. It seems that the earliest cannon emerged almost simultaneously in Europe and in China in the early 1300s. These guns were small, inaccurate, and produced less firepower than catapults and trebuchets. The cannon's awesome sound, however, fascinated many Europeans who experimented systematically with both guns and powder.[81]

A key European innovation was the "corning" of gunpowder, first in England in the 1370s and across Europe by the 1420s.[82] The powder was mixed with water or other liquids and pressed into solid sheets, which were broken into pellets and tumbled to wear down sharp edges. The pellets ignited more slowly than powder but then exploded all together with enormous force. The size and number of cannon also increased almost year by year. A single giant cannon belonging to the city of Nuremberg in 1388 required 12 horses to haul. At this time, gunners could fire only around five shots a day. By the 1420s, some could manage over one hundred.

Now cannon began to play an important role in siegecraft. Some large armies deployed 100 cannon, many firing stone balls of 100 pounds or more. Even so, as late as the 1420s, a well-equipped castle armed with its own cannon could still defend against any siege, so long as relief came in a reasonable time.[83] Within a few decades, however, warfare was turned upside down. Henceforth, great powers with the resources to build and coordinate effectively a large number of artillery pieces could lay waste to any fortifications, subdue any foe insufficiently equipped with cannon, and dominate the battlefield anywhere on the European continent.

Advances in technology made these changes possible.[84] Gunsmiths increased the ratio of length of barrel to ball size. Reinforced gun barrels could be extended to around eight feet in length, which increased firepower, accuracy, and rapidity of firing (since longer cannon overheated less). Balancing the tubes on trunnions near their center of gravity allowed for easy adjustment of gun elevation. Mounted on two-wheeled carriages, the cannon could be moved readily by a single team of strong horses. Finally, iron cannon balls were introduced. They not only packed a far greater punch than stone balls but could also be reused. The increasing skill of gunsmiths also gradually brought down the cost of cannon production.

An "artillery revolution" now transformed the political landscape of Europe. The richest states invested heavily in firearms of all types and sizes. By the 1440s, for example, the French military spent two-thirds of its budget on gunpowder weaponry. They soon crushed the same English fighters who for an entire century had routed them time and again in battle. It had taken Henry V (r. 1413–22) 4 years to conquer the northern part of Normandy after his signal victory at Agincourt. By contrast, Charles VII of France (r. 1422–61) spent only 1 year (1449–50) recovering that territory. In fact, faced with Charles's mighty artillery, most of the English strongholds surrendered without a fight. To further his aims, in 1439 Charles had increased taxes and founded Europe's first standing army—locally garrisoned companies numbering some 25,000 soldiers. Such forces gave an advantage to centralized monarchies, made possible the development of political absolutism, and contributed to the decay of feudal institutions and customs.

The year 1453 marked the emergence of the world's first "gunpowder empires."[85] In that year, French forces, armed with hundreds of cannon, as well as thousands of bows and crossbows, destroyed the last English resistance in southwestern France at Castillon, putting an end to the Hundred Years' War—and to England's possession of territory on the Continent (except for Calais, which it lost in 1558). Two months before, the Ottoman Empire of Mehmed II had accomplished an even more awesome feat—the sack and subjection of Constantinople.

In the mid-1300s, the Ottomans had established the region's first standing army since antiquity, the Janissary Corps.[86] This infantry elite probably comprised no more than 5,000 soldiers in the mid-1400s, but they were highly disciplined

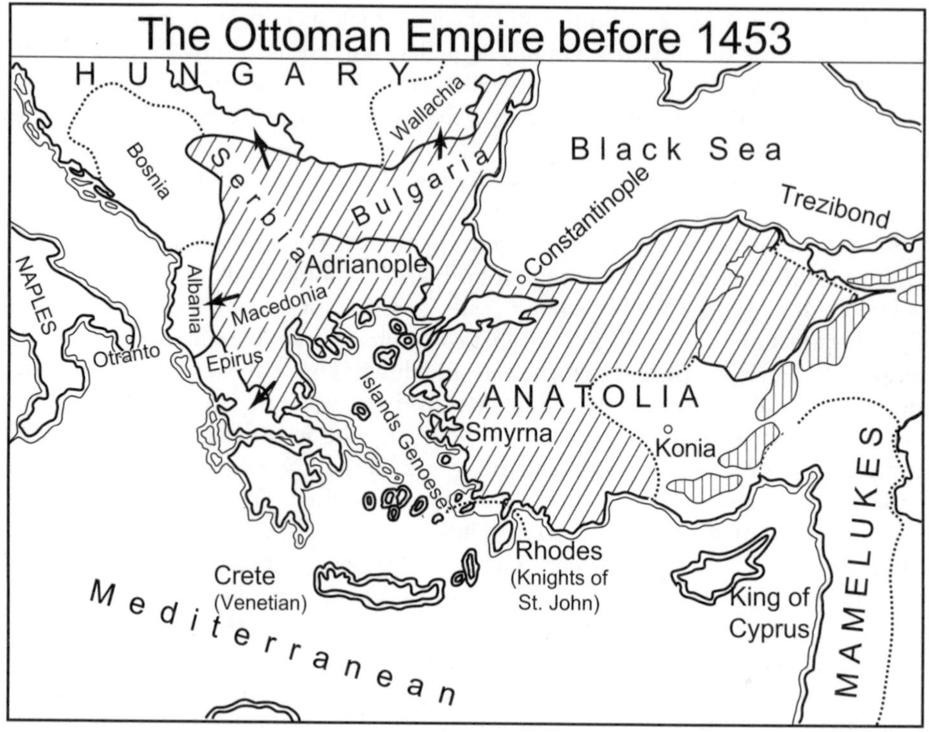

MAP 4.3 *Even before the capture of Constantinople in 1453, the Ottoman Empire encompassed much of Asia Minor and the Balkans.*

and resourceful. Recruited almost exclusively from conquered Christian peoples, especially in the Balkans, they joined light cavalry and other infantry units to form the massive army of 80,000 men that laid siege to Constantinople in 1453.[87] That venerable city's fortifications included four miles of walls and a vast ditch facing land and nine miles of walls facing the sea, all punctuated by a hundred towers.[88] The Ottomans gained expertise in cannon forging from captured Central Europeans, in particular, Hungarians. With their assistance, at the siege of Constantinople massive cannon were cast, one measuring 26 feet in length.[89] The once great Byzantine state that had stood proudly for a thousand years now crumbled and was absorbed by the rising Ottoman Empire (see Map 4.3).[90]

This state faced no sustained, powerful alliance in any direction yet enjoyed easy access to Europe by water and land. The robust Ottoman naval forces practically transformed the Danube River and its major tributaries into military highways leading into Central Europe.[91] Suleiman the Magnificent used these routes to besiege and conquer Belgrade (1521) and Mohács in southern Hungary (1526).[92] The sultan's forces were stopped only at Vienna in 1529. Thenceforth, he concentrated on gaining possessions in the Aegean Sea until his death in 1566.

Other Muslim powers also began adopting gunpowder technology. The Venetians imported cannon into Persia in the 1470s in order to establish a counter-force east of the Ottoman Empire. After the Safavid Dynasty reinvigorated Persia in the early 1500s, it threatened the Ottomans, though Suleiman seized Baghdad from them in 1535. He also armed the Uzbeks and the Khan of Crimea with gunpowder ordnance.[93] Muslim and Christian gunsmiths manufactured firearms in Indian coastal cities sometime after 1500. Within decades, artillery and handheld guns formed a standard element in Mughal armed forces. Even so, the Muslim world failed to keep pace with technological developments in Europe.

European political fragmentation created hothouse conditions for innovation and almost constant warfare.[94] By the 1450s, field artillery was coming into its own, sparking a boom in metal production and a new "bronze age."[95] Charles the Bold (r. 1467–77) of Burgundy, fabulously wealthy thanks to far-flung possessions in Flanders and eastern France, assembled vast artillery forces, comprising some 400 cannon at the Battle of Morat (1476). In one of the last instances for a half-century when a small state could withstand such firepower, however, the Swiss Confederation defeated Charles in a series of three battles ending at Nancy (1477) where he died in combat.[96]

Since artillery was now the decisive element in battle, however, and because only big states could afford the spiraling cost of outfitting gigantic artillery forces, henceforth only the big states could thrive. For the first time in many centuries, the advantage lay with offensive powers. Since the larger states could pay for more guns, they could conquer more territory. Controlling more land meant the ability to gather more taxes and thus to buy more artillery. In numeric terms, the largest central governments doubled their tax revenues between 1450 and 1500.[97]

The two biggest winners, aside from the Ottoman Empire, were Spain and France. In the 10 years after 1482, Spanish forces destroyed the last Islamic stronghold on the Iberian Peninsula at Grenada. In 1494, Charles VIII of France launched a lightning conquest of Naples, precipitating the Italian Wars.[98] After a crushing defeat by the French at Seminara in 1495, the brilliant Spanish general Gonzalo Fernández de Córdoba invented the "tercio," in which square blocks of tightly arrayed pikemen were flanked and protected by rectangular masses of men armed with arquebusiers.[99] Since the muzzle-loading arquebus was rather cumbersome, crossbows remained a strong competitor until the 1500s. Córdoba's heavy reliance on arquebusiers nevertheless caught a far larger French army off guard at the Battle of Cerignola in 1503 and marked the beginning of a "combined-arms revolution."[100] Able to both charge and defend, the Spanish *tercio* found emulators across Europe.

Sieges, long avoided as costly and often indecisive, multiplied as France and Spain exploited their advantage in gunpowder ordnance. As if to prove that each innovation engendered a countervailing breakthrough in early modern European warfare, however, the Italians, who had lagged behind in the gunpowder revolution, soon achieved ingenious advances in the art of fortification.

Already in 1500, during a war with Florence, the Pisans discovered that hastily constructed, sloping earthen ramparts could absorb the shock of cannon balls.[101] With war being waged on Italian soil by Europe's most powerful states, some brilliant minds devoted themselves to matters of defense. In 1529, Michelangelo was placed in charge of designing and building Florence's fortifications.[102] The fortifications whose construction he supervised boasted elaborate bastions designed for the emplacement of defensive firearms. They withstood a siege by Imperial forces for ten months before Florence surrendered because its people could fight no longer.

These and other designs by Italian architects and engineers again revolutionized warfare. The *trace italienne* combined three main elements.[103] First, wide, flat ramparts were armed with cannon. Second, polygonal protruding towers able to thwart attackers along a 180-degree radius punctuated the ramparts. These features combined to minimize blind spots or dead areas for attack. Finally, a wide ditch and a low, sloping, generally earthen wall surrounded the inner fortifications. Within a few decades, the *trace italienne* had reestablished the advantage of defensive warfare. Even lesser states could afford this new technology. By the 1570s, the new fortifications—along with extraordinary tenacity and much desperate fighting—enabled the small though wealthy northern provinces of the Netherlands to withstand the massive firepower of the richest state in Europe, the Habsburg Empire (see Chapter 10).[104] Charles V's dream of unifying all Europe under his rule foundered on this and other obstacles.

What an extraordinary career the humble explosive powder thus made. Yet note an important distinction. Invented in China, gunpowder had only a minor impact on Chinese society and politics until the arrival of British gunboats in 1839 (see Chapter 13). By contrast, it swayed the fortunes of other Eurasian lands before heavily armed European merchant-warriors sailed to the four corners of the earth. The Chinese culture, given its devotion to the ideal of historical continuity, found ways to maintain stability while integrating novelties that radically transformed European culture.

Revolution in the nature and scale of war

The populations and wealth of Europe continued to increase, providing more "sinews of war." Among the stimuli of economic growth were vibrant international trade (see Chapters 5 and 9) and a boom in iron production. In the 1540s, the English learned to forge cannon from iron. The epicenter of cannon production nevertheless remained in the Low Countries, thanks to their great concentration of blast furnaces.[105] Moral, ideological, confessional, and protonationalist fervor also made the early-modern wars of Europe bloodier, longer, and far more costly. Gradually, only the biggest states, along with the few highly integrated and efficient smaller states, could survive.

Bright minds brought critical thinking and mathematical precision to military affairs. The main European armies by the 1550s were specialized. Each of the three main branches performed clearly delineated roles. The job of light cavalry was to charge, fire their pistols, and retreat. The infantry trained as fusiliers, grenadiers, and sappers, among other tasks. Specific artillery units were designed for field or siege warfare. Armies also mobilized and trained specialists of many kinds, including surgeons, engineers, carpenters, wagon-makers, and masons.[106] The most effective commanders divided their men into smaller and smaller units—paring the 3,000-man Spanish *tercios* down to 550-man Dutch units.[107]

Modern military training and drill began with Maurice of Nassau, Prince of Orange (1567–1625), a gifted commander and strategist.[108] He started with scholarly research into Roman military success. He then experimented in the field. This work enabled Maurice to reorganize the Dutch army completely. First, he divided it into smaller units in order to improve control, loyalty to officers, and solidarity among soldiers. Second, he instituted rigorous discipline and almost continuous drill. Soldiers learned to load their guns systematically, to function with their fellows in unison and at command, and especially to march in regularized patterns semiautomatically. Third, like Roman soldiers, they constantly dug earthen fortifications, which kept them both safer during battle and out of trouble during peacetime. Such training tapped into a subconscious source of sociability, rendering the soldiers unquestioningly obedient, ready for self-sacrifice, and utterly dedicated to comrades and officers, irrespective of social origin. European governments found they could conscript destitute men and drill them into excellent soldiers.[109]

Maurice also instituted the standardization of weaponry and volleying in ranks.[110] Having carefully studied the available models of arquebus and larger-bore muskets, in 1599 he ordered arms makers in Holland to produce guns only to requested specifications. This made repairs easier and brought down the overall cost of firearms. Yet they remained slow to reload, making it possible for an enemy to break one's lines before all the guns were ready for a second volley. In the 1560s—only two decades after Portuguese merchants had introduced firearms to Japan—the Japanese warlord Oda Nobunaga had an inspiration. What if the marksmen staggered their fire? What if they lined up in ranks, the first ones firing and then retreating to reload while the next rank discharged their guns, and so on? This method may have spread to Europe. At any rate, in the 1590s Maurice adopted a similar tactic, with as many as six ranks of marksmen and intense training in countermarch to the back of the ranks for reloading. By 1604, armies in both Europe and the Ottoman Empire had embraced it.[111]

A peculiarity of most European military forces in this age was their immediate and wholesale adoption of all such advances.[112] The systematic rotation of soldiers across the vast Habsburg lands and the voluntary movement of mercenaries among Europe's armies fostered the rapid transfer of military knowledge and technologies. So did the proliferation of illustrated military treatises—more than ever before thanks to the printing revolution (see Chapter 6).[113] Among the most important volumes was one by Maurice's cousin Johan Lodewijk (1607), which described training in minute detail. It demonstrated, for example, how marksmen should pass through 42 distinct positions as they fired and reloaded their weapons in unison.[114] Translations and pirated versions immediately appeared in several European languages.[115]

War in Europe had become as much a science as an art, its nature more industrial than chivalric, its scale immense, a matter of survival and no longer sport. States had an interest in gaining more territory, which meant more population, more revenue, and consequently bigger armies. Government grew more centralized, as bureaucracies became more efficient at tax collection and administration.[116] Of course, each state was unique, following its own path. Taxation, for example, was controlled by the crown in France and Spain but by representative institutions in England, the Dutch Republic, and Poland. Each state coped as best it could in the menacing international environment. Some rulers chose to crush representative institutions and throw off trammels on their power.

The Thirty Years' War (1618–48) tested the staying power of the major European states and forced the emergence of modern armies.[117] The Holy Roman Empire began the war with 20,000 men at arms but 15 years later was fielding over 150,000, thanks to the entrepreneurial efforts of Albrecht von Wallenstein (1583–1634). The combined peak strength of the two sides was roughly 1 million soldiers. To maintain so many fighting men, each power drew heavily upon the resources of the societies involved. Civilian populations, especially in the German lands, suffered heavy taxation and military requisitioning, quartering of soldiers, and massive destruction of property. Most horrifying was the human tragedy. Some 4 million people died from pestilence, famine, destruction of the built environment, and combat, as the well-articulated military "organisms" collided violently for three decades.

The relationship between state and society changed in Europe. When France entered the war in 1635, Louis XIII deployed *intendants* throughout the realm.[118] These officials imposed heavy taxes, often collected by regular soldiers. A further tax increase in 1647 set off a rebellion (the Fronde). The rebels not only achieved none of their aims; the regional estates and *parlements* emerged weaker. "Absolutism" had triumphed in France. Louis XIV (r. 1643–1715) authorized his minister of finance, Jean-Baptiste Colbert (from 1665), to develop a systematic plan for promoting the national economy. Called "mercantilism," it involving subsidies and tax breaks to favored industries and businesses, the importation of skilled workers and professionals, using colonies as closed markets, infrastructural investments (roads, bridges, and canals), and the promotion of international trade by instituting state shipping insurance and other measures.[119] Louis XIV's ulterior motive in adopting all these policies was war.

It would be wrong, however, to suggest that "absolutism" implied unlimited royal prerogatives. In practice, the power of European monarchs, even during the so-called period of absolutism (roughly 1650–1750), was always limited by various forces and institutions, including the landed nobility, chartered towns, self-governing bodies at the regional and local level, representative institutions, law courts, and the church. Monarchs had to respect custom and to act within the law. Rarely could they violate the person or property of secular and ecclesiastical elites. In some spheres, in particular war and foreign policy, they were less constrained than in others, for example, in regard to raising taxes.[120] Yet even the most ardent defenders of absolute monarchy like Jacques-Bénigne Bossuet categorically rejected despotism as a great evil. In Bossuet's view, a true monarch, while wielding absolute authority, rules justly, protects the person and property of his subjects, respects custom, and adheres to the law. A despot, by contrast, rules by personal whim and treats his subjects as slaves.[121]

Of course, monarchical power was more expansive in some countries than others. The rulers of Russia and the Ottoman Empire faced much weaker restraints on their power—because society in those countries was weaker. Nor did absolute rule emerge first in Europe. On the contrary, it is as old as civilization and far more common than limited government. If one defines an absolute monarchy as one in which sovereignty is vested in a single person,[122] then the endurance record for such a polity would have to go to China. Yet even there, where the intermediate institutions and society in general placed far weaker limits on the power of the emperors, the latter could not rule without regard to custom, morality, common beliefs, and people's expectations for economic prosperity and stability. One scholar argues persuasively that the most decisive check on the Chinese emperors were frequent popular rebellions—2,106 in just over 2,000 years, each one averaging 7 years and involving 226,000 participants—which resulted in the overthrow of several dynasties.[123]

In the age of absolutism, European monarchs sometimes adapted the institutions and practices of successful polities like China. Indeed, Voltaire and other Enlightenment thinkers actively promoted European imitation of what they considered the highly rational Chinese civil service.[124]

Europe's extreme case of bureaucratic absolutism was Brandenburg-Prussia.[125] Over the course of his long reign, Frederick William, the Great Elector (r. 1640–88), imposed higher taxes, reduced the authority and power of the Estates, undermined the rule of law, strengthened the institution of serfdom, and established a 40,000-man standing army. Peasants east of the Elba River became like chattel. Within a century, the entire country was like a training school for soldiers, bowed under crushing taxation, with private and corporate interests subordinated to the state but society infused with a collective spirit of honor and duty. By 1760, amid the Seven Years' War, 1 in 14 Prussians served in the army, compared to 1 in 86 in France.[126]

Not all of Europe succumbed to the absolutist tendency. The Polish nobles retained control of taxation, the judiciary, the mint, and even royal succession. They persistently refused to countenance military reforms. Thus, by the early 1700s Poland alone among the Central European states lacked an infantry-centered army. When Poland's neighbors combined at the end of the century to carve it into oblivion, nothing stopped them.[127]

A few major states avoided both the twin threats of absolutism and military impotence. Sweden might have veered into the former under Charles XII (r. 1697–1718) had the army not remained loyal to the constitution and had Charles not lost the Great Northern War.[128] England stood down several attempts to entrench various forms of absolutism (see Chapter 10). The Dutch Republic avoided any such threat. In other words, the European states confronted the threats and opportunities of military revolution in a variety of ways.

Yet across Europe military prowess developed in similar ways, involving ceaseless analysis and imitation of successful methods of warfare, rational planning, technological and tactical innovation, and increased spending. Consider Europe's reaction to the reforms of King Gustavus Adolphus of Sweden (r. 1611–32).[129] He reduced the size and weight of his infantry's muskets and armed them with paper cartridges for rapid loading. Instead of squares, like the Spanish *tercios*, he arranged his highly disciplined fighters in thin, but long lines, up to six men deep. This "linear" tactic remained the European standard until World War I. The father of modern field artillery, Gustavus deployed small, highly mobile cannon in three standardized calibers. He trained his cavalry, who also bore pistols, to charge with sabers extended. Finally, and perhaps most important, he trained his infantry, cavalry, and artillery to fight tightly together in the field. The rest of the European powers quickly adopted most of King Gustavus's reforms.

The innovations continued. Toward the end of the century, nearly all European armies adopted flintlock muskets, which were safer and more efficient than matchlocks, and equipped them with socket bayonets. This simple device enabled marksmen to defend themselves in the face of a charging enemy and thus obviated the need for pikemen in infantry formations. Rapidly increasing population (from 118 million in 1700 to 187 million in 1800), steady economic growth, and vastly enhanced output of iron and steel greatly increased the resources available to the European armed forces. Russia alone, for instance, produced 125,000 handguns from 1700 to 1710.[130] War materiel deployed by Europeans surged. One English general, posted on the Caribbean island of St Lucia in 1780, requested 600,000 musket cartridges, 200,000 flints, 2,400 cannon shot, and 12,000 barrels of powder, among other items.[131] All Europe, as well as the American colonies, continued to accelerate the pace of their military development decade by decade and almost year by year.

* * *

One can trace the origins of Western military supremacy back to ancient Greece's formidable democratic citizen soldiery.[132] It is also possible to contend that the culture of ancient Greece and modern Europe produced highly different fighting forces with little to no continuity between them.[133] Yet one can scarcely deny that by the eighteenth century Europe had achieved a military preeminence that the Western world maintains to the present day.

To varying degrees, many non-Western powers continued or began to Westernize their armed forces, including the Khanate of Crimea, the Ottoman Empire, Persia, India, Japan, Russia, and China. Firearms diffused all over the globe, from North America to New Zealand and from Africa to Southeast Asia.[134] Even so, in the face of European innovation, the other great civilizations fell further and further behind.

Despite impressive military triumphs in 1711–15, some serious efforts at reform, and the recruitment of European military experts over the next several decades, the Ottoman Empire gradually lost its great-power status.[135] Japan was producing thousands of muskets by the 1570s, but government restrictions soon forbade anyone but samurai to own guns or even swords. Even books on military technology were banned. Japan turned in on itself. China, by far the richest, most populous, and mightiest state in the world, at least on paper, failed to keep pace. The inventor of gunpowder relied on big infantry forces rather than firepower to defend against the yearly incursions by Mongol raiders in 1550–66.[136] In the 1620s, thanks in part to artillery provided by European Jesuit missionaries, Ming forces managed to hold back Manchu invaders. Within two decades, however, they had conquered most of China, thanks in part to massive internal turmoil in the country, and had established a new ruling dynasty, the Qing. The number and quality of gunpowder weaponry increased over subsequent decades, yet neither China nor any Asian power modernized their military forces as rapidly as the Europeans.[137]

Europe's ability to project power abroad had been expanding rapidly as well. In fact, sea power constituted the West's greatest military triumph. The European land armies were pushed back or threatened by the Ottoman land forces until the late 1600s.[138] During a series of subsequently more and more devastating conflicts on European soil, however, their firepower, tactics, training, and logistics stupendously improved.[139] Even sooner, the European navies came to dominate the "seven seas" and faced no rival in the world until the rise of the United States. Centuries before the West's mastery of the seas, Europeans were driven by the desire for exotic wares, a spirit of adventure, and sheer curiosity out into the world as explorers, merchants, travelers, and conquerors. The next chapter tells this story.

QUESTIONS FOR REFLECTION

How did iron democratize warfare?

How can one account for the ferocity of European warriors?

When and why did mounted warriors come to predominate in Europe?

How did war contribute to the development of representative government in Europe?

Why did gunpowder weaponry favor large states?

What is meant by the "combined-arms revolution"?

Why did gunpowder not lead to a military revolution in China?

How did European armies become more specialized and why?

How did knowledge about advances in warfare spread in early modern Europe?

Chapter 5 Chronology

Late fifth century:	Clovis establishes Frankish Merovingian dynasty
Eleventh century:	Italian merchants travel to southern and eastern Mediterranean
1096:	First Crusade to Holy Land launched
Twelfth century:	Up to 200,000 German settlers migrate across Elbe-Saale line
1192:	By Charter of Dublin, King of England voluntarily limits his powers
Thirteenth century:	Cistercian order sets up 1,400 chapters
1200:	800 bishoprics exist throughout Europe
1236:	400,000 volumes of scholarship captured when Córdoba falls to Christians
1244:	Permanent recapture of Jerusalem by Muslims
1270:	Pisan merchants create portolan charts
1291:	Muslims recapture Acre, putting end to Crusades in the Levant
1298:	Marco Polo writes account of the Far East while imprisoned
1299:	Ottoman Empire founded
1350:	Fifteen royal titles held by ten families in Europe, all but three of Frankish origin
1406:	Ptolemy's *Geographia* translated from Greek to Latin
1415:	Portuguese capture Ceuta
1488:	Bartolomeu Diaz rounds the southern coast of Africa
1492:	Columbus discovers Caribbean islands
1494:	Treaty of Tordesillas divides lands outside Europe between Spain and Portugal
1497:	Vasco da Gama sails from Portugal to India and back
1510:	Portuguese capture Goa
Early 1500s:	Cannon become standard weapons in naval warfare
1537:	Bartolomé de Las Casa's writes about plight of Native Americans

1571:	Spanish traders and colonists found Manila
1595:	Holland reaches East Indies and begins trading empire
1602:	United East India company first publically traded, multinational LLC
1714:	Spain concedes *asiento* (right to trade slaves) to England
1756–63:	Seven Years' War

5

Discovery of the world

Since our ancestors first trod the earth or from the time a baby is born, we humans hunger for knowledge of the world. As one evolutionary geneticist put it, "No other mammal moves around like we do. . . . There's a kind of madness to it."[1] Mere survival or a desire for better living conditions has driven most of our seeking, but pure curiosity is never absent. Among the first to marvel at the lands beyond their borders were the ancient Greeks. Herodotus (fifth-century B.C.) was the first person to write systematically about the known world of his day, often from first-hand experience.[2] His voyages took him to Egypt, Libya, the Middle East, Mesopotamia, Persia, the Black Sea region, the Caucasus, the Balkans, throughout Greece, and perhaps to India (see Map 5.1). His *Histories* (inquiries) comment on peoples in all these regions and their history, customs, achievements, ways of life, beliefs, and political and social arrangements; on geographical features; on local flora and fauna; and on natural phenomena. Many travelers followed in his footsteps over the centuries. Few could fill his shoes. Among the modern peoples who rose to the challenge of knowing their world, none could compare with the Europeans. Their drive to survey, examine, comprehend, encompass, fathom, and ultimately dominate every corner of the globe was unparalleled in human history and constituted a transformation of man's relationship to geographic space.

Migrations

Like all of the earth's continents, Europe was peopled by wanderers who originally came from Africa. At the end of the last Ice Age, around 10000 B.C., Europe's population probably did not exceed 100,000. The Neolithic Revolution (stone tools, pottery, weaving, metal-working, and agriculture) of the 5th millennium B.C., combined with immigration from the Middle East, caused the population to surge to 2 million by 3000 B.C.[3] In this period, early Europeans erected thousands of huge stone monuments in Iberia, France, the British Isles, and Scandinavia. Some rose before the pyramids of Egypt. Many of the stones weighed several tons and were transported from great distances, testifying to highly efficient social organization. The builders left no written records, however, so it is impossible to know for certain the purpose of the monuments.

Migrants from the east, as well as from Iberia, continued to settle in Europe, albeit slowly.[4] Since all the "indigenous" agriculturalists of Europe had to move

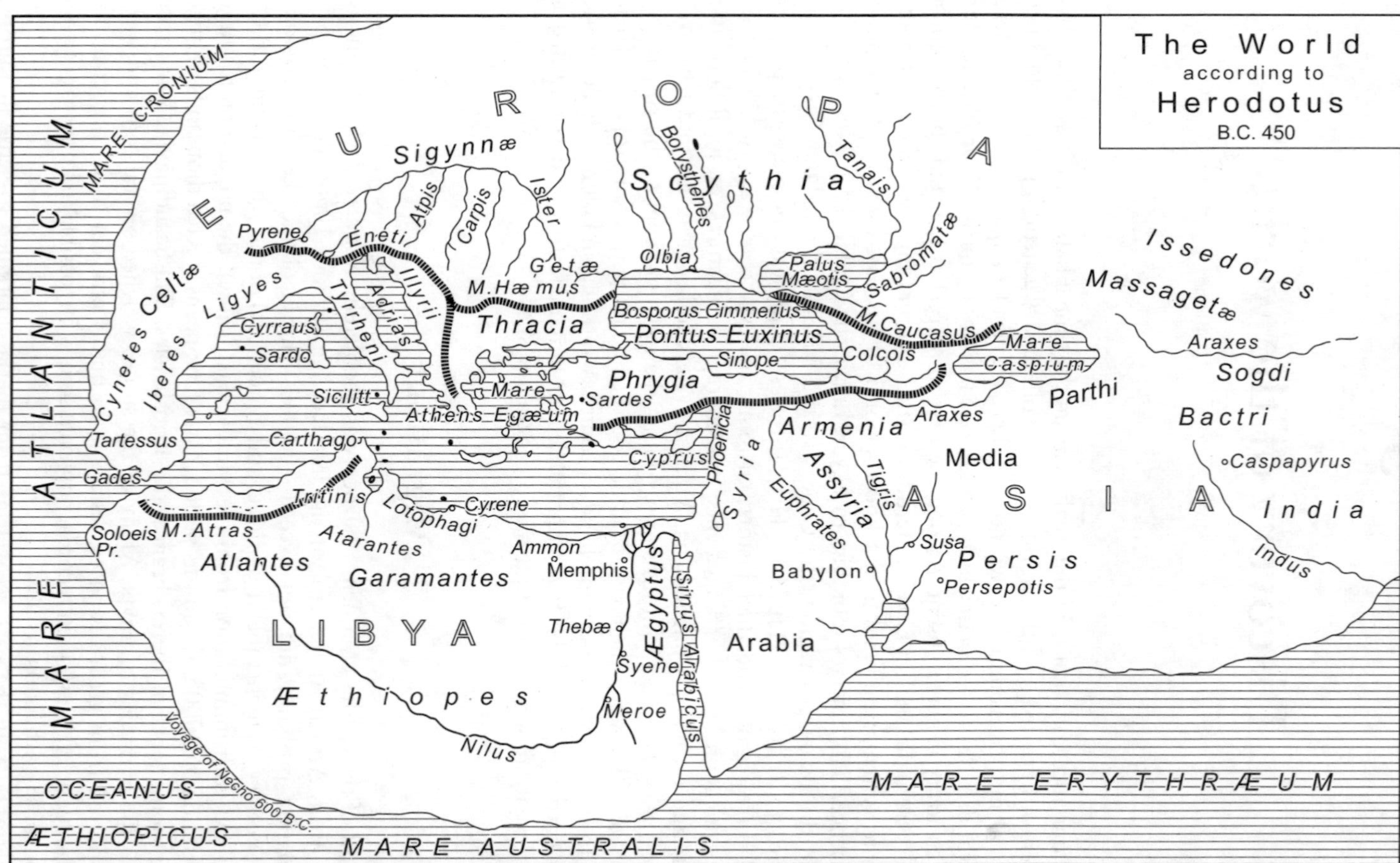

MAP 5.1 *The world according to Herodotus: Representing his travels throughout North Africa and Eurasia.*

every few years in search of fertile soil, it would have been difficult for any one group to distinguish in-migration from simple migration within the continent. Not all Europeans at this stage worked the land; many were still hunters and gatherers. Most of the newcomers, who wandered into Europe between 3000 and 1000 B.C., spoke Indo-European languages.

Among the most important early immigrants were the Celts. Spread across the continent, from the British Isles to Anatolia (today's Turkey) and from the Carpathian Mountains to Portugal, they were technologically sophisticated, employing wheels, plows, and battle-axes.[5] Slavs settled in the east, and Germanic peoples in the north. Others were drawn into the fertile and geographically diverse southeast edge of the continent, today's Greece and vicinity. There the Minoan civilization, centered on Crete, flourished for over a thousand years after 2700 B.C.[6] Probably around the start of the second millennium, the earliest Greeks adopted their future homeland, establishing the warlike Mycenaean civilization by the 1600s B.C.[7] Even earlier, the pugnacious Hittites diffused through Thessaly and then crossed into Anatolia.[8] A former Hittite dependency may have been the Greeks' foe in the semilegendary siege of Troy. Smaller migrations of mostly Indo-European peoples continued for centuries.

Pivotal was the fifth-century A.D. "Barbarian Invasion," when waves of raiders pressed against the frontiers of the Roman Empire and helped precipitate its collapse.[9] Aside from the most famous tribes—the Visigoths who sacked Rome in 410 and the Huns, whose chieftain Attila (406–53) forged an empire stretching from Central Asia to Europe—the intruders included Ostrogoths, Vandals, Lombards, Alemanni, Burgundians, Bulgars, Alans, Frisians, Saxons, and Franks. Most were Germanic, but some were of Iranian, Turkic, and Slavic origin, and all had mingled with various linguistic and ethnic groups. The fall of Rome enabled hundreds of thousands to flood into Europe, contributing to its peculiar cultural dynamism.[10]

Internal colonization

The Germanic leaven may also account for the internal colonization of Europe after the fall of the Carolingian Empire in the 800s. The most significant colonizers were the Vikings, discussed in Chapter 4, who established colonies in many peripheral areas, and the Franks, who dominated Europe's heartland. In fact, by the eleventh century the term "Franks" came to mean Latin Christians in general, particularly those engaged in colonizing and settling new lands.[11]

The Franks had originally settled in the region of modern-day Belgium in the 200s A.D. The most prominent early Frankish clan were the Salians. Allies of Rome, they helped throw back an assault by Attila's Huns in 451. Some of them migrated into Gaul (today's France). Of these, the founder of the Merovingian dynasty, Clovis (r. 481–511), conquered or pushed back several neighboring tribes, including the Burgundians, Thuringians, Alemanni, and Visigoths. More warlord than king, he established his capital at Paris, converted to Catholicism (from Paganism), and forged an immense rulership stretching from southern Gaul to northern Germany.[12] Upon his decease, the Merovingian lands dispersed among his successors and were re-gathered and re-dispersed several times before the rise of the Carolingians. Though Charlemagne's empire soon collapsed, the Franks persisted in colonizing Europe.

In the vanguard rode aristocratic Frankish knights, seeking territory, fiefs, glory, retinues, titles, and crowns. They were by all accounts—those of their apologists and of their enemies—the fiercest, most bloodthirsty warriors yet witnessed within the Mediterranean or European region. Relentlessly savage, tireless in battle, brave in the face of hopeless odds, the grimmest of adversaries—such an image they propagated in chronicles, histories, stories, and song.[13]

The most successful warriors usually came of prolific families. They also drew sustaining wealth from Europe's rich heartland. Yet boasting a successful and illustrious lineage was insufficient. Only by pledging one's loyalty to a greater lord, in exchange for fiefs or a share in the spoils of conquest, and by gaining the fealty of lesser knights on similar but inverted terms, could any one lord hope to advance in the expansionist drama. Skill, craftiness, daring, and ruthlessness all played important roles, but so too did blind luck. Accidental death in battle, premature illness from contagion, missteps by one's lord, or infertility in the bedchamber could easily dash the upward trajectory of an aristocratic house. Only success in battle and in marriage politics could ensure its continuation. No knight would for long follow his lord without a steady flow of land and loot.

Along with valor and fierceness, the Franks possessed a technological superiority in the face of nearly all their enemies. The crossbow, the heavy cavalry charge, and sophisticated siegecraft were especially formidable against the relatively backward Baltic peoples, though even their Muslim foes could marvel at several dozen heavily armored mounted knights racing with lances extended against a defensive line. And wherever the Franks pushed their frontiers outward, they systematically built castles as both defensive and offensive bases.[14]

The most successful Frankish houses crowned their expansionist endeavors quite literally with crowns. If the expected prize of conquest was fiefs, the one most hoped for was a royal domain. Among the thrones in dispute were the many new kingdoms that emerged after the millennium in Castile, Portugal, Bohemia, and Sicily. No warrior elites could best the Franks. In 1350, Latin Christendom boasted 15 royal titles borne by 10 ancestral families. Only three—those of Sweden, Denmark, and Poland—did not descend from the Franks.[15]

All the ventures of the Frankish raiders exhibited both predatory and constructive elements. Though many were invited as fighters, military experts, and lords of unsettled lands—for example, to Scotland, Pomerania, and Denmark—most seized new territory by force of arms. Yet as they sallied forth on quests of valor, both pious and purely secular, they endowed religious houses and founded towns, both back home and in new lands. They imposed the ways and means of feudal society, including the fief as a reward for military service and homage as a sign of fealty to a lord.[16] They dotted the landscape with networks of estates, constructed mills, built castles, produced documentary records, expanded commercial relations and coinage, spread Latin Christianity with its distinctive liturgy and rites, and facilitated the establishment of ecclesiastical institutions.

As the Franks extended their territory, bishoprics followed. Starting in 948, for example, Otto I encouraged the establishment of several along the northern and eastern frontiers of the Holy Roman Empire in newly conquered Slav lands. By the turn of the millennium, a Polish church with its own archbishopric, as well as several Hungarian and Bohemian bishoprics, ensured that all three peoples would look west to Rome for spiritual and cultural leadership. Similar scenarios unfolded in the Scandinavian lands, the Baltic region, the British Isles, Spain, Sicily, southern Italy, the Balkans, the Crimea, and even parts of the Near East. By the year 1200, Latin Christendom boasted some 800 bishoprics, the largest concentration in Italy and southern France—some dating to Roman times, but many recently founded all along the borderlands of the Carolingian core.[17]

The expansion of the Latin Church throughout Europe was sometimes imposed through force of arms, especially in the face of militant resistance by pagan Slavs or Muslims. Yet the millennium, as discussed in Chapter 3, was a time of fervent lay devotion, enthusiastic ecclesiastical renewal, the proliferation of new churches and monasteries, the rebuilding and renovation of existing ones, undulating movements of popular and elite piety, and apocalyptic episodes of mystical awakening.[18] Religious ardor of immigrants and colonizers surely stirred the hearts of natives in all the border regions of Europe and stimulated spiritual growth and conversion.

Lordly colonizers encouraged peasants, artisans, traders, and clergy to follow them and put down roots. Most were agricultural workers drawn to wild regions by promises of land grants and favorable economic and legal conditions.[19] In exchange for a commitment to settle relatively permanently and to clear and improve the land, most migrants received freedom from servile labor obligations, status as hereditary leaseholders, and a reduction or even a temporary waiver of normally required rent payments and tithes during the first years of relocation. Lords of every stature, including kings, granted such concessions to attract settlers to newly conquered lands. Entire rural settlements received charters endowing them with the status of "free villages," a status similar to that of towns receiving charters of liberty (see Chapter 2). This was a great boon to the migrants, because lords in Europe and elsewhere typically insisted on their supremacy and their subjects' complete inferiority. Devolving even relatively modest power to migrating peasants proved a wise policy from the perspective of European development. The immigrant agricultural workers, aggressive and resourceful, spread the use of efficient agricultural and industrial methods, including the heavy plow, the three-field crop rotation, water and windmills, and the cultivation of cash crops.[20]

The lords gained enormously from the peasants' transformation of forests, prairies, and even swamps into valuable agricultural land. The Frankish aristocrats themselves focused more and more on the profitability of all their ventures. They began keeping financial records, commissioning surveys of their estates, and reading technical manuals on estate management.[21] The seeds or even the foundations of a commercialized agricultural economy were steadily being laid.

It is impossible to know with any accuracy the number of settlers who migrated from Latin Christendom's heartland to unsettled core areas and its periphery, though one scholar estimates that the number of German settlers alone who crossed the Elbe-Saale line in the twelfth century was around 200,000.[22] If so, then probably several million established new lives in outlying regions.

The colonists and settlers imagined and represented themselves as bringing culture and civilization to barbarous hinterlands even though most people in these places had lived for centuries according to established customs. The same discrepancy existed at the level of larger settlements, many of which long predated the Western incursions into Europe's frontier areas. Danzig (Gdansk), for example, had thrived for centuries as an economic center before its official founding in 997.[23] By this point, dense trade routes and flourishing commercial relations characterized the southern Baltic shoreline.

When Frankish and other princes conferred charters of liberty on the larger towns (or even rural settlements) and implanted legal systems in them, they increased their prestige, raised the status of all the inhabitants, and created a magnet for further migration. As Lord of Ireland, installed by his father King Henry II of England, Prince John granted a charter to Dublin in 1192 conferring on its citizens impressive privileges. These included immunity from certain lawsuits, exemption from various fines and road tolls, the right to form guilds and to institute commercial monopolies, and the right freely to dispose of all the space within the city limits.[24] In a word, Prince John, like dozens of other lords throughout Europe, voluntarily limited his own power to interfere in the lives and activities of his subjects. A constitutional transformation was clearly underway.

Many rural settlements in Europe's peripheral zones also received urban charters, and thereby privileges and immunities, in the first centuries after the millennium. Such charters were often intended to attract settlers to frontier areas and to build up bulwarks against reconquest by those peoples recently expelled or defeated, for example, Muslims in Spain or Baltic pagans in Eastern Europe.

Charters of liberties and legal systems tended to follow established patterns and to mirror existing norms of various "mother cities." Thus, the legal traditions of Magdeburg and Lübeck, which derived ultimately from original mother cities further west, served as the model for hundreds of chartered settlements throughout Eastern Europe.[25] These towns then sometimes reproduced their own "daughter cities" further still. Thus, for example, Halle, a dependency of Magdeburg in Saxony, became the model for numerous towns in Silesia to the east. Some mother cities kept up a legal superintendence over their widely dispersed daughter cities. In nearly every case, there began to emerge a commercial mentality that prized explicit rules, contractual relations, financial incentives, rights, exchange, and mutual profit. Peasants as well as lords shared in this new worldview and way of life.

Theirs was not, however, a purely rationalistic, practical, lucre-oriented mindset. As discussed above, these centuries also witnessed intensified religious fervor and spiritual renewal. Millions of ordinary people went on pilgrimages, took part in mass penitential movements, fell into a wide variety of "heresies," and swelled the ranks of monastic orders, the Cistercians and the mendicants especially.

The new religious orders spread widely across Europe and deeply into its periphery, aiding to spread Western customs, values, institutions, rites, and technology. Chains of Cistercian monasteries stretched from France in nearly every direction—"from Portugal to Sweden, from Ireland to Estonia, and from Scotland to Sicily," in the words of one scholar.[26] Technological masters in the fields of agriculture, mechanics, and metallurgy, the Cistercians diffused their expertise across the continent.[27] The mendicant orders also played a key role in internal colonization. Their administrative sophistication, absolute mobility, high education level, and ability to function in any context made them nimble culture-bearers. Within a century of their founding in the early 1200s, the Franciscans alone had set up over 1,400 chapters.[28]

Europeans across the continent were on the move, founding urban centers and increasing population density decade by decade. It can be said that the geographical area covered by Latin Christendom doubled between 950 and 1350.[29] The Norman French colonized Ireland and other Celtic regions. Frenchmen wandered across the Pyrenees. Spaniards settled or resettled lands seized from the Muslims in southern Iberia. Germans spread throughout Eastern Europe and the Baltic region. Everywhere ethnic and linguistic clashes occurred. In most places the colonizers had their way, imposing their language and customs, establishing their dominance. Hostility and even disgust smoldered and flared up on both sides. Grudges set in. Just as often, colonizers and natives learned and borrowed from each other, resented but also admired each other.

Increasingly, administrative and ecclesiastical advancement in the literate, rationalistic, and knowledge-oriented European world required higher education. Thus, more and more scions of aristocratic families in Europe's periphery joined in the "academic pilgrimage," attending the few existing universities in the heartland, such as those in Paris, Bologna, and Oxford.[30] There they acquired similar habits of mind, linguistic expertise, legal training, philosophical approaches, and experiences. Returning home, they helped Westernize and colonize their native lands.

In all such colonization of peripheral and backwater regions of Europe, public and private interests and actors consistently took part. This movement was propelled as much from the grass roots as from the halls of power, both secular and ecclesiastical. Influence and authority were articulated through hundreds of offices, institutions, confraternities, and associations at every level of society. Europe was beginning to prove itself more capable of coordinating extensive and intensive activity within a politically and religiously fragmented context than was any other civilization. No endeavor demonstrated this trend better than the military campaigns by which Western Christians hoped to defend the things most precious to them—church and faith.

The Crusades

Compared with the greatest geopolitical and economic powers at the millennium, especially China and the Islamic world, Europe was an almost insignificant developing region. Yet it was impressively dynamic, gradually more outward looking, and eager to explore and assimilate foreign customs, ideas, technologies, and even values.[31] The Crusades marked a turning point in Europe's relationship with the wider world (see Map 5.2).[32] Aside from territory gained (at least temporarily) and trade routes opened in the Middle East, Iberia, and the Baltic region, Europe benefited from the capture of precious cultural treasures, for example, in the looting of Constantinople in 1204.[33] The crusaders learned to organize giant logistical undertakings involving thousands of men and animals transported thousands of miles over land and water and to coordinate these activities among men of diverse mother tongues and native cultures.[34] Even so, the greatest legacies of the Crusades were probably cultural and psychological. Encountering the brilliant urban civilizations of the Islamic and Byzantine worlds stimulated the Occidentals' desires for exotic wares and commodities, challenged their self-perceptions, stretched their imaginations, and spurred their interest in other cultures.

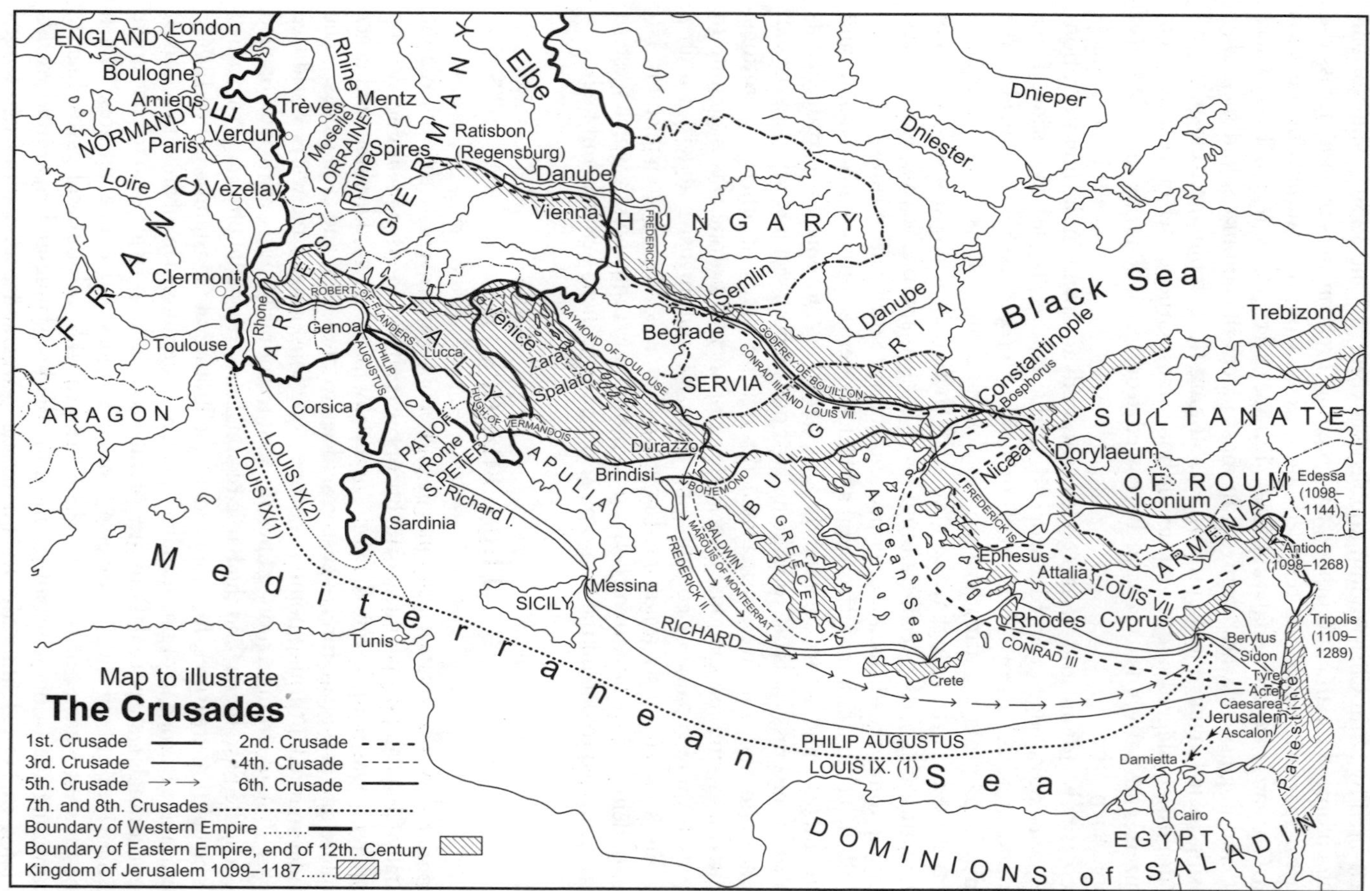

MAP 5.2 *Though they ultimately ended in failure, the Crusades marked a turning point in Europe's relationship with the wider world.*

Pope Urban II preached crusade throughout 1095, most forcefully in November at Clermont in France. He had in mind a just cause: the defense of the Eastern Church, which had been withstanding withering assaults by Islamic fighters, and the recovery of Christianity's most holy places, especially Jerusalem, from Muslim captivity. For centuries, pilgrims had sojourned to the city of Christ's Passion.[35] Reports of their mistreatment by the conquering Muslims strengthened the pope's resolve. He promised remission of sins to every person who "took up the cross" but only "out of pure devotion and not for the purpose of gaining honor or money."[36] The response to this and other summons was great. As many as 100,000 marched toward Jerusalem. While many sought adventure or glory, the overtly confessed aim of all was the "business of Jesus Christ."[37] The decision could not have been taken lightly, since those departing expected to be gone for at least a year. They generally sold all they had, gathered up as much money as possible, and bid farewell to everyone back home.

A prelude to the First Crusade began in early 1096 when thousands of poor men, women, and children marched eastward without awaiting the main crusader army. Led by a charismatic preacher, Peter the Hermit, and some knights without renown, they divided into three or four principal hosts and made their way to Constantinople—massacring Jews along the way.[38] Against the advice of Emperor Alexius, they ventured onward. Most died at the hands of superior Turkish forces. One is surprised not at their fate but that they should have marched idealistically across nearly 2,000 miles of unknown and often hostile territory. In a world dominated by political hierarchy, warlords, clear lines of authority, and in a few places centralized government, masses of ordinary people simply never coalesced into relatively orderly legions with clear purposes and relatively strong cohesiveness. Here is proof of the Europeans' unusual independence of mind, capacity for corporate action, and lust to experience the new.

The real First Crusade began in early 1097, when a proper army of over 60,000 men, including at least 6,000 knights, departed in three main groups from the mostly Frankish parts of Europe. Each group also comprised many poor, sick, and infirm. No king joined the enterprise. With logistical support and supplies from Emperor Alexius in exchange for pledges to return to him recovered Byzantine lands, the crusaders set off from Constantinople in spring 1097. Luckily for them, the Muslim rulers of the Middle East were weakened by power struggles. Even so, it took all their strength, discipline, and cooperation to fight for more than 2 years along the southern coast of Turkey and down the eastern Mediterranean shore. They captured Antioch (June 1098) and Jerusalem (July 1099), along with many other towns and fortresses in between. The crusaders established four "states" in the region, including the Principality of Antioch and the Kingdom of Jerusalem. It was a stunning success. Many crusaders now returned home; others remained to settle. Still more citadels fell to them, including Acre (1104), Beirut (1110), and Tyre (1124).[39]

Europeans exulted. God, they were sure, had blessed their endeavors. When Jerusalem was returned to Christian control, Western Europe experienced such a powerful wave of piety that conflicts and wars ceased for a time and yet more people took vows to lead a godly life.[40] Religious and secular writers in Europe blamed the Muslims' military defeats on alleged religious infidelity and atrocities against Christians (conveniently forgetting all the atrocities by Christians against Muslims).[41]

The papacy authorized the creation of several military religious orders (the Templars, the Hospitallers, and others) to assist with the crusading effort. Some grew rich and powerful.[42] Popes promised remission of sins to fighters for Christ in Spain, Germany, the Baltic region, and against Albigensian heretics in southern France.[43] Numerous European kings, beginning with King Sigurd of Norway in 1110, led crusades to the eastern Mediterranean, to Egypt, and to North Africa. A few crusades involved unexpected conquests, including the Second (Lisbon in 1147) and the Fourth (Constantinople, in 1204). One saint, Francis of Assisi, even ventured unarmed into the court of the Egyptian Sultan Malik al-Kamil in 1219, at the height of the Fifth Crusade, hoping to convert him to Christianity. He failed, but so did the crusade.[44]

Indeed, after the First Crusade, success in the Middle East eluded the Europeans and their enthusiasm waned. Ultimately, the only crusades crowned with success were the reconquest in Spain[45] and—not technically a crusade—the colonization of northeastern Europe by Germans.[46] In the Middle East, Islamic forces gradually swept away the crusaders and their states, recapturing Jerusalem temporarily and then definitively in 1244. The fall of Acre in 1291 spelled the end of the Latin territories.[47] The bright papal vision of establishing Jerusalem as the holy capital of a theocracy never materialized, and indeed the papacy's prestige gradually fell, as the Crusades failed or were patently exploited for political or even economic ends.

Yet contact with Islamic civilization, whose accomplishments far exceeded those of Latin Christendom, was powerful and lasting. In all, millions of people expanded their mental horizons, explored new lands, discovered for themselves the falsity of anti-Muslim prejudices,[48] savored novel cultural offerings, discovered exotic social and economic patterns, and befriended or even married very alien individuals indeed.[49]

World travelers

For centuries, Europeans had ventured beyond the bounds of their heartland, most eagerly to visit the Christian sacred places. Around 400 A.D., for example, the Frankish nun Egeria traveled to the Holy Land and left a lengthy account of her journey.[50] Some traveled seeking adventure, for example, the Anglo-Saxon monk St Willibald (700?–787?) who spent 7 years traveling to all the major holy places in the Near East.[51] Dozens more narratives were set down in subsequent centuries, in an uninterrupted line of pilgrimage.[52] From around 1350, these accounts grew more secular, more focused on the customs of the inhabitants of the Holy Land and the observations of the pilgrims. Presumably many Europeans were gaining a more humanistic disposition.

Some European travelers sought learned texts and scholars. Gerbert of Aurillac (ca. 945–1003), a mathematician, inventor, scholar, teacher, and later pope (Sylvester II), spent several years in Spain studying Arabic works of mathematics and science translated into Latin.[53] He was probably the first scholar to introduce Hindu-Arabic numbers, the astrolabe, and the abacus to Europe. Constantine the African (ca. 1020–85), who was born in Carthage, traveled throughout the Middle East and even India. He converted to Christianity, became a Benedictine monk, and settled in Italy where he prolifically translated scientific, especially medical, works.

A half-century later, Adelard of Bath lived among Muslims in Sicily, the Near East, and Andalusia, apparently even pretending to be Muslim in order to gain access to texts and scholars.[54] By 1122, he returned to England and translated philosophical, mathematical, and scientific works from Arabic, including Euclid's *Elements*, and published his own philosophical writings.[55] The rest of the century witnessed dozens of Europeans making secular pilgrimages to the Muslim world, learning Arabic, and translating hundreds of scholarly and scientific works.

Islamic scholars had avidly translated and studied the scholarly works of Greeks, Persians, and Indians. Yet few visited Europe or carefully studied the growing output of scholarship in Latin.[56] At the millennium, the Europeans may well have had precious few treasures of culture or learning to offer.[57] Century by century, however, they acquired and produced a vast fund of them; still non-Christians did not come.[58]

Muslims sojourned extensively, usually on Hajj, and wrote many travel narratives.[59] Abu Said, who hailed from Siraf on the Persian Gulf, penned one in 915 A.D.[60] Ibn Jubayr, a native of Valencia, traveled three times to the eastern Mediterranean region, including to lands seized by the crusaders, and left a narrative of his first journey (1182–85).[61] Probably the most well-traveled man before the modern age was Ibn Battuta, a Berber from Tangier.[62] Between 1325 and 1345, he wandered throughout the Muslim world in Africa and Asia and wrote a lengthy account of his voyages. Of Christian countries, he visited only Bulgaria, which was soon to be conquered by the Ottoman Empire. Surprising is the relative lack of interest in travel narratives among Muslim readers, at least compared to the thirst for the genre in Europe. It seems strange, too, that Islamic voyagers steered clear of Christian, especially Latin Europe.

The Islamist Bernard Lewis points out that Muslims would have faced persecution in medieval Europe, as did Jews, and that the absence of mosques, bathhouses, and established Muslim communities would have impeded free travel within Christendom.[63] Yet one assumes that people intent on exploring exotic and innovative societies could have overcome these obstacles. Another scholar points out that Muslims played a key commercial role throughout the eastern two-thirds of Eurasia, with large numbers of expatriates in the major Chinese cities.[64] Even so, it seems that passionate curiosity about the wider world gradually became a peculiarly European phenomenon.

A great number of Europeans traveled to the east, and the accounts they penned enjoyed great popularity back home. From 1247 to 1253 alone, four Europeans journeyed to the court of the Great Khan in Mongolia, and two, Giovanni da Pian del Carpine (ca. 1180–1252) and Willem van Rubroeck (ca. 1220–93), left detailed travel accounts without overly fanciful embellishment.[65] Most famously, in 1271 Marco Polo journeyed with his father and brother to the court of Kublai Khan in present-day Beijing with a papal mission to report in particular on the state of Christianity in East Asia. They remained for two decades, engaging in commerce and fulfilling official duties for the Khan. In his book later dictated in prison, Polo accurately reported on people, places, flora, and fauna.[66] It enjoyed great popular success and survives in some 150 different manuscripts.[67] This and other such travel accounts helped Italians and other Europeans in the thirteenth century to gain a broadly cosmopolitan understanding of the known world.[68] Educated men and women were henceforth at least dimly aware of all the great civilizations, both contemporary and historical.

Global traders

International trade had flourished since ancient times across Eurasia.[69] India and China had traded relatively intensively with the Roman Empire, but cycles of trade can be traced back even further in time.[70] Commerce along the famed Silk Road linking China and western Eurasia flowed more or less continuously.[71] From a thousand years ago, Chinese traders settled profitably throughout Southeast Asia, while Muslims exercised a hegemonic commercial role from East Africa to China.[72] In other words, when the Europeans began to enter the Eurasian universe of trade, it had been thriving for many centuries.

The Italians, in particular, were drawn to explore the world in the interest of commerce. Venetian merchants had served as intermediaries between the Muslim and Byzantine East and the Latin West beginning at the latest in the 700s. By the ninth century, their main items of commerce were fish, salt, and slaves mostly transported to the Muslim world. The sale of slaves was condemned by emperor and pope, as was the sale of wood, given its strategic importance. The Venetian merchants ignored such prohibitions: they were traders first and foremost. Slaves and wood were sold to Muslims for gold and silver with which to buy luxury goods from Constantinople.[73]

By the second half of the eleventh century, sea-borne merchants from Venice, Pisa, and Genoa were landing all along the eastern and southern Mediterranean coast, buying and selling goods, establishing trading colonies, and plundering vulnerable settlements.[74] They played decisive roles in the Crusades, supplying maritime transport, logistical assistance, and commercial expertise in exchange for trading concessions in the crusader states.[75] All three Italian merchant powers negotiated commercial access throughout the Mediterranean, irrespective of the religious faith of established powers, Latin, Greek, or Muslim. They competed fiercely among themselves, Venice gaining from the sack and conquest of Constantinople in 1204,[76] Genoa from Byzantium's reconquest of Constantinople in 1261. The Genoese went on to set up trading posts and colonies on the southern and eastern Black Sea coast.[77]

The Italians built and sailed the biggest and best ships in the Mediterranean. In the twelfth and thirteen centuries, their "round ships" usually bore two (sometimes three) lateen (triangular) sails, sported two decks, and displaced around 200 tons fully loaded.[78] By the mid-thirteenth century, the Venetians and Genoans each possessed a couple of ships rated at 500 deadweight tons. These were huge ships for Europe, given that the *Santa Maria* was rated at 100 and the *Mayflower* at 180 tons. The typical warships of the time were bireme galleys. Very long but narrow, they were powered by 12 to 18 sets of oars on each side of the ship.[79]

A "nautical revolution" of the late 1200s transformed shipping and maritime commerce in the Mediterranean.[80] For centuries, mariners determined position by reference to the stars. Because of unpredictable weather, including frequent winter winds, fog, clouds, and rain, most ships remained docked for half the year, from October to April. Gradually seafarers devised more reliable navigational methods. First, they plotted distances and directions between all the ports of the Mediterranean into "port books." By 1250, the data were integrated into a single book for the entire sea. Drawing on all this information, in 1270 someone in Pisa drafted a marine chart with grid lines measuring about three feet across. Called a "portolan chart," it depicted all the coasts and islands of the Mediterranean Sea accurately and to scale.[81]

Around the same time, mariners figured out how to fix a magnetized needle so it could pivot freely as dictated by the Earth's magnetic field. Chinese inventors had devised the first compass over two centuries before and had used the device to aid in navigation from the early 1100s. Whether the Europeans made their discovery independently or by diffusion from China, the instrument was a key element in "dead reckoning" navigation (as opposed to "live reckoning" by the stars).[82] Another important element was the traverse table, which permitted calculating change in longitude. When one tossed a log attached to a rope into the water to give an approximate sense of the ship's speed, it became possible to determine roughly one's position at any time of day or night and any season of the year.[83] These breakthroughs enabled ships to double their effective utility and perhaps doubled their economic output.

Ship design and naval architecture also underwent major changes.[84] In the decades around 1300, ships grew larger, stouter, and nimbler. Triremes (with three rowers on each side instead of two) began to replace biremes. By the 1350s, some galleys sported as many as 200 oars.[85] Being wider, they could carry far more cargo, though still less than round ships. The bigger crew could also help fight off pirates, a perennial trouble. The trireme's main advantage was keeping to a schedule, since it did not depend solely on wind power. Italian round ships from the early 1300s often added one or two square sails and an extra deck in imitation of northern European cogs. Taller construction created an advantage for archers who could dominate the enemy from above. Square sails required fewer men to adjust for shifts in the wind than did triangular sails. Saving labor meant saving money and increasing profit.

The governments of Venice and Genoa, being dominated by merchants, actively promoted commerce by founding state-sponsored shipyards (e.g. the Arsenal in Venice), organizing convoys, creating war fleets to open up trade in hostile waters, systematically selecting the best shipping routes, establishing shipping schedules, and encouraging the use of bigger, more efficient vessels.[86]

Genoese vessels sailed through the straits of Gibraltar, into the rough and dangerous waters of the Atlantic, and up to Iberian and northern European ports as early as 1277. In subsequent decades, they established regular trade routes. A few decades later, the Venetians followed suit.[87] European shipping lanes stretched from the Sea of Azov, through the entire Mediterranean, along the North Atlantic coast, and the length of the Baltic Sea. They even bore the majority of Muslim pilgrims from Spain and northwest Africa to Egypt. Italian sailors dominated all these passages for several reasons. They were excellent businessmen with the best financial infrastructure, instruments, and methods. They deployed advanced European military technology. The northern coasts of the Mediterranean enjoyed more favorable currents and wind patterns than those on the southern littoral. Most of the Mediterranean islands, being closer to its northern coast, fell more readily to European, especially Italian, colonizers.[88] The Genoese, in particular, were ruthless merchants. They were also daring mariners. In spring 1291, the Genoans Vandino and Ugolino Vivaldi sailed out into the Atlantic Ocean, apparently seeking a passage to India. They were never seen again.[89]

For a couple centuries prior, vibrant commercial networks had united China, the Indian Ocean, Persia, the Middle East, and North Africa into the first global trading system.[90] Europe was now slowly connecting to this larger outside commercial world through Egypt and the Middle East. The prizes included spices—pepper, nutmeg,

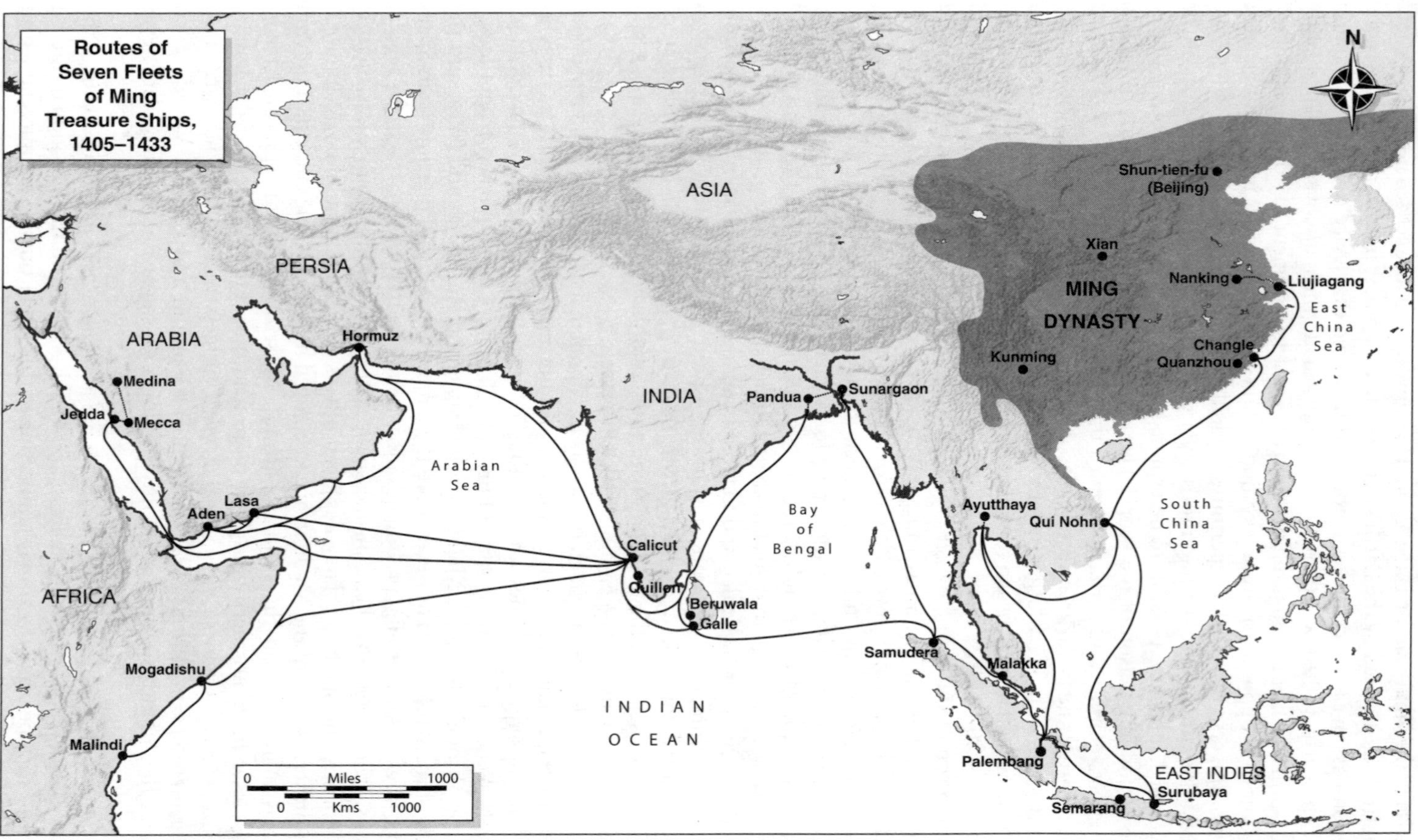

MAP 5.3 *In 1405–33, the Chinese-Muslim eunuch, Zheng He, sailed seven fleets of ships throughout Asian waters to display China's grandeur.*

cinnamon, ginger, and cloves—medicines, porcelain, sugar, and silks. Despite demographic catastrophe following the Mongol conquests of the 1200s (China's population plunged from 115 million in 1200 to 85 million in 1300),[91] the Pax Mongolica created favorable conditions for East–West trade.[92]

The collapse of the Mongol Empire after the Black Death struck Eurasia (1340s) disrupted international trade and caused further demographic calamity. The population of Europe plummeted from 80 million in 1330 to 60 million in 1400, and demographic loss on the steppe must have been great, though even approximate figures are unavailable. The fall of the Mongols witnessed rebellions and possibly outbreaks of the plague, driving China's population down from 85 to 75 million (1340–80).[93] In the midst of these troubles, a Muslim carrying forward Genghis Khan's legacy ripped through half of Asia, bringing destruction to India, the Middle East, and Persia. Tamerlane (1336–1405) forged an empire centered on Samarkand and stretching from northern India to the Black Sea.[94] His empire did not outlast him, but the bitter memory of thousands slaughtered in its making surely did.

A profound contraction in economic activity affected Eurasia. The trade routes of Central Asia, in particular, languished. New powers emerged from the wreckage. The Ming Dynasty (1368–1644), seeking to return China to its ancient traditions, reestablished the civil service exam, set up military garrisons throughout the country to maintain political control, and weakened the social position of commercial elites. On land, the Chinese military attacked Burma and conquered Vietnam (1407).[95] From 1405 to 1433, seven fleets of hundreds of enormous "treasure ships" sailed throughout the Indian Ocean under the command of the Muslim eunuch Zheng He, calling in all major ports along the African and Asian coasts (see Map 5.3).[96] Their purpose was to prove the greatness and might of China, to establish diplomatic contacts, to take control of foreign commerce from private traders and pirates, and to extend the emperor's tribute system. After Zheng's death in 1433, the expeditions ended, the ships were destroyed, and decrees forbade sailing beyond China's coastal waters.[97] High politics and fear of Mongol incursions turned China's rulers inward.

Two other significant powers emerged in this period. The Ottoman Empire, founded in 1299 by Osman I (1258–1326), expanded from a slender arc of lands verging the Sea of Marmara in the mid-1300s to engulf most of Anatolia and half the Balkans a century later (see Map 4.3 above).[98] This dynamic state drew heavily on European military technology and threatened Europe on both land and sea for two more centuries, but concentrated on ruling a big empire and never displayed a profound curiosity about the wider world. To the south arose another warrior state, Mamluk Egypt.[99] After the Mongols sacked Baghdad in 1258, a succession of Mamluk warlords controlled most of the territory from Syria to Egypt and therefore most of the trade passing between Europe and Asia for more than two centuries.

Seafarers and explorers

In 1450, vast regions of the globe remained unexplored for inhabitants of the Old World, including three continents and two oceans. Three civilizations had the capacity to open up the oceanic frontiers. One seized the moment. For centuries,

Islamic merchants had dominated the lucrative Indian Ocean trade. Minarets and prayers to Allah rose across North and East Africa, the Middle East, the Balkans, Central Asia, much of South Asia, and parts of East Asia, right down into Indonesia. This was the most widely flung civilization the world had ever known. Yet the highly skillful Muslim mariners never ventured into the Atlantic or Pacific Oceans. The most inventive people, until then, the Chinese, could obviously have sailed to every corner of the globe had they willed it. Still, the Chinese neither crossed nor explored the Pacific Ocean. It seems that the deeply rooted Confucian ethos stifled interest in fully applying inventions and hindered close associations between scholars and artisans.[100]

Europeans in the Age of Exploration were animated not only by a lust for the spices and treasures of the East but also by an abiding desire to know the world. This contrasted markedly with Chinese attitudes.[101] Europeans had known of unusual animals since the Middle Ages, though they typically interpreted them in relation to beliefs about themselves or about fantastic legends and stories. And many scholars sought to avoid idle curiosity, following the teaching of St Augustine.[102] By the Renaissance, however, Europeans had acquired an insatiable thirst for novelty. Strange fauna topped the list. Middle Eastern sultans kept vast zoological gardens and from time to time bestowed exotic specimens on European rulers. The collections in Florence in the second half of the fifteenth century were especially impressive. In 1486, the Mamluk sultan of Egypt presented to Lorenzo the Magnificent a giraffe as a goodwill offering. The beast wandered the streets freely to public delight and acclaim. Poets sang its praises; artists painted its portrait, one inserting its image in a depiction of the Magi.

The way a gift-giraffe was received in early Ming China could scarcely have been more different. In 1414, the king of Bengal sent one to the Chinese Emperor. Ordinary people exulted, but the Confucian elites expressed neither surprise nor curiosity. Having consulted learned scrolls, they identified the odd beast as a unicorn, "the foremost of the 360 creatures living on land."[103] Its appearance was interpreted, in conjunction with other favorable signs, as an especially good omen attesting to the benevolence of the Yongle Emperor (r. 1402–24). The giraffe, situated within a known semiotic matrix, pointed to the central symbol of Chinese self-identification. It led nowhere outside China. Everything, it seems, had its place; nothing induced wonder or bewilderment. For the Florentines, in their naiveté, the giraffe betokened worlds to discover and explore. Certainly, European mariners, including such Florentines as Amerigo Vespucci, were soon to embark upon world-transforming journeys.

Key mental shifts made them possible. Ever since Pythagoras, Western thinkers had imagined the Earth as spherical. Yet they had disagreed whether insuperable obstacles divided its inhabitable parts. As early as 1267, however, Roger Bacon claimed that only a narrow stretch of ocean separated Iberia from India. A French theologian and cardinal, Pierre d'Ailly, reiterated this theory in *Imago mundi* (1410). Equally, if not more, important in transforming the Renaissance worldview was Ptolemy's *Geographia*. Translated from Greek into Latin in 1406 and diffused widely from 1475, it described the Earth as mathematically proportional.[104] Ptolemy's imposition of grid lines enabled geographers to determine precisely any location and to conceptualize the world as homogeneous and continuous. Within two decades,

European cartographers began to construct globes. In the final decades of the fifteenth century, the boldest mariners had begun to view the oceans less as impediments than as highways. Some discussed projects of circumnavigation.[105]

Improved naval construction from the late 1300s made such projects feasible. Iberian shipwrights fused elements of Mediterranean and Atlantic shipbuilding technology to produce the ancestor of fully rigged sailing ships. The first European oceangoing vessels were carracks (also called "naus").[106] They boasted three (later four) masts rigged with square sails fore and lateens aft. Strong and stout, they could withstand rough seas and carry sufficient provisions for long voyages. Caravels, with two or three masts and lateen sails aft and jib sails attached to a bowsprit, like schooners, were nimbler and better able to navigate in shallow waters. Portuguese, Italian, and Spanish seafarers used both types of ship as they sailed down the African coast and into the Atlantic Ocean in the second half of the 1400s. Navigational technology, close familiarity with trade winds and currents, and the astonishing bravery of their skippers enabled small flotillas of ships to sail literally into the unknown. Cannon fixed aboard ships meant they had little to fear from most human foes.

The first recorded instance of firearms installed on ships was an English vessel in 1337. Burgundy had deployed armed vessels during the Lombard Wars in the 1420s and 1430s.[107] By mid-century, some war galleys began to sport forward-mounted guns, though crossbow fire, ramming and boarding the enemy ship, and diversionary tactics like ripping its sails with grappling hooks remained the standard methods of fighting in the Mediterranean.[108] Carracks and caravels, being fitted with side-mounted guns, could engage the enemy from a distance, thus neutralizing those methods. As the cannon mounted on European sailing ships grew bigger, by around 1500, they were installed on sliding carriages to absorb the recoil. Mounting the guns lower on the hull, made possible by watertight, retractable lids covering the gun ports, also increased stability.[109] By the 1520s, most European (and Ottoman) oceangoing ships were nearly unconquerable floating fortresses.[110]

Superior technology did not always drive successful exploration but was sometimes its result as mariners demanded innovations and improvements in ship building to meet specific challenges they encountered at sea. The new designs often gave those who adopted them a decisive edge against rivals who failed to keep pace. A curious fact about European states and entrepreneurs is that they feverishly copied each other's ship-building technology in every manner possible, including by theft and capture.

The first global seafaring power was tiny Portugal.[111] With a population of only 1 million, isolated from most of Europe, bordered by its historic enemy, Spain, yet with a lengthy Atlantic coastline, Portugal sent most of the greatest mariners of the fifteenth century into the open sea. They sailed for glory, seeking profits, hoping to encounter long-lost Christian settlements, and in a very few instances, at least in the early years, sought to convert native peoples. Portuguese sailors were the first to sail down the West African coast, around the Cape of Good Hope, and to reach India by ship from Europe. They explored the Malay and Indonesian archipelagoes, sighted Australia, and traded with China and Japan. They "discovered" Brazil. Their ventures opened vast uncharted maritime expanses, yielded astonishing fortunes, and won an empire on three continents.

The main goal of the Portuguese mariners was to find a passage to India in order to cut out the Arab and Turkish middlemen who controlled the existing trade routes. Aristocrats dominated Europe, but merchants enjoyed more prestige and influence than in other major cultures. Benedetto Cotrugli (1416–69), a diplomat and merchant who served at the court of Naples for 15 years and first codified the principles of double-entry bookkeeping, gave voice to a widespread sentiment in Europe when he wrote that merchants were viewed as model citizens and the greatest promoters of the common good.[112] Merchants often viewed their work as entirely compatible with serving God. Indeed, company books often opened with a prayer for success in business and the health and safety of its workers.[113] It was surely a powerful stimulus to dare to believe that the Lord sanctioned one's ventures, as the majority of Europe's seafarers apparently did.

The first great European patron of the maritime arts was a brother of the King of Portugal, Prince Henry the Navigator (1394–1460).[114] In a chivalric test in 1415, Henry led an assault on Ceuta, a port and commercial center on the African side of the Strait of Gibraltar. Henry immediately realized the great wealth in gold, pepper, and slaves to be had from controlling trans-Sahara commerce. He thus hired the best cartographers and outfitted scores of ships for exploration. The contrast was stark with the Chinese rulers who not only did not support Chinese overseas traders and voyagers but also considered them traitors.[115]

The first Portuguese discovery, made by accident in 1419, was the Madeira archipelago, 450 miles off the coast of Morocco. Portuguese settlers began to establish themselves on the main islands, Madeira and Porto Santo, almost immediately. In 1427, Henry's mariners discovered the Azores, 900 miles due west of Lisbon; in 1434, sailed past Cape Bojador, a place of doom for many ships because of treacherous winds and currents; in 1444, landed on the coast of Senegal; and in 1456, reached the Cape Verde Islands, 200 miles out in the Atlantic.[116] Meanwhile, dozens of mercantile expeditions, mostly private, had followed in the explorers' wake, bringing back gold and slaves. Slave trading in Lisbon and sugar plantations on the island of Madeira were yielding enormous profits by the 1450s.[117] Muslims continued to dominate the East African human trafficking, but henceforth Europeans monopolized that infernal commerce on the West African coast. The wealth and glory to be had from maritime exploration drew hundreds more explorers and thousands more merchants southward along the African coastline. By 1488, Bartolomeu Diaz reached the southern tip of Africa, proving that ships from Europe could reach the East (see Map 5.4).

The next decade witnessed two of the greatest human achievements of all time. Both might have been credited to Portugal, had King João II not declined (twice) to fund the venture of the Genoese Christopher Columbus. João II's experts all assured him that the transoceanic distance to India far exceeded Columbus's estimate of 2,400 miles. They were right, of course: Columbus ended up sailing over 4,000 miles to the Bahamas alone where he and his crew first landed in the New World. The rest of the story—three subsequent voyages involving the discovery of the main Caribbean islands and the coast of Central America—is well known. Suffice it to say that dozens more mariners followed in his wake to explore, map out, exploit, and settle all the lands of the New World (see Map 5.4).

The discoveries of Vasco da Gama (1469?–1524), though far less celebrated than those of Columbus, were in the short term more consequential.[118] In midsummer

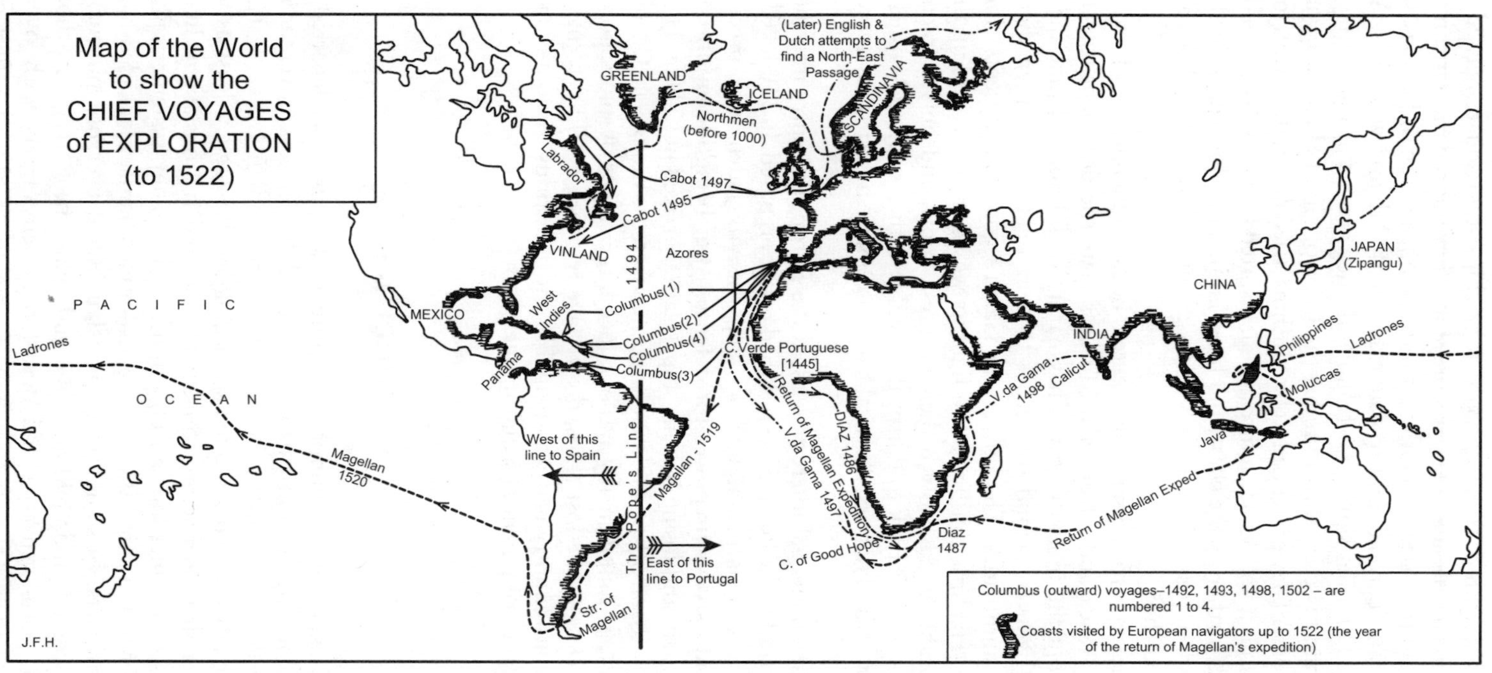

MAP 5.4 *Voyages by explorers opened up new trade routes and worlds to Europeans.*

1497, he set sail with 170 men aboard four ships: two square-masted *naus*, one caravel with lateen sails, and a larger store ship. They hugged the African coast until Sierra Leone and then steered southwest into the open sea in order to avoid adverse coastal winds and currents and to catch the South Atlantic westerlies. After three months and 6,000 miles sailing far from land, they arrived at the southern African coast. Gama and his crew then rounded the Cape of Good Hope and sailed up the East African coast. They pretended to be Muslims, tried negotiation with local rulers, fired hellish cannon volleys when threatened, resorted to piracy occasionally, won an ally in Malindi further up the coast, and hired an Indian pilot. This skilled navigator guided the ships across the Arabian Sea to Calicut on India's Malabar coast, where they dropped anchor.

Calicut, the region's commercial center, boasted merchants of every known religion from Africa and all of Asia. Muslims were the dominant traders, as they were throughout the Indian Ocean. They naturally did not welcome the European intruders and worked behind the scenes to sour relations between them and the ruling Hindu authorities. The poverty of Gama's goodwill presents simply made matters worse. His little flotilla had to fight its way out of port and up the coast of India. Unfavorable winds slowed their progress home, and only a fraction of the original sailors made it back to Portugal alive. Nevertheless, King Manuel showered Gama with favors and honors. Portugal had won a place in history that few countries ever achieve.

Entrenched commercial interests resisted the Europeans' entry into the lucrative Indian Ocean trade. The Portuguese returned better prepared. In 1500, Pedro Álvares Cabral and crew departed aboard 13 ships heavily laden with precious goods for trading and massive firepower for defense. After being blown off course, thus discovering Brazil, and losing half his ships, Cabral arrived in Calicut. His reception was disastrous (over 50 of his men were massacred), though in Cochin, further down the coast, he found an ally and obtained large cargos of spices, porcelain, and cotton cloth. Despite the lost ships, the voyage returned a 100 percent profit. The excitement of his countrymen was palpable and infectious. A gold-rush mentality gripped thousands of potential seafaring merchants.

Conquerors

Dozens more expeditions comprising hundreds of ships soon departed eastward, each one heavily armed and often commanded by fearless adventurers. Within 15 years, the Portuguese had seized control of the Indian Ocean.[119] The Indians, Muslims, and Chinese had mastered science and technology at least as well as the Europeans, yet their merchants could not withstand the onslaught, like so many gas molecules expanding into an unconfined space. They systematically harassed and captured Muslim ships, drove out Muslim merchants, blockaded harbors, and seized Muslim ports. In some cases, they slaughtered everyone on board Muslim ships—men, women, and children. Time and again the Portuguese, though vastly outnumbered, outmaneuvered and devastated their targets with overwhelming cannonades. In early 1509, for example, Francisco de Almeida's fleet of 18 ships completely destroyed a fleet five times as big off the Gujarati port of Diu. As they advanced, the Portuguese established forts, warehouses, and settlements.[120]

The greatest Portuguese naval strategist—the greatest in world history until then—was Alfonso de Albuquerque (1453–1515), a brilliant and learned nobleman.[121] Before anyone else, he grasped that sea power depended not only on force of arms and fighting capacity but just as much on the control of strategic bases and on the deployment of vigorous merchant shipping fleets. During his 6 years as "viceroy of India," starting in 1509, he worked tirelessly to establish strongholds at all choke points on maritime routes and along all important shipping lanes of the Indian Ocean. The hub of the Portuguese empire was Goa, on the west coast of India, which he captured in 1510. His successful amphibious assault on Malacca the following year gave Portugal control of the extraordinarily important Strait of Malacca, the principal shipping lane linking the Indian and Pacific Oceans. In 1515, Albuquerque established a Portuguese base on Hormuz Island at the mouth of the Persian Gulf by the strategically valuable Strait of Hormuz. These and other ports and forts gave Portugal at the time of his death in 1516 almost full control of commercial shipping in the Indian Ocean. Rarely in world history had so few men accomplished so much.

How can one explain the triumph of tiny Portugal—and by extension of each of the seafaring states of Europe—in the face of often much larger enemies, in unfamiliar environments, thousands of miles from home, and usually spectacularly outnumbered in the field?[122] Europe's balanced political fragmentation fostered intense military competition and the development of the most powerful war machines the world had ever seen. Also, the purpose of fighting and conquering for most peoples of the world was to seize people in order to enslave them. The Europeans did not reject slavery in practice, except in Europe itself, but their main objective everywhere was expanding their trading relations and acquiring territory. They therefore tended to fight with more indiscriminate violence than most of their adversaries. Finally, the opportunities for personal enrichment through overseas expansion, conquest, international trade, and colonization were so fabulous that they probably filled European merchant-warriors with prodigious confidence and drove them to extreme feats of boldness.

Over the next few decades, Portuguese merchants established bases in the Maluku (Spice) Islands just west of New Guinea, received the unprecedented permission to set up a trading post in China (Macau), became middlemen in the Sino-Japanese trade, and conquered the coastal regions of Ceylon. Still, their network of trading bases did not translate into military control throughout the region. In fact, the Portuguese colonists faced opposition from both indigenous peoples and rival Europeans. Chief among them were the Spanish.

In 1493 and 1494, Pope Alexander VI had divided the western hemisphere, right down the middle of the Atlantic, into Spanish and Portuguese colonial regions (see Map 5.4).[123] Cabral's discovery of Brazil placed it on Portugal's side of the ledger. Another Portuguese mariner, Ferdinand Magellan (1480–1521), on his path-breaking voyage around the world in 1522, discovered and claimed the Philippines on behalf of his sponsor, the Spanish crown. Henceforth, all the continents were known to be linked by oceans, humankind acquired a fully global perspective, and every corner of the earth beckoned for exploration. As the Spanish empire rose to stunning heights, Portugal's entered into decline while remaining one of the biggest in history. In the late 1500s, Portugal was forced into a union with Spain under Philip II.[124]

In the New World, the Spanish forged an immense empire. The only relatively sophisticated civilizations in the western hemisphere, those of the Aztecs and Incas, were far behind Europe technologically. They had invented neither the wheel nor a system of writing, though the script of the once great Mayan civilization remained in use in isolated places.[125] Iron was unknown to them. The only large domesticated animals in the pre-Columbian Americas were Andean camelids (llamas and alpacas). Everywhere else, humans were the only beasts of burden.

When the Spanish arrived in the New World armed with guns, crossbows, and steel-edged weapons, riding horses, sailing ships, and capable of fighting in tightly disciplined formation, the natives could withstand them only with the most overwhelming of odds. Many natives, whether in rejection of their own rulers or wishing to join the winning team, became allies of the intruders. The native populations and cultures fell before the Spanish conquistadores everywhere they appeared. Yet, as Alfred Crosby has noted, "when Columbus brought the two halves of this planet together, the American Indian met for the first time his most hideous enemy: not the white man nor his black servant, but the invisible killers which those men brought in their blood and breath."[126]

Cut off from the Afro-Eurasian land continuum for millennia, the Native Americans had developed no immunity against such diseases as smallpox and measles, which for them proved lethal. Scholars agree universally on these points but dispute vehemently two others. First, how many people inhabited the Americas in 1492? Thirty or forty years ago, relatively little controversy surrounded the answer to this question—roughly 14 million from the Arctic to Tierra del Fuego.[127] Beginning in 1966, a few scholars advanced far higher numbers, ranging to 50 or even 100 million. Many, though not all, scholars have now joined the revisionists.[128] Taking a position in this debate automatically affects how one views the post-Columbian population loss. Scholars agree that by 1600 the native population of the Americas had fallen to roughly 11.5 million. If the high point in 1492, therefore, had been 14 million, then the total human destruction was on the order of 18–20 percent—or fewer than died in Europe during the Black Death (some 30 percent).[129] On the other hand, if the original population total had been 100 million, then the population destruction within a century of contact with Europeans was close to 90 percent—a veritable holocaust.

One widely respected scholar, David Stannard, in fact, has used that exact term. In *American Holocaust*, he draws an explicit comparison to Jews who died in transit to the death camps or in other ways unrelated to direct Nazi extermination. He thus argues that

> the natives of Hispaniola and Mexico and Peru and Florida and Virginia and Massachusetts and Georgia and Colorado and California and elsewhere who died from forced labor, from introduced disease, from malnutrition, from death marches, from exposure, and from despair are as much victims of the Euro-American genocidal race war as were those burned or stabbed or hacked or shot to death, or devoured by hungry dogs.[130]

He asserts further: "The destruction of the Indians of the Americas was, far and away, the most massive act of genocide in the history of the world."[131]

Was it really genocide? According to the U.N. Convention on Genocide, only the intentional destruction of a people, in whole or in part, qualifies as genocide.[132] Scholars have brought to light a few cases of Europeans intentionally spreading smallpox among native peoples. There may have been other such cases, of course, though some were apparently made up.[133] On a large scale, this would have constituted genocide. Other scholars have pointed to the driving of whole peoples hundreds and even thousands of miles from their homelands—like nearly 17,000 Cherokee forced to march the "Trail of Tears" in 1838, causing some 8,000 deaths.[134] This was deeply callous but presumably not the intentional destruction of peoples.

Another scholar argues that European concepts of property rights and of economic efficiency were used to justify the seizure of nearly all the land on the two American continents. In the European mind, people who failed to make their land as productive as possible did not deserve to possess it. At first the American and Canadian governments resisted this push and tried to apply legal norms and to follow specific procedures, but "landhunters, grazers, and squatters" overwhelmed the system, and by the second half of the nineteenth century the governments were actively displacing the natives and distributing their land to people of European ancestry (see Chapter 14).[135] Obviously, people cannot easily survive as a people without any land to call their own.

The historian Alfred Crosby has argued persuasively that human migrants have always carried with them their entire biota—plants, animals, and diseases—and have always wreaked havoc on the places and peoples they encountered, unless they were destroyed or subdued by them. The Europeans' arrival in the New World with their pathogens, weeds, and small and large animals (in particular, rats and horses) was among the more catastrophic of such encounters. Together with the colonizers themselves, he writes, they "made a revolution more extreme than any seen on this planet since the extinctions at the end of the Pleistocene."[136] The extinctions in question were the destruction of most of the large mammals of the Americas soon after human migrants crossed over from Asia at the end of the last Ice Age. A similar catastrophe had befallen Australia some 40,000 years ago and Eurasia earlier still. In other words, destructively transforming their environments is what human migrants sometimes do. Crosby considers metaphorically the two waves of migrants—from Asia 11,000 years ago and from Europe after 1492—as "two waves of invaders of the same species, the first acting as the shock troops, clearing the way for the second wave, with its more complicated economies and greater numbers.[137]

While conquerors plundered, maimed, enslaved, and killed, a few missionaries developed new ways of seeing the native peoples. The philosophical doctrine of John Mair (1467–1550), a Scottish humanist teaching in Paris, had justified the conquerors' actions. Drawing on Aristotle's *Politics*, Mair described the native peoples as incapable of mastering their passions and therefore psychologically unfit for a life of freedom. Spanish lawyers and theologians seized upon this claim, though evidence gathered by missionaries in the field and careful study of the Aztec, the Inca, and the Mayan civilizations were beginning to undermine it.

The Dominicans Francisco de Vitoria (ca. 1492–1546), a leading Catholic theologian and philosopher, and Bartolomé de Las Casas (1484–1566), as well as the Jesuit José de Acosta (1539–1600), the latter two with years of experience as missionaries in Latin America, argued vigorously that all mankind descended from a common human ancestor created and endowed with reason by God and that the very idea of "natural slavery" of such beings made no sense. Empirical data of a wide variety of cultural levels observed among native populations led them, in particular Acosta, to posit a theory that all humans evolve through specific stages of cultural development, the highest being conversion to Christianity. The theory gained wide acceptance by Spanish officials. Further, a papal bull of 1537 denounced as heresy the idea that Native Americans were irrational and laws adopted in 1542 significantly improved their lot.[138] Europe's political diversity fostered competing ideas, which, in this case, laid the foundation for a philosophically grounded system of human rights for all persons.

Spain became the dominant naval power in the Pacific, especially after the founding of Manila in 1571.[139] During the late sixteenth and early seventeenth centuries, hundreds of thousands of pounds of silver flowed yearly into the gigantic Chinese economy from mines in Japan and South America (transshipped either via Manila or European cities).[140] Most important was Potosí (today in southwestern Bolivia), which quickly developed into one of the world's biggest cities despite its elevation of 13,420 feet.[141] Merchants exchanged the bullion for a profusion of silk, spices, porcelain, and other luxury goods.

Chinese demand for silver drove global trade and European world exploration. Some scholars argue further that silver imports to China made profitable the establishment of plantations in the New World. In short, without the voracious Chinese economy, they claim, Europe would have continued to stagnate as it had throughout the Middle Ages.[142] It seems just as likely that massive imports of silver helped China avoid an economic slump in the early 1500s and that a decline in silver imports in part brought down the Ming Dynasty in 1644.[143] The Europeans' discovery of the New World, their mercantile dynamism, business acumen, and extraordinary innovativeness also made possible the emergence of a world economy in the sixteenth century. Moreover, by far the biggest beneficiary of the exploitative mining of New World silver—Spain—remained relatively underdeveloped, while economic and industrial innovation surged forward in Northern Europe. China persisted as the world's single biggest economy, but the global trading system centered on Europe (see Chapter 9).

Military and political struggles among the European states now spilled across the globe. By 1600, only Antarctica and Australia (first sighted in 1606) were unknown to them and avoided becoming their battleground. Even the seas witnessed continual fighting among these powers, as the weaker and poorer preyed on the ships of the current victor.[144]

The rising star, Holland, reached the East Indies in 1595 and within a few decades established strong positions in the Indonesian archipelago, Ceylon, Formosa, and on the Indian coast, driving out many European competitors. The most efficient world traders, with a government controlled by merchants, the Dutch soon dominated the commerce in precious Asian commodities. Their United East India Company, founded in 1602, was the world's first publicly traded, limited-liability, multinational firm.[145] Like a sovereign state, the company had the right to field military forces, declare war, conclude treaties, establish settlements, and construct fortresses.[146] It helped Dutch commercial development that its government supported but did not interfere with the country's private business interests, unlike the Portuguese and Spanish governments.[147] The company often used brutal methods—including the massacre of natives—to seize control of the Asian spice trade. Especially important was Dutch control over the Moluccan Islands, and in particular, the ten tiny Banda Islands, the sole producers in the world of cloves, nutmeg, and mace. Naturally, Holland's European rivals sought to break its hold on them.

England's first ships entered the Indian Ocean in 1591, and like the Dutch they quickly took over many Portuguese trading posts.[148] Major confrontation with the Dutch in the Banda Islands almost led to war, until both countries signed a treaty of economic cooperation in Asia in 1619.[149] Further wars with England and with France gradually sapped the power of the Dutch Republic, but for most of the seventeenth century, its "Golden Age," Holland dominated world trade.

Thwarted in Indonesia, the English oriented their trading efforts toward India and America. They negotiated outposts and settlements along the Indian coastline beginning in 1612 but did not establish any formal administrative control beyond these small confines until well into the 1700s. In the early 1600s, English merchants with government backing established several profitable colonies on Caribbean Islands devoted to the production of sugar and dependent on enslaved African labor. Colonies in North America and fur-trading operations in what would become Canada also increased the wealth of enterprising Englishmen, if not always the home country itself. A series of wars, fought largely over colonial possessions and the control of overseas trade, pitted England against Spain, then Holland, and finally France. The English emerged victorious from each conflict, gaining huge territorial advantages especially from the Seven Years' War (1756–63) in North America, the Caribbean, and India.[150] The French conquest of Holland in 1795 allowed the British to seize valuable Dutch colonies, including Malacca, Padang (Sumatra), and the Cape Colony. By this point, Great Britain was the world's preeminent colonial power, as it would remain for well over a century.[151] Its mariners also continued world exploration, for example James Cook (1728–79), the first European to encounter Australia and the Hawaiian Islands, to circumnavigate New Zealand, and to cross the Antarctic Circle.

Among the concessions granted by Spain as a result of the War of the Spanish Succession (1701–14) was the *asiento*, or the right to import slaves to Spanish America. English merchant-shippers played a key role in the slave trade, transporting as many as 3.5 million African slaves to the Americas, or one-third of the total, until Parliament abolished the practice in 1807.[152]

For centuries, Muslim conquerors and traders had captured or sold millions of slaves from western, Saharan, and eastern Africa.[153] They were set to work in domestic service, agriculture, and mineral extraction, as well as in higher callings like the military and civil service in Muslim lands, and in the non-Muslim kingdoms of Uganda, Benin, and Dahomey. Slaves were woven into the fabric of these societies.[154]

European merchants, whose own societies prohibited the institution of slavery, created a unique, highly innovative, extraordinarily profitable, but also radically dehumanizing slave-driving system.[155] The main use of slave labor was on plantations devoted to the cultivation and processing of sugar, cotton, and tobacco. Sugar was the first valuable American commodity. Columbus introduced sugarcane to the New World on his second voyage.[156] Sugar mills sprouted up by the dozen throughout the Caribbean basin within a few decades. As the native populations declined, slaves were imported from Africa.[157] Beginning on islands in the eastern Atlantic Ocean, the plantation system reached its apogee of utility and barbarity in the Caribbean. Of the 10 or so million Africans who survived the Atlantic crossing to the New World from 1500 to 1900, roughly 4 million ended up in the Caribbean and four more million in Brazil and Guiana. Poor conditions for enslaved laborers in the Caribbean region led to exceptionally high levels of mortality.[158]

The scholarly debate about whether capital accumulated from the Caribbean slave-based plantation system made possible the Industrial Revolution can be left aside until Chapter 11. For now, suffice it to say that Europeans opened up sea passages across all the oceans, created a truly global economy, developed relatively efficient means of extracting fabulous wealth from previously impoverished lands, and introduced a few new, and astonishingly popular, products and commodities to the wider world, including tobacco, coffee, and cocoa (see Chapter 9).

These new products were part of the so-called Columbian Exchange of plants and animals between the New and Old Worlds.[159] Often overlooked in discussions of this issue, however, are the immense contributions going from Europe to the Americas. Of course, New World products enormously enhanced nutrition in Europe and beyond. It suffices to mention potatoes, corn, beans, peppers, peanuts, tomatoes, cashews, pineapples, squash, and turkeys. The potato in particular, which can grow well in poor soils and provides the highest caloric output per acre of any staple, as well as several vitamins and minerals necessary for human health, slowly became a mainstay of the European diet and in the short term probably added to Europe's advantages vis-à-vis Asia.[160] Rubber, which is native to South America, proved an invaluable industrial product.

The range of natural additions flowing in the other direction was far greater. One can start with domestic livestock, including cattle, horses, swine, chickens, goats, and sheep. Then there were the world's two most valuable insects, whose handiwork man harvests, the bee and the silkworm. The list of comestible plants is at least twice as long as the American contribution. It included all the staple grains aside from corn; almonds and walnuts; apples, bananas, peaches, pears, and citrus fruits; beets, cabbage, carrots, lettuce, and peas; and coffee and tea. Of plants yielding industrial products, one can name flax and hemp. (Though cotton is native to both hemispheres, sophisticated cotton textile production developed first in India.)[161]

The astonishing aspect of this story is how one small and recently backward region of the world—Europe—brought all these products, peoples, countries, and continents together, bound them into one worldwide marketplace, one interconnected network of port cities—Quebec, New Orleans, Halifax, Boston, New York, Williamsburg, Savannah, Charleston, Kingston, Havana, Lima, Buenos Aires, Cape Town, Bombay, Madras, Calcutta, Batavia, and Manila, among many others—all dominated by the West.[162]

Other civilizations of the world, especially China, Korea, Japan, the Ottoman Empire, and Mughal and Maratha India, possessed the material resources, entrepreneurial energy, technological attainments, and military prowess to have explored the globe first or at least to challenge the Europeans on the high seas. Yet none, aside from the Ottomans in the Indian Ocean, ever attempted.[163] The Ottoman Empire remained a powerful force in the eastern Mediterranean until the late 1600s.[164] The other great Eurasian civilizations, apparently content to cultivate their own territory and immediate environs, never ventured into the broader oceanic realms and gradually declined technologically and militarily. Meanwhile, the major European maritime powers went from strength to strength.

By the late 1600s, France, England, and Holland all funded large, well-equipped navies. France's Royal Academy of Science, founded in 1666, was intended in large part to promote naval progress through the consolidation of advances in cartography, chemistry, and engineering. By 1690, Louis XIV's navy boasted 100,000 sailors and 9,000 cannon. Early in the next century, 14 two-decker British ships carried 74 guns apiece, part of the biggest, most effective, most efficiently funded, and best equipped and staffed navy in the world.[165] Following the Seven Years' War, Britain and China were the two greatest powers of the age—one outward reaching, the other inward looking. Whereas the Chinese Empire constituted a single, grand, and ancient realm, however, Britain was only one of a half-dozen dynamic and expansive European powers. By 1775, the Europeans—if one includes Russia, which conquered most of Siberia between 1581 and 1661—controlled one-third of the earth's land surface and dominated all its oceans.[166]

* * *

One key feature of Western civilization by this period was the sociability of Europeans at all social levels. They simply exchanged ideas, traveled, shared inspirations, conversed widely, worked together, and forged collaborative bonds and institutions far more than peoples in other cultures. Francisco Pizarro, who overthrew the Inca Empire, had consulted with Hernán Cortés, the conqueror of Mexico, before his second expedition to Peru. Cortés later advised Charles V in his campaign against Algiers in 1541. Magellan had fought under Albuquerque in the siege of Malacca—before discovering and claiming the Philippines for Spain. Cooperation, consultation, coordination, and comparing methods thus alternated with competition, but all such cases inspired and spread the fruits of innovation.[167]

The culture of cooperation and competition infused every social and political element of European society. Scholars and sailors, merchants and mercenaries, travelers and tradesmen all moved relatively easily from state to state, pursuing monetary gain, searching for masters to teach them the mysteries of their craft, fleeing religious persecution, or pursuing enticements from enterprising statesmen. Nearly every people of Europe contributed to the general advancement of knowledge, learning, science, and invention. The Dutch dominated cartography and lens crafting, the Portuguese spearheaded open-sea navigation, and the Italians were the premier early bankers and financial innovators. The greatest contribution of the Germans, surely, was printing. No other single breakthrough so radically transformed the world of learning and information—as well as of practice and action. The mass production of maps, geographical atlases, and travel accounts, for example, helped transform the European urge to travel into the Age of Discovery. Printing in fact brought on advances in nearly every sphere of life in the Western world.

QUESTIONS FOR REFLECTION

What legal rights did charters of liberty give to towns?

What impact did the Crusades have on Europe?

How did early travelers from Islamic countries differ from those from Europe?

How did the rise and fall of the Mongol Empire impact the Eurasian economy?

Why did slavery develop in European colonies?

Explain what is meant by the sociability of Europeans in the early modern period.

Chapter 6 Chronology

3000 B.C.:	Scribes first begin to use symbols to represent sounds (cuneiform)
~1500:	Proto-Caananite alphabetic writing emerges
1000:	Papyrus usage spreads throughout eastern Mediterranean
1031 A.D.:	University of Córdoba library destroyed, along with its 400,000 volumes
1100:	Paper introduced to Europe through Sicily and Spain
1300:	Woodblock printing spreads across Europe
1400:	Paper succeeds as dominant writing material in Europe
1450s:	Johannes Gutenberg invents printing press and prints Bible
1460:	First vernacular version of Bible printed in German
1481:	Vatican library houses 4,500 titles, many of them extremely rare codices
1501:	260 towns in 17 countries hold 1,120 print shops
1530:	Technical writing becomes common
1537:	King Francis I decrees royal library should receive copy of every book printed in France
1539:	New World's first book produced in Mexico City
1550–59:	First compilation of several travel stories printed in Italy
Early seventeenth century:	Royal Library of France rivals earlier Alexandria and Córdoba
1729:	Early printing press in Muslim world opened but does not last

6

Explosion of the printed word

Until the advent of printing, a single book could cost more than a laborer's wages for a year or, in a documented case occurring in 1074, could fetch the price of an entire vineyard.[1] Medieval university professors "read" their subjects, meaning they literally read texts aloud to students who could not afford to own them. Books in general were rare. University libraries possessed relatively few and usually bound them with chains to walls, shelves, or tables, or kept them in special coffers under lock and key. Borrowing a book often required leaving collateral of equal value.[2] Even so, monasteries not infrequently threatened with excommunication any person who failed to return a book. As late as the early 1600s, the rules of the Bodleian Library at Oxford University demanded a pledge to handle the books carefully and to report misuse by other patrons.[3] Failure to return any volume entailed a fine double its worth.[4] In today's marketplace, such a fine would be astronomical. In 2004, a fourteenth-century East Anglian psalter sold for £1.7 million.[5]

Around the mid-fifteenth century, however, books became easier to reproduce. Instead of thousands per year in Europe, mechanical devices were soon manufacturing millions.[6] The prices consequently fell. Over the following centuries, output and price continued to move in inverse relationship. Nowadays, presses around the world spew out some 10 billion books every year—all thanks to the labors of a south-German craftsman with entrepreneurial talent and ambition.[7] Of course, his invention did not emerge from thin air, as this chapter will show.

Icon, token, symbol

Language is the *sine qua non* of humanity. When our ancestors began to communicate with words, they became human. For many tens of thousands of years, man conversed and stored up information almost exclusively with speech and memory. The stories they told could fill volumes, but no volumes existed. Elders, shamans, and priests initiated and trained apprentices. Yet an entire culture could be lost through one tragic misfortune. In fact, of the earliest cultures almost nothing remains today. The first obvious representations, perhaps symbolic, of things that humans fixed materially are stupendously beautiful cave paintings at Chauvet in southern France, created some 32,000 years ago.[8] Beginning 24,000 years later, humans in the Middle East fashioned clay tokens with signs or symbols.[9] None of these artifacts represents a means of sustained communication. None permitted people to transmit complex messages. They were generally as vague as Romantic program music and no more able to convey precise meaning than Mussorgsky's *Pictures at an Exhibition* (1874) could really suggest visiting an art gallery to a listener who knew nothing of the composer's intention.

Then over 5,000 years ago, a system of writing began to emerge.[10] Its cradle was in Mesopotamia, between the Tigris and Euphrates Rivers. Sumerian priests and scribes kept a reckoning of valuable objects, accounts, and religious sacrifices by inscribing marks on clay tablets. Or as one scholar has asserted, "Writing was devised, purely and simply, as a solution to an account-technical problem."[11] At some point, the symbolic marks took on a standard wedge shape. In around 3000 B.C., in Jemdet Nasr, not far from the modern city of Baghdad, the symbols began to represent linguistically meaningful sounds. One mark could thus denote both an object and a monosyllabic word. Unmoored from its pictographic origins, cuneiform blended together words, syllables, meanings, and sounds. The scribes now had the means to record tales, feats, and speculation, yet none did—or at least, nothing of the sort remains. At the turn of the third millennium, few still spoke Sumerian. The new dominant people in the region, the Semitic Akkadians, adopted its writing system. Others, in particular the Assyrians, followed.[12]

The story of ancient Egyptian, the world's other oldest written language, was similar. It emerged around the same time as Sumerian and developed a more obviously pictographic style.[13] The hieroglyphs also came to stand for sounds, syllables, and words. A parallel cursive form also emerged. These scripts were extraordinary complex. Since Egyptian scribes wrote on stone, instead of small clay tablets, the scope of their compositions was often far greater than in Mesopotamia. Even so, only the narrowest elite, a tiny fraction of the elite, mastered it. The same can be said of the Chinese pictographic script, which developed in the Shang period, after 1500 B.C.[14]

A simpler form of writing was fully developed around 1000 B.C. in the Middle East. It apparently derived from a much earlier set of Egyptian hieroglyphs, which stood for consonants but were not typically used to form words. By an unknown process of transmission, the concept of letters passed down to Phoenicia.[15] The Phoenicians, a Semitic people who dominated trade and shipping in the eastern Mediterranean, apparently devised the first alphabet. It comprised 22 letters, one per consonant, with no vowels. Unlike written language, which emerged independently in Mesopotamia and Central America (in the 200s B.C.), but possibly also in Egypt and China, the alphabet appeared only this one time. All other alphabets stem from it. The Greek alphabet—named after its first two letters, alpha and beta—added vowels, an important element in Indo-European languages.[16]

Alphabets made writing vastly easier. The tiny Ancient Greek civilization accumulated a body of scientific, philosophical, and literary writings at the time of its flourishing to rival, and probably to surpass, in range and depth if not in absolute quantity, all the vast output of Ancient China but with a population more than ten times smaller.[17] It also transmitted much of ancient Near Eastern literature, learning, wisdom, and lore that otherwise might have been lost, a vitally important contribution to civilization. Perhaps its relatively straightforward and uncomplicated writing system made all this possible.

Papyrus, scroll, codex

The book is one of the great inventions of mankind. It stores nearly everything we know of the world, of the past, of our hopes and dreams as humanity. Yet the great stories, epics, poems, lore, and professions of faith that have come down to us from ancient times were originally written on clay tablets or stone. While each method marked a radical breakthrough in information storage, neither readily facilitated communications or the dissemination of knowledge.

The first portable writing material was made from a grass-like plant that grew abundantly in the Nile delta.[18] Ancient Egyptians used *Cyperus papyrus*, a member of the sedge family, to make boats, sandals, rope, mats, and other practical items. As early as 5,000 years ago, artisans found that the plant would also yield a kind of paper. First they sliced the plant stem's white pith into thin strips, laid them in a row, slightly overlapping, on a piece of cloth, and overlaid more strips at right angles on the first layer. Then, covered by a second sheet of cloth, the strips would undergo heavy pressure until dry. A natural adhesive, inherent to the plant, would bind the strips into sheets, which were glued edge to edge to form rolls.

Papyrus for writing spread throughout the eastern Mediterranean region from around the start of the first millennium B.C. The Greeks adopted it as early as the sixth century. The written culture of Hellenistic civilization, spread in the wake of Alexander's conquests from Persia to Alexandria to Rome, was penned on millions of papyrus scrolls. As late as the eleventh-century A.D., papyrus was still in use in Sicily. Many works of classical antiquity and the early Christian centuries survive on papyrus.[19]

A second lightweight writing material, parchment, was fashioned by ancient Egyptians from dried animal skin as early as 2500 B.C.[20] It also spread widely across the Middle East and the Hellenistic world. Nearly all of the earliest extant Old Testament manuscripts have come down to us on parchment. During the second-century B.C., Greek artisans in eastern Anatolia developed much thinner, more refined parchment. This material is still called "pergamon" (spelled variously) in many languages after the Hellenistic kingdom where it first appeared. Within a few hundred years, it began to rival papyrus outside Egypt, continuing to grow finer and thinner. (The most refined material is usually called "vellum.")[21]

The use of papyrus had diminished in the Mediterranean region by the millennium, but now a new medium appeared and stole its name.[22] Chinese artisans had crafted the material from various plant fibers more than 2,000 years ago.[23] It had spread throughout the Muslim world by the millennium and then diffused into Europe via Spain and Sicily starting in the 1100s. Parchment guilds and upholders of propriety opposed paper manufacturing. In Europe, shredded and pulped rags, usually discarded undergarments, provided paper's main content. Peter the Venerable (ca. 1092–1156), an abbot of Cluny who commissioned a huge translation project of Islamic texts, decried the use of such "vile material" for the making of sacred books.[24] Nevertheless, paper was far easier, faster, and cheaper to make than vellum, and it gradually came to dominate the market.

Double-sided parchment, as well as paper, made possible another refinement. Craftsmen stacked individual sheets and bound them at one end. They then affixed them to a casing, usually also made of animal skin. After some experimentation, large sheets (quires) folded down to page size replaced piles of pages. Thus was born the "codex," or leaf book, essentially the book as we know it today.[25] Scholars debate when it first appeared. Nearly all the documents dating from ancient Egypt survive on sheets or rolls of papyrus. Books depicted in Imperial Roman art, for example, are not bound volumes, but scrolls. Yet archeological and some literary evidence indicates that papyrus and parchment codices began to have limited use in the time of Augustus Caesar (r. 27 B.C.–14 A.D.), the first Roman Emperor.

Christians, it seems, were the first to adopt the medium in large number. Codices were less expensive than papyrus rolls, could contain longer texts, and were far easier to use for reference purposes.[26] The early Christians constantly disputed with pagans and Jews on the basis of philosophical and religious texts, in particular, the Old Testament. Imagine them winding and rewinding lengthy scrolls hunting, for example, for signs bearing witness to the coming of Christ. The shift to codices would have simplified these efforts enormously. Codices could also be made much smaller than scrolls, to the advantage of itinerant missionaries.[27] The success of the codex followed—and perhaps helped—that of Christianity. By the time Emperor Theodosius I proclaimed Christianity as the official religion of the Roman Empire in 380, the codex had become the predominant form for books in the Roman world.

Medieval Europeans improved writing and codices in two fundamental ways. First, monks illuminated thousands of ancient and revered texts with lovely illustrations and ornamentation.[28] A small number of illuminated manuscripts descend from antiquity, but the vast majority has been handed down from the medieval period when monks lovingly copied and recopied cherished texts.[29] They probably saved many books from destruction by illiterate warlords who presumably attributed more value to illustrated volumes than to ones filled only with text. (Alas, monks also condemned to slow obliteration those texts they failed to copy, like most works by Marcus Varro, a celebrated Roman author.) A second valuable advance concerned orthography. In ancient times, scribes had written only uppercase letters and had rarely put spaces between words. Several centuries after the birth of Christ, lowercase letters had emerged, though only for informal use and not mixed with uppercase. During the Carolingian Renaissance, a more standardized and reader-friendly script—the Caroline miniscule—appeared with capital letters used only for emphasis and words separated by spaces.[30] These formalities made documents and literary works more accessible to people unable to devote a lifetime to mastering quirky ancient forms of writing.

Libraries

Codices possessed another advantage over scrolls. The books' spines could readily display bibliographical information. Stacked flat on shelves, they were easy to store, classify, and retrieve. Catalogs in codex form also enormously simplified navigation among large collections. These features greatly facilitated the efforts of collectors and librarians, though significant libraries had previously existed.

Scribes in the ancient Near East, from at least four and one-half thousand years ago, had maintained collections of tablets, mostly administrative records.[31] By at least the thirteenth-century B.C., some documents stored in the Hittite capital Hattusa displayed colophons, like title pages. A catalog listed most titles—predominantly concerning religion—in the collection, though haphazardly. The Assyrian king Ashurbanipal (r. 668–627 B.C.) established in his capital Nineveh the world's first library in any generally understood sense. Gathered together from many sources, it contained roughly 1,500 titles, mostly of religious, mythological, magical, and linguistic-reference texts, as well as some literary and scientific works (especially dealing with medicine and astronomy). Its main purpose, it seems, was to enable the king to verify recommendations made to him by counselors expert in the study of omens and signs.

The Greeks created the first large libraries of a more clearly scholarly purpose.[32] The first significant one belonged to Aristotle (384–322 B.C.). Extraordinary in both scope and size, it apparently provided the basic layout and classification system for the world's greatest early library.[33] Founded around 300 B.C., the library of Alexandria was comprehensive and public. Any scholar could work among its roughly 500,000 papyrus rolls. They covered all of Greek learning, every practical art, and translations from many places and languages. The Ptolemaic rulers of Egypt were ruthless book collectors. They paid astronomical sums, seized books from ships docked in their harbors, and ordered scribes to copy every book available in the near Mediterranean world.[34] Librarians at Alexandria invented alphabetization in order to classify their massive collection.[35] A scholar working at the library, Callimachus, compiled a 120-volume bibliographical survey of Greek writers and their works housed at Alexandria.[36] The survey was divided and subdivided by topic and probably followed the classification scheme of the library. Scholars working at the library invented such invaluable tools as the authoritative text edition, the commentary, and the systematic grammar book.[37]

The library of Alexandria was destroyed partially in 48 B.C. and fully around 270 A.D.[38] For many centuries thereafter, few book repositories in the world could even meekly rival it. Yet literacy expanded during Hellenistic and Roman times. Many ordinary people read avidly. Wealthy Greeks and Romans often collected books. Cicero amassed a library big enough to require permanent staff. Many well-to-do Romans hoarded books merely for the status they conferred. The Stoic philosopher Seneca (4 B.C.–65 A.D.) complained of personal libraries stuffed to the ceiling with choice scrolls, like bathrooms outfitted with lavish accessories. Rome's first public library, divided into Greek and Latin sections, was built soon after Caesar's assassination in 44 B.C. Others followed, three by Augustus' death in 14 A.D., all apparently with spacious reading rooms. The largest of all was the library of the Forum of Trajan, built in 112–113 A.D, though even it had only around 20,000 papyrus rolls.[39] Libraries were many but relatively small—for example, in public baths.[40] Subsequent Roman emperors bestowed sumptuous libraries on provincial capitals throughout the empire. Yet none held especially large collections. The decline and fall of Rome naturally entailed the neglect and abandonment of most Roman libraries.[41]

The Byzantine and Islamic successors to Rome greatly outshone the mother city in this regard. The Imperial library of Constantinople boasted 120,000 volumes by the fifth century, though it was apparently badly damaged by a fire in 471. Private libraries also flourished.[42] The construction of paper mills in Baghdad starting in 794 dramatically lowered the cost of books. The main library at Baghdad, with vast collections of Greek, Indian, Egyptian, and Persian literature and scholarship translated into Arabic, served as a model for the entire Islamic world.[43] Baghdad itself boasted dozens of smaller collections, fed by over 100 booksellers in 891. Scholars compiled glossaries and dictionaries for all the main branches of learning. Masters certified scribes as competent to transcribe specific books. A century later, the Umayyad caliph al-Hakam II (r. 961–76) founded in Córdoba what would become the first serious rival to Alexandria. It ultimately contained some 400,000 volumes, all carefully inscribed with bibliographical data and catalogued in 44 volumes. The city also boasted the greatest book market in the Western world in the late 900s. This preeminence waned, however, when doctrinaire interpretations of Quranic teachings swept across North Africa and the Middle East after rise of the Fatimid Caliphate in 909. Books were burnt in many places. In 1031, fundamentalist insurgents toppled the Andalusian Umayyad dynasty. By some accounts, they destroyed the great library of Córdoba. Christian warriors began their reconquest from the north, seizing Toledo in 1085. Córdoba itself fell in 1236. The Mongols sacked Baghdad in 1258, destroying most of its libraries in 1 week.

Other world libraries require a brief mention. Although Indian civilization dates into the farthest antiquity, no evidence supports the existence of libraries in ancient times.[44] The priestly class closely guarded religious lore and passed it down orally. Buddhism and Jainism, which both emerged in the sixth-century B.C. in opposition to Hinduism, developed written culture. The Buddhist center of learning at Nalanda in the far northeast attracted scholars and religious seekers from as far as China. Its extensive collections included works of secular learning. Unfortunately, Muslim conquerors destroyed them around 1200. Jain monasteries instituted manuscript collections beginning in the late 700s in order to protect and preserve sacred texts, though not to make them available to readers. In subsequent centuries, Jain merchants and kings established a plethora of libraries devoted mostly though not solely to religious works.[45] A few royal libraries contained a much wider range of works. Although hundreds of thousands of manuscripts were preserved until modern times, they remained scattered and did not contribute to a flourishing of scholarship and science.

The same cannot be said of China. Over the centuries, scholars and scribes produced vast quantities of written matter. Emperors and government officials commissioned the gathering of these writings into extravagant compilations, often running to hundreds or (in later years) many thousands of volumes, and deposited them in official libraries. Despite bouts of autocratic intolerance—Emperor Qin Shi Huang (r. 221–210 B.C.) ordered the obliteration of nearly every book then existing—and frequent destruction during civil wars, fires, and internal strife, book production and collecting continued century by century. The core works were the Confucian classics, the ideological foundation of the emperors' authority. Thus, each time a central collection perished, officials spared no expense to recopy as much as possible from private libraries. Since every member of the Confucian elite was expected to be a scholar, private collections were numerous. One scholar counted 500 private libraries, of both individual collectors and academies, during the Qing.[46] Yet private collectors typically refused to grant access to their books, following the old adage "To loan a book is unfilial."[47]

The Imperial government maintained official collections both in the capital and throughout the country.[48] Beginning with the Yongle Emperor (r. 1403–22), the central government produced numerous "palace editions" of the Confucian classics, the writings of neo-Confucian philosophers, and other canonical texts and sent them free of charge to every school in the country. These books often constituted a large proportion of the schools' libraries. The main collection of the Tang Dynasty comprised more than 80,000 volumes (but only roughly 4,000 titles) by the mid-600s. An Imperial library began to emerge around this time.[49] Woodblock printing flourished during the Song Dynasty. The output of books must have been astronomical, since a single printer could produce 1,000 pages daily. Yet repeated catastrophes, including destruction and plunder during the Jurchen and Mongol conquests, kept the Imperial library's collection from growing. At its highest point during the Song, in 1220, the library reached only 60,000 volumes. In other words, it seems that only libraries in the Mediterranean world attained any sustained, massive scale. And only in Europe did such efforts reach a tipping point beyond which accumulation built upon accumulation.

Reaching that point was long and arduous. Early Christian thinkers maintained serious reference libraries in Alexandria, Jerusalem, and Caesarea, the latter holding some 30,000 volumes into the 300s and that at Jerusalem surviving till 618.[50] When Muslims conquered the entire region a few decades later, the centers of Christian learning shifted to Byzantium and Europe.

Nearly all European monasteries maintained libraries. In fact, without the copying and recopying by monks of ancient texts countless numbers would have perished. The Rule of St Benedict played a key role in this work by prescribing the pursuit of knowledge and the preservation of books.[51] As one monk wrote in 1170, "A monastery without a library is like a castle without an armory."[52] Individual scholars, secular lords, and eventually professionals and merchants also gathered book collections. Yet no single collection anywhere in Europe exceeded 1,000 volumes. By the early Renaissance, scholars were scouring the continent for the most accurate texts of works by classic authors. Private libraries, for example those of Petrarch (1304–74) and Cosimo de' Medici (1389–1464), grew to substantial proportions.[53] Cosimo placed the humanist intellectual Tommaso Parentucelli (1398–1455) in charge of his public collection. As Pope Nicholas V, Parentucelli founded the Vatican library. By 1481, it housed around 3,500 titles and was by far the best-endowed library of Europe.[54] If not for a quantum breakthrough, the libraries of Alexandria and Córdoba might never have been matched.

The printing revolution

The ancient Egyptians had learned to carve images and symbols into wooden blocks and to stamp them on clay. The Han Chinese, some 2,000 years later, contrived to spread ink on carved blocks or on engraved-metal plates and to stamp text and images on silk. In the late 900s, Chinese printers used woodblocks to print the entire Buddhist canon on paper (in 130,000 pages).[55]

A century later, a Chinese artisan learned to craft individual characters from clay. He could arrange and rearrange them for imprinting texts. This was movable type, a huge step forward technologically.[56] Korean printers designed metal type and produced a 50-volume compendium in 1234. Yet neither system saved labor, since preparing the type for thousands of individual characters took immense efforts. Emperor Sejong (r. 1418–50) presided over the alphabetization of the Korean language, theoretically making possible a printing revolution.[57] Yet he prohibited the mass production of books and the commercialization of book printing. Even without mechanical printing, however, it seems that the Chinese book market remained far more developed than Europe's.[58]

Tin-covered wood-block printing emerged in the Islamic world around the ninth or tenth century and enabled itinerant peddlers to sell amulets decorated with supposedly handwritten Quranic inscriptions. Called "tarsh," this printing method remained on the margins of society but may have been used to manufacture tarot cards, among the first printed objects to appear in Europe.[59] It may also have introduced Europeans to wood-block printing, which spread quickly in Europe after 1300 for the production of pamphlets, calendars, and other printed matter.[60]

By the mid-1400s, all the necessary elements were in place for a quantum transformation of printing in Europe.[61] Paper was relatively cheap, widespread, and of the perfect weight and texture. Chinese paper, by contrast, was too fine to suffer the pressure of heavy printing equipment. All European languages are alphabetical. Fashioning movable type made practical sense for two dozen letters but not for many thousands of complex Chinese characters, at least in those days. Lacking a taste for wine and olives, the Asians had not devised screw-based presses. That technology had existed in Europe for thousands of years. Finally, printing efficiently turned out to require highly sophisticated technical skills, lots of experimentation with materials and techniques, and big infusions of capital. In other words, its inventor had to be simultaneously a skilled craftsman, a dogged scientist, and an entrepreneur of talent. Such a man grew up in Mainz at the convergence of the rivers Main and Rhine.

The father of Johannes Gutenberg (ca. 1398–1468) was a well-to-do merchant. He owned a farm, interest income from an annuity paid by the city, and a country estate by marriage. He was also a patrician of the town.[62] Yet Mainz itself was in economic distress and was prone to bouts of civil unrest during this period with patricians and guildsmen often at each other's throats.[63]

Gutenberg himself was a goldsmith but not prosperous. He inherited no properties. His annuities were at risk. Yet he was tremendously ambitious. In 1434 he relocated to Strasbourg, a more vibrant and affluent city of 25,000 one hundred miles south.[64] There he apparently conceived the idea of moveable-type printing and worked secretly for several years to achieve a series of technical breakthroughs.[65] One was a letter punch, made of hard metal, used to strike matrices in softer metal. Each matrix was set in a handheld mold into which molten metal was poured. This required a special alloy, combining lead with one-quarter antimony and roughly 15 percent tin. The resultant mix—Gutenberg's own invention—flowed well, solidified quickly, and held sharp, hard edges. When cooled, the halves of the mold were separated, and a silver rectangle, an inch and a half long, fell out. At one end, a letter or symbol protruded; at the other, the base. Each piece of type fit next to another in lines, then were stacked by lines in a frame to create an entire page.

As Gutenberg discovered, however, casting letters of different sizes and fitting the type and spacing properly in the lines was an extremely touchy job. Though the

German alphabet had only 30 letters, when one added capitals, punctuation marks, spaces, ligatures, and other variations, each typeface required some 300 different punches. Of course, that was nothing compared to tens of thousands for the Chinese characters.

There were many other details he had to attend to. Merely inking the type and pressing it manually against a sheet of paper did not make a sharp impression. The operation required a heavy mechanical press, one that applied uniform pressure across an entire page. And what ink should Gutenberg use?[66] Black by itself would not do. He also needed at the very least blue and red in order to compete with the scribes. He must have experimented endlessly with various mixes and textures of rare and common substances to find inks that would take just right without smudging or running. An oil-based ink produced the best results. It helped also to dampen the paper carefully and uniformly before imprinting it. Then of course he had to dry each sheet separately. These were just some of the problems Gutenberg needed to resolve.

As the Hundred Years' War threatened to spill over into Strasbourg in 1444, Gutenberg disappeared from historical view, perhaps settling in Frankfurt. Traces of his existence resurfaced in Mainz in 1448. His sister had died, making the ancestral Gutenberg house available to him.[67] With a loan of 800 gulden (later doubled) from a Strasbourg businessman named Johann Fust and a half-dozen assistants, he established a workshop. In 1450, they ran off a brief Latin grammar book by Aelius Donatus called the *Ars Grammatica*. Printed in the standard heavy Gothic lettering, it sold very well. In fact, over the next several years it came out in at least 24 editions and thousands of copies. They may also have published a 750-line German poem the *Sybelline Prophecies* that used the mythological prophetess Sybil to criticize papal corruption. When Constantinople fell to the Turks in 1453, the pope authorized issuing letters of indulgence to raise money for a defense of Cyprus. Gutenberg's shop printed hundreds of them.[68] Other small jobs followed. Yet the revolutionary of printing envisioned bigger undertakings.

The monks who copied most of Europe's Bibles, despite their best efforts and even with the greatest devotion, could not avoid making little mistakes. Sometimes they changed the meaning of passages with a slip of the quill. In others, they altered the text to fit what they believed was correct.[69] Thus, humanistic theologians and clergymen advocated providing all monks and priests with access to well-translated and edited Bibles.[70]

Gutenberg set up a second workshop, found a Latin Bible to copy, letter for letter, and designed a new typeface. The project required thousands of calfskins. Punch operators turned out tens of thousands of pieces of type. Teams of printers set up four separate presses. Each compositor worked with three different frames to avoid idling. Gutenberg soon added two more presses. Quantity was important, but quality more so. He wanted to make his Bible not just as accurate as the best in Europe but also more beautiful. How else would he entice buyers for a machine-produced sacred book? For one thing, he justified the right margin, something beyond the capacity of scribes. The new Bible, printed in 2 columns and 42 lines per page, yielded 1,282 pages with 3 million characters in 2 volumes. (Illuminators also added some decorative details by hand.) In roughly 2 years, his team produced some 180 copies. A single scribe in that time probably would have completed only one.

A team of roughly 20—the number of printers working in Gutenberg's shop—could have inscribed no more than 20, or one-ninth Gutenberg's actual total.[71] Of course, once the type was set, a second edition could be run off in less time still. The credit for this breakthrough remains Gutenberg's, but control over its use immediately slipped from his hands.

In 1455, when the operation was about to become profitable, Fust won a lawsuit against Gutenberg for failure to pay the interest punctually on his debt. Fust received the larger of the two print shops. He also hired away several of Gutenberg's staff, including his assistant, Peter Schöffer.[72] In 1457, they published the Mainz Psalter, a beautifully printed collection of psalms, Bible passages, prayers, religious poems, and other liturgical texts. Gutenberg had invented the medium, yet Fust and Schöffer stole all the credit. In fact, they drew attention to themselves on the title page by appending the first printed colophon and the first printer's logo. They then went on to publish several more books and made a killing. After Fust died, Schöffer soared from height to height, an international publishing phenomenon until his death in 1503.[73]

Gutenberg, by contrast, took on minor jobs, sold his expertise to other printers, and tried to carry on his work, but fate kept hounding him. In 1462, amid political struggles between the pope and the archbishop of Mainz, the father of printing was driven from the city and had to settle with relatives in the countryside. Happily, he did not die in obscurity and penury like some inventive geniuses. In 1465, the archbishop of Mainz appointed him a gentleman of the court and bestowed on him a pension, a court uniform, and tax-free payments in kind (big annual gifts of grain and wine). He was set for life. Unfortunately, he enjoyed these privileges for only three more years. Of course, his name will go on as long as man walks the earth. Only scholars will remember Fust or Schöffer.

Publishing boom

Meanwhile, other members of the original Gutenberg team opened print shops. In 1458, King Charles VII sent an industrial spy to learn the technique and establish it in France. Gutenberg himself shared the mysteries of his trade with many aspirants. At first, Germans dominated the business, but it soon spread throughout Europe. In the 1470s, presses appeared in Venice, Paris, Kraków, Aalst (Flanders), and London.[74] By 1501, entrepreneurs in 260 towns across 17 European countries were operating 1,120 print shops, employing well over 10,000 printers as far west as Lisbon and as far north as Stockholm—a pan-European phenomenon (see Map 6.1). By 1480, Italy had become the center of printing in Europe. In less under 50 years, publishers had produced nearly 30,000 titles in upward of 20 million copies. Scholars later dubbed these early books—published until 31 December 1500—*incunabula*, meaning "the swaddling clothes" (the infancy) of printing. Roughly one-half of these books were religious, mostly in Latin. Nearly all the great works of Latin antiquity appeared, mostly in Italy. Books also came out in many vernacular languages, as well as in Hebrew. Between 140 and 200 million more books came out during the following century.[75]

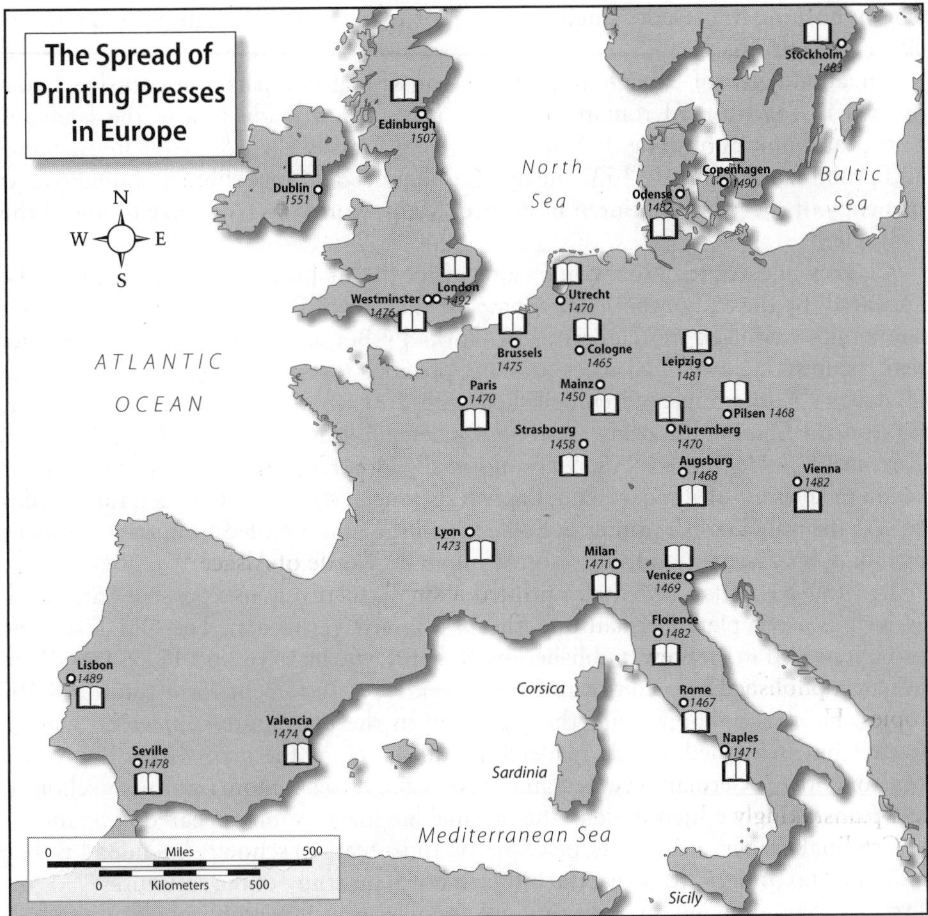

MAP 6.1 *Invented in 1450 by Johannes Gutenberg, the printing press had spread to 260 other towns throughout Europe by 1501.*

Venice had the largest concentration of print shops, numbering at least 109 according to a careful tabulation.[76] Many Greeks fleeing Constantinople after the Ottoman conquest in 1453 settled there, bringing hundreds of Greek manuscripts.[77] One enterprising scholar, Teobaldo Manucci (b. 1449), or Aldus Manutius in Latin, conceived an exciting project: to publish all the classic works of ancient Greece.[78] In 1490, he settled in Venice and began printing beautiful, technically accurate, painstakingly prepared, conveniently small, and inexpensive volumes. Seeking editorial assistance, he founded an association of lovers of Greek learning. The Aldine press also published Latin classics, for which they adopted the Caroline minuscule and added punctuation marks, such as the colon and semicolon. To keep costs down, Aldus issued press runs of 1,000 or even 1,500, instead of the more usual 200–300. By 1515, the year of his death, he had given the world a large portion of the works of 28 classic authors, including 5 volumes by Aristotle.

The publishing house continued its work for many years, though pirated editions cut into its profits.[79]

An abundance of French printers, by providing compact, inexpensive books printed in easy-to-read roman and italic types, soon made France the leader in European book publishing. It helped that King Francis I (r. 1515–47) loved books and promoted printing. In 1537, he decreed that his own royal library should receive one copy of every book printed in France. Many world libraries later followed this example.[80]

Classics and contemporary literature of all the major European languages also appeared. By the end of the 1400s, some 50 editions of Dante's *Divine Comedy* had come out—and even more editions of works by Boccaccio and Petrarch.[81] A wide readership suddenly gained access to these precious texts. In 1476, a German edition of *Aesop's Fables* appeared embellished with 200 woodcut illustrations.[82] William Caxton, the first English printer and bookseller, published Chaucer's *The Canterbury Tales* in 1477. He printed some 90 books in all, 74 in English. He, more than anyone, began the process of standardizing English spelling and grammar. In fact, for decades, he was the only English printer in England; all the others hailed from the Continent, including his assistant and successor, Wynkyn de Worde of Alsace.[83]

In 1460–61, Johann Mentelin printed a small, relatively inexpensive Latin Bible as well as a complete German one, the first in any vernacular. The Old Testament soon appeared in Hebrew, published by Italian Jews. In 1516 and 1519, Desiderius Erasmus published two editions of the Greek New Testament for a total of 3,500 copies. He was unhappy with the result, given the inaccurate sources he worked from,[84] but it reached a wide readership and served as the main Greek source for Martin Luther's German New Testament (see Chapter 7). A more rigorously scholarly and painstakingly edited Bible in the original languages soon appeared in Spain.

Cardinal Francisco Ximénez de Cisneros and a team of scholars intended for their monumental project "to revive the hitherto dormant study of the scriptures."[85] From 1502 to 1517, drawing on every original and well-translated biblical text they could lay hands on, they compiled and published the six-volume Complutensian Polyglot Bible.[86] The Old Testament consists of the original Hebrew and parallel translations into Latin (the Vulgate of St Jerome) and Greek (the early Greek Septuagint), along with an ancient Aramaic translation and its own Latin translation at the bottom. The New Testament includes the original Greek plus a parallel Latin translation. An extra volume contains various dictionaries, glossaries, and other study aids. By far the most rigorously accurate and scientifically useful Bible conceivable at the time, it was produced in only 600 copies. Far more cumbersome than the Erasmus edition, it had consequently a far smaller impact except among scholars: Erasmus himself revised his own version using the Complutensian Polyglot.

Readers hungered for the great texts of Christianity beyond the Bible. St Augustine's *City of God* came out in 19 editions before 1500.[87] The first edition (1467), published near Rome, was a masterpiece of early printing. The reading interests of Christian seekers included contemporary writing as well. The best-selling book by far during the infancy of printing was a popular religious devotional work by the mystic Thomas à Kempis called *De imitatione Christi* (The Imitation of Christ). Between 1471 and 1500, it ran through 99 editions.[88]

Printing also made it possible to add technical and artistic illustrations. According to one scholar, some one-third of all books published before 1500 were illustrated.[89] The impact of making thousands of images widely available is not to be underestimated. Ptolemy's *Geographia*, an atlas of the world known to the ancient Romans, including most of Eurasia and north Africa plotted on gridlines, was printed several times from 1477.[90] Its maps and analytical apparatus helped cartographers to think systematically about geographical representation. Columbus apparently preferred the *Imago mundi* (1460), by Pierre d'Ailly, which he studied carefully and took with him on his journey across the Atlantic.[91] Albrecht Dürer published a number of books of illustrations, mostly religious. He also authored theoretical works, on geometry, fortifications, and the artistic representation of the human body.[92] Art and science thus influenced each other.

Illustration proved invaluable for scientific books and technical manuals.[93] Semipopular illustrated encyclopedias summarizing and systematizing scientific, geographic, and theological knowledge appeared in both Latin and vernacular languages across Europe. Among important early specialized works were *De Triangulis omnimodus* (1464), a textbook on trigonometry by Johannes Müller von Königsberg; *De re militari* (1472), a treatise on military affairs by Roberto Valturio; a manual on Gothic construction by a late fifteenth-century German master mason named Lorenz Lechler; and Georgius Agricola's *De re metallica* (1501), the first book devoted to mineralogy.[94] Technical writing came forth in torrents after around 1530 on every conceivable subject, from music and dance to agriculture and accounting. The enormous benefit Europeans received was not solely the prodigious expansion of learning. The publishing boom also established connections between the artisans' world and that of high culture. Craftsmen, men of the law, scholars, intellectuals, and aristocrats all came together—figuratively—over many of the same books.

Europeans displayed an insatiable appetite for the exotic and the novel. Travel literature, more than any other genre, catered to this desire.[95] Among the most copied in manuscript was John Mandeville's *Voyage d'Outre-mer* (1350). Despite heavy plagiarism and whopping inaccuracies, it survives in 300 manuscripts and 90 editions printed from 1475 to 1600. The second half of the sixteenth century witnessed a proliferation of more reliable, first-hand travel accounts. Among the most popular was by a German soldier, Hans Staden, who had visited Brazil. His *True Story and Description of a Country of Wild, Naked, Grim, Man-eating People in the New World, America* ran through four editions in 1 year (1557). The reading public went on to devour dozens more editions in diverse translations. Around the same time, an Italian named Giambattista Ramusio hit upon a clever idea: the publication of tales by a variety of travelers. His *Raccolta delle Navigationi e Viaggi* (3 volumes; 1550–59) brought knowledge of Marco Polo's journeys, among others, to a wide readership. The books' success inspired many others to compile similar works—for example, Theodore de Bry's multivolume *The Great Travels*, which he published in Latin and German beginning in 1590.

Richard Hakluyt (ca. 1552–1616) merits a special mention.[96] An ordained priest and personal secretary to English statesmen, his passion was promoting the English colonization of America. He intended his first book, *Divers Voyages* (1582), to demonstrate that the English deserved glory for their early explorations but needed encouragement to continue in the wake of other adventurers. He presented his next tome (1584) to Elizabeth I to gain her support for English colonization in Virginia. Once that operation began, after her death, he continued to promote official sponsorship. Meantime, he edited and published numerous travel narratives, most famously his *The Principal Nauigations, Voiages, Traffiques and Discoueries of the English Nation* (1598–1600). He carefully analyzed the original texts and, in his later years, rejected those whose veracity he could not reasonably verify. He also encouraged others to publish many travel narratives, including an English translation of *The History and Description of Africa* by Leo Africanus.

One final genre of publication to note is historical. In these decades, scholars compiled and printed enormous collections of historical documents in all the lands of Europe. The Franciscan Peter Crabbe, who published a collection of church records in 1528, claimed he had worked in more than 500 libraries.[97] Europeans were cataloguing, preserving, and reclaiming their heritage. In part because of such efforts, and of course thanks also to the printing revolution, the history of no other civilization is so well documented. Scholars not only gathered and published historical materials but also subjected them to exhaustive critical analysis, employing the methods of philologists and jurists.

Étienne Pasquier (1529–1615), for example, rejected all legends about France. Official chronicles claimed that the founders of the French monarchy, the Franks, had descended rather circuitously from the Trojans. Pasquier demonstrated systematically that no ancient author had ever heard of the Franks. Indeed, their first historical mention dated to the fourth century. Drawing on a learned German philologist, he then showed that the Franks comprised several Germanic tribes who had settled in the Rhine Delta. In brief, Pasquier resolved "to say nothing of importance without proof."[98] Given the state of available primary sources, he accepted his inability to reach unassailable conclusions on many issues. Those who came after, he expected, would build upon his humble foundations. His main job, as he saw it, was to demolish naive suppositions and baseless assertions of chroniclers.

In the century following Gutenberg's breakthrough, printing spread to Europe's farthest extremities and to its settler colonies in the wider world. The first book came off a press in the New World in Mexico City in 1539.[99] Muscovite Russia's first printed books appeared in the 1560s, though printing developed so slowly that in the entire seventeenth century only some 500 printed titles were published, because of both low consumer demand and tight official control, which continued until the late eighteenth century.[100] In 1593, Spanish colonists in the Philippines, employing Chinese Catholics with expertise in wood-block printing, put out the first book in Southeast Asia. In 1604, Dominican friars in Manila began to print with movable type.[101] The Englishman Stephen Daye constructed and operated the first printing press in North America in Cambridge, Massachusetts, in 1638, 2 years after Harvard College (then called "New College") was founded.[102]

Strange to say, printing did not spread easily beyond Europe and its colonies. In spite of Jewish refugees publishing Hebrew books in Constantinople and Cairo in the late 1400s and early 1500s, and the Quran even appearing in Arabic in Italy by 1500, the technology stopped cold at the frontiers of the Islamic world. The Muslims had wealth, a high level of scholarship, a large output of paper, expertise in chemistry, knowledge of wine presses, and an alphabetic script, yet for some 300 years throughout the Dar al-Islam only one Muslim put mechanical printing briefly into use before it finally spread across the Middle East beginning in 1784.[103] How can one explain this resistance to change? Surely one factor was a traditional mistrust of written texts or an abiding faith in immediate, oral learning and intellectual exchange.[104] Socrates, after all, refused to write down his wisdom. Another reason was feelings of horror at errors or sloppiness that could and did creep into printed texts, especially the Quran.[105] In any event, rejecting the printing revolution doubtless stifled intellectual development, cultural renewal, religious reform, and scientific advancement. The same had to be true of East Asia, where peoples who had invented the earliest movable-type printing systems—China and Korea—failed to adopt mechanical printing presses until 400 years after its invention by Gutenberg. In fact, Westerners published the first newspapers in China and Japan in the mid-1800s.[106]

Although the European religious authorities imposed some enhanced restrictions on publishing starting in 1529 (see Chapter 7), books continued to pour out in torrents from thousands of presses across Europe. Tens of millions of printed books were already in the public domain by 1500, and their number grew exponentially, giving Europeans access to a far greater range of printed matter than any other people in history.

As the number of books increased, rulers, scholars, and religious authorities instituted more libraries to house them. The Royal Library of France had a printed catalog by 1622 listing some 6,000 titles, both manuscript and print, and subdivided by language. The library expanded greatly under Louis XIV. An important librarian of his reign, Nicolas Clément, implemented a system of classification by subject, from art to science, which remained in use until 1996. In the early 1700s, the collection held around 80,000 printed volumes and 16,000 manuscripts.[107] Finally, a European library was closing in on the holdings of ancient Alexandria and Umayyad Córdoba. Since multiple "volumes" in those early repositories presumably often comprised a single title, the Royal Library had probably already reached parity with them. Certainly by 1818, in part thanks to confiscations from religious congregations and aristocratic families, the re-christened "Bibliothèque Nationale" reached 800,000 books and manuscripts and continued to grow and grow (it now has well over 10 million volumes).[108] Never before in human history had so much learning and knowledge been stored up systematically in one place with free and relatively convenient access to all. (As early as 1720, the general public gained regular access to the collections.) Of course, all the main Western countries were also building up, historically speaking, unprecedented libraries.

Organizing information grew far easier thanks to printing. Full alphabetization, though invented in antiquity, now gradually replaced the thematic organization and cataloguing of knowledge.[109] This was especially valuable as the amount of information exploded. Also importantly, one could easily add an alphabetical index to any book, increasing public access to all branches of knowledge. In the gradual development of political participation, for example, the indexing of law books and legal digests played an important role. John Rastell and his son William compiled several indispensable legal aides, in particular the first law dictionary, *Expositiones terminorum legum Anglorum*, which went through at least 29 editions after its first publication in 1527, and *A Collection of All the Statutes (from Magna Carta to 1557)*.[110] The value of these works for the understanding and application of the law in England should not be underestimated.

Public access to general knowledge had a stupendous impact on European society, culture, and politics. For example, the rise in the confidence and sense of power that knowledge brings gave birth to a new intellectual attitude. This spirit, which one scholar has called the "style of Paris," involved not only rationalism, skepticism, empiricism, and curiosity but also sympathy toward peoples of different cultures.[111]

The French botanist Pierre Belon (1517–64) embodied this intellectual persona exquisitely.[112] Enjoying the financial and political support of influential prelates, Belon traveled with a diplomatic mission to the Levant in 1546. He undertook expeditions for 3 years, conducting painstaking observations and research into natural history, archeology, and even anthropology in Greece, Turkey, Palestine, Egypt, and the Greek islands. His investigations often astonish by their rigor and meticulousness. In order to verify ancient claims for the medicinal properties of Lemnos clay, he carefully analyzed many samples purchased in Constantinople, and then, on the island of Lemnos itself, interviewed some 600 people of every craft and rank. The term "observations"—the title of the book he published upon returning home—defined his main activity. He reported only what he had seen with his own eyes. Although he consciously sought to retrace the steps of ancient naturalists, he did not hesitate to refute any of their assertions he found baseless. Belon also displayed an admirable affinity toward people of other cultures and religions. He expressed particular admiration for Jews. He had much praise for the Turks he encountered and took exception only to their culinary traditions. The large, dense book he published in French in order to reach the widest possible audience enjoyed great popularity. Evidently many educated French people desired knowledge about even the most arcane aspects of the world beyond Christendom.

***

All of the transformations described so far were cumulative. This tendency was especially true of the invention of printing. No other single breakthrough can be as directly credited with initiating so much revolutionary change. It is fair to say that without printing none of the revolutions investigated in the following chapters could have occurred. The gathering together of all known information into readily available, all but pocket-sized instruments of transmission radically altered the very nature of culture, scholarly cooperation, and technological advancement. After the invention of the mass-produced book, the world would never be the same.

It is worth pausing to mention that every technological breakthrough, beginning with the mastery of fire, has carried with it a dark side. This is especially true of the extraordinary and unprecedented advances of Europe and the West during the past 500 years or so. In some cases, the evils have been obvious, for example, in the development of Western firepower from the gunpowder revolution to the atomic age or in the discovery of the Americas, which resulted in the death of tens of millions.

Yet even the printing revolution was not an unalloyed good.[113] Printing made possible both modern medicine and the proliferation of war-mongering journalism, child pornography, and hate-filled propaganda.

QUESTIONS FOR REFLECTION

How did writing first emerge?

In what sense was the alphabet democratic?

Where were the greatest libraries in medieval times and why?

Why did movable-type printing not take off in China?

How did printing help in the development of science and technology?

Where, beyond Europe, did printing first spread?

Chapter 7 Chronology

1209:	Albigensian crusade
1229:	Church decree bans possession of vernacular religious books
1296:	Pope Boniface VIII clashes with Philip the Fair of France
1305:	Clement V moves Papal Curia to Avignon
Early fourteenth century:	Giotto begins shift toward new style of art
1384:	John Wyclif completes first English-language translation of Bible
1410:	First excommunication of Jan Hus
1414–18:	Council of Constance
1415:	Jan Hus executed by decision of Council of Constance
1420–31:	Anti-Hussite Crusades
1447:	Nicholas V, a humanist, becomes Pope
1467:	St Augustine's *City of God* first printed
1476:	Sixtus IV establishes formal practice of indulgences
Sixteenth century:	Literacy rates begin to increase rapidly
1504:	Michelangelo sculpts *David*
1512–17:	Fifth Lateran Council
1516:	Tetzel sells indulgences near Saxony
1517:	Martin Luther begins preaching 5 *solas*, makes public 95 theses in Wittenberg
1518–25:	Estimated one-third of all books printed in Germany are by Luther
1519:	Zwingli begins preaching his reformed theology
1520:	Papal Bull orders destruction of Luther's works
1521:	Luther excommunicated
1525:	Estimated one-third of Holy Roman Empire espouses reform doctrines

1529:	Sweden switches to Lutheranism, Denmark and Norway follow
1534:	Church of England established
1535:	John Calvin flees to Switzerland
1540:	Jesuit order established
1545–63:	Council of Trent meets in three sessions
1555:	Peace of Augsburg
1560:	Scotland accepts Presbyterianism
1572:	St Bartholomew's Day massacre
1598:	Edict of Nantes

7

The Reformation

"I defy the Pope, and all his laws," bellowed William Tyndale to a learned cleric, "and if God spares my life, ere many years, I will cause a boy that driveth the plow, shall know more of the Scriptures than thou dost."[1] A literary genius who gave us dozens of ringing phrases like "the powers that be,"[2] Tyndale completed his translation of the New Testament from Greek into English in 1525, but not in England. Official persecution had driven him into a wandering exile for the rest of his life. Back home, the thousands of copies of his translation smuggled through English and Scottish ports found eager buyers. Persecuted by secular and ecclesiastical authorities, Tyndale was condemned as a heretic and executed in 1536, his dead body incinerated publicly.[3]

Why this extreme reaction to the translation of the Bible? Was not England a Christian country, and did not the church authorities encourage the spreading of the faith? In reality, they considered "a little knowledge" to be a dangerous thing. Ordinary people, unschooled in the profound mysteries of Christian doctrine, might make erroneous interpretations. They needed the clergy to guide them in the faith and keep them on the straight path to salvation. Individuals were considered incapable of interpreting Scripture for themselves and therefore of finding salvation directly.[4] The complete rejection of this worldview is the simplest way of characterizing the Reformation.

The Renaissance

The discovery, translation, and publication of hundreds of texts by Aristotle, Plato, and Ptolemy, as well as by such brilliant Islamic scholars as Averroes and Avicenna, had challenged the outlook and altered the mentality of medieval European intellectuals. What mattered to them above all were ideas. Thinkers in the Renaissance also cared about how ideas were expressed. They eagerly studied Latin and Greek grammar, rhetoric, poetry, ethics, and history.[5] Such "humanists" wanted to think like the ancient Romans.

Renaissance humanists revived older literary forms. Some sought to rival the Latin masters in the composition of poetry in Latin. Many engaged in extensive and learned correspondence with colleagues across Europe.[6] The scholastic philosophers, like Aquinas, Scotus, and Ockham, by contrast, wrote fewer and much more businesslike letters. The individual personality mattered little to them. The concrete and differentiated person to the humanists, however, was an object of enduring interest. Some, for example, conducted dialogues with deceased poets. An intellectual community encompassing vast realms of time and space thus emerged.[7]

Thinkers, such as Petrarch (1304–74), while usually remaining devout Christians, gradually began to place a greater emphasis on the creative and intellectual capacities of humankind.[8] Yes, faith was the highest ideal, but human reason enables man to comprehend the universe and therefore makes him great far beyond all other creatures, as Pico della Mirandola (1463–94) argued. In his early 20s, Pico knew Latin, Greek, Hebrew, and Arabic and had carefully read philosophical and mystical writings in all of them. At 23, he challenged any scholar in Europe to debate him on 900 propositions concerning religion, philosophy, science, and magic—in his words, "everything knowable." He even offered to pay their travel expenses to Rome.[9] His *Oration on the Dignity of Man* (1486), often considered a manifesto of Renaissance humanism, asserted that man chooses his own destiny—brutish or angelic—whereas by nature animals are brutish, and angels obedient to God.[10]

Other scholars, including Leonardo Bruni (1370–1444), pushed humanism away from faith. He authored a history of Florence, often called the first book of modern historical scholarship, which divided history into three periods: Antiquity, Middle Ages, and the Modern Age.[11] This implied a radical break with the religious chronology in which Christ's Crucifixion was the central moment. Bruni and other Renaissance historians began to interpret all of human activity and endeavor—including language, ideas, artistic expression, traditions, and customs—as historically conditioned. Bruni also argued that the most meaningful life was not contemplative (as both Aristotle and Aquinas asserted) but one of civic engagement.

Most humanists rejected the approach and outlook of their intellectual predecessors, the scholastic philosophers and theologians. The universities, where the latter flourished, almost entirely excluded the study of literature. Sacred doctrine was reduced to theology, a mere subject among others. Erasmus denounced the scholastics as engaging in sterile and uninspiring debates about technical and unessential matters. Their disputes, conveyed in an arid and complicated jargon, or at best a merely systematic droning of point and counterpoint, abstracted from deeply experienced faith, from the living Gospel. What truly mattered to the humanists, who developed no systematic philosophy, was texts that set one's heart and soul on fire, be they filled with rhetorical brilliance like the works of Cicero and Seneca or, as most of the humanists agreed, earthshaking power like writings of the Church Fathers or the Bible.[12]

The greatest break, thus, came not so much in content as in style. The shift to humanism was most clear in the plastic arts. Artistic expression in medieval times often seemed stiff and lifeless because the medieval mind considered the indwelling spirit of greater importance than physical things themselves.[13] The revolution in painting wrought by Giotto in the early 1300s precisely consisted in dwelling on the loveliness of natural things (see Chapter 2). Gradually, European artists developed a deep appreciation for the human form and the uniqueness of human faces.[14] In all of history, only the Greeks and Romans had thought to depict them realistically. By the early 1500s, when Leonardo, Michelangelo, Botticelli, and Raphael were all active, Italian artists had not only achieved a similar mastery, but had also gone beyond it. Michelangelo's *David* (1504), for example, both represents a human physique with stunning technical accuracy and suggests that man can be greater than what his normal capacities would allow. David, who has just killed Goliath, displays an extraordinary boldness befitting the humanists' understanding of mankind.[15]

Graphic perspective and architecture progressed too. The medieval mind collapsed and distorted time and space. Scenes from diverse moments in time might be depicted on one canvas, or three sides of a building represented all at once on another. Again, objective appearance mattered less than conveying full details or other specific content. Filippo Brunelleschi (1377–1446), a pathbreaking Florentine architect, invented linear perspective, by means of which parallel lines are represented as converging toward a vanishing point far in the distance.[16] Brunelleschi used this concept in designing such important buildings as the Church of Santo Spirito (1434–82) and the dome of the Cathedral of Florence (1419–36). Yet as a recent study has argued, "Perspective was not only an artist's or architect's tool, it also was a way of examining and recording the natural world." Thus, art became a science. Renaissance artists and scientists often worked closely together leading to ever-more accurate depictions of natural phenomena.[17]

The church warmly embraced the new arts and humanism itself. The deeply learned scholar, Cardinal Bessarion (1403–72), was a humanist. He translated works by Aristotle, revived interest in Plato, and sought to reconcile the two philosophers.[18] (He also greatly admired Western technological innovation.)[19] Several popes were humanists. In fact, many religious reformers considered the "princes of the church" simply too much of this world. In many cases, this was no exaggeration.

Worldly theologians

Rome as ever was a cesspool of sin and vice at the height of the Italian Renaissance. While Raphael and Michelangelo painted divine frescoes on the walls of the papal chambers, prostitutes and beggars filled the streets outside. Popes and cardinals were widely known to frequent brothels and to keep lovers.[20] Throughout Christendom, ambitious elites used the wealth, power, and prestige of the church for their own ends. Albrecht of Brandenburg, for example, a Hohenzollern and therefore an ancestor of the future Prussian kings, managed to gain appointment to two archbishoprics by age 24 in 1514. The canonical limits were age 30 and one see at a time. Never mind, wealth and connections overcame these obstacles.[21] Generations of reformers had decried the deep-rooted corruption in the church.

Many popes played this game, including Leo X (r. 1513–21) who was reputed to have said, upon his election to the Holy See, "Since God has given us the papacy, let us enjoy it."[22] Others were decidedly humanistic in outlook. Nicholas V (r. 1447–55) undertook sumptuous building projects, commissioned frescoes by Fra Angelico and other great artists, filled the Vatican Library (mentioned in Chapter 6) with fresh translations from the Greek (both pagan and Christian), and continued to pursue his intellectual passions.[23]

The most dramatic scandals occurred in the fourteenth century. As noted in Chapter 3, a power struggle between France and Rome resulted in the papacy moving to Avignon in southern France in 1309. The so-called Babylonian Captivity of the papacy ended in 1378, when Urban VI was elected pope in Rome. Five months later, however, the Western Schism began when the French cardinals picked Clement VII.

All the secular rulers of Europe had to decide which pope—and which ecclesiastical hierarchy—to back. Things got even worse when a council of cardinals in Pisa in 1409 elected a third pope, Alexander V.

Among the specific ills condemned by reformers were indulgences. Early medieval clergy had prescribed substitutes for the penances prescribed by canon law, for example, allowing penitents to sing 50 psalms kneeling instead of fasting for a day.[24] Pilgrimages to holy places could also replace specified penances.[25] Pope Urban II made a quantum departure in 1095, however, when he offered a plenary indulgence—full remission of sins—to all who joined the First Crusade, so long as they confessed their sins earnestly.[26] In 1187, Gregory VIII went further still. He granted plenary indulgence to anyone who sent another on crusade or who supported the effort materially. Similar indulgences were later granted for participation in military campaigns against pagans and heretics. Following a century-long grassroots tradition, in 1476 Sixtus IV began formally granting indulgences to the dead on behalf of living benefactors of the church.[27] Expiating sins had become a financial transaction.

The church raised vast sums selling indulgences. Pope Leo X launched a big campaign in 1515 to complete the Basilica of St Peter. Yet elite opinion was turning against the practice. Thus, Frederick the Wise of Saxony forbade the sale of indulgences in his realm. In 1516 just outside Saxony, however, Johann Tetzel began offering exculpation for the most heinous crimes in exchange for defined sums of money but without contrition on the part of the giver.[28] An explosion of condemnation erupted, rending Christendom asunder.

Voices from below

Calls for reform and renewal in the church were nothing new. In essence, they began even before the church began, since Christianity descends from the Hebrew prophetic tradition. Especially numerous were preachers and mystics calling for spiritual rejuvenation from medieval times down to the extraordinarily popular *The Imitation of Christ* (1420–27) by Thomas à Kempis,[29] who asserted over and over that we can accomplish nothing of value without God.[30] Visionaries also repeatedly decried sins and corruption in the institutional House of God.

Peter Waldo (ca. 1140–1218) anticipated many innovations of the Reformation itself.[31] A rich French merchant, he experienced spiritual conversion in his early 20s. He gave his wealth to the poor, took a vow of poverty, and preached that all Christians should do the same. The Holy Scripture, he argued, provides an infallible guide in all spiritual matters. So he commissioned a Lyonnais priest to translate the four Gospels from Latin into the local dialect. As noted above, the church vehemently opposed translating Scripture. Around 1200, for example, Pope Innocent III warned of a great danger should any "simple and unlearned person . . . presume to attain to the sublimity of Holy Scripture." His agents burned all the Waldensian Bibles they laid hands on. A church decree of 1229 even banned the possession by nonclergy of any religious books in the vernacular languages.[32]

Despite papal condemnations and excommunications, a large following flocked to Waldo. Calling themselves the Poor of God, they denounced corruption in the established Church and commissioned both men and women to preach the Gospel to all people. The movement spread to northern Spain and Italy, many regions of France, and the German-speaking lands. In various localized forms, it later merged into some streams of the Reformation.[33]

Many other offshoots of Christianity swelled to prominence in this period. The Cathars arose in the Rhineland in the mid-1100s and spread to France and Italy. A Manichaean doctrine that rejected the material world as inherently evil, Catharism had little in common with the Waldensians. The established church launched a campaign against the Cathars (the Albigensian Crusade) in 1209, and then rooted them out by means of the Inquisition over the following century and a half.[34]

Far closer to Waldo, and also prefiguring the Reformation in many ways, was John Wyclif (ca. 1330–84), a prominent English philosopher and logician educated and employed at Oxford.[35] The Bible, he argued, was a direct and faithful emanation from God. The true church comprises the elect, those predestined for eternal salvation. Yet no man, he claimed in an era of increasing urban literacy, was "so rude a scholar but that he might learn the words of the gospel according to his simplicity."[36] Together with several Oxford colleagues, therefore, Wyclif undertook a word-for-word translation of the Holy Book, the first in English, which they finished in 1384.

Wyclif and his supporters, often called "Lollards," advocated a lay priesthood, rejected the church hierarchy and priestly power, challenged clerical celibacy, denied the doctrine of transubstantiation (whereby the bread and wine of the Eucharist actually become the Body and Blood of Christ), objected to the veneration of the cross and other material objects, and favored the taxation of church properties.[37] Despite the heretical nature of these doctrines, Wyclif and his followers enjoyed the protection of King Edward III's son and of the University of Oxford, at least until the Peasants' Revolt of 1381. Beginning in 1401, however, numerous Lollards were burnt at the stake for refusing to repudiate their beliefs. The movement went underground, though it too reemerged with the rise of Protestantism.

King Richard II's marriage to Anne of Bohemia in 1382 spread Wyclif's ideas to the Czech lands where they strongly influenced the Czech philosopher and theologian Jan Hus (ca. 1372–1415).[38] He and other reformers at the University of Prague vehemently denounced corruption and opulence in the church and emphasized simplicity, spiritual purity, and the exclusive authority of the Bible. In 1410, the Archbishop of Prague excommunicated Hus. In 1412, for denouncing the sale of indulgences, Pope Gregory XII also excommunicated him. King Wensceslas IV of Bohemia, who stood to gain a portion of the proceeds from sales of indulgences, recommended that Hus explain his beliefs before the Council of Constance.

It is ironic that the very council that condemned Hus to the pyre had emerged from a philosophical doctrine attributing ultimate authority in church governance to church councils.[39] Conciliarism derived in large part from the work of Marsilius of Padua. His *The Defender of the Peace* (1324) denied the divine establishment of the papacy and argued that all legitimate government—secular or ecclesiastical—requires popular consent.[40] The book was burned immediately and the author condemned as a heretic. Yet his ideas lived on. Dietrich of Niem (d. 1418), quoting Marsilius liberally but without attribution (or only to call him "a great theologian of modern times"),[41] argued that popes and bishops should be subject to secular courts of justice.

Dietrich played a leading role at the Council of Constance (1414–18).[42] It was a vast gathering with, at various times, the participation of hundreds of ecclesiastical and secular leaders and emissaries. A majority of the delegates, voting by "nation" (France, Germany, Spain, Italy, and England), ruled that the council's authority stemmed directly from God, that in regard to matters of faith and church governance its judgment was supreme, and that even the pope had to obey its decrees. The body deposed all three men then claiming the papacy and elected a new one, Martin V. Further decrees provided for a general council every 10 years with supreme authority in regard to spiritual and ecclesiastical matters.[43]

A second goal of the delegates, perhaps the chief one of the German speakers, was to cleanse the church of corruption. They agreed on several specific points, mostly aimed at lessening the influence of wealth in ecclesiastical affairs. These efforts came to naught, as did the hope for conciliar preeminence, for Martin and his successors cooperated with secular authorities to reassert absolutist rule.[44]

The third purpose of the council was the persecution of heretics. The council condemned several dozen teachings of Wyclif, ordered the destruction by fire of all his books, and decreed the removal of his remains from consecrated ground in England. A select commission interrogated Hus on two points. The first concerned his advocacy of offering both bread and wine to the laity during Holy Communion, instead of only bread according to church tradition. The second related to Hus's agreement with Wyclif's teachings. Significantly, Hus refused to abjure them unless they were refuted by Holy Writ, a move that prefigured Luther's own defense a century later. Although Emperor Sigismund had promised Hus his full protection, he was burned to death at the stake.[45] They obliterated Hus but unleashed a civil war.

The Hussites attacked Catholics and their churches throughout Bohemia. Following an assault on Hussites in July 1419, a mob led by John Zizka seized the town hall and cast several city leaders out an upper window—the infamous first Defenestration of Prague.[46] For the next decade, the Hussites fought boldly, creatively, and effectively. They deployed handheld firearms, simple but effective defensive techniques, and well-articulated infantry formations, keeping their foes constantly off balance.[47] The Hussites launched repeated incursions into neighboring Germanic lands. Wherever they went, they advocated the right to preach the Word of God freely, to receive both bread and wine at Communion, and to strip the clergy of secular power.[48]

An agreement reached at a church council in Basel in 1433 brought the Hussites back into the Catholic fold but allowed Bohemian priests to continue serving both bread and wine to communicants.[49] Thus, even before the Reformation shattered the unity of Western Christendom, an independent church with unconventional organization and practices existed within its very bosom.

Movements aimed at church reform thus emerged in many different places across Europe. Those involved for the most part believed in the capacity of individual believers to discern the truth, to judge rightly without reference to any established hierarchy or authority, and, in concert with one another, even to lay down the law on church governance. All these struggles seemed largely in vain, however, when Pope Julius II convened the Fifth Lateran Council in 1512–17, having packed it with cardinals opposed to conciliarism. Together they reasserted the supremacy of papal authority.[50] Little did they expect a tidal wave of reformism just around the corner. The printing revolution provided a means to get the reformists' message out to millions. Humanism helped make their case more persuasive.

The humanistic movement in Germany, along with critical interpretation of texts and the return to classical antiquity, involved a strong anti-Roman and anti-papal element. Dozens of scientists, physicians, scholars, poets, and philosophers contributed to its development. Several, who knew first-hand the moral depravity and anti-German prejudice in Rome, brought back and circulated anonymous antipapal lampoons.[51] Papal greed, corruption, and political and cultural imperialism, many contended, kept the German-speaking peoples from achieving their full potential. Conrad Celtis (1459–1508), founder of a learned society and Poet Laureate of the Holy Roman Empire, perhaps more than anyone helped stimulate the emergence of Germanic—and anti-Roman—national consciousness.[52] In an address of 1492 to the students of the University of Ingolstadt, he urged the Germans to rise to the level of the Italians in learning and letters.[53] Such patriotic humanism over the next several decades helped justify criticism and defiance of Rome by religious reformers. It also apparently influenced the man who launched the Reformation.

Luther

Born in a small Saxon town in 1483 to harsh and demanding parents, Martin Luther studied the liberal arts in high school and college and then began a program in law and philosophy at Erfurt.[54] A fearful young man, at age 21 a lightning bolt struck near him during a thunderstorm. Terrified to the quick, he swore to take monastic vows should he escape alive. A man of his word, he joined the cloistered Augustinian monastery in Erfurt. Ordained a priest, he continued his studies and was made a professor of theology. He also became a regional director of his monastic order and the prior of his monastery while still teaching. Thus over-burdened, he alternated between laxity and extreme asceticism and spiritual devotion, often followed by profound despair.

Among the ideas that racked him with doubt was how to achieve salvation.[55] At the heart of the matter lay two central Christian paradoxes. First, if man has free will, then he can choose to love and serve God. If he is fundamentally corrupted by Original Sin, however, then he cannot possibly choose aright. Second, the distance between God and man is infinite, so no amount of good deeds can bridge the gap. Therefore, we can be justified, or made right with God, only by His grace. Here came Luther's terrifying yet comforting eureka-moment: on our own, we are damned, but through divine grace we are saved. Stunning. Thus, one of Luther's central propositions was simply this: *sola gratia*.

Luther summed up a second key belief as *sola fide*, or "faith alone." The church taught that faith and "good works" together justify a Christian. Luther argued on the contrary that only faith could do so. Once the soul is transformed by grace, it will naturally perform good deeds, but the deeds do not actually help bring about the transformation. He considered *sola fide* to be the doctrine "on which the church stands or falls."[56] He meant that the church could achieve nothing more worthy in the world than to constitute a community of faithful people and to help cultivate their faith in God.

Yet where did faith come from? *Sola scriptura*. Luther meant that God had revealed Himself to mankind through the Bible. By reading these holy texts, Luther argued, any believer can find all the truth and meaning of his relationship with God. This doctrine was revolutionary. It implied a corollary: *solus Christus* or "through Christ alone." In other words, man can reach God directly without the mediation of priests. In fact, since Scripture was relatively straightforward in its meanings, at least according to Luther, one did not have to be a theologian in order to comprehend it. The naive faith of children and an openness to Scripture alone leads to salvation. Priests in the Lutheran tradition would continue to tend their flocks yet without any attribution of transformative power.

Never before in human history had a set of doctrines so empowered ordinary people. Luther basically argued that every living person had direct and immediate access to the greatest treasure of Christendom and of all human life—religious faith. Whereas the church limited teaching and preaching to clergy, Luther claimed that each person should read, interpret, and be transformed by the Bible individually.

Politically, these doctrines had several implications. First, the church comprised not institutions and officials but only an invisible community of believers. The "papal monarchy" that emerged in the Middle Ages was thus a travesty. For the papal doctrine of the Two Swords, Luther substituted that of the Two Realms: one of politics and law, the other faith and grace.[57] Luther and other reformers expected rulers in the Earthly Realm to shoulder big responsibility, for example, by instituting poor relief and education.[58] Beyond that, they should employ all their human capacities to promote the common good: a doctrine recalling the hopes Plato placed in the "philosopher kings" in his *Republic*. (Neither thinker believed, as Enlightenment thinkers later would, that one should not entrust too much power to any individual—see Chapter 10.)

Luther began to go public with his views in fall 1517. According to the traditional account, he nailed a list of 95 propositions to the door of Wittenberg's castle church.[59] He emphasized the necessity of true repentance, questioned the pope's capacity to remit sins, condemned the sale of indulgences, and urged the convocation of a church council to discuss these matters. Some compelling evidence suggests that he had sent his list confidentially to the Archbishop of Mainz who in turn had probably sent it to Rome for consideration. Meanwhile, some printer had got hold of the document, translated it into German, and flooded the market, so to speak.

Almost instantly, Luther's bold deed reached the whole of Germany. As a writer of genius, he kept his name before the public over the next several years with a torrent of sermons, articles, pamphlets, polemics, treatises, and leaflets in both German and Latin. In Wittenberg alone, some seven print shops soon existed to publish the works of Luther and his colleagues.[60] Some of Luther's sermons came out in 20 editions in the course of 2 or 3 years. By one calculation, roughly 20 percent of all the pamphlets printed in Germany from 1500 to 1530 bore Luther's name.[61] By another reckoning, printers sold some 300,000 copies of Luther's 30 publications in the period 1517–20.[62] According to one scholar, "he dominated to a degree that no other person to my knowledge has ever dominated a major propaganda campaign and mass movement since. Not Lenin, not Mao Tse-tung, not Thomas Jefferson, John Adams, or Patrick Henry."[63]

Luther's literary production made handsome profits for hundreds of printers across the German-speaking lands and fortunes for those closest to the source in

Wittenberg.[64] The political fragmentation of the Empire, combined with the avid desire of these craftsmen to earn money, made controlling the booming output impossible.

A confrontation with the church was unavoidable.[65] Thanks to Frederick of Saxony, Luther avoided arrest. In summer 1519, he publicly debated the learned theologian, Johann Eck (1486–1543), for 4 weeks straight. Eck then intensified his attacks on Luther, demanding that his works be burned. In July 1520, Leo X threatened Luther with excommunication should he fail to renounce his views within 60 days.[66] Far from any retraction, Luther lashed out with a scathing diatribe against the church leaders, calling for violence against them. The emperor, kings, and princes, he argued, should

> gird themselves with force of arms to attack . . . these monsters of perdition, these cardinals, these popes, and the whole swarm of the Roman Sodom, who corrupt youth and the Church of God. Why do we not rather assault them with arms and wash our hands in their blood?[67]

Luther explained later that, as a Christian, he abhorred bloodshed and therefore meant these words figuratively. Yet he never managed to live them down.[68]

Over the next several months, Luther published three fundamental texts of the Reformation. His *Address to the Christian Nobility of the German Nation* denounced corruption and abuse of power in the church. Most importantly, Luther argued that the laity were "all consecrated as priests by baptism" and therefore possessed spiritual independence, authority over the church, and the right to reform it.[69] *The Babylonian Captivity of the Church*, published in October 1520, rejected four of the traditional sacraments, preserving only Baptism, Eucharist, and Penance. Luther also demanded a dramatic reinterpretation of the Eucharist.[70] It was not a reenactment of Christ's passion, he argued, since Christ had sacrificed himself once for all time, but rather a communing with Him.[71] The treatise's vindictive tone and Luther's comparison of the pope to the Antichrist alienated many supporters of the reform movement, including Erasmus.[72] Finally, in November Luther came out with *On the Freedom of a Christian*. "A Christian," he claimed, "is a perfectly free lord of all, subject to none. A Christian is a perfectly dutiful servant of all, subject to all."[73] Despite the deferential cover letter to Pope Leo X, which he appended to the tract, the pontiff repudiated it.[74]

Luther was nothing if not a provocative polemicist. At the very end of November, he offered a point-by-point rebuttal of the pope's condemnation of his doctrines. In regard to point number 18, for example, he jocularly and tauntingly averred that

> I was wrong, I admit it, when I said that indulgences were "the pious defrauding of the faithful." I recant and I say, "Indulgences are the most impious frauds and imposters of the most rascally pontiffs, by which they deceive the souls and destroy the goods of the faithful.[75]

The German-speaking lands were by now in turmoil. Every attempt to publicly excommunicate Luther and burn his writings had provoked anger and even riots. Several authorities dragged their feet to avoid bloodshed. In mid-December, in the company of a rebellious crowd of professors, students, and citizens, Luther burned *Exsurge Domine*, the pope's threat of excommunication, and a book of canon law, because as he later wrote "it makes the pope a god on earth." On 3 January 1521, the pope excommunicated Luther.[76]

Later in January, the Holy Roman Emperor Charles V convened the Estates of the Holy Roman Empire in Worms, a town on the Rhine River, to evaluate Luther's ideas.[77] Two thousand people turned out to welcome Luther. Heir to an ancient lineage, Charles ruled over lands stretching across South America and Europe. Luther, a miner's son, stood before him. He refused to repudiate his publications but apologized for their often harsh tone. Famously, he asserted:

> "I am bound by the Scriptures I have quoted and my conscience is captive to the Word of God. I cannot and I will not retract anything, since it is neither safe nor right to go against conscience. I cannot do otherwise, here I stand, may God help me. Amen."

On 25 May, the diet issued the Edict of Worms, a formal condemnation of Luther, his works, and anyone daring to aid or abet him. He escaped only because Frederick the Wise arranged his concealment in the spectacular Wartburg Castle in Thuringia. There Luther translated the New Testament (his Old Testament, translated with collaborators, followed a decade later) into a version of German that became the standard for educated people for five centuries.

Social and political transformations

Tradition and authority were now under assault in the German-speaking lands. Priests said the mass in the vernacular; priests, monks, and nuns sloughed off their vows of chastity and married; the faithful received wine during Communion; some ate meat on fast days; others smashed sacred images; princes challenged the authority of prelates; and ordinary people openly defied secular rulers and landlords.[78] Luther's German Bible fostered the rise of national consciousness.[79] Grassroots change was moving swiftly in many directions.

The transformation of the mass made a huge difference in ordinary people's lives. A key purpose of the Papal Revolution had been to mark the secular and especially the monastic clergy as truly elect and to separate them from the mass of believers. Their vows of chastity made them alone worthy to touch the sacred Eucharistic elements. In forsaking the carnal pleasures, they gained in return the greatest human ecstasy—to commune directly and regularly with the Most Holy. The rules were strict. Only the celebrant could taste of the cup. The communicants could receive the bread but not touch it with their unchaste fingers. Priests could celebrate mass alone. The laity had first to confess their sins before approaching the altar. In general, they were not encouraged to take Communion more than once a year.[80] Luther and his supporters tore down all these walls. The Eucharist, they insisted, was a shared experience of believers that bound them both together and to God.[81]

Luther sought both to keep up the movement's velocity and to direct its throbbing impulses in proper channels. He railed in open letters against the continued sale of indulgences and approved the marriage of priests and monks. He rejected monasticism as unbiblical and asserted that all people are equally priests.[82] Everyone, even the humblest person can serve God, can have a calling, not merely those with a "spiritual vocation."[83] Since the mass was not a sacrifice or a propitiation, but a thanksgiving to God and a shared experience with fellow believers, Luther deplored the practice of priests saying masses for single individuals or for the dead.[84] It is difficult to overemphasize how much Luther's efforts to transform the church focused on empowering the majority of Christians, on leveling society in the realm of religious life.

These changes in religious practice provoked consternation and even violence. Through the second half of 1521 and early 1522, students and townspeople in Wittenberg jeered at unreformed believers, seized mass books, and destroyed religious imagery and depictions including crucifixes. Iconoclastic riots were inspired, among others, by Luther's senior colleague at Wittenberg, Andreas Karlstadt (1486–1541), on the premise that "God is a spirit" and must be worshiped in spirit only.[85] In February 1522, Frederick publicly called upon the reformers to exercise caution, to use persuasion rather than force, and to try to build consensus for the changes. "We have gone too fast," he warned.[86]

In the midst of such turmoil, three men arrived from nearby Zwickau claiming prophetic powers. They rejected the authority of the Bible and infant baptism and preached the slaughter of the "ungodly." The end of the world was near, they promised, and the Kingdom of God at hand. A loyal following quickly arose.[87] Who could possibly stand up to them?

Luther returned to Wittenberg in March 1522. He also urged moderation. It had taken him 3 years of mental and spiritual efforts to develop his reformist ideas, he argued. Could ordinary people achieve the same in three months?

> Do you suppose that abuses are eliminated by destroying the object which is abused? Men can go wrong with wine and women. Shall we then prohibit and abolish women? The sun, the moon, and stars have been worshiped. Shall we then pluck them out of the sky? Such haste and violence betray a lack of trust in God.[88]

Sermons like this restored calm in Wittenberg and lifted the Zwickau preachers' spell. Luther now realized that leading people to salvation, to loving Christ and one's neighbors had to be accomplished while maintaining order and encouraging civic responsibility.[89] Foremost, he urged people to view their trade and station in life as a source of joy. Just as the shepherds, after seeing the Lord of the universe lying in a manger, returned to their sheep, so the baker, the cook, and the weaver all play an essential role in society yet partake in the great mystery of all creation.[90] The greatest cook is God himself, for He makes the Sun to bring forth all good things to eat.[91]

Other leaders grew more radical. The Swiss reformer, Ulrich Zwingli (1484–1531), demanded the purification of Christian worship. In 2 weeks in 1525, his supporters cleared all the churches in Zurich of adornments and whitewashed their walls. Two years later, they destroyed all the organs. For Zwingli, Holy Communion merely commemorated Christ's Passion. This conclusion led almost inevitably to the abolition of the mass as such and its replacement by a gathering to hear readings from Scripture and commentary thereon. At the Marburg Colloquy in 1529, Zwingli and Luther agreed on every theological point except the nature of the Eucharist. Also unlike Luther, Zwingli was prepared to shed blood reform the church. He in fact died by the sword, defending Zurich in 1531 against an alliance of Catholic cantons.[92]

The Anabaptists, who also emerged in Switzerland, rejected war, refused to swear oaths, and forswore private possessions, drinking, carousing, and bodily adornments. Among the Anabaptists (and their offshoots like the Amish and Mennonites) arose the first pacifist movements and "peace churches." Their most divergent belief was that Christians should consciously choose baptism. The church should therefore not baptize infants. The city council of Zurich denounced these ideas and indeed criminalized the re-baptism of adults in 1526. The following year the city executed Felix Manz by drowning him—in a mockery of his ideas about baptism—for breaking this law, the first of some 2,000 Anabaptist martyrs throughout Europe.[93]

The Reformation took a violent turn in many places. In 1522, aristocratic reformers launched a military campaign against Catholic "princes of the church." The "Knights' Revolt" ended disastrously when the Archbishop of Trier proved a worthy fighter with powerful supporters. Pro-Catholic forces then pursued the revolt's leader, Franz von Sickingen (1481–1523), to his formerly impregnable castle and with artillery reduced its walls to rubble within 1 week.[94]

Discontent was also rife at the opposite end of the social spectrum. The life of peasants had progressively worsened for a century and more, sparking sporadic unrest and rebellion. Their discontent had many causes.[95] The Europe-wide growth of bureaucracy resulted in increased taxes for which the countryside received few benefits. The adoption of Roman law, which aimed at rationalizing administrative systems, undermined the peasants' traditional access to common lands that Germanic customary law had ensured. An increase in population resulted in a decline in living standards. Finally, the abundant production of silver in recently opened German mines accelerated the shift to a money economy, threatening age-old peasant folkways.[96] For all these reasons, massive peasant revolts had broken out periodically in Europe in the late Middle Ages. The French Jacquerie of 1358, for example, resulted in over 30,000 deaths.[97]

The spread of Reformation teachings reached deeply into the countryside. By 1525, according to one estimate, roughly one-third of the peasants of the Holy Roman Empire had espoused the doctrines of Luther, Zwingli, and other reformers.[98] Many envisioned utopian communities governed by the Gospel and advocated grassroots control over the election of priests, the administration of ecclesiastical justice, and the collection and management of the tithes. As a money economy replaced labor services, peasant communities across northern Europe had gained some administrative independence. They now also sought religious autonomy and control. They were often willing to pay more to increase the availability of sacramental and pastoral services, but they wanted a say in their administration.[99]

For several decades, isolated peasant rebellions had broken out in many of the German lands over high taxes and other forms of oppression. Peasant activists and lay preachers, like Hans Böheim of Niklashausen, attracted large followings in the final decades of the 1400s but were routinely suppressed. After the turn of the century, Swiss and German peasants formed more cohesive rebel organizations, which launched armed revolts. All of them were crushed militarily. From around 1509, lower-class town dwellers in many German lands complained of mismanagement by city councils and demanded a larger say in civil government. In late 1524, rural and urban discontents began to coalesce into a vast rebellion, which one historian has called a "Revolution of the Common Man," with outbreaks in dozens of places across the German lands.[100]

This movement ultimately encompassed a territory of over 30,000 square miles stretching from the Swiss Alps to Saxony. The rebels started by demanding redress for specific grievances but soon aimed to overturn the feudal order itself. Luther's doctrine of the "priesthood of all believers" touched their hearts. The movement's leaders published dozens of pamphlets. The most famous was *The Twelve Articles*, which came out in early 1525 and quickly ran through 25 editions.[101] It demanded the right to appoint pastors, to regulate taxation according to biblical principles, to gain access to formerly common pasture and woodlands, and to end serfdom and oppression by secular and ecclesiastical lords. Luther denounced elite hard-heatedness and exhorted both sides to peace and reconciliation.[102]

The insurgencies, often well organized and armed, grew steadily, reaching a crescendo in April and May. Under the leadership of the learned theologian and fiery preacher, Thomas Müntzer (ca. 1488–1525), thousands of peasants terrorized traditional believers, destroying a dozen monasteries in the region of Mühlhausen in central Germany. Luther now changed his tune. In a tract of 6 May, he urged the princes "to smite, slay, and stab" the rebels, since "nothing can be more poisonous, hurtful, or devilish than a rebel."[103] Nine days later, the princes slaughtered Müntzer's armed band at Frankenhausen and then tortured and executed him. Within two more weeks, the rebellion had been crushed nearly everywhere. In all, some 100,000 people lost their lives in less than a year of struggle.[104]

The princes made some concessions to the peasants and townsfolk but resolved never again to allow the religious transformation to slip from their control. Luther himself concluded that only law and reason—not theology or even the Gospel—could serve as the guiding principles of governance.[105] The only hope for benevolent governance, it seemed to Luther, were God-fearing Christian princes ruling in the interest of the common good.

Christendom shattered

Yet who could best define the common good? At the Diet of Speyer in 1529, Charles V demanded a restoration of the old faith in his vast lands.[106] A minority of Lutheran princes and leaders of imperial cities, knowing that the Catholic faith augmented Charles's power over them, issued a protestation, earning them the pejorative label "Protestants." In their lands, the reforms continued.[107]

Battle lines were drawn. The adherents to the Augsburg Confession, a statement of Lutheran beliefs issued in 1530,[108] formed a defensive league and marshaled philosophical and legal arguments to justify armed resistance to the emperor. Fighting continued for decades, with the Protestants mostly on the losing end. In 1550, theologians and pastors issued the Magdeburg Confession, the first official Protestant justification of religious resistance to authority. It retained legitimacy for centuries, right down to the Confessing Church's struggle against Adolf Hitler.[109] Five years later, Catholic and Protestant princes agreed to the Peace of Augsburg, which established the right of each to impose his faith upon his realm, the right of subjects to emigrate for reasons of conscience, and the right of secular princes to retain most confiscated church property. It also recognized Lutheranism (but not Anabaptism) as a legitimate denomination of Christianity and established religious pluralism but did not abolish allegiance to the empire. Charles's hope for a united Catholic Europe ended; so did Luther's goal to reform and not split apart Christendom.[110]

Most of the Germanic lands north of Bavaria adopted Lutheranism. In Scandinavia, Catholicism was completely uprooted. The kings of Denmark and Sweden realized that the reformed faith would empower them to seize ecclesiastical property, to undermine the authority of bishops, to take control of the universities, and to increase their power generally.[111] King Gustavus Vasa (r. 1523–60), who led Sweden to independence from Denmark in 1523, imposed Lutheranism—with the agreement of a diet of nobles—in 1527. King Christian III of Denmark (r. 1534–59) fought a civil war against the Catholics in 1534–36 and established a national Lutheran church in 1537 with himself as *de facto* supreme head. In the same year, he imposed the doctrine in Norway, a province of Denmark.

A third giant of the Reformation, after Luther and Zwingli, also established himself in Switzerland. Born and raised in France, John Calvin (1509–64) received an excellent religious, legal, and humanistic education, including a mastery of Latin, Greek, and Hebrew.[112] Around 1533, a powerful spiritual experience convinced him that only faith can reconcile us to God. In 1535, anti-Protestant persecution drove him to Basel. There he published the *Institutes of the Christian Religion* (1536), the fundamental theological statement of Calvinism.[113] He settled in 1541 in Geneva, which had recently voted "to live according to the gospel and the Word of God."[114] He soon established a polity strongly influenced by Christian principles.

Calvin's Ecclesiastical Ordinances set out in detail institutional organization, church hierarchy, and rules for proper conduct, both civil and religious.[115] Improper conduct included adultery, cursing, dancing, playing games of chance, absence from regular worship, singing "indecent" songs, and relapses to Catholicism. Elders and an ecclesiastical court enforced these rules with punishments including jail time and excommunication (denying access to Holy Communion). Though some Genevans opposed Calvin's Puritanism, most accepted it enthusiastically. Between 1550 and 1562, some 7,000 Protestants settled in Geneva, practically doubling the population. The immigrants usually possessed valuable skills and educational attainments. Most considered Geneva a close approximation of the city of God.[116]

What was to become the distinctive doctrine of Calvinism, predestination, flowed logically from Luther's conviction that grace alone ensures salvation.[117] If our own acts and achievements can play no role in reconciling us to God, then only His mercy saves us. But since not all are saved, then He must choose an "elect" by some mysterious calculus. If so, since God is eternal, then He must know His elect from the beginning of time.[118] Calvin expected that this article of faith would comfort those of his followers who faced persecution throughout Europe.

Into the kingdom of Calvin's birth, dozens of his disciples traveled secretly, on pain of death, to spread the new Gospel message from Geneva. They and other couriers transported a massive number of reformist imprints, including the Bible in French—banned by French law in 1526.[119] The French monarchs had little to gain from embracing the reform. The concordat of Bologna of 1516 gave them significant control over the clergy.[120] Strong central control and regulation of printing in France made spreading dissident imprints far harder than in the politically divided German lands. Furthermore, the Catholic Church in France was an essential element in the people's national consciousness. The response of Catholic intellectuals to the new ideas was swift and often effective.

Even so, by 1561 France had more than 2,000 reformed congregations. The translation of the Psalms into French and set to rousing music stirred the hearts of hundreds of thousands of converts. The new faith enjoyed great success among artisans, shopkeepers, businessmen, and the nobility. In fact, roughly half of the French nobility and a quarter of the urban population adopted the new faith. Catholic intellectuals and officials fought back, however, leading to the first of several French wars of religion (1562–63).[121] Decisively outnumbered, the Protestants never came close to actually triumphing. By the time of the St Bartholomew's Day massacre of 1572, which resulted in the death of some 20,000 Protestants throughout the country, the new faith was already in decline. Catholic leaders across Europe celebrated the massacre. In 1598, King Henry IV felt secure enough to issue the Edict of Nantes, which granted the Calvinists almost full religious freedom but abridged their civil and political rights.

Calvinism spread to more countries than did Lutheranism (see Map 7.1). The execution of some 1,500 Protestants in the Habsburg Netherlands between 1540 and 1570, combined with heavy taxation, spurred the Dutch to revolt. Embracing the reformed faith accompanied the emergence of national consciousness and inspired a struggle of national liberation. They won their struggle for several reasons. First, they were blessed with princes of enormous talent, including Maurice of Nassau, the military innovator discussed in Chapter 4. Second, tens of thousands of skilled and fervently believing Calvinist refugees migrated into the northern provinces from the largely Catholic south. Finally, the reformers drew upon powerful intellectual articulations of the moral right and obligation to oppose rulers denying the true faith.[122]

Although the Calvinist leaders hoped to establish a religious and civil order similar to that of Geneva, the Dutch Republic instead became a haven of religious toleration welcoming persecuted minorities from around the continent including Jews.[123] Among the forms of toleration they extended to Protestant minorities was exemption from military service, first granted by William I of Orange (1533–84). This early instance of conscientious objection gradually spread to other Protestant countries, though it became a movement only later in the American colonies.[124] Even Socinians—who rejected the doctrine of the Trinity—found refuge in the Dutch Republic. The main goal of Dutch society, it seemed, was to make money and to devote oneself to financial, cultural, and technological innovation.[125]

The beginnings of the Reformation in England are linked, as noted above, with William Tyndale, who translated the New Testament into plain and accessible English and had 3,000 copies printed in Worms in 1526.[126] Despite official persecution, most of the copies quickly found their buyers, often at very low prices. A hand-copied Bible in those days cost more than £30—15 times the annual wages for a laborer. Tyndale's Bible often went for around 1 week's pay. In the next 3 years, Tyndale ordered 18,000 more copies. He also published numerous works by Luther. Protestant book publishing did not take off in England in the sixteenth century because of effective censorship, yet Protestantism triumphed. Two main factors explain this turn of events.

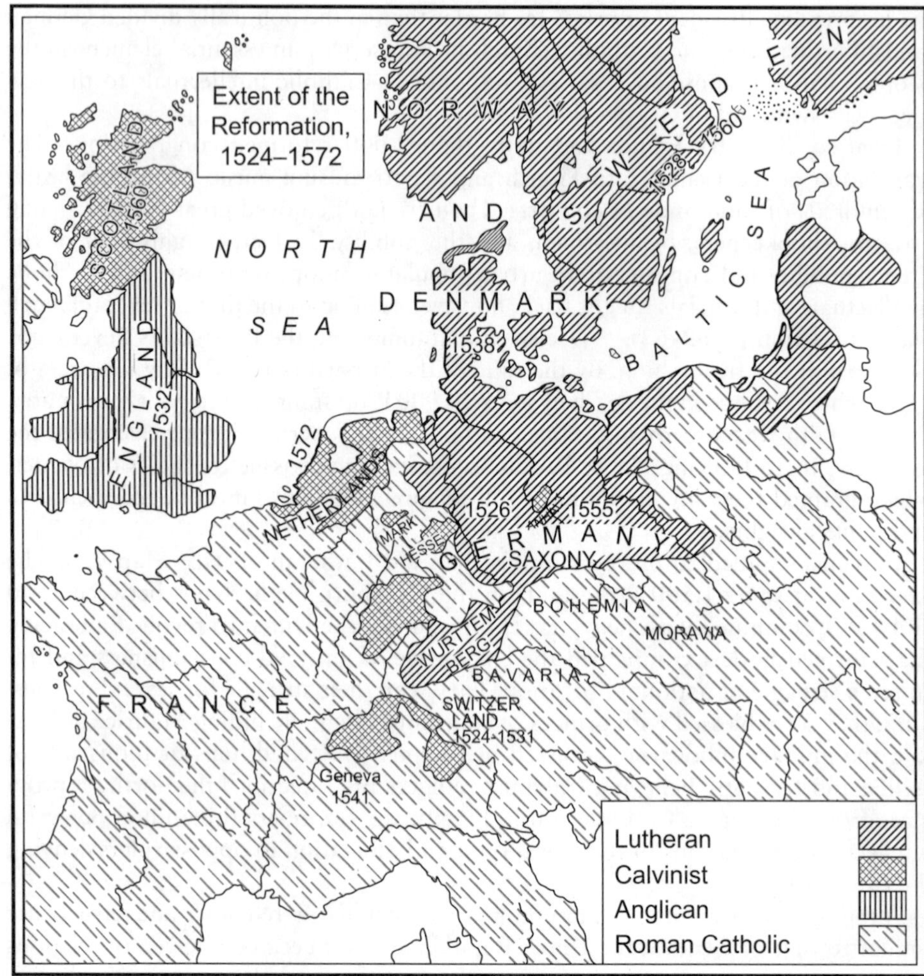

MAP 7.1 *The Reformation divided Christianity as Lutheranism, Calvinism, and Anglicanism uprooted Catholicism in many regions of Europe.*

Anticlericalism was strong in English society.[127] Disgust at the abuse of ecclesiastical power and wealth by such notorious "princes of the church" as the Lord Chancellor, Cardinal Wolsey, inspired *Supplication for Beggars* (1529) by the London lawyer Simon Fish, who urged confiscating ecclesiastical property and stripping clerics of their secular power. As on the Continent, such proposals enticed the cash-strapped and power-hungry English monarch.

In 1527, Henry VIII asked the Pope to annul his marriage to Catherine, an aunt of Charles V. Because of a canonical technicality and for fear of Charles, the Pope refused.[128] Beginning in 1529, therefore, what came to be known as the Reformation Parliament adopted a series of laws reducing the power and privileges of the clergy and papal authority in England.[129] In 1531, the Commons affirmed the king as their "only and supreme lord and, as far as the law of Christ allows, even supreme head."[130] The following year, Henry forbade the church to issue canon laws without his permission. In 1534, the Act of Supremacy deleted the words "as far as the law of Christ allows,"[131] and the Treasons Act prescribed death for anyone who denied the king's supremacy over of the Church of England. On the basis of this law, the reformer and humanist Thomas More, the author of *Utopia* (1516), met his death.[132] Because of his divorce from Catherine, authorized by the Archbishop of Canterbury, the Pope excommunicated Henry and the archbishop.

Thomas Cromwell, Henry's principal advisor, presided over the dissolution of England's monasteries during 5 years beginning in 1536. Most of their vast lands were sold or gifted to members of the nobility, bringing huge financial resources to the crown (rather quickly squandered on war, patronage, and splendor) and creating a powerful vested interest in the new status quo.[133] During these years, radical ideas and practices of the Reformation spread widely. Iconoclasm, religious disputes, and violence broke out across the realm.[134] Henry and his advisers, in contrast, reaffirmed many traditional Catholic practices relating to the sacraments, clerical celibacy, confession, and belief in transubstantiation, often applying bloody punishments to those who rejected them.

Protestants encountered broad toleration under Edward VI (r. 1547–53)—Zwinglians flocked to England—and bloody persecution at the hands of Mary I (r. 1553–58).[135] Anglicanism as such was born during the long reign of Elizabeth I (r. 1558–1603). The Church of England retained the vestments, the hierarchical structure, and some features of the mass (wafers instead of bread, a toleration of the belief in transubstantiation) of the Catholic Church. It nevertheless adopted the vernacular language, authorized clerical marriage, greatly simplified church ornamentation, rejected many "fond" (i.e., foolish) traditions of Catholicism including purgatory, and instituted Holy Communion of the two kinds (i.e., bread and wine) for the laity. The Elizabethan compromise was a true *via media* both in religion and politics.[136] None of these changes could have been instituted without the cooperation and participation of Parliament, which thereby cemented its power and status in England. Persecution of Catholics occurred in England but mostly because of their perceived links with foreign powers. Puritanism, which owed more to Calvin than to Luther, gained much influence in England during Elizabeth's reign.

Calvinism found an even wider following in Scotland.[137] Long-standing dynastic, political, and economic ties provided channels through which reformist ideas spread into the country. John Knox (ca. 1513–72), the principal Scottish reformer, for example, spoke fluent French and preached in reformed congregations in France. He also resided in Geneva for several years in the 1550s. In 1560, amid a popular rebellion and thanks to military and diplomatic support from England, the Scottish Reformation Parliament voted to establish Protestantism in Scotland.[138] The reformers destroyed nearly every stick of church ornamentation, leaving only austere white walls.[139] A new branch of Christianity emerged, Presbyterianism, which spread to all the English-speaking lands and beyond. Calvinism itself won a big following in Hungary.[140]

For several decades before Luther challenged Rome to reform, a movement for renewal had been underway in the church. It focused on personal spiritual growth through prayer, meditation, self-discipline, and ethical self-improvement. An extreme example of this tendency was Girolamo Savonarola (1452–98), the austere

Dominican fighter against priestly corruption and popular immorality who set up a Christian republic in Florence.[141]

The first institutional Catholic renewal began during the pontificate of Adrian VI (r. 1522–23). A former professor of theology, he advocated the rooting out of corruption in the church, an attitude that won him few supporters among Christendom's worldly theologians. He also discovered, much to his horror, that abolishing the sale of clerical benefices and offices would drastically weaken papal finances. Most Italians considered him a prig and a barbarian for his disinterest in the delights of high culture and the treasures of classical antiquity.[142]

Subsequent popes undertook repressive measures to stamp out Protestantism. The most infamous was the Inquisition. At this stage, it functioned regionally, for example, the Roman Inquisition and the notorious Spanish Inquisition.[143] These offices had a checkered history that often depended on who was in charge. In an age when torture used to extract confessions and the execution of criminals were routine judicial procedures, the methods and sentences of the Inquisition were often rather mild. Apparently what frightened defendants most was the shame and humiliation they would face if found guilty.[144]

The church had initially hailed the advent of printing as a means to increase the number and accuracy of sacred books or to produce letters of indulgence.[145] When printing began to threaten the integrity and authority Catholicism, however, the ecclesiastical authorities sought to tighten their control over the printed word. Pope Paul III decreed in 1543 that the printing of each and every book required the express permission of the church. Paul IV established the first list of prohibited books in 1559. It banned works by both Protestants and humanists like Boccaccio and Erasmus. (The Index was abolished only in 1966.)[146] Ironically, the list inadvertently drew attention to forbidden books.[147] In any event, the political fragmentation of Europe made it relatively easy to circulate banned imprints.

The Society of Jesus emerged not in direct response to the Reformation but as part of the movement for personal spiritual renewal within the church.[148] Following devastating injuries in battle and a spiritual awakening during convalescence, Ignatius of Loyola (1491–1556) pledged to devote his life to the service of Christ. His outlook combined the Renaissance appreciation for the value of the individual with the medieval ideal of the perfection of the soul. He devoted the next dozen years to study and wrote *Spiritual Exercises*, which served as the spiritual guidebook for the Jesuits, a religious order established by Paul III in 1540. Devoting themselves to education and apostolic mission to the world, they counted 1,000 members by the time of Loyola's death in 1556.

The Council of Trent, which met between 1545 and 1563 because of intervening political events, established Catholic orthodoxy. It affirmed that the Roman Church was the ultimate interpreter of both tradition and Scripture, that individual Christians participate in their own salvation, that the seven Sacraments shed Grace on those who receive them, and that the laity should receive only the bread during communion.[149] As for reforms, they voted to institute the Catholic Catechism, to raise education standards for priests, to ban political appointments of bishops, and to obligate them to play a more active role in religious life.

The main emphasis in the Catholic Church was not on corporate worship but on individual spirituality. The great exemplars of this time were not hymn-writing reformers like Luther but mystics penetrating to the heart of spiritual life through asceticism and rigorous self-discipline like St Teresa of Avila (d. 1582) and St John of the Cross (d. 1591). Artistic representations captured such mystical experiences in great works like "Christ on the Cross" by El Greco (d. 1614) and Bernini's "St. Teresa in ecstasy" (1646), which depicts her in a state that could just as easily be carnal as spiritual exaltation. The highly austere religious Order of Capuchins founded in Italy in 1528, followed by the Capucines for women in 1538, captured this spirit in institutional form.[150]

The Catholic Church patronized an explosion of exuberance in art, architecture, and music. The vast canvases of Peter Paul Rubens (1577–1640) exuded optimism and energy. A learned Renaissance man, he attended mass every day.[151] Throughout Catholic Europe, huge and often ornately ornamented churches arose. The Jesuits built many—24 in Bavaria alone in 1580–1650. In Rome, they hired the great Renaissance composers Palestrina and de Victoria to teach their students. At the 74 Jesuit high schools in Europe, Asia, and South America, students followed rigorous programs of music and dance. This was almost like a conscious thumbing of the nose at the more austere Protestants who banned dancing outright. The same could be said of the mass itself, which the Catholic Church lovingly and ostentatiously preserved as the central feature of their worship.[152]

The foundations of modern rights

The Reformation's most profound contribution to the development of Western civilization was not religious renewal, but the end of all central authority in Europe. Unlike other major cultures, Europe never had a single political authority. Further, from the time of Jesus himself, Christian leaders had contested the right of the secular rulers to dictate to them. Just after the millennium, the Papal Revolution had split Christendom into two powers: one fragmented and secular, the other unified and ecclesiastical. This duality of authority provided shelter for myriad secular and religious institutions and associations. Gradually, secular rulers began to challenge papal supremacy in ecclesiastical affairs. The religious revolution launched by Luther ended that supremacy forever. Europe was now both politically and religiously pluralistic. A third pole of authority—aside from that of church and state—also gained recognition: individual conscience.

Foremost in facilitating the collapse of papal supremacy was the enormous expansion of printing and literacy. Luther himself recognized the power of the printing revolution, which he called "God's highest and extremist act of grace, whereby the business of the Gospel is driven forward."[153] So much so, argued John Foxe (1517–87), an English Protestant author, "that either the pope must abolish knowledge and printing or printing at length will root him out."[154] By the time Luther died in 1546, over 3,400 editions of the Bible in whole or in part had appeared in High German and another 430 in Low German, for a total of about 1 million copies.[155] Given a population in the Holy Roman Empire of roughly 19 million, probably one in three or four families could own a copy of the Good Book. Again, thanks to Luther, more and more people felt inspired to learn to read. Certainly, the German-speaking lands had an advantage over all other regions of Europe with their 92 centers of printing in the sixteenth century compared to 60 Italy, 53 in France, and 27 in the Low Countries. Moreover, the printing industry was completely decentralized in the German lands.[156] Abolishing knowledge and printing there was next to impossible. The proliferation of schools had the same effect.

For centuries, monasteries and cathedrals had maintained small educational institutions for training monks and priests.[157] In the early Middle Ages, nearly all literate people in Europe bore clerical status. From the early 1300s, monasteries increasingly hired masters to teach Latin to bright boys of poor circumstances.[158] Non-monastic religious communities founded schools in the 1400s throughout the Dutch and German lands. Cathedral schools, collegiate churches, chantries, guilds, hospitals, and public grammar schools also offered Latin instruction to young people not pursuing clerical vocations. Tuition was often free. Girls constituted a tiny minority of both teachers and pupils, though the proportion varied from place to place. In 1380, for example, women made up fully one-third of grammar-school instructors in Paris and its suburbs, for a total of 21 out of 62.[159] This proportion seems to have far exceeded that in any English town.

Schools multiplied rapidly after 1500. First, humanists persuaded Europe's elites that studying classical literature constituted the best means to acquire both learning and virtue.[160] Second, the printing revolution, by dramatically lowering the cost of books, made it far easier for urban and religious communities to found and maintain thousands of new schools. Finally, transmitting a particular understanding of the faith became an urgent necessity in both Protestant and Catholic countries.

Municipal public schools shaped the European elites for generations.[161] Many of the teachers were Protestant, even in France, at least until Jesuits took over most public schools in the later 1500s. They taught manners, morals, and nonaristocratic values. Tuition was mostly free, subsidized by the municipal authorities, though students from out of town had to pay for room and board. In most places girls could attend, though everywhere only a small number did. Many teachers shaped behavior through persuasion and shaming rather than corporal punishment. Students often gained a healthy appreciation of talent and merit, though a strong emphasis fell upon respect for authority.

Scholars debate just how much the schools opened the pupils' minds.[162] Some clearly did a marvelous job, for example, in training Michel de Montaigne (1533–92) and other brilliant humanists who challenged every received idea.[163] Yet it seems that the purpose of most public schools was to impose conformity, acceptance of authority, support for the existing order, and the affirmation of hierarchy and status. The rote learning of passages from ancient authorities in dead languages could not automatically open the mind to new ways of thinking. The emphasis on assiduously studying the rules of grammar probably also conditioned the mind to accept and project authority. Surely most secular and ecclesiastical authorities had this in mind when they drafted minutely detailed pedagogical regulations and curricula throughout Europe but especially in the German-speaking lands. Yet perhaps one should not draw a stark contrast between one type of education that opened minds and another that disciplined them. Europe's classical schools produced both brilliant, unorthodox, creative, and innovative minds and rigorously trained, intellectually skilled, and mentally disciplined elites. This combination must have contributed powerfully to Europe's development.

Literacy rates had been slowly rising since late medieval times. In the German lands, roughly 1 in 20—and perhaps one in three urban males—could read.[164] The Reformation caused these numbers to spike.[165] Increasingly, lay people could understand and even prepare documents in Latin. More and more nonreligious literate men were bearing witness in court, acting as representatives of the clergy, and performing other duties requiring expert literacy and status in society. The multiplication of schools certainly helped, though much literacy was acquired in the home. Literacy rose especially dramatically in the Holy Roman Empire, Scotland, Sweden, and Switzerland. In 1686, the Lutheran Church in Sweden established strict rules making marriage and taking Holy Communion dependent on literacy. By the 1740s, in the southwestern diocese of Skanör, 91 percent of males and 93 percent of females could read.[166] In most places in Europe, however, class, gender, and urban–rural differences remained. About the only region on earth where such distinctions vanished was eighteenth-century Colonial New England.

The contrast with China was striking. The land that had invented printing, both woodblock and moveable-type, had enjoyed a vibrant book market for centuries, and had devoted vast energy to learning did not experience a dramatic increase in literacy until the twentieth century. The extremely demanding preparations for the civil service examination, practically the only path to public success in China, and the persistence of a single universal written language that few could master kept literacy the preserve of a narrow elite, whereas in Europe a minimal "functional literacy," especially in the vernacular languages, gradually expanded.[167]

The ideas and practices of the Reformation also led to theories about limiting established authority. Martin Luther was not the first European intellectual to claim the primacy of conscience, but his formulation exerted a great political impact.[168] Yet both Calvin and Luther viewed the state in absolutist terms, especially a state that upheld the true church in their view. To such a state, one owed full obedience.[169] In a few localities, however, the Reformation engendered significant instances of religious and political toleration. The first such place was the Netherlands.

Around 1600, a professor of theology named Jacob Arminius (1560–1609) publicly advocated religious tolerance and challenged Calvin's teachings. His followers lost their bid for political protection from the urban oligarchs of the United Provinces and were forced to flee.[170] Yet their congregations continued to meet without leaders and engaged in "free prophecy"—letting the Holy Spirit direct their prayer and utterances. This "Collegiant" movement spread throughout the Netherlands from 1620 to 1650. For the most part, its members were tolerated. Indeed, since the late 1500s, thousands of radical Protestants—chiefly Anabaptists, Spiritualists, and Evangelical Rationalists—had been flocking to the Netherlands and in particular to Holland, the most religiously tolerant land in all of Europe. The ruling Dutch Reformed oligarchs disapproved of their beliefs and practices but turned a blind eye to them so long as they remained private. More than anything else, the oligarchs wished to avoid any disturbances and therefore disruptions to commercial life.[171] The Collegiant movement, which upheld absolute freedom of thought and expression, attracted many radicals. Scholars have called this movement the Second Reformation.

The religious fragmentation of Europe enabled dissenters to find safe havens.[172] Already in the early 1400s, English Lollards had sought refuge in Scotland. In the mid-1500s, Geneva and England offered asylum to Protestants. A century later, during the English Revolution and Civil Wars (see Chapter 10), thousands of English Protestants fled to the Low Countries. Hugo Grotius put forward a legal justification of this policy in *De jure belli ac pacis* (1625), the seminal book on international law. (As an Arminian, he had found refuge in Paris in 1621). Friedrich Wilhelm (1620–88), the Elector of Brandenberg, institutionalized this practice in 1685 by granting safe haven to French Huguenots after the revocation of the Edict of Nantes in 1685. Similar laws followed in other countries, including England (1708) and the English colonies of North America.

Lutheran jurists and theologians also developed arguments justifying resistance to rulers thwarting the free exercise of one's faith. The so-called constitutional theory of resistance found its initial formulation in the late 1520s (but was anticipated by aristocrats who had rebelled against Louis XI of France in 1465). This doctrine asserted that an authoritative government official "ought by God's mandate to resist" a "superior magistrate" who oppresses "the true worship of God."[173] This argument found a central place in the Magdeburg confession of 1550. A second line of argumentation was the so-called private-law theory of resistance.[174] When a ruler fails to fulfill the responsibilities of his office, then he ceases to be a power ordained by God, and can be opposed as a private individual. Calvinist theorists were soon propounding similar arguments all around Europe—in France, the Netherlands, England, and Scotland.[175] Calvin and his followers also developed a theory and practice of popularly elected magistrates with the authority to check the power of rulers.[176]

The Englishmen John Ponet (ca. 1514–56) and Christopher Goodman (1520–1603) argued further that any private citizen has the right to resist unjust authorities. They hold this right thanks to God's covenant with humankind, which makes it "the duty of every man" to "declare himself enemy to that which so highly provokes the wrath of God."[177] Such arguments formed the foundation, a century later, of John Locke's *Two Treatises of Government*. Yet Locke considered political resistance a moral right and not a religious duty. The Huguenots provided the link between these two theoretical developments when the St Bartholomew's Day massacre of 1572 pushed them to justify theoretically a full-scale revolution within France (see Chapter 10). Ironically, in order to make their case, radical Calvinist theorists drew heavily upon scholastic theologians like Aquinas, the codifiers of Roman law, and leading conciliarists, in other words, Catholic thinkers.[178] Clearly, the intellectual foundations of resistance to authority in Europe were manifold and robust.

The self-confident, articulate, and well-organized Calvinist minorities who vociferously and successfully demanded rights in various European countries could not then, philosophically speaking, deny toleration and therefore rights to others.[179] As Lynn Hunt has argued regarding the later development of human rights, rights by their very nature, have "a tendency to cascade."[180] The general attitude of Christians in medieval and early modern Europe toward people who were different—heathens, Jews, Turks, and heretics—was of course deplorable. Later in his life, Luther joined in that inhumane chorus, yet in 1523 in a tract called *That Jesus Christ was Born a Jew* he argued that there would be nothing wrong even with marrying a non-Christian, since each such person "is just as much a man or a woman—God's good creation—as St. Paul, St. Peter, and St. Lucy."[181] Similarly, Luther's emphasis on universal literacy and the doctrine of the priesthood of all the baptized suggested that every individual had equal rights within the community, even if Luther did not draw out this logical conclusion. Reformation thought was full of radical ideas and principles whose logical implications—both good and bad—did not immediately come to the fore.

Brad S. Gregory has recently analyzed some of the negative implications.[182] By insisting that the interpretation of Scripture alone is the key to discovering truth, he argues, the reformers opened the door to a veritable Babel of truth claims and to violent conflicts over religious doctrine. Only the separation of church and state, it seemed, could ensure the development of peaceful social life. Religion thus became a largely private matter and governments gradually usurped all the power formerly divided between the secular and spiritual realms. Science with its formidable demonstrative capacity has led by extension to a widespread belief that God cannot exist and that there are no moral certainties in the universe. Most people in modern societies agree that everyone deserves rights, but no one can explain why, given the lack of common metaphysical foundations. Further, just as religion became a private matter, so did morality, with the result that the powerful human impulse of acquisitiveness could no longer be resisted by public religious condemnation. Ultimately, Western societies became obsessed with making and consuming material things, which now threatens the environment with catastrophe.

* * *

If political fragmentation helps account for the dynamism, innovativeness, transformative power, and material success of Europe before 1500, then it seems likely that the continuation of these features was made possible in part by the cultural and theological fragmentation brought about by the Reformation, whose main result was the demolition for a large portion of Europeans of the institution and belief system that had held politically fragmented Europe together for centuries—Roman Catholicism. In subsequent transformations, other authorities would fall as well. Among these were kings and received ideas about the nature of the universe. The following chapter recounts the dethronement of the Earth from its traditional central position in the universe. Luther himself gave a boost to this development by rejecting Aristotle and other classical authorities and by insisting on interpreting primary evidence using his own intellectual faculties,[183] two key ingredients of the Scientific Revolution.

QUESTIONS FOR REFLECTION

What distinguished Renaissance humanists from scholastic philosophers?

Why was translating the Bible into vernacular languages such a big deal?

Why did the Lutheran doctrine empower ordinary people so enormously?

How and why did the Reformation turn violent?

How did Calvinism differ from Lutheranism?

How did Calvinism in Holland foster the development of religious toleration?

How did the Reformation strengthen the movement toward individual rights?

How did the Reformation influence literacy?

Chapter 8 Chronology

1258:	Mongol capture of Baghdad
1300:	False Geber discovers sulfuric acid
1315:	Mondino dei Liuzzi lays out principles of dissection
1317:	Pope John XXII prohibits practice of alchemy
1471:	Ficino translates *Corpus Hermeticum*
1531:	Galen's anatomical treatise rediscovered, becomes standard
1533:	First chair of botany in Europe established
1543:	Andreas Vesalius writes *On the Structure of the Human Body*; Copernicus publishes *On the Revolutions of the Heavenly Spheres*
1560:	Academy of Mysteries of Nature founded in Naples
Late sixteenth century:	Microscope invented
1609:	Kepler Johannes publishes *New Astronomy*
1619:	Kepler Johannes publishes *Harmonices Mundi*
1614:	Francis Bacon publishes *New Atlantis*
1616:	Galileo begins his clashes with church
1620:	Francis Bacon publishes *Novum Organum*
1637–41:	René Descartes writes *Discourse on Method* and *Meditations on First Philosophy*
1660:	Royal Society of London founded
1687:	Newton states his three universal laws of motion
1751:	Benjamin Franklin publishes treatise on electricity
1755–97:	A dozen new elements successfully identified
1869:	Dmitrii Mendeleev conceives periodic table

8

Scientific revolutions

We expect bold, even arrogant men and women to make revolutions. It is not always so. Charles Darwin, a modest, self-effacing man, prey to frequent and severe bouts of illness during most of his adult life, single-handedly altered our understanding of the natural world more than any other human being. For 20 years, he built up evidence to prove a radical new theory—so radical, he admitted jokingly to a friend, "it is like confessing a murder."[1] What we call Darwinism implied that species were not immutably created by God, that all living things have descended from a single ancestor, and that evolution has occurred gradually by means of the "natural selection" of random genetic mutations, a process therefore requiring no supernatural causation and involving no determinism or teleology. In other words, nothing has evolved necessarily or toward a specific goal.[2] These tenets of evolutionary biology, which most educated people share today, are not incompatible with religious faith—ask Francis Collins, a distinguished scientist, the director of the National Institutes of Health, and a devout Christian.[3] Yet they have undermined the religious faith of many millions of people.

Ironically, modern science—a fundamentally new way to understand how nature works, combining experimental methods, the application of mathematical hypotheses to nature, rigorously logical thinking, the geometrization of space, systematic classification, and an astonishing receptivity to new ways of interpreting the world—may have emerged among Europeans in large part because of their belief that God created a rational, lawful, stable universe capable of being understood by human reason.

Artistic geniuses, while influenced by predecessors and contemporaries, bring to life unique and inimitable visions of reality. The creations of a poet or sculptor may stand unsurpassable for all of time. The development of science is altogether different. Although scientific knowledge and insights can be lost, for example when texts perish and cultures die out, human understanding of the natural world has mostly accumulated century by century and from culture to culture—from ancient Babylon, Egypt, India, and China and from ultimately every scientific tradition passed down, studied, interpreted, and built upon.[4] Without this steady accumulation of knowledge and practice—now slower, now more abundant—Isaac Newton could not have justly claimed: "If I have seen further it is only by standing on the shoulders of giants."[5] No poet today rivals Homer, yet the scientific knowledge of any school child exceeds that of Democritus.[6] Modern science emerged in early modern Europe from a high intensity of exploration and information sharing by a vast and interconnected intellectual community drawing on millennia of scientific understanding.

Ancient and medieval roots

Scholars in ancient Egypt and Mesopotamia discovered patterns in the heavens and on earth, kept detailed records of the movements of the stars and other heavenly bodies, developed complex number systems, and devised sophisticated and accurate calendars. Yet they understood the workings of nature mythologically, as caused by divine intervention.[7] The early Greek philosophers, by contrast, devised explanations for natural phenomena without recourse to the personal agency of deities.[8] The pre-Socratic thinkers wanted to know what things were made of, how they moved, and how they changed over time. They argued that all things stemmed from a basic substance and defined it variously as earth, water, air, or fire. On the one hand, they posited an underlying unity of reality, which could make a rational explanation possible for what existed and happened. On the other hand, they looked for concrete manifestations of these principles. Thus, for example, Anaxagoras (ca. 500–428 B.C.) explained earthquakes as caused by water bursting into subterranean hollows, and Anaximenes (fl. 585–528 B.C.E) as avalanches of subterranean earth. One may contrast these materialistic theories with interpretations centered on imagined interactions of "yin" and "yang" put forward by early Chinese thinkers.[9]

Other ancient Greek thinkers, in particular the Pythagoreans, argued that at the foundation of all things lay numbers. They meant that one can understand reality in terms of mathematical relationships.[10] The harmonic proportions the Pythagoreans discovered in musical tones exemplified for them the inner numeric harmony and orderliness of the universe. Centuries later, a similar insight contributed to Europe's scientific revolution.

Meanwhile, Plato and Aristotle achieved the first systematic understanding of the natural world. Plato argued that a rational being had created all things according to rational principles but no longer influences their motions and actions. Like the Pythagoreans, he considered mathematics the unchangeable language of reality. Yet he also conceived the cosmos as "ensouled," or infused with divine meaning and purpose.[11] Aristotle was more down to earth. He agreed with his teacher Plato that purposiveness inheres in all reality but only because each thing has its own specific nature. Each therefore deserves study. Among the subjects he investigated systematically were logic, botany, zoology, physics, cosmology, psychology, metaphysics, ethics, political theory, esthetics, rhetoric, poetry, theater, and music.[12] He advanced bold interpretations even about invisible forces he could not understand and distant objects he could not touch. Everything, in his mind, could be explained. Between them, Plato and Aristotle set the boundaries of nearly all subsequent philosophizing about the natural world, at least in the Near East and Europe, until the early modern period.

A few lesser Greeks made signal contributions to our understanding of nature. Democritus (ca. 460–370 B.C.) and Epicurus (341–270 B.C.) developed the theory that invisible, unbreakable, indivisible, and eternal atoms moving through an eternal void constitute all things by forming and reforming the substances of nature.

Purely mechanical, their movements lacked purpose.[13] Euclid, in addition to laying the foundations of geometry, applied geometric calculations to understand visual perspective. Archimedes (ca. 287–212 B.C.), one of history's greatest mathematicians, wrote a theoretical explanation of the functioning of the lever, invented the screw-pump, and formulated methods for calculating complex areas and approximating the number pi. Ptolemy of course developed a sophisticated astronomical conception of the solar system placing Earth at the center.[14] Though false, this model reigned supreme until overthrown definitively by Newton.

Greek scholars achieved breakthroughs in medicine as well.[15] Hippocrates of Kos (ca. 450–370 B.C.) and his followers developed a holistic, preventive method of preserving health. Proper diet and lifestyle they considered the essential means for maintaining harmony among the key bodily fluids. One century later, Herophilus of Chalcedon (ca. 330–260 B.C.) and his students at the Alexandrian medical school founded the disciplines of anatomy and physiology, thanks to human dissection, which had been and remained taboo in most cultures. Galen of Pergamum (ca. 129–200 A.D.) achieved an understanding of the nervous system, circulatory system, and general human anatomy that remained unsurpassed for over 1,000 years. Western Christians displayed little interest in Greek and Roman learning until the later Middle Ages.

At the other end of Eurasia, a powerful Chinese scientific tradition also emerged. The followers of the philosopher Mozi (ca. 470–391 B.C.) made advances in logic, mathematics, and geometrical optics.[16] The movement was suppressed several centuries later, and most of their writings were lost, but a tradition remained of applying scientific knowledge to practical matters like civil engineering, astronomy, meteorology, cartography, and the early detection of earthquakes.[17] These branches of learning developed steadily in China over the following 2,000 years, though discontinuities in transmission meant that scientists often had "to reinvent the wheel," so to speak.[18] An early understanding of magnetism led to the invention of a rudimentary compass some 2,000 years ago and a more sophisticated one proper for navigation a thousand years later. Chinese alchemists made continuous progress in understanding the properties of organic and inorganic substances in their search for elixirs of life.[19] Unburdened by the Galenic prohibition against using minerals and animal by-products for medicinal purposes, researchers discovered a wide range of pharmacological remedies, some unfortunately fatal.[20] The Chinese scientific approach remained largely empirical, however, and rarely led to systematic explanations or hierarchical structures of knowledge.[21]

Muslim scholars synthesized learning from across Eurasia and made signal contributions to mathematics, medicine, astronomy, optics, and, most importantly, chemistry. Jabir ibn Hayyan (ca. 721–815) methodically described chemical operations like calcination, reduction, sublimation, distillation, and crystallization and their application to such industrial processes as metallurgy and glassmaking.[22] He also concluded that the fundamental constituents of all metals are rarefied forms of sulfur and mercury. When combined in the right proportion, he argued, they produce gold. This theory inspired alchemists to achieve innumerable advances in the understanding of chemical reactions and properties, though Avicenna (ca. 980–1037) provided a detailed refutation of the possibility of metallic transmutation. Jabir's most illustrious successor, Muhammad ibn Zakariya al-Razi (865–925), devised a classification of minerals into six divisions, which included four "volatile substances," seven metals, and eleven salts.[23] Gradually, however, scientific research in the Muslim lands grew more speculative and less experimental and fell into decline after the Mongol conquest of Baghdad in 1258. A few Muslim scholars made great advances, especially in astronomy, which kept up a rich scholarly and speculative tradition for centuries. The work of Ibn al-Shatir (1304–75), Ali Qushji (1403–74), and other astronomers seems almost certain to have influenced Copernicus—even made his breakthroughs possible.[24] Yet this fact is crucial as well: such Muslim thinkers contributed to a series of extraordinary scientific advancements in early modern Europe but not in the Islamic world.

The bulk of Greek learning had also entered European libraries via translation from Arabic and original texts.[25] A few of Aristotle's claims posed a severe challenge to Christian beliefs, for example, that the universe is eternal and that the soul cannot exist after death. Aquinas's work of synthetic reconciliation did not please everyone but certainly shielded ancient Greece's foremost scientific thinker from blanket condemnation. It also opened the door to minutely analyzed interpretations and reinterpretations of Greek thought.

As discussed in Chapter 3, scholastic philosophers intensively debated a wide variety of questions concerning God, the universe, nature, the mind, and ethics. They often tested implausible, provocative, and innovative hypotheses. Since hundreds—and ultimately thousands—of scholars were working at dozens of institutions of higher learning across Europe, sharing ideas, learning from one another, moving from place to place, and critiquing new ideas as they appeared, they gradually reached a critical mass of discovery.[26]

For example, a team of logicians and mathematicians at Merton College, Oxford University, in the second quarter of the fourteenth century, defined velocity as intensity of motion, a striking new interpretation. Just as a color can be more or less bright, they reasoned, motion can be more or less swift. They also defined uniformly accelerated velocity (constant acceleration) in the same way as modern physics. They went on to formulate several theorems, like the "Merton rule" that an object will travel the same distance in the same time whether accelerating uniformly or moving steadily at a rate half the speed of the accelerating body's ultimate velocity. Other scholars verified these results or built on their foundation. Thus, Nicolas Oresme (ca. 1323–82) of the University of Paris devised geometrical proofs for the Mertonian principles.[27]

The development of physical science owes an enormous debt to medieval thinkers, nearly all of whom were priests or monks, like Oresme. He rejected Aristotle's view that heavy objects are drawn toward the Earth's center and light objects toward the "sublunary region," arguing instead that objects lose weight the farther they move from the Earth's center. Again refuting Aristotle, he hypothesized that the Earth moves (and not the Sun). To those who objected that things would fly off the Earth as it spun, he reasoned that since everything spins together nothing falls off. Another scholar active in Paris, Jean Buridan (ca. 1300–60), revised the Aristotelian theory of projectile motion. Drawing on an idea passed down from the Hellenistic Near East through Islamic natural philosophers, he argued that projectiles move not because of a continuous external force but because a force, at the time of launching, becomes internal to the object.[28] He called this force "impetus" and concluded that only resistance could diminish its effect.[29] This idea was strikingly close to the modern conceptualization of inertia.

By this point, intellectual ferment, rigorous scholarship, diversity of approaches, and a fever to explore distinguished Europe from all other possible rivals in the world. The Islamic Golden Age had ended. Isolated advances in astronomy and mathematics continued but never again reached a critical mass of development. The rich and powerful Muslim empires that emerged over the next couple centuries—the Ottoman, Safavid, and Mughal—were traditional agrarian states with only weakly developed intellectual communities and priestly classes under the secular authority of the rulers.[30] The Indian religions—Buddhism, Jainism, and Hinduism—emphasized withdrawal from earthly concerns and otherworldly passivism. Some mathematicians continued to accomplish brilliant and path-breaking work, but pure contemplation attracted most of the gifted minds, and systematic inquiry was comparatively rare.[31] As for China, the Confucian literati cared little for science, while the Ming court opposed and severely limited foreign trade and exploration. Learned scholars and natural philosophers abounded but for the most part depended for their livelihoods on a strictly centralized bureaucratic system.[32]

In general, the world's other great civilizations lacked the freewheeling criticism and inquiry, the diversity of patrons and funding sources, and the avid thirst for knowledge and delight in novelty that characterized Europe in the late medieval and Renaissance periods. In fact, people of no other culture in the world then or at any time before so freely adapted concepts, practices, ideas, institutions, theories, technologies, inventions, terminology, and products as did Europeans already in this age, a trend that intensified and expanded in the coming two centuries. Combining this extraordinary openness to the accomplishments of others with a feverish intellectual enthusiasm and a rigorous and systematic approach to learning and knowledge, Europe laid the foundation for a qualitative transmutation of the human understanding of the natural world.

Methods and approaches

Neither Plato nor Aristotle developed science in the modern sense. Plato used a deductive method of arriving at the truth by arguing from general principles to particular cases. Aristotle marshaled evidence from concrete and detailed observations in order to formulate hypotheses in various branches of natural philosophy. Aristotle's ultimate goal, however, was to enunciate first principles and ultimate causes, not to explain mundane natural phenomena. The supreme model of science, he believed, was geometry. Yet the rules and premises of mathematics (and logic) describe only conceptual reality—not actual physical existence. They can serve as tools for organizing and interpreting observations of physical reality, as indeed scientists in the early modern period discovered (see below). Yet mathematics and logic cannot by themselves yield empirically falsifiable knowledge about the natural world, or what we call science.[33]

Jurists in medieval Europe's law schools contributed sociologically, methodologically, and institutionally to the later emergence of modern science.[34] Using the scholastic method, as noted in Chapter 3, they sought to reconcile disparate laws and customs in force across Europe with fundamental religious and philosophical texts. Like modern scientists, medieval jurists developed a code of conduct involving objectivity and integrity, methodical skepticism, openness to new ideas, and the assumption that their task is not to seek final answers but ever more adequate approximations to the truth. They thus developed a coherent body of knowledge, which systematically accounted for specific instances in terms of general principles derived from concrete observation, creative hypotheses, and the verification of each hypothesis through further observation and the study of historical cases. Scholars in philosophy, medicine, and theology soon applied similar methods in their own disciplines.

Most scholars now agree that medieval and Renaissance practitioners of "magic" stumbled upon genuine scientific breakthroughs.[35] Early Christians, from the New Testament through St Augustine, viewed all magic as evil. Some ancient Greek and Roman authors, by contrast, reported on manifestations of "natural magic," or wonders of nature—physical objects or phenomena allegedly exhibiting miracle-working properties. Lemnos clay, which Pierre Belon investigated, was a notable example.[36] Muslim and medieval Christian authors passed down such claims, which enjoyed much interest in Europe. Marsilio Ficino (1433–99), an influential humanistic philosopher who first translated the complete works of Plato into Latin, and Nicolas Oresme both meticulously studied natural magic.[37]

Especially influential was Ficino's translation in 1471 of the *Corpus Hermeticum*, a collection of Greek texts from the second and third centuries A.D.[38] Dealing with alchemy, astrology, numerology, ancient wisdom, and other esoteric subjects, Ficino's volume went through two dozen editions in a half-century. His treatise on magic, *De vita coelitus comparanda*, of 1489, enjoyed similar success. Drawing on Neoplatonist thought, Avicenna, obscure Muslim thinkers, and Aquinas, he argued that a person who understood the secret natural connections among terrestrial, celestial, and divine things could manipulate them to his own ends. In Ficino's words,

> Using natural objects, natural magic captures the beneficial powers of the heavenly bodies to bring good health. . . . Just as the farmer tempers his field to the weather to give sustenance to man, so this wise man, this priest, for the sake of man's safety tempers the lower objects of the cosmos to the higher. [Natural magic] puts natural materials in a correct relationship with natural causes.[39]

As a physician, Ficino sought to use hidden or inexplicable powers in physical and celestial objects to treat his patients. As a Christian priest, however, he carefully respected strict distinctions made by Aquinas between, say, amulets intended to traffic with demonic intelligences and those merely possessing natural curative powers.

That occult (hidden) forces existed in nature was indisputable for Ficino and most other natural philosophers going back to antiquity. The electric ray, which can stun its prey with an electric shock, furnished a case in point. Ancient physicians, while having no understanding of the nature of its sting, used the fish to treat pain.[40] So long as natural philosophers could devise no nonmagical explanation of this effect—something they began to manage only in the 1700s—the ray stood as a proof of magical forces in nature.

Belief in natural magic inspired the research of thousands of alchemists in medieval and Renaissance Europe. Following ancient Greek and Golden Age Islamic theories and practices, some deriving from ancient India and China, they expected to apprehend the inner essence of things and to transform nature—for example, to transmute base metals into gold or to concoct a potion restoring youth.[41] Such hopes justified numberless efforts to experiment with diverse substances and spurred European alchemists, following their Islamic predecessors, to pave the way toward modern chemistry.

Among significant advances achieved through alchemy was the isolation of the element arsenic by St Albertus Magnus (ca. 1200–80) and around 1300 the discovery of sulfuric acid by False Geber, a Spanish monk who adopted the name of an eighth-century Muslim alchemist. This was a huge breakthrough, because until then scholars had known about only very weakly corrosive acids, like acetic acid distilled from vinegar.[42] Some scholars consider this the most important step forward in chemistry since the discovery of how to separate iron from iron ore 3,000 years before.[43] False Geber also discovered strong nitric acid. These acidic compounds enabled alchemists to dissolve substances, to form precipitates, to isolate elements, and to create salts. Around the same time, Arnaldus de Villa Nova (1235–1311), a physician of Catalan origin who translated many scientific works from Arabic, discovered carbon monoxide and first distilled pure alcohol, which he found to have preservative and antiseptic qualities. Some alchemists abused their practice, for example, selling false gold for real, leading Pope John XXII to prohibit alchemy in 1317.[44] Even so, alchemical investigations continued.

The next important figure in the advance of chemistry was Paracelsus (1493–1541). He and his followers rejected logic, mathematics, the Aristotelian elements, Galenic humoral medicine, and scholastic thought generally—in a word, abstract approaches. They argued instead for a careful study of the "Book of Nature" through observation and experiment. As practicing physicians, many Paracelsians sought chemically based treatments for diseases, especially the virulent new forms of venereal disease then gripping the continent. Traditionalists vociferously defended Galenic medicine. Partisans of the "chemical philosophy" responded in kind. One of them, Robert Fludd (1574–1637), propounded a mystical vision of the unity of man with all things and of cosmic harmony, in which mathematics had no place.[45]

Mathematics provided a third transformative way to understand the world.[46] Johannes Kepler (1571–1630) replied to Fludd in his *Harmonices mundi* (1619) and other works.[47] Using mathematics, he argued, one can describe physical reality and in general the natural order more accurately than using qualitative constructs. Kepler was thus also arguing against Plato and Aristotle who had preferred to describe, analyze, grasp intuitively, and seek to apprehend the essence of things—in part using mathematics—rather than to quantify them. Thousands if not millions of Europeans since the high Middle Ages, however, had been engaged precisely in a vast though uncoordinated project of measuring, assigning numeric value, and in general quantifying nearly every conceivable object, condition, state, and process.

Johannes de Muris (1290–1351) devised a system of musical notation that determined the relative duration of each note by its shape and size. A century later, Benedetto Cotrugli codified the principles of bookkeeping. In between these two points and then beyond, mathematicians lent their skills to warfare, to the voyages of discovery, to architecture and engineering, to clock making, to the plastic arts (Fra Luca Bartolomeo de Pacioli, a professor of mathematics, helped Leonardo with spatial calculations)[48]—to myriad objects and activities. The printing revolution made widely accessible powerful mathematical tools, such as logarithms and Cartesian coordinates.[49] This approach to the world distinguished European society perhaps more than any other. Other societies had made breakthroughs in mathematics and had applied them to practical matters. Yet in none had the power of numbers and measurement so pervaded the culture, so empowered artisans and professionals, and so increased efficiency and output.

The most prescient thinkers realized they were ushering in a new era. It would not merely rival the achievements of the ancient world, as the Renaissance humanists thought hopefully of their epoch, but would reach almost unimaginable heights of intellectual achievement. Little wonder the word "new" appeared in the titles of major books—for example, Francis Bacon's *New Organon* (1620). He opposed his "new method" to Aristotle's purely logical *Organon*, which more than any other text guided scholastic thinking. Bacon wished to forge a new path, though one drawing on the best existing approaches.[50] He divided all natural philosophers into empiricists and rationalists.

> Empiricists, like ants, simply accumulate and use; Rationalists, like spiders, spin webs from themselves; the way of the bee is in between: it takes material from the flowers of the garden and field; but it has the ability to convert and digest them. This is not unlike the true working of philosophy; which does not rely solely or mainly on mental power, and does not store the material provided by natural history and mechanical experiments in its memory untouched but altered and adapted in the intellect. Therefore much is to be hoped from a closer and more binding alliance (which has never yet been made) between those faculties (i.e. the experimental and the rational).[51]

In simplest terms, it was insufficient merely to observe and catalog, like Aristotle, or to develop grand theories, like Plato. Enhancing human understanding of the natural world required both.

More than that, natural philosophers needed to shed their own prejudices about reality and to see everything as if with new eyes. "We more often need to pay attention to known things," Bacon argued, "than to get information about unknown things."[52] Researchers should therefore plan their observations and experiments in advance. Above all, they should maintain detailed laboratory notebooks in which to inscribe data answering a host of questions. Among these might be "what is lost and disappears; what remains and what accrues; what expands and what contracts; what is combined, what is separated; what is continuous, what interrupted; what impels, what obstructs; what prevails, what submits; and several other questions."[53]

Innovative thinkers devised new ways of analyzing and organizing knowledge in every field of endeavor. Johann Dryander (1500–60), one of the first anatomists in history to draw anatomical illustrations from his own dissections, argued for a "mathematical" model of knowledge enabling scholars to discern fact from fiction in 1557.[54] The humanist Petrus Ramus (1515–72) developed a method for organizing knowledge that resembled the game of "twenty questions," but with defined lines of inquiry from the most general to the most particular. His student, Theodor Zwinger (1533–88), later published an account of his travels (*Methodus apodemica*), in which he sets forth a method for properly organizing the potentially vast data culled from observations and experiences. Other scholars wrote similar treatises around the same time.[55]

Thousands of "Renaissance men" kept abreast of advances in many different fields, dabbled themselves in several, conducted practical scientific experiments, corresponded broadly across Europe, and year by year increased the intellectual ferment of the continent. For example, over 1,000 at least vaguely scientific books appeared in Germany alone every year in the late 1500s. Few scholarly advances occurred within university walls, which suffered from scholastic rigidity and religious orthodoxy (Lutheran universities, for example, had to adhere to the Augsburg Confession).[56]

The need for institutionalized means for the exchange of ideas therefore engendered a new kind of scholarly association, the learned society.[57] In 1560, Giambattista della Porta (1535–1615), who wrote an encyclopedia on "natural magic," founded the Academy of the Mysteries of Nature in Naples. Anyone could join who had made some discovery in natural philosophy. A half-century later, Francis Bacon argued that "the path to science is not, like that of philosophy, such that only one man can tread it at a time."[58] In his *New Atlantis* (1614), he advocated establishing institutes staffed by dozens of specialized researchers. Within a few decades, scientists like Robert Boyle (1627–91) were meeting regularly in an "invisible college" that formed the basis for the Royal Society of London (1660). The deeply pious Boyle himself conducted research simultaneously in chemistry, medicine, physics, mechanics, and agriculture.[59] Above all, he pursued only useful, practical knowledge. Over and over, he stressed the necessity to publish the results of each and every experiment, in order to establish a paper trail that others could follow. And voilà, in 1665 the world's first two learned journals began to appear in print, the French *Journal des sçavans* and the *Philosophical Transactions* of the Royal Society.

The most radical philosophical approach was the "methodical doubt" of René Descartes (1596–1650). Educated at a Jesuit high school in northwestern France, he wandered for years before settling in the Dutch Republic in 1628. In two of his major works, *Discourse on Method* (1637) and *Meditations on First Philosophy* (1641), he ruminated on how we obtain knowledge. "From time to time I have found that the senses deceive," he lamented, "and it is prudent never to trust completely those who have deceived us even once."[60] For example, a stick plunged into water falsely appears to be broken. Similarly, a piece of wax has specific characteristics as reported by the senses until a flame transforms its external appearance. The mind insists, however, that the substance remains wax. Therefore, one can trust the understanding more than the senses. Yet much knowledge the understanding possesses derives from unreliable sources. In order to sort fact from fiction, he determined to doubt everything he had ever learned.[61]

He concluded after much effort that he could know only one thing for certain: *Cogito, ergo sum*, or "I am thinking therefore I exist."[62] This proposition permitted Descartes to develop an alternative to the Aristotelian conception of physical reality as defined by such qualities as hot, cold, wet, and dry. Instead he argued that reality consists of two sharply distinct phenomena—*res cogitans*, or thinking things, and *res extensa*, or extended things.[63] The fundamental characteristics of the latter are length, breadth, and depth. One can precisely measure these aspects of any body, along with their shape, position, and motion, opening the door to a mathematical physics. Descartes's pathbreaking work in linking algebra and geometry also facilitated this development.[64] Finally, his division of all things into mind or body—only humans combine the two, though awkwardly—set the stage for mechanistic and materialistic worldviews.[65] This outlook made it possible to view nature as a field for experimentation and action and led to prodigious achievements in the sciences but in the long run also tended to foster the development of nihilistic beliefs.

In no other region of the world could one find anything like the European intellectual ferment, institutionalized scholarly research, abundance of philosophical approaches, interconnectedness of learned men and women, cross-fertilization of applied and theoretical sciences, or profusion of means and venues for sharing the fruits of research.[66]

China had for centuries been the richest, best organized, and most powerful civilization in the world. The agricultural system fed by far the largest population in history (though not without demographic catastrophes and popular rebellions).[67] The government was efficient and intrusive. Chinese physicians practiced an ancient and relatively effective holistic medicine. Artisans and builders maintained a highly developed material culture in dozens of thriving cities. Artists and writers produced a torrent of sophisticated works. Scholars compiled enormous editions of classic literature. The economy involved trade throughout East Asia and the Indian Ocean region.[68] Chinese scientists made brilliant but often isolated discoveries in the study of magnetism, optics, and mathematics. Armies of scholars accumulated vast stores of knowledge about the natural world but only rarely pieced it together into explanatory systems.[69] Why did Chinese thinkers favor empirical over theoretical approaches? As noted in Chapter 1, most intellectually gifted Chinese devoted extraordinary efforts to pass the civil service examinations. Success typically involved literary creativity and striking juxtapositions but not theoretical brilliance or imagination. Intellectuals also remained hamstrung by the neo-Confucian orthodoxy.

During the Song Dynasty, the philosopher Zhu Xi (1130–1200) synthesized into an organic worldview key principles of Confucian, Buddhist, and Taoist thought.[70] Zhu's philosophy was almost Platonic, combining emphasis on the moral cultivation of the individual person with a metaphysical conception of natural reality. The universe, he argued, is made up of *li*, or principle, and *ch'i*, or material force. *Li* manifests itself as humanity, righteousness, propriety, and wisdom. Material force consists of a complex interplay of yin and yang, which express themselves concretely in the five material agents: metal, wood, fire, water, and earth. All things are made up of a complicated mix of ying, yang, and the five agents. Zhu advocated "the study of things," though it seems the things he had in mind had more to do with the moral and human realms than the natural world. Zhu's neo-Confucian synthesis became China's official doctrine and the "Four Books," which he compiled and edited from among ancient Confucian texts, when added to the "Five Classics" compiled by Confucius himself, formed the core reading for the Imperial examination system for hundreds of years until its abolition in 1905.[71]

A few thinkers challenged this orthodoxy. Wang Yang-ming (1472–1529), a statesman-general, deplored unreflective Chinese rote learning. He argued that man has an innate ability to distinguish good from evil and that all moral understanding and all our knowledge of the world is acquired through experience. Understanding oneself and striving to lead a moral life, he claimed, are the primary ends of man.[72] During the early Qing, Gu Yanwu (1630–82) denounced what he considered the vague and abstruse metaphysical theorizing of the official philosophy and the endless discoursing by scholars on such topics as "the refined and the undivided."[73] The rigidity of Chinese thought, he lamented, had made both officials and scholars unable to address real-life social and political problems, leading to the collapse of the Ming Dynasty. Gu therefore advocated pursuing knowledge "of practical use to society," seeking ways to reduce distress and poverty in the world. The movement he founded gradually evolved into an antiquarian preoccupation with classical Confucian texts.

Thus, as Europe was embarking on an almost total transformation of our understanding of nature and reality, the best Chinese minds remained walled in by philosophical orthodoxy. Muslim scholars and researchers from Persia to Iberia made almost numberless contributions to the advancement of science and learning until the twelfth century and then all but stopped. Astronomy was the only natural science in the Islamic world that continued to develop into the early modern period.[74] Scholars and thinkers of the other great cultures of the world also remained isolated, stifled, and largely unproductive.

Life science

Late medieval European natural philosophers made their first serious advances in the field of anatomy. For more than 1,500 years, since the work of physicians at the Alexandrian school of medicine, it seems that no one on earth practiced the dissection of human corpses.[75] Postmortem dissection for forensic purposes became a common procedure in fourteenth-century Europe, but most physicians had little understanding of anatomy and tended, like the Muslims whose works they often read in translation, to treat disease without understanding how the body functions. Only one brief treatise by Galen, on the digestive organs, had been translated into Latin by this time. Armed with this work, Mondino dei Liuzzi (ca. 1270–1326), a professor of medicine at the University of Bologna, laid out the principles of dissection in a textbook of 1315.[76] He also incorporated dissection classes into his curriculum. As Mondino read from his textbook, a surgeon would point to the relevant organs and body parts. This practice became standard in most late medieval medical schools. In fact, even after Galen's principle treatise, *On the Use of the Parts*, was translated and published in 1322, most scholars and physicians continued to prefer Mondino's treatise. It appeared in a printed edition in 1476, followed by 27 more by 1600. Getting beyond Mondino became difficult.

Among the first dissenters was Leonardo da Vinci. Like other Italian artists, he had carefully studied animal and human anatomy and performed dissections.[77] He also read Galen and vehemently criticized Mondino in 1506. The publication of Galen's long-lost treatise, *On Anatomical Procedures* (1531) proved a turning point. Whereas Mondino began with the viscera, Galen started with the skeleton and then moved to the muscles, nerves, veins, and arteries of the arms and legs before proceeding to the internal organs, which he divided according to function. Galen quickly became the new authority. Other researchers built on his achievements.

Andreas Vesalius (1514–64) stood out among them.[78] A professor at the University of Padua and later court physician to Charles V and Philip II, he revolutionized the teaching of human anatomy. First, he conducted public and private dissections himself instead of relying on a demonstrator. He dissected both humans and animals, seeking contrasts and similarities. Second, he tested every claim by Galen and noted many inaccuracies. Finally, he incorporated detailed illustrations into his teaching and publications. *On the Structure of the Human Body* (1543) included nearly 100 illustrations, sumptuously executed by artists of Titian's celebrated workshop. The work made dozens of significant anatomical and physiological advances, especially concerning the circulatory and nervous systems. It was revolutionary in its uniting of art, science, and the latest technological innovations.[79]

Across Europe, knowledge of plants and animals increased exponentially. The University of Padua medical school established a chair in botany in 1533; several others followed elsewhere. In the 1530s and 1540s, German Protestant botanists published encyclopedic surveys of known plants, including their habitats and medicinal properties, based on both ancient authors and extensive field research and accompanied by many hundreds of detailed illustrations. Otto Brunfels (ca. 1488–1534) commissioned illustrations of such accuracy and realism that they included the roots, surface detail, and leaves and flowers viewed from diverse angles.[80] The Italian botanist, Luca Ghini (1490–1556), established a collection of dried plants, an herbarium, at the University of Bologna. By the time of his death, herbaria were being maintained throughout Europe. Systematic botanical gardens also appeared in several cities during the second half of the sixteenth century.[81] There was nothing coincidental about these scholars' Protestantism. A major point of the Reformation, after all, was to challenge authority and to go to the sources.

Two Swiss Protestants, the botanist Conrad Gesner (1516–65) and Georg Bauer, often called "Agricola" (1494–1555),[82] undertook a systematic study of "fossils," meaning anything dug from the ground. They analyzed, catalogued, categorized, and described gems, rocks, metals, hardened fluids like amber, and fossils proper. Gesner also urged cooperative research on fossils and appended to *A Book on Fossil Objects* (1565) a catalog to an existing collection of specimens, which fostered the development of more such collections around Europe. Both scholars considered the possibility that fossils stemmed from prehistoric living things, though neither embraced this idea. For devout Christians and biblical literalists, it would have caused too much cognitive dissonance.

Gesner also produced the first major European work on zoology, *Historiae animalium* (1551–58), which ran to around 4,500 pages. Drawing mostly on the work of ancient Greek and Roman predecessors, he also worked from first-hand observations.[83] The Italian naturalist, Ulysses Aldrovandus (1522–1605), planned an 11-volume study, for which he personally furnished the volumes on birds, insects, and lower-order animals. (Three colleagues completed the work). Such scholars were "Renaissance men." Gesner is considered the father of systematic bibliography and modern botany. He also wrote and published on pharmacopeia, medicine, metallurgy, fossils, and theology.[84] By Renaissance scholarly standards, Gesner's prolixity was unexceptional. Most of the authors who figure in the rest of this chapter could boast a similarly varied and abundant output. In general, only Copernicus, who published very little in his lifetime and focused largely on one subject, stood out as unusual.[85]

Year by year, scholars and natural philosophers advanced their understanding of the natural world, publishing immense numbers of treatises, encyclopedias, compendia, and other scholarly works and communicating directly with one another through dense networks of intellectual exchange. Human knowledge expanded more systematically, intensively, and expansively than ever before in history. If scholars made significant breakthroughs during the Islamic Golden Age every decade or two, in the Renaissance era scientific advances occurred nearly every year. For example, in 1545 Ambroise Paré initiated the practice of tying off an artery to stop bleeding. The following year, Girolamo Fracastoro hypothesized that microscopic agents spread infectious diseases. In 1551, Pierre Belon described similarities between different animal species.[86] These were only advances in the life sciences; their frequency has increased ceaselessly until the present time. David Landes has called this process the "routinization of discovery."[87]

Of course, knowledge had to accumulate before natural philosophers could bring about paradigm-shifting achievements.[88] In the life sciences, two of the most significant shifts concern the circulatory system and modern scientific classification.

The Arab Muslim polymath, Ibn al-Nafis (1213–88), had described pulmonary circulation, whereby blood is enriched with oxygen and returns to the heart.[89] Even European scholars with the greatest anatomical knowledge like Leonardo and Vesalius, however, adhered to Galen's belief that "veinous" blood flowed from the liver, where it was produced, to the rest of the body and also into the right ventricle of the heart.[90] Thence, some "veinous" blood supposedly passed through what in fact is an impermeable wall, the septum, into the left ventricle. There, Galen claimed that air, pumped directly from the lungs, transformed it into "arterial" blood, which flowed to the brain and, via the nerves, to other vital organs. A few later physicians, including the Protestant Michael Servetus who was burned at the stake in 1553, understood the function of pulmonary circulation, but even they continued to uphold the overall Galenic system. Breaking free from its straitjacket proved impossible, until the work of William Harvey (1578–1657).

After graduating from Cambridge University, Harvey spent 5 years studying medicine at the University of Padua, which boasted a long tradition of experimental anatomy and a high level of intellectual freedom. In 1602, he settled in London where he practiced medicine and was named a Fellow of the Royal College of Physicians. After 14 years of painstaking experimentation and observation of both animal and human anatomy, he concluded that blood circulates in two closed systems. (He published his findings in 1628.) First, the heart pumps blood through the lungs, which enrich it with oxygen; then, it pumps the enriched blood throughout the body via the arteries. The depleted blood returns to the heart through the veins, and the process starts over. Simple and elegant, Harvey's theory both described reality and radically altered the whole of physiology, since a proper understanding of the circulatory system led to a more accurate comprehension of the respiratory, digestive, and other bodily systems. A scientific revolution in medicine was underway.

Medical knowledge increased partly thanks to new instruments. The most important physical instrument was the microscope. Invented in the late 1500s, it enabled researchers to examine and understand fine details of anatomy. The one piece of the puzzle Harvey had not grasped was how blood passes from the veins to the arteries through microscopic capillaries. Employing a crude microscope, Marcello Malpighi (1628–94) discovered them in 1661.[91] More important still, the Dutch scholar Antoni van Leeuwenhoek (1632–1723) used the device to discern various microorganisms beginning in 1674. Within a decade, he had observed and accurately described the function of spermatozoa and had isolated bacteria. Another Dutchman, Jan Swammerdam (1637–80), discovered red blood cells.[92]

Conceptual instruments also contributed to the advance of medical science. In 1596, the Swiss botanist Gaspard Bauhin (1560–1624) published a classification of some 6,000 plant species using a system of binomial nomenclature that divided organisms by genera and species.[93] Some 140 years later, Carolus Linnaeus (1707–78), a Swedish botanist and zoologist, developed a sophisticated and elaborate method of biological classification.[94] He divided all living things into two kingdoms (plants and animals), which he divided further, in ascending order of specificity, into classes, orders, genera, and species. The tenth edition of his *Systema Naturae* classified 4,400 species of animals and 7,700 of plants. His method of taxonomy enabled researchers to organize and understand the vast information accumulating about the biological realm by relating each organism to similar ones and by means of a simple and stable system of identifying labels. The Linnaean method epitomized the rational, systematic, and utilitarian approach of natural philosophy in the era of Scientific Revolution.

Cosmology

Coming to terms with the movement of our own planet proved extraordinarily difficult for people of all times and places. Common sense and our own experience tell us that our Earth is stable and that the objects in the heavens move around it. In the far distance, the fixed belt of the starry zodiac unfolds its storied pictures in the course of 12 months, while the planets move at their own pace in the same direction, west to east.[95] Yet, upon close inspection, they appear to move in strange ways. Every year or two, each planet, according to its own immutable timetable, slows down, stops, and moves in the opposite direction for a time, before returning to its original path. Stargazers and astronomers in all cultures, it seems, noted these anomalies, though generally without offering philosophical, much less scientific, explanations.

Ancient Greeks wrestled more fruitfully with these conundrums than any other people. Philolaus (c. 480–385 B.C.), a disciple of Pythagoras, claimed that the Earth, the Moon, the Sun, the five planets, and the fixed stars—farthest of all—rotated round a "central fire" that remained unseen because the inhabited part of the Earth was always turned away from it.[96] As Greek travelers visited distant regions, like the Ganges in the East, yet returned with no sightings of the "central fire," subsequent Pythagoreans dropped that concept. Heraclides Ponticus (387–312 B.C.), a student of Plato, though a follower of Pythagoras, posited the rotation of the Earth on its own axis. Of all the planets, Mercury and Venus traced the most erratic pathways, though always apparently close to the Sun. Heraclides therefore argued that the two inner planets must in fact revolve around the Sun. Aristarchus (310–ca. 230 B.C.), born like Pythagoras on the island of Samos, went much further. He placed the Sun at the center of our world, though the treatise in which he propounded this view is now lost. According to Archimedes, however, he "supposed that the fixed stars and the sun are immovable, but that the Earth is carried round the sun in a circle."[97] The rest of the planets followed circular orbits around the Sun as well. Yet for nearly 1,800 years, astronomers rejected Aristarchus's heliocentric theory. Unmooring the Earth in a vast universe probably frightened the ancient mind more than it could bear.

Aristotle's model proved more reassuring. He divided the cosmos into the sublunary region below the Moon, where all things—made of earth, water, air, and fire—decay and change, and the incorruptible superlunary realm. Earth, being the heaviest element, finds its place at the center of the cosmos.[98] The lightest element, fire, moves naturally in the opposite direction, upward. Combinations and recombinations of the four elements account for all change and all things in the sublunary realm. The heavens, made of an immutable substance called "aether," consist of a series of concentric, invisible, rotating spherical shells, or spheres. Attached to each, at the appropriate interval, are the Moon, the Sun, a planet, or the fixed belt of distant stars. A "prime mover" residing beyond the starry firmament imparts to the outermost sphere a constant impetus. As in a set of interconnected gears, the impetus then passes from sphere to sphere. Nothing exists beyond the unmoved mover.

Despite its elegance and simplicity, the model failed to account for obvious astronomical activity. Aside from regressions, there was also the problem of variable brightness. Venus, Mars, and Jupiter in particular wax and wane in intensity, belying Aristotle's claim that the heavens never change. He nevertheless adopted a complicated system of 55 nesting concentric spheres, several for every planet, each rotating on an axis tilted this way and that, in order to represent the planet's anomalous motion. To improve upon this system, since by now the whole point of astronomy was to prove the uniform circular motion of all heavenly bodies, nearly 400 years later Ptolemy invented an even less realistic conceptual model.[99] He imagined the celestial bodies attached to "epicycles" or smaller rotating spheres attached to the larger spheres already described. In some cases, he devised epicycles attached to epicycles. Altogether these devices, along with the geometrical trick of placing the axes of the wandering orbs off center from their spheres, accounted for all celestial motion, though not the planets' variations in luminosity. The model also divorced the cosmos from sublunary physical reality, offered no scientific explanation of how the celestial realm actually functioned, and indeed was never taken to represent actual physical processes. Still, the Ptolemaic system remained the world's dominant relatively scientific cosmological model for nearly 1,500 years.

After a "dark age" from the fall of Rome to the Carolingian Renaissance, when some scholars believed the universe and the Earth were shaped like the Holy Tabernacle that Moses built,[100] the Ptolemaic system again predominated. The medieval mind added many more levels to reality, imagining a "great chain of being," with no empty places, stretching from minerals, through a hierarchy of living things and up, past the crystalline spheres of the heavens, to a hierarchy of angels and, ultimately, God.[101] Man, given his dual nature, had a foot in both realms. From the millennium, serious astronomers knew and even accepted the planetary theory of Heraclides. Yet they also affirmed a naïve geocentrism. Similarly, maps depicting a rectangular Earth existed in parallel with highly detailed portolano charts in use among mariners.[102] Holding two radically incompatible visions of the same reality proved acceptable for centuries yet remained like a ticking time bomb ready to blow apart the medieval worldview.

Several dogmas stood in the way of a cosmological breakthrough, including the belief that "heavenly bodies" move uniformly and in perfect circles, that physicists and astronomers study entirely different subjects, that mathematics does not apply to natural philosophy, and that the natural state of all objects is rest. A succession of three brilliant innovators—Copernicus, Kepler, and Galileo—broke free from these dogmas and cleared a path for Newton's grand synthesis. Each innovator played a key role, though none was exactly an unalloyed hero.[103]

Nicolaus Copernicus (1473–1543) was timid, even obsequious, resentful and often sour, extremely conservative, and miserly.[104] He had few friends and tended to push well-wishers away. After 12 years of study, including 9 in Italy, he took up various sinecures back in Prussia, giving him plenty of leisure for his studies. A philosopher and mathematician, rather than a scientist, he spent little time observing the heavens and drew most of his data from ancient astronomical works. In 1514, he circulated among several acquaintances a "Little Commentary" that sought to improve the Ptolemaic model by forcing it to conform to its own principle of uniform circular motion. He achieved this end by means of several new ideas, among them that the planets revolve around the Sun, the Earth rotates on an axis, and the stars stand at an extremely far distance from the solar system. The model was vastly simpler and thus more elegant than the Ptolemaic, which presupposed myriad objects moving around the Earth instead of a rotating Earth only giving the impression of such movement. The trouble was, he could not prove that the Earth was in fact moving.[105]

Meanwhile, he spent this next 15 or so years trying to demonstrate the accuracy of his claims using mathematics. Although leading scholars and Catholic prelates urged him to publish his work, he refused, fearing ridicule. Finally in 1543, a scholarly admirer arranged for the publication of Copernicus's masterwork, *On the Revolutions of the Heavenly Spheres*, which appeared just in time for its author to receive it into his hands and then expire. A Lutheran theologian, Andreas Osiander, who oversaw the final stages of publication, added an unauthorized preface denying that the book's claims were more than hypotheses. Whatever Copernicus himself thought of the preface, if he even read it, it suggested to readers that no true revolution had taken place.[106] Although numerous scholars carefully read the text, it had no immediate earth-shattering effect. The church prohibited it only in 1616, more than 70 years after its publication, and 7 years after Galileo greatly improved the telescope and began making observations supporting the Copernican theory.[107]

Ironically, Copernicus remained largely in thrall to the Aristotelian explanation of physical reality, while several scholars at Oxford and Paris over 100 years before had made serious advances in the study of motion, momentum, and acceleration, achievements he either ignored or rejected as unorthodox. He did not posit an infinite universe, a revolutionary concept foreign to Aristotle, yet his doctrine implied it. The lack of a clear and firm center left the universe decentralized and anarchic. All this was far from Copernicus's intention. As Kepler later commented, "Copernicus tried to interpret Ptolemy rather than nature."[108] Either way, he helped launch a revolution he never wanted.

About Johannes Kepler, an obsessive recorder of facts and details, we know almost infinitely more than about the timid Copernicus.[109] His father, a mercenary soldier who brutalized his family, disappeared when Kepler was 17. His quarrelsome mother, who was later tried as a witch, often disappeared with her husband. Several brothers and uncles also led the lives of vagabonds. A sickly child, Johannes suffered multiple and continuous ailments. He constantly wrangled and made enemies. Yet he somehow managed to sublimate his family's wandering streak into an inspired and even reckless pursuit of philosophical and scientific truth.

A visionary, at age 24 Kepler thought he grasped the mathematically proportionate relationships between the planets, their orbits, and their distances from the Sun, which he correlated with the five "Platonic" solids, the only perfectly symmetrical geometric solid objects conceivable.[110] The fact that there were only five solids and five intervals between the six (known) planets meant to him that God must have ordained geometry and the cosmos to fit seamlessly together. His conception, which proved entirely false, nevertheless spurred him to decades of assiduous and ceaseless mental exercise and the perfecting of his mathematical skills. "What else can the human mind hold but numbers and magnitudes?" he wrote in 1599. "These alone we apprehend correctly, and if piety permits to say so, our comprehension is in this case the same as God's, at least insofar as we are able to understand it in this mortal life."[111] Precisely this tool enabled him to tackle several thorny problems of astronomical physics, problems that in most cases no other thinkers had ever posed.

The mystical speculation in Kepler's first book, *The Sacred Mystery of the Cosmos* (1596), repelled modern thinkers like Galileo. Indeed, few who read it recognized the genius of its author. Among those who did was the Danish aristocratic stargazer Tycho Brahe (1546–1601).[112] A court astrologer whose patrons lavishly supported his construction and large-scale staffing of sophisticated and well-equipped observatories, first in Denmark and then in Bohemia, he obsessed over the accuracy of observations and measurements. Correcting errors in ancient and modern astronomical tables consumed much of his efforts. The realization that astronomy required precise and systematically recorded data constituted his main contribution to science. Careful observations enabled him to demonstrate the occurrence of celestial changes, such as the sudden appearance of new stars. Kepler realized he desperately needed those data.

The opportunity arose in 1600 when Brahe invited Kepler to join his team in Bohemia, for he probably sensed that no one else could build a new model of the universe from his vast but undigested mountain of data. Only 18 months later, after the master's death and his own appointment as Imperial Mathematician, did Kepler get his hands on the gold mine. The resultant *New Astronomy* (1609), in 900 large-format pages bursting with calculations, demonstrated purely physical explanations of planetary motion.[113] Each planet, he argued, is pulled simultaneously away from and toward the Sun by two unseen forces. (Naming them—gravity and inertia—and understanding their exact nature had to wait for Newton.) Kepler also formulated his first two laws of planetary motion, indeed the first two scientific laws in history. The first—that the planets trace elliptical and not perfectly circular orbits—was a huge disappointment to him as a traditionalist. Yet facts are facts, and Kepler above all sought the truth. (The second law describes the regularity of any planetary orbit despite fluctuating velocity.) A new science and a new conception of the universe, one ruled by laws of physics and not geometry, were emerging.

Ten years later, Kepler published another major work, *The Harmony of the Worlds*. It both propounded the third law of planetary motion and argued for a deep mathematical harmony within all of physical reality, including the celestial realm. In fact, the law itself exemplifies that harmony. It describes a proportional relationship between the mean distance from, and the period of orbit around, the Sun of any two planets. For Kepler, the value of this discovery as well as that of his other two laws consisted in its contribution to a mystical understanding of the universe.[114]

The assault on the heavens received a powerful boost when an Italian physicist and mathematician used the newly invented telescope for systematic stargazing. A brilliant thinker and gifted inventor, Galileo Galilei (1564–1642) possessed a fully modern mind without any tendency toward metaphysics, mysticism, or the blind acceptance of authority.[115] In 1610, he published a short but potent text, *A Message from the Stars*, in which he claimed, in a crisply factual manner, to have observed four new planets (actually moons orbiting Jupiter) and a host of new stars in the firmament. The Aristotelian worldview was collapsing further.

Galileo's fortunes rose and fell. Influential prelates and Jesuit astronomers confirmed and praised his discoveries in regard to the imperfect surface of the Moon and the movement of objects in the supralunary realm.[116] Yet most Aristotelian prelates, and there were many, opposed his scientific ideas.[117] In a publication of 1613, which described sunspots as evidence of physical changes of the Sun, for the first time he publicly advocated the Copernican system. Public and private discussions immediately drew out the implications of this position. Galileo therefore publicly denied that science in any way was at variance with Holy Scripture or the faith. "Sacred Scripture and nature both derive from the Divine Word," he wrote, "the former as dictated by the Holy Spirit and the latter as the faithful executrix of God's commands."[118] In 1615, Roberto Bellarmino, a foremost theologian and influential cardinal, went so far as to admit the Copernican model's superiority to that of Ptolemy. Still, he insisted—correctly—that it remained a hypothesis.[119] Adjusting our interpretation of Holy Scripture, therefore, required more scientific proof that it correctly described reality. (The Book of Joshua records that God commanded the Sun—not the Earth—to cease moving.)

His reputation on the line, Galileo, against the advice of his wisest supporters, forced a showdown with the Holy See in 1616. Although the church never officially declared the immobility of the Earth an article of faith, it did condemn the Copernican system as "false and altogether opposed to holy Scripture."[120] So long as one did not advocate it as scientific truth, however, one could escape censure. Galileo himself had to pledge not to defend the doctrine publicly (or not to discuss it at all; the evidence is unclear).

In 1623, to Galileo's great fortune, one of his ardent supporters was elected pope as Urban VIII. After a series of warm conversations with the pontiff, Galileo felt emboldened to publish an adamant defense of the Copernican theory, the *Dialogue Concerning the Two Chief World Systems*, in which he seemed to represent his friend the pope as dull-witted. When the book appeared, the pope quickly realized he had been insulted and became enraged.[121] Brought before the Inquisition on suspicion of heresy in 1633, Galileo denied that he had ever intended to defend the Copernican system in the *Dialogue*, an obvious falsehood.[122] Yet realizing they had him cornered, he ultimately recanted and pledged to "abjure, curse, and detest" his views on heliocentrism. Condemned for the rest of his life to house arrest in his villa outside Florence with a lovely view of the hills of Tuscany[123]—he spent not a single day imprisoned—he worked fruitfully in dynamics, mechanics, and kinematics.

In these fields, working as "an entrepreneurial scientist," Galileo developed a "new philosophy of nature" that became the model for scientific research in the seventeenth century.[124] In the *Discourses and Mathematical Demonstrations Relating to Two New Sciences*, published in the Netherlands in 1638, Galileo laid out the results of his application of mathematics and experimentation to common physical materials, objects, and processes. Much of this work disproved core tenets of Aristotelian physics. He argued, in his law of falling bodies, that only wind resistance or other sources of friction prevent objects of every size and mass from falling and accelerating at the same rate. His law of projectile motion provided a mathematical description and prediction of any projectile's parabolic (in reality elliptical) trajectory, depending on the speed and angle with which it is projected and the force of gravity bearing down on it. He also discovered the principle of inertia.[125] Along with Kepler, Galileo had formulated with mathematical precision the first laws of science.

It is worth pausing to note that the tensions between the Jesuits and Galileo had a direct impact on the development of modern science in China. When Jesuit scholars introduced mathematical astronomy beginning the 1630s, many Chinese astronomers eagerly embraced the new approach. Yet further advances achieved by Galileo were not communicated to them, and so they did not undertake a broader systematic quantification of physical phenomena. Moreover, Chinese astronomers linked the European methods they did embrace to traditional Chinese astronomic conceptions. In other words, a scientific revolution occurred in seventeenth-century China, but it did not fundamentally transform Chinese society.[126]

What astonishing courage it must have taken to untether the Earth from its central position in the universe and to imagine it and the other planets hurtling through open space against all sensory evidence, the weight of tradition, the assertions of Scripture, and the authority of the greatest philosophers who ever lived! Copernicus, Kepler, Brahe, and Galileo, against all those forces of inertia and flawed creatures that they were, brought humanity to the verge of a radically new and scientifically accurate understanding of the physical world. Though each was a genius in his own way, none achieved these accomplishments in isolation but did so in the context of a society dynamically questioning all things, systematizing all things, investigating all things, and therefore constantly advancing human knowledge and understanding.

These efforts culminated in the work of Isaac Newton (1643–1727), who definitively overthrew the Aristotelian conception of the physical universe.[127] A brilliant mathematician who invented calculus (at the same time as but independently from Gottfried Leibniz) and an inventor who devised the first reflecting telescope, he also avidly practiced alchemy and numerology. Probably his belief in occult forces enabled him to make the fantastic conceptual leap necessary to formulate his law of universal gravitation, or the mutual attraction of all physical objects at a distance. Indeed, the idea that the Sun could transmit sufficient force to hold the Earth in its orbit across 93 million miles space "without the mediation of something else, which is not material" was to Newton himself "inconceivable."[128] Yet he mathematically demonstrated precisely this conclusion, as well as three universal laws of motion (relating to inertia, acceleration, and action and reaction), in his *Philosophiae Naturalis Principia Mathematica* (1687).[129] By applying all four principles, one can explain the behavior of all physical objects larger than an atom and moving more slowly than the speed of light.

Thus, Newton established both the scientific discipline of classical mechanics and a mechanistic conception of the universe without any day-to-day necessity of divine intervention. Here was the irrefutable proof demanded by churchmen to justify the adoption of the Copernican theory. Scholars throughout Europe welcomed the book enthusiastically, and he quickly achieved the status of an intellectual demigod, especially in England, though not all scholars accepted all of his conclusions.[130] For several decades, most French scientists preferred the Cartesian theory that vortices, like whirlpools spinning in the "aether," kept the planets moving in their orbits.

The manifest success of Newton's experimental method and his scientific achievements dramatically increased the prestige of natural philosophy, charged Europe's intellectual climate with optimism, and inspired a craze for scientific study and research. From 1692, popularizers made Newton's ideas accessible to a wider reading public, first in England and then on the Continent. In the early 1700s, lecture courses in "experimental philosophy" and experimental displays in coffeehouses were all the rage in London.[131] Entrepreneurs advertised the courses in London's dozen or so newspapers, targeting tradesman, students, and society elites, including women. Numerous professional scientists made a handsome living feeding this appetite.[132] The most popular subjects were Newton's *Principia* and *Opticks*, but audiences also liked lectures on Boyle's air-pump experiments.

Demystifying nature: Chemistry and electricity

Robert Boyle, a passionate alchemist, laid early foundations of the modern discipline of chemistry.[133] A careful and systematic empiricist, he performed countless experiments. Alchemists typically shrouded their work in secrecy, but not Boyle. He recorded and published elaborate details of his experiments—including meticulous descriptions of procedures, equipment, and observations. The invention of a mercury barometer in Italy and an air pump in Germany enabled Boyle to meticulously investigate the nature of air.[134] In 1660, he published the results of a series of 43 experiments, demonstrating that air has weight and exerts pressure and that the absence of air impedes combustion and harms diverse living creatures but does not affect magnetism, the transmission of sound, or the movement of pendulums. A second edition of the study, published in 1662, set out Boyle's law: that the volume of a gas varies inversely to the pressure exerted on it.

The previous year, in *The Sceptical Chymist*, Boyle had argued against the ancient Greek belief that four basic elements—earth, fire, air, and water—constitute all things. His research had convinced him that one can neither combine those elements to form any substance nor extract them from another substance. Instead, he pointed to

> certain primitive and simple, or perfectly unmingled bodies; which not being made of any other bodies, or of one another, are the ingredients of which all those called perfectly mixt bodies are immediately compounded, and into which they are ultimately resolved.[135]

He apparently did not understand these elements in the modern sense, although researchers were slowly isolating actual chemical elements (e.g. phosphorus was discovered in 1667).[136]

Equally important, Boyle devised valuable and effective research methods. He invented chemical analysis—procedures to test the chemical content of substances.

For instance, he used ammonia to test for copper, silver nitrate to test for salt in water, and was able to test for 30 different components in mineral water. He also invented a reliable means to test for acidity and alkalinity.[137] He urged other researchers to use his methods to investigate physical substances, not for the advancement of medicine or alchemy but in order to further develop chemistry as a science.

Hundreds of researchers took up this challenge in a dozen European countries, from the German Johann Joachim Becher (1635–82), who first formulated the phlogiston theory of combustion, to the Russian Mikhail Lomonosov (1711–65), who rejected it on the basis of experimental evidence.[138] The greatest was a rich and powerful French aristocratic banker, beheaded at the height of the French Revolutionary Terror, Antoine-Laurent Lavoisier (1743–94).[139] He demonstrated that the hitherto mysterious process of combustion resulted from a chemical combination of substances with a constituent element of air, which he called oxygen. He also showed the role of oxygen in rusting metal and in animal respiration. Except for experiments taking place in a vacuum, he noted, researchers always had to take into account the possibility of chemical reactions to gaseous components within air. Most importantly, he demonstrated that matter is neither gained nor lost during chemical reactions and thus formulated the law of conservation of mass.[140]

European scientists cooperated intensively and built on one another's work, constituting a subset of the intellectual community called the Republic of Letters.[141] Laboratories across Europe were now buzzing with activity.[142] Researchers discovered and isolated a dozen elements in a dozen different places: magnesium in Scotland (1755); hydrogen in England (1766); barium, chlorine, and manganese in Sweden (1774); beryllium and chromium in France (1797); tellurium in Hungary (1789); tungsten in Spain (1783); yttrium in Finland (1794); and zirconium in Prussia (1789), to name only some.[143] In 1808, John Dalton (1766–1844) published an atomic theory of elements and chemical reactions. He argued that specific atoms, each with a distinct atomic weight, make up the elements and combine to form chemical compounds and therefore all material substances. Thus, chemical reactions do not destroy atoms but merely rearrange them.[144] Amedeo Avogadro (1776–1856) distinguished further between atoms and molecules. Research by the Swedish chemist Jöns Jacob Berzelius (1779–1848) corroborated Dalton's theory. In 1828, he published a table of the relative atomic weights of known elements and invented the system of chemical notation still in use today, but with small modifications (e.g., H^2O stood for water). Finally, in 1869 the Russian Dmitrii Mendeleev (1834–1908) devised a periodic table of elements, which arranged them according to ascending atomic weight and similarity of chemical properties.[145] Mendeleev correctly predicted the discovery of numerous additional elements and made space for them in his table.

One could list dozens and even hundreds of more breakthroughs in chemistry and in other scientific disciplines, whose number steadily multiplied. Science also broadened geographically. Researchers discovered the element platinum in South America and zirconium in minerals brought back from Ceylon (Sri Lanka), and, in 1676–78, Edmond Halley led a scientific expedition to the South Atlantic where he set up an astronomical and meteorological observatory on the island of St Helena.[146] Researchers outside of Europe also began to make scientific breakthroughs. Most occurred in the British North American colonies and subsequent United States. One non-European in the eighteenth century stood out as the "Newton of the Age."

When contemporaries referred in this way to Benjamin Franklin (1706–90), they meant the Newton of the *Opticks* who conducted an enormous range of experiments and formulated a vast number of hypotheses about the properties, effects, actions, and reactions of all sorts of natural phenomena.[147] Elected a fellow of the Royal Society of London without the obligation to pay the membership dues—an unprecedented honor—and one of only eight foreign associates of the French Academy of Sciences, Franklin was celebrated in his lifetime and his scientific papers were avidly read all across Europe. What can explain this level of achievement in a man born and raised outside of Europe who received only 2 years of formal schooling?

The short answer is that Franklin used Newtonian experimental methods to develop a relatively complete understanding of a topic in physics about which Newton knew very little.[148] He demonstrated that electricity in general and all electrical phenomena in particular were manifestations of a single "fluid," composed of particles that are attracted to most particles of matter. Electrification, he argued, involves only the redistribution of electric "fluid" (charge) already existing in objects, not the creation (or destruction) of any electric "virtue" or charge.[149] Here Franklin had hit upon the law of conservation of charge. A body that receives excess electric "fluid" becomes charged "plus" or "positive"; one that loses some of its natural charge, "minus" or "negative." His theory explained the mysterious functioning of the recently invented Leyden Jar and proved that its two conductors necessarily had opposite but equal charges. He also hypothesized correctly that lightning is a form of electricity. In general, his theory explained such phenomena as conduction, insulation, electrostatic induction, grounding, and electrical attraction and repulsion. Franklin's treatise on electricity, which first appeared 1751, represented the cutting edge in experimental method, from the formulation of theoretical concepts and the design and implementation of experiments, through the crafting, testing, and modification of hypotheses, to the interpretation and presentation of results.

Franklin's accomplishments demonstrate that the European scientific method was transferable to the rest of the world, though in the short term only one non-European region adopted successfully this powerful tool—the United States of America.[150]

The Enlightenment

Meanwhile, from St Petersburg to Philadelphia, scholars and statesmen sought to transfer the principles of the Scientific Revolution to nearly every aspect of life. They applied rationalism, skepticism, constructive criticism, systematic thinking, and methodical problem solving to politics, social issues, the law, economics, and business.[151] They challenged tradition, authority, prejudice, intolerance, and custom. Among the hundreds if not thousands of ways and means to improve life and society that emerged from these efforts were such powerful new concepts as the political separation of powers, human rights, the emancipation of women, limited government, and making punishment fit the crime, to name only a few.

Scholars and statesmen, often working together, demanded and sought the compilation of information regarding nearly everything. In 1716, for example, the French regent, Philip, Duke of Orleans, ordered a study into the mineral resources of the whole of France.[152] At the end of the century, the geologist William Smith completed his first attempt at what one author has called "the map that changed the world," a geological survey of the whole of England, Wales, and part of Scotland indicating the predominant mineral types throughout.[153] One can mention the encyclopedia edited by Denis Diderot (1751–72) in 35 volumes with 71,818 articles—all alphabetized—and 3,129 illustrations. Nothing even remotely as comprehensive had ever appeared anywhere in the world.[154] Perhaps even more impressive was the 113-volume *Descriptions des Arts et Métiers* (1761–88), which contained a vaster range of technical and technological information. Expert knowledge became systematized, catalogued, and codified mathematically and graphically for every branch of learning and endeavor in thousands of publications often running through dozens of editions and translations.[155]

Ways and means of exchanging information also proliferated over the course of the century. The number of journals and newspapers grew exponentially. Books became more and more available through inexpensive editions, lending libraries,

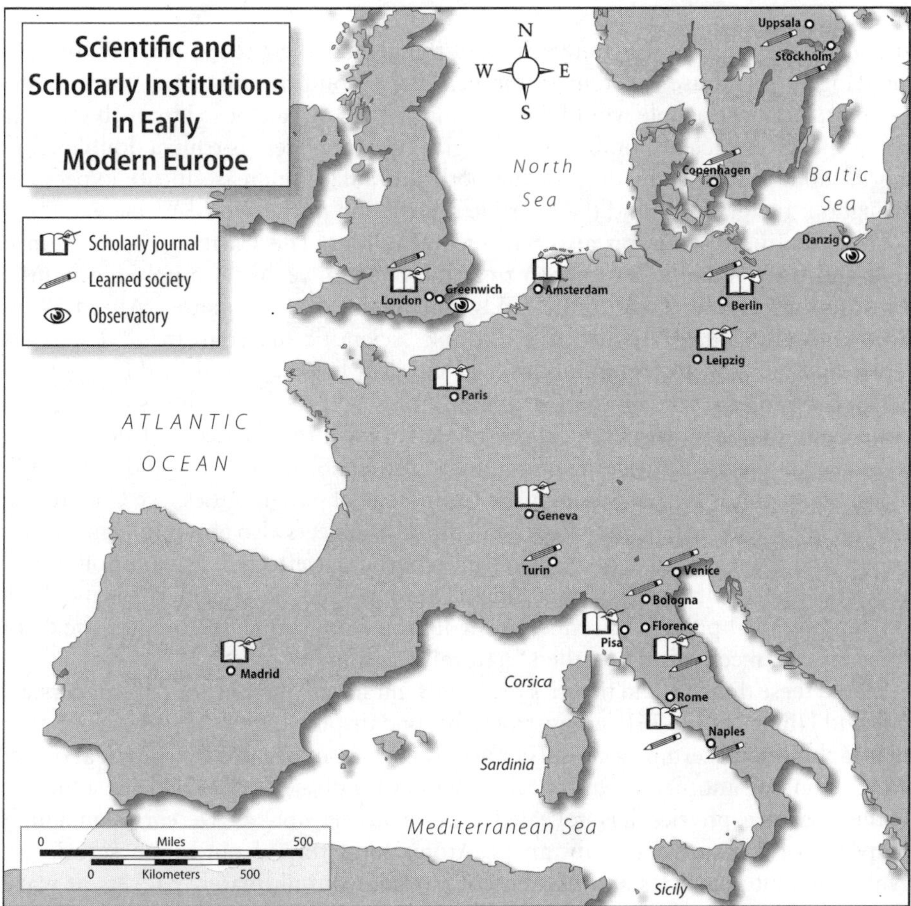

MAP 8.1 *The number of learned societies multiplied all across Europe during the Enlightenment.*

and stocks of reading material in the burgeoning coffeehouses and cafés of Europe's major cities, leading to what one scholar has called a "reading revolution," in which people ceased reading a few books over and over and instead began reading extensively.[156] Educated elites increasingly formed clubs and voluntary associations, including salons, debating societies, and Freemasonic lodges (see Chapter 14).[157] The number of learned societies multiplied all across Europe, including many in small towns and provincial localities (see Map 8.1). Women, though a distinct minority, played a role in all of these endeavors and a leading one in the salons.[158]

The intensification of rational and systematic thinking about society, work, leisure, and life itself inevitably increased the efficiency and effectiveness of institutions, organizations, methods of operation, and businesses. In a word, people of the West—now meaning Europeans and Americans—grew more and more practically skilled and knowledgeable and therefore more powerful and ultimately more rich.

The dark side of modern science

Of course, the more power humans wield the greater their scope for working evil. The dangers for abuse inherent in the printing revolution might not seem readily apparent, but most people would quickly think of the threats posed by such scientific achievements as nuclear bombs and biological warfare. Here is truly a double-edged sword: modern science made possible both a dramatic increase in life expectancy throughout the planet[159] and the horrible destruction of the World Wars.

The Scientific Revolution also had mental fallout. The Cartesian separation of mind and body made it possible to treat the physical realm in purely mechanistic terms, as observable, measurable, and controllable bits of matter. Alfred North Whitehead (1861–1947) called this outlook "scientific materialism."[160] It enabled Kepler and Newton to formulate laws of physical behavior, and in their footsteps followed hundreds and ultimately millions of scientists busily investigating how a multitude of things work or can be made to work in practice.[161] Knowledge of physical and chemical processes and effects also enabled tinkerers and technicians to develop methods for harnessing their technological potentialities (see Chapters 11 and 12). The scientific tendency to treat all things as objects also powerfully influenced biology and the social sciences.[162] Darwin in particular effected a revolution in how modern people comprehend living things. They emerged, he argued, through a blind and unintentional process of branching evolution from simple to complex life forms by means of a mechanism he called "natural selection."[163]

Yet did these thinkers and theories really account for all of reality or truly understand it? David Hume (1711–76) demonstrated beyond dispute over 200 years ago that we are incapable of discerning a causal connection between the effects of physical objects acting upon one another, if we conceive them as totally self-contained substances.[164] Further, particle physics has revealed that reality is not, as Descartes imagined, composed of self-sufficient substances. Atoms have turned out, upon scrutiny, to break down into particles and particles of particles and ultimately packets or waves of energy all constantly moving and changing and interacting with one another.[165] Thus, every physical object, every Cartesian extended thing, proves a mere congeries of forces. This includes all living things, which evolved over hundreds of millions of years, thanks to trillions of purely random genetic variations, the "fittest" of which are "selected" by their capacity to adapt. Not surprisingly, countless modern people have concluded that it is impossible to believe in anything.[166] Chapter 13 will address how this question played out socially and culturally.

* * *

Why did modern science develop first in Europe? Why, in other words, did Europeans first devise a rigorously scientific method of studying nature, involving an extravagant openness to new knowledge and ideas, careful observation, systematic classification of data, the application of mathematics to natural phenomena, the formulation and testing of hypotheses, a faith in the rationality of the universe, and an inveterate optimism that its secrets can be unlocked and understood?

Scholars have put forward potential explanations. Some point to Christian theology, according to which God created a rational, lawful, stable universe.[167] Given this worldview, all man had to do was to try to discover its laws, something required by one's obligation to worship the Creator. Thus, Copernicus, Kepler, Newton, and apparently even Galileo sought to discover regularity in the universe as evidence of God's majesty. Other religions, by contrast, posit a willful or arbitrary creator or indeed no creator at all. Of course, not all Christians promoted scientific research. Some medieval theologians and seventeenth-century puritans considered scientific inquiry presumptuous. Yet far, far more Muslim thinkers, starting with al-Ghazali, held that view down the centuries.[168]

The Christian faith also holds that God became incarnate as a human and "dwelt among us (John 1:14)," suggesting dramatically the intrinsic worth of the material world. It certainly seems important that nearly all Christian thinkers have affirmed that reality exists independently from our will, or that of the Creator. Buddhism and Daoism, by contrast, emphasize the illusory character of matter and our need to transcend it in order to achieve enlightenment. Daoist alchemists made important technological breakthroughs, like gunpowder, but neither Daoists nor Buddhists achieved any significant scientific advancements in premodern times, despite the curious affinity of some of their teachings with esoteric aspects of modern science.[169]

Other historians emphasize the legal and juridical heritage of Europe.[170] Whereas the ancient Greeks developed the concept and practice of impersonal, blind legality and justice, and the Romans codified and systematized them, the Chinese, despite all their manifest and admirable cultural accomplishments, felt little need for more than criminal and penal law. Yet a systematic approach to the law in medieval Europe helped pave the way to important advances in the methods of natural philosophy.

Another scholar has argued that scientific advances require the separation of fact from value and moral life from physical reality, something Europeans managed gradually to achieve during the medieval period, if not earlier.[171] By contrast, neo-Confucian doctrines, which dominated most East Asian societies, blended these things, making it difficult to isolate either one as an object of rigorous investigation.

One way to understand these contrasts is to think about origins. The West received part of its scientific heritage from the Mesopotamian and Egyptian civilizations but only through the mediation of Greece and Rome, which marked a dramatic rupture from that base. By contrast, the Chinese and Indian cultures retain even to this day direct ties to their ancient heritages without any mediation through other civilizations.[172] Another point worth making is that China had slowly advanced to a great height of achievement over the course of nearly 2,000 years and then grew complacent. When Europe, thanks to heavy borrowing from other peoples, brought about the Scientific and Industrial Revolutions in the early modern period, neither China nor any other culture could readily assimilate these massive changes.[173]

Finally, experimentation, tinkering, and other dabbling in the mechanical arts carried a social stigma in many developed human societies, even the most dynamic and creative ones. Chinese inventors, through the Song Dynasty, were among the most innovative and prolific in history, yet the Confucian elites often held in contempt experiments and tinkering, so that many technological achievements were forgotten or underappreciated. Of course, an aristocratic disdain for manual occupations was widespread in medieval and early modern Europe, especially in the less advanced regions. It was surely not a coincidence that the countries in which inventors and scientists were held in the greatest esteem were also those where commercial, political, and industrial revolutions first broke out.

QUESTIONS FOR REFLECTION

Contrast ancient Greek and ancient Chinese explanations of natural phenomena.

Why was Aristotle both a help and a hindrance to scientific development?

Which features of medieval European society fostered scientific inquiry?

How did Kepler use mathematics to understand nature?

What was the "methodical doubt" of René Descartes?

Why did Chinese thinkers favor empirical over theoretical approaches?

What did medieval European thinkers mean by the "great chain of being"?

Why did Robert Boyle insist upon publishing elaborate details of his experiments?

Why did modern science arise in Europe instead of in the Islamic world or in China?

Chapter 9 Chronology

1270s:	Italian merchants begin to spread risk by dividing costs between many investors
1300:	Distillation process takes off in Europe
1347–51:	Black Death devastates Europe
Fifteenth century:	Medici banks established by collaboration of Medici partnerships
Early sixteenth century:	Chocolate arrives in Europe via Spain
Sixteenth century:	Growth of chartered companies
1520:	Portuguese first plant sugarcane in Brazil
1543:	Potato first imported to Europe
1571:	London's Royal Exchange opens
1592:	Dutch elites vote for religious moderation and toleration
Early seventeenth century:	Newspapers begin to appear and quickly multiply in number
1600:	2,000 tons of pepper arrives annually in Europe, increases to 5,000 by 1680
1602:	Dutch East India Company founded
1615:	Coffee spreads to Vienna, then to rest of Europe
1668:	15,000,000 lbs. of tobacco imported to Europe, up from 2,500 50 years before
1694:	Bank of England created
Late seventeenth century:	Fire and life insurance develop in London
1713:	Treaty of Utrecht
1720s:	Big companies begin to trade on both London and Amsterdam stock exchanges
1750:	European population doubles in following century
1792:	New York Stock & Exchange Board founded, later becomes NYSE
1807:	United Kingdom abolishes slave trade
From 1830s:	Banking revolution sweeps Europe
1840s:	Artificial fertilizer first developed

9

Commercial revolutions

Imagine a country where setting up a business that requires the employment of just one worker can require 207 steps and nearly a year of intense effort; or where one can secure the right to lease a plot of state-owned land only by wending one's way through 65 bureaucratic hurdles taking on average 2 years of work. Unfortunately, according to the Peruvian economist Hernando de Soto, in vast regions of the globe most people face just such obstacles.[1] When legally registering a piece of state-owned land in places like the Egyptian desert can take up to 14 years, no wonder millions of people from Brazil to the Philippines never even try to establish legal ownership and instead squat. This is a tragic shame, not only because a squatter's home can be bulldozed without warning but also because it cannot be borrowed against, cannot serve as a source of funding for entrepreneurship. It is therefore, in de Soto's term, "dead capital." Such extra-legal and untitled real estate may have constituted over 9 trillion dollars in 1997, more than the total GDP of the European Union or the United States.[2] What a waste!

Legal protections of property and business owners throughout Europe, by contrast, began to emerge in the Middle Ages.[3] (A system of property rights began to emerge even earlier in China, which surely helps to explain its great economic success.)[4] In this favorable environment, artisans, entrepreneurs, merchants, and financiers ever more boldly devised ways to accumulate capital and to maximize their wealth. Just as European physicians shifted from blaming the stars after the main outbreak of the Plague to investigating concretely its manifestations and prescribing specific remedies and preventive measures, merchants and traders adapted their businesses to the ever-changing conditions of economic life. They made financial concessions to their employees whose labor had grown more valuable, established hundreds if not thousands of regional commercial fairs all across the continent, placed a greater emphasis on high-end commodities and goods, invested in labor-saving technologies, and adopted strategies of increased specialization. At the macro level, capital steadily accumulated and interest rates declined. At the level of consumer demand, an ever-larger segment of the population hungered for exotic products from the farthest corners of the globe.

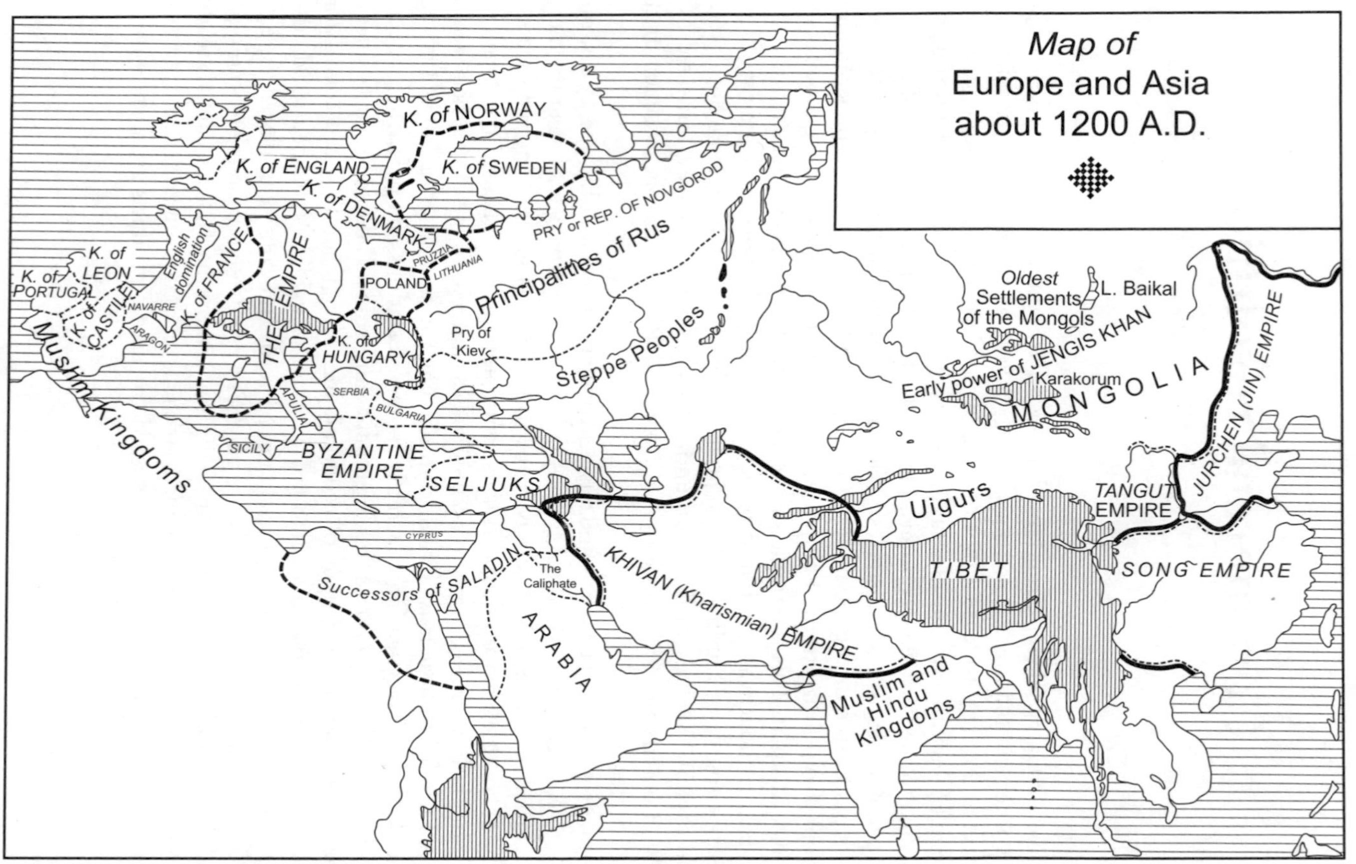

MAP 9.1 *In their desire for exotic commodities Europeans traveled across Eurasia to obtain them.*

Commodity fetishes

It is hard to believe yet true that the greatest economic boom in world history and indeed the entire rise of the West stemmed in part from Europeans' desire for comestible substances with no nutritional value. From pepper and nutmeg in the Middle Ages to sugar and tobacco in the early modern period, seeking means to spice up otherwise bland lives drove millions to buy, trade, hunt down, import, and fight over commodities that could not grow in Europe. In the effort to understand the expansion of wealth and power in Europe, one explanation generally overlooked is precisely this: had these commodities thrived naturally at the western end of the Eurasian land mass, then perhaps China would have risen to colonize it (see Map 9.1).

Persistent legends notwithstanding, medieval Europeans did not use spices to preserve meat or to mask its putrefaction.[5] Cooks on the contrary added dozens of exotic ingredients, often in odd combinations from the point of view of current culinary traditions, such as cinnamon, cloves, and ginger used together in meat dishes. In time, increased availability permitted some spices to filter down the food chain, as it were. By the 1300s, even many peasants could afford pepper, while the rich consumed veritable mountains of costly spices. When George, Duke of Bavaria-Landshut, married Jadwiga, Princess of Poland, in 1475, the festivities required 386 pounds of pepper, 286 of ginger, 207 of saffron, 205 of cinnamon, 105 of cloves, and 85 nutmeg.[6] Presumably much of this more than half-ton of precious vegetable matter went to revelers as gifts. But note: this celebration antedated the return to Portugal by Vasco da Gama with his vast cargo of pepper by some quarter century. Europeans clearly had the ability to obtain large quantities of exotic spices and had the taste for commodities that enlivened their material existence. Yet they wanted more.

Pepper in particular flooded the market over the next two centuries, its trade dominated first by the Portuguese and then by the Dutch. From his second voyage to India, da Gama returned with 1,700 tons of spices, mostly pepper, about as much as Venice had been importing annually.[7] In other words, the availability of spices skyrocketed in Europe. Soon, pepper became a common commodity, available to nearly everyone. In fact, by the seventeenth century, spices in general became too ordinary for many sophisticated cooks, especially in France. Bringing out the natural and subtle flavors in foods became the aim of refined European cuisines.[8]

The next big consumer craze was sugar, which "conquered the world."[9] Native to the Bengal coast, sugarcane had spread to Persia, the Mediterranean coast, and China hundreds of years before. Portuguese traders planted it in Brazil around 1520, and its cultivation flourished within a few decades. By the 1570s, Europeans were devouring the sweet substance.

To feed the insatiable demand for the "white gold," entrepreneurs devised new industrial complexes in Brazil and many islands of the Caribbean,[10] leading to a "sugar revolution."[11] At the center of this development lay the plantation, a highly sophisticated system of processing the precious white crystals. Plantation economies involved several transformative features. They yielded huge profits, attracting significant investments of capital. The plantations became the world's largest and most productive industrial concerns until then. They necessitated big labor inputs, hence the importation of slaves from Africa. The cultivation of sugarcane, being enormously lucrative, drove out all other crops, forcing the importation of foodstuffs.

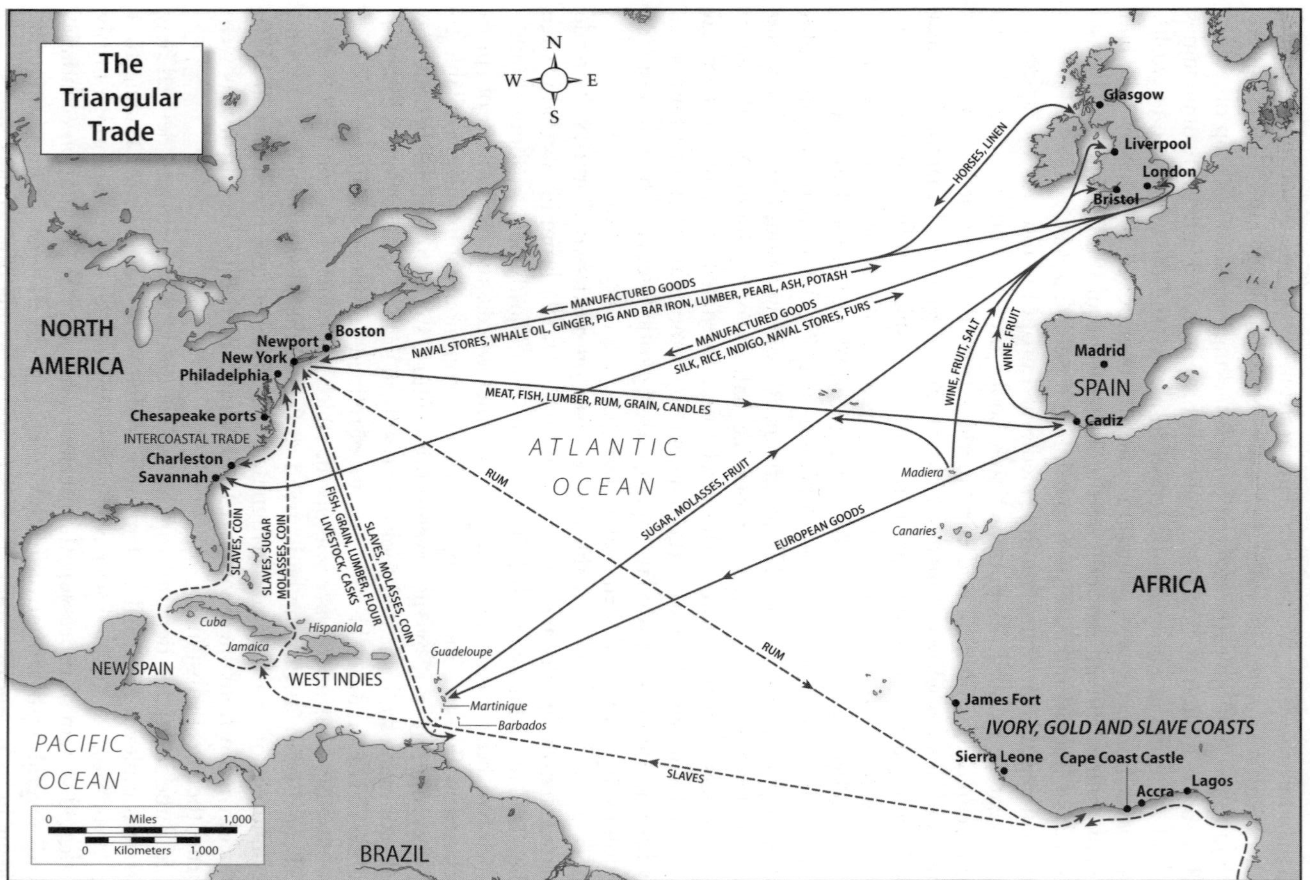

MAP 9.2 *The triangular trade was the result of the European obsession to maximize profits, as no ship was to sail without a full cargo.*

Thus emerged the grim reality of triangular trade (see Map 9.2), itself a sign of the European merchants' obsession with maximizing profits: no ship, they concluded, should ever set sail without a full cargo. The Caribbean planters grew fabulously rich. So great became the volume of trade and the magnitude of profits that numerous scholars link the industrial revolution to capital accumulation made possible by Europe's colonies and slave economies (see Chapter 11).

The contrast with the role sugar played in China's economy is instructive. Although Chinese artisans and entrepreneurs developed innovative techniques for the cultivation and production of sugar, it did not exert a significant dietary impact.[12] By contrast, Europeans, especially from the 1700s, added it to a wide range of foods, including cereals, puddings, and rice milk.[13] Perhaps the Chinese culture was simply more balanced, less a prey to fads and crazes. Europeans, by contrast, jumped from one to another.

One developed all across Eurasia: hard liquor beverages. Perhaps invented in Persia or even China a few centuries before (the word "alcohol" itself is Arabic in origin), medieval European alchemists learned about the distillation process around 1100 and began producing various forms of "aqua vitae" from the 1300s, the first from wine, such as brandy, and then from diverse fruits, vegetables, and grains, as well as from sugar.[14] Initially used mostly for medicinal purposes, these alcoholic beverages soon gained cultural relevance, as each people created one or more "national" liquors. The production and trade in brandy began to take off in the late 1500s, mostly on the Atlantic coast and dominated by Dutch entrepreneurs. Throughout the 1600s, the production spread inland and increased dramatically in volume, while the price fell just as steeply. Consumption shot up, too, especially among soldiers.

All the other exciting new commodities came from other continents. Three were stimulating drinks: coffee, tea, and chocolate.[15] A product of the New World, chocolate reached Spain in the early 1500s, where its popularity remained greatest, though the ancient Aztec treat slowly gained a following among aristocrats and courtiers in other countries, and a few shops serving hot chocolate sprang up in London in the mid-1600s.[16] Teahouses appeared in a far greater number around the same time. Within a century, Europeans were importing some 7,000 tons of the leaf every year from China.[17] Whereas tea enjoyed its greatest popularity in the northern climes of Europe where the vine did not flourish, coffee took the entire continent by storm. Unlike tea, whose use in China had an ancient lineage, the career of coffee apparently began no earlier than 1470, in Aden, on the Horn of Africa.[18] Having conquered most of the Islamic world, coffee appeared in Venice in around 1615, then spread to other major cities, meeting with its greatest success in Paris in the late 1600s. The first Parisian coffeehouse, established to imitate those of Constantinople, which in the 1560s had more than 600, opened in 1672. Within 4 years, several proprietors formed their own association. In other words, the café culture of France was fast on its way to fruition. By 1700, both France and England boasted thousands of such emporia.[19] To feed the demand, European entrepreneurs established coffee plantations from Indonesia to South America.

Tea and coffee, soon the most popular drinks in Europe, played a civilizing role, though in different ways. Beginning in around the 1690s, women presided over afternoon tea in England, the Netherlands, and the English colonies of North America, ritualistically affirming their control over the domestic sphere.[20] The British and the

Dutch were, it seems, the first people in the world to add sugar to tea as part of this practice. The tea ritual, it has been argued, marked a shift in the ascription of status in northern Europe and its settler colonies from dependence on one's birth to the level of one's respectability as measured by self-control, temperance, and household order.[21] Women were even welcome at London's tea gardens, which in fact often catered to them.[22] Coffee, by contrast, was a man's drink. For the most part, only men gathered in coffeehouses, for leisure, for business, and to exchange ideas. Both drinks clearly helped shape European culture in the early modern period.

Another plant with stimulative properties, tobacco, exerted if anything an even greater sway over Europeans in these same centuries.[23] Columbus witnessed Caribbean natives smoking its leaves on his first voyage. Within a century, tobacco had gained—ironically—a solid reputation as a miracle cure for a vast range of diseases and ailments, from headaches to tumors. It also had a growing number of users seeking pleasure. Soon, however, the weed attracted enemies, including James I of England, who denounced it as dangerous to one's health, unseemly, immoral, and economically wasteful. Many governments in northern Europe banned tobacco, starting in 1630, and imposed small fines for failure to comply. Yet public opposition, ever-widening use, and the realization that taxing the weed could provide significant revenues caused the abandonment of all such laws by around 1700. For England in particular, whose American colonies lacked precious metals and exotic spices, trade in tobacco proved a great boon. Imports from the Chesapeake region rose from 2,500 pounds in 1616 to 15 million pounds in 1668–69—all taxed but half of it re-exported to other European countries.[24] The people—and their governments—were hooked.

Why did Europeans feverishly seek out and integrate into their way of life all of these inessential commodities? Surely their appetite for novelty and their willingness to adopt new customs are the main reasons. Coffee gained popularity in much of the Muslim world before conquering Europe. The Japanese adopted tea from their neighbor, but it enjoyed less success in the rest of East Asia. Nor did East Asians, by and large, add sugar to their tea.[25] Introduced by Europeans beginning in the Philippines, tobacco spread rapidly throughout Asia and the East and North African coasts. Many Asians adopted elaborate means for smoking the leaf, including finely carved pipes and hookahs. Chocolate, by contrast, did not catch on anywhere in Asia (aside from the Philippines).[26] The essential point is not to belittle the openness and adaptability of other cultures[27] but simply to note the willingness to try new things, bordering on recklessness, that characterized European societies.

Agricultural revolution

Europeans of the early modern period did not only fritter their income away on "unnecessary" commodities. Their agricultural workers and traders achieved remarkable improvements in diet, food output, and alimentary variety. In some regions, food production consistently outpaced human consumption. Such abundant output had occurred a number of times previously, for example, Western Europe in the twelfth and thirteenth centuries or Imperial China from 1680 to 1780.[28] In every such case, however, the additional mouths ultimately strained the system's ability to provide adequate food, and demographic catastrophe followed. In early modern Europe, by contrast, agricultural production gradually took on a pattern of growth that consistently met human need. Basically, from the 1620s in England and Holland famine struck no more, a boon that gradually spread to the rest of Europe.[29] Moreover, from the 1730s further increases in food production led to a demographic increase and a century later, a population explosion. Within one century, beginning in 1750, the European population grew from around 142 to 265 million. Unlike in previous expansions, when population increases always pushed up food prices, after 1800, in England at least, the two indices began to move in opposite directions. The so-called Agricultural Revolution, which soon spread to the rest of Europe, made this decoupling possible.

This transformation of the European agrarian economy defies easy description. For decades, scholars have argued over when it began and which elements specifically characterized it.[30] In fact, many sectors and regions experienced changes at radically different paces and in different ways. Selective breeding in late medieval England, for example, had already increased the size of cattle by the early 1500s. The "enclosure" of farmland in England, meaning both the physical consolidation and separation of fields and the transition from the medieval system of common landholding to a system of private property rights, took 300 years to work itself out beginning around 1500.[31] Scholars have estimated that enclosed farmland was from 13 to 100 percent more productive than open fields.[32] Cultivators of the land also spent centuries introducing nitrogen-fixing fodder plants, adding lime to improve the nitrogen intake of soil, draining wetlands, clearing forests, planting new mixes of food crops, devising efficient methods of alternating crops, and adopting strategies of agricultural specialization. The effects of these improvements included, in England and Wales for example, steadily improving diets, expanding grain exports after around 1675, and a doubling of the population to 6 million between 1540 and 1700.[33]

No single new crop had a bigger impact than the potato.[34] Native to the Andean highlands, it grew faster, easier, and more abundantly than the grain crops. Gradually, the potato found its way into the diet of ordinary Europeans, beginning mostly in the western German-speaking lands in the mid-1600s and then in France after the Great Famine of 1709.[35] Governments and rulers began to promote its cultivation. In 1744, for example, Frederick the Great distributed free seed potatoes and planting instructions. In 1773, Antoine-Augustin Parmentier published a study demonstrating scientifically the virtues of the potato, leading the way to its conquest of France in the following decades.[36] By the early 1800s, millions of Europeans, especially in northern countries, subsisted almost exclusively on potatoes. Even the horrific potato famine of 1845–49, which affected much of northern Europe but of course especially Ireland, did not undermine its popularity.

The success of the potato in Europe exemplifies several important trends. Exploration and colonial expansion clearly benefited the continent by introducing valuable new plants. (Corn, though not as important, enjoyed much popularity in the Balkans.)[37] Early modern Europeans exhibited a remarkable openness to new foodstuffs. Government officials systematically promoted agricultural improvements. Scientists carefully analyzed the nutritive value of crops, conducted experiments to find the best methods of cultivation, and widely published their results.

Scientific innovation contributed enormously to the improvement of agriculture. As early as the sixteenth century, inventors published designs for seed drills (invented by the Chinese centuries before),[38] though they caught on in a big way in England only from the early 1800s. Experts in husbandry like the Englishman Arthur Young (1741–1820) tirelessly advocated experimentation, which he claimed "is the rational foundation of all useful knowledge: let everything be tried."[39] Associations of farmers developed from the late 1700s to disseminate useful information, maintain libraries, and host lectures and expositions.[40] Again, as in nearly every field of human endeavor, Europeans sought to rationalize and systematize agriculture using the most ingenious methods. The single most important breakthrough was John Bennet Lawes's discovery and commercialization of artificial superphosphate fertilizer in the early 1840s.[41]

The gradual breakdown of medieval economic regulations also stimulated more production. Rules and decrees restricting market relations had stifled growth for centuries, though in ways varying from place to place.[42] They fixed prices, sought to root out fraud, established standard weights and measures, imposed market tolls, strictly limited the times and places for trading, licensed or even banned the activities of middlemen and other traders, and determined how much each purchaser could buy. All of these regulations aimed to protect consumers and to prevent the enrichment of merchants.

Yet as economic activity in Europe expanded and agricultural output increased, traders found ways to circumvent the regulations, and in many places they fell into disuse or were repealed. As Europe's cities grew, their alimentary needs expanded well beyond what their immediate regions could provide. From the 1500s to the 1800s, markets developed on the local, then regional, national, and international levels. Merchants developed networks of contacts; sources of information about supply, demand, and prices; expert knowledge of modes of transport and local regulations; and methods and sources of credit.[43]

Europeans were also beginning to take control of reproduction. From at least the sixteenth century, especially in northwestern Europe, people began to marry later than people in other cultures, roughly age 24 for women and 26 for men.[44] No one coordinated this change, nor can any scholar account for it.[45] Perhaps it stemmed from a desire to avoid demographic catastrophe,[46] though E. L. Jones has argued that the major Asian peoples responded to their (admittedly more frequent and devastating) natural disasters by keeping fertility high.[47] In any event, delaying marriage until mature adulthood allowed individuals and couples to lay the foundations of a prosperous livelihood by affording time to acquire skills, property, and capital.[48] Recent scholarship suggests that in roughly the same period, many, though fewer, Chinese also limited population growth but did so by radically different means: in particular, female infanticide.[49] Yet presumably delaying marriage resulted in greater capital accumulation, both material and human, since marrying later meant having more time for school, apprenticeships, and inheriting the family trade or farm before establishing one's own household.

Pooling resources

Changes in the law made it easier for Europeans to manage risk and therefore take more chances. The standard form of business in the Middle Ages in both Europe and the Middle East was the partnership.[50] The partners, usually few in number and nearly always related by blood, joined together for specific ventures and disbanded upon their completion. In order to launch a new enterprise, they typically had to renegotiate from scratch. Despite these restrictions, partnerships provided a way to pool capital and spread risk among several participants. By the mid-eighth century, at least three or four centuries before anything comparable in Europe, Muslim financiers accepted deposits, lent money, and issued bills of exchange. Yet banks did not emerge, nor did merchants pool large amounts of capital. This state of affairs persisted until the nineteenth century, when the first joint-stock company appeared in the Middle East.[51] Similarly, Chinese merchants operated pawnshops during the Tang era. Private merchants and then the government itself issued paper currency from the Song dynasty and into Ming times. Moreover, the government-issued currency was the world's first "fiat money," legal tender that had value without any material backing.[52] Yet China's financial innovation hit a ceiling just as Europe's was taking off.

Islamic inheritance law explains the slow emergence of big Muslim companies.[53] The Quran requires that two-thirds of a deceased person's property be divided among numerous near and distant relations, thus ensuring the dispersal of most estates among many heirs. While this rule enhanced the economic security of women, it also prevented the accumulation of riches and the rise of powerful aristocracies. In Europe, despite regional variations, the law typically limited inheritance to nuclear families and did not clearly spell out who should inherit property. In fact, from the Middle Ages, the very un-Islamic practice of primogeniture spread in Europe, until by the sixteenth century it was dominant in most of northern Europe. This practice made possible the accumulation of a very large number of relatively stable concentrations of private wealth. Unlike in the Islamic world, where power and privilege depended almost exclusively on political favor, wealthy European aristocratic and mercantile families derived a large part of their power and influence from assets that monarchs could not touch.

This distinction starkly influenced the evolution of business in the two regions. Imagine two partnerships, each comprising five partners, one in the Islamic world and the other in a European country recognizing primogeniture. One partner dies in each case. In the European country, in every likelihood, the deceased partner has left his share of the business to the son he has been grooming to succeed him. Although the original business contract has ended, the designated heir has every reason to sign on to a new partnership with the original terms. The venture thus continues. In a country without primogeniture, by contrast, the deceased partner might have numerous heirs, any one of whom could refuse to renew the contract or could demand the sale of any asset owned at the time of death, in order to receive his or her share. The Muslim custom of polygamy, which often resulted in well-to-do men siring many children, inevitably increased this likelihood. Out of prudence, therefore, Muslim entrepreneurs tended to keep their partnerships small.[54] This in turn prevented them from creating economies of scale, pooling extensive resources, and achieving further organizational innovations.

When the commercial boom began to gather steam in the century or two after the millennium in Europe, merchants adapted the partnership model to a variety of new opportunities. Italian financiers already in the thirteenth century formed durable partnerships often lasting several years and involving participants unrelated by blood. A century later, Francesco di Marco Datini forged an entire constellation of businesses across Europe all headed by different partnership arrangements and answering back to him. Several of the partners, that is, part owners, had risen through the ranks via promotion. As noted in Chapter 3, Datini maintained control over the sprawling organization by means of highly sophisticated accounting methods.[55]

Muslim entrepreneurs failed to develop such complex partnerships, yet for centuries in the South Asian and East African markets they had more than rivaled their less-developed indigenous competitors.[56] As European merchants came out onto the world stage in beginning in the 1500s, however, their more sophisticated business methods enabled them to outclass most of their Muslim competitors. European entrepreneurs frequently combined elements of various models by means of side contracts. A partnership could thus gain greater longevity, or minority shareholders of corporations could win protections against majorities. Overall, the range of possibilities enabled merchants and financiers to find more and more efficient means to share risk, amalgamate resources, and pursue business opportunities.

Innovations in medieval European law permitted the formation of entirely new business entities, as well. Jurists, drawing on Roman and canon law, recognized as lawful "corporate persons," entities with all the rights of an individual to own property, testify in court, bring lawsuits, and conduct any legal or other business, yet without the normal limitation on human longevity: such institutions could in principle persist indefinitely.[57] Many guilds, universities, religious communities, and cities obtained this legal designation. A good example is the City of London, which, first incorporated in the 1100s, still owns one-quarter of the land within its jurisdiction. Some business concerns also achieved this status, such as the still-existing Aberdeen Harbor Board, which dates to 1136.[58] Yet few profit-oriented companies formed as corporations until legal changes of the nineteenth century (see Chapter 11).

Far more numerous in the early modern period were companies chartered by monarchs seeking to exploit resources overseas. Already in 1347, the Swedish king granted a charter to the copper-mining company, Stora Kopparberg.[59] Yet the heyday of the chartered company began two centuries later. Most of them received some form of monopoly rights over trade with a specific region, sometimes in exchange for granting a stake in the enterprise to the charter-granting monarch. Usually, anyone could buy shares in the company, their liability being restricted to the capital invested. In other words, business failure or bankruptcy could not entail stripping an investor of any further assets. By shielding those assets from risk, the limited-liability company encouraged the well to do to stake a portion of their wealth in risky ventures, thus fueling a wide range of entrepreneurial activity. The Muscovy Company, chartered in 1555, was the first of the new breed, which included others focusing on the Levant, Africa, Virginia, Hudson's Bay, and of course the East and West Indies. These firms quickly gained impressive size. In 1592, for example, 53 merchants joined forces in the Levant Company. Such firms commanded extensive resources. In 1620, the English East India Company deployed up to 40 heavily armed ships traveling in convoys and transporting a wide array of goods from England to many Asian countries and back. By 1700, the firm employed more than 350 people at its headquarters in London. Pooling risk made sense, since long-distance commercial voyages often met with disaster, including the loss of one or more ships and the death of many crew members.

The importance of officially chartered companies in the economic development of early modern Europe has led several scholars to contend that government support for business in Europe was a major contributor to the rise of the West.[60] Not only did Western rulers and government officials create a favorable legal environment for business, they often also actively promoted world exploration and commercial expansion, including, for example, providing military protection to merchants. In other parts of Eurasia, by contrast, merchants typically enjoyed scant cooperation and often faced outright hostility from their respective governments. As Immanuel Wallerstein has argued, an emperor cannot behave like an entrepreneur seeking to increase the wealth of a particular region or state within his empire. "For an empire pretends to be the whole." He continues: "It cannot enrich its economy by draining from other economies, since this is the only economy."[61] Of course, the monarchs of the European countries forging overseas commercial empires were acting precisely as entrepreneurs all fiercely competing with one another. Again, the political fragmentation of Europe fostered innovative development.

Scholars have debated the role of Protestantism in the development of capitalism.[62] The commercial revolution took place largely in Protestant countries; even in Catholic France, Protestants (and to a lesser extent Jews) dominated high finance. Yet Luther and Calvin both deplored focusing on commerce, wealth seeking, lending at interest, and all forms of greed. At the same time, however, they rejected idleness and monasticism and praised hard work.[63] "Let the birds teach us a lesson," Luther adviced.[64] Of course, European townspeople did not need Luther to tell them to put their shoulders to the wheel. For centuries, urban life had seen the intensification of economic, political, and cultural activities. Laziness and city living did not go together. Townspeople in Europe had increasingly adopted a systematic, analytical, autonomous, and individualistic attitude. Since nearly all merchants of the time devoutly practiced Christianity, they inevitably applied their outlook to matters of faith. Thus, an equally valid historical question would concern the role of capitalism in the development of Protestantism.[65] While it seems likely that merchants and urban dwellers in China, India, and the Islamic world developed similarly rationalistic and practical approaches to both commerce and faith,[66] since towns nowhere outside of Europe achieved a similar level of political and economic autonomy,[67] their inhabitants could not exert a similarly powerful influence in the religious sphere.

Religion and politics concretely affected the emergence in Holland of the new type of company and its revolutionary means of capitalization.[68] In 1592, Amsterdam's political and economic elites (they were one and the same) voted in favor of religious moderation and tolerance and for "the cultivation of peace and harmony."[69] The Seven Dutch Provinces of the North, led by Holland, had by then achieved remarkable prosperity, thanks to efficient trade from the Baltic Sea to the Iberian peninsula in such commodities as grain, lumber, wool, hides, salt, and especially salted herring. In 1565, numerous Dutch partnership companies, often with as many as 100 partners, sailed roughly 700 ships on the Baltic routes alone. The partners themselves often borrowed money from family members or other close acquaintances. Merchants also raised capital by accepting deposits in exchange for interest payments, just like a bank. Those merchants who gained a reputation for honesty, reliability, and success naturally attracted more willing creditors and depositors.

The Spanish capture of Antwerp in 1585 drove some 60,000 Protestants to Amsterdam, who arrived with skills, commercial experience, capital, and international trading connections. In these same years, the Dutch invented the economical and efficient *fluit* ship and adapted windmills for sawing lumber, making it possible to mass-produce such vessels. Dutch merchants gradually extended their commercial ventures throughout the world. They also began trading a wider variety of manufactured goods and commodities, including silks, sugar, porcelain, and spices. Numerous joint-stock companies were founded to outfit convoys of ships and to spread the risk of possible loss (in the years 1595–1601 over one-fifth of all Dutch ships sent to Asia perished). In order to further increase the economies of scale, the Stadholder, Maurice of Nassau, and other political leaders persuaded the directors of these companies in 1602 to form a single, united, and state-sponsored chartered company, the Dutch East India Company (Vereenigde Oost-Indische Compagnie, or VOC for short). It involved more than 1,000 investors, most of course without blood ties to the company's directors.

The VOC marked a commercial breakthrough. It conducted semipermanent business ventures, instead of contracting with different shareholders for each undertaking. (Other firms soon followed suit.)[70] Shares in the company began to trade publicly on the Amsterdam Stock Exchange as soon as it opened its doors in 1611. "Going public" enabled the company to quickly raise the vast sum of 6.5 million guilders.[71] Initial investors had no reason to complain: the share price quickly jumped 15 percent. Those who bought and held did well, too, as the value of the stock tripled in 20 years, while the company paid an average annual dividend over those two decades of 18 percent. Investors clearly expected high dividends, for the company, in times of weak cash flow, paid in quantities of spices or in bonds.[72] The company's success inspired imitation across Europe—from Russia to Portugal.[73]

In order to avoid fluctuations of capital, the VOC required shareholders to invest for a period of 10 years. A secondary market for these shares quickly sprang up, enabling investors to buy and sell them at will. Speculation ensued, involving purchasing shares on credit, frequent buying and selling, and using shares as collateral.[74] There thus emerged a highly efficient, if sometimes risky, system for tapping into the extensive savings of the prosperous Dutch society.

As capital continued to increase, accumulate, and circulate in the consumer, credit, and equity markets of Amsterdam and more broadly the Seven United Provinces, the cost of short-term borrowing steadily declined from 8 percent around 1600, to 6.75 percent in 1608, and down to 5.5 percent in 1619.[75] Such inexpensive credit naturally gave Dutch businesses an advantage over all their rivals in Europe who had to pay significantly higher rates. The development of sophisticated financial derivative products and markets helped investors manage risk and seek higher returns as well.[76]

Dutch merchants and financiers managed to outbid their competitors on nearly every operation. They kept their delivery prices for shipping on average 40 percent below those of their English rivals, thanks to much smaller crews and less expensive ships.[77] On routes with few threats of naval hostility, their ships bore minimal firepower. The crew members themselves contentedly endured the most Spartan conditions. Overall, the Dutch Calvinists, from peasants to bankers, practiced frugality and welcomed austerity.

By mid-century, the Republic, and, in particular, the provinces of Holland and Zeeland, had built up a huge overseas empire.[78] Its dominance of international shipping was unparalleled, with an average annual tonnage of half a million and a reach into nearly every corner of the globe's oceanic surface. Everywhere Dutch mariners and merchant-warriors successfully challenged their competitors. Apparently unconcerned about religious divisions or political rivalries, Dutch merchants traded indiscriminately with both allies and enemies, Christians and Muslims, Catholics and Protestants. Their colonial endeavors were relatively minor, but their commercial operations flourished. From Persia to Japan, Dutch merchants bought, transported, and sold a vast array of manufactured goods and commodities, the bulk of which remained in Asia. By the late 1600s, the Dutch Republic was the richest country in Europe, or, in the words of a contemporary Englishman, "the envy of the present, and may well be the wonder of future generations."[79] Not bad for a small territory with few natural resources.

Therein lies a key feature in the history of economic development. The countries that have succeeded best have often possessed few natural endowments. Genoa and Venice are two obvious cases in point. Holland, given the extent of its commercial triumphs, deserved a medal of special merit. Its land often flooded and required constant efforts to hold back the sea. Its low-lying and damp terrain attracted malaria-bearing mosquitoes. Its minuscule forests provided little timber; its substrata, hardly any stone. Oddly for a great maritime power, the Dutch ports were shallow and could freeze over in winter. Even its windward position on the English Channel, lacking shelter from the prevailing westerlies, was unfavorable.[80] Sometimes a lack of resources can bring out the inventiveness of a people, however, just as an abundance of them can stifle innovation and impede economic progress. Were this not the case, then richly endowed Russia would not suffer under such a burden of poverty, nor would resource-poor Japan have the third-largest economy in today's world.

The story was similar for the world's next commercial leader, England.[81] Some three times more populous (roughly 4.25 million people in 1600) and endowed with more resources than the Dutch Republic, it was far poorer and smaller than France. Yet its merchants, explorers, and colonizers bested the French at nearly every turn. Merchants of the East India Company began, from the 1620s, to establish themselves successfully on the coasts of India and traded goods throughout Asia. English investors, entrepreneurs, merchants, and settlers also established colonial footholds in the New World, in particular, in the Chesapeake region, in Massachusetts, in numerous points in between, in the lesser Antilles, and in Jamaica. Tobacco plantations in the Chesapeake and sugar plantations in the Caribbean yielded huge profits and helped fund further commercial development.

The English Civil Wars (1642–51) slowed commercial development, but the Glorious Revolution of 1688, which divided power between the monarchy and Parliament (see Chapter 10), created highly favorable economic conditions. Already in 1694, the government chartered a private joint-stock company, the Bank of England, to manage the public debt and print currency but also with the right to engage in commercial banking activities.[82] Since the Bank enjoyed the full backing of the English government and could pool financial resources from the entire country, the crown could float vastly more debt—and usually at a lower rate of interest—than any other government in Europe or indeed the world. This contributed to England's military triumphs, in particular, in the Seven Years' War (1756–63), which resulted in territorial gains in Canada, Florida, and key positions in India. The volume of its international trade in fact doubled between 1700 and 1780, in part because British shipping had become the most efficient in the world; its merchant fleet, the largest. Even the independence of its American colonies had little effect on their trading relations with the mother country.[83] The physical control of territory was clearly unnecessary to British prosperity. Presumably just opening connections and creating a network of close international relations between Britain and far-flung regions of the globe stimulated economic development.

Britain's financial sophistication also continued to increase. In 1571, Queen Elizabeth had officially opened London's Royal Exchange where merchants and commodity and stock traders gathered to make deals. In 1698, the stock traders moved to Change Alley, a place teeming with taverns, shops, and coffeehouses.[84] They gravitated in particular to Jonathan's Coffee House. The previous year, John Castaing, who spent a lot of time at Jonathan's, posted on Tuesdays and Fridays the prices of stocks and commodities he had on offer, making it possible for investors to carefully track price fluctuations. This practice quickly caught on.[85] For now, brokers traded shares in some 140 English joint-stock companies, including the Bank of England and the East India Company, but gradually the range and number of such companies increased.

More than anything, financial and commodities exchanges are clearinghouses for information. They enable customers and traders to share valuable data about key aspects of potential business transactions. The more a buyer knows about a given asset, the more informed and profitable decisions he can make regarding its purchase. This has been true for as long as buying and selling have occurred between people—in other words, since even before human civilization. In this period and this region, however, it was becoming more possible than ever before to make informed judgments about financial transactions, to the great benefit of both buyers and sellers.

Deirdre McCloskey has argued further that in this era (beginning in the late 1600s), the northwest European peoples began to view commerce, finance, entrepreneurship, and in general profitable innovation in a more favorable light than at any time or any place previously.[86] The landed aristocrats, intellectuals, great magnates, priests, and other elites, who since time immemorial had dominated human societies, had always looked down upon such activities and stifled them through both contempt and detailed rules and regulations. According to McCloskey, once entrepreneurship began to enjoy wide social esteem, the creative abilities of vast numbers of people throughout society were unleashed. The result was almost constant and extraordinarily beneficial innovation in all segments of society, including business, and the beginning of modern economic growth. This mental or "rhetorical shift," as she calls it, seems indeed to have played an important role in the West's rise to wealth and power, though why the shift occurred is not explained. The evidence marshaled throughout the foregoing chapters suggests that a critical mass of entrepreneurship and innovation had by this point been achieved in Europe such that the peoples best disposed to recognize their power and potential had only to take that added step of publicly affirming them as social goods.

In fact, people in some northwest European societies had become positively crazy over entrepreneurship and innovation. A case in point was the South Sea Company.[87] Founded in 1711, the company assumed the British debt incurred during the War of Spanish Succession (1701–14), gained exclusive trading rights with the Spanish-American colonies, and by the Treaty of Utrecht (1713) received control over the slave trade in the Spanish-American colonies (the *asiento*). Speculation in the company's stock in 1720 drove its price up from just over 100 pounds to more than 1,000 in a matter of months. When the price of shares collapsed in September, thousands of investors, both great and small, lost fortunes. The bursting of the South Sea "Bubble" coincided with that of the French Mississippi Company and more generally with steep declines in share prices in London, Amsterdam, and Paris.

Clearly, the long-term growth of the European economies did not occur without ups and downs.[88] In the seventeenth century alone, one can point to a financial depression of the 1620s, various currency crises, and the so-called tulip mania of 1637.[89] Not surprisingly, scholars carefully investigated both economic development and the gyrations of the business cycle.[90] These first economists, often called "mercantilists," advocated protective tariffs, the promotion of exports, the exploitation of colonies, and other measures designed to ensure a favorable balance of trade. The specifics of their proposals matter less than their faith that man has the capacity to control or at least strongly influence the economy or indeed that there is such a thing as an integrated economy in which a gain in one sector can counterbalance a loss in another. Only in an era experiencing relatively steady economic growth could so many scholars focus on devising ways to promote further development.

More capital markets started to emerge. Late in the seventeenth century, the forerunner of the London Stock Exchange commenced operations, and a century later brokers gathered under a tree on Wall Street to trade stocks. In 1792, 24 of them established the New York Stock & Exchange Board, which evolved into the NYSE.[91] London and New York successively dominated international finance for three centuries. British and American entrepreneurs developed highly efficient financial institutions, which concentrated and efficiently allocated vast financial resources. Their lower costs attracted more capital, creating a virtuous cycle. Since capital availability—liquidity—helps drive economic growth, the financial centers with the most efficient and biggest capital markets triumphed over all others. In time, their scale, efficiency, and transaction speeds increased exponentially.

Despite inevitable booms and busts, stock trading and market growth did not cease. Many large businesses simply found it impossible to avoid selling shares as a means to raise capital. So long as economic activity expanded and the number of companies multiplied, stockbrokers and stock exchanges, as a key means for bringing investors and firms seeking capital together, proved invaluable. The biggest English companies, moreover, traded simultaneously on the stock exchanges of both London and Amsterdam from the 1720s, prefiguring the economic integration of both economies.[92]

Commodity markets and traders played an analogous role and similarly multiplied during the eighteenth century. The Royal Exchange remained their central meeting place, though specialized traders met in nearby coffeehouses, which often bore the names of key trading regions. Brokers gathered at the Jamaica to make deals and share information about commercial opportunities in the West Indies. Those specializing in trade with the American colonies met at the Virginia, and so on.

Scholars have vigorously debated the contributions of colonial possessions to the economic development of the main colonizing states, in particular, Great Britain.

Forcing the North American and Caribbean colonists to purchase finished British goods, to transship commodities produced, say, in Virginia through London, and to pay the same prices as British consumers for products imported from Asia, some argue, placed heavy burdens on the fledgling colonies and enriched the home market.[93] Others point out that laws enabling British consumers to buy products at the lowest price on the world market would have significantly raised their standard of living. Moreover, once one factors in the costs of administration and defense in the colonies borne by London, the net benefits to society as a whole were minuscule. It seems instead that only politically influential business interests profited strongly from the colonial trade. Or as one scholar concluded, "the periphery was peripheral."[94]

The banking revolution

Companies that specialized in aggregating investment capital offered yet another means for pooling economic resources. British financiers led the way.[95] The number of private banks in London increased from fewer than 30 in 1750 to 70 in 1800. These banks received deposits and bills of exchange from hundreds of smaller provincial private banks in Britain's rich agricultural areas and extended credit to bankers in the industrial regions that hungered for capital. The British thus began to challenge Dutch supremacy for domination of the international capital market. Throughout the 1700s, the Dutch financed far more overseas trading ventures and lent more money to sovereign states. By the 1820s, however, the main British banking houses, led by Barings and Rothschilds, had almost completely taken control of the debt issues to European states. In order not to miss out on the action, bankers from around Europe and the United States set up offices in London.

A similar development also occurred in France in the first half of the nineteenth century, when bankers from the provinces, Switzerland, and further afield established themselves in Paris.[96] By the 1820s, only Britain exported more capital. After mid-century, the City of London and Paris ranked number one and two in international banking, though Paris emerged as the biggest creditor to foreign governments and the number one investor in European companies.

These two cities led the way in effecting what one scholar has called a "banking revolution," which swept the entire continent from the 1830s.[97] Thousands of new banks, most of them joint-stock companies, challenged the supremacy of the earlier private banks. Like the private banks they generated capital by taking in deposits. Joint-stock banks had originated in Scotland, though with usually only a small number of shareholders. Laws of 1826 and 1833 ended the ban on this type of bank for England and London, respectively.[98] By 1844, roughly 100 such banks operated in the provinces, along with 5 in London. Each of the London joint-stock banks boasted a capitalization far exceeding that of most private banks, though the latter outnumbered the former by 12 to 1. The English joint-stock banks, again following the Scottish model, set up hundreds of branches all around the country. With the Industrial Revolution generating new wealth in nearly every corner of Britain (see Chapter 11), this network of branch offices made it possible to mobilize the financial resources of what was fast becoming the richest country in the world. The new banks helped channel these resources toward investment opportunities, thus fueling further economic growth.

Simultaneously, British financial entrepreneurs began to set up independent joint-stock banks around the world, from Hong Kong to the Middle East and Latin America. By 1860, they had set up 15 overseas banks with 132 branch offices.[99] These firms aimed to finance trade, mostly with Britain, wherever they operated. They raised capital by offering financial services, in particular, by accepting deposits, to a local clientele. Since much of the world lacked an efficient banking infrastructure, they enjoyed great success.

The banking revolution manifested itself in a variety of ways on the Continent—and in the United States—though none entirely dissimilar from the British model. Their greatest and most important commonalities were to pool the wealth of growing economies, to aggregate for investment purposes vast funds of capital, to encourage savings, and to secure nest eggs for millions of ordinary and well-to-do people. Among other accomplishments, the new banks helped finance the railroad boom throughout Europe and the United States in the second half of the nineteenth century (see Chapter 11).

Merchants in the United Kingdom controlled the largest share of international trade—over 20 percent in 1850 and roughly 25 percent in the 1860s, roughly twice that of its closest competitor, France.[100] London itself remained every bit as much a trading as a financial center. The Port of London, the largest in the world, stretched eastward up the Thames, just on the other side of the Tower of London from the financial district (the City), which existed in large part to provide financial services to London's merchants. These services included lending money, financing international trade, coordinating the movement of goods traded in England or in other parts of the world by London merchants, and maintaining exchanges for all manner of colonial and domestic commodities. They also offered a further invaluable service: insurance.

Spreading risk

Placing an investment can resemble gambling or even, in some cases, Russian roulette. Either way, one runs a risk in the hope of some return—a monetary gain or a thrill. The higher the stakes, the bigger the expected return. When Italian merchant-mariners sailed in pursuit of Levantine riches, they risked a very real possibility of the loss of their ships and cargo and death—more because of piracy than bad weather. The return they hoped for, however, overcame the hesitations of a multitude of entrepreneurs. Yet these men were not fools. As early as the 1270s, Italian merchants spread risk by dividing the cost of funding maritime enterprises between two or more investors.[101] In other cases, a sedentary merchant would partially finance a lesser merchant undertaking an overseas venture with the promise to forfeit his capital in the event of a shipwreck; otherwise, the two participants would share equally in any profit or loss. Italian shipowners frequently extended similar conditions to merchants chartering their ships for overseas ventures.

In the early decades of the 1300s, Italian merchants pioneered maritime insurance with a distinctly modern feel.[102] A wealthy merchant, the underwriter, would contract to indemnify a shipment of merchandise—or the ship itself—against possible loss in exchange for a premium set at a fraction of its value, in numerous cases between 11 and 18 percent, depending on distance, route, reports of piracy or warfare, type of vessel, season of the year, and other circumstances. Oftentimes, several underwriters each assumed a portion of a given risk. In such cases, insurance brokers collected pledges from as many underwriters as required to cover the potential loss. In the next century, competition drove down the premiums, which naturally promoted more overseas trade.

Other seafaring peoples, in particular, the Flemish and Dutch, followed the Italians' lead. Judges and port officials, sometimes in consultation with Italian merchants, established precedents and rules concerning standard provisions of maritime insurance. For example, insurers were not liable if a ship perished while still in port or before the signing of an insurance contract.[103] England lagged in developing marine insurance but led the way in insuring property.

The Commercial Revolution drove a construction boom in the major trading centers of Europe. Individuals, firms, and institutions built lavish houses, sprawling warehouses and factories, grand exchanges, guildhalls, offices, workshops, stores, drinking emporia, and banking establishments—to say nothing of a vast number of ordinary homes.[104] London's population in particular surged from roughly 130,000 in 1600 to over 500,000 in 1700. To keep up with the demand for new construction, investors, speculators, real estate agents, and builders accumulated and shared their expertise in "pattern books" that recommended how best to finance, buy, sell, lease, and assess the value of immovable property.[105] These books provided an invaluable service in a market lacking systematic public records or annual data concerning housing starts, units sold, mortgages signed, and other pertinent information. Despite the obvious difficulties of navigating this market, by the later 1600s estimates suggest that one-quarter of all households of London owned real estate. True, many people built houses without permits, yet generally speaking the common law recognized these homes as property. The owners could lease out or mortgage them for use as an investment vehicle. In other words, what might otherwise have remained "dead capital" yielded a value well beyond the initial outlay and thus greatly increased the already fast-expanding wealth of Londoners, enabling them to invest in further goods and services, including new and existing businesses.[106]

In September 1666, the Great Fire of London laid waste to over 13,000 houses, several dozen parish churches, 44 headquarters of trade associations, the Royal Exchange, and the Custom House. Not surprisingly, it spurred financiers to apply the marine-insurance model to the risk of fire. After all, they had plenty of experience in spreading risk via partnerships and joint-stock companies.

Among the first purveyors of fire insurance was Nicholas Barbon (c. 1640–1698).[107] Within a decade, his company established London's first fire brigade, whose job was to fight fires that broke out in properties he insured. In 1706, the Sun Fire Office began to insure commercial assets and personal property as well as buildings themselves.[108] Other large companies emerged over the next couple of decades. Most offered marine, fire, and life insurance. They quickly developed such methods for assessing risk as employing surveyors to inspect the location, construction, and soundness of buildings and physicians to perform physical examinations on customers seeking life insurance. They also sought to ascertain the moral character (the so-called "moral hazard") of prospective clients: is he or she likely to take undue risks?[109] Fire insurance developed quickly in the Electorate of Brandenburg (backed at first by state compulsion) and within several decades in the rest of northern Europe.[110]

The range of risks that early modern Europeans incurred on a daily basis would appall most inhabitants of today's developed countries. Periodic epidemics, times of poor harvests, the lack of police forces, the arbitrary powers of government officials, frequent fires, the dangers of travel—the list is almost endless. Take the concept of property rights. Unlike in most parts of the world then and, unfortunately, even today, people owned title to most landed and built property in most countries and regions of Europe. Yet clear title to any piece of property might prove difficult to obtain in the absence of systematic land registries and public records of real estate transactions.[111] Without such official repositories, which began to appear here and there from the early 1600s (e.g. in Scotland), one could not easily know whether any liens or encumbrances attached to a parcel of land or a house. Hidden encumbrances apparently led to a majority of lawsuits regarding real estate in London. According to the author of one pattern book, the only means by which to avoid legal pitfalls was to "deal with an honest man."[112]

Sharing information

The desire to spread enlightenment, to share knowledge as it became available, and in general to foster transparency and efficiency in every field of endeavor drove a huge variety of activities in this era. Scientists and thinkers published thousands of monographs, scholarly journals, and reference works. Travelers, mariners, and cartographers set out their knowledge of geography and navigation in portolan charts, globes, atlases, maps, and travel guides. Experts in dozens of fields wrote and published pattern and other how-to books. Financiers, traders, and investors "read" prices and shared information about supply and demand by studying the indices in stock and commodity exchanges. They also turned to venues that gained widespread popularity in the seventeenth century: periodicals and coffee shops.

Newspapers began to appear in European cities in the very early 1600s. Amsterdam, with its dynamic mix of transient merchants, quickly became home to the most vibrant periodical press.[113] Semiprivate, specialized newsletters and transcriptions of official documents (called "separates" in England) also appeared and avoided censorship more easily than newspapers.[114] All sorts of publications were available at the fast proliferating coffeehouses throughout Europe—London alone boasted some 2,000 by 1700—where men gathered to exchange ideas and information about business, finance, international affairs, and politics. As one scholar asserted, coffeehouses "became not just a place of discourse but a library where journals could be studied by a news-hungry public."[115] Further, many periodicals got their start in coffeehouses. Edward Lloyd, who owned a coffee shop in the City from 1688 to 1726, provided a weekly news bulletin of information on ships and shipping for merchants and insurance underwriters who frequented his shop.[116]

In commerce, the more accurate, reliable, and consistent information one possesses about supply, demand, prices, opportunities, risks, financing, potential profits, and other aspects of business, the more intelligent and prudent decisions one can make and the more successful one's investments and operations are likely to be. Traders and entrepreneurs from time immemorial have sought and used information critical to their undertakings. The range and accuracy of such information available to the business interests of Holland and Great Britain in this era, along with much greater access to capital, effected what scholars have called a "financial revolution."[117] These developments made it difficult for financiers and entrepreneurs in the rest of Europe—and next to impossible for those elsewhere—to compete with the major banks and trading companies of Amsterdam and London.

* * *

The main problem in other places was not a lack of wealth, business acumen, trading experience, or even knowledge of sophisticated financial instruments. Bills of exchange, after all, had been issued, discounted, and even traded for centuries. Yet nowhere before had entrepreneurs and financiers figured out how to transform concrete assets into large numbers of abstract, tradable, collateralized, and capital-generating instruments. The aggregate sum of real property, business concerns, agricultural output, and available natural resources of France probably exceeded those of Great Britain; those of China did many times over. Moreover, France had a robust banking industry, with more than 70 houses in 1780. It also had a modest stock exchange founded in 1721.[118] Yet financiers in neither country had mastered the art of so efficiently linking together thousands and ultimately hundreds of thousands of investors, of tapping the abundant wealth of their compatriots and of moneyed individuals, companies, and institutions so as to fund vast undertakings on the order of international conflicts or trading operations with global scope. Doubtless, the Chinese government could have raised adequate funds through its tax farmers to conduct any military or entrepreneurial activity on a European—if not far grander—scale. Presumably its treasure fleets of the early 1400s exceeded the logistical and financial burdens of the Seven Years' War. The point, however, is that the Chinese, for all their business skill, lacked the legal and social protections for business and entrepreneurship, relatively unencumbered regulatory environment, and financial sophistication of the British and Dutch—and after 1800, the French—to double, triple, and more the investing and purchasing power of their vast wealth. Such a financial revolution in Beijing could easily have kept China in the top economic position for centuries to come. Instead, while China and other great powers fell into relative decline, Europe achieved all-round economic supremacy. One outcome of this ascendancy was destructive: worldwide imperialism (see Chapter 13); another was beneficial: struggles for political liberation.

The enormous expansion of wealth and economic power of European business people inevitably led to their demanding and seeking an increased political role. Riches, property, business skills, financial influence, and other economic attributes confer on those who possess them a sense of self-worth and dignity. Such people are used to deciding important matters for themselves efficiently, intelligently, and successfully. Yet in most human societies, government officials, political satraps, and other grandees minutely regulated and otherwise interfered in every economic activity or worse—confiscated property and harassed merchants. A merchant's only salvation often lay in paying bribes, seeking patrons, and other humiliating activities.

In early modern Europe, however, secure property rights, legal protections for business interests, influential financial institutions, and the accumulation of relatively stable fortunes empowered substantial groups of individuals to challenge the monopoly on political power exercised by rulers and government officials.

QUESTIONS FOR REFLECTION

Why is the legal protection of property so important for economic development?

What was the social role of tea and coffee in Western societies?

How did scientific innovation contribute to the improvement of agriculture?

How did medieval regulations affecting agricultural markets impede development?

How did the limited liability of chartered companies promote entrepreneurship?

Does the possession of vast natural resources necessarily lead to wealth?

Why did the commercial revolution not happen in China or in the Islamic World?

Chapter 10 Chronology

800:	Charlemagne crowned emperor
Late eleventh century:	First successful experiments in self-government begin in Italy
1159:	John of Salisbury publishes *Policraticus*
1188:	Alfonso IX of Leon calls Cortes (proto-parliament)
Thirteenth century:	Peasants begin to rise in bargaining power and landownership
1215:	Magna Carta signed
1291:	Swiss cantons gain de facto autonomy
1312:	Pope abolishes Knights Templar
1324:	Marsilius of Padua writes *Defender of the Peace*
1460:	University of Basel founded
1499:	Swiss cantons gain de facto independence from Holy Roman Empire
1513:	Machiavelli writes *The Prince*
1568–1648:	Eighty Years' War (Dutch War of Independence)
1572:	St Bartholomew's Day Massacre
1615:	French Estates-General no longer summoned
1648:	Peace of Westphalia; Charles I executed
1658:	Stuart dynasty reinstalled in England, 2 years after death of Oliver Cromwell
1670s:	Slaves first introduced in large numbers to English colonies
1686:	James II establishes Dominion of New England
1689:	England passes Act of Toleration and Bill of Rights; Glorious Revolution
1700–50:	Economic output of English colonies expands 500 percent
1776–83:	American War of Independence
1787:	Constitutional Convention convenes in Philadelphia

1789:	Estates-General called in France; revolution begins
1792:	French Republic declared; King Louis XV imprisoned
1794:	Reign of Terror ends on 27 July

10

Political revolutions

John of Salisbury fled to France in 1163, following a dispute with King Henry II. He vehemently took the side of the Archbishop of Canterbury, Thomas Becket, against Henry's efforts to subordinate the church. John returned to England in 1170 and was close by when four of Henry's knights entered Canterbury Cathedral and murdered Becket. Consecrated bishop of Chartres in 1176, he died of natural causes 4 years later.[1] Given this brief biography, one might be surprised to learn that John published an argument in favor of tyrannicide, the assassination of unjust rulers.[2] A humanistic philosopher who eagerly quoted pagan writers, John went so far as to claim that members of society have a moral obligation to remove a tyrant or else count as his accessories. How could he get away with expressing such a view publicly? Were not legitimate rulers beyond criticism on any basis? Apparently not in Europe.

More than in any other region of the world, Europe enjoyed favorable circumstances for the emergence of liberty and political pluralism. Foremost and fundamentally, political fragmentation made it impossible for any ruler to dominate the continent. Vast, enduring, centralized empires on the Chinese, Mughal, or Ottoman model could not arise there. Like Confucianism and Islam, Christianity provided indispensable cultural cement yet also, uniquely among the great religious teachings, a philosophical basis for challenging and further fragmenting political authority. Beyond these fundamentals, all the transformations discussed in earlier chapters contributed to the dispersal of power among individuals, institutions, organizations, and communities. Entrepreneurs and financiers, printers and guild masters, scientists and scholars, property owners and city fathers, prelates and ministers all exercised authority and boasted rights. More than in any other society of the world—then or before—individuals and collectives limited the power of princes and offered the potential for creating a *system* of limited government if only significant numbers could band together and act in concert.

Foundations of liberty

Europe's geography favored political fragmentation. Two great rivers and their valleys—the Yangtze and Yellow—dominate China; controlling them enabled its rulers to dominate the country. In contrast, no water routes unified Europe and consequently none offered an easy pathway to political centralization.[3] When the Romans unified the Mediterranean region, which is only partly European, they brought civilization—roads, aqueducts, efficient government, a system of law, a great language, and, from the late empire, a universal religion, Christianity—to southern Europe. Upon these foundations, medieval Europe emerged.

After the collapse of Roman supremacy and the rise of dozens of regional warlords, the continent's economic activity, population, means of communication, intellectual attainments, and technological innovation sharply declined. Europe divided into four distinctive regions, none linked to any other except by the Christian faith and occasional royal intermarriage.[4] The core area for centuries was the Italian peninsula. Its key enclave was the Papal States, conquered from a vestige of Byzantium in 756 by the Frankish king, Pepin the Short. They spread from Rome into narrow confines but projected influence and pretensions well beyond their small size. The most sophisticated urban cultures of Europe, outside of Italy, persisted along the Mediterranean littoral, in particular, in Catalonia, Languedoc, and Provence. The northern heartland, the focus of much future development, emerged on either side of the Rhine River. These lands, where Charlemagne gathered his empire around 800, grew into France and Germany.[5] Century by century thereafter warriors and missionaries migrated east, drawing Slavs and other peoples into the European orbit. Finally, an arc of peripheral lands further west and north—northern Spain, England, Ireland, Scotland, and Scandinavia—also gradually adopted Christianity.

Europe's politico-religious make-up differed markedly from those of the great empires to its southeast. A single emperor ruled Byzantium, while four apostolic patriarchs (in Constantinople, Jerusalem, Antioch, and Alexandria) divided religious authority.[6] The Abbasid Caliphs, simultaneously religious and secular leaders, reigned over vast lands from north Africa to Persia until the devolution of power to regional lords in the tenth century.[7] For centuries in Europe, by contrast, the papacy supplied the only intellectual, administrative, and even political unity. All other politics were truly local.

The range of authorities astonishes by its diversity. Monasteries, especially those founded on the Rule of St Benedict, exercised great administrative and spiritual autonomy. The Rule also instituted a form of democracy in each community by empowering the monks to elect their abbots (to whom they nevertheless owed absolute obedience) and forbidding abbots from discriminating among the monks in their charge.[8] The Cluniac and Cistercian monasteries, discussed in Chapter 3, also enjoyed significant political autonomy, often answering only to the pope. Bishops, too, wielded secular authority founded on spiritual power. In some areas of conduct, for example, in imposing the Peace and Truce of God from around the millennium, they could dictate to knights and other lords. Threats of excommunication and warnings of eternal damnation or displays of holy relics of deceased saints carried enormous persuasive power. Of course, the more secular lords feared the prospects of hell, the more bountiful their bequests to local religious institutions. Greater wealth increased prestige and majesty and made it possible to buy more relics.[9] Finally, the military religious orders, like the Knights Hospitaller, the Templars, and a dozen others, which formed during the Crusades, enjoyed extensive political influence. The Templars, by seeking to facilitate pilgrimages and crusades to the Holy Land, pioneered the use of letters of credit, accumulated enormous financial and landed assets, and built an international financial empire.[10]

The Germanic, Celtic, Slavic, and other tribes that ruled much of Europe during early medieval times often made decisions collectively at "folkmoots," sometimes involving all freemen. These assemblies decided war, passed judgments, and elected kings, of which hundreds reigned across Europe in pre-Carolingian times. As they slowly consolidated their power, most kings continued the tradition of summoning councils, with names like Witenagemot or Althing, to advice them.[11] The earliest included only knights and other lords, often the king's closest followers, and met usually only to wage war.[12]

In time, other members of society joined the king's summons. In 1188, Alfonso IX of Leon in northwestern Iberia convoked the first such assembly, the Cortes, with three estates representing the nobles, clergy, and commons (or "third estate").[13] As discussed in Chapter 4, rulers summoned such representative institutions in order to secure the loyalty of their subjects during succession or other crises, in support of war, or to increase revenue.[14] By the thirteenth century, what German scholars call the Ständestaat, or "polity of the estates," in which rulers shared power with the three major social components, had emerged throughout much of the continent.[15]

Also during the Middle Ages, regional assemblies of individual social categories—such as urban dwellers, clergy, notables, or even peasants—emerged without any official sanction. Moreover, urban and other communities often formed confederations for economic or political purposes. Most, like the royally summoned assemblies, gradually declined, but not all: for example, the Swiss and Dutch confederations (see below).[16] Folk councils and local alliances gathered for decision making throughout the world then and before, but none outside Europe evolved into institutional forms such as these.

The rise of autonomous chartered towns, described in Chapters 2 and 5, also limited the power of rulers and lords. They differed dramatically from urban centers in other cultures.[17] Most European towns governed themselves and constituted centers of power through the banding together and the pooling of resources by otherwise powerless individuals. All urban inhabitants enjoyed exemption from feudal dues and other obligations. Nearly all gained their livelihood from manufacturing and commerce. Many also took up the necessary burdens of self-government and defense. Cities as incorporated communities elected officials, kept records, imposed taxes, built high walls, and maintained militias. Over time, their administration gained in complexity. By 1450, the urban government of Frankfurt am Main divided into 18 distinct committees.[18] Yet, except for a few Italian city-states, most looked to local and regional rulers—princes, kings, bishops, dukes—to administer justice between the towns and other political actors, to mint coins, and to keep good order in the wider realms of territory in the midst of which individual towns lay. In order to secure these benefits, most urban communities sided with territorial rulers in their political struggles with feudal lords.

Within the city walls, tradesmen and merchants banded together into craft associations or guilds. Such institutions defended the interests of members, defined and upheld standards of production and measurement, and fought for other regulations favorable to their trade.[19] When in the early modern period the guilds generally hampered industrial and economic development by stifling innovation,[20] creative entrepreneurs often simply moved their operations outside the city walls where the guilds could not dictate to them.[21] Guilds thrived in early modern India and China as well, as discussed in Chapter 2, but in neither place did they wield political power or influence. Nor did towns in these countries, many of them thriving metropolises, gain corporate status or join together to form urban leagues, as in the case of the Hansa in northern Europe.

Other "constituted bodies" besides towns added to the clout of the third estate, including universities, religious foundations and orders, and in France and other nearby lands *parlements*, judicial bodies with the right to register all royal edicts. When the European universities, like the craft guilds, began to stifle wide-ranging inquiry, the more innovative scholars and thinkers pursued their intellectual activities outside the universities.[22] They corresponded with each other across the continent, founded scholarly journals, and joined learned societies. This was a key feature of European culture: that individuals and communities continuously looked for innovative ways to organize themselves and their activities. By contrast, the Islamic and Chinese societies were far more austere, with very few intermediary bodies standing between the ruler and the ruled. As one scholar has argued, "strong arbitrary powers and weak infrastructural ones . . . tend to go together."[23]

The European peasantry, which comprised the largest component of the third estate, enjoyed no direct representation in any national or regional diet or assembly of estates except that of Sweden, thanks to the relatively great power of free Swedish peasants.[24] Battles between kings and nobles, however, often resulted in increased rights for peasants and other commoners, as the main contenders sought to win supporters within the third estate.[25] Regional parliaments emerged in several places, for example, France.[26] These bodies tended to impede or at least weaken the development of national assemblies.

The fragmentation of political authority in Europe made it impossible, at least by the standards of the great authoritarian empires like the Chinese and Ottoman, and certainly on a continent-wide basis, for rulers to impose intellectual and political conformity, to levy crushing taxes, or to stifle innovation.[27] In most places, people with initiative and drive could flee political and religious persecution, experiment in nearly every aspect of life, and evade overly high taxes.

Political battles played out in many ways depending on shifting constellations of interests. Kings eagerly summoned assemblies of estates looking for allies in their struggles with the nobility, which everywhere in Europe dominated the countryside. Occasionally, to their surprise, towns joined forces with nobles. Philip the Fair convened France's first national assembly in 1302 to unite towns and nobles with the monarchy against the papacy in a struggle for control of the French Church. Pressure he thus brought to bear forced the pope in 1312 to abolish the Knights Templar, whose immense assets in France Philip immediately seized.[28] A century later, the French kings began to undermine the power of the national estates until they ceased meeting altogether after 1614. The vibrancy of regional assemblies in France surely contributed to this development. A like scenario unfolded in most countries of Europe.

Even as the assemblies of estates declined, they left behind a beneficial legacy. The personal, arbitrary power of rulers had diminished. The separation of powers between church and state had become more concrete and regulated. Rapacious local feudal lords had lost their right to plague townspeople and villagers—or at least, for the most part, willingly gave up this practice. Laws and fiscal policies that aimed to facilitate commercial relations developed. Finally, elites had begun to feel an allegiance to institutions and laws rather than individual rulers or dynasties.

On this basis, national consciousness began to develop, first in France and England and somewhat later in the Netherlands and Sweden.[29]

Much of the distinctive European experience of politics in the early modern period rested on a foundation of private property rights. Nobles dominated the European countryside largely thanks to their ownership of land. In societies where grandees held land without secure property rights—but only at the pleasure of rulers—in the Ottoman Empire, for example, they could never gain general political influence as an estate or other corporate entity. Their power stemmed only from their favor at court, their success in battle, or other contingent conditions. It therefore remained temporary. European aristocrats, by contrast, constituted a collective political force whose individual members possessed status and influence that monarchs could contest and strive to undermine but rarely repudiate. Tradition and law undergirded their social position, but without their often-vast tracts of landed property to serve as power bases, the European nobility could not have limited and even contested royal prerogatives and authority as they so often successfully did.[30] Likewise, the wealth-generating property of urban communities gave them the wherewithal to negotiate the immunities and exemptions from taxation that placed them outside the control of secular rulers. Even the European peasantry enjoyed its relatively high status, thanks to land-ownership rights. (The same was true of China's peasants but not its other social orders.)[31] Nobles in borderland regions, in particular, offered grants of freely held land to attract laborers, as noted in Chapter 5. From the 1200s to the 1400s, peasants gained in bargaining power and landowning rights all across Western Europe. Ownership confers power, and since property was more divided among diverse social categories in Europe than in other great civilizations, power itself was more dispersed and rulership more limited.

Status, rights, and power in Europe also stemmed from autonomously existing, rule-governed, legitimately constituted offices throughout society. Rights and duties inhered in officeholders, by virtue of their holding specific offices within recognized corporate bodies, such as guilds, urban communities, and universities.[32] Explicit rules specified the procedures for acceding to any such office. Failure to follow them scrupulously made one illegitimate. The contrast with the Islamic world could not have been starker. Muslims attained responsible offices by proving their worth as individuals. Children, women, or incapacitated people therefore rarely served in high office. On the face of it, this system seems a more efficient means of political selection. In reality, it opened the door to power struggles, violence, and arbitrary rule, since politics at every level depended more on individual will than on institutional rules and norms. The complex system that emerged in Europe fostered a respect for the rule of law at every level of society.

Even European rulers felt obligated to obey the law. This conception of the law as superior even to duly constituted political power derived from the twelfth-century Italian jurist Gratian's understanding of natural law, in which "princes are bound by and shall live according to their laws."[33] They could change old laws but only by following established legal procedure. As late medieval European rulers sought to reassert their authority, they found support among legal experts who gradually rose to form the nobility of the robe. This powerful new element of the aristocracy naturally reinforced the idea of *rex infra legem*, or "the king under the law."[34]

By the early 1400s, as noted in Chapter 7, some European political theorists argued that representatives of duly constituted bodies could more efficiently and more legitimately exercise leadership than individual rulers. Such conciliarists asserted that pluralistic decision making usually achieved superior results by encouraging rational argumentation and reconciling diverse points of view. Nevertheless, the weight of tradition soon won the day in most of Europe.

Within a century, a rigidly hierarchical papacy reasserted itself, the Medicis made themselves masters of Florence, Charles V began to establish the greatest European empire since Charlemagne, and authoritarian monarchs emerged in many other countries besides, foremost among them in France. It was the age of gunpowder revolution (see Chapter 4). Raising huge military forces required vast sums of money and enormous bureaucracies to collect them.[35] Pointing to the obvious geopolitical dangers—previously thriving regional powers like Livonia, Novgorod, and Burgundy simply disappeared from the map—rulers nearly everywhere demanded and received enhanced powers, undermined traditions of local self-government, and imposed heavier and heavier taxation (which remained very light by today's standards). In a few corners of the continent, however, the traditions of self-government persisted.

Those traditions benefited from several centuries of European theorizing about the nature of government and its limits. Among the earliest and most remarkable medieval political philosophers was John of Salisbury (c. 1120–1180). A bishop and frequent emissary from the Archbishop of Canterbury to Rome, he was one of the most learned men of his age. As mentioned above, he articulated a defense of tyrannicide.[36]

Every society, he claimed, is like a living organism, with diverse faculties, organs, and members. John conceived the ruler as the brain, the clergy as the soul, the king's council as the heart, the royal judges and local administrators as the senses, the financial officials as the stomach and intestines, the two hands as the tax collector and the soldier, and the feet as the artisans and peasants. As in a living organism, every body part must work harmoniously with the others, each bears responsibility for crucial functions, and ultimately all must work together toward the common good. A ruler who shirks this responsibility offends against justice itself and against God's will. Members of society should tolerate such injustice up to a point and should pray that it might cease, but when it does not they have a moral obligation to kill the tyrant. John, it seems, did not have in mind a specific living tyrant but simply formulated a universal principal of just government.[37] (The third-century B.C. Confucian thinker, Mencius, had advanced a similar idea, but it developed no further.)[38]

The idea of tyrannicide conflicted with much contemporaneous thinking on the nature of politics. Most writers before him, following St Paul and St Augustine, had considered government a curse or punishment that man deserved because of his sinful nature.[39] The translation of Aristotle's *Politics* in 1260, with his conception of the state as a positive and creative force, challenged this view.[40] St Thomas Aquinas blended this idea with the optimistic Christian vision of God bringing salvation to man in history. By measuring the laws promulgated by our rulers against the Natural Law that the Creator has inscribed in our minds man can judge the extent to which these laws are just, that is, whether they promote the common good of society. In various writings, therefore, St Thomas justified the murder of a tyrannical usurper, the deposing, by a duly constituted representative body, of a tyrant who abuses rightful authority, and even insurrection against tyranny, for unjust laws are "acts of violence" against the community.[41] For a pillar of Roman Catholic theological thought for hundreds of years to defend such rebellious activity is nothing short of extraordinary. One can scarcely imagine its parallel in the other great civilizations.

Protestant theorists advanced still more vehement justifications of resistance to unjust rule, as discussed in Chapter 7. Some incorporated elements of natural law theory, Roman and canon law, and Roman republican ideals into their arguments and downplayed the religious reasons for opposing tyranny, in order to win a broader basis of support. Yet even the work that recent scholarship has singled out as exemplary of this "secular turn," Philippe du Plessis-Mornay's *Vindiciae contra tyrannos*, supplies five times more references to biblical than to secular texts and justifies killing tyrants primarily as obstacles to achieving salvation through Christ.[42] In fact, Mornay argues that every godly person, by virtue of his or her covenant with God, has the right to liberate the church from an unjust ruler—since all humans are brothers and children of God, and tyrants harm everyone and hinder the fulfillment of the divine plan. Mornay's book ran through dozens of Latin editions and translations into vernacular languages in the later sixteenth century.

All of the foregoing customs, traditions, institutions, rules, political entities, ideas, and values, as well as accidents of geography and history, contributed to the development of republican ideals and polities in early modern Europe.

Early European self-government

In a continent plagued by almost constant warfare and powerful states bent on conquest, preserving a smaller land's territorial integrity without ceding all fiscal and military power to a single ruler required both pluck and luck. A few states enjoyed the luxury of natural defenses. Clever diplomacy could win defensive allies. Ingenuity and assiduous military training enabled even relatively poor and small polities to resist the great powers throughout the late medieval and early modern period. A thriving economy also benefited smaller states by enabling them to fund big military budgets. Only those few states boasting a solid combination of these characteristics avoided the continent-wide trend toward absolutism. They preserved a remnant of republican ideals and traditions of self-government and laid the foundation for a series of political revolutions that swept the continent and established political participation, pluralism, and freedom as Western hallmarks.

The first successful European experiments in self-government after antiquity occurred in northern Italy, beginning in the late eleventh century. The leading citizens in Padua, Florence, Pisa, Siena, Genoa, Arezzo, Milan, and other urban communities gradually established elective councils headed by officials called *podestà* and endowed with supreme executive and judicial authority. Written documents typically guaranteed these arrangements.[43] Thus arose the Italian city-states or, as some scholars prefer, city-republics. All male heads of household who paid taxes and resided permanently in a given city had the right to vote. Italian Renaissance political theorists, drawing heavily on the writings of classical Roman authors like Cicero, clearly spelled out the role of citizens, as electors who normally pursued their own self-interest, and of rulers, who acted merely as their agents or administrators of justice. Republicanism, as they conceived it, involved freedom from arbitrary rule and the right of the most "worthy" and virtuous citizens to take part in the political process. Virtue in this context implied a public spirit and a willingness to place the common good above one's own private affairs.

Since noblemen tended to dominate the councils, other members of society sometimes banded into associations and formed their own counsels. These came into conflict with, and sometimes pushed aside, the official ones. Conflicts naturally ensued. The pre-humanist Italian writer, Giovanni da Viterbo, lamented around 1250 that "practically every city nowadays is divided within itself, with the result that the effects of good government are no longer felt."[44] Several decades later, Marsilius of Padua argued in his *Defender of the Peace* (1324) that the people acting as a whole, through elected representatives, would be able to adopt laws that more adequately met the needs of all—and would more willingly be obeyed—than could any ruler or oligarchy. He asserted further that elected officials must serve the common good or face removal from office.[45] By the time Marsilius finished his masterwork, however, elective government was giving way in Padua and other city-republics to hereditary rule.

What had gone wrong? Marsilius and other thinkers had placed too much confidence in their civic leaders. The Florentine political theorist Niccolò Machiavelli (1469–1527) explained the fundamental problem in his *Discourses on Livy* (completed c. 1518).[46] The three main forms of government, as described by Aristotle—monarchy, aristocracy, and democracy—tend to degenerate over time, respectively, into despotism, oligarchy, and mob rule, which itself usually gives way again to monarchy. People, he averred, are usually selfish, lazy, mistrustful, and unlikely to seek the common good without compulsion. They also pursue diverse interests, depending on their wealth, sources of livelihood, and status. A political system that elevates one social category—the powerful, the middling sorts, or the poor—will necessarily shortchange the others. A system that promotes all the main interests of society will create less political friction and will achieve greater stability and a higher level of general satisfaction. Machiavelli pointed in particular to the mixed government of Republican Rome with its consuls, Senate, and tribunes of the people. Such a political system, involving overt competition, required liberty. Yet in the dangerous world he inhabited, the defense of the polity from external threats often required strong—even despotic—central leadership. Thus, in *The Prince* he provided instructions for rulers wishing to build strong states.

The northern Italian city-republics bequeathed a valuable legacy in dozens of seminal texts advancing arguments for the first time since classical antiquity in favor of self-government.[47] Many actors in subsequent political struggles in Europe and the wider world found inspiration in these texts. Also important was the continued flourishing of one city-republic, Venice, into the eighteenth century. Aristocratic families dominated the polity, but they displayed great civic-mindedness, avoiding the internecine conflicts of the other Italian city-republics. A mixed form of government, which divided power among the Great Council, the Senate, and the doge (chief magistrate), largely satisfied Machiavelli's criteria. A jealous resistance to papal authority, resulting more than once in diplomatic tension, embodied an ideal of the subordination of church to the state. Together these attributes served to inspire political reformers in northern Europe, and especially in Holland and England.[48]

As discussed in Chapter 4, three Swiss cantons gained *de facto* autonomy in 1291 from the House of Habsburg, which had been attempting to impose more direct rule in the region. By 1300, they had "developed a political autonomy which was unprecedented and astonishing."[49] Over the following six decades, five more cantons joined them, most importantly the free imperial cities of Zurich and Bern with their extensive adjacent territories.[50] Forming not a polity but a "jumble of alliances,"[51] in the words of one historian, they nevertheless used successful battles, astute diplomacy, hard-to-besiege mountainous terrain, and brilliant military tactics to resist continuous efforts at encroachment by the Habsburg emperors and other rulers fearful of the bad example the Swiss were setting for their own subjects. A dread example indeed: within a decade of the victorious Battle of Sempach, serfdom was abolished within the three original cantons. Decade by decade, from the 1450s, other cantons joined them under various terms of association, increasing their efforts at cooperation but still remaining fiercely independent on local matters. Thanks to diplomatic maneuvering, in a context of France, Habsburg Austria, and Burgundy all vying to outsmart and outgun one another, in 1474 the Swiss Confederation won an absolute renunciation of feudal claims on their territory from Sigismund, Duke of Further Austria, in the name of the Habsburg Empire. Meanwhile, the confederates expanded their territory to the north, south, and east, both through diplomacy and conquest. A series of victorious battles in the Burgundian Wars, in particular, at Grandson and Morat in 1476, secured Swiss independence from Habsburg overlordship. A treaty of 1499, following the Swabian War, gave the Confederation *de facto* independence from the Holy Roman Empire as well.

The 13 confederated cantons (by 1513), along with several other associated towns, cantons, and territories, governed themselves autonomously, with little interference from the others. Nevertheless, a political assembly, called the Tagsatzung, emerged in the fourteenth century. Composed of two representatives each from the cantons, by 1400 it was meeting at least a few times annually in order to negotiate common policies and to settle intercantonal disputes.[52] Several of the major cities, including Basel and Zurich, where guildsmen shared political influence with urban patricians, enjoyed relatively democratic governance. Free landholding also gradually increased in the rural areas. The confederation's relatively vibrant economy involved the export of cheeses, textiles, and mercenaries. The University of Basel, founded in 1460, became a major center of humanistic learning, attracting such scholars as Erasmus and Paracelsus and such church reformers as Calvin and Zwingli.[53]

The Swiss Confederation formalized its political independence at the conclusion of the Thirty Years' War in 1648, a status that continues until the present day. Yet a small number of patrician families came to dominate each of the cantons, inhibiting popular political participation and stifling economic and technological innovation.[54] Moreover, the famed Swiss mercenaries hired into military service across Europe drained the country of manpower and led to social disruption when bands of soldiers returned. Finally, the combined arms and gunpowder revolutions (see Chapter 4) put an end to Swiss military prowess.[55] The Swiss remained prosperous but not a commercial, financial, or military power like the Dutch.

Geography probably favored the emergence of self-government in the seven northern provinces of the Netherlands.[56] The sandy, marshy, waterlogged land did not lend itself to the consolidation of large estates. Draining swamps and maintaining dikes required collective and therefore relatively egalitarian efforts. In the sixteenth century, the entire Netherlands could boast only 12 accredited noble families, a few of them major landowners and mostly concentrated in the ten southern provinces. Moreover, their status, wealth, and influence were in decline.[57] Indeed, middle-class urban dwellers (burghers) controlled the provincial estates, administrative offices, and law courts. The provincial estates of Holland, by far the strongest, had only one aristocratic member.

The Holy Roman Emperor, Charles V, inherited the Low Countries in 1506, ruled them through a succession of regents, and negotiated their liberation from feudal obligations through the Pragmatic Sanction of 1549.[58] He intended to root out Protestantism and to centralize these diverse lands, each with its own laws, customs, and political institutions, as the "Seventeen Provinces." Charles also sought to divide and rule over the various provincial estates, the constituent elements of each estate, and the Estates-General, always aiming to increase taxation in his ceaseless efforts to finance war.[59] He repeatedly pressured the representatives of Brabant, for example, to disregard their oath to uphold the charter of liberty, the Joyeuse Entrée, granted by Duke John III in 1354. Year by year, however, Charles, and then his son and successor, Philip II (from 1556), met with proud resistance in all 17 provinces. The constitutional organization of the provinces impeded easy domination. If only one of the 17 rejected a settlement, even after prolonged negotiations, then any deal fell through and required renegotiation.

Philip, who spoke neither Dutch nor French, felt none of his father's sympathy for the Dutch people. He therefore pressed the centralizing project harder, persecuted Protestantism more vehemently, and sought to extract even more taxes. Tensions built for a decade involving minor disturbances and general discontent. Spanish officials and their supporters feared that the Dutch hoped to turn the king into a figurehead. In 1566, an iconoclastic movement burst out, with Calvinists destroying "idolatrous" statues and images in churches across the Netherlands.[60] In August, Philip sent the Duke of Alba with 10,000 troops to crush the rebellion. He set up a special court that put to death over 1,000 alleged rebels and even some staunchly Catholic nobles who had committed no greater "crime" than tolerating Protestants. These acts divided the country and sparked the Eighty Years' War or Dutch Revolt (1568–1648).

It consisted of a series of protracted and bloody rebellions and battles, often spearheaded by radical Calvinists.[61] The movement's key political leader and military commander in the first two decades was William I of Orange, the stadtholder (the military but not political leader) of the provinces of Holland, Zeeland and Utrecht. He obtained French, English, and even Ottoman support against the Habsburgs. Dutch—and English—naval forces harried and seized Spanish commercial ships throughout the Spanish Main and beyond. (The ill-starred Spanish Armada aimed to punish England for such acts.) William resorted to a clever weapon in 1572–73: breaking open dikes in order to surround most of Holland and Zeeland with water. Finally, in 1579 the 17 provinces divided into 10 in the south that remained Catholic, loyal to Spain, and dominated by aristocrats; and 7 in the north, where Calvinism, the middle class, and commerce ruled (see Map 10.1).

Europe's first professional, salaried, meticulously trained army now emerged in the north. The typical aristocratic officer placed honor above all else. The soldiers' job in the Dutch army, by contrast, was to win battles not seek glory. Until then, soldiers contemptuously refused to dig their own trenches; the Dutch soldier carried a shovel as standard equipment.[62]

MAP 10.1 *In 1579, seven northern Dutch provinces seceded from Spain and joined forces to resist Spanish domination.*

In 1581, the Estates-General of the seven northern provinces declared their independence from Philip as a tyrant and an oppressor of Dutch liberties. Their attempts to elect a prince from outside the Netherlands as a figurehead ruler failed miserably. The Duke of Anjou had to be driven out for attempting to seize absolute power, and the Earl of Leicester fled of his own accord.[63] In 1587, therefore, the Estates appointed Maurice of Nassau, the stadtholder of Holland and Zeeland and the brilliant military innovator discussed in Chapter 4. The following year, the seven provinces proclaimed themselves a republic. Maurice for the most part acted as their main political and military leader until his death in 1625, though local, town, and provincial governments handled most administrative responsibilities. In fact, one can seriously question whether there was a Dutch state at all.[64] The Peace of Westphalia (1648), which ended the Thirty Years' War, finally recognized the independence of the Republic of the United Provinces.

The Dutch Republic had already commenced its career as the greatest commercial power of the world with the biggest fleet of ships, the most trading connections, the heftiest concentration of capital, and the most efficient financial system, as discussed in Chapter 9. Few countries in the world could rival the tiny Dutch Republic in the seventeenth century for achievements in the arts, science, and intellectual life.[65] The country's prosperity and toleration attracted and nurtured a host of geniuses: in philosophy, Descartes and Baruch Spinoza (1632–77); in science, the physicist and mathematician Christiaan Huygens (1629–95) and Anton van Leeuwenhoek; and in painting, artists of talent almost too numerous to list, including Rembrandt and Vermeer. Dozens more fled their homelands seeking refuge, from the royalist Thomas Hobbes to the theorist of limited government John Locke.

The Dutch did not make a revolution. They preserved from medieval times a form of constitutionally limited self-government. During the early modern period, urban mercantile elites dominated politics. Their fabulous wealth and efficient capital markets enabled the merchant-oligarchs to fund a lengthy war of independence without imposing heavy taxation, innovation-stifling political centralization, or an ever-expanding bureaucracy, which most European rulers found unavoidable in this age of almost constant and exorbitantly expensive warfare. While not exactly revolutionary in the normal political sense, this Dutch achievement was extremely radical: the establishment of a republican, federal state with a high level of religious and political toleration, governmental decentralization, and economic efficiency and stability yet without the need to overthrow existing political, economic, and social systems and structures.[66] The first great European political revolution required such an upheaval.

The English revolutions

During the early Middle Ages, Germanic tribes repeatedly invaded the British Isles by boat. In this manner, William, Duke of Normandy, conquered England in 1066, despoiled the native aristocracy, centralized the institutions of governance, and built defensive fortifications throughout the country. For over six hundred years, no foreign power again successfully invaded the insular land. Therefore, its rulers found it unnecessary to maintain a standing army. In an age of military revolution, this was unheard of. The absence of a standing army had two important political effects. First, the English monarchs had less need to build up a complex and intrusive bureaucracy. Second, they found it harder to impose laws against the will of the elites.

England's system of law also limited royal power. When the continental governments and professors of law created new legal codes, institutions, and jurisprudence based largely on Roman law, as discussed in Chapter 3, English rulers and jurists maintained the common law, incorporating only some of the organizational features of Roman law.[67] Under common law, judges enjoyed great flexibility in deciding cases and appeals. Sometimes they interpreted acts of Parliament. Other times they followed the interpretations of other judges. In still other cases they developed principles of law—often called "case law" or "precedents"—with no statutory basis whatsoever. Over time, the common law became dense, complex, highly particularistic, and often completely outside the reach of the English monarchs. By contrast, the entirely rationalistic Roman law, which continental jurists strived continuously to reconcile with royal edicts, facilitated the development of absolutism.[68]

Common law favored the emergence of an admirable institution, the trust.[69] Like a corporation, it had the legal rights of a person in perpetuity. Yet unlike a corporation, one did not need official permission to create a trust. The English formed trusts for charitable purposes, to bequeath assets to heirs other than first-born sons, to shelter wealth on behalf of women, and to create a broad array of institutions. By the 1700s, hundreds of prestigious gentlemen's clubs, learned societies, political associations, and religious denominations (including Catholic, Jewish, and dissenting Protestant) functioned as trusts. Many business enterprises began and persisted as trusts, among them the London Stock Exchange and several big insurance firms discussed in Chapter 9. The very Inns of Court—the training and professional associations of all English lawyers—have existed from medieval times as trusts. Since their members possessed great wealth and power, they could easily have arranged incorporation. They preferred to maintain their independence.

In medieval times, ecclesiastical and secular elites occasionally imposed legal or constitutional limits on the monarchs' power. In 1100, for example, William the Conqueror's designated successor William Rufus died while the next in line, Robert of Normandy, was on crusade in the Holy Land. When their younger brother Henry claimed the throne, he did so from a position of weakness and therefore had to agree to promulgate the Charter of Liberties. By this document, Henry promised to end recent oppressive policies toward the church and the great families of the realm, including the imposition of new taxes and arbitrary fines and the interference in marriage choice and lawful inheritance.[70] For the most part, however, Henry failed to keep his promises.

A century later, in 1215, the authority of another English king plummeted, thanks to serious military reversals in France and new taxes imposed to recoup his losses. Facing a revolt of the barons led by the Archbishop of Canterbury at an assembly described a few decades later as a "parliament,"[71] King John (r. 1199–1216) limited royal power still further, by the "Great Charter" or Magna Carta. This constitutional monument provided for the convocation of a "great council" of barons without the king's summons, for the abolition of some unpopular taxes, and for the right of merchants and other travelers to come and go freely, among other clauses. Perhaps most significant, it stated that "No free man may be arrested or imprisoned or disseised or outlawed or exiled, or in any way brought to ruin, nor shall we go against him nor send others in pursuit of him, save by the legal judgment of his peers or by the law of the land." Within a few decades, English jurists interpreted the phrase "the law of the land" as meaning that the law limited the king's power.[72] The Great Charter's main provisions and its spirit of limiting royal power established a foundation of English constitutional law—and of the king's subordination to the law—for many centuries. For now, however, royal charters authorizing the incorporation of towns imposed a more effective and immediate check on monarchical power.[73]

Meanwhile, the outbreak of the Hundred Years' War with France obliged King Edward III (r. 1327–77) to promise the Great Council that all new taxes would require the consent of the Lords and Commons in Parliament and that only that body could annul statutes it enacted.[74] Even so, for centuries the English monarchs remained the senior partner in this power-sharing arrangement.

The English monarchs also gradually relegated the Roman papacy to the status of junior partner—sooner and more vigorously than other European rulers. King Edward I struck the first blow with the Statute of Provisors (1306), which forbade any religious authority to export abroad money or objects of value gathered through taxation or other impositions.[75] A second statute of the same name, promulgated in 1350, prohibited the pope from appointing bishops without local input. Other statutes followed, all aimed at curtailing political and economic influence in England by the papacy or its agents. The most famous of these decrees, the Statute of Praemunire issued in 1392 by Richard II (r. 1377–99), made it a grave crime to receive an ecclesiastical office or a judgment in matters relating to England from any "alien," meaning quite specifically Rome.[76] These laws of praemunire, which had remained in full force, justified Henry VIII's rebellion against the papacy, as described in Chapter 7.

Before Henry turned to Parliament for backing in his struggle to free the English Church and himself from Roman tutelage, England had seemed on a path away from parliamentary monarchy. From 1485 until 1529, Parliament had met only 11 times—roughly every 4 years—in sessions lasting an average of 10 or 11 weeks each. Henry VIII had summoned the body only four times from his accession to the throne in 1509 until the Reformation Parliament, which sat almost continuously from 1529 to 1534.[77] By justifying the king's break with Rome, Parliament established itself in principle as a partner with the monarch.[78]

Over the next several decades, the prerogatives of Parliament slowly increased. If Thomas More, acting as speaker in 1523, humbly requested that members be allowed to speak freely in Parliament,[79] three decades later Elizabeth I recognized the members' freedom of speech as a "right in practice."[80] Although Elizabeth contested the right of Parliament to initiate legislation, especially in ecclesiastical matters, she accepted its right to participate in the enactment of all new laws. Sir Thomas Smith, a professor of law, Member of Parliament, ambassador to France, and adviser to the queen, argued in his *The Commonwealth of England* (1583) that "the most high and absolute power of the realm of England consisteth in the Parliament."[81] Scholars disagree about how far Parliament's authority expanded under the Tudors,[82] yet it is clear that a truly dramatic break forward occurred only under the next dynasty, that of the Stuarts.

When Elizabeth died childless in 1603, the English throne passed to James VI, King of Scots (r. 1567–1625). In *The True Law of Free Monarchies* (1598), he had asserted the divine right of kings to rule without answering to anyone save God alone.[83] Yet James I of England came to power with the royal coffers empty.[84] Whatever his pretensions to political absolutism, he lacked the power to impose new taxes without the consent of Parliament. Instead, he sold aristocratic titles and crown lands.[85]

His son, Charles I, who acceded to the throne in 1625, also professed a belief in absolutism. He married the daughter of the French king, a staunch Catholic who refused to convert to Anglicanism. The suspicious gentry leaders of Parliament voted to grant the king only provisionally and for 1 year the right to impose import and export tariffs ("tonnage and poundage"), instead of the customary right to impose them for life.[86] A confrontation with the king prompted the Commons to let the bill lapse entirely, thus depriving the king of a big source of income. Considering himself unbound by parliamentary decision, Charles continued to collect the monies without it and extracted involuntary loans from grandees of the realm and ordered the arrest and imprisonment of those who refused to pay. When their lawyers petitioned the Court of King's Bench for writs of *habeas corpus*, the king replied that he had the right to order the arrest of any person for reasons of state.

In 1628, Charles again summoned Parliament in order to secure funding. The assembly devoted most of its efforts to debating and adopting the "Petition of Right."[87] Drawing on constitutional law stretching back to Magna Carta, the legislators banned the billeting of troops in private homes, the imposition of forced loans, declarations of martial law in peacetime, depriving prisoners of their right of *habeas corpus*, and levying taxes without the consent of Parliament. In order to gain that consent, especially amid disastrous military campaigns against France and Spain, Charles agreed to sign the document, believing he could simply ignore its provisions. He then went on to rule without calling Parliament for 11 years, having made peace with France and Spain. He also levied various taxes without following the letter of tradition and persecuted religious dissenters. Discontent grew widespread.

A turning point came in 1640, when a rebellion over Charles's meddling in Scotland's religious affairs threatened an invasion of England.[88] Charles summoned Parliament, desperately seeking revenue, but quickly dissolved the assembly when it focused its attention on royal abuses. Following disasters on the battlefield, he again called Parliament. The Long Parliament sat for 13 years. It demanded accountability from the king's staff, apportioned to the king only adequate funding to maintain his household, and passed statutes—with Charles's assent—by which Parliament had to convene at least one 50-day session every 3 years and could not be dissolved without its consent. In early 1642, Charles fled London and began to raise forces loyal to him. In response, parliamentarians also set about gathering an army. The two sides first clashed in September 1642, a royalist victory.

Devout Calvinists—Puritans and radical Presbyterians—came to dominate Parliament, as well as its military forces, after radicals drove out monarchists and other upholders of the former establishment.[89] They created a full-time professional soldiery, the New Model Army.[90] Oliver Cromwell (1599–1658), a Puritan of the middling gentry, proved its most able commander. He led the parliamentary "roundheads" in a series of victories against the royalist "cavaliers" through two successive phases of the Civil War (see Map 10.2), amid shifting alliances with Scottish and Irish forces, culminating in August 1648 in the utter defeat of the royalists. Five months later, a specially constituted High Court of Justice found Charles guilty of treason and ordered his execution. Nothing remotely like this had occurred in European history—a legitimately ruling monarch removed from office for specific crimes and publicly beheaded.

The remaining parliamentarians declared a "Commonwealth," or a republic. It continued policies first undertaken in 1642, such as banning theatrical performances, excise taxes replacing feudal dues, reduced government intervention in the economy, securing the toleration of dissenting Protestant denominations, and rooting out ornamentation and music from Anglican churches.[91] In 1653, Cromwell was granted

MAP 10.2 *Areas controlled by Parliamentary forces and forces loyal to the King at the end of 1643 during the English Civil War.*

many attributes of kingship as "Lord Protector" for life. He repeatedly overpowered royalist insurgencies in Ireland and Scotland and an incursion into England itself. Yet neither Parliament nor Cromwell rose above the law, trampled the institutions of self-government, established a large bureaucracy, or attempted to abolish Parliament outright. Still, Cromwell's intrusive Puritanism and heavy taxation inclined the country to support the restoration of the Stuart dynasty in 1660, 2 years after Cromwell's death.

Parliament determined that Charles II would require a minimum annual income of 1.2 million pounds but then failed to ensure him secure means to acquire it.[92] In the later years of his reign, however, England's strong economic growth and curtailed involvement in European wars enabled Charles to achieve relative financial independence. In fact, he seldom called Parliament and seemed to be moving toward absolutism, like most of Europe.[93] When Charles died without issue in 1685, his younger brother acceded to the throne as James II.

Parliament granted the new king a generous annual allowance. In return, he ignored the body for the rest of his reign.[94] He also ruled as a pro-Catholic absolutist. He allowed Catholic officers to serve as regimental commanders, rigged elections to return candidates favorable to his policies (a ploy in which his brother had also dabbled), and dismissed numerous judges who disagreed with his positions (something Charles had also done though on a lesser scale). A rebellion at the start of his reign enabled him to treble the number of royal troops to nearly 20,000; he then further increased it to over 29,000 by the end of his reign. This was a Continental-style standing army that in the eyes of many Englishmen threatened their liberties. So did the slowly growing professional bureaucracy.[95] In 1687, James issued a Declaration for the Liberty of Conscience, which granted toleration for Catholics and dissenting Protestants. This and other acts partially disestablished the Anglican Church.[96] In order to carry his reforms further, James orchestrated the dismissal of hundreds of officials opposed to them, ordered the postal service to distribute pro-government propaganda and to monitor opposition imprints, and forbade Anglican priests to criticize the Catholic Church from their pulpits.

The birth in June 1688 of a son and heir, whom James and Queen Mary would surely raise in the Catholic faith, provided grounds for extreme alarm among leading Protestants, including many aristocrats, traditionalists, and conservatives, especially as most of them associated Catholicism with political absolutism.[97] Concerned elites therefore invited Prince William III of Orange, the husband of James's daughter Mary, to invade England.[98] William pledged just before launching his attack to restore "the whole Constitution of the English government."[99] William's landing in November with 20,000 men spurred many Protestant royalists to defect. James fled abroad. A "Convention Parliament" ruled that James had abdicated his throne and therefore that it could be offered to William and Mary.

Thus occurred the Glorious Revolution. In unprecedented acts of civic self-assertiveness, its leaders deposed a king, established a constitutional monarchy, and imposed strict limits on the ruler.[100] Sadly, 20,000 people lost their lives, many in Scotland and Ireland (though ten times more perished during the English Civil War).[101] The Declaration of Rights of February 1689 enunciated alleged abuses of the king, prohibited a standing army,[102] made Parliament a coequal legislator, required parliamentary consent for new taxes, affirmed the right to petition the monarch and to bear arms (for Protestants), and banned cruel and unusual punishments.[103] Participation in political life remained restricted to a thin layer of propertied men, but many of the enunciated rights applied to a far wider swath of society. In December, Parliament reiterated these principles in the Bill of Rights, adding a prohibition on the monarch professing Catholicism. Some of these provisions were radically new, in particular, the exclusion of James's son from succession to the throne, the outlawing of a permanent standing army, and the placing of all acts of Parliament beyond the monarch's power to abrogate.

William and Mary adopted numerous policies that reinforced the restrictions on their power.[104] They appointed bishops who believed in the limited nature of royal authority and in religious toleration. They supplemented the Act of Toleration (May 1689), which granted freedom of worship to all Protestants, by offering their personal protection to other religious minorities, including Catholics and Jews.[105] In foreign policy, they maintained a staunch alliance with the tolerant and politically free Dutch Republic and declared war on absolutist France. William and Mary also supported the development of manufacturing, following the advice of economic theorists who viewed that sector as the key to future prosperity, and withdrew support from the monopolistic East India Company. Despite continued political tensions, the new monarchs managed to unite nearly the entire country after decades of strife, mutual suspicion, enmity, and civil war.[106] Most people apparently came to believe that the King in Parliament justly represented the interests of the whole of England (and following the Act of Union of 1707, the whole of Scotland).

The opponents of absolutist monarchy, often called "Whigs," justified the establishment of limited government by appealing to reason, natural law, religious teaching, history, and common sense.[107] They cited Scripture, noting that neither Saul nor David ruled by hereditary right. They pointed to Magna Carta's frequent reissuing and reaffirmation over the centuries. The "ancient constitution" of England, whereby monarchs had always pledged to uphold the law and to judge impartially, loomed large in their arguments, as did such customary limitations on the English monarchs as parliamentary consent being necessary to impose new taxes.

The most thoughtful Whig theorist was the philosopher John Locke (1632–1704). His *Two Treatises of Government*, published anonymously in December 1689 though written a decade before, rejected the widely believed divine right to rule and propounded instead a contractual theory of government in which popular consent justifies the sovereign authority.[108] He began with two principles. First, God created all people free and equal. Second, in the state of nature, which Locke posited as a theoretical construct, following Thomas Hobbes (1588–1679), no individual could legitimately wield power or authority over another. Therefore, civil government could arise only with the consent of the governed. However, they would grant their consent only in exchange for some good or service. Hobbes, a pessimist greatly affected by the violence of the Civil War era, believed that individuals yielded all their sovereignty to a ruler in order to gain protection from violence. Locke, an optimist who trusted in the sociability of man, argued that government emerged for the more positive purpose of defending people's life, liberty, and property. Only insofar as the ruler guarantees those things can he legitimately claim the right to rule. Government and the state, therefore, exist only to serve their subjects and not the other way around. In other terms, absolute monarchy is inconsistent with civil society because government exists to prevent any individual—including rulers—from wielding the absolute power we all gave up when we left the state of nature.

Other Whig theorists and politicians stopped short of Locke's contractual conception of government, which many feared could lead to a democratic republic. Yet all opposed unlimited monarchy and advocated representative government and the political participation of men of wealth. Their views had triumphed.

Calvinists, in particular English Puritans, played a crucial role in achieving this success. These men and women espoused, individually or collectively, several radical principles in regard to politics.[109] First, they advocated its complete reformation, including all laws and institutions. "A new heaven and a new earth" (Rev. 21:1) is what many aspired to. During the publishing boom in the years of Civil War and early Interregnum, when censorship all but collapsed, Puritans published more than 10,000 pamphlets advocating legal reforms.[110] Second, Calvin had affirmed the God-given right and even duty of "lower magistrates" to oppose tyrants. The Calvinist emphasis on Original Sin and man's inherently selfish nature led logically to the idea of a written constitution aimed at placing limits on individuals, including rulers. Third, Calvinists even more than Lutherans cherished individual conscience and affirmed their collective rights to defend it, even against all the established powers of the world. The Puritan political figures during their struggles against the Stuart kings willingly faced prison, fines, loss of professional opportunity, torture, and even death rather than compromise their principles and submit to a power they considered tyrannical. These brave people in the long run helped win the struggle for civil rights in the Western world.

The American Revolution

The English Revolution had immediate repercussions in its American colonies, sparking the colonists' first rebellion.[111] In 1686, King James II had established the Dominion of New England in America, an administrative union eventually encompassing the English colonial provinces from what is now Maine to New Jersey. Interference in political, religious, and economic matters by the Dominion Governor in Chief Edmund Andros (1637–1714) naturally angered the colonists. Having learned about the Glorious Revolution, therefore, they rose up and overthrew Andros in Boston.[112] This act of rebelliousness was not surprising: leading colonists professed the same radical Calvinist reformism as many English revolutionaries.

English explorers had established a first colony on Roanoke Island off the coast of Virginia—named for Elizabeth, the virgin queen—in 1585.[113] All of its 108 original inhabitants perished awaiting provisions. Twenty-two years later, in 1607, a private joint-stock company founded Jamestown, the first continuous English presence in North America. The settlers elected Captain John Smith (ca. 1579–1631) president of the Jamestown council in 1608, probably the first instance of popular democracy in the Americas. Three years later, his successor Sir Thomas Gates established the first American legal code (with strong Puritan overtones—including obligatory Sabbath observance). In 1616, the colonists began to export tobacco. In 1619, the first General Assembly of Virginia, divided into an upper and a lower chamber, met at Jamestown Church. A new governor, Sir George Yeardley, and six elected councilors acted as the government. They studied and modified and then adopted the law code, just like Parliament back home, only freer and more sovereign.

A "second America" began to emerge in that same year, unfortunately, when 20 Africans arrived aboard a Dutch ship. Impressed into domestic servitude, they could in principle receive their freedom after paying off their indenture. Soon, however, Virginia planters began to purchase chattel slaves, which gradually became the foundation of the state's economy.[114] Thus emerged in the same place at around the same time the foundations of the freest human society on earth, yet where a minority would live in the direst bondage. Pico della Mirandola's claim that man's destiny ranges from bestial atrocity to angelic purity truly found embodiment here.

Meanwhile, around 450 miles to the north as the crow flies, an entirely different English settlement began with the landing of the *Mayflower* at New Plymouth in 1620. Not male adventurers seeking gain, but 41 families, including 35 Puritan nonconformists who considered England hopelessly corrupt and aspired to found a godly and just society. The Virginia Company had granted them land and the authority to govern themselves.[115] During the transatlantic crossing, the 41 heads of household signed a "compact," a religious and political contract based on God's covenant with the Israelites but also drawing on the Calvinist ideal of covenanted communities and the emerging philosophical concept of the social contract.[116] Thousands more settlers followed—some 20,000 in the 1630s alone—not to visit and return home but to build a new and unique shrine, "a city upon a hill," with the help of Providence.[117] They too—or at least the "godly" freemen—governed themselves and all certainly read the Bible and interpreted it for themselves. They elected their pastors and decided parish business in community with no bishops to rule over them.

When political or ecclesiastical governance—they usually coincided—proved burdensome or unpalatable to some minority, it could migrate further afield and establish a colony to its liking.[118] Thus, Roger Williams (1603–83) founded the new settlement of Rhode Island with extensive freedom of worship, the separation of church and state, unfettered competition among denominations, the political participation of all free inhabitants, and humane treatment of the Native peoples.[119] Each colony had its own character. A broad swath of territory running from New York to Delaware started out as Dutch colonies until they fell to the English as a result of the Second Anglo-Dutch War (1664–67).[120] Many Catholics settled in Maryland as did religious dissenters of various denominations.[121] All the main branches of Protestantism were represented in the colonies, along with scattered Jewish congregations and people attending no church.[122] Dutch, German, Irish, Scotch, Welsh, Swiss, and French immigrants also established themselves throughout. Politically, the colonies had in common two things: self-government and broad-based political participation. In 1636, the Massachusetts colonists instituted a "Pilgrim Code of Laws" that functioned like a constitution. Within a decade or so, all of the colonies had adopted similar foundational documents.[123]

This land, rich beyond measure in the humbler natural resources yet long neglected by the colonizing powers for its lack of gold and silver, attracted an abundance of skilled men: carpenters, joiners, glass makers, potters, shoemakers, silversmiths, and countless other tradesmen. Before the Revolution, at least half of all immigrants arrived as indentured servants or redemptioners who had to work off the cost of their passage for five or more years before becoming freemen.[124] Merchants in the colonies inspected them like livestock and offered them better or worse contracts depending on their health, strength, apparent talents, and skills. After paying off their masters, most could make a far better living in America than back home and the majority worked for themselves. Unlike everywhere else on the planet, ordinary people could obtain good land either for nothing or for a pittance. From the seaboard, settlers pushed slowly inland toward an ever-moving frontier, founding towns and hamlets as they went. Investors bought, sold, and speculated in land parcels with wild abandon.[125] Slaves spread slowly throughout the southern colonies (their number reached 78,000 in 1727),[126] forming a foundation of their economies.

The scarcity of labor also fostered experiments with mechanization. Water-powered sawmills produced a vast supply of lumber. By 1760, shipwrights were turning out 300 to 400 ships annually.[127] Despite decrees from London forbidding manufacturing in the colonies, they produced many other goods, including bar iron, cloth, and furniture. The American economy grew rapidly—from 4 percent as big as Britain's in 1700 to 40 percent in 1775. In the same years, the population increased tenfold, from 250,000 to 2.5 million. The colonies' per capita income was probably the highest in the world.[128] People ate well, including lots of protein, making them bigger and healthier than Europeans on average. Most could be described as middle class.

Institutions, culture, and urbanization all developed apace. Philadelphia, the city second in the British Empire only to London, hosted a lending library (1731), a volunteer fire company (1736), a learned society (1743), and a college (1751). By 1763, the colonies boasted some two dozen weekly newspapers.[129] In no other colonial society of the day could one find such a proliferation of periodicals.[130]

Starting in the late 1600s and early 1700s, the crown again tried to assert its control over the colonies, revoking or refusing to renew charters and establishing a Board of Trade and Plantations (1696).[131] Yet since London did not pay the salaries of governors—in principle, crown agents in the new world—or, except very rarely, send inspectors to monitor their work, the colonists continued to govern themselves. The victories of English constitutionalism, especially the Glorious Revolution, seemed to many colonists their victories, too.[132] Gradually, from the early 1700s, the lower chambers throughout the colonies negotiated, proclaimed, or seized political control from the governors and upper chambers. Since most adult white males had the vote, the assemblies could not impose rules rejected by a majority of the population. It is not surprising, therefore, that the American colonists bore the lightest burden of taxation of any people of European culture.[133]

Although Puritanism had declined as a social force by the early 1700s, religion remained vibrant.[134] Revival movements erupted from time to time, often on the frontier, involving not only charismatic preachers from diverse national backgrounds, but also a few brilliant thinkers like Jonathan Edwards (1703–58). Edwards, a polymath who entered Yale at age 13 and graduated first in his class, taught that the essence of God is love, that we can choose freely to receive that love, and that it alone can transform us and the world. He inspired such itinerant preachers as George Whitefield (1714–70), an Englishman who traveled back and forth across the colonies during seven tours in the 30 years after 1740, stirring up "the Great Awakening." Other powerful voices joined the chorus, including John Wesley (1703–91) who returned to England where he founded the Methodist movement. Many preached under the open air. With deep conviction, they elicited frequently emotional responses. Greatly influenced by German pietism, the movement affected vast numbers of colonists, instilling in them a sense of their personal relationship with God, the radical equality and worth of all people, and the greater importance of religious experience over institution and doctrine. Not that most preachers appealed only to the feelings. On the contrary, logic and argument constituted a big part of their success. They convinced hundreds of thousands of colonists of the need for spiritual renewal by "convicting" both the heart and the mind.

Thus, decades before the American Revolution, the American colonists had experienced a profound transformation of their understanding of self and society. Many began to see themselves as a people, as Americans, as perhaps uniquely blessed by the Creator, but also as endowed by him with inalienable rights, and as destined to accomplish great things. The Great Awakening was therefore a hugely formative development in the history of the American people. One can even argue that it made the revolution possible.[135]

A global war, precipitated on the margin of the civilized world, indirectly brought about the American Revolution.[136] The French and Indian War (1754–63), a part of the larger Seven Years' War (1756–63), began with a skirmish near present-day Pittsburgh when Virginia militiamen led by George Washington attacked a French encampment, killing a dozen Frenchmen. The war ended disastrously for France, which had to give up its North American colonies, several islands of the Caribbean, and key positions in India. Securing victory, however, drove up the British debt from £60 to £133 million. The British crown endeavored to extract payment for the cost of maintaining 10,000 British soldiers in North America and began to meddle more in colonial governance. Unfortunately for the British, the main factor ensuring the colonists' loyalty had been fear of the French. With them safely out of the picture, why should the Americans tolerate outside interference?

In late 1763, the king prohibited migration of colonists west of the Allegheny Mountains.[137] The colonists simply ignored this decree (see Map 10.3). London hired more tax collectors in the colonies and ordered the strict collection of customs duties, which the colonists had largely avoided until then. The Stamp Act of 1765, which imposed a tax on all legal documents and imprints (except books), provoked an outcry of indignation throughout the colonies. As Englishmen, many argued, the colonists should not pay taxes they had not consented to. Crowds took to the streets in town after town, in some places attacking the homes of tax collectors. Delegates from most of the colonies gathered in October in New York City to denounce the law. Hundreds of merchants pledged to boycott British goods. Parliament voted to repeal the Act in February 1766 though also, by means of the Declaratory Act, affirmed the absolute right of the British Parliament to legislate for the colonies. Duties (taxes) imposed on numerous commodities in 1767 provoked more unrest and boycotts. The strongest resistance occurred in Boston, where in 1770 a unit of redcoats fired at a rebellious crowd, killing five.

A war in which the media played a crucial war had begun—one that the highly literate and ingenious Americans were supremely prepared to wage.[138] The barrage of publications included illustrated broadsheets, carefully researched historical treatises, inflammatory tracts, and philosophical disquisitions, like Thomas Jefferson's *Summary View of the Rights of British America* (1774).[139]

Following Locke, Jefferson argued that merit and not birth should determine social status, so kings and aristocrats deserve no special right to govern. He went on to emphasize the primacy of individual rights, in particular, the right to life and liberty, with which the Creator endows, all people. These rights, he claimed, give each society sovereign legislative power. English tradition and the long-standing practice of self-government in the colonies also buttressed the Americans' right to independence.

The colonists had not only powerful arguments, habits of effective self-rule, and up-to-date technologies of communication, but also great leaders of every type. Aside from intellectuals like Jefferson and John Adams, there were fiery orators like Patrick Henry, the cosmopolitan and practical Renaissance man Benjamin Franklin, and the brilliant organizer and charismatic leader with nerves of steel, George Washington. It was quite extraordinary that men of such talent united to accomplish one grand purpose far from the centers of civilization.

A succession of incidents, conflicts, and battles followed—the Boston Tea Party (1773), the battles of Lexington and Concord (1775), and many atrocities committed by British soldiers, including the burning of towns and the killing of women and children.[140] Thomas Paine (1737–1809), an Englishman who arrived in Philadelphia in 1774, described these horrors in great detail in *Common Sense*, which came out in January 1776. He denounced King George as a tyrant and demanded nothing less than a complete break with Britain. As if directly responding to his appeal, in June the second Continental Congress directed Jefferson and others to draft a formal Declaration of Independence. The words "all men are created equal" remained in the unanimously adopted final version, but most southern delegates forced the removal of an explicit acknowledgment of the evil of slavery. Politically, the Declaration severed all ties to the King and Britain and appealed to the world community for recognition and acceptance.

After 2 years of difficult fighting back home, Franklin managed in 1778 to drum up invaluable support in Paris.[141] Rich merchants sent dozens of ships laden with supplies, the government forged cannon for the rebels and deployed several thousand soldiers, and aristocratic officers lent their services. Frenchmen thus gleefully seized

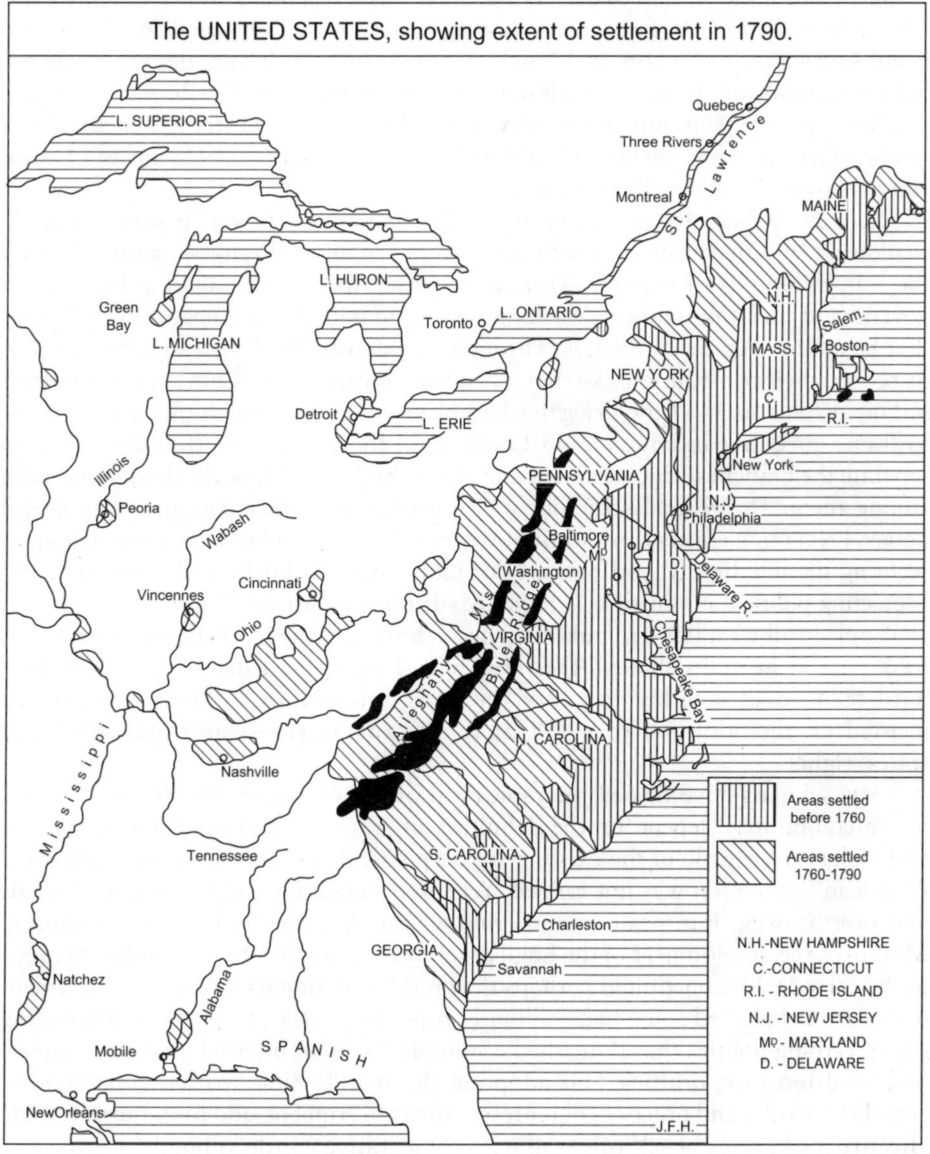

MAP 10.3 *The 13 American colonies before and after George III became king of Great Britain in 1760.*

the opportunity to avenge their defeat a decade and a half earlier. The Spanish and Dutch also helped. By 1782, with British forces defeated or cornered, (temporary) French naval dominance of the Eastern Seaboard's coastal waters assured, and a Franco-Spanish fleet poised to invade England, Britain sued for peace.

The Treaty of Paris (1783) granted full independence to the United States and, furthermore, the right to expand their settlements westward, shoving aside the Native peoples and, in the southern states, dragging their slaves with them (see Map 10.3). An abolitionist movement gained steam throughout the North, involving laws and lawsuits, which put an end to slavery here and there, beginning in Pennsylvania and Massachusetts in 1780. Few voices, however, were raised on behalf of the Native peoples, thousands of whom had fought for the British.[142] Britain, despite losing the colonies, fared well. It kept Gibraltar, held its positions in the Caribbean and India, continued profitable trading relations with the Americans, and strengthened its hold in Canada, to which some 60,000 to 80,000 loyalists emigrated.[143] Spain and France emerged from the war with massive debts.

The new polity that emerged from the wreckage of war proved radically egalitarian.[144] Education and worldly success would determine status. During the war, thousands of ordinary citizens had risen to positions of responsibility in government and the military. Washington, a committed republican, refused pleas that he accept dictatorial powers. Throughout the war all of the states had written or revised their constitutions, so that when the Constitutional Convention convened in Philadelphia in 1787 the delegates had plenty of experience thinking about how to frame government. Drawing on Locke and Montesquieu, the framers aimed to separate the branches of government and to institute a system of checks and balances among them. The federal structure was intended to further decentralize political power. Preventing concentrations of power was meant to achieve their main goals—securing the life, liberty, and property of individuals, as Locke had envisaged, and protecting political minorities, as James Madison emphasized.[145]

People in all 13 states—in public squares, churches, tiny hamlets, and big cities—took part in heated debates—the most wide-ranging and democratic in history until then—over whether to ratify the new constitution.[146] Many participants insisted on the adoption of a Bill of Rights guaranteeing both individual and states' rights.

Some scholars have denied the radicalism of the American Revolution.[147] One's interpretation may depend on the definition of "radical." If it implies vast carnage and violent overthrow of the existing social, political, and economic order, then the American Revolution was not radical. Yet surely sundering existing political bonds and overthrowing European colonial rule for the first time in history was radical. Moreover, the development of the English colonies in America from their foundations in the early 1600s constituted perhaps the most revolutionary political achievement in history. It involved some half-million Europeans crossing an ocean and founding self-governing polities that flourished economically in an undeveloped and sparsely inhabited territory, drafting and adopting the world's first written constitutions, establishing rules and practices of representative government, and founding relatively effective institutions of self-rule—all with comparatively little killing.[148]

Others have contended that the American revolutionaries were hypocrites who betrayed the ideals of the Declaration of Independence and thus committed "treason against the hopes of the world," in the words of one scholar.[149] A recent study by Michal Jan Rozbicki has argued, by contrast, that the founders were not hypocrites at all but rather believed in a more traditional conception of liberty. In their minds, liberty was a privilege that could be enjoyed only by some members of society—the ones most fit to represent and lead the broader people. He claims that the American provincial elites feared losing their privileges in the context of tighter controls from London and therefore articulated a vision of liberty, equality, and independence that would enable them to maintain their privileged status but would not raise the majority of their fellow countrymen to a higher level. Yet once the vision had been proclaimed, extoled, and enshrined in the governing documents of the new republic, other members of society demanded to partake of those same privileges.[150]

Owning landed property worth 40 pounds or having an income of 40 shillings yearly and being a white male were required for voting in most states in 1789.[151] Gradually, such property restrictions were replaced by a taxpayer qualification or were even dropped entirely. In many states, new immigrants could vote in federal elections—a right that very few of them had enjoyed back in Europe. Finally, during the Jacksonian Era of the 1830s the franchise broadened still further (though generally it was now restricted to citizens). By 1855, something like universal white male suffrage (in many states even for noncitizens) had been achieved, largely without a struggle.[152] In no other country did so broad a range of ordinary people exercise political rights. Thus, whatever the intentions of the founders, the results were undeniable: the foundation of a republic in which ideals of liberty and equality were proclaimed and gradually extended to more and more people. Unfortunately, blacks and women remained disfranchised, and winning the vote for them would require far more efforts and even bloodshed (see Chapter 14).

The logic of successful political revolution throughout history has led to the gradual expansion of rights and participation. Elites may have started the early revolutions, but by enunciating principles of liberty and rights they have opened the door to demands for greater inclusiveness. Political principles are either universal or not principles at all. There is no fundamental logic to excluding specific categories of people from rights once they are proclaimed as "endowed" by the Creator.

Why was the American Revolution so successful? Unlike the European countries or the Latin American colonies, the British colonies had no deeply rooted traditional institutions—an aristocracy, a state church, feudal rights, entrenched guilds, a centralized bureaucracy, and a monarch reining in their midst. Naturally, no terrible violence was needed to overthrow them. Moreover, in the absence of such institutions, the colonists needed to rule themselves or fall into anarchy. Like the most advanced European societies—the Dutch Republic and the British constitutional monarchy—the Americans developed a high level of economic, political, social, and cultural pluralism, indeed a higher level than in those or any other societies in the world.

Why did North America become amazingly innovative while South and Central America did not? The Latin American colonies developed and prospered earlier, but by 1750 per capita incomes were roughly the same both north and south of the Rio Grande, and they were twice as high in the north in 1820 and five times higher in 2000.[153] Geography surely helped the gap to widen: a north–south geographic axis noted in Chapter 1, especially one that crosses the equator, does not favor easy migration or the free exchange of ideas and goods. More important, presumably, were the reasons for

European colonization—to found "cities on a hill" and commercial enterprises in the north but quite often to seek glory, riches, or government offices in the south, where state institutions fostered the concentration of wealth and power in a narrow colonial elite.[154] Also significant was who did the colonizing: the most advanced Europeans in the north, but among the European peoples least committed to innovation and experimentation in the south. Nor were peoples south of the Rio Grande accustomed to governing themselves. Entrenched traditional institutions fought violently against political and social change. Therefore, the wars of liberation from Spain and Portugal were bloody and protracted.[155] Entrenched institutions also played an important role in the country where the next major political revolution broke out.

France and the revolutionary tradition

The French Revolution, while involving immense turmoil, violence, and bloodshed, yielded few notable accomplishments. The French population did not achieve self-government, gain permanent civil rights or significant political participation, or even establish so much as a constitutional monarchy, much less a republic, except very briefly. Nor did the revolutionary upheaval contribute much to economic development: the agricultural sector, despite the abolition of feudal dues and internal custom tolls, remained fairly backward and aimed largely at subsistence. Manufacturing and trade benefited from the dismantling of the guild system, the introduction of patents and the metric system, and the creation of a unified internal market, yet commerce continued to center on small-scale operations, and habits of protectionism remained strong. Government interference in business affairs and administrative centralization actually grew stronger. Finally, the severing of commercial ties with Britain impeded industrialization.[156] What happened then?

Most importantly, unlike the American colonists the French had no experience of self-government except at the local and regional levels, and unlike the British they lacked a national representative institution. Their Estates-General had last met in 1614. Interlocking ruling elites monopolized most of the power, wealth, prestige, and authority in France. The monarchs claimed absolutist powers and divine right to rule. Tens of thousands of aristocratic families (compared to only 220 British peers) controlled vast riches, set the cultural tone of the country, and benefited from numerous legal privileges. A huge number of wealthy commoners joined their ranks by purchasing government offices (the right to exercise some official functions in exchange for fees) and landed estates. They thus gained exemption from billeting soldiers, serving in the military, hanging or flogging (save in treason cases), and most taxes. They also enjoyed the right to own government offices and to pass them on to heirs. Further, French lords could extract various monetary, service, and material payments from their peasants. Finally an established Catholic Church dominated the country's educational system, disposed of enormous revenues, wielded power at the highest levels of government, and sought to impose religious orthodoxy across the land, with government officials sometimes fiercely persecuting Protestants as late as the mid-1700s. Scholars have called this nexus of power relationships, grounded in tradition and custom, the *ancien régime*.[157] People felt and expected deference toward authority, allegiance to specific places and the person of the king (but not abstractions like the nation), and rootedness in the soil.

Ancien régime France was rich.[158] Europe's best network of roads and canals, largely built in the eighteenth century, dramatically shortened travel times and cut transportation costs. France continued to dominate the manufacturing of luxury goods in Europe.[159] French merchants maintained a chokehold on Europe's trade with the Middle East and saw the value of their commercial activities in the Atlantic triangular trade expand enormously. In fact, France's international traders represented the country's most innovative business people. Some made fortunes, especially in the slave trade and the importation of commodities from the Caribbean.[160]

Yet financial constraints slowed economic development. France had no central bank, no well-developed stock exchange, few private banks, and almost no joint-stock companies. Business remained largely a family affair with few economies of scale.[161] Industrial enterprises operated here and there but with vastly less mechanical equipment than in Britain. Moreover, entrepreneurs often reinvested their profits not in further business ventures but in land (sometimes with attendant seigneurial rights), government offices, and state bonds, seeking either a steady monetary return or social status. Ironically, it was often members of the nobility who poured capital into business ventures.[162] Many scholars descry a convergence of interests and characteristics of the moneyed elites of both mercantile and aristocratic origins. Yet neither group displayed exceptional dynamism as a whole. Nor did the agricultural sector experience much innovation in the 1700s. In general, France remained economically backward compared to Britain and the Dutch Republic.

What France lacked in economic dynamism it made up for with intellectual vibrancy. The Enlightenment, discussed in Chapter 8, flourished in France as nowhere else. Hundreds of social critics gathered in salons where the grandest nobles rubbed shoulders with brilliant commoners to discuss ideas, policies, current events, and other worldly matters.[163] Most such intellectuals, or philosophes, rejected the established church as obscurantist, corrupt, and intolerant. Nearly all decried government abuses and the arbitrary exercise of power, but not necessarily monarchy as such. Nor did most advocate democracy, universal education of the masses, or broadly based political and intellectual pluralism.[164] Even so, the ideas of the philosophes gradually trickled down to the 50 percent of French males who could read by 1780. Would-be philosophes made a living by publishing "gutter literature."[165] Among their writings were scandal sheets denouncing in great detail—though not always accurately—the sexual behavior of the royal family, aristocratic grandees, and other elites. It seems that many ordinary people came to believe the most outrageous tales of depravity among their "social betters."

Neither government officials nor the king closed their minds entirely to new ideas and innovations. Yet they often worried about their effect on ordinary people and so maintained a strict and highly intrusive system of censorship.[166] Even such celebrated thinkers as Diderot, Rousseau, and Voltaire spent time in prison, in exile, or hiding from the police. Yet government officials and even members of the court occasionally sheltered political dissidents, promoted their work, or stymied the censors. Naturally, entrepreneurs smuggled forbidden literature, which enjoyed great commercial success, from Switzerland and Holland. So government repression served more to alienate intellectuals than to stifle the spread of their ideas. Over time, the intellectuals claimed the ability—better than the king himself or his officials—to discern and advocate the collective good of the French people. They shared this attitude with legal professionals, especially members of the *parlements* (regional law courts with the power to ratify royal edicts).[167]

Specific government policies fed the opposition tendencies. Public opinion turned strongly against the king and his government when they embraced France's former archenemy Austria in 1756 and then lost shamefully in the Seven Years' War. Other diplomatic humiliations followed, most spectacularly the first Partition of Poland by Austria, Russia and Prussiain 1772.[168] The emasculation of the *parlements* in 1771 by Louis XV not only provoked a sustained public uproar but came to naught when Louis XVI restored the institutions to their former status in 1774.[169] The new king proved weak, indecisive, uncharismatic, and certainly unfit to manage the grave crisis in state finances precipitated by French support of the American Revolution. Land hunger and a declining standard of living among the lower orders of society, coupled with bad weather and poor harvests in the mid-1780s, fostered social violence and embittered large segments of the population, especially in the fall and winter of 1788–89.[170]

A succession of controllers-general (finance ministers) struggled to resolve the desperate situation. As in England, the government could not raise taxes without the consent of representatives, but unlike across the Channel no representative body existed to give its consent. So, Louis summoned an ad hoc "Assembly of Notables" in 1787 (the first time such a body had met since 1626), which rejected his appeal for new taxes. He then called the Estates-General in 1789.[171]

The king hoped this body would agree to raise taxes. Instead it simply arrogated to itself legislative power as the National Assembly and the right to draft a constitution. In August, it proclaimed the Declaration of the Rights of Man and the Citizen, which established human rights more universally than the American revolutionaries. Then, in the face of popular rebellion and the hesitancy of many officers and soldiers to crush it, the revolutionary leaders grew more radical. By 1790, they had seized church property; abolished the religious orders, the nobility, and the *parlements*; and demanded that the clergy swear allegiance to the state.[172] Violence marked the year 1792, as the leadership declared "revolutionary war" and militant crowds seized the king, murdered his guards, and massacred over 1,000 prisoners, priests, and other "counterrevolutionary elements" in September.[173] Soon thereafter, the National Convention declared France a republic. Three months later, after a brief trial, the king was executed. Price controls, restrictions on private property, and other government regulations aimed at enforcing social equality simply stifled economic activity. A "reign of terror" began in September of the following year, in the midst of military defeats, leaving tens of thousands dead across the country by the time Robespierre himself became its last victim on the night of 27 July 1794. A campaign of "dechristianization" ran parallel to the Terror. Laws forbade displaying crosses, ringing church bells, and celebrating mass; a new calendar abolished Sundays and Christian holidays; mobs ransacked churches and held "festivals of reason" in them; and government officials arrested, deported, and massacred priests.

One cannot but marvel at this astonishing turn of events. Surely not a single delegate to the Estates-General in May 1789 could have foreseen or approved this outcome. Nearly all hoped for moderate reforms involving more efficient government, free trade, equality before the law, religious toleration, an end to arbitrary rule, and the defense of civil rights—including the absolute right to liberty and property. Then successive elections brought more and more radical leaders to the fore. As the government continuously failed to improve economic conditions for ordinary people, they naturally demanded that somebody do something. One policy both popular and feasible was the escalation of violence against internal "enemies" allegedly preventing the achievement of the social progress most people expected from the revolution. In many places, however, political and religious repression provoked counterrevolutionary agitation and rebellion, creating a vicious cycle. In order to save the Revolution, the revolutionary leadership abandoned many of its key principles.[174]

Unfortunately, the policies and activities of the revolutionary leadership promoted economic stagnation and even decline. The manufacturing sector contracted all over France: for example, in the years after 1789, Marseille's industrial production plunged 75 percent. Overseas trade suffered almost as much, falling from 25 percent of France's gross physical product to only 9 percent in 1796.[175] As commercial activity diminished, people fled the major cities. Although the Revolution might have stimulated agricultural production, since it expanded private land ownership at the expense of the church, output in fact probably declined. In the end, aristocratic landowners and government officials benefited most from the revolution, far more than industrialists, entrepreneurs, or merchants, though the abolition of seigneurial rights by a decree of 11 August 1789, was doubtless a precondition of later democratic advancement in France.

The main actors in the English and American Revolutions had sought to ratify, institutionalize, or at most build upon long-standing practices, habits, rules, and experiences. Eminently practical men, they strived to accomplish the feasible and the reasonable. They had exercised political authority for many decades and demanded to continue in that path. They claimed concrete and specific rights—freedom from taxation without representation, the billeting of soldiers in private homes, and royal meddling in judicial affairs, to name crucial ones—and enforced those claims. Many French revolutionary leaders, by contrast, at least during the Revolution's most radical phase, hoped and sought to change the world: to root out repression everywhere, to overthrow and destroy the deeply rooted *ancien régime*, to raise up perfectly virtuous citizens, to build a society founded on reason and equality, and even to do away with religion entirely.[176] This wide-ranging transformation foundered in part on the opposition of a large proportion of French society, millions of whom hesitated about or rejected outright one or other element in the revolutionary program. Several of these elements, moreover, seem incompatible. A consideration of the revolutionary slogan—liberty, equality, fraternity—sheds light on this problem.

Upholding individual liberty, especially the right to dispose of one's property, proved hard to square with the level of social equality expected by many revolutionary leaders and ordinary people. Fraternity, or pledging allegiance to the nation instead of the monarch, in the minds of many revolutionaries also required the renunciation of claims to full individual liberty. The difficulty of harmonizing these three revolutionary goals helped cause the Revolution's "skidding out of control."[177]

Beyond the terror and revolutionary war, Napoleon conquered most of Europe in the name of revolution (see Map 10.4). The French armies abolished noble privileges and serfdom and everywhere imposed the Napoleonic code—perhaps the Revolution's

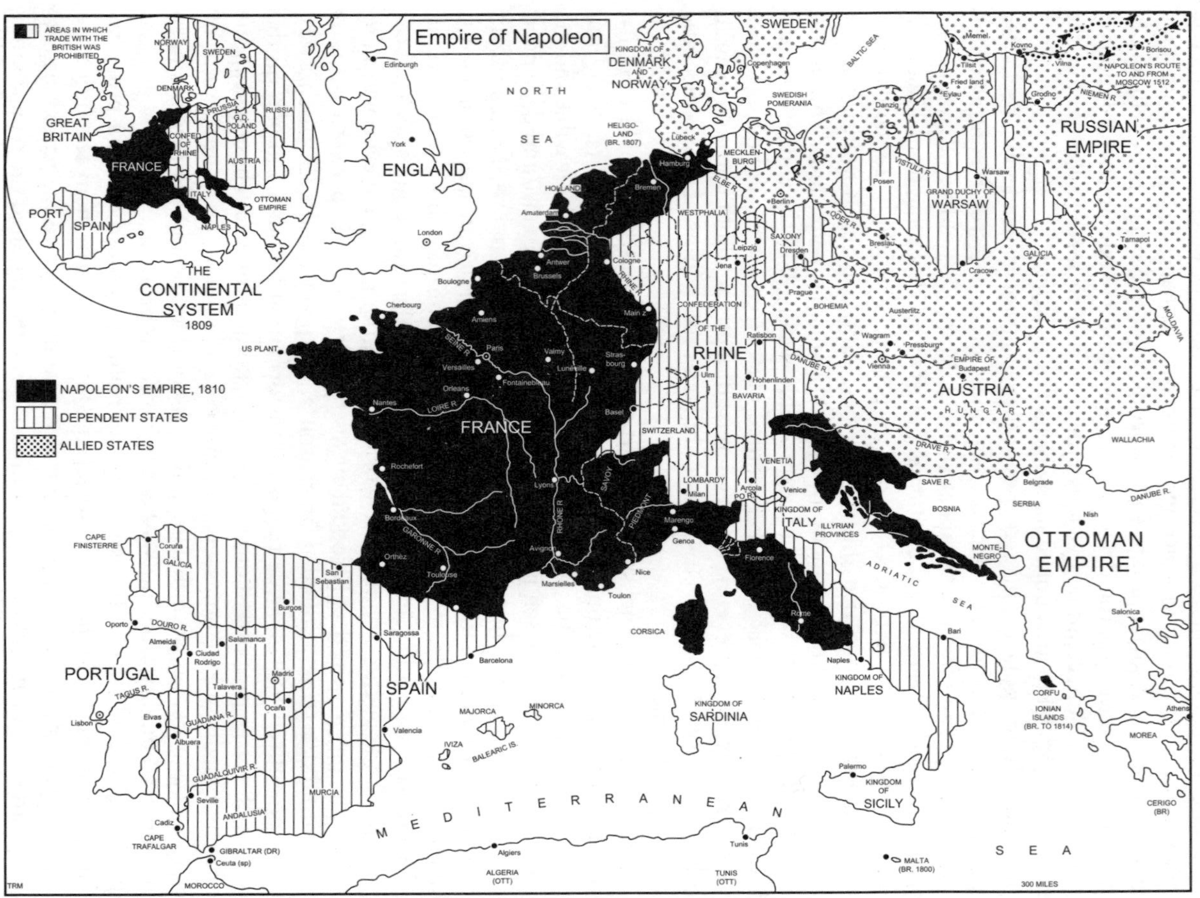

MAP 10.4 *Napoleon spread the French Revolution to most of Europe, abolishing noble privileges and serfdom and imposing the Napoleonic code.*

most enduring legacy, along with the metric system.[178] More than anyone or anything, argues David Jordan, Napoleon institutionalized the revolution and gave it "time to take root in France."[179] Also important were revolts in the Caribbean inspired by the French and American Revolutions, especially the massive, bloody, and successful 1791 rebellion against the system of slavery on Saint-Domingue, which led to the French revolutionaries' abolition of slavery in 1794 (a decree rescinded later by Napoleon) and the creation of an independent Haiti in 1804.[180] Yet what remained after a grand coalition of European countries put an end to the revolutionary wars in 1815 was not a new type of polity, an industrialized economy, or a society enjoying defensible civil rights but rather a new set of ideas, a mentality of crusading for social justice, and a tradition of contesting established authority and seeking to overturn the political status quo. As one scholar has expressed this idea, no beliefs, institutions, rulers, customs, or laws "needed to be accepted anymore as set in the nature of things."[181]

This revolutionary tradition led to repeated instances in nineteenth-century Europe of social upheaval, wars of liberation, and political subversion. Waves of revolutionary violence crashed across the continent in 1830 and 1848 yet fell far short of the aspirations that animated them. Serfdom and seigneurial institutions were swept away throughout Central and Eastern Europe. Constitutional government was instituted and retained in some countries, including Prussia and Piedmont-Savoy. More importantly, mass political participation in clubs, organizations, demonstrations, and voting set a precedent that peoples across Europe would seek to make their birthright.[182] Within several decades, most European countries achieved such goals, originally proclaimed universally by the French revolutionaries, as universal male suffrage, the right to free speech and assembly, constitutional government, and popular sovereignty. These and even more radical aims became worldwide ambitions.

The political activists inspired by French revolutionary ideals and practices divided into three main currants. Those emphasizing liberty evolved into advocates of classical liberalism. Their supreme values included political participation, the right to property, limited government, individual responsibility, and equality before the law. Others, who considered social and economic equality the highest social goods, developed various streams of socialist thought and practice. A third movement elevated allegiance to the nation above all other ideals. National consciousness motivated partisans of this revolutionary strain to fight for national liberation, to forge nation-states, and to create patriotic communities in which millions of people stood ready to sacrifice their lives for the good of the nation. These three modern ideologies—liberalism, socialism, and nationalism—have proved the most powerful intellectual constructs for motivating individual and collective action in the modern world. They have inspired the formation of national states, revolutionary takeovers, and economic globalization across the planet. No other political ideals from any other culture can claim such a legacy.

Rebellions, palace coups, and the overthrow of governments had occurred throughout history in nearly every culture. As noted in Chapter 4, massive popular rebellions broke out in China nearly annually during the 2,000 years before the Revolution of 1911–12. Popular revolts and elite takeovers were commonplace in the Ottoman capital Istanbul from the seventeenth through the nineteenth century.[183] In fact, rebellion and revolution were frequent all across Eurasia in the early modern period.[184] Yet only in the revolutions discussed in this chapter did the rebels put forward concrete, constitutionally oriented, and wide-ranging political ends, and only in England and the United States did they do so successfully. Their successes inspired subsequent imitation, first in France and later across the planet. The results were sometimes fruitful, as in the wars of liberation throughout Latin America. In other cases, they were ultimately catastrophic, as in Russia in 1917 and China in 1949 (see Chapter 13).

* * *

While the French revolutionaries dragged their country and most of Europe into over two decades of upheaval and world war, another revolution was unfolding across the Channel and in the newly independent United States. The Industrial Revolution transformed the economic life of Anglo-America, then Europe, and eventually the world. The scarcity of physical energy—for millennia man could harness only wind, water, and muscle power—had prevented the achievement of steady economic growth. A series of innovations resolved this problem by harnessing the almost limitless supply of energy locked away in coal, a humble sedimentary rock.

QUESTIONS FOR REFLECTION

Which "constituted bodies" stood between individuals and the state in medieval Europe?

What role did Calvinism play in the struggle for Dutch self-government?

What were the main achievements of the Glorious Revolution?

How did Whig political thinkers like John Locke view the nature of government?

What was the Great Awakening and how was it important?

Why did North America become more innovative than South and Central America?

What was the greatest legacy of the French Revolution?

Chapter 11 Chronology

Thirteenth century:	Coal consumption for industry begins to rise in England
1279:	Fall of Chinese Song dynasty
1474:	Venice begins to develop patent law
1666:	Great Fire of London
1688:	Glorious Revolution
Early eighteenth century:	Newcomen steam engine first designed and produced
1700:	London's population now 575,000
1709:	Abraham Darby effectively uses coal-derived coke for smelting
1750:	Coke-fired iron smelting becomes standard
1764:	Spinning Jenny invented
1769:	Water-powered spinning frame and Boulton & Watt steam engine invented
1780s:	Henry Cort invents iron puddling process
1785:	Edmund Cartwright invents power loom
1787:	World's first steam-powered boat launched
Late eighteenth century:	Josiah Wedgwood industrializes production of ceramics
1800:	Watt patent on steam engines expires
1813:	Boston Manufacturing Company of Waltham founded
1815:	Diffusion of industrial technology begins
1819:	US Supreme Court rules corporations possess inherent rights
1820–60:	Economic growth greatly outpaces population growth in advanced regions of the West
1830:	First major rail line established between Liverpool and Manchester
1831:	Industrial workers now 41 percent of workforce in Britain
1844:	Joint Stock Companies Act

1850s:	Limited liability granted to companies in United States, France, United Kingdom
1860:	Population of London now 3,188,485
Nineteenth century:	Expansion of railroads greatly boosts economic growth

11

Industrial Revolution

From the Egyptian pyramids to the first steam engines nearly 4,000 years later, human and animal labor power—augmented with rollers, levers, sledges, or wheeled carts—were the only means of hauling on land. The Neolithic people who built Stonehenge in three phases from 3100 to 1500 B.C. managed to drag over 20 miles dozens of giant stone monoliths—some 30–50 tons—and to assemble them into a perfect circle with seven-ton lintels hoisted atop the others.[1] The first locomotives, with their capacity to pull 90 tons of coal at 15 mph, finally enabled humans to best that record in the 1830s. Only then could we achieve modern economic growth.

During nearly the entire existence of humankind, economies grew only very slowly, occasionally, and for short periods of time. Here or there some ingenious artisan conceived a new agricultural method, increasing output. For a generation or at most several, the population lived well and multiplied. Yet inevitably the extra mouths, indigenous elites, or external predators—and the need to defend against them—consumed the surplus, driving the standard of living back down again. So, too, did unavoidable climatic misfortunes and natural disasters. Even during such times of economic flourishing as Song China, medieval Europe, or Tokugawa Japan (1603–1868), the annual growth of economic output probably did not much exceed 0.2 percent and in any event ceased entirely after a century or two.[2] Europe's economy may have grown during the thousand years before 1700 at roughly 0.11 percent annually. At that rate, an economy's size doubles approximately every 630 years.[3]

Modern economic growth—an average annual increase in output of at least 1–2 percent—boggles the mind in historical context. The numerous technological, agricultural, institutional, infrastructural, and intellectual innovations described in Chapter 2 did not enable medieval Europeans to achieve a sustained economic growth rate of even 0.5 percent, much less the four or five times higher figure realized in Great Britain by the mid-nineteenth century, which the economies of the United States and Germany significantly bested in the following decades.[4] Such a leap forward could not come from nowhere; it required a long gestation process. Indeed, centuries of innovation and revolutionary transformation had made it possible. So did integrating and building on those advances.

Accumulation of resources

All human cultures have devised ingenious methods for ensuring survival. Each one has also contributed ideas, traditions, institutions, inventions, and other breakthroughs, though not all of these have come down to present times. Nor indeed have all formerly existing cultures themselves persisted. In recent millennia, the peoples of sub-Saharan Africa have bequeathed only a modest legacy to the world. Yet who can fail to consider their first legacy—the emergence of *Homo sapiens sapiens* on earth—the most momentous of all contributions to human development? Yet if all cultures have contrived ways of adapting to the world, great civilizations have risen only thanks to the continuous, long-term integration of adaptations into an entire way of life, an organic whole. The ancient Egyptians built a civilization of great achievements continuing for nearly 3,000 years.[5] Today, however, little remains aside from awe-inspiring artistic and architectural remnants and scientific and mathematical principles absorbed and passed down by the ancient Greeks. The legacies of Greece and Rome, while far greater, also have long outlived the civilizations themselves. In fact, few of history's great cultures have reached the present day intact. One of the few is China.

No other culture has endured as long China as a vital, thriving, supremely innovative community and polity. A modified version of its written language has remained in use for over 3,000 years.[6] A succession of rulers, despite periodic breakdowns and crises, have unified the vast lands watered by the Yellow and Yangtze River valleys and created favorable conditions for lengthy periods of intense cultural flourishing. Take the Song period, for example.

Chinese society under the Northern and Southern Song Dynasties (960–1279) attained one of the highest levels of civilization in human history. Artists executed marvelously realistic sculptures and paintings, including accurate renderings of architecture and machinery requiring an expert knowledge of mathematics and engineering,[7] though they did not achieve an understanding of true perspective.[8] Song innovations in technology astonish by their diversity and significance. Among the more notable advances include the double-gated canal lock, gunpowder weapons, sophisticated sailing ships, the discernment of true north, water-driven mechanical clocks, and ceramic moveable type printing.[9]

Artisans in the Northern Song period (960–1127) also smelted iron with mineral coal for fuel and constructed ventilation devices to evacuate noxious gases from mine shafts and blast furnaces to refine the ore.[10] In the West, by contrast, coke-fired iron smelting began in 1709 (see below). Although recent scholarship has questioned earlier assumptions about aggregate output,[11] it still seems possible that China's total yearly iron production in the period 1064–78 nearly equaled Europe's total production in the early 1700s.[12] Following the Jurchen and Mongol invasions in the twelfth and thirteenth centuries, Chinese iron production collapsed.[13]

The shifting fortunes of the iron industry exemplify a broader problem in the history of China. While core elements of Chinese technology endured, advancement occurred unevenly. The elaborate astronomical clock devised by Su Song (1020–1101) perished during the Jurchen invasion. Sophisticated mechanical clocks did not appear in China again until their introduction by Europeans centuries later.[14] After the discovery of gunpowder, it took Chinese artisans some 300–400 years to develop rudimentary firearms such as flame-throwers, arrow-launchers, handheld guns, and primitive cannon.[15] Once Europeans learned the formula from the Mongols in the mid-1200s, however, they were forging cannon of almost unimaginable destructiveness in less than two centuries.[16] Here one sees an early example of the accelerating pace of change in Europe.

It is hard to compare China and Europe around 1200 or 1300. Did Chinese achievements in art and sculpture and impressively lofty pagodas bespeak a more creative or refined culture than did the conception and building of dozens of immense Gothic cathedrals reaching for the heavens and illuminated through many thousands of square feet of stained glass (21,500, for example, in the roughly 170 windows of the Cathedral of Chartres)?[17] Or did the intellectual attainments of the vast cohort of literati officials all brilliantly versed in the classics of Confucianism and avid dabblers in poetry and painting surpass those of Europe's university professors and clerical elite? Did it matter that urban elites in Europe exercised political rights, wielded power autonomously, and presided over vital social microcosms whereas those in China did not? Can one even compare China's vastly bigger domestic market, industrial output, and population with Europe's smaller, more fragmented, commercially driven economy? Chinese jurists compiled and maintained a penal code far more extensive than anything in Europe, yet lacked the detailed civil law emerging at this time at the other end of Eurasia. Chinese writers composed a vast output of literary and philosophical works, yet none achieved a lucid exposition of a hundred topics, both practical and esoteric, like St Thomas Aquinas. Europe's political fragmentation led many rulers to share some of their power with groups of their subjects, something the vastly more powerful Chinese emperors would not have dreamed of. Finally, no Chinese elites successfully challenged the political and cultural status quo by making reference to ideals, beliefs, and values, as European religious reformers did in the Papal Revolution or in early modern political revolutions.

Most scholars would no doubt qualify China's attainments in the three centuries after the millennium as far superior, grander, and more refined than Europe's—as would travelers with experience in both lands, such as Marco Polo. Who could blame them? Polo marveled at Hangzhou, the capital of the Southern Song Dynasty until the recent Mongol conquest (1279) and the largest city in the world for several more decades. He found paved streets, a well-maintained network of subterranean sewers, public baths fed by hot springs, markets stocked with unimaginable abundance, enormous public parks, the large and majestic Imperial Palace, regularly scheduled night patrols, and a system for the registration of all inhabitants.[18] No European city could boast such amenities for another several hundred years. Of course, achieving them in China had taken well over a millennium. Meanwhile, Europe had already begun its path toward revolutionary transformation.

Century by century, Europeans increased their institutional sophistication and technological development; their level of knowledge and ability to store, process, and disseminate information; their capacity to work together and organize social networks; their mastery of the art of war; their rationalization of economic methods and transactions; their understanding of the natural world; their sense of individual and corporate rights; their challenges to established authorities, traditions, beliefs, and customs; their quantification and measurement of things; their mechanization of manufacturing processes; and their application of a systematizing mindset to life.

These changes prepared the ground for the mechanization of production and the emergence of modern economies in late eighteenth- and nineteenth-century Europe.

Other societies naturally made strides in some or even all of these areas but with less velocity and intensity. Nor did Europe suffer such world-shattering disruptions as the Mongol conquest or such impediments to further innovation and development as the discouragement by Muslim religious authorities of philosophical inquiry from the twelfth century or the official closing of the Chinese and Japanese societies to outside influences from the fifteenth. On the contrary, Europe grew ever more open to the world and innovative. Whereas thousands of Europeans visited China for business, exploration, scientific and cultural pursuits, or missionary work in 1500–1800, only 200 or 300 Chinese, mostly Christian converts, traveled to Europe, typically to Rome or Naples.[19] By this time, Europe's intellectual climate fostered collaboration across the continent and an expansive accumulation of cultural resources. The development of patent law in Venice from 1474, apparently the first in world history, played an important role in stimulating inventiveness, by increasing the precision of technical description and preserving details of technological advances.[20]

The printing revolution, combined with perspective drawing, made possible the accurate transmission of precise technical knowledge, which in previous times had likely slipped into oblivion for want of means to preserve it. These streams of development began to yield rich fruit by the eighteenth century, as thousands and thousands of inventors, designers, entrepreneurs, scientists, artists, professionals, dilettantes (a term that enters the English language in 1748), artisans, professors, engineers, and other amateurs and experts shared and exchanged knowledge, skills, experience, and visions.[21] As detailed in Chapter 8, learned societies and journals united scholars for exchanges of ideas, while universities, clubs, newspapers, popular publications, and lecture series brought the latest breakthroughs to the attention of the wider public. Knowledge continued to advance in the other great civilizations but in more compartmentalized ways.

In China, for example, scholars engaged in philosophical inquiry felt a traditional aristocratic scorn for people who worked with their hands; they also rarely interacted with artisans and technical experts.[22] By contrast, Cardinal Nicholas of Cusa (d. 1464), while devoting most of his mighty intellectual labors to theology, philosophy, mathematics, and the law, played important political and diplomatic roles and also wrote extensively about astronomy and physics, touching on even such mundane issues as corrective lenses.[23] Europe's brightest minds grew ever more practically oriented during the three centuries leading to the Enlightenment. A quintessential thinker of that era, Denis Diderot, insisted on making public even the most workaday technical expertise.[24] He and like-minded "public intellectuals" excluded the very idea of looking down upon knowledge whatever its provenance.

Tsar Peter the Great (r. 1682–1725) had exactly the same attitude beginning with his early experiences among Western Europeans in the "German Settlement" outside Moscow. He devoted his reign to transforming Russia by importing and adapting a wealth of scientific, technological, cultural, and managerial (but not political or constitutional) expertise. Russia thus became the world's first "developing country" and by 1900 one of the great European powers.[25] Probably other entrepreneurial and energetic rulers of the time could have Europeanized their countries in this way, yet none did until Japan following the Meiji Restoration (1868). It doubtless helped that Russia shared important cultural traits with Europe, but a vast gulf of incomprehension divided Eastern and Western Christianity. Only an utterly determined absolutist ruler like Peter, it seems, could impose so many alien ways on his people.

Meanwhile, specialists and handymen in Europe accumulated, in the words of one scholar, vast treasuries of "useful knowledge."[26] Such valuable information included the properties of every known material, the best practices in diverse trades and industries, the effects of temperature and pressure on gases and material substances, the proper uses of chemicals and chemical compounds from home to shop to field and battalion, and how to measure nearly anything and then to record the resultant data. Individually, these men and women sought practical outcomes for specific purposes; collectively, however, they seemed engaged in advancing the common good. Certainly, leading intellectuals of the age—Voltaire, Adam Smith, Cesare Beccaria—aimed at improving the human condition. Indeed, John T. Desaguliers, a celebrated English scientist and inventor of French Huguenot origin, argued in the 1730s that science should "make Art and Nature subservient to the Necessities of Life."[27]

From the time of Nicholas of Cusa, more and more women and men of learning traveled widely, corresponded extensively, and spoke multiple languages. Specialists designed and employed sophisticated scientific instruments; compiled and read handbooks, encyclopedias, dictionaries, textbooks, and newsletters; and translated the latest technical and literary works into all the main European languages. Educated and practically minded people advanced human knowledge and understanding in tandem across Europe yet nowhere so much as in Great Britain in the eighteenth century.

Perfect conditions

Joseph Banks (1743–1820), an English explorer and botanist who headed the Royal Society for 42 years, corresponded with leading entrepreneurs. Joseph Priestley (1733–1804), an English scholar, theologian, scientist, grammarian, political theorist, and historian who first isolated oxygen and invented soda water, married Mary Wilkinson, the daughter and sister of successful industrialists. He also frequented the Lunar Society, an informal club that brought together prominent scientists, businessmen, and intellectuals in Birmingham from the 1770s.[28] Among those who attended, aside from such luminaries as Erasmus Darwin (a noted naturalist and the grandfather of Charles Darwin), were James Watt (1736–1819), a Scottish inventor who designed the first mechanically efficient and economically viable coal-fired steam engine; and Matthew Boulton (1728–1809), an English manufacturer who financed and managed the production of Watt's engine.[29] Over the next quarter century, Boulton and Watt marketed some 450 steam engines, thus harnessing a revolutionary new source of power and endowing ordinary manufacturers with the building capacity of pharaohs.

Over the course of the seventeenth century, England had evolved from an almost entirely agrarian to one of the most urbanized countries in the world. London, much the biggest city, grew from some 75,000 to 120,000 inhabitants in 1550 to between 490,000 and 575,000 in 1700—roughly one-tenth of the total population

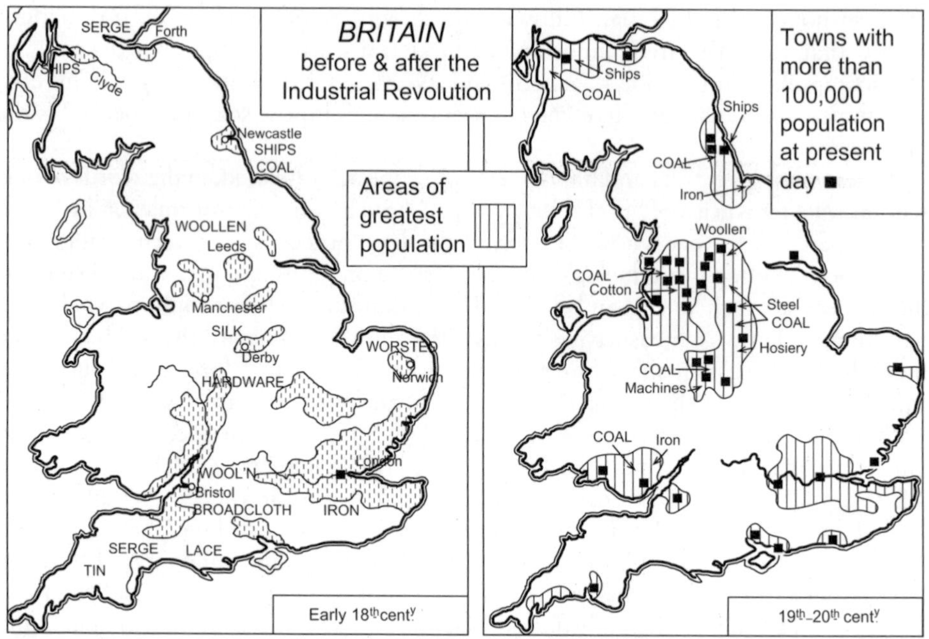

MAP 11.1 *The Industrial Revolution increasingly concentrated population in industrial centers and therefore cities.*

of England and Wales and bested on a global scale probably only by Beijing (roughly 1,000,000), Ayutthaya in Siam (possibly over 1,000,000), and Constantinople (roughly 700,000).[30] Also by 1700, another half-dozen English cities exceeded 10,000 inhabitants—Norwich, Bristol, Exeter, York, Manchester, Newcastle, and Great Yarmouth—while two dozen more hovered between 5 and 10,000 (see Map 11.1).[31] New manufacturing concerns emerged across the country, specializing, beyond the traditional textile sector, in the production of sugar, glass, pottery, iron, and ships. Miners extracted ever-larger quantities of coal, lead, iron ore, and tin.[32]

Commercial activity increased steadily, too. Shops of all kinds opened in cities big and small. Builders constructed a huge number of houses from brick and stone especially after London's Great Fire of 1666. Ordinary people living even in small towns and villages avidly purchased items only the rich could afford in the earlier 1600s, like mirrors, books, clocks, pottery, linens, curtains, and silverware.[33] Opportunities for leisure abounded, including spas and resorts, parks with concession stands, and more than a thousand coffee shops in London alone. Regularly scheduled stagecoach lines connected both major and minor towns over an expanding network of roadways. The mail service grew more efficient, adopting the postmark in the early 1660s and in the 1670s guaranteeing same-day mail delivery within greater London.[34] In 1680, an entrepreneur, William Dockwra (1635–1716), established an elaborate and popular private postal system in London, but the crown shut him down for infringing on the monopoly rights of the General Post Office.[35] An army of entrepreneurs everywhere in England sought to reap a harvest from the increasing wealth and disposable income of the population. Men could make fortunes.

The ambitious sought to invent, purvey, confect, build, display, or finagle anything and everything that the buying public might wish. A vibrant and growing internal market gave birth to consumer culture, just as it had in the Dutch Republic.

Whereas nearly all the countries of Europe suffered an economic downturn during most of the seventeenth century, economic growth continued in England and especially the Dutch Republic, probably thanks to their integration into international trading networks.[36] Despite continuing Dutch preeminence in international commerce, moreover, England was fast catching up, achieving first place sometime after 1700. Its overall foreign trade then quintupled during the eighteenth century.[37]

Other factors favored industrial development in Great Britain as well. All across Europe, in fact in nearly every village and town, small-scale entrepreneurs—often peasants, both male and female, working in the off-seasons—mined, wove, fished, spun, brewed, smithed, manufactured, sewed, pickled, sawed, forged, distilled, crafted, and otherwise fashioned goods for nearby markets and middlemen with connections to more distant ones.[38] The members of the landless lower classes, who engaged in most of this work, often moved from place to place, seeking employment opportunities. The English seem to have displayed greater entrepreneurship and geographical mobility than other peoples of Europe, partly because the enclosure movement beginning in the sixteenth century had pushed hundreds of thousands of peasant farmers off the land and driven them to hunt for employment elsewhere and partly thanks to greatly increased agricultural output, which liberated from the plow a huge number of laborers. A declining mortality rate in Britain in the second half of the eighteenth century, probably due in part to the introduction of smallpox inoculation and improvements in hygiene, made this cohort bulge still larger.[39] The country's high population density, compact geography, and relatively dense network of rivers and canals greatly lowered transportation costs.

Not only did intellectuals, scientists, inventors, and entrepreneurs associate easily with one another; members of the landed gentry and even the nobility had a tradition of pursuing adventurous callings in the Royal Navy, merchant marine, and business.[40] "Well born" younger sons, excluded from inheritance by strictly applied laws of primogeniture, often embarked upon these occupations with the blessing of their elders. An aristocratic contempt for occupations that dirtied one's hands or required feverish activity and hard work constituted a powerful impediment to economic development for centuries the world over. This prejudice afflicted the elites of Great Britain perhaps less than those of any other European country besides the Netherlands. Furthermore, economic interest often bound mercantile, landed, and governmental elites together. Sheep growers depended on the price of wool on the international market, as did tax collectors. London merchants, moreover, frequently lent large sums to the crown, further strengthening this nexus of interdependency.

The Glorious Revolution of 1688 did not spark a commercial or economic revolution in England, which by that point already had a relatively developed financial system and set of social structures involving extensive wage labor, social and geographical mobility, urbanization, and widespread entrepreneurship.[41] Yet the climate of political stability brought about by the agreement of king and property owners (represented by Parliament) inspired investors, innovators, and entrepreneurs to risk their capital, time, and effort in ever bolder—and as it turned out, ever more profitable—business ventures.[42]

Finally, rich deposits of coal and mineral ore, often concentrated together throughout England, Scotland, and Wales, along with fast running waterways in many places, combined to furnish both sources of energy and raw materials for the coming industrial boom. Coal and iron ore abounded in other regions of Europe—for example, in Silesia, the Ruhr, and the Ural Mountains—and indeed of the world—the eastern Gangetic plain, northern China, and western Pennsylvania. In this regard, Great Britain enjoyed a distinct advantage over the Dutch Republic but not necessarily over potential rivals elsewhere on the planet.

Scholarly disputes

From the plenteous diversity of favorable conditions for industrial development in Great Britain, some historians have singled out two for special mention, as its allegedly primary causes: namely, coal and colonies. For some specialists, the slave trade in particular furnished its start-up capital. Other scholars have credited the great Asian civilizations with making that development possible in the first place. Therefore, before describing the Industrial Revolution's main stages, it seems appropriate to confront these contentions.

Janet L. Abu-Lughod argued two decades ago that a global system of commercial relations thrived in the century before the Black Death across the Eurasian continuum, from the English Channel to the Yellow Sea.[43] Within this "world system," China and the Middle East played dominant, but Europe subordinate, roles. Each developed sophisticated financial, technological, and infrastructural innovations. All appeared on the cusp of a revolutionary economic transformation until natural or man-made disasters or trends—the Black Death or the turning inward of the Ming rulers—left only Europe able to colonize the Americas and thus to finance the emergence of commercial and industrial revolution. Of course, a relatively similar level of "proto-capitalism" at the extreme ends of Eurasia does not mean equal chances of achieving actual modern economic growth any more than successful "proto-industrialization" in both Russia and England in 1750 meant each had a similar likelihood of engendering an industrial revolution. A decade later, Andre Gunder Frank argued that a unified global economy, centered on Afro-Asia, continued to flourish after 1500. Again, Europe remained peripheral to this system and broke into its richest markets only thanks to silver imported from the Americas.[44]

Kenneth Pomeranz, in a far more detailed study, sought to demonstrate that as late as 1800 China, especially the Lower Yangtze Delta, remained as prosperous, commercially innovative, infrastructurally connected, and economically developed as Europe.[45] Moreover, he argues, China's political elites interfered far less in market relations than did Europe's, chartered firms like the Dutch East India Company with state-sanctioned monopoly powers having no counterparts in China. Britain's small geographical area and relatively limited human and natural resources drove its entrepreneurs to extract coal from the ground and food and raw materials from the New World. Pomeranz applies here the concept of "ghost acreage," coined by Georg Borgstrom and developed further in a 1980 book by William R. Catton.[46] Timber and food imports thus substituted for millions of acres of forest and cropland that

Britain lacked.[47] Coal, once the Industrial Revolution got underway, furnished a vast army of "ghost labor."[48]

Pomeranz implies but does not demonstrate that British consumers obtained sugar and cotton at lower prices from the Americas than Chinese or other consumers paid on world or domestic markets. In reality, sugar and like commodities often fetched higher prices in Great Britain than elsewhere in the world. Nor does Pomeranz show that slave labor in the Americas cost less than free labor in India or China. Since in the early modern period the price of food correlated directly with the price of labor, and since food cost less to produce in India or China than in the Americas or Europe, then it seems likely that labor costs remained lower in the great Asian countries.[49] One could therefore conclude that Chinese and Indian entrepreneurs had less incentive to mechanize production, though Pomeranz denies that.[50]

Other important factors Pomeranz fails to emphasize sufficiently include China's impressive territorial expansion in the eighteenth century, which exceeded England's, especially once it lost the American colonies.[51] He might also have investigated England's vastly higher ratio of domestic animals to humans. The 6 million Britons in 1695, for example, possessed around 1.2 million horses whose labor power probably equaled that of 6–12 million male laborers, vastly expanding the country's labor power and productivity.[52] The much greater abundance of manure produced by the country's livestock increased agricultural output, per capita consumption, and urbanization.[53] Yet even a sixfold increase in the land available to the Europeans per capita—as calculated by E. L. Jones—could not have augmented the Western standard of living by a factor of 16 in the past 200 years, as Deirdre McCloskey would argue.[54] Moreover, the Russians and Mongols—and many other peoples in history—multiplied the size of their territory exponentially without engendering the modern world or any other great transformations and without even greatly increasing their standard of living.[55]

Moreover, British entrepreneurs could not just reach out and snatch up coal and colonies. They still had to mine the coal and harness its transformative power, discover new lands and implant societies in them thousands of miles from home, integrate raw materials and industrial processes on three continents into sophisticated commercial operations, and finally market manufactured goods across the globe competing with established producers throughout Eurasia. Britons, and in short order Americans and other Europeans, achieved these breakthroughs, setting themselves and the broader West on a path of revolutionary transformation. The Chinese and the Indians did not.

Eric Williams (1911–81), who later served as the first Prime Minister of Trinidad and Tobago, claimed that capital accumulation fed by slavery and the slave trade financed the Industrial Revolution and that the British Parliament abolished the slave trade in 1807 only because it had grown less profitable.[56] Numerous scholars carried forth this thesis, undergirding it with facts and figures.[57] Among their findings: several leading industrialists in both Great Britain and New England made their first fortunes in the slave trade, cotton production yielded around half of American exports by the mid-nineteenth century, cheap slave labor made possible rapid economic development of the colonies, the colonies contributed substantially to the standard of living of the mother countries (especially the higher consumption of sugar), and the slave-based economies absorbed a large proportion of the cotton-cloth production in both countries.

Other specialists have advanced counterarguments. First, much of the earnings from slave trading remained in the hands of traders or circulated in local economies. Second, only a very small proportion of the wealth of slavers living in Britain "trickled down" to the rest of society.[58] Third, the slave trade remained highly profitable on the eve of its abolition;[59] in fact, it was at its high point of volume and prices for slaves.[60] Fourth, the English plantation economies in the late seventeenth and early eighteenth centuries contributed only modestly to the metropolitan income and gross product.[61] Even Barbados, the world's biggest sugar producer, constituted the equivalent of a small English county, economically speaking. A century later, the sugar industry added perhaps only 2.5 percent to British national income. At its apogee at the end of the 1700s, the slave trade probably accounted for under 3 percent of British shipping tonnage.[62]

In general, it seems that the British colonies contributed only modestly to capital accumulation during the early stages of industrialization in Great Britain. More importantly, Deirdre McCloskey has argued persuasively that no capital accumulation was necessary to launch the Industrial Revolution, since no large investments were involved until the mid-nineteenth-century railroad boom.[63] Anyway, if capital accumulation really mattered to economic development, the greatest colonial accumulator of gold and silver, Spain, should have industrialized first, instead of stagnating until the twentieth century. Similarly, conquerors throughout history have massively exploited other societies, yet none ever managed to launch rapid economic growth.

It seems, similarly, that foreign trade in general did not drive industrialization. British exports and imports more than quadrupled over the course of the eighteenth century, while the country's population only doubled.[64] Yet throughout that time neither any single item of trade nor any particular trading partner proved indispensable. The century's almost continuous wars repeatedly disrupted trade and forced the substitution of various goods and markets for others. Nor is it certain that foreign trade increased the consumption and standard of living of most Britons. At any rate, the value added to the British economy by trade with foreign countries definitely comprised a modest proportion of total economic output.[65] Further, if trade alone could drive industrialization, why did not the intense and extensive trading networks of the early modern Indian Ocean region lead the most developed Asian economies to industrialize?[66]

Rather than one or two factors, it seems far more likely that a host of favorable conditions facilitated the mechanization of production. Such factors included a system of interlocking and mutually dependent networks for exchanging capital, land, labor, commodities, ideas, and innovative technologies. It seems incontestable that in the early modern world Europe, and in particular Great Britain, boasted a more robust, diverse, and efficient set of such networks than any other country or region. Merely possessing wealth—for example, coal and colonies—does not automatically translate into innovation. One needs first to discover how to use it in innovative ways. That precisely was the European contribution to the making of the modern world.[67] To claim, as Robert Marks does, that "the British were fortunate to develop a usable coal-fueled steam engine,"[68] suggests that luck sufficed to bring about the Industrial Revolution. In reality, more than luck went into its development.

Chains of innovation

For centuries, Europeans had produced iron in a variety of traditional ways—mostly by direct smelting of iron ore in bloomeries in the south and by a two-stage process using blast furnaces in the north—but in each case with charcoal as the source of heat.[69] Specialized tradesmen produced charcoal by slowly heating wood to high temperatures but in the presence of low oxygen levels (pyrolysis). It took roughly ten tons of charcoal to produce one ton of hot iron—and ten tons of wood to derive one ton of charcoal. Not surprisingly, deforestation gradually became a problem in many regions of Europe.

From the 1200s, hearths, forges, and limekilns began to consume ever-larger quantities of coal in England.[70] Over the following three centuries, craftsmen developed new ways to harness the energy within the mineral for a variety of industrial processes, including glassmaking, pottery-firing, brewing, dye-making, and smelting nonferrous metals. Gradually, English tradesmen acquired more valuable skills and knowledge than in any other European country about ovens, kilns, and forges; the properties of diverse types of coal; and which kinds of fuel—wood, charcoal, coal, peat, or coke—worked best for a variety of industrial uses. Such experience and expertise enabled an English Quaker named Abraham Darby (1678–1717) to make an important technological breakthrough.

In 1709, after diverse earlier business ventures, Darby established a blast furnace in Shropshire in the West Midlands.[71] Blast furnaces, which usually ran on charcoal, exceeded bloomeries in size but, most importantly, achieved higher temperatures by means of bellows injecting blasts of air from below. Darby knew about burning coke, thanks to his earlier apprenticeship with a malt-mill maker, and he rightly believed that coke, which colliers derived from coal through a process of pyrolysis, would prove a more efficient heating agent than charcoal. Darby commercially produced household ironware, though coke smelting became the industry standard only around 1750 in Great Britain and much later on the Continent because of technical difficulties posed by the varieties of available coal.

Meanwhile, craftsmen and entrepreneurs developed other new technologies.[72] Around 1710, Thomas Newcomen (1664–1729), a lay Baptist preacher, devised a functional steam-powered engine that he marketed for pumping out the water that frequently flooded mine shafts throughout the country.[73] Within a few years, Darby's system of iron casting allowed outfitting Newcomen engines with larger pistons and thus increased their horsepower. These innovations dramatically increased the supply of coal and other minerals over the following decades.[74]

Something amazing began to happen in eighteenth-century Britain. Take a look at any list of inventions throughout history. The first major technological innovations occurred every thousand years or so. Eventually, depending on one's criteria, they began to emerge century by century. By the 1500s, as noted in Chapter 8, scientific breakthroughs took place every year or two. In the 1700s, British engineers and inventors achieved that frequency in technology, though often by incorporating and improving innovations first developed on the Continent.[75] Why the time lag? Science involves understanding nature and the world. Technology transforms them. To do so, detailed knowledge, skills, and extensive experience are necessary. Now, for the first time in history, human beings were reaching a point of incessant, constantly accelerating, and mutually reinforcing scientific and technological advancement.

Woolen textiles remained Britain's largest manufacturing and export commodity in the first half of the eighteenth century. Ordinary people produced the cloth in their homes—"cottage industry"—using handlooms and spinning wheels. Very slowly, however, cotton, a softer and more comfortable fabric, woven into vivid and beautiful patterns by expert cloth makers in India, gained popularity among all social classes. Home-based English weavers began to produce cotton cloth as well, though they could not compete profitably with their Indian competitors, given the low cost of labor in India.[76] Cravings for the lovely new fabrics—madras, calico, chintz, muslin—as well as continuous technological innovation and entrepreneurs seeking their fortunes combined to transform the industry.

The mechanization of textile production required many steps.[77] John Kay (1704–80) of Bury in northwest England contributed the first breakthrough in 1733. His "flying shuttle" enabled a single worker, instead of two, to run a hand-operated loom. The weavers hated it, however, fearing for their jobs. Moreover, a bottleneck now appeared: the ability to weave more cloth created a need for more yarn or thread. It so happened that around that time a Huguenot refugee from France, Lewis Paul (d. 1759), along with his partner, John Wyatt (1700–66), an English carpenter and inventor, devised a mechanism using rollers for spinning—drawing out and twisting—fiber into thread. The partners' efforts to set up commercial spinning mills unfortunately met with scant success. Meanwhile, Paul obtained a patent in 1748 for a hand-driven carding machine to complete an initial stage in preparing cotton fiber for spinning.

Intrigues, swindles, and injustice surrounded the next development in the story.[78] Two inventors, James Hargreaves (1720–78) and Thomas Highs (1718–1803), both claimed credit in 1764 for devising a "spinning jenny," a machine that processed several threads at once. Highs enlisted another John Kay, this one a clockmaker from Lancashire, to build the device. A few years later, Kay met Richard Arkwright (1733–92) and confided to him the secrets of the spinning jenny. Arkwright, it turned out, possessed abundant business acumen but few scruples. In 1769, he patented a water-powered spinning machine, called the spinning frame, and with funds provided by wealthy associates set up the first water-powered spinning factory in 1771. Over the following decade, Arkwright built several more factories employing hundreds of workers. By his death, he had amassed a huge fortune, totaling £500,000, despite a court having overturned his patents on the grounds of theft of intellectual property.

Several other innovations quickly followed, some minor, including new methods for bleaching, dying, and impressing patterns into the fabric; others further mechanized textile production. In 1779, Samuel Crompton (1753–1827) invented what he called a "spinning mule," which mechanically spun thread thick enough to sustain large-scale production.[79] Five years later, Edmund Cartwright (1743–1823), an English clergyman, made a still more momentous leap forward with his power loom, which he patented in 1785. This device combined all of the elements for manufacturing cloth into a single mechanical operation. Unfortunately, the mechanism worked very inefficiently. In particular, the thread frequently broke. The resolution of these problems had to await several innovations introduced by William Radcliffe (1761?–1842) in the water-powered cotton-weaving factory he established in Lancashire in 1789.[80] Thus, between 1785 and 1822, British cotton textile output increased tenfold.[81] Crucially, every invention was followed by a host of innovations improving its basic design, which often led to new inventions and further innovations. It was an awesomely virtuous cycle, one that has continued to the present day.

In these same years, Josiah Wedgwood (1730–95) industrialized the production of the second most popular manufactured imports from Asia, ceramic pottery.[82] Born into a family of potters in the Midlands of England, from a young age he repeatedly tested different materials, firing techniques, and glazing methods and by age 28 began keeping meticulous records of all his experiments. In time, he designed strikingly beautiful patterns, textures, colors, bas-reliefs, and imprinted figures into both delicate and extremely solid and durable lines of pottery, jewelry settings, cameos, and other decorative objects, some inspired by ancient Egyptian, Greek, and Roman motifs. In 1762, he met a classically educated and well-traveled businessman named Thomas Bentley (1731–80) who became his business partner. A personal friend of Joseph Priestley and an acquaintance of Benjamin Franklin, he brought many contacts and connections to the firm, which came in handy for lobbying Parliament, for example, to approve the building of canals linking the Staffordshire potteries with the port cities of Liverpool and Hull. Mission accomplished.

The partners steadily expanded their business, divided the production of different types of earthenware among specialized workshops, opened showrooms in several cities, including London, adopted the latest technological innovations, built workmen's cottages around their factory, paid for a rudimentary worker-sickness fund, set up a school to train apprentices in drawing and modeling, and introduced the world's first clocking-in system. They also developed innovative marketing techniques. In 1771, the firm sent unsolicited samples of their wares to some 1,000 members of the German aristocracy. The gamble paid off, as most of these potential customers took the bait. The following year, Wedgwood became one of the first companies to brand its merchandise, by impressing its name into every item sold. They also avidly sought—sometimes at a loss—custom orders from aristocrats and members of the royal family in Britain, considering them "legislators in taste" with the ability to bestow valuable celebrity sanction.[83] The firm kept prices relatively high but offered such appreciated services as free shipping to anywhere in England, replacement coverage for items damaged during transport, and a money-back guarantee, apparently the first such instance of this still popular policy. Wedgwood cultivated an upper-class clientele Europe, the New World, Turkey, and even China. By 1783, nearly 80 percent of the firm's output went to foreign customers.[84]

Meanwhile, other inventors and entrepreneurs improved the production of iron and steam engines.[85] John Wilkinson (1728–1808), the brother-in-law of Joseph Priestley, expanded the family ironworks in northern Wales and established a second one in Shropshire in 1757. There he used raw coal for iron casting and developed a machine for boring cannon barrels and steam-engine cylinders. Numerous entrepreneurs experimented in the following decades with iron-casting methods. The puddling process, developed in the 1780s by Henry Cort (1740–1800), consumed less fuel and dramatically increased output. In 1779, several entrepreneurs, led by Abraham Darby III (1750–91), began constructing the first cast-iron bridge ever built. Two years later, the engineering marvel spanned 100 feet across—and rose 60 feet above—the River Severn in Shropshire. In the end, the project swallowed up nearly 400 tons of iron. Engineers used iron to build vertically as well, constructing five- and six-story buildings in the 1790s.[86]

Power generation increased dramatically. Many hundreds of Newcomen engines, improved in minor ways over the decades, continued to function all over England and the Continent into the early years of the nineteenth century, some of them, beginning in the 1780s, driving crankshafts attached to power looms and other mechanical devices.[87] By 1778, Boulton and Watt had perfected a new type of steam engine that functioned five times more efficiently and consumed 75 percent less coal. A new model on the market 5 years later could drive rotary machinery more effectively than the Newcomen engine. By 1800, they had produced nearly 500 engines, most of which powered textile mills. Soon thereafter, Watt's patent expired, opening the door to dozens of improvements, innovations, and new designs. In numeric terms, the cost of producing one kilowatt of power fell from £5,000 in 1760 to around £1,000 in 1810.[88] Simultaneously, craftsmen developed a variety of machine tools for metalworking, including lathes, planers, and milling machines all enabling machinists to mass-produce an enormous variety of useful and decorative items.

Inventors harnessed coal power for more and more uses. William Murdoch (1754–1839), a Scottish engineer and employee at the Boulton and Watt foundry, devised a lighting system that burned gas derived from coal. By the 1810s, utility companies had installed lighting grids in London and by the 1820s, in Paris.[89] Murdoch also invented a self-propelled steam carriage in 1784. Three years later, John Fitch (1743–98), an American inventor, launched the world's first steam-powered boat on the Delaware River.[90] In 1807, another American, Robert Fulton (1765–1815), began the world's first regularly scheduled steamboat service (between New York City and Albany).

A dozen engineers and inventors over the next two decades, in both the United States and Great Britain, devised high-pressure steam engines, installed them on locomotives, built small routes of iron rails, and launched intercity railroad services.[91] The first regularly scheduled passenger service opened in September 1830 running between Liverpool, a port city in the west, and Manchester, a major textile-manufacturing center 35 miles inland. Constructing this route required huge feats of engineering, including a tunnel more than a mile long bored beneath Liverpool itself, several dozen bridges and viaducts, blasting through many rocky hills, and devising a means to cross an immense peat bog.[92] Within a few decades, engineers in Great Britain, the United States, and the Continent managed to lay rail lines between all the major cities.

Starting manufacturing ventures until this point, as noted above, had required relatively little capital. Most British entrepreneurs financed their operations through personal savings, borrowing from family members, and joining forces with a few partners. Arkwright, Darby (all three of them), Wedgwood, and Boulton and Watt had all organized their businesses as modestly sized partnerships.[93] They eschewed limited-liability companies as requiring a lower level of commitment from investors; they wanted to place binding personal obligations on their business associates. Yet setting up a railroad line, even a very short one, demanded vast outlays of cash and an innovative business organization.

Chartered corporations had long enjoyed popularity in the American colonies.[94] Starting with America's oldest corporation, Harvard University (chartered in 1636), hundreds of municipalities, churches, businesses, and utilities functioned as corporations. Yet government tended to regulate these entities very closely, sometimes revoking charters arbitrarily, which made them a less than ideal business form, until the Supreme Court ruled in 1819 that corporations possess inherent private rights. In response, the American state governments, as well as Parliament in Britain, eased restrictions on them. With the rise of railroads, Parliament issued a couple of dozen charters of incorporation every year. The Joint Stock Companies Act of 1844 made it possible simply to register corporations, leading to the creation of hundreds of new companies. Meanwhile, laws in the United States and France granted corporations limited liability, forcing Parliament to follow suit in 1856. Then the floodgates opened: over the next 6 years, entrepreneurs set up nearly 25,000 limited-liability companies in Great Britain alone.[95] Investors naturally felt more comfortable backing a company if creditors could not demand their last penny in the event of bankruptcy.

Limited-liability corporations had two profound effects on Western society. First, they constituted the first major new political actors, autonomous institutions, and concentrations of power since the rise of towns in medieval Europe. They existed within society and exerted a powerful influence on it yet remained largely independent of government. Second, for the first time in history thousands of business organizations existed that could attract into the marketplace a substantial portion of a country's wealth and could allocate it rationally according to the best rate of return in tens, and soon hundreds, of thousands of diversified ventures. Many businesses naturally went bankrupt—over 30 percent of those formed in Britain between 1856 and 1883.[96] Yet the failure of even many tiny pieces in the ever-expanding and awesomely variegated commercial mosaic could not permanently disrupt, much less destroy, the fabric of an economic system growing ever more responsive to consumer demand, efficient in the allocation of resources, and productive in the organization of labor and entrepreneurial talent. The number and range of investors increased year by year, as more and more people made bets on the future, aspired to increase their wealth, and believed in a life of ever-growing prosperity. The age of free enterprise was beginning to dawn.

Non-Western societies joined this development rather late. The Ottoman parliament, for example, legalized corporations only in 1908, by which point dozens of foreign corporations, headquartered in Paris or London, already operated within the empire.[97]

Railroads radically transformed the way humans traveled and transported goods. For thousands of years, people had ambled along at a few miles per hour, with occasional faster bursts. They walked, rode on the backs of animals, rowed, or sailed. Even the fastest ships-of-the-line could attain a speed of no more than 14 knots (or 16 miles per hour) and usually cruised much slower because of the irregularity of the winds.[98] Now, suddenly, people were traveling at 25–30 miles per hour. The speed and hauling power of the railroads increased within a few years to 60 mph for passenger trains and hundreds of tons of freight.[99] The cost savings generated by Britain's rail transport may have equaled between 1.5 and 20 percent in 1830–70, depending on whose numbers one believes.[100]

Railroad companies transformed business practices. They not only put to work vast amounts of capital, but also created huge economies of scale and new organizational techniques necessary for managing the transportation of millions of passengers and tons of freight across thousands of miles of track all according to finely calibrated schedules.[101] The larger companies, by mid-century, employed 50 or more managers, nearly all inspired with an ethos of professionalism and exactitude. Their numbers grew and grew over the following decades. The more innovative among them developed complicated fare and scheduling algorithms, organizational charts, and other techniques of rational management.[102] The railroads' need for raising capital for all practical purposes created the New York Stock Exchange, which went from trading a couple of hundred shares a day in the 1830s, to hundreds of thousands in the 1850s.

By 1845, nearly 2,500 miles of track united the industrial centers, ports, extractors of natural resources, and agricultural regions of Great Britain, expanding to roughly 9,000 miles in 1860.[103] Linking all the corners of the country required some amazing feats of engineering. The Royal Albert Bridge, for example, which began service in 1859, stretched nearly a half-mile across the Tamar River, connecting Devon and Cornwall. Already in 1830, Great Britain produced roughly four-fifths of the total global output of 30 million tons of coal. Forty years later, this number had surged to 110 million tons and still accounted for roughly half the total world production.[104] This was a revolution in energy. By mid-century, the English and Welsh population of some 18 million consumed roughly 50 Mtoe (million tons of oil equivalent) or only 50 percent less than the 300 million inhabitants in all of Qing China.[105] This energy fueled a vast increase in industrial production. Pig iron produced in Britain increased from 700,000 tons in 1830 to nearly 4 million tons in 1870. Overall, Britain exported more goods in 1870 than France, Germany, and Italy combined.[106]

Britain had become the "workshop of the world." The number of cotton textile factories in Lancashire, England's main textile-producing county, nearly doubled from 676 in 1835 to 1,235 in 1850. Most of these firms employed a relatively small number of workers, on average around 150, and remained in the hands of families and a limited number of partners.[107] Stiff competition drove a large number of firms out of business, creating a secondary market for textile machinery, which continuously inspired other entrepreneurs to seek their fortunes in the business. Already in 1800, people working in industry, commerce, and services produced over half of Britain's national economic output.[108] By 1831, more Britons worked in industry than in any other sector of the economy (41 percent).[109] The urban population grew rapidly, comprising half the country's population by 1850, as factories attracted ever more laborers. Manchester, the textile town par excellence, grew from around 25,000 in 1772 to 367,232 in 1851. Other major industrial centers like Leeds, Birmingham, and Sheffield also added population at a rapid pace.[110] London, however, dwarfed them all—and indeed every city in the history of the world by a wide margin—reaching 3,188,485 souls in 1861.[111]

Undoubtedly, coal fueled and accelerated the Industrial Revolution in Great Britain. One wonders, however, whether British entrepreneurs and innovators might have launched this transformation even without it. After all, most ironmasters did not abandon charcoal until late in the 1700s. Just as crafty English cannon-forgers substituted cast-iron for bronze in the 1500s, given the lack of copper deposits in England (see Chapter 4), thus turning a liability into an advantage since cast-iron cannon cost less, would not British industrial entrepreneurs in the early 1800s have found practical alternatives, such as more wind and water power or the importation of wood and coal from the Continent? They almost certainly would have, because ingenuity, cross-fertilization of scientific and technical expertise, favorable social and economic conditions, and dynamic entrepreneurship appear to have mattered more to Britain's industrial transformation than the merely convenient juxtaposition of coal and iron ore deposits throughout the country. A consideration of the spread of industrialization to the Continent tends to support this view.

Diffusion

From the late 1700s, the British Parliament prohibited the emigration of skilled tradesmen and the export of sophisticated machinery.[112] The French Revolutionary and Napoleonic Wars did a better job of impeding such transfers. Certainly they slowed the industrialization of continental Europe (though reforms imposed by France in many countries laid the groundwork for fast economic development—as noted in Chapter 10). After 1815, however, impeding industrial and technology transfer proved difficult in an open society where individuals enjoyed civil rights. Entrepreneurs and governments in Europe and the United States used licensing, apprenticeship, and industrial espionage to gain access to cutting-edge technology. Also, British engineers, contractors, skilled workers, managers, foremen, and even industrialists emigrated in their hundreds and thousands to Belgium, France, Germany, and the United States. Entrepreneurs and innovators in these countries quickly established mechanized production systems in factories and added to them valuable innovative processes, methods, and devices—such as the Jacquard weaving loom, the wet spinning of flax invented by de Girard, and Krupp's steel-casting process—which British industrialists adopted and adapted in their own firms.[113] In 1842, the British government repealed the last of its prohibitions on technology and skilled labor transfers and embarked upon a policy of free trade.[114]

For the most part, each European country developed an industrial sector in its own way.[115] In Belgium and Germany, for example, coal, iron, and engineering played a bigger role than textile manufacturing. Swiss entrepreneurs built cotton-spinning factories around Zurich but mostly concentrated on the labor-intensive manufacturing of such goods as clocks, watches, and scientific instruments. Switzerland as a whole, while never fully industrializing, developed into a highly commercialized society with a very high per capita national income. French industrialists took advantage of their skilled labor force and concentrated on the production of luxury goods, for example, silk cloth, for which France boasted a large consumer market. Sweden's iron industry expanded; its export of raw materials such as lumber, iron ore, and pulp increased; and a mechanized textile industry emerged. Industrialization lagged in Southern and Eastern Europe, developing robustly only beginning around 1900, for example, in Italy and Russia.

Despite different rates of growth, one can argue that Europe as a whole, thanks to centuries of innovation and transformation, gave birth to the Industrial Revolution. For one thing, within four decades of British railroad development, the major countries of Europe had laid 50,000 miles of track linking the more highly developed regions and cities of the Continent (see Map 11.2).[116] Industrial development crossed state lines in other ways, as well: France and Belgium shared a huge coalfield; France and Germany, large iron ore deposits; and Prussia, Austria, and Russia, both. Moreover, the more developed countries had backward regions (northern Scotland and the mountainous cantons of Switzerland), while the less-developed countries often had more advanced regions (Catalonia and Bohemia).[117] Those countries that did not industrialize early or along British lines (like Holland and Denmark) nevertheless experienced dramatic and continuous economic growth and broad commercialization. Indeed, compared to other regions of the world, where few countries managed to industrialize before the twentieth century, one can justifiably consider all of Europe a single socioeconomic sphere with sufficiently compatible sets of preconditions for radically faster economic development than ever seen before on earth.

The first non-European country to industrialize became a world leader during the nineteenth century. Labor scarcity and abundance of land characterized the economy of the United States of America. These factors steered many American farmers away from grain cultivation, which involved a high level of labor seasonality, and toward the production of meat, dairy products, and other agricultural commodities, providing a healthier diet for the population than in Europe.[118] Those workers who engaged in manufacturing tended to labor full-time and year-round in factories or workshops, both mechanized and nonmechanized, at a far higher rate than in Britain, where cottage industry continued to account for a large portion of the labor force until

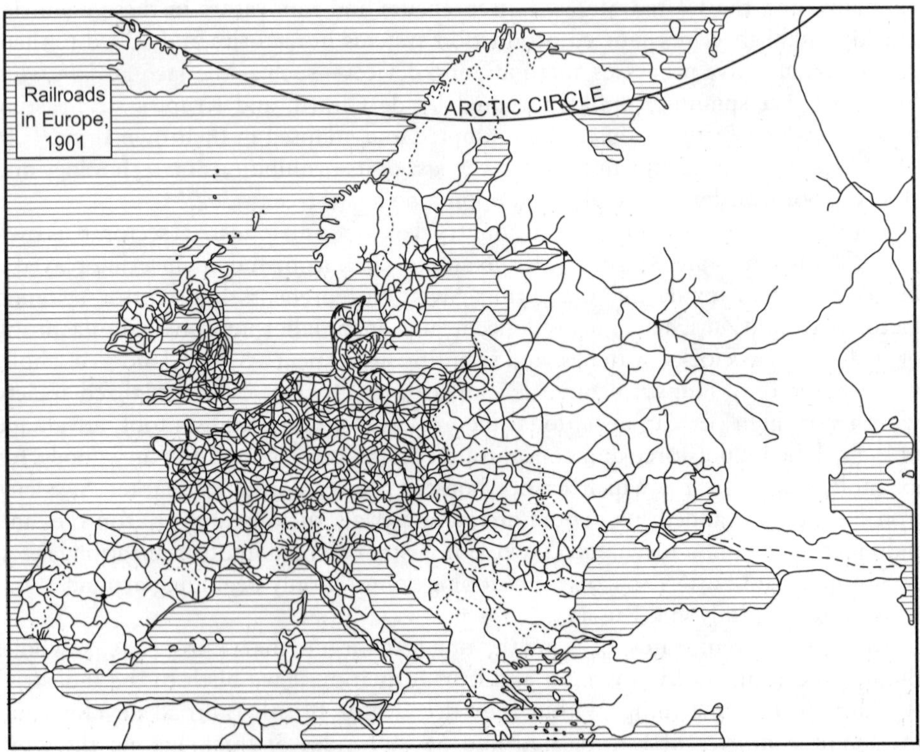

MAP 11.2 *Railroads transformed travel and the transportation of goods as Europe became increasingly interconnected.*

well into the nineteenth century. American labor scarcity naturally pushed up labor costs and spurred a more intensive search for labor-saving devices and methods than anywhere in Europe and prompted entrepreneurs to allocate their workers in the most efficient ways possible. They created economies of scale, introduced the specialization of labor and standardization of parts, and developed and adopted new productive technologies earlier and at a faster rate than in Europe.

By the 1820s and 1830s, some foreigners began to talk about the "American system of production." Several elements, most of them originating in Europe,[119] went into this process.[120] The assembly of firearms from interchangeable parts began in France in the 1770 and was pursued further over the following decades by manufacturers, such as Eli Whitney (1765–1825), the inventor of the cotton gin.[121] From around 1814, Eli Terry of Connecticut (1772–1852) commenced the mass production of clocks using interchangeable parts and standardized methods of assembly.[122] The scarcity of labor in the early American Republic spurred entrepreneurs to develop these methods systematically. Specialized woodworking tools—Thomas Blanchard (1788–1864) invented several, like the irregular turning lathe—facilitated the fashioning of ever more standardized parts. Inventions followed one after the other in all branches of manufacturing. Blanchard's first mechanical innovation (1806) produced 500 tacks per minute, each one entirely like the others.[123]

Among the first important high-volume consumer goods produced by the American system were shoes. As production by unskilled workers using a division of labor and standardized materials crowded out skilled artisans making shoes by hand, prices fell and enabled the average consumer to buy more footwear. Throughout the country, the per capita output of shoes increased from 2.1 in 1840 to 3.5 in 1850. In other words, it nearly doubled in only 10 years—without large infusions of capital or the widespread introduction of machinery.[124]

New England entrepreneurs dominated American textile manufacturing. Samuel Slater (1768–1835), an English engineer, brought the latest technology to the United States in 1789 and teamed up with the Quaker merchant Moses Brown (1738–1836) to establish near Providence the first water-powered cotton-spinning mill in the New World.[125] Slater hired local families, for whom he built dwellings adjacent to his factory, each member accomplishing specific tasks. He joined with more partners and established two new factories in 1799. By 1815, one of them ran 5,170 spindles. Entrepreneurs throughout the region and in New York and New Hampshire hired mechanics and managers with experience acquired in Slater's operation, thus carrying the "Rhode Island system" further afield.

Although Slater and others had fully mechanized thread production, as late as 1810 nearly everyone in New England still produced their own cotton cloth at home. Even factories employed handlooms, at least until around 1815. Francis Cabot Lowell (1775–1817), a member of a prominent Boston family with a Harvard education and formidable business experience, carried industrial textile production in America to the next level.[126] In 1810, he visited textile factories in Lancashire, England, and committed to his photographic memory the design, layout, and operation of power looms and other industrial equipment. In 1813, he joined with partners to form the Boston Manufacturing Company of Waltham, which received the right to incorporate and to raise up to the astonishing sum of 400,000 dollars by selling shares in the company.[127] Twelve investors, including Lowell, began with an initial capitalization of 100,000 dollars. The firm carefully mapped out and developed business strategy, including meticulous accounting, a hierarchical corporate management structure, attentive organization of labor, the pursuit and adoption of the latest technological advances, lobbying (successfully, it turned out) for a protective tariff, a focus on manufacturing affordable cloth, and vertically integrated production from spinning thread to weaving cloth. They proposed and accomplished a dramatic early industrial development—the world's first fully integrated textile mill. The company offered high wages to intelligent and well-educated young women from good families and lodged them in clean and well-maintained boardinghouses, to which they later added a library, church, and store. The "mill girls," according to contemporary visitors, dressed very well and exuded an air of self-respect.[128]

All of the company's careful preparations rewarded its initial investors handsomely. Sales soared from around 51,000 dollars in 1817 to over 260,000 dollars in 1820, making the company the largest textile manufacturer in the country.[129] In 1817, the firm built a separate machine shop and began selling power looms and other equipment. They also expanded textile operations, building an entire factory community in the early 1820s, naming the new town (incorporated in 1826) after the now-deceased Lowell. Within a few decades, Lowell surpassed all other American cities as an industrial center. Already in 1835, investors opened rail service between Boston and Lowell, the first major railroad in Massachusetts. The industrial revolution in America went roaring forward.

The economic output of the entire country grew at a blistering rate of about 4 percent a year on average, quintupling the size of the economy from 1820 to 1860.[130] Population growth could not keep up, so wages increased, and disposable income nearly doubled. Manufacturers invested heavily in capital stock and increased their output of consumer goods. Factories grew larger, and manufacturing labor productivity increased at a healthy 2–3 percent clip. Agriculture also became more productive, thanks to the development of labor-saving devices—some invented by Americans, like polished-steel plowshares and the mechanical reaper (see Chapter 12). Farmers gradually planted more and more for a railroad-driven national market. As the agricultural sector increased its output per worker, millions of people migrated from the countryside to cities on the Eastern Seaboard whose population rose sevenfold in 1820–60. The population of the Midwest grew even faster, so eastern investors scrambled to build road, canal, and rail lines linking their major cities with the Midwestern hinterlands. An integrated, industrializing national economy began to develop.

* * *

No non-European countries managed to replicate this feat, at least in the short term. As time went on—in fact, decade by decade and even year-by-year—the rest of the world fell further behind the peoples and countries of the West.

From the vantage point of even the mid-eighteenth century, when some Europeans, like Voltaire,[131] apparently viewed China as more advanced than their continent, this outcome made little sense. Did not the quality and overall output of India's cotton textile industry or China's production of silk cloth and porcelain and other ceramic goods vastly exceed those of Europe? The agricultural sectors of both countries also outproduced Europe, resulting in larger populations and perhaps a higher caloric intake per person.[132] China's bureaucracy, many believed, surpassed that of any contemporary state.

In reality, these "obvious" facts must have been either untrue or beside the point. The central Chinese government throughout the Qing period, for example, according to most recent research, has turned out rather small, inefficient, underfunded (on a per capita basis), and far less concerned with promoting national development than, say, the government of Louis XIV. More to the point, it seems unlikely that the European takeoff could have sprung from socioeconomic foundations similar to those of China or India.[133] As suggested earlier in this chapter, industrialization probably required a long period of gestation and a host of favorable conditions relating not only to material but also to cultural, intellectual, and social circumstances and indeed to many habits of behavior and attitude that apparently emerged more or less simultaneously throughout Europe and in some of Europe's diaspora communities overseas, in particular, in the United States. Why they did so may remain a conundrum.

Yet once the process began, as it clearly had by the mid-nineteenth century, the tempo of acceleration rose to a more and more furious rate. Invention bred innovation. Clever process inspired brilliant instrument. Efficient machine spawned time-saving method. A technological revolution had begun and has never ceased. The Industrial Revolution proved merely an incubator of this even more revolutionary transformation.

Since humans mastered fire, our greatest technological and conceptual breakthroughs have involved both promise and danger. Even human language for all its extraordinary power as a medium of communication leads us inevitably into manifold conceptual errors, some catastrophic, because of its—and our—imperfections. All of the transformations so far discussed had a "dark side," since each one has increased human power and therefore created more opportunities for abuse. Military prowess and navigational skill, for example, enabled Europeans to conquer two entire continents. And the Reformation, which above all sanctioned the personal spiritual authority of millions of ordinary believers, unleashed decades' long civil wars across Europe. Yet the Industrial Revolution so intensified this trend that for the first time a distant question of "sustainability"—whether or not one can continue to increase growth and production indefinitely—emerged. Could one explore every corner of the planet, publish endless new book titles, limitlessly question religious doctrine, turn the natural world into a mere object of study, commodify every good and service, devolve political power to ever-broader layers of society, and continuously subdivide the labor force without threatening the very cohesiveness of human society?

Voices in the early nineteenth century warned against the dangers of industrialization. "Luddites" and other artisans protested against machines replacing skilled labor and employers driving down prices and wages in an endless spiral of competition.[134] Poets and artists decried overly rational approaches to life and nature; "We murder to dissect," cautioned William Wordsworth (1798). Others lamented the "dark satanic mills" of industry (William Blake 1808) or sang a "Song for the Luddites" (Lord Byron 1816).[135] Aristocrats mourned the passing of bucolic rural paradises as cities expanded and spread into farmland. Social theorists began denouncing economic exploitation and devising plans for utopian societies.[136] From the beginning, therefore, many thoughtful people felt ambivalent about the power of technology unleashed in the Industrial Revolution. Despite their concerns, technological transformation accelerated and massively increased Western power, wealth, and standards of living.

QUESTIONS FOR REFLECTION

What is modern economic growth and when did it first begin?

What distinguished Europeans' attitudes toward innovation?

What scholarly dispute centers on the question of "coal and colonies"?

Which commercial ventures began to require vast inputs of capital?

What effects did the limited-liability corporation have on Western society?

How did railroad companies transform business practices?

Why did the pace of innovation keep accelerating?

What were the "dark sides" of industrialization and how did people react to them?

Chapter 12 Chronology

1770s:	Great increase in labor productivity begins
1800:	World's first battery
1810:	Peter Durand patents canning process
1825:	Erie Canal opens
1830:	Cyrus McCormick takes over family manufacturing of mechanical reapers
1831:	First demonstrations of electromagnets
1836:	Samuel Morse creates first telegraph prototype
1839:	Charles Goodyear invents vulcanized rubber
1843:	Joseph Dart invents grain elevator
1857:	Bessemer process greatly reduces price of steel
1867:	Chicago's meatpacking industry begins
1870s:	Business strategy of vertical integration begins
1874:	Thomas Edison creates Menlo Park research laboratory
1875:	Alexander Graham Bell invents telephone
1880:	First electrical elevators
1882:	World's first hydroelectric power plant built in Appleton, Wisconsin
1885:	Chicago's Home Insurance Building, world's first skyscraper, built; first viable motorcars
1886:	Nikola Tesla creates Alternating Current (AC) electricity system
1888:	Electric streetcars first built
Mid-1890s:	Guglielmo Marconi creates first workable wireless apparatus
1899:	World's first entirely synthetic medication, aspirin, invented
1903:	Orville and Wilbur Wright launch first successful airplane
1913:	Moving assembly line innovation first used by Ford Motor Company
1928:	Penicillin discovered
1936:	Public television broadcasts begin
1946:	World's first electronic computer created
1947:	Invention at Bell Labs of transistor

12

Technological Revolution

On 26 August 1895, at 7:30 in the morning, the world's biggest hydroelectric generator began operation just upriver from Niagara Falls.[1] It transformed into electricity the tremendous kinetic energy of millions of gallons of water plunging through massive hydraulic shafts carved deep into the rock below. Within a few years, the Niagara Falls Power Company had added 20 more dynamos for a total output of 100,000 hp and 75 megawatts of AC electric power. Nothing like it had ever been attempted. Engineers from General Electric and Westinghouse overcame a host of obstacles, creating the first wide-area power-delivery system, supplying vast quantities of energy first to a nearby aluminum manufacturer and then to Buffalo, New York, 22 miles away. Soon the city boasted the nation's cheapest electricity and became the world's biggest electrochemical producer.[2] The promoters had not expected to revolutionize this industry, but they did. The age of abundant and inexpensive energy available for almost infinite uses was dawning.

Food production

Agriculture formed the understructure of nearly every economy in history. For the past 10,000 years, nearly all people on earth have grown food, mostly only to feed themselves and their families. Farming improvements took place gradually, in Europe especially in Britain and the Netherlands, as noted in Chapter 9, slowly boosting the output of grain and meat starting in the 1500s. Farmers began in large numbers to plant for the market, as the consolidation of landholding, improved methods, and new technologies increased their productivity. Scholars still debate when the greatest increases in crop yields occurred—some argue before 1770, others say only after 1800.[3] In fact, labor productivity mattered more than bushels per acre.[4] After all, farmers in China and India achieved very high crop yields using labor-intensive methods.[5] Technological and scientific revolution in the West, on the contrary, liberated vast armies of laborers from the land by dramatically increasing labor productivity beginning in the first half of the nineteenth century.

As in the textile or iron-making sectors, innovations in farming built upon and mutually influenced each other. Unlike in those sectors, however, farmers and scientists devised both mechanical and biological improvements. For decades, historians attributed to agricultural implements primacy in explaining the revolution in output. Recent scholarship has suggested that inventors devoted vastly more efforts to unlock secrets of nature through seed selection, hybridization, research into fighting pests, irrigation, crop rotations, fertilizers, and animal breeding. To take just one example, the two-ton American ox, Brother Jonathan, made a far bigger splash at the 1839 London exposition than the McCormick reaper at the Crystal Palace in 1851.[6] Still, both types of advances contributed enormously to raising agricultural productivity during the past 200 years. They also had a synergetic effect on each other.

Just as increased spinning capacity created a bottleneck resolved only by the mechanization of weaving, so increased crop yields demanded better harvesting techniques. Thus, for example, artisans from about the 1770s in Europe and the United States attached long wooden "fingers" to scythes, creating grain cradles, which enabled farmers to cut and stack grain in one operation. The tool required a bit more skill to use than did a scythe but significantly reduced labor requirements.[7]

During these same years, first in Great Britain but soon also in the United States, inventors developed more effective plows. Charles Newbold (b. 1780) of New Jersey, for example, patented a cast-iron plow with share and moldboard all in one piece in 1797. In 1814, Jethro Wood of New York (1774–1834) added standardized parts, so that a farmer who broke his plowshare or moldboard could replace either instead of buying a new plow. John Deere (1804–86), a blacksmith who settled in Illinois in the 1830s, added polished-steel plowshares, which cut easily through the heavy prairie soil.[8] Of course, with farmers now able to plant more acreage than ever before—according to one estimate, the new plows freed up one horse in three—they needed a new breakthrough in harvesting.

Cyrus McCormick (1809–84) supplied it. He grew up in the Shenandoah Valley in northwestern Virginia.[9] His father had developed a relatively sophisticated mechanical reaper but without commercial success and handed the project over to him in 1830. Seventeen years later, he moved to Chicago and built a factory. A gifted entrepreneur, McCormick developed an effective business model, incorporating trained sales staff, fixed prices, an installment plan for payment, a money-back guarantee, and advertising campaigns. His engineers continuously improved on the initial design, so that at the world's fair in Paris in 1855 it worked three times faster than available European models. No wonder American farmers undersold their European competitors, often even in the face of high tariffs and import duties. Other companies added mechanisms for binding the harvested crops in bundles, first with wire (1872) and then with string (1880), innovations that all the major players incorporated into their designs.[10]

Ingenious tinkerers invented many other farm implements during these decades, including horse-drawn hayrakes in the 1820s, wheat-planters in the 1830s, corn-planters and hay-mowing machines in the 1840s, self-governing windmills for pumping water in the 1850s (rendering most farmers at least partly energy independent), mobile steam-powered tractors and threshing machines in the 1860s, barbed wire in the 1870s (making it possible for ranchers to take control of their grazing land), and horse-drawn combine harvesters in the 1880s.[11] Decade by decade, clever innovators improved the design and function of these and many other time-and labor-saving devices. By the 1890s, the entire American agricultural economy had become intensely mechanized and commercialized—more than any other in history.[12]

At the same time, American farmers and agricultural experts filled countless journals and newsletters with articles about biological innovations.[13] How much ink could one spill about a reaper? Plant cultivation, fighting diseases, choosing the right seeds, irrigation, raising prize-winning livestock—these were topics one could write about endlessly.

Thanks to ceaseless innovation, American agricultural productivity soared. Producing 100 bushels of wheat required some 250–300 man-hours in 1830 but only 40–50 in 1890—an improvement by a factor of five to seven. During roughly the same years (1839–1909), American farmers increased their wheat production from 85 million to 640 million bushels.[14] They achieved this feat in part by scouring the world for more productive strains of wheat, by careful seed selection, and by expanding the areas of cultivation farther and farther north, something again made possible through seed selection.[15] The number of labor-hours needed to grow and harvest 100 bushels of corn fell from 276 in 1840 to 147 in 1900.[16]

High productivity naturally resulted in high wages, far higher than in Europe or anywhere else in the world. One Irish observer who traveled in the United States wrote in 1850 that any immigrant could save enough money in a year to head out west and buy an 80-acre farm. Moreover, the California Gold Rush of 1849, involving the most prolific gold mines in history, fueled an economic boom worldwide and led to two dozen more gold rushes in Canada, the United States, and Australia over the following three decades.[17] No wonder a flood of immigrants poured into the country, mostly from Britain, Ireland, and Germany. By 1854, the number of new entrants swelled to 427,833, the highest level of immigration per capita in the nation's history.[18] (Unfortunately, the increasing population and movement westward of millions of settlers prompted statesmen like Andrew Jackson to "remove" native peoples forcibly from their homelands in the east and, beginning in 1851, to resettle them on reservations; see Chapter 14.)[19]

An ingenious government policy helped spur the agricultural boom. The Homestead Act of 1862, part of Abraham Lincoln's campaign platform, promised free of charge up to 160 acres of undeveloped land outside the original 13 colonies to anyone who settled on it for at least 5 years and met certain other criteria. Partly thanks to this law, the number of farms in America grew from 2 million in 1862 to over 6 million in 1910, and the quantity of farmland increased by roughly 15,000,000 acres each year. By 1934, some 1.6 million farmers (and crafty businessmen) had taken possession of homesteads comprising around 270,000,000 acres (420,000 sq mi), an area larger than the entire combined territory of France and Imperial Germany.[20] Law had thus wrought a revolution, devolving more land and ultimately more wealth to more ordinary people more quickly than ever before or since in human history.

When the Erie Canal opened in 1825, linking Albany to Buffalo and thence across the Great Lakes to the entire Midwest, farmers throughout the region could easily ship their output to the Eastern Seaboard and Europe. Grain flooded into Buffalo, increasing from 112,000 to over 2 million bushels a year between 1835 and 1841. How to process it? Typically, burlap sacks were carted and ferried and hauled and piled up one by one. In 1843, businessman Joseph Dart (1805–57) of Buffalo built a massive wooden storage bin, into which a steam-powered and belt-driven bucket loader conveyed grain from ships and barges.[21] Thus stocked, his grain elevator could offload grain by force of gravity through chutes into barges bound for Albany. Other Buffalo merchants quickly copied Dart's design, and by 1860 these distributors could store a combined 1.5 million bushels. No other port in the world at this time handled more grain. Within a few years, hundreds of merchants operated grain elevators in

Brooklyn and Chicago, too, truly linking the Midwest with the world in the most efficient way possible at that time.[22]

Chicago had been growing rapidly into the great Midwestern metropolis. In 1848 alone, a canal route opened between Lake Michigan and the Mississippi River, rail service linked Chicago with Galena, Illinois, on the bank of the Mississippi, steam-powered grain elevators began functioning, and the Chicago Board of Trade commenced operations as the world's first futures and options exchange—made possible by the birth of the telegraph (see below).[23] The Board of Trade established rules and procedures for selling and buying existing—and future—grain and livestock on paper. Less than a decade later, it devised a wheat-grading system, enabling processors to exchange grain of a specific grade for tradable warehouse receipts. By 1861, Chicago's merchants handled 50 million bushels of grain yearly, up from only 2 million a decade before.[24]

Chicago became the grain capital of the nation, but meatpacking defined it even more. In 1865, nine railroad companies collaborated in the opening of vast new stockyards southwest of the city center where innovative techniques of meat processing industrialized the business.[25] Starting with the transplanted New Yorker Philip Danforth Armour (1832–1901), in 1867, meat packers in Chicago set up slaughterhouses with steam-driven overhead trolley systems. The devices carried suspended carcasses slowly past 125 or 150 stationary workers who carved, hacked, and otherwise disassembled hogs and other beasts—up to several thousand a day in a given factory.

Armour and the other major firms—Swift, Hammond, and Morris—also innovated in the preservation and delivery of meat. Gustavus Swift (1839–1903), who had started his own butchery at age 16 and migrated to Chicago from Massachusetts in 1875, grasped that the rapidly expanding railroad system made possible commercial distribution networks on a national scale.[26] After all, the Union Pacific and Central Pacific Railroad companies had completed the first transcontinental railway in 1869; overall, 167,191 miles of track crisscrossed the country in 1890 and 249,992 miles in 1910 (see Map 12.1).[27] By the 1880s, freight could move from Philadelphia to Chicago in two days or less, instead of the 3 weeks it had taken in the 1840s. Swift wisely developed a fleet of refrigerator railroad cars, which in 1881 delivered 3,000 beef carcasses weekly to Boston. His competitors quickly followed suit.[28]

Swift created one of the world's first vertically integrated business organizations.[29] Until the 1870s, most industrial companies only manufactured products. They did not purchase directly their raw materials or secure control or rights to them, produce the parts for their production needs, or market their finished output themselves. Instead, they paid commissioned agents to handle all these operations. Starting in the 1880s, Swift and his brother Edwin built a large-scale regional distribution network, set up subsidiary meat-packing divisions in several western and Midwestern cities all with cold-storage warehouses, established a centralized purchasing unit, and invested in stockyards. The other meat packers—at least the ones that also built nationwide enterprises—adopted similar business structures. During the same years, firms producing such products as cigarettes, flour, and farm machinery—like Cyrus McCormick—pursued similar patterns of development. This business model integrated operations from raw materials and production to marketing and distribution and even, in many cases, servicing, financing, advertising, and special delivery systems.

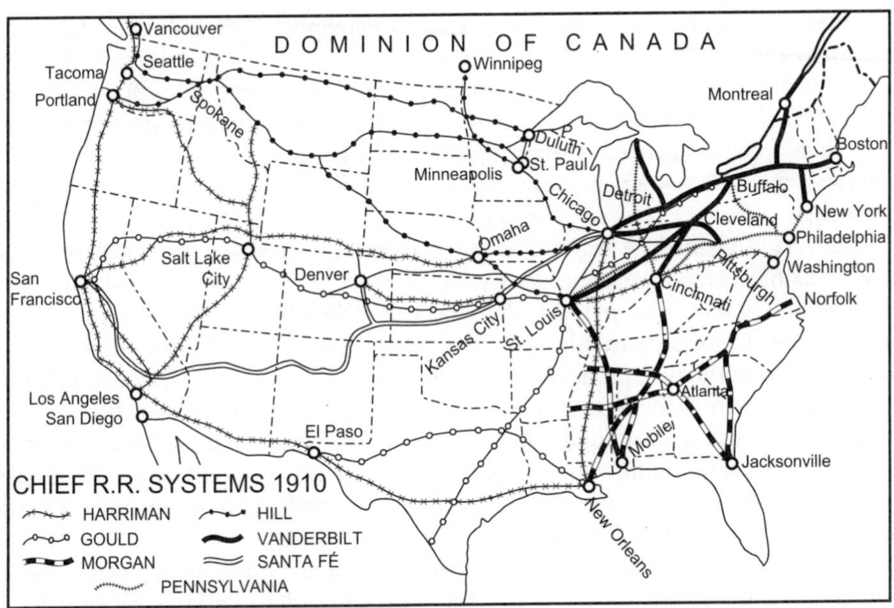

MAP 12.1 *Nearly 250,000 miles of railroad track in 1910 made possible commercial distribution on a national scale in the United States.*

Once the integrated meatpacking firms had achieved economies of scale in purchasing, manufacturing, and distribution, the more successful ones like Armour and Swift diversified their product lines. They began with dressed meats—pork, lamb, veal, beef—and moved on to processed, canned, and pickled meat products. Their professional staff figured out how to transform every last scrap of livestock into a wide variety of salable products, including oleomargarine, brushes, violin strings, soap, glue, fertilizer, combs, buttons, and animal feed. By 1920, meat processors could extract 41 by-products from a single steer.[30]

Other food-processing companies developed integrated business structures, for example, the Minneapolis-based wheat milling firms, General Mills and Pillsbury.[31] In the 1870s, combining and perfecting the latest methods from France, Germany, and Hungary, they erected colossal mills—the biggest in the world—running dozens of fully automated iron, steel, and porcelain rollers (instead of millstones). In 1899, the mills in Minneapolis produced far more flour than the next nine largest flour-producing cities in the United States combined: 14,291,780 barrels. Of that vast mountain of flour, fully 97 percent left the state and one-third found markets abroad. The export of American food and food products expanded greatly from 1870 to 1900, though it constituted at most one-quarter of the total output.[32]

American consumers benefited from flour's falling prices. With a dollar they could buy 15 pounds in 1872 but 34 pounds in 1897. They enjoyed similar savings on other products, the dollar fetching 43 percent more rice over that same period, 114 percent more sugar, 62 percent more mutton, 60 percent more butter, and 42 percent more milk. Thus, people's standard of living rose dramatically.[33]

Living and working conditions were worst for laborers employed in American factories, especially in the decades before and after 1900. In big cities, sanitation was often practically nonexistent in lower-class neighborhoods, industrial and street accidents were epidemic, wages were low, and work hours were long.[34] Over the next few decades, however, thanks to stupendous economic growth nationwide, wages increased significantly.[35] Moreover, large firms introduced policies of "welfare capitalism" that improved their employees' living conditions.[36] Urban life for American workers remained harsh, but it was probably better than anywhere else on earth.

As the land yielded its fruits ever more abundantly, innovators began to devise new kinds of preserved and processed foods. From the early Scientific Revolution, geniuses like Francis Bacon and Leibniz bent their intellects to the problem of food preservation. Bacon apparently even died from a pulmonary infection contracted while experimenting with using snow as a preservative.[37] By the early 1600s, European scientists had discovered microbial life and began to speculate that bacteria could cause putrescence in food. But whence came bacteria? Some scholars proposed "spontaneous generation." The Italian scientist Lazzaro Spallanzani (1729–99) proved in 1765, however, that microbes can only multiply if already present. He also showed that heat could kill them.[38]

Around the same time, having experimented meticulously with diverse means of preserving fruits, vegetables, soups, and meat in bottles and jars, the Frenchman Nicolas Appert (1749–1841) hit upon the same concept.[39] He kept careful records, maintained the highest standards of hygiene and cleanliness, and used only the freshest ingredients. Having settled on boiling sealed jars at high temperature, which killed bacteria that could cause spoilage, he opened a successful business in 1804 outside Paris. In 1810, Peter Durand, an Englishman with Huguenot origins and connections across the Channel, patented a canning process involving metal cans. It did not immediately take off in Britain, so Durand patented the method in the United States in 1818. In the late 1840s, Allen Taylor and Henry Evans devised machinery for the mass production of metal cans. A decade later, John Landis Mason (1832–1902) invented the glass mason jar for home canning.[40]

William Underwood (1787–1864) founded the most successful early company—one that still thrives—in Boston. He canned mustard and other condiments, then added pickles, marmalade, and later fish and seafood to his line. Underwood sold most of his products to pioneers settling the western United States and made a fortune supplying the Union Army during the Civil War. Gail Borden (1801–74) patented condensed milk in 1856 and also prospered selling canned foods during the conflict.[41]

For many decades in Europe, mostly only soldiers and sailors ate canned foods, given their poor flavor and texture, though France's sardine canneries produced 100,000 tins a year in 1836—and 50 million in the 1880s.[42] Sumptuous displays of canned fare at London's Crystal Palace Exhibition in 1851 thrilled visitors and might have sparked a boom in the product continent wide but for knowledge that tins of meat regularly putrefied and contained disgusting animal remains.[43]

European and American food producers began to experiment and innovate more and more. Small family businesses in England mass-produced brightly decorated tins of biscuits (cookies)—over 50 million pounds a year by the late 1870s. The Fry family chocolate firm in Bristol, England, invented and began marketing chocolate bars in 1847, adding dozens of items to their product list, including chocolate

Easter eggs in 1873.[44] In 1870, Underwood's sons patented a process for grinding, seasoning, and canning meats that they called "deviling," which remains popular. In 1889, the Pearl Milling Company of St Joseph, Missouri, launched the world's first ready-mix processed food, a pancake mix, soon called Aunt Jemima's.[45] Two decades before, a Philadelphia pharmacist named Charles Elmer Hires (1851–1937) began to market a new "temperance drink" he called root beer. It quickly gained popularity in America but never much caught on abroad.[46] In 1885, another pharmacist, John Stith Pemberton (1831–88), of Columbus, Georgia, invented Coca Cola as a cure-all tonic.[47] Sold in bottles from 1894, in subsequent decades it took the entire world by storm—rather like tea and coffee a couple of centuries before, but now nature's existing repertory no longer constrained inventive man.

John Harvey Kellogg (1852–1943), the Seventh-day Adventist director of a sanitarium in Battle Creek, Michigan, invented the world's first commercially successful breakfast cereal—corn flakes—in 1894.[48] His brother, Will Keith Kellogg (1860–1951), after initial collaboration, founded a firm in 1906 that evolved into the Kellogg Company. Meanwhile, a visitor to the sanitarium, Charles William Post (1854–1914), had founded his own cereal company in 1897 and marketed Grape Nuts as his first product. Their successes led to many other experiments with puffing, flaking, and toasting of grains. Innovation in advertising, packaging, and marketing enabled these firms to shake up the entire industry, in fact to help create an entirely new food-processing industry. From the turn of the century, food companies advertised more than any other business sector.

An explosion of processed and scientifically engineered foods followed over the next decades—including baking powder, dried milk and eggs, powdered and flavored gelatin, and packets of soup and gravy mixes. A Japanese-American inventor, Satori Kato, formulated in 1901 and a Belgian-British-American inventor, George Constant Louis Washington (1871–1946), successfully marketed instant coffee beginning in 1910.[49] "Iceberg" lettuce, a crisp varietal cultivated without dark greens or bitterness so as to stay fresh for weeks, appeared on the market in 1903.[50] James Lewis Kraft (1874–1953) invented a pasteurized processed "cheese food" in 1915 and sold some 6 million pounds to the US Army during World War I.[51] A grandson of the original Underwood, thanks to intensive collaboration with a scientist at the Massachusetts Institute of Technology in the late 1890s, showed that heating canned foods at higher temperatures would kill all harmful bacteria and prevent the continued occasional swelling and even explosions of canned products.[52] Their publications benefited the entire industry, which by 1910 turned out some 3 billion cans of food, a few with product labels still familiar today, like Heinz, Campbell's, Van Camp's, and of course Underwood.[53] As a result, by the mid-1920s, few middle-class American women still spent their summers putting up fruits and vegetables. "Food technologists" employed by all the big, vertically integrated and hyper-rational firms ceaselessly developed new products from the same traditional raw materials—according to one calculation, some 1,500 different products were extracted from the noble wheat kernel.[54] Meanwhile, sales departments promoted their adoption by millions of families across America and, gradually, the world.

Purely scientific investigations revolutionized crop yields, though only gradually. Intensive study of the properties of plant heredity by Gregor Mendel (1822–84) in the mid-nineteenth century and by Charles Darwin (1809–82) on plant hybrids in the 1870s prompted William J. Beal (1833–1924), a professor at Michigan Agricultural College (now Michigan State University), to develop by 1880 a higher-yielding hybridized strain of corn through cross-fertilization.[55] By the 1930s, most American farmers had converted to hybrid corn and achieved up to 35 percent higher yields than those using open-pollinated varieties. Overall, technological innovation drove down the number of man-hours needed to sow, cultivate, and harvest 100 bushels of wheat and 100 bushels of corn in the American Midwest from 190 hours in 1930 to 10 hours in 1987.[56]

Icehouses and iceboxes gained popularity in America from the mid-nineteenth century, but the high cost of ice slowed their expansion for industrial use. Australian inventors in the 1870s developed compressed-gas coolers making possible trans-oceanic shipments of meat from Argentina, Australia, and the United States. Clarence Birdseye (1886–1956) used this technology but coupled with ancient lore.[57] While working as a naturalist in Labrador in 1912–15, he learned from the Inuit that fish and meat frozen quickly at extremely low temperatures kept their freshness and quality for months thereafter. He commercialized the process throughout the 1920s and sold his patents to General Foods in 1929, which in 1930 brought out an extensive product line under the Birds Eye brand, including frozen meat, fish, seafood, vegetables, and fruits.

From the invention of sliced bread in 1928 by Otto Rohwedder (1880–1960) of Des Moines to gas ranges that outnumbered coal or wood burners by 1930, all sorts of technological improvements continued to change the way people fed themselves. Grocery chain stores had gained a huge market share, with A&P operating over 3,000 stores in 1915 and a whopping 13,961 stores by 1925.[58] Homemakers avidly tried out new recipes discovered in magazines designed for them specifically, like *Ladies Home Journal* and *Good Housekeeping*.[59] Eating habits that people today in developed countries would recognize began to put down roots. Even fast-food restaurant chains and franchises began to sprout up, starting in 1921 with White Castle and A&W.[60] By 1933, Americans bought 80 percent of their bread presliced.[61]

Intellectuals and culinary snobs have bewailed the advent of "industrial alimentation," the loss of traditional meal-taking, processed foods lacking taste and nutritional value, the replacement of fresh food with fast food, and vegetables engineered more for the convenience of shippers than for the enjoyment of consumers.[62] No doubt, fresh and natural strawberries surpass those frozen, canned, or genetically modified in flavor and texture. And, in the long run, obesity and diabetes have become immense public health problems. Yet surely frozen or canned are preferable to none at all. The critics of modern gastronomic ways cannot easily deny, moreover, the numerous advantages brought to contemporary life by technology and entrepreneurship. For one thing, there is the explosion in the quantity of available food, in the range of choices and styles of eating, and in the convenience with which people can nourish themselves. Pouring cereal and milk into a bowl takes vastly less time than cooking bacon and eggs or even porridge—and it is as healthy as the latter and more so than the former. Just as important, these new domestic traditions have gained for hundreds of millions of people greater control over their cultural destiny, enabling them to select or invent a huge variety of lifestyles, from traditional to anti-traditional or combinations of both. The productiveness of the new farming methods also offered millions of immigrants to the United States the chance to own their own land and their own business. All these transformations wrought social revolutions that Chapter 14 will explore in detail.

Harnessing thunderbolts

While inventors, entrepreneurs, managers, and scientists transformed how and what people ate in the West (but especially in America), others brought about revolutions in nearly every other facet of material existence. These changes mostly occurred in parallel, though figuring out how to exploit the power of electrons began earliest.

After Franklin's research, scholars and scientists throughout the West investigated the properties of electricity.[63] Charles-Augustin de Coulomb (1736–1806) defined mathematically the attraction and repulsion caused by static electricity. Luigi Galvani (1737–98) proved in 1792 that a form of electric current animates the nervous systems of animals. His colleague Alessandro Volta (1745–1827) constructed in 1800 the world's first battery; it produced constant electric current. In the same year, two Englishmen, William Nicholson (1753–1815) and Anthony Carlisle (1768–1842), used a battery to decompose water into hydrogen and oxygen, the first recorded instance of electrolysis. In 1820, Hans Christian Ørsted (1777–1851), a Dane, demonstrated that electric current produces a magnetic field.

Among the early investigators, an Englishman with little formal schooling but a brilliant knack for experimentation, Michael Faraday (1791–1867), advanced human understanding of electricity and electromagnetism more than anyone.[64] He proved, for example, the unitary nature of all the various forms of electricity—work that won him membership in over 70 scientific societies around the Western world. Most important from a practical point of view, in 1821 he demonstrated how electromagnetism could induce circular motion in metal objects, an insight that led later in the century to electric motors.

Meanwhile, electricity powered a communications revolution. Joseph Henry (1797–1878), the first director of the Smithsonian Institution, took the invention of an electromagnet by the Englishman William Sturgeon (1783–1850) and increased its potency by tightly coiling insulated wire hundreds of times around a piece of iron and passing an electric current through it.[65] In 1831, he devised an electromagnet weighing less than 60 pounds that supported a weight exceeding two tons. Back in 1821, André-Marie Ampère (1775–1836) had proposed to use electrical current to send encoded signals across wires, yet no inventor had managed to configure such a device because of the tendency of electrical current to lose force over even relatively short lengths of wire. Through his experiments, Henry discovered that a battery connected in series increases the electrical driving force (voltage). He went on to construct a telegraphic mechanism but only used it for classroom demonstrations.[66]

It did not take long for entrepreneurs to harness the potential of the new device. Scientists in Germany experimented with short-distance telegraphic services, but two British inventors, Charles Wheatstone (1802–75) and William Cooke (1806–79), established the world's first commercial service in 1839. The system gained popular acclaim in 1845 when its use enabled the police to capture a murderer, John Tawell (1784–1845), within hours of his crime.[67] The previous year, thanks to congressional funding, Samuel Morse (1791–1872), a Yale graduate and successful painter, sent a message via telegraph from Washington, D.C., to Baltimore. He obviously did not invent the technology, but he did more than anyone to make it viable, not least because of his user-friendly binary code.[68]

Telegraphic services spread quickly throughout the major European countries and the United States. Within 8 years, some 20 American companies operated across 17,000 miles of telegraph lines running along railroad rights of way and linking cities from the Eastern Seaboard to the Midwest and down to New Orleans using the Morse Code. The web of lines expanded swiftly and in every direction. By 1862, they extended 150,000 miles worldwide, including 48,000 in the United States.[69] By then, the Western Union Telegraph Company had come on line, and the New York Associated Press (not the predecessor of today's AP) had established its wire service.[70] Links ran to California (1861), London (1866), India (1870), and Australia (1872) (see Map 12.2). The invention especially benefited business, its main patron. For the first time in history, businessmen could coordinate moneymaking operations across vast distances in real time, fabulously boosting efficiency and productivity and spurring further innovation. Swift could not have built his vertically integrated empire without the telegraph, nor could his imitators in a dozen other industrial sectors.

The general newspaper business flourished too, as journalists strived to bring out local and international news as fast as possible in the simplest ("telegraphic") language. People had access to more information about more topics of current events than ever before. Speculation and rumors about such events naturally declined precipitously.[71] Politicians had to choose their words more carefully, a phenomenon simply intensified today when an indiscreet utterance caught on a digital video recorder can doom a political campaign, as former Sen. George Allen discovered to his chagrin in 2006.[72]

Major technical improvements in the early 1870s—making it possible to send one and then two messages simultaneously back and forth—rendered the breakthrough all the more world changing. The man responsible for these improvements, perhaps the single greatest inventor in history, channeled the new energy in myriad pathways.

Thomas Alva Edison (1847–1931) grew up home-schooled by his mother in Port Huron, Michigan.[73] A telegraph operator from age 17 and an inveterate tinkerer, he filed his first patent—for an electric vote recorder—at 21 and made a small fortune from his invention of a stock-ticker 2 years later. In fact, Edison proved a shrewd businessman, fierce competitor, and brilliant manager, as well as a gifted innovator. His phonograph (1877), while superseded by the gramophone of Emile Berliner (1851–1929), was the world's first recording device and marks the commencement of the home-entertainment industry. Soon, ordinary people could listen to their favorite music at will, just like princes and magnates of old. Edison's motion-picture camera (1891) opened wondrous vistas of popular visual experience and of course launched one of the great and most distinctively modern industries. In all, Edison obtained 1,093 US patents plus many more in other countries. How could one man have accomplished so much?

After Edison sold the rights to his quadruplex telegraph to Western Union in 1874 for 30,000 dollars, he created the world's first industrial research laboratory in Menlo Park (now called Edison), New Jersey. He staffed an immense facility

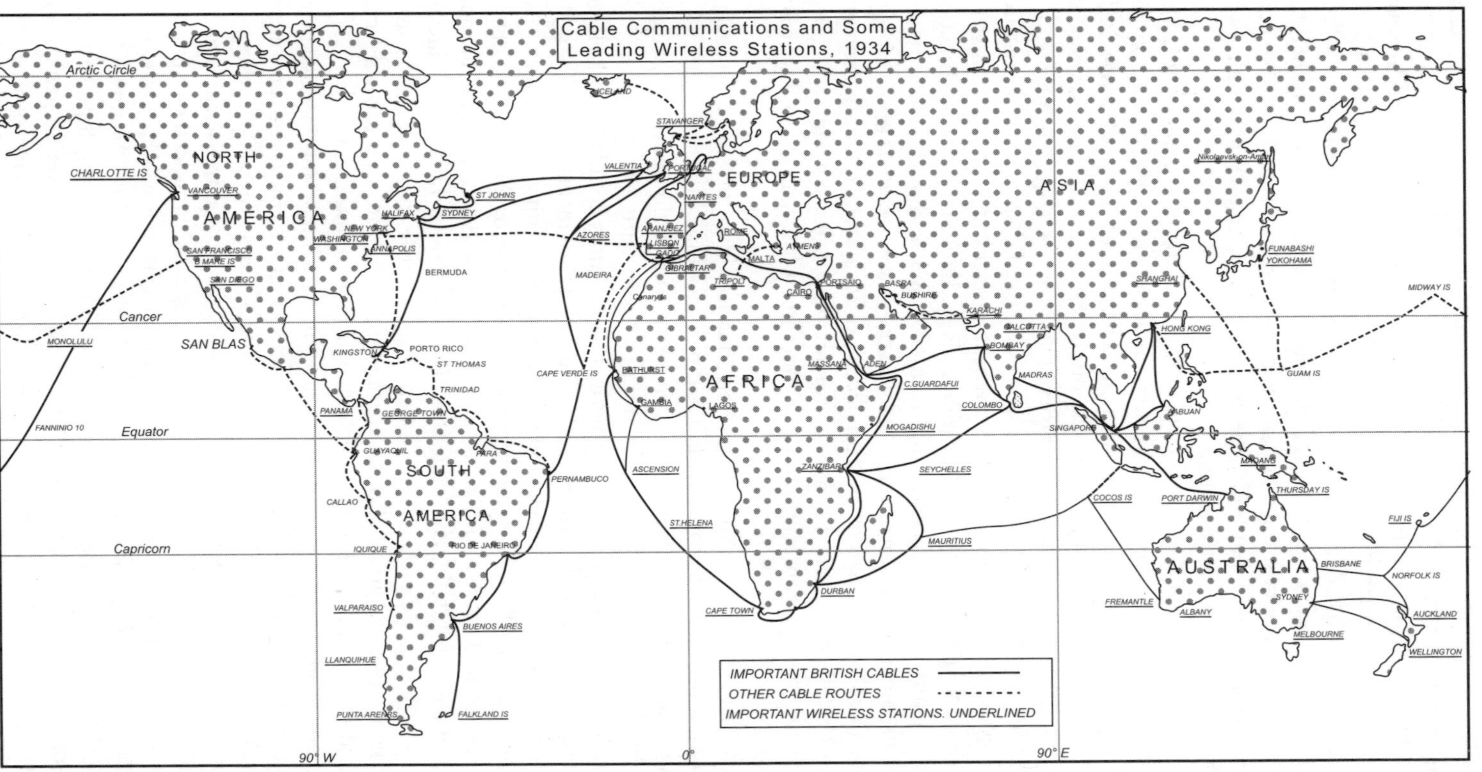

MAP 12.2 *The network of cables expanded steadily decade by decade.*

occupying two city blocks with numerous technicians and engineers and furnished it with tens of thousands of chemicals, materials, research instruments, and tools of all kinds.[74] Here, Edison and his team, who mostly acted as his research assistants, made their greatest contributions to human development, including a commercially viable electric light bulb (1877) and a system for generating and distributing electrical power (1880). These advances dispelled the gloomy darkness that man had known for long portions of the day since he had trod the earth. Light—beaming, flashing, brilliant, or soft and gentle, but under the power of each person with a light switch—this had the Western inventor wrought.

Edison himself founded the first electric utility, the Edison Illuminating Company, in 1880, and 2 years later he (or his agents) launched the world's first commercial electric-power plants at Holborn Viaduct in London and on Pearl Street in lower Manhattan.[75] They delivered 110 volts direct current (DC) to several dozen customers using steam-powered generators. The projects required massive capital outlays and huge efforts of engineering. In New York, Edison had to bury 100,000 feet of wiring to deliver the power, invent a workable electric meter, and construct six steam-powered dynamos, each one four times bigger than any other yet functioning. Even so, the plant delivered power only to a six-block radius and lost money for 2 years. Subsequently, Edison established electrical service in several more cities on the East Coast, while dozens of firms licensed his system for power generation around the United States and Europe. Unfortunately, direct current, which Edison insisted vehemently on promoting, can only operate at low-voltage and therefore at short distances, within a mile or two.

Meanwhile, a brilliant Serbian-American engineer and inventor, Nikola Tesla (1856–1943), a onetime employee of Edison, had developed the more efficient and versatile alternating current (AC) system.[76] A generator could deliver AC current at extremely high voltage, then it could be ramped down with a transformer to levels appropriate for home or business use. By this method, a utility could transmit electricity over very long distances. In 1888, Tesla found employment with Westinghouse Electric & Manufacturing Company in Pittsburgh and a staunch supporter in George Westinghouse (1846–1914).[77] Westinghouse had invented the railway air brake in 1869 at age 22, had made a fortune as this indispensable device became the industry standard, and had mounted a challenge to Edison in 1886 by building an alternative AC power generation and distribution system. After a battle royal, Westinghouse won the day. When Edison General Electric merged with Thomson-Houston Electric to form General Electric in 1892, they switched over to AC equipment.

Electric power generating plants got a huge boost from serial improvements by dozens of engineers, mathematicians, and scientists in several countries on water-wheel designs. The first important breakthrough came in 1826, when Benoît Fourneyron (1802–67) developed an efficient outward-flow impulse turbine, whose curved blades driven by high-pressure jets of water greatly enhanced power delivery. Thanks to further improvements, the device gained continuously in force, reaching 800 hp in one unit installed by the Paris water works in 1854.[78] Meanwhile, James B. Francis (1815–92), an English immigrant to Massachusetts, developed an inward-flow reaction turbine with even greater mechanical efficiency (over 90 percent). Later in the century, electrical engineers harnessed both types of turbine for hydroelectric power generation throughout the world.

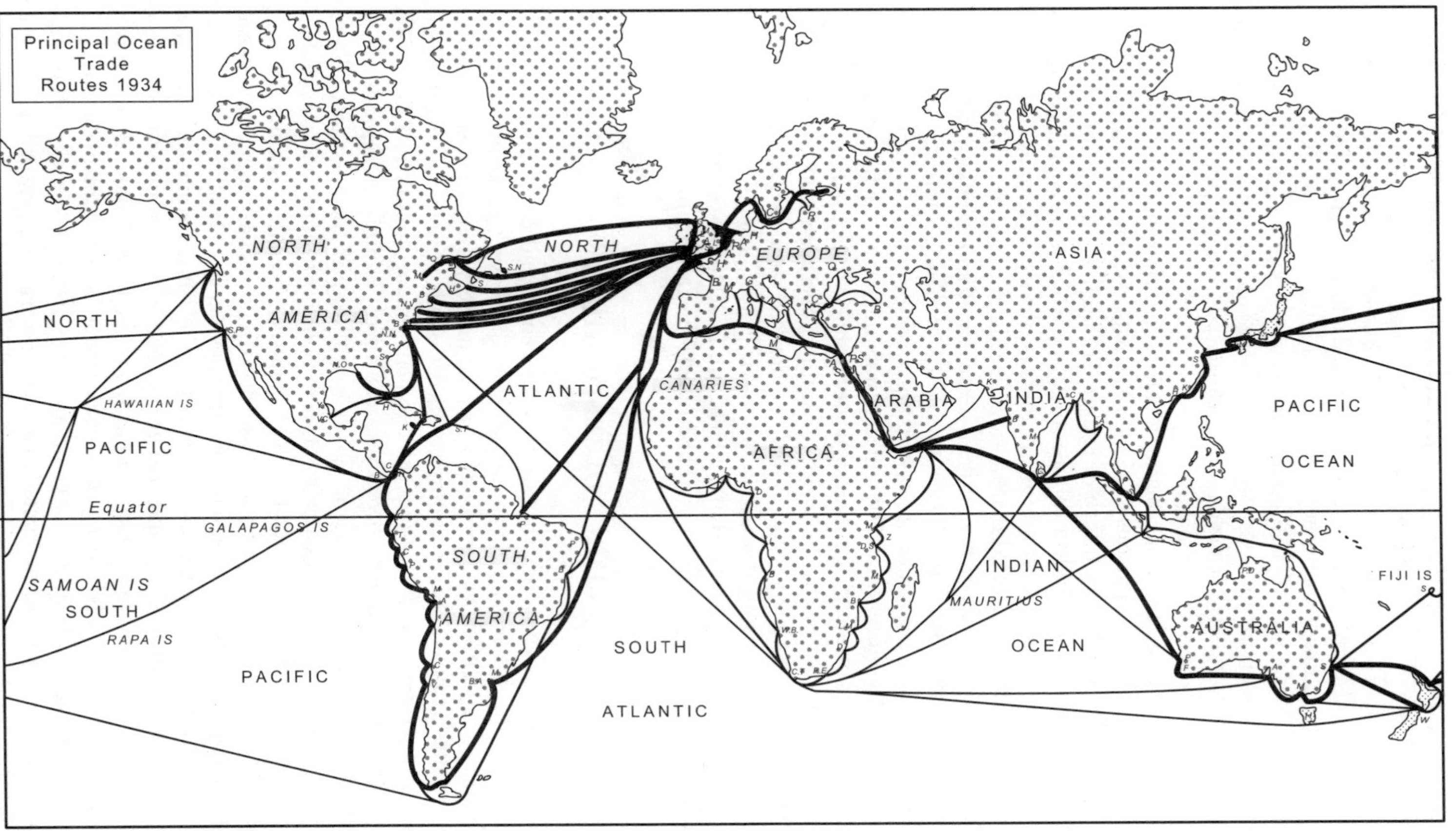

MAP 12.3 *The steam-driven turbine engine revolutionized commercial shipping.*

One of the first—if not the first—hydroelectric plants in the world began operation on the Fox River at Appleton, Wisconsin, in 1882, running a patented "Elmer" turbine to generate DC current under license from Edison.[79] A decade and a half later, Tesla designed and Westinghouse built, with financial backing from J. P. Morgan and other investors, ten massive Fourneyron turbines on the US side of Niagara Falls to produce, as noted above, 100,000 hp and 75 megawatts of AC electric power—by far the world's greatest generating capacity.[80] In the long run, however, the Francis turbine came to dominate the field—for instance, powering China's Three Gorges Dam, the world's biggest.[81]

Two years after Edison began generating electricity using Watt-and-Boulton-style steam engines, Charles A. Parsons (1854–1931), a British engineer and the son of an earl, invented a steam-driven turbine engine. Traditional steam engines generated energy by reciprocal (back-and-forth) piston action, which crankshafts converted to the rotary motion needed to turn most mechanical devices. Turbines, already more efficient by themselves, delivered that motion directly and therefore more efficiently still. Parsons built the first turbine-driven steamship, the *Turbinia*, which in 1897 attained the astonishing speed of 34.5 knots (39.7 mph).[82] Soon, the British government commissioned turbine engines for all its warships, including the first turbine-powered battleship, HMS *Dreadnought* (1906), at 21 knots (24 mph) the fastest warship on the high seas. The same year, the enormous ocean liners *Lusitania* and *Mauretania*, began service, clocking nearly 24 knots (27.6 mph) average speed on transatlantic crossings. The new engine revolutionized commercial and military shipping (see Map 12.3). It also contributed mightily to electric-power generation. By the 1920s, coal-fired steam turbines operated at 100,000 hp. In 1943, the world's largest unit, installed in Chicago, produced 280,000 hp and 215 megawatts of electricity.[83]

Flashes of inspiration

Inventors throughout the nineteenth century conceived and developed dozens and even hundreds of devices aimed at saving labor, increasing efficiency, expanding manufacturing capacities, and performing an immense variety of tasks. From the mid-nineteenth century, Americans proved exceptionally inventive, in part because of labor scarcity and in part because of excellent patent laws. The Patent Office Act of 1836 required inventors to register detailed plans and descriptions of their innovations, which enabled other innovators to build upon their advances. Patents certified for novelty became tradable assets, an incentive to innovation available in no other country.[84] Similarly, since no other country's patent procedures provided such detailed descriptions and analysis of novelty, US patents automatically gained a "presumptive right to its claims, and immediately a value in the market."[85] Obtaining a patent, moreover, cost far more in France and the United Kingdom than in the United States, where ordinary people had greater access to legal protection for their innovations.[86] No wonder the number of patents in the United States began to surge in the 1860s, reaching 20,000 per year three decades later.[87] A mania of invention gripped the country, as thousands of clever tinkerers strained to make a fortune by devising socially useful and commercially viable discoveries. In the words of Abraham Lincoln, patent law "added the fuel of interest to the fire of genius."[88]

Describing all such devices for even a decade of the nineteenth century would fill many pages, but a few notable ones deserve mention, including the revolver (1836), Daguerreotype photography (1839), the vulcanized rubber pneumatic tire (1845), elevator safety brakes and the bicycle (1861), dynamite (1866), paper-strip photographic film and the mechanical cash register (1884), and the machine gun (1885), among so many others.[89] The person who first conceived an invention, first built it, or who refined it significantly might ultimately get the credit, but nearly every innovation required the work of many hands and the inspiration of many minds.

A dozen inventors across Europe and the United States tinkered for several decades with designs for typing until Christopher Sholes in Milwaukee, Wisconsin, developed a commercially viable typewriter in 1868, which the Remington Corporation soon began to market.[90] The device transformed business, record keeping, and the processing of documents. A similar scenario unfolded with the sewing machine, though Americans logged nearly all of the early developments and launched most of the early manufacturers in the 1850s and 1860s.[91] Thanks to innovation in design, sales, distribution, marketing, and service, the Singer Company completely dominated the worldwide market by 1900, selling over 500,000 machines annually.[92] These devices revolutionized the production of garments, both commercially and in the home. Henceforth, more and more people could clothe themselves according to comfort, taste, preference, and fashion.

Electric motors created an explosion of innovative possibilities. Tesla deserves the credit for this breakthrough.[93] Working at the Westinghouse industrial laboratories in Pittsburgh, in 1888 he devised the first practical multiphase AC electric motor (all previous electric motors had used DC current, which made them far less versatile and efficient). A few years later, Westinghouse brought out a rotary fan running Tesla's motor.[94] It powered a welter of other new devices in the following years. H. Cecil Booth (1871–1955), a British civil engineer, patented the first electric vacuum cleaner in 1901. In 1907, an American janitor, James Spangler (1848–1915), built a model with rotary brushes and sold his patent to W. H. Hoover (1849–1932), who forged a commercial empire and established the world's best-known brand in the business.[95] Within a few decades, entrepreneurs and inventors launched dozens of electric-motor-driven appliances and electric household devices, including coffee grinders (1898), air conditioners (1902), washing machines and electric mixers (1908), refrigerators (1914), handheld hair dryers (1920), blenders and electric kettles (1922), dishwashers (1927), can openers (1931), and many more. A huge market opened up in the United States as electric service steadily fell in price and spread to more and more homes—70 percent by 1930.[96]

Businesses producing electric laborsaving devices frequently marketed them as "electric servants," which, as a General Electric advertisement suggested in 1917, one could depend on "to do the muscle part of the washing, ironing, cleaning and sewing."[97] The same firm also promoted its innovations as "hygienic, uniform and economical"—in other words, as even superior to human servants.[98] One can only with great difficulty dispute such claims, no matter how self-interested, by industrial firms seeking to transform Western households. Electric appliances undoubtedly made women's work vastly easier, actually empowered them in the sense of conferring on them control over powerful devices, freed up more of their time for other pursuits (though higher standards of cleanliness and household management swallowed some of the extra time), and helped promote women's liberation (see Chapter 14).

Electric motors transformed not only the household and business, but also urban life, industry, and society more broadly. Steam-powered elevators operated from the mid-nineteenth century in industrial work sites. In 1854, Elisha Graves Otis (1811–61), an American craftsman and inventor, showed off a safety elevator at the New York World's Fair by cutting the rope holding the platform he stood on and, to gasps from the crowd, plunged only a few inches before the automatic brake saved his life. His elevator business skyrocketed.[99] In 1880, the inventor and industrialist Werner von Siemens (1816–92) assembled the first electric-motor-powered elevator.[100] Over the following decade, numerous inventors, government inspectors, and manufacturers improved the speed, safety, convenience, and efficiency of electric elevators.[101] They now made it possible radically to transform cityscapes, especially in America.

In 1857, Henry Bessemer (1813–98), an English engineer and inventor, devised a method that dramatically reduced the cost of producing steel. During the Civil War, an American mechanical engineer, Alexander Lyman Holley (1832–82), redesigned the Bessemer process, increasing its efficiency and laying the foundation for the swift growth of the American steel industry.[102] Abundant and inexpensive steel, coupled with efficient electric elevators and reinforced concrete (invented in France in the 1850s), encouraged architects and engineers, first in Chicago and then in New York, to build up instead of out.[103] Chicago's Home Insurance Building, erected on a steel skeleton frame but without exterior load-bearing masonry walls, rose 12 stories in 1885. Over the next few decades, architects and investors vied with each other to see who could outbuild the others.[104] At first, Chicago dominated when its Masonic Building soared 21 stories in 1895. Then New York took the lead, with the 47-story Singer Building (1908), the 60-story Woolworth Building (1919), and the awesome 102-story Empire State Building (1931) with its 67 high-speed electric elevators.[105]

Vertical development made sense for two main reasons. Water and rapid urban development hemmed in the two core areas where tall buildings first reached for the skies. More importantly, the captains of the new, vertically integrated industries wanted not only their often vast management teams, but also allied business services—printing, accounting, advertising, and the like—under one roof and of easy access.[106] They naturally found it more convenient to move by elevator from floor to floor in a high-rise than throughout some vast one-story edifice or from building to building.

Engineering genius combined with steel enabled city planners to master their environments in other spectacular ways. From the 1,500-foot tubular steel Eads Bridge spanning the Mississippi River at St Louis (1868–74) to the triumphal 1,600-foot steel-cable suspension bridge linking Brooklyn and Manhattan (1869–83), daring entrepreneurs and visionary engineers apparently found few challenges too daunting to tackle.[107]

Electric motors helped transform the urban environment in another fundamental way. In most big cities in Europe and America, horse-drawn trams ran on steel rails. Electric motors could in theory drive several cars at once while eliminating hundreds and thousands of horses from city streets. The first successful design was by Frank Sprague (1857–1934), a manufacturer of high-speed elevators who had worked for Edison. In 1880, he devised a system for transmitting electricity from overhead cables through a flexible arm attached to the roof of streetcars.[108] In late

1887, he won a lucrative but daunting contract to build a 12-mile street railway system operating 40 cars in hilly Richmond, Virginia. An inveterate optimist with astonishing determination, Sprague overcame a dozen obstacles and had the system up and running early in 1888. Two years later, Edison bought him out and took part in a scramble to build electric streetcar networks throughout America and Europe—22,576 miles of track and 987 urban railway systems completed in the United States alone by 1902.[109] Over the following decade, interurban electric railways, especially in the American East and Midwest, also flourished.

Entrepreneurs began to harness electric motors for industrial uses starting in 1894.[110] In fact, nearly any factory using water or steam power could function more efficiently on electricity. One could build such factories anywhere and not only near a large source of water. Moreover, whereas a single giant steam engine delivered power to all the machines in an entire factory by means of innumerable belts, often running up several floors, every machine powered by electricity could have its own motor and factories could therefore be built all on one level making it vastly easier to transport materials throughout the structure. The absence of high-tension belts, which could snap, made the work place vastly safer.[111] Most plants ran AC current, though DC proved more effective for steel-rolling operations. Industrial power generation surged in the decade after 1899 from 16,891 motors putting out a half-million hp to 388,854 motors producing 4,817,140 hp.[112] Finally, small electric motors made it possible to design and build a wide variety of hand tools—saws, drills, planers, sanders, routers, and the like—rendering crafts- and tradesmen immensely more productive.

Electricity also made voice transmission possible. Thanks to designs by Alexander Graham Bell (1847–1922) and others, in 1904 thousands of independent companies had established local telephone exchanges across the United States and Europe.[113] In 1907, some 5.5 million telephones operated in the United States.[114] Americans living in big cities had already taken to using the device for personal communications, something that horrified European visitors.[115] Long-distance lines emerged slowly, linking New York with Chicago in 1892, with Denver in 1911, and with San Francisco (thanks to electronic amplifiers) in 1915. The various telephone systems functioned in parallel without connections between them, so that subscribers often had to purchase telephone service from more than one carrier, at least until AT&T began to impose monopoly control from 1913. The development of automatic switchboards made it possible to dial local calls directly in most places beginning in the early 1920s. Convenient and widespread telephony became a part of everyday life.

If steam engines conferred on a handful of industrialists the power of pharaohs and enabled ordinary people to travel at "lightning speed" across land and sea, electricity endowed them with previously unimaginable capacities and opened to them awesome vistas. It illuminated their world more brilliantly than any king's in former times, enabled them to chill and preserve food at will, to scale tall buildings in an instant, and to record sounds and sights bygone artists could only dream of, and provided comforts of cooling and heating at the flip of a switch that no human had ever experienced—in a word, harnessing electric current radically empowered mankind. Electrical devices also made possible the West's next great technological development—one at least as world changing if not more so—the mass-produced automobile.

Explosions in a box

As early as the seventeenth century, the French scientist Denis Papin (1647–ca. 1712) conceived of an engine driven by gunpowder exploding in a cylinder.[116] Over the next century and a half, dozens and perhaps even hundreds of inventors developed this idea, substituting various inflammable gases and liquids for gunpowder, until Nikolaus Otto (1832–91), a German tinkerer, built a practical four-stroke internal combustion engine in 1876. It compressed and combined coal-derived "illuminating gas" with air to produce a powerful explosion on every third stroke. Whereas steam engines wasted a lot of energy burning fuel, generating steam, and transmitting the resultant power, the exploding fuel of the Otto engine delivered all its energy directly to a piston-driven crankshaft. By 1900, some 200,000 of them powered small factories, printing shops, pumping stations, and electrical generators throughout the West, especially in the United States, Great Britain, and Germany. Hundreds of inventors worked to perfect the design, adding electric ignition systems, experimenting with liquid fuels, figuring out the proper fuel-air mixture, and ultimately building a model sufficiently light and powerful to drive a carriage.

Major advances toward the automobile took place in Germany beginning in the 1880s. Gottlieb Daimler (1834–1900) worked for years as production manager for Otto until he launched his own firm in 1882, taking with him the brilliant engineer and inventor, Wilhelm Maybach (1846–1929). Together in 1885, they—and quite independently Karl Benz (1844–1929)—built the first viable motorcars.[117] Many other firms throughout Europe and the United States entered the field, bringing intense competition. In 1893, Maybach built a device—the carburetor—that sprayed a fine jet of gasoline into the cylinder on the first, or intake, stroke. Meanwhile, Benz invented a spark ignition system. In 1902, Robert Bosch (1861–1942) and his chief engineer, Gottlob Honold (1876–1923), invented an efficient ignition system driven by an electrical magneto with a high-voltage spark plug capable of igniting hundreds of times per minute.

Another clever invention that appeared in the same year as Daimler's and Benz's automobiles gave their development a solid boost. The "safety" bicycle, put on the market in 1885 by the English inventor John Kemp Starley (1854–1901), became very popular and thus created a big demand for smoother roads and whetted consumers' appetites for more powerful mechanical vehicles.[118] As bicycles developed, they spurred valuable technical advances directly relevant to the automobile industry, including steel-tube framing, ball and roller bearings, wire-spoked wheels, pneumatic tires, and chain-driven drive trains. Many bicycle manufacturers, in fact, tried to manufacture motorcycles and automobiles.

The automobile industry rocketed forward after the turn of the century. In 1903, Henry Ford (1863–1947) founded the Ford Motor Company. Five years later, he put his Model T on the market. The following year, American car manufacturers broke the 100,000 mark and, 5 years after that, the million mark.[119]

Many firms incorporated major and minor technical improvements, like transmission systems and the "steering knuckle" (1902), which allowed the front wheels to pivot while the axle remained fixed.[120] The following decade witnessed key advances in automotive development. The electric starter, devised by Charles F. Kettering (1876–1958) in 1912, made it possible for anyone to start an automobile easily and conveniently.[121] The following year, Vincent Bendix (1881–1945) invented the Bendix drive, a clutching mechanism that enabled the electric starter to disengage from an engine after ignition.[122] Many other innovations followed, including hydraulic four-wheel brake systems. American inventors, scientists, and entrepreneurs brought to life all of these advances and many more besides.[123]

The concept of "scientific management," developed after 1900 by another American, Frederick Winslow Taylor (1856–1915), contributed to mass-production systems.[124] The method consisted in observing, analyzing, simplifying, and standardizing the tasks of workers. The overall purpose was to find the "One Best Way" to accomplish any job. Taylor, perhaps most famously, analyzed worker performance with "time and motion studies." Frank Gilbreth (1868–1924), another American, took such analyses to a higher level. Using an open-shutter still camera, he photographed workers accomplishing their tasks with small lights attached to their arms and hands. Gilbreth would then study each photo in the series looking for useless movements. Such studies transformed the workplace, making it more and more efficient and driving down the costs of production 10 or even 20 fold. As labor became more productive, wages increased dramatically, raising the standard of living of nearly the entire society. Even relatively unskilled workers could become highly paid machine operators, the largest occupational group in every industrial country between 1910 and 1940. Simultaneously, the number of trained managers increased, opening up a vast number of white-collar jobs.

These studies influenced Ford's revolutionary development of the assembly-line production model.[125] So did, it seems, the Chicago meat-packing industry's "disassembly line" and probably his employment at a Detroit power station, which taught him the importance of continuous flow in the production process.[126] Every element of this new system had existed for years—interchangeable parts, conveyor belts, specialization of work, high precision of output, and scientific management—Ford simply combined them in a systematic and creative way. His goal: to produce high-quality, durable, mechanically simple vehicles at low cost. Ford began in 1913 with a moving assembly line, manned by 29 workers, who drove down the time to assemble a magneto from 18 minutes to 5. Within a year, Ford's employees constructed a chassis along a line 250 feet long in 90 minutes instead of over 12 hours.[127] With the prospect of unimaginable success before him, Ford boosted his employees' minimum wage to 5 dollars a day—up from an average of 2.25 dollars.[128] Other companies had no choice but to follow suit.

The output of Model T's expanded phenomenally from only 170,000 in 1912 to 10 million in 1924, while the price fell from 850 dollars in 1908 to only 290 dollars in 1924. Now, Ford was producing half the cars in the world.[129] To keep up with Ford's demand for parts, suppliers had to adopt the assembly line—as, of course, did the competition. Ford's vertically integrated business controlled many elements of supply and distribution, creating huge cost savings and vast economies of scale. Ford's successes drove him to innovate in areas beyond car manufacturing. Thus, his company invented a method for pouring glass into a continuous sheet and moving it along a workbench for rolling, grinding, polishing, and cutting into standard sizes of plate glass.[130] In the 1920s, the steel industry adopted a similar method for rolling out sheet steel. Soon, workers were assembling consumer goods of all kinds on conveyor belts, again to huge cost savings and price decreases.[131]

Ford's competitors counterattacked with clever designs, frills, lots of optional features, annual changes in styling, and a hierarchy of brands for "every purse and purpose," for example, in the case of General Motors, from Chevrolet to Cadillac. By 1929, GM turned out more cars than any other company in America—32.3 percent of the US total.[132] (American companies as a whole accounted for 85 percent of world production in that year.)[133] The whole enterprise fueled a boom in consumer spending, as workers earned more money and could afford more goods, further stimulating economic growth, in a virtuous cycle of advancement. By emphasizing advances in styling and marketing over continuous technological improvements, however, the American automobile industry paved the way toward its eventual decline, though that outcome lay far in the future.[134]

Mass production made it possible to increase the number of gasoline-powered tractors from around 10,000 in 1910 throughout the United States to nearly 90,000 in 1917.[135] Fewer horses and mules to feed meant more land for food crops. Outfitted with dozens of farm implements and steadily improved by further technological innovations, tractors and other farm machinery cut in half the time spent on most field operations. Further mechanization of farms freed up labor for participation in other sectors of the economy.

Commercial vehicles, in particular trucks, had developed more slowly than automobiles, but World War I demonstrated their worth and spurred further development.[136] If only 1,400 trucks and buses had plied the roads in America in 1905, their number exceeded 1 million by 1920.[137] The figures continued to increase year by year, thanks to Goodyear's invention of a pneumatic tire for trucks in 1916,[138] buses designed specifically to transport people in the 1920s, the rapid expansion of highway networks, and serial improvements to diesel engines in both Europe and the United States. Commercial trucks drew people in even the remotest locations into the broader economy, and large diesel buses gave lower-income people more options for travel and transport.

More efficient, cheaper to operate, less temperamental, longer-lived, and able to pull far heavier loads than gas-powered internal combustion engines, the diesel engine revolutionized the entire world of large vehicles.[139] From fire trucks to tanks, from locomotives to submarines, and from ocean liners to cargo ships, they all gradually converted to diesel. Diesel locomotives, which came into widespread use in the 1940s, cost up to 30 percent less to operate on an annual basis than steam engines. They were more versatile, too, and so fewer were needed for the same amount of work. Ships gained substantial extra cargo space, thanks to the elimination of both coalbunker and the crew formerly needed to run the fire-room. Operators in all large transportation branches realized similar savings and efficiencies, increasing the overall wealth of all Western societies.

One final triumph made possible by the internal combustion engine remains to mention—flight.[140] For several decades before 1903, inventors, scientists, engineers, and mathematicians had demonstrated and tested its feasibility, gathered and assembled materials, and attempted hundreds of designs and constructions in the hope of soaring into the heavens. Wilbur (1867–1912) and Orville (1871–1948) Wright spent 7 years designing and testing a gasoline-powered bi-plane with a carefully designed propeller and—their most important innovation—a wing and rudder mechanism enabling a pilot to control its movements on three axes. Starting with a 59-second flight at Kitty Hawk on 17 December 1903 (their third that day), man began to master the skies. In 1909, Louis Blériot (1872–1936) flew across the English Channel, spurring other pilots to attempt ever more daring records and engineers to develop faster, larger, and more powerful aircraft.[141] The next big advance came with the design and production of gas turbine or turbojet engines in Germany and Great Britain, in 1939 and 1941, respectively, as a necessity of war.[142]

The age of the brilliant craftsmen-inventor was waning and that of university-trained scientific researchers was commencing. In the clearest sign of this shift, German—and then many other Western—universities shifted their focus from teaching to pure and applied research. Neither of the Wright brothers had graduated from high school. By contrast, Rudolf Diesel (1858–1913), who graduated from the Technical University of Munich with highest honors, designed and built his engine from principles of thermodynamics.[143] He first deduced theoretically that ultrahigh compression could cause a fuel-and-air mixture to ignite before he proceeded to the drawing board. The emergence of electrical engineering programs in European and American universities beginning in 1882 and an increase in the number of students majoring in mechanical, electrical, and later chemical engineering to tens of thousands by the 1920s ensured a large pool of technical expertise.[144] (The Massachusetts Institute of Technology offered the world's first 4-year chemical engineering curriculum in 1888.)[145] Clever tinkering, experimentation, and flashes of insight could resolve many electrical and mechanical challenges but few of those posed by the far more complex, yet ultimately highly rewarding, realms of chemistry and electronics, in which technological revolutions had already begun.

Revolutions in chemistry

The industrial production of valuable chemical substances like sulfuric acid began in Western Europe in the mid-eighteenth century. New products often emerged from existing industries, as when sulfuric acid combined with common salt was found to yield sodium sulfate, a key ingredient in detergents. In the nineteenth century, chemists isolated chemical elements through electrolysis and devised such processes as electroplating and the production of aluminum.[146] In seeking improvements to the manufacture of aluminum, a Canadian engineer working in North Carolina hit upon a commercial method for producing calcium carbide in 1892. This discovery proved an industrial and scientific boon, because three decades earlier Friedrich Wöhler (1800–82) had figured out how to hydrolyze calcium carbide to produce acetylene, a key source of organic chemicals. In other words, researchers and technical experts advanced man's mastery of chemical processes and properties in every direction with many lucrative industrial applications.

Chemists and entrepreneurs concocted entirely new substances throughout the nineteenth century. In 1839 in Massachusetts, Charles Goodyear (1800–60), after years of experiments that ruined him financially and landed him in debtors' prison, figured out how to give shape and solidity to latex by heat- and pressure-treating it with sulfur.[147] "Vulcanized" rubber proved an excellent material for manufacturing rain gear, weatherproofing and insulating materials, and eventually tires. (Goodyear died many years before an entrepreneur founded the tire company that bears his name.)[148]

An American inventor, John Wesley Hyatt (1837–1920), patented the first industrial plastic, celluloid, in 1869 and 1870. Produced by a mixture of nitrocellulose, camphor, and common solvents, it worked best as a thin film, in particular, in photography and for motion pictures.[149] Dozens of chemists labored from mid-century seeking a way to produce fiber from nitrocellulose, succeeding only in the 1890s with a product that came to be known as rayon.[150]

Leo Baekeland (1863–1944), a Belgian who earned a PhD in chemistry, taught at the university level, and then emigrated to the United States, invented another commercially significant early plastic.[151] After selling his patented Velox photographic paper to Kodak for 1 million dollars, he developed a method in 1909 for converting carbolic acid and formaldehyde into a cheap, strong, durable, and purely synthetic plastic that he called Bakelite. Advertised as "the material of a thousand uses," it was fashioned into cups, plates, billiard balls, combs, jewelry, and many other objects, including telephones and electrical insulators because it resists heat and does not conduct electricity. Baekeland, unlike so many inventors, became a multimillionaire. Over the following decades, researchers discovered dozens more plastic and other synthetic substances, including polyethylene, styrene, polystyrene, vinyl polymers, nylon, and silicone.[152]

More and more, professional chemists—particularly in Germany—made most of the advances. Research laboratories at universities and government-funded institutes worked systematically through all the known elements and substances beginning in the 1820s.[153] Many studied the by-products of the coal-distillation process, including August von Hofmann (1818–92), a brilliant and passionate scientist, who headed London's Royal College of Chemistry for nearly two decades.[154] In 1856, an 18-year-old student at the college, William Henry Perkin (1838–1907), discovered inadvertently that a chemical reaction with aniline, a by-product of coal tar, yielded a bright purple synthetic dye. It was an awesome breakthrough, because the color was beautiful—in fact the height of fashion in Paris and London at the time—and organic dyes in that hue faded much faster. More enterprising than his mentor, Perkin made a fortune. He also contributed advancements in medicine, perfume, food technology, explosives, and photography.[155] Other researchers quickly synthesized several more dye colors. Within a half-decade, 29 companies in Europe marketed synthetic dyes, all priced vastly lower than the organic compounds they replaced.[156]

Since British firms held patents to several popular dyes and given Britain's huge coal reserves and dominance of the textile industry, they might also have become the world's leading manufacturers. They failed, however, to exploit their advantages. Instead, three German companies (Bayer, BASF, and Hoechst) established giant industrial plants on the Rhine River, which achieved economies of scale, driving down the price of a kilogram of dye from 100 marks in the early 1870s to only 9 marks in 1886.[157] They also exploited economies of scope, with Bayer alone producing over 2,000 different synthetic dyes in 1913. The successful firms developed vertical integration involving vast distribution and supply networks. Bayer fielded an army of salesmen with training in chemistry to serve their global customer base of 25,000 in 1902. They also divided their production facilities into several specialized departments—managing sales, purchasing, patents, accounting, and statistics—each with its own research and development teams, all overseen by professionalized administrative units.[158] The organization rose hierarchically from specialized laboratories and production floors to a pinnacle of senior management officers—a model that many successful firms throughout the West imitated in the pre-World War I years.

Chemists and engineers achieved important practical breakthroughs in many areas of research.[159] The development of powerful new explosives—nitroglycerin (1847), TNT (1863), and most important of all dynamite, which Alfred Nobel (1833–96) patented in 1867—proved a huge boon to the mining, construction, oil production, and armaments industries.[160] Chemical pulping methods developed in the United States using sulfites (1867) and in Germany using sulfates (1879) made it possible to dramatically ramp up paper production.[161] In combination with mechanical breakthroughs like the lightning-fast rotary printing press (1847) and the automatic type-setting machine (1886), it fueled a new printing revolution—this one enabling people in Western societies to buy a wide variety of books and periodicals.[162] Alloys involving common and rare metals yielded an array of useful materials, such as "stainless steel" marketed by the German firm Krupp beginning in 1914.[163]

An entirely new and world-changing branch of industrial chemistry, pharmaceuticals, made its debut in 1899 when either Felix Hoffman (1868–1946) or Arthur Eichengrün (1867–1949)—scholars are unsure to whom the credit is due—created aspirin (acetylsalicylic acid), the world's first entirely synthetic medication, while working for the Bayer Company in Germany.[164] Aspirin made a fortune for Bayer, though another drug that Hoffman synthesized, heroin, enjoyed far less legitimate commercial success.[165]

A decade later, Paul Ehrlich (1854–1915) developed the concept of chemotherapy. He and his research team at the University of Göttingen systematically modified the compound arsanilic acid in over 600 experiments until, in 1909, they invented arsphenamine, marketed as Salvarsan, an effective treatment for syphilis and the first modern chemotherapeutic agent. (He went on to win the Nobel Prize in medicine.)[166] Most subsequent pharmaceutical research followed this approach. Over the following decades, scientists, engineers, veterinarians, and physicians worked in dozens and then hundreds of research laboratories—supported by governments, businesses, and universities—to synthesize an astonishing variety of medications, hormones, vitamins, and other health-enhancing substances. The discovery of penicillin in 1928 by the Scottish scientist and later Nobel laureate Alexander Fleming (1881–1955) led to a pharmaceutical revolution beginning in the 1940s.[167] The result was medical care, for the first time in history, able systematically to cure diseases.[168]

Researchers found dozens more efficient and inexpensive processes for manufacturing chemical products, spurring enormous new output. The Belgian Ernest Solvay (1838–1922) made a fortune manufacturing sodium carbonate, a compound necessary for glass- and soap-making, and licensing his procedure to companies in Europe and the United States.[169] Others, especially Germans, found clever new ways to manufacture ammonia, chlorine, nitric acid, caustic soda, sulfuric acid, and many other chemical substances essential for producing fertilizer, detergents, bleaching powder, and petroleum distillates. Before World War I, the big German firms completely dominated chemical production.[170] After the war, however, American firms began to catch up in pharmaceuticals, electrochemicals, synthetic fertilizers, and petrochemicals, in part thanks to the United States government's expropriation during the war of US-based German chemical firms.[171]

The petroleum industry began in the mid-nineteenth century when researchers discovered a way to use sulfuric acid to refine crude oil into a lamp fuel, which the Canadian geologist and entrepreneur Abraham Gesner (1797–1864) named kerosene.[172] For the next half-century, Imperial Russia's oil fields in and around Baku produced the bulk of the world's oil output. With the discovery of oil in western Pennsylvania in 1859, the United States became a major producer. In 1865, American entrepreneurs built the first pump-driven oil pipeline—a key technological breakthrough. Within a few years, John D. Rockefeller (1839–1937) began to forge an oil-refining business that grew into the Standard Oil Trust, a giant, vertically integrated organization.[173] In 1879, other developers built the first long-distance pipeline over the Allegheny Mountains. Two years later Standard Oil followed suit, and for nearly two decades it dominated the American market in oil production and refining. Then, on 10 January 1901, in southeastern Texas, the prodigious "Spindletop" well sparked an oil boom that brought dozens more firms into the market and catapulted the United States into the top position in world production. The discovery temporarily drove the price of oil down to $.03 per barrel.[174] The era of inexpensive motor fuel had begun.

Aside from automotive fuel, petroleum supplied a host of other products, thanks to petrochemical research by major companies. Union Carbide led the way when, in 1920, its researchers discovered a method for extracting ethylene—a key ingredient in dozens of substances like polyethylene and vinyl—from natural gas liquids.[175] The petrochemical industry surged after World War II, with all the major oil companies using petroleum by-products like benzene and propylene to produce plastics, pharmaceuticals, solvents, detergents, adhesives, lubricants, synthetic fibers, pesticides, paint, varnish, synthetic rubber, and dyes.[176]

In the United States and Germany, research and development in the chemical industries spiked. In America, from 1921 to 1946 the percentage of scientists working on chemistry research at the 200 biggest firms rose from roughly 5 to just over 30 percent (petroleum research, the next biggest category, rose from under 2 to nearly 29 percent).[177] This research paid off in the postwar years with veritable revolutions in petrochemical and pharmaceutical production. As big firms realized bulging profits from these revolutions, especially in the United States, they plowed large sums back into research and development, fueling continued American dominance and more and more industrial breakthroughs.

Taken together, ever-more efficient and productive industrial manufacturing of machinery, motor vehicles, chemicals, pharmaceuticals, rubber, metals, processed and packaged foods, plastics, electrical equipment, appliances, ships, airplanes, weapons, locomotives, textiles, synthetic materials—in a word, the entire panoply of modern, mass-produced goods and commodities—defined and characterized the twentieth century and in the process dramatically increased the wealth and power of the West (and rapidly westernizing Japan). Never before had any countries or region or civilization risen to preeminence in so many fields so quickly. Technology had made this rise possible. It seemed that nothing in the natural world could stop the West's progress.

Even the invisible realms revealed their secrets to Western researchers. In 1895, the German physicist Wilhelm Röntgen (1845–1923) discovered X-rays, for which other scientists and inventors quickly found practical uses, such as medical diagnosis and testing the soundness of metals.[178] In *The Interpretation of Dreams* (1899), Sigmund Freud (1856–1939) proposed a method for systematically analyzing the unconscious mind.[179] Then in 1905, Albert Einstein (1879–1955) enunciated his special theory of relativity, a major step toward unlocking the awesome power of atoms.[180] Within four decades, European and American scientists had designed and built nuclear fission weapons and reactors, though governments and societies used the weapons only twice and derived only a fraction of world energy needs from nuclear reactors, mostly because of public concerns about dangers inherent in harnessing nuclear energy.

Using scientific expertise to unleash powerful chemical reactions was not without its own drawbacks. The contamination of natural environments with toxic chemicals, such as dioxins (polychlorinated dibenzodioxins) and PCBs (polychlorinated biphenyls), occasionally resulted in the poisoning of human populations.[181] Here and there, entire communities exposed to dangerous chemical substances had to be evacuated, for example from Love Canal, New York, in the late 1970s.[182] Not surprisingly, the DuPont Corporation dropped its slogan "Better Living Through Chemistry" in 1982.[183] One of the worst industrial disasters in history occurred 2 years later at a Union Carbide pesticide plant in Bhopal, in northcentral India, when a large quantity of toxic gases escaped. Exposure to the gases killed up to 15,000 people and injured another half-million.[184] Industrial chemistry still contributes mightily to maintaining the modern lifestyle, but few well-informed people today believe its contributions pose no risks to the environment or to health.

If industrial production largely characterized the Western and ultimately the world economy in the twentieth century, then one can argue plausibly that the mastery of unseen forces, the description of reality through encoding, data processing, algorithms, networks and interconnections, and the transmission and manipulation of information constituted the latest wave of revolutionary transformation in the West and beyond.

Electronics and information revolutions

In the 1860s, a Scot, James Clerk Maxwell (1831–79), perhaps the greatest physicist in history after Newton and Einstein, demonstrated theoretically in four mathematical equations that light, magnetism, and electricity all radiate as electromagnetic waves.[185] He also predicted the existence of radio waves as part of a broader electromagnetic spectrum. Two decades later, Heinrich Hertz (1857–94) produced in the laboratory electromagnetic radiation at various wavelengths but at lower frequencies than light. Several inventors attempted practical applications of radio transmission before Guglielmo Marconi (1874–1937) built a workable wireless apparatus—a transmitter, a receiver, and a grounded antenna—in the mid-1890s. Year by year, adding improvements to his basic design, he extended the distance of transmission, reaching 1,700 miles in 1901 in Newfoundland with his historic reception of a radio signal broadcast from Cornwall across the Atlantic Ocean. Dozens of inventors and researchers throughout the West (as well as in Russia) advanced every aspect of radio technology.

Marconi established the world's first wireless communication company in 1897 and gained contracts with the British, Italian, and other navies. Telefunken in

Germany and General Electric, American Telephone and Telegraph, and Westinghouse in the United States soon challenged the leader. Yet no one made any money in the absence of further technological breakthroughs. In 1907, Lee de Forest (1873–1961), drawing on the work of many pioneers, not least Thomas Edison, devised a three-electrode vacuum tube (a triode), which could produce, detect, and amplify radio waves.[186] Its full potential was not realized, however, until researchers at GE and AT&T developed high-vacuum tubes in 1912–13. The improved device made possible transcontinental telephone service and voice transmission by radio across the Atlantic in 1915 (see Map 12.2 above). Many researchers in Europe and the United States worked tirelessly during the World War to resolve problems of static, modulation, and amplification. The power of transmitting tubes increased from 25 watts in 1915 to 250 watts in 1918 and up to 10 kilowatts in 1921.

In 1920, Westinghouse began the first regularly scheduled radio broadcasts from KDKA in Pittsburgh using amplitude modulation, or AM. The public went wild, with consumers snatching up receivers and merchants eager to underwrite programming. The previous year, the US Navy had engineered the purchase by GE of the American Marconi Company and the creation of the Radio Corporation of America, or RCA, in order to ensure American dominance in the emerging wireless telecommunications industry. The new company quickly became the world leader in commercializing radio broadcasting and receiving. Companies and entrepreneurs rushed to license radio stations around the United States—556 by the end of 1923. Radio receivers sold by the million. Entertainment and news broadcasting proliferated. By late 1922, David Sarnoff (1891–1971), RCA's brilliant 31-year-old vice president, had established more than 200 distribution outlets around the country. In 1926, he launched the country's first radio broadcasting network, the National Broadcasting Company (NBC), with 19 stations in 1926 and 103 a decade later. The network brought in substantial income but so did RCA's licensing of radio and vacuum tube technology throughout the industry. Radio broadcasting companies and services quickly formed around the world, including a first competitor in the United States, the Columbia Broadcasting System (CBS), in 1927.

All three of the big American electronics companies maintained high-power research laboratories. Charles Steinmetz (1865–1923) had developed the first truly modern research laboratory in the electrical industry for GE in Schenectady, New York, back in 1900. It brought together scientists and experts in a wide variety of fields both to collaborate and to pursue independently the systematic application of science to technological development. AT&T's Bell Labs and Westinghouse's Pittsburgh laboratory followed suit. Collectively, employing dozens of researchers, including numerous PhDs, they made dramatic strides in bringing about successive generations of technological revolution. Vladimir Zworykin (1888–1982), a refugee from the Russian Civil War who found a job with Westinghouse, brought together and developed the essential elements of television in 1928.[187] Two years later, Sarnoff lured him away to head up television research at RCA's new laboratories in Camden, New Jersey. The invention at Bell Labs in 1947 of the transistor—a semiconductor device without tubes that amplifies and switches radio and other electronic signals—led to the gradual transformation of the entire electronics industry, including solid state equipment, integrated circuits, the miniaturization of parts, and ultimately microprocessors.[188]

The major corporations did not dominate all technological research and breakthroughs in these years. Philo Farnsworth (1906–71), who spent his first 12 years living in a log cabin in Utah and remained a largely independent inventor and entrepreneur, made important contributions to the development of television, radar, and electron microscopy.[189] Edwin Armstrong (1890–1954), a professor at Columbia University, invented FM radio in a basement laboratory.[190] Also, in the 1920s American and European amateur radio operators developed shortwave radio broadcasting and receiving, which had powerful potentialities for radar and long-distance telecommunications links.[191]

Public television broadcasts commenced in London in 1936, though broadscale commercialization began only after World War II. Sarnoff tenaciously pursued color television technology, while his competitors dropped out of the running in the face of enormous technical difficulties. In 1959, RCA made its first profit with the new technology and then dominated the world market in the production and licensing of color-television tubes and components.[192] When, starting in 1965, RCA diversified into computer technology and nonelectronic consumer goods, it lost its edge at a moment when Japanese companies, thanks to their licensing of American transistor patents and intensive practical research, began to emerge as world leaders in consumer electronics. Year by year, Matsushita increased its market share worldwide with the Panasonic and Quasar brands. In 1968, Sony introduced the Trinitron television tube—by far the best in the world. Matsushita developed the industry standard video-cassette recorder (VCR) in the early 1970s, and Sony brought out its Walkman in 1979, coming to dominate the market for compact disc players in the 1980s and for DVD players from the late 1990s. Sony, with a lot of help from the Dutch firm Philips, in the words of a leading business historian, "digitalized the world."[193] No other firms in any other countries could effectively compete with the triumphant Japanese.

What an astonishing accomplishment within a mere century for a country previously closed to the outside world! Japan's systematic adaptation of Western science, technology, political institutions, market economy, and even values, while maintaining its own traditional culture and spirit, beginning with the Meiji Restoration in 1868, marked the most dramatic and rapid transmutation of a society in all of human history. Key leaders, including public intellectuals like Fukuzawa Yukichi (1835–1901), recognized that in order to produce, say, 1,000 warships Japan needed to built a vast social, economic, intellectual, and technological infrastructure, involving 10,000 merchant ships, 100,000 navigators, and a huge number of sailors, merchants, and experts in maritime science.[194] The country, moreover, needed to achieve similar feats simultaneously in several dozen spheres of activity. The country's first clear triumphs came in military affairs. Within a few decades, Japan had defeated a great European power in the Russo-Japanese War (1904–05) and had begun its career of imperialism culminating in the territorial acquisition of Manchuria, parts of eastern China, and most of Southeast Asia. Defeat in World War II, followed by constitutionally imposed demilitarization, forced the Japanese to channel their extraordinary talents into technological and business expansion—the first non-Western country to do so successfully. If their economic growth was on the low end of the developed countries in 1900–50, it achieved a blistering 7.1 percent annual GDP growth in 1950–87—a rate 62 percent higher than the next contenders,

Germany and Canada.[195] In the latest frontier—information technology—they have proved just as powerful a challenger to Western hegemony as in consumer electronics.[196]

Yet the world of innovation remains fluid, constantly in flux. Starting in 2001, the American company Apple, having essentially invented the personal computer, revolutionized the consumer electronics industry by launching the Apple Store, the iPod, iTunes, the iTunes Store, the iPhone, the iPad, and iCloud. By August 2011, Apple had become the most valuable company in the world. Walter Isaacson, who also wrote biographies of Benjamin Franklin and Albert Einstein, concluded that Steve Jobs, the driving force behind these breakthroughs, was one of history's greatest technological and entrepreneurial innovators, alongside Edison and Ford.[197]

Man has sought means to calculate and to process data for thousands of years, beginning with the abacus first developed in ancient Mesopotamia and then achieving more sophistication in the mid- to later 1600s with the invention in the British Isles of the slide rule, in France of the gear-driven mechanical adding machine, and in Germany of a mechanical multiplier.[198] The development of precision engineering in the nineteenth century—tools and gauges calibrated to within 0.00001 of an inch—enabled inventors to devise ever-more powerful calculators and data-processing machines. In particular, the American Herman Hollerith (1860–1929) developed electric "tabulating" machines able to process large volumes of data by encoding them as patterns of holes punched into cards. These machines proved invaluable in compiling United States Census data in 1890 and 1900.[199] His company evolved into International Business Machines, or IBM, for most of its history a world leader in computer technology.

In collaboration with IBM and Harvard University, Howard Aiken (1900–73) designed the world's first actual computer, the Automatic Sequence Controlled Calculator, or Mark I, which was unveiled in 1944.[200] The immense electricity-powered device—it measured 50 by 8 feet—functioned mechanically and could process decimal numbers up to 23 places and multiply 2 11-place numbers in 3 seconds. Two years later, on behalf of the United States military, John Mauchly (1907–80) and J. Presper Eckert (1919–95) of the University of Pennsylvania launched the first electronic computer—it had 18,000 radio tubes and could tackle the same multiplication problem as the Mark I in 3000ths of a second. Over the next two decades, innovators replaced radio tubes with transistors, added integrated circuitry, steadily miniaturized components, developed more and more sophisticated binary-digit codes (or programs) to run operations, and devised a host of peripheral equipment—storage devices, printers, networking—creating astonishingly powerful systems for data processing.

In 1964, the main player internationally, IBM, commercialized its System/360 mainframe computer, a series of machines of varying size, speed, and memory capacity all running the same operating software and using compatible peripherals. A major gamble, the S/360 succeeded fabulously, quickly becoming the industry standard. Its chief architect, Gene Amdahl (1922–), left IBM in 1970 and joined forces with Fujitsu, which gave it and other Japanese firms state-of-the-art technology and helped launch them on a powerful challenge to IBM.[201] One by one, meanwhile, European computer makers dropped out of the running, leaving only Japanese and American companies. The latter brought out supercomputers in the 1960s and microcomputers in the 1970s.

Then IBM revolutionized the entire industry.[202] In 1981, it launched relatively inexpensive, mass-produced personal computers running nonproprietary components (like Intel microprocessors) and a simple but powerful operating system licensed from a then obscure firm, Microsoft. Sales skyrocketed as consumer demand exploded. The IBM PC—both the originals and the clones—became the industry and world standard. Entrepreneurial and inventive focus henceforth shifted from computer platforms to microchips, networks, software, and the internet, fields that American companies dominated at the start of the twenty-first century. The next frontier in information technology may be "quantum computing," which aims to use the properties of sub-atomic particles to process data at speeds many times faster than the fastest computers of today.[203]

The other major area of extraordinary technological advancement in the twenty-first century is genetics, itself an information technology. Having mapped out the genome, the complete DNA blueprint, for many living beings, including humans, scientists have gone on essentially to design a bacterial genome, to insert it into a bacterial cell, and to get it to reproduce itself just like any other bacterium.[204] With the cost of genetic sequencing diminishing faster than that of microprocessor technology, genetic engineering promises to radically transform medicine and all the other subfields of biology. The rewards, and perhaps also the risks, seem staggering.

* * *

The leading edge of technological development, which catapulted the Western societies to the highest standards of living, the greatest economies of scale and efficiency, and the most tremendous concentrations of wealth and power the world had ever seen, passed within a century from heavy industries and manufacturing to processing information, cybernetics (the analysis of systems and organizations in order to make them more efficient), and making connections among ideas and data. In other words, the West's most creative minds turned their focus from the concrete, material, and noisy to the conceptual and ethereal. Western societies and firms remained capable of designing and manufacturing a wide variety of products—natural and processed foods, refined tools, electrical devices, motorized vehicles, air- and spacecraft, sophisticated chemicals and pharmaceuticals, consumer electronics, and computer hardware—though non-Western, especially Asian, countries produced a large proportion of them, thanks to lower labor costs.

Technological innovation by the end of the second millennium proved most fruitful in electronic applications, however, rather than in concrete electronic products as such. Firms like IBM and Intel continued to increase the efficiency and speed of microprocessors—the so-called Moore's law, formulated by Gordon Moore (1929–), the co-founder of Intel, that computer power would double every 2 years has in fact held true.[205] Many of the most powerful and profitable advances in the decade before and after the turn of the third millennium exploited the potentialities of "cyberspace"—Google, Amazon, iTunes, eBay, Facebook, and Netflix.

Yet one of the prime movers of the computer revolution, Bill Gates, now foresees a convergence of information, electronics, and mechanical technologies leading to "a future in which robotic devices will become a nearly ubiquitous part of our day-to-day lives. . . . We may be on the verge of a new era, when the PC will get up off the desktop and allow us to see, hear, touch, and manipulate objects in places where we are not physically present." (Japan is currently the world's biggest producer and consumer of robots.)[206] This new technological revolution is already making a big impact in warfare and promises to transform the lives of many if not most people in the developed countries of the world.[207]

The story of Western innovation and advancement has consisted largely in an ever-increasing mastery of knowledge and information. Europeans and then Americans and other peoples of the West acquired, stored, organized, shared, and exploited more knowledge about the world, nature, man, and abstract ideas than any other civilization or culture in history, vastly more. They used this mental prowess to gain mastery over the physical realm, to increase their wealth and power, and to raise the standard of living of most people in the West and then also in the wider world. The effects of these changes—both negative and positive—are described in the following two chapters.

QUESTIONS FOR REFLECTION

How did changes in agriculture contribute to industrialization?

Where were wages highest in the world in the nineteenth century and why?

What is meant by a vertically integrated business organization?

How did efficient patent law contribute to innovation?

How did electric motors make factories more efficient?

What is "scientific management" and how did it contribute to economic development?

How did higher education begin to contribute to the technological revolution?

Why were the big German pharmaceutical firms so successful?

What products were made possible by petrochemical technology?

How did Japanese firms come to dominate the consumer electronics industry?

Chapter 13 Chronology

1842:	Treaty of Nanjing ends First Opium War
1848:	Publication of *Communist Manifesto*
1858:	British Raj (formal rule) begins in India
1868:	Meiji Restoration in Japan
1870–71:	Franco-Prussian War
1881:	Terrorist assassination of Alexander II
1884–85:	Conference of Berlin sets ground rules of Scramble for Africa
1894–95:	Sino-Japanese War
1896:	Ethiopia wins Battle of Adowa against Italy
1898:	British massacre Sudanese in Battle of Omdurman
1904–05:	Russo-Japanese War
1911:	Amundsen's team reaches South Pole
1912–13:	Balkan Wars
1914–18:	World War I
1917:	Russian Revolution
1919:	Treaty of Versailles
1921:	Soviet New Economic Policy; famine breaks out in Russia
1922:	Mussolini comes to power
1928:	Soviet Five-Year Plan and Collectivization begin
1933:	Hitler comes to power
1939–45:	World War II
1949:	Chinese Communists come to power
1950–53:	Korean War
1962:	Cuban Missile Crisis
1973:	Vietnam War ends
1991:	The USSR collapses; the Cold War ends

13

Crises of the West

In mid-1840, some 4,000 British and Indian troops in 50 ships, including 4 armed steamers, arrived off Canton, the only Chinese port open to foreigners, and blockaded the entrance to the Pearl River. They then sailed northeast, capturing and blockading positions along nearly the entire Chinese coast. Negotiations initially led nowhere. The following year, British forces captured more ports, destroyed forts, and sank numerous Chinese boats. Following a winter lull, the British seized Shanghai in June 1842 and Zhenjiang further up the Yangtze in July, thus threatening Nanjing. The Chinese sued for peace. By the Treaty of Nanjing, China ceded Hong Kong, one of the world's best deepwater harbors but then nearly deserted, opened four more ports to British traders, accorded them favorable trading terms and the right to trial by their own courts (extraterritoriality), and promised an indemnity of 20 million dollars. These rights soon expanded further and extended to all the main Western countries.[1] Thus, a country of 28 million brought the great Chinese Empire with 16 times more people (435 million) to its knees.[2]

No one would call the First Opium War just. The United Kingdom had been running a large trade deficit for decades with the Chinese, who coveted almost nothing British merchants had to offer. Officially, the Chinese government treated all foreign peoples as tributaries of the Chinese Emperor. In the late eighteenth century, British traders discovered a strong taste in China for opium, which they began to supply to Chinese merchants in ever-growing quantity. (Much was also produced inside China.)[3] By the 1830s, use of the drug was contributing to major social problems and a trade imbalance in Britain's favor. When a Chinese official in 1839 seized opium valued at between 10 and 20 million dollars and destroyed it, the British retaliated militarily.[4] Chinese artisans and engineers were apparently capable of meticulously copying Western military technology, yet most officials rejected wholesale imitation as humiliating.[5] The war was unpopular in Britain and the United States, but it showed that even the greatest non-Western country until then was no longer a match for Europe's premier naval power.[6]

Imperialism

When Europeans first ventured by ship into the Indian Ocean, the splendor of Chinese and Indian civilizations awed them. Only their weaponry seemed inferior.[7] Europeans had been able to colonize the Americas largely because of the pathogens they carried. By contrast, few Europeans could survive contact with diseases endemic in sub-Saharan Africa. They established outposts on the coasts of Africa and Asia and of course came to dominate international maritime trade because of their better ships and guns. If they considered themselves superior to other peoples, however, it was mostly because of their belief that divine revelation had given them possession of transcendent truth.[8]

Even before Europeans set out into the wider world, in large part to circumvent Muslim control of the Asian luxury trade, the Ottoman Empire had begun expanding at their doorstep. In the second half of the fourteenth century, Ottoman control extended deep into the Balkans. An elite professional military force, centering on the Janissary Corps recruited from converted Christian prisoners, enabled a succession of sultans to conquer the remnants of the Byzantine Empire, Greece, Serbia, and Bosnia in the fifteenth century and Egypt, North Africa, Croatia, Romania, Hungary, and part of Ukraine in the early sixteenth century. They besieged Vienna in 1529 and again in 1683. They maintained a powerful navy in the Eastern Mediterranean and a significant naval presence in the Indian Ocean into the sixteenth century.[9] Yet unlike the European powers, they never built an overseas colonial empire.

Throughout the eighteenth century, the European powers fought one another incessantly, mostly on their continent but also in North America and the Caribbean, as well as in Asia, where they gained a foothold.[10] The British East India Company began to rule formally over small territories in India from the mid-1700s and extended its control throughout most of India a century later, thanks in part to incessant conflicts between local rulers in the subcontinent. Formal British rule began in 1858.[11] By then, nearly all of Latin America had gained independence from Spain and Portugal. The Portuguese retained narrow coastal dominance in southeastern and southwestern Africa, the Dutch controlled parts of Indonesia and the southern coast of Africa, Spain retained scattered colonies, and France had outposts on the African coast. Britain had the only large overseas empire. It stretched from Canada to New Zealand.[12]

A massive overseas migration of Europeans flowed into not only current and former British colonies, but also South America—perhaps the largest human resettlement in history: up to 50–60 million people in the nineteenth century alone.[13] They built what Alfred Crosby calls Neo-Europes—regions with sparse indigenous populations and ecological conditions similar to those in Europe, including the United States, Canada, Australia, New Zealand, Uruguay, and Argentina. The human, plant, and animal intruders displaced natives in most of these places and established world powerhouses of agricultural production. In 1982, these countries accounted for 30 percent of all agricultural exports and far higher percentages of such staples as wheat (72 percent).[14]

By the late eighteenth century, Europeans came to believe that science and technology set them apart from other peoples. Thousands of philanthropists and missionaries eagerly sought to bring science, technology, literacy, hygiene, and civilization in general to non-Western peoples. The mid-century British Victorians, pointing to their own success—an annual increase in real income in 1851–78 of 27–30 percent—optimistically believed they could bring civilization and prosperity to the entire world by spreading free trade, private enterprise, and Christian morality.[15] As one scholar has concluded, "From early in the nineteenth century the notion that it was the Europeans' destiny and duty to develop the resources of the globe was included in the mixture of humanitarian sentiment, cultural arrogance, and self-serving rationalization that advocates of imperial expansion blended into the civilizing-mission ideology."[16]

Steadily increasing technological precision and efficiency enabled Westerners to control time, space, their bodies, and nature more and more skillfully. Foreign cultural attainments that a few decades prior had impressed European travelers now seemed trifling or inept.[17] By the late 1800s, many educated and ordinary Western people came to believe in their inherent cultural if not biological superiority. Theorists and researchers buttressed racial stereotyping with allegedly scientific proofs using such now discredited disciplines as craniology.[18]

Sadly, humans tend to exclude and mistreat people different from themselves. The most successful societies typically believe in their own superiority. For centuries, the Chinese elites viewed their civilization as the world leader and all others as its humble tributaries. When the British envoy to China refused to fall on his face ritualistically before the Qianlong Emperor in 1793, the court expressed outrage.[19] Many Muslims also have believed their civilization to be greater than all others. As late as 1949, Hassan al-Banna (1906–49), the Egyptian founder of the Muslim Brotherhood, argued that the Islamic religion was "infinitely more accomplished, more pure, more glorious, more complete, and more beautiful than all that has been discovered up till now by social theorists and reformers."[20] So the peoples of the West were not unique in their cultural arrogance.

The most obvious sphere of Western superiority was military. From the eighteenth century, no Western power worried about military threats from any non-Western country or region. In the following century, Western power could scarcely be stopped. Japan, which feverishly adopted Western technology and practices in the late nineteenth century, was the exception that proved the rule, defeating Russia in 1904–05.[21] It became possible for Western (or Westernized) societies, organized into nation-states, a revolutionary new type of polity,[22] to impose their will on nearly any people on the planet and more decisively so as the decades wore on. The *Pax Britannica*, the British naval domination, as well as British efforts to maintain geopolitical balance among European powers, helped prevent a major war from breaking out in Europe for a century (1815–1914).[23]

Yet their bellicose spirit did not diminish—on the contrary. Ideologies and worldviews placing struggle at the center of human existence dominated the second half of the nineteenth century. Previous Western theories of human development, culminating in that of Hegel (1770–1831), had emphasized the action of a transcendent power in moving the world toward a higher level.[24] By 1848, however, Karl Marx was distilling a new outlook in his *Communist Manifesto* in which he argued, "The history of all hitherto existing society is the history of class struggles."[25] In the following decades, Social Darwinists viewed human life as a struggle for survival. Friedrich Nietzsche rejected Christianity as a religion for slaves and extolled the virtues of the "superman" to come. Eugenicists advocated using science in order to maintain a "purified race."[26] Militarists in all the great European powers preached an arms race and pushed their compatriots toward war.[27]

Western adventurers raced to the remaining uncharted localities. The Scottish missionary David Livingstone walked thousands of miles throughout Africa exploring, establishing missions, and fighting against the slave trade from 1841 to his death in 1873. When he died, his devoted servants carried his body 1,500 miles to the coast.[28] Livingstone and others competed to find the source of the Nile. Efforts to visit the remotest localities and to discover the most stupendous geographical features captivated the public's attention.[29] For many decades, dozens of intrepid voyagers vied to reach the poles. On 6 April 1909, the American Robert Peary planted several flags at the North Pole. (His claim was later contested.) The Norwegian Roald Amundsen, who had previously navigated the Northwest Passage and was now hoping to focus on the North Pole, abruptly reoriented his energies, attaining the South Pole in December 1911, a 900-mile overland trek up 10,000 feet of elevation in some of earth's most punishing weather. A month later, British naval officer Robert Scott and his team arrived to find they had been beaten to the goal. Crushed and dejected, the men all perished on the way back to their ship.[30] The episode illustrates the deadly seriousness of such ventures for audacious Westerners.

Others advocated territorial expansion. Justifications put forward were many. Military officials wanted strategic ports. Abolitionists aimed to root out slavery. Missionaries desired a freer hand for proselytizing. Humanitarians hoped to spread education and medical services. Journalists were eager for dramatic stories. Businessmen expected to corner some market. Government officials envisaged self-aggrandizement. Economics, far from the main driving force, was often only an ex post facto argument for retaining colonies.[31] Yet colonies almost never paid for themselves, enriching only some individuals or companies, and did not magically enable merchants to gain access to commodities they could not have otherwise acquired through open trading. (India was an exception; a self-supporting colony, it actually made money for the British government through taxes.) For example, British investors typically earned more from domestic trade and industry than from colonial ventures.[32] Thus, European governments tended to resist calls for direct imperialist action.

This tendency began to change in the late nineteenth century. Statesmen sought to acquire colonies partly because "a great power must have colonies."[33] Germany, Italy, France, the United States, and Japan all to some extent seized foreign territory for this reason, and the Austro-Hungarian and Russian Empires strived to maintain or extend their territory to avoid falling behind. Competition among the major Western powers (and Japan) led to serious tensions and often conflicts where their territories or colonial possessions met. Not that this situation was unusual, historically speaking. "The history of the world," writes John Darwin, "is an imperial history, a history of empires," since the resources necessary for state building have been unevenly distributed.[34] Consolidating human and natural endowments made enormous sense in earlier ages of inefficient systems of exchange. In the late nineteenth century, however, modern technology and efficient markets made it possible for the Western powers to acquire whatever they needed by means of normal commercial relations. Yet the fear of losing one's position in a menacing international hierarchy and the ideal of a "civilizing mission" spurred the zealous competition for colonies dubbed "the New Imperialism."[35]

It culminated in the Scramble for Africa.[36] The discovery of gold and diamonds in South Africa beginning in 1869 deepened tensions between the British and the Afrikaners. The 1870s brought a worldwide economic slump that sharpened commercial rivalries between the European great powers. In 1876, King Leopold II of Belgium started to transform the Congo into a proprietary colony.[37]

France immediately laid claim to adjacent territory. Italy and Germany, recently unified as countries, were also eager to become colonial powers. Egypt, now independent from Ottoman rule, fell into debt to European investors.[38] To pay them back, in 1875 it sold a large share of the Suez Canal (opened in 1869) to the British government. France vied with Britain for control over the surrounding Egyptian territory. Britain invaded Egypt in 1882 to crush native unrest and protect the canal, which vexed the French. All of these conflicting interests sparked a frenzied struggle for control in Africa, the continent least able to resist European incursions.[39]

The colonial powers signed hundreds of bilateral agreements and treaties with one another and with local African leaders in the 1880s demarcating (artificial) borders. In many cases, the African leaders did not realize the extent to which they were giving up sovereignty. In 1884–85, the Conference of Berlin established ground rules for the colonizers. They had to demonstrate "efficient administration," for example, and had to legitimize their conquests, hence the treaties. They also pledged to put an end to slavery and the slave trade in Africa (though Leopold's company so mistreated its workers that the Belgian Parliament bought the colony from him in 1908).[40] The partition and formal rule of nearly the whole of Africa involved economic, infrastructural, administrative, and other forms of development but also the subordination of Western ideals of human rights, the rule of law, and the promotion of human improvement to the requirements of colonial rule. To say the least, few African countries emerged from the process well equipped for success in the modern world.[41]

Abyssinia (Ethiopia) alone among African countries maintained its independence, thanks to shrewd balance of power geopolitics and the adoption of modern technology and institutions. At the Battle of Adowa in 1896, Ethiopian forces crushed an attacking Italian army—the first defeat of a modern Western power by a non-Western people.[42]

China's defeat in the Sino-Japanese War of 1894–95 did not lead to a "scramble for China," largely because of growing US interests in China and the Pacific and its successful insistence on an Open Door policy of equal access to the Chinese market. Official resistance to the kind of wholesale reform that had enabled Japan to modernize quickly was overcome once the Imperial government fell in 1911, but the collapse of China into competing regional power bases led to civil war and further stagnation.[43] Meanwhile, the imperialist powers chipped away at China's border territories and tributaries. France established colonial role in Indochina thanks in part to the Sino-French War of 1884–85.[44] Similarly, Britain seized the tributary state Burma, and Russia, while expanding its territory dramatically into Central Asia and the Far East, also encroached on China.[45]

Colonial expansionism entailed many vicious acts of violence. One can mention, among many other instances, the machinegun massacre of some 11,000 Sudanese by British forces at the Battle of Omdurman in 1898,[46] the more than 20,000 Filipino rebel soldiers killed by American conquerors in 1899–1902 (not counting up to 200,000 civilians who may have died from famine, disease, and other causes),[47] and the merciless and relentless slaughter of as many as 50,000 Herero people in South-West Africa (today's Namibia) in 1904 by an apparently psychopathic German officer.[48] For many Westerners, it seemed that the rules of decency and humanity, which they considered foundational values of their civilization, did not apply to their dealings with non-Western peoples.

Japan was the only non-Western country, as noted in Chapter 12, to successfully adapt Western technology and institutions and indeed to achieve a level of development equal to that of the major Western countries. The commencement of this advance was seemingly inauspicious. In 1853, American gunboats sailed into Tokyo Bay and demanded that the country open to commercial relations. Following intensive domestic struggle, samurai warlords toppled the government and returned the emperor to power in 1867 in what came to be known as the Meiji Restoration. Only four decades later, Japan seized Taiwan and Korea and had broken free from the unequal treaties imposed by the Western powers and regained sovereignty over its economic policy.[49]

Still, in comparison with the main European imperialists, the Japanese were bit players. By 1913, according to one calculation, the world empires ranged in size from Britain's 32 million and France's 11 million to Japan's 297,000 km^2. The 8 European colonial powers, while constituting only 1.6 percent, of the earth's landmass, controlled nearly half of the rest, or 41.3 percent (see Map 13.1).[50]

How was this possible and what benefit did it bring to Europe? According to Jack Goldstone, "It was not colonialism and conquest that made possible the rise of the West, but the reverse—it was the rise of the West (in terms of technology) and the decline of the rest that made possible the full extension of European power across the globe."[51] It seems that Goldstone has isolated only one of many reasons for both imperialism and the West's rise. These include an unprecedented ability to manage and share information, to unlock the secrets of nature, to coordinate human activity, to foster and intensify individual initiative, to discover and adapt diverse ideas and resources, and to build and maintain institutions that promote all of these things.

Ironically and tragically, all of the feverish imperialist endeavors brought very little of positive value to the aggressive powers, as mentioned in Chapter 9. For one thing, European investors obviously considered their colonies the least desirable place to send capital. The British, for example, invested roughly 4 billion pounds abroad in 1865–1914. Over 30 percent went to the United States and Canada. Nearly 19 percent went to Latin America. Four British colonies in the developing world (India, South Africa, Egypt, and Rhodesia) received around 17 percent. Only tiny fractions of the rest (roughly 34 percent) were invested in dozens of other countries.[52] A key problem was that most of the developing countries in Asia, Africa, and even much of Latin America lacked basic transportation, communications, legal, and market infrastructure necessary to accommodate large investments of capital."[53]

In the period 1871–1913, some one-third of Britain's national income came from overseas, about half from nonservice exports. Again, very little of this trade involved territories acquired during the Scramble for Africa. In fact, all the dependent colonies absorbed only between 15 and 21 percent of British exports.[54] India's cotton textile industry mechanized rapidly from the 1870s and by 1910 was seriously contesting British dominance. Moreover, Britain traded far less with India than with France, Germany, or the United States and exported only 14 percent of all manufacturing exports to its "jewel in the crown," India.[55] British investments in the colonies provided slightly higher returns than in Britain proper, but investments in nonimperial countries, like the United States and South America, yielded a bit more still.[56]

Nor, it seems, did imperialism greatly enrich the other colonial powers, though scholars have studied them far less closely. We know that Europe's colonies absorbed

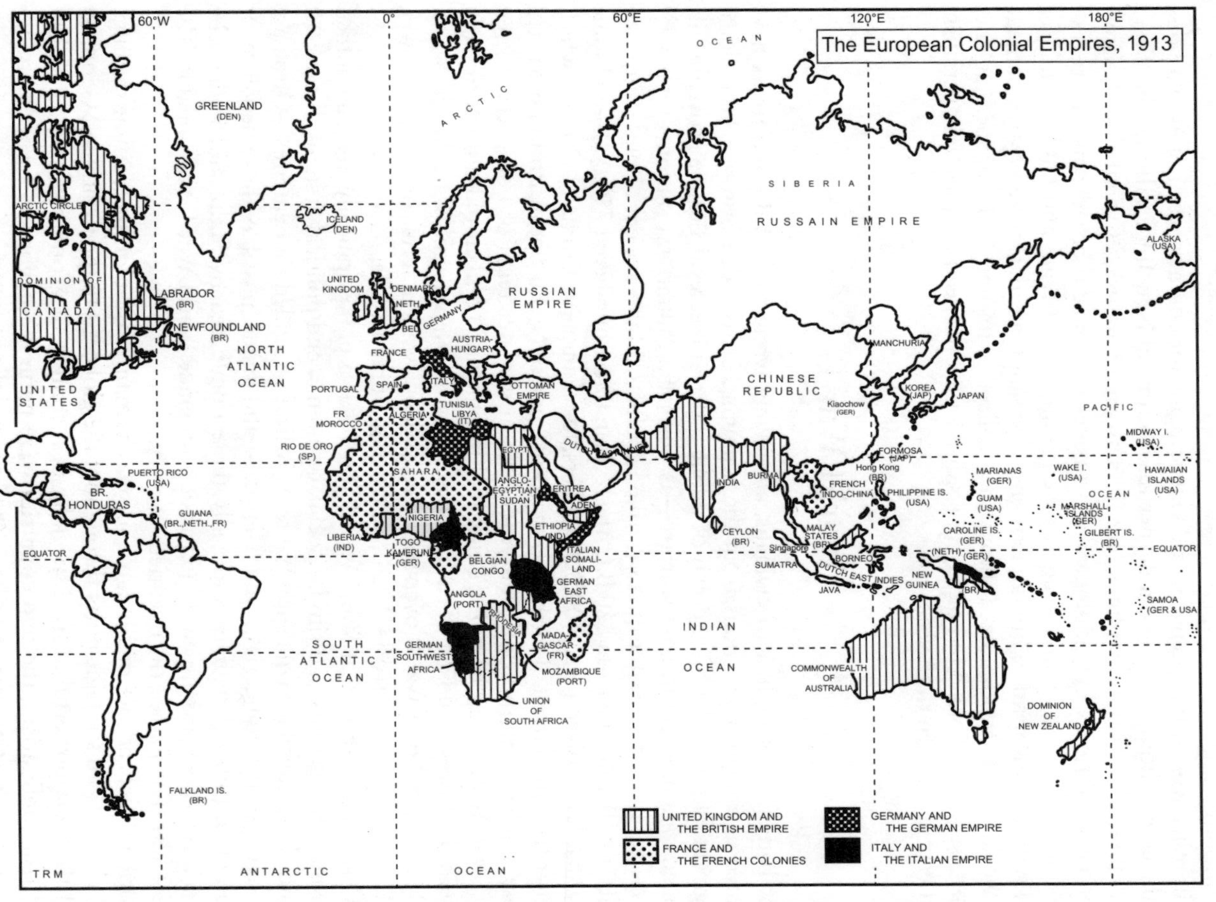

MAP 13.1 *By 1913, eight European powers controlled nearly half of the earth's landmass.*

only 15 percent of the continent's total exports, but it is unclear whether the colonies were a net plus or minus for most of the imperialist powers. Certainly, some sectors of the colonial societies benefited—the military establishments and investors (but not so much entrepreneurs)—yet few if any of the broader populations gained significantly.[57]

In other words, the intense worldwide struggle for colonies was not even a boon to the competitors. Was there a deeper reason for the New Imperialism? The West's raw physical power, apparent scientific mastery of nature, efficient and dynamic economy, and myriad technological advantages provoked a broader moral crisis of Western civilization involving aggressive ideologies justifying and lauding violence and struggle as central to human existence. Sigmund Freud, shocked by the carnage of World War I, hypothesized about the "collective insanity" of Europe.[58] It does indeed seem as if some kind of psychosis drove the European peoples to imperialism and war at the turn of the century.

World War I

Epic battles, the slaughter of civilians, and laying waste to settled populations have figured in human interactions from the beginning of recorded history. The political fragmentation and the breakdown of public order in medieval Europe proved fertile ground for almost continuous warfare—as well as for military revolution—yet not for an increase in the size of armies or armed conflicts. Many ancient armies comprised well over 100,000 men—in 220 B.C. the Roman forces numbered 750,000—and some great battles involved up to 400,000 soldiers, for example at Gaixia (203 B.C.), which led to the establishment of the Han Dynasty in China.[59] No European army approached those numbers until nearly 2,000 years later, in the later reign of Louis XIV.[60] Even the Seven Years' War, the world's first multicontinental conflict, did not enormously exceed the forces deployed in earlier wars. Only the Napoleonic Wars, World War I, and especially World War II overshadowed previous wars in terms of scale, firepower, and, in the case of the World War II, destruction of human life.

Once called the "Great War," World War I was a philosophically absurd conflict. The main belligerents had similar social, economic, and political systems. It took 10 million lives, called into question Western civilization, ended four empires—Ottoman, Russian, Austro-Hungarian, and German—and made possible the emergence of totalitarian political regimes, especially those dominated by Stalin and Hitler. The latter's absolute commitment to expansionism made World War II unavoidable. The Great War thus shaped the twentieth century.

Britain's dependence on foreign trade was its main reason for maintaining the huge Royal Navy and strategic ports throughout the globe.[61] On the Continent, Germany had the most powerful army. Especially in a context of geopolitical expansionism and rising militarism, the two countries were natural antagonists.[62] The lightning-fast Franco-Prussian war of 1870–71 had created the pretext for German unification but left France humiliated and fearful of renewed attack. A defensive alliance with Russia in 1894 was France's belated response. Austria and Germany (and Russia)—recently and incompletely reformed absolutist monarchies—were natural partners, but Austria was a weak state composed of numerous ethnic minorities hoping for political autonomy and thus a weak ally. Moreover, Austria was deeply embroiled in the complex and tense Balkan Peninsula. Had the German leaders known of Britain's secret defensive agreements with France, catastrophe might have been averted.[63]

Numerous events peripheral to Europe increased tensions between the European powers. A *coup d'état* in Belgrade in 1903 brought to power a government committed to territorial expansion. The Russo-Japanese War of 1904–05 provoked a revolution further underscoring Russia's geopolitical weakness. Tensions in 1905 and 1911 between Germany and France over the control of Morocco drew Britain closer to France. In 1908, Austria-Hungary cleverly maneuvered Russia into approving Austria's annexation of Bosnia to howls of protest by Serbia. After that slap in the face, Russia would feel honor bound to defend Serbia in future conflicts. In 1912, when the Ottoman Empire was defending Libya from an Italian invasion, the Balkan League (Bulgaria, Serbia, Greece, and Montenegro) drove the Turks almost entirely out of the region. Its members fought the Second Balkan War the following year to contest the spoils.[64]

On the eve of the World War, France, Germany, Russia, and even Austria-Hungary all had big land armies, sustained by rapidly increasing expenditures, longer terms of military training and service, and widespread public backing. These forces deployed sighted rifles deadly accurate up to 500 meters (over a quarter mile), field artillery capable of firing explosive shells up to 5 miles at 20 rounds per minute, mobile siege guns with a range of over 25 miles, and machine guns able to fire 600 rounds per minute.[65] In fact, one regiment of field guns in 1914 could focus more firepower in 1 hour than all the combatants involved in the entirety of the Napoleonic Wars.[66] Military strategists and statesman considered a protracted war involving such awesome weaponry unthinkable and so planned for a short conflict. Few in authority expected a bigger and more grueling version of the terrible American Civil War.[67] Tragically, that is what they got.

It began with the terrorist assassination in Sarajevo of the heir to the Austrian throne in late June 1914. The Austrian government issued a humiliating ultimatum to Serbia, which had shadowy connections to the organization behind the murder.[68] Germany had given the infamous diplomatic "blank check" to Austria—its willingness to back even a declaration of war on Serbia, which ensued on 28 July. Politically unable to overlook the challenge to Serbia's sovereignty, the Russian tsar mobilized his country's armed forces. Two days later, the German Kaiser ordered mobilization of his forces and on 3 August launched an invasion of France through the territory of neutral Belgium. Having guaranteed that country's neutrality, the United Kingdom declared war on Germany the following day.[69]

It seems that most Europeans willingly embraced what years of militaristic and survival-of-the-fittest rhetoric had advocated. And why not? The troops, most believed, would be home by Christmas.[70] In reality, the Germans got bogged down in northeastern France and for the next 4 years the two sides dug in—literally. In opposing trenches, along a line stretching over 400 miles, millions of soldiers lived or died with rain, snow, rats, lice, and mud. Repeatedly their commanders sent them against the barbed wire, landmines, and machine guns of the enemy. They also attempted several vast, coordinated, and meticulously planned offensives involving the discharge of millions of explosive shells, yet the front lines scarcely moved. And that was only one military theater.[71] On the 900-mile-long Eastern Front, the

Russians managed to advance significantly against Austria a few times, until extra German troops were redeployed east to halt them. Beginning in mid-1915 and accelerating toward the end of the war, Germany made deep inroads into Russian territory. Those were the main and decisive theaters of battle, but combat occurred in many other places, including the Middle East (the Ottoman Empire sided with the Central Powers), throughout the Balkans, between Austria-Hungry and Italy (after Italy entered the war in May 1915), and against Germany's colonies in Africa and the Pacific.

Such total war placed extraordinary demands and stresses on each belligerent society. Everywhere governments restricted liberty, regulated or took control of the economy, and mobilized vast support efforts on the home front.[72] Millions of women flooded into factory and office jobs. Voluntary associations helped coordinate logistics, supply, public health, and services to military personnel. Taxes grew heavy; inflation raged. By 1916, war weariness was gripping all the participating societies.[73]

Germany (and the Central Powers) might well have won the war had it not provoked the United States by sinking passenger ships with Americans aboard and promising the southwestern states to Mexico in exchange for military support. With America involved, German defeat was mostly a foregone conclusion. First, the United States proved capable of building merchant ships faster than German submarines could sink them. Second, fresh American troops were pouring into Europe by early 1918 at a rate of 300,000 a month.[74] German efforts to stir up anti-British Jihadism in the Middle East, had they been successful, might have tipped the balance back. Certainly it helped when the Bolsheviks, whom the German high command had supported, came to power and immediately sued for peace in late 1917 and then pulled Russia out of the war in March.[75] The peace of Brest-Litovsk gave Germany one-third of European Russia, yet half a year later the war was over and the Central Powers lay in ruins.

The Treaty of Versailles, signed in June 1919, stripped Germany of all its conquests including overseas colonies, transferred lands long-possessed by Germany, for example, to Poland and Denmark, imposed onerous reparations payments, demilitarized the left and right banks of the Rhine River on its western border, and strongly curtailed its military capacity. Austria-Hungary was completely broken up into three new countries (Austria, a severely reduced Hungary, and Czechoslovakia) and parts of four others (Poland, Italy, Yugoslavia, and Romania). The Ottoman Empire lost all of its territory except Anatolia and the Straits.[76]

For years scholars have debated which of the belligerent powers deserves more blame for precipitating the war. Scholars have pointed the finger at Germany,[77] Britain,[78] and most recently Russia.[79] German militarism—perhaps especially that of Kaiser Wilhelm II—probably drove Europe into war more than any other factor. Yet the broader context must be kept in mind. In the course of a few decades, the leading Western peoples carved up an entire continent and parts of another, conducted an aggressive arms race, positively reveled in ideologies of struggle, and then marched off to battle and fought mercilessly for four straight years on three continents. The horrible carnage was not unprecedented—some 25 million died in the Taiping armed rebellion, part of a series of popular revolts in China (1850–73) that nearly brought down the Qing Dynasty.[80] Yet the destruction of the World War called into question Western culture and values in ways the Chinese unrest did not.

The European empires, especially Britain's, expanded during and after the war, for example, in the Middle East and Africa. Yet overall Europe came out a loser. Nearly all of the 10 million dead were Europeans. The built environment suffered terribly, especially in France, where some 850,000 buildings were demolished or badly damaged.[81] Their economies were bled white, and trade was disrupted. Japan and above all, the United States, emerged as powerful global competitors in markets previously dominated by the main European powers and as major international creditors, with America now the world's largest.[82]

A huge number of survivors came out of the war maimed both physically and psychologically.[83] Society had changed in many ways, especially in Europe. Mores became more permissive. Government intervened more in economic life. Politics grew more secular. The welfare state developed rapidly.[84]

The carnage, destruction, irrationality-driven combat, and apparent futility of the war led many Western intellectuals to question their culture's devotion to science and technology, the idea of progress, Western claims to moral superiority, mankind's rational control over its own destiny, the idea that Europeans had risen above "the savages," and in general the foundations of Western civilization.[85] Artists expressed such doubts in creative styles like abstract Expressionism, Dadaism, and Surrealism.[86] One can argue that the war tragically fulfilled the insight of artists such as Igor Stravinsky—whose 1913 premier of pagan-themed *The Rite of Spring* scandalized Parisian ballet lovers—that technology and rapid economic growth were pushing European culture toward some apocalypse.[87] Other intellectuals like Herman Hesse sought "alternatives to the 'wounded' civilization of Europe" in Eastern culture and mysticism.[88]

Yet most ordinary people, educated elites, and even intellectuals in Britain, France, and Germany found spiritual and cultural means of coming to terms with their losses that reconnected with traditional forms and enabled them to remain hopeful about their civilization and values.[89] Moreover, the majority of at least British literature was quite patriotic and traditional in style, content, and outlook. Film throughout Europe and America tended to render the war heroic and even romantic, at least until the powerfully antiwar film *All Quiet on the Western Front* (1930).[90] The tragic losses experienced by tens of millions of survivors in the major European countries convinced most people that another major war was to be avoided at all cost. The League of Nations, founded in 1919 to preserve world peace, was just one expression of this determination. Sadly, leaders of regimes brought to life by the war had other ideas.

Totalitarian ideologies

One can plausibly interpret the rise of the totalitarian dictatorships of the twentieth century as rebellions against Western values: individual freedom, democracy, political and economic decentralization, the rule of law, and the free and open pursuit of every form of knowledge and self-expression.[91] The achievements of Western civilization thus provoked powerful counter-ideologies aimed at overthrowing it. These ideologies emphasized a traditional unity of rulership, a communitarian ideal, and a collectivist vision of social justice. Nazism, moreover, added a reversion to tribalism. No other civilization has ever changed the world so much as to call forth such catastrophically destructive ruling counter-ideologies.

The first to emerge was Bolshevik Communism. In the nineteenth and early twentieth centuries, the Russian government was the most repressive and absolutist in Europe. Following the disastrous Crimean War (1853–56), Tsar Alexander II embarked upon the Great Reforms, which freed the servile half of Russia's population, established institutions of local self-government, and created an independent judiciary. Thus, advances typically imposed on rulers from below in the West occurred in Russia by top-down fiat.[92] Radical intellectuals pressed for further change. Some, called "Populists," went out among the peasantry hoping to inspire rebellion. When their efforts failed, in the mid-1870s, some of them forged the world's first conspiratorial terrorist organization, People's Will. In 1881, they succeeded in killing the "Tsar Liberator." His son, Alexander III, crushed the revolutionary intelligentsia with harsh repression and launched an industrialization drive that, in the 1890s, resulted in exceptionally high economic growth.[93]

The expansion of industry, commerce, railroads, education, the professions, and other elements of modern life fostered social dislocation and discontentment. Factory workers began to unite; intellectuals founded Marxist, liberal, and populist political organizations; extremely rapid population growth in the countryside gave rise to "land hunger." The new tsar, Nicholas II (r. 1894–1917), though a weak leader, promised his father to uphold political absolutism. Geopolitical expansion in the Far East led to ignominious defeat by Japan in 1904–05. In the midst of the war, political revolution nearly toppled the government. Nicholas felt compelled to adopt civil rights legislation and to institute a parliament (the Duma).[94] To some extent these were half measures, yet they marked an important turning point for Russia. If not for the disastrous World War, the country might have continued to evolve politically and economically in a Western direction.[95]

The demands of total war placed an especially heavy strain on Russia with it's weakly developed middle class, financial and communications infrastructure, bureaucratic institutions, and civil society. Popular discontent and even mutinies broke out in all the belligerent countries, but in Russia they brought the regime crashing down. Street demonstrations protesting bread shortages broke out in Petrograd on 8 March 1917.[96] A week later, the tsar abdicated. Power was now shared between the liberal Provisional Government lacking an electoral mandate but enjoying the support of educated people and the Petrograd Soviet, to which most workers and soldiers felt loyal. As the war continued disastrously over the summer, more and more socialists entered the government. Only the Bolsheviks promised peace. In October, they seized power in the name of the Soviets (worker, peasant, and soldier councils). Probably they enjoyed at this point at least the tacit support of most ordinary people.

They could have formed a broad socialist governing coalition but instead created a one-party dictatorship, nominally sharing power until summer with a small number of Left Socialist-Revolutionaries. They proclaimed an end to the war, all land to the peasantry, self-determination of national minorities, and rule of the lower classes. In practice, however, their rejection of other political parties precipitated a civil war, the need to provision the cities and army drove them to confiscate grain, minorities were integrated under centralized control, and the Soviets, trade unions, and factory committees were all soon dominated by authoritarian Bolsheviks.[97] A secret police with wide powers, the Cheka, was set up in December. It and the Red Army, created in mid-1918, were the two most efficient institutions in early Bolshevik Russia.

Those who opposed the new regime—most educated people, the church, former officers, and ultimately most peasants and even many workers—never formed a united front and therefore lost the Civil War.[98] The liberal, conservative, and socialist opposition had been defeated by 1920. Grain seizures continued, though, provoking lower-class rebellion into 1921. The Bolshevik leadership therefore proclaimed the New Economic Policy (NEP) in early 1921, which replaced the confiscations with a fixed tax and legalized small-scale trade. (Tragically, it was too late to avert a famine that left some 5 million dead.)[99] By 1927, the country was approaching its prewar economic output.[100] To compensate for their "retreat" on the "economic front," Lenin and the Bolshevik leadership tightened their political control, even banning "factions" within their own party.[101]

A power struggle following Lenin's death in 1924 pitted advocates of slow, partially market-based economic development against those in favor of rapid industrialization.[102] The Bolsheviks were Marxists. They rejected private property, the free market, and what they called bourgeois liberties, which they believed only rich people could enjoy.[103] Building socialism was their main goal. As Marx taught, that required a high level of industrial development. So here was a dilemma: Russia was growing more prosperous under the NEP but only thanks to free economic exchange and the emergence of well-to-do farmers and traders. Achieving socialism required industrialization, but there were insufficient financial resources to fund it. After all, the Bolsheviks had repudiated the former government's financial obligations to the outside world. They had also confiscated every last bit of wealth from former property owners (individuals, government agencies, religious organizations, private institutions, and voluntary associations).[104] The only way to industrialize now was either slowly, by allowing the peasantry and small-scale entrepreneurs to enrich themselves and thus pay for industrialization through taxes, or to mercilessly squeeze the only large population group in the country: the peasantry.

Joseph Stalin, a brilliant political operator and ruthless tactician, came out on top of the political succession struggle, thanks in part to his advocacy of rapid development.[105] That was certainly what the party militants who had won the Civil War desired above all else. They had not shed so much blood to see private interests thrive in Russia.

In 1928, the party launched Russia's first Five-Year Plan aimed at radically increasing the output of coal, iron, steel, and electricity. Simultaneously, a policy of "collectivizing" the entire Russian peasantry was undertaken.[106] The peasants lost their land, their livestock, and the right to leave their villages at will and were forced to give up most of their output to the state. Those who resisted were branded "kulaks," or "rich peasants." Some 2 million were exiled in boxcars and resettled and forced to work in distant places. Millions more were driven from their homes. Many were executed or died from the poor conditions of transport or labor.[107] Inordinate grain confiscations, along with the slaughter of livestock by peasants unwilling to hand it over to government officials, provoked a second major famine in Soviet Russia. It raged in 1932–33 and caused some 6 million deaths, a large proportion in Ukraine, leading many commentators but relatively few scholars to charge intentional genocide.[108] Unlike in 1921, however, the peasantry did not revolt—how could they

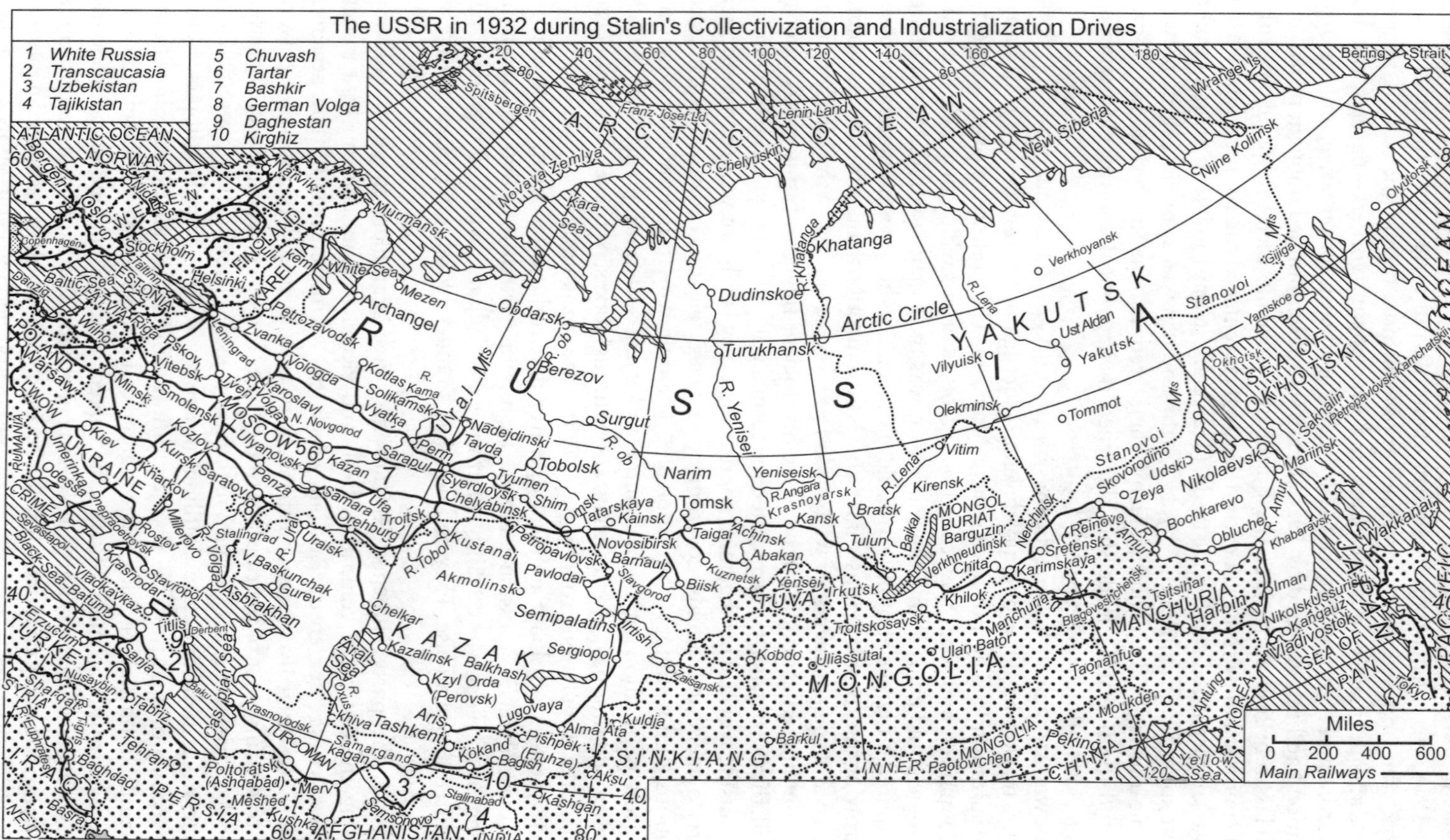

MAP 13.2 *Comprehending one-sixth of the earth's landmass and extending across eleven time zones, the USSR was the world's largest country.*

in the face of such ferocious repression and suffering?—nor did the party leadership retreat. On the contrary, they pressed forward with rapid industrialization and paid for it largely through agricultural confiscation (see Map 13.2).

These policies obviously caused hardship throughout society. The economic drive emphasized heavy industry at the expense of consumer goods. Millions of peasants flooded into the cities for factory work, yet practically no new housing was built.[109] People unused to the strict rhythms of industrial labor suffered endless accidents on the job. The results of the 5-year plans were quite impressive, but they always fell short of the published targets. In other words, there was plenty of trouble, but who could be blamed? Certainly not the party, which was in charge of everything yet was considered infallible. In this context, the Great Terror broke out.

"Show trials" had been used in 1922 against socialist opponents and religious leaders and in 1928 against "bourgeois specialists," especially engineers, alleged to have committed acts of industrial sabotage. A series of three sham trials in 1936–38 found dozens of major Bolshevik leaders guilty of utterly implausible crimes, including collaborating with foreign powers for more than a decade to overthrow the Soviet government.[110] In summer 1937, moreover, an order was issued to imprison and execute specific quotas of "enemies of the people" throughout the country. Police officials, accustomed as were all Soviet citizens to the expectation of over-fulfilling every plan, repressed far more people than officially required. According to government statistics, more than 680,000 people perished.[111] Among the victims were people from all walks of life, but an especially high proportion of educated elites, including many thousands of officers.

Soviet foreign policy was driven in large part by hostility to the Western capitalist powers. Ideologically, the Bolshevik leaders believed that their socialist society must struggle and ultimately triumph against them. Yet backward and largely agrarian Russia, in Marxist terms, needed their technical and financial help to advance toward socialism. Thus, the Bolsheviks desperately hoped revolution would occur in Europe. In 1919, they founded the Communist International, or Comintern, to promote revolution throughout the world.[112] Its members were required to place the interests of the Soviet Union above those of their own countries and to subvert their own governments. It is not surprising that these policies provoked fear wherever they were implemented, leading to "red scares" in most major countries.

The clearest beneficiaries of the widespread panic induced by communist subversion were anti-communist political organizations.[113] Fascism almost certainly could not have come to power in Italy in 1922, for example, were it not viewed by broad segments of Italian society as a credible counterforce to violent communist activists. Mussolini's movement combined anti-capitalist rhetoric, attacks on property, violence against socialists and communists, the idealization of modern technology, radical intellectual opposition to "decadent" bourgeois society, and calls for nationalistic unity. Unlike in Russia, where war and revolution had destroyed the already weakly developed institutions of civil society, in Western Europe revolutionary activists could not hope to come to power without the support of existing political, economic, military, religious, social, cultural, and other influential elites and institutions. Radicals on the left could not win such support, but it was the peculiar genius of rightwing extremists in Italy and later in Germany to forge a broad-based movement that appealed to disgruntled elements throughout society.[114]

Mussolini did not fight his way to power by force of arms (though his Fascist squads killed dozens of people), much less by electoral means. His so-called March on Rome was a fiasco, and before coming to power his party never received more than 35 out of 535 seats in parliament.[115] He ascended to office entirely because of King Victor Emmanuel III who, fearing the much more electorally successful socialists, selected him to serve as prime minister in 1922. Mussolini pursued cautious and conservative policies in order to retain the support of the political establishment, but feeling pressure from his party base, in 1925–27 he closed opposition periodicals and organizations, instituted strict censorship, dissolved opposition parties, and established tight control over labor organizations and local administration. In a word, he established a one-party dictatorship.[116]

A decade after Mussolini, Hitler came to power in a similar way. A skillful demagogue able like Mussolini to play upon the fears of broad segments of German society, Hitler enjoyed far greater success at the ballot box. In parliamentary elections of July 1932, his National Socialist, or Nazi, party captured 37 percent of the vote. Although the Nazi party slipped in the election of 6 November, on 30 January the aged President Hindenburg appointed Hitler Chancellor of Germany, fearing the leftists more than the Nazis. Here and in Italy, a decade before, the political establishment believed they could control these upstarts, among the first lower-class men to achieve power in major European countries.[117]

Hitler spilled more blood than Mussolini establishing his rule—hundreds killed rather than dozens—yet both shared power with establishment elites and maintained many existing institutions and governmental structures.[118] The contrast with Communist Russia was stark. The Bolsheviks completely dismantled or severely repressed most of the existing institutions that remained after the February Revolution, including the law courts, institutions of local self-government, the army, the navy, and the officer corps, institutions that retained considerable autonomy under Mussolini and Hitler.[119] Crushing all potential centers of power, rather than accommodating with some of them, was naturally far bloodier. In each of the first 5 years of their rule, the Bolsheviks executed at least 28,000 people (not counting those killed during Civil War battles).[120] In contrast, the worst early Nazi bloodbath—the Night of the Long Knives on 30 June 1934—left fewer than 100 people dead[121] and largely strengthened the existing German military.

The Communist and Nazi states functioned differently in other ways too. Early Nazi rhetoric was staunchly anticapitalist and anti-property, but when the Nazis came to power they worked closely with leading business interests. Most top Nazis, including Hitler, were staunch atheists or at least militantly anti-Christian, and they closely watched and harassed the clergy and churches but did not crush them.[122] Censorship was strict, but in Nazi Germany much of the press was allowed to continue to function. Indeed, all of these elements of civil society—business and the market, faith and religion, and means of public expression—while often meticulously regulated did not face annihilation or near annihilation as in Soviet Russia.[123]

Yet the two regimes exhibited some striking similarities. Charismatic leaders advancing revolutionary programs of completely transforming the world dominated both. Thousands of ideologically fervent activists ready to use violent repression backed them. The essential institutions of modern liberal democracy—free and fair elections, broad-based political participation, civil rights—were absent. The political authority of ruling party elites was all embracing in both systems, the life of every member of society hanging from the whim of the supreme leaders.[124] In other words, what was most distinctive about modern Western society was precisely what both Soviet Communism and Nazism vehemently excluded. Yet those polities were not throwbacks to an earlier ethos. In both, modern technology flourished but normative morality was disparaged.[125] (The communist leaders advocated Western ideals of liberation though not consistently.)

Political parties and movements hostile to democracy, individualism, the rule of law, the separation of powers, and constitutionalism were particularly successful and virulent in Russia and Germany, and to a lesser extent Italy, in the 1920s and 1930s, but they also flourished in many other parts of Europe. Between the wars, authoritarian regimes also replaced constitutional government in Spain, Portugal, Greece, and much of Eastern Europe. Moreover, authoritarian parties enjoyed considerable success in several other European countries.[126]

Overall, fascist parties flourished best in those countries with the weakest institutions of self-government and civil society. Also, countries that industrialized later were able to skip steps, borrow technology from abroad, and thus compress the pace of development, causing greater social dislocation, which made them more susceptible to fascist revolution.[127]

Perhaps the most consequential similarity shared by Communism and Nazism was their apparent commitment to "permanent revolution."[128] Constant radical movement forward seems to have been essential to both for retaining popular and activist support, though they diverged in the nature of the momentum. Overthrowing or severely repressing nearly all existing laws, institutions, voluntary associations, and traditions was obviously going to provoke hostile reactions. In fact, the leading Bolsheviks considered violence, terror, and even civil war inevitable.[129] "Constructing socialism" in a territory comprising one-sixth of the earth's landmass was surely a gargantuan and to some extent never-ending task. So were creating a "racially pure" society and bringing about Nazi world domination. The Nazis sought to achieve these goals by infiltrating committed activists into the existing socioeconomic and administrative systems and inculcating their racist values to young people.[130] The Nazis intended to destroy whole categories of people, in particular, Jews and the disabled, and to launch grandiose military conquest. The Bolsheviks aimed to root out "class enemies." The two ideologically driven rivals both clashed and collaborated. In the swath of Eastern Europe that separated them, which Timothy Snyder has called the "bloodlands," they destroyed some 14 million lives in 1933–45, not counting combat deaths.[131]

Both radical agendas were Western-inspired in the sense that they aimed to transform the world as dramatically as Western civilization had done in the previous centuries. They also employed much of the latest technology and science. Yet they were also anti-Western in important ways. The Western transformations had been made possible by liberating human creativity and initiative, freeing people up to coordinate their efforts at will, prizing innovation in every aspect of life, and placing fewer and fewer limits on the pursuit of "impossible dreams." The Communist and Nazi dictatorships, by contrast, sought to mobilize and coordinate entire populations for the attainment of centrally determined plans and goals. Their leaders and parties were preponderant; the individual, nearly without value.

Systematically and carefully, Hitler built up Germany's military capacity and tackled modest aims until it was obvious no one could oppose him. Having secretly begun to rearm the country, in 1935 he reintroduced conscription, flouting a key provision of the Versailles Treaty.[132] The following year, he sent troops unopposed into the legally demilitarized Rhineland. He then launched a Four-Year Plan of military preparation. He also began supplying military assistance to the right-wing forces of Franco in Spain. In 1937–38, he removed many conservatives from senior government and military positions (though without violence), because he assumed they would resist his policies of military aggression. Believing most Germans to be unenthusiastic about militarism, he proceeded cautiously. In March 1938, having engineered the appointment of a Nazi as Austrian chancellor, Hitler sent an invasion force across the border. It met with no resistance. In April, rampant voter intimidation yielded 99.75 percent support in an Austrian plebiscite for union with Germany. Full annexation ensued.[133] Again the other European powers did nothing. In September, Hitler organized a meeting with the prime ministers of France and Britain in Munich to discuss Germany's desire to annex German-speaking regions of Czechoslovakia. They approved this demand. A few months later, German troops occupied the entire Czech region. These easy victories increased Hitler's popularity at home.

The second transformative Nazi goal—anti-Jewish repression—was also underway. In 1935, the Nuremberg Laws stripped Jews of all civil and even social rights; for example, they were not allowed to marry or engage in sexual relations with "Aryan" Germans. On 9 and 10 November 1938—exactly 20 years after the German surrender—the Nazi leadership coordinated attacks against Jewish businesses, synagogues, and homes in hundreds of communities throughout Germany and Austria.[134] Storm troopers and other activists killed 91 Jews, arrested and sent some 30,000 to concentration camps, burned more than 1,000 synagogues, and damaged or destroyed over 7,000 businesses. The victims received no help from police or firefighters, were unable to collect any insurance payments, and had to pay a huge fine. For Hitler, the Jews of Germany and the world were to blame for Germany's humiliation in World War I. In his mind, he would make them pay for their alleged treachery.

On 30 January 1939, the sixth anniversary of the Nazi ascent to power, Hitler verbally linked the two central Nazi goals. Germany's economic troubles, he claimed, stemmed directly from a lack of *Lebensraum*, that is, insufficient territory to accommodate the growing German population. Given his country's militaristic buildup and annexation of two foreign countries the previous year, one would assume that he was planning to seize yet more land. Yet, like a child "hiding" a toy in his hand and asking his parent where it has disappeared to, the Nazi leader, claiming prophetic powers, warned that if a new world war should break out, it would lead to "the annihilation of the Jewish race in Europe."[135] Although Hitler had asserted in 1919 that "The removal of the Jews altogether" should be the "final aim" of any patriotic German government,[136] this was his first public reference to his diabolical plan since he had assumed power. In the next few years, he referred over and over to his "prophecy"—but as having occurred on 1 September—the date when his military forces invaded Poland and precipitated World War II.[137] Clearly the two "operations" were closely intertwined in his worldview.

World War II

If World War I was philosophically senseless, World War II was unavoidable. The belligerents in the first war had relatively little to fight over, certainly nothing over which to destroy 10 million lives. In 1939, by contrast, two governments in Europe were militantly hostile to Western values and, each in its own way, ideologically committed to territorial expansion. The leaders of neither Soviet Russia nor Nazi Germany could imagine living cooperatively and in nonviolent economic competition with the Western Democratic peoples, who by their very institutions and way of life were deemed ideological enemies. Mussolini with his dreams of empire strengthened Hitler's hand, albeit modestly. Moreover, Imperial Japan was hell-bent on territorial expansion. It had invaded Manchuria in 1931, launched a full-scale war against China in 1937, and unsuccessfully attacked the Soviet Far East in 1938–39 (see Map 13.3).[138] These actions resulted in painful US-imposed economic sanctions.[139] An interesting twist was the mutual admiration of Stalin and Hitler for each other, despite their countries' official enmity.[140]

Therefore, the nonaggression pact they signed in August 1939 was far less bizarre than it seemed to the world at the time.[141] A secret protocol stipulated the division of Poland, the Baltic States, and Finland between the two powers. Hitler lost no time, launching an invasion of Poland on 1 September. Two days later, France and Britain declared war on Germany. In a further 2 weeks, the Soviet Union attacked from the east. By the end of the month, the two aggressors had divided the country between them. In the winter, the USSR defeated Finland, but with difficulty. A few months later, Germany easily overran Denmark, Norway, Belgium, the Netherlands, Luxembourg, and France, which on 22 June ceded its northern half directly to Germany and installed a subservient puppet government in the south. (The previous day Italy had invaded a small portion of southern France.) Such triumphs increased public support for the Nazis, including among the previously skeptical but now enthusiastic military leadership.[142] Germany milked the captured lands of resources, labor, and industrial production, increasing its fighting capacity and maintaining a high standard of living back home.[143] With Switzerland, Sweden, Spain, Portugal, and Ireland neutral, the only significant European power opposed to Germany was Britain. Consequently, the Nazis launched three months of bombing raids, known as the Battle of Britain. It failed, leaving a lone outpost of freedom and democracy on the continent.

The war soon extended to the periphery of Europe and beyond. Italy had already conquered Abyssinia in 1936 and Albania in 1939. Now, in September 1940, Mussolini attacked Egypt from bases in Libya (German troops had landed in North Africa in the spring).[144] Later that month, Germany, Italy, and Japan formed a military pact. In October, Italy attacked Greece. Nothing succeeds like success, and within the next several months Slovakia, Hungary, Romania, and Bulgaria joined the Axis Powers. In April, Germany joined the Greek offensive and led its allies in an invasion of Yugoslavia. On 22 June, Hitler launched a massive attack involving 3.5 million men against Soviet Russia, divided into 3 main forces along a 1,800-mile front. In 2 days, the Germans had destroyed 3,922 Soviet planes.[145] Within a few months, they had captured or killed over 2 million Soviet troops and were at the gates of Leningrad, Moscow, and Rostov in the south.[146] With the Axis

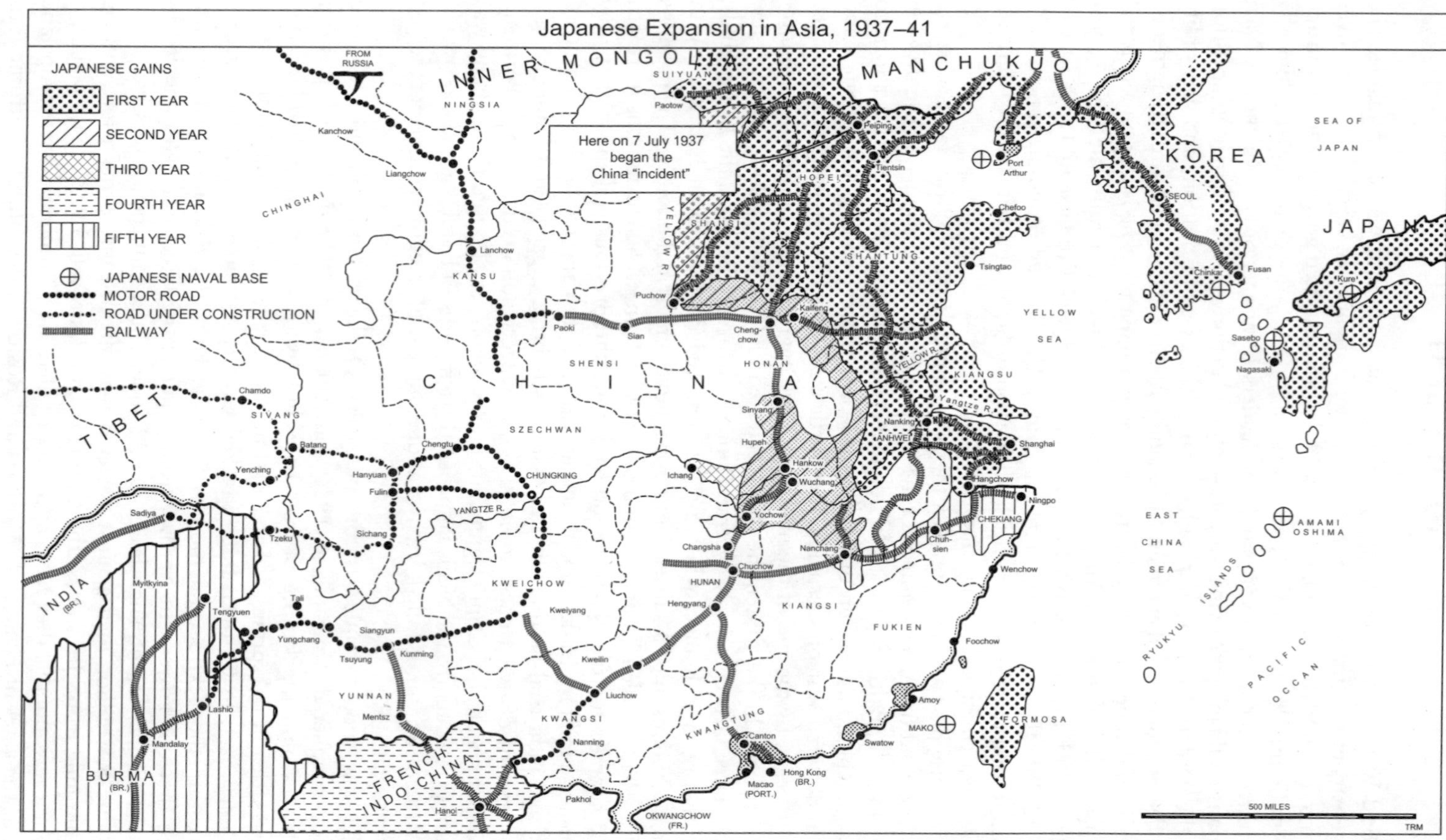

MAP 13.3 *Beginning in 1937, Japan expanded its territory in China and Southeast Asia.*

powers in almost complete control of Europe and the British Empire isolated and its resources stretched to the limit, the grandiose Nazi visions of world domination seemed close to fulfillment.

As the war intensified, so did Hitler's murderous plans to "purify the Aryan race." Again, the two projects were connected. Territorial expansion was intended to free up living space; the removal of "undesirable" people would improve it.

Soon after the outbreak of war in 1939, the Nazis undertook their top secret T-4 program, which aimed to murder disabled children and then expanded to (both physically and mentally) disabled adults. Following public disquiet in 1940–41, reflected in protests by religious leaders, the program was pursued more furtively but with greater intensity. It had so far taken some 70,000 lives; even more would die in the next 3 years. Some killing methods developed for the program were redeployed in the Final Solution.[147]

The conquest of western Poland, with its large Jewish population, intensified the "Jewish problem" for the Nazis. Henceforth, Jews were required to wear a yellow Star of David (a policy extended to the entire Reich in August 1941).[148] Special SS troops, *Einsatzgruppen*, were dispatched in the wake of regular military forces (as they had been in 1938 in Czechoslovakia) to "combat anti-German elements." Their orders were to kill insurgents, educated elites, nobles, priests, and Jews. Regular military forces occasionally took part and regularly cooperated in this work. Local ethnic minorities often assisted as well. The squads typically shot their victims, though gas vans first used in the T-4 program were later employed as well.[149]

It was in the USSR that these special troops wreaked the most damage. Following a plan laid out in advance by Hitler, they began killing adult males, targeted women and children beginning in August and September, and massacred entire Jewish communities from September to October.[150] By the end of 1941, they had slaughtered a half-million Jews. During the course of the war, they killed roughly 2 million people, including 1.3 million Jews.[151] This policy, and three others adopted soon after the invasion, pointed toward the Holocaust. First, individual Nazi officials in the Baltic States and Eastern Poland, on their own initiative but sure of finding favor in Berlin, began the mass murder of whole Jewish communities, including women and children. Second, in September 1941 at Auschwitz, 600 Soviet POWs were put to death using the insecticide Zyclon-B. Third, convoys of Jews from Germany to the East, including some "part Jews" and Jews married to "Aryans," were on a few occasions butchered, but largely in secret and apparently without Berlin's prior knowledge.[152] In late fall, construction began on extermination units in Belzec near Lublin and Chelmno near Lodz. A small number of Jews were murdered at the Chelmno camp starting on 8 December.[153]

The final decision to root out and destroy all of European Jewry was taken in mid-December 1941 in the context of several dramatic events. First, Germany suffered its first serious retreat—from Rostov. Several days later, on 5–6 December, Soviet troops launched a successful counteroffensive outside Moscow. In Libya, British forces pushed back Rommel's *Afrika Korps* on 7–8 December.[154] On 7 December 1941, the Japanese bombed US naval installations at Pearl Harbor in Hawaii—killing over 2,000 and destroying or damaging 5 battle ships. (Japan then expanded furiously in Southeast Asia, conquering the Philippines, Indochina, Thailand, Burma, Malaya, the Dutch East Indies, and Singapore within a few months.)[155] On the 11th, Italy and Germany joined their ally Japan in declaring war on the United States.[156] (Hitler had always planned to fight the United States but needed the support of a big navy, which Japan provided.)[157]

At a meeting of senior Nazi leaders on 12 December 1941, Hitler recalled his "prophecy" about the annihilation of the Jews. Now, he said, "those responsible for this bloody conflict will have to pay for it with their lives."[158] Senior Nazi officials worked out details of this policy over the next several days.[159] The Wannsee Conference of party and state officials, originally scheduled for 9 December but which met on 20 January, was likely an effort to coordinate actions already underway in various localities and to apply to them the highest party sanction.[160] The Foreign Ministry had basically already agreed to the rounding up of Jews from throughout Europe and their execution in the East, so long as these efforts did not incite diplomatic protests.[161] The key thing that was decided was the fate of German Jews (but not "half Jews" or Jews married to non-Jews), until then a largely protected category. Within two months, many of those already on hand in Riga and Minsk had been executed. In May, many more began arriving in the East for extermination.[162]

A policy of institutionalized killing was made possible by the establishment, beginning in early 1942, of five additional extermination units within existing concentration camps, all of them located in Polish territory. (Fear of public opposition and meddling by scrupulous government officials doubtless kept the sites outside of Germany.) At all six death camps—Chelmno, Belzec, Sobibor, Treblinka, Majdanek, and Auschwitz-Birkenau—some 3 million Jews and many tens of thousands of Gypsies, or Roma, and other non-Jews perished.[163] This was only a fraction of the 11 million prisoners (including up to 6 million Jews) who died in thousands of camps throughout German-controlled lands during the war (see Map 13.4).[164] Even when military retreat forced the abandonment of the killing centers, merciless Nazi guards marched hundreds of thousands of prisoners westward for further use as slave labor; up to one-third died in transit.[165]

Many Europeans felt a deep antipathy toward the Jews because of their cultural differences, great success in modern times (thanks in large part to their devotion to learning), and strong associations with both capitalism and socialism. Even thousands of highly educated German professionals—doctors, lawyers, engineers, and scientists—took an active part in the extermination programs; in fact, the Holocaust could not have happened without them.[166] Those who took part in the killing were motivated by racism, careerism, peer pressure, cajoling by superiors, and desire for better material conditions. Heavy use of alcohol lowered many executioners' moral inhibitions.[167]

While the slaughter was taking place, the Nazi war effort was stalling and then collapsing. Bombing raids by Britain and the United States wrought extraordinary devastation in Germany in the final 2 years of the war, destroying around 5 million dwellings.[168] In May 1943, Allied troops expelled Axis forces from North Africa and in July began landings in Sicily. Two weeks later, the king deposed Mussolini, and in September Italy surrendered. Germany then installed the former dictator as a puppet in the north (partisans shot him in April 1945). By now, Soviet forces were advancing relentlessly westward (see Map 13.5). In June 1944, the Western allies liberated Rome and then launched a massive amphibious offensive in northwest France—D-Day—involving 5,000 ships, 50,000 vehicles, 11,000 planes, and 150,000 soldiers

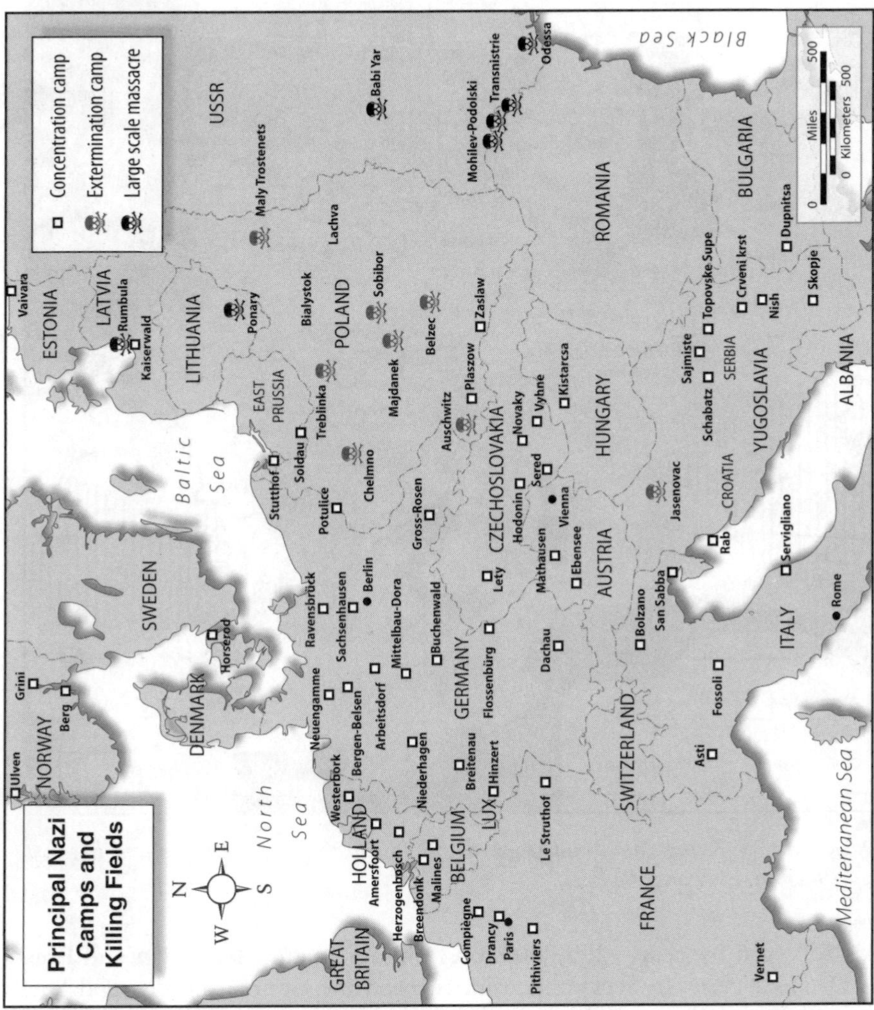

MAP 13.4 *Thousands of camps in Nazi Germany and its conquered territories housed millions of prisoners.*

MAP 13.5 *By 1943, the Allies had stopped the advance of the Germans and began to pressure them in Italy and the East.*

(quickly followed by nearly 200,000 more). In late August, American and British troops liberated Paris. In September, they reached the German border, and Soviet troops were outside Warsaw. In April 1945, the Allies were encircling Berlin. On the 30th, Hitler and some of his closest associates committed suicide. Germany surrendered in early May.[169]

The war in the Pacific was far from over, however. Following intensive fighting from island to island, including the loss of 7,000 US Marines in February on Iwo Jima, American forces had reached Okinawa several hundred miles south of Japan. On 1 April, they commenced a gargantuan assault. Ordered to fight to the death, over 100,000 Japanese soldiers gave their lives, including some 1,900 suicide-pilots (kamikazes). In 6 weeks of combat, the Americans, now reinforced by the Royal Navy, suffered over 10,000 deaths.[170] Massive bombing raids throughout Japan, which killed some 330,000 people, had no impact on the leaders' resolve to keep fighting. On the contrary, they threw all their efforts into preparing to defend tooth and nail against an expected ground offensive.[171] American intelligence services had broken the main Japanese code and therefore knew in detail these intentions. Official reports estimated that an overall offensive would cost at the very least 100,000 American lives—and perhaps as many as 1 million—and far, far more Japanese dead; senior commanders began to hesitate about invading.[172]

By midsummer, however, President Truman, who had succeeded the deceased President Roosevelt in April, could deploy a weapon whose explosive force was equal to the combined bombing capacity of 1,000 B-29 Superfortresses. The only problem was, only two atomic bombs were available for combat use. What if they failed to compel surrender? Truman bluffed, suggesting America had an endless supply.[173] He also faced a second difficulty. Back in February, FDR had promised Stalin Japanese territory in exchange for help winning the war in the Pacific.[174] Now that Germany was defeated, and the atomic bomb had been invented, such a concession seemed superfluous. Preventing Soviet takeover of Japanese territory, according to one historian,[175] may have partly motivated Truman's use of one bomb on 6 August 1945, though presumably saving American lives was the main factor. Despite the complete destruction of the first target city, Hiroshima—and perhaps 70,000 dead instantaneously—the Japanese government held firm. Two days later, the USSR declared war on Japan. According to Tsuyoshi Hasegawa, this act frightened the Japanese leadership more than the atomic bombing itself.[176] Still they did not surrender. On 9 August, an American B-29 dropped the only other available atomic bomb (another one could be ready by 21 August). Now the Japanese leadership began to talk. American conventional bombing was suspended on 11 August. On 14 August, the emperor agreed in principle to surrender. (That night a group of officers attempted a coup to prevent surrender, but their plot failed.) Despite some loose ends in Southeast Asia and China, World War II was over.[177]

In all, some 60 million people had died, including roughly 26 million Soviets (mostly civilians) and at least 15 million Chinese.[178] Additionally, perhaps 21 million people were displaced by the end of the war in Europe alone.[179] Approximately two million Soviet POWs were returned home, where many suffered further mistreatment, including execution or exile to labor camps.[180] A further 20 million people were left homeless in Germany, as well as 25 million in the USSR, where 70,000 villages, 1,700 towns, and 32,000 factories had been destroyed.[181] No event in history had caused so much havoc in a mere half-dozen years.

The Cold War

Yet a new conflict had already begun. A fear of Soviet conquest of Japanese territory was only one source of tension. The Western Allies were certainly willing to grant Stalin large swaths of land along his Western border and even a huge sphere of influence running across a half-dozen countries in Eastern Europe, given the extraordinary suffering of the Russian people and heroic efforts of its military. What they did not bargain for, however, was the imposition of Soviet-style dictatorships without any possibility of popular political participation or civil rights.[182] It seems hard to believe that the former allies could have maintained cordial relations under such circumstances.

Scholars explain the onset of the Cold War variously. Some trace postwar tensions back to prior hostilities, starting when the Bolsheviks pulled out of World War I, leaving their allies in the lurch, followed by the allies landing troops on Soviet territory both to prevent military equipment falling into German hands and to support anti-Bolshevik forces. From then until they joined forces in World War II, the Western democracies and the Soviet Union were, if not enemies, then at least not friends.[183] One can point to dozens if not hundreds of negative policies and actions on both sides. For example, the Soviet Union funded political subversion in every Western country, and the United States did not recognize Soviet Union diplomatically until 1933. Even during the war, tensions between the allies often flared up, as when Stalin castigated the Western Allies for failing to invade France until June 1944, while his country was fighting desperately on the Eastern Front.[184]

Other scholars point to diplomatic mistakes, instances of saber rattling, and missed opportunities. For example, in September 1945 the United States ended the Lend-Lease program, which had given the USSR 10 billion dollars in supplies and equipment during the course of the war.[185] Stalin felt insulted; after all, his country was in ruins and could have used help rebuilding. It is also possible to emphasize Stalin's personal role as a paranoid, ruthless dictator,[186] or to consider the Stalinist political system to have been "the greatest threat to liberal values on a global scale."[187]

Indeed, a political system founded on free enterprise is not readily compatible with one founded on communist principles. In a capitalist economy, the free interplay of market relations and private ownership of property defines a huge range of interactions among people both domestically and abroad. Exchanges of goods, services, and information occur largely without the intermediary of central governments. Businesses and nonprofit organizations in such countries compete among themselves to win customers and followers. In a communist system, by contrast, the central government and party leadership direct or try to control all significant economic, political, social, and cultural exchanges.[188] One obvious result is an inefficient and uncompetitive economy. After World War II, the United States was able to compete peacefully with its two recent archenemies—Japan and Germany—which within a few decades, because of their free-market economies, became the second and third richest societies in the world. The USSR, in contrast, produced almost no goods or services salable on the international market. Economic competition was therefore impossible. Yet its leadership was ideologically committed to competition for world preeminence with the capitalist West. The only available means of competition, aside from such relatively trivial pursuits as sports and high culture, in which the Soviets enjoyed enormous success, was military. For this reason, the USSR became oriented above all toward military supremacy.[189]

The Soviet government steadily increased its military spending until by the late 1970s it had achieved relative parity with the United States—not just in conventional forces, which had been its strength since the war, but also in ballistic missiles, in a massive blue water navy, in air power, and in nuclear weaponry. During its final decades of existence, Soviet military expenditures totaled at least 25 if not

40 percent of GDP (by contrast, American military spending was under 10 percent). In addition, perhaps 30 or 40 percent of the labor force contributed to military purposes.[190] Military culture was pervasive. Virtually all Soviet children received civil defense training in elementary school and basic, along with some specialized military training, in secondary school. (Girls typically learned different skill sets.) As part of their military-patriotic instruction, most students—both boys and girls—also played *zarnitsa* ("lightning"), a competitive "war game" organized by real military instructors. The games grew more serious and realistic in the higher grades.[191] After graduation, most young men completed their 2-year military service. Those who went on to college typically underwent reserve officer training. Nearly all males up to the age of 50 were subject to potential mobilization from the reserves. In addition, tens of millions of Soviet youth aged 14 and older joined the paramilitary sport club for cooperation with the three military branches (DOSAAF).[192] In other words, it was as if the Soviet military were an integral part of every ordinary Soviet citizen's life.

The mighty Soviet military was showcased every year in gigantic parades on Red Square in Moscow to commemorate the October Revolution and the 9 May victory over the Nazis. First, military bands and thousands and thousands of soldiers and veterans marched vigorously past the Soviet leadership perched on the Lenin Mausoleum. Hundreds and hundreds of tanks, field artillery, rocket launchers, missile carriers of all sizes, jeeps, and armored personnel carriers followed them.[193] Clearly the parades were intended to intimidate Soviet citizens (who were not even allowed to view the parade in person without special authorization),[194] to project the country's superpower status to the wider world, and ultimately to highlight the one truly great accomplishment of the Soviet system. (Despite all these efforts, the Soviet military may never even have achieved qualitative parity with the West.)[195]

Indeed, the entire Cold War may be characterized as an ongoing standoff between the two sides. The American testing and then use of atomic weapons shocked Stalin, but within 4 years the Soviets also had the atomic bomb. It then took them less than a year after the Americans built a hydrogen bomb to detonate one of their own in summer 1953.[196] In the immediate postwar years, Soviet military forces in Europe remained preponderant; only the American "nuclear umbrella" counterbalanced them. When the Soviets expanded their nuclear arsenal, most Western Europeans welcomed the installation of small-scale battlefield or "tactical" nuclear weapons.[197]

Disagreements between Moscow and Washington over specific policies in Western and Eastern Europe occasionally reached the boiling point in the years after the war. Fearing that Greece and Turkey might fall under Soviet control, President Truman in March 1947 declared support for "free people who are resisting attempted subjugation by armed minorities or by outside pressures."[198] The Truman Doctrine implied an intention to resist the spread of communism by means of military and economic aid. Stalin wanted Germany to remain prostrate, an understandable desire, given that Germany had invaded Russia twice in the previous three decades. The Western allies wanted a militarily weak but economically strong Germany, which also made sense since economic hardship had contributed to the rise of Hitler. The Soviets rejected the American Marshall Plan for the economic recovery of Europe, announced later in 1947, and refused to allow the Eastern European countries to take part. This program, which came with few strings attached, led to a spectacular economic boom in Western Europe in the 1950s.[199]

Discussion of forming a Western military alliance in early 1948 and the creation of a separate German currency in the Western zones of occupation on 18 June led Stalin to blockade West Berlin six days later. For nearly a year, the United States and Britain supplied the beleaguered city by airlift with 277,569 flights carrying everything from food to coal.[200] Fear of Soviet hostility pushed numerous European countries to join NATO, a US-led Atlantic defense organization created in April 1949—a development Stalin had wished above all to avoid.[201] Although the "Soviet Bloc" counterpart—the Warsaw Pact—was not instituted until 1955, an implacable standoff henceforth dominated geopolitics in Europe.

Since nuclear weapons made armed confrontation between the two superpowers almost inconceivable, a series of "proxy wars" broke out around the globe for the next four decades. The first such conflict took place in Korea. In June 1950, Communist North Korea, with Soviet logistical and military support, invaded pro-US South Korea.[202] The United Nations authorized a US-led coalition to help the South Korean military repulse the attack. By September, however, the coalition had been beaten back to a small enclave at the south of the Korean Peninsula. Within a month, a counteroffensive pushed the North Koreans northward almost to the Chinese border, unleashing a powerful Chinese intervention. (Communists had taken power in China in 1949.) The conflict was extremely bloody on both sides. American forces dropped 635,000 tons of bombs (plus 32,557 tons of napalm), more than in the entire Pacific theater in World War II. Nearly every major North Korean city suffered massive damage.[203] Physical destruction in South Korea was probably as horrific; 51 percent of industry, one-fifth of homes, 47 percent of railroads, and 80 percent of power plants were ruined.[204] More tragic was the loss of life—perhaps 600,000 Chinese troops and over 2 million Koreans.[205]

The war had two positive results. First, the carnage and close brush with Armageddon—President Truman apparently considered using atomic weapons then categorically rejected the idea—brought forcefully home to both sides that a "hot war" must be avoided at all cost. Second, South Korea was stabilized politically and economically and, despite the terrible destruction of the war, within a few decades became economically self-sufficient with a favorable balance of trade, respect for civil rights, and established democratic institutions. By 2005, it was one of the 12 most developed, richest, and technologically advanced economies and the most "wired" country in the world, with 72 percent of households enjoying broadband connections. In contrast, North Korea has remained an impoverished, isolated military dictatorship with industrial equipment valued at 2 billion dollars (compared with 489 billion dollars in the South).[206] During these decades, the United States maintained a "nuclear umbrella" over Korea and its former enemy Japan, enabling both to prosper with limited military spending.[207] This was an extraordinary success story of Western anti-communist military intervention. Sadly, the interventions multiplied, while the successes dwindled.

Fear of communist subversion prompted the United States to support anti-communist insurgents on nearly every continent, while desire to stir up trouble for the West led the Soviets to support anticolonial and other independence movements throughout the developing world. In 1953, US agents helped overthrow the democratically elected reformist prime minister of Iran, Mohammad Musaddiq, whose government had nationalized the British-controlled oil industry in 1951.

The American government, fearing Soviet involvement, cut short a promising development in democratic politics.[208] Similarly, the following year, a covert US operation overthrew the democratically elected President of Guatemala, Jacobo Arbenz, a social reformer who had received only limited Soviet support.[209] The United States did not in every instance thwart movements for reform and independence in the Third World. For example, in 1956 it pressured the Israelis, French, and British to abandon their efforts to wrest back control of the Suez Canal, following its nationalization by the President of Egypt, Gamal Abdel Nasser. Yet justified horror at the results of every communist takeover—economic ruin, political terror, one-party dictatorship, and the abolition of civil rights—led the American government to react violently (though usually secretly) at each hint of potential Soviet involvement.[210]

During the 1950s, however, the Soviet Union was not deeply involved in global subversive operations. Instead, most of its energies were focused on rebuilding the Soviet built environment, solidifying control in Eastern Europe, and crushing occasional rebellions or efforts at liberalization there. Uprisings were violently suppressed in East Germany in 1953 and in Poland and Hungary in 1956.[211]

Tensions between East and West reached a critical point beginning in 1957, when the Soviet Union launched Sputnik, the first man-made satellite, into planetary orbit. The following year, NATO went forward with plans to strengthen the German military capacity as a means of defense against preponderant Eastern Bloc conventional forces.[212] In 1959, Fidel Castro led a revolutionary takeover in the American client state of Cuba, 90 miles away from the US coast. The systematic nationalization of businesses and landed property, along with close trade and diplomatic relations with the Soviet Union established in 1960, deeply worried President Eisenhower. Also in 1960, the Soviet military shot down a U2 spy plane violating its sovereign territory, which soured diplomatic relations. At a Communist Party rally in Moscow in January 1961, Nikita Khrushchev pledged Soviet support for "wars of national liberation," which he insisted would help bring about the worldwide victory of communism. In April, the United States helped a group of Cuban émigrés attempt the overthrow of Castro. The Bay of Pigs invasion failed miserably. In August 1961, the East German government, naturally with Soviet support, built a heavily fortified wall around the entirety of West Berlin in order to stop the flood of émigrés from the east to the west (as many as 3 million had fled since 1949).[213]

These tensions and confrontations reached their climax in 1962. The conflict over Berlin had not fully subsided when the Soviet military began to install nuclear missiles on the island of Cuba in October. The United States quickly discovered the operation, and President Kennedy imposed a blockade of the island and demanded the removal of the missiles. Khrushchev agreed in exchange for an American pledge not to invade Cuba and to remove US missiles stationed in Turkey.[214]

The superpowers never again came so close to World War III; their leaders were too afraid of nuclear catastrophe. Yet they competed vigorously in the "space race"—the Americans won that contest with their moon mission of 1969—and in the Olympic Games, where the Soviets triumphed with six wins to five in the total medal count from 1948 to 1988.

Indirect military confrontations also proliferated. The biggest, most tragic, and for the Americans most disastrous was the Vietnam War. After the World War, the French colony divided into the Soviet- and Chinese-backed North and the

Western-backed South. As in Korea, the North Vietnamese leaders attempted to take control of the South, and first France and then the United States opposed them. In this context in 1954, President Eisenhower articulated the "domino theory" (already implied in the Truman Doctrine)—that communist takeover in one country would lead to communist takeover in all nearby countries. Starting in 1964, American involvement escalated. The troop level peaked in 1968 at 500,000. During the war, the US Air Force dropped 7.8 million tons of bombs throughout Indochina—five times more than the Western Allies had dropped on Germany in all of World War II. (The United States worked hard to avoid loss of life; wartime bombing killed nearly 600,000 Germans but only 50,000 North Vietnamese).[215] In all, the United States spent some 200 billion dollars and lost 58,000 lives; the Vietnamese, both North and South, lost over 1 million. For reasons that are still being debated by scholars,[216] the United States signed a peace treaty in 1973 and withdrew.

Two years later, the Communist North conquered the South and imposed a dictatorship. Over 1 million people were sent to "reeducation camps," further wars broke out between Vietnam and Cambodia and Vietnam and China, and a genocidal massacre of perhaps 1.6 million people was carried out by the communist leadership under Pol Pot of Cambodia. In addition, over 2 million people fled the region, seeking refuge across the globe.[217] Doubtless American involvement helped make these tragedies possible, though most likely they would not have occurred had the United States won the war.

The 1970s were also a time of domestic trouble in the West. Excessive American spending in Vietnam sparked an economic crisis, compounded by a surge in the price of oil beginning in 1973. All of the Western countries experienced "stagflation," a combination of high inflation and unemployment. In the United States, the Watergate scandal brought down President Richard Nixon in 1974 amid shocking revelations of law breaking.[218] During these same years, the USSR dramatically expanded its military reach, supporting anti-Western movements in Angola, Mozambique, El Salvador, Nicaragua, the Philippines, Ethiopia, and elsewhere. Anti-American revolutionary governments took power in Ethiopia, Afghanistan, Nicaragua, and Iran, and the Soviet military invaded Afghanistan in order to prop up its client state. It certainly seemed to Soviet leaders and KGB operatives that the world was "going their way."[219]

Yet the exact opposite happened—not Soviet triumph, but Soviet collapse in just over a decade. Without a military defeat or a civil war or even a significant domestic crisis, one of the world's two superpowers simply imploded like a house of cards.[220] How this happened says a lot about the nature of the communist system. In a word, it was the mirror opposite of the Western civilization it emerged to challenge.

Most importantly, the USSR did not evolve organically, gaining and growing constantly from the interactions of its citizens and through contacts with the outside world. The enforcement of one orthodox interpretation of the truth—Marxism-Leninism—hindered the emergence of new ideas in political, economic, social, and cultural life. Innovation was tolerated only if it did not threaten this orthodoxy or the Communist Party's monopoly of power. Whereas in the West businesses and independent organizations of all kinds engage each other directly and with little government interference both domestically and abroad, in the Soviet Union, where independent organizations scarcely existed, most formal interactions were mediated and indeed made possible by government agencies. Scholars and cultural elites enjoyed more contacts with the outside world than other elements of Soviet society, but even these interactions were tightly regulated and even monitored by the secret police.[221] Nor did the USSR gain much from its widely flung allies. For example, maintaining relations with Cuba cost the Soviet Union and Eastern Bloc countries heavy subsidies.[222] (Ironically, communist misconceptions of the nature of modern economics cost Cuba dearly. When the Castro regime nationalized the Bacardi Company, it seized the factories but not the trademarks, which were infinitely more valuable.)[223]

Soviet economic inefficiency and aversion to individual initiative and uncontrolled innovation had led by the early 1980s to demographic, ecological, and economic catastrophes. Infant and adult mortality were on the rise.[224] Health problems of a wide variety were increasing. Air and water pollution were becoming serious problems—vastly more serious than in any Western country.[225] The Soviet economy was also declining. The policy of detente begun in the 1970s enabled the USSR and Eastern Bloc countries to borrow billions of dollars and therefore to import a lot of Western goods, but they exported only raw materials to the West and only limited goods and commodities to the wider world. As a result, the Soviet Bloc stagnated while the Western countries steadily grew in prosperity.[226]

After Stalin's death, political terror ended and repression eased. Yet society was not allowed to evolve autonomously. Religious oppression prevented reform within the church. Official policies of "fraternal relations among peoples" prevented people from dealing with the demons of bigotry; even after the fall of communism, most Russians remained deeply hostile toward ethnic minorities. Women, who had enjoyed significant emancipation during the early Bolshevik regime, had to work outside the home and bear heavy traditional burdens of housework.[227] The early Soviet leaders implemented radical Western ideals of liberation and transformation, but within a couple of decades politics, economics, and culture became frozen in time, so that a visitor to the USSR as late as 1990 could encounter many aspects of life that had not changed much since the late 1950s.

Mikhail Gorbachev came to power in 1985 hoping to reform the political and economic systems. He discovered that adopting policies and values that enabled the West to prosper—freedom of information, association, conscience, speech, physical movement, and economic initiative, and the right to political participation and private property—completely undermined the Soviet system, which was based upon central control, tight restrictions on information, and a hermetically closed society. Once people could find out for themselves just how fabulously well people lived in the West, how inefficient and corrupt their economy was, how many privileges their leaders enjoyed, and how much terror and destruction the people and environment had suffered, most people completely lost faith in Soviet Communism.[228] New leaders quickly emerged to challenge the system.[229] Since Gorbachev himself no longer believed in using force to preserve the Soviet Union, it simply collapsed. When it did, the Cold War ended.

China's story was different. Its leaders began to liberalize China's economy in 1978, enabling the country gradually to compete economically, while they retained firm political control. This was possible largely because the rural sector could return to individual production and serve as a foundation for further development.[230] By contrast, the Soviet peasantry had almost completely forgotten the old ways. In other words, a communist system could survive and prosper by imitating Western economic methods but not by adopting Western political practices and values. In the long run, it seems, unconstrained contacts with non-communist peoples and ways of life threatened the existence of communism.

The Western world, by contrast, absorbed and adapted a wide variety of ideas, values, institutions, and breakthroughs from communist societies. Even aspects seemingly most threatening often ended up strengthening the flexible Western countries.[231] The list is long of social, political, legal, and institutional innovations (often imperfectly implemented in the Soviet Union itself) adopted in Western countries, frequently as part of an effort not to fall behind the apparently progressive Communist Bloc. One can mention laws and policies on job security, subsidized child care, paid maternity leave, universal medical care, legalized abortion, equality of women, subsidized housing, and simplified divorce proceedings. Western countries also embraced Soviet innovations in international law, such as prosecuting national leaders for war crimes, treating guerrilla fighters as regular soldiers, defining aggressive war as unlawful, and viewing one's territorial waters as extending 12 miles. Similarly, constant Soviet criticism of Western colonialism and American racial discrimination was one factor driving policymakers in Europe to liberate their colonies (though American criticism, colonial rebellion, and economic unsustainability played more important roles)[232] and in America to improve the treatment of blacks.[233] The Western countries benefited from these policy changes. Real per capita income of the former colonial powers increased sharply after they lost their colonies.[234] Less overt racism in America made the society more moral and improved the lives of millions of blacks and other minorities (though their status and success often remained precarious).[235]

* * *

This book has argued consistently that all humans are inherently and fundamentally creative. Every moment of our lives—waking or sleeping—we create unique personal experiences from multiplicitous sensory data and memories. In other words, we create as easily as we breathe.[236] How extensively we create beyond forging our experiences depends on our scope for free expression. All sorts of factors can limit that scope, including individual talent, tradition, social or political oppression, peer pressure, and cultural norms. The greater openness of scope, the greater the freedom of action, the more abundantly we will create. The peoples of the West were not inherently more creative, but they built up and lived in societies affording them far greater latitude for creativity—for trying new things, for innovating. And innovate they did to the extent of radically transforming their societies and the world around them. The more we create and innovate, the greater the opportunity for doing both evil and good. Neither outcome is predetermined. It would not do to restrict people's room for self-expression in order to prevent the rise of a Hitler, since those restrictions could very likely also prevent the emergence of an Albert Einstein, a Mother Theresa, or a Martin Luther King, Jr. Indeed, the greatest story in the West for the past two centuries has been the gradual integration of more and more members of society into public, cultural, economic, and political life, and the resultant development of a more just and prosperous society, as discussed in the following chapter.

QUESTIONS FOR REFLECTION

What motivated the New Imperialism?

How did World War I call into question the foundations of Western civilization?

Compare and contrast Communism and Nazism.

What caused the Cold War?

Why did the Soviet Union collapse?

Chapter 14 Chronology

1600:	Europe achieves unparalleled levels of urbanization
Early 1800s:	Common interest voluntary associations proliferate
1824:	British repeal of Combination Acts allows voluntary associations to form
1833:	Parliament bans slavery in United Kingdom and its possessions
1847:	American Medical Association founded
1849:	Elizabeth Blackwell becomes world's first female medical doctor
1850s:	Western women gain admission to college
1865:	US 13th amendment abolishes slavery and enforces equal rights
1869:	Knights of Labor, America's first labor union, formed
1870:	US Naturalization Act of 1870 restricted immigration to whites and blacks
1878:	American Bar Association founded
1886:	American Federation of Labor formed
1900:	Western literacy rates reach 90 percent
1919:	US 19th amendment gives women right to vote
1940:	93.5 percent of urban dwellings in United States had running water, 83 percent with private toilets
1943:	Bracero Program begins large-scale Mexican immigration to United States
1950:	Half of all American homes had central-heating; 40-hour work week becomes national average
1952:	US Congress repeals Chinese Exclusion Act
1954:	*Brown v. Board of Education* overturns *Plessy v. Ferguson* (1896)
1960:	US percentage of college educated population doubles compared to 20 years prior
1963:	None of top 200 nonfinancial firms in United States privately owned
1964:	Civil Rights legislations makes racial discrimination and segregation illegal

14

Social Revolutions

In January 1896 at age 65, Isabella Bird commenced a journey from Shanghai up the Yangtze River and into places in western China rarely visited by foreigners.[1] An inveterate English traveler, whom an acquaintance described as displaying an "absolute unconsciousness of fear," she had already visited Canada and the United States—her first trip at age 22—Australia and New Zealand, Egypt and Persia, Japan and Korea, Kurdistan and Morocco.[2] Generally mingling with the local populations and eschewing Westerners, she roamed widely and systematically took measurements of temperature, altitude, and barometric pressure and recorded detailed geographical, botanical, political, and cultural observations. These materials formed the basis of a dozen best-selling travel narratives and won her an appointment as a fellow of the Royal Geographical Society in London, the first woman ever. This uncommon woman, only one of many dozen British and American female travelers who explored the globe throughout the eighteenth and nineteenth centuries,[3] symbolized as well as anything the multifaceted transformation of Western society and culture brought on by the revolutions described in this book.

The revolutionary middle class

The idea of a "revolutionary middle class" seems to many intellectuals an absurdity. Scholars and social critics in the West for almost two centuries have heaped scorn on the lowly "bourgeoisie," calling them philistines and reactionaries, denouncing their alleged materialism, hedonistic values, and lack of social conscience.[4] Such thinkers, numerous though usually not dominant, have typically idealized members of the lower classes, especially manual laborers and factory workers (and sometimes peasants) with their supposed earnest simplicity, closeness to nature, physicality, or, according to Marxists in the case of "proletarians," world historical destiny. Perhaps such mental laborers disdain the middle social ranks to deflect attention from their own middle-class roots or even out of hidden admiration for the aristocracy that for centuries set the social and cultural tone of the West. Do not the special qualities of the nobleman—the sophistication, the lack of material concerns, the willingness to set one's very life at naught for what one believes in—dramatically outshine the tawdry commercial virtues of the burgher?[5]

Until recently, peasants have formed the core populations of every European country and indeed of every country in the world. They contributed heavily to the material survival of every culture and civilization, yet few innovated, conceived powerful new ideas, or developed means for human advancement. At the other end of the social scale, aristocrats, who like the peasants occupied a fixed place in society because of their birth, unlike them constituted Europe's ruling elite from its earliest days until recent times. They also played at least minor roles in all of Europe's transformations of the past ten centuries. They naturally participated heavily in the Papal Revolution (though Gregory VII himself was apparently the son of a blacksmith) and the Military Revolution (though burghers and prosperous farmers brought about the infantry revolution). And one can name dozens if not hundreds of significant figures of aristocratic background in Europe's development into the world's most powerful civilization, from Thomas Aquinas to Tycho Brahe and from the baron de Montesquieu to Sir Charles Algernon Parsons (the inventor of the steam turbine).

Yet the people who lived and died within the social spectrum wedged between the tillers of the soil and the men of arms shaped the modern West—and therefore the modern world—more than any other social group. From the merchants, artisans, and bankers of the medieval commercial revolution to the primary movers of nearly every subsequent major transformation—the rise of towns, printing, the Reformation, modern science, constitutional government, industrialization, and the technological revolutions—the vast majority of innovators and revolutionaries hailed from urban life, from the middle class, from the bourgeoisie.

Their social station made this possible. The peasantry, living at the edge of subsistence and bound to the soil and traditional farming methods, only very rarely experimented, for fear of starvation. Aristocrats by contrast enjoyed material security and leisure. Many readily embraced adventure. Several noteworthy explorers boasted noble origins. Yet most of Europe's innovations had little to do with adventure and everything to do with a painstaking development of new processes, the invention of mechanical devices, the accumulation of information, the systematic mastery and sharing of knowledge, and brain-numbing experimentation—activities only a few aristocrats had the stomach for. Urban and commercial life prepared the bourgeoisie for exactly these endeavors. Tradition, noble obligations, and the key aristocratic virtue—honor—did not constrict their outlook and willingness to try new things. Thus, century after century, while the vast majority of Europeans worked the land and its tiny but powerful elite ruled and bore arms, a slowly growing urban population laid the groundwork for the West's emergence as a great civilization.

It seems likely that in the other great civilizations artisans, merchants, and urban dwellers also contributed more innovations than people of other social categories because of their practical orientation, access to capital and other resources, interactions with a wide variety of like-minded people, moneymaking opportunities, and relative freedom from invention-stifling values and traditions. European society ultimately distinguished itself, it seems, mostly because its cities and urban populations enjoyed more political and economic autonomy and therefore could reap ever more abundant fruits of innovation. Market-oriented mental laborers and artisans multiplied and soon came to make up a larger proportion of society. By 1600, most European countries had achieved levels of urbanization that China did not match until two centuries later.[6] In fact, from the early modern period no country of the world could match them. (Japan's level of urbanization, though still falling short, probably came closest, which may help to account for its stunning material successes from the late nineteenth century.)

The European (and North American) middle classes, certainly by the late nineteenth century, played a crucial role in Western society. Presumably, the wealthy played an even greater role. Yet throughout the twentieth century, at least in the United States, a large proportion of men and (increasingly) women business leaders emerged directly from the middle class.[7] Moreover, even most factory workers considered themselves part of the middle class.[8] Statistically, the number of people enjoying comforts and conveniences unimaginable for any but the very rich in past centuries steadily increased in the United States and the wider West.[9]

One key aspect of Western societies, at least since the early modern period, has consisted in sociability. As noted in Chapter 11, from the late eighteenth-century innovation-minded intellectuals, industrialists, engineers, and the mechanically inclined—sometimes irrespective of social class or estate—gathered periodically to exchange ideas and think through projects. Members of the middle class nearly always organized such gatherings. The famous Parisian hostess Madame Marie Geoffrin (1699–1777), who drew together dozens of French intellectuals for wide-ranging and apparently highly fertile discussions, had solidly bourgeois origins.[10] Indeed, in every corner of Europe and in the United States, especially from the early 1800s, hundreds and gradually thousands of voluntary associations formed to bring together sometimes the most diverse groups so long as they shared common interests.[11] (Members of the lower classes, because of poverty and discrimination, took less part in such ventures, and the rich and powerful did not need to form big associations to get things done.)[12] Their purposes ranged from purely intellectual and cultural to practical and economic, from idealistic and pleasure seeking to political and reformist.

Masonic lodges, among the first prominent voluntary associations, gained significant memberships during the early to mid-eighteenth century. They functioned not only as social clubs but also as rationalistic alternatives to church attendance, with rituals and other pious activities.[13] In the second half of the century, hundreds and even thousands of reading clubs sprang up around Europe.[14] Some of the earliest societies formed to spread the Christian Gospel, such as the London Missionary Society (1795), the New York Bible Society (1809), and the American Baptist Home Mission Society (1832). Many also wished to promote Christianity but placed a bigger emphasis on helping others, for example, the YMCA (1844) and the Salvation Army (1865).[15] Some emphasized promoting health worldwide, like the International Committee of the Red Cross (1863). Still others aimed at camaraderie and self-help, like the Elks (1868). Many others arose for specific purposes relating to the improvement of society, such as promoting temperance and abolishing slavery, cruelty to animals, prostitution, poverty, and vices of every kind. This is what scholars have termed "civil society," and what everyone else simply calls "society."[16]

Depending on the club or organization, men (though very seldom women) of even antagonistic or at least discordant religious faiths, political views, ethnic backgrounds, and social classes would regularly gather for their appointed activities or duties. In fact, the organizations' popularity stemmed in part from their apparent ability to promote social harmony in an age of rapid change.[17]

The modern voluntary associations traced their origins to mutual aid societies or fellowships, like the Odd Fellows, that had emerged from among the guilds in medieval times and had grown fairly common in the eighteenth century. They probably also drew inspiration from coffee shops as places of camaraderie and semiformal gathering.[18] The speed of the new associations' proliferation astonishes. Many commentators believe they enjoyed particular success in the early American republic. Alexis de Tocqueville (1805–59), who traveled across America in 1831–33, certainly thought so. Having listed a wide variety of purposes to which voluntary associations were put—including the establishment of schools, hospitals, seminaries, churches, and prisons—he notes, "In every case, at the head of any new undertaking, where in France you would find the government or in England some territorial magnate, in the United States you are sure to find an association."[19] Often these fellowships outnumbered public institutions. In Massachusetts and Maine, for example, every year in the 1820s ordinary people founded 70 new associations. In at least some places, one-third or more of the population of small and medium towns belonged to some organization or other.[20]

Tocqueville, a brilliant social analyst and historian, believed that the trajectory of Western history since medieval times was toward greater and greater social and political equality. Indeed, he wrote his magnificent two-volume survey of American life in order to understand that trajectory better, since he concluded that America had become the future of the West. In a society in which people are mostly equal economically and politically, they need more than in any other type of society to join together for common purposes, or else they will fall under the domination of a central government. The Americans rose to that challenge by creating a society with the greatest grassroots social, political, and economic activism in history. As he commented, "Thus the most democratic country in the world now is that in which men have in our time carried to the highest perfection the art of pursuing in common the objects of common desires and have applied this new technique to the greatest number of purposes."[21]

Voluntary associations enjoyed less success in most European countries in part because of government persecution, but they still proliferated mightily. Most associations excluded broad categories of people, such as women, the lower classes, Jews, or, in the case of the United States, African-Americans.[22] It is a sign of the robustness of Western societies, however, that many of these excluded minorities founded their own associations.[23] For example, women in America established a huge number aimed at self-development and community service.[24]

Members of Western societies formed networks of social agency in order to impart rationality, organization, efficiency, and practicality to all aspects of life while enjoying human fellowship. Throughout history, people had usually contributed to the life of society in their narrow areas of expertise. Farmers sowed and reaped. Soldiers fought. Craftsman built and repaired. Judges decided cases. A weaver for the most part could not help design a better waterwheel. Yet every person may have insights to share on nearly any topic. A genius of modern Western society lay in sanctioning the participation of tens of millions of people in resolving social problems and opening channels for the free exchange of ideas. Inevitably, a society that brings into play the intelligence, creativity, and inspiration of vastly more of its members will prove far more innovative and successful in nearly every endeavor than one that does not. Even voluntary associations formed solely to foster self-improvement, amusement, or camaraderie—choirs, gymnastics clubs, and literary societies, for example—enhanced social capital by promoting human interconnection.

Professional associations deserve a special mention. University training throughout the West—especially in graduate and professional schools—became more systematic and formalized in the late nineteenth century. Graduate programs with established research protocols, peer-reviewed scholarship, and methodical training of professionals became the academic standard. In the United States more than in any other country, university education was open to the middle class and helped reinforce its dominance of American society.[25] Professionals and scientific and technical experts commanded high salaries, social prestige, and cultural and political influence. The associations they founded—for example, the American Medical Association (1847) and the American Bar Association (1878)—reinforced and further legitimated their position and that of the middle class in Western society.[26]

During the same years, industrial laborers throughout the West, who typically worked in harsh conditions, also banded together in voluntary associations, many of them secret because of antilabor laws. Great Britain first legalized labor organizations with the repeal of the Combination Acts in 1824, though many legal restrictions remained.[27] The development of railroads made it easier to organize national and even international labor associations. The first broad-based American organization, the Knights of Labor, emerged in Philadelphia in 1869 as a secret society that admitted both women and (from 1878) African-Americans and sought to inculcate in all wage laborers a sense of class solidarity.[28] Meanwhile, the American Federation of Labor, founded in 1886, organized workers by craft, eschewed violence, and successfully emphasized collective-bargaining agreements and constructive political activism.[29] (Sadly, most US labor organizations discriminated against blacks.)[30] Powerful labor parties emerged in Germany (1875) and Great Britain (1900). All such organizations gradually drew ever-larger segments of population into social, economic, and political life.

Associational activity in all the Western countries continued to deepen and expand until by 1900 it permeated nearly every aspect of society, including rural areas, urban laborers, and even the European colonies. Many organizations that formed between 1900 and 1920 still play a vital role in today's Western societies, including the Wandervögel back-to-nature youth organization in Germany (1901), Scouting (1907), and the Rotary (1905), Kiwanis (1915), and Lions (1917) clubs.[31] According to one estimate, in 1900 1 in 5 (or even 1 in 3) American men belonged to one more of the country's 70,000 fraternal lodges.[32] One marvels that so many Western people should have taken an active role in the social, economic, and cultural life of their countries at a time when even most European men did not yet have the vote. Yet they ran their hundreds of thousands of associations democratically.[33] Never before in history had formalized political life involved practically entire populations.

Other developments in the West in these years also helped people to share information and make connections. A mass-circulation press began to emerge in the 1830s. For example, the *New York Sun* sold an average of 40,000 copies a day in 1840.[34] The telegraph wire services made such newspapers truly informative. Sports reporting, crime stories, society gossip, and other human-interest topics increased readership. Technological developments described in Chapter 12—the rotary press, Linotype, and cheap wood-pulp-based newsprint—enabled publishers to feed the insatiable demand for news.[35] The *Sun* sold 220,000 copies reporting on the highly disputed presidential election of 1876. Literacy soared in England, France, and the

United States (for native-born whites) to over 90 percent during these decades.[36] By 1904, the United States had 2,452 daily newspapers with a combined daily circulation of almost 20 million.[37] Nearly 600 US cities had more than one daily newspaper.[38] The biggest-circulation newspaper in the world, the London *Daily Mail*, sold 1 million copies in 1902.

The telephone also connected members of the middle class and ultimately promoted democracy. Certainly, the Bell system's founder and first president, Gardiner Hubbard (1822–97), intended it that way.[39] From the late 1860s, he had hoped to break the hammerlock of the business-oriented Western Union Company over the telegraph. The telephone, he believed, would place a revolutionary technology directly in the hands of middle- and upper-class people. He was right. By 1880, the United States had roughly 300 telephone exchanges. The service exploded only after the turn of the century, but it had already begun to fulfill Hubbard's expectations.

Bringing in one-half of humanity

As discussed in Chapter 2, European women had enjoyed a higher social status from medieval times than the women of other civilizations. They suffered no enforced debilitations like the traditional Chinese foot-binding practice and were not expected to throw themselves upon the funeral pyre of their deceased husbands as in India. The idea of a learned woman like Christine de Pizan (1363–c.1434) regularly lecturing to groups of male scholars would have struck the educated elites of any other society in the early modern period as a gross absurdity.[40] Certainly, a Turkish diplomat who visited Vienna in 1665 considered baffling the spectacle of the emperor showing respect to random women.[41] For two more centuries, Northwest European and Colonial American women overall remained significantly less literate than men—on the order of one-third versus two-thirds—and vastly less literate outside northwest Europe,[42] though the situation was far worse beyond Europe: even elite women in early modern China were not taught to read.[43]

Few women studied Latin in early modern Europe, and none attended university, yet many elite women received a brilliant education at home and took a serious part in the life of the mind.[44] The Englishwoman Margaret Cavendish wrote prolifically, including on natural philosophy, and her romance *The Blazing-World* (1666) represents one of the first examples of science fiction writing. In Germany, women comprised roughly 14 percent of all astronomers in 1650–1710, though no woman received an invitation to join any European scientific organization until the election of Mary Somerville and Caroline Herschel in 1835 to London's Royal Astronomical Society.[45] Ironically, just over half a century before, Empress Catherine the Great (r. 1762–96) had appointed the energetic Princess Yekaterina Dashkova (1743–1810), who had lived in Scotland for 6 years and was strongly influenced by leading members of the Scottish Enlightenment, to head the St Petersburg Academy of Sciences and the Russian Academy. Under her leadership, Russia's first etymological dictionary (in six volumes) was published between 1789 and 1794.[46]

By this point in Western history, a movement for the political advancement of women had emerged. Mary Wollstonecraft, a British philosopher and early feminist, argued in her *Vindication of the Rights of Woman* (1792) that women deserve the same rights as men, including an equal education, because, she claimed, they have equal intellectual abilities.[47] Since English female writers practically invented the modern novel in the first half of the 1800s—think of Jane Austen, George Eliot (Mary Ann Evans); and Charlotte, Emily, and Anne Brontë—they did not take long to prove her point. Beginning in the 1850s, society recognized as much, too. Across Europe and the United States, women began to gain admission to college (though often only in special "ladies' programs"). A few colleges for women were founded, such as Vassar College (1865) and Girton College at Cambridge University (1869). The land-grant colleges established in the United States from 1862 also admitted women.[48] In 1870, women made up 21 percent of all college students in America, a number that soared to nearly 40 percent in 1910 and just over 47 percent in 1920.[49] (European women entered college more slowly.)

Higher education opened many new doors to employment for women, as did changing social attitudes and further rapid economic growth. From the 1820s, thousands of "proper" young women had worked in the textile industry in New England. Many "mill girls" of Lowell, Massachusetts, edited or contributed to literary magazines, such as the *Lowell Offering* (1840–45).[50] By mid-century, women, especially in America, pushed vigorously against social boundaries. Elizabeth Blackwell (1821–1910), an English immigrant, for example, studied medicine on her own and then sent application after application to medical schools until the Geneva Medical College in Geneva, New York, admitted her. In 1849, she graduated first in her class, the first formally trained female medical doctor in the world.[51] In New York City, she founded a private practice, an infirmary for the poor, a training school for nurses, and a medical college for women (1868).

Women did not yet flock into the labor force, though changing technology drew in significant numbers. In 1890, women constituted 19 percent of the American labor force (up to 25 percent in 1930).[52] By 1900, thanks to the typewriter, thousands of women found jobs as typists and stenographers. Ten years later, thousands more worked as telephone operators, a predominantly female occupation. These technologies enabled a "decent" girl to find respectable work living on her own without a husband or father to care for her.[53] As these skilled jobs opened up to women, more and more attended high school. (By 2010, women made up just over 50 percent of the American workforce and the majority of professional workers in several developed countries.)[54] Drawing on the talents of so many women promoted economic growth and further swelled the middle class. A few women also began to play a transformative role in various sectors of the economy. For example, Gabrielle "Coco" Chanel (1883–1971) completely changed the world of fashion and haute couture, and was the first woman to build an international commercial empire.[55]

Long years of enthusiastic and creative voluntary work had prepared women for economic and political activity. For 30 years, thousands of fervent Christian abolitionist women contributed the bulk of efforts to raise money, write and distribute antislavery propaganda, organize lectures and public debates, circulate petitions, promote "free produce" movements, and appeal to lawmakers.[56] Abolitionism probably also constituted the world's first well-organized social force in which women played an integral role.

Women reformists—first in America in the early 1800s and then in the British Isles and Scandinavia—took up other causes such as fighting against prostitution, working to improve public health and sanitation, and especially promoting temperance.[57] The movement gained strength after the Civil War, with such organizations as the Woman's Christian Temperance Union, founded in Illinois in 1873 and the British Women's Temperance Association founded 3 years later. Women organized protest meetings, lecture tours, prayer vigils, petition campaigns, and even acts of vandalism. The cause triumphed in America in 1919 when 36 of the 48 states ratified the Eighteenth Amendment to the US Constitution banning the "manufacture, sale, or transportation of intoxicating liquors."[58] Unlike the definitive abolition of the slave trade in Great Britain (1807) and slavery in the United States (1865), however, a further constitutional amendment overturned Prohibition in 1933. The idealism in this crusade had proved misplaced. One cannot make the same claim about the greatest achievement of the women's movement: suffrage.

Women had enjoyed substantial political and civil rights in medieval and Renaissance Europe. In England they could serve as custodian of a castle or as sheriff, attend the king in council, or vote for city and town assemblies and some local officials (such as knights of the shire)—though they exercised these rights usually only as property owners or heads of household.[59] They had also wielded enormous influence and power as abbesses of great convents.[60] True, women's property rights in England were gradually curtailed from the 1500s, as the common law crowded out the other legal systems (ecclesiastical, manorial and borough, and equity).[61] (A series of laws in the United States and Great Britain, starting with the 1848 Married Women's Property Act of New York, ended this discriminatory practice.)[62] Women property owners received modern political rights for the first time when the Constitution of New Jersey, adopted in 1776, defined voters as "adult inhabitants" who owned property valued at 50 pounds. Such women participated vigorously in New Jersey's political life until 1807, when legislation restricted the right to vote to male property owners.[63] Similar laws and customs existed in Europe. The English Reform Bill of 1832, for example, clearly spelled out that only men who owned property could cast ballots.[64]

The women's suffrage movement emerged around mid-century in both Great Britain and the United States, spearheaded for the most part by Quaker abolitionists and temperance leaders.[65]

Foreign visitors repeatedly described American women as "independent," "self-sufficient," and "strong-minded."[66] Tocqueville wrote: "If anyone asks me what I think the chief cause of the extraordinary prosperity and growing power of this nation, I should answer that it is due to the superiority of their women."[67] In other words, if women in any country of the world were going to obtain the right to vote in the nineteenth century, then American women were among the most likely candidates. Laws did enfranchise women in Wyoming territory (1869), Utah territory (1870), Washington territory (1883), Colorado (1893), and Idaho (1896). Within two decades, nearly every state had granted women some or even full voting rights (in presidential, municipal, or primary elections) (see Map 14.1).[68] Yet they lacked full nationwide voting rights.

Intellectuals, both male and female, had much to do with legitimating the suffrage movement and bringing about its triumph. The philosopher John Stuart Mill (1806–73), for example, advocated women's rights throughout the 1860s with his mighty pen and as a Member of Parliament.[69] Laws established women's suffrage only decades later, however: in New Zealand (1893), Australia (1902), Finland (1906),

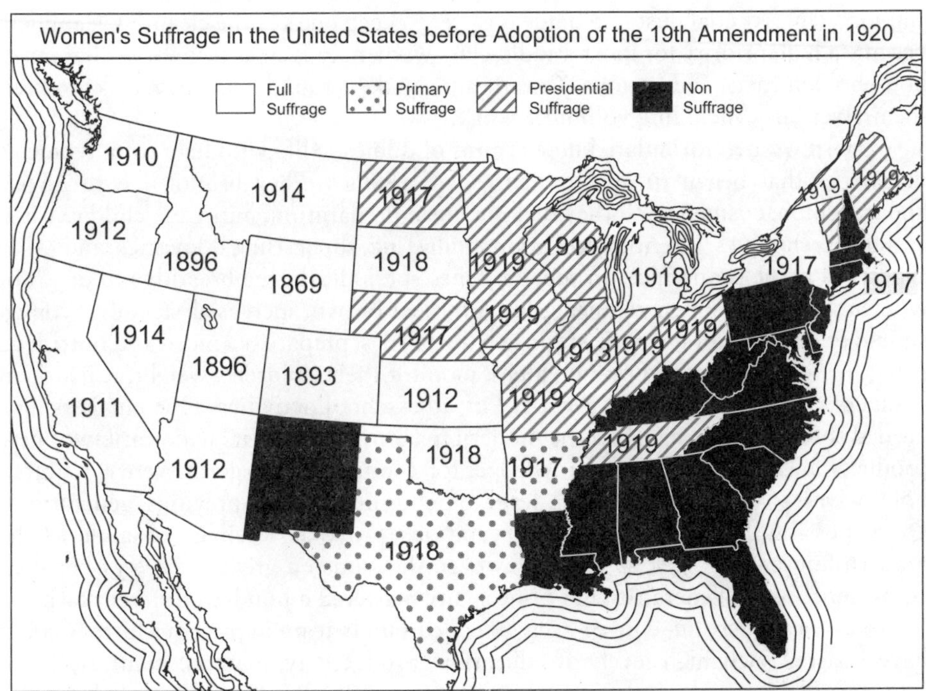

MAP 14.1 *Even before the 19th Amendment enfranchised women, many states had already granted women some or even full voting rights.*

Norway (1913), and most other countries of the West during or soon after World War I (though in France not until 1944).

Changes in society and culture had slowly induced fundamental change in the roles and position of women. As the industrial economy boosted prosperity, leading to higher wages for factory work, more and more men throughout the West could become sole breadwinners, enabling their wives to devote themselves full-time to homemaking and child rearing. The displacement by mechanization of jobs traditionally fulfilled by women—for example, spinning thread at home—also promoted this trend, as did the idealization of "domesticity."[70] This concept encompassed the faith that women could create a safe and pure haven, sheltered from the harshness of public and commercial life. As education, already widely available and public, became compulsory for children in the final decades of the nineteenth century,[71] an expectation of living this ideal spread from the upper to the lower classes in most Western societies, though only gradually.

All of these changes had a huge impact on family life. For one thing, women had fewer children. Throughout northwest Europe, their fertility rates fell between 1890 and 1920 by over 10 percent. Also, the nuclear family steadily became the Western norm.[72] As noted in Chapter 12, electrical and other labor-saving devices, along with processed foods and household products, reduced the drudgery of housework. Safe electric irons, introduced in 1892, and powdered detergent, which came on the market in Britain in 1899, eliminated two of the worst chores—handling and fire-heating a heavy solid iron and scraping and boiling bars of laundry soap. Electric stoves eliminated messy coal dust and made it easier to keep one's home clean.[73] Cleanliness became a high priority for most middle-class women. In fact, as technology lightened household burdens, industrious Western homemakers found many new tasks to keep themselves busy, including volunteer work.

Western women formulated new visions of domestic life with help from women's magazines that began to appear in the late 1800s.[74] They brimmed with advice about fashion, cosmetics, clothes-making, meal preparation, nutrition, child rearing, cleaning techniques, interior decoration, budgeting, supervising domestics, and other aspects of home economics. To judge by these periodicals, the breadth and depth of women's chores, though requiring less physical brawn, increased steadily. Women should prepare infant formula, sterilize baby bottles, prepare balanced and nutritious meals, instill religious and moral values, monitor their children's weight, teach them manners, and enroll them in a variety of after-school activities. Homemakers also needed shrewdness to navigate the modern marketplace with its wide variety of new products. Increased scientific knowledge, for example about germ theory, required housewives to aim for a higher level of cleanliness than previous generations. Quite possibly, these heightened expectations provoked feelings of guilt in the modern housewife.[75] Just as likely, however, she gained a greater sense of her own competence—as a generalist who of necessity mastered a hundred different tasks.

No average husband–wife or even extended-family team in previous history could have boasted such high levels of education, productivity, material comfort, social influence, or disposable income. Armed with motor-driven, electric-powered, electronic, and gas-fired devices, both adult members of household in their respective spheres of activity—home, workplace, volunteering, and grassroots politics—contributed more to society than their ancestors could have imagined doing. They also reaped fantastic material rewards from the burgeoning cornucopia of consumer goods.

Living like lords and ladies

Popular magazines and advertising promoted the rising middle class's desire for new products and helped develop consumer culture.[76] The range of product choices available to an ever-growing bulk of population would have astonished people of earlier times. Department stores offered lovely and even opulent surroundings, attentive service, and a huge variety of goods with fixed prices—so no haggling.[77] People could decorate their homes almost like aristocrats of old, though with mass-produced wallpaper, ceramics, furniture, and other accessories. Starting in 1900, just about anyone in Europe or America could afford the one-touch Brownie camera marketed by Kodak for one dollar.[78] Capturing one's environment, loved ones, and special moments gave each person with a camera the power to create a sense of stability, to hold on to one's world, and to pass along artifacts to succeeding generations, something permitted only to the rich in former times.

Consumer culture drove an entertainment boom. The range of musical styles invented in America from the 1890s to the present day astonishes.[79] African-Americans contributed strongly to many of them, including jazz (and allied forms like ragtime, Dixieland, and swing), blues, Depression-era protest songs, and rock. Most of these musical styles involved crossing racial lines, perhaps most notably in the 1950s by

Elvis Presley (1935–77), who interpreted African-American music for white audiences (racism limited the commercial success of black artists). African-Americans single-handedly developed several other genres, including gospel, soul, Motown, spirituals, and hip hop. Other Americans created country, bluegrass, musicals, folk rock, pop, grunge, alternative, and many more. For centuries, elites in the West had dominated music's creation and enjoyment, as it grew ever more complex and abstract. At the start of the twentieth century, experiments by European composers with dissonance and brutal polyrhythms alienated many concertgoers just when popular music began to take off. Since then, through more and more sophisticated production and marketing techniques, American (and British) popular music came to dominate the vast and dynamic worldwide popular music market.[80]

Cinema also took the world by storm. The invention of the motion picture camera and projector in the late nineteenth century gave rise to a motion picture industry in Europe and America from the early 1900s.[81] When World War I interrupted European production, Hollywood seized the dominant position. By the mid-1920s, 20 studios were churning out 800 feature films a year, or over three-quarters of global output. Worldwide moviemakers defined themselves either as "anti-Hollywood"—including many in Europe—or imitators, like India's "Bollywood." Together they entertained billions.

People in the West enjoyed dramatic improvements in plumbing and electrification, especially in the United States. By the end of the 1920s, a large proportion of American homes—61 percent of those in Zanesville, Ohio, in 1926—had hot and cold running water—filtered and chlorine-treated—and a bathroom with a recessed enameled bathtub, tiled floors and walls, a single-unit toilet, and an enameled sink.[82] In 1940 across the United States, 44 percent of homes had electric refrigerators and 54 percent had gas or electric ranges. By 1950, 70 percent also enjoyed hot and cold running water.[83] (In the mid-1950s, most European homes did not yet even have cold running water.)[84] Again, for millennia the rich had enjoyed indoor plumbing and hot and cold running water; ordinary people had not.

The ancient Romans invented central heating systems, which circulated air beneath the flooring of baths, major public buildings, and the homes of the wealthy. This amenity, often simplified, continued in limited use in the Middle East after the decline and fall of Rome. A similar arrangement apparently emerged in early China and Korea. Greenhouses and then hospitals and public buildings began to install piped hot-water heating systems in Europe and then the United States beginning in the late eighteenth and early nineteenth centuries. Steam heating systems soon followed. Slowly, these systems grew relatively widespread, reaching the majority of upper middle-class homes in Muncie, Indiana, by 1924. One decade later, it seems that the entire middle class of Muncie enjoyed this amenity.[85] The census of 1950 indicated that roughly half of all American homes had central heating.[86] (In France, for example, only a tiny fraction did.)[87] Never before in history had so many people enjoyed such comfort.

Extraordinary improvements in the quality and accessibility of lighting further increased well-being. From candles to whale oil in the eighteenth, through gas and kerosene in the nineteenth, and on to electric light in the twentieth century, artificial illumination plummeted in cost and soared exponentially in efficiency—by a factor of thousands. Just to take one example, the United Kingdom today consumes around 25,000 times more light than in 1800.[88]

Suburbia, the swaths of low-density neighborhoods surrounding urban centers, has come in for harsh criticism. The large houses, broad lawns, and lengthy commutes all waste natural resources. The materialistic, shopping-oriented culture dulls the mind and corrupts the spirit. The inhabitants have fled their less fortunate brethren, leaving them to stagnate and their problems to fester.[89] Yet surely the denizens of suburbia generally seek only to build for themselves a version of the good life within financial reach. Moreover, since ancient times people have longed to retire from the noise, congestion, pollution, and dangers of the city to a bucolic retreat endowed with natural beauty, a slower pace of life, and room enough to calm one's nerves.[90] Unfortunately, for most of history only the rich could afford such luxury.

In Great Britain, the ground zero of industrialization, almost half the population dwelled in cities by 1840, a level of urbanization achieved in the rest of Europe and in the United States several decades later.[91] This concentration of productive capacity led to the generation of sufficient wealth and technological innovation—first electric trains and trams and then cars—to enable many people in Western countries to dwell in neighborhoods with relatively large free-standing houses, each adorned with informal gardens.

The process began in England, first in London and then in other industrial centers like Manchester and Liverpool, as members of the middle class and then also factory workers pushed out into suburban and more distant exurban belts. Similar trends ensued in the environs of major cities on the Continent and, later still, in the United States. After the turn of the century, this movement gained strength, reaching flood proportions in America, especially out west, during the Roaring Twenties.[92] By the end of the decade, most people in the region surrounding Los Angeles lived in single-family homes and owned automobiles. The population of Detroit followed closely behind. Abundant shopping facilities and other amenities served the new communities—by 1935, some 75 percent of all of Chicagoland's retail outlets operated outside the city center.[93] These trends continued for the next several decades, especially after World War II, in the United States and to a lesser extent in Europe.

A managerial revolution helped fuel suburbanization and increased the status and wealth of millions of middle-and upper-level employees of industrial and service-oriented companies throughout the Western world.[94] The business moguls of the late nineteenth century—like John D. Rockefeller in the oil business, Cornelius Vanderbilt in railroads, and Andrew Carnegie in steel—built up economies of scale, speed, and scope that drove down their costs, lowered prices to the consumer, and forced their competitors to adopt this business model—vertical integration and multidepartmental organization. This structure required ever-larger pools of highly educated managers. No one entrepreneurial genius, no matter how gifted, could effectively control all the workings of a major modern company involving thousands of laborers, sophisticated technologies, and vast financial operations.

The multidivisional firm had a modular structure: one could quickly set up a new division to manage any new product, service, or operation. More and more thought and analysis went into developing, coordinating, and rationalizing business operations. Competition among firms grew intense. New divisions emerged to tackle problems that arose, thanks to intensive investigation and analysis—for example, marketing research, brand management, and worker motivation.[95]

The expertise of "white-collar" workers—achieved on the job and at the proliferating business schools—boosted their salaries. These "company men" formed an elite caste within society. The "man in the gray flannel suit," with his white shirt and tie, strict work ethic, and staunch loyalty to his firm set the standard for meritocratic advancement in America. He also constituted most of the brains of industrial capitalism.[96] Maligned by intellectuals for their alleged narrowness of mind and overweening preoccupation with material things, American managers built themselves into a powerful bulwark of the middle class even as they helped build their firms into the dominant economic forces of the world in the middle decades of the twentieth century. By 1963, not a single one of the 200 biggest nonfinancial firms in America was privately owned, and in only five did a family or group exercise majority control through shareholding.[97] Hundreds of thousands of managers ran them and thousands of other companies. In most cases, they blazed learning pathways, developed sophisticated functionalities, and built up organizational capabilities that enabled each company to vie with its competitors, to develop new products and operations, and in general to adapt to the constantly shifting circumstances of economic, social, and political life.[98]

Tens of millions of white-collar workers continued decade by decade to increase their personal attainments and contributions to society.[99] The number of Americans who had completed at least 1 year of college grew from roughly 8 million in 1940—dividing into equal proportions of men and women, though more men graduated—to around 17 million in 1960. (All the higher-education statistics for America greatly exceeded those for any other Western country.)[100] Fewer women—even college graduates—entered the workforce, however. Thus, in 1960, only 39 percent of recent female graduates were employed, nearly half as teachers. Of course, the higher education of those who stayed home must have had a big impact on their families and social environments.

As in previous decades, Americans and indeed people throughout the West joined clubs, took an active part in community life, and volunteered their time for the advancement of benevolent causes, especially through churches and synagogues. They also gained expertise within the household. Many women took classes in (or followed how-to books) on sewing, gardening, knitting, cooking, and other aspects of home economics. They acquired and put to use diverse kitchen appliances. Millions learned to make clothing from patterns, using the electric sewing machines that appeared in more and more homes. Many mastered the art of entertaining and carefully studied the rules of etiquette. Some took academic classes at local colleges. Nearly all helped with their children's homework. Men often learned to make at least minor repairs around the house and garage, usually acquiring a wide variety of hand and power tools. Typically at least one spouse took responsibility for the family's personal finances and, though less frequently, investing. As the average US work week diminished from 66 hours in 1850, to 50 hours in 1909, and down to 40 hours in 1950, and as workers enjoyed a large increase in holidays and vacation time, they had even more time for hobbies, travel, and other leisure activities, a large proportion sponsored by employers and religious organizations.[101] Some of these undertakings required training and study. Overall, people's competency levels in a wide variety of domains increased steadily during the postwar years.

Some scholars have discerned a gradual "proletarianization" of white-collar workers.[102] Undoubtedly, as more and more people entered the formerly upper reaches of the middle class, their level of independence, use of creativity on the job, and comparative remuneration within the economic hierarchy could only decline. Yet such critics surely fail to recognize that for the first time in history a comparatively large—perhaps even majority—share of the population in numerous countries had attained a level of material comforts, leisure opportunities, sophisticated competencies, and social status that in even relatively recent times only a minority—and throughout most of human history only a tiny minority—had enjoyed. This was truly a revolution.

One can fret that the expansion of education and the broadening of cultural access have led to a general "dumbing down" of discourse and a certain shallowness of life-feeling.[103] Thus, for example, newspapers changed from a densely literary medium to a semi-visual one with one- or two-sentence paragraphs, while orchestras often neglect serious programming, and operas add projected subtitles. Yet such losses of depth have perhaps been a small price to pay for enabling vastly more people to take part in the life of the mind.

The greatly enlarged middle class has also contributed an invaluable political benefit to modern Western societies. In traditional social arrangements, a tiny elite typically controls most wealth and power, while nearly everyone else makes do with crumbs. Living at the edge of subsistence, as most humans throughout history have done, gives one little stake in the social order and necessarily renders political and social institutions unstable. In modern developed societies by contrast, most people, even when their wealth and power may seem puny by comparison with the rich, feel socially and therefore politically committed to the established order. Extensive civil and political rights in Western societies reinforce this commitment, making violent social upheaval far less prevalent than in other societies.

Of course, satisfaction and happiness in human life often come only with difficulty. Doubtless some white-collar workers and their wives—and probably more as the years rolled by—regretted missed opportunities or chafed at restrictions on their independence or self-realization.[104] In a general sense, people have always exercised some free will in regard to their lives. Even a peasant or a slave can decide to accept his fate or rebel, to live virtuously or without integrity, and to behave generously or unkindly. At the same time, rules, customs, habits, and traditions have limited the range of choices for most people on earth. The social revolutions of the West, however, began to erode these constraints. What had seemed natural and even necessary to one's parents gradually began to appear optional. Career choices and lifestyle possibilities gradually began to expand and multiply. A "generation gap" opened between parents and children, youth and authorities. Formerly dutiful company men began to look out for themselves. Wives and daughters challenged their positions of inferiority within the family and society, reaching parity with men in college attendance and a high proportion of participation in the labor force (77 percent of women age 35 to 44) in 1989.[105] By 2010, women in America made up more than half of the labor force, strongly outnumbered men as graduates from college and professional schools, held a majority of managerial jobs, and earned more than men as CEO's of big companies.[106]

Like women, oppressed and disrespected ethnic, racial, and religious minorities demanded equal treatment. For many of the same reasons that permitted Western societies to bring about the series of revolutions described so far in this book, they also managed to address these challenges, or at least to weather them, relatively successfully.

Ending discrimination

It seems unlikely that any human society has avoided discrimination based on religious, ethnic, cultural, or racial differences. The very word for "slave" in the Sumerian language meant "person of another country" and "barbarian" referred to a person speaking no Greek.[107] Tribally constituted communities—for most of human history the vast majority of people on earth—define membership and its boundaries very strictly. Those who belong systematically exclude those who do not. In the most cruel and tragic recent instance, in the African country of Rwanda in 1994, ethnic Hutus killed some 800,000 people, mostly ethnic Tutsis.[108]

The Roman Empire made the world's first major and sustained departure from this primeval norm.[109] Drawing in part on the Hellenistic philosophical tradition of Stoicism (founded in the third-century B.C.), which posited a universal reason inhering in all things, Roman jurists developed a complex and sophisticated system of law encompassing the vast array of peoples subjected to their rule and even elaborated a "law of the nations," or *jus gentium*, applicable to those outside its scope. As Cicero (106–43 B.C.), the Roman philosopher and statesman, wrote hopefully, "there will not be different laws at Rome or at Athens, . . . but one eternal and unchangeable law will be valid for all nations and for all times."[110] Of course, the Roman legions committed terrible atrocities against some of those nations. Yet the concept of Roman citizenship as open to a wide variety of inhabitants of the empire retained its force for centuries. St Paul, a Hellenized Jewish tent-maker and religious leader from Tarsus, a Roman provincial capital in what is now south-central Turkey, demanded and received his transfer from the authorities of Caesarea in Palestine, sometime between 58 and 60 A.D., to a court in Rome on the basis of his Roman citizenship.[111]

This tradition, coupled with universalist prophetic tendencies in Judaism,[112] permeated Christianity beginning with the missionary voyages of St Paul, who proclaimed that there "is neither Jew nor Greek, slave nor free, male nor female, for you are all one in Christ Jesus" (Gal. 3:28). This promise helps explain Christianity's spread within a few centuries throughout the Mediterranean region, into Europe, and even south of the Sahara and into Persia.[113] The Christians preached universal salvation, though only to those who believed in Christ. A similar belief animated the rise and rapid spread of Islam a half-millennium later. The Quranic tradition of *dhimma*, or legal protection afforded to believers of other recognized faiths (at first Judaism and Christianity, but later also Zoroastrianism and others), while not removing all legal and social disabilities, established a practice of limited religious toleration.[114] Throughout the Islamic world, large populations of non-Muslims could pay an annual tax and then live their lives and even rise in service to the local ruler, for the most part without the crushing persecution non-Christians typically faced in the medieval and early modern West.

Acceptance of others, however, stems at least as much from active curiosity as from passive toleration. Here, it turns out, Christian Europeans, beginning in the

Middle Ages, distinguished themselves from other peoples, aside from the ancient Greeks. Already in 1143, the English scholar Robert of Ketton translated the Quran into Latin.[115] As discussed in Chapter 5, European scholars had lived and studied in Muslim lands for over a century by that point. Their Muslim counterparts did not follow suit, not even when the Europeans began to rival and then surpass them in intellectual attainments in the later Middle Ages.

Practically no Muslims traveled in Christian Europe, studied its languages, took an interest in its literature, or wrote treatises on its political, social, or economic life—activities that Europeans pursued passionately in reverse. Several geographers described some aspects of Western Europe, though apparently only a few actually had any first-hand experience of these lands, for example, the tenth-century author Ibrahim ibn Yaqub al-Israili.[116] Most Muslim travelers preferred to sojourn in the East. Thus, in the tenth century Ibn Fadian visited the Islamic Bulgar people on the Volga River and left a detailed account of them, Vikings, and possibly Slavs who traded with them, but he ventured no further west.[117] Another interesting case was al-Hasan al-Wazzan, a Moroccan who was kidnapped in 1518 and taken to Rome. He converted to Christianity, became known as Leo Africanus, and wrote a 900-page description in Italian of people, places, and things in Africa. Published in 1550, it became a bestseller and was translated into several European languages. Yet after al-Wazzan returned to Africa, he apparently did not write about his travels in Europe.[118] During their nearly 800-year rule of parts of Iberia (Spain and Portugal), scarcely any Muslims exhibited detailed scholarly interest in the cultures, languages, or history of the rest of Europe.[119] Even the admirably up-to-date world map prepared in 1513 by Piri Reis, an Ottoman admiral, languished in the sultan's palace, and no complete copy remains.[120] Exploring the wider world did not become a passion for Muslims. (Muslim authors began to take an interest in the West in the 1800s.)[121]

From at least the early sixteenth century, numerous European intellectuals began to use their detailed knowledge and experiences of other cultures as ammunition for critiques of their own societies. Critics from Peter Martyr d'Anghiera (1457–1526) to Bartolomé de Las Casas decried what they considered the greed, cruelty, and narrow-mindedness of the Spanish conquerors in the New World.[122] Others, like Pierre Belon and Michel de Montaigne (1533–92), imagined the customs and institutions of other lands superior—less unfair or more pure—to their own.[123] In the seventeenth and eighteenth centuries, many European intellectuals, like Leibniz and Voltaire, admired the well-ordered and rationally minded Chinese monarchy.[124]

European institutions of higher learning had established scholarly chairs for the study of Arabic in Paris (1538) and Cambridge (1633).[125] Collections of Islamic books developed systematically from the fifteenth century in major and even minor European countries.[126] Partly this was aimed at "knowing one's enemy," but the result was detailed knowledge.[127] Serious scholarly interest by Europeans in other cultures and civilizations broadened and deepened. Popular writers also wrote many often highly sympathetic books about the great non-Western cultures.[128] Yet the objects of this assiduous intellectual curiosity still did not repay the compliment.

The European thirst for knowledge about humankind, attitude of self-criticism, and religious tolerance starting after the religious wars gave birth during the Enlightenment to a passionate promotion by some intellectuals of the equality of all persons and even peoples, no matter their religious, ethnic, gender, and racial distinctions.[129]

This process began in specific localities, such as the seventeenth-century Dutch Republic, where Catholics, Jews, and radical Protestants all lived largely unmolested.[130] Dutch influence in turn helped make New Amsterdam (New York) a radically tolerant and diverse city from its earliest days.[131] Other places of toleration also emerged in the English colonies, in particular Rhode Island, which Roger Williams founded in 1636 as a refuge for religious dissenters, as discussed in Chapter 10. Perhaps more important, the Maryland Toleration Act of 1649 established the freedom of worship for all Christians—even Catholics—so long as they believed in the Trinity.[132] Although the Act remained in force less than 40 years,[133] it established a precedent as the first legal guarantee in history—not merely a protection dependent on the goodwill of rulers or magistrates—of religious freedom. As such it served as a forerunner of the first amendment of the US Constitution. These and other laws that emerged throughout the West went radically beyond the Islamic provision of *dhimma*, which afforded protection but not equal rights to religious minorities. Gradually, other minorities gained protections and rights in Western countries.

The Christian exhortation to "love one another" and to "be a servant to others" played a crucial role in the struggles for extending human rights to oppressed minorities and, in particular, in the fight against slavery.

Throughout nearly all of history, most human societies have accepted and justified the institution of slavery. The world's greatest religious and philosophical thinkers of ancient and medieval times took it for granted.[134] Racially based slavery had deep roots in the Islamic and Chinese civilizations, though less so in ancient Greece or Rome or in India from the Buddhist period. Although the rise of feudalism in medieval Europe engulfed and largely blunted the harsher elements of chattel slavery, that institution continued to flourish in Iberia where warring Christians and Muslims enslaved prisoners seized in their bitter conflict. It flourished, too, in Constantinople. In the later medieval and early Renaissance periods, Genoese and Venetian merchants dominated the slave trade throughout the eastern Mediterranean, and the grave labor shortage brought about by the Black Death (1347–51) gave rise to some renewed slave-owning, particularly in northern Italy. Nevertheless, the entire commerce died out within Europe by around 1600.[135] From the mid-1400s, however, the Portuguese established slave-based plantations in Madeira, the Azores, and other Atlantic islands.[136] By then, many European towns and then whole countries (France and England, in particular) had established the principle that any slave could gain his or her freedom by residing in their territory.[137] One found the starkest contrast to this practice and the sharpest distinctions between slave and free in North America—the site of history's greatest struggle over the institution of slavery.[138]

That struggle began intellectually with the French political philosopher Jean Bodin (1530–96), the first major thinker in history to condemn slavery on philosophical grounds.[139] In developing a theory of an organic state, he refused to conceive of any member of society as excluded from the body politic and therefore as not subject to the will of the sovereign. Using the powerful logic of Peter Ramus, he demolished every argument in favor of slavery. He also showed with enormous erudition that throughout history slavery had everywhere engendered inhuman treatment, degradation, dissension, and rebellion. Among early modern political thinkers, however, Bodin had few allies.[140] Neither Hugo Grotius, nor Thomas Hobbes, nor John Locke rejected slavery as an institution, though each defined relatively narrow grounds for its continued existence. Even many Enlightenment thinkers—including Voltaire, Kant, and Hume—refused to condemn slavery, though Montesquieu asserted that human bondage deviated from natural law, and Adam Smith believed that it impeded moral and economic progress. Though still few in number in the eighteenth century, these European minds deserve praise for their efforts to invalidate the ancient yet deplorable practice.[141]

Evangelical Christianity, especially in Great Britain and the United States, proved far more powerful than any philosophical arguments, for it inspired the most passionate opposition to slavery.[142] Quakers were the staunchest crusaders.[143] In 1775 in Philadelphia, the Quaker immigrant from France, Anthony Benezet (1713–84), organized the world's first antislavery society, the Society for the Relief of Free Negroes Unlawfully Held in Bondage.[144] Quaker activists in the American colonies exhorted masters to free their slaves, prohibited their members from involvement in any facet of slavery, organized abolitionist associations, submitted antislavery petitions to the legislatures in the American colonies, and pressed for similar efforts in Great Britain. It helped their cause that Quakers in both countries maintained perhaps the world's most reliable communications network, thanks to both continuously itinerant missionaries and fabulous commercial success. Scholars have pointed to industrial development coinciding with antislavery activism and industrialists standing to gain from an expansion of the labor market, but it seems that most activists were motivated primarily by moral principles.[145] Other Christians, in particular Methodists and Mennonites, joined with them in forming the backbone of abolitionism.

The first legal milestone came when the French revolutionaries out of purely humanistic concerns abolished slavery at home and in the French colonies in 1794, though this law remained in force only until 1802.[146] The powerfully eloquent evangelical Christian William Wilberforce and his allies enjoyed the first permanent successes when the British Parliament abolished the slave trade in 1807 and made participation in it a felony in 1811. In 1833, just before Wilberforce's death, Parliament outlawed slavery in most of the British Empire. Over the next half-century, all the existing and former European colonies in the New World abolished slavery. Thus, Europeans took an ancient and universal but evil institution, dragged it down to its lowest conceivable level of inhumanity and degradation, and then rejected the practice root and branch for philosophical and religious reasons.

The American and French revolutionary traditions, as discussed in Chapter 10, affirmed, in words of the French Declaration of the Rights of Man of 1789, that each person is endowed with "natural, unalienable, and sacred rights." No other civilization or culture had ever made such a sweeping and bold claim. Although no society immediately enforced it, each of the Western countries gradually sought to live up to this ideal.[147]

In recent decades, many scholars have interpreted the nation-state as an "imagined community," which to some has implied its illegitimacy.[148] In reality, this concept has merely rendered explicit a key feature of every human relationship. At some level, even a spouse, a sibling, a colleague, and a friend can only imagine or hope that earnest and unshakable feelings of loyalty stand behind the relationships that they perceive and experience. Therefore, when the spirit of national consciousness legitimated strong imagined relationships over a wide geographical area, as it did ever more powerfully from the late eighteenth century, bonds between people who had never met, professed different religions, spoke different languages, and even looked completely different from one another gradually acquired the force of what people had formerly considered the only natural human relations. In other words, the ideal of universal brotherhood, which stemmed from a fusion of Christian faith and rational Enlightenment thinking, gave birth to societies whose outlook and values required them to overturn every disability and inequality imposed upon their members by tradition, custom, or prejudice.

Historically, even petty criminals have faced harsh punishments. In most traditional conceptions of justice, committing a crime challenged and dishonored the ruler's authority. Only public executions and floggings, apparently, could reassert its prestige.[149] Since trained police forces existed nowhere until the nineteenth century, few criminals actually faced prosecution. Alleged criminals, when occasionally captured, often faced horrific punishments—to frighten others and thus to deter crime. Judicial torture—as part of the investigative process—was widely practiced in Europe until gradually abolished, first in Prussia in 1754 and in subsequent decades elsewhere.[150]

The Enlightenment in general brought a more rational, practical, and humane approach to crime fighting. In *On Crimes and Punishments* (1764), Cesare Beccaria argued that each punishment should both fit the crime and strike with certainty.[151] Since only a trained police force could catch criminals systematically, the modern Western states instituted such forces, starting with Great Britain in the 1820s. As punishment became more certain, it also grew more lenient. Public executions disappeared nearly everywhere in Europe between 1770 and 1870,[152] and by 1820 the American states had abolished capital punishment except for grave crimes.[153] Western reformers, often influenced by evangelical Christians, also devised methods of incarceration aimed at rehabilitating criminals. The United States became the Mecca for prison reform, attracting visitors from Europe.[154] Reformers experimented with such innovations as single-cell incarceration, solitary confinement, instruction in hygiene and other elements of civilized life, enforced exercise, pervasive silence, strict discipline, productive work, and vocational and academic training. These new prison regimens—which taxpayers willingly funded—did not eliminate crime from society, as the reformers eagerly hoped, yet to some extent they treated criminals humanely.

A similar story unfolded for the mentally ill. Before an era of reform began in the later eighteenth century, victims of mental illness were chained, beaten, ill nourished, and scarcely treated for their afflictions. The French physician Philippe Pinel (1745–1826) led the way in Paris by establishing relatively humane conditions at the mental wards of two large hospitals—removing the inmates' shackles, for example.[155] Legislation throughout the Western world—such as the British Lunacy Act of 1845, spearheaded by the devoutly Christian seventh Earl of Shaftesbury (1801–85)—led to a proliferation of mental hospitals and specialized medical personnel and treatments.[156] For many decades, these institutions often remained overcrowded and harshly impersonal. Yet they represented a humanitarian impulse to include within the human community people with some of the most intractable problems.

The mid-twentieth-century pharmaceutical revolution (as noted in Chapter 12) finally made possible relatively effective treatments for mental illness.[157] By the

1960s, "community psychiatry" created conditions for medicated patients to lead relatively productive lives on their own or in group homes.[158]

The public reform movement in Western countries, beginning in the first half of the nineteenth century, aimed to protect the vulnerable (women and children in particular), improve public health through clean drinking water and sewage systems, ameliorate the conditions of labor, expand education, and create opportunities for the support and self-reliance of the poor.[159] They fell short in nearly every case. The poor continued to suffer, laborers to work unconscionably long hours and often in unsafe conditions, and drinking water to carry infectious diseases. Yet in every case the efforts remained noble and in the long run reached lofty goals.

Immigrants to Western countries—in particular to the United States—gradually, though often very slowly, gained acceptance in their new homelands. The 22 million Europeans who departed for non-US shores typically migrated in national waves, Spaniards and Italians to Brazil and Argentina, Britons to Canada and Australia. They mostly fit in well. The range of immigrants to the United States—some 35 million from 1820 to 1920—varied far more dramatically.[160] Irish and German immigrants predominated up to 1860; Italians and a wide variety of Central and Eastern Europeans, among them many Jews, did so thereafter. Within these waves, over 2 million Scandinavians and another 2 million or so Greeks, Dutch, Portuguese, French, Swiss, and Turks also arrived. Newcomers generally faced systematic discrimination and hostility, especially the Irish and those not from northwestern Europe. Conflicts frequently arose among them, notably between the Irish and Germans. They nearly all started at the bottom rungs of society and gradually worked their way up. Most came to feel at home—though in 1880–1930 one-quarter to one-third of European immigrants returned to Europe permanently.[161]

Feeling at home, loving America, and achieving impressive worldly success was unfortunately not always enough to ensure acceptance. Thus, the Ivy League universities imposed quotas on Jews for undergraduate admissions from the 1920s through the 1950s and excluded them from the professorate until the late 1940s.[162] Restrictive residential covenants in many localities continued to exclude Jews from a variety of communities into the 1970s.[163] Nor has anti-Semitism disappeared entirely even today. Gradually, however, the very small but highly successful minority of Jews in America went on to many triumphs, bringing their extraordinary talents to science, the arts, business, entrepreneurship, and nearly every other walk of life. In fact, Jews have enjoyed greater success in the United States than anywhere else on earth, much to the country's benefit.[164] Why? America ultimately exhibited to a rare degree the West's radical openness to people of different backgrounds.

Asian immigrants received the worst treatment. From the gold-rush years to the late 1800s, some 370,000 Chinese embarked for the United States.[165] They faced hostility and even violence from white laborers who often considered them unfair competition. Most elite Americans of the time considered the Chinese an "inferior race" with alien customs and habits making them incapable of assimilating to the American way of life. Accordingly, the Naturalization Act of 1870 specified that only "white persons and persons of African descent" could apply for American citizenship. Though intended to target the Chinese, over time the law applied to Turks, Japanese, and East Indians. Twelve years later, the Chinese Exclusion Act prohibited the immigration of Chinese laborers (but not of teachers, students, merchants, and travelers). The Geary Act of 1892 imposed further restrictions on Chinese residents, in particular, the obligation to carry residency permits. The Chinese population steadily declined from its peak of 107,488 in 1890. (When China became an ally in World War II, Congress repealed the Chinese Exclusion Act.)[166]

During the four decades from 1880 to 1920, roughly 275,000 Japanese made the United States their home and faced similar discrimination and ill-treatment. Under diplomatic pressure, the Japanese government agreed to issue no passports to laborers planning to work in the continental United States. (Many Japanese continued to migrate to Hawaii.) Following Imperial Japan's attack on Pearl Harbor, the federal government interned over 100,000 Japanese in concentration camps as potential traitors. (Congress issued an apology in 1988 followed by restitution payments to each internee.)[167]

Low quotas instituted in the early 1920s kept out most non-Europeans.[168] The only exception was several hundred thousand Mexicans allowed to take temporary low-skill jobs under the Bracero Program in 1943–64. Many faced terrible discrimination.[169]

The Immigration and Nationality Act of 1965 threw the US borders open to non-Europeans. Over the next 35 years, some 10 million immigrants arrived from nearly every country on earth, roughly half from Mexico.[170] Discrimination and scorn continued to plague them, especially those whose appearance and customs differed most from the native born. Yet over time, again, the status and success of most immigrants increased—though Mexicans in particular established vast, linguistically self-sufficient, but often economically disadvantaged communities.

Societies throughout history have discriminated against newcomers. The countervailing progress made in Western countries, and particularly in America, although painfully slow and still incomplete, constitutes a humane, rational, and ultimately fruitful development. As this book has argued, a key source of Western success has been the ability to draw upon an ever-larger pool of human talent. The most successful society, and perhaps also the morally best one, will always integrate the maximum possible human diversity with the maximum of ever-evolving principles of orderliness. Immigration in the West has therefore proved both a boon and a triumph. One cannot, however, say as much about America's treatment of its Native- and African-American minorities.

Scholars have estimated the number of native peoples living in pre-Columbian North America at between one and 18 million. They spoke some 200 distinct languages and comprised hundreds of tribes and communities, some relatively sophisticated and developed like the Iroquois Confederation. Contact with diseases unwittingly borne by Europeans devastated the native populations, which plunged to 600,000 in 1800 and 237,000 by 1890.[171] White Americans treated the natives in diverse ways. James Fenimore Cooper (1789–1851) depicted them with dignity in countless stories, though few other writers followed his example.[172] Devout Christians in considerable number sympathized with them and some tried to help them adapt to American life. Most people, including George Washington and Thomas Jefferson, viewed them as "savages" incapable of improving the vast lands they occupied.[173]

Given the whites' hostility, the native cultures stood little chance of surviving, much less thriving.[174] The Supreme Court ruled in *Johnson v. M'Intosh* (1823) that the United States government had the right to compel native tribes to sell their land in a process resembling eminent domain.[175] The Indian Removal Act of 1830 paved the way for the forced migration westward of tens of thousands of Native Americans. Thousands died or were killed along the way. Gradually, starting in 1851, the government resettled native peoples on dozens and eventually a few hundred reservations, partly to preserve their ancestral ways of life and to protect them from encroachment by settlers. Tragically, migrating European settlers continued to carry diseases lethal for the natives, hunted their game to near extinction, and provoked a series of bloody "Indian wars."[176]

Beginning in the late 1800s, the federal government attempted to improve the lives of Native Americans, though without success. The Dawes Act (1887), for example, attempted to assimilate native peoples to the American way of life, by promising to each family a sizable farm (160 acres) and schooling for their children.[177] In practice, however, the land they received was often poor, many natives were unable or unwilling to farm, or they simply lacked the necessary capital and equipment. The welfare of natives continued to stagnate. The Indian Reorganization Act of 1934 increased social services to them yet without major improvements in their standard of living. In 2000, the Assistant Secretary for Indian Affairs of the Department of the Interior issued a formal apology on behalf of his agency (but not the federal government) for nearly two centuries of mistreatment and what he described as "ethnic cleansing."[178] Australia, Canada, and New Zealand have offered fuller apologies and more significant forms of compensation.[179] Yet what a phenomenal loss of talent from millions of people who, had they been welcomed earlier, could have contributed so much!

The story of African-Americans is far different. For over two centuries, European settlers in North America enslaved and oppressed Africans. In the first half of the nineteenth century, abolitionists had fought against the practice. Peaceful means of eradicating it proved impossible, however, and the most wrenching and destructive war in American history was fought, pitting the agrarian, slave-owning South against the industrial and ultimately far more powerful North (see Map 14.2).

Following the conflict, the three so-called Reconstruction Amendments, adopted starting with the Thirteenth Amendment (1865), abolished slavery, made African-Americans full-fledged citizens, and established equal rights—including the right to vote—for all Americans.[180] In 1867, the US Army oversaw state elections throughout the South in which freed blacks took part as both voters and candidates. The resulting biracial state governments expanded public education, developed railroads, and promoted economic growth.[181] The "original sin" of institutionalized slavery in America, which for nearly a century had made a mockery of the stirring words of the Declaration of Independence, "all men are created equal," seemed on the path toward expiation. Alas, after federal troops left the South in 1877, Southern Democrats gradually restricted the civil liberties of African-Americans through a system of rules known as "Jim Crow."[182] By means of policies and customs, both overt and covert, nearly all southern blacks lost their right to vote, to choose where they wished to live, to send their children to the better schools, to shop and dine and even worship as they pleased, to attend most colleges and universities, to advance professionally according to their merits, and in general to become full-fledged members of American society.

African-Americans fared better in the North, where approximately 1.5 million migrated between 1910 and 1930, though even there they faced terrible discrimination,

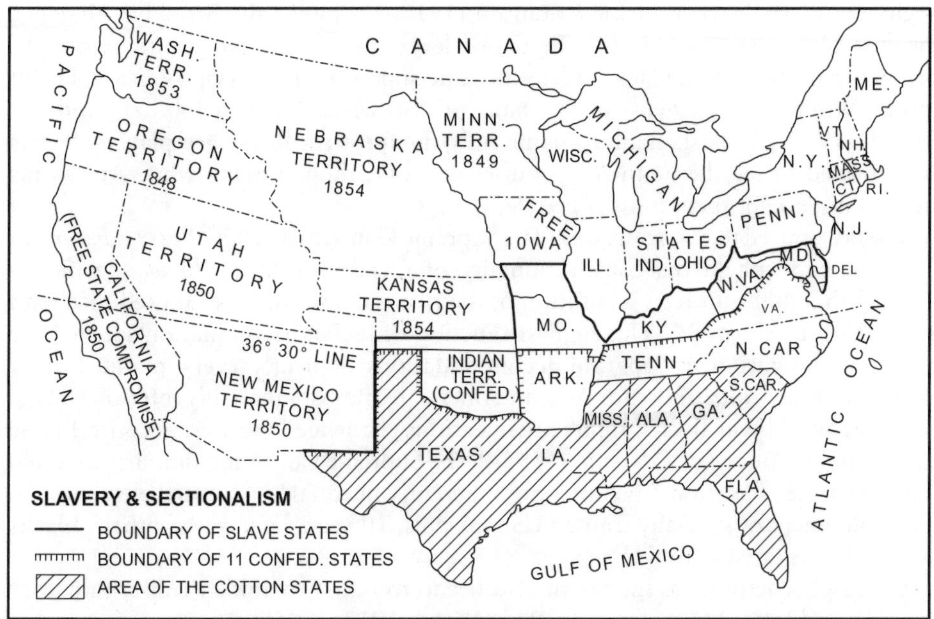

MAP 14.2 *The Mason-Dixon line divided the free states in the north and the slave states in the south. Though a few slave states were above this line, only Virginia joined the Confederacy.*

including exclusion from the better neighborhoods (and therefore schools), from many jobs and job promotions, and from clubs and voluntary associations.[183] Few gained admission to the best colleges. White supremacism gripped American society.[184]

An important debate in moral philosophy stems from the views of Socrates and Aristotle. At the risk of grossly oversimplifying, Socrates believed that a person needed only to grasp the truth about any situation in order to act ethically. For this reason, he urged everyone to "know thyself" and to reflect constantly.[185] Aristotle, by contrast, argued that correct moral training from a young age held the key to ethical behavior.[186] Developing a just society probably requires both approaches. A few examples from American sports history may serve to prove this point.

When white boxers declined to fight the African-American Jack Johnson (1878–1946), they as much as admitted their fear that a black man might prove superior to any white challenger.[187] When Johnson, all smiles and good humor, won the world-heavyweight boxing championship in 1908 and then defended it in a celebrated fight against the former champion Jim Jeffries (1875–1953) in 1910, he proved that point beyond the shadow of a doubt. Henceforth, the white man throughout the West knew intellectually, that is, in a Socratic sense, that his alleged superiority in every sphere of human achievement had been a sham. Yet assimilating this lesson required a lengthy period of Aristotelian training.

The social tectonics began to shift during World War II. With more than 1 million African-Americans in uniform, some military bases desegregated—for example, Fort Benning in George—though full racial integration came only during and after the Korean War.[188] Gradually, the American armed forces became one of the most racially integrated institutions in the country. Professional sports grew equally well integrated, beginning in 1947 when Jackie Robinson (1919–72) joined the Brooklyn Dodgers, the first black man to play for the major leagues since the nineteenth century.[189] Beginning in the 1950s, black athletes became superstars in every professional team sport—Willie Mays (1931–) in baseball, Jim Brown (1936–) in football, and Bill Russell (1934–) in basketball, to name only the most revolutionary players. Sports fans thrilled to see these athletic geniuses at work, though many white Americans still did not accept them fully as people.[190]

The law started to change as well. The Supreme Court, in its 1896 *Plessy v. Ferguson* decision, had upheld the constitutionality of racial segregation laws, specifically denying that "the enforced separation of the two races stamps the colored race with a badge of inferiority."[191] This highest sanction of racial discrimination spurred the further proliferation of separate accommodations of nearly every public facility throughout the South, those for African-Americans almost invariably inferior. During and after World War II, civil rights organizations challenged the laws in court. In one case, *Brown v. Board of Education* (1954), the Supreme Court unanimously asserted that "separate educational facilities are inherently unequal."[192] Nevertheless, despite the deployment of specially trained US marshals, 10 years later few southern blacks attended integrated schools.[193]

Civil rights activists in the South also began to refuse to abide by discriminatory customs and laws. Most famously, Rosa Parks (1913–2005) refused to give up her seat on a bus in Montgomery, Alabama, to a white passenger in 1955 and as a result landed in jail.[194] The next day, activists including Martin Luther King, Jr. (1929–68), launched a boycott of the city bus system. It lasted over a year, involved most of the 40,000 African-Americans in the city, and led to repeal of the bus segregation law, though only when the Supreme Court in *Browder v. Gayle* (1956) rendered such laws unconstitutional. Civil-rights legislation, in particular the Civil Rights Act of 1964, made discrimination and segregation illegal in education, employment, and public accommodations on the basis of "race, color, religion, sex, or national origin."[195] The Voting Rights Act of the following year made it illegal to restrict the right to vote on the basis of race through such means as poll taxes or literacy tests. Consequently, by 1969 black voter registration in the former Confederate states had increased from 24.4 to 60.7 percent. In the words of one scholar, "Black voters had become a political factor, especially in the black belt areas of the Deep South where they had been barely visible as registered voters before the Voting Rights Act."[196]

All of these efforts had repercussions throughout society. Harvard, Princeton, and Yale Universities, for example, had admitted all together only 15 black students in 1960 but, after President Kennedy urged them in 1962 to "make a difference," their total enrollments of black students shot up to 284 in 1970.[197] Across the country, black college enrollment doubled in the 5 years after 1967 to 727,000 or 18 percent of all college-age blacks (compared with 26% of whites).[198] Gradually, discrimination eased, and African-Americans joined the middle class in ever-larger numbers. If only 20 percent had graduated high school in 1960, over 50 percent had by 1980.[199] Forty-three percent owned their own homes in 1990, compared to 34.5 percent in 1950.[200] Decade by decade, the proportion of African-Americans in the professions and in positions of leadership in government and business increased, until Colin Powell could serve as Secretary of State from 2001 to 2005 and Condoleezza Rice could succeed him. Then in 2008, a majority of the American electorate, including 54 percent of young white voters and 43 percent of white voters overall, felt sufficient respect for Barack Obama to elect him their president.[201] Race prejudice has not disappeared entirely from the country, but the shift in white attitudes toward African-Americans over the previous century had been dramatic.

Yet perhaps enumerating all these successes merely begs the question of how much more success earlier civil-rights legislation could have ensured—and how much pain, suffering, failures, losses, and other misfortunes it might have avoided. These questions concern not only African-Americans but also the whole of American society. This book has, in its most general sense, argued that openness, pluralism, a thirst for knowledge and sharing information, a commitment to rationality and the rule of law, respect for persons, and individual initiative are precisely the values that enabled the West to rise.[202] The inclusion and actualization of the broadest range possible of human talent, drive, ability, and passion furnish a recipe for both social harmony and success. America's failings in this regard have cast a pall over its otherwise admirable development. This holds true in other cases of discrimination and unjust treatment of racial and ethnic minorities. Given the immense social, cultural, economic, and political contributions of Asians in recent decades, for example, one can only ponder with deep regret what might have been had Congress never adopted the Chinese Exclusion Act.

The same can be said of all the European and other Western countries. Some, at various periods in their history, discriminated less on the basis of race, treated their native peoples better, or welcomed immigrants more warmly than did the Americans. Yet all excluded ethnic, cultural, religious, and racial minorities from mainstream institutions and opportunities—or worse—and thus inevitably wasted precious human talent.[203]

Explosion of rights

The final decades of the last millennium saw the Western societies, from a sense of responsibility, from painful awareness of their failures to address legitimate past grievances, or under pressure from protesters and dissidents, grant an extraordinary range of liberties, efforts at restitution, and expressions of acceptance toward persons, behaviors, and lifestyles previously deplored or rejected. Meanwhile, members of society tested, pushed against, and assaulted the limits of the permissible.

An important stimulant in these developments was the philosophical approach called "Postmodernism."[204] Like the Surrealists after World War I, postmodernist thinkers questioned key principles of Western culture. Their leading lights flourished in Paris in the 1960s and 1970s. Jacques Derrida argued that humans live in and experience not an objective reality but only a tight meshwork of language. We speak and think metaphorically, not realistically. Nor are our stories, what we tell each other—even the greatest works of fiction—our own. No incontestable criteria enable us to evaluate specific interpretations; thus, one should adopt an attitude of "play" and "openness." According to Michel Foucault, however, there are underlying intellectual structures, which determine how we think about the world and usually advantage the powerful. Even who we are is conditioned or constructed by various "discourses of power." Modern societies are not really free, claimed Foucault, since rules and laws minutely regulate human behavior.[205] Presumably most citizens believe that such norms make densely populated modern Western societies livable and that such societies are still freer than most others. People in the West also tend still to consider themselves relatively autonomous individuals responsible for their actions. Postmodernist refutations of scientific claims to objectivity and political neutrality have enjoyed even less success in the public mind. Yet their critiques of social norms and structures oppressing minorities and marginalized social groups struck a powerful chord in societies already steadily moving toward ending discrimination. "Identity politics" and broad liberation movements in Western societies in recent decades owed a lot to the "postmodernist turn."

A "sexual revolution," made possible in part by the invention and marketing of effective artificial birth control methods, in particular the birth control pill, which came on the market in the United States in 1960, took the Western world by storm.[206] Millions of people pushed aside or rejected mores and norms that had stood for decades if not centuries, as they experimented with new lifestyles. "Free love," often involving sexual encounters with strangers, was widely promoted in the late 1960s as a beautiful, natural, and powerful form of self-expression.[207] Sex emerged into the public domain and stimulated endless discussion and experimentation. For example, research into human sexuality by William Masters (1915–2001) and Virginia Johnson (1925–2013) showed that most women can experience orgasms and in some cases multiple times. Court cases and legislation allowed the publication of books and magazines formerly banned as obscene. Readers snatched up dozens of "how-to" sex books like *The Sensuous Woman* (1969). Singles bars opened by the thousand in the 1970s, making random encounters possible.[208]

Throughout the Western societies, new attitudes toward sexuality took hold and radically changed family life, popular culture, and the process of courtship. The number of divorces per year shot up from under 10 per 1,000 married women in the United States in 1960 to over 22 in the late 1970s, thanks in part to the adoption of no-fault divorce laws in most states. The divorce rates for most other Western countries increased by factors of from 2 to 5 during these years.[209] The number of out-of-wedlock births in the United States also increased dramatically, from less than 4 percent of all births in 1940 to nearly 34 percent in 1994.[210]

Homosexual men and women began to demand recognition of their lifestyle as acceptable to the broader community and to fight against laws banning homosexual activity.[211] These efforts soon bore fruit, for example, when the American Psychiatric Association removed homosexuality from its official list of mental disorders in 1973. By the 1980s, most Western societies had adopted at least a relatively accepting attitude. Within another decade or so, they had also extended at least tolerance to those choosing to undergo sex reassignment surgery.[212]

In time, activists demanded the abolition of every form of discrimination. Some campaigned against "sexism" or treating men and women differently. Thus, in most Western countries, women won the right to enter the military or to serve as firefighters. Ethnic jokes became frowned upon as insensitive. Others rejected "ageism," or disability based on age. Still others claimed rights for animals.[213] Anti-cruelty and animal-welfare movements and organizations had begun to emerge in 1822 in the United Kingdom and gained philosophical power from writers like Henry S. Salt (1851–1939) before resulting in significant legislative protections for animals in the

1960s.[214] Activists seeking to guarantee for nonhuman hominids the right to life and freedom won their first major victory when the Spanish parliament passed a resolution in 2008 guaranteeing such rights to great apes.[215]

Young people furnished much of the energy in these struggles. They became a political force in the late 1960s when their protests weakened public support for the Vietnam War in America and, in conjunction with a general strike, nearly toppled the French government in May 1968.[216] The extraordinary affluence of postwar Western societies often meant that youths had money to spend, which gave them a sense of independence and self-sufficiency. Young people questioned traditions, customs, institutions, and authority. Millions decried militarism, environmental degradation, and economic exploitation, blaming such problems on the "older generation."

The position of children and young people changed dramatically. Postwar baby booms throughout the West gave this cohort strength in numbers. They became a major marketing target for businesses, given their increasing disposable income and the willingness of parents to spend more and more money on them. To an ever-greater extent, elements of popular entertainment—music, television shows, and movies—catered specifically to them. Corporal punishment, a key disciplining method used by parents and teachers for centuries, became illegal in many Western societies and frowned upon in all.[217] The relationships of authority between young people and parents, teachers, and other social figures weakened, and the social hierarchies, which they had formerly maintained, flattened.

Informality gained throughout the West at the expense of authority and hierarchy. Polite forms of address, such as "Mr." or "Sir," often fell by the wayside.[218] Even languages and cultures with the built-in formality of the tú-usted distinction have developed the custom of (relatively) quickly passing on to the less formal pronoun. In many countries, work acquaintances and service personnel began to use their interlocutors' first names. Even officials and politicians in high office gradually adopted the practice, as when in 2006 President George W. Bush addressed the British Prime Minister with the phrase, "Yo, Blair!" Or when Prime Minister Gordon Brown referred to the American president in 2009 as "Barack." Both incidents provoked minor scandals that presumably could not have even occurred a few decades before or, even today, outside the "Anglosphere." The personal titles "Mrs." and "Miss" fell into desuetude, though their replacement, "Ms.," enjoys far less use than its predecessors. In some countries, like Germany, formal titles retain more importance, though even there people switch to first names and the familiar pronoun "du" far more quickly than in the past. The same holds true throughout the Nordic countries and most of the rest of Europe.

People began dressing less formally as well. Obligatory hats for men and gloves for women went out in the 1960s apparently never to return. Some feminists gave up wearing brassieres, but while this act of defiance gained the status of custom in some societies, it did not in most. Many businesspeople and government employees still uphold formal dress codes—suit and tie or at least jacket and tie for men and business suit for women—but "business casual" outfits of slacks and shirts or skirts and blouses have made big inroads into American places of employment—43 percent according to a Gallup poll of 2007, compared to only 9 percent wearing formal business attire.[219] Employers in Silicon Valley near San Francisco, during the dot-com boom-times of the 1990s, led the way toward more informal dress codes. Even the formerly richest man in the world, Bill Gates (1955–), the founder of the colossal Microsoft Corporation, frequently shows up at highly formal venues without a tie.

* * *

A new world, it seems, has been dawning: a world of informality of human behavior but of extraordinary access to formally organized information and knowledge, of previously unimaginable toleration of others and of people's ability to reinvent themselves and redefine their environments, of constant interconnections of billions of people across the earth but also still of potentialities for the physical destruction of both nature and human societies, and of hopes without end that science and technology can resolve these and other problems we humans grapple with. The transformative Western civilization made all these things possible, for better or worse.

QUESTIONS FOR REFLECTION

How did the "associational life" of Western societies contribute to democracy?

What roles did the middle class play in Western development?

How did women gain more power in Western societies?

How was the European attitude toward other cultures unusual?

In what sense were Europeans more self-critical than other peoples?

Why are openness and pluralism so important for human development?

Conclusions:

A new type of society

In 1976, two college dropouts, Steve Jobs (1955–2011) and Steve Wozniak (1950–), created a business in Jobs's parents' garage with start-up capital amassed from selling a Volkswagen van and two HP calculators.[1] Four years later, they launched the biggest initial public stock offering since Ford went public in 1956. On that day they made themselves and 300 other investors millionaires. Their company? Apple, maker of what may be considered the first personal computer, the Apple II (launched in 1977)—affordable, user-friendly, small but relatively powerful, useable right out of the box, with high-resolution color graphics, a floppy-disk drive, a keyboard, and built-in software. The following year, IBM successfully challenged Apple's dominance of the PC market. Yet those two visionaries—the charismatic Jobs and the shy but brilliant engineer and inventor Wozniak, both inveterate pranksters—changed the world of technology, putting extraordinary power to process information in the hands of everyman. Not Big Blue—IBM—but two young computer geeks.

Innovation has played a critical role in human development from the earliest times. Continuous efforts to adapt to changing environments have enabled humankind to increase its mastery, from the discovery of fire to the World Wide Web. In each case, our fund of useful knowledge has grown. Early humans taught one another through example and gradually by means of language, as their mental capacities increased through evolution. Our more recent ancestors learned to use numbers, to write language, to organize long-distance trade networks, to philosophize, and to develop connections to transcendent reality. From all of these endeavors they set down descriptions, explanations, arguments, prophecies, exhortations, and compendia of knowledge they considered precious. Sometimes, however, people failed to preserve these treasures or the threads of innovation broke.

The great civilizations flourished because they developed important skills or mastered powerful knowledge. They declined or entered stasis by failing to continue to adapt. Yet the most powerful knowledge is not necessarily the most sophisticated or profound. When the Mongols sacked Baghdad in 1258, they possessed vastly less knowledge and skill than the conquered except in horsemanship and war. Human development follows no clear patterns. Any sphere of learning or action can prove unexpectedly crucial for advancement. Therefore, pursuing knowledge in every direction can only benefit a society. Probably no tinkerer could have devised an efficient steam engine without a scientific understanding of the properties of gases.[2] For this reason, societies that encourage to the greatest extent the pursuit of learning, information sharing, human interaction, reflection, publication, scientific investigation, and scholarly inquiry will almost certainly achieve more innovation, a higher standard of living, and a greater concentration of power than similar societies that do not.

Apple was not the first big American electronics company founded in a garage. A half-century earlier, Bill Hewlett (1913–2001) and Dave Packard (1912–96) had founded in Packard's garage what is still one of the biggest information technology companies in the world.[3] Many other entrepreneurs followed in their footsteps. Bill Gates dropped out of college to pursue a business-venture in software writing, a passion from his early teenage years.[4] In fact, the entire dot-com revolution consisted in undercapitalized but brilliantly inventive entrepreneurs figuring out new ways to exploit the power and promise of information technology. More recently Sergey Brin (1973–) teamed up with Larry Page (1972–)—they graduated from college but suspended their doctoral studies—to develop the world's most powerful information-processing system, Google.[5] Brin, who left Russia as a child, almost certainly would not have helped bring this astounding firm into the world had he stayed in his parents' homeland. Russia does not lack brilliant and innovative minds; unfortunately, the political and economic environment often makes it hard for them to flourish.

All these cyber-entrepreneurs resembled Edison in their ingenuity, determination, and individual initiative but differed from him in their higher level of formal education and, for the most part, the breadth of their vision. Also, whereas something like the frontier spirit animated Edison, entrepreneurs like Jobs—who traveled to India and converted to Buddhism—felt the influence of various countercultural movements of the 1960s and 1970s.[6] Many "computer geeks" of the time hoped that information technology would transform the world, open up its power to everyone, break down all barriers between people, and bring about a sociopolitical revolution, empowering the poor, common laborers, the elderly, students, and minorities.[7] Many programmers designed—and continue to design—software open to all users without charge—"shareware"—and ultimately internet platforms as public services, like the ubiquitous and awesomely powerful Wikipedia.

The revolution they and others in the computer business brought about achieved all these things and more. As a moneymaking venture, information technology has exceeded even the wildest hopes of the most unbridled dreamers. Also, any ordinary person with an internet connection can now access massively more intellectual content than the greatest scholars of times past.

Such a mastery of knowledge or at least information is the culmination of centuries of Western development. From the legal compendia of the twelfth century to the theological and philosophical *summae* of the thirteenth, from the profusion of mechanically reproduced books on every imaginable subject of the fifteenth century to the specialized handbooks and treatises a century later, from the mathematically informed scientific studies of the seventeenth century to the all-encompassing encyclopedias and newspapers of the eighteenth and right down through the scientific and technological knowledge making it possible to build machines and harness the forces of nature in the past 200 years—the rise of the West has been an information revolution coming to fuller and fuller fruition for 1,000 years.

This revolution has propelled more and more technological breakthroughs. Not only do scientists in every field use ever more powerful computers to process data from their experiments and to test their theories; some fields of study have begun to exhibit accelerated transformations similar to information technology itself. Scientists sequenced the first 1 percent of the human genome in seven and a half years and the other 99 percent in less than half that time. The HIV retrovirus took 5 years to sequence; SARS took only 31 days.[8] In other words, technological progress has grown exponentially. According to the inventor, entrepreneur, and futurist Raymond Kurzweil (1948–), important elements of the life sciences have already become information technologies. He predicts that energy production will soon follow. Even if his views prove overly optimistic, one cannot deny that the pace of technological change has so far accelerated radically.

The information revolution has transformed people's lives in ways big and small. Any ordinary person with a video camera—even those built into many cell phones—can break dramatic news stories and even influence the course of politics by uploading clips to YouTube. Millions of people with an internet connection can now work at home, "telecommuting," as employers, especially in Western Europe, are willing to negotiate "flextime."[9] Powerful but inexpensive computers have also made it easier for people to become self-employed and thereby gain more autonomy and control over their lives. In 2006, 21 million people in the United States owned their own businesses, accounting for 17 percent of all employment.[10] Many were "micro-businesses" employing no outside personnel but often following the Hollywood model of bringing together teams of specialized workers only for specific projects. An entrepreneur wanting to develop a logo can nowadays solicit proposals through a business-connections website like LogoMyWay and may, within seven days, choose from among 100 or more designs from around the world. Flexibility is key, something entirely inherent in the information revolution and in the internet itself. Indeed, many of the most successful companies of recent years have manufactured nothing, possess very little physical plant, and even lack a storefront. Critics may well decry these new enterprises as impersonal, yet some of them—like MySpace, Facebook, Twitter, Ning, and many others—actually enable hundreds of millions of people to make connections and stay in touch with one another. These connections surely differ from face-to-face contacts but still possess enormous social and cultural significance, and value as well.

Ultimately, Western—and especially American—development has enabled people to define themselves, to create their own identity, to reimagine the world in a variety of new ways, "to write the script of your own life."[11] Throughout most of history and in most places on earth even today, one's caste, tribe, family position, gender, and a host of traditions and social norms limit the parameters of one's life path. Despite these impediments, people accomplish wonderful things, and many doubtless achieve their full potential. Yet the West has offered conditions and possibilities for more people to achieve this than ever before. One could multiply examples like that of Sergey Brin almost *ad infinitum*. Sixty-two immigrants to the United States won Nobel Prizes in science from 1946 to 2009. How many would have done so in their homelands? The vast research funding available in America has had a lot to do with it, of course, but so has the immense diversity of research opportunities. In the years 2005–09, 21 Nobel laureates in science (out of a total of 37) had conducted most of their research in the United States.[12] These 21 had worked at 18 different institutions—seven public universities in five states, seven private universities, and two public and two private research laboratories. No other country in the world offers even a quarter as many relatively independent venues for scientific research.

If one had to pick a single feature of Western civilization that helps to explain its extraordinary innovativeness and stunning accomplishments over the past thousand years, one could scarcely go wrong in pointing to decentralization of authority. I mean not only political or governmental authority,[13] but economic, social, and cultural authority as well. Another way to phrase this is to say that the West has exhibited an extraordinary range and effectiveness of private initiatives. The central authorities of all the major and minor civilizations of history have been capable of undertaking huge and complex projects—the Egyptian and Aztec pyramids, the Great Wall and treasure fleets of China, the conquests of Alexander the Great, or the maintenance of religious conformity across the vast Islamic world. Only Western cultures, however, accomplished enterprises approaching those in magnitude largely through private initiative. One can point to the early modern world exploration, the printing revolution, the founding of countless new religious denominations, extraordinarily fruitful scientific and technological collaborations, the Industrial Revolution, the laying of telegraph and telephone cables all across the earth, and the forging of commercial networks linking together every city and village on the planet. Scholars of the world-systems school emphasize that such undertakings required public–private collaboration or even the co-optation of the state by private interests.[14] That is certainly true in some or perhaps even many cases. Yet, as the respected economic historian Joel Mokyr points out, the British "government played a remarkably modest role in fostering the Industrial Revolution."[15] Even in the classic Western case of state-driven economic development—building the German railroad network—private initiative played a big role.[16] In no other civilization has the capacity for both cooperative undertakings and individual self-expression been more fully realized.

Two broad historical developments explain the West's lack of centralized control. First, after the fall of Rome, no rulers established long-term political dominance. Second, individuals, communities, associations, institutions, and societies throughout the West emerged as bulwarks of order and agents opposed to the countervailing forces of warlordism, absolutism, authoritarianism, dictatorship, and totalitarianism. A political stalemate, an extraordinary balance of powers, resulted. Consequently, no European polity had the power to fully dominate its society.

Dozens of factors contributed to the state of political equilibrium in Europe. The Middle Ages brought the struggles for moral authority between church and state, the emergence of semiautonomous urban communities, and the empowerment of weaker political actors by the infantry revolution. The early modern period contributed the printing press, the shattering of Christendom, the rise of multinational companies, and the emergence of institutions of scientific research. The modern era dawned with philosophically informed battles for independence and self-government, the proliferation of self-organizing associations and political parties, social movements aimed at transforming the world, the extraordinarily efficient "invisible hand" of the market, and the harnessing by independent entrepreneurs of awesome new machines and systems—right down to today's World Wide Web, which is especially vibrant and largely escapes centralized control in Western countries (though authoritarian governments in countries like China strive to control it).[17] Over the course of the centuries, in other words, dozens of centrifugal forces in Western societies have given millions of people vast opportunities for invention and self-realization.

None of this is meant to deny that elite patronage and government funding, from ancient times down to the transistor, the internet, and the human genome project, have made possible many advances in science and technology. The key distinction to note, however, is just how much latitude innovators in the modern West have enjoyed compared to those in other places and times. Yes, Congress largely funded the successful test of America's first telegraphic prototype in 1844.[18] Yet Morse and the other founders of telegraphy invented their devices, laid their plans, and built their systems with little government interference. Congress even refused to buy Morse's telegraph system, much to his chagrin. That did not stop it from becoming a wildly successful private enterprise.

For a half-millennium after the year 1000, Europeans absorbed priceless treasures of learning and wisdom from the great Eurasian civilizations. Then for the next few hundred years, nearly all the world's most significant technological innovations came from the West. Not that no non-Western cultures developed highly sensible and rational approaches to social, political, and economic matters. The Nobel Prize-winning economist Amartya Sen has pointed to enlightened historical actors in many past cultures.[19] It seems, however, that the extraordinary successes of the modern West completely overshadowed them. In the past half-century or so, however, the vector has shifted again, though slowly. Relatively Westernized postwar Japanese entrepreneurs began to challenge the West with "lean manufacturing," ultrahigh quality consumer goods, and technological breakthroughs.[20] Interactions and mutual impacts benefited both cultures by drawing 100 million more consumers and potential innovators into dialogue with the already-developed world. Now, as we enter into the third millennium, 2 or 3 billion more people seem poised to add their talent, energy, creativity, and thirst for a better life to the global search for the most effective and efficient means of using resources. The whole world will benefit from this synergy.

Already in 2006–08, the number of Brazilian, Indian, Chinese, and Russian firms on the *Financial Times* list of the world's 500 biggest companies jumped from 15 to 62.[21] Because the markets in those countries are so huge and their available talent pools so vast, Western multinational companies have been rushing to build not just factories there but also dozens of giant research centers, branches employing hundreds of thousands of "mental workers," and even global headquarters—for example, Cisco East in Bangalore, India. Entrepreneurs and innovators in these countries are developing new business practices, adapting and refining Western models, inventing new technologies, and improving on existing ones.[22] Such borrowing (like earlier Western borrowing) can enable societies to "skip stages" and today is enabling China to achieve the fastest pace of economic growth in history.[23]

To take a specific case in India of innovative development, Dr Devi Shetty has dramatically lowered the cost of heart surgery and other complicated medical procedures by adopting processes reminiscent of those by which Henry Ford revolutionized the production of automobiles.[24] The quality of his results surpasses that achieved in the average American hospital because the high volume of surgeries allows Dr Shetty's team to gain enormous specialized experience. Yet his hospital in Bangalore charges an average of 2,000 dollars for open-heart surgery instead of the 10 to 50 times more demanded in American hospitals. Western business theorists have dubbed this approach "frugal innovation."[25] It is pushing down costs and increasing efficiencies throughout the fastest-growing emerging markets. Managers and professors of business in the developed world are now scrambling to apply its principles to their own work. East and West and North and South are thus fruitfully engaged in learning from each other through the sorts of decentralized processes that enabled the West to rise in the first place.

Such widespread collaboration has surely contributed to the recent decline in armed conflict, which Joshua Goldstein believes to be "at an all-time low."[26] He adduces several further reasons for the drop, including the end of the Cold War, the spread of democracy, and successful United Nations peacekeeping efforts. Also important has been the change in Western attitudes toward war. A majority of Europeans rejects the idea of using warfare as "a continuation of political intercourse with a mixture of other means," in the often incorrectly quoted words of Carl von Clausewitz (1780–1831),[27] and indeed prefers to avoid war at almost any cost.[28] Most Americans, who in all their wars have lost only half as many lives as France did in World War I, remain more willing to project military power. The United States spent 40.6 percent of all defense spending in the world in 2003. Yet this constituted only 4 percent of GDP—less than half of peak Vietnam era spending—and paid mostly for sophisticated military technology, not troops (only 8 percent of the world total).[29] A key purpose of US military power is protecting international markets and the roughly 50 countries America is obligated by treaty to defend.[30] Overall, Americans refuse to fight without humanitarian or national-security justifications and in recent conflicts have strived to minimize civilian deaths. In other words, all the Western peoples have grown less warlike and more humane in their international relations during the past few decades.

Yet perhaps all the development and growth of recent times—made possible by Western innovation and making possible a dramatic rise in the standard of six-sevenths of the earth's population[31]—is leading to environmental catastrophe. Is it possible that a materially comfortable lifestyle for the vast majority of humanity could overtax our planet's resources?[32]

Recent decades have witnessed the annual destruction of tens of thousands of species across the globe.[33] Marine capture fisheries, by severely depleting stocks of fish in the middle of the food chain, have driven dozens of important larger aquatic life-forms to extinction in coastal waters—most species of sea turtles, whales, manatees, sea cows, codfish, sharks, rays, and many others. Such disasters, combined with chemical runoff, have contributed to the emergence of vast algal blooms and hundreds of resultant "dead zones," like the giant one covering 8,000 square miles beyond the Mississippi Delta.[34] Human disruptions of natural habitats threaten with extinction hundreds of thousands if not millions of species worldwide.[35]

The theory of man-made global warming—that carbon dioxide and other greenhouse gases released into the atmosphere will steeply raise the Earth's temperature—deserves special mention. The atmospheric concentration of carbon has increased since the preindustrial age from roughly 280 to close to 400 parts per million.[36] Higher levels of atmospheric carbon probably account for the past century's 1°C rise in surface temperature. Many scientists predict a dramatically accelerated increase, as the carbon level continues to rise, to as much as 6 or 7°C per doubling of atmospheric carbon. Such an outcome would effect catastrophic ecological transformations. Yet recent evidence—for example, surface warming has been flat during the past 15 years—suggests that the next several decades may see a more moderate increase, perhaps no more than 3°C, a change that could still occasion serious environmental havoc.[37]

The lesson is clear: human behaviors associated with technological development may result in ecological trauma.

Environmental conditions are particularly bad in many developing countries. Overgrazing, population growth, and drought have combined in Africa and Asia to expand desert regions dramatically.[38] Lake Chad and the Aral Sea, along with many other formerly thriving bodies of water, have nearly disappeared.[39] Forest cover has diminished rapidly, for example, in Brazil (8.1 percent between 1990 and 2005) and Haiti (9.5 percent); meanwhile, the whole of Africa lost 8 percent of its forests in the 1990s alone.[40] This problem in turn has caused soil erosion, landslides, and the destruction of biodiversity.

Ironically, further economic and technological development may be the only means to resolve these crises.[41] For example, biotechnology offers means of fertilizing crops and controlling pests without contaminating the environment with dangerous toxins.[42] Also, the advanced developed countries have led the way toward environmental protection. For example in the United States, the period 1976–97 saw steep declines in the emission of major air pollutants, from nitrogen dioxide (29 percent) to lead (97 percent), despite the fact that production and consumption increased dramatically during those years.[43] America's carbon and energy intensity (the amounts of carbon and energy needed to produce $1 of GDP) declined more sharply than did those of most European countries in 1980–2006: 43.6 and 42 percent, respectively.[44] So, Americans are growing more efficient in the ways they use energy, but the Europeans (and Japanese) consume less of it per person.[45] They drive fewer and smaller cars and use more public transportation. They also produce more renewable energy (such as solar, wind, geothermal, and biomass). For example, Germany generated 14 percent of its electricity from renewables in 2007 (compared to 6 percent in the United States).[46] Finally, economic development has enabled China—since 2009 the world's biggest energy consumer[47]—to become a world leader in renewable energy.[48] Moreover, as noted above, entrepreneurs in developing countries are contributing to sustainability with "frugal innovation."

The best news is that our Earth is resilient and can recover from ecological harm. Most developed countries have regained forest cover in recent decades.[49] Thus, in 1990–2005 the total forest cover increased 1.5 percent in the United States and 6 percent in Switzerland.[50] International covenants and national statutes now restrict fisheries in many parts of the world and in some places have resulted in the partial restoration of some species, including haddock, yellowtail, and scallops.[51] The expected increase in global fish production by fish farms from 35 million tons—one-quarter of global fishery output—in 2000 to 70 million tons in 2015 will doubtless further ease pressure on our oceans.[52] Thanks to changes in government policies and industrial production, numerous dead zones have either disappeared or shrunk, for example, in the Black Sea, San Francisco Bay, and the North Sea.[53]

Such progress is of utmost importance. The phenomenal profusion of species on Earth—estimated at between 5 and 100 million, only around 2 million so far described—is not merely an esthetic or scientific marvel. All of these creatures, most of them microbial, are interdependent. Some, like many bacteria, apparently share DNA across the entire planet and thus form something like a "super-organism."[54] All others, aside from man, interact locally or regionally. Furthermore, they depend upon complex ecosystems, each one involving hundreds of factors—soil, organic matter, diseases and pathogens, water, climate, weather, natural disasters, elevation, atmospheric chemistry—and billions of living things comprising an intricate food web of mutual dependency. Alter or destroy any factors or life-forms and one automatically affects many if not all others, albeit perhaps only imperceptibly.[55] In a more and more interdependent world, an ecological model may well be the best one for human development and interaction.

As argued in the Prologue, Western civilization developed through organic interaction with its environment, through an uncommon openness to outside influences, and by enabling individuals and communities within its boundaries to express their creative potential more fully than at any other time or place in history. More than other civilizations, it invested humans with rights and liberties, evolved an ethics of toleration, emphasized the rule of law, developed institutions of political participation and self-government, endowed individuals and communities with spiritual authority, created institutions and procedures for building up and sharing information, and a host of other means of empowerment.[56] (Eventually Western societies endowed both children and animals, if not with rights, then with extensive protections.)[57] These very qualities, and only they, I have argued, can explain the West's modern success.

Why and how did these qualities emerge? Presumably the Christian faith was a key factor, given its profound importance to Western civilization. Yet in recent decades many people throughout the West, especially in Europe, profess no religious faith.[58] Americans remain more fervently religious,[59] as they apparently have for at least 200 years,[60] though even in the United States a high proportion of educated elites profess atheism or agnosticism; only a tiny fraction of members of the National Academy of Sciences, for example, believed in God in 1998.[61] As shown throughout this book, Christian faith, spiritual movements, and institutional religion contributed powerfully, if often only thanks to major struggles, to the development of values that most people today would consider essential to the flourishing of the West—tolerance, openness, a spirit of innovation, the affirmation of the sacred value of each human person, and the search for truth that accords with science and experience.

These Western values are now embodied in robust institutions—constitutions, independent judiciaries, systems of checks and balances, the rule of law, defined property rights, and representative democracy—that protect the rights of individuals and communities and the interests of majorities and minorities. The free-enterprise system, which emerged partly thanks to this matrix of values and institutions, has made it possible for society to "domesticate" and co-opt even many of its harshest critics. The radical political activist in the 1960s and early 1970s, Jerry Rubin (1938–94) subsequently became a successful businessman.[62] Similarly, the Black Panther Bobby Seale (1936–) wrote a cookbook and marketed his own barbecue sauce. The hope of becoming wealthy exerts on many people, especially the most ambitious, a forceful pull.[63]

Yet not every radical can be domesticated. Hitler took strong Western institutions and completely subverted Western values. The Bolshevik leadership took praiseworthy Western values and built them into totalitarian institutions. Avoiding such pitfalls and continuing the extraordinary Western odyssey surely require a more substantial foundation than good institutions and values.

The emphasis in traditional religions on mysteries and childlike faith has put off millions of highly educated people in the West. Anything that cannot be proven scientifically or observed empirically, they believe, has no meaning or value. Yet some things that they themselves typically rank highly also fall into that category. How can one prove scientifically that each living thing and certainly each human person has intrinsic value? How can I prove that my wife or best friend is loyal to me? Can anyone show that human life is meaningful? In fact, no one can prove any of these propositions scientifically. Yet nearly every person, even the most staunchly atheistic, strongly believes in each of them.[64] This being the case, should not each person, and certainly everyone devoted to the life of the mind, seek to understand on what basis he or she does so? Does it not make sense, in other words, to find a metaphysical ground upon which our values and institutions can rest?

As a historian and a student of philosophy, my interpretations of the past are guided by an underlying philosophy of history, as they are for any historian, whether consciously or unconsciously. I believe my philosophical outlook should meet three fundamental criteria. It must contradict neither science nor human experience (is therefore coherent), must ascribe intrinsic value to all things and especially to all living things (is therefore comprehensive or universal), and must make sense of the biggest moral and philosophical questions that human beings have asked about their place in the world (is therefore metaphysical).[65]

It is not my place as a historian to promote a particular philosophical or religious outlook, but it does seem appropriate to wonder if our civilization can continue to thrive without some approach that makes it possible to render coherent our unavoidable faith in the meaningfulness of life, our moral intuition that all of nature—especially living creatures—has intrinsic worth and deserves protection, and finally our certainty that rational inquiry into everything that can be known must be pursued. We inherited these values and ideals from the Judaeo-Christian and Hellenistic traditions and as a civilization have believed in them for centuries. Will it be possible to inspire and undergird continued Western development within a framework of sustainability without such a comprehensive and coherent religious or philosophical vision?

In recent years, scholars have heatedly debated which of the current global centers of power will gain (or retain) hegemonic status in our emerging multipolar world (though some thinkers argue that a "dewesternizing" process will result in a yet more radical decentralization of power).[66] The main contenders are the United States,[67] the European Union,[68] and China.[69] The United States and Europe have been the biggest world economic powers for at least 200 years and the major technological innovators for 500. In 2010, they were home to nearly every country on the planet with the highest gross national income per capita (China was ranked number 121).[70] They diverge in interesting ways. Europe's social safety nets are denser; America is more innovative. China had the world's largest economy for several hundred years before the Western ascendancy and was the greatest technological innovator for nearly 2,000 years prior. Today it is four times more populous than the United States. It also has the second-biggest economy and is projected to achieve first place by 2027.[71]

Yet the contenders all confront significant problems. China is encircled by powerful but not always friendly neighbors. Its standard of living is very low, and popular unrest is widespread and ongoing across the country.[72] The government is actively impeding public debate, the resolution of social problems, and innovation by strictly controlling the internet.[73] Europe also faces uneasy relations with countries to its east and south,[74] and ethnic and religious hostility plagues the continent.[75] The major European countries are, moreover, quite inhospitable to entrepreneurship.[76] Unlike China, which runs a big government surplus, most European countries and the United States carry a large burden of government debt.[77] The United States has an exceptionally large prison population.[78] Finally, primary and secondary education in America, once the envy of the world, has fallen woefully behind in performance, especially among blacks.[79] For each of the rivals, therefore, maintaining current status or rising to higher levels of success and well-being are not a given.

As this book has argued, the world's biggest economies and indeed all human cultures will thrive best when they create conditions for the flourishing of individual and collective initiative, self-expression, innovation, and creativity. Which country or region will lead or dominate is less important, therefore, than that each of them maintain, adopt, or adapt the Western recipe of success—decentralized authority, the affirmation of individual rights and liberty, the pursuit of truth in all its forms, toleration of differences, the rule of law, respect for property, openness to novelty, and unimpeded access to information and knowledge.

QUESTIONS FOR REFLECTION

What factors caused the great civilizations to flourish or to decline?

Give some examples of the acceleration of the information revolution.

How has decentralized authority contributed to the strength of Western civilization?

How are non-Western countries now beginning to contribute to global innovation?

NOTES

Prologue

1 See the eyewitness account excerpted in William Stearns Davis (ed.), *Readings in Ancient History: Illustrative Extracts from the Sources*, 2 vols. (Boston: Allyn and Bacon, 1912–13), Vol. II: *Rome and the West*, 365–6.

2 Syed Ameer Ali, *The Life and Teachings of Mohammed: Or, The Spirit of Islam* (London: W. H. Allen & Company, Limited, 1891), 557–8.

3 See Valerie Hansen, *The Open Empire: A History of China to 1600* (New York: W.W. Norton & Company, 2000), 264, 270–1, 282.

4 See J. Bradford De Long and Andrei Shleifer, "Princes and Merchants: European City Growth before the Industrial Revolution." *The Journal of Law and Economics* 36 (October 1993): 671–702 (here: 677).

5 See Helen H. Robbins, *Our First Ambassador to China; An Account of the Life of George, Earl of Macartney, with Extracts from His Letters, and the Narrative of his Experiences in China, as Told by Himself, 1737–1806, from Hitherto Unpublished Correspondence and Documents* (London: J. Murray, 1908), 395–6.

6 See Marco Polo, *The Travels of Marco Polo*, trans. Ronald Latham (London: Penguin, 1958).

7 On early modern material culture in South and East Asia, see Kenneth Pomeranz, *The Great Divergence: Europe, China, and the Making of the Modern World Economy* (Princeton: Princeton University Press, 2000), 143–65.

8 Jared Diamond, *Guns, Germs, and Steel: The Fates of Human Societies* (New York: W.W. Norton & Company, 1997), 139–42, 159–60.

9 For summaries of these views, see Jonathan Daly, *Historians Debate the Rise of the West* (forthcoming).

10 Andre Gunder Frank, *ReORIENT: Global Economy in the Asian Age* (Berkeley: University of California Press, 1998), xxv.

11 The most lucid book in this vein is Pomeranz, *The Great Divergence*.

12 A recent study divides scholars into "short-termers" and "long-termers" on this basis. See Ian Morris, *Why the West Rules—For Now: The Patterns of History and What They Reveal About the Future* (New York: Farrar, Straus and Giroux, 2010), 13–21.

13 The anti-Eurocentrist literature is large. See, for example, Samir Amin, *Eurocentrism*, trans. Russell Moore and James Membrez (New York: Monthly Review Press, 1989); Rajani Kannepalli Kanth, *Against Eurocentrism: A Transcendent Critique of Modernist Science, Society, and Morals* (New York and Basingstoke, UK: Macmillan, 2005).

14 For a recent study in this vein, see Daron Acemoglu and James Robinson, *Why Nations Fail: The Origins of Power, Prosperity, and Poverty* (New York: Crown Business, 2012).

15 See, for example, John A. Hall, *Powers and Liberties: The Causes and Consequences of the Rise of the West* (Oxford: Oxford University Press, 1985).

16 An eloquent advocate of this perspective is David Landes, *The Wealth and Poverty of Nations: Why Some Are so Rich and Some so Poor* (New York: W. W. Norton & Company, 1998).

17 This interpretation is developed by Charles Birch and John B. Cobb, Jr., in their *The Liberation of Life: From the Cell to the Community* (Cambridge and New York: Cambridge University Press, 1981).

18 Regarding innovative behavior among birds and primates, see Raymond L. Neubauer, *Evolution and the Emergent Self: The Rise of Complexity and Behavioral Versatility in Nature* (New York: Columbia University Press, 2012), 74–8.

19 Hansen, *The Open Empire*, 371.

20 Ibid., 407–9.

21 See E. L. Jones, *The European Miracle: Environments, Economies, and Geopolitics in the History of Europe and Asia*, 3rd edn (London and New York: Cambridge University Press, 1981), ch. 6 and Afterword to the Third Edition.

22 See Christopher Dawson, *Religion and the Rise of Western Culture* (New York: Sheed & Ward, 1950).

23 For the first formulation of this concept, see Marshall G. S. Hodgson, "The Great Western Transmutation," in *Rethinking World History: Essays on Europe, Islam, and World History*, ed. Edmund Burke (Cambridge: Cambridge University Press, 1993b).

24 Marshall Hodgson, "Historical Method in Civilizational Studies," in ed. Burke, in *Rethinking World History*, 77.

25 See Norman Davies, *Europe: A History* (New York: Oxford University Press, 1996), 10–12.

26 See M. E. Yapp, "Europe in the Turkish Mirror," *Past & Present* 137 (November 1992): 134–55. As late as 1945, the poet T. S. Eliot asserted that above all Europe's Christian tradition informed its culture. See Davies, *Europe*, 9.

27 See Yapp, "Europe in the Turkish Mirror," 142–54 (quotation: 148).

28 See Tzvetan Todorov, "European Identity," trans. Nathan Bracher, *South Central Review* 25 (Fall 2008): 3–15 (here: 4–5).

29 See Davies, *Europe*, 15.

30 See Benjamin H. Isaac, *The Invention of Racism in Classical Antiquity* (Princeton: Princeton University Press, 2004).

31 See Cemil Aydin, *The Politics of Anti-Westernism in Asia: Visions of World Order in Pan-Islamic and Pan-Asian Thought* (New York: Columbia University Press, 2007).

32 See, for example, Morris, *Why the West Rules*.

33 See Davies, *Europe*, 19–26.

34 See, in particular, Gilbert Allardyce, "The Rise and Fall of the Western Civilization Course." *The American Historical Review* 87 (June 1982): 695–725.

35 See Peter N. Stearns, *Western Civilization in World History* (New York and London: Routledge, 2003), 11–13 (quotation: 13).

36 See Norbert Elias, *On Civilization, Power, and Knowledge: Selected Writings*, eds. Stephen Mennell and Johan Goudsblom (Chicago and London: University of Chicago Press, 1998), ch. 3.

37 See, for example, Stearns, *Western Civilization in World History*, 31–2; Keith Chandler, *Beyond Civilization: The World's Four Great Streams of Civilization: Their Achievements, Their Differences and Their Future* (Bloomington, IN: Indiana University Press, 2001), 4–6.

38 See Jan-Erik Lane, *Globalization and Politics: Promises and Dangers* (Aldershot, UK and Burlington, VT: Ashgate Publishing, 2006), 77–88; Stearns, *Western Civilization in World History*, 32–4.

39 See Samuel P. Huntington, *The Clash of Civilizations and the Remaking of World Order* (New York: Simon & Schuster, 1996), 41–2.

40 See Arnold J. Toynbee, *A Study of History*, abridgement of Volumes I–VI by D. C. Somervell (Oxford: Oxford University Press, 1946), 34.

41 See William H. McNeill, *The Shape of European History* (New York and London: Oxford University Press, 1974), 42.

42 See John L. Esposito (ed.), *The Oxford Dictionary of Islam* (Oxford and New York: Oxford University Press, 2003), 62–3.

43 See Ibrahim Abu-Lughod, *The Arab Rediscovery of Europe: A Study in Cultural Encounters*, intro. Rashid Khalidi (London: Saqi Books, 2011).

44 See Yapp, "Europe in the Turkish Mirror," 140.

45 See Huntington, *The Clash of Civilizations*, 41–2.

46 See Benjamin Barber, *Jihad vs McWorld: Terrorism's Challenge to Democracy* (New York: Ballantine Books, 1996), 4.

Chapter 1

1 See Gregory Curtis, *The Cave Painters: Probing the Mysteries of the World's First Artists* (New York: A.A. Knopf, 2006).

2 Quoted in Mark Pagel, *Wired for Culture: Origins of the Human Social Mind* (New York: W.W. Norton & Company, 2012), 111.

3 Jared Diamond, *Guns, Germs, and Steel: The Fates of Human Societies* (New York: W.W. Norton & Company, 1997), ch. 1.

4 The literature is vast. For intelligent overviews, see Alan Barnard, *Social Anthropology and Human Origins* (Cambridge: Cambridge University Press, 2011); Douglas Palmer, *Seven Million Years: The Story of Human Evolution* (London: Weidenfeld & Nicolson, 2005); Chris Stringer, *The Origin of Our Species* (London: Allen Lane, 2011).

5 See S. Savage-Rumbaugh and R. Lewin, *Kanzi: An Ape at the Brink of the Human Mind* (New York: Wiley, 1994).

6 For details on the evolution of humankind, see Richard G. Klein, *The Human Career: Human Biological and Cultural Origins*, 3rd edn (Chicago: University of Chicago Press, 2009); Bernard A. Wood, *Human Evolution: A Very Short Introduction* (New York: Oxford University Press, 2005).

7 See Michael C. Corballis, "The Gestural Origins of Language." *The American Scientist* 87 (March–April 1999): 138–45; idem., "The Evolution of Language." *Annals of the New York Academy of Sciences* 1156 (March 2009): 19–43.

8 See Johan Goudsblom, *Fire and Civilization* (London: Penguin, 1992).

9 See, for example, Barnard, *Social Anthropology and Human Origins*, 44.

10 On this question, see Benoît Dubreuil, *Human Evolution and the Origins of Hierarchies: The State of Nature* (New York: Cambridge University Press, 2010).

11 On the emergence and spread of *H. sapiens*, see Hua Liu, Franck Prugnolle, Andrea Manica, and François Balloux, "A Geographically Explicit Genetic Model of Worldwide Human-Settlement History." *The American Journal of Human Genetics* 79 (2006): 230–7.

12 According to one study, however, the behavior of Neanderthals differed little from that of *H. sapiens*. See Donald O. Henry, Harold J. Hietala, Arlene M. Rosen, Yuri E. Demidenko, Vitaliy I. Usik, and Teresa L. Armagan, "Human Behavioral Organization in the Middle Paleolithic: Were Neanderthals Different?" *American Anthropologist*, New Series 106 (March 2004): 17–31.

13 See Steven J. Mithen, *The Singing Neanderthals: The Origins of Music, Language, Mind, and Body* (Cambridge: Cambridge University Press, 2006), and Philip Lieberman, *Eve Spoke: Human Language and Human Evolution* (New York: W.W. Norton & Company, 1998).

14 See Charles Hartshorne, *Creative Synthesis and Philosophic Method* (London: SCM Press, 1970), 95.

15 See David Martel Johnson, *Three Prehistoric Inventions That Shaped Us* (New York: Peter Lang Publishing, 2011), 122.

16 Some scholars reject the dominant "Out-of-Africa" hypothesis and instead argue that Africans mated with more primitive humans on other continents. See Klein, *The Human Career*, 627–31; Pamela R. Willoughby, *The Evolution of Modern Humans in Africa: A Comprehensive Guide* (Lanham, MD: AltaMira Press, 2007), ch. 5.

17 On the development of prehistoric technology, see Klein, *The Human Career*, 672–3.

18 See, for example, Stringer, *The Origin of Our Species*, 116–37.

19 Curtis, *The Cave Painters*, 14–16.

20 Pieces of ochre engraved with apparently abstract designs and dating to 77,000 years ago in a cave on the Indian Ocean coast of South Africa were reported in 2002. See Barnard, *Social Anthropology and Human Origins*, 14; Palmer, *Seven Million Years*, 159–61.

21 Some scholars argue for a more gradual development over the past 250,000 years. See Stringer, *The Origin of Our Species*, 123–5.

22 See G. K. Chesterton, *The Everlasting Man* (Garden City, NY: Image Books, 1955), 37–8.

23 See his *Three Prehistoric Inventions That Shaped Us*, 171–2. For a profound and wide-ranging reflection on the spiritual meaning of the "human revolution," see Brendan Purcell, *From Big Bang to Big Mystery: Human Origins in the Light of Creation and Evolution* (Dublin: Veritas Publications, 2011).

24 See Peter LaFrenière, *Adaptive Origins: Evolution and Human Development* (New York and Hove, UK: Taylor & Francis Group, 2010), 84–5.

25 On the Neanderthals and their displacement by *H. sapiens*, see Merlin Donald, *Origins of the Modern Mind: Three Stages in the Evolution of Culture and Cognition* (Cambridge, MA: Harvard University Press, 1991), 203–7. On their smaller social groupings, see Ann Gibbons, "Grisly Scene Gives Clues to Neanderthal Family Structure." *Science* (20 December 2010), http://news.sciencemag.org/sciencenow/2010/12/grisly-scene-gives-clues-to-nean.html (accessed on 13 June 2013).

26 See Diamond, *Guns, Germs, and Steel.*

27 See Charles Gates, *Ancient Cities: The Archaeology of Urban Life in the Ancient Near East and Egypt, Greece, and Rome*, 2nd edn (Abingdon, UK and New York: Routledge, 2011), 17.

28 A good introduction to the emergence of civilization remains William H. McNeill, *The Rise of the West: A History of the Human Community* (Chicago: University of Chicago Press, 1963).

29 See Xueqin Li, Garman Harbottle, Juzhong Zhang, and Changsui Wang, "The Earliest Writing? Sign Use in the Seventh Millennium BC at Jiahu, Henan Province, China." *Antiquity* 77 (March 2003): 31–44.

30 See, for example, Barry J. Kemp, *Ancient Egypt: Anatomy of a Civilisation* (Abingdon, UK and New York: Routledge, 2006); J. N. Postgate, *Early Mesopotamia: Society and Economy at the Dawn of History* (London and New York: Routledge, 1992).

31 See Martin Bernal, *Black Athena: The Afroasiatic Roots of Classical Civilization*, 3 vols. (New Brunswick, NJ: Rutgers University Press, 1987–2006).

32 See, for example, Mary R. Lefkowitz and Guy Maclean Rogers (eds), *Black Athena Revisited* (Chapel Hill: The University of North Carolina Press, 1996).

33 See Jack Goody, *The Logic of Writing and the Organization of Society* (Cambridge: Cambridge University Press, 1986); Guy Maclean Rogers, "Multiculturalism and the Foundations of Western Civilization," in *Black Athena Revisited*, eds. Lefkowitz and Rogers.

34 Historians debate their origins. See, for example, Michal Artzy, "On Boats and Sea Peoples." *Bulletin of the American Schools of Oriental Research* 266 (May 1987): 75–84.

35 See P. Rietbergen, *Europe: A Cultural History* (London and New York: Routledge, 1998), 28–9.

36 Peter Watson, *Ideas: A History of Thought and Invention, from Fire to Freud* (New York: HarperCollins, 2005), 69–70.

37 On early writing, see Steven R. Fischer, *A History of Reading* (London: Reaktion Books, 2004) and John Man, *Alpha Beta: How 26 Letters Shaped the Western World* (New York: Headline, 2002). On the context in which alphabetic writing emerged, see Walter Burkert, *The Orientalizing Revolution: Near Eastern Influence on Greek Culture in the Early Archaic Age*, trans. W. Burkert and M. E. Pinder (Cambridge: Cambridge University Press, 1992), especially 6–17.

38 Karl Jaspers, *Way To Wisdom: An Introduction to Philosophy*, 2nd edn, trans. Ralph Manheim (New Haven: Yale University Press 2003), 98–101 (here: 98). Scholars dispute whether Zoroastrianism emerged when Jaspers supposes or earlier.

39 On the emergence of monotheism among the ancient Israelites, see Robert Karl Gnuse, *No Other Gods: Emergent Monotheism in Israel* (Sheffield: T&T Clark, 1997).

40 Thus argues Herbert Butterfield, *The Origins of History*, ed. Adam Watson (New York: Basic Books, 1981), 89–90. The uniqueness of the ancient Israelites went further in this regard: their detailed historical memory reached further back in their ethnic development than any other people in the ancient world. See ibid., 94.

41 See, for example, Landes, *The Wealth and Poverty of Nations*, 58–9.

42 See Bernal, *Black Athena*, vol. 1: *The Fabrication of Ancient Greece, 1785–1985*, 103.

43 On early Greece, see Jonathan M. Hall, *A History of the Archaic Greek World, ca. 1200–479 BCE* (Malden, MA: Blackwell Publishers, 2007); on classical Greece, see

Sarah B. Pomeroy, Stanley M. Burstein, Walter Donlan, and Jennifer Tolbert Roberts, *Ancient Greece: A Political, Social, and Cultural History*, 2nd edn (New York: Oxford University Press, 2008). For a sprightly overview, see Thomas Cahill, *Sailing the Wine-Dark Sea: Why the Greeks Matter* (New York: Doubleday, 2003).

44 On Hellenistic civilization, see Peter Green, *The Hellenistic Age: A Short History* (New York: The Modern Library, 2007); Pomeroy et al., *Ancient Greece*.

45 Horace, Epistle to Augustus, *The Second Book of the Epistles of Horace*, http://www.authorama.com/works-of-horace-9.html (accessed 13 June 2013).

46 See Thomas W. Africa, *The Immense Majesty: A History of Rome and the Roman Empire* (Wheeling, IL: Harlan Davidson, 1991).

47 On Roman law, see H. Patrick Glenn, *Legal Traditions of the World: Sustainable Diversity in Law*, 2nd edn (Oxford: Oxford University Press, 2004), ch. 5.

48 See Phillip Nemo, *What Is the West?* (Pittsburgh: Duquesne University Press, 2004), 24–7.

49 See Denis Twitchett and Michael Loewe (eds), *The Cambridge History of China*, vol. 1: *The Ch'in and Han Empires, 221 BC–AD 220* (Cambridge: Cambridge University Press, 1987).

50 See Hansen, *The Open Empire*.

51 See Geoffrey Ernest Richard Lloyd, *Adversaries and Authorities: Investigations Into Ancient Greek and Chinese Science* (Cambridge: Cambridge University Press, 1996), 212.

52 The Babylonians discovered this concept, but it was lost when their civilization collapsed. See Stanislas Dehaene, *The Number Sense: How the Mind Creates Mathematics*, rev. edn (New York: Oxford University Press, 2011), 86–7.

53 On the Tang, see Denis C. Twitchet (ed.), *The Cambridge History of China*, vol. 3, pt. 1: *Sui and T'ang China, 589–906 AD* (Cambridge: Cambridge University Press, 1980).

54 On Chinese technological advances, see Joseph Needham, *The Grand Titration: Science and Society in East and West* (London: Allen & Unwin, 1969); Colin A. Roman (ed.), *The Shorter Science and Civilisation in China: An Abridgement of Joseph Needham's Original Text* (Cambridge and New York: Cambridge University Press, 1978–81).

55 On the Song, see Denis Twitchett and Paul Jakov Smith (eds), *The Cambridge History of China*, vol. 5: *The Sung Dynasty and its Precursors, 907–1279* (Cambridge: Cambridge University Press, 2009).

56 See Robert Hartwell, "A Revolution in the Iron and Coal Industries during the Northern Sung." *Journal of Asian Studies* 21 (February 1962): 153–62.

57 See Denis Twitchett and Frederick Mote (eds), *The Cambridge History of China*, vols. 7–8: *The Ming Dynasty, 1368–1644* (Cambridge: Cambridge University Press, 1988–98).

58 On Chinese "stagnation," see Derk Bodde, *Chinese Thought, Society, and Science: The Intellectual and Social Background of Science and Technology Pre-modern China* (Honolulu: University of Hawaii Press, 1991); Mark Elvin, *The Pattern of the Chinese Past* (Stanford: Stanford University Press, 1973). For an opposing view, see Gang Deng, *The Premodern Chinese Economy: Structural Equilibrium and Capitalist Sterility* (London and New York: Routledge, 1999).

59 See Paul F. Cressey, "The Influence of the Literary Examination System on the Development of Chinese Civilization." *The American Journal of Sociology* 35 (September 1929): 250–62.

60 See Ssu-yu Teng, "Chinese Influence on the Western Examination System." *Harvard Journal of Asiatic Studies* 7 (1942–43): 267–312.

61 See Walter Scheidel (ed.), *Rome and China: Comparative Perspectives on Ancient World Empires* (Oxford and New York: Oxford University Press, 2009).

62 See Jack A. Goldstone, "Efflorescences and Economic Growth in World History: Rethinking the 'Rise of the West' and the Industrial Revolution." *Journal of World History* 13 (2002): 323–89.

63 On comparing ancient Greece and China, see Lloyd, *Adversaries and Authorities.*

64 See Lloyd, *Adversaries and Authorities*, 220.

65 See Malati Shrikhande, "Taxila: The Seat of Learning in Ancient India," in *Encyclopaedia of Higher Education: The Indian Perspective*, 5 vols. vol. 1: *Historical Survey—Pre-Independence Period*, eds. Suresh Kant Sharma and Usha Sharma (New Delhi: Mittal Publications, 2005).

66 See Vincent A. Smith, *The Oxford History of India*, 4th edn, ed. Percival Spear (Oxford: Oxford University Press, 1981), 117–37; Romila Thapar, *Early India: From the Origins to AD 1300* (Berkeley and Los Angeles: University of California Press, 2004), 178–84; Amartya Sen, *Development as Freedom* (New York: A.A. Knopf, 1999), 235–6.

67 See Smith, *The Oxford History of India*, 164–84; Thapar, *Early India*, 282–7; R. S. Sharma, *India's Ancient Past* (New Delhi: Oxford University Press, 2005), chs. 24–5.

68 See Bruce B. Lawrence, "The Eastward Journey of Muslim Kingship: Islam in South and Southeast Asia," in *The Oxford History of Islam*, ed. John L. Esposito (Oxford: Oxford University Press, 1999), 404–11; John F. Richards, *The Mughal Empire* (Cambridge and New York: Cambridge University Press, 1993), chs. 1–3. For primary source accounts, see Shireen Moosvi, *Episodes in the Life of Akbar: Contemporary Records and Reminiscences* (New Delhi: National Book Trust, 1994).

69 Statistic cited in Giorgio Riello, "The Globalization of Cotton Textiles: Indian Cottons, Europe, and the Atlantic World, 1600–1850," in *The Spinning World: A Global History of Cotton Textiles, 1200–1850*, eds. Giorgio Riello and Prasannan Parthasarathi (Oxford: Oxford University Press, 2009), 265.

70 Despite a powerful IT industry, however, India has lagged behind China in internet business and innovation. See "Indian Technology: The Screen Revolution." *The Economist* (16–22 March 2013): 63–5.

71 See Karen Armstrong, *Buddha* (New York: Viking, 2001).

72 By "universal religion" I mean one open to all people, in which proselytizing plays a major role, not one actually encompassing all people.

73 See E. Zuercher, *The Buddhist Conquest of China: The Spread and Adaptation of Buddhism in Early Medieval China*, 2 vols. (Leiden: E.J. Brill, 1972).

74 Taoism, an indigenous philosophical school of thought and way of life, often linked to a traditional polytheistic pantheon, provided a lens through which Buddhism was interpreted and integrated into Chinese religious life. Throughout China's history, these spiritual approaches mutually influenced each other.

75 See Kim Plofker, *Mathematics in India* (Princeton: Princeton University Press, 2009).

76 See Arun Bala, *The Dialogue of Civilizations in the Birth of Modern Science* (Basingstoke, UK: Palgrave Macmillan, 2008), 67–72.

77 On Byzantium, see John Haldon, *Byzantium: A History* (Stroud, UK: Tempus, 2000).

78 This section draws on Marshall G. S. Hodgson, *The Venture of Islam: Conscience and History in a World Civilization*, 3 vols. (Chicago: University of Chicago Press, 1974); Fred M. Donner, "Muhammad and the Caliphate: Political History of the Islamic Empire Up to the Mongol Conquest," in *The Oxford History of Islam*, ed. John L. Esposito (Oxford: Oxford University Press, 1999); Jonathan P. Berkey, *The Formation of Islam: Religion and Society in the Near East, 600–1800* (Cambridge: Cambridge University Press, 2003).

79 See Jane I. Smith, "Islam and Christendom: Historical, Cultural, and Religious Interaction from the Seventh to the Fifteenth Centuries," in *The Oxford History of Islam*, ed. Esposito, 312.

80 See, for example, Avigdor Levy, *The Sephardim of the Ottoman Empire* (Princeton: Princeton University Press, 1992).

81 See Mayeul de Dreuille, *From East to West: A History of Monasticism* (Leominster, UK and New York: Gracewing Publishing, 1999).

82 See, for example, Lawrence Rosen, "Theorizing from Within: Ibn Khaldun and His Political Culture." *Contemporary Sociology* 34 (November 2005): 596–9.

83 On the ancient Mesopotamian roots of many economic techniques and instruments of later times, see Goody, *The Logic of Writing and the Organization of Society*, ch. 2.

84 See Janet L. Abu-Lughod, *Before European Hegemony: The World System A.D. 1250–1350* (New York: Oxford University Press, 1989), pt. 2; David Abulafia, "Asia, Africa and the Trade of Medieval Europe," in *Trade and Industry in the Middle Ages*, 2nd edn, eds. M. M. Postan, Edward Miller, and Cynthia Postan (Cambridge: Cambridge University Press, 1987).

85 See Abraham L. Udovitch, *Partnership and Profit in Medieval Islam* (Princeton: Princeton University Press, 1970).

86 See Maya Shatzmiller, *Labour in the Medieval Islamic World* (Leiden, The Netherlands and New York: E.J. Brill, 1994), ch. 5.

87 See Majid Fakhry, *A History of Islamic Philosophy*, 3rd edn (New York and Chichester, UK: Columbia University Press, 2004), x.

88 See Seyyed Hossein Nasr, *Islamic Philosophy from its Origin to the Present: Philosophy in the Land of Prophesy* (Albany: State University of New York Press, 2006), 44–5.

89 On the development of science in Islamic societies, see Ahmad Dallal, "Science, Medicine, and Technology: The Making of a Scientific Culture," in *The Oxford History of Islam*, ed. Esposito.

90 See *Al-Ghazali's Path to Sufism: His Deliverance from Error, al-Munqidh min al-Dalal*, trans. R. J. McCarthy, pref. David Burrel, intro. William A. Graham (Louisville, KY: Fons Vitae of Kentucky, 2000).

91 See Massimo Campanini, "Al-Ghazzali," in *History of Islamic Philosophy*, 2 vols., eds. Seyyed Hossein Nasr and Oliver Leaman (London and New York: Routledge, 1999), 1: 258–9.

92 See Dallal, "Science, Medicine, and Technology," in *The Oxford History of Islam*, ed. Esposito, 171–82; Robert M. Haddad, "Philosophical Theology and Science in Medieval Christianity and Islam: A Comparative Perspective." *The Journal of the Historical Society* 8 (September 2008): 349–93 (here: 370–3).

93 Abderrahmane Lakhsassi, "Ibn Khaldun," in *History of Islamic Philosophy*, eds. Nasr and Leaman, 1: 354.

94 Diamond, *Guns, Germs, and Steel*, 19–22.

95 See Robert O. Collins and James M. Burns, *A History of Sub-Saharan Africa* (Cambridge and New York: Cambridge University Press, 2007).

96 William McNeill emphasizes this point throughout his *The Rise of the West.*

97 See M. Paul Lewis (ed.), *Ethnologue: Languages of the World*, 16th edn (Dallas, TX: SIL International, 2009), 19.

98 See Graham Connah, *African Civilizations: An Archaeological Perspective*, 2nd edn (Cambridge: Cambridge University Press, 2001).

99 See Diamond, *Guns, Germs, and Steel*, 53.

100 See Collins and Burns, *A History of Sub-Saharan Africa.*

101 See Diamond, *Guns, Germs, and Steel*, 389.

102 See, for example, Geoffrey W. Conrad and Arthur A. Demarest, *Religion and Empire: The Dynamics of Aztec and Inca Expansionism* (New York: Cambridge University Press, 1984).

103 See Alfred W. Crosby, Jr., *The Columbian Exchange: Biological and Cultural Consequences of 1492*, Thirtieth Anniversary ed. (Westport, CT: Praeger, 2003).

104 See Ed Morales, *The Latin Beat: The Rhythms and Roots of Latin Music, from Bossa Nova to Salsa and Beyond* (Cambridge, MA: Da Capo Press, 2003).

105 Charles C. Mann makes this point in *1491: New Revelations of the Americas Before Columbus* (New York: A.A. Knopf, 2005), 123.

106 See Erik Hildinger, *Warriors of the Steppe: A Military History of Central Asia, 500 B.C. to A.D. 1700* (Cambridge, MA: Da Capo Press, 2001), 1.

107 For earlier developments, see also Jeannine Davis-Kimball, Vladimir A. Bashilov, and Leonid T. Yablonsky (eds), *Nomads of the Eurasian Steppes in the Early Iron Age* (Berkeley: University of California Press, 1995).

108 On the Mongol Empire, see David Morgan, *The Mongols*, 2nd edn (Malden, MA: Blackwell Publishers, 2007).

109 Abu-Lughod emphasizes this point in *Before European Hegemony.*

110 See Paul Johnson, *A History of the Jews* (London: HarperCollins, 1987).

111 See Butterfield, *The Origins of History*, 89–97.

112 Against such beliefs, St Augustine of Hippo devoted much of his *Concerning the City of God against the Pagans*, trans. Henry Bettenson, intro. John O'Meara (London and New York: Penguin Books, 1984).

113 Johnson, *A History of the Jews*, 173–4.

114 See Lawrence Palmer Briggs, *The Ancient Khmer Empire* (Philadelphia: American Philosophical Society, 1951).

115 Jared Diamond, *Collapse: How Societies Choose to Fail or Succeed* (New York: W.W. Norton & Company, 2005), ch. 2.

116 On the Great Buddha, see Delmer M. Brown, "Introduction," in *The Cambridge History of Japan*, vol. 1: *Ancient Japan*, ed. Delmer M. Brown (New York: Cambridge University Press, 1993), 43.

117 See Sonoda Koyu with Delmer M. Brown, "Early Buddha Worship," in *Ancient Japan.*

118 See William H. McCollough, "The Heian Court, 794–1070," in *The Cambridge History of Japan*, vol. 2: *Heian Japan*, eds. Donald H. Shively and Willam H. McCollough (New York: Cambridge University Press, 1999), 82–8.

119 See Ishii Sumumu, "The Decline of the Kamakura Bakufu," in *The Cambridge History of Japan*, vol. 3: *Medieval Japan*, ed. Kozo Yamamura (Cambridge: Cambridge University Press, 1990), 131–48.

120 For the period 1550–1800, see *The Cambridge History of Japan*, vol. 4: *The Early Modern Period*, ed. John W. Hall (Cambridge: Cambridge University Press, 1991).

121 See Jeremy Black, *Kings, Nobles and Commoners: States and Societies in Early Modern Europe, a Revisionist History* (London and New York: I.B. Tauris, 2004), 181.

122 W. G. Beasley, "The Foreign Threat and the Opening of the Ports," in *The Cambridge History of Japan*, vol. 5: *The Nineteenth Century*, ed. Marius B. Jansen (Cambridge: Cambridge University Press, 1989).

123 See Alan Macfarlane, *The Making of the Modern World: Visions from the West and East* (Houndmills, UK and New York: Palgrave Macmillan, 2002), 190.

124 The idea of "core areas of civilization" is developed in Marshall G. S. Hodgson, "Cultural patterning in Islamdom and the Occident," in *Rethinking World History: Essays on Europe, Islam, and World History*, ed. Edmund Burke, III (Cambridge: Cambridge University Press, 1993a), 126–70.

125 David Cosandey credits the West's success to this favorable "thalassography." See *Le secret de l'Occident: Du miracle passé au marasme présent* (Paris: Arléa, 1997).

126 See E. L. Jones, *The European Miracle: Environments, Economies, and Geopolitics in the History of Europe and Asia*, 3rd edn (London and New York: Cambridge University Press, 2003), ch. 2.

127 See Michael McCormick, *Origins of the European Economy: Communications and Commerce A.D. 300–900* (New York: Cambridge University Press, 2001).

128 See C. H. Lawrence, *Medieval Monasticism: Forms of Religious Life in Western Europe in the Middle Ages*, 3rd edn (Harlow, UK: Longman, 2001).

129 See Peter Brown, "'Mohammed and Charlemagne' by Henri Pirenne." *Daedalus* 103 (Winter 1974): 25–33.

130 See Joanna Story (ed.), *Charlemagne: Empire and Society* (Manchester and New York: Manchester University Press, 2005).

131 Christopher Dawson, *Religion and the Rise of Western Culture* (New York: Sheed & Ward, 1950), 23.

132 This idea is advanced by Marshall Hodgson, an acquaintance with whose magisterial three-volume *The Venture of Islam* I owe to my wife, Sofia Villafuerte.

Chapter 2

1 Quoted in Bertold Spuler, *History of the Mongols: Based on Eastern and Western Accounts of the Thirteenth and Fourteenth Centuries*, trans. Helga and Stuart Drummond (Berkeley and Los Angeles: University of California Press, 1972), 120–1.

2 David Morgan, *The Mongols*, 2nd edn (Malden, MA: Blackwell Publishers, 2007), 72.

3 On these trends, see Robert S. Lopez, *The Commercial Revolution of the Middle Ages, 950–1300* (Cambridge: Cambridge University Press, 1976). Regarding the stupendous achievement of Gothic architecture, see Robert Mark, "Structural Experimentation in Gothic Architecture: Large-scale Experimentation Brought Gothic Cathedrals to a Level of Technical Elegance Unsurpassed Until the Last Century." *American Scientist* 66 (September–October 1978): 542–50.

4 See Paul Freedman and Gabrielle M. Spiegel, "Medievalisms Old and New: The Rediscovery of Alterity in North American Medieval Studies." *The American Historical Review* 103 (June 1998): 677–704.

5 See, for example, his *On the Medieval Origins of the Modern State* (Princeton: Princeton University Press, 1970).

6 This and subsequent paragraphs rely on Michael Moïssey Posta (ed.), *The Agrarian Life of the Middle Ages*, vol. 1 of *The Cambridge Economic History of Europe*, 2nd edn (Cambridge: Cambridge University Press, 1966), ch. 3.

7 See Lopez, *The Commercial Revolution of the Middle Ages*, 28.

8 Some doubt has been cast on the concept of a worldwide Medieval Warm Period, but the temperatures in Europe seem to have risen significantly in parts of the eleventh and twelfth centuries. See Thomas J. Crowley and Thomas S. Lowery, "How Warm Was the Medieval Warm Period?" *Ambio* 29 (February 2000): 51–4.

9 See Jared Diamond, *Guns, Germs, and Steel: The Fates of Human Societies* (New York: W.W. Norton & Company, 1997), 77.

10 On the shift from oxen to horses as draft animals in medieval Europe, see John Langdon, *Horses, Oxen and Technological Innovation: The Use of Draught Animals in English Farming from 1066–1500* (Cambridge: Cambridge University Press, 1986), 4–21.

11 Thomas Malthus, *An Essay on the Principle of Population* (London: J. Johnson, 1798), ch. 7, par. 20, http://www.econlib.org/library/Malthus/malPop3.html#VII.20 (accessed 13 June 2013).

12 See Cormac Ó Gráda, *Famine: A Short History* (Princeton: Princeton University Press and Oxford, 2009), 25–38.

13 See, for example, Elspeth Whitney, *Medieval Science and Technology* (Greenwood, CT: Greenwood Press, 2004), 114–16.

14 See John M. Hobson, *The Eastern Origins of Western Civilization* (Cambridge: Cambridge University Press, 2004), 201–5.

15 On the violence and instability of premillennial Europe, see Thomas N. Bisson, *The Crisis of the Twelfth Century: Power, Lordship, and the Origins of European Government* (Princeton: Princeton University Press, 2008).

16 See Fredric L. Cheyette, "Some Reflections on Violence, Reconciliation, and the 'Feudal Revolution,'" in *Conflict in Medieval Europe: Changing Perspectives on Society and Culture*, eds. Warren Brown and Piotr Górecki (Aldershot, UK and Burlington, VT: Ashgate Publishing, Ltd., 2003), 250–9.

17 See Thomas N. Bisson, "The Problem of Feudal Monarchy: Aragon, Catalonia, and France." *Speculum* 53 (July 1978): 470.

18 The classic treatment is François Louis Ganshof, *Feudalism*, 3rd edn, trans. Philip Grierson (New York: Harper Torchbooks, 1996).

19 See Elizabeth A. R. Brown, "The Tyranny of a Construct: Feudalism and Historians of Medieval Europe." *The American Historical Review* 79 (October 1974): 1063–88; Susan Reynolds, *Fiefs and Vassals: The Medieval Evidence Reinterpreted* (Oxford: Oxford University Press, 1994), 11–12.

20 For a description of such proceedings, see "Feudal Documents (11th–13th Centuries)," in *Sources of the West: Readings in Western Civilization*, 4th edn, 2 vols., ed. Mark A. Kishlansky (New York: Longman, 2001), vol. 1, 154–8.

21 Even German society under the Nazis, though intimidated, brutalized, and oppressed, remained vibrant and strong, allowing the triumph of a relatively tolerant and pluralistic social order after World War II.

22 Scholars of very different outlooks often agree in emphasizing this point. See, for example, Diamond, *Guns, Germs, and Steel*, 430; Nathan Rosenberg and L. E. Birdzell, Jr., *How the West Grew Rich: The Economic Transformation of the Industrial World* (New York: Basic Books, 1986), 136; Niall Ferguson, *Civilization: The West and the Rest* (London: Penguin Books Ltd, 2010), 38.

23 See Hugh Thomas, *The Slave Trade: The Story of the Atlantic Slave Trade, 1440–1870* (New York: Simon & Schuster, 1997), 34–6.

24 See George Huppert, *After the Black Death: A Social History of Early Modern Europe*, 2nd edn (Bloomington, IN: Indiana University Press, 1998), 112–16.

25 See Lester K. Little, *Religious Poverty and the Profit Economy in Medieval Europe* (Ithaca: Cornell University Press, 1978), 7.

26 See Janet L. Abu-Lughod, *Before European Hegemony: The World System A.D. 1250–1350* (New York: Oxford University Press, 1989), ch. 2.

27 The phrase comes from Lopez, *The Commercial Revolution of the Middle Ages*.

28 See Aidan Southall, *The City in Time and Space* (Cambridge and New York: Cambridge University Press, 1998), chs. 2–3.

29 See Southall, *The City in Time and Space*, ch. 4.

30 See Huppert, *After the Black Death*, chs. 2–3.

31 On the guilds, see Southall, *The City in Time and Space*, 109–19.

32 See Carlo M. Cipolla, *Before the Industrial Revolution: European Society and Economy, 1000–1700*, 2nd edn. (New York and London: W.W. Norton & Company, 1980), 146–7.

33 By 1300, roughly 10 percent of Europeans lived in towns, but around 20 percent in Flanders, Brabant, and northern Italy. See Paul Bairoch, Jean Batou, and Pierre Chèvre, *La population des villes européennes: Banque de données et analyse sommaire des résultats, 800–1850* (Geneva: Librairie Droz, 1988), 259.

34 See Eric H. Mielants, *The Origins of Capitalism and the "Rise of the West"* (Philadelphia: Temple University Press, 2007).

35 On Chinese cities and guilds, see Southall, *The City in Time and Space*, 38–44, 125–58.

36 See Hobson, *The Eastern Origins of Western Civilization*, 61–70.

37 Marshall Hodgson, *The Venture of Islam: Conscience and History in a World Civilization*, 3 vols. (Chicago: University of Chicago Press, 1974), 93.

38 The early history of European guilds is presented in Antony Black, *Guild & State: European Political Thought from the Twelfth Century to the Present* (New Brunswick, NJ: Transaction Pub., 2003), pt. 1.

39 Giovanni Boccaccio, *The Decameron*, trans. Mark Musa and Peter Bondanella (New York: Penguin Group, 1982), 18.

40 Hodgson, "Cultural patterning in Islamdom and the Occident," 159.

41 See Philip C. C. Huang, "Review: Development or Involution in Eighteenth-Century Britain and China? A Review of Kenneth Pomeranz's 'The Greater Divergence: China, Europe, and the Making of the Modern World Economy.'" *The Journal of Asian Studies* 61 (May 2002): 501–38 (in particular: 34).

42 See Adam Robert Lucs, "Industrial Milling in the Ancient and Medieval Worlds: A Survey of the Evidence for an Industrial Revolution in Medieval Europe." *Technology and Culture* 46 (January 2005): 1–30.

43 Terry S. Reynolds, *Stronger Than a Hundred Men: A History of the Vertical Water Wheel* (Baltimore and London: The Johns Hopkins University Press, 1983), 51–4; Lynn White, Jr., *Medieval Technology and Social Change* (London: Oxford University Press, 1962b), ch. 3.

44 William D. Phillips, Jr., *Slavery from Roman Times to the Early Transatlantic Trade* (Minneapolis: University of Minnesota Press, 1985), ch. 3.

45 Reynolds, *Stronger Than a Hundred Men*, 109–14.

46 See Paolo Malanima, *Pre-Modern European Economy: One Thousand Years, 10th–19th Centuries* (Leiden: E.J. Brill, 2009), 72–4; Reynolds, *Stronger Than a Hundred Men*, 173–7.

47 See Reynolds, *Stronger Than a Hundred Men*, 69–94, 136.

48 Also important for increasing textile production were the European adaptation of spinning wheels from India and horizontal looms from the Middle East. See Giorgio Riello and Prasannan Parthasarathi, *The Spinning World: A Global History of Cotton Textiles, 1200–1850* (Oxford and New York: Oxford University Press, 2009), 3.

49 Joel Mokyr, *The Lever of Riches: Technological Creativity and Economic Progress* (Oxford and New York: Oxford University Press, 1990), 35. For speculation on why water power was far less exploited in China and the Islamic world, see Reynolds, *Stronger Than a Hundred Men*, 114–21.

50 See Lynn White, Jr., "The Act of Invention: Causes, Contexts, Continuities and Consequences." *Technology and Culture* 3 (Autumn 1962a): 486–500 (here: 499).

51 Landes, *The Wealth and Poverty of Nations*, 46–7.

52 See Cipolla, *Before the Industrial Revolution*, 222.

53 See David Landes, *Revolution in Time: Clocks and the Making of the Modern World*, rev. edn (Cambridge, MA: Harvard University Press, 2000).

54 See Joseph Needham, Wang Ling, and Derek J. de Solla Price, *Heavenly Clockwork: The Great Astronomical Clocks of Medieval China*, 2nd edn. with suppl. by John H. Combridge (Cambridge and New York: Cambridge University Press, 1986); Joseph Needham, *Time and Eastern Man* (London: Royal Anthropological Institute of Great Britain & Ireland, 1965); Endymion Wilkinson, *Chinese History: A Manual*, rev. edn. (Cambridge, MA: Harvard University Press, 2000), 198–206.

55 See Landes, *The Wealth and Poverty of Nations*, 51.

56 See David A. King, "On the Role of the Muezzin and the Muwaqqit in Medieval Islamic Society," in *Tradition, Transmission, Transformation: Proceedings of Two Conferences on Pre-modern Science Held at the University of Oklahoma*, eds. F. J. Ragep, Sally P. Ragep, and Steven John Livesey (Leiden: E.J. Brill, 1996).

57 Bernard Lewis, *The Muslim Discovery of Europe* (New York: W. W. Norton & Company, 2001), 233. See also Bernard Lewis, *What Went Wrong? Western Impact and Middle Eastern Response* (Oxford: Oxford University Press, 2002), 129–31.

58 On the increasing accuracy of Western timekeeping, see Norman Davies, *Europe: A History* (New York: Oxford University Press, 1996), 1250.

59 See Lopez, *The Commercial Revolution of the Middle Ages*.

60 The following section draws on John Mickelthwait and Adrian Wooldridge, *The Company: A Short History of a Revolutionary Idea* (New York: Modern Library, 2003).

61 See Subhi Y. Labib, "Capitalism in Medieval Islam." *The Journal of Economic History* 29 (March 1969): 79–96.

62 See James Franklin, *The Science of Conjecture: Evidence and Probability before Pascal* (Baltimore and London: The Johns Hopkins University Press, 2001), 259–63.

63 As quoted in François Crouzet, *A History of the European Economy, 1000–2000* (Charlottesville, VA: University of Virginia Press, 2001), 33. On the medieval "price revolution," see David Hackett Fischer, *The Great Wave: Price Revolutions and the Rhythm of History* (New York and Oxford: Oxford University Press, 1996), 17–30.

64 See John M. Hobson, "What Have the Muslims Ever Done for Us? Islamic Origins of Western Civlization," in *The Challenge of Eurocentrism: Global Perspectives, Policy, and Prospects*, ed. Rajani Kannepalli Kanth (New York: Palgrave Macmillan, 2009), 221; Jack Goody, *The Logic of Writing and the Organization of Society* (Cambridge: Cambridge University Press, 1986), ch. 2.

65 See Edwin S. Hunt, *The Medieval Super-Companies: A Study of the Peruzzi Company of Florence* (Cambridge and New York: Cambridge University Press, 1994).

66 See Martin Allen, "Italians in English Mints and Exchanges," in *Fourteenth Century England*, vol. 2, ed. Chris Given-Wilson (Woodbridge, UK and Rochester, NY: Boydell & Brewer Incorporated, 2002).

67 See Mielants, *The Origins of Capitalism*, 28–9.

68 See, for example, Janet L. Abu-Lughod, *Before European Hegemony: The World System A.D. 1250–1350* (New York: Oxford University Press, 1989).

69 See David Gaimster, "A Parallel History: The Archaeology of Hanseatic Urban Culture in the Baltic c. 1200–1600." *World Archaeology* 37 (September 2005): 408–23.

70 See Erwin Panofsky, Introduction, in *Abbot Suger on the Abbey Church of St.-Denis and Its Treasures*, ed. Erwin Panofsky (Princeton: Princeton University Press, 1946), 18–36.

71 See Eugen Rosenstock-Huessy, *The Driving Power of Western Civilization: The Christian Revolution of the Middle Ages*, pref. Karl W. Deutsch (Boston: Beacon Press, 1950), 74–6. On draft animals in medieval Europe, see Mokyr, *The Lever of Riches*, 35–8.

72 Peter Draper, "Islam and the West: The Early Use of the Pointed Arch Revisited." *Architectural History* 48 (2005): 1–20.

73 See Louis Grodecki, Anne Prach, and Roland Recht, *Gothic Architecture*, trans. I. Mark Paris (New York: H. N. Abrams, 1985), 7–14.

74 See Robert Bork, "Rock, Spires, Paper: Technical Aspects of Gothic Spires," in *Villard's Legacy: Studies in Medieval Technology, Science, and Art in Memory of Jean Gimpel*, ed. Marie-Thérèse Zenner (Aldershot, UK and Burlington, VT: Ashgate Publishing, Ltd, 2004), 135n1, 146–7.

75 A storm (or perhaps an earthquake) in 1549 brought down the spire of the Lincoln Cathedral, and a windstorm of 1561toppled Old St Paul's. See Bork, "Rock, Spires, Paper," 146–7.

76 Hackett Fischer, *The Great Wave*, 13.

77 See William W. Kibler (ed.), *Medieval France: An Encyclopedia* (New York: Garland Publishing, 1995), 171.

78 See Rik Van Nieuwenhove, *An Introduction to Medieval Theology* (Cambridge: Cambridge University Press, 2012), 250.

79 See Martin Cook, *Medieval Bridges* (Princes Risborough, UK: Shire Publications, 1998), 27–38.

80 See Meg Lota Brown and Kari Boyd McBride, *Women's Roles in the Renaissance* (Westport, CT: Greenwood Press, 2005), 210–20.

81 See Roger Boase, "Arab Influences on European Love-Poetry," in *The Legacy of Muslim Spain*, eds. Salma Khadra Jayyus and Manuela Marín (Leiden, the Netherlands: E.J. Brill, 1992).

82 See Roger Boase, *The Origin and Meaning of Courtly Love: A Critical Study of European* Scholarship (Manchester: Manchester University Press, 1977).

83 Landes, *Wealth and Poverty of Nations*, 413.

84 See Amy Kelly, *Eleanor of Aquitaine and the Four Kings* (Cambridge, MA: Harvard University Press, 1950).

85 On Blanche and other influential medieval women, see Kathleen Nolan, *Capetian Women* (Basingstoke, UK and New York: Palgrave Macmillan, 2003).

86 See, for example, Esther S. Lee Yao, *Chinese Women: Past and Present* (Mesquite, TX: Ide House, 1983).

87 See Huppert, *After the Black Death*, 131.

88 See the many examples in Helen M. Jewell, *Women in Late Medieval and Reformation Europe: 1200–1550* (New York: Palgrave, 2007).

89 Quoted in *Love's Trinity: A Companion to Julian of Norwich*, trans. John-Julian, commentary Frederick S. Roden (Collegeville, MN: Liturgical Press, 2009), x.

90 See Adam S. Cohen, *The Uta Codex: Art, Philosophy, and Reform in Eleventh-Century Germany* (University Park, PA: Perm State University Press, 2000), 188–9.

91 See C. M. Millward and Mary Hayes, *A Biography of the English Language*, 3rd edn (Boston: Wadsworth, 2012), 214.

92 See J. J. Clarke, *The Tao of the West: Western Transformations of Taoist Thought* (London and New York: Routledge, 2000), 114; Stephen Owen, "The Cultural Tang, 650–1020," in *The Cambridge History of Chinese Literature*, vol. 1: *To 1375*, eds. Kang-i Sun Chang and Stephen Owen (Cambridge: Cambridge University Press, 2010), 524.

93 In a standard Chinese anthology of Tang era poets, roughly one in ten poets listed were women, as cited in John Minford and Joseph S. M. Lau (eds), *An Anthology of Translations: Classical Chinese Literature*, vol. 1: *From Antiquity to the Tang Dynasty* (New York, Chichester, UK and Hong Kong: Chinese University Press, 2000), 956.

94 See Michael A. Fuller and Shuen-Fu Lin, "North and South: The Twelfth and Thirteenth Centuries." *The Cambridge History of Chinese Literature* 1 (2010): 1469–71.

95 See Introduction to Volume II, in *The Cambridge History of Chinese Literature*, vol. 2: *Since 1375*, eds. Kang-i Sun Chang, Stephen Owen (Cambridge: Cambridge University Press, 2010), xxviii.

96 See Jonathan Berkey, "Women in Medieval Islamic Society," in *Women in Medieval Western European Culture*, ed. Linda E. Marshall (New York and London: Garland Publishing, 1999), 108–9.

97 See Maya Shatzmiller, "Aspects of Women's Participation in the Economic Life of Later Medieval Islam: Occupations and Mentalities." *Arabica* 35 (March 1988): 36–58

(quotation: 52); idem., *Labour in the Medieval Islamic World* (Leiden: E.J. Brill, 1994).

98 See Maya Shatzmiller, *Her Day in Court: Women's Property Rights in Fifteenth-Century Granada* (Cambridge, MA: Harvard University Press, 2007).

99 See Merry E. Wiesner, *Women and Gender in Early Modern Europe*, 2nd edn (Cambridge and New York: Cambridge University Press, 2000), 89–90.

100 See Merry E. Wiesner, *Early Modern Europe, 1450–1789*, 2nd edn (Cambridge and New York: Cambridge University Press, 2013), 122.

101 See Valerie J. Hoffman, "Oral Traditions as a Source for the Study of Muslim Women: Women in the Sufi Orders," in *Beyond the Exotic: Women's Histories in Islamic Societies*, ed. Amira El Azhary Sonbol (Syracuse, NY: Syracuse University Press, 2005), 366.

102 Berkey, "Women in Medieval Islamic Society," 109–10.

103 Ibid., 110.

104 Quoted from Dante Alighieri, *The Divine Comedy*, trans. Henry F. Cary, vol. 20 of The Harvard Classics (New York: P.F. Collier & Son Co., 1909), 13.

105 See W. Montgomery Watt, Introduction, *The Faith and Practice of Al-Ghazālī*, trans. W. Montgomery Watt (Oxford: Oxford University Press, 1998); Robert M. Haddad, "Philosophical Theology and Science in Medieval Christianity and Islam: A Comparative Perspective." *The Journal of the Historical Society* 8 (September 2008): 349–93 (here: 359–63).

106 See Derk Bodde, *Chinese Thought, Society, and Science: The Intellectual and Social Background of Science and Technology Pre-modern China* (Honolulu: University of Hawaii Press, 1991), 82–92, 129–32, 242–4.

107 Neo-Confucian thinkers like Zhu Xi (1130–1200) developed powerful philosophical concepts, conceiving of everything as composed of *qi*, or what we might call matter-energy, and *li*, or organizing principle, a subtle distinction compatible with modern scientific conceptions. See Daniel K. Gardner, trans. and ed., *The Four Books: The Basic Teachings of the Later Confucian Tradition* (Indianapolis and Cambridge, MA: Hackett Publishing Co., 2007), 86.

108 See Rodney Stark, *For the Glory of God: How Monotheism Led to Reformations, Science, Witch-hunts, and the End of Slavery* (Princeton: Princeton University Press, 2003).

109 Stark, *For the Glory of God*, 137.

110 This paragraph draws on Donald Jay Grout, *A History of Western Music*, 3rd edn, Shorter and Claude V. Palisca (New York and London: W.W. Norton & Company, 1981), especially chs. 3 and 4.

111 See D. Kern Holoman, *Berlioz: A Musical Biography of the Creative Genius of the Romantic Era* (Cambridge, MA: Harvard University Press, 1989), 308–11.

112 See Lewis, *What Went Wrong?*, 128–9.

113 This paragraph relies on Michael Levey, *From Giotto to Cézanne: A Concise History of Painting* (London: Thames and Hudson, 1968), especially ch. 1.

114 See Marc Gotlieb, "The Painter's Secret: Invention and Rivalry from Vasari to Balzac." *The Art Bulletin* 84 (2002): 469–90 (here 469–70).

115 For an interesting contrast, see Julia K. Murray, *Mirrors of Mortality: Narrative Illustration and Confucian Ideology* (Honolulu: University of Hawaii Press, 2007).

Chapter 3

1 The scene is described in Thomas Frederick Tout, *The Empire and the Papacy, 918–1273* (London: Rivingtons, 1903), 131–2.

2 See Lawrence Boadt, *Reading the Old Testament: An Introduction* (Mahway, NJ: Paulist Press, 1984), 126–8.

3 See Robert Karl Gnuse, *No Other Gods: Emergent Monotheism in Israel* (Sheffield: Sheffield Academic Press, 1997).

4 See James K. Beilby and Paul Rhodes Eddy (eds), *The Historical Jesus: Five Views* (Downers Grove, IL: InterVarsity Press, 2009).

5 See Rodney Stark, *The Rise of Christianity: A Sociologist Reconsiders History* (Princeton: Princeton University Press, 1996).

6 Quoted from Sarah Ruden, *Paul among the People: The Apostle Reinterpreted and Reimagined in His Own Time* (New York: Pantheon Books, 2010), xix.

7 See Stark, *The Rise of Christianity*, ch. 5.

8 Statistic supplied in Ralph Martin Novak, Jr., *Christianity and the Roman Empire: Background Texts* (Harrisburg, PA: Trinity Press International, 2001), 103. On the early spread of Christianity, see Martin Goodman, *Mission and Conversion: Proselytizing in the Religious History of the Roman Empire* (Oxford and New York: Oxford University Press, 1994); Ramsay MacMullen, *Christianizing the Roman Empire: A.D. 100–400* (New Haven: Yale University Press 1984).

9 Cited in Robert M. Haddad, "Philosophical Theology and Science in Medieval Christianity and Islam: A Comparative Perspective." *The Journal of the Historical Society* 8 (September 2008): 349–93 (here: 352).

10 Cited in Haddad, "Philosophical Theology and Science in Medieval Christianity and Islam," 353.

11 See John W. O'Malley, *Four Cultures of the West* (Cambridge, MA: Harvard University Press, 2004), 79–83.

12 See Ramsay MacMullen, *Christianity and Paganism in the Fourth to Eighth Centuries* (New Haven: Yale University Press 1997).

13 Kathleen G. Cushing, *Reform and the Papacy in the Eleventh Century: Spirituality and Social Change* (Manchester and New York: Manchester University Press, 2005), 57.

14 See James Harvey Robinson, *Readings in European History*, 2 vols. (Boston: Ginn and Company, 1904–1906), vol. 1, 72.

15 On the theory of the "two swords," see David VanDrunen, *Natural Law and the Two Kingdoms: A Study in the Development of Reformed Social Thought* (Grand Rapids, MI: W. B. Eerdmans Pub. Co., 2010), 32–41.

16 Saint Augustine, *The City of God*, ed. Vernon J. Bourke (Garden City, NY: Image Books, 1958).

17 C. H. Lawrence, *Medieval Monasticism: Forms of Religious Life in Western Europe in the Middle Ages*, 3rd edn (Harlow, UK: Longman, 2001).

18 Phyllis Tickle, *The Divine Hours: Prayers for Autumn and Wintertime: A Manual for Prayer* (New York: Doubleday Religious Publishing Group, 2006), vii.

19 Lynn White, Jr., *Machina ex Deo: Essays in the Dynamism of Western Culture* (Cambridge, MA: Harvard University Press, 1968), 65.

20 See Terry S. Reynolds, *Stronger Than a Hundred Men: A History of the Vertical Water Wheel* (Baltimore and London: Johns Hopkins University Press, 1983), 32–4.

21 See Lawrence, *Medieval Monasticism*, ch. 2.

22 See MacMullen, *Christianity and Paganism.*

23 See Richard Tarnas, *The Passion of the Western Mind: Understanding the Ideas That Have Shaped Our World* (New York: Ballantine Books, 1991), 120–54, 171–90.

24 See Jude P. Dougherty, *The Logic of Religion* (Washington, DC: The Catholic University Press, 2003), 26–7.

25 See Tom Streeter, *The Church and Western Culture: An Introduction to Church History* (Bloomington, IN: Indiana University Press, 2008), ch. 7; William R. Cook and Ronald B. Herzman, *The Medieval World View: An Introduction* (New York: Oxford University Press, 1983), 59–71.

26 See Cook and Herzman, *The Medieval World View*, 123–31.

27 See MacMullen, *Christianity and Paganism.*

28 Quoted from Peter Brown, *Through the Eye of a Needle: Wealth, the Fall of Rome, and the Making of Christianity in the West, 350–550 AD* (Princeton and Oxford: Princeton University Press, 2012), 523–4.

29 See Carole E. Straw, *Gregory the Great: Perfection in Imperfection* (Berkeley: University of California Press, 1988); Cook and Herzman, *The Medieval World View*, 142–7.

30 See Roger Collins, "Charlemagne's Imperial Coronation and the Annals of Lorsch," in *Charlemagne: Empire and Society*, ed. Joanna Story (Manchester and New York: Manchester University Press, 2005), 55.

31 See Cook and Herzman, *The Medieval World View*, 183–94.

32 See Stefan Heid, *Celibacy in the Early Church: The Beginnings of a Discipline of Obligatory Continence for Clerics in East and West*, trans. Michael J. Miller (San Francisco, CA: Ignatius Press, 2000).

33 See H. E. J. Cowdrey, *The Cluniacs and the Gregorian Reform* (Oxford: Oxford University Press, 1970).

34 See Christopher Dawson, *Religion and the Rise of Western Culture* (New York: Sheed & Ward, 1950), 18–21.

35 See Giles Constable, *The Reformation of the Twelfth Century* (Cambridge: Cambridge University Press, 1996), 3.

36 Constable, *The Reformation of the Twelfth Century*, 6.

37 See John Haldon and Leslie Brubaker, *Byzantium in the Iconoclast Era, c. 680–850* (New York: Cambridge University Press, 2011).

38 See William E. Phipps, *Clerical Celibacy: The Heritage* (London and New York: Continuum, 2004), 126.

39 Catherine E. Boyd, "The Gregorian Reform," in *The Gregorian Epoch: Reformation, Revolution, Reaction?* ed. Schafer Williams (Boston: Heath, 1964), 75–6.

40 See Cushing, *Reform and the Papacy in the Eleventh Century*, 14.

41 See Susan Wood, *The Proprietary Church in the Medieval West* (Oxford and New York: Oxford University Press, 2006), 300–1.

42 On the Peace of God, see Cushing, *Reform and the Papacy in the Eleventh Century*, ch. 3.

43 See Thomas Head, "The Development of the Peace of God in Aquitaine (970–1005)." *Speculum* 74 (July 1999): 656–86 (here: 656).

44 This paragraph draws on Cushing, *Reform and the Papacy in the Eleventh Century*, 41–9.

45 See Colin Morris, *The Papal Monarchy: The Western Church from 1050 to 1250* (Oxford: Oxford University Press, 1989).

46 See Uta-Renate Blumenthal, *The Investiture Controversy: Church and Monarchy from the Ninth to the Twelfth Century*, trans. by the author (Philadelphia: University of Pennsylvania Press, 1988).

47 See Norman Cohn, *The Pursuit of the Millennium: Revolutionary Millenarians and Mystical Anarchists of the Middle Ages* (Oxford: Oxford University Press, 1970).

48 Cushing, *Reform and the Papacy in the Eleventh Century*, 91.

49 See ibid., 22–4.

50 On these points, see ibid., 121–4.

51 On the powerful dualism in Christian thought, see Tarnas, *The Passion of the Western Mind*, 120–54; H. D. McDonald, "Biblical Teaching on Personality," in *Psychology and Christian Integration*, eds. Daryl H. Stevenson, Brian E. Eck, and Peter C. Hill (Batavia, IL: Christian Association for Psychological Studies, 2007), 166–8.

52 See Cowdrey, *The Cluniacs and the Gregorian Reform*.

53 See Blumenthal, *The Investiture Controversy*, 70–9.

54 On Leo, see *The Papal Reform of the Eleventh Century: Lives of Pope Leo IX and Pope Gregory VII*, trans. and annotated by I. S. Robinson (Manchester: Manchester University Press, 2004).

55 See Timur Kuran, "The Rule of Law in Islamic Thought and Practice: A Historical Perspective," in *Global Perspectives on the Rule of Law*, eds. James J. Heckman, Robert L. Nelson, and Lee Cabatingan (New York: Cavendish Publishing, 2010), 71–89.

56 See H. Patrick Glenn, *Legal Traditions of the World: Sustainable Diversity in Law*, 2nd edn (Oxford: Oxford University Press, 2004).

57 The following paragraphs draw on Harold J. Berman's magisterial *Law and Revolution: The Formation of the Western Legal Tradition* (Cambridge, MA: Harvard University Press, 1983), chs. 2–3.

58 See John J. Contreni, "The Carolingian Renaissance," in *Renaissance Before the Renaissance: Cultural Revivals of Late Antiquity and the Middle Ages,* ed. Warren Treadgold (Stanford, CA: Stanford University Press, 1984).

59 The liberal arts were divided into the Trivium (grammar, rhetoric, and logic) leading to the Quadrivium (geometry, arithmetic, astronomy, and theoretical and mathematical aspects of music). In practice, most schools focused on grammar and rhetoric. See David L. Wagner (ed.), *The Seven Liberal Arts in the Middle Ages* (Bloomington, IN: Indiana University Press, 1983). The idea of the liberal arts, while originating in late antiquity, probably arrived in the Latin West via Islam. See Joel L. Kraemer, *Humanism in the Renaissance of Islam: The Cultural Revival during the Buyid Age* (Leiden: E.J. Brill, 1993), 2–5, 9.

60 See Édouard Jeauneau, *Rethinking the School of Chartres*, trans. Claude Paul Desmarais (Toronto: University of Toronto Press, 2009), ch. 2.

61 See Harold J. Berman, "The Origins of Western Legal Science." *Harvard Law Review* 90 (March 1977): 894–943.

62 See Berman, "The Origins of Western Legal Science," 917–19.

63 A good summary of these developments is in ibid., 899–906.

64 The Latin term *universitas* applied to all guilds but stuck in the case of those devoted to education.

65 See Stephen C. Ferruolo, "The Twelfth-Century Renaissance," in *Renaissance Before the Renaissance*, ed. Treadgold, 131; Peter Landau, "The Development of Law," in *The New Cambridge Medieval History*, vol. 4: *c. 1024-c. 1198*, ed. David Luscombe et al. (New York: Cambridge University Press,1995), 126–7.

66 For a detailed list, see Norman Davies, *Europe: A History* (New York: Oxford University Press, 1996), 1248.

67 See Toby E. Huff, *The Rise of Early Modern Science: Islam, China, and the West*, 2nd edn (Cambridge: Cambridge University Press, 2003).

68 On the law of waqf, see George Makdisi, *The Rise of Colleges: Institutions of Learning in Islam and the West* (Edinburgh: Edinburgh University Press, 1981), 35–74.

69 See Makdisi, *The Rise of Colleges*, 75–82.

70 See Jonathan Berkey, *The Transmission of Knowledge in Medieval Cairo: A Social History of Islamic Education* (Princeton: Princeton University Press, 1992), chs. 2–4; idem., *The Formation of Islam: Religion and Society in the Near East, 600–1800* (New York: Cambridge University Press, 2003), 226–30.

71 See Timothy Brook, "Edifying Knowledge: The Building of School Libraries in Ming China." *Late Imperial China* 17 (June 1996): 93–119; Jan L. Hagman, "Schools and Civil Service in the Ming Dynasty," in *Hawai'i Reader in Traditional Chinese Culture*, eds. Victor H. Mair et al. (Honolulu: University of Hawaii Press, 2005).

72 See Huff, *The Rise of Early Modern Science*, 228–9.

73 See George Makdisi, "Madrasa and University in the Middle Ages." *Studia Islamica* 32 (1970): 255–64.

74 See Timur Kuran, "The Provision of Public Goods under Islamic Law: Origins, Impact, and Limitations of the Waqf System." *Law & Society Review* 35 (2001): 841–98.

75 Alan Macfarlane argues that English individualism emerged independently from this struggle. See *The Origins of English Individualism. The Family, Property, and Social Transition* (New York: Wiley, 1978).

76 For an early instance, see Greta Austin, *Shaping Church Law Around the Year 1000: The Decretum of Burchard of Worms* (Farnham, UK and Burlington, VT: Ashgate Publishing, 2009).

77 See Landau, "The Development of Law," 120.

78 On Gratian's efforts, see Landau, "The Development of Law," 128–32.

79 Quoted in Berman, *Law and Revolution*, 923.

80 See Berman, *Law and Revolution*, chs. 9–14.

81 On the common law, see Berman, *Law and Revolution*, 434–59; Glenn, *Legal Traditions of the World: Sustainable Diversity in Law*, 2nd edn (Oxford: Oxford University Press, 2004), 434–58.

82 For such comparisons, see Glenn, *Legal Traditions of the World*.

83 See Berman, *Law and Revolution*, 542–3.

84 On the trust, see Alan Macfarlane, *The Making of the Modern World: Visions from the West and East* (Basingstoke, UK and New York: Palgrave Macmillan, 2002), 263–72.

85 See Monica M. Gaudiosi, "The Influence of the Islamic Law of Waqf on the Development of the Trust in England: The Case of Merton College." *University of Pennsylvania Law Review* 136 (April 1988): 1231–61.

86 Quoted in Berman, *Law and Revolution*, 521.

87 See Harold J. Berman, *Law And Revolution, II: The Impact of the Protestant Reformations on the Western Legal Tradition* (Cambridge, MA: Harvard University Press, 2003), 33.

88 See Cushing, *Reform and the Papacy in the Eleventh Century*, 130.

89 On this rhetoric, see Cushing, *Reform and the Papacy in the Eleventh Century*, ch. 6.

90 This and the next paragraph draw on Cushing, *Reform and the Papacy in the Eleventh Century*, ch. 4; Blumenthal, *The Investiture Controversy*, ch. 4; Brian Tierney, *The Crisis of Church and State, 1050–1300: With Selected Documents* (Toronto: University of Toronto Press, 1988), 53–73.

91 It is reproduced in Sidney Z. Ehler and John B. Morrall (eds), *Church and State through the Centuries: A Collection of Historic Documents with Commentaries* (London: Burns & Oates, 1988), 43–4.

92 See Blumenthal, *The Investiture Controversy*, ch. 5.

93 See Morris, *The Papal Monarchy*, chs. 7–8.

94 See Anne J. Duggan, "Conciliar Law 1123–1215: The Legislation of the. Four Lateran Councils," in *The History of Medieval Canon Law in the Classical Period, 1140–1234: From Gratian to the Decretals of Pope Gregory IX*, eds. Wilfried Hartmann and Kenneth Pennington (Washington, DC: CUA Press, 2008), 335.

95 See Morris, *The Papal Monarchy*, ch. 17.

96 See Duggan, "Conciliar Law," 313, 343.

97 For two primary sources on the Inquisition, see Henry Bettenson and Chris Maunder (eds), *The Documents of the Christian Church*, 4th edn (New York: Oxford University Press, 2011), 140–2.

98 Richard Landes makes this point in "Economic Development and Demotic Religiosity: Reflections on the Eleventh-Century Takeoff," in *History in the Comic Mode: The New Medieval Cultural History*, eds. Rachel Fulton and Bruce Holsinger (New York: Columbia University Press, 2007).

99 See Sarah Hopper, *To Be A Pilgrim, The Medieval Pilgrimage Experience* (Stroud: Sutton, 2002); Rosamund Allen, *Eastward Bound: Travel and Travellers, 1050–1550* (Manchester: Manchester University Press, 2004).

100 See J. van Herwaarden, *Between Saint James and Erasmus: Studies in Late-medieval Religious Life: Devotions and Pilgrimages in the Netherlands*, trans. Wendie Shaffer (Leiden: E.J. Brill, 2003), 212, 233.

101 See Clive Foss, "Pilgrimage in Medieval Asia Minor." *Dumbarton Oaks Papers* 56 (2002): 129–51; Colin Morris, *The Sepulchre of Christ and the Medieval West: From the Beginning to 1600s* (New York: Oxford University Press, 2005).

102 William H. McNeill, *The Shape of European History* (New York and London: Oxford University Press, 1974), 42.

103 See Peter Rietbergen, *Europe: A Cultural History* (London and New York: Routledge, 1998), 114–18.

104 See Constance Hoffman Berman, "Medieval Agriculture, the Southern French Countryside, and the Early Cistercians. A Study of Forty-Three Monasteries." *Transactions of the American Philosophical Society*, New Series 76, 5 (1986): i-179.

105 See Morris, *The Papal Monarchy*, ch. 10.

106 Statistic cited in Peter Turchin and Sergey A. Nefedov, *Secular Cycles* (Princeton: Princeton University Press, 2009), 57.

107 See Ronald G. Witt, *The Two Latin Cultures and the Foundation of Renaissance Humanism in Medieval Italy* (New York: Cambridge University Press, 2012).

108 Ferruolo, "The Twelfth-Century Renaissance," 128.

109 See Étienne Gilson, *History of Christian Philosophy in the Middle Ages* (New York: Random House, 1955).

110 See Herwaarden, *Between Saint James and Erasmus*, 146.

111 See Jerry L. Walls, *Purgatory: The Logic of Total Transformation* (Oxford and New York: Oxford University Press, 2012), ch. 1.

112 See Ronald C. Finucane, *Miracles and Pilgrims: Popular Beliefs in Medieval England* (New York: Palgrave Macmillan, 1995).

113 See Ferruolo, "The Twelfth-Century Renaissance"; Norman F. Cantor, *The Civilization of the Middle Ages: A Completely Revised and Expanded Edition of Medieval History, the Life and Death of a Civilization* (New York: HarperCollins, 1993), ch. 14.

114 Gilson, *History of Christian Philosophy in the Middle Ages*, 144.

115 See John Marenbon, *Medieval Philosophy*, vol. 3 of *Routledge History of Philosophy* (London and New York: *Routledge*, 1998), 226–7.

116 See Cook and Herzman, *The Medieval World View*, 119.

117 David C. Lindberg, *Science in the Middle Ages* (Chicago: University of Chicago Press, 1980), 38–9.

118 See Majid Fakhry, "Philosophy and Theology: From the Eighth Century C.E. to the Present," in *The Oxford History of Islam,* ed. John L. Esposito (Oxford and New York: Oxford University Press, 1999), 287.

119 By contrast, it seems that none of the major Islamic philosophers cited his Christian counterparts approvingly.

120 See George Makdisi, *The Rise of Colleges: Institutions of Learning in Islam and the West* (Edinburgh: Edinburgh University Press, 1981), 245–60.

121 See John F. Wippel, "The Parisian Condemnations of 1270 and 1277," in *A Companion to Philosophy in the Middle Ages*, ed. Randall Curren (Malden, MA and Oxford: Blackwell Publishers, 2002), 66.

122 See Seyyed Hossein Nasr, *An Introduction to Islamic Cosmological Doctrines: Conceptions of Nature and Methods Used for its Study by the Ikhwan Al-Safa, Al-Biruni, and Ibn Sina* (Albany: State University of New York Press, 1993), 185; Fakhry, "Philosophy and Theology," in *The Oxford History of Islam*, ed. Esposito, 302.

123 On these differing views, see Ferruolo, "The Twelfth-Century Renaissance," 132–4.

124 See Brian Davies, *The Thought of Thomas Aquinas* (Oxford: Oxford University Press, 1993); Marie-Dominique Chenu, *Aquinas and His Role in Theology* (Collegeville, MN: The Liturgical Press, 2002).

125 See Saint Thomas Aquinas, *Summa Theologica*, 22 vols., trans. fathers of the English Dominican province (New York: Benziger Brothers, 1911–25).

126 The document is published in Arthur Hyman, James J. Walsh, and Thomas Williams (eds), *Philosophy in the Middle Ages: The Christian, Islamic, and Jewish Traditions*, 3 edn (Indianapolis and Cambridge, MA: Hackett Publishing Co., 2010), 541–50.

127 Aquinas was canonized in 1323 and declared a Doctor of the Church in 1567.

128 See Lindberg, *Science in the Middle Ages*, 107.

129 Armand Augustine Maurer, *The Philosophy of William of Ockham in the Light of Its Principles* (Toronto: Pontifical Institute of Medieval Studies, 1999), 150, 177.

130 See Haddad, "Philosophical Theology and Science in Medieval Christianity and Islam," 349–93.

131 See, for example, Thomas A. Brady, Jr., "The Rise of Merchant Empires, 1400–1700: A European Counterpoint," in *The Political Economy of Merchant Empires: State Power and World Trade, 1350–1750*, ed. James D. Tracy (Cambridge: Cambridge University Press, 1991), 123–32.

132 See, for example, Malcolm Lambert, *The Cathars* (Oxford: Oxford University Press, 1998).

133 See Lambert, *The Cathars*, 40.

134 See, for example, Edward Peters, *Inquisition* (New York: Free Press, 1988); Morris, *The Papal Monarchy*, 470–6.

135 See Daniel H. Nexon, *The Struggle for Power in Early Modern Europe: Religious Conflict, Dynastic Empires and International Change* (Princeton: Princeton University Press, 2009), 80–1.

136 Thomas A. Brady, Jr., makes this argument in "The Rise of Merchant Empires."

137 See Cantor, *Civilization of the Middle Ages*, 395–7.

138 See Jim Bradbury, *The Capetians: Kings of France, 987–1328* (London and New York: The University of Michigan, 2007), 47–50, 78, 123–4, 298.

139 Ralph Francis Bennett makes this argument in "The Gregorian Program," in *The Gregorian Epoch: Reformation, Revolution, Reaction?* ed. Schafer Williams (Boston: Heath, 1964), 45.

140 See C. J. Nederman, "Aristotelianism and the Origins of 'Political Science' in the Twelfth Century." *Journal of the History of Ideas* 52 (1991): 179–94.

141 See Samuel Edward Finer, *The Intermediate Ages*, vol. 2 of *The History of Government from the Earliest Times*, 3 vols. (Oxford: Oxford University Press, 1997), ch. 8.

142 See Gianfranco Poggi, *The State: Its Nature, Development, and Prospects* (Stanford: Stanford University Press, 1990), 40–2.

143 See Thomas N. Bisson, "The Military Origins of Medieval Representation." *The American Historical Review* 71 (July 1966): 1199–218. On the earliest English assemblies, see also R. F. Trehane, "The Nature of Parliament in the Reign of Henry III," in *Historical Studies of the English Parliament*, vol. 1: *Origins to 1399*, eds. E. B. Fryde and Edward Miller (Cambridge: Cambridge University Press, 1970).

144 See Tierney, *The Crisis of Church and State*, 180–94.

145 The full text of the papal bull *Unam Sanctam* is printed in Tierney, *The Crisis of Church and State*, 188–9 (quotation: 189).

146 See Bernard Schimmelpfennig, *The Papacy*, trans. James Sievert (New York: Cambridge University Press, 1992), ch. 9.

147 James A. Brundage, *The Medieval Origins of the Legal Profession: Canonists, Civilians, and Courts* (Chicago and London: University of Chicago Press, 2008), 123, 265, 271, 349, 492.

148 See Cantor, *Civilization of the Middle Ages*, ch. 17.

Chapter 4

1 Jean Froissart, *The Chronicles of England, France and Spain, and the Adjoining Countries*, trans. Thomas Johnes, 2 vols. (London: W. Smith, 1844), vol. 1, 165.

2 On the battle, see Andrew Ayton and Philip Preston (eds), *The Battle of Crécy, 1346* (Woodbridge, UK: Boydell, 2005).

3 Froissart, *The Chronicles of England*, 166.

4 The first paragraphs of this section draw upon R. Ernest Dupuy and Trevor N. Dupuy, *The Harper Encyclopedia of Military History: From 3500 B.C. to the Present*, 4th edn (New York: Harper Resource, 1993) and William H. McNeill, *The Pursuit of Power: Technology, Armed Force, and Society since A.D. 1000* (Chicago: University of Chicago Press, 1982), ch. 1.

5 See Chs. 1 and 2 by Sidney Smith, in *The Cambridge Ancient History*, vol. 3: The Assyrian Empire, eds. J. B. Bury, S. A. Cook, and F. E. Adcock (Cambridge: Cambridge University Press, 1965).

6 On the rise of Macedonia, see Frank E. Adcock, *The Greek and Macedonian Art of War* (Berkeley: University of California Press, 1957); Peter Green, *Alexander of Macedon, 356–323 B.C.: A Historical Biography* (Berkeley and Los Angeles: University of California Press, 1991).

7 On China's early history, see Valerie Hansen, *The Open Empire: A History of China to 1600* (New York: W.W. Norton & Company, 2000).

8 See Geoffrey Parker (ed.), *The Cambridge History of Warfare* (Cambridge: Cambridge University Press, 2005b), part 1; J. F. C. Fuller, *A Military History of the Western World*, vol. 1: *From the Earliest Times to the Battle of Lepanto* (New York: Funk and Wagnalls Company, 1954), chronicles 3–8.

9 Regarding the gradual decline of Rome, see Chester Starr, *A History of the Ancient World* (New York: Oxford University Press, 1965), chs. 30–2.

10 See Helen Nicholson, *Medieval Warfare: Theory and Practice of War in Europe, 300–1500* (Basingstoke, UK and New York: Palgrave Macmillan, 2004), 51.

11 See Philippe Contamine, *War in the Middle Ages*, trans. Michael Jones (New York: Blackwell, 1986), 22–9.

12 See Nicholson, *Medieval Warfare*, 100.

13 McNeill, *The Pursuit of Power*, 64n2.

14 See Geoffrey Parker, "Europe and the Wider World, 1500–1750: The Military Balance," in *The Political Economy of Merchant Empires: State Power and World Trade, 1350–1750*, ed. James D. Tracy (Cambridge: Cambridge University Press, 1991), 167–8.

15 See H. B. Clarke, "The Vikings," in *Medieval Warfare: A History*, ed. Maurice Keen (Oxford: Oxford University Press, 1999); Else Roesdahl, *The Vikings*, trans. Susan M. Margeson and Kirsten Williams (London: Penguin, 1998).

16 See McNeill, *The Pursuit of Power*, 20.

17 Nicholson, *Medieval Warfare*, 102–4; Contamine, *War in the Middle Ages*, 27.

18 On medieval castles, see Nicholson, *Medieval Warfare*, 81–6.

19 See McNeill, *The Pursuit of Power*, 68.

20 See Nicholson, *Medieval Warfare*, 102–3.

21 See Clifford J. Rogers, "The Military Revolutions of the Hundred Years' War." *The Journal of Military History* 57 (April 1993): 246.

22 See Christon I. Archer et al., *World History of Warfare* (Lincoln, NE: University of Nebraska Press, 2002), 146. See also Andrew Ayton, "Arms, Armour, and Horses," in *Medieval Warfare*, ed. Keen, 188.

23 Maurice Keen, Introduction, in *Medieval Warfare*, ed. Keen, 7.

24 See Nicholson, *Medieval Warfare*, 107–8.

25 John Gillingham, "An Age of Expansion, c. 1020–1204," in *Medieval Warfare*, ed. Keen, 32.

26 See Nicholson, *Medieval Warfare*, 31.

27 Contamine, *War in the Middle Ages*, 48.

28 Rogers, "The Military Revolutions of the Hundred Years' War," 247.

29 See Stuart Croft, *Strategies of Arms Control: A History and Typology* (Manchester and New York: Manchester University Press, 1996), 24.

30 See Nicholson, *Medieval Warfare*, 3.

31 Ibid., 64.

32 See Peter Heath, "War and Peace in the Works of Erasmus: A Medieval Perspective," in *The Medieval Military Revolution: State, Society, and Military Change in Medieval and Early Modern Europe*, eds. Andrew Ayton and J. L. Price (London and New York: I.B. Tauris, 1995), 130–1.

33 Contamine, *War in the Middle Ages*, 43.

34 See Nicholson, *Medieval Warfare*, 81–6.

35 See Gillingham, "An Age of Expansion," 81.

36 On the trebuchet, see Paul E. Chevedden, "The Invention of the Counterweight Trebuchet: A Study in Cultural Diffusion." *Dumbarton Oaks Papers* 54 (2000): 71–116; Nicholson, *Medieval Warfare*, 93–5.

37 George Lane, *Genghis Khan and Mongol Rule* (Indianapolis, IN: Hackett Publishing Company, Inc, 2009), 39–40.

38 Gillingham, "An Age of Expansion," 89.

39 R. L. C. Jones, "Fortifications and Sieges in Europe," in *Medieval Warfare*, ed. Keen, 165–6, 185.

40 See E. L. Jones, *The European Miracle: Environments, Economies, and Geopolitics in the History of Europe and Asia* (London and New York: Cambridge University Press, 1981), 161.

41 Norman Housley, "European Warfare, c. 1200–1320," in *Medieval Warfare*, ed. Keen, 127–8.

42 See Hunt and Murray, *A History of Business in Medieval Europe*, 99–104.

43 See Nicholson, *Medieval Warfare*, 47.

44 See Housley, "European Warfare," 131–2; McNeill, *The Pursuit of Power*, 67.

45 McNeill discusses this in *The Pursuit of Power*, 77–9.

46 See McNeill, *The Pursuit of Power*, 74.

47 See George C. Kohn (ed.), *Encyclopedia of Plague and Pestilence: From Ancient Times to the Present*, 3rd edn (New York: New York University Press, 2008), 31.

48 See Joseph P. Byrne, *The Black Death* (Westport, CT and London: Greenwood Press, 2004), 58–62.

49 See Janet L. Abu-Lughod, *Before European Hegemony: The World System A.D. 1250–1350* (New York: Oxford University Press, 1989), ch. 11.

50 Byrne, *The Black Death*, 62–6. For a selection of primary sources, see Rosemary Horrox, trans. and ed., *The Black Death* (Manchester and New York: Manchester University Press, 1994).

51 See McNeill, *The Pursuit of Power*, 72.

52 See Edwin S. Hunt and James M. Murray, *A History of Business in Medieval Europe* (Cambridge: Cambridge University Press, 1999), 134.

53 This paragraph draws on Hunt and Murray, *A History of Business in Medieval Europe*, ch. 7.

54 See Ibid., 239–40.

55 See Ibid., 213.

56 See Ibid., 245.

57 See Jacob Strieder and Mildred L. Hartsough, *Jacob Fugger the Rich: Merchant and Banker of Augsburg, 1459–1525*, eds. Norman Scott and Brien Gras, trans. Mildred L. Hartsough (New York: Beard Books, 2001).

58 See Hunt and Murray, *A History of Business in Medieval Europe*, 170.

59 See McNeill, *The Pursuit of Power*, 65–6.

60 See John Stone, "Technology, Society, and the Infantry Revolution of the Fourteenth Century." *The Journal of Military History* 68 (April 2004): 361–80 (here: 369).

61 John Stone argues persuasively that socioeconomic developments fueled the infantry revolution. See his "Technology, Society, and the Infantry Revolution of the Fourteenth Century."

62 See Randall Fegley, *The Golden Spurs of Kortrijk: How the Knights of France Fell to the Footsoldiers of Flanders in 1302* (Jefferson, NC and London: McFarland, 2002); Clifford J. Rogers, "The Age of the Hundred Years' War," in *Medieval Warfare*, 137–42.

63 See J. F. Verbruggen, *The Art of Warfare in Western Europe during the Middle Ages from the Eighth Century to 1340*, 2nd edn (Woodbridge, UK: The Boydell Press, 1997), 179–80.

64 See Rogers, "The Military Revolutions of the Hundred Years' War," 247.

65 See Rogers, "The Age of the Hundred Years' War," 144.

66 See Guilmartin, "The Military Revolution," 304.

67 For background on the Swiss foot soldiers, see Verbruggen, *The Art of* Warfare, 112–15.

68 See Brian M. Downing, *The Military Revolution and Political Change: Origins of Democracy and Autocracy in Early Modern Europe* (Princeton: Princeton University Press, 1992), 61–2.

69 See Rogers, "The Age of the Hundred Years' War," 143n; Rogers, "The Military Revolutions of the Hundred Years' War," 249.

70 Andrew Ayton, "The English Army at Crécy," in *The Battle of Crécy*, eds. Ayton and Preston, 183–9; Bertrand Schnerb, "Vassals, Allies, and Mercenaries: The French Army before and after 1346," in ibid., 269–70.

71 Michael Prestwich, "The Battle of Crécy," in *The Battle of Crécy,* eds. Ayton and Preston, 151–3.

72 See Rogers, "The Age of the Hundred Years' War."

73 See Nicholson, *Medieval Warfare*, 58.

74 See David Bell, *The First Total War: Napoleon's Europe and the Birth of Warfare as We Know It* (New York: Houghton Mifflin, 2007), 35–6.

75 See John Kautsky, *The Politics of Aristocratic Empires* (New Brunswick, NJ: Transaction Publishers, 1997), 363.

76 This section draws on Thomas N. Bisson, "The Military Origins of Medieval Representation." *The American Historical Review* 71 (July 1966): 1199–218; Downing, *The Military Revolution and Political Change.*

77 Rogers, "The Military Revolutions of the Hundred Years' War," 253.

78 See P. S. Lewis, *Essays in Later Medieval French History* (London and Ronceverte, WV: The Hambledon Press, 1985), 106.

79 Rogers, "The Military Revolutions of the Hundred Years' War," 253–4.

80 See Joseph Needham, *Science in Traditional China: A Comparative Perspective* (Cambridge, MA: Harvard University Press, 1981), ch. 2; Jack Kelly, *Gunpowder: Alchemy, Bombards, and Pyrotechnics: The History of the Explosive That Changed the World* (New York: Basic Books, 2004).

81 See McNeill, *The Pursuit of Power*, 83.

82 Ibid., 83–8; Jones, "Fortifications and Sieges in Europe," 180–2; Maurice Keen, "The Changing Scene: Guns, Gunpowder, and Permanent Armies," in *Medieval Warfare,* ed. Keen, 273–4.

83 Rogers, "The Military Revolutions of the Hundred Years' War," 261.

84 See, for example, Keen, "The Changing Scene," 273–5; Rogers, "The Military Revolutions of the Hundred Years' War," 258–61, 267–72; McNeill, *The Pursuit of Power*, 86–8.

85 See Rogers, "The Military Revolutions of the Hundred Years' War," 272–3; McNeill, *The Pursuit of Power*, 95; Keen, "The Changing Scene," 273.

86 Guilmartin, "The Military Revolution," 304–5; Mesut Uyar and Edward J. Erickson, *A Military History of the Ottomans: From Osman to Atatürk* (Santa Barbara, CA: Praeger Security International/ABC-CLIO, 2009), ch. 1.

87 Keen, "The Changing Scene," 280; Uyar and Erickson, *A Military History of the Ottomans*, 32–6.

88 See Jones, "Fortifications and Sieges in Europe," 179n.

89 Keen, "The Changing Scene," 273–4.

90 See Jonathan Harris, *The End of Byzantium* (New Haven: Yale University Press 2010).

91 John F. Guilmartin, Jr., "The Military Revolution: Origins and First Tests Abroad," in *The Military Revolution Debate: Readings on the Military Transformation of Early Modern Europe*, ed. Clifford J. Rogers (Boulder: Westview Press, 1995), 319.

92 Jeremy Black, *War and the World: Military Power and the Fate of Continents, 1450–2000* (New Haven and London: Yale University Press 1998), 18–19; Uyar and Erickson, *A Military History of the Ottomans*, 73–4.

93 Black, *War and the World*, 21–3, 29–30.

94 For a list of the principal European wars from the fifteenth to the eighteenth centuries, see Davies, *Europe*, 1266–7, 1282–3.

95 McNeill, *The Pursuit of Power*, 86.

96 See Keen, "The Changing Scene," 284–6; Jeremy Black, *The Cambridge Illustrated Atlas of Warfare: Renaissance to Revolution, 1492–1792* (New York: Cambridge University Press, 1996), 148–50.

97 See Rogers, "The Military Revolutions of the Hundred Years' War," 275.

98 See Guilmartin, "The Military Revolution," 306–7.

99 On the *tercio*, see Henry Kamen, *Spain's Road to Empire: The Making of a World Power, 1492–1763* (London: Penguin Books, 2002), 163.

100 See Guilmartin, "The Military Revolution," 307–8.

101 Ibid., 307.

102 William E. Wallace, " 'Dal disegno allo spazio': Michelangelo's Drawings for the Fortifications of Florence." *The Journal of the Society of Architectural Historians* 46 (June 1987): 119–34; McNeill, *The Pursuit of Power*, 89–91.

103 See Mahinder S. Kingra, "*Trace Italienne* and Military Revolution, 1567–1648." *The Journal of Military History* 57 (July 1993): 431–46.

104 See Jan Glete, *War and the State in Early Modern Europe: Spain, the Dutch Republic and Sweden as Fiscal-Military States, 1500–1660* (London: Routledge, 2002).

105 Rogers, "The Military Revolutions of the Hundred Years' War," 270.

106 Nicholson, *Medieval Warfare*, 58.

107 See Dennis E. Showalter and William J. Astore, *Soldiers' Lives Through History: The Early Modern World* (Westport, CT: Greenwood, 2007), 63–4.

108 See Geoffrey Parker, "The Limits to Revolutions in Military Affairs: Maurice of Nassau, the Battle of Nieuwpoort (1600), and the Legacy." *The Journal of Military History* 71 (April 2007): 331–72.

109 See McNeill, *The Pursuit of Power*, 126–36; idem., *Keeping Together in Time: Dance and Drill in Human History* (Cambridge, MA: Harvard University Press, 1995), 128–31.

110 Parker, "The Limits to Revolutions in Military Affairs," 332–47.

111 Ibid., 358–9.

112 See McNeill, *The Pursuit of Power*, 123.

113 See Frank Tallett, *War and Society in Early-Modern Europe, 1495–1715* (London and New York: Routledge, 1992), 39–43.

114 See Olaf van Nimwegen, *The Dutch Army and the Military Revolutions, 1588–1688*, trans. Andrew May (Woodbridge, UK and Rochester, NY: Boydell Press, 2010), 102–3.

115 A modern treatise on training and tactics had appeared in China in 1562, but it seems to have spawned no imitations. See William H. McNeill, "Ch'I Chi-kuang," in *The Reader's Companion to Military History*, eds. Robert Cowley and Geoffrey Parker (New York: Houghton Mifflin, 1996), 83; McNeill, *Keeping Together in Time*, 125.

116 John A. Lynn, "The Trace Italienne and the Growth of Armies: The French Case." *The Journal of Military History* 55, 3 (July 1991): 297–330.

117 See C. V. Wedgewood, *The Thirty Years' War* (New York, 1961); Geoffrey Parker (ed.), *The Thirty Years' War*, 2nd edn (London and New York: Cambridge University Press, 2006).

118 See James B. Collins, *The State in Early Modern France* (Cambridge and New York: Cambridge University Press, 1995).

119 See Glenn J. Ames, *Colbert, Mercantilism, and the French Quest for Asian Trade* (DeKalb, IL: Northern Illinois University Press, 1996).

120 Jeremy Black, *Kings, Nobles and Commoners: States and Societies in Early Modern Europe, a Revisionist History* (London and New York: I.B. Tauris, 2004), 3–8.

121 See Jacques-Bénigne Bossuet, *Politics Drawn from the Very Words of Holy Scripture*, ed. Patrick Riley (Cambridge: Cambridge University Press, 1990), 263–70.

122 See Black, *Kings, Nobles and Commoners*, 4.

123 Gang Deng, *The Premodern Chinese Economy: Structural Equilibrium and Capitalist Sterility* (London and New York, 1999), 245; Kent G. Deng, "Development and Its Deadlock in Imperial China, 221 B.C.–1840 A.D." *Economic Development and Cultural Change* 51 (January 2003): 479–522 (statistics: 504).

124 See D. E. Mungello, *The Great Encounter of China and the West, 1500–1800* (Lanham, MD: Rowman & Littlefield, 2005), 128.

125 See Downing, *The Military Revolution and Political Change*, ch. 4.

126 Statistics in Downing, *The Military Revolution and Political Change*, 95.

127 On Poland's plight, see Downing, *The Military Revolution and Political Change*, ch. 6.

128 See Downing, *The Military Revolution and Political Change*, 187.

129 See Geoffrey Parker, *The Military Revolution: Military Innovation and the Rise of the West, 1500–1800* (New York: Cambridge University Press, 1996), ch. 2; Michael Roberts, *Gustavus Adophus: A History of Sweden, 1611–1632*, 2 vols. (London: Longmans Green, 1953–1958).

130 See Black, *War and the World*, 90.

131 Ibid., 159.

132 See, for example, Victor Davis Hanson, *The Western Way of War: Infantry Battle in Classical Greece* (New York: A.A. Knopf, 1989); idem., *Carnage and Culture: Landmark Battles in the Rise of Western Power* (New York: Anchor Books, 2001).

133 See John Lynn, *Battle: A History of Combat and Culture* (Boulder, CO: Westview Press, 2003).

134 See Black, *War and the World*, 156; Iqtidar Alam Khan, *Gunpowder and Firearms: Warfare in Medieval India* (New Delhi: Oxford University Press, 2004); Kenneth Chase, *Firearms: A Global History to 1700* (Cambridge: Cambridge University Press, 2003).

135 See Jonathan A. Grant, "Rethinking the Ottoman 'Decline': Military Technology Diffusion in the Ottoman Empire, Fifteenth to Eighteenth Centuries." *Journal of World History* 10 (Spring 1999): 179–201.

136 On Japan and China, see Black, *War and the World*, 50–2.

137 See Chase, *Firearms*, ch. 6.

138 See Carlo Cipolla, *Guns, Sails, and Empires: Technological Innovation and the Early Phases of European Expansion 1400–1700* (New York: Pantheon Press, 1965), 140.

139 See, for example, David Chandler, *The Art of Warfare in the Age of Marlborough* (New York: Hippocrene Books, 1976); Christopher Duffy, *The Army of Frederick the Great* (New York: Hippocrene Books, 1974); Gunther E. Rothenburg, *The Art of Warfare in the Age of Napoleon* (Bloomington, IN: Indiana University Press, 1980).

Chapter 5

1 Quoted in David Dobbs, "Restless Genes." *National Geographic* (January 2013): 45.

2 See Herodotus, *The Histories*, trans. Walter Blanco, eds. Walter Blanco and Jennifer Tolbert Roberts (New York and London: W.W. Norton & Company, 1992); James S. Romm, *Herodotus* (New Haven and London: Yale University Press 1998); Justin Marozzi, *The Way of Herodotus: Travels with the Man who Invented History* (Cambridge, MA: Harvard University Press, 2008).

3 See Martin Richards, "The Neolithic Invasion of Europe." *Annual Review of Anthropology* 32 (2003): 135–62.

4 See Richards, "The Neolithic Invasion of Europe," 135.

5 See Bettina Arnold and D. Blair Gibson, *Celtic Chiefdom, Celtic State: The Evolution of Complex Social Systems in Prehistoric Europe* (Cambridge: Cambridge University Press, 1995).

6 See John C. McEnroe, *Architecture of Minoan Crete: Constructing Identity in the Aegean Bronze Age* (Austin, TX: University of Texas Press, 2010).

7 See Louise Schofield, *The Mycenaeans* (London and Los Angeles: J. Paul Getty Museum, 2007).

8 See Trevor Bryce, *The Kingdom of the Hittites* (Oxford: Oxford University Press, 1998).

9 See Peter Heather, *Empires and Barbarians: The Fall of Rome and the Birth of Europe* (New York: Oxford University Press, 2009).

10 See Christopher Dawson, *Religion and the Rise of Western Culture* (New York: Sheed & Ward, 1950).

11 See Robert Bartlett, *The Making of Europe: Conquest, Colonization, and Cultural Change, 950–1350* (Princeton: Princeton University Press, 1993), 102–5.

12 See Raymond Van Dam, "Merovingian Gaul and the Frankish Conquests," in *The New Cambridge Medieval History*, vol. 1: *c.500–c.700*, ed. Paul Fouracre (Cambridge: Cambridge University Press, 2005).

13 See Bartlett, *The Making of Europe*, 85–90.

14 Ibid., 60–9.

15 Ibid., 40.

16 Ibid., 43–51.

17 See Bartlett, *The Making of Europe*, 6.

18 See Richard Landes, "Economic Development and Demotic Religiosity: Reflections on the Eleventh-Century Takeoff," in *History in the Comic Mode: The New Medieval Cultural History*, eds. Rachel Fulton and Bruce Holsinger (New York: Columbia University Press, 2007), 106.

19 See Landes, "Economic Development and Demotic Religiosity," 110–11.

20 See Bartlett, *The Making of Europe*.

21 Ibid., 121.

22 Cited in ibid., 144.

23 Ibid., 169.

24 See Roger Osborne, *Civilization: A New History of the Western World* (New York: Pegasus Books, 2006), 172.

25 See Bartlett, *The Making of Europe*, 173–6.

26 See Terryl Nancy Kinder, *Cistercian Europe: Architecture of Contemplation* (Grand Rapids, MI: W.B. Eerdmans Pub. Co., 2002), 37. See also Janet Burton and Julie Kerr, *The Cistercians in the Middle Ages* (Woodbridge, UK: The Boydell Press, 2011), 21–55, 96–7.

27 See Burton and Kerr, *The Cistercians in the Middle Ages*, 156–81, 189.

28 See Bartlett, *The Making of Europe*, 259.

29 Ibid., 292.

30 See Hilde de Ridder-Symoens, "Mobility," in *Universities in the Middle Ages*, vol. 1 of *A History of the University in Europe*, ed. H. de Ridder-Symoens (Cambridge: Cambridge University Press, 1992), 280–302.

31 William H. McNeill advances this claim in *The Rise of the West: A History of the Human Community* (Chicago: University of Chicago Press, 1963), 558–9.

32 See Jonathan Phillips, *Holy Warriors: A Modern History of the Crusades* (New York: Random House 2009); Christopher Tyerman, *God's War: A New History of the Crusades* (Cambridge, MA: Harvard University Press, 2006).

33 See Tyerman, *God's War*, 553.

34 See John H. Pryor (ed.), *Logistics of Warfare in the Age of the Crusades* (Aldershot, UK and Burlington, VT: Ashgate Publishing, 2006).

35 See Colin Morris, *The Sepulchre of Christ and the Medieval West: From the Beginning to 1600s* (New York: Oxford University Press, 2005).

36 Quoted in Edward Peters, *A Modern Guide to Indulgences: Rediscovering This Often Misinterpreted Teaching* (Chicago: University of Chicago Press, 2008), 6.

37 As quoted in Rebecca Rist, *The Papacy and Crusading in Europe, 1198–1245* (London and New York: Continuum, 2009), 90.

38 See Kenneth M. Setton and Marshall W. Baldwin, *A History of the Crusades: The First Hundred Years* (Madison, WI: University of Wisconsin Press, 2006), 258–83.

39 See Jonathan Phillips, *The Crusades, 1095–1194* (Harlow, UK: Longman, 2002), chs. 2–3.

40 See Thomas F. Madden, *The New Concise History of the Crusades* (Lanham, MD and Oxford: Rowman & Littlefield, 2005), 34–5.

41 See Penny Cole, "'O God, the Heathen Have Come into Your Inheritance' (Ps. 78.1): The Theme of Religious Pollution in Crusade Documents, 1095–1188," in *Crusaders and Muslims in Twelfth-Century Syria*, ed. Maya Shatzmiller (Leiden, New York and Köln: E.J. Brill, 1993).

42 On the military orders, see Phillips, *The Crusades*, ch. 5.

43 See Rist, *The Papacy and Crusading in Europe*, 5–7, 13, 171–3.

44 See William R. Cook and Ronald B. Herzman, *The Medieval World View: An Introduction* (New York: Oxford University Press, 1983), 299.

45 See Michael Brett and Elizabeth Fentress, *The Berbers* (Oxford and Cambridge, MA: Blackwell, 1996), 113.

46 See Hermann Aubin, "The Lands East of the Elbe and German Colonization Eastwards," in *The Cambridge Economic History of Europe: The Agrarian Life of the Middle Ages*, ed. Michael Moïssey Postan (Cambridge: Cambridge University Press, 1966).

47 See Helen J. Nicholson, *The Crusades* (Westport, CT: Greenwood Press, 2004a), 9–18.

48 See Francesco Gabrieli (ed.), *Arab Historians of the Crusades* (Berkeley and Los Angeles: University of California Press, 1969), 73–84; Daniel W. Brown, *A New Introduction to Islam*, 2nd edn (Chichester, UK and Malden, MA: Blackwell Publishers, 2009), 224–5.

49 See Stephen C. Ferruolo, "The Twelfth-Century Renaissance," in *Renaissance Before the Renaissance: Cultural Revivals of Late Antiquity and the Middle Ages*, ed. Warren Treadgold (Stanford, CA: Stanford University Press, 1984), 137.

50 George E. Gingras, trans., *Egeria: Diary of a Pilgrimage* (New York: Newman Press, 1970).

51 On St Willibald and other pilgrims, see John Wilkinson, *Jerusalem Pilgrims Before the Crusades* (Warminster, UK: Aris & Phillips, 2002).

52 See Clive Foss, "Pilgrimage in Medieval Asia Minor." *Dumbarton Oaks Papers* 56 (2002): 129–51; Jennifer Speake (ed.), *Literature of Travel and Exploration: An Encyclopedia* (New York: Fitzroy Dearborn, 2003).

53 On Gerbert, see David C. Lindberg, *Science in the Middle Ages* (Chicago: University of Chicago Press, 1980), 37.

54 See Cathy Cobb and Harold Goldwhite, *Creations of Fire: Chemistry's Lively History From Alchemy to the Atomic Age* (New York: Plenum Press, 1995), 74.

55 See Charles Burnett, ed. and trans., *Adelard of Bath, Conversations with his Nephew: On the Same and the Different, Questions on Natural Science, and On Birds* (Cambridge: Cambridge University Press, 1998).

56 See Ibn Warraq, *Defending the West: A Critique of Edward Said's* Orientalism (Amherst, NY: Prometheus Books, 2007), 63–5.

57 Bernard Lewis, *The Muslim Discovery of Europe* (New York: W.W. Norton & Company, 2001), 91.

58 See Olivia Remie Constable, "Muslims in Medieval Europe," in *A Companion to the Medieval World*, eds. Carol Lansing and Edward D. English (Chichester, UK: Blackwell Publishing Ltd, 2009), 319–21.

59 See Fathi A. El-shihibi and Sparrow Hansard, *Travel Genre in Arabic Literature: A Selective Literary and Historical Study* (New York: Dissertation.com, 2006).

60 See Paul Zumthor and Catherine Peebles. "The Medieval Travel Narrative." *New Literary History* 25 (Autumn 1994): 809–24.

61 See Lewis, *The Muslim Discovery of Europe*, 97–8.

62 See Ibn Battuta, *The Travels of Ibn Battuta: In the Near East, Asia and Africa, 1325–1354*, trans. and ed. Rev Samuel Lee (Mineola, NY: Dover Publications, 2004 [1829]).

63 See Lewis, *The Muslim Discovery of Europe*, 91.

64 See Janet L. Abu-Lughod, *Before European Hegemony: The World System A.D. 1250–1350* (New York: Oxford University Press, 1989), 304–11, 336–7.

65 See Leonardo Olschki, *Marco Polo's Asia: An Introduction to His "Description of the World" Called "Il milione,"* trans. John A. Scott, rev. by author (Berkeley: University of California Press, 1960), 59–66.

66 See Olschki, *Marco Polo's Asia*, 117–20.

67 See David Buisseret (ed.), *The Oxford Companion to World Exploration*, 2 vols. (New York: Oxford University Press, 2007), 165.

68 See John Larner, *Marco Polo and the Discovery of the World* (New Haven and London: Yale University Press 1999), ch. 9.

69 See Jack Goody, *The East in the West* (Cambridge: Cambridge University Press, 1996), chs. 2–3.

70 See Andre Gunder Frank and Barry K. Gills (eds), *The World System: Five Hundred Years or Five Thousand?* (London and New York: Routledge, 1993).

71 See Susan Whitfield, *Life Along the Silk Road* (Berkeley and Los Angeles: University of California Press, 1999).

72 See Abu-Lughod, *Before European Hegemony*; Charles H. Parker, *Global Interactions in the Early Modern Age, 1400–1800* (New York: Oxford University Press, 2010), chs. 3–4.

73 See Frederic C. Lane, *Venice: A Maritime Republic* (Baltimore: The Johns Hopkins University Press, 1973), 7–8.

74 See Abu-Lughod, *Before European Hegemony*, ch. 4.

75 Felipe Fernández-Armesto, "Naval Warfare after the Viking Age, c. 1100–1500," in *Medieval Warfare: A History*, ed. Maurice Keen (Oxford: Oxford University Press, 1999), 248.

76 See John F. Guilmartin, Jr.,"The Military Revolution: Origins and First Tests Abroad," in *The Military Revolution Debate: Readings on the Military Transformation of Early Modern Europe*, ed. Clifford J. Rogers (Boulder: Rowman & Littlefield, 1995), 322.

77 See Bartlett, *The Making of Europe*, 187.

78 Ibid., 189.

79 See Lane, *Venice*, 46.

80 See Edwin S. Hunt and James M. Murray, *A History of Business in Medieval Europe* (Cambridge: Cambridge University Press, 1999), 69.

81 See Geoffery Vaughan Scammell, *The World Encompassed: The First European Maritime Empires, c. 800–1650* (Berkeley: University of California Press, 1981), 206–7.

82 See Guilmartin "The Military Revolution," in *The Military Revolution Debate*, ed. Rogers, 305.

83 See Hunt and Murray, *A History of Business in Medieval Europe*, 50.

84 See Nathan Rosenberg and L. E. Birdzell, Jr., *How the West Grew Rich: The Economic Transformation of the Industrial World* (New York: Basic Books, 1986), 81–5.

85 See Lane, *Venice*, 122.

86 Ibid., 124–5.

87 See John E. Dotson, "Everything is a Compromise: Mediterranean Ship Design, Thirteenth to Sixteenth Centuries," in *The Art, Science, and Technology of Medieval Travel*, eds. Robert Bork and Andrea Kann (Aldershot, UK, Burlington, VT: Ashgate Publishing, 2008), 38.

88 See John Gillingham, "An Age of Expansion, c. 1020–1204," in *Medieval Warfare*, ed. Keen, 66.

89 See Abu-Lughod, *Before European Hegemony*, 189.

90 See K. N. Chaudhuri, *Trade and Civilisation in the Indian Ocean: An Economic History from the Rise of Islam to 1750* (Cambridge: Cambridge University Press, 1985).

91 Earl H. Pritchard, "Thoughts on the Historical Development of the Population of China." *The Journal of Asian Studies* 23 (November 1963): 3–20 (here: 18).

92 This is the main subject of Abu-Lughod, *Before European Hegemony*.

93 Pritchard, "Thoughts on the Historical Development of the Population of China," 19.

94 See Jane Burbank and Frederick Cooper, *Empires in World History: Power and the Politics of Difference* (Princeton: Princeton University Press, 2010), 113–14.

95 Vietnam regained its independence in 1428.

96 See Andre Gunder Frank, *ReORIENT: Global Economy in the Asian Age* (Berkeley: University of California Press, 1998), 99.

97 Wen-yuan Qian makes this point in *The Great Inertia: Scientific Stagnation in Traditional China* (London and Dover, NH: Croom Helm, 1985), 112.

98 See H. Inalcik, "The Rise of the Ottoman Empire," in *A History of the Ottoman Empire to 1730*, ed. M. A. Cook (Cambridge: Cambridge University Press, 1976).

99 See R. Stephen Humphreys, "Egypt in the World System of the Later Middle Ages," in *The Cambridge History of Egypt*, vol. 1: *Islamic Egypt, 640–1517*, ed. Carl F. Petry (Cambridge and New York: Cambridge University Press, 1998), 452–6.

100 See Derk Bodde, *Chinese Thought, Society, and Science: The Intellectual and Social Background of Science and Technology in Pre-modern China* (Honolulu: University of Hawaii Press, 1991), 222–3.

101 See Erik Ringmar, "Audience for a Giraffe: European Expansionism and the Quest for the Exotic." *Journal of World History* 17 (2006): 375–97.

102 See *The Confessions of St. Augustine*, trans. and ed. John K. Ryan (Garden City, NY: Image Books, 1960), 264–6.

103 Quoted in Ringmar, "Audience for a Giraffe," 391.

104 See Scammell, *The World Encompassed*, 229.

105 See John M. Headley, "The Sixteenth-Century Venetian Celebration of the Earth's Total Habitability: The Issue of the Fully Habitable World for Renaissance Europe." *Journal of Modern History* 8 (Spring 1997): 1–27.

106 See Scammell, *The World Encompassed*, 146.

107 Helen Nicholson, *Medieval Warfare: Theory and Practice of War in Europe, 300–1500* (Houndmills, UK and New York: Palgrave Macmillan, 2004b), 159.

108 Fernández-Armesto, "Naval Warfare after the Viking Age," 237.

109 Guilmartin, "The Military Revolution," 305.

110 See Palmira Johnson Brummett, *Ottoman Seapower and Levantine Diplomacy in the Age of Discovery* (Albany: State University of New York Press, 1994), ch. 4.

111 See M. D. D. Newitt, *A History of Portuguese Overseas Expansion, 1400–1668* (London: Routledge, 2005).

112 See Benedetto Cotrugli, "On the Dignity and Office of Merchants," in *The Traditions of the Western World*, ed. J. H. Hexter et al. (Chicago: University of Chicago Press, 1967), 274–5.

113 Hunt and Murray, *A History of Business in Medieval Europe*, 69.

114 See Peter Edward Russell, *Prince Henry "The Navigator": A Life* (New Haven: Yale University Press 2000).

115 See Jonathan D. Spence, *The Search for Modern China*, 2nd edn (New York and London: W.W. Norton & Company, 1999), 119.

116 See Russell, *Prince Henry "The Navigator,"* chs. 4–5.

117 See Ibid., ch. 10.

118 See Glenn J. Ames, *Vasco da Gama: Renaissance Crusader* (New York: Pearson/ Longman, 2005).

119 See Carlo Cipolla, *Guns, Sails, and Empires: Technological Innovation and the Early Phases of European Expansion 1400–1700* (New York: Pantheon Books, 1965), 137.

120 Daniel R. Headrick, *Power over Peoples: Technology, Environments, and Western Imperialism, 1400 to the Present* (Princeton: Princeton University Press, 2010), 62–73.

121 See Glenn J. Ames, *The Globe Encompassed: The Age of European Discovery, 1500–1700* (Upper Saddle River, NJ: Pearson Prentice Hall, 2008), 32–5.

122 See Immanuel Wallerstein, *The Modern World-System I. Capitalist Agriculture and the Origins of the European World-Economy in the Sixteenth Century* (New York: Academic Press Inc., 1974), 47–52.

123 See Bailey Wallys Diffie and George Davison Winius, *Foundations of the Portuguese Empire, 1415–1580* (Minneapolis, MN: University of Minnesota Press, 1977), 173–4.

124 See Jeremy Black, *War and the World: Military Power and the Fate of Continents, 1450–2000* (New Haven and London: Yale University Press 1998), 45–7.

125 See Robert J. Sharer with Loa P. Traxler, *The Ancient Maya*, 6th edn (Stanford: Stanford University Press, 2006), 120–37.

126 See Alfred Crosby, *The Columbian Exchange: Biological and Cultural Consequences of 1492* (Westport, CT: Greenwood Publishing Co., 1972), 31.

127 See, for example, Colin McEvedy and Richard Jones, *Atlas of World Population History* (Harmondsworth, UK: Penguin, 1978), 272.

128 See, for example, Woodrow Borah, "The Historical Demography of Aboriginal and Colonial America: An Attempt at Perspective," in *The Native Population of the Americas in 1492*, ed. William M. Denevan, 2nd edn (Madison, WI: University of Wisconsin Press, 1992); Massimo Livi-Bacci, "The Depopulation of Hispanic America after the Conquest." *Population and Development Review* 32 (June 2006): 199–232.

129 Compare Figures 1.2 and 4.2 in McEvedy and Jones, *Atlas of World Population History*. See also ibid., 25, 272.

130 See David E. Stannard, *American Holocaust: Columbus and the Conquest of the New World* (New York: Oxford University Press, 1992), 255. See also Russell Thornton, *American Indian Holocaust and Survival: A Population History Since 1492* (Norman, OK: University of Oklahoma Press, 1987).

131 Stannard, *American Holocaust*, x.

132 See John B. Quigley, *The Genocide Convention: An International Law Analysis* (Aldershot, UK, and Burlington, VT: Ashgate Publishing, 2006), 10.

133 See Alfred Jay Bollet, *Plagues & Poxes: The Impact of Human History on Epidemic Disease* (New York: Demos Medical Publishing, Inc., 2004), 78; Stiffarm and Lane, "The Demography of Native North America," 32–3. Hugh A. Dempsey cites authentic and fictional cases in "Smallpox: Scourge of the Plains," in *Harms' Way: Disasters in Western Canada*, eds. Anthony W. Rasporich and Max Foran (Calgary: University of Calgary Press, 2004), 35–7.

134 See Stiffarm and Lane, "The Demography of Native North America," 34–6; Thornton, *American Indian Holocaust and Survival*, 107–9.

135 John C. Weaver, *The Great Land Rush and the Making of the Modern World, 1650–1900* (Montreal and Kingston: McGill-Queen's University Press, 2006), 264.

136 Alfred Crosby, *Ecological Imperialism: The Biological Expansion of Europe, 900–1900* (Cambridge: Cambridge University Press, 1986), 271.

137 Crosby, *Ecological Imperialism*, 280.

138 See Livi-Bacci, "The Depopulation of Hispanic America after the Conquest," 202–3.

139 See Black, *War and the World*, 63.

140 See William Atwell, "Ming China and the Emerging World Economy, c. 1570–1650," in *The Cambridge History of China*, vol. 8: *The Ming Dynasty, 1368–1644*, pt. 2, eds. Denis Twitchett and Frederick Mote (Cambridge: Cambridge University Press, 1998), 388–99.

141 See Lewis Hanke, *The Imperial City of Potosí: An Unwritten Chapter in the History of Spanish America* (The Hague: Nijhoff, 1956).

142 See, for example, Dennis O. Flynn and Arturo Giráldez, "Born with a 'Silver Spoon': The Origin of World Trade in 1571." *Journal of World History* 6 (Fall 1995): 201–21; Frank, *ReOrient*, 277.

143 See William S. Atwell, "International Bullion Flows and the Chinese Economy circa 1530–1650." *Past and Present* 95 (May 1982): 68–90; idem., "Another Look at Silver Imports into China, ca. 1635–1644." *Journal of World History* 16 (December 2005): 467–89.

144 See Virginia W. Lunsford, *Piracy and Privateering in the Golden Age Netherlands* (Basingstoke, UK: Palgrave, 2005).

145 See John Mickelthwait and Adrian Wooldridge, *The Company: A Short History of a Revolutionary Idea* (New York: Modern Library, 2003), 19–21.

146 See Maarten Prak, *The Dutch Republic in the Seventeenth Century: The Golden Age* (Cambridge: Cambridge University Press, 2005), 116–19.

147 See Prak, *The Dutch Republic in the Seventeenth Century*, 106–8.

148 See Black, *War and the World*, 48.

149 See Vincent C. Loth, "Armed Incidents and Unpaid Bills: Anglo-Dutch Rivalry in the Banda Islands in the Seventeenth Century." *Modern Asian Studies* 29 (October 1995): 705–40.

150 See Black, *War and the World*, 125–8.

151 On British overseas expansion, see *The Oxford History of the British Empire*, 5 vols. (Oxford and New York: Oxford University Press, 1998), vols. 1–2.

152 See Stanley L. Engerman, "The Slave Trade and British Capital Formation in the Eighteenth Century: A Comment on the Williams Thesis." *The Business History Review* 46 (Winter 1972): 430–43 (here: 436).

153 See J. Alexander, "Islam, Archaeology, and Slavery in Africa." *World Archaeology* 33 (June 2001): 44–60.

154 See, for example, James F. Searing, *West African Slavery and Atlantic Commerce: The Senegal River Valley, 1700–1860* (Cambridge: Cambridge University Press, 1993).

155 See David Eltis and Stanley L. Engerman, "The Importance of Slavery and the Slave Trade to Industrializing Britain." *The Journal of Economic History* 60 (March 2000): 123–44; William Darity, "British Industry and the West Indies Plantations." *Social Science History* 14 (Spring 1990): 117–49.

156 See Lawrence A. Peskin and Edmund F. Wehrle, *America and the World: Culture, Commerce, Conflict* (Baltimore: Johns Hopkins University Press, 2012), 20–1.

157 See Kenneth F. Kiple, *The Caribbean Slave: A Biological History* (New York: Cambridge University Press, 2002; Patrick Manning, "The Slave Trade: The Formal Demography of a Global System." *Social Science History* 14 (Summer 1990): 255–79.

158 Jeremy Black argues, however, that the Europeans probably used less coercion and paid higher prices than the Muslim slave traders. See his *Kings, Nobles and Commoners: States and Societies in Early Modern Europe, a Revisionist History* (London and New York: I.B. Tauris, 2004), 173.

159 See Crosby, *The Columbian Exchange*.

160 See John Reader, *Potato: A History of the Propitious Esculent* (New Haven and London: Yale University Press 2009).

161 See Beverly Lemire, *Cotton* (Oxford and New York: Oxford University Press, 2011), 10–20.

162 Jeremy Black makes this point in *Kings, Nobles and Commoners*, 157.

163 On Ottoman military successes, see Jeremy Black, *War and the World*, 18–44, 102–5.

164 See Burbank and Cooper, *Empires in World History*, ch. 5.

165 See Black, *War and the World*, 127–8.

166 Geoffrey Parker, "The Limits to Revolutions in Military Affairs: Maurice of Nassau, the Battle of Nieuwpoort (1600), and the Legacy." *The Journal of Military History* 71 (April 2007): 331–72 (here: 332).

167 Guilmartin advances this argument in "The Military Revolution," 302–3.

Chapter 6

1 David E. Wellbery, Judith Ryan, and Hans Ulrich Gumbrecht, *A New History of German Literature* (Cambridge, MA: Belknap Press, 2004), 30.

2 Michael H. Harris, *History of Libraries in the Western World*, 4th edn (Lanham, MD: Scarecrow Press, 1999), 100, 110.

3 The pledge is reproduced here: Theodore W. Koch, "Some Old-Time Old-World Librarians," in *Library Daylight: Tracings of Modern Librarianship, 1874–1922*, ed. Rory Litwin, intro. Suzanne Stauffer (Duluth: Library Juice Press, 2006), 148–9.

4 Frederick Andrew Lerner, *The Story of Libraries: From the Invention of Writing to the Computer Age* (New York: Continuum, 2001), 71–5.

5 Maev Kennedy, "Battle to Save Rare 14th Century Psalter for the Nation," *The Guardian* (9 September 2004), http://www.guardian.co.uk/uk/2004/sep/09/artsandhumanities.arts1 (accessed 13 June 2013).

6 See Elizabeth L. Eisenstein, *The Printing Press as an Agent of Change: Communications and Cultural Transformations in Early Modern Europe*, 2 vols. (Cambridge: Cambridge University Press, 1979), vol. 1, 45–8.

7 See John Man, *Gutenberg: How One Man Remade the World with Words* (New York: John Wiley, 2002), 4.

8 See Gregory Curtis, *The Cave Painters: Probing the Mysteries of the World's First Artists* (New York: A.A. Knopf, 2006), 16.

9 See Keith Devlin, *Mathematics: The Science of Patterns: The Search for Order in Life, Mind, and the Universe* (New York: Scientific American Library, 1997), 11–12.

10 See Albertine Gaur, *A History of Writing*, 2nd edn (London: Barrie and Jenkins Ltd., 1987), 48–51, 65–7.

11 See D. T. Potts, "Before Alexandria: Libraries in the Ancient Near East," in *The Library of Alexandria: Centre of Learning in the Ancient World*, ed. Roy MacLeod (London and New York: I. B. Tauris, 2005), 20.

12 See John Man, *Alpha Beta: How 26 Letters Shaped the Western World* (New York: Headline, 2000), ch. 2.

13 See Gaur, *A History of Writing*, 60–5.

14 See Man, *Alpha Beta*, chs. 2–3.

15 On this process, see Gaur, *A History of Writing*, 88–92.

16 See Man, *Alpha Beta*, ch. 8; Gaur, *A History of Writing*, 118–21.

17 See Geoffrey Ernest Richard Lloyd, *The Ambitions of Curiosity: Understanding the World in Ancient Greece and China* (New York: Cambridge University Press, 2002).

18 See A. Wallert, "The Reconstruction of Papyrus Manufacture: A Preliminary Investigation." *Studies in Conservation* 34 (February 1989): 1–8; Donald P. Ryan, "Papyrus." *The Biblical Archaeologist* 51 (September 1988): 132–40.

19 David Diringer, "Early Hebrew Writing." *The Biblical Archaeologist* 13 (December 1950): 74–95.

20 Raymond P. Dougherty, "Writing upon Parchment and Papyrus Among the Babylonians and the Assyrians." *Journal of the American Oriental Society* 48 (1928): 109–35.

21 See John William Bradley, *Illuminated Manuscripts* (Chicago: University of Chicago Press, 1909), 6–8.

22 Victor W. Von Hagen, "Paper and Civilization." *The Scientific Monthly* 57 (October 1943): 301–14.

23 On the Chinese origins of paper, see Tsuen-Hsuin Tsien, *Written on Bamboo and Silk: The Beginnings of Chinese Books and Inscriptions*, afterward by Edward L. Shaughnessy (Chicago and London: University of Chicago Press, 2004), ch. 7. Mayan paper, made from tree bark around 500 A.D., later diffused to the Toltecs and Aztecs. See Victor Wolfgang Von Hagen, *The Aztec and Maya Papermakers* (Mineola, NY: Dover Pub., 1999), 11.

24 Von Hagen, "Paper and Civilization," 313.

25 C. C. McCown, "Codex and Roll in the New Testament." *The Harvard Theological Review* 34 (October 1941): 219–49.

26 On the codex generally, see Casson, *Libraries in the Ancient World*, ch. 8.

27 Electronic media have now come full circle, as we "scroll" through our e-books. I am grateful to Steven Marks for reminding me of this fascinating development.

28 See Bradley, *Illuminated Manuscripts*.

29 See Eisenstein, *The Printing Press as an Agent of Change*, vol. 1, 12–15.

30 See Rosamond McKitterick, "Script and Book Production." in *Carolingian Culture: Emulation and Innovation*, ed. Rosamond McKitterick (Cambridge: Cambridge University Press, 1994), 221–34.

31 This paragraph draws on Casson, *Libraries in the Ancient World*, ch. 1.

32 See Casson, *Libraries in the Ancient World*, chs. 2–4.

33 See R. G. Tanner, "Aristotle's Works: The Possible Origins of the Alexandria Collection," *The Library of Alexandria,* ed. MacLeod.

34 See Edward Alexander Parsons, *The Alexandrian Library: Glory of the Hellenic World: Its Rise, Antiquities, and Destructions* (Amsterdam, London and New York: Elsevier Press, 1952), 163.

35 They alphabetized only the first letter of each word, so all the alphas would be together randomly. Full alphabetization first occurred around 200 A.D. but did not spread widely until the high Middle Ages. See Lloyd W. Daly, *Contributions to a History of Alphabetization in Antiquity and the Middle Ages* (Brussels: Latomus, 1967), 95–6.

36 See Parsons, *The Alexandrian Library*, 207.

37 See Casson, *Libraries in the Ancient World*, 38–9, 45.

38 Casson, *Libraries in the Ancient World*, 45–7.

39 John Willis Clark, *The Care of Books: An Essay on the Development of Libraries and their Fittings, from the Earliest Times to the End of the Eighteenth Century* (Cambridge: Cambridge University Press, 1901), 12–21.

40 Casson, *Libraries in the Ancient World*, 85–9.

41 Ibid., ch. 7.

42 Harris, *History of Libraries in the Western World*, 71–6; Allen Kent and Harold Lancour (eds), *Encyclopedia of Library and Information Science*, vol. 1 (New York: Marcel Dekker, 1968), 408–11.

43 Lerner, *The Story of Libraries*, ch. 5; C. Prince, "The Historical Context of Arabic Translation, Learning, and the Libraries of Medieval Andalusia." *Library History* 18 (July 2002): 73–87.

44 See D. N. Marshall, *History of Libraries: Ancient and Medieval* (New Delhi: Oxford & IBH Publishing Company, 1983), ch. 8.

45 John E. Cort, "The Jain Knowledge Warehouses: Traditional Libraries in India." *Journal of the American Oriental Society* 115 (January–March 1995): 77–87.

46 Endymion Wilkinson, *Chinese History: A Manual*, rev. edn (Cambridge, MA: Harvard University Press, 2000), 266.

47 Quoted in Joseph McDermott, "The Ascendance of the Imprint in China," in *Printing and Book Culture in Late Imperial China*, eds. Cynthia J. Brokaw and Kai-wing Chow (Berkeley: University of California Press, 2005), 92.

48 This paragraph draws on McDermott, "The Ascendance of the Imprint in China."

49 See John H. Winkelman, "The Imperial Library in Southern Sung China, 1127–1279: A Study of the Organization and Operation of the Scholarly Agencies of the Central Government." *Transactions of the American Philosophical Society,* New Series 64, 8 (1974): 1–61.

50 Casson, *Libraries in the Ancient World*, 137–9.

51 Ernest A. Savage, *Old English Libraries: The Making, Collection and Use of Books During the Middle Ages* (Teddington, UK: Echo Library, 2006), 14.

52 Quoted in Brian Moynahan, *The Faith: A History of Christianity* (New York: Doubleday Religious Publishing Group, 2002), 136.

53 See Harris, *History of Libraries in the Western World*, 121–4.

54 Ibid., 124.

55 See Wilkinson, *Chinese History*, 450n7.

56 On Chinese printing, see Cynthia J. Brokaw, "On the History of the Book in China," in *Printing and Book Culture in Late Imperial China*, eds. Brokaw and Chow, 8–11.

57 Pow-key Sohn, "Early Korean Printing." *Journal of the American Oriental Society* 79 (April–June 1959): 96–103; Man *Gutenberg*, 111–13.

58 See Brokaw, "On the History of the Book in China," 11.

59 See Richard W. Bulliet, "Medieval Arabic Tarsh: A Forgotten Chapter in the History of Printing." *Journal of the American Oriental Society* 107 (July–September 1987): 427–38.

60 Man, *Gutenberg*, 89.

61 Robert Friedel, *A Culture of Improvement: Technology and the Western Millennium* (Cambridge, MA: MIT Press, 2007), 115.

62 On the early man, see Thomas J. Misa, *Leonardo to the Internet: Technology and Culture from the Renaissance to the Present* (Baltimore: The Johns Hopkins University Press, 2004), 20; Stephan Füssel, *Gutenberg and the Impact of Printing*, trans. Douglas Martin (Aldershot, UK and Burlington, VT: Ashgate Publishing, 2005), 11–12; Man, *Gutenberg*, 25–9.

63 See Füssel, *Gutenberg and the Impact of Printing*, 10; Man, *Gutenberg*, 30–1.

64 Ibid., 12–15; Man, *Gutenberg*, 56–8.

65 See Misa, *Leonardo to the Internet*, 21–2; Füssel, *Gutenberg and the Impact of Printing*, 13–18; Man, *Gutenberg*, 122–33.

66 See Man, *Gutenberg*, 133–6; Füssel, *Gutenberg and the Impact of Printing*, 16–17.

67 Ibid., 142–60; Füssel, *Gutenberg and the Impact of Printing*, 21–32.

68 See Eisenstein, *The Printing Press as an Agent of Change*, vol. 1, 60.

69 See Laura Light, "The Bible and the Individual: The Thirteen-Century Paris Bible," in *The Practice of the Bible in the Middle Ages: Production, Reception, and Performance in Western Christianity*, eds. Susan Boynton and Diane J. Reilly (New York: Columbia University Press, 2011), 231–2.

70 See Man, *Gutenberg*, 152.

71 Ibid., 164–78; Füssel, *Gutenberg and the Impact of Printing*, 18–25.

72 On Fust and Schöffer, see Man, *Gutenberg*, 185–95; Füssel, *Gutenberg and the Impact of Printing*, 18–25, 52–6.

73 See Man, *Gutenberg*, 243; Füssel, *Gutenberg and the Impact of Printing*, 568.

74 On the early spread of printing, see Füssel, *Gutenberg and the Impact of Printing*, 59–70; Lotta Helinga, "The Gutenberg Revolutions," in *A Companion to the History of the Book*, eds. Simon Eliot and Jonathan Rose (Oxford and Malden, MA: Blackwell Publishers, 2007).

75 Statistics in Elizabeth Eisenstein, "Some Conjectures about the Impact of Printing on Western Society and Thought: A Preliminary Report." *Journal of Modern History* 40 (1968): 8.

76 Augustus Pallotta, "Venetian Printers and Spanish Literature in Sixteenth-Century Italy." *Comparative Literature* 43 (Winter 1991): 20–42 (here: 22).

77 Donald M. Nicol, *Byzantium and Venice: A Study in Diplomatic and Cultural Relations* (Cambridge: Cambridge University Press, 1992), 419–20.

78 See Martin Lowry, *The World of Aldus Manutius: Business and Scholarship in Renaissance Venice* (Ithaca: Cornell University Press, 1979).

79 See Christopher May, "The Venetian Moment: New Technologies, Legal Innovation and the Institutional Origins of Intellectual Property," in *Intellectual Property Rights: Critical Concepts in Law*, vol. 3, ed. David Vaver (Abingdon, UK and New York: Routledge, 2006), 20; S. H. Steinberg, *Five Hundred Years of Printing*, 3rd edn (Hamondsworth, UK and Baltimore: British Library, 1974), 141.

80 See Robert Jean Knecht, *The Rise and Fall of Renaissance France, 1483–1610*, 2nd edn (Oxford and Malden, MA: Blackwell Publishers, 2001), 171.

81 Deborah Parker, *Commentary and Ideology: Dante in the Renaissance* (Durham, NC: Duke University Press, 1993), 132.

82 See Edward Hodnett, *Francis Barlow: First Master of English Book Illustration* (Berkeley: University of California Press, 1978), 67.

83 See Norman Blake, *Caxton and His World* (London: André Deutsch, 1969).

84 See Jaroslav Pelikan, "The Other Face of the Renaissance." *Bulletin of the American Academy of Arts and Sciences* 50 (April 1997): 52–63 (here: 58–9); Alistair Hamilton, "Humanists and the Bible," in *The Cambridge Companion to Renaissance Humanism*, ed. Jill Kraye (New York: Cambridge University Press, 1996).

85 Quoted in Steinberg, *Five Hundred Years of Printing*, 98.

86 Pelikan, "The Other Face of the Renaissance," 61–2; Hamilton, "Humanists and the Bible," in *The Cambridge Companion to Renaissance Humanism*, ed. Kraye.

87 Pelikan, "The Other Face of the Renaissance," 55.

88 Statistic cited in Philip G. Altbach and Edith S. Hoshino (eds), *International Book Publishing: An Encyclopedia* (New York: Fitzroy Dearborn Publishers, 1995), 160.

89 See Steinberg, *Five Hundred Years of Printing*, 158.

90 See Alan G. Hodgkiss, *Discovering Antique Maps*, 5th edn (Princes Risborough, UK: Shire Publications Ltd, 1996), 32.

91 See Edward Grant, *God and Reason in the Middle Ages* (Cambridge: Cambridge University Press, 2001), 340.

92 See Walter L. Strauss (ed.), *The Complete Engravings, Etchings and Drypoints of Albrecht Durer* (Miseola, NY: Courier Dover Publications, 1972), viii.

93 See William A. Locy, "The Earliest Printed Illustrations of Natural History." *The Scientific Monthly* 13 (September 1921): 238–58.

94 See Wilber Applebaum (ed.), *Encyclopedia of the Scientific Revolution: From Copernicus to Newton* (New York: Garland Publishing, 2000).

95 See Paul Zumthor and Catherine Peebles. "The Medieval Travel Narrative." *New Literary History* 25 (Autumn 1994): 809–24.

96 See Peter C. Mancall, *Hakluyt's Promise: An Elizabethan's Obsession for an English America* (New Haven: Yale University Press 2007).

97 Lerner, *The Story of Libraries*, 86.

98 See George Huppert, *The Style of Paris: Renaissance Origins of the French Enlightenment* (Bloomington, IN: Indiana University Press, 1999), ch. 5 (here: p. 63).

99 Sabrina Alcorn Baron, Eric N. Lindquist and Eleanor F. Shevlin (eds), *Agent of Change: Print Culture Studies after Elizabeth L. Eisenstein* (Amherst, MA: University of Massachusetts Press, 2007), 216.

100 Gary Marker, "Russia and the 'Printing Revolution': Notes and Observations." *Slavic Review* 41 (1982): 269–81.

101 See Damon L. Woods, *The Philippines: A Global Studies Handbook* (Santa Barbara, CA: ABC-CLIO, 2006), 30–1.

102 Samuel Adams Drake, *The Making of New England* (Scituate, MA: Digital Scanning, Inc, 2001 [1896]), 216–17.

103 Bernard Lewis, *The Muslim Discovery of Europe* (New York: W.W. Norton & Company, 2001), 50. See also George N. Atiyeh, "The Book in the Modern Arab World: The Cases of Lebanon and Egypt," in *The Book in the Islamic World*, ed. George N. Atiyeh (Albany: State University of New York Press, 1995).

104 See Francis Robinson, "Technology and Religious Change: Islam and the Impact of Print." *Modern Asian Studies* 27 (February 1993): 229–51 (here: 236–9).

105 See Muhsin Mahdi, "From the Manuscript Age to the Age of Printed Books," in *The Book in the Islamic World*, 1–2.

106 See Albert A. Altman, "Korea's First Newspaper: The Japanese *Chosen Shinpo*." *The Journal of Asian Studies* 43 (August 1984): 685–96.

107 Sidney L. Jackson, *Libraries and Librarianship in the West: A Brief History* (New York: McGraw-Hill, 1974), 197.

108 Noémie Lesquins, "Bibliothèque Nationale de France," in *Encyclopedia of Library and Information Science*, 4 vols., 2nd edn, ed. Miriam A. Drake (New York: Marcel Dekker, 2003), vol. 1, 329–30.

109 See Bill Katz, *Cuneiform to Computer: A History of Reference Sources* (Lanham, MD and Folkestone, UK: Scarecrow Press, 1998), 3.

110 Miles Oscar Price and Harry Bitner, *Effective Legal Research: A Practical Manual of Law Books and Their Use* (Boston: Prentice-Hall, 1953), 221.

111 See Huppert, *The Style of Paris*.

112 Ibid., ch. 1.

113 For concerns about mechanical printing expressed by some early Western commentators, see Elizabeth L. Eisenstein, *Divine Art, Infernal Machine: The Reception of Printing in the West from First Impressions to the Sense of an Ending* (Philadelphia and Oxford: University of Pennsylvania Press, 2011), 7, 45–7, 88, 92, 96, 143.

Chapter 7

1 David Daniell, *William Tyndale: A Biography* (New Haven: Yale University Press 1994), 79.

2 Daniell, *William Tyndale*, 1.

3 Ibid., 382.

4 See Lesley Janette Smith and Jane H. M. Taylor (eds), *Women, the Book, and the Godly: Selected Proceedings of the St. Hilda's Conference*, 1993 (Woodbridge, UK and Rochester, NY: Boydell & Brewer, 1995), 2–4.

5 See Nicholas Mann, "The Origins of Humanism," in *The Cambridge Companion to Renaissance Humanism*, ed. Jill Kraye (New York: Cambridge University Press, 1996); Charles G. Nauert, Jr., *Humanism and the Culture of Renaissance Europe* (Cambridge: Cambridge University Press, 1995), ch. 1.

6 Gideon Burton, "From Ars dictaminis to Ars conscribendi epistolis: Renaissance Letter-Writing Manuals in the Context of Humanism," in *Letter-Writing Manuals and Instruction from Antiquity to the Present*, eds. Carol Poster and Linda C. Mitchell (Columbia, SC: University of South Carolina Press, 2007).

7 John W. O'Malley, *Four Cultures of the West* (Cambridge, MA: Harvard University Press, 2004), 103–4, 149–53.

8 Interestingly, he discovered the importance of the Scriptures only after he reached 40; he termed this a "damnable lateness." See Alistair Hamilton, "Humanists and the Bible," in *The Cambridge Companion to Renaissance Humanism*, ed. Kraye, 100.

9 *Syncretism in the West. Pico's 900 Theses (1486): The Evolution of Traditional Religious and Philosophical Systems*, trans. S. A. Farmer (Tempe, AZ: Medieval and Renaissance Texts and Studies, 1998), x–xi.

10 Pico della Mirandola, *On the Dignity of Man*, excerpted in *The Traditions of the Western World*, ed. J. H. Hexter et al. (Chicago: University of Chicago Press, 1967), 302–5.

11 On Bruni's historical work, see Nauert, *Humanism and the Culture of Renaissance Europe*, 30–3.

12 See O'Malley, *Four Cultures of the West*, 160–1; Nauert, *Humanism and the Culture of Renaissance Europe*, 4, 56.

13 See Max Dvorák, "The New Relationship to Nature," in *Modern Perspectives in Western Art History: An Anthology of Twentieth-Century Writings on the Visual Arts*, ed. W. Eugène Kleinbauer (New York: Holt, Rinehart and Winston, 1971), 399–400.

14 Norman Davies makes this point in *Europe: A History* (New York: Oxford University Press, 1996), 479. See also Joanna Woods-Marsden, *Renaissance Self-Portraiture: The Visual Construction of Identity and the Social Status of the Artist* (New Haven: Yale University Press 1998).

15 See Jonathan W. Zophy, *A Short History of Renaissance and Reformation Europe: Dances over Fire and Water*, 2nd edn (Upper Saddle River, NJ: Prentice Hall, 1999), 113.

16 See M. Kemp, *The Science of Art: Optical Themes in Western Art From Brunelleschi to Seurat* (New Haven: Yale University Press 1992); Nauert, *Humanism and the Culture of Renaissance Europe*, 77–80.

17 Daniel D. Cavalcanti et al., "Anatomy, Technology, Art, and Culture: Toward a Realistic Perspective of the Brain." *Neurosurg Focus* 27 (September 2009): 1–22 (here: 2, 6).

18 James Hankins, *Plato in the Italian Renaissance*, 2 vols. (Leiden and New York: E.J. Brill, 1990), vol. 1, 208, 216–25.

19 A. G. Keller, "A Byzantine Admirer of 'Western' Progress: Cardinal Bessarion." *Cambridge Historical Journal* 11 (1955): 343–8.

20 See, for example, Charles L. Stinger, *The Renaissance in Rome* (Bloomington, IN: Indiana University Press, 1998), 28.

21 See Carter Lindberg, *The European Reformations*, 2nd edn (Chichester, UK and Malden, MA: Blackwell Publishers, 2010), 80.

22 As quoted in William Samuel Lilly, *The Claims of Christianity* (New York: D. Appleton and Co., 1891), 191.

23 See Innocenzo Venchi et al. (eds), *Fra Angelico and the Chapel of Nicholas*, photo. Alessandro Bracchetti et al. (Vatican City State: Edizioni Musei Vaticani, 1999);

Michael H. Harris, *History of Libraries in the Western World*, 4th edn (Lanham, MD: Scarecrow Press, 1999), 124.

24 William John Kubelbeck, *The Sacred Penitentiaria and its Relations to Faculties of Ordinaries and Priests* (Somerset, OH: Rosary Press, 1918), 114.

25 See Diana Webb, *Pilgrims and Pilgrimage in the Medieval West* (London and New York: I. B. Tauris, 1999), 14–16.

26 See Jean Richard, *The Crusades, c.1071–c.1291* (Cambridge: Cambridge University Press, 1999), 23–4.

27 See J. van Herwaarden, *Between Saint James and Erasmus: Studies in Late-Medieval Religious Life: Devotions and Pilgrimages in the Netherlands*, trans. Wendie Shaffer (Leiden: E.J. Brill, 2003), 58.

28 Lindberg, *The European Reformations*, 71–3.

29 See David L. Larsen, *The Company of the Preachers: A History of Biblical Preaching from the Old Testament to the Modern Era* (Grand Rapids, MI: W. B. Eerdmans Pub. Co., 1998), 107–38.

30 See William C. Creasy, trans., *The Imitation of Christ by Thomas a Kempis: A New Reading of the 1441 Latin Autograph Manuscript*, 2nd edn (Macon, GA: Mercer University Press, 2007).

31 See Gabriel Audisio, *The Waldensian Dissent: Persecution and Survival, c.1170–c.1570*, trans. Claire Davison (Cambridge: Cambridge University Press, 1999).

32 Smith and Taylor (eds), *Women, the Book, and the Godly*, 2–4 (quotation: 4).

33 Audisio, *The Waldensian Dissent*, chs. 8–9.

34 See Malcolm Lambert, *The Cathars* (Oxford: Oxford University Press, 1998).

35 See Stephen Edmund Lahey, *John Wyclif* (Oxford: Oxford University Press, 2009); Henry Hargreaves, "The Wycliffite Versions," in *The West from the Fathers to the Reformation*, ed. G. W. H. Lampe, vol. 2 of *The Cambridge History of the Bible*, 3 vols. (Cambridge: Cambridge University Press, 1969).

36 Quoted in Neil R. Lightfoot, *How We Got the Bible*, rev. 3rd edn (Grand Rapids, MI: W. B. Eerdmans Pub. Co., 2003), 175.

37 See John Stacey, *John Wyclif and Reform* (Philadelphia: Westminister Press, 1964); Anne Hudson, *The Premature Reformation: Wycliffite Texts and Lollard History* (Oxford and New York: Oxford University Press, 1988); Richard Rex, *The Lollards: Social History in Perspective* (New York: Palgrave, 2002).

38 See Lindberg, *The European Reformations*, 44; Jean W. Sedlar, *East Central Europe in the Middle Ages, 1000–1500* (Seattle: University of Washington Press, 1994), 183–7, 389, 418–19, 472.

39 See Antony Black, "The Conciliar Movement," in *The Cambridge History of Medieval Political Thought c.350–c.1450*, ed. J. H. Burns (Cambridge: Cambridge University Press, 1988).

40 See Marsilius of Padua, *The Defender of the Peace*, ed. Annabel Brett (Cambridge: Cambridge University Press, 2006).

41 See Paul E. Sigmund, Jr., "The Influence of Marsilius of Padua on XVth-Century Conciliarism." *Journal of the History of Ideas* 23 (July–September 1962): 392–402 (here: 394).

42 Sigmund, Jr., "The Influence of Marsilius of Padua," 393–4.

43 Lindberg, *The European Reformations*, 46–7.

44 Ibid., 49.

45 See Frank K. Flinn, *Encyclopedia of Catholicism* (New York: Infobase Pub., 2007), 182.

46 Sedlar, *East Central Europe in the Middle Ages*, 186.

47 See Maurice Keen, "The Changing Scene: Guns, Gunpowder, and Permanent Armies," in *Medieval Warfare: A History*, ed. Maurice Keen (Oxford: Oxford University Press, 1999b), 279.

48 See Sedlar, *East Central Europe in the Middle Ages*, 186–7.

49 See F. Donald Logan, *A History of the Church in the Middle Ages*, 2nd edn (Abingdon, UK and New York: Routledge, 2013), 311.

50 See Lindberg, *The European Reformations*, 325.

51 See Kurt Stadtwald, *Roman Popes and German Patriots: Antipapalism in the Politics of the German Humanist Movement from Gregor Heimburg to Martin Luther* (Geneva: Librairie Droz, 1996), 60–70.

52 See Lewis W. Spitz, "The Philosophy of Conrad Celtis, German Arch-Humanist." *Studies in the Renaissance* 1 (1954): 22–37 (here: 29–33).

53 See the address in Kenneth R. Bartlett and Margaret McGlynn (eds), *Humanism and the Northern Renaissance* (Toronto: Canadian Scholars' Press, 2000), 73–86.

54 This paragraph draws on Roland Bainton, *Here I Stand—A Life of Martin Luther* (New York: Abingdon-Cokesbury Press, 1950), chs. 1–2; Lindberg, *The European Reformations*, 54–9. See also Martin Brecht, *Martin Luther: His Road to Reformation, 1483–1521*, trans. James L. Schaaf (Minneapolis: Fortress Press, 1993a).

55 See Bainton, *Here I Stand*, ch. 3; Lindberg, *The European Reformations*, 66–70.

56 Quoted in Martin Brecht, *Martin Luther: The Preservation of the Church, 1532–1546*, trans. James L. Schaaf (Minneapolis: Fortress Press, 1993c), 180.

57 On the doctrine of the two realms, see Oswald Bayer, *Martin Luther's Theology: A Contemporary Interpretation*, trans. Thomas H. Trapp (Grand Rapids, MI: W. B. Eerdmans Pub. Co., 2008), ch. 14.

58 Lindberg, *The European Reformations*, ch. 5.

59 Bainton, *Here I Stand*, 60–7; Lindberg, *The European Reformations*, 82.

60 Lindberg, *The European Reformations*, 35.

61 See Mark U. Edwards, *Printing Propaganda and Martin Luther* (Minneapolis: Fortress Press, 2005), 1–2.

62 Cited in Eisenstein, *The Printing Press as an Agent of Change*, 303.

63 Edwards makes this claim in *Printing Propaganda and Martin Luther*, xii.

64 See Andrew Pettegree and Matthew Hall, "The Reformation and the Book: A Reconsideration." *Historical Journal* 47 (December 2004): 785–808 (here: 787–8).

65 See the highly detailed chronology of events in C. Scott Dixon, *The Reformation in Germany* (Oxford: Oxford University Press, 2002), xix–xii.

66 Brecht, *Martin Luther: His Road to Reformation*, 299–323; Lindberg, *The European Reformations*, 80–3.

67 As quoted in Bainton, *Here I Stand*, 115.

68 Bainton, *Here I Stand*, 115–16.

69 The text is published in Henry Bettenson and Chris Maunder (eds), *The Documents of the Christian Church*, 4th edn (New York: Oxford University Press, 2011), 204–9 (here: 206).

70 See the document in Bettenson and Maunder (eds), *The Documents of the Christian Church*, 209–12.

71 See Robert C. Croken, *Luther's First Front: The Eucharist as Sacrifice* (Ottawa: University of Ottawa Press, 1990), 22–8.

72 Bainton, *Here I Stand*, 105–10.

73 See Martin Luther, *On Christian Liberty*, trans. Harold John Grimm and William Lambert (Minneapolis: Fortress Press, 2003), 2.

74 Bainton, *Here I Stand*, 84, 127; Eric W. Gritsch, *A History of Lutheranism* (Minneapolis: Fortress Press, 2002), 25–6.

75 Bainton, *Here I Stand*, 127–8.

76 See Heiko Augustinus Oberman, *Luther: Man Between God and the Devil*, trans. Eileen Walliser-Schwarzbart (New Haven: Yale University Press 2006), 186; Bainton, *Here I Stand*, 121–8 (quotation on p. 128).

77 This paragraph draws on Gritsch, *A History of Lutheranism*, 28–35; Lindberg, *The European Reformations*, 83–5 (quotation: 84).

78 See, for example, Lindberg, *The European Reformations*, 92–8; Dixon, *The Reformation in Germany*, 111.

79 See Dixon, *The Reformation in Germany*, 31; Bainton, *Here I Stand*, 156.

80 Ibid., 38.

81 See Gritsch, *A History of Lutheranism*, 24–5.

82 Lindberg, *The European Reformations*, 94; Bainton, *Here I Stand*, 156.

83 Bainton, *Here I Stand*, 180–90.

84 See Brecht, *Martin Luther: His Road to Reformation*, 381.

85 Quoted in Carter Lindberg, *The Third Reformation: Charismatic Movements and the Lutheran Tradition* (Macon, GA: Mercer University Press, 1983), 62. See also Lindberg, *The European Reformations*, 102–3.

86 Quoted in Bainton, *Here I Stand*, 162.

87 Lindberg, *The European Reformations*, 101; Dixon, *The Reformation in Germany*, 87–8.

88 Quoted in Bainton, *Here I Stand*, 165.

89 Martin Brecht, *Martin Luther: Shaping and Defining the Reformation, 1521–1532*, trans. James L. Schaaf (Minneapolis: Fortress Press, 1993b), 59–65.

90 Lindberg, *The European Reformations*, 94.

91 See Brecht, *Martin Luther: His Road to Reformation*, 358.

92 This paragraph draws on Carlos M. N. Eire, *War Against the Idols: The Reformation of Worship from Erasmus to Calvin* (Cambridge: Cambridge University Press, 1986), 72–86; Lindberg, *The European Reformations*, 181–6.

93 See R. Ward Holder, *Crisis and Renewal: The Era of the Reformations* (Louisville: John Knox Press, 2009), 104; Sigrun Haude, "Anabaptism," in *The Reformation World*, ed. Andrew Pettegree (London and New York: Routledge, 2000), 48.

94 See Bainton, *Here I Stand*, 101; Peter George Wallace, *The Long European Reformation: Religion, Political Conflict, and the Search for Conformity, 1350–1750* (Basingstoke, UK and New York: Palgrave Macmillan, 2004), 86.

95 See Peter Blickle, "Communal Reformation and Peasant Piety: The Peasant Reformation and Its Late Medieval Origins." *Central European History* 20 (September–December 1987): 216–28.

96 George H. Waring, "The Silver Miners of the Erzgebirge and the Peasants' War of 1525 in the Light of Recent Research." *The Sixteenth Century Journal* 18 (Summer 1987): 231–47.

97 See Michael Alford Andrews, *The Birth of Europe: Colliding Continents and the Destiny of Nations* (London: BBC Books, 1991), 159.

98 Blickle, "Communal Reformation and Peasant Piety," 217.

99 Blickle makes this argument in "Communal Reformation and Peasant Piety," 226.

100 Carter Lindberg thus entitles a subsection of *The European Reformations*, 158–68.

101 Lindberg, *The European Reformations*, 155–6.

102 Brecht, *Martin Luther: Shaping and Defining the Reformation*, 190–4; Lindberg, *The European Reformations*, 155–6.

103 As quoted in Lindberg, *The European Reformations*, 158.

104 Bainton, *Here I* Stand, 215–20; Wallace, *The Long European Reformation*, 86–8.

105 See Lindberg, *The European Reformations*, 159.

106 See Oberman, *Luther: Man Between God and the Devil*, 359–60; Lindberg, *The European Reformations*, 220.

107 See Wallace, *The Long European Reformation*, 115–16; Lindberg, *The European Reformations*, 227–32.

108 See Theodore G. Tappert, trans. and ed., *The Augsburg Confession* (Minneapolis: Augsburg Publishing House, 1980).

109 Lindberg, *The European Reformations*, 216–18.

110 Wallace, *The Long European Reformation*, 125–6; Lindberg, *The European Reformations*, 230–2.

111 See Diarmaid MacCulloch, *The Reformation: A History* (New York: Viking, 2004), 262–70; Wallace, *The Long European Reformation*, 150–1.

112 On Calvin, see Wallace, *The Long European Reformation*, 102–6; MacCulloch, *The Reformation*, 195–8, 230–61; Lindberg, *The European Reformations*, ch. 10.

113 The standard modern translation is John Calvin, *Institution of the Christian Religion*, trans. Ford Lewis Battles (Atlanta: John Knox Press, 1975).

114 As quoted in Lindberg, *The European Reformations*, 241.

115 See John Witte, Jr., *From Sacrament to Contract: Marriage, Religion, and Law in the Western Tradition* (Louisville: Westminster/Knox, 1997), 81–2.

116 See Lindberg, *The European Reformations*, 249–51.

117 Lindberg, *The European Reformations*, 252–3; David Bagchi and Steinmetz, David C. (eds), *The Cambridge Companion to Reformation Theology* (Cambridge: Cambridge University Press, 2004), 118–20.

118 This doctrine is expounded in the 1559 edition of the *Institutes*. See John Calvin, *Institutes of the Christian Religion*, trans. Henry Beveridge (Grand Rapids, MI: W. B. Eerdmans Pub. Co., 1989), book 4, ch. 21.

119 Andrew Pettegree, *The French Book and the European Book World* (Leiden: E.J. Brill, 2007), 92–3, 312; Lindberg, *The European Reformations*, 257–8.

120 This and the next paragraph draw upon Lindberg, *The European Reformations*, ch. 11; Patrick Collinson, *The Reformation: A History* (New York: Random House Publishing Group, 2006), 86–96.

121 William T. Cavanaugh argues persuasively that separating politics from religion is anachronistic in this era and that the modern state was the primary cause of these wars. See his *The Myth of Religious Violence: Secular Ideology and the Roots of Modern Conflict* (Oxford and New York: Oxford University Press, 2009).

122 See Winthrop S. Hudson, "Democratic Freedom and Religious Faith in the Reformed Tradition." *Church History* 15 (September 1946): 177–94.

123 See Andrew Fix, "Radical Reformation and Second Reformation in Holland: The Intellectual Consequences of the Sixteenth-Century Religious Upheaval and the Coming of a Rational World View." *The Sixteenth Century Journal* 18 (Spring 1987): 63–80.

124 See Charles C. Moskos and John Whiteclay Chambers II, "The Secularlization of Conscience," in *The New Conscientious Objection: From Sacred to Secular Resistance*, eds. Charles C. Moskos and John Whiteclay Chambers II (New York: Oxford University Press, 1993), 10–11.

125 R. Po-Chia Hsia and Henk van Nierop (eds), *Calvinism and Religious Toleration in the Dutch Golden Age* (New York: Cambridge University Press, 2002); Willem Frijhoff, "How Plural Were the Religious Worlds in Early Modern Europe? Critical Reflections from the Netherlandic Experience," in *Living with Religious Diversity in Early-Modern Europe*, eds. C. Scott Dixon, Dagmar Freist, and Mark Greengrass (Farmham, UK and Burlington, VT: Ashgate Publishing, 2009).

126 On Tyndale, see Daniell, *William Tyndale*; Lindberg, *The European Reformations*, 299–301.

127 See Lindberg, *The European Reformations*, 294–6.

128 On Henry's reformation, see G. W. Bernard, *The King's Reformation: Henry VIII and the Remaking of the English Church* (New Haven: Yale University Press, 2005). On the Reformation in England broadly, see A. G. Dickens, *The English Reformation*, 2nd edn (London: B.T. Batsford, 1989).

129 See Stanford E. Lehmberg, *The Reformation Parliament 1529–1536* (Cambridge: Cambridge University Press, 1970).

130 Quoted in David Gordon Newcombe, *Henry VIII and the English Reformation* (New York: Routledge, 1995), 45.

131 As quoted in Lacey Baldwin Smith, *Fools, Martyrs, Traitors: The Story of Martyrdom in the Western World* (Evanston, IL: Northwestern University Press, 1999), 167.

132 See Lindberg, *The European Reformations*, 303.

133 See Dickens, *The English Reformation*, 74–8; Richard Lachmann, *Capitalists in Spite of Themselves: Elite Conflict and Economic Transitions in Early Modern Europe* (New York: Oxford University Press, 2000), 100–7.

134 See Dickens, *The English Reformation*, 252.

135 See Lindberg, *The European Reformations*, 308–9; Dickens, *The English Reformation*, ch. 12.

136 Ibid., 310–15; Dickens, *The English Reformation*, ch. 14.

137 Ibid., 316–20; MacColloch, *The Reformation*, 368–71.

138 See Clare Kellar, *Scotland, England, and the Reformation 1534–1561* (Oxford and New York: Oxford University Press, 2003), 185–219, 221–3.

139 See D. McRoberts, "Material Destruction Caused by the Scottish Reformation," in *Essays on the Scottish Reformation 1513–1625*, ed. David McRoberts (Glasgow: Burns, 1962).

140 David P Daniel, "Calvinism in Hungary: The Theological and Ecclesiastical Transition to the Performance Faith," in *Calvinism in Europe, 1540–1620*, eds. Andrew Pettegree, Alastair Duke, and Gillian Lewis (Cambridge: Cambridge University Press, 1994).

141 MacColloch, *The Reformation*, 88–90; Lindberg, *The European Reformations*, 321–3.

142 See Stinger, *The Renaissance in Rome*, 13; Lindberg, *The European Reformations*, 325.

143 See, for example, Edward Peters, *Inquisition* (Berkeley and Los Angeles: University of California Press, 1989); Henry Kamen, *The Spanish Inquisition: A Historical Revision* (New Haven: Yale University Press 1998).

144 See William Monter, *Frontiers of Heresy: The Spanish Inquisition from the Basque Lands to Sicily* (Cambridge: Cambridge University Press, 1990), xiii.

145 See Elizabeth L. Eisenstein, *Divine Art, Infernal Machine: The Reception of Printing in the West from First Impressions to the Sense of an Ending* (Philadelphia and Oxford: University of Pennsylvania Press, 2011) 13, 33.

146 On the Inquisition and lists of prohibited books (Index Librorum Prohibitorum), see Paul F. Grendler, "Printing and Censorship," in *The Cambridge History of Renaissance Philosophy*, eds. Charles B. Schmitt and Quentin Skinner (Cambridge: Cambridge University Press, 1988); Lindberg, *The European Reformations*, 328–33; Wallace, *The Long European Reformation*, 127.

147 See Eisenstein, *Divine Art, Infernal Machine*, 49.

148 See John Patrick Donnelly, *Ignatius of Loyola: Founder of the Jesuits* (New York: Pearson/Longman, 2004); Lindberg, *The European Reformations*, 333–8.

149 See R. Holder, *Crisis and Renewal: The Era of the Reformations* (Louisville, KY: Westminster John Knox Press, 2009), 190–208; Lindberg, *The European Reformations*, 338–44.

150 See Lindberg, *The European Reformations*, 336–7; Barbara B. Diefendorf, *From Penitence to Charity: Pious Women and the Catholic Reformation in Paris* (New York: Oxford University Press, 2002), 118–31.

151 See O'Malley, *Four Cultures of the West*, 227–8.

152 Ibid., 225–9.

153 As quoted in Doug Underwood, *From Yahweh to Yahoo!: The Religious Roots of the Secular Press* (Urbana, IL: University of Illinois Press, 2002), 36.

154 As quoted in Joseph Black and Joseph Laurence Black (eds), *The Broadview Anthology of British Literature: The Renaissance and the Early Seventeenth Century*, 2nd edn (Toronto: Broadview Press, 2010), 97.

155 See Lindberg, *The European Reformations*, 35.

156 These statistics are presented in Pettegree and Hall "The Reformation and the Book," 793–5.

157 See A. G. Little, "Theological Schools in Medieval England." *The English Historical Review* 55 (October 1940): 624–30.

158 See John Nelson Milson, "Schools and Literacy in Later Medieval England." *British Journal of Educational Studies* 11 (November 1962): 16–27.

159 Milson, "Schools and Literacy in Later Medieval England," 25.

160 O'Malley makes this claim in *Four Cultures of the West*, 154, 163–4.

161 This paragraph draws on George Huppert, *Public Schools in Renaissance France* (Urbana: University of Illinois Press, 1984).

162 See, for example, Gerald Strauss, "Liberal or Illiberal Arts?" *Journal of Social History* 19 (Winter 1985): 361–7.

163 Such humanists are discussed in George Huppert, *The Style of Paris: Renaissance Origins of the French Enlightenment* (Bloomington, IN: Indiana University Press, 1999).

164 See Edwards, *Printing, Propaganda, and Martin Luther*, 38.

165 See H. G. Haile, "Luther and Literacy." *PMLA* 91 (October 1976): 816–28.

166 Statistics in Rab Houston, "Literacy and Society in the West, 1500–1850." *Social History* 8 (October 1983): 269–93.

167 See Cynthia J. Brokaw, "On the History of the Book in China," in *Printing and Book Culture in Late Imperial China*, eds. Cynthia J. Brokaw and Kai-wing Chow (Berkeley: University of California Press, 2005), 13–14.

168 See Lindberg, *The European Reformations*, 352.

169 See Anders Schinkel, *Conscience and Conscientious Objections* (Amsterdam: Amsterdam University Press, 2007), 406–7.

170 On this struggle, see Fix, "Radical Reformation and Second Reformation in Holland."

171 See Fix, "Radical Reformation and Second Reformation in Holland," 65.

172 This paragraph draws on Atle Grahl-Madsen, "The European Tradition of Asylum and the Development of Refugee Law." *Journal of Peace Research* 3 (1966): 278–89.

173 Quoted in Quentin Skinner, *The Foundations of Modern Political Thought,* vol. 2: *The Age of Reformation* (Cambridge: Cambridge University Press, 1978), 208.

174 See Skinner, *The Foundations of Modern Political Thought*, vol. 2, 201–23.

175 For France, see Paul Saenger, "The Earliest French Resistance Theories: The Role of the Burgundian Court." *The Journal of Modern History* 51 (December 1979): D1225–D49.

176 See John Calvin, *Institution of the Christian Religion*, 310. Calvin argued forcefully that Christians have a strict duty to obey all established authorities, as God's agents on Earth, except if such obedience should "lead us away from obedience" to God. See ibid., 284–311 (quotation: 310).

177 See Skinner, *The Foundations of Modern Political Thought*, vol. 2, 223–4, 234–7 (quotation: 237).

178 On the radical Calvinist theorists, see Skinner, *The Foundations of Modern Political Thought*, vol. 2, 320–3. On the theoretical right to resist, see ibid., ch. 9.

179 See Hudson, "Democratic Freedom and Religious Faith in the Reformed Tradition," 178.

180 See Lynn Hunt, *Inventing Human Rights: A History* (New York and London: W.W. Norton & Company, 2007), 147.

181 As quoted in Lindberg, *The European Reformations*, 365.

182 See Brad S. Gregory, *The Unintended Reformation: How a Religious Revolution Secularized Society* (Cambridge, MA: Harvard University Press, 2012).

183 See Lindberg, *The European Reformations*, 63–4.

Chapter 8

1 See Ralph Colp, Jr., "'Confessing a Murder'": Darwin's First Revelations about Transmutation." *Isis* 77 (March 1986): 8–32.

2 See Ernst Mayr, "Darwin's Influence on Modern Thought." *Scientific American* (July 2000): 79–83.

3 See Francis Collins, *The Language of God: A Scientist Presents Evidence for* Belief (New York: Free Press, 2006). For a stimulating debate on the relationship of faith and science, see Donald C. Dennett and Alvin Plantinga, *Science and Religion: Are They Compatible?* (New York: Oxford University Press, 2011).

4 See, for example, Jack Goody, *The East in the West* (Cambridge: Cambridge University Press, 1996), 224, 233–4.

5 As quoted in Robert King Merton, *On the Shoulders of Giants: A Shandean Postscript* (Chicago and London: University of Chicago Press, 1993), 1.

6 Joseph Needham makes this argument in *Science in Traditional China: A Comparative Perspective* (Cambridge, MA: Harvard University Press, 1981), 8.

7 See David Lindberg, *The Beginnings of Western Science: The European Scientific Tradition in Philosophical, Religious, and Institutional Context, 600 BC. to AD. 1450* (Chicago: University of Chicago Press, 1992), ch. 1.

8 One can nevertheless argue that most pre-Socratic Greek philosophers had a visionary or even spiritual approach to reality. See Seyyed Hossein Nasr, *Islamic Philosophy from its Origin to the Present: Philosophy in the Land of Prophesy* (Albany: State University of New York Press, 2006), 1–4.

9 Details and argument from Wen-yuan Qian, *The Great Inertia: Scientific Stagnation in Traditional China* (London and Dover, NH: Croom Helm, 1985), 75–6.

10 See Bryan E. Penprase, *The Power of Stars: How Celestial Observations Have Shaped Civilization* (New York: Springer, 2011), 110–12.

11 On Plato's thought, see Robert G. Turnbull, *The* Parmenides *and Plato's Late Philosophy* (Toronto: University of Toronto Press, 1998), 21, 186, 190.

12 On the methods and works of Aristotle, see Richard McKeon, Introduction, in *The Basic Works of Aristotle*, ed. Richard McKeon (New York: Random House, 1941); Lindberg, *The Beginnings of Western Science*, ch. 3.

13 Lindberg, *The Beginnings of Western Science*, 27–34, 70–81.

14 On Hellenistic scientific thought, see George Sarton, *Hellenistic Science and Culture in the Last Three Centuries B.C.* (New York: Dover Pub., 1987).

15 See Lindberg, *The Beginnings of Western Science*, chap. 6; Sarton, *Hellenistic Science and Culture*, chs. 8–9, 22.

16 On the Mohists, see Joseph Needham, *The Grand Titration: Science and Society in East and West* (London: George Allen & Unwin, Ltd., 1969), 220–42, 325–6.

17 See, for example, Laura Hostetler, *Qing Colonial Enterprise: Ethnography and Cartography in Early Modern China* (Chicago and London: University of Chicago Press, 2001).

18 See Needham, *The Grand Titration*, chs. 1–2. On the problem of interrupted chains of scientific discovery in China, see Qian, *The Great Inertia*, 59–62.

19 See Joseph Needham and Gwei-Djen Lu, *Science and Civilisation in China*, vol. 5 *Chemistry and Chemical Technology*, pt. 2: *Spagyrical Discovery and Invention: Magisteries of Gold and Immortality* (Cambridge: Cambridge University Press, 1974).

20 On Chinese medicine, see also Nathan Sivin, "Science and Medicine in Imperial China: The State of the Field." *The Journal of Asian Studies* 47 (February 1988): 41–90.

21 See Qian, *The Great Inertia*, 102; Nathan Sivin, "Why the Scientific Revolution Did Not Take Place in China – or Didn't It?" in *Science in Ancient China: Researches and Reflections* (Aldershott, UK; Brookfield, VT: Variorum, 1995), 48.

22 On the contributions of Muslims to proto-chemistry, see Eric John Holmyard, *Makers of Chemistry* (Oxford: Oxford University Press, 1931), sections 16–25; Arthur John Hopkins, *Alchemy, Child of Greek Philosophy* (New York: Columbia University Press, 1934).

23 Robert M. Haddad, "Philosophical Theology and Science in Medieval Christianity and Islam: A Comparative Perspective." *The Journal of the Historical Society* 8 (September 2008): 349–93 (here: 371–2).

24 See Jonathan Lyons, *The House of Wisdom: How the Arabs Transformed Western Civilization* (New York: Bloomsbury Press, 2009); George Saliba, *Islamic Science and the Making of the European Renaissance* (Cambridge, MA: MIT Press, 2007); F. J. Ragep, "Copernicus and His Islamic Predecessors: Some Historical Remarks." *History of Science* 45 (March 2007): 65–81.

25 On the impact on medieval thought of ancient texts, see Edward Grant, *The Foundations of Modern Science in the Middle Ages* (Cambridge: Cambridge University Press, 1996), chs. 2, 4–6.

26 See Toby E. Huff *The Rise of Early Modern Science: Islam, China, and the West*, 2nd edn (Cambridge: Cambridge University Press, 2003), 228–9; Harold J. Berman, "The Origins of Western Legal Science." *Harvard Law Review* 90 (March 1977): 894–943 (here: 939–40).

27 See Lindberg, *The Beginnings of Western Science*, 300–6.

28 On Oresme and Buridan, see Lindberg, *The Beginnings of Western Science*, 282–5; Arthur Koestler, *The Sleepwalkers: A History of Man's Changing Vision of the Universe* (London: Arkana, 1989), 202.

29 See Maurice P. Crosland (ed.), *The Science of Matter: A Historical Survey* (Amsterdam: OPA, 1992), 105–6.

30 Daniel Chirot advances this argument in "The Rise of the West." *American Sociological Review* 50 (April 1985): 181–95 (here: 189). See also Stephen F. Dale, *The Muslim Empires of the Ottomans, Safavids, and Mughals* (Cambridge and New York: Cambridge University Press, 2010).

31 On early Indian mathematics, see C. B. Boyer, *A History of Mathematics*, 2nd edn, rev. by Uta C. Merzbach (New York: John Wiley & Sons, 1991), ch. 12.

32 See Needham, *The Grand Titration*, 31–7.

33 On the crucial importance of ancient Greek thought for conceptualizing a study of nature driven by argumentation and evidence, see A. C. Crombie, *Styles of Scientific Thinking in the European Tradition: The History of Argument and Explanation Especially in the Mathematical and Biomedical Sciences and Arts*, 3 vols. (London: Duckworth, 1994), vol. 1, 3–22.

34 See Berman, "The Origins of Western Legal Science," 930–43.

35 See Brian P. Copenhaver, "Astrology and Magic," in *The Cambridge History of Renaissance Philosophy*, eds. Charles B. Schmitt and Quentin Skinner (Cambridge: Cambridge University Press, 1988), 264–300.

36 See George Huppert, *The Style of Paris: Renaissance Origins of the French Enlightenment* (Bloomington, IN: Indiana University Press, 1999), 13–14.

37 See Richard Kieckhefer, "The Specific Rationality of Medieval Magic." *The American Historical Review* 99 (June 1994): 813–36.

38 This paragraph draws on Richard G. Olson, *Science and Religion, 1450–1900: from Copernicus to Darwin* (Baltimore: The Johns Hopkins University Press, 2004), 34–45.

39 As quoted in Olson and Olson, *Science and Religion, 1450–1900*, 39.

40 See Vivian Nutton, *Ancient Medicine* (New York: Routledge, 2004), 172–3.

41 See Michela Pereria, "Alchemy and Hermeticism: An Introduction to This Issue." *Early Science and Medicine* 5 (2000): 115–20.

42 This paragraph draws on N. C. Datta, *The Story of Chemistry* (Hyderguda, Hyderabad, India: Universities Press, 2005), 54–6; Holmyard, *Makers of Chemistry*, sections 19, 26–9.

43 Kate Kelly makes this point in *The History of Medicine: The Middle Ages, 500–1450* (New York: Facts On File, 2009), 29.

44 See M. R. McGuire, *Technology, Crime and Justice: The Question Concerning Technomia* (Abingdon, UK and New York: Routledge, 2012), 40.

45 This paragraph draws on Allen G. Debus, "Chemists, Physicians, and Changing Perspectives on the Scientific Revolution." *Isis* 89 (March 1998): 66–81.

46 On the contributions of other Eurasian cultures to the development of mathematics in Europe, see Arun Bala, *The Dialogue of Civilizations in the Birth of Modern Science* (New York: Palgrave Macmillan, 2006), chs. 7 and 11.

47 This and the next paragraph rely on Alfred W. Crosby, *The Measure of Reality: Quantification and Western Society, 1250–1600* (New York: Cambridge University Press, 1996).

48 See Kirsti Andersen, *The Geometry of an Art: The History of the Mathematical Theory of Perspective from Alberti to Monge* (New York: Springer, 2007), 93–4.

49 See Elizabeth L. Eisenstein, *Divine Art, Infernal Machine: The Reception of Printing in the West from First Impressions to the Sense of an Ending* (Philadelphia and Oxford: University of Pennsylvania Press, 2011), 94.

50 See Madeline M. Muntersbjorn, "Francis Bacon's Philosophy of Science: Machina Intellectus and Forma Indita." *Philosophy of Science* 70 (December 2003): 1137–48.

51 See Francis Bacon, *The New Organon*, eds. Lisa Jardine and Michael Silverthorne (Cambridge: Cambridge University Press, 2000), 79.

52 See Bacon, *The New Organon*, 92.

53 Ibid., 106.

54 On Dryander, see Eve M. Duffy and Alida C. Metcalf, *The Return of Hans Staden: A Go-between in the Atlantic World* (Baltimore: The Johns Hopkins University Press, 2012), ch. 3.

55 On Zwinger and Ramus, see Justin Stagl, *A History of Curiosity: The Theory of Travel 1550–1800* (Chur, Switzerland: Harwood Academic Publishers, 1995), 55–70.

56 See Steven Matthews, *Theology and Science in the Thought of Francis Bacon* (Aldershott, UK and Burlington, VT: Ashgate Publishing, 2008), 3–6.

57 This paragraph draws on William Eamon, "From the Secrets of Nature to Public Knowledge," in *Reappraisals of the Scientific Revolution*, eds. David C. Lindberg and Robert S. Westman (Chicago: University of Chicago Press, 1990).

58 As quoted in Geoffrey Parker, "The Future of Western Warfare," in *The Cambridge History of Warfare*, ed. Geoffrey Parker (Cambridge: Cambridge University Press, 2005a), 419.

59 On Boyle, see Michael Hunter, *Boyle: Between God and Science* (New Haven: Yale University Press 2009).

60 René Descartes, *Meditations on First Philosophy: With Selections from the Objections and Replies*, ed. John Cottingham (Cambridge: Cambridge University Press, 1996), 12. This paragraph draws on his First and Second Meditations.

61 See Stephen Gaukroger, *Descartes: An Intellectual Biography* (Oxford: Oxford University Press, 1995), 309–20.

62 René Descartes, *A Discourse on the Method*, trans. Ian Maclean (Oxford: Oxford University Press, 2006), 28. This phrase is often translated as "I think therefore I am."

63 Descartes develops this idea in his Sixth Meditation.

64 See William R. Shea, *The Magic of Numbers and Motion: The Scientific Career of Rene Descartes* (Canton, MA: Science History Publications, 1991).

65 See Gaukroger, *Descartes*, 269–89.

66 See Steven J. Harris, "Networks of Travel, Correspondence, and Exchange," in *The Cambridge History of Science*, vol. 4: *Early Modern Science*, eds. Katharine Park and Lorraine Daston (Cambridge: Cambridge University Press, 2006).

67 See Gang Deng, *The Premodern Chinese Economy: Structural Equilibrium and Capitalist Sterility* (London and New York: Routledge, 1999), 85–7, 220–46.

68 See Andre Gunder Frank, *ReORIENT: Global Economy in the Asian Age* (Berkeley: University of California Press, 1998), 108–16, 218–25.

69 See Derk Bodde, *Chinese Thought, Society, and Science: The Intellectual and Social Background of Science and Technology Pre-modern China* (Honolulu: University of Hawaii Press, 1991).

70 See Yuheng Bao, Ben Liao, and Letitia Lane, *Renaissance in China: The Culture and Art of the Song Dynasty, 907–1279*, pref. by Letitia Lane (Lewiston, NY: Edwin Mellen Press, 2006), 14–21.

71 See Paul F. Cressey, "The Influence of the Literary Examination System on the Development of Chinese Civilization." *The American Journal of Sociology* 35 (September 1929): 250–62.

72 See Warren G. Frisina, "Are Knowledge and Action Really One Thing?: A Study of Wang Yang-ming's Doctrine of Mind." *Philosophy East and West* 39 (October 1989): 419–47.

73 See a key excerpt in Wm. Theodore de Bary et al. (eds), *Sources of Chinese Tradition* (New York: Columbia University Press, 1960), 608–11.

74 See "Astronomy," in *The Islamic World: Past and Present*, 3 vols., ed. John L. Esposito (Oxford and New York: Oxford University Press, 2004), vol. 1, 55.

75 See Roger French, *Dissection and Vivisection in the European Renaissance* (Aldershot, UK and Brookfield, VT: Ashgate Publishing, 1999).

76 On the re-emergence of anatomical dissection, see Daniel D. Cavalcanti et al., "Anatomy, Technology, Art, and Culture: Toward a Realistic Perspective of the Brain." *Neurosurg Focus* 27 (September 2009): 1–22.

77 Cavalcanti et al., "Anatomy, Technology, Art, and Culture," 11.

78 On Vesalius and the context of his work, see Harold J. Cook, "Medicine," in *The Cambridge History of Science: Early Modern Science*, eds. Park and Daston.

79 See Cavalcanti et al., "Anatomy, Technology, Art, and Culture," 13–15.

80 See Carmen Nekrasz and Claudia Swan, "Art," in *The Cambridge History of Science: Early Modern Science*, eds. Park and Daston, 780, 780n21.

81 See Paula Findlen, "Anatomy Theaters, Botanical Gardens, and Natural History Collections," in *The Cambridge History of Science: Early Modern Science,* eds. Park and Daston.

82 Agricola also founded geology and mineralogy as scientific disciplines.

83 See Paula Findlen, "Natural History," in *The Cambridge History of Science: Early Modern Science,* eds. Park and Daston.

84 On Gesner, see Wilbur Applebaum (ed.), *Encyclopedia of the Scientific Revolution from Copernicus to Newton* (New York: Gardland Pub., 2000), 413–14.

85 For this insight, see Koestler, *The Sleepwalkers*, 145.

86 On these three breakthroughs, see Applebaum (ed.), *Encyclopedia of the Scientific Revolution*, 127–8, 374, 745.

87 David Landes, *The Wealth and Poverty of Nations: Why Some Are so Rich and Some so Poor* (New York: W.W. Norton & Company, 1998), 204.

88 The idea of scientific paradigm shifts was first articulated in Thomas S. Kuhn, *The Structure of Scientific Revolutions*, 3rd edn (Chicago and London: University of Chicago Press, 1996), 18–20, 43–51.

89 John B. West, "Ibn al-Nafis, the Pulmonary Circulation, and the Islamic Golden Age." *Journal of Applied Physiology* 105 (December 2008): 1877–80.

90 The remainder of this paragraph and the following one draw upon Herbert Butterfield, *The Origins of Modern Science, 1300–1800* (New York: Free Press, 1957), ch. 3.

91 See Butterfield, *The Origins of Modern Science*, 65.

92 On the early discovery of microorganisms, see Findlen, "Natural History," 465.

93 On Bauhin's and similar contemporaneous work, see Findlen, "Natural History," 455–64.

94 See Tore Frangsmyr (ed.), *Linnaeus: The Man and His Work* (Berkeley: University of California Press, 1983).

95 See, for example, Dinah L. Moché, *Astronomy: A Self-Teaching Guide,* 7th edn (Hoboken, NJ: John Wiley & Sons, 2009).

96 On Philolaus, see Carl A. Huffman, *Pythagorean and Presocratic: A Commentary on the Fragments and Testimonia with Interpretive Essays* (Cambridge: Cambridge University Press, 1993); Lindberg, *The Beginnings of Western Science*, 86–104.

97 As quoted in Koestler, *The Sleepwalkers*, 51.

98 See Mary Louise Gill, *Aristotle on Substance: The Paradox of Unity* (Princeton: Princeton University Press, 1989), ch. 2.

99 See Michael J. Crowe, *Theories of the World from Antiquity to the Copernican Revolution*, 2nd rev. edn (Mineola, NY: Dover Publications, 2001), ch. 4.

100 See Valérie Shrimplin, *Sun-Symbolism and Cosmology in Michelangelo's Last Judgment* (Kirksville, MO: Truman State University Press, 2000), 13.

101 See Arthur O. Lovejoy, *The Great Chain of Being: A Study of the History of an Idea* (Cambridge, MA: Harvard University Press, 1936).

102 As noted in Koestler, *The Sleepwalkers*, 103–4.

103 See William Donahue, "Astronomy," in *The Cambridge History of Science: Early Modern Science*; H. Floris Cohen, *How Modern Science Came into the World: Four Civilizations, One 17th-Century Breakthrough*, eds. Park and Daston (Amsterdam: Amsterdam University Press, 2010).

104 See Owen Gingerich and James H. MacLachlan, *Nicolaus Copernicus: Making the Earth a Planet* (Oxford: Oxford University Press, 2005).

105 See Maurice A. Finocchiaro, *Defending Copernicus and Galileo: Critical Reasoning in the Two Affairs* (New York: Springer, 2010), 23–33.

106 See Finocchiaro, *Defending Copernicus and Galileo*, 35.

107 Ibid., xv, 45–6.

108 As quoted in Koestler, *The Sleepwalkers*, 203.

109 On Kepler, see Crowe, *Theories of the World*, ch. 8.

110 This is discussed in detail in James R. Voelkel, *Johannes Kepler and the New Astronomy* (New York: Oxford University Press, 1999), 30–3, 88–9.

111 As quoted in Crosby, *The Measure of Reality*, 126.

112 On the Tychonic system, see Crowe, *Theories of the World*, ch. 7.

113 Alexandre Koyré, *The Astronomical Revolution: Copernicus, Kepler, Borelli*, trans. R. E. W. Maddison (Paris and Ithaca: Cornell University Press, 1973), 183.

114 See André Charrak, "The Mathematical Model of Creation According to Kepler," in *Mathematics and the Divine: A Historical Study*, eds. T. Koetsier and Luc Bergmans (Amsterdam: Elsevier, 2005).

115 See Peter Machamer, "Galileo's Machines, His Mathematics, and His Experiments," in *The Cambridge Companion to Galileo*, ed. Peter Machamer (Cambridge: Cambridge University Press, 1998), 54. On Galileo's achievements, see Crowe, *Theories of the World*, ch. 9. For a recent authoritative biography, see J. L. Heilbron, *Galileo* (Oxford and New York: Oxford University Press, 2010).

116 Galileo's run-ins with the ecclesiastical authorizes is discussed in "Galileo and the Church," in *Encyclopedia of the Scientific Revolution,* ed. Applebaum; William R. Shea and Mariano Artigas, *Galileo in Rome: The Rise and Fall of a Troublesome Genius* (Oxford and New York: Oxford University Press, 2003).

117 See J. L. Heilbron, Introduction, in Galileo Galilei, *Dialogue Concerning the Two Chief World Systems: Ptolemaic and Copernican*, ed. and trans. Stillman Drake (New York: Modern Library, 2001), xxiii.

118 As quoted in Shea and Artigas, *Galileo in Rome*, 57. For the case that Galileo believed that "theology and science are inseparable," see Pietro Redondi, "From Galileo to Augustine," in *The Cambridge Companion to Galileo,* ed. Machamer, 201.

119 See Michael Sharratt, *Galileo: Decisive Innovator* (Cambridge: Cambridge University Press, 1994), 118.

120 As quoted in "Galileo and the Church," in *Encyclopedia of the Scientific Revolution,* ed. Applebaum, 394.

121 See Shea and Artigas, *Galileo in Rome*, 100–12; Heilbron, Introduction, xxiii.

122 See John Henry, "Religion and the Scientific Revolution," in *The Cambridge Companion to Science and Religion*, ed. Peter Harrison (Cambridge: Cambridge University Press, 2010), 39–40.

123 James Reston, Jr., *Galileo: A Life* (New York: HarperCollins, 1994), 271.

124 See Machamer, "Galileo's Machines," 53–5.

125 See John Henry, *The Scientific Revolution and the Origins of Modern Science*, 2nd edn (Basingstoke, UK and New York: Palgrave Macmillan, 2002), 23–4.

126 See Sivin, "Why the Scientific Revolution Did Not Take Place in China," 62–4; Benjamin A. Elman, *On Their Own Terms: Science in China, 1550–1900* (Cambridge, MA: MIT Press, 2005), 63–149.

127 On Newton, see Michael White, *Isaac Newton: The Last Sorcerer* (Reading, MA: Perseus Books, 1999).

128 As quoted in Gerald James Holton and Stephen G. Brush, *Physics, the Human Adventure: From Copernicus to Einstein and Beyond* (New Brunswick, NJ: Rutgers University Press, 2001), 152. According to Einstein's general theory of relativity of 1915, gravitation is an intrinsic property of the space-time continuum and not an instance of unmediated action at a distance.

129 See Butterfield, *The Origins of Modern Science*, 164–70.

130 See J. B. Shank, *The Newton Wars and the Beginning of the French Enlightenment* (Chicago: University of Chicago Press, 2008).

131 See P. Fontes da Costa, "The Culture of Curiosity at The Royal Society in the First Half of the Eighteenth Century." *Notes and Records of the Royal Society of London* 56 (May 2002): 147–66 (here: 152–3); Shank, *The Newton Wars*, ch. 2.

132 See Jeffrey R. Wigelsworth, *Selling Science in the Age of Newton: Advertising and the Commoditization of Knowledge* (Farnham, UK and Burlington, VT: Ashgate Publishing, 2010), chs. 3–5.

133 See William R. Newman, "From Alchemy to 'Chymistry," in *The Cambridge History of Science: Early Modern Science*, eds. Park and Daston.

134 This paragraph relies on John B. West, "Robert Boyle's Landmark Book of 1660 with the First Experiments on Rarified Air." *Journal of Applied Physiology* 98 (2005): 31–9.

135 For an excerpt from Boyle's study, see Crosland (ed.), *The Science of Matter*, 143–6 (quotation: 145).

136 J. V. Golinski, "A Noble Spectacle: Phosphorus and the Public Cultures of Science in the Early Royal Society." *Isis* 80 (March 1989), pp. 11–39 (especially 18–19).

137 Marie Boas Hall, *Robert Boyle and Seventeenth-Century Chemistry* (Cambridge: Cambridge University Press, 1958), ch. 4.

138 On the phlogiston theory, see Crosland (ed.), *The Science of Matter*, 134–5.

139 See J. B. Gough, "Lavoisier and the Fulfillment of the Stahlian Revolution." *Osiris*, 2nd Series, 4 (1988): 15–33.

140 See his statement of the theory in Crosland (ed.), *The Science of Matter*, 136.

141 See Dena Goodman, *The Republic of Letters: A Cultural History of the French Enlightenment* (Ithaca: Cornell University Press, 1994), 15–23.

142 See Pamela H. Smith, "Laboratories," in *The Cambridge History of Science: Early Modern Science*, eds. Park and Daston.

143 For details on their discovery, see John Emsley, *Nature's Building Blocks: An A–Z Guide to the Elements* (Oxford: Oxford University Press, 2001).

144 For Dalton's view on the conservation of matter, see Crosland (ed.), *The Science of Matter*, 136–7.

145 See Paul Strathen, *Mendeleyev's Dream: The Quest for the Elements* (London: Hamish Hamilton, 2000).

146 See Alan H. Cook, *Edmond Halley: Charting the Heavens and the Seas* (Oxford: Oxford University Press, 1998).

147 See I. Bernard Cohen, "Benjamin Franklin: An Experimental Newtonian Scientist." *Bulletin of the American Academy of Arts and Sciences* 5 (January 1952): 2–6.

148 This paragraph also draws upon Michael Brian Schiffer, *Draw the Lightning Down: Benjamin Franklin and Electrical Technology in the Age of Enlightenment* (Berkeley: University of California Press, 2003).

149 For Franklin's statement of his theory of electrical "fluid," see Crosland (ed.), *The Science of Matter*, 181–2.

150 It is striking that no scientist even remotely as eminent emerged in Latin America, despite the fact that European settlement, printing, and higher education began there a century earlier than in North America.

151 A short but reliable overview is Margaret C. Jacob, *The Enlightenment: A Brief History with Documents* (Boston: Bedford/St. Martin's, 2001).

152 See D. Headrick, *When Information Came of Age: Technologies of Knowledge in the Age of Reason and Revolution, 1700–1850* (New York: Oxford University Press, 2000), 178.

153 See Simon Winchester, *The Map That Changed the World: William Smith and the Birth of Modern Geology* (New York: HarperCollins, 2001).

154 See Peter Watson, *Ideas: A History of Thought and Invention, from Fire to Freud* (New York: HarperCollins, 2005), 529–31.

155 See Headrick, *When Information Came of Age.*

156 James Van Horn Melton discusses this development in *The Rise of the Public in Enlightenment Europe* (Cambridge: Cambridge University Press, 2001), ch. 3.

157 See Stefan-Ludwig Hoffmann, *Civil Society, 1750–1914* (Houndmills, UK: Palgrave Macmillan, 2006), ch. 1; Mary Ann Clawson, *Constructing Brotherhood: Class, Gender, and Fraternalism* (Princeton: Princeton University Press, 1989), ch. 2.

158 See Monique Frize, *The Bold and the Brave: A History of Women in Science and Engineering* (Ottawa: University of Ottawa Press, 2009), 67, 99 and passim; Steven Kale, *French Salons: High Society and Political Sociability from the Old Regime to the Revolution of 1848* (Baltimore: Johns Hopkins University Press, 2004).

159 See Kenichi Ueda, *Life Expectancy and Income Convergence in the World: A Dynamic General Equilibrium Analysis* (Washington, DC: International Monetary Fund, 2008).

160 See Alfred North Whitehead, *Science and the Modern World*, 2nd edn (Cambridge: Cambridge University Press, 1932), 22, 47, 99.

161 Cartesian dualism could lead to researchers viewing animals as entirely without feeling, but Descartes himself did not profess this view. See John Cottingham, "'A Brute to the Brutes?: Descartes' Treatment of Animals." *Philosophy* 53 (October 1978): 551–9.

162 See, for example, Claude Bernard, *An Introduction to the Study of Experimental Medicine*, trans. Henry Copley Greene, intro. Lawrence J. Henderson (1927; New York: Dover Pub., 1957).

163 See Mayr, "Darwin's Influence on Modern Thought," 79–83.

164 See David Hume, *An Enquiry Concerning Human Understanding*, ed. Tom L. Beauchamp (New York: Oxford University Press, 1999).

165 See Mark P. Silverman, *Quantum Superposition: Counterintuitive Consequences of Coherence, Entanglement, and Interference* (Berlin and Heidelberg: Springer, 2010), 3–10.

166 In reality, the claim that "there is no meaning" logically contradicts itself, or there could be no point to state it. See Schubert M. Ogden, *The Reality of God, and Other Essays* (Dallas, TX: Southern Methodist University Press, 1992), 34–41.

167 Rodney Stark makes this argument in *For the Glory of God*.

168 See Huff, *The Rise of Early Modern Science*, 113–15.

169 See Fritjof Capra, *The Tao of Physics: An Exploration of the Parallels between Modern Physics and Eastern Mysticism*, 4th edn (Boston: Shambala Publications, 1999); Donald S. Lopez, Jr., *Buddhism and Science: A Guide for the Perplexed* (Chicago and London: University of Chicago Press, 2008).

170 See, in particular, Harold J. Berman, *Law and Revolution: The Formation of the Western Legal Tradition* (Cambridge, MA: Harvard University Press, 1983).

171 Alan Macfarlane advances this contention in *The Making of the Modern World: Visions from the West and East* (Basingstoke, UK and New York: Palgrave Macmillan, 2002), 224.

172 See Christopher Dawson, *Religion and the Rise of Western Culture* (New York: Sheed & Ward, 1950), 26–7.

173 A. C. Graham makes this point for China in "China, Europe and the Origins of Modern Science: Neeham's The Grand Titration." *Asia Major* 16 (1971): 178–96 (especially 194–6). For the Islamic world and other early developed cultures, see Marshall Hodgson, "The Great Western Transmutation," in *Rethinking World History: Essays on Europe, Islam, and World History*, ed. Edmund Burke (Cambridge: Cambridge University Press, 1993).

Chapter 9

1 See Hernando De Soto, *The Mystery of Capital: Why Capitalism Triumphs in the West and Fails Everywhere Else* (New York: Basic Books, 2000).

2 See M. Dutta, *China's Industrial Revolution and Economic Presence* (Singapore: World Scientific, 2006), 104.

3 See David D. Haddock and Lynne Kiesling. "The Black Death and Property Rights." *The Journal of Legal Studies* 31 (June 2002): S545–S87. Broadly, see Nathan Rosenberg and L. E. Birdzell, Jr. *How the West Grew Rich: The Economic Transformation of the Industrial World* (New York: Basic Books, 1986).

4 See Gang Deng, *The Premodern Chinese Economy: Structural Equilibrium and Capitalist Sterility* (London and New York: Routledge, 1999), 8, 50–61.

5 See Paul Freedman, "The Medieval Taste for Spices," *Historically Speaking* (September–October 2008a).

6 Statistics in Paul Freedman, *Out of the East: Spices and the Medieval Imagination* (New Haven: Yale University Press 2008b), 6.

7 See Freedman, *Out of the East*, 133; Anthony R. Disney, *Twilight of the Pepper Empire: Portuguese Trade in Southwest India in the Early Seventeenth Century* (Cambridge, MA: Harvard University Press, 1978), ch. 3.

8 See Jack Turner, *Spice: The History of a Temptation* (New York: A.A. Knopf, 2004), 137–40; Freedman, *Out of the East*, 216–22.

9 See Kenneth Pomeranz and Steven Topik, *The World That Trade Created: Society, Culture, and the World Economy, 1400 to the Present*, 2nd edn (New York: M.E. Sharpe, 2006), 126.

10 This paragraph draws on Sidney W. Mintz, *Sweetness and Power: The Place of Sugar in Modern History* (New York: Penguin, 1985).

11 See B. W. Higman, "The Sugar Revolution." *The Economic History Review*, New Series 53 (May 2000): 213–36.

12 Jan De Vries, *The Industrious Revolution: Consumer Behavior and the Household Economy, 1650 to the Present* (New York: Cambridge University Press, 2008), 155–6; Higman, "The Sugar Revolution," 227.

13 See Mintz, *Sweetness and Power*, 19, 129–43.

14 See R. J. Forbes, *A Short History of the Art of Distillation: From the Beginnings up to the Death of Cellier Blumenthal* (Leiden: E.J. Brill, 1948; reprinted 1970), especially 95–106.

15 On these beverages, see Bennett Alan Weinberg and Bonnie K. Bealer, *The World of Caffeine: The Science and Culture of the World's Most Popular Drug* (New York and London: Routledge, 2002).

16 See Sophie D. Coe and Michael D. Coe, *The True History of Chocolate* (New York: Thames and Hudson, 1996).

17 See Jean Louis Flandrin, Massimo Montanari, and Albert Sonnenfeld (eds), *A Culinary History*, trans. Clarissa Botsford (New York: Penguin, 1999), 390.

18 Flandrin, Montanari and Sonnenfeld (eds), *A Culinary* History, 386–9; John Crawford, "History of Coffee." *Journal of the Statistical Society of London* 15 (April 1852): 50–8.

19 See Adrian Johns, "Coffee Houses and Print Shops," in *The Cambridge History of Science*, vol. 4: *Early Modern Science*, eds. Katharine Park and Lorraine Daston (Cambridge: Cambridge University Press, 2006).

20 See Ross W. Jamieson, "The Essence of Commodification: Caffeine Dependencies in the Early Modern World." *Journal of Social History* 35 (Winter 2001): 269–942 (here: 84–6).

21 See Woodruff D. Smith, "Complications of the Commonplace: Tea, Sugar, and Imperialism." *Journal of Interdisciplinary History* 23 (Autumn 1992): 259–78 (here: 275–8).

22 Weinberg and Bealer, *The World of Caffeine*, 172–3.

23 This paragraph draws on Joel Best, "Economic Interests and the Vindication of Deviance: Tobacco in Seventeenth Century Europe." *The Sociological Quarterly* 20 (Spring 1979): 171–82; Jordan Goodman, *Tobacco in History: The Cultures of Dependence* (London: Routledge, 1993).

24 Best, "Economic Interests and the Vindication of Deviance," 178.

25 See Mintz, *Sweetness and Power*, 109.

26 Weinberg and Bealer, *The World of Caffeine*, 254.

27 See Pomeranz and Topik, *The World That Trade Created*, 127; Kenneth Pomeranz, *The Great Divergence: Europe, China, and the Making of the Modern World Economy* (Princeton: Princeton University Press, 2000), 152–61.

28 Jack A. Goldstone discusses these cases in "Efflorescences and Economic Growth in World History: Rethinking the 'Rise of the West' and the Industrial Revolution." *Journal of World History* 13 (2002): 323–89.

29 See Cormac Ó Gráda, *Famine: A Short History* (Princeton and Oxford: Princeton University Press, 2009), 36, 38.

30 See Mark Overton, *Agricultural Revolution in England: The Transformation of the Agrarian Economy, 1500–1850* (Cambridge: Cambridge University Press, 1996), 1–9.

31 On the development of the enclosure movement, see Overton, *Agricultural Revolution in England*, ch. 4; Eric Kerridge, *The Agricultural Revolution* (New York: A. M. Kelley, 1968).

32 J. R. Wordie, "The Chronology of English Enclosure, 1500–1914." *The Economic History Review*, New Series 36 (November 1983): 483–505 (here: 504–5).

33 See Kerridge, *The Agricultural Revolution*, 332–6.

34 See William L. Langer, "American Foods and Europe's Population Growth, 1750–1850." *Journal of Social History* 8 (Winter 1975): 51–66; John Reader, *Potato: A History of the Propitious Esculent* (New Haven and London: Yale University Press, 2009).

35 See Tom Standage, *An Edible History of Humanity* (New York: Walker, 2009), 120.

36 See "American Foods and Europe's Population Growth," 55.

37 Ibid., 60.

38 See John M. Hobson, *The Eastern Origins of Western Civilization* (Cambridge: Cambridge University Press, 2004), 201–5.

39 As quoted in Jules N. Pretty, *Regenerating Agriculture: Policies and Practice for Sustainability and Self-Reliance* (Washington, DC: Joseph Henry Press, 1995), 183.

40 See Overton, *Agricultural Revolution in England*, 130.

41 See Elizabeth H. Oakes (ed.), *Encyclopedia of World Scientists*, rev. edn (New York: Facts on File, 2007), 430.

42 See S. R. Epstein, "Regional Fairs, Institutional Innovation, and Economic Growth in Late Medieval Europe." *The Economic History Review*, New Series 47 (August 1994): 459–82.

43 See Janet L. Abu-Lughod, *Before European Hegemony: The World System A.D. 1250–1350* (New York: Oxford University Press, 1989), chs. 2–3.

44 For England, see L. R. Poos, *A Rural Society After the Black Death: Essex, 1350–1525* (Cambridge: Cambridge University Press, 1991).

45 See Wally Seccombe, *A Millennium of Family Change: Feudalism to Capitalism in Northwestern Europe* (London: Verso, 1992).

46 See George Huppert, *After the Black Death: A Social History of Early Modern Europe*, 2nd edn (Bloomington, IN: Indiana University Press, 1998), 12–13.

47 See E. L. Jones, *The European Miracle: Environments, Economies, and Geopolitics in the History of Europe and Asia*, 3rd edn (London and New York: Cambridge University Press, 2003), 16–20.

48 Jones advances this contention in *The European Miracle*, 15–16.

49 See Pomeranz, *The Great Divergence*, 41.

50 This paragraph draws on John Mickelthwait and Adrian Wooldridge, *The Company: A Short History of a Revolutionary Idea* (New York: Modern Library, 2003); Edwin S. Hunt and James M. Murray, *A History of Business in Medieval Europe, 1200–1550* (Cambridge: Cambridge University Press, 1999).

51 See Timur Kuran, "The Absence of the Corporation in Islamic Law: Origins and Persistence." *The American Journal of Comparative Law* 53 (Fall 2005): 785–834 (here: 785).

52 See William N. Goetzmann and K. Geert Rouwenhorst, "Introduction: Financial Innovations in History," in *The Origins of Value: The Financial Innovations that Created Modern Capital Markets*, eds. William N. Goetzmann and K. Geert Rouwenhorst (Oxford and New York: Oxford University Press, 2005), 7–11; Valerie Hansen and Ana Mata-Fink, "Records from a Seventh-Century Pawnshop in China," in ibid.; Richard Von Glahn, "The Origins of Paper Money in China," in ibid.

53 This paragraph relies on Timur Kuran, "The Islamic Commercial Crisis: Institutional Roots of Economic Underdevelopment in the Middle East." *The Journal of Economic History* 63 (June 2003): 414–46; Timur Kuran, *The Long Divergence: How Islamic Law Held Back the Middle East* (Princeton and Oxford: Princeton University Press, 2011).

54 See Kuran, "The Absence of the Corporation in Islamic Law," 816–17.

55 Hunt and Murray, *A History of Business in Medieval Europe*, 156.

56 See Abu-Lughod, *Before European Hegemony*, chs. 6–7.

57 See Rosenberg and Birdzell, Jr., *How the West Grew Rich*, 192.

58 On these early corporations, see Mickelthwait and Wooldridge, *The Company*, 12–13.

59 This paragraph is based upon Mickelthwait and Wooldridge, *The Company*, 12–17.

60 See, for example, Immanuel Wallerstein, *The Modern World-System I. Capitalist Agriculture and the Origins of the European World-Economy in the Sixteenth Century* (New York: Academic Press, 1974); Eric H. Mielants, *The Origins of Capitalism and the "Rise of the West"* (Philadelphia: Temple University Press, 2007).

61 Stated in Wallerstein, *The Modern World-System I*, 60.

62 The first scholar to raise this question was Max Weber in *The Protestant Ethic and the Spirit of Capitalism*, trans. Talcott Parsons, intro. Anthony Giddens (New York: C. Scribner, 1958).

63 Carter Lindberg makes these points in *The European Reformations* (Cambridge, MA: Harvard University Press, 1996), 372.

64 Quoted in Roland Bainton, *Here I Stand: A Life of Martin Luther* (New York: Abingdon-Cokesbury Press, 2007), 190.

65 Samir Amin develops this idea in *Eurocentrism*, trans. Russell Moore (New York: Monthly Review, 1989), 86–7.

66 As Jack Goody argues persuasively in *The East in the West* (Cambridge: Cambridge University Press, 1996), chs. 1–2.

67 As Mielants shows throughout *The Origins of Capitalism and the "Rise of the West"*.

68 This paragraph and the subsequent one draw on Carl Bangs, "Dutch Theology, Trade, and War, 1590–1610." *Church History* 39 (December 1970): 470–82.

69 As quoted in Bangs, "Dutch Theology, Trade, and War," 473.

70 See Mickelthwait and Wooldridge, *The Company*, 20.

71 See Jan De Vries, *Economy of Europe in an Age of Crisis, 1600–1750* (Cambridge: Cambridge University Press, 1976), 132.

72 See Roy S. Freedman, *Introduction to Financial Technology* (Amsterdam and Boston: Elsevier/Academic Press, 2006), 3.

73 See Goetzmann and Rouwenhorst, "Introduction: Financial Innovations in History," in *The Origins of Value*, 14.

74 See Oscar Gelderblom and Joost Jonker, "Completing a Financial Revolution: The Finance of the Dutch East India Trade and the Rise of the Amsterdam Capital Market, 1595–1612." *The Journal of Economic History* 64 (September 2004): 641–72 (here: 659–64).

75 See Gelderblom and Jonker, "Completing a Financial Revolution," 663.

76 See Oscar Gelderblom and Joost Jonker, "Amsterdam as the Cradle of Modern Futures and Options Trading, 1550–1615," in *The Origins of Value*.

77 See Rodney Stark, *The Victory of Reason: How Christianity Led to Freedom, Capitalism, and Western Success* (New York: Random House, 2005), 145.

78 This paragraph relies on Geoffery Vaughan Scammell, *The World Encompassed: The First European Maritime Empires, c. 800–1650* (Berkeley: University of California Press, 1981), ch. 7.

79 As quoted in Scammell, *The World Encompassed*, 420.

80 See Dorothy Denneen Volo and James M. Volo, *Daily Life in the Age of Sail* (Westport, CT: Greenwood Press, 2002), 37.

81 This paragraph and the next draw on Scammell, *The World Encompassed*, ch. 9.

82 The Bank of Amsterdam, founded in 1609, acted as a clearinghouse for foreign currencies and rarely lent money. See Larry Allen, *The Global Financial System 1750–2000* (London: Reaktion, 2001), 160–1.

83 Scotland and England combined in 1707 to form the United Kingdom of Great Britain.

84 See Richard Dale, *The First Crash: Lessons from the South Sea Bubble* (Princeton: Princeton University Press, 2004), 30–1.

85 See Larry Neal, *The Rise of Financial Capitalism: International Capital Markets in the Age of Reason* (Cambridge: Cambridge University Press, 2002), 32–4.

86 See Deirdre McCloskey, *Bourgeois Dignity: Why Economics Can't Explain the Modern World* (Chicago: University of Chicago Press, 2010).

87 This paragraph draws on Dale, *The First Crash*.

88 See Charles F. Kindleberger, *Manias, Panics, and Crashes: A History of Financial Crises* (New York: Basic Books, 1978).

89 See Jan De Vries and A. M. van der Woude, *The First Modern Economy: Success, Failure, and Perseverance of the Dutch Economy, 1500–1815* (Cambridge: Cambridge University Press, 1997), 54.

90 On the development of economic thought, see Gianni Vaggi and Peter Groenewegen, *A Concise History of Economic Thought: From Mercantilism to Monetarism* (Houndmills, UK and New York: Palgrave Macmillan, 2003).

91 On these episodes, see Jatinder N. D. Gupta and Sushil Kumar Sharma, *Creating Knowledge Based Organizations* (Hershey, PA and London: Idea Group, 2004), 83.

92 See Larry Neal, "The Integration and Efficiency of the London and Amsterdam Stock Markets in the Eighteenth Century." *The Journal of Economic History* 47 (March 1987): 97–115.

93 Kenneth Pomeranz makes this argument in *The Great Divergence*, 24–5, 296–7.

94 Patrick K. O'Brien, "European Economic Development: The Contribution of the Periphery." *Economic History Review* 35 (1982): 1–18 (here: 18). See also, McCloskey, *Bourgeois Dignity*, chs. 26–7.

95 See Charles P. Kindleberger, *A Financial History of Western Europe*, 2nd edn (New York and Oxford: Oxford University Press, 1993); Youssef Cassis, *Capitals of Capital: A History of International Financial Centres, 1780–2005*, trans. Jacqueline Collier (Cambridge: Cambridge University Press, 2006).

96 See Rondo Cameron, *France and the Economic Development of Europe: Evolution of International Business, 1800–1945* (Princeton: Princeton University Press, 1961).

97 See Cassis, *Capitals of Capital*, 42–54.

98 Ibid., 43.

99 Statistics cited in Cassis, *Capitals of Capital*, 44.

100 See Ranald Michie, "The City of London and International Trade, 1850–1914," in *Decline and Recovery in Britain's Overseas Trade, 1873–1914*, eds. D. C. M. Platt, A. J. H. Latham and Ranald Michie (Basingstoke, UK: Macmillan, 1993).

101 See Florence Edler De Roover, "Early Examples of Marine Insurance." *The Journal of Economic History* 5 (November 1945): 172–200.

102 This paragraph draws on Hunt and Murray, *A History of Business in Medieval Europe*, 60–2, 158–9; Rosenberg and Birdzell, *How the West Grew Rich*, 115–19.

103 See De Roover, "Early Examples of Marine Insurance," 198–200.

104 This paragraph relies on William C. Baer, "The Institution of Residential Investment in Seventeenth-Century London." *The Business History Review* 76 (Autumn 2002): 515–51.

105 Other pattern books, a species of how-to guides, answered questions on trade, credit, and kindred topics. See Baer, "The Institution of Residential Investment," 524.

106 As noted at the start of this chapter, the problem of "dead capital" is the main concern of De Soto, *The Mystery of Capital*.

107 On Barbon, see Philip S. James, "Nicholas Barbon—Founder of Modern Fire Insurance." *The Review of Insurance Studies* 1 (June 1954): 44–7.

108 For more details, see Harry M. Johnson, "The History of British and American Fire Marks." *The Journal of Risk and Insurance* 39 (September 1972): 405–18.

109 See Robin Pearson, "Moral Hazard and the Assessment of Insurance Risk in Eighteenth- and Early-Nineteenth-Century Britain." *The Business History Review* 76 (Spring 2002): 1–35.

110 This matter is illuminated in Reinhold A. Dorwart, "The Earliest Fire Insurance Company in Berlin and Brandenburg, 1705–1711." *The Business History Review* 32 (Summer 1958): 192–203.

111 See Baer, "The Institution of Residential Investment," 533–7.

112 As quoted in Baer, "The Institution of Residential Investment," 537.

113 See Brendan Dooley and Sabrina A. Baron (eds), *The Politics of Information in Early Modern Europe* (London and New York: Routledge, 2001).

114 On the separates, see Ian Atherton, "'The Itch Grown a Disease': Manuscript Transmission of News in the Seventeenth Century," in *News, Newspapers, and Society in Early Modern Britain*, ed. Joad Raymond (London and Portland, OR: Frank Cass, 1999).

115 See Dale, *The First* Crash, 7.

116 Regarding Lloyd, see Christopher Baker (ed.), *Absolutism and the Scientific Revolution, 1600–1720: A Biographical Dictionary* (Westport, CT: Greenwood Press, 2002), 233.

117 See, for example, Oscar Gelderblom and Joost Jonker, "Completing a Financial Revolution: The Finance of the Dutch East India Trade and the Rise of the Amsterdam Capital Market, 1595–1612." *The Journal of Economic History* 64 (September 2004): 641–72; P. G. M. Dickson, *The Financial Revolution in England: A Study in the Development of Public Credit 1688–1756* (London: Macmillan, 1967).

118 See Cassis, *Capitals of Capital*, 25.

Chapter 10

1 See C. Nederman, *John of Salisbury* (Tempe, AZ: Arizona Center for Medieval and Renaissance Studies, 2005).

2 See Cary J. Nederman, "A Duty to Kill: John of Salisbury's Theory of Tyrannicide." *The Review of Politics* 50 (Summer 1988): 365–89.

3 See Daniel Chirot, *How Societies Change* (Thousand Oaks, CA: Pine Forge Press, 1994), 59–62.

4 See by J. M. Roberts, *The Penguin History of Europe* (London: Penguin, 1996), 122–3.

5 On the Carolingian Empire, see Marios Costambeys, Matthew Innes, and Simon MacLean, *The Carolingian World* (Cambridge: Cambridge University Press, 2011).

6 On Byzantium, see Jonathan Shepard (ed.), *The Cambridge History of the Byzantine Empire c. 500–1492* (Cambridge: Cambridge University Press, 2008).

7 See D. Sourdel, "The 'Abbisid Caliphate," in *The Cambridge History of Islam*, Vol. 1A: *The Central Islamic Lands from Pre-Islamic Times to the First World War*, eds. P. M. Holt, Ann K. S. Lambton, and Bernard Lewis (Cambridge: Cambridge University Press, 1970).

8 See Samuel Wells, *Christian Ethics: An Introductory Reader* (Chichester, UK: Wiley-Blackwell, 2010), 39.

9 See Kathleen G. Cushing, *Reform and the Papacy in the Eleventh Century: Spirituality and Social Change* (Manchester and New York: Manchester University Press, 2005), 46–50.

10 See Peter Edbury, "Warfare in the Latin East," in *Medieval Warfare: A History*, ed., Maurice Keen (Oxford: Oxford University Press, 1999), 95.

11 See Harold J. Berman, "The Background of the Western Legal Tradition in the Folklaw of the Peoples of Europe." *The University of Chicago Law Review* 45 (Spring 1978): 553–97 (especially 555–67).

12 See Thomas N. Bisson, "The Military Origins of Medieval Representation." *The American Historical Review* 71 (July 1966): 1199–218.

13 See Joseph F. O'Callaghan, "The Beginnings of the Cortes of Leon-Castile." *The American Historical Review* 74 (June 1969): 1503–37.

14 See Wim Blockmans, "Representation (Since the Thirteenth Century)," in *The New Cambridge Medieval History*, vol. 7: *c. 1415-c. 1500*, ed. Christopher Allmand (Cambridge: Cambridge University Press, 1998), 38–53.

15 See Gianfranco Poggi, *The Development of the Modern State: A Sociological* Introduction (Stanford, CA: Stanford University Press, 1978), especially ch. 3.

16 See Blockmans, "Representation (Since the Thirteenth Century)," 32–4, 53–60.

17 See, for example, Nathan Rosenberg and L. E. Birdzell, Jr., *How the West Grew Rich: The Economic Transformation of the Industrial World* (New York: Basic Books, 1986), 61–2.

18 See Brian M. Downing, "Medieval Origins of Constitutional Government in the West." *Theory and Society* 18 (March 1989): 213–47.

19 See S. R. Epstein (ed.), *Guilds, Innovation and the European Economy, 1400–1800* (New York: Cambridge University Press, 2008).

20 See Sheilagh Ogilvie, "Rehabilitating the Guilds: A Reply." *The Economic History Review*, New Series 61 (February 2008): 175–82.

21 Eric Mielants discusses this process in *The Origins of Capitalism and the "Rise of the West"* (Philadelphia: Temple University Press, 2007), 38–9.

22 See John W. O'Malley, *Four Cultures of the West* (Cambridge, MA: Harvard University Press, 2004), 117–21.

23 See John A. Hall, *Powers and Liberties: The Causes and Consequences of the Rise of the West* (Oxford: Oxford University Press, 1985), 78, 103.

24 Thomas Munck, *Seventeenth Century Europe: State, Conflict, and the Social Order in Europe, 1598–1700* (Houndmills, UK and New York: Macmillan, 1989), 266.

25 See Jeremy Black, *Kings, Nobles and Commoners: States and Societies in Early Modern Europe, a Revisionist History* (London and New York: I.B. Tauris, 2004), 87.

26 See Peter Shervey Lewis, *Essays in Later Medieval French History* (London and Ronceverte, WV: The Hambledon Press, 1985), chs. 2, 8–10.

27 See Black, *Kings, Nobles and* Commoners, 181.

28 See William Chester Joran, "The Capetians from the Death of Philip II to Philip IV," in *The New Cambridge Medieval History*, vol. 5: *c. 1198-c. 1300*, ed. David Abulafia (Cambridge: Cambridge University Press, 1999), 307, 310.

29 See Abida Shakoor, *Origins of Modern Europe: Medieval National Consciousness*, eds. Q. Z. Hasan and Hajira Kumar (Delhi: Aakar Books, 2004), ch. 1.

30 This paragraph draws on Richard Pipes, *Property and Freedom* (New York: Vintage, 1999), ch. 2. See also Douglass C. North and Robert Paul Thomas, *The Rise of the Western World: A New Economic History* (New York: Cambridge University Press, 1973).

31 See Gang Deng, *The Premodern Chinese Economy: Structural Equilibrium and Capitalist Sterility* (London and New York: Routledge, 1999), 8, 20–1, 33, 50–61, 70–4, 140–5.

32 Marshall G. S. Hodgson develops this idea in "Cultural Patterning in Islamdom and the Occident," in Hodgson, Marshall G. S. *Rethinking World History: Essays on Europe, Islam, and World History*, ed. Edmund Burke, III (Cambridge: Cambridge University Press, 1993).

33 As quoted in Harold J. Berman, *Law and Revolution: The Formation of the Western Legal Tradition* (Cambridge, MA: Harvard University Press, 1983), 145.

34 See Berman, *Law and Revolution*, 276, 293.

35 See Hillay Zmora, *Monarchy, Aristocracy, and the State in Europe, 1300–1800* (New York: Routledge, 2001).

36 See also Cary J. Nederman and Catherine Campbell, "Priests, Kings, and Tyrants: Spiritual and Temporal Power in John of Salisbury's Policraticus." *Speculum* 66 (July 1991): 572–90.

37 See J. Van Laarhoven, "Thou Shalt not Slay a Tyrant! The So-called Theory of John of Salisbury," in *The World of John of Salisbury*, ed. M. Wilkes (Oxford: Oxford University Press, 1984).

38 See *Mencius*, trans. D. C. Lau (Harmondsworth: Penguin, 1970).

39 See James V. Schall, *At the Limits of Political Philosophy: From "Brilliant Errors" to Things of Uncommon Importance* (Washington, DC: Catholic University of America Press, 1996), 92–3.

40 See William R. Cook and Ronald B. Herzman, *The Medieval World View: An Introduction* (New York: Oxford University Press, 1983), 255.

41 Edward Ruben, "Judicial Review and the Right to Resist." *Georgetown Law Journal* 96 (2008): 61–118 (here: 72–5).

42 See Anne McClaren, "Rethinking Republicanism: Vindiciae, Contra Tyrannos in Context." *The Historical Journal* 49 (March 2006): 23–52.

43 See Quentin Skinner, "The Italian City-Republics," in *Democracy: The Unfinished Journey, 508 BC to AD 1993*, ed. John Dunn (Oxford: Oxford University Press, 1992).

44 As quoted in Quentin Skinner, "The Italian City-Republics," 58.

45 On Marsilius, see Quentin Skinner, *The Foundations of Modern Political Thought*, vol. 1: *The Renaissance* (Cambridge: Cambridge University Press, 1978), 61–5; Cary J. Nederman, *Worlds of Difference: European Discourses of Toleration, c. 1100-c. 1550* (University Park, PA: Pennsylvania State University Press, 2000), ch. 5.

46 On these ideas, see David Held, *Models of Democracy* (Stanford, CA: Stanford University Press, 1996), 40–5. See also Skinner, "The Italian City-Republics," 64–9.

47 Held makes this point in *Models of Democracy*, 32.

48 Scott Gordon, *Controlling the State: Constitutionalism from Ancient Athens to Today* (Cambridge, MA: Harvard University Press, 1999), 137–63.

49 See Roger Sablonier, "The Swiss Confederation," in *The New Cambridge Medieval History*, vol. 7, 653.

50 On these developments, see Sablonier, "The Swiss Confederation," 645–56; Bruce Gordon, *The Swiss Reformation* (Manchester and New York: Manchester University Press, 2002), 6–24; Oliver Zimmer, *A Contested Nation: History, Memory and Nationalism in Switzerland, 1761–1891* (Cambridge: Cambridge University Press, 2003), 21–8.

51 Quoted from Gordon, *The Swiss Reformation*, 11.

52 See Zimmer, *A Contested Nation*, 24.

53 See Gordon, *The Swiss Reformation*, 38–40.

54 See Sablonier, "The Swiss Confederation," 657–9, 667.

55 See Gordon, *The Swiss Reformation*, 40–2.

56 The next few paragraphs draw upon Brian M. Downing, *The Military Revolution and Political Change: Origins of Democracy and Autocracy in Early Modern Europe* (Princeton: Princeton University Press, 1992), ch. 9; Gordon, *Controlling the State*, ch. 6.

57 See H. F. K. Van Neirop, *The Nobility of Holland: From Knights to Regents 1500–1650* (Cambridge: Cambridge University Press, 1993), 12; M. D. Feld, "Middle-Class Society and the Rise of Military Professionalism: The Dutch Army, 1589–1609," in *The Military-State-Society Symbiosis*, ed. Peter Karsten (New York and London: Garland Publishing, 1998), 48–9.

58 See G. Griffiths, *Representative Government in Western Europe in the Sixteenth Century: Commentary and Documents for the Study of Comparative Constitutional History* (Oxford: Oxford University Press, 1968), 302.

59 On the Estates General of the Low Countries, see Griffiths, *Representative Government in Western Europe in the Sixteenth Century*, 298–318.

60 See Jonathan I. Israel, *The Dutch Republic: Its Rise, Greatness, and Fall, 1477–1806* (Oxford: Oxford University Press, 1995), 547.

61 See Geoffrey Parker, *The Dutch Revolt* (London and New York: Penguin books, 1988).

62 See Feld, "Middle-Class Society and the Rise of Military Professionalism," 51–2.

63 See Griffiths, *Representative Government in Western Europe in the Sixteenth Century*, 313–17; E. H. Kossmann and A. F. Mellink (eds), *Texts Concerning the Revolt of the Netherlands* (Cambridge: Cambridge University Press, 1974), 29–49.

64 See Jan Glete, *War and the State in Early Modern Europe: Spain, the Dutch Republic and Sweden as Fiscal-Military States, 1500–1660* (London and New York: Routledge, 2002), 123–35.

65 See Maarten Prak, *The Dutch Republic in the Seventeenth Century: The Golden Age*, trans. Diane Webb (Cambridge: Cambridge University Press, 2005).

66 On the failed efforts of the House of Orange to establish monarchical rule in the Dutch Republic during these years, see Herbert H. Rowen, *The Princes of Orange: The Stadholders in the Dutch Republic* (Cambridge and New York: Cambridge University Press, 1988).

67 See Berman, *Law and Revolution*, 434–58; H. Patrick Glenn, *Legal Traditions of the World: Sustainable Diversity in Law*, 2nd edn (Oxford: Oxford University Press, 2004), 434–58.

68 See Ellis Sandoz, *A Government of Laws: Political Theory, Religion, and the American Founding* (Columbia, MO: University of Missouri Press, 2001), 29–30.

69 On the English trust, see Alan Macfarlane, *The Making of the Modern World: Visions from the West and East* (Houndmills, UK and New York: Palgrave Macmillan, 2002), 263–72.

70 See Christopher Brooke, *From Alfred to Henry III, 871–1272* (New York: W.W. Norton & Company, 1961), 159–60.

71 On the early development of Parliament, see Chapter 4; R. F. Trehane, "The Nature of Parliament in the Reign of Henry III," in *Historical Studies of the English Parliament*, vol. 1: *Origins to 1399*, eds. E. B. Fryde and Edward Miller (Cambridge: Cambridge University Press, 1970).

72 See Brooke, *From Alfred to Henry III*, 219–23 (quotation: 221).

73 See Gordon, *Controlling the State*, 230.

74 See George Holmes, *The Later Middle Ages, 1272–1485* (New York: T. Nelson, 1962), 86–8.

75 On these statutes, see R. H. Helmholz, *The Oxford History of the Laws of England*, vol. 1: *The Canon Law and Ecclesiastical Jurisdiction from 597 to the 1640s* (Oxford and New York: Oxford University Press, 2004), 177–80.

76 The text of the statute is available in Oswald J. Reichel, *The See of Rome in the Middle Ages* (London: Longmans, Green, and Co., 1870), 462–7.

77 See Michael A. R. Graves, *The Tudor Parliaments: Crown, Lords and Commons, 1485*–1603 (London and New York: Longman, 1985), 41.

78 J. S. Roskell argues this in "Perspectives in English Parliamentary History," in *Historical Studies of the English Parliament*, vol. 2: *1399 to 1603*, eds. E. B. Fryde and Edward Miller (Cambridge: Cambridge University Press, 1970), 322.

79 See Edmund Fryde, Introduction, in *Historical Studies of the English Parliament*, 2:22; J. E. Neal, "The Commons' Privilege of Free Speech in Parliament," in ibid.

80 See F. W. Maitland, *The Constitutional History of England*, ed. H. A. L. Fisher (Cambridge: Cambridge University Press, 1908), 255.

81 As quoted in G. R. Elton, *The Tudor Constitution: Documents and Commentary*, 2nd edn (New York: Cambridge University Press, 1982), 266.

82 On these debates, see Roskell, "Perspectives in English Parliamentary History."

83 See Gordon, *Controlling the* State, 245–7. The text is available in James I, *The True Law of Free Monarchies; and, Basilikon Doron*, eds. Daniel Fischlin and Mark Fortier (Toronto: Centre for Reformation and Renaissance Studies, 1996).

84 G. P. V. Akrigg, *Jacobean Pageant: Or, the Court of King James I* (Cambridge, MA: Harvard University Press, 1962), 85–6.

85 The next few paragraphs draw partly upon Barry Coward, *The Stuart Age: England, 1603–1714*, 4th edn (Harlow, UK and New York: Pearson Longman, 2012).

86 See Linda S. Popofsky, "The Crisis over Tonnage and Poundage in Parliament in 1629." *Past & Present* 126 (February 1990): 44–75.

87 The text is available in C. Warren Hollister, ed., *Landmarks of the Western Heritage*, 2 vols. (New York: Wiley, 1967), vol. 1, 501–4.

88 See G. E. Aylmer, *Rebellion or Revolution? England, 1640–1660* (Oxford and New York: Oxford University Press, 1986).

89 See David Underdown, *Pride's Purge: Politics in the Puritan Revolution* (Oxford: Oxford University Press, 1971); J. C. Davis, "Religion and the Struggle for Freedom in the English Revolution." *The Historical Journal* 35 (September 1992): 507–30.

90 See Ian Gentles, *The New Model Army in England, Ireland, and Scotland, 1645–1653* (Oxford and Cambridge, MA: Harvard University Press, 1992).

91 See Aylmer, *Rebellion or Revolution?* 108–16, 121. On the Puritans' religious policies, see Blair Worden, *God's Instruments: Political Conduct in the England of Oliver Cromwell* (Oxford and New York: Oxford University Press, 2012).

92 See Coward, *The Stuart Age*, 293.

93 See Geoffrey Holmes, *The Making of a Great Power: Late Stuart and Early Georgian Britain, 1660–1722* (London and New York: Longman, 1993), 88–92, 165–6.

94 See Holmes, *The Making of a Great Power*, 166–7.

95 Ibid., 167–74; Steven Pincus, *1688: The First Modern Revolution* (New Haven and London: Yale University Press 2009), chs. 4–7.

96 See Holmes, *The Making of a Great Power*, 169–70, 182–5.

97 See Julian Hoppit, *Land of Liberty? England 1689–1727* (Oxford: Oxford University Press, 2002), 2.

98 On these events, see Holmes, *The Making of a Great Power*, ch. 12; Pincus, *1688*, 224–37.

99 An abbreviated text of his Declaration is available in Steven C. A. Pincus, *The Glorious Revolution, 1688–1689: A Brief History with Documents* (Boston: Bedford/St. Martin's, 2006), 39–43 (here: 43).

100 On the unfolding of these events, see Hoppit, *Land of Liberty?*, ch. 2.

101 On the violence of the revolution, see Pincus, *1688*, ch. 9.

102 See Lois G. Schwoerer, *"No Standing Armies!" The Antiarmy Ideology in Seventeenth-Century England* (Baltimore: John Hopkins University Press, 1974).

103 See the text in Pincus, *The Glorious Revolution*, 69–71 (quotation: 70).

104 See Holmes, *The Making of a Great Power*, ch. 13.

105 On religious developments, see Pincus, *1688*, ch. 13.

106 See Hoppit, *Land of Liberty?*, ch. 5.

107 See, for example, Holmes, *The Making of a Great Power*, 137–42; Pincus, *1688*, 293.

108 See John Locke, *Two Treatises of Government*, ed. Peter Laslett, student ed. (Cambridge and New York: Cambridge University Press, 1988).

109 See Skinner, *The Foundations of Modern Political Thought*, vol. 2: *The Age of Reformation*, part 3.

110 On the publishing boom during the Civil War years, see David Zaret, *Origins of Democratic Culture: Printing, Petitions, and the Public Sphere in Early Modern England* (Princeton: Princeton University Press, 2000), ch. 7.

111 On early American history, see Alan Taylor, *American Colonies: The Settling of North America* (New York: Viking, 2001).

112 On colonial New England generally, see Joseph A. Conforti, *Saints and Strangers: New England in British North America* (Baltimore: The Johns Hopkins University Press, 2006).

113 On these developments, see Frederic W. Gleach, *Powhatan's World and Colonial Virginia: A Conflict of Cultures* (Lincoln, NE: University of Nebraska Press, 1997). On the economic development of the American colonies, see April Lee Hatfield, *Atlantic Virginia: Intercolonial Relations in the Seventeenth Century* (Philadelphia: University of Pennsylvania Press, 2004).

114 See Edmund S. Morgan, *American Slavery, American Freedom: The Ordeal of Colonial Virginia* (New York and London: W.W. Norton & Company, 1975); Betty Wood, *Slavery in Colonial America, 1619–1776* (Lanham, MD: Rowman & Littlefield, 2005).

115 See Sydney E. Ahlstrom, *A Religious History of the American People*, 2nd edn (New Haven: Yale University Press 2004), 105–6.

116 On the idea and practice of covenanted communities, see Edward Vallance, *Revolutionary England and the National Covenant: State Oaths, Protestantism, and the Political Nation, 1553*–1682 (Woodbridge, UK: Boydell Press, 2005).

117 The quotation, spoken by John Winthrop (1587/8–1649), a long-serving governor of the Massachusetts Bay Colony, is paraphrased from the New Testament (Mat 5:14-15). See Conforti, *Saints and Strangers*, 2–3, 40–1.

118 Paul Johnson makes this point in Paul Johnson, *A History of the American People* (New York: HarperCollins, 1997), 46–50.

119 See Ahlstrom, *A Religious History of the American People*, ch. 11.

120 See Jaap Jacobs, *The Colony of New Netherland: A Dutch Settlement in Seventeenth-Century America* (Ithaca: Cornell University Press, 2009).

121 See Ahlstrom, *A Religious History of the American People*, 109.

122 Ibid., 4.

123 See Gordon, *Controlling the State*, 286.

124 See Ran Abramitzky and Fabio Braggion. "Migration and Human Capital: Self-Selection of Indentured Servants to the Americas." *Journal of Economic History* 66 (December 2006): 882–905; Christopher L. Tomlins. *Freedom Bound: Law, Labor, and Civic Identity in Colonizing English America, 1580–1865* (New York: Cambridge University Press, 2010), 29–35.

125 See John C. Weaver, *The Great Land Rush and the Making of the Modern World, 1650–1900* (Montreal: Mcgill-Queen's University Press, 2006), ch. 4.

126 Statistic in Johnson, *A History of the American People*, 74.

127 Statistic in ibid., 92.

128 See James T. Lemon, "Colonial America in the Eighteenth Century," in *North America: The Historical Geography of a Changing Continent*, 2nd edn, eds. Thomas F. McIlwraith and Edward K. Muller (Lanham, MD: Rowman & Littlefield Publishers, 2001), 121, 143–4.

129 See David A. Copeland (ed.), *Debating the Issues in Colonial Newspapers: Primary Documents on Events of the Period* (Westport, CT: Greenwood Press, 2000), viii.

130 See, for example, *The Cambridge History of Latin America*, vol. 2: *Colonial Latin America*, ed. Leslie Bethell (Cambridge: Cambridge University Press, 1984), 701.

131 See Alvin Rabushka, *Taxation in Colonial America* (Princeton: Princeton University Press, 2008), 302–4.

132 See Gordon, *Controlling the State*, 288.

133 See Rabushka, *Taxation in Colonial America*, 14; Appendix: Tax Burdens in the American Colonies, 1714, in ibid.

134 This paragraph draws on Thomas S. Kidd, *The Great Awakening: The Roots of Evangelical Christianity in Colonial America* (New Haven and London: Yale University Press 2009).

135 Paul Johnson argues thus in *A History of the American People*, 116–17.

136 See Jeremy Black, *War for America: The Fight for Independence 1775*–1783 (New York: St. Martin's Press, 1991).

137 This paragraph draws on Robert Middlekauff, *The Glorious Cause: The American Revolution, 1763–1789* (Oxford and New York: Oxford University Press, 2005). See also Ray Raphael, *A People's History of the American Revolution: How Common People Shaped the Fight for Independence* (New York: New Press, 2002).

138 See, for example, Richard Buel, Jr., "Freedom of the Press in Revolutionary America: The Evolution of Libertarianism," in *The Press and the American Revolution*, eds. Bernard Bailyn and John B. Hench (Worcester: American Antiquarian Society, 1980).

139 See Thomas Jefferson, *A Summary View of the Rights of British America* (New York: Scholars' Facsimiles and Reprints, 1971).

140 See Gordon S. Wood, *The American Revolution: A History* (New York: Modern Library, 2002).

141 See Don Higginbotham, *The War of American Independence: Military Attitudes, Policies, and Practice, 1763–1789* (Boston: Northeastern University Press, 1983).

142 See Johnson, *A History of the American People*, 168–71; Wood, *The American Revolution*, 118–19, 127–34.

143 See Wood, *The American Revolution*, 113.

144 See Gordon S. Wood, *The Radicalism of the American Revolution* (New York: A.A. Knopf, 1991).

145 See Gordon, *Controlling the State*, 297–317.

146 See Michael Allen Gillespie and Michael Lienesch, Introduction, in *Ratifying the Constitution*, eds. Michael Allen Gillespie and Michael Lienesch (Lawrence, KA: University Press of Kansas, 1989), 1–2; Wood, *The Radicalism of the American Revolution*, 258.

147 For example, see John Patrick Diggins, *On Hallowed Ground: Abraham Lincoln and the Foundations of American History* (New Haven and London: Yale University Press, 2000), 44–61.

148 See, however, Richard M. Brown, "Violence and the American Revolution," in *Essays on the American Revolution,* eds. Stephen G. Kurtz and James H. Hutson (Chapel Hill: University of North Carolina Press, 1973).

149 See Paul Finkelman, "Jefferson and Slavery: 'Treason Against the Hopes of the World,'" *Jeffersonian Legacies*, ed. Peter S. Onuf (Charlottesville, VA: University Press of Virginia, 1993). See also Leonard W. Levy, *The Origins of the Bill of Rights* (New Haven: Yale University Press 1999); Michael Zuckerman, "Rhetoric, Reality, and the Revolution: The Genteel Radicalism of Gordon Wood." *The William and Mary Quarterly*, Third Series, 51 (October 1994): 693–702.

150 See Michal Jan Rozbicki, *Culture and Liberty in the Age of the American Revolution* (Charlottesville and London: University of Virginia Press, 2011).

151 Women could vote until 1807 in New Jersey, and free black men could vote in several states in the Early Republic. See Sally L. Kitch, *The Specter of Sex: Gendered Foundations of Racial Formation in the United States* (Albany: State University of New York Press, 2009), 181–8; Gordon S. Wood, *The Idea of America: Reflections on the Birth of the United States* (London: Penguin, 2011), 207.

152 See Alexander Keyssar, *The Right to Vote: The Contested History of Democracy in the United States* (New York: Basic Books, 2000), 28–33, Tables A.1, A.2, and A.3.

153 Angus Maddison, *The World Economy*, 2 vols. (Paris, 2006). The author lists seven main reasons for the disparate development of North and South America. See ibid., 1:109–10.

154 See Daron Acemoglu, Simon Johnson, and James A. Robinson, "The Colonial Origins of Comparative Development: An Empirical Investigation." *The American Economic Review* 91 (December 2001): 1369–401; Daron Acemoglu and James Robinson, *Why Nations Fail: The Origins of Power, Prosperity, and Poverty* (New York: Crown Business, 2012), especially ch. 1; Douglass C. North, William Summerhill, and Barry R. Weingast, "Order, Disorder and Economic Change: Latin America vs. North America," in *Governing for Prosperity*, eds. Bruce Bueno de Mesquita and Hilton L. Root (New Haven and London: Yale University Press 2000).

155 For astute observations on the early development of Latin America, see Alexis de Tocqueville, *Democracy in America*, trans. George Lawrence, ed. J. P. Mayer (Garden City, NY: Doubleday, 1969), 162–70, 226, 280, 305–8.

156 See Florin Aftalion, *The French Revolution: An Economic Interpretation* (Cambridge: Cambridge University Press, 1990), 191–4.

157 On the French *ancien régime* (or Old Regime), see William Doyle, *The Ancien Régime*, 2nd edn (Basingstoke, UK: Palgrave Macmillan, 2001); idem., ed., *The Oxford Handbook of the Ancien Regime* (Oxford: Oxford University Press, 2012); idem., ed., *Old Regime France, 1648–1788* (Oxford: Oxford University Press, 2001b).

158 See Joel Félix, "The Economy," in *Old Regime France*, ed. Doyle.

159 See Robert Fox and Anthony John Turner (eds), *Luxury Trades and Consumerism in Ancien Régime Paris: Studies in the History of the Skilled Workforce* (Brookfield, VT: Ashgate Publishing, 1998).

160 See Pierre H. Boule and D. Gillian Thompson, "France Overseas," in *Old Regime France,* ed. Doyle.

161 See Roger Price, *The Economic Modernisation of France, 1730–1880* (New York and Toronto: Halsted Press, 1975).

162 See Simon Schama, *Citizens: A Chronicle of the French Revolution* (New York: A.A. Knopf, 1989), 118–19.

163 See Dena Goodman, *The Republic of Letters: A Cultural History of the French Enlightenment* (Ithaca: Cornell University Press, 1994).

164 See Peter Gay, *The Enlightenment: An Interpretation*, vol. 2: *The Science of Freedom* (New York: A.A. Knopf, 1969), 36; Thomas Munck, "Enlightenment," in *Old Regime France*, ed. Doyle.

165 See Robert Darnton, *The Literary Underground of the Old Regime* (Cambridge, MA: Harvard University Press, 1982).

166 See Robert Darnton, *The Forbidden Best-Sellers of Prerevolutionary France* (New York: W.W. Norton & Company, 1996).

167 See Schama, *Citizens*, 103–8.

168 See Bailey Stone, *The Genesis of the French Revolution: A Global-Historical Interpretation* (Cambridge: Cambridge University Press, 1994).

169 See J. F. Bosher, *The French Revolution* (New York and London: W.W. Norton & Company, 1988), 85–91.

170 See Bosher, *The French Revolution*, 6–13, 124–5.

171 See Schama, *Citizens*, 238–47.

172 See Bosher, *The French Revolution*, 142–6.

173 The remainder of this paragraph draws on D. M. G. Sutherland, *France, 1789–1815: Revolution and Counterrevolution* (New York: Oxford University Press, 1986), chs. 5–6.

174 See David Andress, *The Terror: The Merciless War for Freedom in Revolutionary France* (New York: Farrar, Straus and Giroux, 2005).

175 Statistics cited in T. C. W. Blanning, *The French Revolution: Aristocrats Versus Bourgeois?* (Atlantic Heights, NJ: Humanities Press International, 1987), 45–8.

176 For a discussion of these contrasts, see John Markoff, "Violence, Emancipation, and Democracy: The Countryside and the French Revolution." *The American Historical Review* 100 (April 1995): 360–86.

177 This phrase was coined in François Furet, *Interpreting the French Revolution*, trans. Elborg Forster (Cambridge: Cambridge University Press, 1981), 129.

178 See William Doyle, *The French Revolution: A Very Short Introduction* (Oxford and New York: Oxford University Press, 2001a), 10.

179 See David P. Jordan, *Napoleon and the Revolution* (Houndmills, UK, and New York: Palgrave Macmillan, 2012), 10.

180 See Lester D. Langley, *The Americas in the Age of Revolution, 1750–1850* (New Haven: Yale University Press, 1996), chs. 4–6; David Patrick Geggus and Norman Fiering (eds), *The World of the Haitian Revolution* (Bloomington, IN: Indiana University Press, 2009).

181 Quoted from Doyle, *The French Revolution*, 75.

182 See Jonathan Sperber, *The European Revolutions, 1848–1851*, 2nd edn (Cambridge: Cambridge University Press, 2005), 273–80.

183 See Edhem Eldem, "Istanbul," in *Encyclopedia of the Ottoman Empire*, eds. Gabor Agoston and Bruce Masters (New York: Facts on File, 2009), 288.

184 See Jack A. Goldstone, *Revolution and Rebellion in the Early Modern World* (Berkeley and Los Angeles: University of California Press, 1991).

Chapter 11

1 See James E. McClellan III and Harold Dorn, *Science and Technology in World History: An Introduction* (Baltimore: Johns Hopkins University Press, 2006), 23–5.

2 See Jack A. Goldstone, "Efflorescences and Economic Growth in World History: Rethinking the 'Rise of the West' and the Industrial Revolution." *Journal of World History* 13 (2002): 323–89.

3 Statistic cited in Thomas K. McCraw, Introduction, in *Creating Modern Capitalism: How Entrepreneurs, Companies, and Countries Triumphed in Three Industrial Revolutions*, ed. Thomas K. McCraw (Cambridge, MA: Harvard University Press, 1995), 1.

4 See Solomos Solomou, *Phases of Economic Growth, 1850–1973: Kondratieff Waves and Kuznets Swings* (Cambridge: Cambridge University Press, 1987), ch. 3.

5 See Toby Wilkinson, *The Rise and Fall of Ancient Egypt* (New York: Random House, 2010).

6 On early Chinese development, see Valerie Hansen, *The Open Empire: A History of China to 1600* (New York: W.W. Norton & Company, 2000).

7 See Heping Liu, "'The Water Mill' and Northern Song Imperial Patronage of Art, Commerce, and Science." *The Art Bulletin* 84 (December 2002): 566–95.

8 See Joseph Needham, *Science and civilisation in China*, vol. 4: *Physics and physical technology*, pt. 3: *Civil Engineering and Nautics* (Cambridge: Cambridge University Press, 1971), 111–19.

9 For a detailed list of Chinese inventions, see Simon Winchester, *The Man Who Loved China: The Fantastic Story of the Eccentric Scientist Who Unlocked the Mysteries of the Middle Kingdom* (New York: HarperCollins, 2008), Appendix I.

10 See Kenneth Pomeranz, *The Great Divergence: Europe, China, and the Making of the Modern World Economy* (Princeton: Princeton University Press, 2000), 65.

11 See Donald B. Wagner, "The Administration of the Iron Industry in Eleventh-Century China." *Journal of the Economic and Social History of the Orient* 44 (2001): 175–97.

12 See Robert Hartwell, "A Revolution in the Chinese Iron and Coal Industries During the Northern Sung, 960–1126 A.D." *Journal of Asian Studies* 21 (February 1962): 153–62.

13 See William H. McNeill, *The Pursuit of Power: Technology, Armed Force, and Society since A.D. 1000* (Chicago: University of Chicago Press, 1982), 32.

14 See Joseph Needham, *Science in Traditional China: A Comparative Perspective* (Cambridge, MA: Harvard University Press, 1981), 15–21; David Landes, *Revolution in Time: Clocks and the Making of the Modern World*, rev. edn (Cambridge, MA: Harvard University Press, 2000), 15–28.

15 See Joseph Needham et al., *Science and Civilization in China*, vol. 5: *Chemistry and Chemical Technology*, pt. 7: *Military Technology: The Gunpowder Epic* (Cambridge: Cambridge University Press, 1986).

16 See McNeill, *The Pursuit of Power*, 83–90.

17 Statistic cited in Donald Langmead and Christine Garnaut, *Encyclopedia of Architectural and Engineering Feats* (Santa Barbara, CA: ABC-CLIO, 2001), 64.

18 See Marco Polo, *The Travels of Marco Polo*, trans. Ronald Latham (London: Penguin, 1958), 213–23.

19 See D. E. Mungello, *The Great Encounter of China and the West, 1500–1800*, 2nd edn (Lanham, MD: Rowman & Littlefield, 2005), 81. See also Wolfgang Franke, *China and the West*, trans. R. A. Wilson (Columbia: University of South Carolina Press, 1967).

20 Christine MacLeod, *Inventing the Industrial Revolution: The English Patent System, 1660–1800* (Cambridge: Cambridge University Press, 1988), 11.

21 See Joel Mokyr, "The Intellectual Origins of Modern Economic Growth." *The Journal of Economic History* 65 (2005): 285–351.

22 See Derk Bodde, *Chinese Thought, Society, and Science: The Intellectual and Social Background of Science and Technology Pre-modern China* (Honolulu: University of Hawaii Press, 1991), 222–35.

23 See Erich Meuthen, *Nicholas of Cusa: A Sketch for a Biography*, trans. David Crowner and Gerald Christianson (Washington, DC: Catholic University of America Press, 2010).

24 See John R. Pannabecker, "Representing Mechanical Arts in Diderot's 'Encyclopédie.'" *Technology and Culture* 39 (January 1998): 33–73 (here: 34).

25 See James Cracraft, *The Revolution of Peter the Great* (Cambridge, MA and London: Harvard University Press, 2003).

26 See Joel Mokyr, *The Gifts of Athena: Historical Origins of the Knowledge Economy* (Princeton: Princeton University Press, 2002), ch. 1.

27 Quoted in Mokyr, *The Gifts of Athena*, 42.

28 Benjamin Franklin formed a discussion group for journeymen in Philadelphia even earlier (1727). See Deirdre McCloskey, *Bourgeois Dignity: Why Economics Can't Explain the Modern World* (Chicago: University of Chicago Press, 2010), 392.

29 See Robert E. Schofield, *The Lunar Society of Birmingham: A Social History of Provincial Science and Industry in Eighteenth-Century England* (Oxford: Oxford University Press, 1963).

30 Statistics cited in Liên Luu, *Immigrants and the Industries of London, 1500–1700* (Burlington, VT: Ashgate Publishing, 2005), 34; George Modelski, *World Cities: -3000*

to 2000 (Washington, DC: Faros, 2003), 66–7. It is also worth noting that Beijing constituted only about one one-hundred-fiftieth of China's total population.

31 Statistics supplied by C. G. A. Clay, *Economic Expansion and Social Change: England 1500–1700* (New York: Cambridge University Press, 1984), 169.

32 See Richard Brown, *Society and Economy in Modern Britain 1700–1850* (London: Routledge, 1990), ch. 5.

33 See François Crouzet, *A History of the European Economy, 1000–2000* (Charlottesville, VA: University of Virginia Press, 2001), 96.

34 See Steven C. A. Pincus, *The Glorious Revolution, 1688–1689: A Brief History with Documents* (Boston: Bedford/St. Martin's, 2006), 9–10.

35 See Frank Staff, *The Penny Post, 1680–1918* (London: Lutterworth Press, 1964), 34–49.

36 See Andre Gunder Frank, *ReORIENT: Global economy in the Asian Age* (Berkeley: University of California Press, 1998), 231.

37 See Phyllis Deane and W. A. Cole, *British Economic Growth, 1688–1959*, 2nd edn (Cambridge: Cambridge University Press, 1967), 83.

38 See Gay L. Gullickson, "Agriculture and Cottage Industry: Redefining the Causes of Proto-Industrialization." *The Journal of Economic History* 43 (December 1983): 831–50.

39 See Thomas McKeown and R. G. Brown, "Medical Evidence Related to English Population Changes in the Eighteenth Century." *Population Studies* 9 (November 1955): 119–41; Peter Razzell, "The Growth of Population in Eighteenth-Century England: A Critical Reappraisal." *The Journal of Economic History* 53 (December 1993): 743–71.

40 Brian Lavery, *Nelson's Navy: The Ships, Men, and Organisation, 1793–1815* (London: Conway Maritime Press Ltd, 1989), 90; Richard Grassby, *The Business Community of Seventeenth-Century England* (Cambridge: Cambridge University Press, 1995), 158–9.

41 Steven Pincus advances this argument in *1688: The First Modern Revolution* (New Haven and London: Yale University Press 2009), 90.

42 See Pincus *1688*, ch. 12.

43 See Janet L. Abu-Lughod, *Before European Hegemony: The World System A.D. 1250–1350* (New York: Oxford University Press, 1989).

44 See Frank, *ReORIENT*.

45 See Kenneth Pomeranz, *The Great Divergence: Europe, China, and the Making of the Modern World Economy* (Princeton: Princeton University Press, 2000).

46 Georg Borgstrom, *The Hungry Planet: The Modern World at the Edge of Famine* (New York: Collier Books, 1967), ch. 5; William R. Catton, *Overshoot: The Ecological Basis of Revolutionary Change* (Urbana, IL: University of Illinois Press, 1982), 38–45.

47 See also E. L. Jones, *The European Miracle: Environments, Economies, and Geopolitics in the History of Europe and Asia* (London and New York: Cambridge University Press, 1981), ch. 4.

48 For critical assessments of Pomeranz's book, see P. H. H. Vries, "Are Coal and Colonies Really Crucial? Kenneth Pomeranz and the Great Divergence." *Journal of World History* 12 (Fall 2001): 407–46; C. C. Philip Huang, "Review: Development or Involution in Eighteenth-Century Britain and China? A Review of Kenneth Pomeranz's 'The Great Divergence: China, Europe, and the Making of the Modern World Economy'." *The Journal of Asian Studies* 61 (May 2002): 501–38.

49 See Stephen Broadberry and Bishnupriya Gupta, "The Early Modern Great Divergence: Wages, Prices and Economic Development in Europe and Asia, 1500–1800." *Economic History Review* 59 (February 2006): 2–31.

50 See Pomeranz, *The Great Divergence*, 38–53.

51 See Jeremy Black, *War and the World: Military Power and the Fate of Continents, 1450–2000* (New Haven and London: Yale University Press 1998), 10.

52 J. A. Chartres, "The Marketing of Agricultural Produce," in *The Agrarian History of England and Wales*, vol. 5: *1640–1750*, eds. H. P. R. Finberg, Joan Thirsk, and Stuart Piggott (Cambridge: Cambridge University Press, 1985), 446.

53 On the benefits to Europeans of possessing abundant livestock, see E. L. Jones, *The European Miracle: Environments, Economies, and Geopolitics in the History of Europe and Asia* (London and New York: Cambridge University Press, 1981), 3–4, 9–18.

54 Jones, *The European Miracle*, 82; McCloskey, *Bourgeois Dignity*, 1–6, 34, 48–50, 210.

55 The territory of Muscovy expanded 320-fold (from some 17,800 to roughly 5.7 million square miles) in the period 1300–1700. See Lawrence N. Langer, *Historical Dictionary of Medieval Russia* (Lanham, MD: Scarecrow Press, 2002), 12.

56 See Eric Williams, *Capitalism and Slavery*, intro. Colin A. Palmer (Chapel Hill and London: The University North Carolina Press, 1994 [1944]). See also Heather Cateau and S. H. H. Carrington (eds), *Capitalism and Slavery Fifty Years Later: Eric Eustace Williams–A Reassessment of the Man and His Work* (New York: Peter Lang Publishing, 2000).

57 See, in particular, Robin Blackburn, *The Making of New World Slavery: From the Baroque to the Modern, 1492–1800* (London and New York: Verso, 1997); Joseph E. Inikori, *Africans and the Industrial Revolution in England: A Study in International Trade and Economic Development* (Cambridge: Cambridge University Press, 2002).

58 See David Eltis and Stanley L. Engerman, "The Importance of Slavery and the Slave Trade to Industrializing Britain." *The Journal of Economic History* 60 (March 2000): 123–44; David Richardson, "The British Empire and the Atlantic Slave Trade, 1660–1807." in *The Oxford History of the British Empire*, vol. 2: *The Eighteenth Century*, ed. P. J. Marshall (Oxford and New York: Oxford University Press, 1998); McCloskey, *Bourgeois Dignity*, ch. 26.

59 See Roger T. Anstey, "Capitalism and Slavery: A Critique." *The Economic History Review*, New Series 21 (August 1968): 307–20; Kenneth Morgan, *Slavery and the British Empire: From Africa to America* (Oxford and New York: Oxford University Press, 2007), 81.

60 See David Eltis, *The Rise of African Slavery in the Americas* (Cambridge: Cambridge University Press, 2000), 162.

61 See Stanley L. Engerman, "The Slave Trade and British Capital Formation in the Eighteenth Century: A Comment on the Williams Thesis." *The Business History Review* 46 (Winter, 1972): 430–43; Eltis and Engerman, "The Importance of Slavery and the Slave Trade"; R. P. Thomas and D. N. McCloskey, "Overseas Trade and Empire, 1700–1860," in *The Economic History of Britain since 1700*, vol. 1: 1700–1860, eds. Roderick Floud and Donald McCloskey (Cambridge: Cambridge University Press, 1981), 97–9.

62 Statistics supplied by Eltis and Engerman, "The Importance of Slavery and the Slave Trade," 129, 132.

63 See McCloskey, *Bourgeois Dignity*, 153.

64 See Kenneth Morgan, *Bristol and the Atlantic Trade in the Eighteenth Century* (Cambridge: Cambridge University Press, 1993), 2.

65 See Elise S. Brezis, "Foreign Capital Flows in the Century of Britain's Industrial Revolution: New Estimates, Controlled Conjectures." *The Economic History Review*, New Series 48 (February 1995): 46–67.

66 McCloskey makes this point in *Bourgeois Dignity*, 201.

67 See Joel Mokyr, "The New Economic History and the Industrial Revolution," in *The British Industrial Revolution: An Economic Perspective*, ed. Joel Mokyr (Boulder, CO: University of Colorado Press, 1999). See also McCloskey, *Bourgeois Dignity*.

68 See Robert B. Marks, *The Origins of the Modern World: A Global and Ecological Narrative* (Lanham, MD: Rowman & Littlefield, 2002), 101.

69 See Chris Evans and Göran Rydén, Introduction, *The Industrial Revolution in Iron: The Impact of British Coal Technology in Nineteenth-Century Europe*, eds. Chris Evans and Göran Rydén (Burlington, VT: Ashgate Publishing, 2005), 1.

70 See John Hatcher, *Before 1700: Towards the Age of Coal*, vol. 1 of *The History of the British Coal Industry* (Oxford: Oxford University Press, 1984), chs. 1–2, 12.

71 See Michael W. Flinn, with David Stoker, *1700–1830: The Industrial Revolution*, vol. 2 of *The History of the British Coal Industry*, 239–40.

72 The most authoritative study remains Charles Singer et al. (eds), *A History of Technology*, vol. 4: *The Industrial Revolution, 1750–1850* (New York and London: Oxford Clarendon Press, 1958).

73 See Eugene S. Ferguson, "The Steam Engine Before 1830," in *Technology in Western Civilization*, eds. Melvin Kranzberg and Carroll W. Pursell, Jr. (New York: Oxford University Press, 1967); John Kanefsky and John Robey, "Steam Engines in 18th-Century Britain: A Quantitative Assessment." *Technology and Culture* 21 (April 1980): 161–86; T. K. Derry and Trevor I. Williams, *A Short History of Technology: From the Earliest Times to A.D. 1900* (Oxford: Oxford University Press, 1960), 311–19.

74 See Joel Mokyr, *The Lever of Riches: Technological Creativity and Economic Progress* (New York: Oxford University Press, 1990), 988; Abbott Payson Usher, *A History of Mechanical Inventions* (Boston: Beacon Press, 1959), 346–54.

75 See A. E. Musson and Eric Robinson, *Science and Technology in the Industrial Revolution* (Manchester: Manchester University Press, 1969), ch. 2; Derry and Williams, *A Short History of Technology*, 104–8.

76 See Abbot Payson Usher, "The Textile Industry, 1750–1830," in *Technology in Western Civilization*, eds. Kranzberg and Pursell. On the emergence of cotton textile manufacture, see O. I. May and K. E. Lege, "Development of the World Cotton Industry," in *Cotton: Origin, History, Technology, and Production*, eds. C. Wayne Smith and Joe Tom Cothren (New York: John Wiley & Sons, 1999).

77 See Trevor Griffiths, Philip A. Hunt, and Patrick K. O'Brien, "Inventive Activity in the British Textile Industry, 1700–1800." *The Journal of Economic History* 52 (December 1992): 881–906; Derry and Williams, *A Short History of Technology*, ch. 19.

78 See Mokyr, *The Lever of Riches*, ch. 5.

79 Ibid., 97–104; Griffiths, Hunt, and O'Brien, "Inventive Activity in the British Textile Industry," 889.

80 See Beverly Lemire, *Cotton* (Oxford and New York: Oxford University Press, 2011), 91.

81 See Michael Adas, *Machines As the Measure of Men: Science, Technology, and Ideologies of Western Dominance* (Ithaca and London: Cornell University Press, 1989), 135.

82 See Nancy F. Koehn, "Josiah Wedgwood and the First Industrial Revolution," in *Creating Modern Capitalism*, ed. McCraw.

83 See Koehn, "Josiah Wedgwood and the First Industrial Revolution," 40.

84 Statistic supplied by Koehn, "Josiah Wedgwood and the First Industrial Revolution," 42.

85 See Chris Evans, "The Industrial Revolution in Iron in the British Isles," in *The Industrial Revolution in Iron,* eds. Evans and Rydén, 15–28.

86 See Adas, *Machines as the Measure of Men*, 135.

87 See Manfred Weissenbacher, *Sources of Power: How Energy Forges Human History*, 2 vols in 1 (Santa Barbara, CA: ABC-CLIO, 2009), 199–205.

88 See Roger Fouquet, *Heat, Power and Light: Revolutions in Energy Services* (Cheltenham, UK and Northampton, MA: Edward Elgar, 2008), 120.

89 See John Griffiths, *The Third Man: The Life and Times of William Murdoch 1754–1839* (London: A. Deutsch, 1992); Leslie Tomory, *Progressive Enlightenment: The Origins of the Gaslight Industry, 1780–1820* (Cambridge, MA: MIT Press, 2012).

90 See Mokyr, *The Lever of Riches*, 88; Derry and Williams, *A Short History of Technology*, 325–9.

91 See Derry and Williams, *A Short History of Technology*, 331–3.

92 See P. J. G. Ransom, *The Victorian Railway and How It Evolved* (London: Heinemann, 1990).

93 See John Mickelthwait and Adrian Wooldridge, *The Company: A Short History of a Revolutionary Idea* (New York: Modern Library, 2003), 41–2.

94 This paragraph draws upon Mickelthwait and Wooldridge, *The Company*, 43–54.

95 See Celia de Anca and Antonio Vazquez Vega, *Managing Diversity in the Global Organization: Creating New Business Values* (Houndmills, UK and New York: Palgrave Macmillan, 2007), 39.

96 Statistic cited in Mickelthwait and Wooldridge, *The Company*, 52.

97 See Timur Kuran, "The Absence of the Corporation in Islamic Law: Origins and Persistence." *The American Journal of Comparative Law* 53 (Fall 2005): 785–834.

98 See Lavery, *Nelson's Navy*, 64.

99 See Ransom, *The Victorian Railway*, 101.

100 See Geoffrey L. Herrera, *Technology and International Transformation: The Railroad, the Atom Bomb, and the Politics of Technological Change* (Albany: State University of New York Press, 2006), 53 (high number); McCloskey, *Bourgeois Dignity*, 169 (low number).

101 See Herrera, *Technology and International Transformation*, 35.

102 Thomas K. McCraw, "American Capitalism," in *Creating Modern Capitalism*, ed. McCraw, 318–19.

103 Statistics cited in B. R. Mitchell, *European Historical Statistics, 1750–1970*, abridged ed. (New York: Columbia University Press, 1978), 315–16.

104 See Jude Wanniski, *The Way the World Works* (Washington, DC: Regnery Gateway, 1998), 187.

105 Goldstone, "Efflorescences and Economic Growth in World History," 323–89 (here: 365).

106 Statistics cited in Wanniski, *The Way the World Works*, 187.

107 See these numbers in Peter Boticelli, "British Capitalism and the Three Industrial Revolutions," in *Creating Modern Capitalism*, ed. McCraw, 62.

108 See Koehn, "Josiah Wedgwood and the First Industrial Revolution," 25.

109 See Crouzet, *A History of the European Economy*, 115.

110 Statistics available in Peter N. Stearns, *European Society in Upheaval: Social History since 1750* (New York: The Macmillan Company, 1967), 112.

111 For data reflecting centuries of growth, see Stephen Codrington, *Planet Geography*, 3rd edn (Sydney: Solid Star Press, 2005), 576. No other city in history had greatly exceeded 1 million population. See Modelski, *World Cities*.

112 See Musson and Robinson, *Science and Technology in the Industrial Revolution*, ch. 6; Charles P. Kindleberger, *Comparative Political Economy: A Retrospective* (Cambridge, MA: Harvard University Press, 2000), 80.

113 See Kindleberger, *Comparative Political Economy*, 125.

114 Kindleberger, *Comparative Political Economy*, 118.

115 This paragraph draws upon Crouzet, *A History of the European Economy*, 116–21.

116 Statistic cited in Crouzet, *A History of the European Economy*, 124.

117 Crouzet makes this point in *A History of the European Economy*, 120.

118 This paragraph is informed by Kenneth L. Sokoloff and David Dollar, "Agricultural Seasonality and the Organization of Manufacturing in Early Industrial Economies: The Contrast Between England and the United States." *The Journal of Economic History* 57 (June 1997): 288–321.

119 See Derry and Williams, *A Short History of Technology*, 355–6.

120 See David A. Hounshell, *From the American System to Mass Production, 1800–1932: The Development of Manufacturing Technology in the United States* (Baltimore: The Johns Hopkins University Press, 1984).

121 See Ken Alder, *Engineering the Revolution: Arms and Enlightenment in France, 1763–1815* (Princeton: Princeton University Press, 1997).

122 Edmund Fuller, *Tinkers and Genius: The Story of the Yankee Inventors* (New York: Hastings House, 1955), 238–9; David R. Meyer, *The Roots of American Industrialization* (Baltimore: The Johns Hopkins University Press, 2003), 83–6.

123 See Fuller, *Tinkers and Genius*, 230; Meyer, *The Roots of American Industrialization*, 231.

124 Meyer, *The Roots of American Industrialization*, 229.

125 See Robert F. Dalzell, *Enterprising Elite: The Boston Associates and the World They Made* (Cambridge, MA: Harvard University Press, 1987), ch. 1; Fuller, *Tinkers and Genius*, 165–78; Meyer, *The Roots of American Industrialization*, 96–9.

126 See Meyer, *The Roots of American Industrialization*, 115–19; Fuller, *Tinkers and Genius*, 177–82.

127 See Dalzell, *Enterprising Elite*, ch. 2.

128 See Hannah Josephson, *The Golden Threads: New England's Mill Girls and Magnates* (New York: Duell, Sloan and Pearce, 1949).

129 Statistics and details available in Chaim M. Rosenberg, *The Life and Times of Francis Cabot Lowell, 1775–1817* (Lanham, MD: Lexington Books, 2011), 294–300.

130 This paragraph draws on data presented in Meyer, *The Roots of American Industrialization*, 126–36.

131 See Jonathan D. Spence, *The Search for Modern China*, 2nd edn (New York and London: W.W. Norton & Company, 1999), 134.

132 See Pomeranz, *The Great Divergence*, 39–40.

133 See, for example, Mark Elvin, *The Pattern of the Chinese Past* (Stanford: Stanford University Press, 1973); Gang Deng, *The Premodern Chinese Economy: Structural Equilibrium and Capitalist Sterility* (London and New York: Routledge, 1999).

134 On the Luddites and other opponents of technological changes in the early nineteenth century, see Stearns, *European Society in Upheaval*, 103–4.

135 In general, it seems many poets of the age felt more animosity toward industrialization than science. See Jacques Barzun, *Classic, Romantic, and Modern*, 2nd edn (Chicago and London: University of Chicago Press, 1961), 64–5.

136 See Frank E. Manuel and Fritzie P. Manuel, *Utopian Thought In The Western World* (Cambridge, MA: Belknap Press, 1979), pt. 5.

Chapter 12

1 See Jill Jonnes, *Empires of Light: Edison, Tesla, Westinghouse, and the Race to Electrify the World* (New York: Random House, 2003), chs. 11–12.

2 See Harold I. Sharlin, *The Making of the Electrical Age: From the Telegraph to Automation* (London and New York: Abelard-Schuman, 1963), 195.

3 See M. E. Turner, J. V. Beckett, and B. Afton, *Farm Production in England 1700–1914* (Oxford: Oxford University Press, 2001).

4 See Gregory Clark, "Yields Per Acre in English Agriculture, 1250–1860: Evidence from Labour Inputs." *The Economic History Review*, New Series 44 (August 1991): 445–60.

5 See Kenneth Pomeranz, *The Great Divergence: Europe, China, and the Making of the Modern World Economy* (Princeton: Princeton University Press, 2000), 13.

6 See Alan L. Olmstead and Paul W. Rhode, *Creating Abundance: Biological Innovation and American Agricultural Development* (New York: Cambridge University Press, 2008), 4.

7 See Peter D. McClelland, *Sowing Modernity: America's First Agricultural Revolution* (Ithaca: Cornell University Press, 1997), 140–3; Carl Crow, *The Great American Customer* (1943; Freeport, NY: Books for Libraries Press, 1970), 64, 184.

8 See McClelland, *Sowing Modernity*, 49–61; Crow, *The Great American Customer*, 68–71.

9 This paragraph draws upon David A. Hounshell, *From the American System to Mass Production, 1800–1932: The Development of Manufacturing Technology in the United States* (Baltimore: The Johns Hopkins University Press, 1984), ch. 4.

10 See Crow, *The Great American Customer*, 188.

11 On these inventions, see Ronald Stokes Barlow, *300 Years of Farm Implements and Machinery, 1630–1930* (Iola, WI: Krause Publications, 2003); Thompson, *The Age of*

Invention, ch. 5; Walter Prescott Webb, *The Great Plains* (Boston: Houghton Mifflin, 1931), 240–4, 270–2.

12 See Vaclav Smil, *Creating the Twentieth Century: Technical Innovations of 1867–1914 and Their Lasting Impact* (Oxford: Oxford University Press, 2005), 293.

13 See Olmstead and Rhode, *Creating Abundance*, 3.

14 Statistics supplied in Olmstead and Rhode, *Creating Abundance*, 20–1.

15 This is the main point of Olmstead and Rhode, *Creating Abundance*, ch. 2.

16 Statistics in United States. Bureau of the Census, *Statistical History of the United States from Colonial Times to the Present* (Stamford, CT: Fairfield Publishers, 1965), 281.

17 See George Fetherling, *The Gold Crusades: A Social History of Gold Rushes, 1849–1929*, rev. edn (Toronto, Buffalo and London: University of Toronto Press, 1997).

18 See Sydney E. Ahlstrom, *A Religious History of the American People*, 2nd edn (New Haven: Yale University Press 2004), 735.

19 See Stuart Banner, *How the Indians Lost Their Land: Law and Power on the Frontier* (Cambridge, MA: Harvard University Press, 2005), ch. 6.

20 See "Teaching With Documents: The Homestead Act of 1862," http://www.archives.gov/education/lessons/homestead-act/ (accessed 14 June 2013).

21 See Francis R. Kowsky, "Monuments of a Vanished Prosperity," in *Reconsidering Concrete Atlantis: Buffalo Grain Elevators*, ed. Lynda H. Schneekloth (Buffalo, NY: The Landmark Society of the Niagara Frontier, 2006), 20–31.

22 See Guy A. Lee, "The Historical Significance of the Chicago Grain Elevator System." *Agricultural History* 11 (January 1937): 16–32; Maury Klein, *The Genesis of Industrial America, 1870–1920* (New York: Cambridge University Press, 2007), 44–5.

23 See Donald L. Miller, *City of the Century: The Epic of Chicago and the Making of America* (New York: Simon & Schuster, 1996), 89.

24 Statistic cited in Miller, *City of the Century*, 108.

25 See Marco D'Eramo, *The Pig and the Skyscraper: Chicago: A History of Our Future*, trans. Graeme Thomson, foreword by Mike Davis (London and New York: Verso, 2003), 30–9.

26 See D'Eramo, *The Pig and the Skyscraper*, 37–8.

27 See United States, Bureau of Foreign and Domestic Commerce, *Statistical Abstract of the United States* (Washington, DC: Government Printing Office, 1913), 300.

28 See Chaim M. Rosenberg, *America At the Fair: Chicago's 1893 World's Columbian Exposition* (Mount Pleasant, SC: Arcadia Pub., 2008), 119–22.

29 See Alfred D. Chandler, Jr., "Integration and Diversification as Business Strategies – An Historical Analysis." *Business and Economic History,* Second Series 19 (1990): 65–73.

30 See D'Eramo, *The Pig and the Skyscraper*, 30–2.

31 This paragraph draws upon Col. George E. Rogers, "History of Flour Manufacture in Minnesota." *Minnesota Historical Collections* 10 (St. Paul, MN: Published by the Society, 1905).

32 The American domestic market, not foreign trade, was the main engine of economic growth, according to Irving B. Kravis, "The Role of Exports in Nineteenth-Century United States Growth." *Economic Development and Cultural Change* 20 (April 1972): 387–405 (here: 404–5).

33 Statistics supplied in Harvey Levenstein, *Revolution at the Table: The Transformation of the American Diet* (Berkeley: University of California Press, 2003), 32.

34 Chicago was notorious in this regard. See James Cracraft, *Two Shining Souls: Jane Addams, Leo Tolstoy, and The Quest For Global Peace* (Lanham, MD: Lexington Books, 2012), 4–6.

35 See William J. Barber, *From New Era to New Deal: Herbert Hoover, the Economists, and American Economic Policy, 1921–1933* (Cambridge and New York: Cambridge University Press, 1985), 46–7.

36 See Michael B. Katz, *In the Shadow of the Poorhouse: A Social History of Welfare in America*, rev. edn (New York: Basic Books, 1996), 186, 194–6.

37 See Sue Shephard, *Pickled, Potted, and Canned: How the Art and Science of Food Preserving Changed the World* (New York: Simon & Schuster, 2001), 219; James Monroe Jay, Martin J. Loessner, and David Allen Golden, *Modern Food Microbiology*, 7th edn (New York: Springer, 2005), 4–6.

38 See Felipe Fernández-Armesto, *Near a Thousand Tables: A History of Food* (New York: Free Press, 2002), 212.

39 See Shephard, *Pickled, Potted, and Canned*, ch. 12. See also Fernández-Armesto, *Near a Thousand Tables*, 212–13; Colin Spencer, *British Food: An Extraordinary Thousand Years of History* (London: Grub Street, 2002), 282.

40 See Andrew F. Smith, *Eating History: 30 Turning Points in the Making of American Cuisine* (New York: Columbia University Press, 2009), 68; Levenstein, *Revolution at the Table*, 28, 36.

41 See Fernández-Armesto, *Near a Thousand Tables*, 213; Smith, *Eating History*, ch. 8.

42 Statistic in Walter Bruno Gratzer, *Terrors of the Table: The Curious History of Nutrition* (Oxford and New York: Oxford University Press, 2005), 108; Shephard, *Pickled, Potted, and Canned*, 241–2.

43 Shephard, *Pickled, Potted, and Canned*, 249–51.

44 See Spencer, *British Food*, 284–6.

45 See Maurice M. Manring, *Slave in A Box: The Strange Career of Aunt Jemima* (Charlottesville: University of Virginia Press, 1998).

46 See Gary J. Allen and Ken Albala (eds), *The Business of Food: Encyclopedia of the Food and Drink Industries* (Westport, CT: Greenwood Press, 2007), 341–2.

47 Bruce S. Schoenberg, "Coke's the One: The Centennial of the 'Ideal Brain Tonic' That Became a Symbol of America." *Southern Medical Journal* 81 (January 1988): 69–74.

48 This story is told in Smith, *Eating History*, ch. 16.

49 See Joel Levy, *Really Useful: The Origins of Everyday Things* (Buffalo: Firefly Books, 2002), 32.

50 See Levenstein, *Revolution at the Table*, 31.

51 See Allen and Albala (eds), *The Business of Food*, 244.

52 See Samuel A. Goldblith, *Samuel Cate Prescott, M.I.T. Dean and Pioneer Food Technologist*, vol. 2 of *Pioneers in Food Science* (Trumball, CT: Food & Nutrition Press, Inc., 1993), ch. 4.

53 Statistic in Levenstein, *Revolution at the Table*, 37.

54 Claim advanced in C. J. K. Henry, "New Food Processing Technologies: From Foraging to Farming to Food Technology." *Proceedings of the Nutrition Society* 56 (1997): 855–63 (here: 857).

55 See Allan G. Bogue, "Changes in Mechanical and Plant Technology: The Corn Belt, 1910–1940." *The Journal of Economic History* 43 (March 1983): 1–25.

56 Clark Archer, "A Medium-Term Perspective on Demographic Change in the American Midlands, 1803–1990," in *Contemporary Rural Systems in Transition*, vol. 2: *Economy and Society*, eds. I. R. Bowler, C. R. Bryant, and M. D. Nellis (Wallingford, UK and Tucson: CABI, 1992), 76.

57 On the development of frozen foods, see Shephard, *Pickled, Potted, and Canned*, ch. 14; Smith, *Eating History*, ch. 18.

58 On A&P and other grocery chains, see Smith, *Eating History*, 176–83.

59 See, for example, Kathleen L. Endres and Therese L. Lueck (eds), *Women's Periodicals in the United States: Consumer Magazines* (Westport, CT: Greenwood Press, 1995); Matthew Schneirov, *The Dream of a New Social Order: Popular Magazines in America, 1893–1914* (New York: Columbia University Press, 1994).

60 See David Gerard Hogan, *Selling 'em by the Sack: White Castle and the Creation of American Food* (New York: New York University Press, 1999).

61 See Stephen Van Dulken, *Inventing the 20th Century: 100 Inventions That Shaped the World from the Airplane to the Zipper* (New York: Simon & Schuster, 2000), 64.

62 See, for example, Fernández-Armesto, *Near a Thousand Tables*, 19, 223–4.

63 See Bern Dibner, "The Beginning of Electricity," in vol. 1 of *Technology in Western Civilization*, 2 vols., eds. Melvin Kranzberg and Carroll W. Pursell (New York: Oxford University Press, 1967); Sanford P. Bordeau, *Volts to Hertz—The Rise of Electricity: From the Compass to the Radio through the Works of Sixteen Great Men of Science Whose Names are Used in Measuring Electricity and Magnetism* (Minneapolis, MN: Burgess Pub. Co., 1982).

64 See Dibner, "The Beginning of Electricity," vol. 1, 446–9; Smil, *Creating the Twentieth Century*, 34.

65 See Sharlin, *The Making of the Electrical Age*, 173.

66 See Thomas Coulson, *Joseph Henry: His Life and Work* (Princeton: Princeton University Press, 1950).

67 See Tom Standage, *The Victorian Internet: The Remarkable Story of the Telegraph and the Nineteenth Century's On-line Pioneers* (New York: Walker and Co., 1998), 33–4, 50–5.

68 On Morse's efforts, see Richard R. John, *Network Nation: Inventing American Telecommunications* (Cambridge, MA: Harvard University Press, 2010), ch. 2.

69 T. K. Derry and Trevor I. Williams, *A Short History of Technology: From the Earliest Times to A.D. 1900* (Oxford: Oxford University Press, 1960), 627.

70 See John, *Network Nation*, 81–2, 95–103; Menahem Blondheim, *News Over the Wires: The Telegraph and the Flow of Public Information in America, 1844–1897* (Cambridge, MA: Harvard University Press, 1994).

71 See Standage, *The Victorian Internet*, 148–58.

72 See Dennis W. Johnson, *Campaigning in the Twenty-First Century: A Whole New Ballgame?* (New York: Routledge, 2011), 25.

73 See Neil Baldwin, *Edison: Inventing the Century* (Chicago and London: University of Chicago Press, 2001), 47–8.

74 See Baldwin, *Edison*, 68–86.

75 Thomas Parke Hughes, *Networks of Power: Electrification in Western Society, 1880–1930* (Baltimore: The Johns Hopkins University Press, 1983), chs. 1–2.

76 On Tesla, see Jonnes, *Empires of Light*, ch. 4.

77 See Quentin R. Skrabec, Jr., *George Westinghouse: Gentle Genius* (New York: Algora Pub., 2007).

78 For the development of turbines, see Abbott Payson Usher, *A History of Mechanical Inventions* (Boston: Beacon Press, 1959), 382–92; Terry S. Reynolds, *Stronger Than a Hundred Men: A History of the Vertical Water Wheel* (Baltimore and London: The Johns Hopkins University Press, 1983), 338–49.

79 See Usher, *A History of Mechanical Inventions*, 403.

80 See Smil, *Creating the Twentieth Century*, 87–8.

81 See John Graham-Cumming, *The Geek Atlas: 128 Places Where Science and Technology Come Alive* (Sebastopol, CA: O'Reilly Media, Inc., 2009), 485–6.

82 See Derry and Williams, *A Short History of Technology*, 337–9; Smil, *Creating the Twentieth Century*, 60–8. Large ships even today can barely exceed that speed. See Frank Osborn Braynard and Robert Hudson Westover, *S.S. United States: Fastest Ship in the World* (Paducah, KY: Turner, 2002).

83 See Usher, *A History of Mechanical Inventions*, 392–400 (statistics: 397–8).

84 See David F. Noble, *America by Design: Science, Technology, and the Rise of Corporate Capitalism* (Oxford: Oxford University Press, 1997), 84–8.

85 Ian Inkster, "Intellectual Property, Information, and Divergences in Economic Development – Institutional Patterns and Outcomes circa 1421–2000," in *The Role of Intellectual Property Rights in Biotechnology Innovation*, ed. David Castle (Cheltenham, UK and Northampton, MA: Edward Elgar, 2009), 417.

86 See B. Zorina Khan, *The Democratization of Invention: Patents and Copyrights in American Economic Development, 1790–1920* (New York: Cambridge University Press, 2005), 49–65.

87 See Lynn G. Gref, *The Rise and Fall of American Technology* (New York: Algora Publishing, 2010), 67.

88 Quoted in Noble, *America by Design*, 84.

89 See, for example, Trevor I. Williams, *History of Invention: From Stone Axes to Silicon Chips*, rev. edn (New York: Checkmark Books, 2000).

90 See Kendall Haven, *100 Greatest Science Inventions of All Time* (Westport, CT: Libraries Unlimited, 2006), 141–3.

91 See Grace Rogers Cooper, *The Sewing Machine: Its Invention and Development* (Washington, DC: Smithsonian Institution Press, 1976), ch. 2.

92 See Louis H. Grossman and Marianne Jennings, *Building a Business Through Good Times and Bad: Lessons from 15 Companies, Each with a Century of Dividends* (Westport, CT: Quorum Books, 2002), 29–32.

93 See Smil, *Creating the Twentieth Century*, 76–9.

94 See Skrabec, *George Westinghouse*, 211.

95 See Carroll Gantz, *The Vacuum Cleaner: A History* (Jefferson, NC and London: McFarland, 2012), ch. 3.

96 See David E. Nye, *Electrifying America: Social Meanings of a New Technology, 1880–1940* (Cambridge, MA: MIT Press, 1992), 16.

97 As quoted in Sara Margaret Evans, *Born for Liberty: A History of Women in America* (New York: Free Press, 1997), 181.

98 As quoted in Spencer, *British Food*, 312.

99 See Jason Goodwin, *Otis: Giving Rise to the Modern City* (Chicago: University of Chicago Press, 2001).

100 See Wilfried Feldenkirchen, *Werner von Siemens, Inventor and International Entrepreneur* (Columbus, OH: Ohio State University Press, 1994), xxii.

101 See Lee Edward Gray, *From Ascending Rooms to Express Elevators: A History of the Passenger Elevator in the 19th Century* (Mobile, AL: Elevator World, 2002), ch. 8.

102 On the development of the steel industry, see Duncan Lyall Burn, *The Economic History of Steelmaking, 1867–1939: A Study in Competition* (Cambridge: Cambridge University Press, 1940).

103 See Carl W. Condit, "Buildings and Construction, 1880–1900," in *Technology in Western Civilization*, eds. Kranzberg and Pursell, vol. 1.

104 Klein, *The Genesis of Industrial America*, 31–2.

105 Sarah Bradford Landau and Carl W. Condit, *Rise of the New York Skyscraper: 1865–1913* (New Haven: Yale University Press, 1996).

106 See Rob Harris, *Property and the Office Economy* (London: Estates Gazette, 2005), 232.

107 Derry and Williams, *A Short History of Technology*, 448–56.

108 See Harold I. Sharlin, "Applications of Electricity," in *Technology in Western Civilization*, eds. Kranzberg and Pursell, vol. 1, 572–4; Hughes, *Networks of Power*, 82–4.

109 Statistics supplied in Sharlin, "Applications of Electricity," 574; Smil, *Creating the Twentieth Century*, 94.

110 See Warren D. Devine, Jr., "Electrified Mechanical Drive: The Historical Power Distribution Revolution," in *Electricity in the American Economy: Agent of Technological Progress*, ed. Sam H. Schurr et al. (New York: Greenwood Press, 1990); Smil, *Creating the Twentieth Century*, 79–80.

111 See Roger Fouquet, *Heat, Power and Light: Revolutions in Energy Services* (Cheltenham, UK and Northampton, MA: Edward Elgar, 2008), 138.

112 See these data in Sharlin, "Applications of Electricity," 577.

113 On the development of the telephone, see John, *Network Nation*, chs. 6–7.

114 Statistics in John, *Network Nation*, 273.

115 See John, *Network Nation*, 269–71.

116 This paragraph draws upon Lynwood Bryant, "The Beginnings of the Internal-Combustion Engine," in *Technology in Western Civilization*, vol. 1, eds. Kranzberg and Pursell.

117 On the developments in this paragraph, see Bryant, "The Beginnings of the Internal-Combustion Engine," 658–61; Smil, *Creating the Twentieth Century*, 125–6.

118 On the bicycle and its impact, see Derry and Williams, *A Short History of Technology*, 390–2; Harold F. Williamson, "Mass Production For Mass Consumption," in *Technology in Western Civilization*, eds. Kranzberg and Pursell, vol. 1, 686–7; Smil, *Creating the Twentieth Century*, 134–5.

119 On Ford and his competitors, see Alfred D. Chandler, Jr. (with the assistance of T. Hikino), *Scale and Scope: The Dynamics of Industrial Capitalism* (Cambridge, MA: Harvard University Press, 1990), 206–9.

120 See John. B. Rae, "The Internal Combustion Engine on Wheels," in *Technology in Western Civilization*, eds. Kranzberg and Pursell, vol. 2, 122.

121 See Smil, *Creating the Twentieth Century*, 124–7.

122 Rae, "The Internal Combustion Engine on Wheels," 127.

123 Thomas P. Hughes argues plausibly that by World War I the United States had become "the most inventive of all nations." See his *American Genesis: A Century of Invention and Technological Enthusiasm, 1870–1970* (New York: Viking, 1989), 7.

124 This paragraph is informed by Hughes, *American Genesis*, ch. 6.

125 On Ford, see Hounshell, *From the American System to Mass Production*, ch. 6.

126 On the influence of meatpacking operations on this development, see Hounshell, *From the American System to Mass Production*, 241.

127 Statistic supplied in Chandler, *Scale and Scope*, 205.

128 See Daniel M. G. Raff and Lawrence H. Summers, "Did Henry Ford Pay Efficiency Wages?" *Journal of Labor Economics* 5, 4, pt 2: "The New Economics of Personnel" (October 1987): S57–S86.

129 Statistics supplied in Thomas K. McCraw and Richard S. Tedlow, "Henry Ford, Alfred Sloan, and the Three Phases of Marketing," in *Creating Modern Capitalism: How Entrepreneurs, Companies, and Countries Triumphed in Three Industrial Revolutions*, ed. Thomas K. McCraw (Cambridge, MA: Harvard University Press, 1995), 274.

130 See Charles Bray (ed.), *Dictionary of Glass: Materials and Techniques*, 2nd edn (London: A&C Black, 2001), 187.

131 See Steven Meyer, "Assembly Line Production," in *Encyclopedia of U.S. Labor and Working-Class History*, 3 vols, ed. Eric Arnesen (New York and Abingdon, UK: Routledge, 2007), vol. 1, 130–1.

132 Data presented in McCraw and Tedlow, "Henry Ford, Alfred Sloan, and the Three Phases of Marketing," 284.

133 See Chandler, *Scale and* Scope, 205.

134 Paul Ingrassia makes this point in *Crash Course: The American Automobile Industry's Road from Glory to Disaster* (New York: Simon & Schuster, 2010).

135 See Reynold M. Wik, "Mechanization of the American Farm," in *Technology in Western Civilization*, eds. Kranzberg and Pursell, vol. 2, 360; Dennis S. Nordin and Roy V. Scott, *From Prairie Farmer to Entrepreneur: The Transformation of Midwestern Agriculture* (Bloomington, IN: Indiana University Press, 2005), 45–6; Smil, *Creating the Twentieth Century*, 143–4.

136 See Vaclav Smil, *Prime Movers of Globalization: The History and Impact of Diesel Engines and Gas Turbines* (Cambridge: Cambridge University Press, 2010).

137 See Rae, "The Internal Combustion Engine on Wheels," 129–31.

138 On Goodyear's breakthrough, see Derry and Williams, *A Short History of Technology*, 527–8.

139 See Smil, *Prime Movers of Globalization*; idem., *Creating the Twentieth Century*, 116–24, 143–4; Bryant, "The Beginnings of the Internal-Combustion Engine," 663–4.

140 This paragraph draws on Smil, *Creating the Twentieth Century*, 145–50; Derry and Williams, *A Short History of Technology*, 396–401.

141 See Thomas M. Smith, "The Development of Aviation," in *Technology in Western Civilization,* eds. Kranzberg and Pursell, vol. 2, 157.

142 See Smil, *Prime Movers of Globalization*, ch. 4.

143 Ibid., 48–50.

144 See Karl L. Wildes and Nilo A. Lindgren, *A Century of Electrical Engineering and Computer Science at MIT, 1882–1982* (Cambridge, MA: MIT Press, 1985).

145 See Nicholas A. Peppas (ed.), *One Hundred Years of Chemical Engineering: From Lewis M. Norton (M.I.T. 1888) to Present* (Dordrecht, The Netherlands: Springer, 1989).

146 On the developments related in this paragraph, see Robert P. Multhauf, "Industrial Chemistry in the Nineteenth Century," in *Technology in Western Civilization*, eds. Kranzberg and Pursell, vol. 1, 472–8.

147 Ancient Mesoamericans apparently discovered a similar process at least 3,500 years ago. See Dorothy Hosler, Sandra L. Burkett, and Michael J. Tarkanian, "Rubber Processing in Ancient Mesoamerica." *Science,* New Series 284 (18 June 1999): 1988–91.

148 Derry and Williams, *A Short History of Technology*, 527–8.

149 John B. Rae, "The Invention of Invention," in *Technology in Western Civilization*, eds. Kranzberg and Pursell, vol. 1, 335.

150 See Multhauf, "Industrial Chemistry in the Nineteenth Century," 482.

151 On Baekeland and his discoveries, see Wiebe E. Bijker, *Of Bicycles, Bakelites, and Bulbs: Toward a Theory of Sociotechnical Change* (Cambridge, MA: MIT Press, 1995), ch. 3.

152 See Fred Aftalion, *A History of the International Chemical Industry: From the "Early Days" to 2000* (Philadelphia: University of Pennsylvania Press, 2001), 149–56.

153 Peter F. Drucker, "Technology Trends in the Twentieth Century," in *Technology in Western Civilization*, eds. Kranzberg and Pursell, vol. 2, 14.

154 See Multhauf, "Industrial Chemistry in the Nineteenth Century," 483–4.

155 See Aftalion, *A History of the International Chemical Industry*, 37; Peter J. T. Morris and Anthony S. Travis, "A History of The International Dyestuff Industry." *American Dyestuff Reporter* 81 (November 1992): 59–100 (here: 61–3); Simon Garfield, *Mauve: How One Man Invented a Color That Changed the World* (New York and London: Faber & Faber, 2000), 8, 23–36.

156 See Peter Watson, *The German Genius: Europe's Third Renaissance, the Second Scientific Revolution, and the Twentieth Century* (New York: HarperCollins, 2011), 358.

157 These and the following statistics are supplied by Chandler, *Scale and Scope*, 26, 475.

158 On Bayer's innovative business organization, see Chandler, *Scale and Scope*, 476–8.

159 On the extraordinary range of these breakthroughs, see Aftalion, *A History of the International Chemical Industry*, chs. 3–4.

160 See Arthur M. Johnson, "Expansion of the Petroleum and Chemical Industries, 1880–1900," in *Technology in Western Civilization*, eds. Kranzberg and Pursell, vol. 1, 675–7; Aftalion, *A History of the International Chemical Industry*, 53–7.

161 See Dept. of Ecology, State of Washington, "Chemical Pulp Mills," http://www.ecy.wa.gov/programs/air/pdfs/pulpmil3.pdf (accessed 14 June 2013).

162 See Derry and Williams, *A Short History of Technology*, 640–8.

163 See Smil, *Creating the Twentieth Century*, 167.

164 See Walter Sneader, "The Discovery of Aspirin: A Reappraisal." *British Medical Journal* 321 (23–30 December 2000): 1591–4.

165 See Mary Ellen Bowden, Amy Beth Crow, and Tracy Sullivan, *Pharmaceutical Achievers: The Human Face of Pharmaceutical Research* (Philadelphia: Chemical Heritage Press, 2003), 10–12..

166 See Aftalion, *A History of the International Chemical Industry*, 45–53.

167 On the foregoing, see Louis Lasagna, "The Pharmaceutical Revolution: Its Impact on Science and Society." *Science* 166 (5 December 1969): 1227–33; Chandler, *Scale and Scope*, 164.

168 See Frank Gonzalez-Crussi, *A Short History of Medicine* (New York: Random House, 2007); William Bynum, *The History of Medicine: A Very Short Introduction* (Oxford and New York: Oxford University Press, 2008), ch. 6.

169 See Aftalion, *A History of the International Chemical Industry*, 57–65, 110–20.

170 Chandler, *Scale and Scope*, 475–8.

171 Kerry A. Chase, *Trading Blocs: States, Firms, and Regions in the World Economy* (Ann Arbor: University of Michigan Press, 2005), 90.

172 See Kendall Beaton, "Dr. Gesner's Kerosene: The Start of American Oil Refining." *The Business History Review* 29 (March 1955): 28–53.

173 See Johnson, "Expansion of the Petroleum and Chemical Industries," 665–9; Smil, *Creating the Twentieth Century*, 291.

174 See Charles A. S. Hall and Kent A. Klitgaard, *Energy and the Wealth of Nations: Understanding the Biophysical Economy* (New York: Springer, 2012), 152.

175 See Aftalion, *A History of the International Chemical Industry*, 129–31.

176 See Chandler, *Scale and Scope*, 180; Aftalion, *A History of the International Chemical Industry*, 214–33; David C. Mowery and Nathan Rosenberg, *Paths of Innovation: Technological Change in 20th-Century America* (Cambridge and New York: Cambridge University Press, 1998), 71–93.

177 See Mowery and Rosenberg, *Paths of Innovation*, 21.

178 See Smil, *Creating the Twentieth Century*, 93–4, 167.

179 See Sigmund Freud, *The Interpretation of Dreams* (New York: Avon, 1965).

180 See Smil, *Creating the Twentieth Century*, 10, 24.

181 See Monica J. Casper, *Synthetic Planet: Chemical Politics and the Hazards of Modern Life* (New York: Routledge, 2003).

182 See Craig E. Colten and Peter N. Skinner, *The Road to Love Canal: Managing Industrial Waste before EPA* (Austin, TX: University of Texas Press, 1996).

183 See Craig Collins, *Toxic Loopholes: Failures and Future Prospects for Environmental Law* (New York: Cambridge University Press, 2010), 81n11.

184 See Ingrid Eckerman, *The Bhopal Saga: Causes and Consequences of the World's Largest Industrial Disaster* (Hyderguda, India: Universities Press, 2005).

185 This paragraph draws on Smil, *Creating the Twentieth Century*, 200–1, 241–54.

186 This and the next two paragraphs are informed by Kenneth Bilby, *The General: David Sarnoff and the Rise of the Communications Industry* (New York: Harper & Row, 1986).

187 These developments are investigated in Albert Abramson, *Zworykin, Pioneer of Television* (Urbana, IL: University of Illinois Press, 1995).

188 See Mowery and Rosenberg, *Paths of Innovation*, 123–8.

189 Regarding Farnsworth, see Evan I. Schwartz, *The Last Lone Inventor: A Tale of Genius, Deceit, and the Birth of Television* (New York: HarperCollins, 2002).

190 See Smil, *Creating the Twentieth Century*, 255.

191 See Frederik Nebeker, *Dawn of the Electronic Age: Electrical Technologies in the Shaping of the Modern World, 1914 to 1945* (Hoboken, NJ: John Wiley & Sons, Inc., 2009), 157–8.

192 For these developments, see Alfred D. Chandler, "How High Technology Industries Transformed Work and Life Worldwide from the 1880s to the 1990s." *Capitalism and Society* 1 (2006): 1–55 (here: 23).

193 The scholar was Alfred D. Chandler in "How High Technology Industries Transformed Work and Life," 37.

194 As reported in Alan Macfarlane, *The Making of the Modern World: Visions from the West and East* (Houndmills, UK and New York: Palgrave Macmillan, 2002), 203.

195 See Angus Maddison, *The World Economy in the 20th Century* (Paris: OECD Publishing, 1989), 15.

196 See Alfred D. Chandler, *Inventing the Electronic Century: The Epic Story of the Consumer Electronics and Computer Science Industries* (New York: Free Press, 2001).

197 See Walter Isaacson, *Steve Jobs* (New York: Little, Brown, 2011), 566.

198 On these developments, see Thomas M. Smith, "Origins of the Computer," in *Technology in Western Civilization*, eds. Kranzberg and Pursell, vol. 2, 310–13.

199 See Smil, *Creating the Twentieth Century*, 262; Chandler, *Inventing the Electronic Century*, 87.

200 These developments are related in Smith, "Origins of the Computer," 316–21.

201 Noted in Chandler, *Inventing the Electronic Century*, 122.

202 On the development of IBM, see Rowena Olegario, "IBM and the Two Thomas J. Watsons," in *Creating Modern Capitalism*; Chandler, *Inventing the Electronic Century*, ed. McCraw, chs. 4–5.

203 See Colin P. Williams, *Explorations in Quantum Computing*, 2nd edn (London: Springer, 2011).

204 See "Genesis Redux: A New Form of Life Has Been Created in a Laboratory, and the Era of Synthetic Biology Is Dawning," *The Economist* (20 May 2010).

205 See the charts on pages 5–6 of Williams, *Explorations in Quantum Computing*.

206 See William D. Hoover, *Historical Dictionary of Postwar Japan* (Lanham, MD: Scarecrow Press, 2011), 260–1.

207 See P. W. Singer, *Wired for War: The Robotics Revolution and Conflict in the Twenty-first Century* (London: Penguin Books, 2009). Quotation in ibid., 7.

Chapter 13

1 Offering favorable trading terms and other enticements had a long history in non-Western foreign policy. See Emrah Sahin, "Ottoman Institutions, Capitulations," in *Cultural Sociology of the Middle East, Asia, and Africa: An Encyclopedia*, vol. 1: *Middle East*, ed. Andrea L. Stanton (Thousand Oaks, CA: SAGE Pub., 2012), 177–9.

2 For an overview, see Jonathan D. Spence, *The Search for Modern China*, 2nd edn (New York and London: W. W. Norton & Company, 1999), 156–62.

3 See Julia Lovell, *The Opium War: Drugs, Dreams, and the Making of China* (Basingstoke and Oxford: Blackwell, 2011), 31.

4 See Spence, *The Search for Modern China*, 119–53.

5 Ibid., 145–9, 160.

6 The magnitude of the defeat was not then acknowledged in China, but starting in the 1990s it became "a key prop for Communist One-Party rule" as a sign of China's "victimization by the West" before the Communist Revolution. See Lovell, *The Opium War*, 11–12.

7 See Michael Adas, *Machines As the Measure of Men: Science, Technology, and Ideologies of Western Dominance* (Ithaca and London: Cornell University Press, 1989), 42–52.

8 See Adas, *Machines As the Measure of Men*, 6–7.

9 See Jason Goodwin, *Lords of the Horizons: A History of the Ottoman Empire* (New York: Henry Holt & Company, 1999); Palmira Brummett, *Ottoman Seapower and Levantine Diplomacy in the Age of Discovery* (Albany: State University of New York Press, 1994).

10 See Jeremy Black, *Warfare in the Eighteenth Century* (London: Cassell, 1999).

11 See Dennis Judd, *The Lion and the Tiger: The Rise and Fall of the British Raj, 1600–1947* (Oxford and New York: Oxford University Press, 2004).

12 See G. V. Scammell, *First Imperial Age: European Overseas Expansion c. 1400–1715* (London and Boston: Unwin Hyman, 1989); Timothy Parsons, *The British Imperial Century, 1815–1914: A World History Perspective* (Lanham, MD and Oxford: Rowman & Littlefield, 1999), 60–8.

13 See Jan Blomme, "Europe, America, and Africa," in *History of Humanity*, vol. 6: *The Nineteenth Century*, ed. Peter Mathias et al. (Paris: UNESCO; Abingdon, UK: Routledge, 2005), 51.

14 See Alfred Crosby, *Ecological Imperialism: The Biological Expansion of Europe, 900–1900* (Cambridge: Cambridge University Press, 1986), (statistics: 3–4).

15 See Ronald Robinson and John Gallagher, with Alice Denny, *Africa and the Victorians: The Climax of Imperialism in the Dark Continent* (New York: St. Martin's Press, 1961), 1.

16 See Adas, *Machines As the Measure of Men*, chs. 2–4 (quotation: 220).

17 Ibid., 241–65.

18 See Stephen Jay Gould, *The Mismeasure of Man*, rev. edn (New York and London: W. W. Norton & Company, 1996), ch. 3.

19 See Alain Peyrefitte, *The Collision of Two Civilisations: The British Expedition to China in 1792–4*, trans. Jon Rothschild (London: Harvill, 1993).

20 As quoted in John J. Donohue and John L. Esposito, *Islam in Transition: Muslim Perspectives* (New York: Oxford University Press, 1982), 60.

21 See J. N. Westwood, *Russia Against Japan, 1904–1905: A New Look at the Russo-Japanese War* (Albany: State University of New York Press, 1986).

22 See, for example, Philip G. Roeder, *Where Nation-States Come from: Institutional Change in the Age of Nationalism* (Princeton: Princeton University Press, 2007).

23 See Rebecca Berens Matzke, *Deterrence Through Strength: British Naval Power and Foreign Policy under Pax Britannica* (Lincoln, NE: University of Nebraska Press, 2011).

24 See Robert Stern, *Routledge Philosophy Guidebook to Hegel and the Phenomenology of Spirit* (London and New York: Routledge, 2002).

25 See Karl Marx and Friedrich Engels, *The Communist Manifesto*, intro. Martin Malia (New York: Penguin, 1998), 8.

26 On these trends, see Jacques Barzun, *Darwin, Marx, Wagner: Critique of a Heritage*, 2nd edn (Chicago and London: University of Chicago Press, 1981), 91–6.

27 See Isabel V. Hull, *Absolute Destruction: Military Culture and the Practices of War in Imperial Germany* (Ithaca: Cornell University Press, 2005), ch. 4.

28 See Tim Jeal, *Livingstone* (New Haven: Yale University Press 1973).

29 See, for example, John Keay, *Mad About the Mekong: Exploration and Empire in South East Asia* (London: Harper Collins, 2005); Alan Moorehead, *The White Nile* (New York: Harper & Brothers, 1960).

30 See John Maxtone-Graham, *Safe Return Doubtful: The Heroic Age of Polar Exploration* (London: Constable, 2000), 284–330.

31 See D. K. Fieldhouse, *Economics and Empire, 1830–1914* (London: Macmillan, 1984).

32 See Kimberly Zisk Marten, *Enforcing the Peace: Learning From the Imperial Past* (New York: Columbia University Press, 2004), 67.

33 See Matthew P. Fitzpatrick, *Liberal Imperialism in Germany: Expansionism and Nationalism, 1848–1884* (New York: Berghahn, 2008), 148.

34 See John Darwin, *After Tamerlane: The Global History of Empire Since 1405* (New York: Bloomsbury Publishing, 2008), 491.

35 See Matthew P. Fitzpatrick (ed.), *Liberal Imperialism in Europe* (New York: Palgrave Macmillan, 2012).

36 See Thomas Pakenham, *The Scramble for Africa: White Man's Conquest of the Dark Continent from 1876–1912* (New York: Avon, 1991); M. E. Chamberlain, *The Scramble for Africa*, 3rd edn (Harlow, UK, 2010).

37 See Adam Hochschild, *King Leopold's Ghost: A Story of Greed, Terror, and Heroism in Colonial Africa* (Boston: Houghton Mifflin Company, 1998).

38 See F. Robert Hunter, *Egypt Under the Khedives, 1805–1879: From Household Government to Modern Bureaucracy* (Pittsburgh: University of Pittsburgh Press, 1984).

39 Parsons, *The British Imperial Century*, 69–79; Jonathan Hart, *Empires and Colonies* (Cambridge and Malden, MA: Blackwell Publishers, 2008), 193–9.

40 See Hochschild, *King Leopold's Ghost*, 257–9.

41 See Olufemi Taiwo, *How Colonialism Preempted Modernity in Africa* (Bloomington, IN: Indiana University Press, 2010).

42 See Bruce Vandervort, *Wars of Imperial Conquest in Africa, 1830–1914* (London: UCL Press, 1998), 156–69.

43 See Spence, *The Search for Modern China*, 215–83.

44 See Pierre Brocheux and Daniel Hémery. *Indochina: An Ambiguous Colonization, 1858–1954*, trans. Ly Lan Dill-Klein et al. (Berkeley: University of California Press, 2009).

45 See Frances V. Moulder, *Japan, China, and the Modern World Economy: Toward a Reinterpretation of East Asian Development ca. 1600 to ca. 1918* (Cambridge: Cambridge University Press, 1977), ch. 4.

46 See John Ellis, *The Social History of the Machine Gun* (New York: Pantheon, 1975), 86–7.

47 Robert Leckie, *The Wars of America*, new and updated ed. (New York: HarperPerenial Publishers, 1992), 574; Stanley Karnow, *In Our Image: America's Empire in the Philippines* (New York: Random House, 1989), 194 (civilians).

48 See Mark Levene, *Genocide in the Age of the Nation State: The Rise of the West and the Coming of Genocide* (London and New York: I.B. Tauris, 2005), 233–6; Sebastian Conrad, *German Colonialism: A Short History*, trans. Sorcha O'Hagan (New York: Random House, Inc, 2012), 84–6.

49 See Carl Mosk, *Japanese Economic Development: Markets, Norms, Structures* (Abingdon, UK and New York: Routledge, 2008), 128–9.

50 David Abernethy, *The Dynamics of Global Dominance: European Overseas Empires, 1415–1980* (New Haven: Yale University Press, 2000), 87.

51 See Jack Goldstone, *Why Europe? The Rise of the West in World History 1500–1850* (Boston: McGraw-Hill Higher Education, 2009), 69.

52 See Irving Stone, *The Global Export of Capital from Great Britain, 1865–1914: A Statistical Survey* (Basingstoke, UK and New York: St. Martin's Press, 1999), 405, 411.

53 Quoted from B. R. Tomlinson, "Economics and Empire: The Periphery and the Imperial Economy," in *The Oxford History of the British Empire*, vol. 3: *The Nineteenth Century*, ed. Andrew Porter (Oxford and New York: Oxford University Press, 1999), 73.

54 See Avner Offer, "Costs and Benefits, Prosperity and Security, 1870–1914," in *The Nineteenth Century*, ed. Porter, 695, 706.

55 Deirdre McCloskey, *Bourgeois Dignity: Why Economics Can't Explain the Modern World* (Chicago: University of Chicago Press, 2010), 234.

56 See Offer, "Costs and Benefits," 699–702.

57 See Guillaume Daudin, Matthias Morys, and Keven H. O'Rourke, "Globalization, 1870–1914," in *The Cambridge Economic History of Modern Europe*, vol. 2, *1870 to the Present*, eds. Stephen Broadberry and Kevin H. O'Rourke (New York: Cambridge University Press, 2010), 24–6.

58 See Theodore Roszak, *The Voice of the Earth: An Essay in Ecopsychology*, 2nd edn (Grand Rapids, MI: W. B. Eerdmans Pub. Co.; Manchester: Manchester University Press 2001), 53–4.

59 See R. Ernest Dupuy and Trevor N. Dupuy, *The Harper Encyclopedia of Military History: From 3500 B.C. to the Present*, 4th edn (New York: Harper Resource, 1993), 79; Paul K. Davis, *100 Decisive Battles: From Ancient Times to the Present* (New York: Oxford University Press, 2001), 43–6.

60 See Guy Rowlands, *The Dynastic State and the Army under Louis XIV: Royal Service and Private Interest, 1661 to 1701* (Cambridge: Cambridge University Press, 2002).

61 See Offer, "Costs and Benefits," 707–10.

62 See Paul Kennedy, *The Rise of the Anglo-German Antagonism, 1860–1914* (London and Boston: George Allen & Unwin, 1980).

63 See William Mulligan, *The Origins of the First World War* (New York: Cambridge University Press, 2010), 101.

64 See Jeremy Black, *The Great War and the Making of the Modern World* (London: Continuum, 2011), ch. 1.

65 See Michael Howard, *The First World War: A Very Short Introduction* (New York: Oxford University Press, 2002), 17–20.

66 Michael Howard, *War in European History* (Oxford and New York: Oxford University Press, 1976), 120.

67 See Irmgard Steinisch, "A Different Path to War: A Comparative Study of Militarism and Imperialism in the United States and Imperial Germany, 1871–1914," in *Anticipating Total War: The German and American Experiences, 1871–1914*, eds. Manfred F. Boemeke, Roger Chickering, and Stig Förster (Cambridge: Cambridge University Press, 1999), 36–7; Adas, *Machines as the Measure of Men*, 365.

68 See Richard C. Hall, "Serbia," in *The Origins of World War I*, eds. Richard F. Hamilton and Holger H. Herwig (Cambridge: Cambridge University Press, 2003), 106–9.

69 See Ian F. W. Beckett, *The Great War, 1914–1918*, 2nd edn (Harlow, UK and New York: Pearson/Longman, 2007), 32–43. See also James Joll, *The Origins of the First World War*, 3rd edn (Harlow, UK and New York: Pearson Education/Longman, 2007).

70 See Beckett, *The Great War*, 55.

71 For details, see Black, *The Great War*; Beckett, *The Great War*; John Keegan, *The First World War* (New York: A. A. Knopf, 1999).

72 For a fascinating description, see Black, *The Great War*, 258–9.

73 On the home fronts, see Beckett, *The Great War*, chs. 7 and 9; Keith Robbins, *The First World War* (Oxford and New York: Oxford University Press, 2002), ch. 5; Howard, *The First World War*, 56–62.

74 See Howard, *The First World War*, 85, 102.

75 See Sean McMeekin, *The Berlin-Baghdad Express: The Ottoman Empire and Germany's Bid for World Power, 1898–1918* (Cambridge, MA: Harvard University Press, 2010).

76 See Beckett, *The Great War*, 551–67.

77 See Fritz Fischer, *Germany's Aims in the First World War* (London: Chatto & Windus, 1967); D. C. B. Lieven, *Russia and the Origins of the First World War* (New York: St. Martin's Press, 1983).

78 See Niall Ferguson, *The Pity Of War: Explaining World War I* (New York: Basic Books, 1999).

79 See Sean McMeekin, *The Russian Origins of the First World War* (Cambridge, MA: Harvard University Press, 2011).

80 See Xiaobing Li, *A History of the Modern Chinese Army* (Lexington, KY: University Press of Kentucky, 2007), 25; Spence, *Search for Modern China*, 167–91.

81 See Hull, *Absolute Destruction*, 262.

82 See Black, *The Great War*, 236–48, 268.

83 See Joanna Bourke, *Dismembering the Male: Men's Bodies, Britain, and the Great War* (Chicago: University of Chicago Press, 1996), ch. 1; Nigel C. Hunt, *Memory, War, and Trauma* (Cambridge and New York: Cambridge University Press, 2010).

84 See Black, *The Great War*, 253–63; Beckett, *The Great War*, 472–4.

85 See Adas, *Machines as the Measure of Men*, 368–80; Beckett, *The Great War*, 617–18.

86 See David Hopkins, *Dada and Surrealism: A Very Short Introduction* (Oxford: Oxford University Press, 2004); Matthew Biro, *The Dada Cyborg: Visions of the New Human in Weimar Berlin* (Minneapolis: University of Minnesota Press, 2009); Annette Becker, "The Visual Arts," in *A Companion to World War I*, ed. John Horne (Chichester, UK and Malden MA: Blackwell Publishers, 2010), 346–50.

87 See Modris Eksteins, *The Rites of Spring: The Great War and the Birth of the Modern Age* (Boston: Houghton Mifflin Co., 1989).

88 See Adas, *Machines as the Measure of Men*, 393–9.

89 See Jay Winter, *Sites of Memory, Sites of Mourning: The Great War in European Cultural History* (Cambridge: Cambridge University Press, 2005).

90 See Beckett, *The Great War*, 619–22, 637–40.

91 Richard Pipes advances this idea in *Russia Under the Bolshevik Regime* (New York: Vintage, 1994), 262–3.

92 See W. Bruce Lincoln, *The Great Reforms: Autocracy, Bureaucracy, and the Politics of Change in Imperial Russia* (DeKalb, IL: Northern Illinois University Press, 1990).

93 See Paul R. Gregory, *Russian National Income, 1885–1913* (Cambridge: Cambridge University Press, 1982), 165.

94 See Abraham Ascher, *The Revolution of 1905: A Short History* (Stanford: Stanford University Press, 2004).

95 See Susan P. McCaffray and Michael Melancon, *Russia in the European Context, 1789–1914: A Member of the Family* (New York and Houndmills, UK: Palgrave Macmillan, 2005).

96 See Rex Wade, *The Russian Revolution, 1917*, 2nd edn (New York: Cambridge University Press, 2005).

97 See Alexander Rabinowitch, *The Bolsheviks in Power: The First Year of Bolshevik Rule in Petrograd* (Bloomington, IN: Indiana University Press, 2007).

98 See Evan Mawdsley, *The Russian Civil War* (New York: Columbia University Press, 2007).

99 See Mawdsley, *The Russian Civil War*, 287.

100 See Mark Harrison, "National Income," in *The Economic Transformation of the Soviet Union*, 1913–1945, eds. R. W. Davies, Mark Harrison, and S. G. Wheatcroft (Cambridge: Cambridge University Press, 1994), 41–2.

101 See Pipes, *Russia under the Bolshevik Regime*, 397–403.

102 See Robert C. Allen, *Farm to Factory: A Reinterpretation of the Soviet Industrial Revolution* (Princeton and Oxford: Princeton University Press, 2003), 51–9.

103 Andrzej Walicki, *Marxism and the Leap to the Kingdom of Freedom: The Rise and Fall of the Communist Utopia* (Stanford: Stanford University Press, 1995), chs. 1–2.

104 See Sean McMeekin, *History's Greatest Heist: The Looting of Russia by the Bolsheviks* (New Haven: Yale University Press, 2009).

105 Robert Service, *Stalin: A Biography* (Cambridge, MA: Harvard University Press, 2005), ch. 20.

106 See Robert C. Tucker, *Stalin in Power: the Revolution from Above, 1928–1941* (New York and London: W. W. Norton & Company, 1990), chs. 4–6.

107 See Norman M. Naimark, *Stalin's Genocides* (Princeton and Oxford: Princeton University Press, 2010), 54–60.

108 See R. W. Davies and Stephen G. Wheatcroft, *The Years of Hunger: Soviet Agriculture, 1931–1933* (New York: Palgrave Macmillan, 2004), ch. 13.

109 See David L. Hoffmann, *Peasant Metropolis: Social Identities in Moscow, 1929–1941* (Ithaca: Cornell University Press, 1994).

110 See William Chase, "Stalin as Producer: The Moscow Show Trials and the Construction of Mortal Threats," in *Stalin: A New History*, eds. Sarah Davies and James Harris (New York: Cambridge University Press, 2005).

111 See Nicolas Werth, "The Mechanism of a Mass Crime: The Great Terror in the Soviet Union, 1937–1938," in *The Specter of Genocide: Mass Murder in Historical Perspective*, eds. Robert Gellately and Ben Kiernan (New York: Cambridge University Press, 2003).

112 See Tim Rees and Andy Thorpe (eds), *International Communism and the Communist International: 1919–43* (Oxford and New York: Oxford University Press, 1998).

113 See Caroline Kennedy-Pipe, *The Origins of the Cold War* (Houndmills, UK and New York: Palgrave Macmillan, 2007), 45–56.

114 See Robert O. Paxton, *The Anatomy of Fascism* (New York: A. A. Knopf, 2004), 4–13.

115 See Bradley Lightbody, *The Second World War: Ambitions to Nemesis* (London and New York: Routledge, 2004), 20; See Paxton, *The Anatomy of Fascism*, 96.

116 See Lightbody, *The Second World War*, 20–1; Paxton, *The Anatomy of Fascism*, 87–90, 109–10.

117 See Paxton, *The Anatomy of Fascism*, 66–8, 92–104.

118 Ibid., 119–28.

119 See Richard Pipes, *The Russian Revolution*, 320–2, 796–800; Allan K. Wildman, *The End of the Russian Imperial Army*, 2 vols. (Princeton: Princeton University Press, 1980–1987); Paxton, *The Anatomy of Fascism*, 133–5.

120 See James Ryan, *Lenin's Terror: The Ideological Origins of Early Soviet State Violence* (Abingdon, UK and New York: Routledge, 2012), 2.

121 See Richard Evans, *The Third Reich in Power* (New York: Penguin Press, 2005), 39.

122 See Evans, *The Third Reich in Power*, 230–56.

123 See Stephen J. Lee, *European Dictatorships, 1918–1945*, 2nd edn (London and New York: Routledge, 2000), 298–308; Paxton, *The Anatomy of Fascism*, 141–7.

124 For comparisons, see Henry Rousso (ed.), *Stalinism and Nazism: History and Memory Compared* (Lincoln, NE and London: University of Nebraska Press, 2004); Richard Overy, *The Dictators: Hitler's Germany and Stalin's Russia* (New York: W. W. Norton & Company, 2004).

125 See Vladimir Tismaneanu, *The Devil in History: Communism, Fascism, and Some Lessons of the Twentieth Century* (Berkeley and Los Angeles: University of California Press, 2012), 2–8.

126 See Paxton, *The Anatomy of Fascism*, 68–78.

127 Ibid., 77–81

128 Paxton analyzes this tendency of fascism in *The Anatomy of Fascism*, 148–58.

129 See Sheila Fitzpatrick, "The Civil War as a Formative Experience," in *Bolshevik Culture: Experiment and Order in the Russian Revolution*, eds. Abbott Gleason, Peter Kenez, and Richard Stites (Bloomington, IN: Indiana University Press, 1985), 59–60.

130 See Evans, *The Third Reich in Power*, ch. 3.

131 See Timothy D. Snyder, *Bloodlands: Europe Between Hitler and Stalin* (New York: Basic Books, 2010), vii–viii.

132 See Evans, *The Third Reich in Power*, ch. 7.

133 See ibid., 111–12, 650–6.

134 See Alan E Steinweis, *Kristallnacht 1938* (Cambridge, MA: Harvard University Press, 2009), 53–61; Michael Berenbaum, *The World Must Know: The History of the*

Holocaust as Told in the United States Holocaust Memorial Museum (Boston: Little, Brown, 1993), 49.

135 See key excerpts in Max Domarus, *The Essential Hitler: Speeches and Commentary*, ed. Patrick Romane (Wauconda, IL: Bolchazy- Carducci, 2007), 186–7, 395–400.

136 Quoted in Ian Kershaw, *Fateful Choices: Ten Decisions That Changed the World, 1940–1941* (London: Penguin Books, 2008), 435.

137 See Kershaw, *Fateful Choices*, 434–5.

138 See Evan Mawdsley, *World War II: A New History* (Cambridge: Cambridge University Press, 2009), ch. 2.

139 On the war's global dimensions, see Roger Chickering, Stig Förster, and Bernd Greiner (eds), *A World at Total War: Global Conflict and the Politics of Destruction, 1937–1945* (Washington, DC: German Historical Institute; Cambridge and New York: Cambridge University Press, 2005); Gerhard L. Weinberg, *A World at Arms: A Global History of World War II*, 2nd edn (Cambridge: Cambridge University Press, 2005).

140 See Norman M. Naimark, *Fires of Hatred: Ethnic Cleansing in Twentieth-Century Europe* (Cambridge, MA: Harvard University Press, 2001), 90.

141 On the war in Europe, see Norman Davies, *No Simple Victory: World War II in Europe, 1939–1945* (New York: Penguin, 2008).

142 See Helmut Langerbein, *Hitler's Death Squads: The Logic of Mass Murder* (College Station, TX: Texas A&M University Press, 2004), 30.

143 See Götz Aly, *Hitler's Beneficiaries: Plunder, Racial War, and the Nazi Welfare State*, trans. Jefferson Chase (New York: Holt, 2007).

144 See Weinberg, *A World at Arms*, 205–15, 224–34.

145 See Von Hardesty and Ilya Grinberg, *Red Phoenix Rising: The Soviet Air Force in World War II* (Lawrence, KS: University Press of Kansas, 2012), 9.

146 See Mawdsley, *World War II*, 147–53. See also Evan Mawdsley, *Thunder in the East: The Nazi-Soviet War, 1941–1945* (London: Hodder, 2005).

147 See Henry Friedlander, *The Origins of Nazi Genocide: From Euthanasia to the Final Solution* (Chapel Hill: University of North Carolina Press, 1995), 78–85, 111–23, 136–63; Bergen *War and Genocide*, 128–33.

148 See Paxton, *The Anatomy of Fascism*, 159.

149 See Christopher Browning, with contributions by Jürgen Matthäus, *The Origins of the Final Solution: The Evolution of Nazi Jewish Policy, September 1939-March 1942* (Lincoln, NE: University of Nebraska Press and Jerusalem: Yad Vashem, 2004), 16–18; Langerbein, *Hitler's Death* Squads, 24–39.

150 See Christian Gerlach, "The Wannsee Conference, the Fate of German Jews, and Hitler's Decision in Principle to Exterminate All European Jews." *The Journal of Modern History* 70 (December 1998): 759–812 (here: 761–2).

151 See Langerbein, *Hitler's Death* Squads, 42–5, 71–3.

152 See Gerlach, "The Wannsee Conference," 769–73.

153 Ibid., 762–3; Bergen *War and Genocide*, 182–3; Berenbaum, *The World Must Know*, 119.

154 See Evan Mawdsley, *December 1941: Twelve Days That Began a World War* (New Haven: Yale University Press 2011), 25–47, 145–51, 160–1.

155 See Mawdsley, *World War II*, 190–13.

156 Ibid., 247–53.

157 See Weinberg, *A World at Arms*, 249–50.

158 Quoted in Gerlach, "The Wannsee Conference," 785.

159 See Gerlach, "The Wannsee Conference," 780–4.

160 See Paxton, *The Anatomy of Fascism*, 159–62; Bergen *War and Genocide*, 153–8, 164; Langerbein, *Hitler's Death* Squads, 48; Gerlach, "The Wannsee Conference," 764.

161 See Gerlach, "The Wannsee Conference," 775–6.

162 Ibid., 795–6, 799–805.

163 See Bergen *War and Genocide*, 182–90; Franciszek Piper, "The Number of Victims," in *Anatomy of the Auschwitz Death Camp*, eds. Yisrael Gutman and Michael Berenbaum (Bloomington, IN: Indiana University Press, 1995), 70–2.

164 See Bergen *War and Genocide*, 196.

165 Ibid., 227–9; Daniel Blatman, *The Death Marches: The Final Phase of Nazi Genocide*, trans. Chaya Galai (Cambridge, MA: Harvard University Press, 2011), 12.

166 See Friedlander, *The Origins of Nazi Genocide*.

167 See Langerbein, *Hitler's Death* Squads, 39–40.

168 See Richard Overy, *The Bombing War: Europe 1939–1945* (London: Allen Lane, 2013).

169 See Weinberg, *A World at Arms*, chs. 12 and 14.

170 See Mawdsley, *World War II*, 411–15.

171 See Barrett Tillman, *Whirlwind: The Air War Against Japan, 1942–1945* (New York: Simon & Schuster, 2010), xvi, 102–3, 134–73, 229, 267.

172 See Robert P. Newman, *Enola Gay and the Court of History* (New York: Peter Lang Publishing, 2004), 6–14; Richard B. Frank, *The End of the Imperial Japanese Empire* (New York: Random House, 1999), 140–8.

173 See Frank, *Downfall*, 253, 269.

174 See Kennedy-Pipe, *The Origins of the Cold War*, 67.

175 See Tsuyoshi Hasegawa, *Racing the Enemy: Stalin, Truman, and the Surrender of Japan* (Cambridge, MA: Harvard University Press, 2005).

176 See Hasegawa, *Racing the Enemy*, 197–8.

177 See Frank, *Downfall*, 302–3; Mawdsley, *World War II*, 426–37; Hasegawa, *Racing the Enemy*, 215–47.

178 See Priscilla Roberts (ed.), *World War II: The Essential Reference* Guide (Santa Barbara, CA: ABC-CLIO, 2012), 29–32; Werner Gruhl, *Imperial Japan's World War Two: 1931–1945* (New Brunswick, NJ: Transaction Publishers, 2007), 19–20; Geoffrey Hosking, *Russia and the Russians: A History*, 2nd edn (Cambridge, MA: Harvard University Press, 2011), 498–9.

179 See Peter Macalister-Smith, *International Humanitarian Assistance: Disaster Relief Action in International Law and Organization* (Dordrecht, The Netherlands: M. Nijhoff, 1985), 35.

180 See Mark R. Elliott, *Pawns of Yalta: Soviet Refugees and America's Role in Their Repatriation* (Urbana: University of Illinois Press, 1982).

181 See Judt, *Postwar*, 16–17.

182 See Vladimir Tismaneanu (ed.), *Stalinism Revisited: The Establishment of Communist Regimes in East-Central Europe* (Budapest and New York: Central European University Press, 2009).

183 See, for example, Tony Judt, *Postwar: A History of Europe Since 1945* (London: Penguin, 2005), 103–4.

184 See Kennedy-Pipe, *The Origins of the Cold War*, 60.

185 See Mawdsley, *World War II*, 337. After the war, this aid was not mentioned publicly in the USSR until the 1970s. See Hedrick Smith, *The Russians* (New York: Times Books, 1985), 327–8.

186 See John Lewis Gaddis, *We Now Know: Rethinking Cold War History* (New York: Oxford University Press, 1997), 25; Gerhard Wettig, *Stalin and the Cold War in Europe: The Emergence and Development of East-West Conflict, 1939–1953* (Lanham, MD: Rowman and Littlefield, 2008), 246.

187 Quoted from Walicki, *Marxism and the Leap to the Kingdom of Freedom*, 400.

188 Walicki, *Marxism and the Leap to the Kingdom of Freedom*, 426–54, 476–94.

189 William T. Lee and Richard F. Staar (eds), *Soviet Military Policy Since World War II* (Stanford: Stanford University Press, 1986).

190 See Martin Malia, *The Soviet Tragedy: A History of Socialism in Russia, 1917–1991* (New York: The Free Press, 1994), 371–2.

191 See Smith, *The Russians*, 323–4; Valerie Sperling, "Making the Public Patriotic: Militarism and Anti-Militarism in Russia," in *Russian Nationalism and the National Reassertion of Russia*, ed. Marlène Laruelle (Abingdon, UK and New York: Routledge, 2009), 229.

192 See Smith, *The Russians*, 325–6, William E. Odom, *The Collapse of the Soviet Military* (New Haven: Yale University Press 1998), 43–4.

193 See Smith, *The Russians*, 289; Stephen L. Webber, "Introduction: The Society-Military Interface in Russia," in *Military and Society in Post-Soviet Russia*, eds. Stephen L. Webber and Jennifer G. Mathers (Manchester and New York: Manchester University Press, 2006), 1.

194 See Smith, *The Russians*, 272.

195 See Tom Gervasi, *The Myth of Soviet Military Supremacy* (New York: Harper & Row, 1986).

196 See David Holloway, *Stalin and the Bomb: The Soviet Union and Atomic Energy, 1939–1956* (New Haven: Yale University Press, 1994).

197 See Robert Ehrlich, *Waging Nuclear Peace: The Technology and Politics of Nuclear Weapons* (Albany: State University of New York Press, 1985), 132–3.

198 See the text in Christine Compston and Rachel Filene Seidman (eds), *Our Documents: 100 Milestone Documents from the National Archives*, foreword by Michael Beschloss (New York: Oxford University Press, 2001), 195–6.

199 See Judt, *Postwar*, 90–9.

200 See Roger G. Miller, *To Save a City: The Berlin Airlift, 1948–1949* (College Station: Texas A&M University Press, 2000), 186.

201 See Wettig, *Stalin and the Cold War in Europe*, 174.

202 See Allan R. Millett, *The War for Korea, 1950–1951: They Came from the North* (Lawrence, KA: University Press of Kansas, 2010), 32, 42.

203 See Bruce Cumings, *The Korean War: A History* (New York: Modern Library, 2010), 159–60.

204 See Young-Iob Chung, *South Korea in the Fast Lane: Economic Development and Capital Formation* (New York: Oxford University Press, 2007), 9.

205 See John Lewis Gaddis, *The Cold War: A New History* (London: Allen Lane, 2005), 50.

206 See Chung, *South Korea in the Fast Lane*, 4, 355, 363.

207 See James L. Schoff, "Changing Perceptions of Extended Deterrence in Japan," *Strategy in the Second Nuclear Age: Power, Ambition, and the Ultimate Weapon*, eds. Toshi Yoshihara and James R. Holmes (Washington, DC: Georgetown University Press, 2012), 100.

208 See John Foran, "Discursive Subversions: *Time* Magazine, the CIA Overthrow of Mussadiq, and the Installation of the Shah," in *Cold War Constructions: The Political Culture of United States Imperialism, 1945–1966*, ed. Christian G. Appy (Amherst, MA: University of Massachusetts Press, 2000).

209 See Piero Gleijeses, *Shattered Hope: The Guatemalan Revolution and the United States, 1944–1954* (Princeton: Princeton University Press, 1991).

210 See, for example, James Callanan, *Covert Action in the Cold War: US Policy, Intelligence and CIA Operations* (New York: I. B. Tauris & Co. Ltd, 2010).

211 See Kevin McDermot and Matthew Stibbe, *Revolution and Resistance in Eastern Europe: Challenges to Communist Rule* (Oxford and New York: Oxford University Press, 2006), chs. 3–4.

212 This paragraph draws on Warren I. Cohen, *The Cambridge History of American Foreign Relations*, vol. 4: *America in the Age of Soviet Power, 1945–1991* (Cambridge: Cambridge University Press, 1993), 121–35.

213 Statistic cited in Judt, *Postwar*, 250.

214 See Aleksandr Fursenko and Timothy Naftali, *One Hell of a Gamble: Khrushchev, Castro, and Kennedy, 1958–1964* (New York: W.W. Norton & Company, 1997).

215 See James P. Harrison, "History's Heaviest Bombing," in *The Vietnam War: Vietnamese and American Perspectives*, eds. Jane Susan Werner and Luu Doan Huynh (Armonk, NY: M. E. Sharpe, 1993), 133. Broadly, see Ronald B. Frankum, Jr., *Like Rolling Thunder: The Air War in Vietnam, 1964–1975* (Lanham, MD: Rowman & Littlefield, 2005).

216 See, for example, Simon Hall, "Scholarly Battles Over the Vietnam War." *The Historical Journal* 52 (September 2009): 813–29.

217 See Nghia M. Vo, *Vietnamese Boat People, 1954 and 1975–1992* (Jefferson, NC and London: McFarland & Co, 2006), 2, 95; Ben Kiernan, *The Pol Pot Regime: Race, Power, and Genocide in Cambodia Under the Khmer Rouge, 1975–79*, 3rd edn (New Haven: Yale University Press 2008), 459.

218 See, for example, Thomas Borstelmann, *The 1970s: A New Global History from Civil Rights to Economic Inequality* (Princeton: Princeton University Press, 2012).

219 See Christopher Andrew and Vasili Mitrokhin, *The World Was Going Our Way: The KGB and the Battle for the Third World* (New York: Basic Books, 2005).

220 See Stephen Kotkin, *Armageddon Averted: The Soviet Collapse, 1970–2000*, updated edn (New York: Oxford University Press, 2008).

221 See Andrea M. Chandler, *Institutions of Isolation: Border Controls in the Soviet Union and Its Successor States, 1917–1993* (Montreal and Buffalo: McGill-Queen's University Press, 1998), 83.

222 See Jorge I. Domínguez, *To Make a World Safe for Revolution: Cuba's Foreign Policy* (Cambridge, MA: Harvard University Press, 1989), ch. 4.

223 See Tom Gjelten, *Bacardi and the Long Fight for Cuba: The Biography of a Cause* (New York: Penguin, 2008).

224 See Wolfgang Lutz, Sergei Scherbov, and Andrei Volkov (eds), *Demographic Trends and Patterns in the Soviet Union before 1991* (London and New York: Routledge, 1994).

225 See Murray Feshbach, and Alfred Friendly, Jr., *Ecocide in the USSR: Health And Nature Under Siege* (New York: Basic Books, 1992).

226 See Richard Crockatt, "Theories of Stability and the End of the Cold War," in *From Cold War to Collapse: Theory and World Politics in the 1980s*, eds. Mike Bowker and Robin Brown (New York: Cambridge University Press, 1993), 74–7.

227 See Barbara Alpern Engel, *Women in Russia, 1700–2000* (Cambridge: Cambridge University Press, 2004), 148–65, 237–9.

228 See Kotkin, *Armageddon Averted*, 68–70.

229 See, for example, Leon Aron, *Boris Yeltsin: A Revolutionary Life* (New York: HarperCollins, 2000).

230 See Loren Brandt, and Thomas G. Rawski (eds), *China's Great Economic Transformation* (New York: Cambridge University Press, 2008).

231 See John Quigley, *Soviet Legal Innovation and the Law of the Western World* (New York: Cambridge University Press, 2007).

232 See, for example, Prasenjit Duara (ed.), *Decolonization: Perspectives from Now and Then* (New York and London: Routledge, 2004).

233 Thomas Borstelmann, *The Cold War and the Color Line: American Race Relations in the Global Arena* (Cambridge, MA: Harvard University Press, 2001).

234 See McCloskey, *Bourgeois Dignity*, 156.

235 See Benjamin P. Bowser, *The Black Middle Class: Social Mobility—and Vulnerability* (Boulder, CO: Lynne Rienner Publishers, 2007).

236 See Charles Hartshorne, *Creative Synthesis and Philosophic Method* (London: SCM Press, 1970), 1–18.

Chapter 14

1 See Isabella Bird, *The Yangtze Valley and Beyond: An Account of Journeys in China, Chiefly in the Province of Sze Chuan and among the Man-tze of the Somo Territory*, intro. Pat Barr (Boston: Beacon Press, 1987).

2 As recounted and quoted in Evelyn Kaye, *Amazing Traveler, Isabella Bird: The Biography of a Victorian Adventurer* (Boulder, CO: University of Colorado Press, 1994), 189.

3 On Western women travelers, see John Gullick (ed.), *Adventurous Women in South-East Asia: Six Lives* (Kuala Lumpur and New York: Oxford University Press, 1995); Shirley Foster and Sara Mills (eds), *An Anthology of Women's Travel Writing* (Manchester and New York: Manchester University Press, 2002).

4 Robert D. Johnston discusses many of these views in *The Radical Middle Class: Populist Democracy and the Question of Capitalism in Progressive Era Portland, Oregon* (Princeton: Princeton University Press, 2003), ch. 1.

5 Deirdre M. McCloskey presents a powerful defense of these virtues in *The Bourgeois Virtues: Ethics for an Age of Commerce* (Chicago: University of Chicago Press, 2006).

6 See Jan de Vries, "Problems in the Measurement, Description, and Analysis of Historical Urbanization," in *Urbanization in History: A Process of Dynamic Interactions*, ed. Ad van der Woude, Akira Hayami, and Jan de Vries (Oxford: Oxford University Press, 1990); Gilbert Rozman, "East Asian Urbanization in the Nineteenth Century: Comparisons with Europe," in ibid.

7 See Anthony J. Mayo, Nitin Nohria, and Laura G. Singleton, *Paths to Power: How Insiders and Outsiders Shaped American Business Leadership* (Boston, MA: Harvard University Press, 2006), 182; Richard L. Zweigenhaft and G. William Domhoff, *The New CEOs: Women, African American, Latino and Asian American Leaders of* Fortune *500 Companies* (Lanham, MD and Plymouth, UK: Rowman & Littlefield Publishers, 2009), 40–1. On Europe, see Michael Hartmann, "Elites and Power Structure," in *Handbook of European Societies: Social Transformations in the 21st Century*, ed. Stefan Immerfall and Göran Therborn (New York: Springer, 2010).

8 See Robert N. Bellah et al., *Habits of the Heart: Individualism and Commitment in American Life* (Berkeley and Los Angeles: University of California Press, 1985), xii.

9 See Paul Ryscavage, *Rethinking the Income Gap: The Second Middle Class Revolution* (New Brunswick, NJ: Transaction Publishers, 2009), 100–8.

10 See Dena Goodman, *The Republic of Letters: A Cultural History of the French Enlightenment* (Ithaca: Cornell University Press, 1994), 53–64.

11 See Johann N. Neem, *Creating a Nation of Joiners: Democracy and Civil Society in Early National Massachusetts* (Cambridge, MA: Harvard University Press, 2008).

12 See Ross McKibbin, *Classes and Cultures: England 1918–1951* (New York: Oxford University Press, 1998), 98–101; Alexis de Tocqueville, *Democracy in America*, trans. George Lawrence, ed. J. P. Mayer (Garden City, NY: Doubleday, 1969), 515.

13 See, for example, Stefan-Ludwig Hoffmann, *Civil Society, 1750–1914* (Houndmills, UK: Palgrave Macmillan, 2006), 11–16; Goodman, *The Republic of Letters*, 253–8; Lynn Dumenil, *Freemasonry and American Culture; 1880–1930* (Princeton: Princeton University Press, 1984); Steven C. Bullock, "The Revolutionary Transformation of American Freemasonry, 1752–1792." *The William and Mary Quarterly*, Third Series, 47 (July 1990): 347–69.

14 See James Van Horn Melton, *The Rise of the Public in Enlightenment Europe* (Cambridge and New York: Cambridge University Press, 2001), 106–15.

15 On these developments broadly, see Hoffmann, *Civil Society*, ch. 2.

16 The classic text is Jürgen Habermas, *The Structural Transformation of the Public Sphere: An Inquiry into a Category of Bourgeois Society*, trans. Thomas Burger (Cambridge, MA: MIT Press, 1991).

17 See Hoffmann, *Civil Society*, 30–3; Mary Ann Clawson, *Constructing Brotherhood: Class, Gender, and Fraternalism* (Princeton: Princeton University Press, 1989).

18 Adrian Johns, "Coffeehouses and Print Shops," in *The Cambridge History of Science*, vol. 3: *Early Modern Science*, eds. Katharine Park and Lorraine Daston (Cambridge: Cambridge University Press, 2006); Melton, *The Rise of the Public in Enlightenment Europe*, 235–51.

19 See Tocqueville, *Democracy in America*, 513.

20 See Hoffmann, *Civil Society*, 30.

21 Tocqueville, *Democracy in America*, 514.

22 See Clawson, *Constructing Brotherhood*, 11.

23 See Hoffmann, *Civil Society*, 34–6.

24 See Anne Firor Scott, *Natural Allies: Women's Associations in American History* (Urbana and Chicago: University of Illinois Press, 1993).

25 See Burton J. Bledstein, *The Culture of Professionalism: The Middle Class and the Development of Higher Education in America* (New York: W. W. Norton & Company, 1976), 296–8, 310–19.

26 See Bledstein, *The Culture of Professionalism*, 84–92.

27 See John McIlroy, *Trade Unions in Britain Today*, 2nd edn (Manchester and New York: Manchester University Press, 1995), 227–8.

28 See Leon Fink, *Workingmen's Democracy: The Knights of Labor and American Politics* (Urbana, IL: University of Illinois Press, 1985).

29 See Julie Greene, *Pure and Simple Politics: The American Federation of Labor and Political Activism, 1881–1917* (Cambridge: Cambridge University Press, 1998).

30 See, for example, Eric Arnesen, *Brotherhoods of Color: Black Railroad Workers and the Struggle for Equality* (Cambridge, MA: Harvard University Press, 2001).

31 See Hoffmann, *Civil Society*, 74; Jeffrey A. Charles, *Service Clubs in American Society: Rotary, Kiwanis, and Lions* (Urbana and Chicago: University of Chicago Press, 1993).

32 Statistics cited in Varda Burstyn, *The Rites of Men: Manhood, Politics, and the Culture of Sport* (Toronto, Buffalo and London: University of Toronto Press, 1999), 62.

33 Stefan-Ludwig Hoffmann makes this point in *Civil Society*, 87.

34 See Walter Russell Mead, *God and Gold: Britain, America, and the Making of the Modern World* (New York: A. A. Knopf, 2007), 159.

35 See David C. Smith, "Wood Pulp and Newspapers, 1867–1900." *The Business History Review* 38 (Autumn 1964): 328–45.

36 Carl F. Kaestle, "Studying the History of Literacy," in *Literacy in the United States: Readers and Reading Since 1880*, ed. Carl F. Kaestle et al. (New Haven: Yale University Press 1991), 18–19, 25.

37 Statistics cited in Robert E. Park, "Urbanization as Measured by Newspaper Circulation." *The American Journal of Sociology* 35 (July 1929): 60–79 (here: 64).

38 See Benno C. Schmidt, Jr., *Freedom of the Press vs. Public Access* (New York: Praeger, 1976), 40.

39 See W. Bernard Carlson, "The Telephone as Political Instrument: Gardiner Hubbard and the Formation of the Middle Class in America, 1875–1880," in *Technologies of Power: Essays in Honor of Thomas Parke Hughes and Agatha Chipley Hughes*, eds. Michael Thad Allen and Gabrielle Hecht (Cambridge, MA: MIT Press, 2001), 35–45.

40 See, for example, Berenice A. Carroll, "Christine de Pizan and the Origins of Peace Theory," in *Women Writers and the Early Modern British Political Tradition*, ed. Hilda L. Smith (Cambridge: Cambridge University Press, 1998).

41 Episode recounted in Bernard Lewis, *What Went Wrong? Western Impact and Middle Eastern Response* (Oxford: Oxford University Press, 2002), 64–5.

42 See R. A. Houston, *Scottish Literacy and the Scottish Identity: Illiteracy and Society in Scotland and Northern England, 1600–1800* (Cambridge: Cambridge University Press, 1985), 59–69.

43 See Craig Clunas, *Superfluous Things: Material Culture and Social Status in Early Modern China* (Cambridge: Cambridge University Press, 1991), 56.

44 See, for example, Alan Cook, "Ladies in the Scientific Revolution." *Notes and Records of the Royal Society of London* 51 (January 1997): 1–12.

45 On these and other (mostly Western) women of science, see Suzanne Le-May Sheffield, *Women and Science: Social Impact and Interaction* (Piscataway, NJ: Rutgers University Press, 2006); Marilyn Bailie Ogilvie, *Women in Science: Antiquity through the Nineteenth Century: A Biographical Dictionary with Annotated Bibliography* (Cambridge, MA: MIT Press, 1988).

46 See A. Woronzoff-Dashkoff, *Dashkova: A Life of Influence and Exile* (Philadelphia: Temple University Press, 2007).

47 See Mary Wollstonecraft, *Vindication of the Rights of Woman* (New York: Dover Publications, 1996).

48 See Frederick Rudolph, *The American College and University: A History*, intro. John R. Thelin (Athens, GA and London: University of Georgia Press, 1990).

49 See the statistical table in Barbara Miller Solomon, *In the Company of Educated Women: A History of Women and Higher Education in America* (New Haven: Yale University Press 1985).

50 See Benita Eisler (ed.), *The Lowell Offering: Writings by New England Mill Women (1840–1845)* (New York: W. W. Norton & Company, 1998).

51 See Pierce Grace, "First Among Women." *British Medical Journal* 303 (21–28 December 1991): 1582–3.

52 Statistics cited in Dayle A. Mandelson, "Women's Changing Labor-Force Participation in the U.S," in *Women and Work: A Handbook*, eds. Paula Dubeck and Kathryn M. Borman (New York and London: Garland Publishing, 1996), 4.

53 See Alice Kessler-Harris, *Out to Work: A History of Wage-Earning Women in the United States*, 20th Anniversary edn (New York: Oxford University Press, 2003), chs. 5–6.

54 See Heather A. Haveman and Lauren S. Beresford, "If You're So Smart, Why Aren't You the Boss? Explaining the Persistent Vertical Gender Gap in Management." *The ANNALS of the American Academy of Political and Social Science* 639 (January 2012): 114–30 (here: 118).

55 See Justine Picardie, *Coco Chanel: The Legend and the Life* (New York: HarperCollins, 2010).

56 See Julie Roy Jeffrey, *The Great Silent Army of Abolitionism: Ordinary Women in the Antislavery Movement* (Chapel Hill: University of North Carolina Press, 1998); James Brewer Stewart, *Holy Warriors: The Abolitionists and American Slavery*, rev. ed (New York: Hill and Wang, 1997).

57 See, for example, Ruth Bordin, *Woman and Temperance: The Quest for Power and Liberty, 1873–1900* (Philadelphia: Temple University Press, 1981); Estelle B. Freedman, *Their Sisters' Keepers: Women's Prison Reform in America, 1830–1930* (Ann Arbor: University of Michigan Press, 1981).

58 As quoted in Richard F. Hamm, *Shaping The Eighteenth Amendment: Temperance Reform, Legal Culture, and the Polity 1880–1920* (Chapel Hill and London: University of North Carolina Press, 1995), 242.

59 See Mary Erler and Maryanne Kowaleski, *Women and Power in the Middle Ages* (Athens, GA: University of Georgia Press,1998); Sandy Bardsley, *Women's Roles in the Middle Ages* (Westport, CT: Greenwood Press, 2007); Meg Lota Brown and Kari Boyd McBride, *Women's Roles in the Renaissance* (Westport, CT: Greenwood Press, 2005).

60 See Silvia Evangelisti, *Nuns: A History of Convent Life 1450–1700* (Oxford: Oxford University Press, 2007); Penelope D. Johnson, *Equal in Monastic Profession: Religious Women in Medieval France* (Chicago: University of Chicago Press, 1991); Bruce L. Venarde, *Women's Monasticism and Medieval Society: Nunneries in France and England, 890–1215* (Ithaca: Cornell University Press, 1997).

61 See Amy Louise Erickson, *Women and Property in Early Modern England* (London and New York: Routledge, 1993), 28–9.

62 See Kathryn Cullen-DuPont (ed.), *The Encyclopedia of Women's History in America* (New York: Da Capo Press, 1998), 153–4.

63 See Judith Apter Klinghoffer and Lois Elkis, "'The Petticoat Electors': Women's Suffrage in New Jersey, 1776–1807." *Journal of the Early Republic* 12 (Summer 1992): 159–93.

64 See Hilda L. Smith, "Women as Sextons and Electors: King's Bench and Precedents for Women's Suffrage," in *Women Writers and the Early Modern British Political Tradition*, ed. Smith, 338.

65 See Edward Raymond Tuner, "The Women's Suffrage Movement in England." *The American Political Science Review* 7 (November 1913): 588–609.

66 Quotations in Paul Johnson, *A History of the American People* (New York: HarperCollins, 1997), 657–8.

67 See Tocqueville, *Democracy in America*, 603.

68 See Alec C. Ewald, *The Way We Vote: The Local Dimension of American Suffrage* (Nashville, TN: Vanderbilt University Press, 2009), 131–2.

69 See, in particular, John Stuart Mill, *The Subjection of Women*, ed. Susan Moller Okin (Indianapolis: Hackett Publishing Company, 1988).

70 On the idea and practice of domesticity, see Nancy F. Cott, *The Bonds of Womanhood: "Woman's Sphere" in New England, 1780–1835*, 2nd edn (New Haven and London: Yale University Press, 1997); Kathryn Kish Sklar, *Catharine Beecher: A Study in American Domesticity* (New York: W. W. Norton & Company, 1976).

71 See, for example, Tracy L. Steffes, *School, Society, and State: A New Education to Govern Modern America, 1890–1940* (Chicago and London: University of Chicago Press, 2012), ch. 4.

72 See Jack Goody, *The European Family: An Historico-Anthropological Essay* (Oxford: Oxford University Press, 2000); Beatrice Gottlieb, *The Family in the Western World from the Black Death to the Industrial Age* (New York: Oxford University Press, 1993).

73 See Ruth Schwartz Cowan, "The 'Industrial Revolution' in the Home: Household Technology and Social Change in the 20th Century," in *Technology and the West: A Historical Anthology from "Technology and Culture,"* eds. Terry S. Reynolds and Stephen H. Cutcliffe (Chicago: University of Chicago Press, 1997).

74 See Amy Beth Aronson, *Taking Liberties: Early American Women's Magazines and their Readers* (Westport, CT: Praeger, 2002); Kathleen L. Endres and Therese L. Lueck (eds), *Women's Periodicals in the United States: Consumer Magazines* (Westport, CT: Greenwood Press, 1995).

75 See Ruth Schwartz Cowan, *More Work for Mother: The Ironies of Household Technology from the Open Hearth to the Microwave* (New York: Basic Books, 1983), 187–8.

76 See Roland Marchand, *Advertising the American Dream: Making Way for Modernity, 1920–1940* (Berkeley: University of California Press, 1985).

77 See Michael B. Miller, *The Bon Marché: Bourgeois Culture and The Department Store, 1869–1920* (Princeton: Princeton University Press, 1981); Bill Lancaster, *The Department Store: A Social History* (Leicester, UK: Leicester University Press, 1995).

78 See Terence P. Moran, *Introduction to the History of Communication: Evolutions & Revolutions* (New York: Peter Lang Publishing, 2010), 176.

79 See Johnson, *A History of the American People*, 698–707; Glenn Appell and David Hemphill, *American Popular Music: A Multicultural History* (Pacific Grove, CA: Cengage Learning, 2006).

80 See David Suisman, *Selling Sounds: The Commercial Revolution in American Music* (Cambridge, MA: Harvard University Press, 2009).

81 See Moran, *Introduction to the History of Communication*, 169–74; Gerald Mast and Bruce F. Kawin, *A Short History of the Movies*, 6th edn (Boston, MA: Prentice Hall, 1996).

82 See Ruth Schwartz Cowan, "The 'Industrial Revolution' in the Home: Household Technology and Social Change in the 20th Century." *Technology and Culture* 17 (January 1976): 1–23 (here: 6–7).

83 See Susan Thistle, *From Marriage to the Market: The Transformation of Women's Lives and Work* (Berkeley and Los Angeles: University of California Press, 2006), 203n9–10.

84 See Tony Judt, *Postwar: A History of Europe Since 1945* (London: Penguin Press, 2005), 339.

85 See Robert S. Lynd and Helen M. Lynd, *Middletown: A Study in Contemporary American Culture* (New York: Harcourt, Brace and Co., 1929), 96.

86 See Theodore Caplow, Louis Hicks, and Ben J. Wattenburg, *The First Measured Century: An Illustrated Guide to Trends in America, 1900–2000* (Washington, DC: American Enterprise Institute, 2001), 99.

87 See Kristin Ross, *Fast Cars, Clean Bodies: Decolonization and the Reordering of French Culture* (Cambridge, MA: MIT Press, 1995), 215n64.

88 See Roger Fouquet, *Heat, Power and Light: Revolutions in Energy Services* (Cheltenham, UK and Northampton, MA: Edward Elgar, 2008), 214–16.

89 See, for example, Paul L. Knox, *Metroburbia, USA* (Piscataway, NJ: Rutgers University Press, 2008), 30–6.

90 Robert Bruegmann makes this point in *Sprawl: A Compact History* (Chicago: University of Chicago Press, 2005).

91 See Jeffrey G. Wiliamson, *Coping with City Growth during the British Industrial Revolution* (New York: Cambridge University Press, 1990), 89.

92 This paragraph draws upon Bruegmann, *Sprawl*.

93 Statistic cited in Bruegmann, *Sprawl*, 37.

94 This paragraph follows Alfred D. Chandler, Jr., *The Visible Hand: The Managerial Revolution in American Business* (Cambridge, MA: Harvard University Press, 1977).

95 See Alfred D. Chandler, "Organizational Capabilities and the Economic History of the Industrial Enterprise." *The Journal of Economic Perspectives* 6 (Summer 1992): 79–100.

96 See C. Wright Mills, *White Collar: The American Middle Classes* (New York: Oxford University Press, 1951), pt. 2.

97 Statistics cited in Robert J. Larner, "Ownership and Control in the 200 Largest Nonfinancial Corporations, 1929 and 1963." *The American Economic Review* 56, pt. 1. (September 1966): 777–87 (here 780).

98 Alfred D. Chandler argues thus in "Learning and Technological Change: The Perspective from Business History," in *Learning and Technological Change*, ed. Ross Thomson (New York: Palgrave, 1993), and Chandler, "Organizational Capabilities."

99 On the rise of white-collar workers, see Olivier Zunz, *Making America Corporate, 1870–1920* (Chicago: University of Chicago Press, 1990); Mark McColloch, *White Collar Workers in Transition: The Boom Years, 1940–1970* (Westport, CT: Greenwood Press, 1983).

100 Statistics cited from United States Census Bureau, Table A1, "Years of School Completed by People 25 Years and Over, by Age and Sex: Selected Years 1940 to 2008," http://www.census.gov/population/socdemo/education/cps2008/tabA-1.csv (accessed 10 December 2009).

101 Statistics from Stephen Moore and Julian L. Simon, "The Greatest Century That Ever Was: 25 Miraculous Trends of the Past 100 Years." *Policy Analysis* 264 (15 December 1999): 1–32 (here: 16).

102 See, for example, Mills, *White Collar*, 249, 290–9.

103 As Brian McNair, Matthew Hibberd, and Philip Schlesinger observe, such concerns span the political spectrum. See their *Mediated Access: Broadcasting and Democratic Participation* (Luton, UK: University of Luton Press, 2003), 5.

104 This was the main point, in regard to middle-class women, of Betty Friedan, *The Feminine Mystique* (New York: W. W. Norton & Company, 1963).

105 Statistic quoted in Suzanne M. Bianchi and Daphne Spain, "Women, Work, and Family in America," in *Sociology of Families: Readings*, ed. Cheryl Albers (Thousands Oaks, CA: Pine Forge Press, 1999), 178.

106 See Haveman and Beresford, "If You're So Smart, Why Aren't You the Boss?" 117–18. See also Hanna Rosin, "The End of Men," *The Atlantic* (July/August 2010).

107 Morris Silver, *Economic Structures of Antiquity* (Westport, CT: Greenwood Press, 1995), 122; Albrecht Dihle, *Greek and Latin literature of the Roman Empire: From Augustus to Justinian* (New York and London: Routledge, 1994), 585.

108 The story of this tragedy is briefly told in René Lemarchand, "Exclusion, Marginalization, and Political Mobilization: The Road to Hell in the Great Lakes," in *Facing Ethnic Conflicts: Toward a New Realism*, ed. Andreas Wimmer et al. (Lanham, MD: Rowman & Littlefield, 2004).

109 This paragraph draws on John C. Headley, *The Europeanization of the World: On the Origins of Human Rights and Democracy* (Princeton: Princeton University Press, 2008).

110 As quoted in Headley, *The Europeanization of the World*, 66.

111 See Joseph M. Callewaert, *The World of Saint Paul* (San Francisco: Ignatius Press, 2011), 158–9.

112 On the prophetic tradition in Christianity, see John W. O'Malley, *Four Cultures of the West* (Cambridge, MA: Harvard University Press, 2004), ch. 1.

113 See Rodney Stark, *The Rise of Christianity: A Sociologist Reconsiders History* (Princeton: Princeton University Press, 1996), ch. 1.

114 On this practice, see Bernard Lewis, *The Muslim Discovery of Europe* (New York: W. W. Norton & Company, 1982), 63–4.

115 See Ibn Warraq, *Defending the West: A Critique of Edward Said's Orientalism* (Amherst, NY: Prometheus Books, 2007), 136–8.

116 See Jane I. Smith, "Islam and Christendom: Historical, Cultural, and Religious Interaction from the Seventh to the Fifteenth Centuries," in John L. Esposito (ed.), *The Oxford History of Islam* (Oxford and New York: Oxford University Press, 1999), 329.

117 Richard N. Frye, trans. and ed., *Ibn Fadlan's Journey to Russia: A Tenth-century Traveler from Baghdad to the Volga River* (Princeton: Princeton University Press, 2005).

118 See Natalie Zemon Davis, *Trickster Travels: A Sixteenth-Century Muslim Between Worlds* (New York: Hill & Wang, 2006).

119 See Warraq, *Defending the West*, 63–9.

120 See Gregory C. McIntosh, *The Piri Reis Map of 1513* (Athens, GA: University of Georgia Press, 2000), xi, 1–9.

121 See Said Bensaid Alaoui, "Muslim Opposition Thinkers in the Nineteenth Century," in *Between the State and Islam*, eds. Charles E. Butterworth and I. William Zartman (Cambridge: Cambridge University Press, 2001), 92–5.

122 See Bartolomé de Las Casas, *A Short Account of the Destruction of the Indies* (London and New York: Penguin, 1992); Warraq, *Defending the West*, 34, 158; Paul S. Vickery, *Bartolome de Las Casas: Great Prophet of the Americas* (New York: Paulist Press, 2006).

123 See George Huppert, *The Style of Paris: Renaissance Origins of the French Enlightenment* (Bloomington, IN: Indiana University Press, 1999); Keith Cameron, *Montaigne and His Age* (Exeter: University of Exeter, 1981).

124 See D. E. Mungello, *The Great Encounter of China and the West, 1500–1800* (Lanham, MD: Rowman & Littlefield, 2005), 83–98, 118–22.

125 See Warraq, *Defending the West*, 45–6, 147.

126 See Stephan Roman, *The Development of Islamic Library Collections in Western Europe and North America* (London and New York: Mansell, 1990).

127 See Smith, "Islam and Christendom," 323–5.

128 See, for example, Mungello, *The Great Encounter of China and the West*, 111–16.

129 See Headley, *The Europeanization of the World*, ch. 2.

130 See R. Po-Chia Hsia and Henk van Nierop (eds), *Calvinism and Religious Toleration in the Dutch Golden Age* (New York: Cambridge University Press, 2002); Willem Frijhoff, "How Plural Were the Religious Worlds in Early Modern Europe? Critical Reflections from the Netherlandic Experience," in *Living with Religious Diversity in Early-Modern Europe*, eds. C. Scott Dixon, Dagmar Freist, and Mark Greengrass (Farmham, UK and Burlington, VT: Ashgate Publishing, 2009). More broadly, see also Perez Zagorin, *How the Idea of Religious Toleration Came to the West* (Princeton and Oxford: Princeton University Press, 2003).

131 Joyce D. Goodfriend, "Practicing Toleration in Dutch New Netherland," in *The First Prejudice: Religious Tolerance and Intolerance in Early America*, eds. Chris Beneke and Christopher S. Grenda (Philadelphia: University of Pennsylvania Press, 2011).

132 See Chris Beneke, "The 'Catholic Spirits Prevailing in Our Country': America's Moderate Religious Revolution," in *The First Prejudice*, eds. Beneke and Grenda,

268; Johnson, *A History of the American People*, 59–601. For an essential excerpt from the document plus commentary, see John J. Patrick and Gerald P. Long (eds), *Constitutional Debates on Freedom of Religion: A Documentary History* (Westport, CT: Greenwood Press, 1999), 14–15.

133 Rescinded in 1654, the act returned to force again during the period 1658–1692. See Patrick and Long (eds), *Constitutional Debates on Freedom of Religion*, 14–15.

134 On the ubiquity of slavery in early history, see David Brion Davis, *The Problem of Slavery in Western Culture* (Ithaca: Cornell University Press, 1966), chs. 1–3.

135 Iris Origo, "The Domestic Enemy: The Eastern Slaves in Tuscany in the Fourteenth and Fifteenth Centuries." *Speculum* 30 (July 1955): 321–66.

136 See Sidney W. Mintz, *Sweetness and Power: The Place of Sugar in Modern History* (New York: Penguin, 1985), 24–30.

137 See Davis, *The Problem of Slavery in Western Culture*, 46, 207. See also Headley, *The Europeanization of the World*, ch. 2.

138 See Edmund S. Morgan, *American Slavery, American Freedom: The Ordeal of Colonial Virginia* (New York and London: W. W. Norton & Company, 1975).

139 This paragraph draws upon Davis, *The Problem of Slavery in Western Culture*, 109–19; David Brion Davis, *The Problem of Slavery in the Age of Revolution, 1770–1823* (New York: Oxford University Press, 1999), 25–7.

140 Some lesser thinkers put forward powerful arguments against slavery. See, for example, John Witte, Jr., "A Demonstrative Theory of Natural Law: Johannes Althusius and the Rise of Calvinists Jurisprudence." *Ecclesiastical Law Journal* 11 (2009): 248–65.

141 See Davis, *The Problem of Slavery in the Age of Revolution*, 47–8.

142 Ibid., 46–7; Davis, *The Problem of Slavery in Western Culture*, chs. 10–12.

143 See Davis, *The Problem of Slavery in Western Culture*, ch. 10; Davis, *The Problem of Slavery in the Age of Revolution*, ch. 5.

144 See Davis, *The Problem of Slavery in the Age of Revolution*, 216, 270–1; Davis, *The Problem of Slavery in Western Culture*, 213–14.

145 Davis, *The Problem of Slavery in the Age of Revolution*, 82. See also Thomas Bender (ed.), *The Antislavery Debate: Capitalism and Abolition as a Problem in Historical Interpretation* (Berkeley: University of California Press, 1992).

146 See Davis, *The Problem of Slavery in the Age of Revolution*, 148–50.

147 See Headley, *The Europeanization of the World*, ch. 2.

148 Benedict Anderson coined the phrase in *Imagined Communities: Reflections on the Origin and Spread of Nationalism* (London: Verso, 1983). See also E. J. Hobsbawm, *Nations and Nationalism since 1780: Programme, Myth, Reality* (Cambridge: Cambridge University Press, 1990).

149 See Peter Spierenburg, *The Spectacle of Suffering: Executions and the Evolution of Repression: From a Preindustrial Metropolis to the European Experience* (Cambridge: Cambridge University Press, 1984).

150 See Lynn Hunt, *Inventing Human Rights: A History* (New York and London: W. W. Norton & Company, 2007), 75–6.

151 See John Hostettler, *Cesare Beccaria: The Genius of "On Crimes and Punishments"* (Hook, UK: Waterside Press, 2011).

152 Spierenburg, *The Spectacle of Suffering*, ch. 6.

153 David J. Rothman, "Perfecting the Prison: United States, 1789–1865," in *The Oxford History of the Prison: The Practice of Punishment in Western Society*, eds. Norval Morris and David J. Rothman (New York: Oxford University Press, 1998), 103.

154 See Rothman, "Perfecting the Prison." See also Randall McGowan, "The Well-Ordered Prison: England, 1780–1865," in *The Oxford History of the Prison,* eds. Morris and David J. Rothman (Oxford: Oxford University Press, 1995).

155 See Gerald Weissmann, "Citizen Pinel and the Madman at Bellevue." *The FASEB Journal* 22 (May 2008): 1289–93.

156 See Kathleen Jones, *A History of the Mental Health Services* (London: Routledge and Kegan Paul, 1972). For a similar story in the early United States, see David J. Rothman, *The Discovery of the Asylum: Social Order and Disorder in the New Republic*, rev. edn (Piscataway, NJ: AldineTransaction, 2002).

157 For a dramatic account of pre-modern psychiatry, see Simon Winchester, *The Professor and the Madman: A Tale of Murder, Insanity, and the Making of the Oxford English Dictionary* (New York: Harpercollins, 1998).

158 See, for example, William R. Breakey (ed.), *Integrated Mental Health Services: Modern Community Psychiatry* (New York: Oxford University Press, 1996).

159 The earliest manifestation of this movement for the most part occurred in nineteenth-century Britain. See E. L. Woodward, *The Age of Reform, 1815–1870*, 2nd edn (Oxford: Oxford University Press, 1962).

160 On this story, see Roger Daniels, *Coming to America: A History of Immigration and Ethnicity in American Life* (New York: Harper Perennial, 2002).

161 See Mark Wyman, *Round-Trip to America: The Immigrants Return to Europe, 1880–1930* (Ithaca: Cornell University Press, 1993), 6.

162 See, for example, Stephen Steinberg, *The Ethnic Myth: Race, Ethnicity, and Class in America* (Boston: Beacon Press, 2001), ch. 9; William G. Palmer, "From Gentleman's Club to Professional Body: The Evolution of the History Department in the United States." *Historically Speaking* 10 (June 2009): 36–8.

163 See Wendy Plotkin, "Restrictive Covenants," in *Antisemitism: A Historical Encyclopedia of Prejudice and Persecution*, 2 vols., ed. Richard S. Levy (Santa Barbara, CA: ABC-CLIO, 2005), vol. 1, 597–9.

164 See Paul Johnson, *A History of the Jews* (New York: HarperCollins, 1987), 278–80, 303–4, 365–8.

165 This paragraph draws on Susie Lan Cassel, *The Chinese in America: A History from Gold Mountain to the New Millennium* (Walnut Creek, CA: Altamira Press, 2002); Gabriel J. Chin, "Segregation's Last Stronghold: Race Discrimination and the Constitutional Law of Immigration." *UCLA Law Review* 46 (1998): 1–74.

166 See Cassel, *The Chinese in America*, 435–6.

167 Statistics and details supplied in Roger Daniels, *Asian America: Chinese and Japanese in the United States since 1850* (Seattle: University of Washington Press, 1988), 115, 216, 241.

168 Regarding these laws, see Daniels, *Coming to America*, 27.

169 On the bracero program, see Daniels, *Coming to America*, 310–11.

170 The details and results of the Act are provided in Daniels, *Coming to America*, 334–87.

171 See J. David Hacker and Michael R. Haines, "American Indian Mortality in the Late Nineteenth Century: The Impact of Federal Assimilation Policies on a Vulnerable Population." *Annales de Demographie Historique* 2 (2005): 17–45.

172 See Johnson, *A History of the American People*, 405–5.

173 See, for example, Anthony F. C. Wallace, *Jefferson and the Indians: The Tragic Fate of the First Americans* (Cambridge, MA: Harvard University Press, 1999).

174 Broadly on government policy, see Francis Paul Prucha, *The Great Father: The United States Government and the American Indians*, 2 vols. (Lincoln, NE: University of Nebraska Press, 1984).

175 Eric Kades, "The Dark Side of Efficiency: Johnson v. M'Intosh and the Expropriation of American Indian." *University of Pennsylvania Law Review* 148 (April 2000): 1065–190.

176 See Stuart Banner, *How the Indians Lost Their Land: Law and Power on the Frontier* (Cambridge, MA: Harvard University Press, 2005).

177 See Frederick E. Hoxie, *A Final Promise: The Campaign to Assimilate the Indians, 1880–1920* (Lincoln, NE: University of Nebraska Press, 2001).

178 See Liz Sonneborn, *Chronology of American Indian History*, rev. edn (New York: Facts On File, 2007), 387–98.

179 See, for example, Valerie Alia, *The New Media Nation: Indigenous Peoples and Global Communication* (New York: Berghahn Books, 2010), 106–8.

180 See Sue Davis and J. W. Peltason, *Corwin and Peltason's Understanding the Constitution*, 17th edn (Belmont, CA: Cengage Learning, 2008), ch. 10.

181 See Eric Foner, *Reconstruction: America's Unfinished Revolution, 1863–1877* (New York: Harper & Row, 1988), ch. 8.

182 See Foner, *Reconstruction*, ch. 12; C. Vann Woodward, *The Strange Career of Jim Crow* (New York: Oxford University Press, 1974).

183 The story of the unprecedented northward migration of millions of African-Americans is told in James R. Grossman, *Land of Hope: Chicago, Black Southerners, and the Great Migration* (Chicago: University of Chicago Press, 1991).

184 See, for example, George M. Fredrickson, *White Supremacy: A Comparative Study of American and South African History* (New York: Oxford University Press, 1981); David H. Jackson, Jr., *Booker T. Washington and the Struggle Against White Supremacy: The Southern Educational Tours, 1908–1912* (New York: Palgrave Macmillan, 2008).

185 On this aspect of the philosophy of Socrates, see Laurence Lampert, *How Philosophy Became Socratic: A Study of Plato's "Protagoras," "Charmides," and "Republic"* (Chicago and London: University of Chicago Press, 2010), 129, 186–200.

186 On this aspect of Aristotle's thought, see Gerard Hughes, *Routledge Philosophy GuideBook to Aristotle on Ethics* (London and New York: Routledge, 2001), ch. 4.

187 This extraordinary story is recounted in Geoffrey C. Ward, *Unforgivable Blackness: The Rise and Fall of Jack Johnson* (New York: A. A. Knopf, 2004).

188 See the officially sponsored study, Morris J. MacGregor, *Integration of the Armed Forces, 1940–1965* (Washington, DC: United States Army, 1981).

189 On this social and cultural triumph, see Joseph Dorinson and Joram Warmund (eds), *Jackie Robinson: Race, Sports, and the American Dream* (Amonk, NY: M. E. Sharpe, 1998).

190 See David Halberstam, *The Fifties* (New York: Ballantine Books, 1993), 692–8.

191 As quoted in Mark Whitman (ed.), *Removing a Badge of Slavery: The Record of Brown V. Board of Education* (Princeton: Princeton University Press, 1993), 14.

192 As quoted in Whitman (ed.), *Removing a Badge of Slavery*, 309.

193 See Robert D. Loevy, "Introduction: The Background and Setting of the Civil Rights Act of 1964," in *The Civil Rights Act of 1964: The Passage of the Law That Ended Racial Segregation*, ed. Robert D. Loevy (Albany: State University of New York Press, 1997), 17–19.

194 For abundant primary source documents, see Stewart Burns (ed.), *Daybreak of Freedom: The Montgomery Bus Boycott* (Chapel Hill, NC: University of North Carolina Press, 1997).

195 See Irene Y. Capozzi (ed.), *The Civil Rights Act: Background, Statutes and Primer* (New York: Nova Pub., 2006).

196 Michael Perman, *Pursuit of Liberty: A Political History of the American South* (Chapel Hill: University of North Carolina Press, 2010), 301–2.

197 See Jerome Karabel, *The Chosen: The Hidden History of Admission and Exclusion at Harvard, Yale, and Princeton: Princeton University Press* (New York: Houghton Mifflin, 2005), 379, 381.

198 See United States, Bureau of the Census, *Current Population Reports: Special Studies*, Issue 46 (July 1973), 3.

199 Statistics supplied in Stephan and Abigail Thernstrom, *America in Black and White: One Nation, Indivisible* (New York: Simon & Schuster, 1997), 190.

200 Data available in Nina M. Moore, *Governing Race: Policy, Process, and the Politics of Race* (Westport, CT: Praeger, 2000), 181.

201 Statistics supplied in Dianne M. Pinderhughes, "Race, the Presidency, and Obama's First Year," in *The Obama Phenomenon: Toward a Multiracial Democracy*, eds. Charles P. Henry, Robert Allen, and Robert Chrisman (Urbana, Chicago and Springfield: University of Illinois Press, 2011), 98.

202 For a similar recent argument, see Daron Acemoglu and James Robinson, *Why Nations Fail: The Origins of Power, Prosperity, and Poverty* (New York: Crown Publishers, 2012).

203 See, for example, Martin MacEwen, *Tackling Racism in Europe: An Examination of Anti-Discrimination Law in Practice* (Oxford and Washington, DC: Berg, 1995); Guðmundur Hálfdanarson (ed.), *Racial Discrimination and Ethnicity in European History* (Pisa: PLUS, Università di Pisa, 2003).

204 This paragraph draws in part on Christopher Butler, *Postmodernism: A Very Short Introduction* (Oxford and New York: Oxford University Press, 2002).

205 See Michel Foucault, *Discipline and Punish: The Birth of the Prison*, trans. Alan Sheridan, 2nd edn (New York: Vintage Books, 1995).

206 See Elaine Tyler May, *America and the Pill: A History of Promise, Peril, and Liberation* (New York: Basic Books, 2010).

207 See Beth Bailey, "The Sexual Revolution: Was It Revolutionary?" in *The Columbia Guide to America in the 1960s*, ed. David Farber and Beth Bailey (New York: Columbia University Press, 2001); Jeffrey Escoffier (ed.), *Sexual Revolution*, photographs by Fred W. McDarrah (New York: Columbia University Press, 2003).

208 See Jan Yager, *Single in America* (New York: Atheneum, 1980), 31.

209 Statistics available in Francis G. Castles and Michael Flood, "Divorce, the Law and Social Context: Families of Nations and the Legal Dissolution of Marriage." *Acta Sociologica* 34 (1991): 279–97.

210 See Mark Abrahamson, *Out-of-Wedlock Births: The United States in Comparative Perspective* (Westport, CT: Praeger, 1998), 35–6.

211 See John D'Emilio, *Sexual Politics, Sexual Communities: The Making of a Homosexual Minority in the United States, 1940–1970*, 2nd edn (Chicago and London: University of Chicago Press, 1998).

212 See Diane Richardson, "Constructing Sexual Citizenship: Theorizing Sexual Rights." *Critical Social Policy* 20 (February 2000): 105–35.

213 See Tom Regan, *The Case For Animal Rights*, updated with a new pref. (Berkeley: University of California Press, 2004).

214 James Turner, *Reckoning with the Beast: Animals, Pain, and Humanity in the Victorian Mind* (Baltimore, MD: The Johns Hopkins University Press, 1980). The Nazis, ironically, adopted history's first and most thoroughgoing series of laws protecting animal welfare beginning in late 1934. See Cyprian Blamires (ed.), *World Fascism: A Historical Encyclopedia*, 2 vols. (Santa Barbara, CA: ABC-CLIO, 2006), vol. 1, 33.

215 On this development, see Chris Impey, *How It Ends: From You to the Universe* (New York: W. W. Norton & Company, 2010), 306–7.

216 For primary sources on these and other events in 1968, see Jeremi Suri, *The Global Revolutions of 1968* (New York: W. W. Norton & Company, 2007).

217 See Bernadette J. Saunders and Christopher Goddar, *Physical Punishment in Childhood: The Rights of the Child* (Chichester, UK: Wiley-Blackwell, 2010), 35–8.

218 On this phenomenon, see "Hi There: Life is Getting Friendlier But Less Interesting. Blame Technology, Globalisation and Feminism." *The Economist* (17 December 2009).

219 For these statistics and commentary, see Joseph Carroll, "'Business Casual' Most Common Work Attire; Women More Likely Than Men to Wear Formal Business Clothing on the Job," Gallup News Service (4 October 2007), http://www.gallup.com/poll/101707/Business-Casual-Most-Common-Work-Attire.aspx (accessed on 18 December 2009).

Conclusion

1 This paragraph draws upon Paul Freiberger and Michael Swaine, *Fire in the Valley: The Making of the Personal Computer*, 2nd edn (New York: Mcgraw-Hill, 2000), chs. 7–8. See also Steve Wozniak, with Gina Smith, *iWoz: Computer Geek to Cult Icon: How I Invented the Personal Computer, Co-Founded Apple, and Had Fun Doing It* (New York: W. W. Norton & Company, 2006).

2 On this linkage, see Joyce Appleby, *The Relentless Revolution: A History of Capitalism* (New York and London: W. W. Norton & Company, 2010), 145–7.

3 See Michael S. Malone, *Bill & Dave: How Hewlett and Packard Built the World's Greatest Company* (New York: Portfolio, 2000).

4 See Marc Aronson, *Up Close: Bill Gates* (New York: Viking, 2009).

5 See David A. Vise and Mark Malseed, *The Google Story: For Google's 10th Birthday* (New York: Random House, 2008).

6 See Walter Isaacson, *Steve Jobs* (New York: Simon & Schuster, 2011).

7 On this idealism, see Bryan Pfaffenberger, "The Social Meaning of the Personal Computer: Or, Why the Personal Computer Revolution Was No Revolution." *Anthropological Quarterly* 61 (January 1988): 39–47; Martin Lister, Jon Dovey, Seth Giddings, Iain Grant, and Kieran Kelly, *New Media: A Critical Introduction* (London and New York: Routledge, 2003), 197.

8 See Interview with Raymond Kurzweil, *The Science Show* (23 February 2008), http://www.abc.net.au/rn/scienceshow/stories/2008/2170327.htm (accessed on 22 December 2009).

9 See Ralph B. Edfelt, *Global Comparative Management: A Functional Approach* (Thousand Oaks, CA: SAGE Pub., 2010), 85.

10 See Michael D. Woods and Glenn Muske, "Economic Development Via Understanding and Growing a Community's Microbusiness Segment," in *Entrepreneurship and Local Economic Development*, ed. Norman Walzer (Lanham, MD: Lexington Books, 2007), 189.

11 Dinesh D'Souza, *What's so Great about America* (Washington, DC: Regnery Publishing, 2002), 83.

12 See Fred Schwarz, "The Uncertainty Principle: America Dominates Science with a Classic American Formula: Freedom." *National Review* (21 December 2009): 26–7.

13 Alexis de Tocqueville usefully distinguished between centralization of government and of administration in *Democracy in America*, trans. George Lawrence, ed. J. P. Mayer (Garden City, NY: Doubleday, 1969), 87–98. In this view, the United States had a decentralized, and France a centralized, administration. It is not this that is being discussed here.

14 See, in particular, Immanuel Wallerstein, *The Modern World-System*, 4 vols. to date (New York: Academic Press, 1974–2011); Eric H. Mielants, *The Origins of Capitalism and the "Rise of the West"* (Philadelphia: Temple University Press, 2007).

15 See Joel Mokyr at http://eh.net/book_reviews/why-europe-grew-rich-and-asia-did-not-global-economic-divergence-1600–1850 (accessed 17 June 2013).

16 See Allan Mitchell, *The Great Train Race: Railways and the Franco-German Rivalry, 1815–1914* (New York: Berghahn, 2000), 68–70.

17 See Xiaoyan Chen and Peng Hwa Ang, "The Internet Police in China: Regulation, Scope, and Myths," in *Online Society in China: Creating, Celebrating, and Instrumentalising the Online Carnival*, eds. David Kurt Herold and Peter Marolt (Abingdon, UK and New York: Routledge, 2011).

18 See Richard R. John, *Network Nation: Inventing American Telecommunications* (Cambridge, MA: Harvard University Press, 2010), 24, 68–74.

19 Amartya Sen, "East and West: The Reach of Reason." *New York Review of Books* 47, 12 (20 July 2000): 33–8.

20 See Arthur Gill, "Lean Manufacturing," in *Exploring Advanced Manufacturing Technologies*, eds. Stephen F. Krar and Arthur Gill (New York: Industrial Press Inc., 2003).

21 See "A Special Report on Innovation in Emerging Markets," *The Economist* (15 April 2010).

22 See, for example, José Eduardo Cassiolato and Virgínia Vitorino (eds), *BRICs and Development Alternatives: Innovation Systems and Policies* (London and New York: Anthem Press, 2009).

23 See Deirdre McCloskey, *Bourgeois Dignity: Why Economics Can't Explain the Modern World* (Chicago: University of Chicago Press, 2010), 113–14.

24 See John D. Kasarda and Greg Lindsay, *Aerotropolis: The Way We'll Live Next* (New York: Farrar, Straus and Giroux, 2011), 267–9.

25 See Navi Radjou, Jaideep Prabhu, and Simone Ahuja, *Jugaad Innovation: Think Frugal, Be Flexible, Generate Breakthrough Growth* (San Francisco: Jossey-Bass, 2012).

26 Quoted from Joshua S. Goldstein, *Winning The War on War: The Decline of Armed Conflict Worldwide* (New York: Dutton/Penguin, 2011), 42.

27 The correct phrasing is supplied by Carl Schmitt, "The Concept of the Political," in *The Weimar Republic Sourcebook*, eds. Anton Kaes, Martín Jay, and Edward Dimendberg (Berkeley and Los Angeles: University of California Press, 1994), 343.

28 See James J. Sheehan, *Where Have All the Soldiers Gone?: The Transformation of Modern Europe* (Boston: Houghton Mifflin, 2008).

29 See Michael E. O'Hanlon, *Defense Strategy for the Post-Saddam Era* (Washington, DC: Brookings Institution Press, 2005), 13–18.

30 See Carla Norrlof, *America's Global Advantage: US Hegemony and International Cooperation* (New York: Cambridge University Press, 2010), 10.

31 On the other seventh, see Paul Collier, *The Bottom Billion: Why the Poorest Countries are Failing and What Can Be Done About It* (New York: Oxford University Press, 2007).

32 See Patricia J. Campbell, Aran MacKinnon, and Christy R. Stevens, *An Introduction to Global Studies* (Malden, MA and Oxford: Blackwell Publishers, 2010), ch. 6.

33 See Michael Novacek, *Terra: Our 100-Million-Year-Old Ecosystem–and the Threats That Now Put It at Risk* (New York: Farrar, Straus and Giroux, 2008).

34 See Jeremy B. C. Jackson et al., "Historical Overfishing and the Recent Collapse of Coastal Ecosystems." *Science* 293 (July 2001): 629–37.

35 See Andy Dobson, "Monitoring Global Rates of Biodiversity Change: Challenges that Arise in Meeting the Convention on Biological Diversity (CBD) 2010 Goals." *Philosophical Transactions: Biological Sciences* 360 (28 February 2005): 229–41.

36 See Kerry Emanuel, *What We Know about Climate Change*, 2nd edn (Cambridge, MA: MIT Press, 2012), 64.

37 See "Climate Science: A Sensitive Matter," *The Economist* (30 March 2013): 77–9.

38 See Rashid M. Hassan, Robert Scholes, and Neville Ash (eds), *Ecosystems and Human Well-Being: Findings of the Condition and Trends Working Group of the Millennium Ecosystem Assessment*, vol. 1: *Current State and Trends* (Washington, Covelo and London: Island Press, 2005), 400–2.

39 See Hassan, Scholes, and Ash (eds), *Current State and Trends*, 555–6, 567, 652.

40 See "Deforestation Figures for Selected Countries," http://rainforests.mongabay.com/deforestation/(accessed on 22 March 2010).

41 See Roger Fouquet, *Heat, Power and Light: Revolutions in Energy Services* (Cheltenham, UK and Northampton, MA: Edward Elgar, 2008), 349–63.

42 See Eric Lichtfouse et al. (eds), *Sustainable Agriculture*, vol. 2 (Dordrecht and Heidelberg: Springer, 2011).

43 For a highly positive account of how Western societies are dealing with environmental issues, see Stephen Moore and Julian Simon, *It's Getting Better All the Time: 100 Greatest Trends of the 20th Century* (Washington, DC: Cato Institute, 2000), 183–206.

44 See Robert Bryce, *Power Hungry: The Myths of "Green" Energy and the Real Fuels of the Future* (New York: Public Affairs, 2010), 140–2.

45 For Japan, see Kent E. Calder, *The New Continentalism: Energy and Twenty-First-Century Eurasian Geopolitics* (New Haven and London: Yale University Press 2012), 184–5.

46 See Steven Hill, *Europe's Promise: Why the European Way Is the Best Hope in an Insecure Age* (Berkeley and Los Angeles: University of California Press, 2010), 158–72.

47 See Calder, *The New Continentalism*, xxxi.

48 See Martin Jacques, *When China Rules the World: The End of the Western World and the Birth of a New Global Order*, 2nd edn (London: Penguin Books, 2012), 211–23.

49 See Pekka E. Kauppi et al., "Returning Forest Analyzed with the Forest Identity." *Proceedings of the National Academy of Sciences* 103 (Fall 2006): 17574–9.

50 See "Deforestation Figures for Selected Countries."

51 See *The State of World Fisheries and Aquaculture 2004* (Rome: Food and Agriculture Organization of the United Nations, 2004), 69–70, 89.

52 See Serge M. Garcia and Richard J. R. Grainger, "Gloom and Doom? The Future of Marine Capture Fisheries." *Philosophical Transactions: Biological Sciences* 360 (29 January 2005): 21–46 (here: 26).

53 See "What Causes Ocean 'Dead Zones'?" *Scientific American* (25 September 2012), http://www.scientificamerican.com/article.cfm?id5ocean-dead-zones (accessed 14 June 2013).

54 This argument is put forward in Sorin Sonea and Léo G. Mathieu, *Prokaryotology: A Coherent View* (Montreal: McGill-Queen's University Press, 2000).

55 See J. R. McNeill, *Something New Under the Sun: An Environmental History of the Twentieth-Century World* (New York: W. W. Norton & Company, 2000).

56 Other cultures were more tolerant in certain periods of their history (e.g., Islam during its Golden Age) yet none developed as extensive a range of safeguards, guarantees, and rights into the modern era as the West.

57 See, for example, Don S. Browning and John Witte, Jr., "Christianity's Contributions to Children's Rights." *Zygon* 46 (September 2011): 713–32.

58 See "Religious Views and Beliefs Vary Greatly by Country, According to the Latest Financial Times/Harris Poll" (20 December 2006), http://www.harrisinteractive.com/news/allnewsbydate.asp? NewsID51131 (accessed 14 September 2010).

59 See John Mickelthwait and Adrian Woodridge, *God Is Back: How the Global Revival of Faith Is Changing the World* (New York: Penguin, 2009), 21.

60 See Thomas Albert Howard, *God and the Atlantic: America, Europe, and the Religious Divide* (Oxford and New York: Oxford University Press, 2011).

61 See Edward J. Larson and Larry Witham, "Leading Scientists still Reject God." *Nature* 394 (1998): 313.

62 On Jerry Rubin, see Ron Chepesiuk, *Sixties Radicals, Then and Now: Candid Conversations with Those Who Shaped the Era* (Jefferson, NC; McFarland & Co., 1995), ch. 12.

63 See Henry Louis Gates, Jr., and Evelyn Brooks Higginbotham, *African American Lives* (New York: Oxford University Press, 2004), 760.

64 See Schubert M. Ogden, *The Reality of God, and Other Essays* (Dallas, TX: Southern Methodist University Press, 1992), 34–41.

65 Charles Hartshorne, probably America's greatest systematic thinker of the twentieth-century, articulates such a philosophy in *Creative Synthesis and Philosophic Method* (London: SCM Press, 1970).

66 See Walter Mignolo, *The Darker Side of Western Modernity: Global Futures, Decolonial Options* (Durham, NC and London: Duke University Press, 2011).

67 See Norrlof, *America's Global Advantage*.

68 See Mark Leonard, *Why Europe Will Run the 21st Century* (New York: Public Affairs, 2005); Hill, *Europe's Promise.*

69 See Jacques, *When China Rules the World.*

70 See The World Bank, *World Development Indicators* (Washington, DC: World Bank, 2012), 20–2.

71 See Jacques, *When China Rules the World*, 16.

72 See Yongshun Cai, *Collective Resistance in China: Why Popular Protests Succeed or Fail* (Stanford: Stanford University Press, 2010).

73 "Special Report: China and the Internet," *The Economist* (6 April 2013): 3–16.

74 See Fabrizio Tassinari, *Why Europe Fears Its Neighbors* (Santa Barbara, CA: Praeger Security International, 2009).

75 See Uwe Backes and Patrick Moreau (eds), *The Extreme Right in Europe: Current Trends and Perspectives* (Göttingen: Vandenhoeck & Ruprecht, 2011).

76 See "European entrepreneurs: Les misérables." *The Economist* (28 July 2012): 19–22.

77 See International Monetary Fund, *Fiscal Monitor: Balancing Fiscal Policy Risks* (Washington, DC: International Monetary Fund, 2012), 14–25.

78 See Todd R. Clear, Michael D. Reisig, and George F. Cole, *American Corrections*, 10th edn (Belmont, CA: Wadsworth Publishing Co Inc, 2012), 463–8.

79 See Linda Darling-Hammond, *The Flat World and Education: How America's Commitment to Equity Will Determine Our Future* (New York and London: Teachers College Press, 2010), 9–10; Richard Fry and Paul Taylor, "Hispanic High School Graduates Pass Whites in Rate of College Enrollment" (9 May 2013), http://www.pewhispanic.org/2013/05/09/hispanic-high-school-graduates-pass-whites-in-rate-of-college-enrollment/ (accessed 3 August 2013).

WORKS CITED IN THIS BOOK

"A Special Report on Innovation in Emerging Markets." *The Economist* (15 April 2010).

Abernethy, David. *The Dynamics of Global Dominance: European Overseas Empires, 1415–1980.* New Haven: Yale University Press, 2000.

Abrahamson, Mark. *Out-of-Wedlock Births: The United States in Comparative Perspective.* Westport, CT: Praeger, 1998.

Abramitzky, Ran and Fabio Braggion. "Migration and Human Capital: Self-Selection of Indentured Servants to the Americas." *Journal of Economic History* 66 (December 2006): 882–905.

Abramson, Albert. *Zworykin, Pioneer of Television.* Foreword by Eric Barnouw. Urbana, IL: University of Illinois Press, 1995.

Abulafia, David. "Asia, Africa and the Trade of Medieval Europe." In *Trade and Industry in the Middle Ages*, 2nd edn. Edited by M. M. Postan, Edward Miller, and Cynthia Postan. Cambridge: Cambridge University Press, 1987.

Abu-Lughod, Ibrahim. *The Arab Rediscovery of Europe: A Study in Cultural Encounters.* Introduction by Rashid Khalidi. London: Saqi Books, 2011.

Abu-Lughod, Janet L. *Before European Hegemony: The World System A.D. 1250–1350.* New York: Oxford University Press, 1989.

Acemoglu, Daron, and James Robinson. *Why Nations Fail: The Origins of Power, Prosperity, and Poverty.* New York: Crown Business, 2012.

Acemoglu, Daron, Simon Johnson, and James A. Robinson. "The Colonial Origins of Comparative Development: An Empirical Investigation." *The American Economic Review* 91 (December 2001): 1369–401.

Adas, Michael. *Machines As the Measure of Men: Science, Technology, and Ideologies of Western Dominance.* Ithaca and London: Cornell University Press, 1989.

Adcock, Frank E. *The Greek and Macedonian Art of War.* Berkeley: University of California Press, 1957.

Africa, Thomas W. *The Immense Majesty: A History of Rome and the Roman Empire.* Wheeling, IL: Harlan Davidson, 1991.

Aftalion, Fred. *A History of the International Chemical Industry: From the "Early Days" to 2000.* Philadelphia: University of Pennsylvania Press, 2001.

Ahlstrom, Sydney E. *A Religious History of the American People*, 2nd edn. New Haven: Yale University Press 2004.

Akrigg, G. P. V. *Jacobean Pageant: Or, the Court of King James I.* Cambridge, MA: Harvard University Press, 1962.

Alaoui, Said Bensaid. "Muslim Opposition Thinkers in the Nineteenth Century." In *Between the State and Islam.* Edited by Charles E. Butterworth and I. William Zartman. Cambridge: Cambridge University Press, 2001, 92–5.

Alder, Ken. *Engineering the Revolution: Arms and Enlightenment in France, 1763–1815.* Princeton: Princeton University Press, 1997.

Alexander, J. "Islam, Archaeology and Slavery in Africa." *World Archaeology* 33, 1 (June 2001): 44–60.
Ali, Syed Ameer. *The Life and Teachings of Mohammed: Or, The Spirit of Islam*. London: W. H. Allen & Company, Limited, 1891.
Alia, Valerie. *The New Media Nation: Indigenous Peoples and Global Communication*. New York: Berghahn Books, 2010.
Alighieri, Dante. *The Divine Comedy*. Translated by Henry F. Cary, vol. 20 of The Harvard Classics. New York: P.F. Collier & Son Co., 1909.
Allardyce, Gilbert. "The Rise and Fall of the Western Civilization Course." *The American Historical Review* 87 (June 1982): 695–725.
Allen, Gary J., and Ken Albala (eds), *The Business of Food: Encyclopedia of the Food and Drink Industries*. Westport, CT: Greenwood Press, 2007.
Allen, Larry. *The Global Financial System 1750–2000*. London: Reaktion, 2001.
Allen, Martin. "Italians in English Mints and Exchanges." In *Fourteenth Century England*, vol. 2. Edited by Chris Given-Wilson. Woodbridge, UK, and Rochester, NY: Boydell & Brewer Incorporated, 2002.
Allen, Prudence. *The Concept of Woman*. Volume 2: *The Early Humanist Reformation, 1250–1500,* Part 1. Grand Rapids, MI: W. B. Eerdmans Pub. Co., 2006.
Allen, Robert C. *Farm to Factory: A Reinterpretation of the Soviet Industrial Revolution*. Princeton and Oxford: Princeton University Press, 2003.
Allen, Rosamund. *Eastward Bound: Travel and Travellers, 1050–1550*. Manchester: Manchester University Press, 2004.
Altbach, Philip G., and Edith S. Hoshino (eds), *International Book Publishing: An Encyclopedia*. New York: Fitzroy Dearborn Publishers, 1995.
Altman, Albert A. "Korea's First Newspaper: The Japanese *Chosen shinpo*." *The Journal of Asian Studies* 43, 4 (August 1984): 685–96.
Aly, Götz. *Hitler's Beneficiaries: Plunder, Racial War, and the Nazi Welfare State*. Translated by Jefferson Chase. New York: Holt, 2007.
Ames, Glenn J. *Colbert, Mercantilism, and the French Quest for Asian Trade*. DeKalb, IL: Northern Illinois University Press, 1996.
—. *Vasco da Gama: Renaissance Crusader*. New York: Pearson/Longman, 2005.
—. *The Globe Encompassed: The Age of European Discovery, 1500–1700*. Upper Saddle River, NJ: Pearson Prentice Hall, 2008.
Amin, Samir. *Eurocentrism*. Translated by Russell Moore. New York: Monthly Review, 1989.
Anca, Celia de, and Antonio Vazquez Vega. *Managing Diversity in the Global Organization: Creating New Business Values*. Houndmills, UK, and New York: Palgrave Macmillan, 2007.
Andersen, Kirsti. *The Geometry of an Art: The History of the Mathematical Theory of Perspective from Alberti to Monge*. New York: Springer, 2007.
Anderson, Benedict. *Imagined Communities: Reflections on the Origin and Spread of Nationalism*. London: Verso, 1983.
Andress, David. *The Terror: The Merciless War for Freedom in Revolutionary France*. New York: Farrar, Straus and Giroux, 2005.
Andrew, Christopher, and Vasili Mitrokhin. *The World Was Going Our Way: The KGB and the Battle for the Third World*. New York: Basic Books, 2005.
Andrews, Michael Alford. *The Birth of Europe: Colliding Continents and the Destiny of Nations*. London: BBC Books, 1991.
Anstey, Roger T. "Capitalism and Slavery: A Critique." *The Economic History Review*, New Series 21 (August 1968): 307–20.
Appell, Glenn, and David Hemphill. *American Popular Music: A Multicultural History*. Pacific Grove, CA: Cengage Learning, 2006.

Applebaum, Wilbur (ed.), *Encyclopedia of the Scientific Revolution from Copernicus to Newton*. New York: Garland Publishing, 2000.
Appleby, Joyce. *The Relentless Revolution: A History of Capitalism*. New York and London: W. W. Norton & Co., 2010.
Aquinas, Saint Thomas. *Summa Theologica*, 22 vols. Translated by the fathers of the English Dominican province. New York: Benziger Brothers, 1911–25.
Archer, Christon I., John R. Ferris, Holger H. Herwig, and Timothy H. E. Travers. *World History of Warfare*. Lincoln, NE: University of Nebraska Press, 2002.
Archer, Clark. "A Medium-Term Perspective on Demographic Change in the American Midlands, 1803–1990." In *Contemporary Rural Systems in Transition*, vol. 2: *Economy and Society.* Edited by I. R. Bowler, C. R. Bryant, and M. D. Nellis. Wallingford, UK, and Tucson: CABI, 1992, 76.
Aristotle. *The Basic Works of Aristotle*. Edited by Richard McKeon. New York: Random House, 1941.
Armstrong, Karen. *Buddha*. New York: Viking, 2001.
Arnesen, Eric. *Brotherhoods of Color: Black Railroad Workers and the Struggle for Equality*. Cambridge, MA: Harvard University Press, 2001.
Arnold, Bettina, and D. Blair Gibson. *Celtic Chiefdom, Celtic State: The Evolution of Complex Social Systems in Prehistoric Europe*. Cambridge: Cambridge University Press, 1995.
Aron, Leon. *Boris Yeltsin: A Revolutionary Life*. New York: HarperCollins, 2000.
Aronson, Amy Beth. *Taking Liberties: Early American Women's Magazines and their Readers*. Westport, CT: Praeger, 2002.
Aronson, Marc. *Up Close: Bill Gates*. New York: Viking, 2009.
Artzy, Michal. "On Boats and Sea Peoples." *Bulletin of the American Schools of Oriental Research* 266 (May 1987): 75–84.
Ascher, Abraham. *The Revolution of 1905: A Short History*. Stanford: Stanford University Press, 2004.
Atiyeh, George N. "The Book in the Modern Arab World: The Cases of Lebanon and Egypt." In *The Book in the Islamic World*. Edited by George N. Atiyeh. Albany: State University of New York Press, 1995.
Atwell, William S. "International Bullion Flows and the Chinese Economy circa 1530–1650." *Past and Present* 95 (May 1982): 68–90.
—. "Ming China and the Emerging World Economy, c. 1570–1650." In *The Cambridge History of China*, vol. 8: *The Ming Dynasty, 1368–1644*, pt. 2. Edited by Denis Twitchett and Frederick Mote. Cambridge: Cambridge University Press, 1998, 388–99.
—. "Another Look at Silver Imports into China, ca. 1635–1644." *Journal of World History* 16 (December 2005): 467–89.
Aubin, Hermann. "The Lands East of the Elbe and German Colonization Eastwards." In *The Cambridge Economic History of Europe: The Agrarian Life of the Middle Ages*. Edited by Michael Moïssey Postan. Cambridge: Cambridge University Press, 1966.
Audisio, Gabriel. *The Waldensian Dissent: Persecution and Survival, c.1170–c.1570*. Translated by Claire Davison. Cambridge: Cambridge University Press, 1999.
Augustine, Saint. *The City of God*. Edited by Vernon J. Bourke. Garden City, NY: Image Books, 1958.
—. *The Confessions of St. Augustine*. Translated and edited by John K. Ryan. Garden City, NY: Image Books, 1960.
Aydin, Cemil. *The Politics of Anti-Westernism in Asia: Visions of World Order in Pan-Islamic and Pan-Asian Thought*. New York: Columbia University Press, 2007.
Aylmer, G. E. *Rebellion or Revolution? England, 1640–1660*. Oxford and New York: Oxford University Press, 1986.
Ayton, Andrew, and Philip Preston (eds), *The Battle of Crécy, 1346*. Woodbridge, UK: Boydell, 2005.

Backes, Uwe, and Patrick Moreau (eds), *The Extreme Right in Europe: Current Trends and Perspectives*. Göttingen: Vandenhoeck & Ruprecht, 2011.

Bacon, Francis. *The New Organon*. Edited by Lisa Jardine and Michael Silverthorne. Cambridge: Cambridge University Press, 2000.

Baer, William C. "The Institution of Residential Investment in Seventeenth-Century London." *The Business History Review* 76, 3 (Autumn 2002): 515–51.

Bagchi, David, and David C. Steinmetz (eds), *The Cambridge Companion to Reformation Theology*. Cambridge: Cambridge University Press, 2004.

Bailey, Beth. "The Sexual Revolution: Was It Revolutionary?" In *The Columbia Guide to America in the 1960s*. Edited by David Farber and Beth Bailey. New York: Columbia University Press, 2001.

Bainton, Roland. *Here I Stand–A Life of Martin Luther*. New York: Abingdon-Cokesbury Press, 1950.

Bairoch, Paul, Jean Batou, and Pierre Chèvre. *La population des villes européennes: Banque de données et analyse sommaire des résultats, 800–1850*. Geneva: Librairie Droz, 1988.

Baker, Christopher (ed.), *Absolutism and the Scientific Revolution, 1600–1720: A Biographical Dictionary*. Westport, CT: Greenwood Press, 2002.

Bala, Arun. *The Dialogue of Civilizations in the Birth of Modern Science*. New York: Palgrave Macmillan, 2008.

Baldwin, Neil. *Edison: Inventing the Century*. Chicago and London: University of Chicago Press, 2001.

Bangs, Carl. "Dutch Theology, Trade, and War: 1590–1610." *Church History* 39, 4 (December 1970): 470–82.

Banner, Stuart. *How the Indians Lost Their Land: Law and Power on the Frontier*. Cambridge, MA: Harvard University Press, 2005.

Bao, Yuheng, Ben Liao, and Letitia Lane. *Renaissance in China: The Culture and Art of the Song Dynasty, 907–1279*, preface by Letitia Lane. Lewiston, NY: Edwin Mellen Press, 2006.

Barber, Benjamin. *Jihad vs McWorld: Terrorism's Challenge to Democracy*. New York: Ballantine Books, 1996.

Barber, William J. *From New Era to New Deal: Herbert Hoover, the Economists, and American Economic Policy, 1921–1933*. Cambridge and New York: Cambridge University Press, 1985.

Bardsley, Sandy. *Women's Roles in the Middle Ages*. Westport, CT: Greenwood Press, 2007.

Barlow, Ronald Stokes. *300 Years of Farm Implements and Machinery, 1630–1930*. Iola, WI: Krause Publications, 2003.

Barnard, Alan. *Social Anthropology and Human Origins*. Cambridge: Cambridge University Press, 2011.

Baron, Sabrina Alcorn, Eric N. Lindquist, and Eleanor F. Shevlin (eds), *Agent of Change: Print Culture Studies after Elizabeth L. Eisenstein*. Amherst, MA: University of Massachusetts Press, 2007.

Bartlett, Kenneth R., and Margaret McGlynn (eds), *Humanism and the Northern Renaissance*. Toronto: Canadian Scholars' Press, 2000.

Bartlett, Robert. *The Making of Europe: Conquest, Colonization, and Cultural Change, 950–1350*. Princeton: Princeton University Press, 1993.

Barzun, Jacques. *Classic, Romantic, and Modern*, 2nd edn. Chicago and London: University of Chicago Press, 1961.

—. *Darwin, Marx, Wagner: Critique of a Heritage*, 2nd edn. Chicago and London: University of Chicago Press, 1981.

Battuta, Ibn. *The Travels of Ibn Battuta: In the Near East, Asia and Africa, 1325–1354*. Translated and Edited by Rev Samuel Lee. Mineola, NY: Dover Publications, 2004 [1829].

Bayer, Oswald. *Martin Luther's Theology: A Contemporary Interpretation*. Translated by Thomas H. Trapp. Grand Rapids, MI: W.B. Eerdmans Pub. Co., 2008.

Beasley, W. G. "The Foreign Threat and the Opening of the Ports." In *The Cambridge History of Japan*, vol. 5: *The Nineteenth Century*. Edited by Marius B. Jansen. Cambridge: Cambridge University Press, 1989.

Beaton, Kendall. "Dr. Gesner's Kerosene: The Start of American Oil Refining." *The Business History Review* 29 (March 1955): 28–53.

Becker, Annette. "The Visual Arts." In *A Companion to World War I*. Edited by John Horne. Chichester, UK, and Malden MA: Blackwell Publishers, 2010.

Beckett, Ian F. W. *The Great War, 1914–1918*, 2nd edn. Harlow, UK, and New York: Pearson/Longman, 2007.

Beilby, James K., and Paul Rhodes Eddy (eds), *The Historical Jesus: Five Views*. Downers Grove, IL: InterVarsity Press, 2009.

Bell, David. *The First Total War: Napoleon's Europe and the Birth of Warfare as We Know It*. New York: Houghton Mifflin, 2007.

Bellah, Robert N., et al. *Habits of the Heart: Individualism and Commitment in American Life*. Berkeley, Los Angeles, and London: University of California Press, 1985.

Bender, Thomas (ed.), *The Antislavery Debate: Capitalism and Abolition as a Problem in Historical Interpretation*. Berkeley: University of California Press, 1992.

Beneke, Chris. "The 'Catholic Spirits Prevailing in Our Country': America's Moderate Religious Revolution." In *The First Prejudice: Religious Tolerance and Intolerance in Early America*. Edited by Chris Beneke and Christopher S. Grenda. Philadelphia: University of Pennsylvania Press, 2011.

Berenbaum, Michael. *The World Must Know: The History of the Holocaust as Told in the United States Holocaust Memorial Museum*. Boston: Little, Brown, 1993.

Berkey, Jonathan. "Women in Medieval Islamic Society." In *Women in Medieval Western European Culture*. Edited by Linda E. Marshall. New York and London: Garland Publishing, 1999.

—. *The Formation of Islam: Religion and Society in the Near East, 600–1800*. Cambridge: Cambridge University Press, 2003.

Berman, Constance Hoffman. "Medieval Agriculture, the Southern French Countryside, and the Early Cistercians. A Study of Forty-Three Monasteries." *Transactions of the American Philosophical Society*, New Series 76, 5 (1986): 1–179.

Berman, Harold J. "The Origins of Western Legal Science." *Harvard Law Review* 90 (March 1977): 894–943.

—. "The Background of the Western Legal Tradition in the Folklaw of the Peoples of Europe." *The University of Chicago Law Review* 45 (Spring 1978): 553–97.

—. *Law and Revolution: The Formation of the Western Legal Tradition*. Cambridge, MA: Harvard University Press 1983.

—. *Law And Revolution, II: The Impact of the Protestant Reformations on the Western Legal Tradition*. Cambridge, MA: Harvard University Press, 2003.

Bernal, Martin. *Black Athena: The Afroasiatic Roots of Classical Civilization*, 3 vols. New Brunswick, NJ: Rutgers University Press, 1987–2006.

Bernard, Claude. *An Introduction to the Study of Experimental Medicine*. Translated by Henry Copley Greene. Introduction by Lawrence J. Henderson. 1927. Reprint, New York: Dover Pub., 1957.

Bernard, G. W. *The King's Reformation: Henry VIII and the Remaking of the English Church*. New Haven: Yale University Press, 2005.

Best, Joel. "Economic Interests and the Vindication of Deviance: Tobacco in Seventeenth Century Europe." *The Sociological Quarterly* 20, 2 (Spring 1979): 171–82.

Bettenson, Henry, and Chris Maunder (eds), *The Documents of the Christian Church*, 4th edn. New York: Oxford University Press, 2011.

Bianchi, Suzanne M., and Daphne Spain. "Women, Work, and Family in America." *Sociology of Families: Readings*. Edited by Cheryl Albers. Thousands Oaks, CA: Pine Forge Press, 1999.

Bijker, Wiebe E. *Of Bicycles, Bakelites, and Bulbs: Toward a Theory of Sociotechnical Change*. Cambridge, MA: MIT Press, 1995.

Bilby, Kenneth. *The General: David Sarnoff and the Rise of the Communications Industry*. New York: Harper & Row, 1986.

Birch, Charles, and John B. Cobb, Jr. *The Liberation of Life: From the Cell to the Community*. Cambridge and New York: Cambridge University Press, 1981.

Bird, Isabella. *The Yangtze Valley and Beyond: An Account of Journeys in China, Chiefly in the Province of Sze Chuan and among the Man-tze of the Somo Territory*. With a new introduction by Pat Barr. Boston: Beacon Press, 1987.

Biro, Matthew. *The Dada Cyborg: Visions of the New Human in Weimar Berlin*. Minneapolis: University of Minnesota Press, 2009.

Bisson, Thomas N. "The Military Origins of Medieval Representation." *The American Historical Review* 71 (July 1966): 1199–218.

—. "The Problem of Feudal Monarchy: Aragon, Catalonia, and France." *Speculum* 53 (July 1978): 460–78.

—. *The Crisis of the Twelfth Century: Power, Lordship, and the Origins of European Government*. Princeton: Princeton University Press, 2008.

Black, Antony. "The Conciliar Movement." In *The Cambridge History of Medieval Political Thought c.350–c.1450*. Edited by J. H. Burns. Cambridge: Cambridge University Press, 1988.

—. *Guild & State: European Political Thought from the Twelfth Century to the Present*. New Brunswick, NJ: Transaction Pub., 2003.

Black, Jeremy. *War for America: The Fight for Independence 1775–1783*. New York: St. Martin's Press, 1991.

—. *The Cambridge Illustrated Atlas of Warfare: Renaissance to Revolution, 1492–1792*. New York: Cambridge University Press, 1996.

—. *War and the World: Military Power and the Fate of Continents, 1450–2000*. New Haven: Yale University Press, 1998.

—. *Warfare in the Eighteenth Century*. London: Cassell, 1999.

—. *Kings, Nobles and Commoners: States and Societies in Early Modern Europe, a Revisionist History*. London and New York: I. B. Tauris, 2004.

—. *The Great War and the Making of the Modern World*. London: Continuum, 2011.

Black, Joseph, and Joseph Laurence Black (eds), *The Broadview Anthology of British Literature: The Renaissance and the Early Seventeenth Century*, 2nd edn. Toronto: Broadview Press, 2010.

Blackburn, Robin. *The Making of New World Slavery: From the Baroque to the Modern, 1492–1800*. London and New York: Verso, 1997.

Blake, Norman. *Caxton and His World*. London: André Deutsch, 1969.

Blamires, Cyprian (ed.), *World Fascism: A Historical Encyclopedia*, 2 vols. Santa Barbara, CA: ABC-CLIO, 2006.

Blanning, T. C. W. *The French Revolution: Aristocrats Versus Bourgeois?* Atlantic Heights, NJ: Humanities Press International, 1987.

Blatman, Daniel. *The Death Marches: The Final Phase of Nazi Genocide*. Translated by Chaya Galai. Cambridge, MA: Harvard University Press, 2011.

Bledstein, Burton J. *The Culture of Professionalism: The Middle Class and the Development of Higher Education in America*. New York: W. W. Norton & Co., 1976.

Blickle, Peter. "Communal Reformation and Peasant Piety: The Peasant Reformation and Its Late Medieval Origins." *Central European History* 20, 3 and 4 (September–December 1987): 216–28.

Blockmans, Wim. "Representation (Since the Thirteenth Century)." In *The New Cambridge Medieval History*, vol. 7: c. *1415-c. 1500*. Edited by Christopher Allmand. Cambridge: Cambridge University Press, 1998, 38–53.

Blomme, Jan. "Europe, America, and Africa." In *History of Humanity*, vol. 6: *The Nineteenth Century*. Edited by Peter Mathias et al. Paris: UNESCO; Abingdon, UK: Routledge, 2005, 51.

Blondheim, Menahem. *News Over the Wires: The Telegraph and the Flow of Public Information in America, 1844–1897*. Cambridge, MA: Harvard University Press, 1994.

Blumenthal, Uta-Renate. *The Investiture Controversy: Church and Monarchy from the Ninth to the Twelfth Century*. Translation by the author. Philadelphia: University of Pennsylvania Press, 1988.

Boadt, Lawrence. *Reading the Old Testament: An Introduction*. Mahway, NJ: Paulist Press, 1984.

Boase, Roger. *The Origin and Meaning of Courtly Love: A Critical Study of European Scholarship*. Manchester: Manchester University Press, 1977.

—. "Arab Influences on European Love-Poetry." In *The Legacy of Muslim Spain*. Edited by Salma Khadra Jayyus and Manuela Marín. Leiden, the Netherlands: E.J. Brill, 1992.

Boccaccio, Giovanni. *The Decameron*. Translated by Mark Musa and Peter Bondanella. New York: Penguin Group, 1982.

Bodde, Derk. *Chinese Thought, Society, and Science: The Intellectual and Social Background of Science and Technology Pre-modern China*. Honolulu: University of Hawaii Press, 1991.

Bogue, Allan G. "Changes in Mechanical and Plant Technology: The Corn Belt, 1910–1940." *The Journal of Economic History* 43, 1 (March 1983): 1–25.

Bollet, Alfred Jay. *Plagues & Poxes: The Impact of Human History on Epidemic Disease*. New York: Demos Medical Publishing, Inc., 2004.

Borah, Woodrow. "The Historical Demography of Aboriginal and Colonial America: An Attempt at Perspective." In *The Native Population of the Americas in 1492*. Edited by William M. Denevan, 2nd edn. Madison, WI: University of Wisconsin Press, 1992.

Bordeau, Sanford P. *Volts to Hertz–the Rise of Electricity: From the Compass to the Radio through the Works of Sixteen Great Men of Science Whose Names are Used in Measuring Electricity and Magnetism*. Minneapolis, MN: Burgess Pub. Co., 1982.

Bordin, Ruth Birgitta Anderson. *Woman and Temperance: The Quest for Power and Liberty, 1873–1900*. Philadelphia: Temple University Press, 1981.

Borgstrom, Georg. *The Hungry Planet: The Modern World at the Edge of Famine*. New York: Collier Books, 1967.

Bork, Robert. "Rock, Spires, Paper: Technical Aspects of Gothic Spires." In *Villard's Legacy: Studies in Medieval Technology, Science, and Art in Memory of Jean Gimpel*. Edited by Marie-Thérèse Zenner. Aldershot, UK, and Burlington, VT: Ashgate Publishing, Ltd, 2004, 135n1, 146–7.

Borstelmann, Thomas. *The Cold War and the Color Line: American Race Relations in the Global Arena*. Cambridge, MA: Harvard University Press, 2001.

—. *The 1970s: A New Global History from Civil Rights to Economic Inequality*. Princeton: Princeton University Press, 2012.

Bosher, J. F. *The French Revolution*. New York and London: W. W. Norton & Company, 1988.

Bossuet, Jacques-Bénigne. *Politics Drawn from the Very Words of Holy Scripture*. Edited by Patrick Riley. Cambridge: Cambridge University Press, 1990.

Boticelli, Peter. "British Capitalism and the Three Industrial Revolutions." In *Creating Modern Capitalism: How Entrepreneurs, Companies, and Countries Triumphed in Three Industrial Revolutions*. Edited by Thomas K. McCraw. Cambridge, MA: Harvard University Press 1995.

Bourke, Joanna. *Dismembering the Male: Men's Bodies, Britain, and the Great War*. Chicago: University of Chicago Press, 1996.

Bowden, Mary Ellen, Amy Beth Crow, and Tracy Sullivan. *Pharmaceutical Achievers: The Human Face of Pharmaceutical Research*. Philadelphia: Chemical Heritage Press, 2003.

Bowser, Benjamin P. *The Black Middle Class: Social Mobility—and Vulnerability*. Boulder, CO: Lynne Rienner Publishers, 2007.

Boyd, Catherine E. "The Gregorian Reform." In *The Gregorian Epoch: Reformation, Revolution, Reaction?* Edited by Schafer Williams. Boston: Heath, 1964, 75–6.

Boyer, C. B. *A History of Mathematics*, 2nd edn. Revised by Uta C. Merzbach. New York: John Wiley & Sons, 1991.

Bradbury, Jim. *The Capetians: Kings of France, 987–1328*. London and New York: The University of Michigan, 2007.

Bradley, John William. *Illuminated Manuscripts*. Chicago: University of Chicago Press, 1909.

Brady, Thomas A., Jr. "The Rise of Merchant Empires, 1400–1700: A European Counterpoint." In *The Political Economy of Merchant Empires: State Power and World Trade, 1350–1750*. Edited by James D. Tracy. Cambridge: Cambridge University Press, 1991, 123–32.

Brandt, Loren, and Thomas G. Rawski (eds), *China's Great Economic Transformation*. New York: Cambridge University Press, 2008.

Bray, Charles (ed.), *Dictionary of Glass: Materials and Techniques*, 2nd edn. London: A&C Black, 2001.

Braynard, Frank Osborn, and Robert Hudson Westover. *S.S. United States: Fastest Ship in the World*. Paducah, KY: Turner, 2002.

Breakey, William R. (ed.), *Integrated Mental Health Services: Modern Community Psychiatry*. New York: Oxford University Press, 1996.

Brecht, Martin. *Martin Luther: His Road to Reformation, 1483–1521*. Translated by James L. Schaaf. Minneapolis: Fortress Press, 1993a.

—. *Martin Luther: Shaping and Defining the Reformation, 1521–1532*. Translated by James L. Schaaf. Minneapolis: Fortress Press, 1993b.

—. *Martin Luther: The Preservation of the Church, 1532–1546*. Translated by James L. Schaaf. Minneapolis: Fortress Press, 1993c.

Brett, Michael, and Elizabeth Fentress. *The Berbers*. Oxford and Cambridge, MA: Blackwell, 1996.

Brezis, Elise S. "Foreign Capital Flows in the Century of Britain's Industrial Revolution: New Estimates, Controlled Conjectures." *The Economic History Review*, New Series 48, 1 (February 1995): 46–67.

Briggs, Lawrence Palmer. *The Ancient Khmer Empire*. Philadelphia: American Philosophical Society, 1951.

Broadberry, Stephen, and Bishnupriya Gupta. "The Early Modern Great Divergence: Wages, Prices and Economic Development in Europe and Asia, 1500–1800." *Economic History Review* 59 (February 2006): 2–31.

Brocheux, Pierre, and Daniel Hémery. *Indochina: An Ambiguous Colonization, 1858–1954*. Translated by Ly Lan Dill-Klein et al. Berkeley: University of California Press, 2009.

Brokaw, Cynthia. "On the History of the Book in China." In *Printing and Book Culture in Late Imperial China*. Edited by Cynthia J. Brokaw and Kai-wing Chow. Berkeley: University of California Press, 2005, 13–14.

Brokaw, Cynthia, and Kai-wing Chow (eds), *Printing and Book Culture in Late Imperial China*. Berkeley: University of California Press, 2005.

Brook, Timothy. "Edifying Knowledge: The Building of School Libraries in Ming China." *Late Imperial China* 17 (June 1996): 93–119.

Brooke, Christopher. *From Alfred to Henry III, 871–1272*. New York: W. W. Norton & Company, 1961.

Brown, A. R. "The Tyranny of a Construct: Feudalism and Historians of Medieval Europe." *The American Historical Review* 79 (October 1974): 1063–88.

Brown, Daniel W. *A New Introduction to Islam*, 2nd edn. Chichester, UK, and Malden, MA: Blackwell Publishers, 2009, 224–5.

Brown, Delmer M. (ed.), *The Cambridge History of Japan*. 1st edn. Vol. 1. Cambridge: Cambridge University Press, 1993.

Brown, Peter. "'Mohammed and Charlemagne' by Henri Pirenne." *Daedalus* 103 (Winter 1974): 25–33.

—. *Through the Eye of a Needle: Wealth, the Fall of Rome, and the Making of Christianity in the West, 350–550 AD*. Princeton and Oxford: Princeton University Press, 2012.

Brown, Richard. *Society and Economy in Modern Britain, 1700–1850*. London: Routledge, 1990.

Brown, Richard M. "Violence and the American Revolution." In *Essays on the American Revolution*. Edited by Stephen G. Kurtz and James H. Hutson. Chapel Hill: University of North Carolina Press, 1973.

Brown, Meg Lota, and Kari Boyd McBride. *Women's Roles in the Renaissance*. Westport, CT: Greenwood Press, 2005.

Browning, Christopher, with contributions by Jürgen Matthäus. *The Origins of the Final Solution: The Evolution of Nazi Jewish Policy, September 1939-March 1942*. Lincoln, NE: University of Nebraska Press, and Jerusalem: Yad Vashem, 2004.

Browning, Don S., and John Witte, Jr. "Christianity's Contributions to Children's Rights." *Zygon* 46 (September 2011): 713–32.

Bruegmann, Robert. *Sprawl: A Compact History*. Chicago: University of Chicago Press, 2005.

Brummett, Palmira. *Ottoman Seapower and Levantine Diplomacy in the Age of Discovery*. Albany: State University of New York Press, 1994.

Brundage, James A. *The Medieval Origins of the Legal Profession: Canonists, Civilians, and Courts*. Chicago and London: University of Chicago Press, 2008.

Bryce, Robert. *Power Hungry: The Myths of "Green" Energy and the Real Fuels of the Future*. New York: Public Affairs, 2010.

Bryce, Trevor. *The Kingdom of the Hittites*. Oxford: Oxford University Press, 1998.

Bryant, Lynwood. "The Beginnings of the Internal-Combustion Engine." In vol. 1 of *Technology in Western Civilization*, 2 vols. Edited by Melvin Kranzberg and Carroll W. Pursell, Jr. New York: Oxford University Press, 1967.

Buel, Richard, Jr. "Freedom of the Press in Revolutionary America: The Evolution of Libertarianism." In The Press and the American Revolution. Edited by Bernard Bailyn and John B. Hench. Worcester: American Antiquarian Society, 1980.

Buisseret, David (ed.), *The Oxford Companion to World Exploration*, 2 vols. New York: Oxford University Press, 2007.

Bulliet, Richard W. "Medieval Arabic Tarsh: A Forgotten Chapter in the History of Printing." *Journal of the American Oriental Society* 107 (July–September 1987): 427–38.

Bullock, Steven C. "The Revolutionary Transformation of American Freemasonry, 1752–1792." *The William and Mary Quarterly*, Third Series, 47 (July 1990): 347–69.

Burbank, Jane, and Frederick Cooper. *Empires in World History: Power and the Politics of Difference*. Princeton: Princeton University Press, 2010.

Burkert, Walter. *The Orientalizing Revolution: Near Eastern Influence on Greek Culture in the Early Archaic Age*. Translated by W. Burkert and M. E. Pinder. Cambridge: Cambridge University Press, 1992.

Burlingame, Roger. "The Beginning of Electricity." In vol. 1 of *Technology in Western Civilization*, 2 vols. Edited by Melvin Kranzberg and Carroll W. Pursell, Jr. New York: Oxford University Press, 1967.

Burn, Duncan Lyall. *The Economic History of Steelmaking, 1867–1939: A Study in Competition*. Cambridge: Cambridge University Press, 1940.

Burnett, Charles, ed. and trans. *Adelard of Bath, Conversations with his Nephew: On the Same and the Different, Questions on Natural Science, and On Birds*. Cambridge: Cambridge University Press, 1998.

Burns, Stewart (ed.), *Daybreak of Freedom: The Montgomery Bus Boycott*. Chapel Hill: University of North Carolina Press, 1997.

Burstyn, Varda. *The Rites of Men: Manhood, Politics, and the Culture of Sport*. Toronto, Buffalo, and London: University of Toronto Press, 1999.

Burton, Gideon. "From Ars dictaminis to Ars conscribendi epistolis: Renaissance Letter-Writing Manuals in the Context of Humanism." In *Letter-Writing Manuals and· Instruction from Antiquity to the Present*. Edited by Carol Poster and Linda C. Mitchell. Columbia, SC: University of South Carolina Press, 2007.

Burton, Janet and Julie Kerr. *The Cistercians in the Middle Ages*. Woodbridge, UK: The Boydell Press, 2011.

Butler, Christopher. *Postmodernism: A Very Short Introduction*. Oxford and New York: Oxford University Press, 2002.

Butterfield, Herbert. *The Origins of Modern Science, 1300–1800*. New York: Free Press, 1957.

—. *The Origins of History*. Edited by Adam Watson. New York: Basic Books, 1981.

Bynum, William. *The History of Medicine: A Very Short Introduction*. Oxford and New York: Oxford University Press, 2008.

Byrne, Joseph P. *The Black Death*. Westport, CT, and London: Greenwood Press, 2004.

Cahill, Thomas. *Sailing the Wine-Dark Sea: Why the Greeks Matter*. New York: Doubleday, 2003.

Cai, Yongshun. *Collective Resistance in China: Why Popular Protests Succeed or Fail*. Stanford: Stanford University Press, 2010.

Cain, P. J., and A. G. Hopkins, "Gentlemanly Capitalism and British Expansion Overseas I. The Old Colonial System, 1688–1850." *The Economic History Review*, New Series 39 (November 1986): 501–25.

Calder, Kent E. *The New Continentalism: Energy and Twenty-First-Century Eurasian Geopolitics*. New Haven and London: Yale University Press, 2012.

Callanan, James. *Covert Action in the Cold War: US Policy, Intelligence and CIA Operations*. New York: I. B. Tauris & Co. Ltd, 2010.

Callewaert, Joseph M. *The World of Saint Paul*. San Francisco: Ignatius Press, 2011.

Calvin, John. *Institution of the Christian Religion*. Edition of 1536. Translated and annotated by Ford Lewis Battles. Atlanta: John Knox Press, 1975.

—. *Institutes of the Christian Religion*. Edition of 1559. Translated by Henry Beveridge. Grand Rapids, MI: W. B. Eerdmans Pub. Co., 1989.

Cameron, Rondo. *France and the Economic Development of Europe: Evolution of International Business, 1800–1945*. Princeton: Princeton University Press, 1961.

Campanini, Massimo. "Al-Ghazzali." In *History of Islamic Philosophy*, 2 vols. Edited by Seyyed Hossein Nasr and Oliver Leaman. London and New York: Routledge, 1999.

Campbell, Patricia J., Aran MacKinnon, and Christy R. Stevens. *An Introduction to Global Studies*. Malden, MA, and Oxford: Blackwell Publishers, 2010.

Cantor, Norman F. *Civilization of the Middle Ages, A Completely Revised and Expanded Edition of Medieval History, the Life and Death of a Civilization*. New York: HarperCollins, 1993.

Caplow, Theodore, Louis Hicks, and Ben J. Wattenburg. *The First Measured Century: An Illustrated Guide to Trends in America, 1900–2000*. Washington, DC: American Enterprise Institute, 2001.

Capozzi, Irene Y. (ed.), *The Civil Rights Act: Background, Statutes and Primer*. New York: Nova Pub., 2006.

Capra, Fritjof. *The Tao of Physics: An Exploration of the Parallels between Modern Physics and Eastern Mysticism*, 4th edn. Boston: Shambala Publications, 1999.

Carlson, W. Bernard. "The Telephone as Political Instrument: Gardiner Hubbard and the Formation of the Middle Class in America, 1875–1880." In *Technologies of Power: Essays in Honor of Thomas Parke Hughes and Agatha Chipley Hughes*. Edited by Michael Thad Allen and Gabrielle Hecht. Cambridge, MA: MIT Press, 2001.

Carroll, Berenice A. "Christine de Pizan and the Origins of Peace Theory." In *Women Writers and the Early Modern British Political Tradition*. Edited by Hilda L. Smith. Cambridge: Cambridge University Press, 1998.

Carroll, Joseph. "'Business Casual' Most Common Work Attire; Women More Likely Than Men to Wear Formal Business Clothing on the Job." Gallup News Service (4 October 2007), http://www.gallup.com/poll/101707/Business-Casual-Most-Common-Work-Attire.aspx. Accessed on 18 December 2009.

Casper, Monica J. *Synthetic Planet: Chemical Politics and the Hazards of Modern Life*. New York: Routledge, 2003.

Cassel, Susie Lan. *The Chinese in America: A History from Gold Mountain to the New Millennium*. Walnut Creek, CA: Altamira Press, 2002.

Cassiolato, José Eduardo, and Virgínia Vitorino (eds), *BRICs and Development Alternatives: Innovation Systems and Policies*. London and New York: Anthem Press, 2009.

Cassis, Youssef. *Capitals of Capital: A History of International Financial Centres, 1780–2005*. Translated by Jacqueline Collier. Cambridge: Cambridge University Press, 2006.

Casson, Lionel. *Libraries in the Ancient World*. New Haven: Yale University Press, 2001.

Castles, Francis G., and Michael Flood. "Divorce, the Law and Social Context: Families of Nations and the Legal Dissolution of Marriage." *Acta Sociologica* 34, 4 (1991): 279–97.

Cateau, Heather, and S. H. H. Carrington (eds), *Capitalism and Slavery Fifty Years Later: Eric Eustace Williams-A Reassessment of the Man and His Work*. New York: Peter Lang Publishing, 2000.

Cavalcanti, D. D., W. Feindel, J. T. Goodrich, T. F. Dagi, C. J. Prestigiacomo, and M. C. Preul. "Anatomy, Technology, Art, and Culture: Toward a Realistic Perspective of the Brain." *Neurosurg Focus* 27 (September 2009): 1–22.

Cavanaugh, William T. *The Myth of Religious Violence: Secular Ideology and the Roots of Modern Conflict*. Oxford and New York: Oxford University Press, 2009.

Chamberlain, M. E. *The Scramble for Africa*, 3rd edn. Harlow, UK: Longman, 2010.

Chandler, Alfred D., Jr. *The Visible Hand: The Managerial Revolution in American Business*. Cambridge, MA: Harvard University Press, 1977.

—. "Integration and Diversification as Business Strategies – An Historical Analysis." *Business and Economic History*, Second Series 19 (1990): 65–73.

—. "Organizational Capabilities and the Economic History of the Industrial Enterprise." *The Journal of Economic Perspectives* 6 (Summer 1992): 79–100.

—. "Learning and Technological Change: The Perspective from Business History." In *Learning and Technological Change*. Edited by Ross Thomson. New York: Palgrave, 1993.

—. *Scale & Scope: The Dynamics of Industrial Capitalism*. Cambridge, MA: Belknap Press, 1994.

—. *Inventing the Electronic Century: The Epic Story of the Consumer Electronics and Computer Science Industries*. New York: Free Press, 2001.

—. "How High Technology Industries Transformed Work and Life Worldwide from the 1880s to the 1990s." *Capitalism and Society* 1 (2006): 1–55.

Chandler, Andrea M. *Institutions of Isolation: Border Controls in the Soviet Union and Its Successor States, 1917–1993*. Montreal and Buffalo: McGill-Queen's University Press, 1998.

Chandler, David. *The Art of Warfare in the Age of Marlborough*. New York: Hippocrene Books, 1976.

Chandler, Keith. *Beyond Civilization: The World's Four Great Streams of Civilization: Their Achievements, Their Differences and Their Future*. Bloomington, IN: Indiana University Press, 2001.

Charles, Jeffrey A. *Service Clubs in American Society: Rotary, Kiwanis, and Lions*. Urbana and Chicago: University of Illinois Press, 1993.

Charrak, André. "The Mathematical Model of Creation According to Kepler." In *Mathematics and the Divine: A Historical Study*. Edited by T. Koetsier and Luc Bergmans. Amsterdam: Elsevier, 2005.

Chartres, J. A. "The Marketing of Agricultural Produce." In *The Agrarian History of England and Wales*. Vol. 5: *1640–1750*. Edited by H. P. R. Finberg, Joan Thirsk, and Stuart Piggott. Cambridge: Cambridge University Press, 1985.

Chase, Kenneth. *Firearms: A Global History to 1700*. Cambridge: Cambridge University Press, 2003.

Chase, Kerry A. *Trading Blocs: States, Firms, and Regions in the World Economy*. Ann Arbor: University of Michigan Press, 2005.

Chase, William. "Stalin as Producer: The Moscow Show Trials and the Construction of Mortal Threats." In *Stalin: A New History*. Edited by Sarah Davies and James Harris. New York: Cambridge University Press, 2005.

Chaudhuri, K. N. *Trade and Civilisation in the Indian Ocean: An Economic History from the Rise of Islam to 1750*. Cambridge: Cambridge University Press, 1985.

Chen, Xiaoyan, and Hwa Ang, Peng. "The Internet Police in China: Regulation, Scope, and Myths." In *Online Society in China: Creating, Celebrating, and Instrumentalising the Online Carnival*. Edited by David Kurt Herold and Peter Marolt. Abingdon, UK, and New York: Routledge, 2011.

Chenu, Marie-Dominique. *Aquinas and His Role in Theology*. Collegeville, MN: The Liturgical Press, 2002.

Chepesiuk, Ron. *Sixties Radicals, Then and Now: Candid Conversations with Those Who Shaped the Era*. Jefferson, NC: McFarland & Co., 1995.

Chesterton, G. K. *The Everlasting Man*. Garden City, NY: Image Books, 1955.

Chevedden, Paul E. "The Invention of the Counterweight Trebuchet: A Study in Cultural Diffusion." *Dumbarton Oaks Papers* 54 (2000): 71–116.

Cheyette, Fredric L. "Some Reflections on Violence, Reconciliation, and the 'Feudal Revolution.'" In *Conflict in Medieval Europe: Changing Perspectives on Society and Culture*. Edited by Warren Brown and Piotr Górecki. Aldershot, UK, and Burlington, VT: Ashgate Publishing, Ltd., 2003, 250–9.

Chickering, Roger, Stig Förster, and Bernd Greiner (eds), *A World at Total War: Global Conflict and the Politics of Destruction, 1937–1945*. Washington, DC: German Historical Institute; Cambridge and New York: Cambridge University Press.

Chin, Gabriel J. "Segregation's Last Stronghold: Race Discrimination and the Constitutional Law of Immigration." *UCLA Law Review* 46, 1 (1998): 1–74.

Chirot, Daniel. "The Rise of the West." *American Sociological Review* 50 (April 1985): 181–95.

Chung, Young-Iob. *South Korea in the Fast Lane: Economic Development and Capital Formation*. New York: Oxford University Press, 2007.

Cipolla, Carlo. *Guns, Sails, and Empires: Technological Innovation and the Early Phases of European Expansion 1400–1700*. New York: Pantheon Press, 1965.

—. *Before the Industrial Revolution: European Society and Economy, 1000–1700*, 2nd edn. New York and London: W. W. Norton, 1980.

Clark, Gregory "Yields Per Acre in English Agriculture, 1250–1860: Evidence from Labour Inputs." *The Economic History Review*, New Series 44, 3 (August 1991): 445–60.

Clark, John Willis. *The Care of Books: An Essay on the Development of Libraries and their Fittings, from the Earliest Times to the End of the Eighteenth Century*. Cambridge: Cambridge University Press, 1901.

Clarke, H. B. "The Vikings." In *Medieval Warfare: A History*. Edited by Maurice Keen. Oxford: Oxford University Press, 1999.

Clarke, J. J. *The Tao of the West: Western Transformations of Taoist Thought*. London and New York: Routledge, 2000.
Clawson, Mary Ann. *Constructing Brotherhood: Class, Gender, and Fraternalism*. Princeton: Princeton University Press, 1989.
Clay, C. G. A. *Economic Expansion and Social Change: England 1500–1700*. New York: Cambridge University Press, 1984.
Clear, Todd R., Michael D. Reisig, and George F. Cole. *American Corrections*, 10th edn. Belmont, CA: Wadsworth Publishing Co Inc, 2012.
"Climate Science: A Sensitive Matter." *The Economist* (30 March 2013): 77–9.
Clunas, Craig. *Superfluous Things: Material Culture and Social Status in Early Modern China*. Cambridge: Cambridge University Press, 1991.
Cobb, Cathy, and Harold Goldwhite. *Creations of Fire: Chemistry's Lively History From Alchemy to the Atomic Age*. New York: Plenum Press, 1995.
Codrington, Stephen. *Planet Geography*, 3rd edn. Sydney: Solid Star Press, 2005.
Coe, Sophie D., and Michael D. Coe. *The True History of Chocolate*. New York: Thames and Hudson, 1996.
Cohen, Adam S. *The Uta Codex: Art, Philosophy, and Reform in Eleventh-Century Germany*. University Park, PA: Perm State University Press, 2000.
Cohen, H. Floris. *How Modern Science Came into the World: Four Civilizations, One 17th-Century Breakthrough*. Edition by Park and Daston. Amsterdam: Amsterdam University Press, 2010.
Cohen, I. Bernard. "Benjamin Franklin: An Experimental Newtonian Scientist." *Bulletin of the American Academy of Arts and Sciences* 5, 4 (January 1952): 2–6.
Cohen, Warren I. *The Cambridge History of American Foreign Relations*, vol. 4: *America in the Age of Soviet Power, 1945–1991*. Cambridge: Cambridge University Press, 1993.
Cohn, Norman. *The Pursuit of the Millennium: Revolutionary Millenarians and Mystical Anarchists of the Middle Ages*. Oxford: Oxford University Press, 1970.
Cole, Penny. "'O God, the Heathen Have Come into Your Inheritance' (Ps. 78.1): The Theme of Religious Pollution in Crusade Documents, 1095–1188." In *Crusaders and Muslims in Twelfth-Century Syria*. Edited by Maya Shatzmiller. Leiden, New York, and Köln: E.J. Brill, 1993.
Collier, Paul. *The Bottom Billion: Why the Poorest Countries are Failing and What Can Be Done About It*. New York: Oxford University Press, 2007.
Collins, Craig. *Toxic Loopholes: Failures and Future Prospects for Environmental Law*. New York: Cambridge University Press, 2010.
Collins, Francis. *The Language of God: A Scientist Presents Evidence for Belief*. New York: Free Press, 2006.
Collins, James B. *The State in Early Modern France*. Cambridge and New York: Cambridge University Press, 1995.
Collins, Robert O., and James M. Burns. *A History of Sub-Saharan Africa*. Cambridge and New York: Cambridge University Press, 2007.
Collins, Roger. "Charlemagne's Imperial Coronation and the Annals of Lorsch." In *Charlemagne: Empire and Society*. Edited by Joanna Story. Manchester and New York: Manchester University Press, 2005, 55.
Collinson, Patrick. *The Reformation: A History*. New York: Random House Publishing Group, 2006.
Colp, Ralph, Jr. "'Confessing a Murder': Darwin's First Revelations about Transmutation." *Isis* 77 (March 1986): 8–32.
Colten, Craig E., and Peter N. Skinner. *The Road to Love Canal: Managing Industrial Waste before EPA*. Austin, TX: University of Texas Press, 1996.

Compston, Christine, and Rachel Filene Seidman (eds), *Our Documents: 100 Milestone Documents from the National Archives*, foreword by Michael Beschloss. New York: Oxford University Press, 2001.
Conforti, Joseph A. *Saints and Strangers: New England in British North America*. Baltimore: The Johns Hopkins University Press, 2006.
Connah, Graham. *African Civilizations: An Archaeological Perspective*, 2nd edn. Cambridge: Cambridge University Press, 2001.
Conrad, Geoffrey W., and Arthur A. Demarest. *Religion and Empire: The Dynamics of Aztec and Inca Expansionism*. New York: Cambridge University Press, 1984.
Conrad, Sebastian. *German Colonialism: A Short History*. Translated by Sorcha O'Hagan. New York: Random House, Inc, 2012.
Constable, Giles. *The Reformation of the Twelfth Century*. Cambridge: Cambridge University Press, 1996.
Constable, Olivia Remie. "Muslims in Medieval Europe." In *A Companion to the Medieval World*. Edited by Carol Lansing and Edward D. English. Chichester, UK: Blackwell Publishing Ltd, 2009, 319–21.
Contamine, Philippe. *War in the Middle Ages*. Translated by Michael Jones. New York: Blackwell, 1986.
Cook, Alan H. *Edmond Halley: Charting the Heavens and the Seas*. Oxford: Oxford University Press, 1998.
Cook, Alan. "Ladies in the Scientific Revolution." *Notes and Records of the Royal Society of London* 51 (January 1997): 1–12.
Cook, Harold J. "Medicine." In *The Cambridge History of Science*. Vol. 3: *Early Modern Science*. Edited by Katharine Park and Lorraine Daston. Cambridge: Cambridge University Press, 2006.
Cook, Martin. *Medieval Bridges*. Princes Risborough, UK: Shire Publications, 1998.
Cook, William R., and Ronald B. Herzman. *The Medieval World View: An Introduction*. New York: Oxford University Press, 1983.
Cooper, Grace Rogers. *The Sewing Machine: Its Invention and Development*. Washington, DC: Smithsonian Institution Press, 1976.
Copeland, David A. (ed.), *Debating the Issues in Colonial Newspapers: Primary Documents on Events of the Period*. Westport, CT: Greenwood Press, 2000.
Copenhaver, Brian P. "Astrology and Magic." In *The Cambridge History of Renaissance Philosophy*. Edited by Charles B. Schmitt and Quentin Skinner. Cambridge: Cambridge University Press, 1988, 264–300.
Corballis, Michael C. "The Gestural Origins of Language." *The American Scientist* 87, 2 (March–April 1999): 138–45.
—. "The Evolution of Language." *Annals of the New York Academy of Sciences* 1156 (March 2009): 19–43.
Cort, John E. "The Jain Knowledge Warehouses: Traditional Libraries in India." *Journal of the American Oriental Society* 115, 1 (January–March 1995): 77–87.
Costambeys, Marios, Matthew Innes, and Simon MacLean, *The Carolingian World*. Cambridge: Cambridge University Press, 2011.
Cotrugli, Benedetto. "On the Dignity and Office of Merchants." In *The Traditions of the Western World*. Edited by J. H. Hexter et al. Chicago: University of Chicago Press, 1967, 274–5.
Cott, Nancy F. *The Bonds of Womanhood: "Woman's Sphere" in New England, 1780–1835*, 2nd edn. New Haven and London: Yale University Press, 1997.
Cottingham, John. "'A Brute to the Brutes?: Descartes' Treatment of Animals." *Philosophy* 53 (October 1978): 551–9.
Coulson, Thomas. *Joseph Henry: His Life and Work*. Princeton: Princeton University Press, 1950.

Cowan, Ruth Schwartz. "The 'Industrial Revolution' in the Home: Household Technology and Social Change in the 20th Century." *Technology and Culture* 17 (January 1976): 1–23.
—. *More Work for Mother: The Ironies of Household Technology from the Open Hearth to the Microwave*. New York: Basic Books, 1983.
—. "The 'Industrial Revolution' in the Home: Household Technology and Social Change in the 20th Century." In *Technology and the West: A Historical Anthology from "Technology and Culture."* Edited by Terry S. Reynolds and Stephen H. Cutcliffe. Chicago: University of Chicago Press, 1997.
Coward, Barry. *The Stuart Age: England, 1603–1714*, 4th edn. Harlow, UK, and New York: Pearson Longman, 2012.
Cowdrey, H. E. J. *The Cluniacs and the Gregorian Reform*. Oxford: Clarendon Press, 1970.
Cracraft, James. *The Revolution of Peter the Great*. Cambridge, MA, and London: Harvard University Press, 2003.
—. *Two Shining Souls: Jane Addams, Leo Tolstoy, and The Quest For Global Peace*. Lanham, MD: Lexington Books, 2012.
Crawford, John. "History of Coffee." *Journal of the Statistical Society of London* 15, 1 (April 1852): 50–8.
Creasy, William C., trans. *The Imitation of Christ by Thomas a Kempis: A New Reading of the 1441 Latin Autograph Manuscript*, 2nd edn. Macon, GA: Mercer University Press, 2007.
Cressey, Paul F. "The Influence of the Literary Examination System on the Development of Chinese Civilization." *The American Journal of Sociology* 35 (September 1929): 250–62.
Crockatt, Richard. "Theories of Stability and the End of the Cold War." In *From Cold War to Collapse: Theory and World Politics in the 1980s*. Edited by Mike Bowker and Robin Brown. New York: Cambridge University Press, 1993, 74–7.
Croft, Stuart. *Strategies of Arms Control: A History and Typology*. Manchester and New York: Manchester University Press, 1996.
Croken, Robert C. *Luther's First Front: The Eucharist as Sacrifice*. Ottawa: University of Ottawa Press, 1990.
Crombie, C. *Styles of Scientific Thinking in the European Tradition: The History of Argument and Explanation Especially in the Mathematical and Biomedical Sciences and Arts,* 3 vols. London: Duckworth, 1994.
Crosby, Alfred. *Ecological Imperialism: The Biological Expansion of Europe, 900–1900*. Cambridge: Cambridge University Press, 1986.
Crosby, Alfred W. *The Columbian Exchange: Biological and Cultural Consequences of 1492*. Westport, CT: Greenwood Press, 1972.
—. *The Measure of Reality: Quantification and Western Society, 1250–1600*. New York: Cambridge University Press, 1996.
Crosland, Maurice P. (ed.), *The Science of Matter: A Historical Survey*. Amsterdam: OPA, 1992.
Crouzet, François. *A History of the European Economy, 1000–2000*. Charlottesville: University of Virginia Press, 2001.
Crow, Carl. *The Great American Customer*. 1943. Reprint, Freeport, NY: Books for Libraries Press, 1970.
Crowe, Michael J. *Theories of the World from Antiquity to the Copernican Revolution*, 2nd rev. edn. Mineola, NY: Dover Publications, 2001.
Crowley, Thomas J., and Thomas S. Lowery. "How Warm Was the Medieval Warm Period?" *Ambio* 29 (February 2000): 51–4.
Cullen-DuPont, Kathryn (ed.), *The Encyclopedia of Women's History in America*. New York: Da Capo Press, 1998.
Cumings, Bruce. *The Korean War: A History*. New York: Modern Library, 2010.
Curtis, Gregory. *The Cave Painters: Probing the Mysteries of the World's First Artists*. New York: A.A. Knopf, 2006.

Cushing, Kathleen G. *Reform and the Papacy in the Eleventh Century: Spirituality and Social Change*. Manchester: Manchester University Press, 2005.
D'Emilio, John. *Sexual Politics, Sexual Communities: The Making of a Homosexual Minority in the United States, 1940–1970*, 2nd edn. Chicago and London: University of Chicago Press, 1998.
D'Eramo, Marco. *The Pig and the Skyscraper: Chicago: A History of Our Future*. Translated by Graeme Thomson. Foreword by Mike Davis. London and New York: Verso, 2003.
D'Souza, Dinesh. *What's So Great About America*. Washington, DC: Regnery Publishing, 2002.
Dale, Richard. *The First Crash: Lessons from the South Sea Bubble*. Princeton: Princeton University Press, 2004.
Dale, Stephen F. *The Muslim Empires of the Ottomans, Safavids, and Mughals*. Cambridge and New York: Cambridge University Press, 2010.
Dallal, Ahmad. "Science, Medicine, and Technology: The Making of a Scientific Culture." In *The Oxford History of Islam*. Edited by John L. Esposito. Oxford: Oxford University Press, 1999.
Daly, Lloyd W. *Contributions to a History of Alphabetization in Antiquity and the Middle Ages*. Brussels: Latomus, 1967.
Dalzell, Robert F. *Enterprising Elite: The Boston Associates and the World They Made*. Cambridge, MA: Harvard University Press 1987.
Daniel, David. *William Tyndale: A Biography*. New Haven: Yale University Press, 1994.
Daniel, David P. "Calvinism in Hungary: The Theological and Ecclesiastical Transition to the Performance Faith." In *Calvinism in Europe, 1540–1620*. Edited by Andrew Pettegree, Alastair Duke, and Gillian Lewis. Cambridge: Cambridge University Press, 1994.
Daniels, Roger. *Asian America: Chinese and Japanese in the United States since 1850*. Seattle: University of Washington Press, 1988.
—. *Coming to America: A History of Immigration and Ethnicity in American Life*. New York: Harper Perennial, 2002.
Darity, William, Jr. "British Industry and the West Indies Plantations." *Social Science History* 14, 1 (Spring 1990): 117–49.
Darling-Hammond, Linda. *The Flat World and Education: How America's Commitment to Equity Will Determine Our Future*. New York and London: Teachers College Press, 2010.
Darnton, Robert. *The Literary Underground of the Old Regime*. Cambridge, MA: Harvard University Press, 1982.
—. *The Forbidden Best-Sellers of Prerevolutionary France*. New York: W.W. Norton & Company, 1996.
Darwin, John. *After Tamerlane: The Global History of Empire Since 1405*. New York: Bloomsbury Publishing, 2008.
Datta, N. C. *The Story of Chemistry*. Hyderguda, Hyderabad, India: Universities Press, 2005.
Daudin, Guillaume, Matthias Morys, and Keven H. O'Rourke. "Globalization, 1870–1914." In *The Cambridge Economic History of Modern Europe*, vol. 2, *1870 to the Present*. Edited by Stephen Broadberry and Kevin H. O' Rourke. New York: Cambridge University Press, 2010, 24–6.
Davies, Brian. *The Thought of Thomas Aquinas*. Oxford: Oxford University Press, 1993.
Davies, Norman. *Europe: A History*. New York: Oxford University Press, 1996.
—. *No Simple Victory: World War II in Europe, 1939–1945*. New York: Penguin, 2008.
Davies, R. W., and Stephen G. Wheatcroft. *The Years of Hunger: Soviet Agriculture, 1931–1933*. New York: Palgrave Macmillan, 2004.
Davis, David Brion. *The Problem of Slavery in Western Culture*. Ithaca: Cornell University Press, 1966.

—. *The Problem of Slavery in the Age of Revolution, 1770–1823*. New York: Oxford University Press, 1999.

Davis, J. C. "Religion and the Struggle for Freedom in the English Revolution." *The Historical Journal* 35 (September 1992): 507–30.

Davis, Paul K. *100 Decisive Battles: From Ancient Times to the Present*. New York: Oxford University Press, 2001.

Davis, Natalie Zemon. *Trickster Travels: A Sixteenth-Century Muslim Between Worlds*. New York: Hill & Wang, 2006.

Davis, Sue, and J. W. Peltason. *Corwin and Peltason's Understanding the Constitution*, 17th edn. Belmont, CA: Cengage Learning, 2008.

Davis, William Stearns (ed.), *Readings in Ancient History: Illustrative Extracts from the Sources*, 2 vols. Boston: Allyn and Bacon, 1912–13.

Davis-Kimball, Jeannine, Vladimir A. Bashilov, and Leonid T. Yablonsky (eds), *Nomads of the Eurasian Steppes in the Early Iron Age*. Berkeley: University of California Press, 1995.

Dawson, Christopher. *Religion and the Rise of Western Culture*. New York: Sheed & Ward, 1950.

de Bary, Wm. Theodore, Wing-tsit Chan, and Burton Watson, with contributions by Yi-pao Mei (and others) (eds), *Sources of Chinese Tradition*. New York: Columbia University Press, 1960.

de Dreuille, Mayeul. *From East to West: A History of Monasticism*. Leominster, UK, and New York: Gracewing Publishing, 1999.

De Long, J. Bradford, and Andrei Shleifer. "Princes and Merchants: European City Growth before the Industrial Revolution." *The Journal of Law and Economics* 36 (October 1993): 671–702.

de Ridder-Symoens, Hilde. "Mobility." In *Universities in the Middle Ages*, vol. 1 of *A History of the University in Europe*. Edited by H. de Ridder-Symoens. Cambridge: Cambridge University Press, 1992.

De Roover, Florence Edler. "Early Examples of Marine Insurance." *The Journal of Economic History* 5, 2 (November 1945): 172–200.

De Soto, Hernando. *The Mystery of Capital: Why Capitalism Triumphs in the West and Fails Everywhere Else*. New York: Basic Books, 2000.

de Tocqueville, Alexis. *Democracy in America*. Translated by George Lawrence. Edited by J. P. Mayer. Garden City, NY: Doubleday, 1969.

De Vries, Jan. *Economy of Europe in an Age of Crisis, 1600–1750*. Cambridge: Cambridge University Press, 1976.

—. "Problems in the Measurement, Description, and Analysis of Historical Urbanization." In *Urbanization in History: A Process of Dynamic Interactions*. Edited by Ad van der Woude, Akira Hayami, and Jan de Vries. Oxford: Oxford University Press, 1990.

—. *The Industrious Revolution: Consumer Behavior and the Household Economy, 1650 to the Present*. New York: Cambridge University Press, 2008.

De Vries, Jan, and A. M. van der Woude. *The First Modern Economy: Success, Failure, and Perseverance of the Dutch Economy, 1500–1815*. Cambridge: Cambridge University Press, 1997.

Deane, Phyllis, and Cole, W. A. *British Economic Growth, 1688–1959*, 2nd edn. Cambridge: Cambridge University Press, 1967.

Debus, Allen G. "Chemists, Physicians, and Changing Perspectives on the Scientific Revolution." *Isis* 89, 1 (March 1998): 66–81.

"Deforestation Figures for Selected Countries," http://rainforests.mongabay.com/deforestation/. Accessed on 22 March 2010.

Dehaene, Stanislas. *The Number Sense: How the Mind Creates Mathematics*. Revised edition. New York: Oxford University Press, 2011.

Dempsey, Hugh A. “Smallpox: Scourge of the Plains.” In *Harms’ Way: Disasters in Western Canada*. Edited by Anthony W. Rasporich and Max Foran. Calgary: University of Calgary Press, 2004, 35–7.

Deng, Gang. *The Premodern Chinese Economy: Structural Equilibrium and Capitalist Sterility*. London and New York: Routledge, 1999.

Deng, Kent G. “Development and Its Deadlock in Imperial China, 221 B.C–1840 A.D.” *Economic Development and Cultural Change* 51 (January 2003): 479–522.

Dennett, Donald C., and Alvin Plantinga. *Science and Religion: Are They Compatible?* New York: Oxford University Press, 2011.

Dept. of Ecology, State of Washington. “Chemical Pulp Mills.” http://www.ecy.wa.gov/programs/air/pdfs/pulpmil3.pdf. Accessed 30 December 2011.

Derry, T. K., and Trevor I. Williams. *A Short History of Technology: From the Earliest Times To A.D. 1900*. Oxford: Oxford University Press, 1960.

Descartes, René. *Meditations on First Philosophy: With Selections from the Objections and Replies*. Edited by John Cottingham. Cambridge: Cambridge University Press, 1996.

—. *A Discourse on the Method*. Translated by Ian Maclean. Oxford: Oxford University Press, 2006.

Devine, Warren D., Jr. “Electrified Mechanical Drive: The Historical Power Distribution Revolution.” In *Electricity in the American Economy: Agent of Technological Progress*. Edited by Sam H. Schurr et al. New York: Greenwood Press, 1990.

Devlin, Keith. *Mathematics: The Science of Patterns: The Search for Order in Life, Mind, and the Universe*. New York: Scientific American Library, 1997.

Diamond, Jared. *Guns, Germs, and Steel: The Fates of Human Societies*. New York: W.W. Norton & Company, 1997.

—. *Collapse: How Societies Choose to Fail or Succeed*. New York: W.W. Norton & Company, 2005.

Dickens, A. G. *The English Reformation*, 2nd edn. London: B.T. Batsford, 1989.

Dickson, P. G. M. *The Financial Revolution in England: A Study in the Development of Public Credit 1688–1756*. London: Macmillan, 1967.

Diefendorf, Barbara B. *From Penitence to Charity: Pious Women and the Catholic Reformation in Paris*. New York: Oxford University Press, 2002.

Diffie, Bailey Wallys, and George Davison Winius. *Foundations of the Portuguese Empire, 1415–1580*. Minneapolis, MN: University of Minnesota Press, 1977.

Diggins, John Patrick. *On Hallowed Ground: Abraham Lincoln and the Foundations of American History*. New Haven and London: Yale University Press, 2000.

Dihle, Albrecht. *Greek and Latin Literature of the Roman Empire: From Augustus to Justinian*. New York and London: Routledge, 1994.

Diringer, David. “Early Hebrew Writing.” *The Biblical Archaeologist* 13, 4 (December 1950): 74–95.

Disney, Anthony R. *Twilight of the Pepper Empire: Portuguese Trade in Southwest India in the Early Seventeenth Century*. Cambridge, MA: Harvard University Press, 1978.

Dixon, C. Scott. *The Reformation in Germany*. Oxford: Oxford University Press, 2002.

Dobson, Andy. “Monitoring Global Rates of Biodiversity Change: Challenges that Arise in Meeting the Convention on Biological Diversity (CBD) 2010 Goals.” *Philosophical Transactions: Biological Sciences* 360, 1454 (28 February 2005): 229–41.

Domarus, Max. *The Essential Hitler: Speeches and Commentary*. Edited by Patrick Romane. Wauconda, IL: Bolchazy-Carducci, 2007.

Domínguez, Jorge I. *To Make a World Safe for Revolution: Cuba’s Foreign Policy*. Cambridge, MA: Harvard University Press, 1989.

Donald, Merlin. *Origins of the Modern Mind: Three Stages in the Evolution of Culture and Cognition*. Cambridge, MA: Harvard University Press, 1991.

Donnelly, John Patrick. *Ignatius of Loyola: Founder of the Jesuits*. New York: Pearson/ Longman, 2004.

Donner, Fred M. "Muhammad and the Caliphate: Political History of the Islamic Empire Up to the Mongol Conquest." In *The Oxford History of Islam*. Edited by John L. Esposito. Oxford and New York: Oxford University Press, 1999.

Donohue, John J., and John L. Esposito. *Islam in Transition: Muslim Perspectives*. New York: Oxford University Press, 1982.

Dooley, Brendan, and Sabrina A. Baron (eds), *The Politics of Information in Early Modern Europe*. London and New York: Routledge, 2001.

Dorinson, Joseph, and Joram Warmund (eds), *Jackie Robinson: Race, Sports, and the American Dream*. Amonk, NY: M.E. Sharpe, 1998.

Dorwart, Reinhold A. "The Earliest Fire Insurance Company in Berlin and Brandenburg, 1705–1711." *The Business History Review* 32, 2 (Summer 1958): 192–203.

Dotson, John E. "Everything is a Compromise: Mediterranean Ship Design, Thirteenth to Sixteenth Centuries." In *The Art, Science, and Technology of Medieval Travel*. Edited by Robert Bork and Andrea Kann. Aldershot, UK, Burlington, VT: Ashgate, 2008, 38.

Dougherty, Jude P. *The Logic of Religion*. Washington, DC: The Catholic University Press, 2003.

Dougherty, Raymond P. "Writing Upon Parchment and Papyrus Among the Babylonians and the Assyrians." *Journal of the American Oriental Society* 48 (1928): 109–35.

Downing, Brian M. "Medieval Origins of Constitutional Government in the West." *Theory and Society* 18 (March 1989): 213–47.

—. *The Military Revolution and Political Change: Origins of Democracy and Autocracy in Early Modern Europe*. Princeton: Princeton University Press, 1992.

Doyle, William. *The French Revolution: A Very Short Introduction*. Oxford and New York: Oxford University Press, 2001a.

— (ed.), *Old Regime France, 1648–1788*. Oxford: Oxford University Press, 2001b.

—. *The Ancien Regime*, 2nd edn. Basingstoke: Palgrave Macmillan, 2001c.

—. *The Oxford Handbook of the Ancien Regime*. Oxford: Oxford University Press, 2012.

Drake, Miriam A. *Encyclopedia of Library and Information Science*, 2nd edn. New York: Marcel Dekker, 2003.

Drake, Samuel Adams. *The Making of New England*. Scituate, MA: Digital Scanning, Inc, 2001 [1896].

Draper, Peter. "Islam and the West: The Early Use of the Pointed Arch Revisited." *Architectural History* 48 (2005): 1–20.

Drucker, Peter F. "Technology Trends in the Twentieth Century." In vol. 2 of *Technology in Western Civilization*, 2 vols. Edited by Melvin Kranzberg and Carroll W. Pursell, Jr. New York: Oxford University Press, 1967.

Duara, Prasenjit (ed.), *Decolonization: Perspectives from Now and Then*. New York and London: Routledge, 2004.

Dubreuil, Benoît. *Human Evolution and the Origins of Hierarchies: The State of Nature*. New York: Cambridge University Press, 2010.

Duffy, Christopher. *The Army of Frederick the Great*. New York: Hippocrene Books, 1974.

Duffy, Eve M. and Alida C. Metcalf. *The Return of Hans Staden: A Go-between in the Atlantic World*. Baltimore: The Johns Hopkins University Press, 2012.

Dulken, Stephen Van. *Inventing the 20th Century: 100 Inventions That Shaped the World from the Airplane to the Zipper*. New York: Simon & Schuster, 2000.

Dumenil, Lynn. *Freemasonry and American Culture, 1880–1930*. Princeton: Princeton University Press, 1984.

Dunn, John (ed.), *Democracy: The Unfinished Journey, 508 B.C. to A.D. 1993*. Oxford: Oxford University Press, 1992.

Dupuy R. Ernest, and Trevor N. Dupuy. *The Harper Encyclopedia of Military History: From 3500 B.C. to the Present*, 4th edn. New York: Harper Resource, 1993.

Dutta, M. *China's Industrial Revolution and Economic Presence*. Singapore: World Scientific, 2006.

Dvorák, Max. "The New Relationship to Nature." In *Modern Perspectives in Western Art History: An Anthology of Twentieth-Century Writings on the Visual Arts*. Edited by W. Eugène Kleinbauer. New York: Holt, Rinehart and Winston, 1971, 399–400.

Eckerman, Ingrid. *The Bhopal Saga: Causes and Consequences of the World's Largest Industrial Disaster*. Hyderguda, India: Universities Press, 2005.

Edbury, Peter. "Warfare in the Latin East." In *Medieval Warfare: A History*. Edited by Maurice Keen. Oxford: Oxford University Press, 1999.

Edfelt, Ralph B. *Global Comparative Management: A Functional Approach*. Thousand Oaks, CA: SAGE Pub., 2010.

Edwards, Mark U. *Printing Propaganda and Martin Luther*. Minneapolis: Fortress Press, 2005.

Ehler, Sidney Z., and John B. Morrall. *Church and State through the Centuries: A Collection of Historic Documents with Commentaries*. London: Burns & Oates, 1988.

Ehrlich, Robert. *Waging Nuclear Peace: The Technology and Politics of Nuclear Weapons*. Albany: State University of New York Press, 1985.

Eire, Carlos M. N. *War Against the Idols: The Reformation of Worship from Erasmus to Calvin*. Cambridge: Cambridge University Press, 1986.

Eisenstein, Elizabeth L. "Some Conjectures about the Impact of Printing on Western Society and Thought: A Preliminary Report." *Journal of Modern History* 40 (1968): 8.

—. *The Printing Press as an Agent of Change: Communications and Cultural Transformations in Early Modern Europe*. New York: Cambridge University Press, 1979.

—. *Divine Art, Infernal Machine: The Reception of Printing in the West from First Impressions to the Sense of an Ending*. Philadelphia and Oxford: University of Pennsylvania Press, 2011.

Eisler, Benita (ed.), *The Lowell Offering: Writings by New England Mill Women, 1840–1845*. New York: W. W. Norton & Company, 1998.

Eksteins, Modris. *The Rites of Spring: The Great War and the Birth of the Modern Age*. Boston: Houghton Mifflin Co., 1989.

Eldem, Edhem. "Istanbul." In *Encyclopedia of the Ottoman Empire*. Edited by Gabor Agoston and Bruce Masters. New York: Facts on File, 2009.

Elias, Norbert. *On Civilization, Power, and Knowledge: Selected Writings*. Edited by Stephen Mennell and Johan Goudsblom. Chicago and London: University of Chicago Press, 1998.

Elliott, Mark R. *Pawns of Yalta: Soviet Refugees and America's Role in Their Repatriation*. Urbana: University of Illinois Press, 1982.

Ellis, John. *The Social History of the Machine Gun*. New York: Pantheon, 1975.

Elman, Benjamin A. *On Their Own Terms: Science in China, 1550–1900*. Cambridge, MA: Harvard University Press, 2005.

El-shihibi, Fathi A., and Sparrow Hansard. *Travel Genre in Arabic Literature: A Selective Literary And Historical Study*. New York: Dissertation.com, 2006.

Eltis, David. *The Rise of African Slavery in the Americas*. Cambridge: Cambridge University Press, 2000.

Eltis, David, and Stanley L. Engerman, "The Importance of Slavery and the Slave Trade to Industrializing Britain." *The Journal of Economic History* 60 (March 2000): 123–44.

Elton, G. R. *The Tudor Constitution: Documents and Commentary*, 2nd edn. New York: Cambridge University Press, 1982.

Elvin, Mark. *The Pattern of the Chinese Past*. Stanford: Stanford University Press, 1973.

Emanuel, Kerry. *What We Know about Climate Change*, 2nd edn. Cambridge, MA: MIT Press, 2012.
Emsley, John. *Nature's Building Blocks: An A-Z Guide to the Elements*. Oxford: Oxford University Press, 2001.
Endres, Kathleen L., and Therese L. Lueck (eds), *Women's Periodicals in the United States: Consumer Magazines*. Westport, CT: Greenwood Press, 1995.
Engel, Barbara Alpern. *Women in Russia, 1700–2000*. Cambridge: Cambridge University Press, 2004.
Engerman, Stanley L. "The Slave Trade and British Capital Formation in the Eighteenth Century: A Comment on the Williams Thesis." *The Business History Review* 46 (Winter 1972): 430–43.
Epstein, S. R. "Regional Fairs, Institutional Innovation, and Economic Growth in Late Medieval Europe." *The Economic History Review*, New Series 47, 3 (August 1994): 459–82.
—. *Guilds, Innovation and the European Economy, 1400–1800*. New York: Cambridge University Press, 2008.
Erickson, Amy Louise. *Women and Property in Early Modern England*. London and New York: Routledge, 1993.
Erler, Mary, and Maryanne Kowaleski. *Women and Power in the Middle Ages*. Athens, GA: University of Georgia Press, 1998.
Escoffier, Jeffrey (ed.), *Sexual Revolution*. Photographs by Fred W. McDarrah. New York: Thunder's Mouth Press, 2003.
Esposito, John L. (ed.), *The Oxford Dictionary of Islam*. Oxford and New York: Oxford University Press, 2003.
"European entrepreneurs: Les misérables." *The Economist* (28 July 2012): 19–22.
Evangelisti, Silvia. *Nuns: A History of Convent Life 1450–1700*. Oxford: Oxford University Press, 2007.
Evans, Chris, and Göran Rydén (eds), *The Industrial Revolution in Iron: The Impact of British Coal Technology in Nineteenth-Century Europe*. Burlington, VT: Ashgate Publishing, 2005.
Evans, Richard. *The Third Reich in Power*. New York: Penguin Press, 2005.
Evans, Sara Margaret. *Born for Liberty: A History of Women in America*. New York: Free Press, 1997.
Ewald, Alec C. *The Way We Vote: The Local Dimension of American Suffrage*. Nashville, TN: Vanderbilt University Press, 2009.
Fakhry, Majid. "Philosophy and Theology: From the Eighth Century C.E. to the Present." In *The Oxford History of Islam*. Edited by John L. Esposito. Oxford and New York: Oxford University Press, 1999, 287.
—. *A History of Islamic Philosophy*, 3rd edn. New York and Chichester, UK: Columbia University Press, 2004.
Farmer, S. A., trans. *Syncretism in the West. Pico's 900 Theses (1486): The Evolution of Traditional Religious and Philosophical Systems*. Tempe, AZ: Medieval and Renaissance Texts and Studies, 1998.
Fegley, Randall. *The Golden Spurs of Kortrijk: How the Knights of France Fell to the Footsoldiers of Flanders in 1302*. Jefferson, NC, and London: McFarland, 2002.
Feld, M. D. "Middle-Class Society and the Rise of Military Professionalism: The Dutch Army, 1589–1609." In *The Military-State-Society Symbiosis*. Edited by Peter Karsten. New York and London: Garland Publishing, 1998, 48–9.
Feldenkirchen, Wilfried. *Werner von Siemens, Inventor and International Entrepreneur*. Columbus, OH: Ohio State University Press, 1994.
Ferguson, Eugene S. "The Steam Engine Before 1830." In *Technology in Western Civilization*. Edited by Melvin Kranzberg and Carroll W. Pursell, Jr. New York: Oxford University Press, 1967.

Ferguson, Niall. *The Pity Of War: Explaining World War I*. New York: Basic Books, 1999.

—. *Civilization: The West and the Rest*. London: Penguin Books Ltd, 2010.

Fernández-Armesto, Felipe. "Naval Warfare after the Viking Age, c. 1100–1500." In *Medieval Warfare: A History*. Edited by Maurice Keen. Oxford: Oxford University Press, 1999.

—. *Near a Thousand Tables: A History of Food*. New York: Free Press, 2002.

Feshbach, Murray, and Alfred Friendly, Jr. *Ecocide in the USSR: Health And Nature Under Siege*. New York: Basic Books, 1992.

Fetherling, George. *The Gold Crusades: A Social History of Gold Rushes, 1849–1929*. Revised edition. Toronto, Buffalo, and London: University of Toronto Press, 1997.

Fieldhouse, D. K. *Economics and Empire, 1830–1914*. London: Macmillan, 1984.

Findlen, Paula. "Natural History." In *The Cambridge History of Science*. Vol. 3: *Early Modern Science*. Edited by Katharine Park and Lorraine Daston. Cambridge: Cambridge University Press, 2006a.

—. "Anatomy Theaters, Botanical Gardens, and Natural History Collections." In *The Cambridge History of Science*. Vol. 3: *Early Modern Science*. Edited by Katharine Park and Lorraine Daston. Cambridge: Cambridge University Press, 2006b.

Finer, Samuel Edward. *The Intermediate Ages*, vol. 2 of *The History of Government from the Earliest Times*, 3 vols. Oxford: Oxford University Press, 1997.

Fink, Leon. *Workingmen's Democracy: The Knights of Labor and American Politics*. Urbana, IL: University of Illinois Press, 1985.

Finkelman, Paul. "Jefferson and Slavery: 'Treason Against the Hopes of the World.'" In *Jeffersonian Legacies*. Edited by Peter S. Onuf. Charlottesville, VA: University Press of Virginia, 1993.

Finocchiaro, Maurice A. *Defending Copernicus and Galileo: Critical Reasoning in the Two Affairs*. New York: Springer, 2010.

Finucane, Ronald C. *Miracles and Pilgrims: Popular Beliefs in Medieval England*. New York: Palgrave Macmillan, 1995.

Fischer, David Hackett. *The Great Wave: Price Revolutions and the Rhythm of History*. New York and Oxford: Oxford University Press, 1996.

Fischer, Fritz. *Germany's Aims in the First World War*. London: Chatto & Windus, 1967.

Fischer, Steven R. *A History of Reading*. London: Reaktion Books, 2004.

Fitzpatrick, Matthew P. *Liberal Imperialism in Germany: Expansionism and Nationalism, 1848–1884*. New York: Berghahn, 2008.

— (ed.), *Liberal Imperialism in Europe*. New York: Palgrave Macmillan, 2012.

Fitzpatrick, Sheila. "The Civil War as a Formative Experience." In *Bolshevik Culture: Experiment and Order in the Russian Revolution*. Edited by Abbott Gleason, Peter Kenez, and Richard Stites. Bloomington, IN: Indiana University Press, 1985, 59–60.

Fix, Andrew. "Radical Reformation and Second Reformation in Holland: The Intellectual Consequences of the Sixteenth-Century Religious Upheaval and the Coming of a Rational World View." *The Sixteenth Century Journal* 18, 1 (Spring 1987): 63–80.

Flandrin, Jean Louis, Massimo Montanari, and Albert Sonnenfeld (eds), *Food: A Culinary History*. Translated by Clarissa Botsford. New York: Penguin, 1999.

Flinn, Frank K. *Encyclopedia of Catholicism*. New York: Infobase Pub., 2007.

Flynn, Dennis O., and Arturo Giráldez. "Born with a 'Silver Spoon': The Origin of World Trade in 1571." *Journal of World History* 6 (Fall 1995): 201–21.

Fogel, Robert William. *The Escape from Hunger and Premature Death, 1700–2100: Europe, America, and the Third World*. Cambridge: Cambridge University Press, 2004.

Foner, Eric. *Reconstruction: America's Unfinished Revolution, 1863–1877*. New York: Harper & Row, 1988.

Fontes da Costa, P. "The Culture of Curiosity at The Royal Society in the First Half of the Eighteenth Century." *Notes and Records of the Royal Society of London* 56 (May 2002): 147–66.

Foran, John. "Discursive Subversions: *Time* Magazine, the CIA Overthrow of Mussadiq, and the Installation of the Shah." In *Cold War Constructions: The Political Culture of United States Imperialism, 1945–1966*. Edited by Christian G. Appy. Amherst, MA: University of Massachusetts Press, 2000.

Forbes, R. J. *A Short History of the Art of Distillation: From the Beginnings up to the Death of Cellier Blumenthal*. 1948. Reprint, Leiden: E. J. Brill, 1970.

Foss, Clive. "Pilgrimage in Medieval Asia Minor." *Dumbarton Oaks Papers* 56 (2002): 129–51.

Foster, Shirley, and Sara Mills (eds), *An Anthology of Women's Travel Writing*. Manchester and New York: Manchester University Press, 2002.

Foucault, Michel. *Discipline and Punish: The Birth of the Prison*. Translated by Alan Sheridan, 2nd edn. New York: Vintage Books, 1995.

Fouquet, Roger. *Heat, Power and Light: Revolutions in Energy Services*. Cheltenham, UK, and Northampton, MA: Edward Elgar, 2008.

Fox, Robert, and Anthony John Turner (eds), *Luxury Trades and Consumerism in Ancien Régime Paris: Studies in the History of the Skilled Workforce*. Brookfield, VT: Ashgate Publishing, 1998.

Frangsmyr, Tore (ed.), *Linnaeus: The Man and His Work*. Berkeley: University of California Press, 1983.

Frank, Andre Gunder. *ReORIENT: Global Economy in the Asian Age*. Columbia: University of South Carolina Press, 1998.

Frank, Andre Gunder, and Barry K. Gills (eds), *The World System: Five Hundred Years or Five Thousand?* London and New York: Routledge, 1993.

Frank, Richard B. *The End of the Imperial Japanese Empire*. New York: Random House, 1999.

Franke, Wolfgang. *China and the West*. Translated by R. A. Wilson. Columbia: University of South Carolina Press, 1967.

Franklin, James. *The Science of Conjecture: Evidence and Probability before Pascal*. Baltimore and London: The Johns Hopkins University Press, 2001.

Frankum, Ronald B., Jr. *Like Rolling Thunder: The Air War in Vietnam, 1964–1975*. Lanham, MD: Rowman & Littlefield, 2005.

Fredrickson, George M. *White Supremacy: A Comparative Study of American and South African History*. New York: Oxford University Press, 1981.

Freedman, Estelle B. *Their Sisters' Keepers: Women's Prison Reform in America, 1830–1930*. Ann Arbor: University of Michigan Press, 1981.

Freedman, Paul. "The Medieval Taste for Spices." *Historically Speaking* (September–October 2008a).

—. *Out of the East: Spices and the Medieval Imagination*. New Haven: Yale University Press, 2008b.

Freedman, Paul, and Gabrielle M. Spiegel. "Medievalisms Old and New: The Rediscovery of Alterity in North American Medieval Studies." *The American Historical Review* 103 (June 1998): 677–704.

Freedman, Roy S. *Introduction to Financial Technology*. Amsterdam and Boston: Elsevier/Academic Press, 2006.

Freiberger, Paul, and Michael Swaine. *Fire in the Valley: The Making of the Personal Computer*, 2nd edn. New York: Mcgraw-Hill, 2000.

French, Roger. *Dissection and Vivisection in the European Renaissance*. Aldershot, UK, and Brookfield, VT: Ashgate Publishing, 1999.

Freud, Sigmund. *The Interpretation of Dreams*. New York: Avon, 1965.

Friedan, Betty. *The Feminine Mystique*. New York W. W. Norton & Company, 1963.

Friedel, Robert. *A Culture of Improvement: Technology and the Western Millennium*. Cambridge, MA: MIT Press, 2007.

Friedlander, Henry. *The Origins of Nazi Genocide: From Euthanasia to the Final Solution*. Chapel Hill: University of North Carolina Press, 1995.

Frijhoff, Willem. "How Plural Were the Religious Worlds in Early Modern Europe? Critical Reflections from the Netherlandic Experience." In *Living with Religious Diversity in Early-Modern Europe*. Edited by C. Scott Dixon, Dagmar Freist, and Mark Greengrass. Farmham, UK, and Burlington, VT: Ashgate Publishing, 2009.

Frisina, Warren G. "Are Knowledge and Action Really One Thing?: A Study of Wang Yang-ming's Doctrine of Mind." *Philosophy East and West* 39 (October 1989): 419–47.

Frize, Monique. *The Bold and the Brave: A History of Women in Science and Engineering*. Ottawa: University of Ottawa Press, 2009.

Froissart, Jean. *The Chronicles of England, France and Spain, and the Adjoining Countries*. Translated by Thomas Johnes, 2 vols. London: W. Smith, 1844.

Froissart, Sir John. *The Chronicles of England, France and Spain*. H. P. Dunster's Condensation of the Thomas Johnes translation. Introduction by Charles W. Dunn. New York: E.P. Dutton, 1961.

Fry, Richard, and Paul Taylor. "Hispanic High School Graduates Pass Whites in Rate of College Enrollment" (9 May 2013), http://www.pewhispanic.org/2013/05/09/hispanic-high-school-graduates-pass-whites-in-rate-of-college-enrollment/ (accessed 3 August 2013).

Fryde, Edmund. "Introduction." In *Historical Studies of the English Parliament*. Vol. 2: *1399 to 1603*. Edited by E. B. Fryde and Edward Miller. Cambridge: Cambridge University Press, 1970.

Frye, Richard N., ed. and trans. *Ibn Fadlan's Journey to Russia: A Tenth-century Traveler from Baghdad to the Volga River*. Princeton: Princeton University Press, 2005.

Fuller, Edmund. *Tinkers and Genius: The Story of the Yankee Inventors*. New York: Hastings House, 1955.

Fuller, J. F. C. *A Military History of the Western World*, vol. 1: *From the Earliest Times to the Battle of Lepanto*. New York: Funk and Wagnalls Company, 1954.

Fuller, Michael A., and Shuen-Fu Lin. "North and South: The Twelfth and Thirteenth Centuries." *The Cambridge History of Chinese Literature* 1 (2010): 1469–71.

Furet, François. *Interpreting the French Revolution*. Translated by Elborg Forster. Cambridge: Cambridge University Press, 1981.

Fursenko, Aleksandr, and Timothy Naftali. *One Hell of a Gamble: Khrushchev, Castro, and Kennedy, 1958–1964*. New York: W. W. Norton & Company, 1997.

Füssel, Stephan. *Gutenberg and the Impact of Printing*. Translated by Douglas Martin. Aldershot, UK, and Burlington, VT: Ashgate Publishing, 2005.

Gabrieli, Francesco (ed.), *Arab Historians of the Crusades*. Berkeley and Los Angeles: University of California Press, 1969.

Gaimster, David. "A Parallel History: The Archaeology of Hanseatic Urban Culture in the Baltic c. 1200–1600." *World Archaeology* 37 (September 2005): 408–23.

Ganshof, François Louis. *Feudalism*, 3rd edn. Translated by Philip Grierson. New York: Harper Torchbooks, 1996.

Gantz, Carroll. *The Vacuum Cleaner: A History*. Jefferson, NC, and London: McFarland, 2012.

Garcia, Serge M., and Richard J. R. Grainger. "Gloom and Doom? The Future of Marine Capture Fisheries." *Philosophical Transactions: Biological Sciences* 360 (29 January 2005): 21–46.

Gardner, Daniel K., ed. and trans. *The Four Books: The Basic Teachings of the Later Confucian Tradition*. Indianapolis and Cambridge, MA: Hackett Publishing Co., 2007.

Garfield, Simon. *Mauve: How One Man Invented a Color That Changed the World*. New York and London: Faber & Faber, 2000.

Gates, Charles. *Ancient Cities: The Archaeology of Urban Life in the Ancient Near East and Egypt, Greece, and Rome*, 2nd edn. Abingdon, UK, and New York: Routledge, 2011.

Gates, Henry Louis, Jr., and Evelyn Brooks Higginbotham. *African American Lives*. New York: Oxford University Press, 2004.

Gaudiosi, Monica M. "The Influence of the Islamic Law of Waqf on the Development of the Trust in England: The Case of Merton College." *University of Pennsylvania Law Review* 136 (April 1988): 1231–61.

Gaukroger, Stephen. *Descartes: An Intellectual Biography*. Oxford: Oxford University Press, 1995.

Gaur, Albertine. *A History of Writing*, 2nd edn. London: Barrie and Jenkins Ltd., 1987.

Gay, Peter. *The Enlightenment: An Interpretation*. Vol. 2: *The Science of Freedom*. New York: A. A. Knopf, 1969.

Geggus, David Patrick, and Norman Fiering (eds), *The World of the Haitian Revolution*. Bloomington, IN: Indiana University Press, 2009.

Gelderblom, Oscar, and Joost Jonker. "Completing a Financial Revolution: The Finance of the Dutch East India Trade and the Rise of the Amsterdam Capital Market, 1595–1612." *The Journal of Economic History* 64: 641–72.

"Genesis redux: A new form of life has been created in a laboratory, and the era of synthetic biology is dawning." 20 May 2010 | From *The Economist* print edition. http://www.economist.com/displaystory.cfm?story_id516163006. Accessed on 30 May 2010.

Gentles, Ian. *The New Model Army in England, Ireland, and Scotland, 1645–1653*. Oxford and Cambridge, MA: Harvard University Press, 1992.

Gerlach, Christian. "The Wannsee Conference, the Fate of German Jews, and Hitler's Decision in Principle to Exterminate All European Jews." *The Journal of Modern History* 70 (December 1998): 759–812.

Gervasi, Tom. *The Myth of Soviet Military Supremacy*. New York: Harper & Row, 1986.

Gill, Arthur. "Lean Manufacturing." In *Exploring Advanced Manufacturing Technologies*. Edited by Stephen F. Krar and Arthur Gill. New York: Industrial Press Inc., 2003.

Gill, Mary Louise. *Aristotle on Substance: The Paradox of Unity*. Princeton: Princeton University Press, 1989.

Gillespie, Michael Allen, and Michael Lienesch (eds), *Ratifying the Constitution*. Lawrence, KA: University Press of Kansas, 1989.

Gillingham, John. "An Age of Expansion, c. 1020–1204." In *Medieval Warfare: A History*. Edited by Maurice Keen. Oxford: Oxford University Press, 1999.

Gilson, Etienne. *History of Christian Philosophy in the Middle Ages*. New York: Random House, 1955.

Gingerich, Owen, and James H. MacLachlan. *Nicolaus Copernicus: Making the Earth a Planet*. Oxford: Oxford University Press, 2005.

Gingras, George E., trans. *Egeria: Diary of a Pilgrimage*. New York: Paulist Press, 1970.

Gjelten, Tom. *Bacardi and the Long Fight for Cuba: The Biography of a Cause*. New York: Penguin, 2008.

Gleach, Frederic W. *Powhatan's World and Colonial Virginia: A Conflict of Cultures*. Lincoln, NE: University of Nebraska Press, 1997.

Gleijeses, Piero. *Shattered Hope: The Guatemalan Revolution and the United States, 1944–1954*. Princeton: Princeton University Press, 1991.

Glenn, H. Patrick. *Legal Traditions of the World: Sustainable Diversity in Law*, 2nd edn. Oxford: Oxford University Press, 2004.

Glete, Jan. *War and the State in Early Modern Europe: Spain, the Dutch Republic and Sweden as Fiscal-Military States, 1500–1660*. London: Routledge, 2002.

Gnuse, Robert Karl. *No Other Gods: Emergent Monotheism in Israel*. Sheffield: T&T Clark, 1997.

Goetzmann, William N., and K. Geert Rouwenhorst. "Introduction: Financial Innovations in History." In *The Origins of Value: The Financial Innovations that Created Modern Capital Markets*. Edited by William N. Goetzmann and K. Geert Rouwenhorst. Oxford and New York: Oxford University Press, 2005, 7–11.

Goldblith, Samuel A. *Samuel Cate Prescott, M.I.T. Dean and Pioneer Food Technologist*. Vol. 2 of *Pioneers of Food Science*. Trumball, CT: Food & Nutrition Press, Inc., 1993.

Goldstein, Joshua S. *Winning the War on War: The Decline of Armed Conflict Worldwide*. New York: Dutton/Penguin, 2011.

Goldstone, Jack A. *Revolution and Rebellion in the Early Modern World*. Berkeley and Los Angeles: University of California Press, 1991.

—. "Efflorescences and Economic Growth in World History: Rethinking the 'Rise of the West' and the Industrial Revolution." *Journal of World History* 13 (2002): 323–89.

—. *Why Europe? The Rise of the West in World History 1500–1850*. Boston: McGraw-Hill Higher Education, 2009.

Golinski, J. V. "A Noble Spectacle: Phosphorus and the Public Cultures of Science in the Early Royal Society." *Isis* 80 (March 1989): 11–39.

Gonzalez-Crussi, Frank. *A Short History of Medicine*. New York: Random House, 2007.

Goodfriend, Joyce D. "Practicing Toleration in Dutch New Netherland." In *The First Prejudice: Religious Tolerance and Intolerance in Early America*. Edited by Chris Beneke and Christopher S. Grenda. Philadelphia: University of Pennsylvania Press, 2011.

Goodman, Dena. *The Republic of Letters: A Cultural History of the French Enlightenment*. Ithaca: Cornell University Press, 1994.

Goodman, Jordan. *Tobacco in History: The Cultures of Dependence*. London: Routledge, 1993.

Goodman, Martin. *Mission and Conversion: Proselytizing in the Religious History of the Roman Empire*. Oxford and New York: Oxford University Press, 1994.

Goodwin, Jason. *Lords of the Horizons: A History of the Ottoman Empire*. New York: Henry Holt & Company, 1999.

—. *Otis: Giving Rise to the Modern City*. Chicago: University of Chicago Press, 2001.

Goody, Jack. *The Logic of Writing and the Organization of Society*. Cambridge: Cambridge University Press, 1986.

—. *The East in the West*. Cambridge: Cambridge University Press, 1996.

—. *The European Family: An Historico-Anthropological Essay*. Oxford: Oxford University Press, 2000.

Gordon, Bruce. *The Swiss Reformation*. Manchester and New York: Manchester University Press, 2002.

Gordon, Scott. *Controlling the State: Constitutionalism from Ancient Athens to Today*. Cambridge, MA: Harvard University Press, 1999.

Gottlieb, Beatrice. *The Family in the Western World from the Black Death to the Industrial Age*. New York: Oxford University Press, 1993.

Gotlieb, Marc. "The Painter's Secret: Invention and Rivalry from Vasari to Balzac." *The Art Bulletin* 84 (2002): 469–90.

Goudsblom, Johan. *Fire and Civilization*. London: Penguin, 1992.

Gough, J. B. "Lavoisier and the Fulfillment of the Stahlian Revolution." *Osiris*, 2nd Series 4, "The Chemical Revolution: Essays in Reinterpretation" (1988): 15–33.

Gould, Stephen Jay. *The Mismeasure of Man*. Revised edition. New York and London: W.W. Norton and Company, 1996.

Grace, Pierce. "First Among Women." *British Medical Journal* 303 (21–28 December 1991): 1582–3.

Graham, A. C., "China, Europe and the Origins of Modern Science: Needham's The Grand Titration." *Asia Major* 16 (1971): 178–96.

Graham-Cumming, John. *The Geek Atlas: 128 Places Where Science and Technology Come Alive*. Sebastopol, CA: O'Reilly Media, Inc., 2009.
Grahl-Madsen, Atle. "The European Tradition of Asylum and the Development of Refugee Law." *Journal of Peace Research* 3, 3 (1966): 278–89.
Grant, Edward. *The Foundations of Modern Science in the Middle Ages*. Cambridge: Cambridge University Press, 1996.
—. *God and Reason in the Middle Ages*. Cambridge: Cambridge University Press, 2001.
Grant, Jonathan A. "Rethinking the Ottoman 'Decline': Military Technology Diffusion in the Ottoman Empire, Fifteenth to Eighteenth Centuries." *Journal of World History* 10 (Spring 1999): 179–201.
Grassby, Richard. *The Business Community of Seventeenth-Century England*. Cambridge: Cambridge University Press, 1995.
Gratzer, Walter Bruno. *Terrors of the Table: The Curious History of Nutrition*. Oxford and New York: Oxford University Press, 2005.
Graves, Michael A. R. *The Tudor Parliaments: Crown, Lords and Commons, 1485–1603*. London and New York: Longman, 1985.
Gray, Lee Edward. *From Ascending Rooms to Express Elevators: A History of the Passenger Elevator in the 19th Century*. Mobile, AL: Elevator World, 2002.
Green, Peter. *Alexander of Macedon, 356–323 B.C.: A Historical Biography*. Berkeley and Los Angeles: University of California Press, 1991.
—. *The Hellenistic Age: A Short History*. New York: The Modern Library, 2007.
Greene, Julie. *Pure and Simple Politics: The American Federation of Labor and Political Activism, 1881–1917*. Cambridge: Cambridge University Press, 1998.
Gref, Lynn G. *The Rise and Fall of American Technology.* New York: Algora Publishing, 2010.
Gregory, Brad S. *The Unintended Reformation: How a Religious Revolution Secularized Society.* Cambridge, MA: Harvard University Press, 2012.
Gregory, Paul R. *Russian National Income, 1885–1913*. Cambridge: Cambridge University Press, 1982.
Grendler, Paul F. "Printing and Censorship." In *The Cambridge History of Renaissance Philosophy*. Edited by Charles B. Schmitt and Quentin Skinner. Cambridge: Cambridge University Press, 1988.
Griffiths, Gordon. *Representative Government in Western Europe in the Sixteenth Century: Commentary and Documents for the Study of Comparative Constitutional History*. Oxford: Clarendon Press, 1968.
Griffiths, John. *The Third Man: The Life and Times of William Murdoch 1754–1839*. London: A. Deutsch, 1992.
Griffiths, Trevor, Philip A. Hunt, and Patrick K. O'Brien. "Inventive Activity in the British Textile Industry, 1700–1800." *The Journal of Economic History* 52 (December 1992): 881–906.
Gritsch, Eric W. *A History of Lutheranism*. Minneapolis: Fortress Press, 2002.
Grodecki, Louis, Anne Prach, and Roland Recht. *Gothic Architecture*. Translated by I. Mark Paris. New York: H. N. Abrams, 1985.
Grossman, James R. *Land of Hope: Chicago, Black Southerners, and the Great Migration*. Chicago: University of Chicago Press, 1991.
Grossman, Louis H., and Marianne Jennings. *Building a Business Through Good Times and Bad: Lessons from 15 Companies, Each with a Century of Dividends*. Westport, CT: Quorum Books, 2002.
Grout, Donald Jay. *A History of Western Music*, 3rd edn, Shorter and Claude V. Palisca. New York and London: W. W. Norton, 1981.
Gruhl, Werner. *Imperial Japan's World War Two: 1931–1945*. New Brunswick, NJ: Transaction Publishers, 2007.

Guilmartin, John F., Jr. "The Military Revolution: Origins and First Tests Abroad." In *The Military Revolution Debate: Readings on the Military Transformation of Early Modern Europe*. Edited by Clifford J. Rogers. Boulder, CO: University of Colorado Press, 1995.

Gullick, John (ed.), *Adventurous Women in South-East Asia: Six Lives*. Kuala Lumpur and New York: Oxford University Press, 1995.

Gullickson, Gay L. "Agriculture and Cottage Industry: Redefining the Causes of Proto-Industrialization." *The Journal of Economic History* 43, 4 (December 1983): 831–50.

Gupta, Jatinder N. D., and Sushil Kumar Sharma. *Creating Knowledge Based Organizations*. Hershey, PA, and London: Idea Group, 2004.

Habermas, Jürgen. *The Structural Transformation of the Public Sphere: An Inquiry into a Category of Bourgeois Society*. Translated by Thomas Burger. Cambridge, MA: MIT Press, 1991.

Hacker, J. David, and Michael R. Haines. "American Indian Mortality in the Late Nineteenth Century: The Impact of Federal Assimilation Policies on a Vulnerable Population." *Annales de Demographie Historique* 2 (2005): 17–45.

Haddad, Robert M. "Philosophical Theology and Science in Medieval Christianity and Islam: A Comparative Perspective." *The Journal of the Historical Society* 8 (September 2008): 349–93.

Haddock, David D., and Lynne Kiesling. "The Black Death and Property Rights." *The Journal of Legal Studies* 31, 2 (June 2002): S545–87.

Haile, H. G. "Luther and Literacy." *PMLA* 91, 5 (October 1976): 816–28.

Halberstam, David. *The Fifties*. New York: Ballantine Books, 1993.

Haldon, John. *Byzantium: A History*. Stroud, UK: Tempus, 2000.

Haldon, John, and Leslie Brubaker. *Byzantium in the Iconoclast Era c. 680–850*. New York: Cambridge University Press, 2011.

Hálfdanarson, Guðmundur (ed.), *Racial Discrimination and Ethnicity in European History.* Pisa: PLUS, Università di Pisa, 2003.

Hall, Charles A. S., and Kent A. Klitgaard. *Energy and the Wealth of Nations: Understanding the Biophysical Economy.* New York: Springer, 2012.

Hall, John A. *Powers and Liberties: The Causes and Consequences of the Rise of the West.* Oxford: Oxford University Press, 1985.

Hall, Jonathan M. *A History of the Archaic Greek World, ca. 1200–479 B.C.E.* Malden, MA: Blackwell Publishers, 2007.

Hall, Marie Boas. *Robert Boyle and Seventeenth-Century Chemistry*. Cambridge: Cambridge University Press, 1958.

Hall, Richard C. "Serbia." In *The Origins of World War I*. Edited by Richard F. Hamilton and Holger H. Herwig. Cambridge: Cambridge University Press, 2003, 106–9.

Hall, Simon. "Scholarly Battles Over the Vietnam War." *The Historical Journal* 52 (September 2009): 813–29.

Hamilton, Alistair. "Humanists and the Bible." *The Cambridge Companion to Renaissance Humanism*. Edited by Jill Kraye. New York: Cambridge University Press, 1996.

Hamm, Richard F. *Shaping the Eighteenth Amendment: Temperance Reform Legal Culture and the Polity, 1880–1920*. Chapel Hill and London: University of North Carolina Press, 1995.

Hanke, Lewis. *The Imperial City of Potosi: An Unwritten Chapter in the History of Spanish America*. The Hague: Nijhoff, 1956.

Hankins, James. *Plato in the Italian Renaissance*, 2 vols. Leiden and New York: E. J. Brill, 1990.

Hansen, Valerie. *The Open Empire: A History of China to 1600*. New York: W.W. Norton & Company, 2000.

Hanson, Victor Davis. *The Western Way of War: Infantry Battle in Classical Greece*. New York: A. A. Knopf, 1989.

Hardesty, Von, and Ilya Grinberg. *Red Phoenix Rising: The Soviet Air Force in World War II*. Lawrence, KS: University Press of Kansas, 2012.

Hargreaves, Henry. "The Wycliffite Versions." In *The West from the Fathers to the Reformation*. Edited by G. W. H. Lampe. Vol. 2 of *The Cambridge History of the Bible*, 3 vols. Cambridge: Cambridge University Press, 1969.

Harris, Jonathan. *The End of Byzantium*. New Haven: Yale University Press, 2010.

Harris, Michael H. *History of Libraries in the Western World*, 4th edn. Lanham, MD: Scarecrow Press, 1999.

Harris, Rob. *Property and the Office Economy*. London: Estates Gazette, 2005.

Harris, Steven J. "Networks of Travel, Correspondence, and Exchange." In *The Cambridge History of Science*. Vol. 3: *Early Modern Science*. Edited by Katharine Park and Lorraine Daston. Cambridge: Cambridge University Press, 2006.

Harrison, James P. "History's Heaviest Bombing." In *The Vietnam War: Vietnamese and American Perspectives*. Edited by Jane Susan Werner and Luu Doan Huynh. Armonk, NY: M.E. Sharpe, 1993, 133.

Harrison, Mark. "National Income." In *The Economic Transformation of the Soviet Union, 1913–1945*. Edited by R. W. Davies, Mark Harrison, and S. G. Wheatcroft. Cambridge: Cambridge University Press, 1994, 41–2.

Hart, Jonathan. *Empires and Colonies*. Cambridge and Malden MA: Blackwell Publishers, 2008.

Hartmann, Michael. "Elites and Power Structure." In *Handbook of European Societies: Social Transformations in the 21st Century*. Edited by Stefan Immerfall and Göran Therborn. New York: Springer, 2010.

Hartshorne, Charles. *Creative Synthesis and Philosophic Method*. London: SCM Press, 1970.

Hartwell, Robert. "A Revolution in the Chinese Iron and Coal Industries During the Northern Sung, 960–1126 A.D." *Journal of Asian Studies* 21 (February 1962): 153–62.

Hasegawa, Tsuyoshi. *Racing the Enemy: Stalin, Truman, and the Surrender of Japan*. Cambridge, MA: Harvard University Press, 2005.

Hassan, Rashid M., Robert Scholes, and Neville Ash (eds), *Ecosystems and Human Well-Being: Findings of the Condition and Trends Working Group of the Millennium Ecosystem Assessment*. Vol. 1: *Current State and Trends*. Washington, Covelo, and London: Island Press, 2005.

Hatcher, John. *Before 1700: Towards the Age of Coal*. Vol. 1 of *The History of the British Coal Industry*. Oxford: Oxford University Press, 1984.

Hatfield, April Lee. *Atlantic Virginia: Intercolonial Relations in the Seventeenth Century*. Philadelphia: University of Pennsylvania Press, 2004.

Haude, Sigrun. "Anabaptism." In *The Reformation World*. Edited by Andrew Pettegree. London and New York: Routledge, 2000, 48.

Haveman, Heather A., and Lauren S. Beresford. "If You're So Smart, Why Aren't You the Boss? Explaining the Persistent Vertical Gender Gap in Management." *The ANNALS of the American Academy of Political and Social Science* 639 (January 2012): 114–30.

Haven, Kendall. *100 Greatest Science Inventions of All Time*. Westport, CT: Libraries Unlimited, 2006.

Head, Thomas. "The Development of the Peace of God in Aquitaine (970–1005)." *Speculum* 74 (July 1999): 656–86.

Headley, John M. "The Sixteenth-Century Venetian Celebration of the Earth's Total Habitability: The Issue of the Fully Habitable World for Renaissance Europe." *Journal of Modern History* 8 (Spring 1997): 1–27.

—. *The Europeanization of the World: On the Origins of Human Rights and Democracy*. Princeton: Princeton University Press, 2008.

Headrick, D. *When Information Came of Age: Technologies of Knowledge in the Age of Reason and Revolution, 1700–1850*. New York: Oxford University Press, 2000.

Headrick, Daniel R. *Power over Peoples: Technology, Environments, and Western Imperialism, 1400 to the Present*. Princeton: Princeton University Press, 2010.

Heath, Peter. "War and Peace in the Works of Erasmus: A Medieval Perspective." In *The Medieval Military Revolution: State, Society, and Military Change in Medieval and Early Modern Europe*. Edited by Andrew Ayton and J. L. Price. London: I. B. Tauris, 1995.

Heather, Peter. *Empires and Barbarians: The Fall of Rome and the Birth of Europe*. New York: Oxford University Press, 2009.

Heilbron, J. L. *Galileo*. Oxford and New York: Oxford University Press, 2010.

Heid, Stefan. *Celibacy in the Early Church: The Beginnings of a Discipline of Obligatory Continence for Clerics in East and West*. Translated by Michael J. Miller. San Francisco, CA: Ignatius Press, 2000.

Heilbron, J. L. "Introduction." In Galileo Galilei, *Dialogue Concerning the Two Chief World Systems: Ptolemaic and Copernican*. Edited and Translated by Stillman Drake. New York: Modern Library, 2001.

Held, David. *Models of Democracy*, 2nd edn. Stanford, CA: Stanford University Press, 1996.

Helinga, Lotta. "The Gutenberg Revolutions." In *A Companion to the History of the Book*. Edited by Simon Eliot and Jonathan Rose. Oxford and Malden, MA: Blackwell Publishers, 2007.

Helmholz, R. H. *The Oxford History of the Laws of England*, vol. 1: *The Canon Law and Ecclesiastical Jurisdiction from 597 to the 1640s*. Oxford and New York: Oxford University Press, 2004.

Henry, C. J. K. "New Food Processing Technologies: From Foraging to Farming to Food Technology." *Proceedings of the Nutrition Society* 56 (1997): 855–63.

Henry, Donald O., Harold J. Hietala, Arlene M. Rosen, Yuri E. Demidenko, Vitaliy I. Usik, and Teresa L. Armagan. "Human Behavioral Organization in the Middle Paleolithic: Were Neanderthals Different?" *American Anthropologist*, New Series 106 (March 2004): 17–31.

Henry, John. *The Scientific Revolution and the Origins of Modern Science*, 2nd edn. Basingstoke, UK, and New York: Palgrave Macmillan, 2002.

—. "Religion and the Scientific Revolution." In *The Cambridge Companion to Science and Religion*. Edited by Peter Harrison. Cambridge: Cambridge University Press, 2010.

Heping Liu. "'The Water Mill' and Northern Song Imperial Patronage of Art, Commerce, and Science." *The Art Bulletin* 84, 4 (December 2002): 566–95.

Herodotus, *The Histories*. Translated by Walter Blanco. Edited by Walter Blanco and Jennifer Tolbert Roberts. New York and London: W. W. Norton & Company, 1992.

Herrera, Geoffrey L. *Technology and International Transformation: The Railroad, The Atom Bomb, and The Politics of Technological Change*. Albany: State University of New York Press, 2006.

Herwaarden, J. van. *Between Saint James and Erasmus: Studies in Late-Medieval Religious Life: Devotions and Pilgrimages in the Netherlands*. Translated by Wendie Shaffer. Leiden: E. J. Brill, 2003.

"Hi There: Life is Getting Friendlier But Less Interesting. Blame Technology, Globalisation and Feminism." *The Economist* (17 December 2009).

Higginbotham, Don. *The War of American Independence: Military Attitudes, Policies, and Practice, 1763–1789*. Boston: Northeastern University Press, 1983.

Higman, B. W. "The Sugar Revolution." *The Economic History Review,* New Series 53, 2 (May 2000): 213–36.

Hildinger, Erik. *Warriors of the Steppe: A Military History of Central Asia, 500 B.C. to A.D. 1700*. Cambridge, MA: Da Capo Press, 2001.

Hill, Steven. *Europe's Promise: Why the European Way Is the Best Hope in an Insecure Age*. Berkeley and Los Angeles: University of California Press, 2010.
Hobsbawm, E. J. *Nations and Nationalism since 1780: Programme, Myth, Reality*. Cambridge: Cambridge University Press, 1990.
Hobson, John M. *The Eastern Origins of Western Civilization*. Cambridge: Cambridge University Press, 2004.
—. "What Have the Muslims Ever Done for Us? Islamic Origins of Western Civlization." In *The Challenge of Eurocentrism: Global Perspectives, Policy, and Prospects*. Edited by Rajani Kannepalli Kanth. New York: Palgrave Macmillan, 2009, 221.
Hochschild, Adam. *King Leopold's Ghost: A Story of Greed, Terror, and Heroism in Colonial Africa*. Boston: Houghton Mifflin Company, 1998.
Hodgkiss, Alan G. *Discovering Antique Maps*, 5th edn. Princes Risborough, UK: Shire Publications Ltd, 1996.
Hodgson, Marshall G. S. *The Venture of Islam: Conscience and History in a World Civilization*. 3 volumes. Chicago: University of Chicago Press, 1974.
—. "Cultural Patterning in Islamdom and the Occident." In *Rethinking World History: Essays on Europe, Islam, and World History*. Edited by Edmund Burke III. Cambridge: Cambridge University Press, 1993a.
—. "The Great Western Transmutation." In *Rethinking World History: Essays on Europe, Islam, and World History*. Edited by Edmund Burke. Cambridge: Cambridge University Press, 1993b.
Hodnett, Edward. *Francis Barlow: First Master of English Book Illustration*. Berkeley: University of California Press, 1978.
Hoffman, Valerie J. "Oral Traditions as a Source for the Study of Muslim Women: Women in the Sufi Orders." In *Beyond the Exotic: Women's Histories in Islamic Societies*. Edited by Amira El Azhary Sonbol. Syracuse, NY: Syracuse University Press, 2005.
Hoffmann, David L. *Peasant Metropolis: Social Identities in Moscow, 1929–1941*. Ithaca: Cornell University Press, 1994.
Hoffmann, Stefan-Ludwig. *Civil Society, 1750–1914*. Houndmills, UK: Palgrave Macmillan, 2006.
Hogan, David Gerard. *Selling 'em by the Sack: White Castle and the Creation of American Food*. New York: New York University Press, 1999.
Holder, R. *Crisis and Renewal: The Era of the Reformations*. Louisville, KY: Westminster John Knox Press, 2009.
Hollister, C. Warren (ed.), *Landmarks of the Western Heritage*, 2 vols. New York: Wiley, 1967.
Holloway, David. *Stalin and the Bomb: The Soviet Union and Atomic Energy, 1939–1956*. New Haven: Yale University Press, 1994.
Holmes, Geoffrey. *The Making of a Great Power: Late Stuart and Early Georgian Britain, 1660–1722*. London and New York: Longman, 1993.
Holmes, George. *The Later Middle Ages, 1272–1485*. New York: T. Nelson, 1962.
Holmyard, Eric John. *Makers of Chemistry*. Oxford: Oxford University Press, 1931.
Holoman, D. Kern. *Berlioz: A Musical Biography of the Creative Genius of the Romantic Era*. Cambridge, MA: Harvard University Press, 1989.
Holton, Gerald James, and Stephen G. Brush. *Physics, the Human Adventure: From Copernicus to Einstein and Beyond*. New Brunswick, NJ: Rutgers University Press, 2001.
Hoover, William D. *Historical Dictionary of Postwar Japan*. Lanham, MD: Scarecrow Press, 2011.
Hopkins, Arthur John. *Alchemy, Child of Greek Philosophy*. New York: Columbia University Press, 1934.
Hopkins, David. *Dada and Surrealism: A Very Short Introduction*. Oxford: Oxford University Press, 2004.

Hopper, Sarah. *To Be a Pilgrim: The Medieval Pilgrimage Experience*. Stroud, UK: Sutton, 2002.

Hoppit, Julian. *Land of Liberty? England 1689–1727*. Oxford: Oxford University Press, 2002.

Hosking, Geoffrey. *Russia and the Russians: A History*, 2nd edn. Cambridge, MA: Harvard University Press, 2011.

Hosler, Dorothy, Sandra L. Burkett, and Michael J. Tarkanian. "Rubber Processing in Ancient Mesoamerica." *Science*, New Series 284, 5422 (18 June 1999): 1988–91.

Hostetler, Laura. *Qing Colonial Enterprise: Ethnography and Cartography in Early Modern China*. Chicago and London: University of Chicago Press, 2001.

Hostettler, John. *Cesare Beccaria: The Genius of "On Crimes and Punishments."* Hook, UK: Waterside Press, 2010.

Hounshell, David A. *From the American System to Mass Production, 1800–1932: The Development of Manufacturing Technology in the United States*. Baltimore: The Johns Hopkins University Press, 1984.

Housley, Norman. "European Warfare, c. 1200–1320." In *Medieval Warfare: A History*. Edited by Maurice Keen. Oxford: Oxford University Press, 1999.

Houston, R. A. *Scottish Literacy and the Scottish Identity: Illiteracy and Society in Scotland and Northern England, 1600–1800*. Cambridge: Cambridge University Press, 1985.

Houston, Rab. "Literacy and Society in the West, 1500–1850." *Social History* 8 (October 1983): 269–93.

Howard, Michael. *War in European History*. Oxford and New York: Oxford University Press, 1976.

—. *The First World War: A Very Short Introduction*. New York: Oxford University Press, 2002.

Howard, Thomas Albert. *God and the Atlantic: America, Europe, and the Religious Divide*. Oxford and New York: Oxford University Press, 2011.

Hoxie, Frederick E. *A Final Promise: The Campaign to Assimilate the Indians, 1880–1920*. Lincoln, NE: University of Nebraska Press, 2001.

Hsia, R. Po-Chia, and Henk van Nierop (eds), *Calvinism and Religious Toleration in the Dutch Golden Age*. New York: Cambridge University Press, 2002.

Huang, Philip C. C. "Review: Development or Involution in Eighteenth-Century Britain and China? A Review of Kenneth Pomeranz's 'The Great Divergence: China, Europe, and the Making of the Modern World Economy'." *The Journal of Asian Studies* 61 (May 2002): 501–38.

Hudson, Winthrop S. "Democratic Freedom and Religious Faith in the Reformed Tradition." *Church History* 15 (September 1946): 177–94.

Hudson, Anne. *The Premature Reformation: Wycliffite Texts and Lollard History*. Oxford and New York: Oxford University Press, 1988.

Huff, Toby E. *The Rise of Early Modern Science: Islam, China, and the West*, 2nd edn. Cambridge: Cambridge University Press, 2003.

Huffman, Carl A. *Pythagorean and Presocratic: A Commentary on the Fragments and Testimonia with Interpretive Essays*. Cambridge: Cambridge University Press, 1993.

Hughes, Gerard. *Routledge Philosophy GuideBook to Aristotle on Ethics*. London and New York: Routledge, 2001.

Hughes, Thomas Parke. *Networks of Power: Electrification in Western Society, 1880–1930*. Baltimore: The Johns Hopkins University Press, 1983.

—. *American Genesis: A Century of Invention and Technological Enthusiasm, 1870–1970*. New York: Viking, 1989.

Hull, Isabel V. *Absolute Destruction: Military Culture and the Practices of War in Imperial Germany*. Ithaca: Cornell University Press, 2005.

Hume, David. *An Enquiry Concerning Human Understanding*. Edited by Tom L. Beauchamp. New York: Oxford University Press, 1999.

Humphreys, Stephen. "Egypt in the World System of the Later Middle Ages." In *The Cambridge History of Egypt*, vol. 1: *Islamic Egypt, 640–1517*. Edited by Carl F. Petry. Cambridge and New York: Cambridge University Press, 1998, 452–6.

Hunt, Edwin S. *The Medieval Super-Companies: A Study of the Peruzzi Company of Florence*. Cambridge and New York: Cambridge University Press, 1994.

Hunt, Edwin S., and James M. Murray. *A History of Business in Medieval Europe, 1200–1550*. Cambridge: Cambridge University Press, 1999.

Hunt, Lynn. *Inventing Human Rights: A History*. New York and London: W. W. Norton & Company, 2007.

Hunt, Nigel C. *Memory, War, and Trauma*. Cambridge and New York: Cambridge University Press, 2010.

Hunter, F. Robert. *Egypt Under the Khedives, 1805–1879: From Household Government to Modern Bureaucracy*. Pittsburgh: University of Pittsburgh Press, 1984.

Hunter, Michael. *Boyle: Between God and Science*. New Haven: Yale University Press, 2009.

Huntington, Samuel P. *The Clash of Civilizations and the Remaking of World Order*. New York: Simon & Schuster, 1996.

Huppert, George. *Public Schools in Renaissance France*. Urbana, IL: University of Illinois Press, 1984.

—. *After the Black Death: A Social History of Early Modern Europe*, 2nd edn. Bloomington, IN: Indiana University Press, 1998.

—. *The Style of Paris: Renaissance Origins of the French Enlightenment*. Bloomington, IN: Indiana University Press, 1999.

Hyman, Arthur, James J. Walsh, and Thomas Williams (eds), *Philosophy in the Middle Ages: The Christian, Islamic, and Jewish Traditions*, 3rd edn. Indianapolis and Cambridge, MA: Hackett Publishing Co., 2010.

Impey, Chris. *How It Ends: From You to the Universe*. New York: W. W. Norton & Company, 2010.

Inalcik, H. "The Rise of the Ottoman Empire." In *A History of the Ottoman Empire to 1730*. Edited by M. A. Cook. Cambridge: Cambridge University Press, 1976.

Ingrassia, Paul. *Crash Course: The American Automobile Industry's Road from Glory to Disaster*. New York: Simon & Schuster, 2010.

Inikori, Joseph E. *Africans and the Industrial Revolution in England: A Study in International Trade and Economic Development*. Cambridge: Cambridge University Press, 2002.

Inkster, Ian. "Intellectual Property, Information, and Divergences in Economic Development – Institutional Patterns and Outcomes circa 1421–2000." In *The Role of Intellectual Property Rights in Biotechnology Innovation*. Edited by David Castle. Cheltenham, UK, and Northampton, MA: Edward Elgar, 2009, 417.

International Monetary Fund. *Fiscal Monitor: Balancing Fiscal Policy Risks*. Washington, DC: International Monetary Fund, 2012.

Interview with Raymond Kurzweil, "The Science Show" (23 February 2008), http://www.aB.C.net.au/rn/scienceshow/stories/2008/2170327.htm. Accessed on 22 December 2009.

Isaac, Benjamin H. *The Invention of Racism in Classical Antiquity*. Princeton: Princeton University Press, 2004.

Isaacson, Walter. *Steve Jobs*. New York: Little, Brown, 2011.

Israel, Jonathan I. *The Dutch Republic: Its Rise, Greatness, and Fall, 1477–1806*. Oxford: Oxford University Press, 1995.

Jackson, David H., Jr. *Booker T. Washington and the Struggle Against White Supremacy: The Southern Educational Tours, 1908–1912*. New York: Palgrave Macmillan, 2008.

Jackson, Jeremy B. C., et al. "Historical Overfishing and the Recent Collapse of Coastal Ecosystems." *Science* 293 (July 2001): 629–37.

Jackson, Sidney L. *Libraries and Librarianship in the West: A Brief History*. New York: McGraw-Hill, 1974.

Jacob, Margaret C. *The Enlightenment: A Brief History with Documents*. Boston: Bedford/St. Martin's, 2001.

Jacobs, Jaap. *The Colony of New Netherland: A Dutch Settlement in Seventeenth-Century America*. Ithaca: Cornell University Press, 2009.

Jacques, Martin. *When China Rules the World: The End of the Western World and the Birth of a New Global Order*, 2nd edn. London: Penguin Books, 2012.

James I. *The True Law of Free Monarchies; and, Basilikon Doron*. Edited by Daniel Fischlin and Mark Fortier. Toronto: Centre for Reformation and Renaissance Studies, 1996.

James, Philip S. "Nicholas Barbon–Founder of Modern Fire Insurance." *The Review of Insurance Studies* 1 (June 1954): 44–7.

Jamieson, Ross W. "The Essence of Commodification: Caffeine Dependencies in the Early Modern World." *Journal of Social History* 35, 2 (Winter 2001): 269–94.

Jaspers, Karl. *Way To Wisdom: An Introduction to Philosophy*, 2nd edn. Translated by Ralph Manheim. New Haven: Yale University Press, 2003.

Jay, James Monroe, Martin J. Loessner, and David Allen Golden. *Modern Food Microbiology*, 7th edn. New York: Springer, 2005.

Jeal, Tim. *Livingstone*. New Haven: Yale University Press, 1973.

Jefferson, Thomas. *A Summary View of the Rights of British America*. New York: Scholars' Facsimiles and Reprints, 1971.

Jeffrey, Julie Roy. *The Great Silent Army of Abolitionism: Ordinary Women in the Antislavery Movement*. Chapel Hill: University of North Carolina Press, 1998.

Jewell, Helen M. *Women in Late Medieval and Reformation Europe: 1200–1550*. New York: Palgrave, 2007.

John, Richard R. *Network Nation: Inventing American Telecommunications*. Cambridge, MA: Harvard University Press, 2010.

Johns, Adrian. "Coffeehouses and Print Shops." In *The Cambridge History of Science*. Vol. 3: *Early Modern Science*. Edited by Katharine Park and Lorraine Daston. Cambridge: Cambridge University Press, 2006.

Johnson, Arthur M. "Expansion of the Petroleum and Chemical Industries, 1880–1900." In vol. 1 of *Technology in Western Civilization*, 2 vols. Edited by Melvin Kranzberg and Carroll W. Pursell, Jr. New York: Oxford University Press, 1967.

Johnson, David Martel. *Three Prehistoric Inventions That Shaped Us*. New York: Peter Lang Publishing, 2011.

Johnson, Dennis W. *Campaigning in the Twenty-First Century: A Whole New Ballgame?* New York: Routledge, 2011.

Johnson, Elmer D., and Michael H. Harris. *History of Libraries in the Western World*, 3rd edn. Metuchen, NJ: Scarecrow Press, 1976.

Johnson, Harry M. "The History of British and American Fire Marks." *The Journal of Risk and Insurance* 39 (September 1972): 405–18.

Johnson, Paul. *A History of the Jews*. New York: HarperCollins, 1987.

—. *A History of the American People*. New York: HarperCollins, 1997.

Johnson, Penelope D. *Equal in Monastic Profession: Religious Women in Medieval France*. Chicago: University of Chicago Press, 1991.

Johnston, Robert D. *The Radical Middle Class: Populist Democracy and the Question of Capitalism in Progressive Era Portland, Oregon*. Princeton: Princeton University Press, 2003.

Joll, James. *The Origins of the First World War*, 3rd edn. Harlow, UK, and New York: Pearson Education/Longman, 2007.

Jones, E. L. *The European Miracle: Environments, Economies, and Geopolitics in the History of Europe and Asia*. London and New York: Cambridge University Press, 1981.

Jones, Kathleen. *A History of the Mental Health Services*. London: Routledge and Kegan Paul, 1972.

Jones, R. L. C. "Fortifications and Sieges in Europe." In *Medieval Warfare: A History*. Edited by Maurice Keen. Oxford: Oxford University Press, 1999.

Jonnes, Jill. *Empires of Light: Edison, Tesla, Westinghouse, and the Race to Electrify the World*. New York: Random House, 2003.

Joran, William Chester. "The Capetians from the Death of Philip II to Philip IV." In *The New Cambridge Medieval History*. Vol. 5: *c. 1198-c. 1300*. Edited by David Abulafia. Cambridge: Cambridge University Press, 1999.

Jordan, David P. *Napoleon and the Revolution*. Houndmills, UK, and New York: Palgrave Macmillan, 2012.

Josephson, Hannah. *The Golden Threads: New England's Mill Girls and Magnates*. New York: Duell, Sloan and Pearce, 1949.

Judd, Dennis. *The Lion and the Tiger: The Rise and Fall of the British Raj, 1600–1947*. Oxford and New York: Oxford University Press, 2004.

Judt, Tony. *Postwar: A History of Europe Since 1945*. London: Penguin Press, 2005.

Kades, Eric. "The Dark Side of Efficiency: Johnson v. M'Intosh and the Expropriation of American Indian Lands." *University of Pennsylvania Law Review* 148, 4 (April 2000): 1065–9.

Kaestle, Carl F., Helen Damon-Moore, Lawrence C. Stedman, and Katherine Tinsley (eds), *Literacy in the United States: Readers and Reading Since 1880*. New Haven: Yale University Press, 1991.

Kale, Steven. *French Salons: High Society and Political Sociability from the Old Regime to the Revolution of 1848*. Baltimore: Johns Hopkins University Press, 2004.

Kamen, Henry. *The Spanish Inquisition: A Historical Revision*. New Haven: Yale University Press, 1998.

—. *Spain's Road to Empire: The Making of a World Power, 1492–1763*. London: Penguin Books, 2002.

Kanefsky, John, and John Robey. "Steam Engines in 18th-Century Britain: A Quantitative Assessment." *Technology and Culture* 21 (April 1980): 161–86.

Kanth, Rajani Kannepalli. *Against Eurocentrism: A Transcendent Critique of Modernist Science, Society, and Morals*. New York and Basingstoke, UK: Macmillan, 2005.

Karabel, Jerome. *The Chosen: The Hidden History of Admission and Exclusion at Harvard, Yale, and Princeton*. New York: Houghton Mifflin, 2005.

Karnow, Stanley. *In Our Image: America's Empire in the Philippines*. New York: Random House, 1989.

Kasarda, John D., and Greg Lindsay. *Aerotropolis: The Way We'll Live Next*. New York: Farrar, Straus and Giroux, 2011.

Katz, Bill. *Cuneiform to Computer: A History of Reference Sources*. Lanham, MD, and Folkestone, UK: Scarecrow Press, 1998.

Katz, Michael B. *In the Shadow of the Poorhouse: A Social History of Welfare in America*. Revised edition. New York: Basic Books, 1996.

Kaye, Evelyn. *Amazing Traveler, Isabella Bird: The Biography of a Victorian Adventurer*. Boulder, CO: University of Colorado Press, 1994.

Kauppi, Pekka E., J. H. Ausubel, J. Fang, A. Mather, R. A. Sedjo, and P. E. Waggoner. "Returning Forest Analyzed with the Forest Identity." *Proceedings of the National Academy of Sciences* 103 (Fall 2006): 17574–9.

Kautsky, John. *The Politics of Aristocratic Empires*. New Brunswick, NJ: Transaction Publishers, 1997.

Keay, John. *Mad About the Mekong: Exploration and Empire in South East Asia*. London: Harper Collins, 2005.

Keegan, John. *The First World War*. New York: A.A. Knopf, 1999.

Keen, Maurice (ed.), *Medieval Warfare: A History*. Oxford: Oxford University Press, 1999a.

—. "The Changing Scene: Guns, Gunpowder, and Permanent Armies." In *Medieval Warfare: A History*. Edited by Maurice Keen. Oxford: Oxford University Press, 1999b.

Kellar, Clare. *Scotland, England, and the Reformation 1534–1561*. Oxford and New York: Oxford University Press, 2003.

Keller, A. G. "A Byzantine Admirer of 'Western' Progress: Cardinal Bessarion." *Cambridge Historical Journal* 11 (1955): 343–8.

Kelly, Amy. *Eleanor of Aquitaine and the Four Kings*. Cambridge, MA: Harvard University Press, 1950.

Kelly, Jack. *Gunpowder: Alchemy, Bombards, and Pyrotechnics: The History of the Explosive That Changed the World*. New York: Basic Books, 2004.

Kelly, Kate. *The History of Medicine: The Middle Ages, 500–1450*. New York: Facts On File, 2009.

Kemp, Barry J. *Ancient Egypt: Anatomy of a Civilisation*. Abingdon, UK, and New York: Routledge, 2006.

Kemp, M. *The Science of Art: Optical Themes in Western Art From Brunelleschi to Seurat*. New Haven: Yale University Press, 1992.

Kennedy, Maev. "Battle to Save Rare 14th Century Psalter for the Nation." *The Guardian* (9 September 2004), http://www.guardian.co.uk/uk/2004/sep/09/artsandhumanities.arts 1 (accessed 13 June 2013).

Kennedy, Paul. *The Rise of the Anglo-German Antagonism, 1860–1914*. London and Boston: George Allen & Unwin, 1980.

Kennedy-Pipe, Caroline. *The Origins of the Cold War*. Houndmills, UK, and New York: Palgrave Macmillan, 2007.

Kerridge, Eric. *The Agricultural Revolution*. New York: A. M. Kelley, 1968.

Kessler-Harris, Alice. *Out to Work: A History of Wage-Earning Women in the United States*, 20th Anniversary edition. New York: Oxford University Press, 2003.

Kershaw, Ian. *Fateful Choices: Ten Decisions That Changed the World, 1940–1941*. London: Penguin Books, 2008.

Keyssar, Alexander. *The Right to Vote: The Contested History of Democracy in the United States*. New York: Basic Books, 2000.

Khan, B. Zorina. *The Democratization of Invention: Patents and Copyrights in American Economic Development, 1790–1920*. New York: Cambridge University Press, 2005.

Khan, Iqtidar Alam. *Gunpowder and Firearms: Warfare in Medieval India*. New Delhi: Oxford University Press, 2004.

Kibler, William W. (ed.), *Medieval France: An Encyclopedia*. New York: Garland Publishing, 1995.

Kidd, Thomas S. *The Great Awakening: The Roots of Evangelical Christianity in Colonial America*. New Haven and London: Yale University Press, 2009.

Kieckhefer, Richard. "The Specific Rationality of Medieval Magic." *The American Historical Review* 99, 3 (June 1994): 813–36.

Kiernan, Ben. *The Pol Pot Regime: Race, Power, and Genocide in Cambodia Under the Khmer Rouge, 1975–79*, 3rd edn. New Haven: Yale University Press 2008.

Kinder, Terryl Nancy. *Cistercian Europe: Architecture of Contemplation*. Grand Rapids, MI: W. B. Eerdmans Pub. Co., 2002.

Kindleberger, Charles P. *Manias, Panics, and Crashes: A History of Financial Crises.* New York: Basic Books, 1978.
—. *A Financial History of Western Europe*, 2nd edn. New York and Oxford: Oxford University Press, 1993.
—. *Comparative Political Economy: A Retrospective*. Cambridge, MA: Harvard University Press, 2000.
King, David A. "On the Role of the Muezzin and the Muwaqqit in Medieval Islamic Society." In *Tradition, Transmission, Transformation: Proceedings of Two Conferences on Pre-modern Science Held at the University of Oklahoma*. Edited by F. J. Ragep and Sally P. Ragep. With Steven John Livesey. Leiden: E. J. Brill, 1996.
Kingra, Mahinder S. "*Trace Italienne* and Military Revolution, 1567–1648." *The Journal of Military History* 57 (July 1993): 431–46.
Kiple, Kenneth F. *The Caribbean Slave: A Biological History*. New York: Cambridge University Press, 2002.
Kitch, Sally L. *The Specter of Sex: Gendered Foundations of Racial Formation in the United States*. Albany: State University of New York Press, 2009.
Klein, Maury. *The Genesis of Industrial America, 1870–1920*. New York: Cambridge University Press, 2007.
Klein, Richard G. *The Human Career: Human Biological and Cultural Origins*, 3rd edn. Chicago: University of Chicago Press, 2009.
Klinghoffer, Judith Apter, and Lois Elkis. "'The Petticoat Electors': Women's Suffrage in New Jersey, 1776–1807." *Journal of the Early Republic* 12, 2 (Summer 1992): 159–93.
Knecht, Robert Jean. *The Rise and Fall of Renaissance France, 1483–1610*, 2nd edn. Oxford and Malden, MA: Blackwell Publishers, 2001.
Knox, Paul L. *Metroburbia, USA*. Piscataway, NJ: Rutgers University Press, 2008.
Koch, Theodore W. "Some Old-Time Old-World Librarians." In *Library Daylight: Tracings of Modern Librarianship, 1874–1922*. Edited by Rory Litwin, introduction by Suzanne Stauffer. Duluth: Library Juice Press, 2006, 148–9.
Koehn, Nancy F. "Josiah Wedgwood and the First Industrial Revolution." In *Creating Modern Capitalism: How Entrepreneurs, Companies, and Countries Triumphed in Three Industrial Revolutions*. Edited by Thomas K. McCraw. Cambridge, MA: Harvard University Press, 1995.
Koestler, Arthur. *The Sleepwalkers: A History of Man's Changing Vision of the Universe*. London: Arkana, 1989.
Kohn, George C. (ed.), *Encyclopedia of Plague and Pestilence: From Ancient Times to the Present*, 3rd edn. New York: New York University Press, 2008.
Kossmann, E. H., and A. F. Mellink (eds), *Texts Concerning the Revolt of the Netherlands*. Cambridge: Cambridge University Press, 1974.
Kotkin, Stephen. *Armageddon Averted: The Soviet Collapse, 1970–2000*. Updated edition. New York: Oxford University Press, 2008.
Kowsky, Francis R. "Monuments of a Vanished Prosperity." In *Reconsidering Concrete Atlantis: Buffalo Grain Elevators*. Edited by Lynda H. Schneekloth. Buffalo, NY: The Landmark Society of the Niagara Frontier, 2006.
Koyré, Alexandre. *The Astronomical Revolution: Copernicus, Kepler, Borelli*. Translated by R. E. W. Maddison. Paris: Hermann; Ithaca: Cornell University Press, 1973.
Kranzberg, Melvin, and Carroll W. Pursell, Jr. (eds), *Technology in Western Civilization*. New York: Oxford University Press, 1967.
Kravis, Irving B. "The Role of Exports in Nineteenth-Century United States Growth." *Economic Development and Cultural Change* 20, 3 (April 1972): 387–405.
Kubelbeck, William John. *The Sacred Penitentiaria and its Relations to Faculties of Ordinaries and Priests*. Somerset, OH: Rosary Press, 1918.

Kuhn, Thomas S. *The Structure of Scientific Revolutions*, 3rd edn. Chicago and London: University of Chicago Press, 1996.

Kuran, Timur. "The Provision of Public Goods under Islamic Law: Origins, Impact, and Limitations of the Waqf System." *Law & Society Review* 35 (2001): 841–98.

—. "The Islamic Commercial Crisis: Institutional Roots of Economic Under development in the Middle East." *The Journal of Economic History* 63, 2 (June 2003): 414–46.

—. "The Absence of the Corporation in Islamic Law: Origins and Persistence." *The American Journal of Comparative Law* 53, 4 (Fall 2005): 785–834.

—. *The Long Divergence: How Islamic Law Held Back the Middle East*. Princeton and Oxford: Princeton University Press, 2011.

Lachmann, Richard. *Capitalists in Spite of Themselves: Elite Conflict and Economic Transitions in Early Modern Europe*. New York: Oxford University Press, 2000.

LaFrenière, Peter. *Adaptive Origins: Evolution and Human Development*. New York and Hove, UK: Taylor & Francis Group, 2010.

Lahey, Stephen Edmund. *John Wyclif*. Oxford: Oxford University Press, 2009.

Lambert, Malcolm. *The Cathars*. Oxford: Oxford University Press, 1998.

Lampert, Laurence. *How Philosophy Became Socratic: A Study of Plato's "Protagoras," "Charmides," and "Republic."* Chicago and London: University of Chicago Press, 2010.

Lancaster, Bill. *The Department Store: A Social History*. Leicester, UK: Leicester University Press, 1995.

Landau, Sarah Bradford, and Carl W. Condit. *Rise of the New York Skyscraper: 1865–1913*. New Haven: Yale University Press, 1996.

Landes, David. *The Wealth and Poverty of Nations: Why Some Are So Rich and Some So Poor*. New York: W. W. Norton & Company, 1998.

—. *Revolution in Time: Clocks and the Making of the Modern World*. Rev. and enl. edn. Cambridge, MA: Harvard University Press, 2000.

Landes, Richard. "Economic Development and Demotic Religiosity: Reflections on the Eleventh-Century Takeoff." In *History in the Comic Mode: The New Medieval Cultural History*. Edited by Rachel Fulton and Bruce Holsinger. New York: Columbia University Press, 2007.

Lane, Frederic C. *Venice: A Maritime Republic*. Baltimore: The Johns Hopkins University Press, 1973.

Lane, George. *Genghis Khan and Mongol Rule*. Indianapolis, IN: Hackett Publishing Company, Inc, 2009.

Lane, Jan-Erik. *Globalization and Politics: Promises and Dangers*. Aldershot, UK, and Burlington, VT: Ashgate Publishing, 2006.

Langdon, John. *Horses, Oxen and Technological Innovation: The Use of Draught Animals in English Farming from 1066–1500*. Cambridge: Cambridge University Press, 1986.

Langer, Lawrence N. *Historical Dictionary of Medieval Russia*. Lanham, MD: Scarecrow Press, 2002.

Langer, William L. "American Foods and Europe's Population Growth 1750–1850." *Journal of Social History* 8, 2 (Winter 1975): 51–66.

Langerbein, Helmut. *Hitler's Death Squads: The Logic of Mass Murder*. College Station, TX: Texas A&M University Press, 2004.

Langley, Lester D. *The Americas in the Age of Revolution, 1750–1850*. New Haven: Yale University Press, 1996.

Langmead, Donald, and Christine Garnaut. *Encyclopedia of Architectural and Engineering Feats*. Santa Barbara, CA: ABC-CLIO, 2001.

Larner, John. *Marco Polo and the Discovery of the World*. New Haven and London: Yale University Press 1999.

Larner, Robert J. "Ownership and Control in the 200 Largest Nonfinancial Corporations, 1929 and 1963." *The American Economic Review* 56, pt. 1 (September 1966): 777–87.

Larsen, David L. *The Company of the Preachers: A History of Biblical Preaching from the Old Testament to the Modern Era*. Grand Rapids, MI: W. B. Eerdmans Pub. Co., 1998.

Larson, Edward J. and Larry Witham. "Leading Scientists still Reject God." *Nature* 394, 6691 (1998): 313.

Las Casas, Bartolomé de. *A Short Account of the Destruction of the Indies*. London and New York: Penguin, 1992.

Lasagna, Louis. "The Pharmaceutical Revolution: Its Impact on Science and Society." *Science* 166 (5 December 1969): 1227–33.

Lau, D. C. *Mencius*. Translated with an introduction by D. C. Lau. Harmondsworth: Penguin, 1970.

Lavery, Brian. *Nelson's Navy: The Ships, Men, and Organisation, 1793–1815*. London: Conway Maritime Press, 1989.

Lawrence, Bruce B. "The Eastward Journey of Muslim Kingship: Islam in South and Southeast Asia." In *The Oxford History of Islam*. Edited by John L. Esposito. Oxford: Oxford University Press, 1999, 404–11.

Lawrence, C. H. *Medieval Monasticism: Forms of Religious Life in Western Europe in the Middle Ages*, 3rd edn. Harlow, UK: Longman, 2001.

Leckie, Robert. *The Wars of America* New and updated edition. New York: HarperPerenial Publishers, 1992.

Lee, Guy A. "The Historical Significance of the Chicago Grain Elevator System." *Agricultural History* 11 (January 1937): 16–32.

Lee, Stephen J. *European Dictatorships, 1918–1945*, 2nd edn. London and New York, Routledge, 2000.

Lee, William T., and Richard F. Staar (eds), *Soviet Military Policy Since World War II*. Stanford: Stanford University Press, 1986.

Lefkowitz, Mary R., and Guy Maclean Rogers (eds), *Black Athena Revisited*. Chapel Hill: The University of North Carolina Press, 1996.

Lehmberg, Stanford E. *The Reformation Parliament 1529–1536*. Cambridge: Cambridge University Press, 1970.

Lemarchand, René. "Exclusion, Marginalization, and Political Mobilization: The Road to Hell in the Great Lakes." In *Facing Ethnic Conflicts: Toward a New Realism*. Edited by Andreas Wimmer et al. Lanham, MD: Rowman & Littlefield, 2004.

Lemire, Beverly. *Cotton*. Oxford and New York: Oxford University Press, 2011.

Lemon, James T. "Colonial America in the Eighteenth Century." In *North America: The Historical Geography of a Changing Continent*, 2nd edn. Edited by Thomas F. McIlwraith and Edward K. Muller. Lanham, MD: Rowman & Littlefield Publishers, 2001.

Leonard, Mark. *Why Europe Will Run the 21st Century*. New York: Public Affairs, 2005.

Lerner, Frederick. *The Story of Libraries: From the Invention of Writing to the Computer Age*. New York: Continuum, 1998.

Lesquins, Noémie. "Bibliothèque Nationale de France." In *Encyclopedia of Library and Information Science*, 4 vols., 2nd edn. Edited by Miriam A. Drake. New York: Marcel Dekker, 2003, vol. 1, 329–30.

Levene, Mark. *Genocide in the Age of the Nation State: The Rise of the West and the Coming of Genocide*. London and New York: I. B. Tauris, 2005.

Levenstein, Harvey. *Revolution at the Table: The Transformation of the American Diet*. Berkeley: University of California Press, 2003.

Levey, Michael. *From Giotto to Cézanne: A Concise History of Painting*. London: Thames and Hudson, 1968.

Levy, Avigdor. *The Sephardim of the Ottoman Empire*. Princeton: Princeton University Press, 1992.

Levy, Joel. *Really Useful: The Origins of Everyday Things*. Buffalo: Firefly Books, 2002.
Levy, Leonard W. *The Origins of the Bill of Rights*. New Haven: Yale University Press, 1999.
Lewis, Bernard. *The Muslim Discovery of Europe*. New York: W. W. Norton & Company, 1982.
—. *What Went Wrong? Western Impact and Middle Eastern Response*. Oxford: Oxford University Press, 2002.
Lewis Gaddis, John. *We Now Know: Rethinking Cold War History*. New York: Oxford University Press, 1997.
—. *The Cold War: A New History*. London: Allen Lane, 2005.
Lewis, M. Paul (ed.), *Ethnologue: Languages of the World*, 16th edn. Dallas, TX: SIL International, 2009.
Lewis, Peter Shervey. *Essays in Later Medieval French History*. London and Ronceverte, WV: The Hambledon Press, 1985.
Li, Xiaobing. *A History of the Modern Chinese Army*. Lexington, KY: University Press of Kentucky, 2007.
Li, Xueqin, Garman Harbottle, Juzhong Zhang, and Changsui Wang. "The Earliest Writing? Sign Use in the Seventh Millennium BC at Jiahu, Henan Province, China." *Antiquity* 77 (March 2003): 31–44.
Lichtfouse, Eric et al. (eds), *Sustainable Agriculture*, vol. 2. Dordrecht and Heidelberg: Springer, 2011.
Lieberman, Philip. *Eve Spoke: Human Language and Human Evolution*. New York: W. W. Norton & Company, 1998.
Lieven, D. C. B. *Russia and the Origins of the First World War*. New York: St. Martin's Press, 1983.
Light, Laura. "The Bible and the Individual: The Thirteen-Century Paris Bible." In *The Practice of the Bible in the Middle Ages: Production, Reception, and Performance in Western Christianity*. Edited by Susan Boynton and Diane J. Reilly. New York: Columbia University Press, 2011, 231–2.
Lightbody, Bradley. *The Second World War: Ambitions to Nemesis*. London and New York: Routledge, 2004.
Lightfoot, Neil R. *How We Got the Bible*. Revised 3rd edn. Grand Rapids, MI: W. B. Eerdmans Pub. Co., 2003.
Lilly, William Samuel. *The Claims of Christianity*. New York: D. Appleton and Co., 1891.
Lincoln, W. Bruce. *The Great Reforms: Autocracy, Bureaucracy, and the Politics of Change in Imperial Russia*. DeKalb, IL: Northern Illinois University Press, 1990.
Lindberg, Carter. *The Third Reformation: Charismatic Movements and the Lutheran Tradition*. Macon, GA: Mercer University Press, 1983.
—. *The European Reformations*, 2nd edn. Chichester, UK, and Malden, MA: Blackwell Publishers, 2010.
Lindberg, David C. *Science in the Middle Ages*. Chicago: University of Chicago Press, 1980.
—. *The Beginnings of Western Science: The European Scientific Tradition in Philosophical, Religious, and Institutional Context, 600 BC. to AD. 1450*. Chicago: University of Chicago Press, 2008.
Lindberg, David C. and Robert S. Westman. *Reappraisals of the Scientific Revolution*. Chicago: University of Chicago Press, 1990.
Lister, Martin, Jon Dovey, Seth Giddings, Iain Grant, and Kieran Kelly. *New Media: A Critical Introduction*. London and New York: Routledge, 2003.
Little, A.G. "Theological Schools in Medieval England." *The English Historical Review* 55, 220 (October 1940): 624–30.
Little, Lester K. *Religious Poverty and the Profit Economy in Medieval Europe*. Ithaca: Cornell University Press, 1978.

Liu, Hua, Franck Prugnolle, Andrea Manica, and François Balloux. "A Geographically Explicit Genetic Model of Worldwide Human-Settlement History." *The American Journal of Human Genetics* 79 (2006): 230–7.

Livi-Bacci, Massimo. "The Depopulation of Hispanic America after the Conquest." *Population and Development Review* 32, 2 (June 2006): 199–232.

Lloyd, Geoffrey Ernest Richard. *Adversaries and Authorities: Investigations Into Ancient Greek and Chinese Science*. Cambridge: Cambridge University Press, 1996.

—. *The Ambitions of Curiosity: Understanding the World in Ancient Greece and China*. New York: Cambridge University Press, 2002.

Locke, John. *Two Treatises of Government*. Edited by Peter Laslett, student edition. Cambridge and New York: Cambridge University Press, 1988.

Locy, William A. "The Earliest Printed Illustrations of Natural History." *The Scientific Monthly* 13, 3 (September 1921): 238–58.

Loevy, Robert D. "Introduction: The Background and Setting of the Civil Rights Act of 1964." In *The Civil Rights Act of 1964: The Passage of the Law That Ended Racial Segregation*. Edited by Robert D. Loevy. Albany: State University of New York Press, 1997, 17–19.

Logan, F. Donald. *A History of the Church in the Middle Ages*, 2nd edn. Abingdon, UK, and New York: Routledge, 2013.

Lopez, Donald S., Jr. *Buddhism and Science: A Guide for the Perplexed*. Chicago and London: University of Chicago Press, 2008.

Lopez, R. S. *The Commercial Revolution of the Middle Ages, 950–1350*. Cambridge: Cambridge University Press, 1976.

Loth, Vincent C. "Armed Incidents and Unpaid Bills: Anglo-Dutch Rivalry in the Banda Islands in the Seventeenth Century." *Modern Asian Studies* 29 (October 1995): 705–40.

Lovejoy, Arthur O. *The Great Chain of Being: A Study of the History of an Idea*. Cambridge, MA: Harvard University Press, 1936.

Lovell, Julia. *The Opium War: Drugs, Dreams, and the Making of China*. Basingstoke and Oxford: Blackwell, 2011.

Lowry, Martin. *The World of Aldus Manutius: Business and Scholarship in Renaissance Venice*. Ithaca: Cornell University Press, 1979.

Lucs, Adam Robert. "Industrial Milling in the Ancient and Medieval Worlds: A Survey of the Evidence for an Industrial Revolution in Medieval Europe." *Technology and Culture* 46 (January 2005): 1–30.

Lunsford, Virginia W. *Piracy and Privateering in the Golden Age Netherlands*. Basingstoke, UK: Palgrave, 2005.

Luscombe, David, and Jonathan Riley-Smith. *The New Cambridge Medieval History*. Vol. 4, c. 1024–1198. Part 1. Edited by David Luscombe and Jonathan Riley-Smith. Cambridge: Cambridge University Press, 2008.

Luther, Martin. *On Christian Liberty*. Translated by Harold John Grimm and William Lambert. Minneapolis: Fortress Press, 2003.

Lutz, Wolfgang, Sergei Scherbov, and Andrei Volkov (eds), *Demographic Trends and Patterns in the Soviet Union before 1991*. London and New York: Routledge, 1994.

Luu, Lien. *Immigrants and the Industries of London, 1500–1700*. Burlington, VT: Ashgate Publishing, 2005.

Lynd, Robert S., and Helen M. Lynd. *Middletown: A Study in Contemporary American Culture*. New York: Harcourt, Brace and Co., 1929.

Lynn, John A. "The Trace Italienne and the Growth of Armies: The French Case." *The Journal of Military History* 55, 3 (July 1991): 297–330.

—. *Battle: A History of Combat and Culture*. Boulder, CO: Westview Press, 2003.

Lyons, Jonathan. *The House of Wisdom: How the Arabs Transformed Western Civilization*. New York: Bloomsbury Press, 2009.

Macalister-Smith, Peter. *International Humanitarian Assistance: Disaster Relief Action in International Law and Organization*. Dordrecht, The Netherlands: M. Nijhoff, 1985.
MacEwen, Martin. *Tackling Racism in Europe: An Examination of Anti-Discrimination Law in Practice*. Oxford and Washington, DC: Berg, 1995.
Macfarlane, Alan. *The Making of the Modern World: Visions from the West and East*. New York: Palgrave Macmillan, 2002.
MacGregor, Morris J. *Integration of the Armed Forces, 1940–1965*. Washington, DC: United States Army, 1981.
Machamer, Peter. "Galileo's Machines, His Mathematics, and His Experiments." In *The Cambridge Companion to Galileo*. Edited by Peter Machamer. Cambridge: Cambridge University Press, 1998, 54.
MacLeod, Christine. *Inventing the Industrial Revolution: The English Patent System, 1660–1800*. Cambridge: Cambridge University Press, 1988.
MacMullen, Ramsay. *Christianizing the Roman Empire: A.D. 100–400*. New Haven: Yale University Press, 1984.
—. *Christianity and Paganism in the Fourth to Eighth Centuries*. New Haven: Yale University Press, 1997.
Madden, Thomas F. *The New Concise History of the Crusades*. Lanham, MD and Oxford: Rowman & Littlefield, 2005.
Maddison, Angus. *The World Economy in the 20th Century*. Paris: OECD Publishing, 1989.
—. *The World Economy*, 2 vols. Paris: Development Centre of the Organisation for Economic Co-operation and Development, 2006.
Mahdi, Muhsin. "From the Manuscript Age to the Age of Printed Books." In *The Book in the Islamic World*. Edited by George N. Atiyeh. Albany: State University of New York Press, 1995.
Mair, Victor H., Nancy Shatzman Steinhardt, and Paul R. Goldin (eds), *Hawai'i Reader in Traditional Chinese Culture*. Honolulu: University of Hawaii Press, 2005.
Maitland, F. W. *The Constitutional History of England*. Edited by H. A. L. Fisher. Cambridge: Cambridge University Press, 1908.
Makdisi, George. "Madrasah and University in the Middle Ages." *Studia Islamica* 32 (1970): 255–64.
—. *The Rise of Colleges: Institutions of Learning in Islam and the West*. Edinburgh: Edinburgh University Press, 1981.
Malanima, Paolo. *Pre-Modern European Economy: One Thousand Years, 10th-19th Centuries*. Leiden: E. J. Brill, 2009.
Malia, Martin. *The Soviet Tragedy: A History of Socialism in Russia, 1917–1991*. New York: The Free Press, 1994.
Malone, Michael S. *Bill & Dave: How Hewlett and Packard Built the World's Greatest Company*. New York: Portfolio, 2000.
Malthus, Thomas. *An Essay on the Principle of Population*. London, 1798, ch. 7, par. 20, http://www.econlib.org/library/Malthus/malPop3.html#VII.20 (accessed 13 June 2013).
Man, John. *Alpha Beta: How 26 Letters Shaped the Western World*. New York: Headline, 2000.
—. *Gutenberg: How One Man Remade the World with Words*. New York: John Wiley, 2002.
Mancall, Peter C. *Hakluyt's Promise: An Elizabethan's Obsession for an English America*. New Haven: Yale University Press, 2007.
Mandelson, Dayle A. "Women's Changing Labor-Force Participation in the U.S." In *Women and Work: A Handbook*. Edited by Paula Dubeck and Kathryn M. Borman. New York and London: Garland Publishing, 1996, 4.
Mann, Charles C. *1491: New Revelations of the Americas Before Columbus*. New York: A.A. Knopf, 2005.

Mann, Nicholas. "The Origins of Humanism." In *The Cambridge Companion to Renaissance Humanism*. Edited by Jill Kraye. New York: Cambridge University Press, 1996.
Manning, Patrick. "The Slave Trade: The Formal Demography of a Global System." *Social Science History* 14, 2 (Summer 1990): 255–79.
Manring, Maurice M. *Slave in A Box: The Strange Career of Aunt Jemima*. Charlottesville: University of Virginia Press, 1998.
Manuel, Frank E., and Fritzie P. Manuel. *Utopian Thought In the Western World*. Cambridge, MA: Belknap Press, 1979.
Marchand, Roland. *Advertising the American Dream: Making Way for Modernity, 1920–1940*. Berkeley: University of California Press, 1985.
Marenbon, John. *Medieval Philosophy*, vol. 3 of *Routledge History of Philosophy*. London and New York: Routledge, 1998.
Mark, Robert. "Structural Experimentation in Gothic Architecture: Large-scale Experimentation Brought Gothic Cathedrals to a Level of Technical Elegance Unsurpassed Until the Last Century." *American Scientist* 66 (September–October 1978): 542–50.
Marker, Gary. "Russia and the 'Printing Revolution': Notes and Observations." *Slavic Review* 41 (1982): 269–81.
Markoff, John, "Violence, Emancipation, and Democracy: The Countryside in the French. Revolution." *The American Historical Review* 100, 2 (April 1995): 360–86.
Marks, Robert B. *The Origins of the Modern World: A Global and Ecological Narrative*. Lanham, MD: Rowman & Littlefield, 2002.
Marozzi, Justin. *The Way of Herodotus: Travels with the Man who Invented History*. Cambridge, MA: Da Capo Press, 2008.
Marshall, D. N. *History of Libraries: Ancient and Medieval*. New Delhi: Oxford & IBH Publishing Company, 1983.
Marsilius of Padua. *The Defender of the Peace*. Edited by Annabel Brett. Cambridge: Cambridge University Press, 2006.
Marten, Kimberly Zisk. *Enforcing the Peace: Learning From the Imperial Past*. New York: Columbia University Press, 2004.
Marx, Karl, and Friedrich Engels. *The Communist Manifesto*. Introduction by Martin Malia. New York: Penguin, 1998.
Mast, Gerald, and Bruce F. Kawin. *A Short History of the Movies*, 6th edn. Boston, MA: Prentice Hall, 1996.
Matthews, Steven. *Theology and Science in the Thought of Francis Bacon*. Aldershott, UK, and Burlington, VT: Ashgate Publishing, 2008.
Matzke, Rebecca Berens. *Deterrence Through Strength: British Naval Power and Foreign Policy under Pax Britannica*. Lincoln, NE: University of Nebraska Press, 2011.
Maurer, Armand Augustine. *The Philosophy of William of Ockham in the Light of Its Principles*. Toronto: Pontifical Institute of Medieval Studies, 1999.
Mawdsley, Evan. *Thunder in the East: The Nazi-Soviet War, 1941–1945*. London: Hodder, 2005.
—. *The Russian Civil War*. New York: Columbia University Press, 2007.
—. *World War II: A New History*. Cambridge: Cambridge University Press, 2009.
—. *December 1941: Twelve Days That Began a World War*. New Haven: Yale University Press, 2011.
Maxtone-Graham, John. *Safe Return Doubtful: The Heroic Age of Polar Exploration*. London: Constable, 2000.
May, Christopher. "The Venetian Moment: New Technologies, Legal Innovation and the Institutional Origins of Intellectual Property." In *Intellectual Property Rights: Critical Concepts in Law*, vol. 3. Edited by David Vaver. Abingdon, UK, and New York: Routledge, 2006, 20.

May, Elaine Tyler. *America and the Pill: A History of Promise, Peril, and Liberation*. New York: Basic Books, 2010.

May, O. I., and K. E. Lege. "Development of the World Cotton Industry." In *Cotton: Origin, History, Technology, and Production*. Edited by C. Wayne Smith and Joe Tom Cothren. New York: John Wiley & Sons, 1999.

Mayo, Anthony J., Nitin Nohria, and Laura G. Singleton, *Paths to Power: How Insiders and Outsiders Shaped American Business Leadership*. Boston, MA: Harvard University Press, 2006.

Mayr, Ernst. "Darwin's Influence on Modern Thought." *Scientific American* (July 2000): 79–83.

McCaffray, Susan P., and Michael Melancon. *Russia in the European Context, 1789–1914: A Member of the Family*. New York and Houndmills, UK: Palgrave Macmillan, 2005.

McClaren, Anne. "Rethinking Republicanism: Vindiciae, Contra Tyrannos in Context." *The Historical Journal* 49 (March 2006): 23–52.

McClellan III, James E., and Harold Dorn. *Science and Technology in World History: An Introduction*. Baltimore: Johns Hopkins University Press, 2006.

McClelland, Peter D. *Sowing Modernity: America's First Agricultural Revolution*. Ithaca: Cornell University Press 1997.

McCloskey, Deirdre M. *The Bourgeois Virtues: Ethics for an Age of Commerce*. Chicago: University of Chicago Press, 2006.

—. *Bourgeois Dignity: Why Economics Can't Explain the Modern World*. Chicago: University of Chicago Press, 2010.

McColloch, Mark. *White Collar Workers in Transition: The Boom Years, 1940–1970*. Westport, CT: Greenwood Press, 1983.

McCollough, William H. "The Heian Court, 794–1070." In *The Cambridge History of Japan*, vol. 2: *Heian Japan*. Edited by Donald H. Shively and Willam H. McCollough. New York: Cambridge University Press, 1999), 82–8.

McCormick, Michael. *Origins of the European Economy: Communications and Commerce A.D. 300–900*. New York: Cambridge University Press, 2001.

McCown, C. C. "Codex and Roll in the New Testament." *The Harvard Theological Review* 34, 4 (October 1941): 219–49.

McCraw, Thomas K. (ed.), *Creating Modern Capitalism: How Entrepreneurs, Companies, and Countries Triumphed in Three Industrial Revolutions*. Cambridge, MA: Harvard University Press, 1997.

McCraw, Thomas K., and Richard S. Tedlow. "Henry Ford, Alfred Sloan, and the Three Phases of Marketing." In *Creating Modern Capitalism: How Entrepreneurs, Companies, and Countries Triumphed in Three Industrial Revolutions*. Edited by Thomas K. McCraw. Cambridge, MA: Harvard University Press, 1995.

McDonald, H. D. "Biblical Teaching on Personality." In *Psychology and Christian Integration: Seminal Works That Shaped the Movement*. Edited by Daryl H. Stevenson, Brian E. Eck, and Peter C. Hill. Batavia, IL: Christian Association for Psychological Studies, 2007.

McDermot, Kevin, and Matthew Stibbe. *Revolution and Resistance in Eastern Europe: Challenges to Communist Rule*. Oxford and New York: Oxford University Press, 2006.

McEnroe, John C. *Architecture of Minoan Crete: Constructing Identity in the Aegean Bronze Age*. Austin, TX: University of Texas Press, 2010.

McEvedy, Colin, and Richard Jones. *Atlas of World Population History*. Harmondsworth, UK: Penguin, 1978.

McGuire, M. R. *Technology, Crime and Justice: The Question Concerning Technomia*. Abingdon, UK, and New York: Routledge, 2012.

McIlroy, John. *Trade Unions in Britain Today*, 2nd edn. Manchester and New York: Manchester University Press, 1995.

McIntosh, Gregory C. *The Piri Reis Map of 1513*. Athens, GA: University of Georgia Press, 2000.

McKeown, Thomas, and R. G. Brown. "Medical Evidence Related to English Population Changes in the Eighteenth Century." *Population Studies* 9 (November 1955): 119–41.

McKibbin, Ross. *Classes and Cultures: England 1918–1951*. New York: Oxford University Press, 1998.

McKitterick, Rosamond. "Script and Book Production." In *Carolingian Culture: Emulation and Innovation*. Edited by Rosamond McKitterick. Cambridge: Cambridge University Press, 1994, 221–34.

McMeekin, Sean. *History's Greatest Heist: The Looting of Russia by the Bolsheviks*. New Haven: Yale University Press, 2009.

—. *The Berlin-Baghdad Express: The Ottoman Empire and Germany's Bid for World Power, 1898–1918*. Cambridge, MA: Harvard University Press, 2010.

—. *The Russian Origins of the First World War*. Cambridge, MA: Harvard University Press, 2011.

McNair, Brian, Matthew Hibberd, and Philip Schlesinger. *Mediated Access: Broadcasting and Democratic Participation*. Luton, UK: University of Luton Press, 2003.

McNeill, J. R. *Something New Under the Sun: An Environmental History of the Twentieth-Century World*. New York: W. W. Norton & Company, 2000.

McNeill, William H. *The Rise of the West: A History of the Human Community*. Chicago: University of Chicago Press, 1963.

—. *The Shape of European History*. New York and London: Oxford University Press, 1974.

—. *The Pursuit of Power: Technology, Armed Force, and Society since A.D. 1000*. Chicago: University of Chicago Press, 1982.

—. "Ch'I Chi-kuang." In *The Reader's Companion to Military History*. Edited by Robert Cowley and Geoffrey Parker. New York: Houghton Mifflin, 1996, 83.

McRoberts, D. "Material Destruction Caused by the Scottish Reformation." In *Essays on the Scottish Reformation 1513–1625*. Edited by David McRoberts. Glasgow: Burns, 1962.

Mead, Walter Russell. *God and Gold: Britain, America, and the Making of the Modern World*. New York: A.A. Knopf, 2007.

Melton, James Van Horn. *The Rise of the Public in Enlightenment Europe*. Cambridge and New York: Cambridge University Press, 2001.

Merton, Robert King. *On the Shoulders of Giants: A Shandean Postscript*. Chicago and London: University of Chicago Press, 1993.

Meuthen, Erich. *Nicholas of Cusa: A Sketch for a Biography*. Translated by David Crowner and Gerald Christianson. Washington, DC: Catholic University of America Press, 2010.

Meyer, David R. *The Roots of American Industrialization*. Baltimore: The Johns Hopkins University Press, 2003.

Meyer, Steven. "Assembly Line Production." In *Encyclopedia of U.S. Labor and Working-Class History*, 3 vols. Edited by Eric Arnesen. New York and Abingdon, UK: Routledge, 2007, vol. 1, 130–1.

Michie, Ranald. "The City of London and International Trade, 1850–1914." In *Decline and Recovery in Britain's Overseas Trade, 1873–1914*. Edited by D. C. M. Platt, A. J. H. Latham, and Ranald Michie. Basingstoke, UK: Macmillan, 1993.

Mickelthwait, John, and Adrian Wooldridge. *The Company: A Short History of Revolutionary Idea*. New York: Modern Library, 2003.

—. *God Is Back: How the Global Revival of Faith Is Changing the World*. New York: Penguin, 2009.

Middlekauff, Robert. *The Glorious Cause: The American Revolution, 1763–1789*. Oxford and New York: Oxford University Press, 2005.

Mielants, Eric H. *The Origins of Capitalism and the "Rise of the West"*. Philadelphia: Temple University Press, 2007.
Mignolo, Walter. *The Darker Side of Western Modernity: Global Futures, Decolonial Options*. Durham, NC, and London: Duke University Press, 2011.
Mill, John Stuart. *The Subjection of Women*. Edited by Susan Moller Okin. Indianapolis: Hackett Publishing Company, 1988.
Miller, Donald L. *City of the Century: The Epic of Chicago and the Making of America*. New York: Simon & Schuster, 1996.
Miller, Michael B. *The Bon Marché: Bourgeois Culture and The Department Store, 1869–1920*. Princeton: Princeton University Press, 1981.
Miller, Roger G. *To Save a City: The Berlin Airlift, 1948–1949*. College Station: Texas A&M University Press, 2000.
Millett, Allan R. *The War for Korea, 1950–1951: They Came from the North*. Lawrence, KA: University Press of Kansas, 2010.
Mills, C. Wright. *White Collar: The American Middle Classes*. New York: Oxford University Press, 1951.
Millward, C. M., and Mary Hayes. *A Biography of the English Language*, 3rd edn. Boston: Wadsworth, 2012.
Milson, John Nelson. "Schools and Literacy in Later Medieval England." *British Journal of Educational Studies* 11, 1 (November 1962): 16–27.
Minford, John, and Joseph S. M. Lau (eds), *An Anthology of Translations: Classical Chinese Literature*, vol. 1: *From Antiquity to the Tang Dynasty*. New York, Chichester, UK, and Hong Kong: Chinese University Press, 2000.
Mintz, Sidney W. *Sweetness and Power: The Place of Sugar in Modern History*. New York: Penguin, 1985.
Misa, Thomas J. *Leonardo to the Internet: Technology and Culture from the Renaissance to the Present*. Baltimore: The Johns Hopkins University Press, 2004.
Mitchell, Allan. *The Great Train Race: Railways and the Franco-German Rivalry, 1815–1914*. New York: Berghahn, 2000.
Mitchell, B. R. *European Historical Statistics, 1750–1970*, abridged edn. New York: Columbia University Press, 1978.
Mithen, Steven J. *The Singing Neanderthals: The Origins of Music, Language, Mind, and Body*. Cambridge: Cambridge University Press, 2006.
Moché, Dinah L. *Astronomy: A Self-Teaching Guide*, 7th edn. Hoboken, NJ: John Wiley & Sons, 2009.
Modelski, George. *World Cities: -3000 to 2000*. Washington, DC: Faros, 2003.
Mokyr, Joel. *The Lever of Riches: Technological Creativity and Economic Progress*. Oxford and New York: Oxford University Press, 1990.
—. "The New Economic History and the Industrial Revolution." In *The British Industrial Revolution: An Economic Perspective*. Edited by Joel Mokyr. Boulder, CO: University of Colorado Press, 1999.
—. *The Gifts of Athena: Historical Origins of the Knowledge Economy*. Princeton: Princeton University Press, 2002.
—. "The Intellectual Origins of Modern Economic Growth." *The Journal of Economic History* 65 (2005): 285–351.
Monter, William. *Frontiers of Heresy: The Spanish Inquisition from the Basque Lands to Sicily*. Cambridge: Cambridge University Press, 1990.
Moore, Stephen, and Julian L. Simon, "The Greatest Century That Ever Was: 25 Miraculous Trends of the Past 100 Years." *Policy Analysis*, 264 (15 December 1999): 1–32.
—. *It's Getting Better All the Time: 100 Greatest Trends of the 20th Century*. Washington, DC: Cato Institute, 2000.

Moore, Nina M. *Governing Race: Policy, Process, and the Politics of Race*. Westport, CT: Praeger, 2000.
Moorehead, Alan. *The White Nile*. New York: Harper & Brothers, 1960.
Moosvi, Shireen. *Episodes in the Life of Akbar: Contemporary Records and Reminiscences*. New Delhi: National Book Trust, 1994.
Morales, Ed. *The Latin Beat: The Rhythms and Roots of Latin Music, from Bossa Nova to Salsa and Beyond*. Cambridge, MA: Da Capo Press, 2003.
Moran, Terence P. *Introduction to the History of Communication: Evolutions & Revolutions*. New York: Peter Lang Publishing, 2010.
Morgan, David. *The Mongols*, 2nd edn. Malden, MA, and Oxford: Blackwell, 2007.
Morgan, Edmund S. *American Slavery, American Freedom: The Ordeal of Colonial Virginia*. New York and London: W. W. Norton and Company, 1975.
Morgan, Kenneth. *Bristol and the Atlantic Trade in the Eighteenth Century*. Cambridge: Cambridge University Press, 1993.
—. *Slavery and the British Empire: From Africa to America*. Oxford and New York: Oxford University Press, 2007.
Morris, Colin. *The Papal Monarchy: The Western Church from 1050 to 1250*. Oxford: Oxford University Press, 1989.
—. *The Sepulchre of Christ and the Medieval West: From the Beginning to 1600s*. New York: Oxford University Press, 2005.
Morris, Ian. *Why the West Rules—For Now: The Patterns of History and What They Reveal About the Future*. New York: Farrar, Straus and Giroux, 2010.
Morris, Norval, and David J. Rothman (eds), *The Oxford History of the Prison: The Practice of Punishment in Western Society*. New York: Oxford University Press, 1998.
Morris, Peter J. T., and Anthony S. Travis. "A History of the International Dyestuff Industry." *American Dyestuff Reporter* 81 (November 1992): 59–100.
Mosk, Carl. *Japanese Economic Development: Markets, Norms, Structures*. Abingdon, UK, and New York: Routledge, 2008.
Moskos, Charles C., and John Whiteclay Chambers II. "The Secularlization of Conscience." In *The New Conscientious Objection: From Sacred to Secular Resistance*. Edited by Charles C. Moskos and John Whiteclay Chambers II. New York: Oxford University Press, 1993, 10–11.
Moulder, Frances V. *Japan, China, and the Modern World Economy: Toward a Reinterpretation of East Asian Development ca. 1600 to ca. 1918*. Cambridge: Cambridge University Press, 1977.
Mowery David C., and Nathan Rosenberg. *Paths of Innovation: Technological Change in 20th-Century America*. Cambridge and New York: Cambridge University Press, 1998.
Moynahan, Brian. *The Faith: A History of Christianity*. New York: Doubleday Religious Publishing Group, 2002.
Mulligan, William. *The Origins of the First World War*. New York: Cambridge University Press, 2010.
Multhauf, Robert P. "Industrial Chemistry in the Nineteenth Century." In vol. 1 of *Technology in Western Civilization*, 2 vols. Edited by Melvin Kranzberg and Carroll W. Pursell, Jr. New York: Oxford University Press, 1967.
Munck, Thomas. *Seventeenth Century Europe: State, Conflict, and the Social Order in Europe, 1598–1700*. Houndmills, UK, and New York: Macmillan, 1989.
Mungello, D. E. *The Great Encounter of China and the West, 1500–1800*. Lanham, MD: Rowman & Littlefield, 2005.
Muntersbjorn, Madeline M. "Francis Bacon's Philosophy of Science: Machina Intellectus and Forma Indita." *Philosophy of Science* 70, 5 (December 2003): 1137–48.
Murray, Julia K. *Mirrors of Mortality: Narrative Illustration and Confucian Ideology*. Honolulu: University of Hawaii Press, 2007.

Musson, A. E. and Eric Robinson. *Science and Technology in the Industrial Revolution*. Manchester: Manchester University Press, 1969.

Naimark, Norman M. *Fires of Hatred: Ethnic Cleansing in Twentieth-Century Europe*. Cambridge, MA: Harvard University Press, 2001.

—. *Stalin's Genocides*. Princeton and Oxford: Princeton University Press, 2010.

Nasr, Seyyed Hossein. *An Introduction to Islamic Cosmological Doctrines: Conceptions of Nature and Methods Used for its Study by the Ikhwan Al-Safa, Al-Biruni, and Ibn Sina*. Albany: State University of New York Press, 1993.

—. *Islamic Philosophy from its Origin to the Present: Philosophy in the Land of Prophesy*. Albany: State University of New York Press, 2006.

Nauert, Charles G., Jr. *Humanism and the Culture of Renaissance Europe*. Cambridge: Cambridge University Press, 1995.

Neal, Larry. "The Integration and Efficiency of the London and Amsterdam Stock Markets in the Eighteenth Century." *The Journal of Economic History* 47, 1 (March 1987): 97–115.

—. *The Rise of Financial Capitalism: International Capital Markets in the Age of Reason*. Cambridge: Cambridge University Press, 2002.

Nebeker, Frederik. *Dawn of the Electronic Age: Electrical Technologies in the Shaping of the Modern World, 1914 to 1945*. Hoboken, NJ: John Wiley & Sons, Inc., 2009.

Nederman, Cary J. "A Duty to Kill: John of Salisbury's Theory of Tyrannicide." *The Review of Politics* 50, 3 (Summer 1988): 365–89.

—. "Aristotelianism and the Origins of 'Political Science' in the Twelfth Century." *Journal of the History of Ideas* 52 (1991): 179–94.

—. *Worlds of Difference: European Discourses of Toleration, c. 1100-c. 1550*. University Park, PA: The Pennsylvania State University Press, 2000.

—. *John of Salisbury*. Tempe, AZ: Arizona Center for Medieval and Renaissance Studies, 2005.

Nederman, Cary J., and Catherine Campbell. "Priests, Kings, and Tyrants: Spiritual and Temporal Power in John of Salisbury's Policraticus." *Speculum* 66, 3 (July 1991): 572–90.

Needham, Joseph. *Time and Eastern Man*. London: Royal Anthropological Institute of Great Britain & Ireland, 1965.

—. *The Grand Titration: Science and Society in East and West*. London: Allen & Unwin, 1969.

—. *Science and Civilisation in China*. Vol. 4: *Physics and Physical Technology*, pt. 3: *Civil Engineering and Nautics*. Cambridge: Cambridge University Press, 1971.

—. *Science in Traditional China: A Comparative Perspective*. Cambridge, MA: Harvard University Press, 1981.

Needham, Joseph and Gwei-Djen Lu. *Science and Civilisation in China*. Vol. 5: *Chemistry and Chemical Technology*. Part 2: *Spagyrical Discovery and Invention: Magisteries of Gold and Immortality*. Cambridge: Cambridge University Press, 1974.

Needham, Joseph, Wang Ling, Lu Gwei-Djen, and Ho Ping-Yü. *Science and Civilization in China*. Vol. 5: *Chemistry and Chemical Technology*. Part 7: *Military Technology: The Gunpowder Epic*. Cambridge: Cambridge University Press, 1986.

Needham, Joseph, Wang Ling, and Derek J. de Solla Price. *Heavenly Clockwork: The Great Astronomical Clocks of Medieval China*, 2nd edn. With suppl. by John H. Combridge. Cambridge and New York: Cambridge University Press, 1986.

Neem, Johann N. *Creating a Nation of Joiners: Democracy and Civil Society in Early National Massachusetts*. Cambridge, MA: Harvard University Press, 2008.

Nekrasz, Carmen, and Claudia Swan. "Art." In *The Cambridge History of Science*. Vol. 3: *Early Modern Science*. Edited by Katharine Park and Lorraine Daston. Cambridge: Cambridge University Press, 2006.

Nemo, Philippe. *What Is the West?* Pittsburgh: Duquesne University Press, 2004.

Neubauer, Raymond L. *Evolution and the Emergent Self: The Rise of Complexity and Behavioral Versatility in Nature*. New York: Columbia University Press, 2012.

Newcombe, David Gordon. *Henry VIII and the English Reformation*. New York: Routledge, 1995.
Newitt, M. D. D. *A History of Portuguese Overseas Expansion, 1400–1668*. London: Routledge, 2005.
Newman, Robert P. *Enola Gay and the Court of History*. New York: Peter Lang Publishing, 2004.
Newman, William R. "From Alchemy to 'Chymistry.'" In *The Cambridge History of Science*. Vol. 3: *Early Modern Science*. Edited by Katharine Park and Lorraine Daston. Cambridge: Cambridge University Press, 2006.
Nexon, Daniel H. *The Struggle for Power in Early Modern Europe: Religious Conflict, Dynastic Empires and International Change*. Princeton: Princeton University Press, 2009.
Nicholson, Helen J. *The Crusades*. Westport, CT: Greenwood Press, 2004a.
—. *Medieval Warfare: Theory and Practice of War in Europe, 300–1500*. New York: Palgrave Macmillan, 2004b.
Nicol, Donald M. *Byzantium and Venice: A Study in Diplomatic and Cultural Relations*. Cambridge: Cambridge University Press, 1992.
Noble, David F. *America by Design: Science, Technology, and the Rise of Corporate Capitalism*. Oxford: Oxford University Press, 1997.
Nolan, Kathleen. *Capetian Women*. Basingstoke, UK, and New York: Palgrave Macmillan, 2003.
Nordin, Dennis S., and Roy V. Scott. *From Prairie Farmer to Entrepreneur: The Transformation of Midwestern Agriculture*. Bloomington, IN: Indiana University Press, 2005.
Norrlof, Carla. *America's Global Advantage: US Hegemony and International Cooperation*. New York: Cambridge University Press, 2010.
North, Douglass C., and Robert Paul Thomas. *The Rise of the Western World: A New Economic History*. New York: Cambridge University Press, 1973.
North, Douglass C., William Summerhill, and Barry R. Weingast. "Order, Disorder and Economic Change: Latin America vs. North America." In *Governing for Prosperity*. Edited by Bruce Bueno de Mesquita and Hilton L. Root. New Haven and London: Yale University Press 2000.
Novacek, Michael. *Terra: Our 100-Million-Year-Old Ecosystem–and the Threats That Now Put It at Risk*. New York: Farrar, Straus and Giroux, 2008.
Novak, Ralph Martin, Jr. *Christianity and the Roman Empire: Background Texts*. Harrisburg, PA: Trinity Press International, 2001.
Nutton, Vivian. *Ancient Medicine*. New York: Routledge, 2004.
Nye, David E. *Electrifying America: Social Meanings of a New Technology, 1880–1940*. Cambridge, MA: MIT Press, 1992.
Ó Gráda, Cormac. *Famine: A Short History*. Princeton and Oxford: Princeton University Press, 2009.
Oakes, Elizabeth H. (ed.), *Encyclopedia of World Scientists*. Revised edition. New York: Facts on File, 2007.
Oberman, Heiko Augustinus. *Luther: Man Between God and the Devil*. Translated by Eileen Walliser-Schwarzbart. New Haven: Yale University Press, 2006.
O'Brien, Patrick K. "European Economic Development: The Contribution of the Periphery." *Economic History Review* 35 (1982): 1–18.
O'Callaghan, Joseph F. "The Beginnings of the Cortes of Leon-Castile." *The American Historical Review* 74 (June 1969): 1503–37.
Odom, William E. *The Collapse of the Soviet Military*. New Haven: Yale University Press, 1998.
Ogden, Schubert M. *The Reality of God, and Other Essays*. Dallas, TX: Southern Methodist University Press, 1992.
Ogilvie, Marilyn Bailie. *Women in Science: Antiquity through the Nineteenth Century: A Biographical Dictionary with Annotated Bibliography*. Cambridge, MA: MIT Press, 1988.

Ogilvie, Sheilagh. "Rehabilitating the Guilds: A Reply." *The Economic History Review*, New Series 61 (February 2008): 175–82.

O'Hanlon, Michael E. *Defense Strategy for the Post-Saddam Era*. Washington, DC: Brookings Institution Press, 2005.

Olmstead, Alan L., and Paul W. Rhode, *Creating Abundance: Biological Innovation and American Agricultural Development*. New York: Cambridge University Press, 2008.

Olschki, Leonardo. *Marco Polo's Asia: An Introduction to His "Description of the World" Called "Il milione."* Translated by John A. Scott. Revised by author. Berkeley: University of California Press, 1960.

Olson, Richard G., and Richard Olson. *Science and Religion, 1450–1900: From Copernicus to Darwin*. Baltimore: The Johns Hopkins University Press, 2004.

O'Malley, John W. *Four Cultures of the West*. Cambridge, MA: Belknap Press, 2004.

Origo, Iris. "The Domestic Enemy: The Eastern Slaves in Tuscany in the Fourteenth and Fifteenth Centuries." *Speculum* 30, 3 (July 1955): 321–66.

Osborne, Roger. *Civilization: A New History of the Western World*. New York: Pegasus Books, 2006.

Overton, Mark. *Agricultural Revolution in England: The Transformation of the Agrarian Economy, 1500–1850*. Cambridge: Cambridge University Press, 1996.

Overy, Richard. *The Dictators: Hitler's Germany and Stalin's Russia*. New York: W. W. Norton and Company, 2004.

—. *The Bombing War: Europe 1939–1945*. London: Allen Lane, 2013.

Owen, Stephen. "The Cultural Tang, 650–1020." In *The Cambridge History of Chinese Literature*, vol. 1: *To 1375*. Edited by Kang-i Sun Chang and Stephen Owen. Cambridge: Cambridge University Press, 2010.

Pagel, Mark. *Wired for Culture: Origins of the Human Social Mind*. New York: W. W. Norton, 2012.

Pakenham, Thomas. *The Scramble for Africa: White Man's Conquest of the Dark Continent from 1876–1912*. New York: Avon, 1991.

Pallotta, Augustus. "Venetian Printers and Spanish Literature in Sixteenth-Century Italy." *Comparative Literature* 43, 1 (Winter 1991): 20–42.

Palmer, Douglas. *Seven Million Years: The Story of Human Evolution*. London: Weidenfeld & Nicolson, 2005.

Palmer, William G. "From Gentleman's Club to Professional Body: The Evolution of the History Department in the United States." *Historically Speaking* 10 (June 2009): 36–8.

Pannabecker, John R. "Representing Mechanical Arts in Diderot's 'Encyclopédie.'" *Technology and Culture* 39 (January 1998): 33–73.

Panofsky, Erwin. "Introduction." In *Abbot Suger on the Abbey Church of St.-Denis and Its Treasures*. Edited by Erwin Panofsky. Princeton: Princeton University Press, 1946.

Park, Robert E. "Urbanization as Measured by Newspaper Circulation." *The American Journal of Sociology* 35, 1 (July 1929): 60–79.

Parker, Charles H. *Global Interactions in the Early Modern Age, 1400–1800*. New York: Oxford University Press, 2010.

Parker, Deborah. *Commentary and Ideology: Dante in the Renaissance*. Durham, NC: Duke University Press, 1993.

Parker, Geoffrey. *The Dutch Revolt*. London and New York: Penguin books, 1988.

—. "Europe and the Wider World, 1500–1750: The Military Balance." in *The Political Economy of Merchant Empires: State Power and World Trade, 1350–1750*. Edited by James D. Tracy. Cambridge: Cambridge University Press, 1991, 167–8.

Parker, Geoffrey. *The Military Revolution: Military Innovation and the Rise of the West, 1500–1800*. New York: Cambridge University Press, 1996.

—. "The Future of Western Warfare." In *The Cambridge History of Warfare*. Edited by Geoffrey Parker. Cambridge: Cambridge University Press, 2005a.

— (ed.), *The Cambridge History of Warfare*. Cambridge: Cambridge University Press, 2005b.

— (ed.), *The Thirty Years' War*, 2nd edn. London and New York: Cambridge University Press, 2006.

—. "The Limits to Revolutions in Military Affairs: Maurice of Nassau, the Battle of Nieuwpoort (1600), and the Legacy." *The Journal of Military History* 71 (April 2007): 331–72.

Parsons, Edward Alexander. *The Alexandrian Library: Glory of the Hellenic World: Its Rise, Antiquities, and Destructions*. Amsterdam, London, and New York: Elsevier Press, 1952.

Parsons, Timothy. *The British Imperial Century, 1815–1914: A World History Perspective*. Lanham, MD, and Oxford: Rowman & Littlefield, 1999.

Patrick, John J., and Gerald P. Long (eds), *Constitutional Debates on Freedom of Religion: A Documentary History*. Westport, CT: Greenwood Press, 1999.

Paxton, Robert O. *The Anatomy of Fascism*. New York: A.A. Knopf, 2004.

Pearson, Robin. "Moral Hazard and the Assessment of Insurance Risk in Eighteenth- and Early-Nineteenth-Century Britain." *The Business History Review* 76, 1 (Spring 2002): 1–35.

Pelikan, Jaroslav. "The Other Face of the Renaissance." *Bulletin of the American Academy of Arts and Sciences* 50, 6 (April 1997): 52–63.

Penprase, Bryan E. *The Power of Stars: How Celestial Observations Have Shaped Civilization*. New York: Springer, 2011.

Peppas, Nicholas A. (ed.), *One Hundred Years of Chemical Engineering: From Lewis M. Norton (M.I.T. 1888) to Present*. Dordrecht, The Netherlands: Springer, 1989.

Pereria, Michela. "Alchemy and Hermeticism: An Introduction to This Issue." *Early Science and Medicine* 5 (2000): 115–20.

Perman, Michael. *Pursuit of Liberty: A Political History of the American South*. Chapel Hill: University of North Carolina Press, 2010.

Peskin, Lawrence A., and Edmund F. Wehrle. *America and the World: Culture, Commerce, Conflict*. Baltimore: Johns Hopkins University Press, 2012.

Peters, Edward. *Inquisition*. Berkeley and Los Angeles: University of California Press, 1989.

—. *A Modern Guide to Indulgences: Rediscovering This Often Misinterpreted Teaching*. Chicago: University of Chicago Press, 2008.

Pettegree, Andrew. *The French Book and the European Book World*. Leiden: E. J. Brill, 2007.

Pettegree, Andrew, and Matthew Hall. "The Reformation and the Book: A Reconsideration." *The Historical Journal* 47, 4 (December 2004): 785–808.

Peyrefitte, Alain. *The Collision of Two Civilisations: The British Expedition to China in 1792–4*. Translated by Jon Rothschild. London: Harvill, 1993.

Pfaffenberger, Bryan. "The Social Meaning of the Personal Computer: Or, Why the Personal Computer Revolution Was No Revolution." *Anthropological Quarterly* 61, 1 (January 1988): 39–47.

Phillips, Jonathan. *The Crusades, 1095–1194*. Harlow, UK: Longman, 2002.

—. *Holy Warriors: A Modern History of the Crusades*. New York: Random House, 2009.

Phillips, William D., Jr. *Slavery from Roman Times to the Early Transatlantic Trade*. Minneapolis: University of Minnesota Press, 1985.

Phipps, William E. *Clerical Celibacy: The Heritage*. London and New York: Continuum, 2004.

Picardie, Justine. *Coco Chanel: The Legend and the Life*. New York: HarperCollins, 2010.

Pico della Mirandola, Giovanni. *On the Dignity of Man*, excerpted in *The Traditions of the Western World*. Edited by J. H. Hexter et al. Chicago: University of Chicago Press, 1967.

Pincus, Steven C. A. *The Glorious Revolution, 1688–1689: A Brief History with Documents*. Boston: Bedford/St. Martin's, 2006.

—. *1688: The First Modern Revolution*. New Haven and London: Yale University Press, 2009.

Pinderhughes, Dianne M. "Race, the Presidency, and Obama's First Year." In *The Obama Phenomenon: Toward a Multiracial Democracy*. Edited by Charles P. Henry, Robert Allen, and Robert Chrisman. Urbana, Chicago, and Springfield: University of Illinois Press, 2011.

Piper, Franciszek. "The Number of Victims." In *Anatomy of the Auschwitz Death Camp*. Edited by Yisrael Gutman and Michael Berenbaum. Bloomington, IN: Indiana University Press, 1995, 70–2.

Pipes, Richard. *The Russian Revolution*. New York: A. A. Knopf, 1990.

—. *Russia Under the Bolshevik Regime*. New York: Vintage, 1994.

—. *Property and Freedom*. New York: Vintage, 1999.

Plofker, Kim. *Mathematics in India*. Princeton: Princeton University Press, 2009.

Plotkin, Wendy. "Restrictive Covenants." In *Antisemitism: A Historical Encyclopedia of Prejudice and Persecution*, 2 vols. Edited by Richard S. Levy. Santa Barbara, CA: ABC-CLIO, 2005, vol. 1, 597–9.

Poggi, Gianfranco. *The Development of the Modern State: A Sociological Introduction*. Stanford, CA: Stanford University Press, 1978.

—. *The State: Its Nature, Development, and Prospects*. Stanford: Stanford University Press, 1990.

Polo, Marco. *The Travels of Marco Polo*. Translated by Ronald Latham. London: Penguin, 1958.

Pomeranz, Kenneth. *The Great Divergence: Europe, China, and the Making of the Modern World Economy*. Princeton: Princeton University Press, 2000.

Pomeranz, Kenneth, and Steven Topik. *The World That Trade Created: Society, Culture, and the World Economy, 1400 to the Present*, 2nd edn. New York: M. E. Sharpe, 2006.

Pomeroy, Sarah B., Stanley M. Burstein, Walter Donlan, and Jennifer Tolbert Roberts. *Ancient Greece: A Political, Social, and Cultural History*, 2nd edn. New York: Oxford University Press, 2008.

Poos, L. R. *A Rural Society After the Black Death: Essex, 1350–1525*. Cambridge: Cambridge University Press, 1991.

Popofsky, Linda S. "The Crisis over Tonnage and Poundage in Parliament in 1629." *Past & Present* 126 (February 1990): 44–75.

Postgate, J. N. *Early Mesopotamia: Society and Economy at the Dawn of History*. London and New York: Routledge, 1992.

Potts, D. T. "Before Alexandria: Libraries in the Ancient Near East." In *The Library of Alexandria: Centre of Learning in the Ancient World*. Edited by Roy MacLeod. London and New York: I. B. Tauris, 2005, 20.

Prak, Maarten. *The Dutch Republic in the Seventeenth Century: The Golden Age*. Translated by Diane Webb. Cambridge: Cambridge University Press, 2005.

Pretty, Jules N. *Regenerating Agriculture: Policies and Practice for Sustainability and Self-Reliance*. Washington, DC: Joseph Henry Press, 1995.

Price, Miles Oscar, and Harry Bitner. *Effective Legal Research: A Practical Manual of Law Books and Their Use*. Boston: Prentice-Hall, 1953.

Price, Roger. *The Economic Modernisation of France, 1730–1880*. New York and Toronto: Halsted Press, 1975.

Prince, C. "The Historical Context of Arabic Translation, Learning, and the Libraries of Medieval Andalusia." *Library History* 18 (July 2002): 73–87.

Pritchard, Earl H. "Thoughts on the Historical Development of the Population of China." *The Journal of Asian Studies* 23, 1 (November 1963): 3–20.

Prucha, Francis Paul. *The Great Father: The United States Government and the American Indians*, 2 vols. Lincoln, NE: University of Nebraska Press, 1984.
Pryor, John H. (ed.), *Logistics of Warfare in the Age of the Crusades*. Aldershot, UK, and Burlington, VT: Ashgate Publishing, 2006.
Purcell, Brendan. *From Big Bang to Big Mystery: Human Origins in the Light of Creation and Evolution*. Dublin: Veritas Publications, 2011.
Qian, Wen-yuan. *The Great Inertia: Scientific Stagnation in Traditional China*. London and Dover, NH: Croom Helm, 1985.
Quigley, John B. *The Genocide Convention: An International Law Analysis*. Aldershot, UK, and Burlington, VT: Ashgate Publishing, 2006.
—. *Soviet Legal Innovation and the Law of the Western World*. New York: Cambridge University Press, 2007.
Rabinowitch, Alexander. *The Bolsheviks in Power: The First Year of Bolshevik Rule in Petrograd*. Bloomington, IN: Indiana University Press, 2007.
Rabushka, Alvin. *Taxation in Colonial America*. Princeton: Princeton University Press, 2008.
Radjou, Navi, Jaideep Prabhu, and Simone Ahuja. *Jugaad Innovation: Think Frugal, Be Flexible, Generate Breakthrough Growth*. San Francisco: Jossey-Bass, 2012.
Rae, John B. "The Internal Combustion Engine on Wheels." In vol. 2 of *Technology in Western Civilization*, 2 vols. Edited by Melvin Kranzberg and Carroll W. Pursell, Jr. New York: Oxford University Press, 1967a.
—. "The Invention of Invention." In vol. 2 of *Technology in Western Civilization*, 2 vols. Edited by Melvin Kranzberg and Carroll W. Pursell, Jr. New York: Oxford University Press, 1967b.
Raff, Daniel M. G., and Lawrence H. Summers. "Did Henry Ford Pay Efficiency Wages?" *Journal of Labor Economics* 5, 4, pt 2: "The New Economics of Personnel."(October 1987): S57–86.
Ragep, F. J. "Copernicus and His Islamic Predecessors: Some Historical Remarks." *History of Science* 45 (March 2007): 65–81.
Ransom, P. J. G. *The Victorian Railway and How It Evolved*. London: Heinemann, 1990.
Raphael, Ray. *A People's History of the American Revolution: How Common People Shaped the Fight for Independence*. New York: New Press, 2002.
Raymond, Joad (ed.), *News, Newspapers, and Society in Early Modern Britain*. London and Portland, OR: Frank Cass, 1999.
Razzell, Peter. "The Growth of Population in Eighteenth-Century England: A Critical Reappraisal." *The Journal of Economic History* 53, 4 (December 1993): 743–71.
Reader, John. *Potato: A History of the Propitious Esculent*. New Haven and London: Yale University Press 2009.
Rees, Tim, and Andy Thorpe (eds), *International Communism and the Communist International: 1919–43*. Oxford and New York: Oxford University Press, 1998.
Regan, Tom. *The Case For Animal Rights*. Updated with a new preface. Berkeley: University of California Press, 2004.
Reichel, Oswald J. *The See of Rome in the Middle Ages*. London: Longmans, Green, and Co., 1870.
"Religious Views and Beliefs Vary Greatly by Country, According to the Latest Financial Times/Harris Poll." http://www.harrisinteractive.com/news/allnewsbydate.asp?NewsID 5 1131. Accessed 14 September 2010.
Reston, James, Jr. *Galileo: A Life*. New York: HarperCollins, 1994.
Rex, Richard. *The Lollards: Social History in Perspective*. New York: Palgrave, 2002.
Reynolds, Susan. *Fiefs and Vassals: The Medieval Evidence Reinterpreted*. Oxford and New York: Oxford University Press, 1994.
Reynolds, Terry S. *Stronger Than a Hundred Men: A History of the Vertical Water Wheel*. Baltimore and London: The Johns Hopkins University Press, 1983.

Reynolds, Terry S., and Stephen H. Cutcliffe (eds), *Technology and the West: A Historical Anthology from Technology and Culture*. Chicago: University of Chicago Press, 1997.

Richard, Jean. *The Crusades, c. 1071-c. 1291*. Cambridge: Cambridge University Press, 1999.

Richards, John F. *The Mughal Empire*. Cambridge and New York: Cambridge University Press, 1993.

Richards, Martin. "The Neolithic Invasion of Europe." *Annual Review of Anthropology* 32 (2003): 135–62.

Richardson, David. "The British Empire and the Atlantic Slave Trade, 1660–1807." In *The Oxford History of the British Empire*. Vol. 2: *The Eighteenth Century*. Edited by P. J. Marshall. Oxford and New York: Oxford University Press, 1998.

Richardson, Diane. "Constructing Sexual Citizenship: Theorizing Sexual Rights." *Critical Social Policy* 20, 1 (February 2000): 105–35.

Riello, Giorgio. "The Globalization of Cotton Textiles: Indian Cottons, Europe, and the Atlantic World, 1600–1850." In *The Spinning World: A Global History of Cotton Textiles, 1200–1850*. Edited by Giorgio Riello and Prasannan Parthasarathi. Oxford and New York: Oxford University Press, 2009.

Rietbergen, P. *Europe: A Cultural History*. London and New York: Routledge, 1998.

Ringmar, Erik. "Audience for a Giraffe: European Expansionism and the Quest for the Exotic." *Journal of World History* 17 (2006): 375–97.

Rist, Rebecca. *The Papacy and Crusading in Europe, 1198–1245*. London and New York: Continuum, 2009.

Robbins, Helen H. *Our First Ambassador to China; An Account of the Life of George, Earl of Macartney, with Extracts from His Letters, and the Narrative of his Experiences in China, as Told by Himself, 1737–1806, from Hitherto Unpublished Correspondence and Documents*. London: J. Murray, 1908.

Robbins, Keith. *The First World War*. Oxford and New York: Oxford University Press, 2002.

Roberts, J. M. *The Penguin History of Europe*. London: Penguin, 1996.

Roberts, Michael. *Gustavus Adophus: A History of Sweden, 1611–1632*, 2 vols. London: Longmans Green, 1953–58.

Roberts, Priscilla (ed.), *World War II: The Essential Reference Guide*. Santa Barbara, CA: ABC-CLIO, 2012.

Robinson, Francis. "Technology and Religious Change: Islam and the Impact of Print." *Modern Asian Studies* 27 (February 1993): 229–51.

Robinson, James Harvey. *Readings in European History*, 2 vols. Boston: Ginn and Company, 1904–1906.

Robinson, Ronald, and John Gallagher, with Alice Denny. *Africa and the Victorians: The Climax of Imperialism in the Dark Continent*. New York: St. Martin's Press, 1961.

Roeder, Philip G. *Where Nation-States Come From: Institutional Change in the Age of Nationalism*. Princeton: Princeton University Press, 2007.

Rogers, Clifford J. "The Military Revolutions of the Hundred Years' War." *The Journal of Military History* 57 (April 1993): 241–78.

— "The Military Revolution in History and Historiography." In *The Military Revolution Debate: Readings on the Military Transformation of Early Modern Europe*. Edited by Clifford J. Rogers. Boulder, CO: University of Colorado Press, 1995.

— "The Age of the Hundred Years' War." In *Medieval Warfare: A History*. Edited by Maurice Keen. Oxford: Oxford University Press, 1999.

Rogers, Col. George E. "History of Flour Manufacture in Minnesota." *Minnesota Historical Collections*. Vol. 10. St. Paul, MN: Published by the Society, 1905, pp. 35–55.

Roman, Colin A. (ed.), *The Shorter Science and Civilisation in China: An Abridgement of Joseph Needham's Original Text*. Cambridge and New York: Cambridge University Press, 1978–81.

Roman, Stephan. *The Development of Islamic Library Collections in Western Europe and North America*. London and New York: Mansell, 1990.

Romm, James S. *Herodotus*. New Haven and London: Yale University Press, 1998.

Rosen, Lawrence. "Theorizing from Within: Ibn Khaldun and His Political Culture." *Contemporary Sociology* 34 (November 2005): 596–9.

Rosenberg, Chaim M. *America At the Fair: Chicago's 1893 World's Columbian Exposition*. Mount Pleasant, SC: Arcadia Pub., 2008.

—. *The Life and Times of Francis Cabot Lowell, 1775–1817*. Lanham, MD: Lexington Books, 2011.

Rosenberg, Nathan, and L. E. Birdzell, Jr. *How the West Grew Rich: The Economic Transformation of the Industrial World*. New York: Basic Books, 1986.

Rosenstock-Huessy, Eugen. *The Driving Power of Western Civilization: The Christian Revolution of the Middle Ages*. Boston: Beacon Press, 1950.

Rosin, Hanna. "The End of Men." The Atlantic Magazine (July/August 2010), http://www.theatlantic.com/magazine/archive/2010/07/the-end-of-men/8135/. Accessed on 28 June 2010.

Roskell, J. S. "Perspectives in English Parliamentary History." In *Historical Studies of the English Parliament*. Vol. 2: *1399 to 1603*. Edited by E. B. Fryde and Edward Miller. Cambridge: Cambridge University Press, 1970.

Ross, Kristin. *Fast Cars, Clean Bodies: Decolonization and the Reordering of French Culture*. Cambridge, MA: MIT Press, 1995.

Roszak, Theodore. *The Voice of the Earth: An Essay in Ecopsychology*, 2nd edn. Grand Rapids, MI: W. B. Eerdmans Pub. Co.; Manchester: Manchester University Press, 2001.

Rothenburg, Gunther E. *The Art of Warfare in the Age of Napoleon*. Bloomington, IN: Indiana University Press, 1980.

Rothman, David J. "Perfecting the Prison: United States, 1789–1865." In *The Oxford History of the Prison: The Practice of Punishment in Western Society*. Edited by Norval Morris and David J. Rothman. New York: Oxford University Press, 1998, 103.

—. *The Discovery of the Asylum: Social Order and Disorder in the New Republic*. Rev. edn. Piscataway, NJ: Aldine Transaction, 2002.

Rousso, Henry (ed.), *Stalinism and Nazism: History and Memory Compared*. Lincoln, NE, and London: University of Nebraska Press, 2004.

Rowen, Herbert H. *The Princes of Orange: The Stadholders in the Dutch Republic*. Cambridge and New York: Cambridge University Press, 1988.

Rowlands, Guy. *The Dynastic State and the Army under Louis XIV: Royal Service and Private Interest, 1661 to 1701*. Cambridge: Cambridge University Press, 2002.

Rozbicki, Michal Jan. *Culture and Liberty in the Age of the American Revolution*. Charlottesville and London: University of Virginia Press, 2011.

Rozman, Gilbert. "East Asian Urbanization in the Nineteenth Century: Comparisons with Europe." In *Urbanization in History: A Process of Dynamic Interactions*. Edited by Advan der Woude, Akira Hayami, and Jan de Vries. Oxford: Oxford University Press, 1990.

Ruben, Edward. "Judicial Review and the Right to Resist." *Georgetown Law Journal* 96 (2008): 61–118.

Ruden, Sarah. *Paul among the People: The Apostle Reinterpreted and Reimagined in His Own Time*. New York: Pantheon Books, 2010.

Rudolph, Frederick. *The American College and University: A History*, 2nd edn, intro. John R. Thelin. Athens, GA, and London: University of Georgia Press, 1990.

Russell, Peter Edward. *Prince Henry "The Navigator": A Life*. New Haven: Yale University Press, 2000.

Ryan, Donald P. "Papyrus." *The Biblical Archaeologist* 51, 3 (September 1988): 132–40.

Ryan, James. *Lenin's Terror: The Ideological Origins of Early Soviet State Violence*. Abingdon, UK, and New York: Routledge, 2012.
Ryscavage, Paul. *Rethinking the Income Gap: The Second Middle Class Revolution*. New Brunswick, NJ: Transaction Publishers, 2009.
Saenger, Paul. "The Earliest French Resistance Theories: The Role of the Burgundian Court." *The Journal of Modern History* 51, 4 (December 1979): D1225–49.
Sahin, Emrah. "Ottoman Institutions, Capitulations." In *Cultural Sociology of the Middle East, Asia, and Africa: An Encyclopedia*, vol. 1: *Middle East*. Edited by Andrea L. Stanton. Thousand Oaks, CA: SAGE Pub., 2012, 177–9.
Saliba, George. *Islamic Science and the Making of the European Renaissance*. Cambridge, MA: MIT Press, 2007.
Sandoz, Ellis. *A Government of Laws: Political Theory, Religion, and the American Founding*. Columbia, MO: University of Missouri Press, 2001.
Sarton, George. *Hellenistic Science and Culture in the Last Three Centuries B.C.* New York: Dover Pub., 1987.
Savage, Ernest A. *Old English Libraries: The Making, Collection and Use of Books During the Middle Ages*. Teddington, UK: Echo Library, 2006.
Saunders Bernadette J., and Christopher Goddar. *Physical Punishment in Childhood: The Rights of the Child*. Chichester, UK: Wiley-Blackwell, 2010.
Savage-Rumbaugh, S., and R. Lewin. *Kanzi: An Ape at the Brink of the Human Mind*. New York: Wiley, 1994.
Scammell, Geoffery Vaughan. *The World Encompassed: The First European Maritime Empires, c. 800–1650*. Berkeley: University of California Press, 1981.
—. *First Imperial Age: European Overseas Expansion c. 1400–1715*. London and Boston: Unwin Hyman, 1989.
Schall, James V. *At the Limits of Political Philosophy: From "Brilliant Errors" to Things of Uncommon Importance*. Washington, DC: Catholic University of America Press, 1996.
Schama, Simon. *Citizens: A Chronicle of the French Revolution*. New York: A. A. Knopf, 1989.
Scheidel, Walter (ed.), *Rome and China: Comparative Perspectives on Ancient World Empires*. Oxford and New York: Oxford University Press, 2009.
Schiffer, Michael Brian. *Draw the Lightning Down: Benjamin Franklin and Electrical Technology in the Age of Enlightenment*. Berkeley: University of California Press, 2003.
Schimmelpfennig, Bernard. *The Papacy*. Translated by James Sievert. New York: Cambridge University Press, 1992.
Schinkel, Anders. *Conscience and Conscientious Objections*. Amsterdam: Amsterdam University Press, 2007.
Schmidt, Benno C., Jr. *Freedom of the Press vs. Public Access*. New York: Praeger, 1976.
Schmitt, Carl. "The Concept of the Political." *The Weimar Republic Sourcebook*. Edited by Anton Kaes, Martín Jay, and Edward Dimendberg. Berkeley and Los Angeles: University of California Press, 1994.
Schmitt, Charles B., and Quentin Skinner (eds), *The Cambridge History of Renaissance Philosophy*. Cambridge: Cambridge University Press, 1988.
Schneirov, Matthew. *The Dream of a New Social Order: Popular Magazines in America, 1893–1914*. New York: Columbia University Press, 1994.
Schoenberg, Bruce S. "Coke's the One: The Centennial of the 'Ideal Brain Tonic' That Became a Symbol of America." *Southern Medical Journal* 81 (January 1988): 69–74.
Schoff, James L. "Changing Perceptions of Extended Deterrence in Japan." In *Strategy in the Second Nuclear Age: Power, Ambition, and the Ultimate Weapon*. Edited by Toshi Yoshihara and James R. Holmes. Washington, DC: Georgetown University Press, 2012, 100.
Schofield, Louise. *The Mycenaeans*. London and Los Angeles: J. Paul Getty Museum, 2007.

Schofield, Robert E. *The Lunar Society of Birmingham: A Social History of Provincial Science and Industry in Eighteenth-Century England*. Oxford: Oxford University Press, 1963.
Schwartz, Evan I. *The Last Lone Inventor: A Tale of Genius, Deceit, and the Birth of Television*. New York: HarperCollins, 2002.
Schwarz, Fred. "The Uncertainty Principle: America Dominates Science with a Classic American Formula: Freedom." *National Review* (21 December 2009): 26–7.
Schwoerer, Lois G. *"No Standing Armies!" The Antiarmy Ideology in Seventeenth-Century England*. Baltimore: John Hopkins University Press, 1974.
Scott, Anne Firor. *Natural Allies: Women's Associations in American History*. Urbana and Chicago: University of Illinois Press, 1993.
Searing, James F. *West African Slavery and Atlantic Commerce: The Senegal River Valley, 1700–1860*. Cambridge: Cambridge University Press, 1993.
Seccombe, Wally. *A Millennium of Family Change: Feudalism to Capitalism in Northwestern Europe*. London: Verso, 1992.
Sedlar, Jean W. *East Central Europe in the Middle Ages, 1000–1500*. Seattle: University of Washington Press, 1994.
Sen, Amartya. *Development as Freedom*. New York: A.A. Knopf, 1999.
—. "East and West: The Reach of Reason." *New York Review of Books* 47, 12 (20 July 2000): 33–8.
Service, Robert. *Stalin: A Biography*. Cambridge, MA: Harvard University Press, 2005.
Setton, Kenneth M. and Marshall W. Baldwin. *A History of the Crusades*, 6 vols. Vol. 1: *The First Hundred Years*, 2nd edn. Madison, MI: University of Wisconsin Press, 2006.
Shakoor, Abida. *Origins of Modern Europe: Medieval National Consciousness*. Edited by Q. Z. Hasan and Hajira Kumar. Delhi: Aakar Books, 2004.
Shank, J. B. *The Newton Wars and the Beginning of the French Enlightenment*. Chicago: University of Chicago Press, 2008.
Sharer, Robert J., and Loa P. Traxler. *The Ancient Maya*, 6th edn. Stanford: Stanford University Press, 2006.
Sharlin, Harold I. *The Making of the Electrical Age: From the Telegraph to Automation*. London and New York: Abelard-Schuman, 1963.
Sharma, R. S. *India's Ancient Past*. New Delhi: Oxford University Press, 2005.
Sharratt, Michael. *Galileo: Decisive Innovator*. Cambridge: Cambridge University Press, 1994.
Shatzmiller, Maya. "Aspects of Women's Participation in the Economic Life of Later Medieval Islam: Occupations and Mentalities." *Arabica* 35 (March 1988): 36–58.
—. *Labour in the Medieval Islamic World*. Leiden, The Netherlands, and New York: E. J. Brill, 1994.
—. *Her Day in Court: Women's Property Rights in Fifteenth-Century Granada*. Cambridge, MA: Harvard University Press, 2007.
Shea, William R. *The Magic of Numbers and Motion: The Scientific Career of Rene Descartes*. Canton, MA: Science History Publications, 1991.
Shea, William R., and Mariano Artigas. *Galileo in Rome: The Rise and Fall of a Troublesome Genius*. Oxford and New York: Oxford University Press, 2003.
Sheehan, James J. *Where Have All the Soldiers Gone?: The Transformation of Modern Europe*. Boston: Houghton Mifflin, 2008.
Sheffield, Suzanne Le-May. *Women and Science: Social Impact and Interaction*. New Brunswick, NJ: Rutgers University Press, 2006.
Shepard, Jonathan (ed.), *The Cambridge History of the Byzantine Empire c. 500–1492*. Cambridge: Cambridge University Press, 2008.
Shephard, Sue. *Pickled, Potted, and Canned: How the Art and Science of Food Preserving Changed the World*. New York: Simon & Schuster, 2001.

Showalter, Dennis E., and William J. Astore. *Soldiers' Lives Through History: The Early Modern World*. Westport, CT: Greenwood, 2007.

Shrikhande, Malati. "Taxila: The Seat of Learning in Ancient India." In *Encyclopaedia of Higher Education: The Indian Perspective*, 5 vols. Vol. 1: *Historical Survey—Pre-Independence Period*. Edited by Suresh Kant Sharma and Usha Sharma. New Delhi: Mittal Publications, 2005.

Shrimplin, Valérie. *Sun-Symbolism and Cosmology in Michelangelo's Last Judgment*. Kirksville, MO: Truman State University Press, 2000.

Sigmund, Paul E., Jr. "The Influence of Marsilius of Padua on XVth-Century Conciliarism." *Journal of the History of Ideas* 23 (July–September 1962): 392–402.

Silver, Morris. *Economic Structures of Antiquity*. Westport, CT: Greenwood Press, 1995.

Silverman, Mark P. *Quantum Superposition: Counterintuitive Consequences of Coherence, Entanglement, and Interference*. Berlin and Heidelberg: Springer, 2010.

Singer, Charles, E. J., Holmyard, A. R. Hall, and Trevor I. Williams (eds), *A History of Technology*. Vol. 4: *The Industrial Revolution, 1750–1850*. New York and London: Oxford Clarendon Press, 1958.

Singer, P. W. *Wired for War: The Robotics Revolution and Conflict in the Twenty-first Century*. London: Penguin Books, 2009.

Sivin, Nathan. "Science and Medicine in Imperial China: The State of the Field." *The Journal of Asian Studies* 47 (February 1988): 41–90.

—. "Why the Scientific Revolution Did Not Take Place in China – or Didn't It?" In *Science in Ancient China: Researches and Reflections*. Aldershott, UK, and Brookfield, VT: Variorum, 1995.

Skinner, Quentin. *The Foundations of Modern Political Thought*, 2 vols. Cambridge: Cambridge University Press, 1978.

—. "The Italian City-Republics." In *Democracy: The Unfinished Journey, 508 BC to AD 1993*. Edited by John Dunn. Oxford: Oxford University Press, 1992.

Sklar, Kathryn Kish. *Catharine Beecher: A Study in American Domesticity*. New York: W. W. Norton & Company, 1976.

Skrabec, Quentin R., Jr. *George Westinghouse: Gentle Genius*. New York: Algora Pub., 2007.

Smil, Vaclav. *Creating the Twentieth Century: Technical Innovations of 1867–1914 and Their Lasting Impact*. Oxford: Oxford University Press, 2005.

—. *Prime Movers of Globalization: The History and Impact of Diesel Engines and Gas Turbines*. Cambridge: Cambridge University Press, 2010.

Smith, Andrew F. *Eating History: 30 Turning Points in the Making of American Cuisine*. New York: Columbia University Press, 2009.

Smith, David C. "Wood Pulp and Newspapers, 1867–1900." *The Business History Review* 38, 3 (Autumn 1964): 328–45.

Smith, Hedrick. *The Russians*. New York: Times Books, 1985.

Smith, Hilda L. "Women as Sextons and Electors: King's Bench and Precedents for Women's Suffrage." In *Women Writers and the Early Modern British Political Tradition*. Edited by Hilda L. Smith. Cambridge: Cambridge University Press, 1998.

Smith, Jane I. "Islam and Christendom: Historical, Cultural, and Religious Interaction from the Seventh to the Fifteenth Centuries." In *The Oxford History of Islam*. Edited by John L. Esposito. Oxford and New York: Oxford University Press, 1999, 329.

Smith, Lacey Baldwin. *Fools, Martyrs, Traitors: The Story of Martyrdom in the Western World*. Evanston, IL: Northwestern University Press, 1999.

Smith, Thomas M. "Origins of the Computer." In vol. 2 of *Technology in Western Civilization*, 2 vols. Edited by Melvin Kranzberg and Carroll W. Pursell, Jr. New York: Oxford University Press, 1967a.

—. "The Development of Aviation." In vol. 2 of *Technology in Western Civilization*, 2 vols. Edited by Melvin Kranzberg and Carroll W. Pursell, Jr. New York: Oxford University Press, 1967b.

Smith, Vincent A. *The Oxford History of India*, 4th edn. Edited by Percival Spear. Oxford: Oxford University Press, 1981.

Smith, Woodruff D. "Complications of the Commonplace: Tea, Sugar, and Imperialism." *Journal of Interdisciplinary History* 23, 2 (Autumn 1992): 259–78.

Smith, Lesley Janette, and Jane H. M. Taylor (eds), *Women, the Book, and the Godly: Selected Proceedings of the St. Hilda's Conference, 1993*. Woodbridge, UK, and Rochester, NY: Boydell & Brewer, 1995.

Sneader, Walter. "The Discovery of Aspirin: A Reappraisal." *British Medical Journal* 321 (23–30 December 2000): 1591–4.

Snyder, Timothy D. *Bloodlands: Europe Between Hitler and Stalin*. New York: Basic Books, 2010.

Sohn, Pow-key. "Early Korean Printing." *Journal of the American Oriental Society* 79 (April–June 1959): 96–103.

Sokoloff, Kenneth L., and David Dollar. "Agricultural Seasonality and the Organization of Manufacturing in Early Industrial Economies: The Contrast Between England and the United States." *The Journal of Economic History* 57, 2 (June 1997): 288–321.

Solomon, Barbara Miller. *In the Company of Educated Women: A History of Women and Higher Education in America*. New Haven: Yale University Press, 1985.

Solomou, Solomos. *Phases of Economic Growth, 1850–1973: Kondratieff Waves and Kuznets Swings*. Cambridge: Cambridge University Press, 1987.

Sonea, Sorin, and Léo G. Mathieu. *Prokaryotology: A Coherent View*. Montreal: McGill-Queen's University Press, 2000.

Sonneborn, Liz. *Chronology of American Indian History*. Rev. edn. New York: Facts On File, 2007.

Sourdel, D. "The 'Abbisid Caliphate.'" In *The Cambridge History of Islam*. Vol. 1A: *The Central Islamic Lands from Pre-Islamic Times to the First World War*. Edited by P. M. Holt, Ann K. S. Lambton, and Bernard Lewis. Cambridge: Cambridge University Press, 1970.

Southall, Aidan. *The City in Time and Space*. Cambridge and New York: Cambridge University Press, 1998.

Speake, Jennifer (ed.), *Literature of Travel and Exploration: An Encyclopedia*. New York: Fitzroy Dearborn, 2003.

"Special Report: China and the Internet." *The Economist* (6 April 2013): 3–16.

Spence, Jonathan D. *The Search for Modern China*, 2nd edn. New York and London: W. W. Norton & Company, 1999.

Spencer, Colin. *British Food: An Extraordinary Thousand Years of History*. London: Grub Street, 2002.

Sperber, Jonathan. *The European Revolutions, 1848–1851*, 2nd edn. Cambridge: Cambridge University Press, 2005.

Sperling, Valerie. "Making the Public Patriotic: Militarism and Anti-Militarism in Russia." In *Russian Nationalism and the National Reassertion of Russia*. Edited by Marlène Laruelle. Abingdon, UK, and New York: Routledge, 2009, 229.

Spierenburg, Peter. *The Spectacle of Suffering: Executions and the Evolution of Repression: From a Preindustrial Metropolis to the European Experience*. Cambridge: Cambridge University Press, 1984.

Spitz, Lewis W. "The Philosophy of Conrad Celtis, German Arch-Humanist." *Studies in the Renaissance* 1 (1954): 22–37.

Spuler, Bertold. *History of the Mongols: Based on Eastern and Western Accounts of the Thirteenth and Fourteenth Centuries*. Translated from the German by Helga and Stuart Drummond. Berkeley and Los Angeles: University of California Press, 1972.

Stacey, John. *John Wyclif and Reform*. Philadelphia: Westminister Press, 1964.

Stadtwald, Kurt. *Roman Popes and German Patriots: Antipapalism in the Politics of the German Humanist Movement from Gregor Heimburg to Martin Luther*. Geneva: Librairie Droz, 1996.

Staff, Frank. *The Penny Post, 1680–1918*. London: Lutterworth Press, 1964.

Stagl, Justin. *A History of Curiosity: The Theory of Travel, 1550–1800*. Chur, Switzerland: Harwood Academic Publishers, 1995.

Standage, Tom. *The Victorian Internet: The Remarkable Story of the Telegraph and the Nineteenth Century's On-line Pioneers*. New York: Walker and Co., 1998.

—. *An Edible History of Humanity*. New York: Walker, 2009.

Stannard, David E. *American Holocaust: Columbus and the Conquest of the New World*. New York: Oxford University Press, 1992.

Stark, Rodney. *The Rise of Christianity: A Sociologist Reconsiders History*. Princeton: Princeton University Press, 1996.

—. *For the Glory of God: How Monotheism Led to Reformations, Science, Witch-hunts, and the End of Slavery*. Princeton: Princeton University Press, 2003.

—. *The Victory of Reason: How Christianity Led to Freedom, Capitalism, and Western Success*. New York: Random House, 2005.

Starr, Chester. *A History of the Ancient World*. New York: Oxford University Press, 1965.

Statistics in United States. Bureau of the Census, *Statistical History of the United States from Colonial Times to the Present*. Stamford, CT: Fairfield Publishers, 1965.

Stearns, Peter N. *European Society in Upheaval: Social History since 1750*. New York: The Macmillan Company, 1967.

—. *Western Civilization in World History*. New York and London: Routledge, 2003.

Steffes, Tracy L. *School, Society, and State: A New Education to Govern Modern America, 1890–1940*. Chicago and London: University of Chicago Press, 2012.

Steinberg, S. H. *Five Hundred Years of Printing*, 3rd edn. Hamondsworth, UK, and Baltimore: British Library, 1974.

Steinberg, Stephen. *The Ethnic Myth: Race, Ethnicity, and Class in America*, 3rd edn. Boston: Beacon Press, 2001.

Steinisch, Irmgard. "A Different Path to War: A Comparative Study of Militarism and Imperialism in the United States and Imperial Germany, 1871–1914." In *Anticipating Total War: The German and American Experiences, 1871–1914*. Edited by Manfred F. Boemeke, Roger Chickering, and Stig Förster. Cambridge: Cambridge University Press, 1999, 36–7.

Steinweis, Alan E. *Kristallnacht 1938*. Cambridge, MA: Harvard University Press, 2009.

Stern, Robert. *Routledge Philosophy Guidebook to Hegel and the Phenomenology of Spirit*. London and New York: Routledge, 2002.

Stewart, James Brewer. *Holy Warriors: The Abolitionists and American Slavery*. Rev. edn. New York: Hill and Wang, 1997.

Stinger, Charles L. *The Renaissance in Rome*. Bloomington, IN: Indiana University Press, 1998.

Stone, Bailey. *The Genesis of the French Revolution: A Global-Historical Interpretation*. Cambridge: Cambridge University Press, 1994.

Stone, Irving. *The Global Export of Capital from Great Britain, 1865–1914: A Statistical Survey*. Basingstoke, UK, and New York: St. Martin's Press, 1999.

Stone, John. "Technology, Society, and the Infantry Revolution of the Fourteenth Century." *The Journal of Military History* 68 (April 2004): 361–80.

Story, Joanna (ed.), *Charlemagne: Empire and Society*. Manchester and New York: Manchester University Press, 2005.
Strathen, Paul. *Mendeleyev's Dream: The Quest for the Elements*. London: Hamish Hamilton, 2000.
Strauss, Gerald. "Liberal or Illiberal Arts?" *Journal of Social History* 19, 2 (Winter 1985): 361–7.
Strauss, Walter L. (ed.), *The Complete Engravings, Etchings and Drypoints of Albrecht Durer*. Miseola, NY: Courier Dover Publications, 1972.
Straw, Carole E. *Gregory the Great: Perfection in Imperfection*. Berkeley: University of California Press, 1988.
Streeter, Tom. *The Church and Western Culture: An Introduction to Church History*. Bloomington, IN: Indiana University Press, 2008.
Strieder, Jacob, and Mildred L. Hartsough. *Jacob Fugger the Rich: Merchant and Banker of Augsburg, 1459–1525*. Edited by Norman Scott and Brien Gras. Translated by Mildred L. Hartsough. New York: Beard Books, 2001.
Stringer, Chris. *The Origin of Our Species*. London: Allen Lane, 2011.
Subhi Y. Labib, "Capitalism in Medieval Islam." *The Journal of Economic History* 29, 1 (March 1969): 79–96.
Suisman, David. *Selling Sounds: The Commercial Revolution in American Music*. Cambridge, MA: Harvard University Press, 2009.
Sumumu, Ishii. "The Decline of the Kamakura Bakufu." In *The Cambridge History of Japan*, vol. 3: *Medieval Japan*. Edited by Kozo Yamamura. Cambridge: Cambridge University Press, 1990, 131–48.
Suri, Jeremi. *The Global Revolutions of 1968*. New York: W. W. Norton & Company, 2007.
Sutherland, D. M. G. *France, 1789–1815: Revolution and Counterrevolution*. New York: Oxford University Press, 1986.
Taiwo, Olufemi. *How Colonialism Preempted Modernity in Africa*. Bloomington, IN: Indiana University Press, 2010.
Tallett, Frank. *War and Society in Early-Modern Europe, 1495–1715*. London and New York: Routledge, 1992.
Tappert, Theodore G., ed. and trans. *The Augsburg Confession*. Minneapolis: Augsburg Publishing House, 1980.
Tarnas, Richard. *The Passion of the Western Mind: Understanding the Ideas That Have Shaped Our World*. New York: Ballantine Books, 1991.
Tassinari, Fabrizio. *Why Europe Fears Its Neighbors*. Santa Barbara, CA: Praeger Security International, 2009.
Taylor, Alan. *American Colonies: The Settling of North America*. New York: Viking, 2001.
Teng, Ssu-yu. "Chinese Influence on the Western Examination System." *Harvard Journal of Asiatic Studies* 7 (1942–43): 267–312.
Thapar, Romila. *Early India: From the Origins to AD 1300*. Berkeley and Los Angeles: University of California Press, 2004.
The State of World Fisheries and Aquaculture 2004. Rome: Food and Agriculture Organization of the United Nations, 2004.
The World Bank. *World Development Indicators*. Washington, DC: World Bank, 2012.
Thernstrom, Stephan, and Abigail Thernstrom. *America in Black and White: One Nation, Indivisible*. New York: Simon & Schuster, 1997.
Thistle, Susan. *From Marriage to the Market: The Transformation of Women's Lives and Work*. Berkeley and Los Angeles: University of California Press, 2006.
Thomas, Hugh. *The Slave Trade: The Story of the Atlantic Slave Trade, 1440–1870*. New York: Simon & Schuster, 1997.

Thomas, R. P., and D. N. McCloskey. "Overseas Trade and Empire, 1700–1860." In *The Economic History of Britain since 1700*. Vol. 1: 1700–1860. Edited by Roderick Floud and Donald McCloskey. Cambridge: Cambridge University Press, 1981.

Thompson, Holland. *The Age of Invention: A Chronicle of Mechanical Conquest*. New Haven: Yale University Press, 1921.

Thornton, Russell. *American Indian Holocaust and Survival: A Population History Since 1492*. Norman, OK: University of Oklahoma Press, 1987.

Tickle, Phyllis. *The Divine Hours: Prayers for Autumn and Wintertime: A Manual for Prayer*. New York: Doubleday Religious Publishing Group, 2006.

Tierney, Brian. *The Crisis of Church and State, 1050–1300: With Selected Documents*. Toronto: University of Toronto Press, 1988.

Tillman, Barrett. *Whirlwind: The Air War Against Japan, 1942–1945*. New York: Simon & Schuster, 2010.

Tismaneanu, Vladimir (ed.), *Stalinism Revisited: The Establishment of Communist Regimes in East-Central Europe*. Budapest and New York: Central European University Press, 2009.

—. *The Devil in History: Communism, Fascism, and Some Lessons of the Twentieth Century*. Berkeley and Los Angeles: University of California Press, 2012.

Tocqueville, Alexis, de. *Democracy in America*. Translated by George Lawrence. Edited by J. P. Mayer. Garden City, NY: Doubleday, 1969.

Todorov, Tzvetan. "European Identity." Translated by Nathan Bracher, *South Central Review* 25 (Fall 2008): 3–15.

Tomlins, Christopher L. *Freedom Bound: Law, Labor, and Civic Identity in Colonizing English America, 1580–1865*. New York: Cambridge University Press, 2010.

Tomlinson, B. R. "Economics and Empire: The Periphery and the Imperial Economy." In *The Oxford History of the British Empire*, vol. 3: *The Nineteenth Century*. Edited by Andrew Porter. Oxford and New York: Oxford University Press, 1999, 73.

Tomory, Leslie. *Progressive Enlightenment: The Origins of the Gaslight Industry, 1780–1820*. Cambridge, MA: MIT Press, 2012.

Tout, Thomas Frederick. *The Empire and the Papacy, 918–1273*. London: Rivingtons, 1903.

Toynbee, Arnold J. *A Study of History*, abridgement of Volumes I–VI by D. C. Somervell. Oxford: Oxford University Press, 1946.

Treadgold, Warren (ed.), *Renaissance Before the Renaissance: Cultural Revivals of Late Antiquity and the Middle Ages*. Stanford, CA: Stanford University Press, 1984.

Trehane, R. F. "The Nature of Parliament in the Reign of Henry III." In *Historical Studies of the English Parliament*. Vol. 1: *Origins to 1399*. Edited by E. B. Fryde and Edward Miller. Cambridge: Cambridge University Press, 1970.

Tsien, Tsuen-Hsuin. *Written on Bamboo and Silk: The Beginnings of Chinese Books and Inscriptions*, afterward by Edward L. Shaughnessy. Chicago and London: University of Chicago Press, 2004.

Tucker, Robert C. *Stalin in Power: the Revolution from Above, 1928–1941* (New York and London: W. W. Norton & Company, 1990).

Tuner, Edward Raymond. "The Women's Suffrage Movement in England." *The American Political Science Review* 7, 4 (November 1913): 588–609.

Turnbull, Robert G. *The* Parmenides *and Plato's Late Philosophy*. Toronto: University of Toronto Press, 1998.

Turchin, Peter, and Sergey A. Nefedov. *Secular Cycles*. Princeton: Princeton University Press, 2009.

Turner, Jack. *Spice: The History of a Temptation*. New York: A. A. Knopf, 2004.

Turner, James. *Reckoning with the Beast: Animals, Pain, and Humanity in the Victorian Mind*. Baltimore: The Johns Hopkins University Press, 1980.

Turner, M. E., J. V. Beckett, and B. Afton. *Farm Production in England 1700–1914*. Oxford: Oxford University Press, 2001.

Twitchet, Denis C. (ed.), *The Cambridge History of China*, vol. 3, pt. 1: *Sui and T'ang China, 589–906 AD*. Cambridge: Cambridge University Press, 1980.

Twitchett, Denis, and Frederick Mote (eds), *The Cambridge History of China*, vols. 7–8: *The Ming Dynasty, 1368–1644*. Cambridge: Cambridge University Press, 1988–98.

Twitchett, Denis, and Michael Loewe (eds), *The Cambridge History of China*, vol. 1: *The Ch'in and Han Empires, 221 BC–AD 220*. Cambridge: Cambridge University Press, 1987.

Twitchett, Denis, and Paul Jakov Smith (eds), *The Cambridge History of China*, vol. 5: *The Sung Dynasty and its Precursors, 907–1279*. Cambridge: Cambridge University Press, 2009.

Tyerman, Christopher. *God's War: A New History of the Crusades*. Cambridge, MA: Harvard University Press, 2006.

Udovitch, Abraham L. *Partnership and Profit in Medieval Islam*. Princeton: Princeton University Press, 1970.

Ueda, Kenichi. *Life Expectancy and Income Convergence in the World: A Dynamic General Equilibrium Analysis*. Washington, DC: International Monetary Fund, 2008.

Underdown, David. *Pride's Purge: Politics in the Puritan Revolution*. Oxford: Oxford University Press, 1971.

Underwood, Doug. *From Yahweh to Yahoo!: The Religious Roots of the Secular Press*. Urbana: University of Illinois Press, 2002.

United States, Bureau of Foreign and Domestic Commerce. *Statistical Abstract of the United States*. Washington, DC: Government Printing Office, 1913.

United States, Bureau of the Census. *Current Population Reports: Special Studies*, Issue 46 (July 1973).

United States, Bureau of the Census. Table A1, "Years of School Completed by People 25 Years and Over, by Age and Sex: Selected Years 1940 to 2008," http://www.census.gov/population/socdemo/education/cps2008/tabA-1.csv. Accessed 10 December 2009.

Usher, Abbott Payson. *A History of Mechanical Inventions*. Boston: Beacon Press, 1959.

Uyar, Mesut, and Edward J. Erickson. *A Military History of the Ottomans: From Osman to Atatürk*. Santa Barbara, CA: Praeger Security International/ABC-CLIO, 2009.

Vaggi, Gianni, and Peter Groenewegen. *A Concise History of Economic Thought: From Mercantilism to Monetarism*. Houndmills, UK, and New York: Palgrave Macmillan, 2003.

Vallance, Edward. *Revolutionary England and the National Covenant: State Oaths, Protestantism, and the Political Nation, 1553–1682*. Woodbridge, UK: Boydell Press, 2005.

Van Dam, Raymond. "Merovingian Gaul and the Frankish Conquests." In *The New Cambridge Medieval History*, vol. 1: *c.500-c.700*. Edited by Paul Fouracre. Cambridge: Cambridge University Press, 2005.

Van Laarhoven, J. "Thou Shalt not Slay a Tyrant! The So-called Theory of John of Salisbury." In *The World of John of Salisbury*. Edited by M. Wilkes. Oxford: Oxford University Press, 1984.

Van Neirop, H. F. K. *The Nobility of Holland: From Knights to Regents 1500–1650*. Cambridge: Cambridge University Press, 1993.

Van Nieuwenhove, Rik. *An Introduction to Medieval Theology*. Cambridge: Cambridge University Press, 2012.

van Nimwegen, Olaf. *The Dutch Army and the Military Revolutions, 1588–1688*. Translated by Andrew May. Woodbridge, UK, and Rochester, NY: Boydell Press, 2010.

Venarde, Bruce L. *Women's Monasticism and Medieval Society: Nunneries in France and England, 890–1215*. Ithaca: Cornell University Press, 1997.

Venchi, Innocenzo, et al. (eds), *Fra Angelico and the Chapel of Nicholas V.* Photographs of the Chapel by Alessandro Bracchetti et al. Vatican City State: Edizioni Musei Vaticani, 1999.

Vandervort, Bruce. *Wars of Imperial Conquest in Africa, 1830–1914*. London: UCL Press, 1998.

VanDrunen, David. *Natural Law and the Two Kingdoms: A Study in the Development of Reformed Social Thought*. Grand Rapids, MI: W. B. Eerdmans Pub. Co., 2010.

Verbruggen, J. F. *The Art of Warfare in Western Europe during the Middle Ages from the Eighth Century to 1340*, 2nd edn. Woodbridge, UK: The Boydell Press, 1997.

Vickery, Paul S. *Bartolome de Las Casas: Great Prophet of the Americas*. New York: Paulist Press, 2006.

Vise, David A., and Mark Malseed. *The Google Story: For Google's 10th Birthday*. New York: Random House, 2008.

Vo, Nghia M. *Vietnamese Boat People, 1954 and 1975–1992*. Jefferson, NC, and London: McFarland & Co, 2006.

Voelkel, James R. *Johannes Kepler and the New Astronomy*. New York: Oxford University Press, 1999.

Volo, Dorothy Denneen, and James M. Volo. *Daily Life in the Age of Sail*. Westport, CT: Greenwood Press, 2002.

Von Hagen, Victor W. "Paper and Civilization." *The Scientific Monthly* 57, 4 (October 1943): 301–14.

—. *The Aztec and Maya Papermakers*. Mineola, NY: Dover Pub., 1999.

Vries, P. H. H. "Are Coal and Colonies Really Crucial? Kenneth Pomeranz and the Great Divergence." *Journal of World History* 12 (Fall 2001): 407–46.

Wade, Rex. *The Russian Revolution, 1917*, 2nd edn. New York: Cambridge University Press, 2005.

Wagner, Donald B. "The Administration of the Iron Industry in Eleventh-Century China." *Journal of the Economic and Social History of the Orient* 44, 2 (2001): 175–97.

Walicki, Andrzej. *Marxism and the Leap to the Kingdom of Freedom: The Rise and Fall of the Communist Utopia*. Stanford: Stanford University Press, 1995.

Wallace, Anthony F. C. *Jefferson and the Indians: The Tragic Fate of the First Americans*. Cambridge, MA: Harvard University Press, 1999.

Wallace, Peter George. *The Long European Reformation: Religion, Political Conflict, and the Search for Conformity, 1350–1750*. Basingstoke, UK, and New York: Palgrave Macmillan, 2004.

Wallace, William E., "'Dal disegno allo spazio': Michelangelo's Drawings for the Fortifications of Florence." *The Journal of the Society of Architectural Historians* 46 (June 1987): 119–34.

Wallerstein, Immanuel. *The Modern World-System I. Capitalist Agriculture and the Origins of the European World-Economy in the Sixteenth Century*. New York: Academic Press, 1974.

Wallert, A. "The Reconstruction of Papyrus Manufacture: A Preliminary Investigation." *Studies in Conservation* 34, 1 (February 1989): 1–8.

Walls, Jerry L. *Purgatory: The Logic of Total Transformation*. Oxford and New York: Oxford University Press, 2012.

Wanniski, Jude. *The Way the World Works*. Washington, DC: Regnery Gateway, 1998.

Ward, Geoffrey C. *Unforgivable Blackness: The Rise and Fall of Jack Johnson*. New York: A. A. Knopf, 2004.

Waring, George H. "The Silver Miners of the Erzgebirge and the Peasants' War of 1525 in the Light of Recent Research." *The Sixteenth Century Journal* 18, 2 (Summer 1987): 231–47.

Warraq, Ibn. *Defending the West: A Critique of Edward Said's Orientalism*. Amherst, NY: Prometheus Books, 2007.

Watson, Peter. *Ideas: A History of Thought and Invention, from Fire to Freud*. New York: HarperCollins, 2005.

—. *The German Genius: Europe's Third Renaissance, the Second Scientific Revolution, and the Twentieth Century*. New York: HarperCollins, 2011.

Watt, W. Montgomery, trans. *The Faith and Practice of Al-Ghazali*. Oxford: Oxford University Press, 1998.

Weaver, John C. *The Great Land Rush and the Making of the Modern World, 1650–1900*. Montreal and Kingston: McGill-Queen's University Press, 2006.

Webb, Diana. *Pilgrims and Pilgrimage in the Medieval West*. London and New York: I. B. Tauris, 1999.

Webb, Walter Prescott. *The Great Plains*. Boston: Houghton Mifflin, 1931.

Webber, Stephen L. "Introduction: The Society-Military Interface in Russia." In *Military and Society in Post-Soviet Russia*. Edited by Stephen L. Webber and Jennifer G. Mathers. Manchester and New York: Manchester University Press, 2006.

Weber, Max. *The Protestant Ethic and the Spirit of Capitalism*. Translated by Talcott Parsons, introduction by Anthony Giddens. New York: C. Scribner, 1958.

Wedgewood, C. V. *The Thirty Years' War*. New York: Anchor, 1961.

Weinberg, Bennett Alan, and Bonnie K. Bealer. *The World of Caffeine: The Science and Culture of the World's Most Popular Drug*. New York and London: Routledge, 2002.

Weissmann, Gerald. "Citizen Pinel and the Madman at Bellevue." *The FASEB Journal* 22 (May 2008): 1289–93.

Weinberg, Gerhard L. *A World at Arms: A Global History of World War II*, 2nd edn. Cambridge: Cambridge University Press, 2005.

Weissenbacher, Manfred. *Sources of Power: How Energy Forges Human History*, 2 vols in 1. Santa Barbara, CA: ABC-CLIO, 2009.

Wellbery, David E., Judith Ryan, and Hans Ulrich Gumbrecht. *A New History of German Literature*. Cambridge, MA: Belknap Press, 2004.

Wells, Samuel. *Christian Ethics: An Introductory Reader*. Chichester, UK: Wiley-Blackwell, 2010.

Werth, Nicolas. "The Mechanism of a Mass Crime: The Great Terror in the Soviet Union, 1937–1938." In *The Specter of Genocide: Mass Murder in Historical Perspective*. Edited by Robert Gellately and Ben Kiernan. New York: Cambridge University Press, 2003.

West, John B. "Robert Boyle's Landmark Book of 1660 with the First Experiments on Rarified Air." *Journal of Applied Physiology* 98 (2005): 31–9.

—. "Ibn al-Nafis, the Pulmonary Circulation, and the Islamic Golden Age." *Journal of Applied Physiology* 105 (December 2008): 1877–80.

Westwood, J. N. *Russia Against Japan, 1904–1905: A New Look at the Russo-Japanese War*. Albany: State University of New York Press, 1986.

Wettig, Gerhard. *Stalin and the Cold War in Europe: The Emergence and Development of East-West Conflict, 1939–1953*. Lanham, MD: Rowman and Littlefield, 2008.

"What Causes Ocean 'Dead Zones'?" (Scientific American 25 September 2012), http://www.scientificamerican.com/article.cfm?id5ocean-dead-zones (accessed 14 June 2013).

White, Lynn, Jr. "The Act of Invention: Causes, Contexts, Continuities and Consequences." *Technology and Culture* 3 (Autumn 1962a): 486–500.

—. *Medieval Technology and Social Change*. London: Oxford University Press, 1962b.

—. *Machina ex Deo: Essays in the Dynamism of Western Culture*. Cambridge, MA: Harvard University Press, 1968.

White, Michael. *Isaac Newton: The Last Sorcerer*. Reading, MA: Perseus Books, 1999.

Whitehead, Alfred North. *Science and the Modern World*, 2nd edn. Cambridge: Cambridge University Press, 1932.

Whitfield, Susan. *Life Along the Silk Road*. Berkeley and Los Angeles: University of California Press, 1999.

Whitman, Mark (ed.), *Removing a Badge of Slavery: The Record of Brown v. Board of Education*. Princeton: Princeton University Press, 1993.

Whitney, Elspeth. *Medieval Science and Technology*. Greenwood, CT: Greenwood Press, 2004.

Wiesner, Merry E. *Women and Gender in Early Modern Europe*, 2nd edn. Cambridge and New York: Cambridge University Press, 2000.

—. *Early Modern Europe, 1450–1789*, 2nd edn. Cambridge and New York: Cambridge University Press, 2013.

Wigelsworth, Jeffrey R. *Selling Science in the Age of Newton: Advertising and the Commoditization of Knowledge*. Farnham, UK, and Burlington, VT: Ashgate Publishing, 2010.

Wik, Reynold M. "Mechanization of the American Farm." In vol. 2 of *Technology in Western Civilization*, 2 vols. Edited by Melvin Kranzberg and Carroll W. Pursell, Jr. New York: Oxford University Press, 1967.

Wildes, Karl L., and Nilo A. Lindgren. *A Century of Electrical Engineering and Computer Science at MIT, 1882–1982*. Cambridge, MA: MIT Press, 1985.

Wildman, Allan K. *The End of the Russian Imperial Army*, 2 vols. Princeton: Princeton University Press, 1980–87.

Wiliamson, Jeffrey G. *Coping with City Growth during the British Industrial Revolution*. New York: Cambridge University Press, 1990.

Wilkinson, Endymion. *Chinese History: A Manual*. Rev. and enl. edn. Cambridge, MA: Harvard University Press, 2000.

Wilkinson, John. *Jerusalem Pilgrims Before the Crusades*. Warminster, UK: Aris & Phillips, 2002.

Wilkinson, Toby. *The Rise and Fall of Ancient Egypt*. New York: Random House, 2010.

William R. Catton, Jr. *Overshoot: The Ecological Basis of Revolutionary Change*. Urbana, IL: University of Illinois Press, 1980.

Williams, Colin P. *Explorations in Quantum Computing*, 2nd edn. London: Springer, 2011.

Williams, Eric. *Capitalism and Slavery*. Introduction by Colin A. Palmer. Chapel Hill and London: The University North Carolina Press, 1994 [1944].

Williams, Trevor I. *History of Invention, Revised Edition: From Stone Axes to Silicon Chips*. Rev. edn. New York: Checkmark Books, 2000.

Williamson, Harold F. "Mass Production For Mass Consumption." In vol. 2 of *Technology in Western Civilization*, 2 vols. Edited by Melvin Kranzberg and Carroll W. Pursell, Jr. New York: Oxford University Press, 1967.

Willoughby, Pamela R. *The Evolution Of Modern Humans In Africa: A Comprehensive Guide*. Lanham, MD: AltaMira Press, 2007.

Winchester, Simon. *The Professor and the Madman: A Tale of Murder, Insanity, and the Making of the Oxford English Dictionary*. New York: HarperCollins, 1998.

—. *The Map That Changed the World: William Smith and the Birth of Modern Geology*. New York: HarperCollins, 2001.

—. *The Man Who Loved China: The Fantastic Story of the Eccentric Scientist Who Unlocked the Mysteries of the Middle Kingdom*. New York: HarperCollins, 2008.

Winkelman, John H. "The Imperial Library in Southern Sung China, 1127–1279. A Study of the Organization and Operation of the Scholarly Agencies of the Central Government." *Transactions of the American Philosophical Society*, New Series 64, 8 (1974): 1–61.

Winter, Jay. *Sites of Memory, Sites of Mourning: The Great War in European Cultural History*. Cambridge: Cambridge University Press, 2005.

Wippel, John F. "The Parisian Condemnations of 1270 and 1277." In *A Companion to Philosophy in the Middle Ages*. Edited by Randall Curren. Malden, MA, and Oxford: Blackwell Publishers, 2002, 66.

Witt, Ronald G. *The Two Latin Cultures and the Foundation of Renaissance Humanism in Medieval Italy*. New York: Cambridge University Press, 2012.

Witte, John, Jr. *From Sacrament to Contract: Marriage, Religion, and Law in the Western Tradition*. Louisville: Westminster/Knox, 1997.

—. "A Demonstrative Theory of Natural Law: Johannes Althusius and the Rise of Calvinists Jurisprudence." *Ecclesiastical Law Journal* 11 (2009): 248–65.

Wollstonecraft, Mary. *Vindication of the Rights of Woman*. New York: Dover Pub., 1996.

Wood, Bernard A. *Human Evolution: A Very Short Introduction*. New York: Oxford University Press, 2005.

Wood, Betty. *Slavery in Colonial America, 1619–1776*. Lanham, MD: Rowman & Littlefield, 2005.

Wood, Gordon S. *The Radicalism of the American Revolution*. New York: A. A. Knopf, 1991.

—. *The American Revolution: A History*. New York: Modern Library, 2002.

—. *The Idea of America: Reflections on the Birth of the United States*. London: Penguin, 2011.

Wood, Susan. *The Proprietary Church in the Medieval West*. Oxford and New York: Oxford University Press, 2006.

Woods, Damon L. *The Philippines: A Global Studies Handbook*. Santa Barbara, CA: ABC-CLIO, 2006.

Woods, Michael D., and Glenn Muske. "Economic Development Via Understanding and Growing a Community's Microbusiness Segment." In *Entrepreneurship and Local Economic Development*. Edited by Norman Walzer. Lanham, MD: Lexington Books, 2007.

Woods-Marsden, Joanna. *Renaissance Self-Portraiture: The Visual Construction of Identity and the Social Status of the Artist*. New Haven: Yale University Press, 1998.

Woodward, C. Vann. *The Strange Career of Jim Crow*. New York: Oxford University Press, 1974.

Woodward, E. L. *The Age of Reform, 1815–1870*, 2nd edn. Oxford: Oxford University Press, 1962.

Worden, Blair. *God's Instruments: Political Conduct in the England of Oliver Cromwell*. Oxford and New York: Oxford University Press, 2012.

Wordie, J. R. "The Chronology of English Enclosure, 1500–1914." *The Economic History Review* 36, New Series (November 1983): 483–505.

Woronzoff-Dashkoff, A. *Dashkova: A Life of Influence and Exile*. Philadelphia: Temple University Press, 2007.

Wozniak, Steve, and Gina Smith. *iWoz: Computer Geek to Cult Icon: How I Invented the Personal Computer, Co-Founded Apple, and Had Fun Doing It*. New York: W. W. Norton & Company, 2006.

Wyman, Mark. *Round-Trip to America: The Immigrants Return to Europe, 1880–1930*. Ithaca: Cornell University Press, 1993.

Yao, Esther S. Lee. *Chinese Women: Past and Present*. Mesquite, TX: Ide House, 1983.

Yager, Jan. *Single in America*. New York: Atheneum, 1980.

Yapp, M. E. "Europe in the Turkish Mirror." *Past & Present* 137 (November 1992): 134–55.

Zagorin, Perez. *How the Idea of Religious Toleration Came to the West*. Princeton and Oxford: Princeton University Press, 2003.

Zaret, David. *Origins of Democratic Culture: Printing, Petitions, and the Public Sphere in Early Modern England*. Princeton: Princeton University Press, 2000.

Zimmer, Oliver. *A Contested Nation: History, Memory and Nationalism in Switzerland, 1761–1891*. Cambridge: Cambridge University Press, 2003.

Zmora, Hillay. *Monarchy, Aristocracy, and the State in Europe, 1300–1800*. New York: Routledge, 2001.

Zophy, Jonathan W. *A Short History of Renaissance and Reformation Europe: Dances over Fire and Water*, 2nd edn. Upper Saddle River, NJ: Prentice Hall, 1999.

Zuckerman, Michael. "Rhetoric, Reality, and the Revolution: The Genteel Radicalism of Gordon Wood." *The William and Mary Quarterly*, Third Series, 51 (October 1994): 693–702.

Zuercher, E. *The Buddhist Conquest of China: The Spread and Adaptation of Buddhism in Early Medieval China*, 2 vols. Leiden: E.J. Brill, 1972.

Zumthor, Paul and Catherine Peebles. "The Medieval Travel Narrative." *New Literary History* 25, 4 (Autumn 1994): 809–24.

Zunz, Olivier. *Making America Corporate, 1870–1920*. Chicago: University of Chicago Press, 1990.

Zweigenhaft, Richard L., and G. William Domhoff. *The New CEOs: Women, African American, Latino and Asian American Leaders of* Fortune *500 Companies*. Lanham, MD, and Plymouth, UK: Rowman & Littlefield Publishers, 2009.

INDEX